*International Directory of*
# COMPANY HISTORIES

# International Directory of

# COMPANY HISTORIES

## VOLUME 116

*Editor*

**Drew Johnson**

**ST. JAMES PRESS**
*A part of Gale, Cengage Learning*

GALE
CENGAGE Learning™

Detroit • New York • San Francisco • New Haven, Conn • Waterville, Maine • London

**International Directory of Company Histories, Volume 116**

**Drew Johnson, Editor**

Project Editor: Miranda H. Ferrara

Editorial: Virgil Burton, Donna Craft, Louise Gagné, Peggy Geeseman, Julie Gough, Sonya Hill, Keith Jones, Matthew Miskelly, Lynn Pearce, Laura Peterson, Holly Selden

Production Technology Specialist: Mike Weaver

Imaging and Multimedia: John Watkins

Composition and Electronic Prepress: Gary Leach, Evi Seoud

Manufacturing: Rhonda Dover

Product Manager: Jenai Drouillard

For product information and technology assistance, contact us at **Gale Customer Support, 1-800-877-4253.**
For permission to use material from this text or product, submit all requests online at **www.cengage.com/permissions.**
Further permissions questions can be emailed to **permissionrequest@cengage.com**

*Gale*
27500 Drake Rd.
Farmington Hills, MI, 48331-3535

LIBRARY OF CONGRESS CATALOG NUMBER 89-190943
ISBN-13:  978-1-4144-4727-8
ISBN-10:  1-4144-4727-2

This title is also available as an e-book
ISBN-13: 978-1-55862-779-6   ISBN-10: 1-55862-779-0
Contact your Gale, a part of Cengage Learning sales representative for ordering information.

BRITISH LIBRARY CATALOGUING IN PUBLICATION DATA
International directory of company histories, Vol. 116
Drew Johnson
33.87409

Printed in México
1 2 3 4 5 6 7 15 14 13 12 11 10

# Contents

# *Preface*

The St. James Press series *The International Directory of Company Histories* (*IDCH*) is intended for reference use by students, business people, librarians, historians, economists, investors, job candidates, and others who seek to learn more about the historical development of the world's most important companies. To date, *IDCH* has profiled more than 11,060 companies in 116 volumes.

## INCLUSION CRITERIA

Most companies chosen for inclusion in *IDCH* have achieved a minimum of US$25 million in annual sales and are leading influences in their industries or geographical locations. Companies may be publicly held, private, or nonprofit. State-owned companies that are important in their industries and that may operate much like public or private companies also are included. Wholly owned subsidiaries and divisions are profiled if they meet the requirements for inclusion. Entries on companies that have had major changes since they were last profiled may be selected for updating.

The *IDCH* series highlights 25% private and nonprofit companies, and features updated entries on approximately 35 companies per volume.

## ENTRY FORMAT

Each entry begins with the company's legal name; the address of its headquarters; its telephone, toll-free, and fax numbers; and its web site. A statement of public, private, state, or parent ownership follows. A company with a legal name in both English and the language of its headquarters country is listed by the English name, with the native-language name in parentheses.

The company's founding or earliest incorporation date, the number of employees, and the most recent available sales figures follow. Sales figures are given in local currencies with equivalents in U.S. dollars. For some private companies, sales figures are estimates and indicated by the abbreviation *est*. The entry lists the exchanges on which the company's stock is traded and its ticker symbol, as well as the company's NAICS codes.

Entries generally contain a *Company Perspectives* box which provides a short summary of the company's mission, goals, and ideals; a *Key Dates* box highlighting milestones in the company's history; lists of *Principal Subsidiaries, Principal Divisions, Principal Operating Units, Principal Competitors*; and articles for *Further Reading*.

American spelling is used throughout *IDCH*, and the word "billion" is used in its U.S. sense of one thousand million.

### SOURCES

Entries have been compiled from publicly accessible sources both in print and on the Internet such as general and academic periodicals, books, and annual reports, as well as material supplied by the companies themselves.

### CUMULATIVE INDEXES

*IDCH* contains three indexes: the **Cumulative Index to Companies**, which provides an alphabetical index to companies profiled in the *IDCH* series, the **Index to Industries**, which allows researchers to locate companies by their principal industry, and the **Geographic Index**, which lists companies alphabetically by the country of their headquarters. The indexes are cumulative and specific instructions for using them are found immediately preceding each index.

### SPECIAL TO THIS VOLUME

This volume of *IDCH* contains entries on multiple African companies of note, such as Kenya's Safaricom Limited, Zambia's Copperbelt Energy, and Libya's Sahara Bank.

### SUGGESTIONS WELCOME

Comments and suggestions from users of *IDCH* on any aspect of the product as well as suggestions for companies to be included or updated are cordially invited. Please write:

The Editor
*International Directory of Company Histories*
St. James Press
Gale, Cengage Learning
27500 Drake Rd.
Farmington Hills, Michigan 48331-3535

St. James Press does not endorse any of the companies or products mentioned in this series. Companies appearing in the *International Directory of Company Histories* were selected without reference to their wishes and have in no way endorsed their entries.

# Notes on Contributors

**Agata Antonow**
A business writer and researcher based in Nova Scotia, Canada. Antonow works with clients all over North America.

**Rhonda Campbell**
Business writer and novelist. Campbell has written for and appeared in several periodicals including *Essence*, *Parade*, and the *Pittsburgh Quarterly*.

**Alicia Elley**
Business writer and librarian currently living in East Texas.

**Aaron Hauser**
Researcher, business writer, and novelist based in Austin, Texas.

**Sara Huter**
A professor of economics. Huter's background also includes risk management in the banking and energy industries with expertise in credit scores. ????

**Paul Ingati**
Business writer and researcher based in Nairobi. Ingati is a specialist in personal finance, business management, business planning, and project management.

**David Larkins**
Professional writer based in Santa Fe, New Mexico, where he contributes to a variety of books and publications. Larkins' most recent book is a collaboration with his father, *Startling Art: Revealing the Art of Dennis Larkins*.

**Ian MacDonald**
Contemporary writer with formal training in technical communications and an advance education in business administration. MacDonald is based in the island city of Richmond, British Columbia.

**Catherine Meyrat**
Business strategist and entrepreneur based in San Antonio. Meyrat received her MBA from Boston University and a has background in journalism, languages, and marketing.

**Diane Milne**
Writer and researcher with a background in the field of education. Milne is currently living in Florida.

**Andrea Newell**
Researcher and business writer currently living in Michigan.

**David Petechuk**
Contributor to business, health care, and various educational publications. Petechuk is the author of a book on ethical issues in transplantation and a book about LSD, which is part of a drug education series targeting a young adult audience.

# List of Abbreviations

€ European euro
¥ Japanese yen
£ United Kingdom pound
$ United States dollar

**A**

**AB** Aktiebolag (Finland, Sweden)
**AB Oy** Aktiebolag Osakeyhtiot (Finland)
**A.E.** Anonimos Eteria (Greece)
**AED** Emirati dirham
**AG** Aktiengesellschaft (Austria, Germany, Switzerland, Liechtenstein)
**aG** auf Gegenseitigkeit (Austria, Germany)
**A.m.b.a.** Andelsselskab med begraenset ansvar (Denmark)
**A.O.** Anonim Ortaklari/Ortakligi (Turkey)
**ApS** Amparteselskab (Denmark)
**ARS** Argentine peso
**A.S.** Anonim Sirketi (Turkey)
**A/S** Aksjeselskap (Norway)
**A/S** Aktieselskab (Denmark, Sweden)
**Ay** Avoinyhtio (Finland)
**ATS** Austrian shilling
**AUD** Australian dollar
**Ay** Avoinyhtio (Finland)

**B**

**B.A.** Buttengewone Aansprakeiijkheid (Netherlands)
**BEF** Belgian franc

**BHD** Bahraini dinar
**Bhd.** Berhad (Malaysia, Brunei)
**BND** Brunei dollar
**BRL** Brazilian real
**B.V.** Besloten Vennootschap (Belgium, Netherlands)
**BWP** Botswana pula

**C**

**C. de R.L.** Compania de Responsabilidad Limitada (Spain)
**C. por A.** Compania por Acciones (Dominican Republic)
**C.A.** Compania Anonima (Ecuador, Venezuela)
**C.V.** Commanditaire Vennootschap (Netherlands, Belgium)
**CAD** Canadian dollar
**CEO** Chief Executive Officer
**CFO** Chief Financial Officer
**CHF** Swiss franc
**Cia.** Compagnia (Italy)
**Cia.** Companhia (Brazil, Portugal)
**Cia.** Compania (Latin America [except Brazil], Spain)
**Cie.** Compagnie (Belgium, France, Luxembourg, Netherlands)
**CIO** Chief Information Officer
**CLP** Chilean peso
**CNY** Chinese yuan
**Co.** Company
**COO** Chief Operating Officer
**Coop.** Cooperative

**COP** Colombian peso
**Corp.** Corporation
**CPT** Cuideachta Phoibi Theoranta (Republic of Ireland)
**CRL** Companhia a Responsabilidao Limitida (Portugal, Spain)
**CZK** Czech koruna

**D**

**D&B** Dunn & Bradstreet
**DEM** German deutsche mark (W. Germany to 1990; unified Germany to 2002)
**Div.** Division (United States)
**DKK** Danish krone
**DZD** Algerian dinar

**E**

**E.P.E.** Etema Pemorismenis Evthynis (Greece)
**EC** Exempt Company (Arab countries)
**Edms. Bpk.** Eiendoms Beperk (South Africa)
**EEK** Estonian Kroon
**eG** eingetragene Genossenschaft (Germany)
**EGMBH** Eingetragene Genossenschaft mit beschraenkter Haftung (Austria, Germany)
**EGP** Egyptian pound
**Ek For** Ekonomisk Forening (Sweden)
**EP** Empresa Portuguesa (Portugal)

**ESOP** Employee Stock Options and Ownership
**ESP** Spanish peseta
**Et(s).** Etablissement(s) (Belgium, France, Luxembourg)
**eV** eingetragener Verein (Germany)
**EUR** European euro

**F**
**FIM** Finnish markka
**FRF** French franc

**G**
**G.I.E.** Groupement d'Interet Economique (France)
**gGmbH** gemeinnutzige Gesellschaft mit beschraenkter Haftung (Austria, Germany, Switzerland)
**GmbH** Gesellschaft mit beschraenkter Haftung (Austria, Germany, Switzerland)
**GRD** Greek drachma
**GWA** Gewerbte Amt (Austria, Germany)

**H**
**HB** Handelsbolag (Sweden)
**HF** Hlutafelag (Iceland)
**HKD** Hong Kong dollar
**HUF** Hungarian forint

**I**
**IDR** Indonesian rupiah
**IEP** Irish pound
**ILS** Israeli shekel (new)
**Inc.** Incorporated (United States, Canada)
**INR** Indian rupee
**IPO** Initial Public Offering
**I/S** Interesentselskap (Norway)
**I/S** Interessentselskab (Denmark)
**ISK** Icelandic krona
**ITL** Italian lira

**J**
**JMD** Jamaican dollar
**JOD** Jordanian dinar

**K**
**KB** Kommanditbolag (Sweden)
**KES** Kenyan schilling
**Kft** Korlatolt Felelossegu Tarsasag (Hungary)
**KG** Kommanditgesellschaft (Austria, Germany, Switzerland)
**KGaA** Kommanditgesellschaft auf Aktien (Austria, Germany, Switzerland)
**KK** Kabushiki Kaisha (Japan)
**KPW** North Korean won
**KRW** South Korean won
**K/S** Kommanditselskab (Denmark)
**K/S** Kommandittselskap (Norway)
**KWD** Kuwaiti dinar
**Ky** Kommandiitiyhtio (Finland)

**L**
**L.L.C.** Limited Liability Company (Arab countries, Egypt, Greece, United States)
**L.L.P.** Limited Liability Partnership (United States)
**L.P.** Limited Partnership (Canada, South Africa, United Kingdom, United States)
**LBO** Leveraged Buyout
**Lda.** Limitada (Spain)
**Ltd.** Limited
**Ltda.** Limitada (Brazil, Portugal)
**Ltee.** Limitee (Canada, France)
**LUF** Luxembourg franc
**LYD** Libyan dinar

**M**
**mbH** mit beschraenkter Haftung (Austria, Germany)
**Mij.** Maatschappij (Netherlands)
**MUR** Mauritian rupee
**MXN** Mexican peso
**MYR** Malaysian ringgit

**N**
**N.A.** National Association (United States)
**N.V.** Naamloze Vennootschap (Belgium, Netherlands)
**NGN** Nigerian naira
**NLG** Netherlands guilder
**NOK** Norwegian krone
**NZD** New Zealand dollar

**O**
**OAO** Otkrytoe Aktsionernoe Obshchestve (Russia)
**OHG** Offene Handelsgesellschaft (Austria, Germany, Switzerland)
**OMR** Omani rial
**OOO** Obschestvo s Ogranichennoi Otvetstvennostiu (Russia)
**OOUR** Osnova Organizacija Udruzenog Rada (Yugoslavia)
**Oy** Osakeyhtiö (Finland)

**P**
**P.C.** Private Corp. (United States)
**P.L.L.C.** Professional Limited Liability Corporation (United States)
**P.T.** Perusahaan/Perseroan Terbatas (Indonesia)
**PEN** Peruvian Nuevo Sol
**PHP** Philippine peso
**PKR** Pakistani rupee
**P/L** Part Lag (Norway)
**PLC** Public Limited Co. (United Kingdom, Ireland)
**PLN** Polish zloty
**PTE** Portuguese escudo
**Pte.** Private (Singapore)
**Pty.** Proprietary (Australia, South Africa, United Kingdom)
**Pvt.** Private (India, Zimbabwe)
**PVBA** Personen Vennootschap met Beperkte Aansprakelijkheid (Belgium)
**PYG** Paraguay guarani

**Q**
**QAR** Qatar riyal

**R**
**REIT** Real Estate Investment Trust
**RMB** Chinese renminbi
**Rt** Reszvenytarsasag (Hungary)
**RUB** Russian ruble

**S**
**S.A.** Sociedad Anónima (Latin America [except Brazil], Spain, Mexico)
**S.A.** Sociedades Anônimas (Brazil, Portugal)
**S.A.** Société Anonyme (Arab countries, Belgium, France, Jordan, Luxembourg, Switzerland)
**S.A. de C.V.** Sociedad Anonima de Capital Variable (Mexico)
**S.A.B. de C.V.** Sociedad Anónima Bursátil de Capital Variable (Mexico)
**S.A.C.** Sociedad Anonima Comer-

cial (Latin America [except Brazil])

**S.A.C.I.** Sociedad Anonima Comercial e Industrial (Latin America [except Brazil])

**S.A.C.I.y.F.** Sociedad Anonima Comercial e Industrial y Financiera (Latin America [except Brazil])

**S.A.R.L.** Sociedade Anonima de Responsabilidade Limitada (Brazil, Portugal)

**S.A.R.L.** Société à Responsabilité Limitée (France, Belgium, Luxembourg)

**S.A.S.** Societe Anonyme Syrienne (Arab countries)

**S.A.S.** Societá in Accomandita Semplice (Italy)

**S.C.** Societe en Commandite (Belgium, France, Luxembourg)

**S.C.A.** Societe Cooperativa Agricole (France, Italy, Luxembourg)

**S.C.I.** Sociedad Cooperativa Ilimitada (Spain)

**S.C.L.** Sociedad Cooperativa Limitada (Spain)

**S.C.R.L.** Societe Cooperative a Responsabilite Limitee (Belgium)

**S.E.** Societas Europaea (European Union Member states

**S.L.** Sociedad Limitada (Latin America [except Brazil], Portugal, Spain)

**S.N.C.** Société en Nom Collectif (France)

**S.p.A.** Società per Azioni (Italy)

**S.R.L.** Sociedad de Responsabilidad Limitada (Spain, Mexico, Latin America [except Brazil])

**S.R.L.** Società a Responsabilità Limitata (Italy)

**S.R.O.** Spolecnost s Rucenim Omezenym (Czechoslovakia

**S.S.K.** Sherkate Sahami Khass (Iran)

**S.V.** Samemwerkende Vennootschap (Belgium)

**S.Z.R.L.** Societe Zairoise a Responsabilite Limitee (Zaire)

**SAA** Societe Anonyme Arabienne (Arab countries)

**SAK** Societe Anonyme Kuweitienne (Arab countries)

**SAL** Societe Anonyme Libanaise (Arab countries)

**SAO** Societe Anonyme Omanienne (Arab countries)

**SAQ** Societe Anonyme Qatarienne (Arab countries)

**SAR** Saudi riyal

**Sdn. Bhd.** Sendirian Berhad (Malaysia)

**SEK** Swedish krona

**SGD** Singapore dollar

**S/L** Salgslag (Norway)

**Soc.** Sociedad (Latin America [except Brazil], Spain)

**Soc.** Sociedade (Brazil, Portugal)

**Soc.** Societa (Italy)

**Sp. z.o.o.** Spólka z ograniczona odpowiedzialnoscia (Poland)

**Ste.** Societe (France, Belgium, Luxembourg, Switzerland)

**Ste. Cve.** Societe Cooperative (Belgium)

T

**THB** Thai baht

**TND** Tunisian dinar

**TRL** Turkish lira

**TTD** Trinidad and Tobago dollar

**TWD** Taiwan dollar (new)

U

**U.A.** Uitgesloten Aansporakeiijkheid (Netherlands)

**u.p.a.** utan personligt ansvar (Sweden)

V

**V.O.f.** Vennootschap onder firma (Netherlands)

**VAG** Verein der Arbeitgeber (Austria, Germany)

**VEB** Venezuelan bolivar

**VERTR** Vertriebs (Austria, Germany)

**VND** Vietnamese dong

**VVAG** Versicherungsverein auf Gegenseitigkeit (Austria, Germany)

W – Z

**WA** Wettelika Aansprakalikhaed (Netherlands)

**WLL** With Limited Liability (Bahrain, Kuwait, Qatar, Saudi Arabia)

**YK** Yugen Kaisha (Japan)

**ZAO** Zakrytoe Aktsionernoe Obshchestve (Russia)

**ZAR** South African rand

**ZMK** Zambian kwacha

**ZWD** Zimbabwean dollar

# ACE Limited

■

Bärengasse 32
Zürich, CH-8001
Switzerland
Telephone: (+41 43) 456-76-00
Fax: (+41 43) 456 76 01
Web site: http://www.acelimited.com

*Public Company*
*Founded:* 1985
*Employees:* 15,000
*Sales:* $15.07 billion
*Stock Exchanges:* NYSE
*Ticker Symbol:* ACE
*NAICS:* 524126 Insurance carriers, property and casualty, direct; 524130 Reinsurance carriers; 524113 Accidental death and dismemberment insurance carriers, direct; 524113 Life insurance carrier; 524210 Life insurance agencies

■ ■ ■

ACE Limited is the parent company of Ace Group and operates worldwide through its headquarters in Switzerland and its offices in Bermuda and New York. The company's products include property and casualty insurance for businesses and personal accident, supplemental health, and life insurance for high-wealth individuals. Through its subsidiary Tempest Re, the company offers reinsurance for property and casualty and life insurance companies. ACE operates more broadly through branches across 50 countries serving clients in over 140 countries. The company has grown quickly through a mixture of new product offerings and aggressive acquisitions of companies with attractive specializations or geographic strengths.

## AN ISLAND FORMATION

In 1985 a consortium of 34 large companies, including General Electric and Merck, joined to form the insurance company ACE Limited. The consortium incorporated ACE in the Cayman Islands and established the headquarters in Hamilton, Bermuda. Both the Cayman Islands and Bermuda offered a tax system less rigid and onerous than the one encountered by companies incorporating in the United States. In addition, for a small island group Bermuda enjoys a population with a high proportion of well-qualified lawyers and accountants. The tax structure and the professional support made the island an ideal environment for insurance companies.

The goal of the company's founders was to pool resources and protect themselves against liability risks. Specifically, the company was to offer excess liability and directors and officers (D&O) liability insurance products. Excess liability insurance, also called umbrella liability insurance, is a policy that covers situations in which the limits of the underlying general liability policy are exceeded. For example, if the general liability policy is for $1 million and there is a claim settlement for $1.5 million the excess liability policy would take care of the additional amount. Directors and officers insurance is a liability policy that pays out to the directors or officers of a corporation when they face losses due to a lawsuit or alleged wrongful acts while serving in their positions with the company.

## COMPANY PERSPECTIVES

We are committed to reinforcing our position as a leader in the global insurance market by always conducting our business in a consistent, disciplined and focused manner. This is the ACE way and it embodies a dedication to providing: Superior client value by committing substantial capital resources and creativity to the assumption and management of risk; Superior shareholder value by managing capital and risks expertly, efficiently and profitably; Superior employee value by creating a rewarding and ethical environment.

Like many insurance companies, ACE sought to use the advantages of the island tax shelter and business environment to financially protect other companies and in essence carry their losses. They were able to give businesses and even other insurance companies room to operate with the risk necessary to do business in their respective nations. When major catastrophes hit, like Hurricane Andrew in 1992 and Hurricane Katrina in 2005, clients could handle the large payouts and still manage to stabilize their bottom line.

In pursuit of becoming the premier source for D&O insurance, the company took over management of Corporate Officers & Directors Assurance, Ltd., (CODA) in 1987. ACE eventually purchased CODA in 1993. That same year ACE completed its initial public offering and was listed on the New York Stock Exchange under the symbol ACL (later changed to ACE).

### BUYING GROWTH

By 1993 ACE had become a small but steady player in the excess liability and D&O liability insurance market, but the company soon faced pressure from its clients to offer more products to satisfy their rather specific needs. In 1994 ACE grew its offerings to include satellite insurance, which covered from prelaunch to launch to sustaining orbit of a space-based satellite; aviation insurance, which covered aspects of airplanes and air flight; excess property insurance, which covered property damage beyond the coverage of a general property damage policy; and financial lines, which could cover various activities of financial institutions.

Even with these new business lines, the company remained a specialty insurance carrier, mainly focused on catastrophic coverage. Then, in 1994, ACE named

Brian Duperreault president & CEO. Duperreault was a proven veteran of the insurance industry. Before coming to ACE he had been with American International Group (AIG) for more than 20 years, during which he worked his way up from an actuarial trainee to become executive vice president of AIG Foreign General Insurance and chairman and chief executive of AIG's American International Underwriters (AIU). Maurice "Hank" Greenberg, president and CEO of AIG, considered Duperreault a prized protégé and the most likely to succeed him until Duperreault left for ACE. According to *Forbes*, Greenberg considered this a betrayal, and it tainted relations between AIG and ACE from that point forward. It did not help that under Duperreault's leadership ACE went after the same high-margin markets that were AIG's speciality.

Duperreault came to ACE with a clear mandate to transform the company from a specialty carrier into a global insurance company. He immediately launched an aggressive round of acquisitions and initiatives to diversify ACE's product lines. One of the first efforts ACE made was to enlarge its footprint in the Lloyd's market. (Lloyd's is not an insurance agency as some think it is. Lloyd's manages a specialist insurance market with over 50 managing agents and over 80 syndicates. Each syndicate specializes in a particular type of insurance and is managed by a managing agent. Managing agents supply capital to fund the Lloyd's market.) In 1996 ACE acquired two of Lloyd's managing agencies, Methuen Group and Ockham Worldwide. Together these acquisitions made ACE one of the largest Lloyd's managing agents in the world. Each acquisition also brought its own particular advantages. The addition of Methuen brought expertise in the aviation market, while Ockham built up ACE's accounting, reporting, and ancillary insurance services.

The next major leap in growth came when ACE set its sights on Tempest Re, a leading Bermuda-based property catastrophe reinsurance company. (Simply put, reinsurance is insurance for insurance companies, which purchase reinsurance to cover excessive losses due to unexpected and significant disasters.) ACE initiated a hostile bid for Tempest Re. According to the *Economist*, at the time there were 15 reinsurance companies on the Bermuda island, together representing a quarter of the world reinsurance market. During the years leading up to ACE's bid, the number of natural disasters had fallen, thereby swelling the coffers of reinsurance companies. These smaller and very profitable reinsurance companies became very enticing to larger specialty insurance companies like ACE.

An AIG affiliate company named IPC Re made a counter bid for Tempest Re. ACE countered and won

## KEY DATES

**1985:** A consortium of 34 companies creates ACE Limited.
**1993:** Company makes its initial public offering and is listed on NYSE.
**1999:** ACE acquires the global property and casualty business of CIGNA Corporation.
**2002:** ACE European Group opens headquarters in London, England.
**2008:** Company moves its place of incorporation to Zürich, Switzerland.

the bidding war in 1996. However, ACE was forced to pay $976 million for Tempest Re, $100 million above its original offer. An analyst wrote in the *Insurance Advocate* that this purchase took ACE to a new level.

The *Insurance Advocate* also noted that the acquisition represented the first step in the consolidation of the property-catastrophe insurance industry. As Lloyd's became less of a dominant player in the 1990s, other companies used their excess cash to fuel acquisitions as a counter to increased competition. With the purchase of Tempest Re, ACE became one of the strongest of these competitors.

On the tail end of integrating Tempest Re into its operations ACE Bermuda joined with XL Insurance Company, Ltd., and Risk Capital Re to form Sovereign Risk Insurance Ltd., in 1997. The joint venture was formed to offer political risk insurance and reinsurance. Political risk insurance covers assets at risk due to political upheaval such as a revolution, coup d'état, or other political changes that can cause a loss. The Sovereign joint venture was a continuation of ACE's expansion into new lines of business and its aggressive push into the reinsurance market.

## GLOBAL EXPANSION ACCELERATES

With the purchase of Tempest Re and the formation of Sovereign, ACE had successfully transitioned from a simple excess insurance company to a multiproduct global player. From there, ACE continued to expand its operations. Again, the company achieved its goals by forming new entities and acquiring existing interests. In 1997 ACE incorporated ACE European Markets and secured licensing to underwrite all 18 classes of nonlife insurance in each member state of the European Union.

The next year, ACE acquired Westchester Specialty Group, Inc., a specialty insurance carrier, for $333 million. This purchase was a critical step for ACE, as it helped the company establish a foothold in the U.S. market. ACE renamed the new subsidiary ACE USA.

Also in 1997, ACE acquired CAT Limited, another Bermuda-based catastrophe reinsurance concern, and integrated it into ACE Tempest Re. This increased ACE's impressive position in the catastrophe reinsurance market.

ACE's next move, the purchase of Insurance Company of North America (INA), drew the ire of its U.S. competitors. INA was CIGNA's highly valuable international property and casualty insurance unit. ACE managed to purchase INA even though U.S. companies such as the Chubb Group and Hartford Financial Services had been eyeing INA's international operations for some time. ACE paid $3.45 billion in cash for INA at premium above the unit's cash value. According to *Forbes*, Chubb and Hartford knew CIGNA would not sell the international operations without attaching the bureaucratic and unprofitable domestic operations. ACE came forward and took both the domestic and international pieces. *Forbes* noted that the domestic unit remained unprofitable, but even so, the deal instantly increased ACE's U.S. market share and made it second in global market presence to AIG. In retribution, ACE's U.S. competitors almost immediately took issue with a lesser-known tax advantage enjoyed by ACE due to its island incorporation. Lawsuits were filed and legislation was proposed to remove the tax rule. ACE could have moved its INA unit, but CEO Duperreault felt it was important for ACE to maintain a U.S. presence. However, this was the beginning of much wrangling over the protection of personal and corporate tax havens in the U.S. political arena.

Despite the cold reception by its competitors ACE had truly moved beyond its status as a niche player. The acquisition of INA raised the company's assets to $30 billion and its employee base to 9,000 covering 47 countries. Another advantage of the INA purchase was that ACE inherited the company's rich history, its first policy having been written in 1792.

ACE continued its successful acquisitions with the purchase of Capital Re, a U.S. company that offered specialty reinsurance for financial guaranty insurance and other financial risks. ACE was already participating in the Sovereign joint venture with Capital Re. At the time, Capital Re was facing a $67 million loss, and ACE agreed to purchase the company for $606 million. ACE's strategy with this purchase was to combine financial instruments and insurance to create products that could be marketed to banks, insurance companies, and corporations globally.

While the successive purchases of Tempest Re, INA, and Capital Re were strategic successes, they did not come without significant integration costs. ACE's operating earnings were dragged down 6 percent in the fourth quarter of 1999. However, the company quickly turned its fortunes around and by September 2000 the company's quarterly net profits rose to $113 million, compared with $69.1 million for the same period in 1999. Gross premiums quadrupled to $2 billion, and net written premiums more than tripled to $1.2 billion for the quarter.

Entering the new millennium ACE continued its expansion across the global market. ACE International acquired a 51 percent shareholding in Egyptian American Insurance Company (EAIC). Sovereign Risk Insurance Ltd., ACE's joint venture with two other companies, was elected to the Berne Union as one of only three private sector political risk insurers to be eligible and approved. (The Berne Union is an association whose members provide insurance or guarantees to protect exporting companies, investors, and financial institutions against political and commercial risks. The goal is to facilitate cross border trade and investment.) In 2002 ACE and Huatai Insurance Company of China announced a strategic partnership to develop new products and services across China. In the same year, ACE European Group opened its new headquarters in London, England. During this time of global expansion ACE changed its ticker symbol on the New York Stock Exchange from ACL to ACE.

By this point, Bermuda had two thriving insurance industries, the reinsurance market, with ACE as a major player, and the captive insurance market. Captive insurance companies are formed and wholly owned by companies, usually industrials, that want to protect themselves against the risks inherent to their particular industries. As with reinsurance companies, locating captive insurance companies offshore in places like Bermuda made economic sense. ACE had already dipped its toe into the captive insurance market, offering consulting and administrative solutions, but not until 2003 did it form its own captive unit, ACE Captive Solutions. The purpose of the new subsidiary was to help clients form their own captive solutions to manage risk and offer ACE's own solutions across its product lines to these companies.

## THE GREENBERG EFFECT & SCANDAL

In 2004 Brian Duperreault relinquished his position of president and CEO. After a decade leading ACE and turning it into a worldwide behemoth he handed the reins over to Evan G. Greenberg. Like Duperreault, Greenberg was a former AIG executive, yet Greenberg's rise to power was more complicated. His father, Maurice "Hank" Greenberg was president and CEO of AIG and had been for 37 years. According to *Forbes*, Hank Greenberg had groomed his two sons, Jeffrey and Evan, as potential successors, but he did not manage his relationships with his sons well. Nor did he manage the relationship between the brothers well, pitting them against each other often and creating resentment. As a result, when Hank Greenberg refused to relinquish his position to either son, each left to take leadership positions with other companies. Jeffrey, a Brown University graduate with a law degree from Georgetown University, became CEO of Marsh & McClennan (MMC), one of the largest insurance brokers in the world. Evan, who attended college but did not earn a degree, left to become vice chairman of ACE.

In October 2004 New York State attorney Eliot Spitzer sued MMC, accusing the company of defrauding its customers by steering business to insurers, including ACE, AIG, Hartford Financial Services, and Munich-American Risk Partners, who allegedly paid the broker special commissions, which were essentially kickbacks. The scandal tarnished the entire industry, but the companies run by the three Greenbergs were singled out for special punishment. Shares of ACE, along with the other companies, plummeted. Jeffrey Greenberg stepped down as CEO of MMC, but Evan and Hank Greenberg remained in their positions.

As president and CEO of ACE, Evan Greenberg continued the Duperreault tradition of enhancing ACE's fortunes through acquisitions, and according to *Business-Week* he also had Duperreault's penchant for poaching AIG executives and wooing away its customers.

Greenberg also continued ACE's worldwide expansion. In 2005 ACE received approvals to provide life insurance in China and Vietnam and commercial property and casualty insurance in Poland and Russia. In 2006 ACE opened an office in South Africa, and branches in Hungary, the Czech Republic, Bahrain, and Peru were opened in 2007. The following year ACE purchased Combined Insurance Company of America for $2.56 billion, doubling its accident and health insurance business. ACE also opened an office in Panama. In 2009 the company opened an office in Turkey.

The battle in the U.S. Congress over tax havens continued throughout these years. By 2008 companies taking advantage of these havens reacted to the economic uncertainty and the poor image being thrust upon them by angry politicians by relocating their headquarters to other countries. ACE was no exception.

ACE relocated its place of incorporation from the Cayman Islands to Zürich, Switzerland, but the company left its executive offices in Hamilton, Bermuda. The move did little to change ACE's position as a global leader in insurance and reinsurance, and nor did it seem likely to slow the company's growth into new markets.

*Aaron Hauser*

## PRINCIPAL SUBSIDIARIES

ACE Global Markets Limited (UK); ACE Group Holdings, Inc. (USA); ACE Group Management and Holding Ltd. (Bermuda); ACE Reinsurance Limited (Switzerland); ACE Services Limited (Cayman Islands); ACE Tempest Life Reinsurance Ltd. (Bermuda); Oasis Insurance Services Ltd. (Bermuda).

## PRINCIPAL COMPETITORS

The Chubb Group; Hartford Financial Services; Markel Insurance Group; Munich Re; Swiss Re; The Travelers Companies, Inc.; XL Capital Ltd.

## FURTHER READING

"Bermuda's Other Triangle," *Economist,* June 15, 1996, p. 68.

Burke, Doris, Barney Gimbel, and Devin Leonard, "Greenberg & Sons," *Fortune,* February 21, 2005, pp. 104–14.

Coolidge, Carrie, "Who's Afraid of Brian?" *Forbes,* May 29, 2000, pp. 90–94.

Hicks, Weston, and Christine Lai, "The Road From Excess: ACE and EXEL Limited," in *Black Book – The Road from Excess: ACE & EXEL Limited.* Cleveland, OH: Sanford C. Bernstein & Co., LLC, 1997, pp. 1–30.

———. "ACE Limited: Building a Diversified Specialty Insurer," *Black Book – Weekly Notes,* 1997, pp. 15–18.

Hogue, Robert D., "ACE Limited Keeps on Buying," *Insurance Advocate,* June 5, 1999, p. 32.

McDonald, Caroline, "Off The Island Despite U.S. Tax Concerns," *National Underwriter,* October 19, 2009, pp. 22–24.

"Transforming ACE into a Global Player," *Business Insurance,* September 18, 2006, pp. 3–24.

# Adecco S.A.

Sägereistrasse 10, P. O. Box Glattbrugg
Zürich, CH-8152
Switzerland
Telephone: (+41 44) 878-88-88
Fax: (+41 44) 829-88-88
Web site: http://www.adecco.com

*Public Company*
*Founded:* 1957
*Employees:* 28,000 (2009)
*Sales:* EUR 14.8 billion ($20.1 billion) (2009)
*Stock Exchanges:* Zürich Euronext
*Ticker Symbol:* ADEN ADO
*NAICS:* 561310 Employment Placement Agencies

∎∎∎

Adecco S.A. is the world's largest temporary employment company. The company has a network of more than 5,500 offices in some 60 countries. Each year the company supplies over 100,000 customers with more than 500,000 temporary and permanent employees.

Geographically, France is Adecco's largest market, accounting for one-third of all revenue in 2008. The North American market (United States and Canada) followed with 13 percent of revenue. In terms of business lines, over half of Adecco's revenue derives from its industrial sector, which accounted for 55 percent of revenue in 2008. The office sector accounted for 22 percent of revenue in that same year.

## FILLING A GAP IN THE 1950S

Adia was founded in Lausanne, Switzerland, in 1957 by Henri-Ferdinand Lavanchy. An independent accountant, Lavanchy got into the employment business when a client asked him to find a worker to fill in quickly on a job. Lavanchy's enterprise remained simply a domestic employment agency for its first four years in business.

In 1961 the company opened its first international office, in Belgium. Adia expanded further the following year, adding an office in Germany. Denmark came on board in 1965, and in 1972 the company expanded overseas, opening an office in Menlo Park, California, its first U.S. outpost. By then, Adia has been joined in Europe by another fast-growing company, ECCO, based in France, and founded in 1964 by Philippe Foriel-Destezet.

In the 1970s Adia became one of the first temporary agencies to offer its workers benefits such as health care and paid vacations. In 1974 Lavanchy recruited Swiss executive Martin O. Pestalozzi to help him run the company. Pestalozzi had spent many years working in the United States for a number of consumer services and manufacturing businesses. Pestalozzi later recalled to *International Management* that when he came aboard at Adia, "all the figures were too small. They all needed several more zeros." Pestalozzi and Lavanchy set out to change this situation through a policy of aggressive acquisitions in countries around the world. During the next 12 years Pestalozzi spent more than half of his time shuttling around the globe, propounding the theory that the temporary employment industry needed to increase its efforts to provide high-quality workers in

## COMPANY PERSPECTIVES

We inspire individuals and organisations to work more effectively and efficiently, and create greater choice in the domain of work, for the benefit of all concerned. As the world's leading provider of HR solutions—a business that has a positive impact on millions of people every year—we are conscious of our global role.

order to improve its credibility. In that time Adia purchased more than 85 companies, tripling its size and operating in more than a dozen countries. This process was aided by the highly fragmented nature of the temporary help industry, which made it easy for a large company to scoop up many small operations.

In the year following Pestalozzi's arrival at the company, Adia entered the French market, and in 1976 the company moved into the British Isles, buying an agency in Ireland. Also in 1976 Adia made an unsuccessful attempt to expand to Brazil. In 1977 the company purchased the Alfred Marks Bureau, Ltd., a venerable British temporary agency, for $3.4 million from its founder's son, Bernard Marks. Aside from the United States, the United Kingdom was the only other market in which Adia franchised offices, in addition to owning them outright.

Expansion continued at a rapid pace throughout the late 1970s and early 1980s, as the company branched out to Austria in 1978 and to Holland in 1979. In that year founder Lavanchy stepped aside as acting chairman of the company to become honorary chairman. He was replaced at the helm by Pestalozzi, who became president and chief operating officer. At that time Adia also sold shares to the public on the Zurich Stock Exchange for the first time. The company's highly valued stock offerings helped to finance further expansion through acquisitions.

The extent of Adia's growth in the second half of the 1970s became clear at the end of the decade, as the company reported revenues and profits three times higher in 1980 than those in 1975. The company's far-flung operations, however, had not spawned a large, multilayered corporate bureaucracy at their center. Operations remained heavily decentralized, as purchased subsidiaries were allowed to continue doing business in much the same way that they had before, to the extent that each made use of its own financial reporting procedures. Although uniform accounting practices were

instituted in the early 1980s, controls in general, at Chairman Pestalozzi's insistence, remained at a minimum. This was signified by the fact that the company's corporate headquarters staff in Lausanne consisted of just 25 people.

### BUILDING A STAFFING GIANT IN THE 1980S

In 1983 the company expanded its North American operations when it opened offices in Canada. Japan came on board in 1985, one year before the company added New Zealand, Spain, and Hong Kong. While Adia continued its international growth, ECCO focused its development largely on its home market, expanding to become a market leader in France by the mid-1980s and by the mid-1990s, the world's second largest staffing services provider, in terms of annual revenues.

Concerned that its steady growth might make Adia the target of an unwanted corporate takeover, Pestalozzi and Adia's other top managers formed Adiainvest S.A., a holding company, in 1985. Adiainvest purchased most of the equity holdings of company founder Lavanchy, giving it effective control of a majority of the company's voting shares. This move guaranteed that the current management could stay in charge of the company it was building.

By 1986 Adia's revenues and earnings had increased dramatically. This dramatic growth was part of an industry-wide phenomenon, as temporary help agencies became the world's third-fastest growing industry in the 1980s. After the economic downturn at the start of the decade, employers trimmed their permanent full-time staffs in an effort to keep their human resources expenditures low. With leaner staffing levels in place across many entire industries, companies looked increasingly to temporary workers to augment their regular staffs for large projects or if business simply picked up. This was in marked contrast to the early years of the temporary employment industry, when short-term workers were used only to fill in for regular employees who were ill or on vacation. In later years, although temporary workers were paid higher hourly wages than full-time employees, this cost was offset by savings on fringe benefits and overhead costs, making temporary help cost-effective.

### EUROPEAN INDUSTRY LEADER: 1986

Benefiting from these changes in the workforce of the developed world, Adia in 1986 reported sales topping $1 billion for the first time. The company became the

## KEY DATES

■

**1957:** Henri-Ferdinand Lavanchy founds Adia.
**1961:** Adia opens office in Belgium.
**1964:** Philippe Foriel-Destezet founds ECCO in France.
**1972:** Adia enters U.S. market with Adia Services Inc.
**1979:** Adia goes public on Swiss stock exchange.
**1984:** Adia Services goes public.
**1996:** Adia and ECCO merge to form Adecco; company acquires ICON Recruitment (Australia).
**1999:** Company acquires Delphi Group Plc., Career Staff Co., and Olsten Corporation.
**2004:** U.S. Securities and Exchange Commission investigates accounting irregularities at Adecco; case is dropped one year later.
**2010:** Company acquires Florida-based MPS Group for $1.3 billion.

European industry leader, with the largest share of the market in three countries: Switzerland, France, and Germany. In addition, its operation in the Netherlands secured a larger share of that country's temporary help business, and the company moved up to fourth place in the United States.

The growth of Adia's profits was also attributable to the company's strong emphasis on quality. Because it stressed high-value services, the company was able to charge more for its temporary workers than some of its competitors, giving it higher earnings. In its quest for quality workers and the high margins they brought, Adia implemented in-house training programs and niche marketing. In the mid-1980s Adia moved strongly into the specialized accounting and word processing fields, providing highly skilled workers to its clients. As an investment in its workforce, Adia subsidiaries provided specialized training in the latest word processing programs to their employees. Alfred Marks, for instance, trained 10,000 secretaries a year on various computer programs at its London headquarters.

The company's broad geographical base helped to insulate Adia from the effects of periodic downturns in the economy on the notoriously sensitive temporary employment industry. The company's extensive U.S. operations acted as a cushion for recessions in the European economy. The U.S. operations were run by Walter Macauley, a former executive with the Manpower

temporary agency who had been recruited to run the U.S. subsidiary Adia Services, Inc., in 1979. In that year the company had sales of $45 million, and it had not yet reached the ranks of the top ten temporary agencies in the country. Adia Services adopted an aggressive two-pronged growth strategy that involved opening company-owned offices in clusters and franchising branches in smaller markets where the company name was little known. As a result of this policy, the company had opened 360 offices by the end of 1987.

In 1984 Adia's U.S. subsidiary went public, offering 1.2 million common shares in conjunction with its Swiss parent company. Also in that year the U.S. subsidiary entered the permanent placement market, following the lead of Adia S.A., which had maintained the activities of a regular permanent employment agency in addition to its temporary business. Adia Services took part in the 1984 Los Angeles Olympics when the company won a contract to hire and coordinate 7,500 transportation workers for the games.

In keeping with Adia's policy of niche marketing, the company's U.S. subsidiary purchased eight companies in 1986 that allowed it to serve various specialized sectors of the employment field. Those businesses, such as Word Processors Personnel Service and Accountants on Call, brought with them higher profit margins on their operations than Adia's general office placement business. The company's $45 million purchase of Nursefinders, a medical staffing concern, launched Adia into the fast-growing health care industry at a time when a shortage of nurses was driving up demand and prices for their services. Each new division retained its own president and headquarters and was allowed to operate independently according to Adia's policy of decentralized control of its acquisitions.

By February 1987 Adia had operations in 16 countries. In August 1987 Adia became involved in the attempt by a British firm to take over U.S. temporary services giant Manpower. Adia offered Manpower some form of business combination that would have allowed the American firm to thwart the hostile takeover attempt, but ultimately Adia bowed out and the deal went through.

In October of that year the value of Adia's 70 percent holdings in U.S. subsidiary Adia Services, Inc., was battered, as the stock dropped dramatically in the sharp plunge suffered by the New York Stock Exchange. Overall, however, 1987 was a good year for Adia Services, as the company reported earnings of $11.4 million, up from $6.2 million the year before. The company purchased another temporary agency at the end of the year, adding Temp World, Inc., to its holdings. It also entered the market for computer professionals with its year-end purchase of Comp-U-Staff.

With more acquisitions, almost half of Adia's U.S. operations were in highly skilled, specialized fields. The company ended 1988 with record profits of $17.6 million, derived from the activities of 520 offices. Although fueled by these steady purchases, Adia experienced slower growth in the late 1980s due to the economy-wide shortage of labor. "The younger workers are shrinking in numbers," Macauley told *Personnel Administrator.* "We have to do a better job of getting the elderly worker back into the work force," he added. In an effort to do so, Adia Services introduced its "Renaissance Program" to entice workers over the age of 48 to take temporary assignments. In addition, the company increased its employee training to make use of people with low skills who might previously not have been in demand. In 1989 Adia Services also bought four more temporary agencies.

As its U.S. unit was expanding through the purchase of companies, Adia added to its worldwide operations. In 1988 and 1989 the company opened offices in three more countries, including Italy. Because Italian laws forbid the operation of a permanent or temporary employment agency such as those Adia operated in other countries, Adia entered the only business open to it in Italy, intermediary between companies wishing to place an advertisement for a new employee and the newspapers where the ad would run. In this limited fashion the company put itself in contact with the Italian labor market. International expansion continued in 1990 when Brazil, Portugal, Greece, Thailand, and Hungary were added. Morocco and Czechoslovakia were subsequently brought on board in 1991 and 1992, respectively.

In January 1989 Adia's managers, through their holding company Adiainvest S.A., sold 40 percent of the company to Inspectorate International S.A., a Swiss conglomerate that provided inspection services, security, and computer leasing. The two companies merged, and Inspectorate's owner, Werner Ray, became a major shareholder in Adia through his stock holding company, Omni Holding AG.

## MARKET LEADERSHIP IN THE 1990S

By the middle of 1990 Adia's U.S. subsidiary was reporting continued economic sluggishness and the implementation of cost-cutting measures. Adia announced that it would increase its holdings in the U.S. company to 80 percent, at an estimated cost of $37 mil-

lion, a move that would allow the U.S. company to take advantage of a tax loophole to significantly lower its tax payments. Despite this measure, economic conditions were difficult for Adia's U.S. franchise holders. A group of franchisees brought a class-action suit against Adia, charging that the company had defrauded them by distributing a falsely optimistic profit plan for its operations. Twenty-two months later a panel of arbitrators ruled that the company was not liable for the franchisees' claims.

Adia's Swiss owners also suffered financial difficulties. These culminated in February 1991 when Ray, Adia's half-owner, was forced to sell a 53 percent voting interest in the company, held by his Omni Holding company, for $612.4 million. The majority stake in Adia was sold to a German retailer, Asko Deutsche Kaufhaus AG, and to Swiss investor Klaus J. Jacobs. The new owners promptly moved to replace the company's managers. In May it was announced that Adia's current chief executive officer, along with former leader Pestalozzi and another member of the company's governing board, would be replaced by Nico Issenmann. Issenmann had previously been an executive with Jacobs's company. The change in leadership took place on June 12, 1991.

By July of that year, Adia's U.S. subsidiary had reported decreasing revenues. One month later its corporate parent did the same, announcing international revenues down nearly 8 percent from the year before, as the economic downturn continued to take its toll. By the second half of the year, Adia's U.S. division had resorted to a wage freeze, layoffs in some areas of operations, and the closing of selected branch offices. The company ended 1991 with profits down 3.6 percent. The change in command of Adia would continue in March 1992 when Macauley, the longtime president of the key U.S. subsidiary, submitted his resignation.

The lingering economic recession, especially severe in Europe, continued to place pressure on the temporary employment market. However, the sector as a whole would benefit from the changing employer-employee relationship. While the workplace in much of Europe remained tightly controlled, in the United States and elsewhere, many employers, caught up in a wave of downsizing efforts, turned increasingly to temporary staffing services providers. As the idea of permanent and even lifetime employment seemed to fade in the United States, companies also looked to temporary staffing companies to provide recruitment and screening services as well, helping to eliminate the costly expense and guesswork of the hiring procedure.

## WORLD NUMBER TWO POSITION: MID-1990S

By the mid-1990s, ECCO's sales had risen to give it the world's number two position, ahead of Adia's number three position, while both trailed industry leader Manpower Inc. Yet ECCO and Adia joined forces in 1996, merging to form Adecco S.A., a company with combined sales of $6.2 billion. Adecco's headquarters were located in Lausanne, Switzerland. ECCO founder Foriel-Destezet and Adia's Klaus J. Jacobs agreed to share the company's leadership, in a revolving chairmanship. This arrangement was resolved in 1999, however, when Jacobs took the vice chairmanship. The company recruited John Bowmer as CEO.

Adecco could claim the world leadership in its industry; however, the company remained number four in the United States, behind Manpower, Kelly Services, and Olsten Corporation. Adecco quickly went on an acquisition drive, boosting its U.S. position with acquisitions including TAD Resources International based in Massachusetts, and Seagate Associates, based in New Jersey, in 1997. The company was also expanding on the global arena, buying up Australia's ICON Recruitment, giving the company a larger share of that region's IT market. In 1999 Adecco's acquisition of Delphi Group Plc, in England, made it a leading world provider to the computer industry; the company also boosted its Asian position with the acquisition of Japan's Career Staff Co.

By the end of 1999, Adecco had reached an agreement to acquire Olsten Corporation for nearly $1.5 billion. The Olsten acquisition not only padded Adecco's world leadership position, it also placed the company in front of Manpower in the United States. By the end of 1999, the company had successfully negotiated the consolidation within its industry sector to claim the leadership position into the new century.

## THE 21ST CENTURY

In 2000 Adecco began trading on the New York Stock Exchange. This action led to some difficulties years later when the Sarbanes-Oxley Act of 2002, created after the collapse of Enron, increased the auditing responsibilities of publicly traded companies. Accounting inconsistencies in Adecco's North American operations prompted the U.S. Securities and Exchange Commission (SEC) to launch an investigation of the company in early 2004. Adecco had to delay reporting its earnings for some months, and while the investigation eventually ended in late 2005 with no charges filed or fines levied, the legal and related costs associated with the inquiry were close to €100 million. The investigation was also a fac-

tor in chairman Bowmer's decision to step down in 2004. Jacobs and Foreil-Destezet became co-chairmen following Bowmer's resignation, with Jacobs assuming the role solely in November 2005.

SEC investigation aside, Adecco grew steadily during the early part of the new decade, with total sales increasing by roughly €1 billion annually from 2003 to 2005. The company continued to expand during this time, with such actions as a 2004 partnership agreement with Fesco Shanghai, a Chinese employment agency. Chinese law placed restrictions on non-Chinese employment companies, so the partnership was required for Adecco to gain access to the massive Chinese labor market.

In 2007 Jacobs stepped down as chairman in favor of Jürgen Dormann, who had been a board member for three years. Rolf Dörig became vice chairman at the same time. Citing low trading levels, Adecco delisted from the New York Stock Exchange that same year. This move did not reduce the company's growth, as earnings reached €21.1 billion in 2007. What did shake Adecco's earning ability was the economic turmoil caused by the meltdown of financial markets in 2008. Earnings dropped that year, to €20 billion.

At the end of 2008, Dormann stepped down as Adecco's chairman and Dörig took over. While 2009 saw global markets recover, the recovery did little to spur job growth, and many countries saw their unemployment rates climb during the year. This deeply affected Adecco's earnings, as there was little need for temporary workers when regular workers were being laid off in high numbers. As might be expected, Adecco's earnings plunged, dropping by 26 percent to €14.8 billion.

Although this decrease was steep, the company scaled back operations and used its position as the world's largest employment company to weather the downturn. Adecco even continued to seek companies to acquire in order to expand its operations. In late 2009 it made an offer of $1.3 billion for the Florida-based MPS Group, a leading employment agency in the Jacksonville area. The deal was approved January 15, 2010. More acquisitions are likely throughout the 2010s as Adecco consolidates and builds upon its position at the top of the employment agency marketplace.

*Robert R. Jacobson*
*Updated, Frank Uhle; Drew D. Johnson*

## PRINCIPAL GEOGRAPHIC DIVISIONS

Australia and New Zealand; France, Switzerland, and India; Germany and Austria; Iberia and South America;

Italy and Eastern Europe; Japan and Asia; North America; Northern Europe; United Kingdom and Ireland.

## PRINCIPAL COMPETITORS

Kelly Services, Inc.; Manpower Inc.; Randstad Holding n.v.; Robert Half International Inc.; SFN Group, Inc.

## FURTHER READING

"Adecco SA Begins Trading on New York Stock Exchange," *Business Wire,* March 16, 2000.

"Adecco Continues to See an Improving Revenue Trend," Adecco Media Relations, March 3, 2010.

"Adecco Delists from New York Stock Exchange (NYSE) and Ends US Reporting Obligations," Adecco Media Relations, May 6, 2007.

"Adecco Improves Gross Margin Despite Weakening Markets," Adecco Media Relations, March 4, 2009.

"Adecco Opens Staffing Services Partnership in China," Adecco Media Relations, July 15, 2004.

"Adecco Said to Face SEC Probe Over Accounting," *Los Angeles Times,* January 14, 2004.

"Adecco to Seek NYSE Delisting," *SOX Center,* April 11, 2007.

Ammerlaan, Nieck, "Adecco Sees Strong 2000," *Reuters,* April 19, 2000.

Arbose, Jules, "Adia's Quality Route to Being World's No. 2 in Temp Help," *International Management,* February 1987.

Bergheim, Kim, "Sociology Degree Proves Useful for Adia's Macauley," *Business Journal-San Jose,* September 21, 1987.

Bernstein, James, "Olsten Sells Out to Competitor," *Newsday,* August 19, 1999, p. 57.

Greising, David, "Temp Agencies Are Praying the Slump Is Just Temporary," *Business Week,* December 11, 1989.

*Key Figures 2008,* About Adecco. www.adecco.com.

Larsen, Peter Thai, "Adecco to Form IT Staffing Giant with £167m Buy," *Independent,* February 5, 1999, p. 19.

"MPS Group Shareholders Approve Adecco's Acquisition,", Adecco Media Relations, January 15, 2010.

"MPS Group to Be Acquired by Adecco," *Jacksonville Business Journal,* October 20, 2009.

Paton, Huntley, "Adia Stands Ready for Boom or Bust," *San Francisco Business Times,* April 18, 1988.

"Rolf Dörig Newly Designated Chairman of the Adecco Group," Adecco Media Relations, November 27, 2008.

# AGL Resources Inc.

—————■—————

Ten Peachtree Place NE
Atlanta, Georgia 30309
U.S.A.
Telephone: (404) 584-4000
Fax: (404) 584-3714
Web site: http://www.aglresources.com

*Public Company*
*Founded:* 1856
*Employees:* 2,469 (Jan. 2010)
*Sales:* $2.317 billion (2009)
*Stock Exchanges:* New York Stock Exchange
*Ticker Symbol* AGL
*NAICS:* 221210 Natural Gas Distribution

■ ■ ■

AGL Resources Inc. is a leading natural gas distribution company in the United States, servicing approximately 2.3 million customers in six states (Georgia, New Jersey, Virginia, Tennessee, Florida, and Maryland). The company conducts its business primarily through the following utilities: Atlanta Gas Light (Georgia); Chattanooga Gas (Tennessee); Elizabethtown Gas (New Jersey); Elkton Gas (Maryland); Florida City Gas (Florida); and Virginia Natural Gas (Virginia). While distribution is the company's primary revenue source, AGL Resources conducts wholesale natural gas services through its Sequent subsidiary and has an

85 percent stake in South Star, a retail natural gas marketer.

## EARLY YEARS: 1856–66

Founded in 1837, Atlanta was still a newly settled town with oil lamps and dirt streets in 1855 when William Helme, a gas industry entrepreneur from Philadelphia, teamed up with the Atlanta City Council to install gas lights along the main street. Helme built a plant to manufacture natural gas from coal and laid three miles of pipeline to fuel 50 new streetlights. Each streetlight cost $21. In 1856 Julius Hayden became the first president of Atlanta Gas Light. Gas lighting became popular and soon spread to Atlanta homes and businesses. The city was happy with its investment and Atlanta Gas Light was booming.

The outbreak of the American Civil War in 1861 hit Atlanta Gas Light hard. Stock held by northern investors, including Helme, became nearly worthless. As the war continued, coal and natural gas were in short supply. Near the end of the war, General William Sherman led the Northern army into Atlanta. The gas plant initially survived the Battle of Atlanta in 1864, but Sherman's soldiers later burned the gas works to the ground, and the company went out of business in the same year.

Atlanta slowly came back to life after the war ended in 1865. Northerners came to the South, and the city began to heal and grow. Former *Atlanta Intelligencer* editor John W. Duncan was elected president of Atlanta Gas Light, and the company underwent extensive repairs, reopening its doors on September 15, 1866.

## COMPANY PERSPECTIVES

■

AGL Resources continues to build on its existing reputation as one of the nation's most efficient operators of natural gas distribution systems. By consistently providing economical and reliable service to our customers, AGL Resources serves all of our stakeholders: customers, regulators, communities, employees and shareholders. It's what we do best.

### NEW USES FOR GAS: 1877–1903

In 1877 Thomas G. Healey, a brick manufacturer and construction executive, became president of Atlanta Gas Light. Healey's first challenge came in 1884 when the Gate City Gas Works emerged and challenged Atlanta Gas Works' sovereignty by claiming that its "water gas" (a synthetically produced mixture of hydrogen and carbon monoxide) was superior to "coal gas." Gas prices plummeted by more than 50 percent within a year. Soon after, the City of Atlanta decided to sell its share of Atlanta Gas Light. After an initial investment of $20,000 in 1855, the city sold its shares in 1887 for $95,642 to fund several building projects, including what would become Georgia Institute of Technology, often referred to as Georgia Tech.

Atlanta Gas Light was dealt another blow in 1888 when the city decided to replace city gas lights with incandescent electric lights. Healey adapted by marketing the recently invented Welsbach Mantle, a combination of incombustible minerals that brightened the gas light. In the midst of this new market competition and the wholesale migration to electric lights, United Gas Improvement Company (UGI), which had already purchased Gate City Gas Works, acquired Atlanta Gas Light in 1889. Instead of facing more competition, this enabled Atlanta Gas Light to continue to grow.

With gas lights dwindling, the next step was to find new uses for gas. Atlanta Gas Light turned its efforts to marketing gas stoves and water heaters. At that time, Atlanta cooks clung stubbornly to their smoky, inefficient coal and wood-burning stoves, but Atlanta Gas Light persisted, offering a reduced rate to customers who switched to gas, and offering installed gas stoves for $10. They made little progress until there was a coal strike in 1902, at which point coal became scarce and extremely expensive. Customers switched to gas stoves in droves and this new business soon far exceeded that of gas lighting. By 1903 Atlanta Gas Light had 122 miles

of gas pipeline, 11,000 customers, and an average daily usage of 1.6 million cubic feet.

### CHANGING HANDS: 1900–30

In the first half of the 20th century, Atlanta Gas Light changed hands many times. In 1903 Atlanta Gas Light was acquired by Georgia Railway and Electric Company (GR&E) which had already centralized Atlanta's steam, street railway, and electric light and power operations. This new monopoly was very unpopular. Politicians and the media protested and called for the utilities to revert to municipal ownership.

During World War I, the U.S. government called on gas utilities to extract Tulol from gas to manufacture TNT. Initially GR&E produced a high-priced, low-BTU product, but when the Railroad Commission demanded that GR&E purchase higher quality gas, the end product improved. After the war ended, GR&E President Preston Arkwright requested, and was granted, three rate increases between 1918 and 1920, again incurring the wrath of politicians and the media. The rate increases were negated in the next few years when the Railroad Commission ordered two rate decreases.

In 1926 Southeastern Power and Light Company acquired GR&E, and it was combined with other Georgia utility holdings to become Georgia Power. Atlanta Gas Light was referred to as the "gas department" of Georgia Power until it was sold to the Central Public Service Corporation of Chicago in 1929. As Atlanta Gas Light passed from owner to owner, changes were also occurring in the gas industry. In 1929 A. E. Pierce, then president of Atlanta Gas Light, successfully acquired the natural gas rights for Atlanta, beating out competitor Southern Natural Gas of Birmingham. That same year, Atlanta Gas Light also moved onto Peachtree Street for the first time. In 1929 Atlanta Gas Light had 487 employees, a fleet of 42 vehicles, and 450 miles of pipeline.

The migration from manufactured gas to cleaner-burning natural gas revitalized Atlanta Gas Light. The company overhauled its old gas lines and created new ones to connect its lines with the Southern Natural Gas lines outside Atlanta. Atlanta Gas Light hired many new workers to convert customers' old gas appliances to accommodate natural gas. As the 1920s came to a close, Atlanta Gas Light was booming.

### INDEPENDENT AGAIN: 1930–47

Just when Atlanta Gas Light was gaining customers and experiencing a huge increase in profits, the Great Depression hit the U.S. economy. Initially, in 1930,

## KEY DATES

**1856:** Atlanta Gas Light builds its first plant.
**1903:** Atlanta Gas Light expands into gas stoves and other appliances.
**1947:** Atlanta Gas Light achieves revenues of $14 million.
**1966:** Atlanta Resources is formed as the holding company for Atlanta Gas Light and other acquisitions.
**2010:** AGL Resources sells its fiber-optic subsidiary AGL Networks to concentrate on its core natural gas businesses.

Atlanta Gas Light customer count rose 15 percent, but it fell in 1931 and 1932. The impact on Central Public Service Corporation was much greater, leading to major reorganization. It moved Atlanta Gas Light from subsidiary to subsidiary, first to United States Electric and Gas Company and then to New York-based Consolidated Electric and Gas.

In 1935 Congress passed the Public Utilities Holding Company Act (PUHCA), which prohibited companies from owning more than one integrated utility system. This legislation ultimately set Atlanta Gas Light free. From 1937 to 1941, a flurry of mergers combined Consolidated Electric and Gas with the Georgia Natural Gas Corporation, Georgia Public Utilities Company, and Macon Gas Company, all under the umbrella of Atlanta Gas Light. The new Atlanta Gas Light entity then served 102,859 customers and 28 cities and towns.

In 1941 the United States entered World War II. Nearly 350 of Atlanta Gas Light's 700 employees left to serve in the war, causing serious labor shortages. Women filled in, taking jobs as meter readers. To keep employees informed, both in service and at home, the Blue Frame newsletter was created.

In 1947, after 58 years of mergers, acquisitions, and parent company control, Atlanta Gas Light was spun off to Consolidated Electric and Gas's preferred shareholders and returned to being an independent, investor-owned utility. At that time, it served 33 incorporated cities, had 123,309 customers, and earned $14 million in revenues.

### POSTWAR BOOM: 1947–70

After the war, Atlanta Gas Light prospered. The economy was healthy and sales of gas-powered appli-ances climbed steadily. Atlanta Gas Light extended its geographic service area, covering more towns and adding more than 35,000 new customers in 1949 and 1950. Company president Rock G. Tabor responded to the booming demand by increasing the amount of gas the company received from Southern Natural Gas and contracting with another pipeline supplier, Transcontinental Gas Pipeline Corporation. Tabor also converted coal gas facilities and built peak-shaving facilities to offset shortages. New pipelines brought natural gas to customers who previously only received manufactured gas, and demand continued to rise.

In 1956, its centennial year, Atlanta Gas served 300,000 customers in 40 Georgia cities, and 74 percent of its stock was owned by Georgia residents. Parties were held all over the state and business continued to grow. By the end of 1957, Atlanta Gas Light had 322,000 customers.

In late 1960 Atlanta Gas Light appointed its first native Georgian president, Wallace L. Lee. Lee brought energy and passion to Atlanta Gas Light, motivating the sales department, emphasizing customer service, and hiring an advertising agency. At a time when the electric industry was aggressively marketing an all-electric home, Lee announced plans for a 150-mile pipeline to bring natural gas to 37 new Georgia communities. Under Lee's direction the company sold new gas-powered appliances, convinced builders to run gas lines to new homes, and cut residential rates.

Atlanta Gas Light acquired the Mid-Georgia and Georgia Natural Gas Companies in 1964, and merged with Savannah Gas Company, the oldest in Georgia, in 1966. By 1970 Atlanta Gas Light had more than 560,000 customers.

### PRICE UPHEAVAL: 1970–89

Inflation and the gasoline shortage in the 1970s halted Atlanta Gas Light's growth and put enormous pressure on the company's finances. Gasoline prices skyrocketed, and earnings plummeted from $1.61 per share in 1969 to $1.01 in 1970. Lee cut costs, tried to cover shortages, and urged consumers to conserve energy, but at the end of his tenure in 1976, circumstances were still dire.

Supply began to increase by the late 1970s, and Atlanta Gas Light saw some growth. However, the Natural Gas Policy Act of 1978, in an attempt to equalize supply with demand and protect consumers from monopoly pricing, drove gas prices up still further. Between 1978 and 1983, wholesale natural gas prices rose 159 percent. In 1985 natural gas prices were completely deregulated and began a long decline, resulting in lower prices in 1992 than in 1984.

Lee was succeeded as president by Joe T. LaBoon, who became CEO in 1980 and chairman in 1985. La-Boon emphasized service and friendliness, instituted an energy assistance program for low-income customers, and reorganized the company to better leverage its growing nonutility operations. By 1986 Atlanta Gas Light had over one million customers. In 1988 Atlanta Gas Light acquired Chattanooga Gas Light Company and began serving customers in Tennessee.

## DEREGULATION: 1990–99

In the 1990s Atlanta Gas Light faced a competitive market where consumers would have a choice of suppliers of natural gas. Although official deregulation was not enacted until 1997, by 1993 Atlanta Gas Light had suffered a $4 million loss when its largest customer, Arcadia Corporation, connected directly to the interstate pipeline and eliminated the utility. This resulted in 700 job cuts and many office closings.

However, Atlanta Gas Light rallied. On March 6, 1996, it created a new parent company, AGL Resources, Inc., which would operate not only Atlanta Gas Light, but its growing number of nonutility subsidiaries, including AGL Investments Inc., and AGL Energy Services Inc. Moving forward, the company would distribute and deliver gas through Atlanta Gas Light and sell and market natural gas through its other interests.

In 1996 the Olympics came to Atlanta, giving Atlanta Gas Light the perfect opportunity to showcase its offerings to an audience around the world. It supplied natural gas-powered vehicles for the marathon races and the Atlanta public bus system. Atlanta Gas Light engineers also worked with a team from Georgia Institute of Technology to design the Olympic torch used for the Olympic ceremonies.

In 1997, after more than 100 years of regulation by the state of Georgia, deregulation was finally enacted. Atlanta Gas Light faced competition from many other marketing companies and was looking for ways to expand its business. Eventually it became a "pipes only" company, moving from selling natural gas to distributing it only.

## THE 21ST CENTURY

The beginning of the 21st century saw AGL Resources becoming a large entity with interests beyond distributing natural gas. While it acquired Virginia Natural Gas and a controlling interest in SouthStar Energy Services, it also formed AGL Networks, a fiber-optic cable company, and Sequent Energy Management, a consulting company, to help large natural gas consumers optimize their assets.

In 2004 the acquisition of Elizabethtown Gas, Florida City Gas, and Elkton Gas spread AGL Resources' presence to six states. Its customer count was over two million. The same year, AGL Resources unveiled a new logo and received the Georgia Business Ethics Award from the Atlanta chapter of the Society of Financial Service Professionals.

In 2006 John W. Somerhalder became president and CEO of AGL Resources, inheriting a healthy, growing company. AGL Resources continued to expand into the natural gas storage market and build gas pipelines.

In 2010, AGL Resources sold AGL Networks to the Colorado-based Zayo Group, thereby concentrating on its core competencies of gas distribution, storage, and consulting. After the Copenhagen Climate Conference in December 2009, greenhouse gas emissions and energy conservation concerns heated up. Since natural gas is the cleanest-burning fossil fuel, AGL Resources predicts that it will play a vital role in the future of the United States as the nation attempts to move toward a low-carbon energy strategy.

*Andrea Newell*

## PRINCIPAL SUBSIDIARIES

Atlanta Gas Light; Chattanooga Gas Light Company; Elizabethtown Gas; Elkton Gas; Florida City Gas; Golden Triangle Storage; Sequent Energy Management; SouthStar Energy Services (85%); Virginia Natural Gas.

## PRINCIPAL COMPETITORS

Atmos Energy Corporation; Enterprise GP Holdings LP; Kinder Morgan Inc.; SCANA Corporation; Sempra Energy; Southern Company; Williams Company, Inc.

## FURTHER READING

Luke, Robert, "Planning a Growth Future: Despite Problems, Utility Believes Good Days Ahead," *Atlanta Journal and Constitution,* September 24, 1989.

"Natural Gas Firms to Compete," *Atlanta Journal and Constitution,* September 14, 1997.

Quinn, Matthew C., "AGL Sees Potential After Gas Deregulation," *Atlanta Journal and Constitution,* September 25, 1997.

Tate, James H., *Keeper of the Flame: The Story of Atlanta Gas Light Company.* Atlanta, GA: Atlanta Gas Light Company, 1985.

"Tremors in the Gas Industry: Different Rules: As Deregulation Comes Down the Pipe, Atlanta Gas and a Group of Industrial Customers Vie to Shape a New System," *Atlanta Journal and Constitution,* December 9, 1995.

# Agricultural Bank of China

No. 69, Jianguomen Nei Avenue
Dongcheng District
Beijing, 100005
China
Telephone: (86) 10 8510 9619
Fax: (86) 10 8510 8557
Web site: http://www.abchina.com

*State-owned company*
*Founded:* 1951 as Agricultural Cooperation Bank
*Employees:* 441,883 (2008)
*Sales:* RMB 211.2 billion ($3.09 billion, 2008)
*NAICS:* 522110 Companies in commercial banking

■ ■ ■

The Agricultural Bank of China (ABC) is a state-owned commercial bank offering personal, commercial, and agricultural financial services across China and internationally. The ABC has over 24,000 branches in addition to 30,000 automatic teller machines (ATMs) across China. Using a state-of-the-art information technology network, the bank is able to provide convenient and efficient services to over 350 million customers. In 2009 the ABC ranked 155 on the *Fortune* Global 500.

## EARLIEST YEARS

In 1951 the Farmers Bank of China and Cooperation Bank joined to form the Agricultural Cooperation Bank. This was the first incarnation of the ABC but would not

be the last. Since the establishment of the People's Republic of China, the ABC has had several deaths and rebirths. The year after the formation of the Agricultural Cooperation Bank the government of China merged the bank with its central bank, the People's Bank of China. Three years later, the ABC enjoyed another short life (about three years) before it was again merged into the central bank in 1955. In 1963 the government formed another agricultural bank but it existed only two years before the government merged it into the central bank. It was not until February 1979 that the government formed the ABC that managed to sustain itself.

## A NEW ABC

The Chinese government founded the ABC in 1979 to support its policy of rural reforms. In particular, the bank was to manage funds and credit to support rural development, rural credit cooperatives, and rural businesses. The ABC quickly ramped up operations as part of its efforts to support state goals. By 1981 the bank had about 2,500 branches and 23,500 operating offices. Also, the bank managed 59,500 rural credit cooperatives. The government created the rural credit cooperatives (RCCs) in the 1950s. Originally, the RCCs were grassroots banks that enabled the state to provide credit to the rural communes. In the 1970s, after the government instituted market-oriented economic reforms, the RCCs became fairly self-sufficient banks providing credit and savings accounts to rural families and enterprises.

The year 1983 brought significant bank restructuring. The government put the People's Bank of

## COMPANY PERSPECTIVES

The ABC is committed to serving agro-related sectors and dedicated to providing first-class financial services to both urban and rural clients. With full international capabilities, an innovative business model, and prudential operations, the Bank provides tailored services to communities both at home and abroad. Based on its large physical and electronic network and diversified products, the ABC is striving to build itself into a modern universal bank with a sustainable development outlook.

China as the central bank over a set of more specialized banks. The specialized banks included the Industrial and Commercial Bank of China (ICBC), the Bank of China, the China People's Construction Bank, and the ABC. The ABC, as before, specialized in loans to agriculture and rural businesses.

Rural loans became 80 percent of the ABC's loan portfolio. This loan portfolio consisted of agricultural loans, loans to rural enterprises, loans to supply and sales cooperatives, and loans for the procurement of agricultural products. These were mostly loans directed to support government policies ("policy loans"). The agricultural loans were to households to support agricultural production. The loans to rural enterprises were to promote growth of township and village enterprises. The supply and sales cooperatives were to support shopping places in the rural areas, something that became less important as market reforms took hold. Lastly, loans for the procurement of agricultural products were intended to support the purchases by state entities of agricultural products such as grain, oil seeds, and cotton. Almost all of these loans were policy loans and did not necessarily make good business sense. Many of these loans resulted in poor performing assets.

In the mid- to late 1980s the ABC began diversifying its business beyond the rural areas. Its involvement in foreign exchanges enabled the ABC to work with township and village enterprises and foreign-invested enterprises to help them grow and expand beyond Chinese borders. The bank helped these enterprises export their products. The bank also expanded into the cities, where it increased lending to state-owned enterprises and offered trust and investment services.

Around 1987 many state-owned entities became concerned about their organizational inefficiencies. The government's market reforms brought incredible growth

but the state-owned operations had not kept pace, mainly because they still operated as an administrative unit of the government. The ABC was no exception. In line with what other state-owned entities were doing, the leaders of the ABC moved towards a more corporate structure. Management would be held to certain performance goals. This included a guarantee to deliver a certain amount of taxes and profits to the government. Also, the bank would strive to reach certain reserve and loan payment goals with regard to the central bank. Lastly, the ABC was to achieve defined efficiency numbers such as deposit growth, utilization of available funds, and loan loss rate.

In 1991 the Chinese Communist Party (CCP) issued its Eighth Five-Year Plan, which covered 1991 to 1995, and it was still apparent that the main purpose of banks, including the ABC, was to further the aims of the Chinese government. The government influence and the policy loan focus of the ABC continued unchanged until banking reform in 1994.

### REFORM AND RETRENCHMENT

In 1993 the government launched a series of reforms, including in banking. The main objective of the 1994 banking reform was to differentiate the roles of each bank. The government created three banks to handle policy loans, while existing banks were to be "commercialized." The commercialized banks were to compete in the open market with the other major banks. The government established the Agricultural Development Bank of China (ADBC) to take over loans related to agricultural and rural development policies. Ultimately, the goal was to transfer all policy loans to the ADBC so that the ABC could concentrate on commercially profitable business. The ABC transferred RMB 186.1 billion worth of agricultural procurement loans to the ADBC. This transfer represented about 28.5 percent of the ABC's total loan portfolio in 1993 and significantly reduced and altered the makeup of its loan portfolio. Also, another major change to the company was the elimination of its supervisory role over the rural credit cooperatives.

During the mid-1990s the ABC instituted several internal reforms to improve profitability. It required that every branch be involved in generating business. Before, the head office, the provincial branches, and the prefectural branches were mainly administrative, overseeing the lower-level branches that were responsible for generating business. After the reform, even the head office in Beijing set up a business department to handle larger clients. The ABC also expanded its intermediary services, which covered mainly asset servicing and transactional functions. As part of a new regional

## KEY DATES

**1951:** Farmers Bank of China and Cooperation Bank merge to form Agricultural Cooperation Bank.

**1952:** Agricultural Cooperation Bank merged into People's Bank of China, the nation's central bank.

**1979:** The People's Republic of China founds a new Agricultural Bank of China (ABC).

**1994:** The Agricultural Development Bank is spun off from the ABC.

**1996:** The Rural Credit Cooperatives is spun off from the ABC.

**2009:** The ABC becomes a joint-stock company.

strategy, the city branches were allowed to have a higher loan-to-deposit ratio. The branches themselves grew in size to handle more customers and their electronic networks took precedence over rural networks. The ABC closed branches that consistently made losses or small profits. Most of these branches were in rural areas.

At the end of the 1990s the government retrenched the ABC's move toward full commercialization. Once again the government saddled the bank with policy loans, transferring RMB 236.6 billion in poverty alleviation and other policy loans from the ADBC to the ABC. The intention was to relieve the ADBC of these loans so it could concentrate on policy loans for agricultural procurement. This move slowed down the market-oriented reforms at the ABC.

### ABC LAGS IN REFORM

Around the end of the 20th century the Chinese government was in active negotiations to join the World Trade Organization (WTO). In preparation for entry to the WTO the government decided to clean up the balance sheets of its state banks before they had to face real market competition. The ABC was treated the same as the other state banks, so a total of RMB 324 billion of bad loans were transferred from the ABC to the Great Wall Asset Management Corporation, which was one of the four asset management corporations set up by the government to take over the state banks' nonperforming loans. Even with this shifting of assets, at the end of the 1990s the ABC was still burdened with a significant number of nonperforming loans.

The Chinese government initiated a new reform effort in 2003. The China Construction Bank, the Bank of China, and the Industrial and Commercial Bank of China underwent significant reforms. The government cleaned up its balance sheets and recapitalized the banks. Then, with the help of strategic investors, the government listed the banks on stock exchanges. In contrast, the ABC underwent none of these reforms, mainly because the amount of capital needed to achieve reform was significantly higher than for the other banks.

Over the previous decade the ABC had managed to expand successfully into the cities, particularly along the coastal areas. It had also moved successfully into some high-profit sectors with loans in the petrochemicals, transport, and telecommunication industries. Even after shutting down half its branches during restructuring, the bank still had the largest coverage of any bank in China. It had 24,900 branches in 2006, and its network was the most comprehensive, covering both rural and urban areas. This made the bank highly attractive to businesses whose operations covered both rural and urban areas.

Despite an effort to concentrate on the cities the bank still had a substantial rural network with over 60 percent of its branches, 51 percent of its staff, 42 percent of its deposits, and 35 percent of its loans in rural counties. The ABC still carried many unprofitable branches in its portfolio. The nonperforming loan ratio (nonperforming loans to total loans) in 2001 was 40 percent. Although the bank had lowered this ratio to 23 percent by 2006 the reduction had more to do with an increase of total loans rather than a reduction in nonperforming loans. The level of capital investment necessary to write off the nonperforming loans and bring the bank up to adequate risk level was estimated to be RMB 800 billion to RMB 1 trillion. In effect, the commercialization efforts in conjunction with the legacy from years as a rural policy institution had made the government's reform efforts a rather daunting challenge.

### A WAY FORWARD

In 2006 the government engaged in a debate on how the ABC should move reform forward. Several solutions were discussed, including a split like the one in 1994 which separated the rural loans into another institution like the ABDC but left the commercial loans with an ABC reformed as a commercial institution. Both institutions could then be recapitalized and listed on stock exchanges in due time. Another solution discussed was to split up the bank into a group of provincial banks, each refocusing its efforts as appropriate for its particular region. In the end, the government decided the ABC should go forward under four principles: Continue to serve the rural areas and support agriculture; Reform the bank as a whole, meaning no splitting of the bank into parts; Operate the bank on a commercial basis, meaning the setting of goals and performance parameters remain; Allow the ABC to choose a time to list on the stock market.

This declaration by party officials did not necessarily solve the problem since points one and three seemed in conflict. The bank was still to maintain its rural business, which was responsible for most of its poorly performing assets while operating on a commercial basis, which required the bank to achieve certain liquidity and profitability goals.

The ABC moved forward on the government's direction through risk management. The main focus of such efforts was the rural areas. The ABC initiated new plans, allowing various branch levels to test out ways to manage risk and deliver better performing loans. Through experimentation the bank tried two different approaches. The first was a microcredit program where a group of households had joint liability for a loan to a business in the community. This was similar to the famous Grameen Bank model started in Bangladesh by Nobel Peace Prize winner Muhammad Yunus. Risk was distributed among the members of the community, who now had an active interest in whether the loan was repaid. The second approach was to offer new services to farmers using information technology. Farmers could use a telephone or the Internet to settle payments. Also, the ABC offered a farmers' credit card that gave farmers easily accessible credit.

In 2008 the ABC instituted both these approaches as a way forward in aligning its rural business with its commercialization goals. The bank used different approaches for the rural and the urban markets. It pushed decision making down to the lower level branches in the rural areas and based the rural credit rating system more on qualitative factors than quantitative (e.g., financial statements). It allowed a certain amount of creativity with regard to collateral for rural loans. Lastly, the ABC simplified the application process for rural borrowers. The results were positive. Rural loans grew after a long period of stagnation, and the bank experienced very few bad loans where it instituted the new strategies.

Seeing the results, the ABC proceeded to the next step in reform, recapitalization. In October 2008 the government injected RMB 130 billion in the ABC. This gave the ministry of finance a 50 percent stake in the bank. However, the bank still had to resolve its nonperforming rural loans. Also, the bank still had to address many factors that were creating burdensome inefficiencies. For instance, it had a large number of employees and more than 24,000 branches, which added to the complexity of its operations. Regardless, the bank was on its way to listing on a stock exchange sometime in the early 2010s. The bank had much to brag about to investors. It had the largest e-banking network in China and the largest number of clients. The bank handled more than 400 million individual deposit accounts and more than 600,000 borrowers.

*Aaron Hauser*

## PRINCIPAL DIVISIONS

Agro-Related Business; BankCards; Corporate Banking; E-Banking; International Business; Personal Banking.

## PRINCIPAL COMPETITORS

Banco Santander; Bank of America Corp.; Bank of China Limited; BNP Paribas; Citigroup, Inc.; China Construction Bank; Crédit Agricole; Dexia Group; Deutsche Bank AG; HSBC Holdings; Industrial & Commercial Bank of China Ltd.; ING Group; J. P. Morgan Chase & Co.; Royal Bank of Scotland; Société Générale; UniCredit Group.

## FURTHER READING

Cheng, Yuk-Shing, "Reforms of the Agricultural Bank of China," *Chinese Economy,* September/October 2009, p. 79–97.

Shih, Victor, "Factions Matter: Personal Networks and the Distribution of Bank Loans in China," *Journal of Contemporary China,* February 2004, p. 3–19.

Xinzhen, Lan, "ABC: Last but Not Least," *Beijing Review,* April 17, 2008, p. 28–30.

Yizhen, Yang, "Foreign-funded Banks: A Grip on Their Holy Grail?" *China Today,* February 2007, p. 26–28.

# The Allstate Corporation

2775 Sanders Road
Northbrook, Illinois 60062
U.S.A.
Telephone: (847) 402-5000
Toll Free: (800) 416-8803
Fax: (847) 836-3998
Web site: http://www.allstate.com

*Public Company*
*Incorporated:* 1931 as Allstate Insurance Company
*Employees:* 36,000
*Total Assets:* $132.65 billion (2009)
*Stock Exchanges:* New York, Chicago
*Ticker Symbol:* ALL
*NAICS:* 524126 Direct Property and Casualty Insurance
    Carriers

■ ■ ■

The Allstate Corporation is the holding company for Allstate Insurance Company, the second-largest property and casualty insurance company by premiums in the United States. In 2008 Allstate controlled about 11 percent of the U.S. home and auto insurance market, second only to State Farm Insurance Companies. While the home and auto markets comprise over 90 percent of Allstate's premiums, the company also offers life, annuity, pension products, and select coverages for small and medium-sized businesses. Allstate's customers are served by 12,300 full-time "captive" (employed only by Allstate) agents, and thousands of independent agents in the United States and Canada.

## FORMED IN 1931

The idea for Allstate came during a bridge game on a commuter train in 1930, when insurance broker Carl L. Odell proposed to his neighbor, Sears, Roebuck and Co. president and CEO Robert E. Wood, the idea of selling auto insurance by direct mail. Odell suggested that selling insurance by mail could sharply reduce costs by eliminating commissions paid to salesmen. The idea appealed to Wood, and he passed the proposal on to the Sears board of directors, whose members were also intrigued by the concept. Allstate Insurance Company, named after an automobile tire marketed by Sears, went into business in April 1931, offering auto insurance by direct mail and through the Sears catalog. Lessing J. Rosenwald was Allstate's first chairman of the board, and Odell was named vice president and secretary.

The company's early success proved Odell and Wood correct with regard to cost-cutting. Selling primarily through the regular Sears catalog, Allstate took in $118,323 in premiums on 4,217 policies in 1931, with a staff of 20 employees based at Sears headquarters in Chicago. Although the company showed underwriting losses in its first two years of operation, by 1933 it earned a profit of $93,000 from 22,000 active policies. That year, the first sale made by an Allstate agent was completed from a Sears booth at the Chicago World's Fair.

In 1934 Allstate opened its first permanent sales office in a Chicago Sears store, marking the beginning of a transition from direct mail to agents as its principal avenue of sales. The use of Sears stores enabled the company to keep a lid on costs even with the added expense of agents' commissions. Allstate's growth through the remainder of the Depression was slow but steady. By 1936 the company's premium volume had reached $1.8 million. Revenue from premiums more than tripled by 1941, reaching $6.8 million from over 189,000 policies in force. In 1943 James Barker was named chairman of Allstate's board.

U.S. participation in World War II slowed Allstate's growth somewhat, since automobile production and usage were curtailed. New legislation, however, helped pave the way for a period of explosive growth that the company would experience after the war's end. In 1941, when only about a quarter of U.S. drivers had auto liability insurance, a law was passed in New York State firmly establishing the financial responsibility of drivers for damage or injuries resulting from auto mishaps. New York's law inspired a flurry of legislation in other states, and by the mid-1950s nearly every state had some sort of financial responsibility law on its books.

## POSTWAR BOOM YEARS

During the 10-year period after World War II, Allstate grew at a phenomenal pace, nearly doubling its size every two years. There were 327,000 Allstate policyholders paying premiums totaling over $12 million in 1945, and by 1955 Allstate's sales had risen to $252 million, with more than 3.6 million policies in force.

Growth was facilitated by a change in the company's structure that was implemented in 1947. That year, Allstate decentralized its operations, adopting a three-tiered structure. Research and policy development were conducted at Allstate's home office. Zone offices were created to interpret company directives, and in turn oversee the regional offices, where the programs were put into effect. Some regions were further organized into district service offices and local sales/service centers. The restructuring extended to the first non-U.S. offices as well. Allstate became an international company in 1953 when its first Canadian office opened. Along with the restructuring, the 1947 introduction of the Illustrator Policy, which simplified

the language of policies and added pictures to enhance customers' understanding of their coverage, facilitated growth.

During the 1950s Allstate became more than an auto insurer. Throughout the decade, Allstate expanded its services to include the entire spectrum of insurance. Personal liability insurance was introduced in 1952. In 1954 Allstate began offering residential fire insurance. Commercial fire, personal theft, and homeowners' insurance were all added in 1957. Through a subsidiary, Allstate Life Insurance Company, life insurance became part of the company's package in 1957 as well. In 1958 personal health and commercial liability insurance were added to the Allstate line. By the end of the decade, boat owners, group life, and group health insurance were all being offered. A new entity, Allstate Enterprises, Inc., was created in 1960 as an umbrella for a variety of noninsurance businesses to come. Among the activities eventually conducted under the Allstate Enterprises banner were a motor club and a number of finance operations, including vehicle financing, mortgage banking, and mutual fund management.

Allstate's well-known slogan, "You're in Good Hands With Allstate," first appeared in 1950 after its creation by the company's general sales manager, Davis W. Ellis. By the end of the decade it was used in the company's first network television advertising campaign, which featured actor Ed Reimers, who would be the voice of Allstate from 1957 until 1979.

Allstate's growth throughout the 1950s paved the way for continued growth over the next few decades. Not only did the company increase its sales volume but it also increased its offerings and its operating space. In 1963 the Allstate Life Insurance subsidiary passed the $1 billion mark in insurance in force, after only six years of operation. By that time, over 5,000 agents were selling Allstate life, automobile, home, and business insurance. Two new subsidiaries, Allstate Insurance Company of Canada and Allstate Life Insurance Company of Canada, were formed the following year. In 1966 the Judson B. Branch Research Center (later renamed the Allstate Research and Planning Center) was opened in Menlo Park, California. The company's home office was moved to a new 723,000-square-foot complex in the Chicago suburb of Northbrook, Illinois, a year later. Meanwhile, Allstate continued to make additional types of insurance available to its customers throughout the decade, including workman's compensation insurance in 1964, surety bonds in 1966, ocean marine coverage in 1967, and a business package policy in 1969.

## KEY DATES

**1931:** Allstate offers auto insurance via direct mail and Sears catalog.

**1934:** Company opens first permanent sales office.

**1950:** The slogan "You're in good hands with Allstate" debuts.

**1953:** First non-U.S. office opens in Canada.

**1973:** Allstate accounts for 30 percent of earnings for parent company Sears.

**1992:** Damage from Hurricane Andrew causes company to post loss.

**1993:** Twenty percent of Allstate sells in an initial public offering.

**1995:** Sears divests itself of remaining control (80%) of Allstate.

**2008:** Global financial meltdown leads to net income loss of $1.68 billion.

## THE 1970S: DIVERSIFICATION AND INTERNATIONAL EXPANSION

By 1970 there were 6,500 Allstate Insurance agents. That year, Allstate unveiled a mutual fund. In 1972 Allstate entered the mortgage banking business by acquiring National First Corporation. The following year, the company purchased PMI Mortgage Insurance Company, marking its entry into that field. Around the same time, Allstate insurance became available through independent agents in rural areas not covered by agents working directly for the company. For 1973 Allstate generated earnings of $203 million, nearly 30 percent of parent company Sears's total.

The 1970s also saw Allstate dramatically increase its presence outside the United States. In 1975 the company entered the Japanese market through a joint venture (Seibu Allstate Life Insurance Company, Ltd.) and purchased Lippmann & Moens, a group of Dutch insurance operations. The remainder of the decade also included the formation of Tech-Cor, Inc., an auto-body research and reclamation firm, in 1976, and the establishment of a Commercial Insurance Division (later called Allstate Business Insurance) to oversee the company's commercial operations in 1978. In the same year a new wholly owned subsidiary, Northbrook Property and Casualty Insurance Company, was formed. Also in 1978, Allstate Reinsurance Co. Limited, a London subsidiary of Allstate International, was incorporated. Two new policies, the Basic Homeowners

Policy and the Healthy American Plan (life insurance), were introduced in 1978 and 1979, respectively.

Allstate was the sixth-largest insurance group in the United States by 1980. At that time, the company was operating 4 zone offices, 31 regional offices, 219 claim-service offices, 687 automobile damage inspection stations, and 2,720 sales/service centers. For 1980 the company reported $450 million in net income on revenue of $6.2 billion, as well as assets of $10.5 billion and 40,000 employees. In 1981 two Dean Witter Reynolds insurance companies, Surety Life Insurance Company and Lincoln Benefit Life Company, became part of the Allstate Life Insurance group. Allstate, Dean Witter, and Coldwell Banker joined forces the following year to form the Sears Financial Network, first appearing in eight Sears stores and later expanding to many other locations.

## THE 1980S: REORGANIZATION OF CORPORATE STRUCTURE

Donald F. Craib, Jr., was named chairman of the board of Allstate in 1982. Under Craib, a major reorganization of Allstate's corporate structure was initiated. The "New Perspective," as it was called, entailed the elimination of zone offices, as well as other streamlining and decentralizing moves. A new, more flexible life insurance plan, the Universal Life policy, was also unveiled that year. By the end of 1983, Allstate's claim staff consisted of 12,500 employees, the largest force in the industry.

In 1985 Allstate rolled out its Neighborhood Office Agent (NOA) program. In its first year, the NOA program placed 1,582 agents in 944 locations. The following year, the company launched an extensive $30 million advertising campaign that included nine new television commercials and the creation of a new tag line: "Leave It to the Good Hands People." The campaign, which extended to print and radio as well, emphasized family protection. For 1986 the company reported income of over $750 million on revenue of $12.64 billion.

A number of business insurance developments took place at Allstate in 1987. First, the company's Commercial Insurance Division and Reinsurance operation were combined under the Business Insurance umbrella. In addition, two new programs were launched in that area. The "Topflight" program created special ties between the company's Northbrook subsidiary and certain independent agents. The STAR-PAK program offered a new business package policy that provided special services such as the delivery of price quotes within five hours. Allstate also launched the Allstate Advantage Program, a three-tiered rating system for auto insurance, in 1987. A new board chairman and chief executive officer, Wayne E. Hedien, was named in 1989.

Throughout the 1980s the company had grown at a rate that could not be supported by its profits. It had roughly doubled its number of premiums during the decade, but in doing so it had burdened itself with a large number of high-risk policyholders. This growth had increased the company's costs both in terms of claims payouts and regular operating expenses. Meanwhile, the company also had to contend with customer backlash against insurance rates, including a court battle in California involving the 1988 passage of Proposition 103, which called for a rollback on premium rates. Allstate's income shrank from $946 million in 1987 to $701 million in 1990. Fiscal concerns relating to Proposition 103 were abated after the California Supreme Court ruled that insurance companies were allowed a fair rate of return.

## THE 1990S: NATURAL DISASTERS AND SPINOFF FROM SEARS

After a solid year in 1991, Allstate suffered losses from Hurricane Andrew, which afflicted serious damage on south Florida in August 1992. This natural disaster led to a net loss for Allstate of $825 million for the year, obscuring an otherwise outstanding year for the company. Subsequently, an insurance crisis developed in Florida. The Florida Legislature was unable to enact a solution the following spring, and Allstate announced a plan to not renew some 300,000 Florida property customers living in areas at high risk for hurricanes. A state-mandated moratorium on nonrenewals was imposed until November 15, 1993. On November 9, 1993, the Florida Legislature approved a catastrophe fund bill designed to protect insurance consumers and the insurance industry from the financial devastation caused by severe hurricanes. The bill enabled Allstate to renew about 97 percent of its Florida property customers in 1994.

In June 1993 20 percent of Allstate was offered to the public. The offering was an extraordinary success, generating $2.4 billion in capital. That sum was the largest ever raised in an initial public offering in the United States to that point. The separation of Allstate from Sears was part of Sears's new focus on its traditional business of merchandising. With newly found financial strength from the successful public offering, Allstate posted impressive numbers for 1993: a record net income of $1.3 billion on revenue of $20.9 billion.

A dip in profits followed in 1994, however, in the wake of another natural disaster which involved massive claims against Allstate. The Northridge, California, earthquake, which struck in January, resulted in claims totaling over $1 billion. In its wake, as had happened following Hurricane Andrew, Allstate (and most other insurers) attempted to stop writing policies for homeowners' insurance in the state, and California eventually passed legislation creating a state Earthquake Authority to help pay future catastrophe claims.

Allstate became completely independent in June 1995, when Sears gave up its 80 percent stake in the company, distributing 350.5 million shares of Allstate stock to its own stockholders. Allstate also streamlined its operations, selling off the PMI Mortgage Insurance subsidiary to raise funds for corporate growth.

Concurrent with the positives of Allstate's independence and financial success, controversies were surfacing on a number of fronts. In Texas, the company's use of Allstate-run law firms to represent claimants in court was questioned, while in California Allstate was accused of falsifying engineering reports to minimize earthquake damage claims. In several other states, attorneys general were investigating allegations that the company was overcharging single car owners for auto insurance. Additional states were examining the practice of Allstate mailing out its "Do I Need an Attorney?" pamphlet to auto accident claimants in an attempt to dissuade them from consulting an attorney. The company fought these and all such actions vigorously.

Allstate, along with a number of other insurance carriers, was also accused of "redlining," or denying insurance, to inner city and minority homeowners. In this case, the company announced it was making changes to its policy guidelines which would improve the opportunity for such customers to obtain insurance.

As Allstate moved into the 21st century, some controversies were resolved. Court rulings and regulations, for example, prompted Allstate to stop sending out its "Do I Need an Attorney?" pamphlet. However, many issues remained.

## THE 21ST CENTURY: INNOVATION AND CHALLENGES

Like most companies during the Information Age, Allstate modified many of its practices to take advantage of improvements in computer technology. For instance, Allstate installed a software program known as Colossus which was designed to evaluate claims by comparing data about a specific claim with data from previous claims of a similar nature. In theory, such software would allow Allstate to come up quickly with a settlement amount in an acceptable range.

Allstate's goal of implementing a program like Colossus was to improve the efficiency of its claims process. The financial results were certainly apparent, as the company earned high profits between 1996 and 2006. However, during this same period claims payouts (as a percentage of premium income) fell from 79 percent to 58 percent for Allstate, and from 64 percent to 55 percent for the property-casualty industry as a whole. This decrease in claims payouts coincided with an increased amount of Internet discussion regarding claims paid by Allstate and other insurance carriers. Some people grumbled that payments were too low, or that they were delayed inordinately. Whether such criticisms were valid is a matter of some debate. However, the combination of higher profits, lower payouts, and the ease with which comments can be posted on the Internet have created a situation where such criticisms spring up regularly. Every time a large calamity occurs, such as Hurricane Katrina in 2005 or California wildfires in 2007, stories surface afterwards regarding policyholders upset about the amount of their settlement.

Insurance companies also have to deal with costly calamities that are not natural disasters. As might be expected, the 2008 global financial collapse caused fiscal trouble for Allstate. The company's property and liability income diminished to a trickle, and the company's financial unit posted a net loss of $1.72 billion in 2008. This led to an overall net loss of $1.68 billion for Allstate. The company bounced back fairly well in 2009, with income from property/liability increasing almost sevenfold from the previous year. Although the financial unit continued to post a net loss, it showed signs of recovery, with losses reduced in 2009 by more than two-thirds. Overall, Allstate returned to profitability in 2009 and entered the 2010s poised to continue its role as a leading insurer.

*Robert R. Jacobson*
*Updated, Frank Uhle; Drew D. Johnson*

## PRINCIPAL SUBSIDIARIES

Allstate Financial Corporation; Allstate Insurance Company; Allstate Insurance Company of Canada (Canada); Allstate Investment Management Company; Allstate Life Insurance Company; Allstate Northern Ireland Limited (Ireland); Castle Key Insurance Company; Encompass Insurance Company; Deerbrook Insurance Company; Kennett Capital Holdings; Signature Motor Club, Inc.; Sterling Collision Centers.

## PRINCIPAL BUSINESS SEGMENTS

Protection (auto, home insurance); Financial (life insurance and other).

## PRINCIPAL COMPETITORS

Farmers Insurance Group of Companies; GEICO; Liberty Mutual Insurance Company; Nationwide Mutual Insurance Company; The Progressive Corporation; State Farm Mutual Automobile Insurance Company; United Services Automobile Association.

## FURTHER READING

Allstate Corporation. Company 10-K, 2009. http://www.sec.gov/edgar.

Berardinelli, David, *From Good Hands to Boxing Gloves: The Dark Side of Insurance*. Portland, OR: Trial Guides, 2008.

Berss, Marcia, "'We Grew Too Fast' (Allstate Insurance Improves Finances)," *Forbes*, February 13, 1995, p. 103.

Boe, Archie R., *Allstate: The Story of the Good Hands Company*. New York: Newcomen Society, 1981.

Bowe, Christopher, "New Thrift Targets 'Disenfranchised' Customers," *Wall Street Journal Europe*, December 17, 1998, p. 25.

Dietz, David, and Darrell Preston. "Home Insurers' Secret Tactics Cheat Fire Victims, Hike Profits," Bloomberg.com, August 3, 2007.

Durgin, Hillary, "Allstate IPO Scores Big," *Crain's Chicago Business*, June 7, 1993, p. 38.

————, "A New Hand Dealt to 1990s Allstate," *Crain's Chicago Business*, December 20, 1993, p. 1.

Flood, Mary, "Allstate Sued over the Use of Lawyers," *Wall Street Journal*, November 11, 1998, p. Tl.

"In Tough Hands at Allstate." *BusinessWeek*, May 1, 2006.

————, "A New Hand Dealt to 1990s Allstate," *Crain's Chicago Business*, December 20, 1993, p. 1.

Opdyke, Jeff D., "How Allstate Tried to Skirt State Laws," *Wall Street Journal*, January 4, 1995, p. Tl.

Seism, Leslie, "Allstate Relaxes Standards on Selling Homeowners' Policies in Poor Areas," *Wall Street Journal*, August 14, 1996, p. A3.

————, "Auto Insurers May Be Facing Slowdown," *Wall Street Journal*, June 5, 1998, p. Cl.

————, "To Avoid Disaster, Allstate Hands Off Home Policies," *Wall Street Journal*, July 11, 1995, p. B4.

Steinmetz, Greg, "Allstate Stock Sale Raises $2.12 Billion," *Wall Street Journal*, June 3, 1993, p. A3.

Stires, David, "SmartMoney Online: Allstate: On Shaky Ground?" *Dow Jones News Service*, May 13, 1998.

Wahl, Melissa, "Allstate President to Be Next Chairman, CEO," *Knight Ridder/Tribune Business News*, September 22, 1998.

*All your protection under one roof ®*

# American Family Insurance Group

600 American Parkway
Madison, Wisconsin 53783
U.S.A.
Telephone: (608) 249-2111
Toll Free: (800) 692-6326
Fax: (608) 243-4921
Web site: http://www.amfam.com

*Private Company*
*Founded:* 1927 as Farmers Mutual Automobile Insurance
    Company
*Employees:* 8,400 (est.)
*Sales:* $6.74 million (2008)
*NAICS:* 524113 Direct Life Insurance Carriers; 524114
    Direct Health and Medical Insurance Carriers;
    524126 Direct Property and Casualty Insurance
    Carriers; 524210 Insurance Agencies and Broker-
    ages; 524128 Other Direct Insurance (except Life,
    Health, and Medical) Carriers

■ ■ ■

The American Family Insurance Group, a *Fortune* 500
corporation since 1996, is a private mutual group that
comprises nine member companies. (In a mutual group,
members contribute funds into a common pool which is
then accessed to cover any specified losses.) Over the
years, American Family has grown from a small mutual
company serving Wisconsin farmers to a highly visible
presence in the Midwestern and Western United States,
expanding its customer base to include homeowners and
the business sector. Although the company specializes in

property and automobile insurance, it also offers life and
health coverage, along with investment and retirement
brokerage services.

## AUTOMOBILES IN THE EARLY TWENTIETH CENTURY

Americans in the early twentieth century were captivated
by the automobile. By the end of the 1920s, mass
production had made automobiles so affordable that the
public was purchasing more than four million cars a
year. Being the owner of a car, however, did not necessarily mean that a person was a competent driver. In
fact, most people took the wheel with no training or
experience at all. Unsurprisingly, as the number of drivers on the roads increased, so did the number of
automobile accidents.

In 1898 Travelers Insurance wrote the first
automobile insurance policy in the United States by
adapting a standard horse-drawn carriage policy to fit
with the specifications of a car. By 1905 a driver could
obtain liability, theft, and fire insurance for an auto. As
the automobile industry gained momentum, insurance
companies began to underwrite standardized policies
based on a car's horsepower, number of cylinders, and
weight. Additionally, many insurance companies began
to offer discounts to people they considered frequent
drivers.

Such policies offered no benefit to farmers, a large
population that was reeling from plummeting farm and
food prices in the post-World War I era. Those farmers
who did own automobiles typically stored them on
blocks for half the year because country roads were

## COMPANY PERSPECTIVES

Our mission is to be the most trusted and valued service-driven insurance company. Our commitment to you is to be fair, helpful, and caring, and to provide ease and convenience when working with us. We strive to provide you industry-leading service, an exceptional claims experience and products that build long-term relationships.

impassable due to snow in the winter and mud in the spring and fall. To insurance agent Herman Wittwer, a fledgling driver himself in the 1920s, the entire insurance situation seemed another blow to the farming community, but one that could be remedied.

### TAKING THE WHEEL: 1927–35

Wittwer, who had grown up in the dairy country of southern Wisconsin, was a traveling salesman for the Wisconsin Automobile Insurance Company of Monroe, Wisconsin. Seeking a way to reduce his time on the road, Wittwer began studying the business conducted by State Farm Mutual Insurance Company, a new company based in Illinois that was growing quickly due to its practice of offering farmers a preferred rate for auto insurance. Wittwer learned from further research that even though Wisconsin farmers owned approximately half of the state's 560,000 automobiles and had fewer accidents than people living in towns and cities, they were not offered any kind of preferred rate by area insurance companies. Wittwer saw the opportunity of an untapped Wisconsin market.

Wittwer partnered with businessman Richard Kalb-skopf in March 1927, and the two men set to work recruiting charter members for the Farmers Mutual Automobile Insurance Company, a mutual company that would sell auto insurance solely to Wisconsin farmers. On October 3, 1927, the first policyholders' meeting of Farmers Mutual was held. Wittwer's plan for handling Farmers Mutual's investments was simply to buy high-quality bonds and hold them until they matured. Many people believed that this approach was too conservative and would never result in any significant financial gain for the company. However, Wittwer's strategy proved shrewd when the stock market crash of 1929 forced a large number of insurance companies that had been more aggressive in their investments out of business.

In 1930 Farmers Mutual recognized its need to move beyond the farm market. Striking a deal with a local cattle owners' insurance carrier, Wittwer helped form the National Mutual Casualty Company, which sold automobile insurance to people who lived in small towns and cities. Three years later, Farmers Mutual and National Mutual merged under the name Farmers Mutual. Next, the company began conducting business in Minnesota. In 1935 Farmers Mutual established State Farm Mutual of Madison to sell windstorm insurance to farmers in the area. (Broadly speaking, a windstorm is a storm with high winds but little rain.) The enterprise rapidly became the leading windstorm coverage provider in the state, inspiring Wittwer to offer burglary and theft insurance as well.

### GOVERNMENTAL INFLUENCE: 1935–45

During the 1930s, the Wisconsin legislature passed various laws that affected both drivers and insurance companies. The most significant of these was a law allowing plaintiffs to name insurance companies as defendants in personal injury and property damage cases. According to the official company history, *Under One Roof: The Story of the Extraordinary Growth of American Family Insurance,* Wittwer openly objected, saying that "the cost of each claim is materially enhanced because of an insurance company's inability to get a fair deal at the hands of a jury." At the same time, state lawmakers introduced an assortment of bills requiring all drivers to carry insurance, forcing insurance companies to accept all applicants.

The insurance industry was finally granted some relief in 1935 when Wisconsin passed its "Judgment Law." This law prohibited drivers who had been found liable in an accident from driving until all claims against them were paid. Income from premiums at Farmers Mutual and its subsidiaries grew by 64 percent after the "Judgment Law" went into effect.

The entry of the United States into World War II brought new challenges to Farmers Mutual. Congress froze prices and wages all over the country, automobile factories were converted to manufacture vehicles for warfare, and Americans were given gasoline ration cards. Farmers Mutual was one of the first companies to modify its private-car classification system to correspond with the ration cards granted by the government, adjusting premiums according to how many miles policyholders should have been able to drive with the amount of gas they received.

## KEY DATES

**1927:** Herman Wittwer establishes the Farmers Mutual Automobile Insurance Company.

**1930:** The National Mutual Auto Insurance Company is formed to conduct business with the general public.

**1933:** Farmers Mutual and National Mutual merge.

**1958:** The company introduces homeowners' insurance and establishes the American Family Life Insurance Company.

**1963:** The name of the company changes to American Family Mutual Insurance Company.

**1970:** American Family merges with American Family General, a windstorm company, and forms a division that offers windstorm, farm fire, and farmowners' insurance.

**2009:** By the end of the first decade of the twenty-first century, American Family expands business operations to Nevada, Idaho, Utah, Washington, and Georgia.

### POSTWAR OPERATIONS: 1946–55

After the war, automobiles flooded the streets as factories resumed production. Americans bought cars in record numbers. Advances in automotive mechanics, such as automatic transmissions, resulted in vehicles that could go faster but cost more to repair. People were so infatuated with speed and power that Cadillac produced an automobile modeled after the P-38 fighter plane. Along with speed and power came accidents, and from 1947 to 1952, Farmers Mutual's cost per claim doubled.

In 1946 the Wisconsin legislature passed a bill that required a driver involved in an accident to present proof of insurance and put down a security deposit to cover damages, or lose the license to drive for 60 days. Consequently, people who had driven for years with no auto insurance applied for coverage in record numbers. Insurers all over the country, Farmers Mutual included, raised premiums in an attempt to counter the number of claims being filed.

In addition to driving up the cost of car repairs, postwar inflation and other factors greatly affected the cost of medical care. This economic factor encouraged Farmers Mutual to diversify further. In 1948 Farmers Mutual began to sell life insurance and sickness and accident (S&A) insurance for the Union Mutual Life Insurance Company. Farmers Mutual added fire insurance to its product offerings in 1950. These new product lines, as well as the company's automobile insurance line, prompted Farmers Mutual to spend the early years of the 1950s providing extensive training to agents so that they would be more versatile and better informed of the insurance industry as a whole.

### EXPANSION DURING DOWNTURN: 1955–65

Between 1955 and 1965, the insurance industry battled potentially devastating underwriting losses due to inflation, rigid government regulation of rates, and fierce competition. The situation was so bleak that by the mid-1960s, insurance providers all over the country had resigned themselves to accepting millions of dollars in underwriting losses. Farmers Mutual/American Family had accumulated $4.4 million in losses during the long downturn.

During the 1950s, state legislatures throughout the United States considered legally requiring drivers to carry automobile insurance. Protesting vehemently, the insurance industry proposed uninsured motorist coverage. This type of insurance would broaden medical coverage and provide death and disability payments to insured drivers who were involved in accidents with uninsured motorists. Resistant at first, Farmers Mutual became a leader in offering protection against uninsured motorists in 1957.

Also in 1957, the Farmers Mutual began offering its own sickness and accident insurance, eventually forming a separate S&A department in 1962. It began to provide homeowners' insurance in 1958. A major change in the organization of Farmers Mutual came that same year, when the company put up $2 million to form a wholly owned subsidiary that would sell life insurance. This new venture was named American Family Life Insurance Company (AFLIC) and was led by chairman Wittwer and president Irving Maurer, the two men who had been the backbone of Farmers Mutual since its earliest days. Within five years, AFLIC's sales had reached $100 million.

In 1961 many insurance companies feared government intervention in the industry once again as the American public became increasingly angered by the growing numbers of drivers unable to afford insurance. After considering their options, the Farmers Mutual board of directors voted to establish a subsidiary that would insure drivers who did not qualify for Farmers Mutual. The American Standard Insurance Company, headquartered in Wisconsin, was launched in 1961. Now, rather than canceling policies (which forced drivers to take their business to competitors), Farmers Mutual could transfer its riskier customers to American

Standard. These drivers could return to Farmers Mutual after a period of safe driving. In addition, American Standard insured young, less experienced drivers until they could qualify for coverage with Farmers Mutual, as well as elderly drivers. American Standard posted $1.3 million in premiums in its first year and soon expanded to offices in Iowa and Minnesota.

## A CHANGING IMAGE

As the reach of Farmers Mutual and its subsidiaries continued to extend, executives recognized the importance of a corporate name that would reflect the company's growth. City-dwelling policyholders outnumbered farming customers two to one by the early 1960s, and Farmers Mutual offered more than automobile insurance. Maurer proposed "American Family Mutual Insurance Company," a name he felt emphasized the company's customer base. Wittwer, however, argued that the company was at heart an organization for farmers. After market research revealed that Maurer's name was well received by the public, Wittwer consented to the change. Policyholders gave final approval to change the company's name to American Family Mutual Insurance Company in 1963.

Before the mid-1960s, Farmers Mutual had encouraged agents to work out of their homes, primarily because home offices reduced an agent's overhead expenses. As the newly renamed American Family Mutual Insurance Company worked to increase visibility, agents began to rent office space in downtown districts and shopping centers. Charlie Ambrosavage, sales promotions manager, and Bob Salisbury, advertising supervisor, spearheaded a cooperative television advertising program that introduced American Family to over two million homes.

On April 6, 1968, Wittwer died after suffering a stroke. Maurer assumed the positions of CEO and chairman of the board of directors. Under his leadership, American Family entered the finance market, and American Family Financial Services (AFFS) was opened in 1969. Within four months, AFFS had $1 million in loans, and by the end of its first year in operation this figure had risen to $2.5 million. American Family further widened its customer base in 1970 when it merged with American Family General, a windstorm insurance company, and formed a division that offered windstorm, farm fire, and farmowners insurance. More than 20 catastrophic storms in 1974 resulted in a $9 million operating loss for American Family.

However, in spite of this setback, the 1970s proved a time of overall prosperity for American Family. It became the nation's fifth-largest mutual auto insurer, and policyholders' surplus totaled $100 million in 1976, a figure that increased to $200 million in 1979. Annual life insurance sales surpassed $1 billion for the first time in the company's history. More agents, better training, and improved products and services continued to attract customers even as high rates of unemployment and the effects of inflation plagued the United States at the end of the decade.

## REMAINING AFLOAT: 1980–90

One advantage American Family had over numerous other insurance companies entering the 1980s was that it did not practice cash-flow underwriting. (Cash-flow underwriters will grant coverage to high-risk customers, discount an insurance product below its true worth, or reduce premiums in order to generate cash.) To compensate for its higher rates, American Family attracted business with new products, such as the L-95 life insurance policy for nonsmokers. American Family also introduced the Gold Star Homeowners policy, which bundled several of the company's most popular coverages, followed by policies for older homes and combined farm/ranch packages. In 1984 AFFS entered the automobile leasing market, while the health insurance division introduced a supplemental Medicare policy in 1985.

In the mid-1980s, most struggling cash-flow companies dramatically increased premiums, laid off employees, closed down agencies, and simply dropped customers with little explanation. The liability coverage market was especially affected when insurers tightened underwriting rules and rates increased anywhere from 500 to 2,000 percent. Restaurants, bars, and school districts were either unable to afford the coverage or unable to find a company willing to provide liability coverage. Once again, American Family capitalized on the shortcomings of cash-flow underwriting. The company adopted the motto "strong, growing, and friendly" as part of its objectives, and American Family's business coverage soon became the fastest-growing product in many of its offices.

Continued economic problems in the 1980s contributed to increased public resentment of insurance carriers, which in turn attracted government attention. The insurance industry as a whole suffered. Many insurance companies filed for bankruptcy, but consumer groups nonetheless accused insurance providers of profiteering. Congress responded to such charges with the Tax Reform Act of 1986, legislation that imposed higher taxes on insurance carriers. In 1987 American Family's taxes rose from $2.6 million to $9.5 million.

The American Family Group faced another setback when the stock market crashed on October 19, 1987.

On this day, known as "Black Monday," the Dow Jones Industrial Average lost more than one-fifth of its value. This plunge resulted in a loss of $57 million for American Family. At the end of 1989, American Family announced $100 million in underwriting losses on auto and homeowners' policies.

## UNDER NEW MANAGEMENT: 1990 TO 2000

In January 1990 Dale Mathwich and Harvey Pierce assumed the respective positions of chairman and president of American Family. Both men believed that one of the first orders of business was to promote American Family's process improvement program as the best way to control costs and facilitate efficiency at every level. The program streamlined operations in a variety of ways, from reducing the flow of paperwork through online communications to cutting telephone costs by installing a system that cut a penny a minute off the thousands of toll-free calls received per month. Each insurance division was charged with initiating fundamental changes to increase overall profits. For instance, a 1992 pilot program implemented in the Minneapolis/St. Paul area allowed American Family to preapprove specific body shops. Policyholders having repair work done at one of these establishments were not required to get estimates from different shops or take their vehicles to an American Family claims center before work could be done. While the program was convenient for customers, it reduced American Family's dependence on costly drive-in claims centers.

In 1994 American Family debuted its catastrophe team (CAT) trailer, a 52-foot disaster-response vehicle that served as a self-contained catastrophe headquarters. Besides office equipment, the trailer was equipped with a satellite dish to help facilitate communications during times of natural disaster. With a response time of less than 24 hours (except for trips to Colorado and Arizona), the CAT trailer allowed American Family representatives to handle policyholders' claims more efficiently than before.

American Family celebrated several milestones in the 1990s. In 1996 American Family debuted at number 403 on the *Fortune* 500, and its rank climbed each subsequent year. In 1997 American Family became the tenth-largest property/casualty insurer in the nation.

## MARKETING IN THE INFORMATION AGE

American Family continued to expand its field operations in the 21st century. The company also became involved in more corporate-sponsored community service activities. For example, it joined with the Green Bay Packers professional football team to sell pink Packers caps, raising more than $1 million for breast cancer treatment, research, and prevention. American Family was the lead donor for the American Family Children's Hospital in Madison, Wisconsin, which celebrated its grand opening in 2007.

Throughout the first decade of the 21st century, American Family broadened its customer base, making sure that agents had multicultural perspectives in their business dealings. In an interview with Tanya Irwin of MediaPost Publications, Linda Bacus, American Family's vice president of marketing, said, "American Family Insurance Group's biggest competitive advantage in a crowded market...[is] customer service."

With this in mind, American Family embarked on a 2009 advertising strategy much different from that of its competitors. As opposed to emphasizing price-driven deals, American Family joined with multiple media partners to produce interactive programs, many based on authentic stories from customers. One of these programs, "In Gayle We Trust," written by Brent Forrester of *The Office,* is an online series with a fictional main character who is an American Family Insurance agent. Supplemented by a Web site where visitors can find tips from a real-life financial expert, "In Gayle We Trust" was streamed 3.5 million times.

Another popular American Family campaign was its Teen Safe Driver Program, revealed in television commercials that began to air in August 2009. The program, explained Bacus, showed "the company's commitment to offering innovative technology, such as an in-vehicle video and audio unit that captures risky teen driving behaviors." Parents and teenagers who had the equipment installed in their vehicles could log on to a Web site for feedback, which included a driving report card, video clips, and a third-party assessment of the teenagers' performance as compared with other young drivers in the nation.

By 2010 the company had offices in 19 states: Arizona, Colorado, Georgia, Idaho, Illinois, Indiana, Iowa, Kansas, Minnesota, Missouri, Nebraska, Nevada, North Dakota, Ohio, Oregon, South Dakota, Utah, Washington, and Wisconsin. The company remained a *Fortune* 500 corporation for the entire first decade, with revenues reaching close to $6.80 million. American Family prided itself on remaining a mutual company for over 80 years, thereby ensuring that its policyholders and owners were one and the same. The mutual company sought to continue its expansion into new markets while retaining its core identity as a mutual company.

*Alicia Elley*

## PRINCIPAL SUBSIDIARIES

American Family Brokerage, Inc.; American Family Financial Services, Inc.; American Family Life Insurance Company; American Family Mutual Insurance Company; American Family Insurance Company; American Family Securities, LLC; American Standard Insurance Company of Ohio; American Standard Insurance Company of Wisconsin; Amfam, Inc.

## PRINCIPAL DIVISIONS

Auto; Home; Health; Life & Annuities; Business; and Farm & Ranch Insurance.

## PRINCIPAL COMPETITORS

Allstate Corporation; Hartford Financial Services; Liberty Mutual Insurance Group; Loews Corporation; Nationwide Mutual Insurance Company; Progressive Insurance; State Farm Mutual Automobile Insurance Company.

## FURTHER READING

American Family Insurance Group, *Under One Roof: The Story of the Extraordinary Growth of American Family Insurance.* Madison, WI: American Family Insurance Group, 1997.

Hampp, Andrew, "American Family Insurance Grows Its Family with Trust," advertisingage.com, February 8, 2010.

Hartley, Deanna, "Customer Satisfaction Through Training," *Chief Learning Officer,* February 2009, p. 44–45.

Irwin, Tanya, "American Family Insurance Focuses on Teens," mediapost.com, August 10, 2009.

Ulfelder, Steve, "Beyond the Suggestion Ox," *Computerworld,* June 27, 2005, p. 66–67.

Wolfe, Daniel, "Breaches," *American Banker,* September 15, 2006, p. 5.

# Ameriprise Financial, Inc.

1099 Ameriprise Financial Center
Minneapolis, Minnesota 55474
U.S.A.
Telephone: (612) 671-2018
Toll Free: (800) 257-8740
Fax: (888) 871-0327
Web site: http://www.ameriprise.com

*Public Company*
*Founded:* 1894 as Investors Syndicate
*Employees:* 9,793 (2009)
*Total Net Revenues* $7.8 billion (2009)
*Stock Exchanges:* New York
*Ticker Symbol:* AMP
*NAICS:* 523920 Portfolio Management; 523930 Investment Advice; 523999 Miscellaneous Financial Investment Activities; 525110 Pension Funds; 525990 Other Financial Vehicles

■ ■ ■

Ameriprise Financial, Inc., a holding company that primarily conducts business through its subsidiaries, is one of the largest financial planning companies in the United States. The company's more than 12,000 financial advisors provide financial planning products, insurance, and asset management to clients, specializing in retirement planning for the wealthy. Ameriprise Financial views its client base as those households with investable assets of greater than $100,000. The range of investment and insurance products and services available focus on helping these affluent clients prepare for the future.

The two brands used by the business in the United States are Ameriprise Financial and RiverSource. Ameriprise Financial is the name used by the company's branded advisor network, as well as some of the company's retail products and services these advisors provide, such as investment advisory accounts, retail brokerage services, and banking products. It is also the name used by the company's personal auto and home insurance products and services that are marketed directly to the consumer.

The RiverSource brand is used for the company's U.S. asset management and annuity products, as well as most of its protection products, including retail and institutional asset management products, retail mutual funds, and life and disability insurance products. International asset management products are sold under the company's Threadneedle brand.

## COMPANY FOUNDING: 1894

As a child, John Elliott Tappan learned a valuable lesson from his mother. She taught him to save his money for a big purchase, rather than spending the funds on small items. Using this advice, he saved enough to buy a pony. Watching people lose their financial stability during a depression in the 1890s taught him that saving was not always enough to promise a comfortable financial future. In 1894, as a 24-year-old Minneapolis lawyer, Tappan established Investors Syndicate, which later became Ameriprise Financial.

According to an August 27, 2001, article in *Publishers Weekly*, "Tappan applied the small town and rural door-to-door sales techniques of life insurance to agricultural banking and eventually branched out into other investment products, including insurance. With products tailored to the needs of small Midwestern investors and borrowers, the company competed successfully with larger and less personal East Coast institutions."

Tappan began with 1,000 investors, each contributing only $5. His goal was to begin a company that would enable its clients to meet their financial goals in order to realize their dreams. Tappan wanted his company to provide insurance and investment products that could meet the unique needs of each customer. This began by creating an investment certificate he called "the face amount certificate." Tappan's face amount certificate was sold at a discount, or purchasers could make small monthly payments. After a period of at least 10 years, the certificate had matured to its $1,000 face value. By establishing a regular savings routine, people were able to provide financial protection for themselves. Tappan's plans for protecting people's finances continued 50 years later with the introduction of the company's first mutual funds, followed by the development of financial planning. This product line would later develop to also include insurance and annuities.

## SUCCESS DURING DIFFICULT YEARS

Tappan's company quickly reached success. In 1914, only 10 years after the company's founding, Investors Syndicate's assets reached $1 million. In 1925, a West Coast entrepreneur named John. R. Ridgeway bought the company from Tappan and his partners. By the following year, the company had $16.27 million in assets under its management.

A few short years later, the stock market crashed. Despite the grim economy created by the Great Depression, the assets managed by the Investors Syndicate increased from $28 million to $153 million. Many at-tribute Investors Syndicate's success during such a period of financial chaos to the fact that the company's bonds were different than those of some investment firms. With no financial regulators at that time, bondholders were unaware of the health of the firms in which they invested. Bonds were often sold with maturity dates that relied on a type of lottery. Rather than following this system, Investors Syndicate incorporated flexible certificate policies that allowed investors to avoid forfeitures by taking advantage of early surrender options if necessary. Also, the company invested in real estate, allowing a greater return on the certificates than was offered by most banks.

During the 1940s, Investors Syndicate became one of the earliest companies to offer mutual funds when it established Investors Mutual. Five years later, in 1945, Investors Selective Fund was introduced as the company's mutual fund affiliate. Its objectives were to provide a stable quarterly income while conserving the value of the investment. Despite the occurrence of World War II, the company prospered during this decade. One factor contributing to its growth was a large force of company salespeople offering financial options to military personnel, many of whom were looking for a home for their savings during this period.

## EXPANDING PRODUCTS AND SERVICES

In 1949 the company name was changed to Investors Diversified Services, Inc. (IDS). During the next two decades, IDS introduced many people to its products and services. According to a March 15, 1983, article in *Financial World*, "IDS, more than anyone, was responsible for spreading the mutual fund gospel during the 1950's and 1960's, as its huge door–to–door sales force fanned out into towns and cities across the country."

The Alleghany Corporation, a company originally founded as a holding company for a family's railroad investments, and later controlled by J. P. Morgan, bought a controlling interest in IDS in 1949. This acquisition helped Alleghany remake itself as a financial force, rather than strictly a railroad company.

Investors Syndicate Life Insurance and Annuity Company, later known as IDS Life Insurance and eventually RiverSource, was formed in 1957. This added life insurance products, and later annuities, to the offerings of IDS. Over the next decade, the sales organization of IDS grew to become a very integrated network of national representatives.

In 1979 IDS became a wholly owned subsidiary of the Alleghany Corporation. Alleghany already owned 44

## KEY DATES

**1894:** Investors Syndicate is founded by John Tappan.

**1940:** Investors Syndicate enters the mutual fund market with Investors Mutual Fund.

**1957:** Investors Syndicate Life Insurance and Annuity Company is formed; the name is later changed to IDS Life Insurance Company.

**1984:** IDS Life Insurance Company is acquired by American Express; the name is eventually changed to American Express Financial Advisors (AEFA).

**2005:** American Express spins off AEFA as an independent, wholly owned company; AEFA is renamed Ameriprise Financial; company stock is introduced on the New York Stock Exchange.

percent of IDS and spent $198 million to buy the remainder of the company. By 1981 IDS was managing $6 billion in mutual funds as well as $11 million in life insurance.

### AN AMERICAN EXPRESS COMPANY

American Express Company (AmEx) bought IDS from Alleghany in 1984 for a purchase price of $780 million in cash and securities. The purchase allowed AmEx to broaden its range of clients. According to a November 20, 1989, article in *Fortune*, the chief executive of AmEx at the time, James D. Robinson, said that purchasing IDS "helped open up the savings and investment side of the equation, where we correctly anticipated growth. Whether consumers spent with the card or saved with IDS, American Express had a chance to win." IDS was renamed American Express Financial Corporation (AEFC). At the time of the sale, IDS had nearly 7,000 independent financial salespeople.

Two years later, the company expanded its hold in the insurance market. In 1986 the Wisconsin Employers Casualty Company of Green Bay was acquired by AEFC. Following the acquisition, AEFC renamed its new purchase IDS Property Casualty Insurance Company. This acquisition allowed AEFC to extend its range of products and services to include property and casualty insurance.

In 1994 assets of the company reached the $100 billion mark. The following year, AEFC changed its

name to American Express Financial Advisors (AEFA). Three years later, in 1998, AEFA bought Securities America, a broker-dealer firm that had 1,200 affiliated brokers. The purchase gave AEFA the opportunity to offer a wider range of services and employment options to its representatives, and allow them access to other financial services.

### CHANGES IN THE 21ST CENTURY

The new century brought a number of changes to AEFA. In 2000 AEFA appointed a new president and CEO. James Cracchiolo had worked with AmEx since 1982, and had served as president and CEO of American Express International Inc, and as president and CEO of American Express Travel Related Services.

In 2002 AEFA acquired Dynamic Ideas, LLC, to become part of RiverSource Investments. Dynamic Ideas specialized in quantitative analysis and portfolio optimization. At the time, Cracchiolo was quoted in *Finance and Commerce* (Minneapolis, Minnesota) as saying the acquisition expanded AEFA's "quantitative capabilities as we look to provide retail and institutional clients with a broad range of quality investment products."

Changes in 2003 expanded AEFA's international presence. During this year, the company acquired a leading British investment firm, Threadneedle, which offered investment management services throughout the United Kingdom, Europe, and the Asia-Pacific region. Following the acquisition, Threadneedle continued to operate under its own brand name.

### AMERIPRISE FINANCIAL

In October 2005 AEFA was spun off from American Express and renamed Ameriprise Financial. The company, which at this point had more than 12,000 advisors and representatives, as well as 2.8 million clients, was traded as a publicly owned company for the first time. As part of the launch of Ameriprise Financial, RiverSource was introduced as the company's money management arm, covering the product, investment, and distribution business.

Unfortunately for the company, 2005 also found Ameriprise Financial in the middle of several actions involving the National Association of Securities Dealers (NASD). In one case, NASD ordered that Securities America, a subsidiary of Ameriprise, pay a large settlement to three retired American Airlines pilots who claimed that a broker of the company misspent their retirement savings by urging them to invest in mutual funds that had high fees and trading costs. The company and the broker were liable for damages and legal fees totaling nearly $9.3 million.

In another case, 32 former Exxon employees claimed that their Ameriprise broker encouraged them to remove money invested in Exxon's investment plan, retire, and invest the same money with Securities America. In this case, NASD required Ameriprise to pay a judgment of $22 million. The company also faced fines during the same year for not supervising sales of 529 of their plans and was ordered to compensate more than 500 customers for this failure in supervision. NASD fined the company $12.3 million for giving preferential treatment to certain mutual fund companies based on the brokerage commissions offered. The Securities and Exchange Commission (SEC) sanctioned Ameriprise for actions related to the same situation.

A milestone came in 2007 when Ameriprise Financial ranked 297 on the *Fortune* 500, marking the company's first appearance on the list. Also during this year, RiverSource introduced a new series of retirement products and services to build brand awareness. However, the year was not all positive as the company also faced more penalties during 2007. Ameriprise was fined by the NASD for brokerage commission violations by Securities America and one of its brokers. The actions were a violation of NASD's rules regarding compensation for mutual funds.

## OPPORTUNITIES FOR GROWTH

During 2008 and 2009, Ameriprise took advantage of several opportunities to add to the company. Ameriprise completed its acquisition of H&R Block Financial Advisors for $315 million in 2008. The purchase of H&R Block Financial, the name of which was changed to Ameriprise Advisors Services, Inc. (AASI), added more than 900 new representatives and advisors to Ameriprise Financial's network. That same year, Ameriprise acquired J. & W. Seligman & Co. , as well as Brecek & Young Advisors, Inc. The acquisition of these two companies expanded the retail distribution and asset management capabilities of Ameriprise Financial.

Acquiring Brecek & Young increased Ameriprise's number of independent advisors by 300, giving the company a total advisor force of approximately 12,500. Acquiring Seligman increased the assets of Ameriprise by about $13 billion. The company anticipated that adding the strong investment teams of Seligman would increase the performance of RiverSource investments, which was struggling during that year. Also, adding the extensive distribution capabilities and established relationships of Seligman enhanced Ameriprise's ability to distribute its RiverSourceproducts outside the company's own advisor force.

## LOOKING TO THE FUTURE

Like many financial companies, Ameriprise suffered losses in 2008 due to the parlous economic climate. The company's net loss was $92 million, but it was able to rebound quickly and post net income of $737 million one year later. In early 2010 the company was close to finishing its acquisition of Columbia Management. Ameriprise planned to combine its U.S. business under the brand of Columbia Management when the transaction was completed. This acquisition illustrated Ameriprise's continued strategy of expanding its financial planning operations both geographically and in terms of products and services.

*Diane Milne*

## PRINCIPAL SUBSIDIARIES

Ameriprise Bank, FSB; Ameriprise Financial Services; Brecek & young Advisors, Inc.; IDS Management Corporation; RiverSource Investments LLC; Sackville Property (GP) Ltd. (UK); Threadneedle Asset Management Ltd. (UK).

## PRINCIPAL DIVISIONS

Advice & Wealth Management; Asset Management; Annuities; Protection; Corporate & Other.

## PRINCIPAL COMPETITORS

Hartford Financial Services Group; Lincoln National Corporation; MetLife, Inc.; Principal Financial Group, Inc.; Prudential Financial, Inc.; State Farm Insurance.

## FURTHER READING

"Alleghany's Delayed–action Bulge: Its IDS Salesmen Upped Their Production by 50%,"*Financial World*, March 15, 1983, p. 48.

"American Express Acquires Dynamic Ideas LLC;," *Finance and Commerce, MN,* 2002.

Gentile, Gary, "American Express Unit Buys Omaha Broker–Dealer in Restructuring Effort," *Investment Dealers' Digest,* 64, no. 6, 1998, p. 14.

"Investing in Middle America: John Elliott Tappan and the Origins of American Express Financial Advisors," *Publishers Weekly,* 248, no. 35, 2001, p. 72.

Jacobson, Robert R. and Christina M. Stansell, "Alleghany Corporation," in *International Directory of Company Histories, Volume 60,* ed. Tina Grant. Detroit: St. James Press, 2004, pp. 13–16.

"John Tappan's Investment Way Worked for Many Cash In: His Innovation and Integrity Led to a Solid Method for

Ordinary Americans to Save Money Even in Dire Conditions," *Investor's Business Daily,* July 8, 2009, p. A04.

Newport, John Paul, "American Express: Service That Sells,"

*Fortune,* November 20, 1989, p. 80.

"With James M. Cracchiolo of Ameriprise Financial Inc.," *Investment News,* 10, no. 45, 2006, p. 35.

**ancestry**.com

# Ancestry.com Inc.

360 West 4800 North
Provo, Utah 84604
U.S.A.
Telephone: (801) 705-7000
Toll Free: (800) 262-3787
Fax: (801) 705-7001
Web site: http://www.ancestry.com

*Public Company*
*Incorporated:* 1983 as Ancestry, Inc.
*Employees:* 620 (2009)
*Revenues:* $224.9 million (2009)
*Stock Exchanges:* NASDAQ
*Ticker Symbol:* ACOM
*NAICS:* 518210 Data Processing, Hosting, and Related
    Services

∎∎∎

The world's largest genealogy network, Ancestry.com helps over one million subscribers research their family histories by granting them access to an extensive collection of historical records that have been digitally reproduced, indexed, and made available online. The company works closely with national, state, and local governments; historical societies; religious institutions; and private collectors to obtain historical archives for use on their Web sites. Used around the world, Ancestry.com regularly introduces new technologies and tools or updates existing ones that facilitate online searches and social networking.

In the United States, Ancestry.com offers two subscription packages, U.S. Deluxe and World Deluxe. The popular U.S. Deluxe plan allows registered users unlimited access to Ancestry.com's entire United States collection of archives, as well as the ability to view digitized images of original documents and communicate with other Ancestry.com members. This service is available on an annual or monthly subscription basis, priced at $155.40 and $19.95 respectively (as of early 2010). Another option for research is the World Deluxe package, which gives unlimited access to Ancestry.com's global content, along with the same benefits as the U.S. Deluxe plan. The World Deluxe package costs $29.95 per month or $299.40 annually. The company's revenues, primarily from subscription fees, have grown approximately 12.5 percent annually, from $140.3 million in 2005 to $224.9 million in 2009.

On Ancestry.com, subscribers can search through birth, baptism, marriage and death records, maps, photographs, newspaper archives, and personal narratives. The collection houses over 180 million immigration records, including passenger lists from ships that arrived at U.S. ports from 1820 to 1960. Another frequently used resource is Ancestry.com's digitized United States Federal Census, available for the years of 1790 to 1930. The company also provides access to specialized databases. Using these, subscribers can search, for example, through collections of military records dating from the seventeenth century to the end of the Vietnam War. Other available databases showcase an African American Collection that includes slave narratives, a Native American Collection showing Indian

Ancestry.com's mission is to help everyone discover, preserve, and share their family history.

four-color magazine supported by outside advertising. *Ancestry Magazine,* which focused on inspiring stories and also taught family historians tips about effective research, quickly became a respected resource for researchers of their family heritages. Examples of articles that appeared in the magazine were "German Immigrants to New York," "On the Trail of the Pony Express," and "Preparing for Your Library Research Trip."

Census Schedules from 1885 to 1940, and a Jewish History Collection that contains lists of Holocaust survivors. With a World Deluxe plan, subscribers can view more than 400 years of records from London churches and the London Metropolitan Archives. International records from Germany, Australia, Canada, France, Italy, and Sweden can be accessed as well.

Ancestry.com also offers a number of other Web sites and products. Modeled after its U.S. site, Ancestry.com's international Web sites provide similar services in the language of the region. Historical records are gathered from local archive sources and digitized in their original form. Besides the United States, Ancestry.com operates country-specific Web sites for Australia, Canada, France, Germany, Italy, Sweden, and the United Kingdom. It is also expanding Jiapu.com, a site that serves China. Approximately one-third of Ancestry.com's total subscribers are located in foreign countries. Other Ancestry.com product and services include Family Tree Maker, Ancestry.com DNA, Ancestry.com Expert Connect, Mundia.com, MyCanvas.com, myfamily.com, RootsWeb.com, and Genealogy.com.

## PUBLISHING OPERATIONS: 1983–94

The roots of Ancestry.com were established in 1983, when Ancestry Publishing was incorporated under the name Ancestry, Inc., in Provo, Utah. The company initially published a genealogy newsletter but soon expanded its business to include various family history titles. In 1984, within a year of its founding, Ancestry won "Best Reference Award" from the American Library Association for *The Source: A Guidebook of American Genealogy,* the company's first published book. In 1992 Ancestry Publishing opened an e-commerce store on the Prodigy Information service, the success of which prompted the company to open additional stores on other private subscriber computer networks such as CompuServe. Among Ancestry's comprehensive library offerings were heritage books, how-to guides, family history preservation books, and historical fiction.

Even as it increasingly published genealogy books, Ancestry continued to distribute its newsletter. In 1994 the company expanded the small publication into a

## TRANSITIONS AND ACQUISITIONS: 1995–2004

Throughout its history, Ancestry, Inc., underwent a number of transitions and acquisitions. In 1995 Ancestry Publishing acquired the Internet Uniform Resource Locater (URL) Ancestry.com, and the Ancestry.com site was officially launched the next year. In 1997 Ancestry, Inc., joined Infobases Incorporated and the Western Standard Publishing Company to create a new Western Standard Publishing Company. One year later, Ancestry, Inc., changed its name to Ancestry.com, Inc., only to change its name once again in the fall of 1999, becoming MyFamily.com, Inc. The company, which was a fast-growing community Web site at the time, introduced the world's first online software allowing multiple users to contribute to their family tree at the same time.

In 2000 MyFamily.com introduced not only new acquisitions to its company profile but also new resources for family history research. In March, for instance, MyFamily.com debuted a free online library of family history instructional materials. In August it began to add images of actual federal census records to its Web site and to generate indexes to those records. By the end of the year, MyFamily.com had acquired Third Age Media, an online media and marketing service primarily for people in their 40s to 60s, and Ah-ha.com, Inc., a local search and performance advertising company. One of its most important acquisitions of the year was that of RootsWeb, a free Internet genealogy community that would function as a division of Ancestry.com into the 2010s.

MyFamily.com added its one billionth record to its Web site in January 2001. In March 2002, the company embarked on a massive project when the U.S. National Archives and Records Administration released the 1930 United States Federal Census to the general public. Within 24 hours of the release, MyFamily.com had added images from the 1930 census to its Web site, and employees were working on indexing every name in the record. This project would be completed by January 2003. In the meantime, MyFamily.com launched www.ancestry.co.uk, a Web site for subscribers in the British

## KEY DATES

**1983:** Ancestry Publishing is incorporated in Utah as Ancestry, Inc.
**1996:** Ancestry.com is launched.
**1999:** Ancestry.com changes its name to MyFamily.com.
**2003:** MyFamily.com purchases Genealogy.com, Familytreemaker.com, and the Family Tree Maker software program from the A&E Network.
**2007:** The company unveils a DNA testing service that allows customers to submit a genetic sample to be analyzed for connections in MyFamily.com's database of family histories.
**2008:** The largest online collection of African American historical records is introduced.
**2010:** Ancestry.com partners with NBC to produce the *Who Do You Think You Are?* television series.

Isles, and set forth creating indexes for Great Britain's census records, beginning with the 1891 census. As 2002 drew to a close, MyFamily.com closed a deal for the acquisition of BigHugs, a service that allowed people to search for living individuals and obtain their contact information.

In 2003 MyFamily.com purchased Genealogy.com, Familytreemaker.com, and the Family Tree Maker software program from the A&E Network. Genealogy.com provided researchers with family and local histories, vital records, and military service records. In 2004 MyFamily.com introduced Family Tree Maker desktop software. For a fee, users could construct their own family tree and make the information available online for other family historians. As of February 10, 2010, subscribers using this product had created more than 14 million family trees comprising almost 1.5 billion profiles. Close to 32 million photographs and scanned documents could be found through MyFamily.com. Subscribers could also use Family Tree Maker to collaborate with other users, upload their own records, and publish family stories for other researchers to view.

### NEW SERVICES: 2005–08

During the next two years, MyFamily.com continued to grow. In 2005 the company acquired Heritage Makers LLC, a Springville, Utah, direct-selling organization that marketed custom published products through in-home

presentations called "Heritage Celebrations" led by Heritage consultants. MyFamily.com launched a Web site for its Canadian subscribers in January 2006, followed by a Web site for Australian customers in July. In November 2006, the name MyFamily.com was changed to The Generations Network, Inc. Under this organization, the largest online collection of African American historical records to date was introduced in 2008, along with the largest collection of U.S. military records.

In 2007 the company unveiled a DNA testing service that allowed customers to submit a genetic sample, obtained with a cheek swab, which would be analyzed and then compared to DNA in Ancestry's database of family histories. Partnering with the lab Sorenson Genomics, The Generations Network claimed that a person could extend his or her family tree by using paternal and maternal DNA lineage tests to find genetic cousins. In early 2009 the cost of the test was lowered from $149 to $79.

The company operated as Generations Network, Inc., until December 5, 2007, at which time it was acquired by Spectrum Equity Investors for $354.8 million. The takeover was coordinated under the name of Generations Holding, Inc., an entity that had been created for the sole purpose of acquiring The Generations Network, Inc. As a result of that transaction, Spectrum and its affiliates held around 67 percent of the company's outstanding shares.

### INCREASED VISIBILITY: 2009 AND BEYOND

In July 2009, Ancestry.com changed its name to Ancestry.com Inc. According to the company's 2009 Form 10-K, this was in order to "better align our corporate identity with the premier branding of Ancestry.com." Family Tree Maker, MyFamily.com, MyCanvas, RootsWeb, Genealogy.com, and Jiapu.com continued to operate under the Ancestry.com umbrella. In the third quarter of 2009, Ancestry.com introduced Mundia.com, a global, multilanguage family history service to reach markets in which the company did not have a local presence. On November 5, 2009, Ancestry.com went public with an Initial Public Offering (IPO) on the NASDAQ. Over seven million shares of common stock were offered at $13.50 per share, leaving Spectrum and its affiliates with approximately 55 percent of the outstanding shares of common stock. Ancestry.com planned to use the money gained from the IPO to repay debts, as well as search for opportunities for mergers and acquisitions that would help strengthen their presence in the market.

Ancestry.com took a significant step toward increasing its visibility in 2009 and 2010. It created national television ads that were scheduled to appear on well-known cable networks and channels AMC, CNN, Fox News, the History Channel, the Lifetime Movie Network, and Hallmark, among others. The "My Story" campaign featured the stories of five Americans who had made life-changing discoveries using Ancestry.com's services. For instance, one vignette described a woman from Chicago who opened a restaurant with a cousin after finding out about their family's tradition of cooking talent. Another told the story of a man who had spent 40 years in vain searching for information about his German great-grandfather. Using Ancestry.com, he found a World War I draft registration card with his great-grandfather's name, which led him to discover that his great-grandfather had immigrated to the United States before World War I, become a U.S. citizen, and been promoted to a captain in the U.S. Merchant Marines before being killed by a German submarine torpedo during World War II. Ancestry.com executives predicted that the 15-, 30-, and 60-second television spots would inspire the everyday person to learn more about his or her heritage.

In March 2010, the series *Who Do You Think You Are?* premiered on NBC, sponsored in part by Ancestry.com. Based on a successful BBC show by the same name, *Who Do You Think You Are?* followed such American celebrities as Sarah Jessica Parker, Spike Lee, Brooke Shields, and Emmitt Smith as they were led on a quest to uncover their genealogical roots. Ancestry.com's product integration deal allowed the company to collaborate with NBC to create a series Web site that allowed people to perform a preliminary family search through Ancestry.com. In a press release issued February 25, 2010, Andrew Wait, senior vice president and U.S. general manager for Ancestry.com, explained, "Through the journeys of these celebrities, we hope millions of Americans will see just how life-changing and rewarding family history can be and begin asking themselves questions about their own roots." The company was hopeful that this type of high-profile exposure would help it

remain the leading online resource for family history and help expand its number of subscribers, both in the United States and abroad.

At the same time it explored other forms of media, Ancestry.com made moves to eliminate the major operations of Ancestry Publishing. The company ceased production of *Ancestry Magazine* in March 2010. On March 23, 2010, Ancestry.com announced a partnership with Turner Publishing, an independent publisher of genealogy titles located in Nashville, Tennessee. According to the agreement, Turner would assume control of the majority of inventory and publishing contracts from Ancestry Publishing. In addition, Ancestry.com granted Turner limited rights to use the Ancestry.com name for publishing and marketing purposes.

*Alicia Elley*

## PRINCIPAL COMPETITORS

FamilySearch.org; Geni.com; Legacy.com.; MyHeritage.com.

## FURTHER READING

"Ancestry.com Goes Public in NASDAQ IPO," wallstreetexposed.net, November 5, 2009.

"Ancestry.com Launches U.S. Military Records Collection," *Worldwide Databases,* July 2007, p. 5–7.

"Ancestry.com Parent Sold for $300 Million," *ZDNet News,* October 17, 2007.

Kundanis, Barb, "Why I Love Ancestry.com," *Library Journal,* October 15, 2008, p. 98.

MacMillan, Douglas, "Ancestry.com Hopes to Stand Test of Time," *BusinessWeek Online,* November 11, 2009, p. 12.

McNamara, Mary, "Review: 'Who Do You Think You Are?' on NBC," *Los Angeles Times,* March 5, 2010.

Ruefenacht, Lisa, "Trace Your Roots," *PC Magazine,* February 2008, p. 44.

# Appaloosa Management L.P.

51 John F. Kennedy Parkway
Short Hills, New Jersey 07078
U.S.A.
Telephone: (973) 701-7000
Fax: ( 973) 701-7055

*Private Company*
*Founded:* 1993
*Employees:* 14 (est.)
*Profits:* $7 billion (est., 2009)
*NAICS:* 525910 Other Investment Pools and Funds

■ ■ ■

Appaloosa Management, L.P.'s Short Hills, New Jersey, office is the company's headquarters; it is also the firm's only office. The company is a small, privately owned stock brokerage firm (more commonly known as a hedge fund) that serves a global clientele. In 2009, during the economic recession that hammered domestic and international financial institutions, Appaloosa Management generated approximately $7 billion in profits. Investing in failing businesses, particularly those that might be positioned for recovery even while they file for bankruptcy or receive federal aid, is the company's forte. Investors in Appaloosa Management include pension funds, insurance companies, commercial banks, financial investment firms, and institutional and individual high net worth investors.

## EARLY GOLDMAN SACHS

Appaloosa Management, L.P., was created by Jack Walton, a former Goldman Sachs asset manager, and David Tepper, a former Goldman Sachs junk bond salesman. Tepper was hired by Goldman Sachs in 1985, a decade prior to the dot-com bubble. According to the *Bloomberg* January 5, 2010, article "Tepper Turns Panic to Profits with $6.5 Billion Hedge Fund Gain," Tepper started out working on Goldman Sachs's high-yield bond desk as a research analyst. Within a year he had not only moved from research to trading, he was heading up Goldman Sachs's high-yield or junk bond desk. The speculative bonds that are generally rated BB or lower due to their high default risk can yield interest rates that are four percentage points higher than interest rates realized through safer government bonds.

Knowing which bonds to invest in was paramount to the balance sheets and continued success of Goldman Sachs. Tepper did this well. In the *Bloomberg* article, and in reference to Tepper's working days at Goldman, Richard Coons, a former Goldman Sachs colleague of Tepper's, stated that Tepper "quickly showed himself to be lead dog."

## TEPPER'S INFLUENCES

The president of Appaloosa Management, David Tepper, was born September 11, 1957, to Harry and Roberta Tepper. Harry Tepper worked as an accountant while Roberta Tepper worked as an elementary school teacher. The Tepper family, with David, Roberta, Harry, and their two other children, lived in a modest red-brick, four-bedroom house in Pittsburgh, Pennsylvania. About his upbringing, David Tepper told his college alma mater, Carnegie Mellon University (where he went to graduate school) that, "We grew up in Pittsburgh. People struggled to get by. We were, or at least we wanted to be, middle class kids."

Although he was an average kid in school when it came to academics, David excelled at football at Peabody High School and later in drama when he attended the University of Pittsburgh. As a child, David loved baseball, a passion that he not only shared with his grandfather but a passion that also revealed early glimpses of David's near photographic memory. About his passion for baseball, Tepper told Carnegie Mellon University, "I knew every player in the major league. You could pull a player's card, and I could tell you the statistics."

It was David's father, Harry, who whet his son's appetite for numbers and investments. Although Harry Tepper's interest in investments never reached the level that his son's did, Harry did make minor investments in the market. While sitting at the dinner table, he would often discuss these and other investments with his family. David listened.

Years before Tepper graduated from college, his father bought him shares in the market. Soon Tepper had a keen interest in stocks, bonds, and other market instruments. As he told Carnegie Mellon University in 2004, he was, "Interested in numbers and averages, like the baseball cards. I had a few hundred shares. Some with Pennsylvania Engineering Company, and some with Career Academies, a company that went bankrupt right after I bought the shares."

David Tepper got his bachelor of arts degree in economics from the University of Pittsburgh in 1978. He worked at the school's fine arts library to help pay for his tuition. He took some of his earnings from his work at the library and invested in the market. It was his hope that he had made the right investments. After all, he needed money to pay his way through college. The first job that Tepper accepted after he graduated from the University of Pittsburgh was at Pittsburgh's Equibank. He worked as a credit analyst in the treasury department. At the time, he was not certain whether he

wanted to pursue a career in law or in financial investments. Nonetheless, just as it had been with the baseball cards that he shared with his grandfather and those early days of investing in the market with his father, his passion for working with numbers prevailed.

Unlike his academic performance in high school, Tepper focused on his studies in graduate school at the Carnegie Mellon University School of Business and earned straight As during his first year at the university. After he graduated from Carnegie Mellon, he went to work at Evergreen Funds (formerly named Keystone Mutual Funds) in Boston, Massachusetts. It would be in Boston that Tepper would meet his wife, Marlene, a Rutgers University graduate who was in Boston working at Wang Laboratories as a project manager. Before the couple wed, Marlene's sister gave her a warning. She advised her sister to be careful that Tepper was not "after her for her money," a bit of advice that often gets a chuckle out of Tepper.

## GOLDMAN SACHS AND PARTNER

Under the leadership of Robert Rubin (who would go on to serve as President Bill Clinton's Treasury Secretary during both of Clinton's presidential terms), David Tepper continued to excel at the investment firm. While both Tepper and he worked at Goldman Sachs, Rubin worked in the fixed income department. Before he left the international investment banking and securities firm in 1992, Rubin would go on to serve as co-chairman at the firm.

Despite the growing profits that Tepper's junk bond desk yielded for Goldman Sachs, Tepper did not make partner. The first time he was passed over for partner, he attributed it to the decline in the junk bond market, a decline that was hastened after First Executive Corporation collapsed and Drexel Burnham Lambert Incorporated (two firms that invested heavily in junk bonds) filed for bankruptcy. The second time Tepper was passed over for partner at Goldman Sachs, the junk bond market had rebounded. In fact, Tepper's desk earned tens of millions of dollars in profit. This time the failure to make partner left a deeper imprint. Tepper began to wonder if he should launch out and start his own investment company.

The year was 1992. His mentor, Rubin, had moved on to enter government work, and Tepper was ready to take his bond-betting skills and become independent. Tepper and a Goldman Sachs colleague, Jack Walton, started Appaloosa Management L.P. with $57 million. A large portion of the start-up money came from professionals Tepper and Walton knew from their days at Goldman Sachs. Initially they wanted to name their

## KEY DATES

**1993:** Appaloosa Management, L.P., is founded.
**1997:** Jin Ho joins Appaloosa Management, L.P., as a general partner.
**2003:** David Tepper, Appaloosa Management, L.P.'s founder, is ranked as the second-highest-paid hedge fund manager in Institutional Investor's Alpha Ranking.
**2004:** David Tepper donates $55 million to Carnegie Mellon Graduate School of Industrial Administration.
**2009:** Appaloosa Management, L.P., generates approximately $7 billion in profits.

company Pegasus, after the winged horse from Greek mythology that was sired by Poseidon, but that name was taken. The two partners settled on Appaloosa instead.

Tepper and Walton started Appaloosa Management early in 1993 and Tepper was named president of the company. By the end of that same year, the company reported a 57.6 percent net gain. A year later, Appaloosa Management had $300 million in assets. Assets under management steadily increased each year for the company from 1993 through 1996. By 1997 Appaloosa Management was managing approximately $850 million.

## MEASURING RISKS AND HEDGING BETS

One early investment for Appaloosa Management came in 1993 when the company bought a stake in Esser Steel Algoma (formerly named Algoma Steel Incorporated). This steel-producing company, founded in 1902 by Francis Clergue in Ontario, Canada, had recently come out of bankruptcy. Betting that the firm would recover, Appaloosa Management bought Esser Steel Algoma shares for roughly 20 cents on the dollar. Later Appaloosa Management sold its shares in the rebounding steel making firm for as much as 80 cents on the dollar. This marked an early example of the firm betting on a distressed company or industry.

The year 1998 was a busy one for Appaloosa Management. The company bought stakes in several businesses across various industries including Mesabi Trust, a mineral royalty trading firm headquartered in New York. In March 1998 Appaloosa Management

bought a stake in Envirotest Systems Corporation, an automotive services firm based out of Sunnyvale, California. It also purchased shares in Aureal Semi-Conductor, Incorporated (formerly named Media Vision Technology, Incorporated) and Imagyn Medical Technologies, Incorporated, a plastics products company headquartered in Newport Beach, California. Grand Union Company, a retail grocery store business based out of Wayne, New Jersey, was another acquisition that Appaloosa Management took on in 1998.

While these domestic investments yielded financial rewards for Appaloosa Management in 1998, the firm's stake in foreign investments did not prove to be equally kind. Russian debt that Appaloosa Management bought in 1998 did not stand up against the odds. Tepper told *Bloomberg* that he thought the Russian government would not default on the debt. It did. For its risks, Appaloosa Management would realize a 29.2 percent loss for the year. Tepper learned from the downturn, but it would not be the last time that he would bank on a government to rescue its failing markets.

In 2001 Appaloosa Management bought stake in several medical firms, including Bio Plexus Incorporated, Vencor Incorporated, and Kindred Healthcare Incorporated. Tepper would serve as director of Kindred Healthcare starting in April 2001. In the deal, Tepper received 2,975,428 shares of common stock in Kindred Healthcare. In regards to another of the healthcare industry acquisitions, Scott Tepper, David's brother, served as vice chairman of Bio Plexus; Scott had helped to build Bio Plexus from the ground up starting with four employees. He began to serve as vice chairman of Bio Plexus in July 2001.

Early in the twenty-first century, David Tepper and his company continued to thrive. In 2004 he and his wife Marlene donated $55 million to the Carnegie Mellon University School of Business, the school that he credited for teaching him about business. For their donation, the university renamed its business school the Carnegie Mellon Tepper School of Business.

As the wheels started to come off the U.S. automobile industry in 2007, Appaloosa Management began to look at buying stake in Delphi Corporation, an international supplier of automotive electronics and technologies. Hours before the deal was set to close, one of Appaloosa Management's affiliate companies, Acquisition Holdings LLC, backed out. *Bloomberg Business Week* reported that Acquisition Holdings stated that Delphi had breached the deal by "entering into talks about an alternative transaction." On May 16, 2008, Delphi filed suit against Appaloosa Management and encouraged its creditors to persuade Appaloosa Management to move forward with the equity deal that was valued at $2.55 billion. A year later, Appaloosa Management was reported to have had a change of heart. In July 2009 the *New York Times* reported that Appaloosa Management was among four bidders that were interested in making an offer for Delphi.

## LOOKING TO THE FUTURE

Hedging bets is Appaloosa Management's business. As the financial markets created panic around the globe starting in late 2007 through 2009, Appaloosa Management bought stock in companies like Bank of America and Citigroup. Appaloosa Management bought the shares with the same confidence that they bought shares in the Russian debt markets in 1998. Appaloosa Management believed that the U.S. government would not let the investment companies default. This time Appaloosa Management was right, and the payoff was rewarding. In 2009 Appaloosa Management generated approximately $7 billion in profits. Tepper was reported to have pocketed between $2.5–$4 billion of that amount. He used some of his fortune to become part owner in his hometown's professional football team, the Pittsburgh Steelers.

In the early 2010s Appaloosa continued to invest in various businesses and holdings. The Securities and Exchange Commission began an investigation of Appaloosa that year over possible short-selling in 2008. While this investigation could potentially negatively impact the company, David Tepper's track record as a hedge fund manager remained one of the strongest in the business.

*Rhonda Campbell*

## PRINCIPAL COMPETITORS

Berkshire Hathaway; Bridgewater Associates Inc.; JP Morgan Chase & Co.; Paulson & Company; Quantum Endowment.

## FURTHER READING

"Appaloosa Management Buys Airlines," seekingalpha.com, February 19, 2010.

Bailey, David, and Soyoung Kim, "Appaloosa Backs Out of Delphi Deal in Blow to GM," *Reuters,* April 4, 2008.

"Creditors of Delphi Corp. Seek to Intervene in Litigation Against Appaloosa Management L.P.," Bloomberg Businessweek, Bloomberg.com, June 2, 2008.

"David Tepper," cityfile.com.

Schwartz, Nelson D., and Louise Story, "Pay of Hedge Fund Managers Roared Back Last Year," *New York Times,* March 31, 2010.

"Stuyvesant Town Foreclosure: Appaloosa Management, Hedge Fund, Seeks Control," Huffington Post.com, April 27, 2010.

Teitelbaum, Richard, "Tepper Turns Panics to Profits with $6.5 Billion Hedge Fund Gain," Bloomberg.com, January 5, 2010.

Wachman, Richard, "Tepper Pips Paulson to Hedge Fund Peak," guardian.co.uk, April 2, 2010.

"Wall Street Wizard David Tepper 'Learns It, Earns It and Returns It' with Record-breaking $55M Gift," *Carnegie Mellon Today,* 1, 2, June 2004.

# Arch Capital Group Ltd.

—■—

**Wessex House, 45 Reid Street**
**Hamilton HM 12,**
**Bermuda**
**Telephone: (441) 278-9250**
**Fax: (441) 278-9255**
**Web site: http://www.archcapgroup.com**

*Public Company*
*Founded:* 1995 as Risk Capital Holdings, Inc.
*Employees:* 1,345 (2010)
*Net income:* $851.1 million (2009)
*Stock Exchanges:* NASDAQ, New York
*Ticker Symbol:* ACGL
*NAICS:* 524126 Direct Property and Casualty Insurance
Carriers; 524128 Other Direct Insurance (except
Life, Health, and Medical) Carriers; 524130 Rein-
surance Carriers.

■ ■ ■

Arch Capital Group Ltd. (Arch Capital, or ACGL) is a
Bermuda-based company that writes insurance and reinsurance for mid-sized to large companies worldwide
with offices in the United States, Canada, Europe,
Australia, and South Africa. ACGL concentrates on two
main underwriting segments: insurance and reinsurance.
ACGL writes insurance and reinsurance for specialty
lines including property, energy, technical risk, aviation,
casualty, general and product liability, workers'
compensation, automobile, construction and surety,
medical professional liability, design professional and
environmental liability, and travel and accident. Its

insurance subsidiaries include Arch Insurance Group
(US), Arch Insurance Canada, Arch Excess & Surplus
Insurance Company, Arch Specialty Insurance
Company, Arch Indemnity Insurance Company, and
Arch Insurance Europe. Arch Capital's reinsurance
subsidiaries also span the globe, including Arch Reinsur-
ance Ltd. (Bermuda), Arch Reinsurance Company
(United States), and Reinsurance Europe Underwriting
Limited.

## BEGINNINGS: 1995–2000

Risk Capital Holdings, Inc., was founded in Delaware
in March 1995. In August 1995, the *New York Times*
reported that the company's first initial public offering
(IPO) failed after investors rejected the stock twice in a
single month. In response to this sluggish demand, Risk
Capital Holdings cut its offering by $40 million (14
percent). In September 1995 it successfully completed
an IPO of its common stock.

In its business plan, Risk Capital planned to use the
funds raised by the stock offering to invest in several of
the insurance companies to which it issued reinsurance.
(When a company offers reinsurance, it contracts with
another insurance company to insure its insurance policies in order to spread the risk so that one company
does not assume all of the financial exposure.) In
November 1995, Risk Capital's wholly owned
subsidiary, Risk Capital Holdings Reinsurance, was
founded in Nebraska. The U.S. economy was booming,
and RCHI's goal was to become a global reinsurance
company with the help of its largest investor, Marsh &
McLennan Capital, Inc., part of the global insurance
brokerage Marsh & McLennan.

## COMPANY PERSPECTIVES

Arch Capital Group seeks to increase shareholder value through three main strategic principles: selectively pursue diverse specialty markets where we can apply our knowledge and expertise; maintain flexibility and responsiveness to allow us to take advantage of market opportunities when they arise; and maintain a disciplined underwriting approach to enable us to select risks and price them appropriately in all phases of the insurance cycle.

Risk Capital Reinsurance engaged in three main types of transactions: reinsurance, various forms of financing (including investments), and a customized combination of reinsurance and financing. Risk Capital believed several factors helped it serve its customers well. As a new company, it could respond to customer needs with more agility and flexibility and less bureaucracy than an older company. Its small staff, supplied with recent technology and motivated by high compensation, worked with more fluidity. Its vast underwriting capacity and diverse investment portfolio allowed Risk Capital to provide reinsurance to more companies. Its management had good relationships with many in the industry, which led to reinsurance and investment opportunities.

In October 1998 Risk Capital Holdings, Inc., formed a new subsidiary, Cross River Insurance Company, which was only licensed to underwrite policies in its home state of Nebraska. This small expansion did little to help the company's bottom line, as, Risk Capital's net income floundered during the last half of the decade, from $4.11 million in 1996, to $2.03 million in 1997, $3.09 million in 1998, and finally posting a loss of $32,436 in 1999.

### NEW OWNER, NEW NAME: 2000

In May 2000 Risk Capital Holdings sold its entire reinsurance holdings to Folksamerica Reinsurance Company (a division of White Mountains Insurance Group). The trade publication *National Underwriter Property & Casualty-Risk & Benefits Management* reported that Risk Capital gave in to pressure from shareholders to sell due to poor earnings and business decisions. In addition, the article claimed that one of the factors Risk Capital banked on to serve its customers, its status as a new company, contributed to its downfall. Customers were more interested in an older, more established firm, in theory, than an unproven new business.

Elizabeth Farrell, an assistant vice president in A.M. Best Company's property-casualty division, commented that Risk Capital's setbacks had caused a loss of confidence by shareholders and the market as a whole. She cited Risk Capital's infancy as the probable cause, stating that a company with only a five-year history was not able to weather these issues as well as a more established company.

After the merger, White Mountains and Folksamerica became Arch Capital Group Inc. (USA). Peter Appel was appointed president, replacing Mark Mosca. Arch Capital Group Ltd. was formed in September 2000 and moved its base to Bermuda to take advantage of more favorable tax laws and an easier entrée into the international reinsurance market. On November 8, 2000, Arch Capital completed a reorganization that put Arch Capital Reinsurance (formerly Risk Capital Holdings) under its umbrella as a wholly owned subsidiary.

### HUGE GROWTH: 2001–05

Beginning in 2001, Arch Capital began creating and purchasing new entities, launching a period of tremendous growth. In May 2001 Arch Capital formed Arch Reinsurance Ltd., a Bermuda-based insurance and reinsurance subsidiary. In June 2001 Arch Capital acquired Arch Risk Transfer Services Ltd., which brought with it Arch Insurance Company (USA), an insurer in all 50 states, Puerto Rico, the U.S. Virgin Islands, and Guam, with an office in Canada. In February 2002 Arch Capital purchased Arch Specialty Insurance Company, an approved excess and surplus lines insurer in 49 states, Puerto Rico, and the U.S. Virgin Islands. (Excess and surplus lines of insurance are employed when standard forms and rates are not applicable. These are typically niche markets.)

In June 2003 came Arch Indemnity Insurance Company, an admitted insurer in 49 states. In August 2003 Constantine "Dinos" Iordanou, already on the board of directors and CEO of Arch Capital Group Ltd (USA), became president and CEO of Arch Capital Group Ltd. (Bermuda). In subsequent years Iordanou continued to grow the company, expanding into Europe, Australia, and South Africa.

Arch Capital's first foray into the European insurance market came in May 2004, when Arch Insurance Company (Europe) Limited, based in London, received approval from the Financial Services Authority in the United Kingdom to begin insurance underwriting activities. During the third quarter of 2004, it began writing a variety of specialty lines in Europe and the UK.

## KEY DATES

**1995:** Risk Capital Holdings founded.
**2000:** Risk Capital Holdings merges with Folk-samerica and becomes Arch Capital Group.
**2005:** Hurricane Katrina and several other natural disasters devastate the insurance market.
**2009:** Constantine Iordanou becomes chairman of the board, in addition to serving as president and CEO.
**2010:** Arch Capital posts first quarter losses after more weather-related disasters including the Chilean earthquake.

## NATURAL DISASTERS AND DEVASTATION: 2005

The worldwide insurance industry is highly competitive but as a whole is subject to the same variations and risk factors. The market fluctuates in waves during which a hard market (high premiums, restrictive underwriting standards, narrow terms and conditions, and underwriting gains) persists for a period of time and is then followed by a soft market (low premiums, loose underwriting standards, broad terms and conditions, and underwriting losses), and back again. In addition, financial results are impacted by many circumstances, including the frequency and severity of claims, catastrophic events and natural disasters, fluctuations in financial markets and interest rates, changes in the law, inflation, and the general economic climate.

Arch Capital continued its expansion plans in early 2005 when Arch Insurance Company (USA) obtained its federal license to begin underwriting in Canada. However, during the latter half of 2005, Arch Capital suffered financial setbacks due to several severe U.S. natural disasters. During the spring and summer of 2005, a drought plagued the Midwest region of the United States, damaging a significant percentage of crops in Arkansas, Illinois, Indiana, Missouri, Ohio, and Wisconsin and causing more than $1 billion in damages.

Beginning in July 2005, a series of devastating storms battered both the United States and the insurance industry. In July Category 3 Hurricane Dennis swept the western Florida panhandle causing flooding and wind damage along the Florida and Alabama coasts, and in Georgia, Mississippi, and Tennessee. Damages totaled more than $2 billion. On August 28 Category 3 Hurricane Katrina hit New Orleans, Louisiana. The storm surge was more than 25 feet, causing the levee system to fail and resulting in more than 1,800 deaths, the most since a hurricane hit south Florida in 1928. It was also the costliest natural disaster in U.S. history to date, with $125 billion in damages.

Over the next two months the storms continued to come. In September Hurricane Rita struck the Texas-Louisiana border, and in October, Hurricane Wilma hit southwestern Florida, each causing more than $16 billion in damages. The insurance industry suffered significant losses, which ultimately led to more stringent rating agency capital requirements for businesses with catastrophe risks. Another unexpected result of the 2005 storms was the deceleration of premium rate decline in many insurance lines, along with marked improvements in market conditions for certain marine and property lines of business. For the 2005 fiscal year, Arch Capital posted a net income of $256.9 million, compared to $316.9 million in 2004.

## RECOVERY AND MORE GROWTH: 2006–09

In 2006 Arch Capital bounced back, earning a Zacks.com #1 best value stock in September and again in December, its value increasing by 10 percent in that time frame. In September Jeffrey Goldstein, formerly of World Bank, was appointed to the board of directors. In November, Arch Capital registered Arch Reinsurance Ltd., the Swiss branch of Arch Re Bermuda, with the commercial register of the Canton of Zurich and began underwriting in Switzerland. In 2007 Arch Capital formed Arch Re Accident & Health ApS (Arch Re Denmark), specializing in accident and health underwriting.

The global economy suffered a significant downturn in 2008, but Arch Capital continued to expand its business. In January Gulf Investment Corporation (GIC) partnered with Arch Capital to form Gulf Reinsurance Limited in the Dubai International Financial Centre. GIC is owned equally by Bahrain, Kuwait, Oman, Qatar, Saudi Arabia, and the United Arab Emirates, the six member states of the Gulf Cooperation Council (GCC). By May, Arch Capital supplied $100 million of funding to Gulf Re, satisfying its joint venture agreement with GIC. Also in 2008, Arch Capital formed Arch Reinsurance Europe Underwriting Limited, underwriting a new line of business in excess workers' compensation and employers' liability insurance, and Arch Re Europe, based in Dublin, Ireland.

In 2009 Arch Capital stretched into Australia and South Africa. Lloyd's Franchise Board and Financial Services Authority (UK) granted approval to establish a managing agent and syndicate at Lloyd's of London. Arch Syndicate 2012 began business during the second quarter of 2009. Two more subsidiaries were formed to underwrite on its behalf, Arch Underwriting at Lloyd's (Australia) Pty Ltd, based in Sydney, Australia, and Arch Underwriting at Lloyd's (South Africa) Pty Limited, based in Johannesburg, South Africa. AUAL Australia opened for business in the fourth quarter of 2009 and AUAL South Africa in the first quarter of 2010. In November Constantine Iordanou was appointed chairman of the board of directors of Arch Capital. That same month, the board of directors authorized Arch Capital to invest up to an additional $1 billion dollars in the company's common shares.

### ANOTHER SETBACK: 2010

In early 2010, the insurance industry was hit again by a group of weather-related catastrophes. In March, Arch Capital announced first-quarter losses due to fallout from the earthquake that struck off the coast of Chile on February 27, a windstorm that swept France and Germany, and hailstorms and floods in Australia. The earthquake caused the most destruction, but all together Arch Capital estimated there was more than $65 million in damages.

After only 10 years, Arch Capital could still be considered a young company, but unlike Risk Capital Holdings, in its ten years it had built a solid track record of good financial decisions and shown consistent growth. The fact that Arch Capital was headquartered in Bermuda might also be an added benefit. The Bermuda Insurance Report 2010 reported that the Bermudian economy remained strong and its large insurance community had proved to be resilient. Despite more losses due to natural disasters, Arch Capital seemed well positioned to weather these setbacks and continue to grow.

*Andrea Newell*

### PRINCIPAL SUBSIDIARIES

Arch Capital Group Inc. (USA); Arch Capital Services Inc. (USA); Arch Europe Insurance Services Ltd. (UK); Arch Excess & Surplus Insurance Company (USA); Arch Indemnity Insurance Company (USA); Arch Insurance Group Inc. (USA); Arch Re Accident & Health ApS (Denmark); Arch Re Facultative Underwriters Inc. (USA); Arch Reinsurance Company (USA); Arch Reinsurance Europe Underwriting Limited (Ireland); Arch Reinsurance Ltd.; Arch Specialty Insurance Company (USA); Arch Underwriting at Lloyd's (UK, Australia, Republic of South Africa).

### PRINCIPAL DIVISIONS

Insurance; Reinsurance.

### PRINCIPAL COMPETITORS

ACE Limited; Allied World Assurance Company; Argo International Holdings, Ltd.; AXIS Capital Holdings Limited; Berkshire Hathaway, Inc.; Chartis, Inc.; Chubb Corporation; Endurance Specialty Holdings Ltd.; Everest Re Group Ltd.; Fairfax Financial Holdings, Ltd.; Hannover Rückversicherung AG; Harbor Point Limited; The Hartford Financial Services Group, Inc.; HCC Insurance Holdings, Inc.; Montpelier Re Holdings Ltd.; Munich Re Group; PartnerRe Ltd.; Platinum Underwriters Holdings, Ltd.; RenaissanceRe Holdings Ltd.; Swiss Reinsurance Company; Transatlantic Holdings, Inc.; The Travelers Companies; Validus Holdings Ltd.; W.R. Berkley Corp.; XL Capital Ltd; Zurich Insurance Group.

### FURTHER READING

"Arch Capital: 1Q Quake, Storm Costs Near $65 Million," *Associated Press*, March 23, 2010.

Aspatore Books Staff, *Inside the Minds: The Insurance Business– Industry Leaders on Managing Risks, Ensuring Investments, and Protecting Assets*. Boston, MA: Aspatore Books, 2004.

"Company News; Another Reinsurer's Initial Offering Runs into Trouble," *New York Times*, August 24, 1995.

"Risk Capital Holdings to Sell Reinsurance Operations to Folksamerica for $361 million," *National Underwriter Property & Casualty-Risk & Benefits Management*, January 24, 2000.

Archipelago Learning

# Archipelago Learning, Inc.

**3400 Carlisle Street, Suite 345**
**Dallas, Texas 75204**
**U.S.A.**
**Toll Free: (800) 419-3191**
**Fax: (877) 592-1357**
**Web site: http://www.archipelagolearning.com**

*Public Company*
*Founded:* 2000 as Study Island Holdings, LLC
*Employees:* 221 (2009)
*Revenue:* $42.77 million (2009)
*Stock Exchanges:* NASDAQ
*Ticker Symbol:* ARCL
*NAICS:* 611710 Educational Support Services

■ ■ ■

Archipelago Learning, Inc., is a subscription-based on-line education company offering standards-based lessons, practice, and assessment to help improve the performance of both educators and students. The company's core product line, Study Island, provides activities to help students in kindergarten through high school master grade-level learning standards, which are specific to their state. Products teach skills in reading, math, language arts, writing, social studies, and science. Products addressing national standards for technological literacy, health, and fine arts are also available.

The company originally developed its products to meet the learning standards of a single state (Ohio) but has since expanded into all 50 states and Washington D.C. Another product line, Northstar Learning, provides remediation, practice, and test preparation activities for post-secondary learners. The majority of Archipelago Learning's revenue is through sales of subscriptions to Study Island, which are generally purchased by individual schools, at a cost of approximately $3 to $10 per student. Usually, schools pay for these subscriptions using general funds, grants, or private donations.

The company offers products that address the increased focus on high academic standards in education, teacher accountability for student progress, and formative assessments used to gauge student learning and drive instruction. The predominance of technology in students' education and personal lives has made Web-based learning tools an effective way to improve educational performance.

## THE INTRODUCTION OF STUDY ISLAND: 2000–01

Study Island was founded in Ft. Lauderdale, Florida, in 2000 by Cameron Chalmers and David Muzzo, who invested $4,000 to launch their new venture. Chalmers, a computer scientist, and Muzzo, an economist and marketer, wanted to develop an online educational program that would help students with a variety of learning styles and abilities master academic content.

Chalmers's and Muzzo's goal for Study Island was to provide activities that would keep students engaged, require them to put effort into their own learning, teach them to overcome academic challenges, build confidence, and help them achieve success. The partners studied research, observed students, and noted learning

## COMPANY PERSPECTIVES

Archipelago Learning provides online high-impact, low-cost educational solutions designed to help educators and students improve performance and do so in a fun and engaging manner.

obstacles in order to develop a product that would best meet the needs of students. Originally, they chose to focus on developing products to address Ohio's academic standards for reading and math, which were being revised and made more challenging at the time. They created the Web application and wrote the academic content that was included in the online activities. The activities allowed students to study by reviewing mini-lessons on various topics, playing interactive games, or taking practice quizzes in the format of multiple choice standardized tests.

When the company's first product was introduced, students and teachers were pleased with the results. Students were engaged in the activities and improving their reading and math skills while having fun. The self-paced programs allowed students to take control of their own learning. Incorrect answers were immediately addressed, allowing students to learn from their mistakes. Teachers were able to customize instruction to meet the needs of individual students and use real-time reporting to monitor progress, tailor instruction, and keep parents and administrators informed of student growth. Within 10 years, about half of all schools in Ohio were using Study Island.

Following the launch of Study Island's products in Ohio, Chalmers and Muzzo introduced the line to schools in Illinois during the same year. By the end of 2000, the company was providing its online educational tools to students in two states and had a total of two employees. The following year, Study Island products were introduced in Texas and Oklahoma. Two field-based educational consultants were hired in Oklahoma and Illinois, and the company's headquarters were relocated to Dallas, Texas. By the end of 2001, Study Island products were being used in four states, and the company had a total of four employees.

### CHANGES IN EDUCATION: 2001

The reauthorization of the Elementary and Secondary Education Act, or ESEA, by the U.S. Congress in 2001 impacted education and the demand for Study Island products. This act, also known as No Child Left Behind, required that states receiving federal funding for education establish high academic standards for students in third grade through high school in the areas of reading, math, and science. The legislation also required states to establish benchmarks at each grade level and monitor students' progress toward these benchmarks each year. The goal of the legislation was that all students show proficiency at grade level by the year 2014.

Many schools were unable to meet Adequate Yearly Progress, or AYP, milestones during the first few years following the reauthorization of ESEA. Consequently, school administrators needed to find tools that would help their students meet the requirements of the new, more stringent academic standards and the annual assessments. The demand for standards-based educational products to help improve students' progress greatly increased, positioning Study Island to expand by offering solutions to the challenges faced by educators and students alike. Since each of the company's products was explicitly designed to address the requirements of a grade-level subject area for a specific state, they were able to offer instruction and review of the skills being assessed for AYP.

### NATIONWIDE EXPANSION: 2002–08

Study Island continued its growth and expansion during the next few years. By the end of 2002, the company's products were being used in a total of seven states, including New York. By the end of 2003, the company was involved in the education of students in 13 states, including California. During 2004 the company focused on enhancing the products available to the states it was currently serving and did not expand into any new states. However, the hiring of several new field-based educational consultants increased the company's employees to 24. The following year, Study Island launched its products in seven new states, including Florida, bringing the total number of states served by the company to 20. By the end of the year, the company employed 35 people.

Not only did Study Island launch its products in three new states during 2006, it also released the beta version of its benchmarking product in four of its current states. The company also developed its inside telephonic/Webinar educational and consultant team and initiated its training department. By the end of the year, the company was serving approximately three million students in 7,800 schools in 23 states, and employed 56 staff members. Also during this year, *Inc.* magazine named Study Island as one of the top small

## KEY DATES

**2000:** Study Island is founded by Cameron Chalmers and David Muzzo.
**2006:** Study Island is named one of the top small businesses of the year by *Inc.* magazine.
**2007:** Providence Equity Partners becomes the majority investor in Study Island.
**2008:** Study Island products are used in all 50 states and Washington D.C.
**2009:** Archipelago Learning is introduced as the corporate name for Study Island and the newly introduced Northstar Learning.

businesses of the year. Annual revenue for the six-year-old company exceeded $10 million.

Study Island continued its rapid growth in 2007. In January, Providence Equity Partners in Rhode Island, a private equity firm, became the majority investor in Study Island. This recapitalization provided the company with extensive financial resources to support continued growth and expansion. A new CEO, Tim McEwen, joined the executive management team. Prior to joining Study Island, McEwen was CEO of Harcourt Achieve, Inc., and president and CEO of Thomson Learning's Higher Education and Lifelong Learning Groups, now Cengage Learning. During 2007 Study Island's products were launched in 12 new states, bringing the company's products to a total of 35 states. By the end of the year, Study Island's staff had doubled from the previous year, with a total of 125 employees. Revenue for 2007 was more than $18 million.

By 2008 Study Island was a leader in online education for students in elementary through high school. By the 2008–09 school year, Study Island products were being used by about 8.9 million students in 21,000 schools in all 50 U.S. states and Washington D.C. In a February 18, 2008, article in the *Oregonian,* a middle school math coach explained that her school used Study Island as an intervention with about 100 struggling students. For approximately one year, these students used the program for nearly an hour every other day over a period of six weeks. These students "gained an average of three points in reading and math on state tests in 2007—considered a significant gain among educators."

During this year, Study Island acquired TeacherWeb. This Web site portal and teacher productivity tool offered educators simple templates for creating Web sites for their classroom, school, or school district. Also during 2008, Study Island was awarded a designation in *District Administration* magazine's Readers' Choice Top 100 Products of the year. (This trade publication focuses on school district administration.) Revenue for Study Island in 2008 was $31,415,000.

### A YEAR OF CHANGE FOR THE COMPANY: 2009

A number of significant changes occurred within the company during 2009. Most notably, Study Island Holdings, LLC, became Archipelago Learnings Holdings, LLC, and Archipelago Learning was introduced as the company's new corporate name and brand identity. The name combined Archipelago, meaning "a group of islands," and the idea of "islands of educational excellence" linked to the company's core product, Study Island, while leaving room for future acquisitions and the development of new product lines.

The Northstar Learning product line was introduced for post-secondary learners in April 2009. These products were similar to those provided by Study Island for school-aged students, and were also based on the belief that increased student effort and engagement leads to improved learning. These online programs were developed to provide instruction, review, practice, assessment, and test preparation for adult learners, and they include products to help test takers prepare for all subject areas assessed on the GED exam. Northstar Learning products were also introduced to help incoming college freshmen review basic math and English skills as well as content in select first and second year math, science, and history college courses. Other products were introduced to help students prepare for health career licensure exams in 10 allied health programs, and to help teachers prepare for the PRAXIS assessments required for certification.

In addition to introducing Northstar Learning in 2009, the company focused on expanding its existing products for high-school level students and adding new products for kindergarten through eighth-grade students. Archipelago Learning also expanded into three provinces in Canada, making its kindergarten through twelfth grade products available outside of the United States for the first time. Study Island Canada products were launched in Ontario, Alberta, and British Columbia.

In October Archipelago Learning sold TeacherWeb to Edline, LLC. Archipelago Learning had previously made an investment in Edline. This investment, as well as the sale of TeacherWeb, allowed Archipelago to focus on further growing Study Island. In an October 31,

2009, press release, McEwen stated, "Divesting Teacher-Web will enable Archipelago Learning to focus on its core standards-based content product lines." He continued, "We are growing rapidly and want to devote our efforts to continually improving products and services for our existing 20,000 school customers and expanding operations to reach even more students and parents in the months and years ahead."

One of the other significant changes in the company took place on November 25, 2009, when Archipelago held an initial public offering (IPO) of its common stock and began trading on the NASDAQ. Prior to the IPO, Archipelago Learning Holdings, LLC, became a wholly owned subsidiary of Archipelago Learning, Inc., as part of the corporate reorganization. Archipelago Learning sold 6.25 million shares during its initial public offering and earned $103.12 million in total gross proceeds. Following this, Providence Equity Partners still owned 48.9 percent of the shares of the company.

## NEW PRODUCTS AND REVIEW OF THE CORE PRODUCT LINE: 2010

In January 2010 Archipelago Learning introduced Study Island SAT to provide SAT preparation for students. Like Study Island's other products, this new line was designed to provide Web-based review. Students review SAT content and strategies at their own pace, and can repeat the program as many times as needed during the one-year subscription period. According to *TendersInfo*, January 27, 2010, McEwan explained, "Many SAT review programs are simply too expensive for schools to provide for all students or for parents to purchase for their children, particularly in these tough economic times. Unfortunately, this results in an unfair advantage for those students from higher socioeconomic homes where parents can afford expensive programs." Study Island SAT was introduced as an affordable, user-friendly option for all students.

In April 2010 the company introduced Study Island ACT, which provided similar benefits to the Study Island SAT program. According to *Globe Newswire*, "A core aspect of Study Island ACT is the use of animated, interactive instructional videos that train students on key test-taking strategies and help them avoid common pitfalls. This approach is designed to be as effective as having a live coach or taking a class."

## THE FUTURE OF EDUCATION AND ARCHIPELAGO LEARNING

In 2010, despite an uncertain economy and the uncertainties in the future of educational laws and funding, Archipelago Learning continued to thrive. According to a company press release, McEwen said, "While the school funding environment remains challenging, this is an exciting time to be involved with the K-12 public education sector. We believe that our Study Island products are well positioned for this dynamic period of educational reform driven by school budget pressures, a rapid shift from print to online digital educational solutions, the integration of curriculum and assessment, and the demand for cost-effective differentiated instruction to improve student performance."

*Diane Milne*

## PRINCIPAL SUBSIDIARIES

AL Midco, LLC; Archipelago Learning Holdings, LLC; Archipelago Learning, LLC.

## PRINCIPAL DIVISIONS

Study Island; Northstar Learning.

## PRINCIPAL COMPETITORS

Cengage Learning; Houghton Mifflin Harcourt Company; John Wiley & Sons, Inc.; The McGraw-Hill Companies, Inc.; Pearson Digital Learning; Reed Elsevier Group; SchoolNet, Inc.; Tom Snyder Productions, Inc.

## FURTHER READING

Archipelago Learning, Inc., "Archipelago Learning, LLC Completes Sale of Teacherweb to Edline, LLC," archipelagolearning.com, October 31, 2009.

"Archipelago Learning, Inc," Bloomberg Businessweek.com.

Blackmun, Maya, "For-Profit Company Teaches to Test," *Oregonian*, February 18, 2008.

Huber, Joe, "Product: Study Island," *Technology & Learning*, 30, no. 9, 2010, p. 22.

"New Study Island ACT Gives Students a Flexible, Affordable Way to Prepare for ACT Exam," *Globe Newswire* April 13, 2010.

"United States: Archipelago Learning Introduces Study Island SAT," *TendersInfo*, January 27, 2010.

# Associated Banc-Corp

1200 Hansen Road
Green Bay, Wisconsin 54304
U.S.A.
Telephone: (920) 491-7000
Toll Free: (800) 236-8866
Fax: (920) 491-7090
Web site: http://www.associatedbank.com

*Public Company*
*Founded:* 1970
*Employees:* 4,784 (2009)
*Sales:* ($285.1 million) (2009)
*Stock Exchanges:* NASDAQ
*Ticker Symbol:* ASBC
*NAICS:* 522110 Commercial Banking

■ ■ ■

Associated Banc-Corp (Associated) is a bank holding company located in Green Bay, Wisconsin, with 300 branches in Wisconsin, Illinois, and Minnesota. Associated is the second-largest bank holding company in Wisconsin, offering banking and wealth management services.

Banking services (loans and deposit products) encompass the largest segment of Associated's revenues. Loan products include home equity loans and lines of credit, mortgage, education, personal, and installment loans. Deposit products include checking, savings, and money market deposit accounts; IRA accounts; certificates of deposit; and safe deposit boxes.

Wealth management services include personal and business insurance products; full-service, online, and discount investment brokerage; trust/asset and investment management; administration of pension, profit-sharing and other employee benefit plans; and estate planning.

## ORIGIN AND GROWTH: 1970–99

During its first 30 years, Associated aggressively pursued acquisitions as its growth strategy, increasing from $240 million in total assets to $12.5 billion by the end of 1999.

Associated Banc-Corp was created by a merger of three of the oldest banks in Wisconsin. Associated Banc-Corp was actually incorporated in 1964, but it remained inactive until 1969 when it received approval from the Federal Reserve to acquire three banks. These banks were First National Bank of Neenah, Kellogg-Citizens National Bank of Green Bay, and Manitowoc Savings Bank. John M. Rose of Kellogg-Citizens became the president of the new entity. He remained in that position for only a short time (until 1975), but he remained active at the bank for much longer, keeping an office at Associated until his death in 2003.

The First National Bank of Neenah was founded in 1861 by Robert Shiells of Edinburg, Scotland. Shiells settled in Milwaukee, Wisconsin, in 1849 after receiving a degree from Dollard College. Shiells was one of the original engineers for the first railway in Wisconsin. Upon the railway's completion, he settled in Neenah and opened a private bank.

## COMPANY PERSPECTIVES

With locations across Wisconsin, Illinois, and Minnesota, Associated Bank is focused on being the preferred provider of financial services for the businesses and individuals in the communities we serve.

Kellogg-Citizens National Bank, originally named Kellogg National Bank, was founded in 1874 by Rufus B. Kellogg. Kellogg was a prominent figure in Green Bay and founded the city's first public library, now named Brown County Library.

The Manitowoc Savings Bank was founded in 1884 by John Schuette. Schuette came from Oldenburg, Germany, and settled in the United States in 1848 with his parents. Schuette also organized the electric light company in 1889 and served as state senator and mayor of Manitowoc.

After combining these three old banks into a new entity, between 1979 and 1996 Associated sought acquisitions to expand its presence and increase its asset base. The first two acquisitions, Kimberly State Bank (1979) and the State Bank of De Pere (1985), were both in Wisconsin. In 1987 Associated purchased the State Bank of Chicago, marking its first move outside Wisconsin. Over the next five years, Associated purchased nine banks in Minnesota, Illinois, and Wisconsin. By 1996 Associated's asset base totaled $4 billion.

It was, however the latter half of the 1990s when Associated achieved the most explosive growth. In 1997 Associated carried out its largest merger to date, merging with First Financial Corp. to create an $11 billion bank. In 1999 Associated carried out five more mergers, further solidifying its foundation in Minnesota and Wisconsin. The acquisitions of Riverside Bank and Windsor Bancshares added five Minnesota branches and $521 million to Associated's portfolio. Three Wisconsin mergers (First National Bank of Sturgeon Bay, Farmers State Bank, and Citizens Bank in Shawano) followed. By the end of the century Associated totaled $12.5 billion in assets.

### RECORD EARNINGS: 2000–05

For the first five years of the 21st century, Associated continued to achieve robust earnings, although it faced challenges including increased interest rate risk and portfolio diversification issues. In 2000 and 2001, Associated carried out efforts to reduce its exposure to interest rate risk. Interest rates, the primary driver of revenue for banks, follow the movements of the Federal Reserve's adjustment of key rates. In 2000 interest rates were at historic lows, squeezing profit margins. Associated balanced its portfolio with fewer mortgage loans and more consumer and business loans. In addition, Associated followed an industry trend by instituting fees for overdrafts, ATM use, and other services. Fee revenue became a major revenue source for Associated in 2001.

Associated continued its growth through acquisitions in the first five years of the century. In 2002 Associated acquired Signal Financial Corporation. Signal Financial Corporation added $1.1 billion in assets to Associated's portfolio and expanded its presence in the Twin Cities and southeastern Minnesota regions. In 2004 Associated purchased First Federal Corp., a move that added in-store banking (banks in supermarkets) to Associated's product mix. In 2005 Associated acquired State Financial Bank, adding 29 banking offices in Wisconsin and Illinois.

Continuing efforts to focus on revenue not tied to the interest rate, Associated focused on its wealth management products with acquisitions of two insurance carriers: CFG Insurance Services of Minnesota in 2003 and Jabas Group of Wisconsin in 2004. The acquisitions added several new lines of business to the company, including medical and dental plans, flexible spending accounts, and business insurance products. At the end of 2004, Associated was the largest insurance company in Wisconsin and one of the top 50 in the United States.

In 2002 Associated announced a change of management, preparing for the retirement of CEO Robert Gallagher at the end of 2003. Gallagher, 61, had been with Associated for over 30 years, holding the CEO title since 2000, having replaced long-time CEO Nick Conlon, who had held the position since 1975. Gallagher's replacement, Paul S. Beideman, came from Mellon Bank, where he had worked for 14 years. Gallagher remained as chairman of the board until 2006 and as a director until April 2009, when he reached the mandatory retirement age.

At the end of 2005, Associated's net earnings of $320 million marked the eighth year of record earnings. Both interest and noninterest income increased significantly. Loans had increased 9.5 percent. As Associated continued into 2006, the company's future looked positive.

## KEY DATES

**1970:** The company is incorporated with the acquisition of three Wisconsin banks.

**1987:** Associated Banc-Corp acquires the State Bank of Chicago, the company's first move outside Wisconsin.

**1997:** Company merges with First Financial Corp., doubling its asset size to $11 billion.

**2004:** Associated acquires First Federal Capital Bank, adding 92 banking offices, including 50 supermarket locations.

**2008:** Associated receives $525 million in TARP funds.

**2009:** Company posts worst financial results in its history due to severe loan losses.

## FIRST SIGNS OF TROUBLE: 2006–07

After eight years of record earnings, Associated's earnings decreased in 2006 and 2007. Although the decreases were slight, Associated found itself continuing the search for revenue sources other than interest income. In 2006 net earnings totaled $316 million, a 1.1 percent decrease from $320 million in 2005. The decrease was due to a net interest income decrease of 0.4 percent and noninterest expenses increasing 3.3 percent. Associated attributed this increase in expenses to a larger operating base from 2005 acquisitions. However, noninterest income increased 1.5 percent. In 2007 net income fell again due primarily to the fall of interest income and the increase of noninterest expenses.

In late 2006 Lisa Binder joined the management team as president and COO. Binder came to Associated from Mid-Atlantic and Midwest regions of Citizens Financial Group, where she was the director of retail banking. Binder and Beideman worked together at Mellon Financial Corp. until 2003 when Beideman left for Associated.

In 2007 Associated continued to experience a challenging environment. While consumer loans increased 51 percent, interest income decreased again. Associated continued to pursue noninterest sources of revenue from noninterest sources, such as brokerage and deposit account fees. Associated made a small acquisition, First National Bank of Hudson, adding eight branches in Wisconsin and $400 million in assets.

The exceptional 51 percent increase in consumer loans may have been a red flag for management. While these loans should have generated significant interest income, instead they set Associated up to experience its most challenging years in its history as the U.S. and world economies suffered, and loan losses increased at unprecedented rates.

## BAILOUT AND RESTRUCTURING

As Associated entered 2008, the banking industry suffered severe setbacks as the real estate and construction industries bottomed out. Furthermore, the automobile industry suffered bankruptcies that trickled throughout the economy. The banking industry, long warned of taking on too many high-risk loans, faced systemwide failure without government intervention.

Although still profitable, in November 2008 Associated applied for and received a $525 million loan from the federal government as a part of the Troubled Asset Relief Fund (TARP), commonly referred to as bailout funds. Associated endured criticism from customers and the community, and was compelled to cancel an annual vacation for its top-performing employees.

The year 2009 proved to be the most difficult in the company's history. As the balance sheet deteriorated, Associated restructured its top management. On May 15, 2009, Lisa Binder, president and COO, abruptly resigned from Associated. Binder was the expected successor to chairman and CEO Paul Beideman. Beideman announced his retirement soon after. In the 2009 annual report, Binder and Beideman's departures were explained as part of a reorganization to thwart financial deterioration. In November Associated announced that Phillip B. Flynn had been chosen as the new CEO and president. Flynn came from Union Bank of San Francisco, where he had served for 30 years, and as president and COO since 2005.

Addressing the company's difficult situation, Flynn stated in the 2009 annual report, "The global, U.S., and our own regional economies have experienced nearly unprecented challenges, and the impact on our company has been severe. Associated Banc-Corp reported its worst financial results ever." Associated reported a net loss of $285 million before taxes. The primary driver of the loss was a $751 million write-off of uncollectable loans. The company attributed the loan losses to the deterioration of its construction and real estate portfolios.

In November 2009 Associated entered into a Memorandum of Understanding (MOU) with the federal government. The MOU required the bank to meet more stringent credit criteria and increase its capital by March 31, 2010. Related to this undertaking,

Associated reviewed its portfolio to revalue loans of most concern, and it wrote off $395 million.

The company faced other hurdles in 2010. On April 2, a lawsuit was filed against Associated, charging that Associated used manipulative practices when assessing overdraft fees. The lawsuit was similar to class-action lawsuits filed against other large banks such as Wells Fargo, Bank of America, and Wachovia.

While Associated was not alone in pursuing and accepting high-risk loans, its position as a diversified financial services entity somewhat absorbed its risk of failure. However, increased government scrutiny and at-risk loans were both significant challenges to overcome. The FDIC, in response to the higher risk of insuring bank deposits, increased its assessment fees in 2009. For Associated, this expense increased from $2.5 million in 2008 to $42 million in 2009.

In the early 2010s, Associated expected to begin returning to its former strength by prioritizing repayment of TARP funds, pursuing growth opportunities, and continuing to review problem loans. Loan losses were expected to remain high, but not as high as in 2009. In addition, Associated generated funds in 2010 with an offering of $478 million in common stock, completed on January 15. Further reorganization efforts included the creation of a new position, chief strategy officer. On February 10, 2010, Associated announced the appointment to that position of Oliver Buechse, formerly chief strategist for Union Bank in San Francisco.

*Sara K. Huter*

## PRINCIPAL SUBSIDIARIES

Associated Bank, National Association; Associated Trust Company, National Association; Banc Life Insurance Corporation; Financial Resource Management Group, Inc.; First Reinsurance, Inc.; IQuity Group, LLC; Kellogg Asset Management, LLC; Riverside Finance, Inc.

## PRINCIPAL DIVISIONS

Banking; Wealth Management.

## PRINCIPAL COMPETITORS

Bank of America Corporation; Marshall & Illsley Corporation; TCF Financial Corporation; U.S. Bancorp.; Wells Fargo.

## FURTHER READING

Browning, Dan, "Judge Dismisses Lawsuit Against Associated Bank; Judge: Associated Bank Had No Duty to Non-customers Who Lost Money in Apparent Fraud Scheme," *Star Tribune,* April 9, 2010.

Landy, Heather, "PEOPLE," *American Banker,* August 28, 2009.

Prestegard, Steve.,"Full Service in the Truest Sense of the Word," *Marketplace,* January 2, 2001.

————, "Associated Banc-Corp Acquires CFG Insurance Services, Inc," *Business Wired,* April 1, 2003.

Treleven, Ed, "Lawsuits Question Overdraft Fees," *Wisconsin State Journal,* April 6, 2010.

# Auchan Group

40, avenue de Flandre
BP 139
Croix, 59964
France
Telephone: (+33) 3 20 81 68 00
Fax: (+33) 3 20 81 69 09
Web site: http://www.auchan.com

*Private Company*
*Founded:* 1903
*Employees:* 243,000 (2009)
*Sales:* EUR 39.67 billion (2009)
*NAICS:* 445110 Supermarkets and Other Grocery (Except Convenience) Stores

■ ■ ■

Auchan is one of the world's top retail and distribution groups. Privately owned by the founding Mulliez family, Auchan also has long held a policy of opening its shares to its employees, who owned 12.3 percent of the company in 2009.

The Group's four primary business segments include hypermarkets, supermarkets, Banque Accord, and Immochan. The Auchan empire is based on the group's 526 hypermarkets, vast stores that combine traditional supermarkets with a department store concept in huge spaces ranging upward to 100,000 square feet. The group's core business interests are represented by the hypermarket segment that accounted for more than 80 percent of revenue in 2009. The supermarket segment represented 17 percent of the

group's revenues that same year. The group's stores trade primarily under the Auchan (hypermarket) and Atac (supermarket) banners in France, where the group posts significant sales, but also under other names on the international scene, primarily in Spain, Portugal, Russia, Poland, and Italy. The company's Banque Accord segment specializes in the provision of financial services. The Immochan segment deals with property development and management.

In addition to Auchan, the Mulliez family also controls various other businesses including Decathlon, the largest sporting goods chain in Europe, and Leroy Merlin, a chain of home improvement superstores. Although company founder Gérard Mulliez retired from active mangement of Auchan in 2006, his son and other relatives continue to lead the retail empire.

## INHERITING THE RETAIL GENE IN THE 1960S

The Mulliez family founded its first company, Phildar, in 1903. At first a manufacturer of textiles, Phildar turned to the retail sector in 1946, when it trademarked the company name and began to develop its Phildar brand name of textiles and knitting and sewing supplies. The company turned toward franchising to expand its distribution network, licensing the first Phildar franchise store in 1956. Phildar grew to become one of the largest textiles distributors in the world, and by the end of the 20th century the company's network included 1,500 stores.

Besides textiles, Phildar also produced Gérard Mulliez, one of French retailing's major figures in the 20th century. A self-proclaimed autodidact, Mulliez never completed high school, but instead went to work, at first in manufacturing, becoming a foreman in the family's textile dye shop before managing the company's knitting factory. At the start of the 1960s, Mulliez decided to go into business for himself. In 1961 Mulliez, then 29 years old, opened his first store, a grocery, in Roubaix, in a neighborhood known as the "haut champs" (or high fields). Pronounced "oh-cham," this first retail location soon gave its name to what was to become the Auchan retail empire.

Mulliez's first store failed, however. Rescued by his family, Mulliez determined to stay in retailing. Taking his inspiration from Edouard Leclerc, the former priest turned founder of the E. Leclerc retail chain, the devoutly Catholic Mulliez adopted Leclerc's discount, self-service supermarket formula. Cutting prices throughout his store, Mulliez soon began to attract a new clientele. By the mid-1960s, the company was ready to expand, taking French retailing to an entirely new level.

In 1967 Mulliez opened the first of a new retailing concept, the hypermarket. This store combined the goods of a typical supermarket with the range of items found in department stores, including everything from musical recordings to furniture, household appliances, and automobile parts. The hypermarket format was quickly emulated throughout France, leading to mammoth stores of up to 100,000 square feet, as large as several football playing fields. The first Auchan hypermarket opened near the Mulliez family's base, in Tourcoing/Roncq in 1967.

The Auchan format was an instant success. In its first year the company posted sales of FRF 70 million and profits of some FRF 300,000. Mulliez quickly began building the Auchan name into one of the country's top retailers. In this, he was helped by a number of factors, from economic to political. The collapse of the long postwar economic boom in France, as the country slipped into the recession brought on by the Arab oil embargo of 1973 to 1974, encouraged consumers to seek out Auchan's discount formula. The

introduction of around 200 company-owned brands, which were priced significantly lower than competing national and international brand name products, helped drive store sales as well. Consumers were also attracted to the modern appeal of these large self-service stores, to the detriment of the country's large class of small boutique shops.

Politicians of the time also greeted the rise of the hypermarket as a way to fight the rampant inflation that was cutting deeply into the country's economy in the 1970s. The large-scale purchasing power of Auchan and rivals such as E. Leclerc, Carrefour, Docks de France, and Casino enabled these stores to maintain relatively low prices. In the 1980s, the transfer of a great deal of planning authority from the national level to the local and regional levels made it possible for communities to clear away a number of planning codes and other obstacles that had prevented the growth of the hypermarket formula. Eager to reap the benefits of the tax revenues and employment opportunities offered by the new huge commercial centers, communities welcomed the new hypermarkets. By the mid-1970s, Auchan's annual sales had topped FRF 2 billion.

Mulliez, who had at first clung to his family's northern France base, launched a new strategy toward the end of the 1970s to transform Auchan into one of the country's top national retailers. In 1977 Auchan began to extend its network of hypermarkets across the country. However, Mulliez avoided raising capital on the public market. Instead, the company, like its competitors, was able to take advantage of a staggered payment structure (up to three months for paying suppliers), using its huge cash flow to finance its expansion. At the same time Auchan began offering stock to its employees, thereby giving them a share of the company. While criticism aimed at the company pointed to the low wages earned by many of its employees, a number of Auchan's employees nonetheless became quite wealthy.

## NATIONAL AND INTERNATIONAL GROWTH IN THE 1980s

With the encouragement of local authorities, France's retailing landscape increasingly turned toward the construction of large commercial centers located on the outskirts of the country's cities and towns. Auchan joined this trend, expanding its number of hypermarkets across the country. At the same time, the company was developing other store formats, including standard supermarkets and smaller grocers, which were located in the country's smaller communities or in urban locations. By the mid-1980s, Auchan had grown to annual sales of more than FRF 20 billion.

## KEY DATES

**1961:** Gérard Mulliez opens first Auchan store.
**1967:** First Auchan hypermarket is established.
**1977:** Company begins employee stock distribution program; launches national expansion.
**1981:** First international store opens in Spain.
**1989:** First store in Italy is opened, and a hypermarket in Houston, Texas, opens for business.
**1996:** Company initiates hostile takeover of Docks de France, as well as of Pao de Agucar (Portugal); opens its first store in Poland.
**1997:** Auchan enters Mexico, Thailand, and Argentina.
**1999:** Company launches new Auchan brand name product range.
**2000:** Auchan begins expanding service and distribution network to Europe and Asia.
**2004:** Auchan Group restructures into four main divisions.
**2009:** Auchan Group registers slight growth despite the global economic crisis.

By then, the Mulliez family had becoming something of a retail empire in France. While Gérard Mulliez built the Auchan chain, other family members were encouraged to explore their own retail initiatives. The flooring and carpeting company, founded by cousin Gonzague Mulliez in 1963, had risen to become France's leading specialist in this category, with 160 large-format stores at the end of the 1990s. Another retail concept, launched by Patrick Mulliez in 1978, was the discount clothing chain Kiabi, which grew to a fashion giant, posting FRF 7.8 billion in sales through more than 170 stores across Europe. Another success story was the company's acquisition of home repair and decoration chain Leroy Merlin, founded in 1923. After acquiring half of Leroy Merlin in 1979, the Auchan group took full control by 1981 and built up its network to more than 100 stores across France and Europe. Meanwhile, the company was enjoying huge success with its Decathlon sporting goods chain, created by family member Michel Leclerc, restaurant group Flunch, and then the electronics and home appliance chain Boulanger, acquired in 1986.

Nevertheless, the Auchan chain continued to drive the family's fortunes, as Auchan began to expand onto the international market in the 1980s. In 1981 the company opened its first store in Saragosse, Spain,

under the Alcampo banner. It then built up that chain to nearly 40 hypermarkets and 90 supermarkets by the end of the 1990s. At the end of the 1980s, Auchan looked toward another southern European market, Italy, where it initiated a partnership with that country's IFIL. Auchan also joined the rush into the vast U.S. market. The company opened several hypermarkets, but by 2003 all had been closed. The U.S. consumer had proven reluctant to adopt the huge hypermarket format, which often required a mile of walking for a single shopping trip.

### CONSOLIDATION: 1991–99

Auchan was facing constraints at home, too. Faced with dwindling sales as the result of the deep economic recession that gripped France during much of the 1990s, Auchan was confronted with a growing backlash against its core hypermarket format. In the early 1990s, increasing numbers of voices were calling for limits on the rate of hypermarket expansion, and, by the mid-1990s, legislation had been passed that effectively stopped the building of new hypermarkets in France. Similar legislation began to appear in Spain and other countries as well.

Auchan, which had built up an empire of 80 hypermarkets, for annual sales worth FRF 64 billion, had taken a position as France's sixth-largest distribution group. However, Auchan's internal expansion in its home market was now severely limited. Only a handful of permits for new hypermarket construction were being granted each year. In addition, the company was under pressure from its larger competitors, particularly Carrefour, Casino, and market leader Leclerc, which enjoyed greater economies of scale. As a result, Auchan felt it had no choice but to make the "defensive" move of launching a hostile takeover of close competitor, and publicly listed, Docks de France, with its chain of Mammouth hypermarkets and Atac supermarkets, as well as 500 U.S.-based Lil'Champ convenience stores. This last chain, heavily in debt, was sold off in 1997.

The highly publicized takeover battle, a rarity in the French business world, sent Docks de France seeking a "white knight" in England (an even greater rarity in France). At last, however, Auchan managed to gain majority control of Docks de France and, in 1997, completed its takeover. The takeover enabled Auchan to double in size, securing its position among France's top retailers. Despite the company's assurances that it would maintain the integrity of Docks de France, Auchan quickly began to dismantle the Docks de France organization, converting its Mammouth signage to Auchan. Auchan then reorganized the entire company along format segments, keeping for the time being the Atac supermarket chain.

The integration of the Docks de France organization took nearly two years to complete and resulted in a new Auchan weighing in at more than FRF 147 billion in sales per year. The company's new size enabled it to pursue continued international expansion. Soon after the Docks de France takeover, the company performed a similar takeover of Portugal's Pao de Aucar, giving it a new leading position in that market. In the late 1990s, the company targeted new strategic growth areas in Central Europe, starting in Poland in 1996, and in Italy, where in 1998 it strengthened its partnership agreement and launched a new phase of Gruppo Auchan openings. Expansion also targeted the vast Asian market, beginning with the opening of stores in Thailand in 1997 and China in 1999. Back home, Auchan was refining its hypermarket concept in line with new consumer trends. The company abandoned its more than 200 brand names, which had ceased to be identified with Auchan by its shoppers, in favor of a single discount Auchan brand. The company similarly launched a new in-house clothing label, replacing its former multilabel offering.

## AUCHAN EXPANDS SERVICE: 2000–03

Auchan Group registered tremendous growth in the first decade of the 21st century with the continued expansion of its network into Central Europe, Eastern Europe, and Asia. In 2000 the Group launched an aggressive marketing and public relations campaign dubbed the *Auchandrive.* Auchandrive was simply a marketing concept that sought to express the company's commitment to excellence and efficiency in service delivery. The Auchan Group adopted the effective marketing and brand-building strategy at a time when it was focusing on retaining its dominance in the Western European markets but also expanding to Central Europe, Eastern Europe, and Asia.

The Group's successful inroads in Asia occurred with the acquisition of Taiwan's RT Mart hypermarkets and partnership with China's RT Mart in 2001. Auchan further launched the *Auchandirect,* an online shopping Web site that targeted customers in Paris, France. The Group's 2001 technological leap was closely followed by the opening of Banque Accord, the company's financial services arm, in Spain and Poland.

Auchan posted another major expansion success in Central and Eastern Europe in 2002 when it opened its first hypermarkets in China and acquired Billa stores, a supermarket chain, in Poland. The Group enhanced its dominance in Western Europe in 2002 with the opening of Accord Italia, the Group's subsidiary of Banque Accord in Italy.

## RESTRUCTURING INTO FOUR DIVISIONS: 2004

The fast pace of growth and expansion of the Auchan Group led to the formal restructuring of the organization into four divisions in 2004. The restructuring process was executed in response to the Group's fast growing diversification into various categories of products and services. Each of the four divisions specialized in the company's distinct categories of interests and operations. The four main divisions established by the group were supermarkets, hypermarkets, Immochan, and Banque Accord.

The supermarket and hypermarket segments were created to focus on the retailing and distribution of the Group's products, while Banque Accord and Immochan were to concentrate on provision of financial services and property management, respectively.

Auchan went on to acquire La Rinascente, a food establishment in Italy, that was formally owned by the Ifil Group. Auchan made another information technology leap in 2005 when it opened the *Chronodrive,* an online portal for ordering and picking up purchased items from selected points in France.

The year 2005 was a busy one for the Auchan Group as it consolidated its presence in Poland and Russia. The group also emphasized the A-tak and Atak supermarket chains in Poland and Russia, respectively. The multibrand marketing approach of Auchan in the Central and Eastern European markets was designed to enhance the market infiltration capacity of the company. The Atak and A-tak supermarket brands helped the company to assert its presence in Poland and Russia, and the company reported increased operations and profit margins in those two countries in 2005. The Group also opened a subsidiary of Banque Accord in Russia.

Major changes were made at the helm of Auchan Group's board in 2006 as Gérard Mulliez passed on the company's leadership mantle to Vianney Mulliez. The entry of Auchan France into the mobile telephony communication sector in 2006 as a virtual service provider and operator was one of the first accomplishments of the company's new leadership under Vianney Mulliez. The company further spread its wings to Romania, where it opened its first hypermarket and created a Banque Accord subsidiary as well.

Auchan signed multiple partnership agreements in 2007 for multiple hypermarket operations with Group Furshet and Enka Group in Ukraine and Russia, respectively. The company proceeded to open its first hypermarket in Ukraine in 2008, the same year in which it entered into a joint venture agreement with Nakheel, a leading retailing company in Dubai.

## GROWTH DESPITE THE GLOBAL ECONOMIC CRISIS: 2009

Weakened global currencies, diminished business prospects, and the collapse of stock prices that characterized the global economic crisis of 2008 and 2009 did not prevent the Auchan Group from registering positive growth in 2009.

During the year, the group opened a total of 46 hypermarket stores as part of its strategic network expansion. Of these stores, 22 were in Europe and 24 were in Asia. Auchan further expanded its presence to the Middle East with a 10 percent acquisition of Dubai-based HyperCorp Ltd's share capital. The acquisition paved the way for the opening of Auchan's first supermarket in Dubai. The presence of Auchan Supermarkets in Central and Eastern Europe was also increased by a total of 19 new units.

According to information contained in Auchan's 2009 financial report, the group experienced growth in its hypermarket, Banque Accord, and Immochan segments. The hypermarket segment increased to EUR 31.9 billion in 2009, a 0.9 percent increase compared to 2008. The Banque Accord and Immochan grew by 4.9 percent and 12.2 percent, respectively.

However, the company's supermarket segment did not register favorable growth in 2009, particularly in Western Europe where it opened 22 new units but closed 28 units. The downturn in the group's supermarket segment was also reflected on its revenue by a 3.2 percent reduction.

At the close of 2009, Auchan had 123 hypermarkets and 286 supermarkets in France while its presence in other parts of Europe had grown to 220 hypermarkets and 453 supermarkets. In Asia, Auchan was mainly based in mainland China and Taiwan where it had 156 and 15 hypermarkets, respectively. In the 2010s the company hoped to improve its presence in emerging markets in order to increase revenues.

*M. L. Cohen*
*Updated, Paul Ingati*

## PRINCIPAL DIVISIONS

Banque Accord; Hypermarkets; Immochan; Supermarkets.

## PRINCIPAL COMPETITORS

Carrefour S.A; Casino Guichard-Perrchon S.A.; E. Leclerc; Guyenne et Gascogne S.A.; ITM Entreprises S.A.; Lidl & Schwarz Stiftung & Co. KG; PPR S.A.

## FURTHER READING

"2009 Results: Firm Performance and Ongoing Growth," Auchan Group Press Release, April 14, 2010.

"Agreement between Auchan Ukraine and Panorama Group: 3 New Hypermarkets in Ukraine," Auchan Group Press Release, September 17, 2009.

"The Four Group Activities," Auchan.com, 2010.

Matlack, Carol, "Gérard Mulliez' Auchan: France's Wal-Mart goes Global," *BusinessWeek,* December 10, 2009.

"Official Opening of the 500th Auchan Group Hypermarket," Auchan Group Press Release, November 23, 2009.

Solovichenko, Maria, "Auchan Revealed as No. 2 Retailer," *Moscow Times,* March 31, 2010.

"2010: 36th Auchan Hypermarket Opened in China," Auchan. com, 2010.

Weisenthal, Joe, "The French Retailer That's Eating Wal-Mart's Lunch in China," *Business Insider,* October 26, 2009.

# Bamburi Cement Limited

Kenya Re Towers
Mara Ragati Road, UpperHill
P.O. Box 10921-00100
Nairobi,
Kenya
Telephone: (+254) 020-2710510
Fax: (+254) 020-2710581
Web site: http://www.bamburicement.com

*Public Company*
*Founded:* 1951
*Employees:* 1,072 (2009)
*Sales:* KES 29.99 billion ($383.7 million, 2009)
*Stock Exchanges:* Nairobi
*NAICS:* 327310 Cement Manufacturing; 712190 Nature Parks and Similar Institutions

∎∎∎

Bamburi Cement Limited (Bamburi) is a leading manufacturer of cement and related building materials in the Eastern and Central African regions but also in the Sub-Saharan African region as a whole. The company's principal cement mining and production activities are in Kenya and Uganda, where the company has an estimated market share of 56 percent and 32 percent, respectively. Bamburi's mining exploits in Kenya are concentrated in the coastal region and in the outskirts of Nairobi City while the operations of the company's subsidiary in Uganda are concentrated in Hima.

Over the years, Bamburi has successfully established a formidable distribution and retail network for its cement products both at the local and international levels. In fact, the company stands out as one of the leading export and foreign earners in Kenya, with Congo, Mauritania, Seychelles, Comoros, Madagascar, Reunion Republic, and Sri Lanka being some of its key export destinations.

Approximately 10 percent of Bamburi's revenue comes from Haller Park, an ecological preserve located at the site of a former quarry. Bamburi is a subsidiary of Lafarge, a global building materials company.

## SCALING THE FOUNDATION: 1951

Bamburi Cement Limited was founded by Felix Mandl in 1951 while Mandl was serving as a director in Cementia Holdings A.G., a Swiss materials firm. Mandl and the new company overcame the challenges of the poor infrastructure network that prevailed during the colonial period in Kenya to set up high-volume cement production in the coastal region of Kenya. Bamburi prospered quickly. In 1954, the company's first year of production, its first production plant in Mombasa started off with a capacity of 140,000 tons annually in a development that subsequently earned revenues of approximately £734,000. It became evident that Bamburi had successfully harnessed the advantages of abundant raw materials and cheap labor to assert the fundamentals of the company's tactical and strategic operations.

Bamburi was solely managed by Cementia Holdings until 1963 when a strategic partnership deal was made with a U.K.-based company, Blue Circle plc. The partnership arrangement between Cementia Holdings and Blue Circle plc was based on equal ownership. The two principal owners of Bamburi then injected more capital into the company throughout the 1960s and successfully expanded its production and operational capacities. Bamburi dominated the materials manufacturing industry in the 1960s because of high demand for cement and limited competition in the cement production industry at the time.

The high costs of capital and equipments required for the exploitation and production of cement meant that there were very few entrants into the industry, a factor that Bamburi capitalized on to become the leading supplier of building materials in both the colonial and postcolonial period in Kenya. The partnership between Cementia Holdings and Blue Circle plc was also a relevant factor behind the operational and production dominance of Bamburi from the 1960s to the late 1980s as the two companies were able to harness and leverage their combined economic and technological capabilities.

## NAIROBI STOCK EXCHANGE: 1970

In 1970 the market capitalization of Bamburi grew significantly following the enlisting of the company's shares at the Nairobi Stock Exchange (NSE) market. The company's highly valued stocks experienced high demand and subsequent stock price increments on their first day of trading at the NSE in September 1970.

The tactical, operational, and strategic activities of Bamburi were managed jointly by the Cementia Holdings and Blue Circle plc until 1989, when Cementia Holdings was acquired by the Lafarge Group. The acquisition was part of Lafarge's $135 million acquisition of Cementia Holding AG's properties across the globe. The entry of Lafarge Group, one of the leading building materials production companies in the world, into the ownership structure of Bamburi enhanced the market leadership potential of the company in the production of cement and clinker in Kenya and the region as whole. (Clinker is a substance that can be ground down at a later stage to produce various types of cement.)

The Lafarge Group injected new knowledge and resource capital in Bamburi and effectively enabled the company to invest massively in capital expansion, product diversification, and exploitation of new cement deposits and reserves. While Lafarge's and Blue Circle's capital and ownership structure of Bamburi was retained at an equal shareholding basis, the company benefited from Lafarge's strategic and capacity advantages associated with economies of scale, technological advancements, and efficient knowledge resources.

Bamburi ventured into the acquisition of other companies in the East Africa region which were dealing with the production of building materials. One such successful acquisition was made by the company in 1999 when it purchased Hima (1994) Uganda Limited, a cement factory based in Western Uganda. Hima Cement Factory was a product of the privatization of the Uganda Cement Industries in 1994, a process in which the state-owned company was subdivided into Tororo Cement and Hima (1994) Uganda Limited. Poor performance of the Uganda Cement Industries was the main contributing factor behind the privatization because the company managed to produce less than 10 percent of its total targeted output of 240,000 tons annually.

The new management of Hima Limited successfully overhauled operations of the company in a move that achieved a production capacity of 170,000 tons annually in 1999. That year Bamburi completed an acquisition process that saw it gain the total ownership of Hima, after which that company's name was changed to Hima Cement Limited. Bamburi enhanced Hima Cement Limited's production capacity and rebranded its products accordingly to suit market demands. Information contained in an article titled "Uganda Government Public Enterprise Reform and Divesture Program: Successful Divesture of Hima Cement Limited," on the docstoc.com Web site, indicated that since 1999, Bamburi has invested more than $13 billion in the modernization of the plant, safety programs, and staff training.

## BAMBURI CEMENT ESTABLISHES HALLER PARK: 1971

Haller Park was jointly established by Dr. Rene Haller and Bamburi in 1971. Haller was a nature conservationist who took the initiative of rehabilitating a quarry that had been left behind by the massive mining activities of Bamburi. Haller Park was the first mining site for Bamburi when the company was founded in 1954. The

<table>
<tr><td colspan="2">

## KEY DATES

</td></tr>
<tr><td>1951:</td><td>Bamburi Cement founded in Kenya.</td></tr>
<tr><td>1970:</td><td>The company lists on the Nairobi stock exchange.</td></tr>
<tr><td>1971:</td><td>Bamburi Cement establishes Haller Park.</td></tr>
<tr><td>1998:</td><td>The company's new grinding plant opens in Nairobi.</td></tr>
<tr><td>2007:</td><td>Fire damages the company's operations in Mombasa.</td></tr>
</table>

quarry had been passively transformed into a nature trail (Bamburi Nature Trail) after the company exhausted the exploitation of limestone. However, it was not until Haller's substantial rehabilitation initiatives that the quarry was fully transformed into a nature and animal park. The park was subsequently renamed Haller Park in recognition of its leading founder.

The rehabilitation process of the park involved planting of indigenous trees as well as maintenance of ponds and swamps within the quarry. Wild animals such as hippopotamuses, tortoises, antelopes, giraffes, and zebras were also introduced. Serval cats and bush pigs could also be found in the park. A good number of wild animals hosted in the park were rescued from zoos and animal orphanages in Kenya. For example, one of the hippos in the park was rescued from a German zoo.

Haller Park has since become a leading model of Bamburi's and Lafarge's environmental conservation initiatives. The company has also been very successful in harnessing the revenue potential of Haller Park as a result of the high number of guests who visit the park. Haller Park accounts for 9 percent of Bamburi's total revenue, a clear indication of the transformation that the rehabilitated quarry has undergone over the years.

## ADDITIONAL GRINDING PLANT IN NAIROBI: 1998

In 1998 the company expanded domestically by opening a new plant for grinding clinker in the Athi River district, within the outskirts of the country's capital city, Nairobi. According to information on the company's Web site, the Athi River district grinding plant had a production capacity of 1 million metric tons of clinker annually. Therefore, Bamburi doubled its production capacity to 2.1 million tons annually in 1998 with the inauguration of the Athi River grinding plant for clinker. The development enhanced the ability of the company to meet the ever-increasing demand for its ce-

ment and associated building materials in Kenya and export destinations around the world.

The Athi River clinker production plant particularly impacted positively on the company's domestic market in Western Kenya and the Ugandan market as well. Customers who previously traveled all the way to the coastal town of Mombasa for the company's cement products now had the convenience of purchasing the same from Nairobi, effectively cutting down on both cost and time. A rail line through the Athi River plant provided the company with adequate access to the country's railway transport network. As such, Bamburi was able to optimize the advantages of the enhanced transport infrastructure and distribution network around Nairobi to gain quick access to markets in the upcountry regions. The clinker grinding plant also enabled the company to extend speed and efficiency in the packing and loading processes for its building materials and products.

## OPPORTUNITIES AND CHALLENGES IN THE 21ST CENTURY

The first decade of the 21st century was extremely eventful for Bamburi in terms of both growth in business opportunities and operational challenges. In 2001 Lafarge successfully completed the purchase and final takeover of Blue Circle plc to gain the principal ownership of Bamburi. The purchase of Blue Circle transformed Lafarge into the world's largest producer of building materials.

In October 2007 Ugandan president Yoweri Kaguta Museveni presided over the commissioning of Hima Cement Limited's new high-capacity production plant in Kasese, Uganda. In her newspaper article titled "Uganda: Hima Cement Starts Shs 185b New Factory," Dorothy Nakawesi stated that the new plant would increase the company's capacity of production to 830,000 tons annually by 2010. During the same event, the chief executive officer of Bamburi's parent company Lafarge confirmed that the completion and commissioning of Hima Limited's additional production facilities included the expansion of the production capacity of clinker by 271,000 tons annually. The enhancement of the cement production and clinker capacity of the Hima Cement factory enabled Bamburi to assert the presence of its diversified building materials and products in the East Africa region.

However, Bamburi experienced a major setback in 2007 when its Mombasa plant caught fire. The company lost properties worth hundreds of millions in Kenya shillings, and it also lost a lot of business opportunities that resulted from disruption of production operations in its largest plant. As a result of the fire, there was panic in the building and construction sector as traders and distributors sought to exploit the impending shortage of cement to ignite unjustifiable upward adjustments of their building products prices.

## BAMBURI CEMENT LIMITED IN 2009

Many industries in Kenya experienced very harsh economic conditions in 2009 following shrinkage in market opportunities for their products, and Bamburi was no exception. Domestically, the company experienced declining market opportunities after the country was hit simultaneously by a long spell of drought, high inflation rates, and diminished credit opportunities. The long droughts affected the capacity of the population to develop economically but also sparked an increase in the cost of electricity. The construction industry was particularly affected because the mortgage foreclosures that had taken precedence during the global economic recession had severely reduced credit opportunities for mortgages and real estate construction. High inflation rates resulted in diminished credit opportunities because banks were lending at exorbitant interest rates. At the international level, the company was affected by decreased demand for cement in the traditionally high-demand markets of Far East countries such as China, Indonesia, and Malaysia.

In 2009 Bamburi also had to contend with a 10 percent increase in the company's direct operating costs compared to the previous year. According to the company's financial director, Joshua Oigara, the ballooning direct operating costs was caused by the effects of inflation on the cost of raw materials, high prices of energy, and weak shilling compared to the major global currencies in the export markets.

However, despite experiencing the economic challenges that were imposed by high inflation domestically and the global economic crisis internationally, Bamburi registered impressive results in 2009. That year the company's sales increased by 9 percent to KES 30 billion, with operating profit and cash equivalents increasing as well. According to a company press release posted on its Web site, Bamburi's chairman, Richard Kemoli, attributed the phenomenal financial results to the "significant measures targeted at containing costs, on the one hand, and the gains of KES 1.2 billion one-off divestment acquired through the sale of company's shares in Athi River Mining (ARM)." The company's business was also boosted by the increased revenue streams from African market destinations and a KES 218 million insurance compensation for the 2007 fire incident.

## FUTURE PROSPECTS

The strategic planning of Bamburi Cement Limited had been oriented toward increased exploitation of limestone deposits in Kenya and the Eastern Africa region as whole. The company continuously sought to expand the market share of its diversified product range in Kenya, Uganda, and Tanzania. The company was also expected to utilize Lafarge Group's global distribution network to achieve a global presence itself.

*Paul Ingati*

## PRINCIPAL SUBSIDIARIES

Hima Cement Limited (Uganda); Bamburi Special Products Limited; Lafarge Ecosystems Limited.

## PRINCIPAL COMPETITORS

Athi River Mining Limited; East African Portland Cement.

## FURTHER READING

Casper, Jennifer, "Lafarge Cement to Buy Plants from Swiss Firm," *Washington Post*, December 18, 1990.

"Larfarge Bamburi Group's Turnover up 9%: Group Returns Strong Results Despite a Challenging Market Environment," Bamburi press release, 2010.

Nakaweesi, Dorothy, "Uganda: Hima Cement Starts Shs 185b New Factory," *Monitor*, October 29, 2007.

"Uganda Government Public Enterprise Reform and Divestiture Program: Successful Divestiture of Hima Cement Limited," docstoc.com, 2010.

# Banco Bradesco S.A.

Cidade de Deus S/N Vila Yara
Osasco, São Paulo 06029-900
Brazil
Telephone: (11) 3684 3702
Toll Free: (800) 704-8383
Fax: (11) 3684 3213
Web site: http://www.bradesco.com.br

*Public Company*
*Incorporated:* 1943
*Employees:* 85,548 (2009)
*Sales:* BRL 8.012 billion ($4.521 billion, 2009)
*Stock Exchanges:* São Paulo: New York; Madrid
*Ticker Symbols:* BBDC; BBD; XXBDC
*NAICS:* 522110 Commercial Banking; 523110 Invest-
    ment Banking & Securities Dealing; 524292 Third
    Party Administration of Insurance & Pension Funds

■ ■ ■

Banco Bradesco S.A. is one of the largest banks in Brazil
and in the world. In 2009 Banco Bradesco's nationwide
and international branch networks had 37,476 service
points serving over 50 million customers, and the bank
managed BRL 506 billion ($285 billion) in total assets.

## HUMBLE BEGINNINGS

The history of Bradesco is a "rags to riches" tale in the
tradition of American Horatio Alger's success stories,
which typically feature a resourceful country boy who
creates a bright future for himself in the big city. Bra-

desco founder Amador Aguiar moved in similar fashion
from the farmlands of Brazil's Ribeiráo Preto region to
the cosmopolitan city of São Paulo. Born in 1904, the
third of 13 children of farm workers, Aguiar went to
work in a printer's shop at the age of 14. After losing a
finger in a printing machine six years later, the young
Brazilian changed jobs and started work as a bank clerk
at Banco Noroeste.

Brazilian banks of the early 20th century paralleled
U.S. banks of the late nineteenth century. They
restricted their services to the wealthy upper classes and
therefore placed themselves in competition for a very
limited clientele. Middle- and lower-class citizens did
not use banks and were not welcome at most financial
institutions. This situation was especially pronounced in
Brazil, where the gap between the classes was even wider
than in the United States.

Aguiar's humble beginnings probably sensitized him
to the inequity of Brazil's banking system. After nearly
two decades as an employee, in 1943 the industrious
Aguiar assumed control of Casa Bancária Almeida e
Companhia (Almeida Banking House), a bank with six
branches and headquarters in Marília. He renamed the
institution Banco Brasileiro de Descontos S.A., which
was later shortened to Bradesco. (The name translates to
"ten-conto bank," a self-effacing reference to an
outdated form of currency. Comparable to "dime savings bank," the name emphasized the institution's appeal
to small-scale savers.)

Aguiar's approach to banking has been compared to
that of Amadeo Peter Giannini, who created the Bank
of America (now Bank of America Corporation) to serve

## COMPANY PERSPECTIVES

Bradesco's primary mission is to provide financial and insurance solutions, products, and services in an adroit, competent fashion, especially through banking inclusion and social mobility promotion, thereby contributing to sustainable development and building long-lasting relationships that create value to shareholders and to society.

the financial needs of "the little fellows" such as area coffee growers. In order to make his target clientele feel welcome, Aguiar made a number of changes in typical banking services. He expanded office hours so that coffee growers and ranchers could do their banking before their work day began. In order to reduce the "intimidation factor" common to many financial institutions, Aguiar moved his managers and loan officers from "cages" at the rear of the bank to more approachable desks near the front doors. The bank even helped its clients learn to write checks, for if an incorrectly endorsed note arrived, Bradesco would call the customer in to correct the document so that the bank could honor it.

Aguiar reformed Bradesco's corporate culture as well, making piety and company loyalty fundamental requirements for hiring and promotion. The work environment was replete with religious references. The company letterhead, for example, featured Bible verses and the phrase "Nos confiamos em Deus," Portugese for "We trust in God." New hires endorsed a "declaration of principles" that described the setting aside of personal interests in favor of the good of the country and the company. A corporate publication emphasized three essential requirements for employees: "punctuality, simplicity, and availability."

According to Lynda Schuster's 1985 interview with Aguiar for the *Wall Street Journal,* promotions in the company were made from within and based on what Aguiar described as "superior moral behavior." In the 1990s all of Bradesco's directors had started out at the company in minor office and clerical positions, and all had at least 15 years of experience at the bank.

The high moral expectations instituted by Aguiar had a legitimate business function. As one top executive commented in the bank's 50th anniversary publication, "a clear ethics code, strictly enforced, neutralizes any conflict potential that the decentralization of the decision-making process might activate." In other words,

the company's policies freed branch managers to make the difficult judgments about extension of loans, mortgages, and lines of business credit, while simultaneously releasing upper-level executives from having to oversee those day-to-day transactions.

Bradesco's mass appeal helped it grow quickly. By 1946 it had expanded sufficiently to warrant the relocation of its headquarters to São Paulo, Brazil's economic capital. The country and Bradesco both enjoyed a period of brisk economic expansion based in large part on burgeoning coffee exports during the 1950s. Bradesco's confidence in its clientele paid off in a big way during this period, as deposits at the bank doubled every month. Less than a decade after its reformation by Aguiar, Bradesco had become Brazil's largest private financial institution.

The bank also diversified into trading during this period, using its growing number of branch offices to distribute products from the more industrialized areas of the country to more isolated regions. This strategy not only endeared Bradesco to the recipients of medicine, fuel, and other benefits of modernization, but also to the industrialists and manufacturers whose sales were boosted by these efforts. The bank also began processing utility payments at this time.

### CITY OF GOD

When Aguiar moved the bank's corporate headquarters to the outskirts of São Paulo in 1953, he named the new location "Cidade de Deus," or "City of God," after a book by the evangelist Saint Augustine. The complex not only featured the standard office buildings, but housing, recreation facilities, hospitals, and schools for the 9,000 employees who worked there. Construction of the compound and support of its inhabitants fostered the growth of a thriving suburb around Cidade de Deus.

Aguiar extended his magnanimity beyond the needs of his employees as well. In 1956 he established The Fundação Bradesco (Bradesco Foundation) to combat illiteracy. Boosted by profits from Bradesco's insurance operations, the program was later expanded to include social services, vocational training, computer equipment, and educational materials. By the early 1990s, the Foundation included 39 schools, 85,000 enrollees, and an annual budget of $30 million. Aguiar's philanthropy earned him the oft-used title "seu," a rural contraction of the honorific "Señor."

In 1962 Bradesco became the first bank in Brazil to make computer automation part of its daily operations, ignoring the Brazilian banking industry's well-established prejudice against new technologies. Notwithstanding the

## KEY DATES

**1943:** Amador Aguiar assumes control of Almeida Banking House and renames it Bradesco.

**1946:** Company relocates headquarters to São Paulo, Brazil.

**1953:** Aguiar moves the headquarters to outskirts of São Paulo and renames new location to mean "City of God."

**1956:** Bradesco Foundation established to combat illiteracy.

**1960s:** Military coup in Brazil; strong national economic growth late in this decade.

**1981:** Aguiar relinquishes executive chairmanship.

**1985:** Bank accommodates to inflation, opens more than one branch per day.

**1986:** Hundreds of branches close once the Cruzado Plan is passed.

**1996:** Company introduces Internet banking system.

**2004:** Banco Bradesco acquires Banco Zigbi, one of many acquisitions this decade.

**2010:** Banco Bradesco inaugurates its floating bank branch.

conventional wisdom, automation proved invaluable in the tumultuous Brazilian economy, which endured triple-digit inflation, rapid currency devaluation, and stagnant gross domestic product growth in the early 1960s. Like other Brazilian banks, Bradesco adapted to this "hyperinflationary" environment, adopting indexing (characterized by Robert M. Bleiberg of *Barron's* as "the widespread use of escalator clauses in financial transactions to minimize the impact of inflation") and issuing daily bank statements so that clients could track their holdings. As one executive reflected in the company history, the daily statement was "an extravagance that impressed people. Some clients considered it an excess but even so understood that the daily statement represented superior service."

A military coup d'état in Brazil in the mid-1960s ushered in a period of government-led economic planning that brought about "the Brazilian miracle" of the late 1960s and early 1970s. The country enjoyed an unprecedented period of prosperity, low inflation, and economic expansion. Bradesco more than doubled its 326-branch system through acquisitions during this period. The two largest of Bradesco's 17 purchases were INCO-Banco Indústria e Comércio de Santa Catarina's 105-branch system in 1967 and Banco da Bahia's 200

branches in 1973. The bank also launched its first credit card, the Cartão Bradesco, during this period. By 1978 the institution claimed over 1,000 branches.

Aguiar stepped down from Bradesco's executive chairmanship in 1981. He remained true to the Spartan work ethic he imposed on his employees, however, and maintained a daily work schedule. The venerable leader retired in 1990 at the age of 86 and died less than a year later.

### AT WORK DAY AND NIGHT

Aguiar was succeeded as chief executive by Lázaro de Mello Brandão, who had started his career with Bradesco in 1942 at the age of 15, when the institution was still the Almeida Banking House. Brandão was as hardworking as his predecessor: he put in 12-hour days and was on call "Dia e Noite" (Day and Night, also a slogan for Bradesco's ATM system). He had been a driving force behind the bank's computerization in the 1960s and its internationalization in the early 1980s.

Triple-digit annual inflation once again raged in Brazil in the early 1980s. Banking customers tried to adapt to the situation with daily transfers of funds to accounts with ever-higher yields. Bradesco and other Brazilian banks' branches increased their services to accommodate this activity. Bradesco's branch system, for example, increased from 1,400 in 1983 to over 1,900 in 1986. In 1985 alone, the bank opened more than one new branch per day. In order to keep its clients informed of events in the fast-moving Brazilian economy, the bank launched "Alô Bradesco," a free, 24-hour consumer complaint, suggestion, and information line, in 1985.

In 1986 the José Sarney administration ratified the "Cruzado Plan," a strategy that was designed to halt inflation and simultaneously boost the economy in Brazil. The country adopted a new fixed-rate currency called the cruzado, instituted price and wage freezes, and even limited banking hours to just five midday hours in order to limit activity. Having reconciled themselves to hyperinflation, many Brazilian banks faced a painful readjustment. Milton Moskowitz noted in the *Global Marketplace* that at Bradesco, "some 80,000 lost their jobs early in 1986, and hundreds of branches were closed."

In order to gradually adapt to the artificially curbed economy, CEO Brandão focused on enhancing productivity through ever-increasing automation. The proliferation of automatic teller machines that offered the full range of traditional bank services diminished the need for employees to work as tellers. In addition, the installation in the early 1990s of a state-of-the-art satellite-based data communications network helped revolutionize the collection of daily transaction records from 200 of Bradesco's branches on the Amazonian frontier. Up to the late 1980s, this information was transmitted through a fleet of boats that traversed the region's estuaries several times each business day.

The bank also "outsourced" several peripheral businesses during this period, including operations as diverse as a cabinet-making division. The company history commented that "self-sufficiency was necessary at a time when services in Brazil were incipient and lacked the means to operate on a large scale." Bradesco did, however, retain ownership of its printing operations, perhaps in homage to the founder's first profession. Through these and other measures, employment at Bradesco was halved, from 146,000 in 1986 to 81,000 in 1994, but assets climbed from $13.6 billion to $15.8 billion during the same period.

The late 1980s and early 1990s also brought a revolution in Bradesco's corporate culture and a deviation from some of Aguiar's strict standards. For example, the board of directors of the company had traditionally worked out in the open. As with the bank's branch managers and tellers, these executives had neither private offices nor even a desk drawer to themselves. The president often personally handled many customer and employee issues. However, during this period of reform, top executives at the home office and in the branches moved into new quarters with private meeting rooms for confidential consultations with clients.

The Brazilian economy was still in turmoil in the early 1990s, which led to more government reforms. Although some analysts questioned the bank's ability to adjust to economic stabilization programs enacted in 1994, Bradesco continued to prosper. In 1993 and 1994, it was the top-rated of Brazil's banks, according to Euro-money, IBCA Limited (London), and Thomson BankWatch Inc. (New York). The company was able to weather the 1990s well enough, and in 1996 even launched the first Internet banking system in Latin America.

## EXPANSION IN BRAZIL AND INTERNATIONALLY: 2000–08

The strategic orientation of Banco Bradesco was largely defined by acquisitions, mergers, divestitures, and takeovers for most of the first decade of the 21st century. In June 2001, for example, the bank acquired the financing unit of Ford-Vehicle from Ford Leasing S. A., a financial services provider that was operated by Ford do Brasil. In a separate strategic move, however, Banco Bradesco sold off its telecommunication networks to Portugal Telecom S. A. in August 2001.

Banco Bradesco experienced increased operational activities in 2002 as it expanded its network and equity interests both in Brazil and internationally. That year the bank expanded its presence in the Brazilian market when it placed the winning bid for Banco do Amazonas, a bank that was previously owned and run by the Brazilian government.

In 2003 Banco Bradesco expanded its asset management interests in Brazil when it entered an agreement to take up the third party fund management segment of Banco JP Morgan S. A. According to information contained in Banco Bradesco's 2003 annual financial statement, the transfer of the third-party funds from Banco JP Morgan S. A. was worth BRL 7 billion.

The purchase of controlling equity interests in Banco Bilbao Vizcaya Argentria Brasil (BBVA) from BBVA S. A. was the other major acquisition of Banco Bradesco in 2003. The transaction involved the transfer of 100 percent of BBVA S.A's share capital to Banco Bradesco in return for ownership of 4.5 percent of Banco Bradesco's ordinary and preference shares that were valued at BRL 530 million. The agreement also granted BBVA an additional BRL 2 billion payout and the right to nominate a member to Banco Bradesco's board of directors.

Banco Bradesco S. A. experienced a series of expansion successes in 2004 which started with the acquisition of Banco Zogbi S. A. and its related subsidiaries. The bank's interests in the acquisition process of the Banco Zogbi S. A. was promulgated through its financial management subsidiary, Banco Finasa S. A. Banco Bradesco further enhanced its domination of Brazil's financial sector in October 2004 when it placed the winning bid for the acquisition of controlling equity stakes in Banco do Estado do Maranhao, an organization formerly run by the Banco Central do Brasil.

Banco Bradesco S. A.'s acquisition string extended into 2005, a year during which the bank added Leader S. A. Administradora de Cartoes de Credito and Morada Distribution Network into its ever-growing list of business units, subsidiaries, and joint venture partners. The acquisition of Leader S. A. Administradora de Cartoes de Credito and Morada Distribution Network secured the bank's strategic targets in its business of processing credit cards and the provision of personal financing services.

## THE FIRST BANK FLOATING BRANCH IN THE WORLD: 2009

Banco Bradesco underwent a change in leadership during 2009 when Luiz Carlos Trabuco Cappi was officially confirmed in the position of CEO, replacing Marcio Artur Laureli Cypriano, who retired. New management or not, the company continued to grow through acquisition, Acquiring Banco Ibi in 2009. In that year the company also set up a bank branch inside a vessel designed to traverse the Solimões River, an innovative strategy for spreading banking services to as many people as possible through mobile banking.

In the 2010s, Banco Bradesco was well placed to continue its dominant position as one of the largest banks in Brazil, and with Brazil's economy experiencing strong growth, prosprects for continued growth appeared favorable.

*April D. Gasbarre*
*Updated, Paul Ingati*

## PRINCIPAL SUBSIDIARIES

Banco Boavista; Banco Bradesco Argentina (99.99%); Banco Bradesco Luxembourg; Bradesco Leasing S.A. Arrendamento Mercantil; Bradesco Securities.

## PRINCIPAL DIVISIONS

Bradesco Corporate; Bradesco Empresas; Bradesco Expresso; Banco Postal; Bradesco Prime; Bradesco Private Banking; Bradesco Varejo.

## PRINCIPAL COMPETITORS

Banco do Brasil S.A.; Banco Santander (Brazil) S.A.; Itaú Unibanco Holding S.A.

## FURTHER READING

"Banco Bradesco S. A. Mergers and Acquisitions," Alacrastore. com, 2010.

"Financial Statements, Independent Auditors' Report, Summary of the Audit Committee's Report and Fiscal Council's Report," Banco Bradesco S. A. 2009.

U.S. Securities and Exchange Commission. "Banco Bradesco S. A.: Report on Economic and Financial Analysis," Washington DC: GPO, 2002.

# BancorpSouth, Inc.

One Mississippi Plaza
201 South Spring Street
Tupelo, Mississippi 38804
U.S.A.
Telephone: (662) 680-2000
Toll Free: (888) 797-7711
Fax: (662) 678-7299
Web site: https://www.bancorpsouthonline.com

*Public Company*
*Founded:* 1876
*Employees:* 4,450 (2009)
*Total Assets:* $13.17 billion (2009)
*Stock Exchanges:* New York
*Ticker Symbol:* BXS
*NAICS:* 521110 Monetary Authorities–Central Bank;
522110 Commercial Banking; 522291 Consumer
Lending; 523110 Investment Banking and Securi-
ties Dealing: 524126 Direct Property and Casualty
Insurance Carriers

■ ■ ■

From a humble origin, BancorpSouth, Inc., has
prospered for over a century to become a thriving
regional bank. The bank offers a wide range of banking
and insurance services in an area well beyond its home
state of Mississippi. In 2009 the bank had 310 branch
offices throughout Mississippi, Tennessee, Alabama,
Arkansas, Texas, Florida, Missouri, and Illinois. BancorpSouth has managed to grow significantly over its
long life mainly through mergers and acquisitions. Also,

due to deregulation the bank has diversified its product
line, becoming a major player in each new arena it has
entered, whether it is insurance or investment
management.

## THE CORNER IN A STORE

On March 31, 1876, the Mississippi state legislature
voted to grant a perpetual charter to Raymond, Trice &
Company, a merchant in Verona, Mississippi. The state
legislature issued the charter as part of its effort to
rebuild the economy after the chaos and devastation
brought by the American Civil War. Mississippi was a
member of the Confederacy during the war and the
Union Army blockade had prevented supplies from
reaching the state. The blockade also brought the state's
central economic driver, the cotton trade, to a complete
halt. Under the charter, Raymond, Trice & Company
set up the bank in the back corner of its store.

The new bank granted loans to landowners to
expand their operations, launch new enterprises, and
buy horses and equipment. The bank also loaned funds
to the community to build schools and other civic
projects. By 1886 the bank had expanded its reach over
a wider area and its shareholders moved the bank to
Tupelo. The city offered better communications between
town and rural communities. The bank was renamed
the Bank of Lee County and shortly afterward was
renamed again as the Bank of Tupelo.

By the beginning of the 20th century the former
Confederate states were on the mend and Mississippi's
cotton fields were profitable. As Mississippi grew, so did
its banks. The Bank of Tupelo merged with the Bank of

Nettleton in 1904 and with the Fulton Bank in 1906. As a result, the Bank of Tupelo developed a stronger presence in northeastern Mississippi. The bank continued to open offices, and by the end of the 1920s it was regarded as the most stable financial institution in Mississippi.

## STRENGTH UNDER ADVERSITY

The 1930s was a time of great turmoil for banks. The Great Depression brought a tidal wave of bank failures. President Franklin Delano Roosevelt and the Congress responded with sweeping banking reform. Southern banks were confronted with economic challenges specific to the South. Agriculture's contribution to the Southern economy declined during the mid-1930s. Small cotton farms gave way to large combines. The region faced inadequate rural housing, the regular flooding of the Mississippi (which displaced thousands of people), and a growing need for serviceable roads and highways. The Bank of Tupelo addressed the regional problems as part of its mission. The bank loaned funds to rebuild the homes destroyed by floods. The bank joined forces with other financial institutions to help fund adequate housing for families in the rural areas of northeastern Mississippi. The Bank of Tupelo's conservative management and loan policies enabled it to survive the worst of the Depression and remain in good standing.

During World War II the Bank of Tupelo sold war bonds to help finance the U.S. war effort. After the war, the Bank of Tupelo joined forces with other Mississippi financial institutions, local development organizations, and such federal agencies as the Appalachian Regional Commission and the Tennessee Valley Authority. Together, they laid plans for a strong economic foundation across northeastern Mississippi. The Bank of Tupelo helped cultivate the growth of small business ventures, retail stores, utility companies, and local school systems. By 1949 the bank had acquired both the Merchants & Farmers Bank of Ecru and the Bank of Sherman.

## A LEADER FOR GROWTH

For 30 years President J. P. Nanney had guided the Bank of Tupelo. His leadership propelled the bank from the status of local institution to regional powerhouse. His cautious financial policies, combined with his commitment to developing an industrial base for the area (he was twice elected mayor of Tupelo), were in large part responsible for the bank's success. By the early 1950s Nanney had hired J. C. Whitehead, Jr., as his handpicked successor. Whitehead, who had graduated from Mississippi State University and whose father had been president of the Fulton Bank since the early 1920s, began his career at the bank as a trust officer. When Nanney died in 1959, Whitehead became president of the bank.

Whitehead led the Bank of Tupelo into the 1960s, a period of unprecedented growth. The bank increased the bank's loan/deposit ratio from 21 percent to 60 percent. The bank used this increase in capital to fund the growth of various industries in northeastern Mississippi. Eventually, the bank found its investments shifting beyond its traditional corner of the state. Whitehead proposed that the bank change its name to better reflect its new statewide focus. After exhaustive discussion among the bank's managers, they chose the name "Bank of Mississippi."

The bank continued to prosper in the 1970s, initiating acquisitions and mergers that resulted in many new financial associates. Customer services were upgraded and communication among the bank's many offices was improved. Most importantly, the bank sharpened its focus on business and industrial development. The bank joined forces with the Community Development Foundation, the Lee County Soil & Water Conservation District, and the Tombigbee River Valley Water Management District to encourage local entrepreneurs and attract national companies. The results of the consortium's efforts were dramatic, yielding economic gains throughout the state. Employment and wages increased, the tax base expanded, and citizens across the state gained greater access to a wider variety of services and products.

One of the most important of the bank's many activities during this period was its involvement in and

## KEY DATES

**1876:** Raymond, Trice & Company receives a perpetual charter to set up a bank in the corner of its store.

**1965:** Company changes its name to Bank of Mississippi.

**1987:** Bancorp of Mississippi merges with First Mississippi National Bank.

**1992:** Merges with Volunteer Bank; Bancorp of Mississippi becomes BancorpSouth, Inc.

**1997:** BancorpSouth lists on New York Stock Exchange.

**2009:** Company's net earnings fall for second consecutive year.

support of the state of Mississippi's educational system. The bank supported programs within the public school system, encouraged and helped to develop curriculum at the community college level, provided loans and scholarships to students attending state universities, and contributed to educational programs at leading colleges and universities throughout the state.

## DEREGULATION BRINGS OPPORTUNITY AND MERGERS

In 1982 the Bank of Mississippi formed a holding company and named it Bancorp of Mississippi. In 1985 the holding company began trading on the NASDAQ under the symbol BOMS. The Bank of Mississippi continued to operate as a separate entity and kept its name. In 1987 the federal government removed restrictions on statewide banking. Before, banks were constrained to a one-hundred-mile radius of a bank's main administrative headquarters. After the repeal, the Bank of Mississippi expanded its presence across the state. Aubrey B. Patterson, Jr., the bank's new president, merged the bank with First Mississippi National. Like the Bank of Mississippi, the First Mississippi National Bank had a long history in the region. It was founded in 1884 in Hattiesburg, Mississippi, under the name Bank of Commerce. The Bank of Commerce became the First National Bank of Hattiesburg. The bank expanded to Biloxi and Jackson and became the First Mississippi National Bank. The merger gave the bank greater access to the Gulf Coast and Jackson markets and provided the bank with the largest market share in the Hattiesburg region. A short time later, the bank acquired both the American Bank of Vicksburg and the Bank of North

Mississippi. After these acquisitions, the Bank of Mississippi was able to serve communities from the Gulf of Mexico to the Tennessee state border.

By 1990 the Bank of Mississippi had grown to over 70 offices and branches covering more than 40 cities and towns. In 1992 the U.S. Congress passed the Federal Interstate Banking Law. The Bank of Mississippi quickly took advantage of the new rules by expanding into Tennessee. The bank merged with Volunteer Bankshares in Jackson, Tennessee. Volunteer Bankshares owned Volunteer Bank, another bank with a long history in the Southern United States. In 1886, around the same time Raymond, Trice & Company and its bank moved to Tupelo, Mississippi, a group of entrepreneurs met in Jackson, Tennessee, at the law offices of Pitts, Hays, and Meeks. They formed the Second National Bank, which would later change its name to Jackson National Bank and then to Volunteer Bank. Soon after the merger of Bank of Mississippi and Volunteer Bankshares, the holding company Bancorp of Mississippi changed its name to BancorpSouth, Inc., to reflect more accurately the company's new regional coverage.

In 1997 BancorpSouth, Inc., listed on the New York Stock Exchange under the symbol BXS. At the same time, BancorpSouth merged the Bank of Mississippi and Volunteer bank into one bank under the name BancorpSouth Bank. BancorpSouth formed BancorpSouth Insurance Services and started offering insurance products to its customers.

In 1998 the bank expanded into Alabama by merging with the Highland Bank in Birmingham, Alabama. In order to handle its explosive growth during the 1990s, BancorpSouth built a new administration and operations facility in Tupelo and established a sophisticated telecommunications system between branches.

At the end of the decade, BancorpSouth made aggressive moves to build up its portfolio of services. It formed BancorpSouth Investment Services to offer equities, bonds, and mutual funds to its customers. The company also made significant steps to expand its insurance division. In 1999 BancorpSouth acquired Stewart Sneed Hewes, Inc., Mississippi's largest insurance brokerage company. Stewart Sneed Hewes was founded in 1905 and specialized in commercial lines of insurance as well as an array of property, casualty, life, health, and employee benefits products and services. At the time it was ranked among the top 100 insurance companies in the nation. In 2000 the bank acquired Pittman Insurance Agency and the Kilgore, Seay and Turner Agency, both large independent agencies based in Jackson, Mississippi. The bank continued to merge with other insurance companies and grow its insurance services.

## THE 21ST CENTURY

BancorpSouth became a regional stalwart in the Southern banking economy. It maintained its social consciousness, investing in the surrounding communities, education, and civic infrastructure. The *Mississippi Business Journal* named BancorpSouth one of the best places to work in 2009.

Accolades aside, the bank suffered from the economic downturn of 2008 and 2009 like many other financial institutions. While total assets remained fairly stable between 2007 and 2009, net income before taxes dropped from $203.9 million (2007) to $174.4 million (2008) and then to $112.8 million (2009). Part of the problem stemmed from write-downs of credit losses, which were $117.3 million in 2009 compared to $22.7 million in 2007. While these write-downs affected BancorpSouth's bottom line, the company entered the 2010s with multiple lines of business and a healthy amount of total assets.

*Aaron Hauser*

## PRINCIPAL SUBSIDIARIES

BancorpSouth Bank; BancorpSouth Insurance Services, Inc.; BancorpSouth Investment Services, Inc.; BancorpSouth Municipal Development Corporation; Century Credit Life Insurance Company; Personal Finance Corporation; Risk Advantage, Inc.

## PRINCIPAL COMPETITORS

Bank of America Corp.; BB&T Corporation; Regions Financial Corporation; SunTrust Banks, Inc.; Trustmark Corporation.

## FURTHER READING

"BancorpSouth Investment Services, Inc. Opens Doors for Business," *Business Wire,* February 24, 1999, 18:34.

"BancorpSouth to Acquire Louisiana's Oldest, Largest Independent Insurance Agency," *PR Newswire,* April 30, 2003, 17:56.

"Bancorp of Mississippi Announces Name Change to BancorpSouth, Inc.,"*Business Wire,* September 28, 1992.

Northway, Wally, "Best Places Winners See Employees as People," *Mississippi Business Journal,* 31, no. 13, March 30, 2009, p. 4.

# Baxter International Inc.

—■—

One Baxter Parkway
Deerfield, Illinois 60015
U.S.A.
Telephone: (847) 948-2000
Toll Free: (800) 422-9837
Fax: (847) 948-3642
Web site: http://www.baxter.com

*Public Company*
*Incorporated:* 1931 as Baxter International Inc.
*Employees:* 49,700 (2009)
*Sales:* $12.56 billion (2009)
*Stock Exchanges:* New York Chicago
*Ticker Symbol:* BAX
*NAICS:* 325411 Medicinal and Botanical Manufacturing; 325412 Pharmaceutical Preparation Manufacturing; 325413 In-Vitro Diagnostic Substance Manufacturing

■ ■ ■

Baxter International Inc. is the world's largest manufacturer and distributor of hospital supplies and a leading provider of medical specialty products. Serving over 5,000 hospitals, Baxter operates in two primary industry segments: medical specialties and medical/laboratory products and distribution. The company's major products and services include dialysis systems, cardiovascular devices, laboratory and surgical equipment, and intravenous and diagnostic systems. Over the course of its history, Baxter has introduced several medical innovations, including blood banks, the first commercial kidney dialysis system, and continuous ambula-

tory peritoneal dialysis (CAPD), a self-administered alternative to hemodialysis in a hospital.

## FOUNDED BY PHYSICIANS

In 1931 two Iowa physicians, Dr. Ralph Falk and Dr. Donald Baxter, launched the Don Baxter Intravenous Products Company to distribute intravenous solutions commercially to hospitals in the Midwest. During this time, only large research centers and university hospitals had the facilities to produce intravenous solutions, which were of variable quality and limited in quantity. Falk and Baxter planned to overcome these problems by manufacturing large, closely controlled supplies of solutions and packing them in evacuated containers. In 1933 the company opened a plant in Glenview, a Chicago suburb. The staff of six employees produced Baxter's complete line of five solutions and packaged them in glass containers. The American Hospital Supply Corporation, also based in Chicago, distributed the Baxter products.

In 1935 Falk bought his partner's interest in the company. Soon thereafter, he established a research and development division and built a second manufacturing facility, in Canada. In 1939 the company introduced the Transfuso-Vac blood collection system, a sterile vacuum-type collection and storage unit for blood. Prior methods allowed blood to be stored for only a few hours, but the Transfuso-Vac provided storage of up to 21 days, giving rise to the practice of blood banking. In 1941 Baxter introduced the Plasma-Vac container, which enabled the medical community to separate plasma from whole blood and store the plasma for later use.

During World War II, Baxter provided blood collection products and intravenous solutions to the U.S. armed forces. The company opened several temporary facilities in order to meet the military's increasing demand, and after the war these operations were consolidated in the Glenview plant. Late in the 1940s, the company moved into a new office and production facility in the Chicago suburb of Morton Grove.

During the 1940s, Willem Kolff, a Dutch physician, was applying dialysis procedures to treatment of kidney failure, and Baxter began making commercial use of his methods in the United States. In 1948 Baxter's product line was expanded to include Fenwal Laboratories' new unbreakable plastic container for blood storage, the precursor to the Viaflex plastic intravenous (IV) bag, a product that would serve as a basis for the development of a plastic delivery system for dialysis solutions. Baxter formed a pharmaceutical specialties division under the name Travenol Laboratories in 1949. This division was responsible for developing and marketing chemical compounds and medical equipment.

The company expanded considerably during the 1950s, opening a facility in Cleveland, Mississippi, which would later produce intravenous and irrigating solutions, needles, dialysis solutions, respiratory therapy products, and many disposable devices used in medical treatment. In addition, Baxter made several important acquisitions during the decade, including Hyland Laboratories of Los Angeles in 1952, as well as Flint, Eaton and Company and Fenwal Laboratories of Boston in 1959. That year, the company also established its international division, which later was divided into two separate divisions, Travenol Europe and the Americas-Pacific Division, both of which established manufacturing facilities in 27 countries and distributed products in more than 100 countries.

One of the most important company developments of the 1950s was the appointment of William B. Graham as Baxter's president and chief executive officer. Named to these posts in 1953, Graham was responsible for the decision to support Dr. Kolff's research effort on the production of artificial kidneys. In 1956 Baxter introduced the first commercially built kidney dialysis system, representing the company's first move into a field in which it would become known as an innovator.

Baxter shares began trading on the New York Stock Exchange in 1961. The company's steady growth during subsequent years prompted shareholders to vote in favor of several two-for-one stock splits. In 1963 Baxter ended its 30-year-old distribution contract with American Hospital Supply and thereafter developed its own sales force. The company also built two Arkansas facilities during this time and acquired Disposable Hospital Products as well as Dayton Flexible Products Company and Cyclo Chemical Corporation. Moreover, Baxter's international operations were making extensive inroads into European markets, especially through the development of its wholly owned subsidiaries.

Several important technological innovations occurred at Baxter during the 1960s and 1970s. The first disposable total bypass oxygenator for open-heart surgery was introduced in 1962, and in 1968 Baxter marketed the Hemofil antihemophilic factor, which was six times as powerful as any similar product offered at that time. The company also developed the Autoplex anti-inhibitor coagulant, another important innovation in the treatment of hemophilia. In 1979 Baxter offered continuous ambulatory peritoneal dialysis as an alternative to hemodialysis for kidney failure. CAPD proved popular as it could be performed at home by the patient, was less costly than hospital treatment, provided more uniform results, and allowed increased patient mobility.

Baxter's sales totaled $242 million in 1972, securing the company a spot on the *Fortune* 500 list. By 1978 sales had quadrupled to $1 billion, and the company could boast an earnings growth rate of 21 percent for the preceding 24 continuous years. During this time, Baxter built a new plant in North Carolina and a new corporate headquarters in Deerfield, Illinois. In a series of acquisitions, the company bought American Instrument Company and Surgitool in 1970, Vicra Sterile Products in 1974, and Clinical Assays in 1976. That year, Baxter shareholders voted to adopt the name Baxter Travenol for the parent company, with Travenol Laboratories as the major domestic operating subsidiary. In 1980 Vernon R. Loucks, Jr., replaced William Graham as president and chief executive officer. He would become chairman seven years later.

During the 1980s, industry analysts predicted a continued strong demand for intravenous solutions and equipment, kidney dialysis equipment, and various blood-derived products, all market areas that Baxter dominated. The company's earnings per share rose

## KEY DATES

**1931:** Baxter International Inc. is incorporated under Delaware law.

**1941:** Baxter introduces the Plasma-Vac container.

**1949:** Baxter forms a pharmaceutical specialties division under the name Travenol Laboratories.

**1956:** Baxter introduces the first commercially built kidney dialysis system.

**1959:** Baxter establishes its international division.

**1961:** Baxter shares begin trading on the New York Stock Exchange.

**1968:** Baxter markets the Hemofil antihemophilic factor.

**1976:** Baxter shareholders vote to adopt the name Baxter Travenol for the parent company, with Travenol Laboratories as the major domestic operating subsidiary.

**1979:** Baxter offers continuous ambulatory peritoneal dialysis as an alternative to hemodialysis for kidney failure.

**1983:** The company forms a partnership with Genentech Inc. to develop, manufacture, and market products in the human diagnostics field.

**1985:** Baxter acquires partner American Hospital Supply Company for $51 per share in cash and securities.

**1993:** Vernon R. Loucks's letter to shareholders acknowledges 1993 losses of $268 million.

**2001:** Several deaths of patients receiving dialysis from Baxter products prompts the company to recall two lines of filters and shut down a factory.

**2009:** Baxter develops a vaccine to the H1N1 virus when the disease is still feared to be a pandemic.

**2010:** The FDA orders Baxter to recall and destroy all 200,000 of its colleague volumetric infusion pumps on the market.

steadily, from $1.86 in 1980 to $2.64 in 1982. Expansion into foreign markets, development of "mini-bags" of pre-mixed drugs, and domination of the CAPD market were all factors favoring the company's continued growth.

Nevertheless, Loucks and other leaders at Baxter believed that the company's continued growth depended on its exploitation of new markets for health care products and services. Under Loucks's guidance, Baxter acquired Medcom Inc., a medical education and information company, in 1982 and subsequently purchased two computer software firms specializing in health management applications. In late 1983 the company formed a partnership with Genentech Inc. to develop, manufacture, and market products in the human diagnostics field.

Loucks also initiated a comprehensive cost-cutting program intended to make Baxter the lowest-cost supplier of medical products and services. Toward that end, Baxter's research and development focused on such cost-cutting products as pre-mixed drugs, rather than the sophisticated, expensive items it had emphasized. Moreover, the new research and development programs, many of which were joint ventures, sought to adapt traditionally expensive products for less costly use in the home.

In 1982, when the federal government announced reductions in the fees it would pay Medicare and Medicaid patients undergoing kidney dialysis treatment, industry observers predicted that Baxter would take the lead in home dialysis methods. Baxter's sales of home dialysis products had risen 40 percent since 1978, when the company introduced CAPD, and the company had also developed a device called an ultraviolet germicidal chamber to reduce the risk of infection from tactile contamination. Although the company seemed well-positioned to gain market share, several factors instead contributed to a poor performance.

At the end of 1983, due to a special charge of $116.1 million after taxes, consolidations involving the closing of three manufacturing facilities, and asset revaluations, Baxter announced that its earnings for the following year were likely to be below the average of previous years. In fact, net sales for 1984 decreased 2.3 percent, net income dropped a precipitous 86.7 percent, and the average price for Baxter common stock declined 29 percent. Moreover, several market trends worked against Baxter. In response to pressure from government and private insurance companies, hospitals sought to control their costs, and demand for Baxter's traditional hospital-oriented products declined sharply. Although the company had anticipated these events and had shifted its research into growth areas, it was unable to offset the slackened demand from hospitals and the resulting competitive pricing in the industry. The high investment in research and development of products for Baxter's new nonhospital products and services had not yet begun to pay off.

One of Baxter's most significant adjustments to changes in the medical industry was its development of a "package deal" of products and services for hospitals. The plan combined the company's traditional products (intravenous supplies, blood therapy products, and hemodialysis and urological goods) with consulting services to help its hospitals reduce costs. Through the plan, Baxter hoped to establish contacts with hospitals engaged in setting up home health care systems. However, to make a profit in home health care, a company had to be able to rely on a large patient pool, particularly because many patients were short-term, and Baxter did not have access to such a pool.

Moreover, Baxter had to bear the expense of maintaining extensive production facilities for the manufacture of its products, particularly intravenous solutions and equipment, while domestic demand for such products decreased. Although demand remained strong in international markets, conducting business in foreign territory proved problematic at times. For example, in 1985, when labor strikes in the Philippines caused turmoil at Baxter's intravenous operation, the company was forced to close its operations there, a withdrawal that cost Baxter its $10 million investment in the facility. Furthermore, in the late 1980s, perceived and real risks of contracting acquired immune deficiency syndrome (AIDS) from blood transfusions depressed the demand for blood therapy products. Although a reliable blood screening test was developed relatively quickly, analysts predicted that a return to earlier levels of use of blood therapy products was unlikely in the near future.

In 1985 Baxter acquired its early partner, American Hospital Supply Company, for $51 per share in cash and securities, through a hostile takeover. Although earnings were diluted by the merger, investors remained confident in the future of the company. Stock rose 35 percent as assimilation of American progressed. With its new name, Baxter International, and new emphasis on high-profit products, including diagnostic equipment and computer software for hospitals, the Baxter-American merger promised increased competition in a crowded market.

Two years later, Baxter acquired Caremark Inc., an alternative site health care business that provided products and services for use outside of hospitals. The purchase doubled Baxter's holdings in that segment, which soon became its fastest-growing business. However, Baxter's traditional hospital customers soon began to resent the threat Caremark posed to their own home health care programs. Moreover, in 1991 a criminal investigation of Caremark for alleged Medicare kickbacks was initiated. Baxter decided to spin Caremark off to shareholders in 1992.

Rumors that the Baxter-American Hospital Supply merger had resulted in difficulties between the divergent corporate cultures seemed to be confirmed in ensuing years, as the firm entered a state of frequent restructuring. Early in 1990, the company announced the largest restructuring in its history, involving the closing of 21 plants, divesting marginal businesses, and laying off about 10 percent of the workforce. The 1990 retrenchment focused largely on Baxter's hospital supply businesses, and the revamp two years later eliminated its alternative site health care business.

During this time, Baxter lost several lucrative contracts, having gained a reputation as a high-cost, high-priced distributor whose practices tended to anger and frustrate hospital purchasing managers. According to an October 1993 *Health Industry Today* article, Baxter's contract with Premier Health Alliance Inc., which represented $32 million in 1992 sales, was not renewed in 1993. Furthermore, the Veterans Administration (VA) proposed to exclude Baxter from bidding on and being awarded contracts for the next year, following allegations by the VA that Baxter knowingly misled and provided false information to the government agency's officials. In a conciliatory measure, Baxter accelerated programs to revamp its sales structure and lines of authority as well as slash executive pay.

In spite of the firm's efforts to improve its reputation, damaging information continued to emerge. In March 1993 Loucks admitted that Baxter had violated laws against aiding the Arab League's boycott of Israel when it sold its Travenol Laboratories Ltd. operations in Israel and entered into a joint venture with the Syrian army. Asserting that such illegal actions were inadvertent, the corporation nevertheless pleaded guilty to federal charges and agreed to pay $6.5 million in fines. Also that year, Baxter was implicated in a lawsuit brought by hemophiliacs infected by HIV-tainted clotting agents, and it took a $700 million charge for divesting some divisions and reorganizing its diagnostics subsidiary. At year's end, President James Tobin quit, and Baxter's stock plunged to a four-year low. Moreover, Baxter's proposed merger with third-ranking Stuart Medical Inc. was terminated, and Stuart quickly engaged another suitor, Owens & Minor Inc. Their combined operations promised to threaten Baxter's top position in medical/surgical supply, as the new company would follow Baxter by only about $300 million in annual revenues.

Loucks's 1993 letter to shareholders acknowledged that the company's "earnings and stock price [had] not performed well," and announced 1993 losses of $268 million. Nevertheless, sales at Baxter had increased every year from 1988 through 1993, with net sales increasing over $400 million from 1992 to 1993. Loucks vowed to "achieve the potential that exists for Baxter International" by emphasizing service, international growth, and technological innovation through its new "Network 2000," a $400 million plan to expand, consolidate, and modernize facilities and operations.

In January 1999 Harry M. Jansen Kraemer, Jr., replaced Vernon R. Loucks, Jr., as chief executive officer. A year later Kraemer became chairman of Baxter's board. Kraemer continued to grow the company through global expansion, acquiring the IV business of Wockhardt Lifesciences, a leading Indian manufacturer of IV solutions, in 2002. The acquisition included manufacturing facilities in several Indian cities, as well as sales and marketing to the major Indian private hospitals and medical centers.

In 2002 Baxter announced its intent to sell off its renal service businesses to focus more on the product side. In 2003 Baxter sold two unprofitable units to DaVita Inc. These were RMS Lifeline, which Baxter founded in 1998 and operated 12 outpatient vascular access clinics, and RMS Disease Management, which formed in 1995 and provided renal patient care management for health care providers and insurance companies. At the same time, Baxter continued to look for growth opportunities and in 2002 acquired Epic Therapeutics, a drug delivery company specializing in injection or inhalation drugs using its proprietary microsphere technology, which releases drugs over a period of time and allows for less frequent drug injections. In 2009 Baxter developed a vaccine for the H1N1 virus. Also known as "swine flu, " the H1N1 virus caused concerns of a possible pandemic, and Baxter was one of several companies to quickly develop a vaccine.

In the first decade of the twenty-first century Baxter International was plagued by tainted or malfunctioning products, lawsuits, and settlements against the company. During 2001 several people receiving dialysis from Baxter products died. Although the cause of the deaths remained unclear, Baxter shut down the factory producing two types of dialysis filters (a common link between the deaths) and issued a worldwide recall. Contaminated ingredients from a supplier in China caused Baxter to recall its popular drug heparin in January 2008 after 19 deaths were linked to the drug in the previous year.

In July 2009 Baxter reached a $2 million settlement with the Kentucky attorney general Jack Conway over its alleged inflation of average prices for its IV solutions that ranged over 1,300 percent more than the real price, which caused Kentucky Medicaid to pay more than it should have. The Baxter settlement was one of a series of lawsuits that Conway filed against 47 pharmaceutical companies. In May 2010 a jury ordered Baxter Healthcare Services to pay $144 million in punitive damages to a Nevada man who contracted Hepatitis C when a clinic reused an anesthetic distributed by Baxter, despite the label clearly stating that it was a single-use product. The verdict may have paved the way for even greater liability for Baxter since the attorney for the plaintiff also represented 40 more people who claimed they contracted the disease the same way.

While Baxter continued to focus on life-saving products that provided an insulation from economic downturns, product recalls posed a threat to its future sales. In May 2010 the FDA ordered Baxter to recall and destroy all 200,000 of its colleague volumetric infusion pumps on the market. Since 1999 the pumps had been recalled several times. The company expected to take a $400 to $600 million pre-tax charge due to the recall.

*April Dougal Gasbarre*
*Updated, Catherine Meyrat*

## PRINCIPAL SUBSIDIARIES

Baxter Healthcare Pty. Ltd. (Australia); Baxter Limited (Japan); Baxter Netherlands Holding B.V.; (The Netherlands); Baxter S.A. de C.V. (Mexico); Baxter World Trade Corporation.

## PRINCIPAL DIVISIONS

BioScience; Medication Delivery; Renal.

## PRINCIPAL COMPETITORS

Bayer HealthCare AG; Becton, Dickinson & Company; CSL Behring GmbH; Johnson & Johnson; Haemonetics Corp.; Talecris Biotherapeutics Holdings Corp.

## FURTHER READING

"Conway Announces $2 million Settlement with Baxter Healthcare," *Business First of Louisville,* July 2, 2009.

Goldstein, Jacob, "FDA Closes in on Heparin Problems." *Wall Street Journal,* March 5, 2008.

Gullo, Karen, "Teva, Baxter Will Fight $500 Million in Damages over Propofol," *Bloomberg Business Week,* May 8, 2010.

Powell, Bill, "Heparin's Deadly Side Effects," *Time,* November 13, 2008.

"S&P Lowers Outlook on Baxter but Maintains Ratings," *Associated Press,* May 6, 2010.

# Bayerische Landesbank

Brienner Strasse 18
Munich, Bavaria 80333
Germany
Telephone: (49) 89 2171-01
Fax: (49) 89 2171-23579
Web site: http://www.bayernlb.de

*State-Owned Company*
*Founded:* 1884 as Landeskultur-Rentenanstalt
*Employees:* 11,821 (2009)
*Revenue:* EUR 2.561 billion ($3.453 billion, 2009)
*NAICS:* 522110 Commercial Banking; 522291 Consumer Lending; 522293 International Trade Financing; 522298 All Other Nondepository Credit Intermediation; 523110 Investment Banking and Securities Dealing;

∎∎∎

Bayerische Landesbank (BayernLB) is a publicly regulated bank based in Munich, Germany, and one of the eight Landesbanken (regional banks) in Germany. It is 94 percent owned by the free state of Bavaria, with the remainder owned by the Sparkassenverband Bayern, the umbrella organization of Bavarian Sparkassen (savings banks). BayernLB is the eighth-largest financial institution in Germany, with assets of EUR 348 billion ($469 billion).

BayernLB's customer base is focused on Mittelstand (mid-market) companies in Bavaria and Germany, with emphasis on sustainable and efficient energy. Products include capital expenditure loans, working capital, and trade financing. International operations have been scaled back considerably, focusing on providing customers in Germany and Eastern Europe. International customers consist of companies in the construction, chemicals, energy, and technology industries.

## INDUSTRIALIZATION AND CASHLESS TRANSACTIONS: 1884–1914

BayernLB was founded in 1972 with a merger of two large banks performing different functions. The first bank, Landeskultur-Rentenanstalt, originated as a government entity meant to industrialize the agricultural production of Bavaria. The second bank, Girozentrale bayerischer Sparkassen, originated in 1914 as a central clearing place for cashless transactions.

In the latter half of the nineteenth century, Germany experienced rapid economic development. Between 1871 and 1910, Germany's population increased by over half, from 40 million to 65 million people. Railways and canals were built to accommodate the movement of people and products. The agriculture industry now had the opportunity to feed more people geographically. In 1884 King Ludwig II instituted the *Landeskultur-Rentenanstalt* (bond agency for land cultivation). The law's purpose was to finance the industrialization of agriculture by modernizing the land's cultivation. The *Landeskultur–Renten–Kommission* (Local Land Commission) was organized to review loan applications and manage the loans.

In 1914, at the beginning of World War I, noncash payments became an important necessity for the

Germans. Bavarian savings banks came together to found the *Giroverband,* a clearing house for *giro,* similar to the U.S. check. Cash-free fund transfer systems had been developed since 1908. In 1914 Germany chose to finance its war efforts with loans, and this development necessitated a centralized clearing location for the most efficient deployment of funds. By 1917 the *Girozentrale bayerischer Sparkassen,* a portion of which would later merge with BayernLB, became fully functional with a full-time management team.

## LANDESKULTUR-RENTENANSTALT: 1904–49

By 1904 Landeskultur-Rentenanstalt had expanded beyond its original mission. While previously the bank's purpose was to finance agricultural projects, the need to finance proejcts that would supply water to rural areas became imperative. Railways and canal projects continued, although many rural villages opposed the industrialization of their communities.

In 1929 Landeskultur-Rentenanstalt, which had until then been an agency of the government, became an independent legal entity. The new entity was able to embark on new opportunities, such as granting loans for housing and land cultivation. After World War II, the bank was a key financial resource for reconstruction and housing in Bavaria. In addition, the reconstruction efforts offered the opportunity of expanding into the energy sector. In 1949 the entity was renamed *Bayerische Landesbodenkreditanstalt* (Bavarian mortgage bank) in order to more accurately describe its function.

## GIROZENTRALE BAYERISCHER SPARKASSEN: 1925–51

In 1925 the clearing association and the savings association of Girozentrale bayerischer Sparkassen separated into two entities. The clearing unit was renamed *Bayerische Gemeindebank (Girozentrale) Öffentliche Bankanstalt.* The name translates to "Bavarian municipal bank under public law." The segmented entity had

expanded its responsibilities to provide long-term lending to municipalities and businesses.

In 1929 the Bayerische Gemeindebank created a new division, *Bayerische Landesbausparkasse,* meaning "Bavarian home loans and savings." In 1951 the bank was granted the right to issue mortgage bonds, with the proceeds allocated to building residential homes.

## THE TWO HALVES MERGE: 1972

On July 1, 1972, Bayerische Gemeindebank and Bayerische Landesbodenkreditanstalt merged and were renamed *Bayerische Landesbank Girozentrale.* As banking was still largely regulated in Germany, the Bavarian Parliament approved the merger by passing the Bayerische Landesbank Act. Half of the new entity's capital came from the Free State of Bavaria. At this time, Bayerische Landesbank became a depository institution to savings banks in Bavaria and expanded into international transactions.

The merger created the second-largest bank under public law in Germany. Loan volume increased fivefold. Nongovernment business (commercial and private) accounted for over 60 percent of the bank's loan business, with public sector work making up the rest.

In the mid–1970s, as a service to the savings banks, the larger *landesbanks* began offering import and export services for the savings banks' commercial customers. Subsidiaries were opened in Luxembourg, Zurich, New York, London, Paris, and Singapore. Representative offices also opened in Vienna, Johannesburg, Toronto, Tokyo, Prague, Budapest, Milan, and Hong Kong. By 1990 the international business segment accounted for 27 percent of Bayerische Landesbank's total assets.

Bayerische Landesbank also ventured into the credit card and airline industries. In 1987 the bank bought a 5 percent stake in German airline Lufthansa. This led to the 1992 offering of a cobranded Visa card, offering airline rewards. Bayerische Landesbank's thrift banks soon began offering Visa cards to their customers. In 1995 the bank participated in a $165 million syndicated loan for Air Canada. In 2000 the bank bought a 46 percent stake in Austrian travel agent chain Ruefa AG, which it sold in 2004.

## EUROPEAN UNION AND WORLD ECONOMY: 2001–05

In 2002 Bayerische Landesbank hired Werner Schmidt, retired chairman of Landesbank Baden-Württemberg (LBBW), a top public-sector bank in Germany. Schmidt was hired to restructure the bank to prepare for European Union (EU) legislation. In part, the EU

## KEY DATES

**1884:** Bavarian King Ludwig II signs a law establishing the Landeskultur-Rentenanstalt (bond agency for land cultivation).

**1914:** Bank representatives found the Giroverband, a central clearing house for check services that endorses a system of commerce using noncash payments.

**1925:** The Girozentrale bayerischer Sparkassen is renamed Bayerische Gemeindebank (Girozentrale) Öffentliche Bankanstalt (Bavarian municipal bank under public law central clearing unit).

**1949:** Landeskultur-Rentenanstalt is renamed Bayerische Landesbodenkreditanstalt (Bavarian mortgage bank).

**1972:** Bayerische Gemeindebank merges with Bayerische Landesbodenkreditanstalt to form Bayerische Landesbank Girozentrale.

**2005:** Bayerische Landesbank changes its name to BayernLB upon the removal of state guarantees.

**2010:** International banker Gerd Häeusler is named CEO of BayernLB.

ordered German banks to remove themselves from state ownership, as the organization violated EU antitrust laws.

At the time of this transition, BayernLB faced other struggles. The world economy was facing a recession due to political unrest, particularly in the Middle East after the terrorist attacks of September 11, 2001, against the United States. In addition, several of the bank's corporate customers were failing. Customers included Enron, WorldCom, Fairchild Dornier, Holzmann, Herlitz, and Kirch Media. In order to generate cash flow, several international offices were sold, and 500 jobs were eliminated. BayernLB also withdrew funding from Lufthansa subsidiary Aero Lloyd, perhaps accelerating its insolvency.

## INTERNATIONAL EXPANSION: 2001–07

In 2005 the Bayerische Landesbank, already known in the press as BayernLB, officially changed its name as such. This name change reflected the restructuring ef-

forts that began in 2002, focused on preparing for the removal of state support.

By 2005, with drastic improvements in financial performance, BayernLB looked to expand into Eastern Europe and Asia. Collaboration with Asian banks and the opening of the German Center in Shanghai marked the Asian expansion, while the founding of an insurance company and purchasing of majority stakes in financial groups marked the Eastern European expansion.

The German Center opened in November 2005. It offered small and mid-sized German businesses ease of entry into the Chinese market, providing office space, local business expertise, and other amenities for German expatriates. (Another German Center was opened in Delhi, India.) In 2006 BayernLB signed strategic collaboration agreements with the Industrial Commercial Bank of China, Shinhan Bank in Seoul, Korea, and ICICI Bank Ltd. in Mumbai, India.

Also in 2006 BayernLB purchased a 60 percent stake in Bulgarian Union Bank. That same year BayernLB partnered with the Versicherungskammer Bayern group, the largest public sector insurer in Germany to found an insurance company in Hungary. In 2007 BayernLB acquired a majority stake in Hypo Group Alpe Adria (HGAA), an international financial group with over 350 banking and leasing offices in central and southeastern Europe. This acquisition would later become the subject of accusations of wrongdoing and severe financial losses for BayernLB.

In 2007 strategic alliances were formed with the Standard Bank of South Africa and Banco Itaú Group in Brazil. These agreements focused on providing financing and liquidity for German enterprises in those areas.

Projects were also pursued in the United States, Russia, and the United Kingdom up through August 2007. However, by the third quarter of 2007, it was apparent that the real estate crisis originating in the United States would resonate throughout the world, affecting financial markets everywhere.

## PROJECT HERCULES: 2008

In March 2008 BayernLB announced that the subprime crisis caused write-downs of EUR 4.3 billion. This led to the resignation of several BayernLB executives, including CEO Werner Schmidt, chief risk officer Gerhard Gribkowsky, and senior vice president of aircraft and ship finance Ruediger Fern. In addition, 5,600 job cuts were announced.

In response to the economic and corporate difficulties, BayernLB requested and received EUR 10 billion in state aid. The State of Bavaria would provide EUR 7 billion in the form of preference shares with voting rights, effectively making BayernLB a state-owned company. The remainder came from the German federal government under a sector-wide bailout program.

In December 2008 BayernLB's executives announced Project Hercules. The bank would exit completely from Asia, although the German Centers in Shanghai and Delhi would remain. Efforts would be focused on Bavaria and selected regions of Europe. Products and activities would be pared down to reduce risk and serve core customers, including institutional clients and savings banks, commercial real estate, and retail customers.

Even with Project Hercules in place, 2009 was a difficult year for the company. Over 8,000 employees were laid off, totaling over 40 percent of the company workforce. Bayern LB took a EUR 3.277 billion writedown on its business, giving the company a net loss of EUR 2.765 billion for the year.

## SCANDAL AND POTENTIAL PRIVATIZATION: 2009 AND BEYOND

On January 25, 2010, investigators with the prosecutor's office in Berlin searched the offices of Deutsche Kreditbank (DKB), a subsidiary of BayernLB. The investigation's intent was to determine if there was any wrongdoing related to the Hypo Group Alpe Adria (HGAA) acquisition of 2007. The investigation focused on the fact that the purchase price of EUR 1.63 billion for just over 50 percent of the company was paid to a group of investors that had, in recent months, bought HGAA shares at a lower price. One of these investors, Franz Pinkl, had been personal friends with BayernLB's CEO Werner Schmidt, and was named CEO of HGAA upon the acquisition. The investigation led to the resignation of CEO Michael Kemmer, Werner's replacement, a participant in the acquisition.

Suspicions mounted when it was discovered that HGAA was experiencing severe losses, undisclosed at the time of the acquisition. To quiet the growing furor, BayernLB sold its 67.1 percent stake in HGAA to the Austrian government for a symbolic price of EUR 1, effectively nationalizing the subsidiary.

Another accusation concerned a sponsorship agreement for construction of Klagenfurt soccer stadium in 2006. BayernLB bank paid EUR 3.7 billion to finance the construction. This project was suspected to be a cover for money-laundering activities.

On January 26, 2010, Gerd Häeusler was approved as the new CEO of BayernLB. Häeusler's objectives were to return BayernLB to sustainable profitability and to make the bank attractive to potential investors. Häeusler had more than 30 years of experience in German and international banking, with leadership experience at the International Monetary Fund (IMF) and RHJ International, an international financial investment firm.

Under such scrutiny, BayernLB severed ties with U.S. bank Goldman Sachs upon the April 2010 announcement that Goldman Sachs faced a lawsuit by the Securities and Exchange Commission (SEC) for fraud. The suit claimed that Goldman incorrectly disclosed a sale of collaterized debt obligations linked to subprime mortgages when it was clear they would not perform. Goldman Sachs had partnered with BayernLB to finance $263 million for the construction of wind farms in Oklahoma and New York. Goldman had also consulted with BayernLB about the possible sale of a stake of BayernLB to a private investor. In fact, BayernLB's CEO, Gerd Häeusler, confirmed that the State of Bavaria would welcome the opportunity to sell its interest in the bank to a private investor at some point in the 2010s.

*Sara K. Huter*

## PRINCIPAL SUBSIDIARIES

Banque LBLux S.A.; Deutsche Kreditbank AG; Landesbank Saar; MKB Bank Zrt.

## PRINCIPAL DIVISIONS

Commercial Real Estate; Large Corporations, Financial Institutions, and the German Public Sector; Mittelstand Companies; Retail.

## PRINCIPAL COMPETITORS

Banco Santander; Bank of America Corp.; BNP Paribas; Deutsche Bank AG; Dexia Group; HSBC Holdings plc; HVB Group; ING Groep N.V.; Royal Bank of Scotland.

## FURTHER READING

"BayernLB CEO Resigns," *Global Banking News,* December 15, 2009.
"BayernLB Retreats from Asia," *Trade Finance,* December 2008, p. 14.
"BayernLB Says Restructuring on Track," *Total Securitization & Credit Investment,* July 20, 2009, p. 47.
"BayernLB to investigate HGAA Purchase Itself – Report," *ADP News Germany,* February 19, 2010.
"BayernLB Wins EU Approval for State Bailout," *Global Banking News,* December 22, 2008.
"Germany's BayernLB Dismisses Chief Risk Officer," *Global Banking News,* April 4, 2008.
Wilson, James, "BayernLB Being Readied for Sale." *Financial Times,* April 16, 2010.

# Botswana Life Insurance Limited

—■—

**Fairground Office Park**
**Block A Plot 50676**
**Gaborone,**
**Botswana**
**Telephone: (267) 3951-564**
**Fax: (267) 3906-386**
**Web site: http://www.botswanalifeinsurance.com**

*Subsidiary of Botswana Insurance Holdings Limited*
*Founded:* 1975
*Employees:* 168 (2009)
*Sales:* BWP 600 million ($84 million, 2009)
*Stock Exchanges:* Botswana
*NAICS:* 524113 Insurance Carriers

■ ■ ■

Botswana Life Insurance Limited (BLIL), a subsidiary of Botswana Insurance Holdings Limited (BIHL), deals with long-term insurance policy products ranging from life insurance to investment assets management. Billed as the oldest insurance company in Botswana, BLIL has a nationwide network with headquarters in the country's capital, Gaborone.

In addition to basic insurance work, BLIL also enters into strategic partnership with microlending institutions to provide secured loans as a way to strengthen its product portfolio. BLIL entered one such collaboration with Letshego, a leading microlending institution in Botswana.

## COMPANY FOUNDING AND EARLY YEARS: 1975–87

Botswana Insurance Company (BIC) came into existence in 1975 when the company's founders registered it as a private company. Botswana Development Corporation and J.H. Minet & Company Limited were the founding owners of the Botswana Insurance Company, with the former commanding the majority shareholding of 51 percent and the latter controlling a 49 percent shareholding. As such, the Botswana Development Corporation controlled and operated the company as its subsidiary.

The insurance company was created to provide a wide range of insurance policy products that included general insurance, underwriting deposit administration schemes, long-term insurance, and management of life and pension funds investments. However, the rolling out of this diversified range of insurance products did not result in immediate concrete business opportunities for BIC, primarily because the company had to wait until 1977 to sell its first life insurance policy.

The slow pace of development of BIC's product portfolio was caused by the lack of adequate regulation of the insurance sector in Botswana, a problem that was finally tackled in 1979 with the promulgation of the First Insurance Act of Botswana.

The First Insurance Act of Botswana largely dealt with creation of operational framework and legal benchmarks in the country's insurance industry. The act provided clear guidelines that placed emphasis on the distinction of the insurance business from other forms of commercial and financial businesses. As such, the promulgation of the First Insurance Act of Botswana was welcome news to the insurance industry, as it allowed insurance companies to enhance their product portfolios with respect to the provisions of the insurance laws.

BIC registered tremendous growth in the 1980s, thanks to the enhanced insurance industry regulations introduced in 1979. The good tidings experienced by the company in the insurance business became evident in 1980 when the company executed its first expansion strategy with the opening of the Francistown branch office. In 1981 BIC ventured into the real estate business by developing a major residential estate, the Tapologo Estate, which consisted of about 100 housing units.

BIC marked a commendable institutional development milestone in 1983 when it opened a new headquarters in Gaborone's Nyerere drive. The opening ceremony of the company's new head office in June 1983 was presided over by the then vice president and finance minister of Botswana, Peter Mmusi, and graced by a host of other high-profile and ranking government officials. Botswana Development Corporation relinquished its controlling stake in the Botswana Insurance Company in 1984 when Sechaba Investment Trust purchased 24 percent of its shares. J.H. Minet & Company Limited followed suit in 1985 when it sold its entire 49 percent shareholding to St. Paul (UK) Limited.

## GOVERNMENT REGULATION AND COMPANY RESTRUCTURING: 1987–94

The promulgation of the Insurance Industry Act (IIA) of 1987 in Botswana introduced new insurance regulations that had far-reaching implications in the operations of insurance companies in the country. This second piece of insurance legislation introduced major amendments to the First Insurance Act of 1979 that were targeted at streamlining the insurance business.

For example, the second act introduced new provisions regarding the underwriting of short-term and long-term policy options, which now had to be run by

separate insurance companies. Developments like this paved the way for the incorporation of Botswana Insurance Holdings Limited (BIHL) in 1990, a company with which BIC developed a subsidiary relationship in the provision of life insurance and asset management products.

The business and investment environment in Botswana received a huge boost in 1991 when the country sanctioned the liberalization of the exchange control in a move that allowed businesses to diversify offshore investments. The enactment of the Insurance Industry Act (IIA) of 1987 and subsequent liberalization of the exchange control ignited changes and modifications in operational strategies in BIC. The company sought to comply with the insurance regulatory benchmark set by the government by splitting its general insurance and life insurance business segments. Accordingly, BIC was split into Botswana General Insurance Limited (BGIL) and Botswana Life Insurance Limited (BLIL).

Whereas BGIL accommodated the company's assets and liabilities associated with the general insurance product, BLIL focused on underwriting life insurance, administration of deposits, and pension schemes. The split of the company's insurance product segments was followed by the conversion of BIC from a private company into a public limited company. Given that BIC had developed a subsidiary relationship with BIHL in 1990, BIHL became responsible for the total share capital issue for both BLIL and BGIL. However, the previous shareholding identity and structure under the BIC was retained in a move that effectively transformed BLIL and BGIL into BIHL's subsidiaries.

The successful restructuring and eventual transformation of the core business activities of BLIL and BGIL was followed by the listing of the parent company BIHL at the Botswana Stock Exchange (BSE) in August 1991. The regulation of the insurance industry had greatly aided BIHL's business, a factor that the company capitalized on to generate sufficient investor interest. Indeed, the high investor interest in the company was confirmed by the oversubscription of its shares by 273 percent during the initial public offering (IPO). The shares also posted an impressive performance on the first day of trading at the BSE. The company's offer of 25 percent of its total shares to the public altered its ownership structure, with the Botswana Development Corporation Limited, St. Paul (UK) Limited, Sechaba Investment Trust Company Limited, and Southern Life Association retaining their shareholding of 17.85 percent, 30.94 percent, 16.2 percent, and 10 percent respectively.

## KEY DATES

**1975:** Botswana Insurance Company is founded.

**1979:** First Insurance Act regulates industry and spurs growth.

**1991:** Parent company Botswana Insurance Holdings Limited lists on the Botswana Stock Exchange.

**1998:** Company's board of directors features Botswanans for the first time.

**2005:** Sanlams acquires majority interest in Botswana Insurance Holdings Limited.

BLIL's parent company, BIHL, underwent numerous operational adjustments and ownership transformations during the remainder of the 1990s. Most of the company's transformations were focused on diversifying and growing its business opportunities. It developed a commercial center in Palapye (Botswana) in 1992 and built another in Maun (Botswana) one year later. In November 1993 BIHL significantly improved its long-term business prospects when it acquired a controlling stake in IGI Botswana Limited, a development that saw the company become the largest life and life insurance company in Botswana. IGI Botswana Limited had its core business interests in composite insurance at the time.

BIHL's share capital base was strengthened in 1993 through a rights issue in which a total of BWP 13.6 million was raised. The success of BIHL's acquisition and product diversification strategies became evident in 1994 when the company posted premium income in excess of BWP 100 million for the first time in its history. BIHL was marked by high-profile divestitures and acquisitions in 1995 when Botswana Development Corporation divested its shareholding interests, and African Life acquired 25 percent of BIHL shares. Consequently, African Life assumed Southern Life's partnership role in technical and operational management.

### LEADERSHIP CHANGES: 1995–99

After serving at the helm of BIHL for more than seven years, the group's chairman, M. O. Molofane, resigned from his post in 1995. The resignation of Molefane followed the divesture of the Botswana Development Corporation's interests from the group. The resignation of Molefane was a major occurrence not only in the company's history but also in Botswana's insurance

industry as a whole. This was because he had presided over the historic transformation of the insurance company from a private company in 1990 into the largest general and life insurance company in Botswana. Molefane successfully maintained a delicate balance amongst the varying interests of the company's investment portfolios as the company's ownership structure kept on changing with every passing year. Indeed, Molefane's strategic leadership and many years of experience in the insurance industry went a long way toward helping BIHL post impressive financial performance and eventually occupy the market leadership position in Botswana's insurance industry.

A new era of leadership in BIHL set in when A. S. Dada was appointed to replace Molefane as the chairman of the group. The first months of Dada's tenure in 1997 were fairly eventful. BLIL opened a new branch office in Palapye, but more importantly, it reset its insurance product portfolio to focus on management of assets, administration of pension funds, and the provision of long-term life insurance products. This development followed St. Paul (UK) Limited's 1997 acquisition of BGIL, the BIHL subsidiary that dealt with general and short-term insurance products.

However, St. Paul (UK) Limited's influence did not last for long as African Life gained a controlling interest of 57.5 percent in BIHL through the acquisition of St. Paul (UK) Limited's shareholding in the company. African Life's acquisition of the controlling stake in BIHL paved the way for the 1998 appointment of new company's directors to BIHL's board. This was a major development in Botswana's corporate history as the new board of directors fronted by African Life included four citizens of Botswana. The continued expansion and growth of the insurance company in 1998 saw its total asset value expand to more than BWP 500 million.

### LONG-TERM INSURANCE PORTFOLIO ENHANCED: 2000–2010

BLIL focused on the differentiation of its long-term insurance policy products with reference to the ever-changing needs in the market. The company's strategic shift in the 21st century involved designing new long-term insurance policy and mortgage products that targeted particular consumer demographic and economic niches. For example, BLIL introduced the Khumo insurance policy in 2001, a policy with set elements such as life coverage of BWP 25,000 and an accidental death benefit for the same amount. The other significant development in BLIL's business strategies was the 2003 replacement and enhancement of its computerized system for the administration of life insurance. Aided by consultancy firm KPMG, the company implemented a business reengineering project, the Tsoseletso project, in 2004. Designed to improve all aspects of the company, the Tsoseletso reengineering project was completed in August 2005.

BLIL and its parent company, BIHL, upgraded their offices in March 2004 when the company relocated its head office to state-of-the-art offices at Fairground. The company underwent another change in its ownership structure in December 2005 when the majority shareholder of BHIL, African Life Insurance, was acquired by Sanlams, a South African financial services company. According to information contained in the BLIL's Web site, the company expanded its insurance product portfolio in 2006 with the introduction of Mmoloki family wealth plans and Motlhokomedi life coverages.

The global financial crisis of 2008 and 2009 saw the company's operating profits reduced by 12 percent to BWP 75.6 million following a slight reduction in its annual business volume. However, the financial results were still impressive because the company's premium revenues grew by 32 percent to reach BWP 622.4 million in 2009. In an article titled "Botwana: BLIL to Venture into Unit Trusts Next Year" on allafrica.com, Wanetsha Mosinyi observed that BLIL stood out as the best-performing subsidiary of the BIHL in 2009 after posting a 51 percent annual growth to BWP 147.3 million in premium income from new business opportunities.

In August 2009 the company unveiled its strategic plans for launching a unit trust product in 2010 as a product diversification and market expansion measure. The company's chief executive officer, Regina Sikalesele-Vaka, asserted that the unit trust element would enhance the company's market hold on life insurance products.

*Paul Ingati*

## PRINCIPAL COMPETITORS

Metropolitan Life of Botswana Limited.

## FURTHER READING

Benza, Brian, "Botswana: Diversification Pays Dividends for BHIL," allAfrica.com, February 20, 2009.

"BIHL: Botswana Share Market," *Bloomberg Business Week,* 2010.

Kgwagaripane, Kgomotso, "Botswana Life Insurance Limited Externalises Its Brands," *Sunday Standard,* September 9, 2009.

Konopo, Joel, "BIHL Records Impressive Results, " *Business Week,* August 21, 2006, p. 21.

Mosinyi, Wanetsha, "Botswana: BLIL to Venture into Unit Trusts Next Year," allAfrica.com, August 28, 2009.

# C.H. Robinson Worldwide Inc.

14701 Charlson Road
Eden Prairie, Minnesota 55347
U.S.A.
Telephone: (952) 937-8500
Toll Free: (800) 323-7587
Fax: (952) 937-6714
Web site: http://www.chrobinson.com

*Public Company*
*Founded:* 1905
*Employees:* 7,347 (2009)
*Sales:* $7.577 billion (2009)
*Stock Exchanges:* NASDAQ
*Ticker Symbol:* CHRW
*NAICS:* 488510 Freight Transportation Arrangement; 422480 Fresh Fruit and Vegetable Wholesalers; 541614 Process, Physical Distribution, and Logistics Consulting Services

■ ■ ■

As one of the leading third-party logistics (3PL) firms in North America, C.H. Robinson Worldwide, Inc., manages the transportation and distribution of materials, parts, supplies, and finished goods for its customers. From a network of 235 offices in North America, Europe, South America, Asia, Australia, and the Middle East, the company reported handling more than 7.5 million shipments in 2009 for more than 35,000 customers. As a third-party logistics company, C.H.

Robinson does not itself own transportation equipment but rather contracts with transportation carriers to coordinate the movement of its customers' freight. About 75 percent of the company's revenues are derived from truckload and less-than-truckload services. The company also generates revenue from intermodal, ocean, and air transport, as well as custom brokerage fees and management fees, information services, and sourcing. C.H. Robinson's sourcing operations (the founding business) comprise one of the largest fresh fruits and vegetables distribution networks in North America. Among the produce distributed by C.H. Robinson are its own lines, marketed under the brands The Fresh 1 and OurWorld Organics, as well as national brand names. C.H. Robinson began as a small brokerage business, functioning as intermediary between buyer and seller. With the development of the interstate highway system in the 1950s, however, the Minnesota company steadily evolved into a full-service transportation management supplier.

## PRODUCE SHIPPING ROOTS

The company traces its origin to the early 1900s, when Charles H. Robinson established a small brokerage firm in Grand Forks, North Dakota, to ship produce to customers throughout the Red River Valley region of northeastern North Dakota and northwestern Minnesota. In May 1905 Robinson formed a partnership with Grand Forks-based Nash Brothers, the forerunner of the Nash Finch Company and the leading wholesaler in North Dakota. The partnership was

## COMPANY PERSPECTIVES

C.H. Robinson helps our customers ship their products around the world, managing the transportation and logistics of all kinds of cargo—from electronics to automobile parts to fresh produce. We also provide our customers with valuable services and resources that drive efficiency into their systems and processes. The items that you purchase and consume every day are a direct result of the supply chain that we've helped keep in motion for the past 100 years.

incorporated as C.H. Robinson Company, and Robinson was named the company's first president. According to popular legend, related by Lee Egerstrom in the *St. Paul Pioneer Press,* Robinson "sold out a couple of years later and ran off with Annie Oakley, the showgirl shootist of Buffalo Bill Cody's Wild West Show fame," dying shortly thereafter in 1909. Historical evidence has shown, however, that if such a relationship existed, it would have concluded before 1905. Moreover, Robinson did not die in 1909, nor were his shares in the company acquired by the Nash brothers and Harry Finch at that time. Nevertheless, by 1913 the partnership had ended, and the principals of the Nash Finch Company were the sole owners of C.H. Robinson Co.

The Robinson subsidiary served primarily as a produce procurement vehicle for Nash Finch and expanded rapidly by establishing branch offices in Minnesota, Iowa, Wisconsin, Illinois, and Texas, places where Nash had established its own warehouses. In 1919 Minneapolis became Robinson's headquarters, from which the company continued to expand until World War II intervened some two decades later.

During the early 1940s, Robinson also faced action by the Federal Trade Commission (FTC), which concluded that the subsidiary and Nash Finch were in violation of the Robinson-Patman Act because of the price advantage Nash received over that of other wholesalers. As later explained in the *Chronicle* in its fall 1988 issue: "Rather than taking the case to court, C.H. Robinson Co. was split into two separate companies. The first company, C.H. Robinson Co., was formed by all offices selling produce to Nash-Finch warehouses, and the ownership of this company was sold to all Robinson employees. The other company, C.H. Robinson, Inc., comprised the remainder of the offices and was still owned by Nash-Finch Co."

## 1960S AND 1970S: MOVING INTO TRUCKING AND BECOMING EMPLOYEE OWNED

Up until this time, Robinson, like its competitors, was limited to rail transport for the majority of its shipments. Massive funding of the interstate highway system was about to alter that. The Federal Highway Act of 1956 catapulted Robinson into the trucking business. Initially working through its Omaha branch office, C.H. Robinson began capitalizing on opportunities for truck brokerage, launching what may have been the first such brokerage operation in the country. This involvement in managing the transport of "exempt" commodities (perishables that were exempt from government regulation) spread to 10 branches by the 1960s. Around mid-decade C.H. Robinson Co. and C.H. Robinson, Inc., consolidated their operations under the name C.H. Robinson Co. Wholesaler Nash Finch still held a minority stake of approximately 25 percent in the brokerage company, with Robinson employees owning the remainder.

This structural arrangement led to a natural conflict of interests, with Nash requesting more Robinson dividends to invest in its own operations and Robinson wishing to retain more earnings in order to accelerate the company's growth. Finally, in 1976, both companies were satisfied when all remaining Nash shares were bought out, and Robinson Co. became an entirely employee-owned business. A year later, D. R. "Sid" Verdoorn was installed as company president and CEO, and Looe Baker was named chairman of the board. "With this new leadership in place," recorded the *Chronicle,* "Robinson remained on its successful path— with a new commitment to data processing, and a continued dedication to the expansion of transportation and produce branch offices."

## 1980S AND EARLY 1990S: EMPHASIZING LOGISTICS

In 1980 the federal government deregulated the transportation industry through the Motor Carrier Act, which effectively broadened competition in the field. Robinson responded by establishing a contract carrier program and promoting itself not only as a purveyor of food products but also as a freight contractor, or middleman sourcing operation, for virtually all shippable goods. In just five years, the company's average annual growth, measured by truckloads, doubled. The company was now posting more than $700 million in sales, with roughly 40 percent generated by truck brokerage and most of the remainder through produce sales. Commenting on Robinson's evident edge in the truck contracting industry, John J. Oslund, of the *Min-*

## KEY DATES

**1905:** Charles H. Robinson joins with Nash Brothers to form a partnership, C.H. Robinson Company, to ship produce to customers in the Red River Valley.

**1913:** With end of partnership, Nash Finch Company (successor of Nash Brothers) gains sole ownership of C.H. Robinson Co.

**Early 1940s:** Company is divided in two, with one company owned by its employees and the other owned by Nash Finch.

**Mid-1960s:** The two successor firms are consolidated under the name C.H. Robinson Co., with Nash Finch owning about 25 percent and employees the remainder.

**1976:** Nash Finch's shares are bought out and the firm becomes entirely employee owned.

**1997:** Company goes public and changes its name to C.H. Robinson Worldwide, Inc.

**2000:** Trans-Consolidated Inc. is acquired, marking C.H. Robinson's entry into a new segment, refrigerated partial truckload shipments for perishable food manufacturers.

**2002:** John P. Wiehoff, president and CFO since 1998, is named CEO, replacing Sid Verdoorn, who served as CEO of the firm since 1977.

**2005:** Purchase of FoodSource Procurement LLC, a provider of produce sourcing and distribution services.

**2006:** C.H. Robinson expands into India with the acquisition of Triune Logistics Pvt Ltd.

neapolis *Star Tribune,* wrote, "Unlike most of its competitors, who are relative newcomers, Robinson has developed its expertise over more than 50 years in the dicey and competitive world of produce delivery."

In January 1988, in a concentrated effort to become a full-service, multiple-carrier provider, the company launched its Intermodal Division (intermodal denotes shipping that involves more than one mode, such as both truck and rail). As explained in the *Chronicle* in its winter 1994 issue, "By combining its truck strengths with the recently improved service of rail carriers, Robinson saves customers significant dollars on long-distance shipments." In a number of subsequent moves, Robinson increasingly solidified its reputation as a well-

rounded, globally positioned transportation and logistics company. For example, in addition to systematically opening a number of new branch offices each year, in 1990 the company expanded its international service through the formation of C.H. Robinson de Mexico. Two years later, international freight forwarding and air freight operations were added through the acquisition of the oldest and largest freight forwarder, C.S. Greene International Inc.

During 1993, a particularly dynamic year for the company, C.H. Robinson made its first foray into the general food and beverage business with the acquisition of New York-based Daystar International Inc., a $40 million distributor of fruit juice concentrates. As Vice President Looe Baker III told Tony Kennedy, in an interview for the *Star Tribune*: "It's a big deal for us, and you'll see us make more moves....[We're] searching for ways to expand into diversified segments of the food market."

During this time, C.H. Robinson continued to rely primarily on a vast network of independent truck operators, who together offered some 730,000 pieces of equipment, from containers on flatcars to refrigerated vans. Nevertheless, the company began to relax its policy of operating as a non-asset-based service firm by acquiring trucking fleets of its own. In early 1993, Robinson bought a trucking operation based in Sioux Falls, South Dakota, in order to service Carlisle Plastics, whose Western Division was also based there. Other fleet purchases, designed "to provide customer-specific service to large, heavy-volume accounts like Frito Lay" and to create greater flexibility for the company, included 100 48-foot refrigerated containers and 90 48-foot insulated containers. During this time, Robinson worked with over 14,000 shippers and moved more than 500,000 separate shipments annually.

Before the end of 1993, the company enhanced its European presence by acquiring a 30 percent stake in Transeco, a French motor carrier; Robinson later acquired the remaining shares for full ownership of Transeco. Other international activity included the opening of offices in Mexico City; Santiago, Chile; and Valencia, Venezuela. In 1994, on the verge of celebrating its 90th anniversary, Robinson expanded its intermodal strategy with two purchases, Atlanta-based Commercial Transportation Services Inc. and Boston-based Bay State Shippers Inc., both for undisclosed amounts. The company also had plans to broaden its The Fresh 1 line to include more value-added items. Annual volume for the 28-item line numbered between six and eight million packages. Careful not to underestimate the potential of the brand, Robinson believed it could yet become "as recognizable to the trade and consumers as the likes of Dole, Del Monte and Chiquita."

## 1995–2000: GOING PUBLIC AND EXPANDING THROUGH ACQUISITIONS

C.H. Robinson continued to expand its logistics capabilities in the late 1990s. In 1995 the company entered the full-service logistics market through the formation of C.H. Robinson Logistics. This new division focused on developing and managing the logistics operations of customers throughout the entire supply chain. Two years later, the company entered the burgeoning market for expedited freight transportation, focusing on full trailerload shipments, through another new division, CHR-Ex.

At this time, the company remained entirely owned by current and former employees. With a number of the shareholders wishing to cash in at least part of their stakes, the company went public in October 1997. An initial public offering that month of about 25 percent of the company, or 10.6 million common shares, sold for $18 per share (which exceeded the expected price of $15 to $17) and generated about $190 million for the 101 people who sold shares. The initial market value of the company, which was at this time renamed C.H. Robinson Worldwide Inc. to reflect its increased international profile, totaled $743 million. Shares began trading on the NASDAQ under the symbol CHRW. Gross revenues for 1997 reached $1.79 billion, while net revenues amounted to $206 million, a 15.1 percent increase over the previous year. (Net revenues were considered by the company to be a more accurate gauge of performance than gross revenues, as they deducted from gross revenues the cost of the transportation contracted for by the company and the purchase price of the products sourced by the company.) Overseas markets accounted for 16 percent of revenues in 1997.

Sid Verdoorn, CEO of the firm since 1977, was named to the additional post of chairman in 1998. John P. Wiehoff, who was named senior vice president and CFO in July 1998, was promoted to president of the company in December 1999. The leaders initiated a string of acquisitions in 1998, as C.H. Robinson continued to seek opportunities for growth and as the transportation industry entered a period of heightened consolidation. During 1998 two acquisitions were completed for Preferred Translocation Systems, a non-asset-based 3PL firm specializing in partial truckloads, and Comexter Group, an Argentinean firm specializing in South American transportation, freight forwarding, trading, and customs brokering. Another overseas acquisition, that of Norminter S.A., was consummated

the following year. Based in Caen, France, Norminter was a non-asset-based third-party logistics company with offices in France, Germany, Spain, and the United Kingdom. Also in 1999, C.H. Robinson acquired Vertex Transportation Inc., which was based in East Rochester, New York, and provided third-party logistics services throughout North America.

The largest of this string of acquisitions came in December 1999 when C.H. Robinson paid about $136 million in cash and stock for American Backhaulers, Inc., a privately held logistics firm based in Chicago. American Backhaulers specialized in over-the-road transportation services and had annual gross revenues of about $285 million. In August 2000 C.H. Robinson entered a new segment of the market through the purchase of Brooklyn Center, Minnesota-based Trans-Consolidated Inc., which was a third-party logistics firm specializing in refrigerated partial truckload shipments for perishable food manufacturers.

## THE 21ST CENTURY: CONTINUED GROWTH

Growth through acquisition played a major part in C.H. Robinson's strategy in the early 21st century, as it consolidated its position domestically and globally. In January 2002 the company acquired Smith Terminal Transportation Services, Inc., one of the largest 3PL providers in Florida. The following year, C.H. Robinson acquired Frank M. Viet GmbH Internationale Spedition, an international freight and forwarding and third-party logistics company based in Hamburg, Germany. Continuing its global expansion, C.H. Robinson announced in June 2004 that it would open seven offices in China, as well as acquire select assets of Dalian Decheng Shipping Agency Co., Ltd. (DDSA). In December 2004 C.H. Robinson acquired US Traffic Inc., a provider of transportation and logistics services. In February 2005 C.H. Robinson expanded its produce division with the acquisition of FoodSource Procurement LLC, a provider of produce sourcing and distribution services. That September, C.H. Robinson purchased, in separate agreements, German and Italian companies. Gebr Hirdes GmbH was a Hamburg-based provider of freight forwarding and distribution, logistics, and warehousing services, and Bussini Transport Srl., based in Milan, provided international freight forwarding, customs brokerage, and domestic truck services.

In 2006 C.H. Robinson acquired two more companies. These were Payne Lynch & Associates Inc., a provider of transportation brokerage services, and Triune Logistics Pvt Ltd, a logistics services provider based in India. In July 2007 C.H. Robinson acquired LXSI Services Inc., a provider of logistics services.

Presiding over this string of acquisitions was John P. Wiehoff, president and CFO since 1999, who was named CEO in 2002, replacing Sid Verdoorn, who had served as CEO of the firm since 1977. The company's board of directors elected Wiehoff, at age 44, as chairman of the board in August 2006.

Not immune to litigation, C.H. Robinson agreed to pay $15 million in April 2006 to settle a suit brought by several current and former female employees alleging sex discrimination. The settlement was covered by the company's liability insurance. The acquisitions continued, with the $51.7 million 2008 purchase of Transera International Holdings Ltd., a project forwarding company headquartered in Calgary, Canada. Transera was one of the largest privately owned project forwarders in North America, with annual gross revenues of about $125 million. Further solidifying its position in the United States, in July 2009 C.H. Robinson acquired International Trade & Commerce, a U.S. customs brokerage company specializing in warehousing and distribution and headquartered in Laredo, Texas. In September 2009, C.H. Robinson bought Rosemont Farms Corp. Inc. and Quality Logistics, two Florida companies that market and transport produce, for $29 million. The purchase secured access to the growing end of produce distribution for the company.

By 2009 C.H. Robinson had grown revenue to $7.58 billion, less than the $8.58 billion in 2008, but better than the prerecession $7.32 billion of 2007. Net income, a better indicator of a company's financial health, remained steady in 2009 at $3.61 million,

almost unchanged from the 2008 net income of $3.59 million. With no debt, strong cash flow, and a motivated workforce that continued to own the bulk of the company stock, C.H. Robinson appeared likely to maintain and solidify its position in the third-party logistics industry.

*Jay P. Pederson*
*Updated, Catherine Meyrat*

## PRINCIPAL SUBSIDIARIES

CHR Aviation LLC; C.H. Robinson International, Inc.; Transera International Logistics Fze. (Dubai); Transera International Logistics Ltd. (Canada).

## PRINCIPAL COMPETITORS

CEVA Group Plc; Con-Way Inc.; CSX Corporation; DHL International GmbH; Echo Global Logistics Inc.; FedEx Corporation; Fritz Corporation; GATX Corporation; Schneider National, Inc.; UPS Supply Chain Solutions.

## FURTHER READING

Anderson, Mitch, "C.H. Robinson Buys Two Produce Firms," *Minneapolis / St. Paul Business Journal,* September 16, 2009.

"C.H. Robinson Organic Produce Brand Backs Sustainable Harvest," *Progressive Grocer,* October 10, 2008.

"C.H. Robinson Worldwide Acquires Transera International," *Trucking Industry News,* August 4, 2008.

Vomhof, John Jr., "C.H. Robinson to Settle Sex-discrimination Suit," *Minneapolis / St. Paul Business Journal,* April 13, 2006.

# CA Inc.

One CA Plaza
Islandia, New York 11749
U.S.A.
Telephone: (631) 342-3550
Toll Free: (800) 225-5224
Fax: (631) 342-6800
Web site: http://www.ca.com/us

*Public Company*
*Founded:* 1976
*Employees:* 13,200 (2009)
*Sales:* $4.271 billion (2009)
*Stock Exchanges:* NASDAQ
*Ticker Symbol:* CA
*NAICS:* 511210 Software Publishers

■ ■ ■

CA, Inc. (formerly Computer Associates), is a major, multinational computer software vendor. Specializing in information technology (IT) software and applications, most of CA's business is conducted in the realm of mainframe and distributed computer systems, the behind-the-scenes processors sometimes referred to as the "plumbing" of the computer industry. At one time the largest software company in the world (surpassing even Microsoft and Oracle), CA remains a major force in the computer software industry, even if it lacks the name recognition of many of its competitors.

Insofar as CA has been in the public eye of late, most of the news has focused around a string of drawn-out legal battles and financial scandals that saw an almost complete turnover in executive personnel and extensive internal restructuring. In the wake of these scandals, CA is now looking to move aggressively into emerging technologies such as cloud computing.

## INCEPTION: 1976

Like many large software companies, CA started out from decidedly modest origins. In many ways, CA's success story is the story of cofounder Charles Wang building his own American Dream. Having immigrated to the United States with his family at the age of eight from Communist China, in 1967 Wang earned a bachelor's degree in mathematics from New York's Queens College. He put his degree to work in the emerging computer industry, heading up sales at Standard Data Corporation.

In the 1970s, after a 1969 mandate from the U.S. government opened up the door for independent companies to compete against IBM, a wave of entrepreneurial software ventures swept the computer industry. In 1976, after his boss turned down a franchise offered by the Swiss company Computer Associates International Ltd. (CAI), Wang, with no venture capital and mostly using credit cards, jumped at the opportunity.

CAI was looking to expand its market into the United States. In partnership with college friend Russell Artzt and the support of a small group of backers, Wang opened CA's first office in Manhattan, New York City. While his partners focused on software development and running the business, Wang put his sales experience to

## COMPANY PERSPECTIVES

We help companies manage information technology (IT) in all environments—mainframe, distributed, virtualized, and cloud—to become more productive and better compete, innovate, and grow their businesses. We apply decades of experience and innovation to develop and deliver software that integrates with other solutions to make a company's technology investments more valuable.

good use, functioning as the company's marketing developer.

From the start, CA's focus was in software to support mainframe computers. The company's first successful program, CA-Sort, a program that allowed mainframes to efficiently sort data, was simply a distributorship deal with CAI. The program had a firm foothold in Europe but was largely unknown in North America. Wang's sales acumen convinced many customers to switch from IBM's data management software to CA-Sort. Since the program was licensed rather than sold, each new customer represented an ongoing revenue stream.

## UNORTHODOX STRATEGIES: 1977–81

With money now flowing in, Wang began hiring new staff and programmers. Significantly for the future of the company, he also began buying up smaller programming firms, marketing their software to existing clients under the CA banner. This strategy, one that among others would distinguish Wang as a maverick in the software industry, would become a hallmark of CA's business model.

In 1978 Wang instituted another unorthodox business strategy when he brought in his brother Tony as the company's legal counsel. Throughout his time at CA, Wang would earn considerable criticism from industry watchdogs for his practice of hiring close family members. Wang, for his part, simply regarded it as "family loyalty."

With CA expanding by leaps and bounds as the 1970s came to a close, Wang and Artzt were able to buy out CAI in 1980. In four years, they had built their fledgling company up into a profitable venture, but they were already looking to take things to the next level.

## AN ACQUISITIVE NATURE: 1981–89

The 1980s were a time of tremendous expansion and success for CA. The company's 1981 initial public offering sold 500,000 shares of stock valued at over $3 million. The next year, the company made a major acquisition, buying Capex, a company specializing in software for computer programmers, in a stock swap for $22 million. The following year, two more companies were added to the CA stable: Stewart P. Orr Associates and Information Unlimited Software, which Wang purchased for $2 million and $10 million, respectively.

Further acquisitions (six in all between 1984 and 1986) strengthened CA's portfolio and set it up for its largest acquisition to date. This was the European company Uccel, which carried the hefty price tag of $830 million. With the Uccel acquisition, CA simultaneously eliminated one of its chief rivals and became the largest mainframe software vendor in the world.

During the mid-1980s CA began to make attempts to gain a foothold in the booming personal computer market. Its acquisition of Integrated System Software Corp. and Software International in 1986 gave the company access to graphics and financial software. Nevertheless, mainframe software remained the company's primary focus, accounting for 70 percent of its revenues in 1986.

By 1989 CA had grown to become a software industry giant. Its acquisition of Uccel had pushed its customer base up over 30,000. Its many other acquisitions over the previous decade meant that the company could market around 200 distinct software programs at a time when Microsoft was only offering 26.

Wang's unconventional strategy had paid off, even in the face of critics who scoffed that the company had merely bought its way to its current position. Be that as it may, Wang displayed a knack for choosing the right companies to add to his quiver. In 1989 CA became the first software company to top one billion dollars in revenue.

## REFOCUSING: 1990–95

Although the previous decade had ended on a high note, CA's rapid growth had left it saddled with a wide range of problems. For instance, Wang often followed an acquisition with massive layoffs. He cut 25 percent of Uccel's staff within five days of the merger. Due to action like this, CA had earned an industry reputation as a "corporate scavenger." Worse, despite committing over half its 4,500-person workforce to sales or sales

## KEY DATES
◼

**1976:** Computer Associates International, Inc., is founded by Russ Artzt, Charles B. Wang, and other colleagues.

**1981:** CA's Initial Public Offering sells 500,000 shares valued at more than $3.2 million.

**1989:** CA revenues reach $1 billion, the first software company to reach that benchmark.

**2002:** Charles Wang resigns as chairman of the board, ending his association with CA.

**2006:** Company officially changes its name to CA, Inc.

support, CA lagged far behind in the field of customer satisfaction.

Despite a high salesperson-to-customer ratio, many customers of companies acquired by CA complained of poor service, or of being unable to find out who their new sales rep was. Other customers, due to overlapping and inefficiencies caused by the company's rapid growth, found themselves with no fewer than four sales reps assigned to their account. All this confusion and inefficiency, combined with a slowdown in mainframe sales, took its toll. The company's growth plummeted from 45 percent in 1989 to 4 percent just one year later.

With so many mounting problems, it was clearly time for streamlining and restructuring. With so many disparate companies brought in, there seemed to be no overarching strategy to CA's growth. In response, in April 1990 CA launched a software strategy titled "Computer Architecture 1990s." A three-pronged approach, the plan focused on applications, database management, and systems management. Furthermore, the strategy called for compatibility between all of CA's programs, an increasing priority in a computer technology environment that was rapidly shifting from mainframe to client-server software. This was a new approach that utilized a local network of computers plugged into a central server rather than a single large mainframe.

The shift from mainframe to personal computers found CA suffering from relative anonymity outside of the business world. Its grab bag of products, developed by dozens of different companies CA had so far acquired, required new software to serve as intermediaries between different programs. Despite refocusing on internal product development and customer satisfaction, as well as trying new strategies like sending out free

samples of programs to interested consumers, CA found it difficult to make inroads in the personal computer market. Supercalc, CA's answer to Lotus 1-2-3 and Microsoft Excel, only managed a 5 percent share of the market, for example.

Unable to compete in the realm of client-server computing on its own, in 1995 CA made what was at the time the largest takeover deal in the history of the software industry: a $1.78 billion acquisition of Legent Corporation, a competitor specializing in client-server software. Thanks to Legent and several other acquisitions, by the mid-1990s about one-third of CA's sales were going to client-server programs. CA further expanded its market when it reached an agreement to license its software to Apple and Unix-based systems. Revenues grew every year throughout the first five years of the decade.

## DIFFICULT TIMES: 1996–2002

Despite the successful refocusing, CA faced serious challenges in the 1990s. The first sign of trouble came with a lawsuit filed in 1991 by CA customer Electronic Data Systems Corporation alleging licensing fraud, breach of contract, and misuse of copyright. CA countersued the next year. It would take four more years before the suit was settled out of court.

Further troubles were to follow. In the wake of the Legent buyout, the U.S. Justice Department put restrictions on CA's ability to acquire further companies. The company's stock was notoriously volatile at this time, and, despite its aggressive pursuit of improving customer service, a survey conducted in 2001 showed a mere 10 percent satisfaction rate among CA's largest clients.

Perhaps the greatest controversy to dog CA as the 1990s came to a close was the issue of executive pay. Despite a slump in revenues, in 1998 Charles Wang, his protégé Sanjay Kumar, and Russell Artzt garnered bonuses totaling nearly $1 billion. Soon after the bonuses, which had been tied to share price, were paid, CA's stock dropped 31 percent in a single day, and some shareholders accused the company's executives of manipulation. A lawsuit was filed, and nearly half the bonuses were returned as a result of the suit's settlement. Unfortunately for CA's executives, this was to prove just the beginning of a dark time in the company's history.

## LITIGATION AND RESTRUCTURING: 2002–06

In 2002 a federal probe conducted by the Department of Justice and Securities and Exchange Commission began to look into CA's accounting practices, specifically whether revenues were misreported in the 1998 and 1999 fiscal years in order to drive up stock revenue and thereby grant Wang, Kumar, and Artzt their bonuses. That same year, four class-action lawsuits were filed on behalf of investors against the company, accusing CA of double-counting revenues and other such creative book-keeping practices. (With 20,000 employees at the end of the 1990s, CA's internal audit division comprised a mere five employees, some part-timers.)

The government probe accused CA of deliberately misreporting revenues in order to meet Wall Street's expectations. As the probe intensified, CEO Sanjay Kumar resigned his post in April 2004. In September of that year a federal grand jury issued an indictment against Kumar and seven other executives on fraud charges. In 2006 Kumar pled guilty to fraud and conspiracy charges, including lying to investigators and authorizing a $3.7 million bribe attempt to buy a witness's silence. In 2007 Kumar was sentenced to 12 years in prison and ordered to pay $800 million restitution to company stockholders. Charles Wang, retired from the company he founded since 2002, was not charged with any crimes.

The fallout from the Kumar trial was predictable. CA stock plummeted 70 percent from its 2000 high, and sales dropped 40 percent. In response to the trial and loss of public and investor confidence, CA instituted a radical restructuring program. The entire upper management and most of the board were replaced, and much tougher accounting controls were instituted.

## NEW EXECUTIVES AND NEW ACQUISITIONS: 2007–10

In the wake of its extensive internal restructuring, in 2005 CA launched a new corporate branding program, titled "Believe Again."

A sign of how far CA had distanced itself from its years under Charles Wang came in 2007, when the company's board issued a 390-page report accusing Wang of engaging in over a decade of accounting fraud. The report, as quoted in a 2007 *New York Times* article, also charged Wang with creating a "culture of fear" in the corporation and with promoting inexperienced, easily manipulated executives to top positions. For his part, Charles Wang issued a statement, quoted in the same *New York Times* article, that he "intend[ed] to vigorously defend [his] good name[,]" was "appalled" by the report, and placed all blame for accounting irregularities on "the crimes of Kumar and his management team[.]"

With its new internal structures in place and the old guard firmly distanced, CA has begun to expand into the emerging field of cloud computing, an Internet-based computing technology that shares resources among a "cloud" of computers in order to deliver information technology to users. Having missed the shift from mainframe to personal and client-server computing, CA was clearly aiming to get in early on this next big shift in IT delivery. Yet in its methodology, it has returned to familiar ground, buying up three cloud computing technology companies at the end of 2009 and beginning of 2010.

Perhaps in part due to its recent surge of acquisitions, CA announced on April 8, 2010, that it would be cutting its workforce by 8 percent. That move came as the latest in a three-year restructuring plan that retrenched 3,100 employees and reduced the company's total expenses by 15 percent. After a decade of litigation and public scandal, with the targeted expansion into emerging technologies and judicious pruning, CA was clearly set to "Believe Again."

*Scott M. Lewis*
*Updated, A. Woodward; David Larkins*

## PRINCIPAL SUBSIDIARIES

Aprisma Holding Inc.; Cendura, L.L.C.; Cheyenne Software, Inc.; MDY Advanced Technologies, Inc.; Uccel Corporation; XOsoft, L.L.C.

## PRINCIPAL COMPETITORS

BMC Software, Inc.; Hewlett-Packard Company; International Business Machines Corporation; Symantec Corp.

## FURTHER READING

Berenson, Alex, "Ex-Executive Agrees to Pay $800 Million in Restitution." *New York Times,* April 13, 2007.

———. "CA Says Its Founder Aided Fraud," *New York Times,* April 14, 2007.

Cowley, Stacy, "Report: CA Probe Focuses on 1998, 1999 Revenue," *Computer World,* May 20, 2002.

Jowitt, Tom, "CA Releases Raft of Admin Tools for 'Lean IT.'," *TechWorld,* May 8, 2009.

"Software Maker Triples Its Profit." *New York Times,* February 1, 2008.

"Wang, Charles B., " in *Business Leader Profiles for Students,* edited by Sheila Dow and Jaime E. Noce. Vol. 1. Detroit: Gale, 2002.

# CenterPoint Energy, Inc.

1111 Louisiana Street
Houston, Texas 77002
U.S.A.
Telephone: (713) 207-1111
Toll Free: (888) 468-3020
Fax: (713) 207-3169
Web site: http://www.centerpointenergy.com

*Public Company*
*Founded:* 1866
*Employees:* 8,810 (2009)
*Revenues:* $8.281 billion (2009)
*Stock Exchanges:* New York; Chicago
*Ticker Symbol:* CNP
*NAICS:* 221122 Electric Power Distribution; 221210
 Natural Gas Distribution

■ ■ ■

As the nation's third-largest combined electricity and gas utility, CenterPoint Energy, Inc., is a *Fortune* 500 public utility holding company that serves approximately five million metered customers. The company operates in five primary businesses: electric transmission and distribution, natural gas distribution, interstate natural gas pipelines, field services, and competitive natural gas sales and services. CenterPoint Energy manages its functions primarily via two wholly owned subsidiaries, CenterPoint Energy Houston Electric, LLC and CenterPoint Energy Resources Corp.

CenterPoint Energy Houston Electric, LLC is a regulated "wires" utility that handles electric transmis-

sion and distribution in the Greater Houston area, which spans around 5,000 square miles and includes over two million customers. Although it delivers power from power plants to homes and businesses, CenterPoint Energy Houston Electric does not generate power or sell power to its customers. Instead, it delivers electricity for 79 retail electric providers via more than 3,700 miles of transmission lines and 47,000 miles of distribution lines. As a wire utility, the company is responsible for operating and maintaining the wires, poles, and electric infrastructure within its service territory.

Under the umbrella of CenterPoint Energy Resources Corp., CenterPoint Energy owns and operates natural gas distribution businesses in Arkansas, Louisiana, Minnesota, Mississippi, Oklahoma, and Texas. CenterPoint Energy Services (CES), its natural gas marketing business, sells unregulated natural gas and related services to some 9,700 industrial, commercial, and wholesale customers located primarily in the eastern half of the United States. CES alone has offices in Illinois, Indiana, Louisiana, Minnesota, Pennsylvania, Texas, and Wisconsin. The Field Services division of CenterPoint Energy Resources Corp. gathers, treats, and processes natural gas from fields in Arkansas, Louisiana, Oklahoma, and Texas, moving it from wellhead to pipeline. Its ServiceStar division installs and maintains remote wellhead monitoring and communications services in Alabama, Arkansas, Colorado, Illinois, Kansas, Louisiana, Mississippi, Missouri, New Mexico, Oklahoma, Texas and Wyoming. In addition, CenterPoint Energy Resources Corp. directs 8,000 miles of interstate pipeline operations in the "mid-continent

## COMPANY PERSPECTIVES

●

At CenterPoint Energy, our vision is "To be recognized as America's leading energy delivery company...and more." To us this means more than just doing business, it means being guided by a set of core values that define who we are and what we believe. At CenterPoint Energy, we're committed to doing business every day with integrity, accountability, initiative and respect—respect for our customers, shareholders, employees, and the communities we serve.

region," an industry term for the fuel-producing and refining region in the nation's heartland.

## HOUSTON UTILITIES

Although CenterPoint Energy was announced as a new holding company on January 18, 2002, the history of CenterPoint Energy dates back to 1866, when the Houston Gas Light Company was formed to supply gas for the city's street lights. Two years later, the company built Houston's first manufactured gas plant on the west bank of the Buffalo Bayou, an operation that made coal gas for distribution to customers. In June 1882, Houston Electric Light & Power was granted a franchise by the Houston City Council. In December of that same year, the company conducted the city's first test of electric lights, which led to the installation of the first electric street lights in Houston in 1884. Competition between Houston Gas Light Company and Houston Electric Light & Power was fierce until Houston Electric Light & Power, which had been experiencing technical and financial difficulties, was acquired by the Houston Gas Light Company in June 1887.

Electric power companies were steadily emerging in other parts of the country as well during the late 1800s. In Minneapolis, for example, the Minneapolis Gas Light Co. provided gas service with gas manufactured from coal or oil at a plant located along the Mississippi River. Fort Wayne Jenny Electric Light Company of Indiana received a franchise to operate in Houston in 1888. Houston investors, however, still believed that the city of Houston needed an independent electric company and chartered the Citizens' Electric Light & Power Company on July 29, 1889. Only three days later, the company bought the franchise rights to Fort Wayne Jenny Electric Light Company, a deal that included all of Fort Wayne's equipment.

Opting not to vie for Houston's electric power market, the Houston Gas Light Company sold its interest in the Houston Electric Light & Power Company in January 1891. As a result, Citizens' Electric became Houston's sole electric power provider. Even so, the company was beset by financial difficulties that forced it to go into receivership, a situation in which the management of a company is handed over to a receiver appointed by a court, on January 7, 1898. Four men were killed when a boiler exploded at the Citizens' Electric's power plant on March 26, 1898, and the plant was completely destroyed by a fire the next day. The property and franchise were sold in 1901 to the newly chartered Houston Lighting & Power Company (HL&P), which served the greater Houston area for the next 80 years.

## ELECTRIC COMPANY GROWTH

The first 30 years of the new century were marked by numerous mergers and acquisitions for HL&P. During these decades, many firsts in Houston's energy industry changed not only how power plants functioned, but also how people lived. In 1922, for instance, the city's first electric traffic signals went into operation. HL&P pioneered the use of natural gas as a boiler fuel in 1926. In 1930 Houston's inaugural lighted baseball game took place on the night of July 22.

On August 16, 1943, HL&P common stock began trading on the New York Stock Exchange, and the company offered its first employee retirement plan in 1945. By 1955 HL&P had installed its 400,000th electric meter in the Houston area, which was growing rapidly. During a special election two years later, Houston voters approved a new 50-year franchise for HL&P. Citizens in the nearby town of Clute followed suit soon after, becoming the first city outside of Houston to grant HL&P a new 50-year franchise.

The beginning of the 1960s brought unexpected financial difficulties for HL&P. On August 11, 1960, a boiler at the company's Webster plant exploded, resulting in damages totaling over $500,000. In response to this incident, HL&P had to increase its rates. On September 11, 1961, Hurricane Carla struck the Texas Coast, causing $1.5 million in damages to HL&P property. Despite these setbacks, HL&P continued to expand its services in supplying energy to Houston, which had a population of one million in 1961, and its surrounding areas. The company's 500,000th customer was connected to power in Houston in 1965. HL&P began a conversion from incandescent to newly improved mercury vapor street lights in June 1965, and the project was completed two years ahead of schedule in 1967.

## KEY DATES

**1866:** Houston Gas Light Company begins operations to supply gas for street lights.

**1887:** Houston Gas Light Company takes over rival Houston Electric Light & Power.

**1891:** Citizens' Electric acquires Houston Electric Light & Power from Houston Gas Light Company.

**1930:** Houston Gas & Fuel, formerly known as Houston Gas Light Company, joins 39 other small gas companies in Texas, Louisiana, and Mississippi to form the United Gas Corporation.

**1961:** Hurricane Carla hits the Texas Coast, causing $1.5 million in damages to Houston Lighting & Power property.

**1974:** United Gas becomes Entex, Inc.

**1997:** Houston Industries merges with NorAm Energy Services to become one of the country's largest integrated energy companies.

**1999:** Houston Industries changes its name to Reliant Energy, Inc.

**2002:** CenterPoint is created as part of the restructuring of Reliant Energy, Inc.

**2009:** The company's first smart meter is installed as part of the Advanced Metering System.

In October 1975 HL&P shareholders established Houston Industries Incorporated in a corporate restructuring plan. According to the agreements of this plan, Houston Industries became the sole owner of all of HL&P's outstanding common stock, as well as the outstanding stock of two of HL&P's former subsidiaries. Each share of common stock of HL&P was converted to one share of Houston Industries stock. The company began trading on the London Stock exchange in 1984.

### GAS COMPANY GROWTH

After splitting from the Houston Electric Light & Power Company in 1891, Houston Gas Light had become Houston Gas & Fuel in 1912. In 1930 Houston Gas & Fuel joined 39 other small gas companies in Texas, Louisiana, and Mississippi to form the United Gas Corporation. United Gas remained one of Houston's leading natural gas providers throughout four decades. In the meantime, other natural gas companies in Arkansas, Louisiana, and Minnesota were expanding their operations, moves that would greatly impact the

gas industry in Houston in the years to come. In 1970 Houston's United Gas Corporation merged with Pennzoil, spinning off the distribution unit as United Gas, Inc. This entity's name was changed to Entex, Inc. in 1974. As Entex, the company acquired the gas distribution properties of former competitor Houston Natural Gas Corporation.

Arkla, Inc., a natural gas company that had been formed in 1934 from the merger of several small companies in Arkansas and Louisiana, purchased Entex in 1988 in the largest acquisition in that company's history. Arkla continued to acquire other gas companies so that its reach expanded to Minnesota, North Dakota, and Nebraska. In 1994 shareholders approved a proposal that Arkla, Inc.'s name be changed to NorAm Energy Corp. This change, they believed, would more accurately reflect the company's presence in the North American market. One year later, NorAm began selling wholesale electric power throughout the nation. NorAm Energy Management was established to oversee retail energy marketing, and the company's gas gathering assets were transferred to NorAm Field Services.

### INTEGRATED ENERGY COMPANY

In a $3.8 billion transaction, Houston Industries acquired NorAm Energy Corp. in 1997. The merger resulted in one of the largest integrated (electric and gas) energy companies in the United States. After Houston Energies changed its name to Reliant Energy Inc. in 1999, its distribution companies became Reliant Energy HL&P, Reliant Energy Entex, Reliant Energy Arkla, and Reliant Energy Minnegasco. The next year, Reliant Energy Inc. announced plans to separate its businesses into regulated and unregulated companies. In 2002 Reliant Energy announced a new holding company, CenterPoint Energy, with the stock symbol CNI that would replace Reliant Energy's REI symbol. Later that year, the Securities and Exchange Commission approved a spinoff in response to Reliant Energy's separation plan, and CenterPoint Energy and Reliant Resources were officially separated. HL&P and Entex both became CenterPoint Energy.

In 2005 CenterPoint's Energy Gas Transmission Company (CETG) and Duke Energy Gas Transmission (DEGT), another Houston-based company, revealed an agreement to cooperate in the evaluation, marketing, and development of a 250-mile pipeline that would connect CEGT's Perryville Hub in northeast Louisiana to DEGT's affiliate pipeline, Gulfstream Natural Gas System. This pipeline would have a transport capacity of at least 700 million cubic feet per day. CenterPoint also worked with fellow utilities in Alabama, Florida, Louisiana, and Mississippi after Hurricanes Katrina and

Rita struck the Gulf Coast in 2005. Combined, the storms caused damages in excess of $92 billion and killed almost 2,000 people. In the aftermath of the hurricanes, CenterPoint dispatched crews from Arkansas, Houston, and Shreveport to work on broken natural gas lines, as well as downed power lines.

## INTELLIGENT GRID TECHNOLOGY

One major focus of CenterPoint Energy in the latter half of the first decade of the 21st century was intelligent grid technology. An intelligent grid, also known as a smart grid, links the transmission and delivery of electricity with communications and computer control to create an automated, highly responsive power delivery system. Smart meters gave CenterPoint the ability to automate meter reading, as well as electric service connection and disconnection. This, in turn, helped reduce the time customers had to wait to have new electric service connected. Smart meters were designed to provide automatic notification to CenterPoint Energy when power outages occurred.

CenterPoint predicted that smart meters would help consumers conserve energy and reduce utility costs. Since the smart meters measure usage in 15-minute intervals, CenterPoint customers could view data showing their consumption habits. The company believed this feature would encourage customers to manage their electric use and its cost closely. Another advantage of a smart meter was that the device could communicate with home appliances integrated with smart technology so that the appliances could be remotely activated to come on during hours when power was less expensive.

On December 18, 2008, CenterPoint was granted approval from the Public Utility Commission of Texas to implement an Advanced Metering System (AMS), approximately 250,000 interactive meters, across its service area. Beginning in March 2009, the project was expected to take five years to complete. On March 23, 2010, CenterPoint Energy announced that it had received a $200 million stimulus grant from the U.S. Department of Energy for its advanced metering system and intelligent grid projects. The company's grant application asked for $150 million to expedite its current installation of smart electric meters, along with the necessary equipment that comprised its AMS. In addition, CenterPoint Energy requested $50 million for the development of a self-healing intelligent grid that would use AMS and other technologies to improve power reliability and efficiency in the Houston area. This funding, the maximum smart grid grant given under the American Recovery & Reinvestment Act of 2009, was

expected to help CenterPoint Energy meet its goal of completing its installation of over two million smart meters in 2012 instead of 2014, as had originally been planned.

Overall sales decreased from 2008 to 2009, caused primarily by a reduction in natural gas sales and services, which went from $4.528 billion to $2.230 billion. Even with this drop, CenterPoint's balance sheet remained strong, and the company had a strong position as the utility service for Houston, one of the nation's fastest growing metropolises.

*Alicia Elley*

## PRINCIPAL SUBSIDIARIES

CenterPoint Energy Field Services, Inc.; CenterPoint Energy Gas Transmission Company; CenterPoint Energy Houston Electric, LLC; CenterPoint Energy Investment Management, Inc.; CenterPoint Energy Resources Corp.; CenterPoint Energy Services, Inc.; Utility Holding, LLC.

## PRINCIPAL DIVISIONS

Electric Transmission and Distribution; Field Services; Interstate Pipelines; Natural Gas Distribution; Natural Gas Sales and Services.

## PRINCIPAL COMPETITORS

American Electric Power Company, Inc.; Dominion Resources, Inc.; Duke Energy; Edison International; Entergy Corp.; Exelon Corp.; FirstEnergy Corp.; Pepco Holdings, Inc.; PG&E Corp.; Public Service Enterprise Group.

## FURTHER READING
Aulbach, Louis F., "The Gable Street Electric Station," *Buffalo Bayou: An Echo of Houston's Wilderness Beginnings,* users.hal-pc.org, April 20, 2010.

Boone, Mike, and Chuck Hackney, "Houston Brings Its Grid Into the Digital Age," *Transmission & Distribution World,* December 2009, p. 36–39.

Carey, John, "Obama's Smart-Grid Game Plan," *BusinessWeek Online,* October 28, 2009, p. 5.

"CenterPoint Energy Files to Deploy up to 250,000 Meters," *Utility Automation & Engineering T&D,* June 2008, p. 14.

Palmeri, Christopher, "Anger in Houston over Post-Ike Power Outage," *BusinessWeek Online,* September 26, 2008, p. 14.

Smith, Jewel, "CenterPoint Succeeds with Program to Include Minority Professional Service Firms," *Natural Gas & Electricity,* July 2008, p. 16–18.

# Charter Communications, Inc.

—■—

12444 Powerscourt Drive
St. Louis, Missouri 63131
U.S.A.
Telephone: (314) 965-0555
Toll Free: (888) 438-2427
Fax: (314) 909-0609
Web site: http://www.chartercom.com

*Public Company*
*Founded:* 1993
*Employees:* approx. 16,700 (2009)
*Sales:* $6.755 billion (2009)
*NAICS:* 4841 Cable and Other Pay Television Services

■ ■ ■

Charter Communications, Inc., (Charter) a *Fortune* 500 company, is one of the largest cable operators in the United States. In addition to delivering cable television services to residential customers, Charter provides telephone and high-speed Internet services to both residential and business customers. Charter serves over five million customers in 27 states. Like all of its major competitors, Charter bundles its services, offering customers packages that include combinations of telephone, television, and Internet services.

## CHARTER GROWS THROUGH ACQUISITIONS: 1993–98

Charter Communications, Inc., was formed in January 1993 by three former executives of St. Louis-based Cen-

com Cable Associates, Inc. Howard Wood was the former president and chief executive officer of Cencom, Barry Babcock was the former chief operating officer of Cencom, and Jerry Kent was Cencom's former chief financial officer. Cencom had been acquired in 1991 by Crown Media Inc., a Dallas-based subsidiary of Hallmark Cards Inc., for an estimated $1 billion. Crown subsequently made an initial investment of several hundred thousand dollars in Charter, and in turn received a 51 percent nonvoting stake in the company. The decision to form Charter was precipitated by Crown's plans to move Cencom's headquarters from St. Louis to Dallas. Babcock became Charter's chairman, and Kent became president, while Wood chaired the management committee.

At first Charter was based in Cencom's offices in west St. Louis County. The company expected to acquire cable properties and began looking around the country. It was also considering such cable-related businesses as telecommunications and video data systems. When Charter was first established, the regulatory environment for cable television was changing. Congress had just passed a new cable bill over President George H. W. Bush's veto, but the Federal Communications Commission (FCC) had not yet established all of the regulations to enforce the new legislation.

In February 1994 Charter announced its first acquisition. It would spend nearly $200 million to acquire 10 cable systems in Louisiana, Georgia, and Alabama. The systems were acquired from the McDonald Group of Birmingham, Alabama, and served about 100,000 subscribers in the Southeast. Charter's strategy at this time was to acquire smaller systems throughout the Southeast and eventually go public.

The price for cable systems jumped dramatically after the regional Bell operating companies (RBOCs) such as Southwestern Bell began buying cable systems in 1993. Southwestern Bell paid about $2,888 per subscriber in a $650 million acquisition in February 1993. The cost of Charter's first acquisition was estimated at about $1,500 to $2,000 per subscriber.

In June 1994 Hallmark Cards sold its Crown Media cable subsidiary to Charter and Marcus Cable for $900 million. Charter purchased the Crown cable systems serving about 270,000 customers in Connecticut, Kentucky, Missouri, North Carolina, and South Carolina. Charter also assumed management of Crown-affiliated cable systems serving another 360,000 subscribers. Marcus acquired the remaining Crown Media cable properties. It was estimated that Charter and Marcus paid about $2,000 per subscriber.

In January 1995 Charter, in partnership with the money management firm Kelso & Co., announced it would acquire Nashville-based Gaylord Entertainment's cable systems serving 180,000 subscribers in California, North Carolina, and South Carolina, for about $370 million. Gaylord selected the Charter-Kelso partnership, CCT Holdings, over Century Communications, with whom it had also been negotiating. The agreement was finalized in April, increasing Charter's cable systems to 850,000 subscribers, and completed in October, by which time Charter had over 900,000 subscribers. The Gaylord family was one of the initial investors in Charter with a 20 percent stake in the company.

In mid-1995 Charter picked up another 29,000 subscribers in northern and central Alabama from CableSouth Inc. for about $50 million. It also acquired Peachtree Cable Systems with 13,000 subscribers in Georgia for $20 million. At the same time the company was bidding for a much larger cable property, Multimedia Inc., which had hired the investment banking firm Goldman Sachs & Co. to auction the company. Multimedia's cable holdings included 125 franchises with 450,000 subscribers, mainly in Kansas, North Carolina, and Oklahoma. Charter's partners in the bidding were Kelso & Co. and Ellis Communications.

They were competing against a group led by the National Broadcasting Co. that included cable giant TCI and others, but Multimedia was sold in 1994 to Gannett Company Inc. for $1.7 billion. At the time Charter was the 15th-largest MSO (multiple system operator) in the United States.

In March 1996 Charter acquired WIBV(AM) serving the St. Louis area for between $1 million and $1.5 million. It was the company's first radio station. In April the company purchased the cable systems it had been managing for Cencom for $211.1 million. The systems served 100,000 subscribers in eight states. In August Charter expanded its share of the Southern California cable market by acquiring CVI Cable for an undisclosed amount. CVI served 67,000 customers in Long Beach and Signal Hill, while Charter had more than 250,000 customers in other Southern California communities.

Charter's 14th acquisition, the 37,000-subscriber Price Cable of Hickory, North Carolina, put it over the one million subscriber mark in February 1997. Between 1993 and 1997 Charter raised more than $2 billion in equity and debt to fund its acquisitions. The company had three or four major financial investors and adopted a different clustering strategy with each partner. The acquisitions involving Kelso & Co. followed an urban clustering strategy, resulting in 230,000 subscribers in St. Louis, 250,000 subscribers in the Los Angeles metropolitan area, and 100,000 subscribers in the Northeast, notably Hartford and New York. Another financial partner, Charterhouse Group International, was used to acquire more than 400,000 subscribers in the southeastern United States.

During 1997 Charter attempted to acquire US West Media Group's 230,000-subscriber cable systems in Minneapolis-St. Paul for $600 million. However, the deal fell through, and in April 1998 the renamed MediaOne Group, a subsidiary of US West, was required to pay Charter between $30 and $50 million to keep the cable systems.

During the second half of 1997 Charter added 70,000 subscribers in Long Beach, California, with the purchase of KC Cable Associates LP for $150 million. In September 1997 Charter announced it would acquire cable systems with 117,000 subscribers in California and Utah from Sonic Communications. The deal closed in May 1998, and Charter moved into the top 10 among MSOs. Other negotiations failed to add to Charter's systems. Charter's bid for a 300,000-subscriber Las Vegas system was topped by Cox Communication's $1.3 billion offer, and Dallas-based Marcus Cable went to the entrepreneur Paul Allen for $2.8 billion.

## KEY DATES

**1993:** Charter Communications, Inc., is formed by three former executives of Cencom Cable Associates, Inc., in St. Louis, Missouri.

**1994:** Charter begins acquiring cable television systems.

**1997:** Charter reaches one million suscribers.

**1998:** Charter is acquired by Microsoft Corp. cofounder, Paul Allen, for $4.5 billion.

**1999:** Charter goes public in November after making more than 10 major acquisitions in one year.

**2000:** Charter acquires Bresnan Communications for $3.1 billion.

**2002:** Class action lawsuits filed against Charter allege that the company engaged in misleading accounting practices and breach of fiduciary duty.

**2003:** Charter sells a portion of its East Coast cable holdings to Atlantic Broadband.

**2005:** Company announces effort to hire new executives amid sustained annual losses.

**2006:** Charter restructures a significant portion of its debt.

**2009:** Charter files for bankruptcy and emerges from Chapter 11 protection.

## PAUL ALLEN MOVES INTO CABLE: 1998–99

Following his purchase of Marcus Cable, Allen bought Charter for $4.5 billion, or about $3,800 per subscriber. Allen's interest in cable properties may have been spurred by Bill Gates's $1 billion investment in 1997 in Comcast. Both Gates and Allen had developed a vision of a "wired world," in which everyone would have a PC at home and at work and be connected by a global network. Cable was now perceived as the best way of implementing that vision by delivering high-speed services over the Internet into U.S. homes.

Kent was named president and CEO of the new company, which combined Charter's 139 cable systems in 17 states with those of Marcus in six states. Babcock became vice chairman, and Wood was named senior adviser. The company's headquarters remained in St. Louis. The combination of Marcus and Charter created the seventh-largest MSO in the United States, with 2.4 million customers. By the end of 1998 Jeffrey Marcus had left Charter to join Chancellor Media, and Babcock

was named chairman. Two top Marcus Cable officials were dismissed following service problems in Fort Worth and other North Texas cities that were blamed on poor management.

In September 1998 Charter reached an agreement with EarthLink, one of the largest independent Internet service providers (ISPs) in the United States, for Earth-Link to offer Internet access over cable modems to Charter's cable customers. The Charter Pipeline service, as it was called, began in 1997 in Southern California. The new agreement would eventually cover Charter's 19-state operating area and give EarthLink a potential market of 1.8 million customers. For 1998 Charter reported a net loss of $535.4 million on revenues of $2.7 billion.

In January 1999 Charter added 68,000 subscribers in Southern California with the purchase of four cable systems from American Cable Entertainment of Stamford, Connecticut. After the acquisition Charter would have more than 500,000 subscribers in the region.

Also in January Charter joined with cable giant TCI Inc. in a $2.4 billion deal to purchase 60 percent of the subscribers of InterMedia Partners, ranked as the 10th-largest MSO. Charter would acquire 400,000 InterMedia subscribers, primarily in the Southeast, for an estimated $1.3 billion. As part of the deal Charter would turn over about 140,000 of its subscribers to TCI. At the time TCI was in the process of being acquired by AT&T.

During February 1999 Charter made several acquisitions and added one million subscribers. By the end of the month it had about 3.33 million subscribers after completing the announced transactions and merging with Marcus Cable. The acquisitions would make Charter the sixth-largest cable operator in the United States. Among the acquisitions were cable systems serving 460,000 subscribers from Rifkin Acquisition Partners and InterLink Communications purchased for an estimated $1.5 billion. Charter also picked up 173,000 subscribers, mostly in central Massachusetts, from New Jersey-based Greater Media Inc., which also sold its cable properties in Philadelphia serving 79,000 subscribers to Comcast. Charter increased its presence in the Southeast by acquiring Renaissance Media Group, a New York partnership serving 130,000 customers near New Orleans, western Mississippi, and Jackson, Tennessee. The price was estimated at $450 million, or about $3,500 per subscriber.

SEC filings that were required before selling $3 billion worth of bonds to pay off higher-interest debt revealed that Allen had personally invested about $4.6 billion to finance $10.6 billion worth of cable acquisitions, making cable Allen's single biggest investment. Allen's personal fortune at the time was estimated at about $22 billion.

In March 1999 Charter confirmed rumors that it was planning an initial public offering (IPO) for the second half of 1999. With 3.4 million subscribers, Charter was the seventh-largest MSO in the United States. The IPO was expected to raise $2 billion to $3 billion. That same month Charter bought a collection of cable systems in the Southeast and Northeast with the $550 million acquisition of New Jersey-based Helicon Cable Communications. The systems served about 171,000 customers in eight states. Charter paid about $3,200 per subscriber. Allen had invested $11.2 billion for cable properties over the past year, with more to follow.

In April the Dallas-Fort Worth cable franchises that had been under Marcus Cable began doing business under their new name, Charter Communications. In May Charter acquired Av-alon Cable TV for $845 million, adding 260,000 subscribers at about $3,250 per subscriber. The acquisition gave Charter 3.9 million customers, taking into account all pending acquisitions. Avalon had acquired most of its subscribers in 1998 from Cable Michigan Inc. when it bought the 220,000-subscriber cable company for $473 million. Charter also acquired a Vista Communications cable system in Smyrna, Georgia, for $125 million.

In May Charter announced it would acquire Falcon Cable TV of Los Angeles for $3.6 billion. The deal would give Charter a total of about five million subscribers and move it up in the rankings from fifth- to fourth-largest MSO. Falcon was the eighth-largest cable operator in the United States with about one million subscribers in 27 states in primarily nonurban areas. It was Charter's ninth acquisition of 1999 and certainly not its last.

Charter's 10th acquisition of 1999 involved Fanch Communications Inc. of Denver. Fanch had 547,000 subscribers, including 308,000 in West Virginia and Pennsylvania, 70,000 in Michigan, and 70,000 in Indiana, Kentucky, Louisiana, and Wisconsin. It was reported that Charter paid $2 billion, or $4,000 per subscriber. The acquisition gave Charter a total of 5.5 million subscribers. Following the acquisition, Charter was the fourth-largest MSO behind AT&T with 16 million subscribers, Time Warner with 12 million, and Comcast with 6.2 million. Adelphia and Cox each had about five million subscribers. Figures include acquisitions pending at the time.

In July Charter was the successful bidder to acquire New York-based Bresnan Communications after the firm began receiving unsolicited offers prior to going public.

The company was founded by cable industry pioneer William J. Bresnan in 1984. It had rebuilt and upgraded most of its systems and offered high-speed Internet service in about half of its markets. Charter's offer of $3.1 billion gave it an additional 690,000 subscribers at a cost of about $4,500 per subscriber, including 298,000 in Michigan, 221,000 in Minnesota, 110,000 in Wisconsin, and 61,000 in Nebraska. The acquisition gave Charter a total of 6.2 million subscribers.

## CHARTER CONTINUES AS A PUBLIC COMPANY

It was the $3.2 billion Bresnan acquisition that fueled speculation that Charter was about to go public. Analysts believed that while Paul Allen had "deep pockets," Charter would need the equity financing that a public stock offering would provide to continue making acquisitions. At the end of July Charter filed documents with the SEC for one of the largest initial public offerings (IPO) ever. The company proposed selling $3.5 billion worth of stock. Up to this time Charter's acquisitions had been financed primarily by Allen borrowing against his $28 billion worth of Microsoft shares. It was estimated that he had committed $11 billion of his own money to finance acquisitions totaling $21.8 billion between March 1998 and mid-1999.

When Charter went public in November 1999, the company raised $3.2 billion by selling 170 million shares, or 60 percent of its equity, at $19 a share. Underwriters had an additional 25 million-share allotment to sell later, which could push Charter's gross to $3.7 billion. In addition to the IPO, Allen infused $750 million of his own money into the company. Following the IPO, Allen retained control of the company through his ownership of Class B securities, which had about 10 times the voting power of the Class A shares available to the public.

Charter's strategy following the IPO was to launch digital cable service in its systems and offer high-speed Internet access through cable modems. At the time of the IPO Charter was heavily leveraged, with its debt level at more than seven times its annual cash flow. The company had $9.4 billion worth of acquisitions pending, including major deals for Falcon Cable TV, Fanch Communications, and Avalon Cable. Once those deals were completed in November 1999, Charter would have to invest heavily in upgrading its systems.

To help develop and execute Allen's vision of a "wired world," he created a consortium called Broadband Partners, consisting of companies in which he had financial interests. In addition to Charter, the consortium included RCN, a company that was dedicated to overbuilding existing cable systems with its own high-speed cable network. Just prior to the Charter IPO, Allen had invested $1.65 billion in RCN. Also part of the consortium were High-Speed Access Corp. and Go2Net. Broadband Partners would work together to develop and deploy content and services to Charter's cable subscribers.

Charter also began swapping customers with other systems to improve the geographic clustering of its systems. In December 1999 it signed a letter of intent with AT&T to swap 1.3 million cable subscribers in St. Louis as well as in Alabama, Georgia, and Missouri. The exchange would make Charter the dominant MSO in its home market of St. Louis, with 500,000 subscribers there that would be combined with subscribers in nearby Illinois for an 800,000-subscriber cluster. Charter said that its St. Louis customers would be the first to be offered advanced services such as cable telephone service, interactive video, and high-speed Internet access. The deal called for Charter to receive a total of 704,000 subscribers from AT&T in exchange for 632,000 Charter customers in California, Connecticut, Kentucky, Massachusetts, Tennessee, and Fort Worth, Texas. Analysts expected more exchanges of customers to take place in the cable industry, since most of the desirable MSOs that were willing to sell had been acquired by the industry's major players.

## GROWING FINANCIAL TROUBLES AND BANKRUPTCY

Despite its successful IPO and continued growth, Charter faced significant financial difficulties throughout the 21st century. In its first post-IPO Annual Report, Charter, recognizing its significant indebtedness, stated, "Our objective is to increase our operating cash flow by increasing our customer base and the amount of cash flow per customer. To achieve this objective…We seek to rapidly integrate acquired cable systems and apply our core operating strategies to raise the financial and operating performance of these acquired systems." Pursuant to its overall strategy to streamline operations, the company was forced to issue additional long-term debt, refinance some of its existing debt, and receive a capital infusion from its parent company. The company also announced its intention to pursue an aggressive program of upgrades to ensure the best, most forward-looking service in the industry.

Even as it attempted to consolidate and streamline, Charter continued to make acquisitions and expensive swaps. In February 2001, Charter made several agree-ments with AT&T Broadband to swap approximately 62,000 customers in Florida for over 500,000 customers in Missouri, Alabama, Nevada, and California, paying for the difference with stock and cash totaling over $2 billion. While continuing to increase its customer base, the company also continued to make efforts to improve service, streamline operations, and increase labor and management efficiency. The company undertook a number of initiatives designed to further these goals. For example, at the end of 2002, Charter began a program to improve operating efficiency and reduce labor costs. The company consolidated three divisions and 10 operating regions into five divisions and reduced its management team by eliminating several layers from its management structure.

In 2002 the company continued the improvement of its services, investing approximately $1.1 billion to complete the upgrade of its cable systems to provide digital video service, higher bandwidth capacity, and two-way communication capability. To finance this upgrade, along with ongoing operations, the company issued additional long-term debt of nearly $1 billion, most of which was used to pay off a portion of the amounts outstanding under revolving credit obligations in order to increase its future capacity for borrowing. That year, the company also restructured its debt to provide for a borrowing capacity of up to $5.2 billion.

Also in 2002, legal difficulties were added to the company's concerns when a class action lawsuit was filed in federal and state courts, alleging that the company had engaged in misleading accounting practices, overstatement of the number of its customers, and a breach of fiduciary duty. The company began to undergo investigation by the U.S. Attorney's Office as well as the Securities and Exchange Commission. The initial optimism that the company could overcome losses by improving efficiency began to wane by the middle of the first decade of the 21st century. Even as early as its 2003 Annual Report, Charter began reporting, "We have had a history of net losses. Further, we expect to continue to report net losses for the foreseeable future. The principal reasons for our prior and anticipated net losses include depreciation and amortization expenses associated with our acquisitions and capital expenditures related to construction and upgrading of our systems, and interest costs on borrowed money." A similar warning appeared in every Annual Report up to the company's bankruptcy filing.

On March 27, 2009, Charter filed with the United States Bankruptcy Court for the Southern District of New York to reorganize under Chapter 11 of the United

States Bankruptcy Code. On May 7, 2009, the company filed a reorganization plan, which was confirmed by the Bankruptcy Court on November 17, 2009, to go into effect on November 30, 2009. Warnings of the bankruptcy began surfacing as early as mid-2008. In July 2008, investment advice Web sites began advising investors to stay away from Charter because of a looming bankruptcy filing. The major symptom of an impending bankruptcy that was cited was the company's debt. As *Seeking Alpha* noted, "The most critical part of the company's balance sheet is its debt level. Charter carries $20 billion in debt, with only $541 million in cash. Their debt grade is low which means they pay a substantially higher interest rate as the potential of default is high. Although Charter generates about $6 billion in annual revenues, most of this money goes to service this debt and company expenses."

Charter faced several challenges in the 2010s, as companies emerging from bankruptcy usually do. However, people were still using Charter's Internet and telephone services, so the company stood poised to return to profitability if it could right its balance sheet over the next few years.

*David P. Bianco*
*Updated, Jack Miller*

## PRINCIPAL COMPETITORS

Time Warner Cable Inc.; Comcast Corporation; Cox Communications Inc.

## FURTHER READING

"Allen Buys More Cable Systems," *Television Digest*, August 3, 1998.

"Charter to pay $144M to settle class action suits." *St. Louis Business Journal*, August 6, 2004.

Charter Communications, Inc., "Annual Report 2003."

Charter Communications, Inc. "Form 10-k: Filed 02/26/10 for the Period Ending 12/31/09."

"Stay Away from Charter Communications: Bankruptcy Filing Looming?" seekingalpha.com, July 16, 2008.

"This Cable Tycoon Can't Stop Buying," *Business Week*, June 7, 1999, p. 42.

# China Southern Power Grid Company Ltd.

No. 6 Huasui Road
Zhujiang Xincheng, Tianhe District
Guangzhou, Guangdong 510623
China
Telephone: (86) 20-3812-1080
Fax: (86) 20-38120189
Web site: http://eng.csg.cn

*Government-owned*
*Founded:* 2002
*Employees:* 130,000
*Company Revenue:* RMB 313.6 billion ($45.92 billion) (2009)
*NAICS:* 22112 Electric Power Transmission, Control, and Distribution

∎ ∎ ∎

China Southern Power Grid Company, Ltd., (CSG) constructs and operates power grids in southern China (Guangdong, Guangxi, Yunnan, Guizhou, and Hainan provinces and regions). The CSG service area is one million square kilometers with a population of 230 million. CSG, along with the State Grid Corporation of China (SGCC), are the two state-owned grid companies responsible for transmitting power for the entire country. CSG distributes many types of power: hydropower, coal-fired power, nuclear power, oil-fired power, gas-fired power, and wind power. CSG is responsible for ensuring a reliable power supply to the five southern provinces it services, promoting the regional power market, planning the development and extension of the power grid, and dispatching power according to power grid operation laws.

## BEGINNINGS: 2002–04

China began its electricity industry reform in 2002, a program aimed at dividing state-owned assets into the separate business entities of electricity generation, transmission, and distribution. The next step was privatization, introducing market competition, and eliminating monopolies. China Southern Power Grid was established in 2002 by combining two existing companies, Guangdong Power Group and Hainan Power Corporation. The goal was to bring more power from the western regions to the underserved Guangdong province by 2005. This forced the price of power down and encouraged residents to use power from the western regions.

Once the electrical system was subdivided into its various entities, the next step was to improve the grid so more power could reach the outlying areas. In February 2004 work began on a $109 million project to lay China's longest submarine electricity cable to transport more power to the southern region. The high-capacity line wound through the south Qiongzhou Straits, linking south China's Hainan Province power system with CSG. Another $206 million project built two transformer substations on either side of the strait to help conduct the higher power capacity. When completed, the new cable would improve not only power capacity but the economic development of the Hainan province.

COMPANY PERSPECTIVES

The company will implement scientific developments to keep pace with progress, and always sieze an opportunity to strengthen and optimize the southern China power grid.

## FINANCIAL TROUBLES: 2004

By April 2004 the Chinese power grids were having financial difficulties and exploring fundraising options, including being listed on domestic or foreign stock markets. At that time, however, listing was not possible unless the Chinese government reformed the electricity pricing to improve profitability for domestic companies and eased restrictions on private and foreign capital to the tightly governed power grids. Both SGCC and CSG were struggling with insufficient capital after investing in the initial improvement and extension of the power grid.

The annual cash flow of the SGCC was estimated to be about $4.0 to $4.2 billion for 2004 to 2010, if the pricing at that time remained unchanged, according to a research report by JP Morgan and the Development Research Centre (DRC). That amount only represented 38 percent of the cost of the planned future investment to expand and upgrade the grid networks. CSG was facing similar financial circumstances. CSG governs power transmission for the five provinces in the south, while SGCC is responsible for the rest of the country.

Amidst this financial squeeze, China was combating a power shortage to outlying areas. The pressure was on to speed up the construction of power generating plants. Stock market listing would provide an infusion of cash, but the Chinese government, at that time, still restricted transmission assets from foreign capital. Since power assets were considered imperative to China's economic security, the government was leery of allowing any foreign control. Even if the government had reversed its position, the power grids did not meet listing requirements due to their weak profitability.

The SGCC reported only a 0.49 percent return on equity, as opposed to 4 to 7 percent for power grids in most other industrialized countries. Sales profit was 0.1 percent, where the national average for all industries in China was 5.1 percent. CSG's numbers were slightly better but still did not fall within the range needed to be listed.

China did not have separate prices for transmission and distribution, and in 2004, only 25 percent of the transmission tariff went to transmission companies, as opposed to 60 percent in other countries. The power-generating companies received the lion's share of the profits, while the transmission companies accumulated staggering debts. Up until 2002, SGCC was using its profits from power generation to finance its transmission construction projects. At the end of 2002, the Chinese government forced SGCC to divest itself of its power-generating companies during the industry restructure.

China needed to continue to expand and upgrade its power grid, so capital for the transmission companies had to come from somewhere. There were two possible methods of generating more profits. The first was to increase competition on the generating side to drive down prices, helping to increase the price margin and keep the end-user prices stable. The other, more likely, possibility was to raise end-user prices. The Chinese government was cautious about taking this route since more than 60 percent of its power consumption was by industrial consumers, and it did not want to slow economic growth by creating an additional financial burden on that customer demographic. To avoid continuing this problem into the future, the government needed to separate the transmission price from the combined electricity price so that grid company profits and expenditures became more transparent and easier to manage.

## MOVING FORWARD: 2004

The first quarter of 2004 saw power shortages in many areas of southern China as the debt-burdened transmission companies could not keep up with increasing demand. In May 2004 CSG signed agreements with power-generating companies to purchase power to meet demand. In addition to purchasing more power, CSG sought help from American power giant General Electric (GE) to improve its transmission capabilities. By June, a peak power consumption period, CSG was proceeding with 12 key projects with the Guangdong Grid Company to keep pace with the rapid growth of the Guangdong economy and resulting demand for power. The projects were expected to improve the power grid foundation, increase power transmission, and alleviate the power shortage in that region.

In September 2004 the China Power Engineering Consulting Group held a conference to discuss the selection of the location of China's first nuclear power plant in an inland region. The plan was to build a total of 27 nuclear power generating sets by 2020, putting two or three into construction each year. In October CSG took a big step forward when it began supplying power to Vietnam using the first high-voltage line to cross the

## KEY DATES

**2002:** China Southern Power Grid is formed.
**2004:** Works begins on China's longest submarine electricity cable to transport more power to the southern regions.
**2004:** China Southern Power Grid begins supplying power to Vietnam.
**2006:** China Southern Power Grid prepares to build the first 800-kilovolt line in the world.
**2008:** China Southern Power Grid forms a partnership with Microsoft.
**2010:** China participates in Copenhagen Climate Change Conference, and China Southern Power Grid explores green power projects.

Chinese border and stretch between China and Vietnam. It was estimated that China would see an annual $7 million profit by selling power to Vietnam.

## SHORTAGES AND GROWTH: 2005–06

As demand and transmission steadily increased, hitting a new high in 2004, CSG turned its attention to developing safety protocols for all department levels, and it published 12 safety production management items by the end of the first quarter of 2005. As power demands continued to increase, CSG committed to investing $3.7 billion to improve its power transmission capacity in the southern provinces. SGCC committed to a similar investment for the rest of the country. Striving to meet demand and eliminate blackouts, both companies were using a large proportion of their investment to construct ultra-high-voltage power grids.

Vietnam continued to buy power from CSG, closing deals with two of its subsidiaries, the Yunnan Electric Power Group Co., Ltd., and the Guangxi Electric Power Group Co. Ltd. This aided the CSG's bottom line, but it did not help China's power shortage issue. By May 2005 experts were predicting that China's summer power shortage may be the highest ever, with the southern provinces hit hardest due to a lack of coal and water supply in the power plants.

As China's economic and industrial growth continued, the demand for power only grew. SGCC and CSG's grid construction projects attempted to keep pace, with both companies investing more and more capital. The remainder of 2005 saw more power outages

as well as a long-term deal to sell more power to Vietnam. With capital needed to fund power projects, 2006 began with a rate increase for domestic customers. A new pricing system for electricity generated by renewable energy was also introduced, as China planned to supply 15 percent of the nation's electricity needs using renewable energy by 2020 (compared to the 2005 level of 7 percent).

In early 2006 CSG began preparations to build the first 800-kilovolt direct transmission line to transport power generated in Yunnan to Guangdong. The line was the first of its kind in the world and one of four lines to be built. China also announced its plans to invest more than RMB 1 trillion ($124.25 billion) in the construction of power grids from 2006 to 2010. This large investment marked a new era of power grid construction in China. In late 2006 China Life, China's largest domestic life insurer, bought 32 percent of CSG, infusing the company with $4.4 billion in new capital for its construction projects.

## INNOVATION AND PARTNERSHIPS: 2007

In April 2007 CSG entered into a partnership with the Microsoft Corporation. CSG would adopt advanced technology to strengthen its competiveness and internal management, while Microsoft increased its brand awareness in China. The year also saw CSG enter into more mutually beneficial partnerships. The company signed an agreement with the Ministry of Railways to build electrified railways. The Agriculture Bank of China (ABC) extended an $8.3 billion credit line to CSG to help fund its power grid construction projects.

## RECOVERY AND RECOGNITION: 2008–10

In late January 2008, China was hit by a severe snowstorm, impacting power grids and economic growth. CSG worked diligently to repair and upgrade power grids to restore power to all regions by early March, well before the end of March deadline imposed by the Chinese government. Due to the heavy losses CSG and SGCC sustained as a result of the storm and their repair efforts, the Chinese government announced substantial subsidies for both companies to help them recover. CSG reported RMB 20 billion in losses and SGCC reported RMB 10.45 billion. In May CSG released its first annual Corporate Social Responsibility report, followed by delivery of emergency supplies to the earthquake-stricken areas in Sichuan.

In late 2008 several global powerhouses were taking an interest in China's ultra-high-voltage projects. Siemens, the ABB Group, AREVA, and GE Energy were among the companies looking to enter China's energy market. Meetings commenced in 2009 and, at 185th on the Global Top 500 list, CSG was growing steadily, financially viable, and finally seeing its ambitious construction projects coming to fruition. In June 2009 the Hainan cable project connecting the five regions was finished and put into operation, its submarine cable the longest in Asia and second-longest in the world.

At the Vietnam International Power Industry Technology and Equipment Exhibition in Hanoi, in November 2009, CSG's booth demonstrated a green power grid and its effect on energy preservation, environment protection, and technology advancement. In meetings directly after the exhibition, upper management discussed low-carbon economy and smart-grid technology. The Chinese government also showed a strong presence at the 2009 Climate Change Conference in Copenhagen in December 2009.

In 2010, in the wake of the Climate Change Conference, the world's governments were focused on climate change and reached a consensus to focus on developing a low-carbon economy, concentrating on lower energy consumption, lower pollution, and lower greenhouse gas emissions. Looking ahead, CSG began committing resources to developing green initiatives, and every employee was encouraged to submit ideas for improving customer service, energy conservation, and emission reduction. As a giant amongst developing countries, it was clear that China wanted to set an example of lowering carbon emissions while still growing economically. There seemed reason to believe that

CSG would play a big part by implementing green power projects while China continued to prosper and show the world that it was possible to be socially responsible and remain financially strong.

*Andrea Newell*

## PRINCIPAL SUBSIDIARIES

CSG International; Dinghe Property Insurance Company, Ltd.; Guangdong Power Grid Company; Guangxi Power Grid Company; Guizhou Power Grid Company; Hainan Power Grid Company; Yunnan Power Grid Company.

## PRINCIPAL COMPETITORS

State Grid Corporation of China.

## FURTHER READING

Ramamurti, Ravi, and Jitendra V. Singh, *Emerging Multinationals in Emerging Markets.* New York: Cambridge University Press, 2009.

Rugman, Alan M., and Simon Collinson, *International Business.* 5th ed. New York: Prentice Hall, 2008.

Rugman, Alan M., and Jonathan P. Doh. *Multinationals and Development.* New Haven, CT: Yale University Press, 2008.

Sauvant, Karl P., Kristin Mendoza, and Irmak Ince, *The Rise of Transnational Corporations From Emerging Markets: Threat or Opportunity (Studies in International Investment).* Northampton, MA: Edward Elgar Publishing, 2008.

Tse, Edward, *The China Strategy: Harnessing the Power of the World's Fastest Growing Economy.* New York: Basic Books, 2010.

# CITIC Pacific Ltd.

**32nd Floor, CITIC Tower**
**1 Tim Mei Avenue**
**Hong Kong, Central**
**China**
**Telephone: (852) 2820 2111**
**Fax: (852) 2877 2771**
**Web site: http://www.citicpacific.com**

*Public Company*
*Founded:* 1979
*Employees:* 30,329 (2009)
*Sales:* HKD 6.525 billion ($838 million, 2009)
*Stock Exchanges:* Hong Kong
*Ticker Symbol:* 00267
*NAICS:* 212210 Iron Ore Mining; 331111 Iron and
    Steel Mills; 531110 Lessors of Real Estate

■ ■ ■

CITIC Pacific Limited is primarily engaged in special steel manufacturing and iron ore mining. The company produced over 6.4 million metric tons of special steel in 2009 for use in automobile (2.8 million tons) and machinery manufacturing. (Special steel refers to steel that has been given special properties such as anti-corrosion or heat resistance.)

However, CITIC is more than just a mining and steel manufacturer. The company has extensive property holdings in Hong Kong and mainland China (over 5 million square meters) and also operates power plants and manages two tunnels that connect Hong Kong to the mainland. CITIC Pacific is 58 percent owned by the

CITIC Group, a state-owned investment group formerly known as China International Trust and Investment Company.

## LAUNCHED BY CHINESE ECONOMIC REFORM IN THE 1980S

The China International Trust and Investment Corporation (CITIC) was established in 1979 as the first step in Deng Xiaoping's "open door policy" of economic reform. Deng chose Rong Yiren to form and lead CITIC, which would become China's primary domestic and foreign investment vehicle. Rong's own history was steeped in capitalism. Before the communist takeover in 1949, the Rongs had been one of Shanghai's wealthiest families, with control over much of that region's textile industry. Most of the Rong family left China when the communists took over, but Rong, who did not himself join the Communist Party, stayed in Shanghai and worked with the new government. Rong, and son Yung Chi-kin, were able to maintain much of their wealth through the 1950s. However, the Cultural Revolution of the mid-1960s saw the family fall from grace. Rong was stripped of his property and Yung was sent off to be "reeducated," doing hard labor on collective farms in remote regions of the country.

The family's fortunes revived with Deng Xiaoping's rise to power. Rong and Yung were rehabilitated in 1972, and their personal property was restored to them. Yung went to Stanford University to study business, and in 1978 he moved to Hong Kong, where he ran a small company that manufactured electronic watch movements. While his father was launching CITIC, Yung was enjoying success as an entrepreneur. Together with a group of Chinese and American friends, Yung invested in a small software company in California. That company merged with another software company, going public in 1984. Yung sold his shares in the company, netting $50 million.

As talks between the British and Chinese governments finalized plans to return Hong Kong to Chinese control, CITIC launched its CITIC Hong Kong investment subsidiary. In 1987 Yung was placed in charge of the new company, with $30 million in start-up funds. From the outset, Yung insisted upon and received a large degree of independence, including the authority to make local investment decisions and to hire his choice of management. This gave Yung a unique position among other Chinese government-controlled companies. Under Yung, CITIC HK bought large shares of two primary Hong Kong businesses, Cathay Airlines and Hong Kong Telecommunications. Named CITIC HK's managing director, Yung was able to make these and other purchases at deeply discounted prices because with China's looming return to control, Hong Kong businesses were eager to establish ties with the government. CITIC HK offered an attractive route to China's State Council, especially once Rong Yiren was named the country's vice president.

CITIC HK operated primarily as a passive investment vehicle. However, China needed to go beyond just regaining governmental control of Hong Kong. It needed to establish itself as a force in the powerful Hong Kong economy, and this meant taking a place in the territory's stock market. Yung took a backdoor to the market in 1990, when CITIC HK bought an inactive but listed holding company, Tylfull Co. Ltd. CITIC HK placed some of its assets, including shares of Cathay and Hong Kong Telecom, into the public company and renamed it as CITIC Pacific Ltd. The company quickly added to its holdings, building its share of Cathay Airlines (Hong Kong's premier international airline) to 12.5 percent. It then acquired 38.3 percent of Hong Kong Dragon Airlines, known as Dragonair, which was partly owned by Cathay and was the premier airline car-

rier along Hong Kong-China routes, and bought 20 percent of Macau Telephone. In addition to these investments, CITIC Pacific quickly established the second of its principal focus markets, buying up HKD 647 million of Hong Kong real estate properties.

## TOP "HONG": 1991–95

CITIC Pacific's ambitions went beyond simply building a portfolio of passive investments, however. In order to gain position in the Hong Kong economy, CITIC Pacific needed to establish itself as one of the territory's "hongs," or trading houses. The four principal hongs, Jardine Matheson, Hutchison Whampoa, Swire Pacific, and Wharf Holdings, were all conglomerates rooted in British control (although Hutchison and Wharf were by then run by Hong Kong entrepreneurs), with interests ranging widely beyond trading into the colony's infrastructure, manufacturing, and real estate. In order to achieve hong status, CITIC Pacific needed to diversify into more active holdings. The company took the first step toward that end in October 1991, when it took a 36 percent share in a consortium organized to make a HKD 7 billion purchase of the private Hang Chong company. Hang Chong, itself a smaller version of a hong, had extensive real estate holdings in Hong Kong, as well as in Japan and the United States. But CITIC Pacific's real interest was in Hang Chong's primary subsidiary, Dah Chong Heng, with food and shipping interests, and a chain of 40 car dealerships that controlled 40 percent of the Hong Kong automobile market. CITIC Pacific's 36 percent interest in Hang Chong quadrupled the company's net assets.

Three months later, CITIC Pacific bought out the other members of the consortium (which included ultimate parent CITIC) and gained a more than 97 percent share of Hang Chong. Under terms of the deal, valued at HKD 3 billion ($385 million), CITIC Pacific also bought an additional 7.8 percent of Dragonair from CITIC, boosting CITIC Pacific's share of the airline to 46.1 percent, for HKD 93 million ($12 million). The company's sales, which had reached HKD 118 million in 1991, skyrocketed to HKD 7.8 billion in 1992. Net profits for the year were up 212 percent, to HKD 1.2 billion.

The move was seen as a major step forward in China's economic stake in Hong Kong. It could also been seen as some assurance that the mainland would honor its commitment to the "one country, two systems" policy that was to govern the return of Hong Kong in 1997. With its large stake in Hong Kong's market, China would be less likely to dismantle the territory's economy. In turn, CITIC Pacific enhanced CITIC's credibility with the international financial

CITIC Pacific Ltd.

# KEY DATES

**1979:** China International Trust and Investment Corporation (CITIC) established to spur economic progress.
**1987:** CITIC opens its China International Trust and Investment Corporation Hong Kong subsidiary.
**1990:** CITIC HK places some telecommunications assets into newly formed CITIC Pacific Limited.
**1991:** CITIC Pacific adds to real estate holdings through acquisition of Hang Chong Company.
**1993:** Company continues to invest in real estate and takes a share in two tunnel projects.
**1996:** CITIC Pacific decreases ownership in Dragonair.
**1997:** Hong Kong reverts back to Chinese control.
**2004:** Company begins major investments in specialty steel companies.
**2006:** CITIC Pacific secures mining rights in Australia.
**2007:** CITIC Pacific secures separate stock exchange listings for principal subsidiaries.

community. Banks were reluctant to lend to the Chinese government, but with CITIC Pacific, China had the opportunity to prove its integrity to investors. At the same time, investments in CITIC Pacific offered a more stable method of investing in the mainland. In January 1993 CITIC Pacific's position as the leading "red chip" (a term given to Hong Kong listed companies that were attractive investments because they were controlled by mainland parent companies, thereby giving investors entry into the mainland's political and economic arenas) enabled it to raise HKD 7.2 billion. By then, however, CITIC Pacific had also turned "blue," after it was added to the territory's Hang Seng Index of blue chip stocks.

CITIC Pacific used that money to purchase a 12 percent share in Hong Kong Telecom from CITIC HK. Under terms of the deal, CITIC HK increased its ownership of CITIC Pacific to 46 percent. CITIC Pacific received a HKD 3.3 billion loan from CITIC HK, as well as controlling shares in two mainland power plants and a 20 percent share in Hong Kong's Chemical Waste Treatment Centre. CITIC Pacific also made a separate purchase of a 51 percent share of the Shanghai Children's Food Factory. In another deal, the company

entered a joint venture with Swire for HKD 2.85 billion real estate purchase in Hong Kong's Yau Yat Chuen area. In June 1993 CITIC Pacific also purchased a 20 percent stake in Chase Manhattan Bank's Manhattan Card Co. Hong Kong credit card business. Apart from further diversifying CITIC Pacific's assets, these deals helped boost the company's market capitalization to HKD 24 billion, placing it in the top 20 of Hong Kong companies. The success of CITIC Pacific was also encouraging other China-backed companies to move into the Hong Kong market, a development that would soon come to haunt CITIC Pacific.

In the meantime, CITIC Pacific continued its aggressive expansion. With sales topping HKD 10 billion for 1993, the company paid HKD 3.06 billion ($390 million) for a 50 percent share of a residential development on Hong Kong's Discovery Bay island. The company was also active on the infrastructure front, paying HKD 104 million ($13.3 million) for 25 percent of the Western Harbour Crossing, a tunnel project linking Hong Kong with the territory's Kowloon airport. The company also acquired 28.5 percent of another Hong Kong tunnel project, the Eastern Harbour Crossing, as well as gaining 50 percent of a mainland tunnel, in Shanghai. These moves were also seen as part of CITIC Pacific's attempt to counter criticism that the company was still not much more than a holding company for passive investments. The company slowed its acquisition growth to concentrate on taking a more active management role in the tunnel projects and its Hang Chong subsidiary. Revenues continued to grow, topping HKD 12 billion in 1994. The diversity of CITIC Pacific's projects, which by then included a joint venture with Japan's Isuzu to build cars and light trucks on the mainland, as well as a 20 percent stake in a joint venture to build an airport railway system, seemed to have finally elevated the company to true hong status.

Not all of CITIC Pacific's critics were convinced, however. Analysts faulted the company for having no clear investment strategy. In addition, the company's trading subsidiary, Dah Chong Hong, in which CITIC Pacific had taken its most active management role, was suffering heavy losses. Nevertheless, the company continued to attract investors, in part because of its close ties with China's government. At the same time, however, the company (and Yung) were widely praised for the company's refusal to exploit the political clout of its parent, relying instead on its own entrepreneurial skills to build the company.

Praise aside, competition from other mainland-backed companies was heating up, and as its position as the premier China investment vehicle came under attack, CITIC Pacific needed to step up its entrepreneurial activities. In 1995 the company began reducing its stake in its more passive holdings, such as Cathay Airlines and Hong Kong Telecom, raising a war chest of some HKD 10 billion. The company's revenues, however, dropped to HKD 10.83 billion for the year, dragged down by Dah Chong Hong's poor performance amid a weak retail market.

## A BLUE CHIP FOR A RED FUTURE

The following year saw CITIC Pacific's first real challenge from another mainland company. China National Aviation Corp. (CNAC), controlled by the mainland's civil aviation agency, which in turn had strong ties to the country's powerful military, announced its intention to establish a third Hong Kong airline. CNAC's ties with China's civil aviation agency would give it a decided advantage in winning important air routes to the mainland's major cities, possibly taking routes away from Dragonair. The move would directly threaten CITIC Pacific, which had been reducing its role in Cathay in favor of boosting its activities in Dragonair.

Meanwhile, the company continued to refocus its business, turning away from minority investments and investing its war chest instead in a new string of infrastructure deals, including purchase of 45 percent of Shanghai's Xu Pu Bridge. The company also added to its infrastructure portfolio with controlling interests in another two mainland power stations. In real estate, the company purchased, for HKD 3.5 billion, the former British naval headquarters site in Central Hong Kong's Tamar Basin in order to build the company's 37-story headquarters.

By May 1996 the situation with CNAC came to a head. In a sudden turnaround, CITIC Pacific agreed to sell a 17.6 percent stake in Dragonair to CNAC. At the same time, however, the company increased its share of Cathay, from 10 percent to 25 percent, for HKD 6.3 billion. Analysts read several implications into the agreement. For one, it was believed that CITIC Pacific had been forced to sell the Dragonair holdings by its parent, CITIC, under direction of China's State Council. The further implication of this was that CITIC Pacific, despite its blue-chip status, continued to operate at the will of the Chinese government. For another, the agreement suggested a potential shift in the Chinese government's power base from the reform-oriented position of the ailing Deng Xiaoping (and Rong Yiren, who himself was 80 years old) to the more left-wing Old Guard, represented by CNAC and its parent, the Civil Aviation Administration of China.

The deal caught the Hong Kong investment community by surprise. Despite the fact that CITIC Pacific had relied on its own business skills, rather than Larry Yung's political ties, to build the company, a shift in the power base was nevertheless seen as harmful to CITIC Pacific's future. In response, the company stepped up its emphasis on its infrastructure portfolio, adding a purchase of 13 water treatment plants in mainland China for HKD 1.26 billion in October 1996. However, at the end of the year, Yung surprised the market again, when he led other members of CITIC Pacific management in buying up 15.5 percent (at a 28 percent discounted price) of the company from CITIC HK. Yung, who took most of the stock, increased his personal share of the company to 18.5 percent, making him the company's second largest shareholder. While some analysts suggested the deal was a way of rewarding Yung for acquiescing in the CNAC agreement, others pointed to the political situation on the mainland. Deng Xiaoping's death was announced in early 1997, suggesting that Yung's political allies were fading. Gaining tighter control of CITIC Pacific placed Yung in a stronger position to steer the company, especially given the imminent return of Hong Kong to Chinese control. (Sovereignty over Hong Kong was formally transferred from Britain to China on July 1, 1997.)

## CITIC PACIFIC EXPANDS BUSINESS: 2000–03

CITIC Pacific registered tremendous growth and expansion throughout the first decade of the 21st century as the company sought to retain its dominance in both Hong Kong and mainland China. In 2000 the company gained significant interests in China's telecommunications industry when it completed the acquisition of Telecom 1616 Group and changed its name to CITIC Telecom 1616 Ltd.

CITIC Pacific also consolidated its stake in Eastern Harbour Crossing in 2000 when it increased its interest from 64.02 percent to 69.38 percent. The Eastern Harbour Crossing was a joint venture that was pioneered by the company with the objective of advancing its interests in the optical fiber cabling and networking in China. The acquisition of 49 percent of Shandong Chenming Xinli Cogeneration Co. Ltd., the full acquisition of Swire Loxley Ltd, and the purchase of CITIC Guoan Ltd's 50 percent interests were the other major network expansion exploits made by CITIC Pacific in 2000. Swire Loxley Ltd was subsequently renamed DCH Healthcare Products Ltd.

In 2001 CITIC Pacific went on to acquire the Sims Trading Company Ltd. in addition to investing in a property management firm in Huang Pu District of Shanghai, the West Garden. The company further spread its wings in Hong Kong's modern information technology sector when it acquired the PSINet Hong Kong Ltd. and subsequently changed its name to CPC-Net Hong Kong Ltd. The company's 2001 technological leap was closely followed by diversification into the power generation industry through the acquisition of a 55 percent controlling stake in Jilin Xinli Power Cogeneration Company Ltd. However, the company made a surprising but strategic move in 2001 when it sold off its 50 percent shareholding in the Chongqing Chang Jiang LJT Bridge in the same year.

The acquisition of the Royal Pavilion and CITIC Square in Shanghai in 2002 elevated CITIC Pacific's position in the property development and management industry. The company's interests in Jilin Xinli Power Cogeneration Company Ltd was increased to 60 percent during a year that the company successfully acquired 50 percent and 51 percent shareholding interests in CITIC Capital Markets Holdings Ltd. and Shanghai CP Guojian Pharmaceutical Company Ltd., respectively. CITIC Pacific also reviewed its share ownership of the Eastern Harbor Crossing in 2002 by increasing its shareholding in the joint venture from 69.38 percent to 70.78 percent.

A major shift in CITIC Pacific's strategic focus in 2003 paved the way for the disposal of the company's entire interests in major construction companies in mainland China that included Yanan East Road Tunnel, Hu Jia Toll Road, Nan Pu Bridge, and Xu Pu Bridge.

## ACQUISITION STRATEGIES: 2004–05

In 2004 CITIC Pacific reverted to its acquisition strategies in a year during which the company also established numerous joint ventures. The 21 percent stake in a joint venture with the North United Power Corporation, a 30 percent joint venture interest with Shanghai Laogang MSW Treatment Company Ltd, an 80 percent joint venture interest with Wuxi Xingcheng Steel Products Company Ltd, and a 71 percent joint venture with Jiangyin Lidian Energy Material Company Ltd were some of the notably valuable joint ventures established by CITIC Pacific in 2004. The company also went on to acquire a 65 percent controlling stake in Sunburst Energy Development Company Ltd. in a move that increased its overall shareholding interests in Ligang Power Station.

The CITIC Pacific's shareholding interests in DCH Healthcare Products Ltd were transferred to Adaltis Inc. in 2004. The company took its acquisition spree to a higher notch with the acquisition of Dongfang Iron and Steel Company Ltd. This was later renamed Hubei Xin Yegang Company Ltd and became one of CITIC Pacific

core business interests. Another big stride in 2004 was the establishment of the Jiangyin Ligang Electric Power Generation Company in mainland China in which CITIC Pacific held a 71 percent contolling stake.

CITIC Pacific experienced an eventful 2005 as it spread its interests to the retailing industry through the acquisition of 35 percent of Wal-Mart East China Stores Company Ltd. The company also reviewed its joint venture interests with Jiangsu Ligang Electric Power Company Ltd under new terms in which it paid an additional RMB 500 million in lieu of adjustments of an existing joint venture into a long-term relationship in accordance with the laws in China. The company disposed of its entire property development interests in Harvest County Ltd in a deal that saw the company receive HKD 880 million in compensation.

## SECURES MINING RIGHTS IN AUSTRALIA: 2006

In March 2006 CITIC Pacific registered a major strategic victory when it entered agreements for potential mining rights in Australia. The mine was in Western Australia and at selected sites that were estimated to be holding more than 6 billion tons of magnetite ore. A deal that allowed CITIC Pacific to extract up to one billion metric tons of magnetite ore was sealed in July 2006.

CITIC Pacific realigned its strategies in 2006 through various agreements that were designed to secure the company's long-term strategies. The company entered numerous agreements to dispose of interests that no longer suited its strategic intents as it entered new strategically viable agreements at the same time. One of the acquisitions made by the company in 2006 was the Shijiazhuang Iron & Steel Company Ltd.

In July 2006 the company entered a mutual agreement to sell its 60 percent interests in Jilin Xinli Power Cogeneration Company Limited to China's Provincial Energy & Communications Corporation. The company also disposed of its 50 percent interest in Festival Walk, a property development and management company.

## SEPARATE STOCK EXCHANGE LISTINGS FOR PRINCIPAL SUBSIDIARIES: 2007

In 2007 CITIC Pacific secured separate listings for CITIC 1616 Holdings Ltd and Dah Chong Hong Holdings Ltd in the Stock Exchange of Hong Kong Ltd. The two companies were CITIC Pacific's principal subsidiaries. The move was designed to help the company in the process of securing its capital base and retaining a competitive advantage over its closest competitors. The company also expanded its joint venture relationship with the Shanghai Shipyard Land Development Project to 50 percent for all the three phases of the project in addition to acquiring 17 vessels for a related project. CITIC Pacific further increased its interests in the Daye Special Steel Company Ltd to 58 percent, effectively cementing its controlling stake in the company.

CITIC Pacific acquired extended rights for the mining of an additional one billion metric tons of magnetite in Western Australia in October 2008. The company also carried on with its acquisition strategies, increasing its shareholding interests in Tongling Xin Yaxing Coking & Chemical Company Ltd to about 93 percent. The company further entered an 85 percent joint venture agreement with Tongling Xin Yaxing Coking & Chemical Company Ltd for coal gas and coke production. In yet another move, the company sold off its 50 percent shareholding interests in Kaifeng Xinli Power Generation Company Ltd. as well as all its shares in Air China Cargo.

## FUTURE PROSPECTS

In the early 2010s CITIC Pacific had great growth potential for expanding its production and sales volume throughout the world. The company was focused on increasing its annual production capacities for special steel and iron to over seven million metric tons and 70 million metric tons, respectively. CITIC Pacific had at its disposal over two billion tons of magnetite deposits to exploit. The advantage provided the company with a solid operational base for its future production targets. It seemed likely that the company's property construction and management segment would experience positive growth as a result of the property boom in mainland China and Hong Kong.

*M. L. Cohen*
*Updated, Paul Ingati*

## PRINCIPAL SUBSIDIARIES

CITIC 1616 Holdings Limited; Dah Chong Hong Holdings Limited.

## PRINCIPAL DIVISIONS

Special Steel; Iron Ore Mining; Property Development.

## PRINCIPAL COMPETITORS

Cheung Kong (Holdings) Limited; Gaungdong Investment Limited; Shanghai Industrial Holdings Limited; Shenzhen Fungyuan Special Steel Company Ltd.

## FURTHER READING

"CITIC Pacific Hit by $US835M Blowout," IBTimes.com, May 12, 2010.

"Company News: CITIC Pacific," mining-journal.com, May 19, 2010.

Ko, Stephen, and Havovi Joshi, "Corporate Governance at CITIC Pacific," *Harvard Business Review,* June 18, 2009.

Wang, Leanne, "Parent Company Bails Out CITIC Pacific," ChinaStakes.com, November 13, 2008.

"0267.HK: Summary for CITIC Pacific," finance.yahoo.com.

CITY NATIONAL BANK
The way up.®

# City National Bank

————— ■ —————

**400 North Roxbury Drive**
**Beverly Hills, California 90210**
**U.S.A.**
**Telephone: (310) 888-6000**
**Toll Free: (800) 773-7100**
**Fax: (310) 888-6940**
**Web site: http://www.cnb.com**

*Public Company*
*Founded:* 1954
*Employees:* 3,019 (2009)
*Assets:* $21.1 billion
*Stock Exchanges:* New York
*Ticker Symbol:* CYN
*NAICS:* 522110 Commercial Banking

■ ■ ■

Under its parent company City National Corporation, City National Bank offers commercial banking services to clients in Southern California, the San Francisco Bay area, Nevada, and New York City. In 2009 City National operated 67 offices, 17 of which were full service regional centers. Operating under the slogan "The Way Up," City National has been recognized by *Barron's* as a leading U.S. wealth management firm for nine consecutive years, from 2001 through 2009.

## CALIFORNIA BEGINNINGS

Alfred Hart, the man who would become City National Bank's founder, was working as a director at Columbia Pictures when he conceived the idea of starting a new bank in Southern California. Familiar with Hollywood's elite through his work at Columbia Pictures, Hart did not have to look far to find a group of wealthy men and convince them that his business idea was a good one. From the outset, City National's aim was to cater to small businesses, prominent entertainers, and other local professionals. Frank Sinatra and Danny Kaye were among Hart's early Hollywood supporters. (In 1963 Hart would help Sinatra raise a $240,000 ransom when Sinatra's son, Frank Jr., was kidnapped.) Outside of Hollywood, Hart talked the bank idea up amongst his friends at the West Los Angeles Hillcrest Country Club. Another early City National supporter was Ben Maltz, a local businessman and philanthropist. (In 2003 the Ben Maltz Gallery was opened in Los Angeles in honor of him.)

With a handful of backers, City National opened for business on January 4, 1954. Hart served as the bank's first president while Maltz was named the bank's first chairman of the board. In 1955 the bank moved its operations to 400 North Roxbury Drive in Beverly Hills, California.

Also in 1955, George Konheim, real estate business owner and president of Buckeye Construction, opened his first account with City National. Konheim went to City National for money to build houses and commercial real estate in the booming Los Angeles market. After Hart checked Konheim's background he agreed to give him the loan. The transaction would connect Hart to the man who would become City National's future chairman of the board and chief executive officer (CEO).

## COMPANY PERSPECTIVES

City National provides entrepreneurs, professionals, their businesses and their families with complete financial solutions on *The way up*. Highly personalized client relationships, combined with a full range of sophisticated financial products—commercial lending, private banking and wealth management capabilities—plus the best talent in the financial industry distinguish City National from its competition. No bank is better able to serve all the financial needs of successful entrepreneurs.

Bram Goldsmith, a University of Illinois graduate and former Army Air Corps member, was Buckeye Construction's financial manager when Konheim received his first loan from the bank. Buckeye Construction would build several of City National's offices, including the building at 400 North Roxbury Drive in 1955. Over the next three years, real estate and other business deals would earn City National the rank of 409th out of 14,000 U.S. banks. In 1958 the Southern California bank's assets were $66 million.

Less than a decade later, City National expanded its range of products and services and entered the international trust and investment arenas. In 1967 the bank first offered its Master Charge services to the public, and in the same year it opened its 24-story Pershing Square complex in downtown Los Angeles. At that time, the complex was the tallest building in the city. Frank Sinatra and actress Rosalind Russell attended the complex's grand opening. Throughout the years, as the bank continued to grow, Goldsmith, Konheim, and Hart would get together for rounds of golf at the Hillcrest Country Club. As of 1985, approximately 65 percent of the country club's members had an account at City National Bank.

### CHANGE AND GROWTH

In the early 1970s, Hart's health started to fail. The founder's physical decline came on the heels of another milestone for the bank, with City National trading stock over the counter for the first time. Prices went at $19.25 per share. Thousands of shares were purchased for a total of more than $2 million.

By 1975 Hart had approached Goldsmith about a buyout. Goldsmith obliged and bought Hart's stake in the bank, which was worth approximately $3.6 million.

In 1975, 21 years after the bank was founded, Goldsmith became City National's chairman of the board and CEO. He would continue in this role for two decades.

Starting with Goldsmith's first year as the bank's CEO, City National opened three new offices: one in Newport Beach, California, and two others in Torrance and Encino. In 1978 City National's assets exceeded $1 billion for the first time. Expansion continued, with the bank opening a new office in La Jolla, in San Diego County.

During Goldsmith's tenure the bank moved to an automated teller network and began to use computerized data processing systems. Goldsmith also focused on growing City National's entertainment accounts. Embassy Productions, Mary Tyler Moore Enterprises, and Lorimar were some of the major movie and television studio houses that did business with City National. Celebrities such as Liza Minnelli, Robert Redford, Cher, and Lucille Ball held accounts at the bank. Goldsmith's combined technological advancement and entertainment industry outreach efforts saw City National's profits increase by 760 percent over the course of his tenure.

City National helped to finance entertainment organizations such as entertainment law firms, talent agencies, production companies, and television "movies of the week." Specialized services for this market included talent and holding escrows, cash management, liquidity, asset and investment management, and foreign exchange contracts. City National also helped finance such movies as *From Here to Eternity*, *Blade Runner*, *Purple Rain*, *Whatever Works*, *Notorious*, and *Our Family Wedding*.

### NEW YORK STOCK EXCHANGE

While his father led the charge at City National, the bank's future president and CEO, Russell Goldsmith (Gram's son) had graduated from Harvard Law School and become a member of City National's board of directors. After graduation from law school, Russell Goldsmith started his own law firm, Sanders, Barnet & Goldsmith. From 1983 to 1985 Goldsmith served as chief operating officer (COO) of Lorimar Incorporated. Beginning in 1986, he served as chairman and CEO at Republic Pictures Corporation.

The year 1990 was a pivotal one for City National. Shareholders and investors would realize increased profits after the company began to trade on the New York Stock Exchange. Two years later, the company made some important personnel changes. California banker George Benter, Jr., served as City National's president and COO beginning in 1992. At the same

## KEY DATES

**1954:** City National Bank is founded.
**1955:** Al Hart is appointed as president of the bank.
**1978:** Total assets top $1 billion for the first time.
**1990:** City National Bank starts to trade on the New York Stock Exchange.
**1995:** City National Bank acquires First Los Angeles Bank, its first major acquisition.
**2009:** City National Bank tops $21 billion in total assets.

time, Frank Pekny, another California banker, served as City National's vice chairman and chief financial officer. Combined, the two men brought five decades of banking experience to City National.

City National's future president, Russell Goldsmith, remained at Republic Pictures Corporation until 1994, a year before he was named chairman and CEO at City National. When asked if he knew when he was growing up that he would eventually take over from his father, Russell told *Los Angeles Business Journal* that he never thought he would be his father's replacement. Asked what it was like to take the helm of City National when he was only 28 years old, Russell replied, "The fact that my family had been with the bank since its inception made it a more logical step." He went on to say that, "I was able to bring candor and the perspective of somebody younger and in touch with the entertainment industry." Under Russell Goldsmith's leadership, not only did City National executives relate more closely with Hollywood's younger generation of movers and shakers, in 1995 the bank also acquired First Los Angeles Bank, its first major firm. The purchase would be one of many in the years to come.

### ERA OF ACQUISITIONS

Midway through the 1990s, City National increased its number of branch offices to 16 and reached $3.3 billion in total assets. The bank also entered a period in which it acquired other firms. After City National acquired First Los Angeles Bank it became the largest independent bank headquartered in Southern California. Less than two years into Russell Goldsmith's tenure, City National made three other acquisitions: Riverside National Bank, Frontier Bank, and Ventura County National Bancorp.

From 1998 to 2000, City National would purchase one or more firms each year. In 1998 City National

acquired Harbor Bank of Long Beach and the San Diego North American Trust Company. With the purchase of the San Diego North American Trust Company, City National began to offer clients 401(k) retirement services. A year later, the bank acquired American Pacific State Bank. It also launched its online banking platform and reached $7.2 billion in total assets.

In 1998, in an effort to ramp up its client services, City National appointed Jan Cloyde as executive vice president of its Banking Services Division. Under Cloyde's guidance, City National would offer innovative products and services to its online cash management systems. As reported in *Business Wire* Jan Cloyde said of the improvements, "We took eight cash management products...and bundled them together into one electronic product that is responsive, convenient, highly functional and uses a minimum of banking jargon." Cloyde went on to say that, "Our system offers three innovative features not found in other online cash management systems." By the end of the twentieth century, many of Los Angeles county's most wealthy residents had an account with City National.

In 2001 City National's total assets reached $10 billion, and the beginning of the new century marked a period of continued growth and expansion. City National's purchase of the Pacific Bank in 2000 helped to expand its branch offices across Northern California. Purchase of Reed, Conner & Birdwell, an investment management firm based in Los Angeles, brought a wealth management platform in-house that allowed City National to offer increased investment services to wealthy individuals and organizations.

As City National worked to assimilate employees from the several recently purchased firms into its culture, the bank redesigned part of its brand. In 2001 City National created a logo that included a six-tiered ladder alongside the words, "City National Bank, The Way Up." As if foreseeing the turbulent mortgage years ahead, City National shrank its non-accrual loans and net charge-offs in 2002. By the close of that year, nonrelationship commercial, purchased media, and telecom loans made up less than 0.25 percent of the bank's total loans.

### CONTINUED INDEPENDENCE

During the heady period when institutions were either gobbling each other up or being gobbled up, City National remained independent. One year after the terrorist atttacks on the United States on September 11, 2001, City National set up an office outside of California for the first time, in New York City. In the same year City National made *Forbes* "Super 500" list for the first time. Before the close of 2002, City National acquired Civic BanCorp, which at the time was an independent business bank with assets worth $510 million. The move would see City National almost double its assets in Northern California. In 2003 City National acquired the asset management holding firm, Convergent Capital Management.

Despite its numerous acquisitions, when City National celebrated its 50th year in business in 2004, the company's vice chairman and CEO, Russell Goldsmith, and the bank's chairman, Bram Goldsmith, told shareholders, "We don't need assets of $1 trillion. City National is not trying to be all things to all people everywhere. Our focus is what sets us apart." The bank's focus on specialized markets had helped it to reap total assets in excess of $14 billion. In subsequent years, bank management renewed its efforts to grow client deposits, particularly in the commercial loan area. Improved wealth, cash, and international bank management services were also on the radar of the bank's management. Treasury Net, a Web-based banking instrument that allowed customers to initiate and complete financial transactions online, would become a key component in this focus.

In 2004 City National moved 800 employees, about one-third of its total staff, into the Los Angeles' ARCO Plaza and Bank of America Tower. The building was renamed City National Tower after City National leased 310,000 square feet of space from the building's owner, Thomas Properties Group. The complex became City National's new downtown Los Angeles regional center.

The following year brought leadership change to City National as Christopher Warmuth was named the bank's president, taking over from George Benter, Jr., who had served in that capacity since 1992. In an effort to expand its business operations outside of the United States, City National formed a joint alliance with the Bank of East Asia Limited, a large, independent Hong Kong bank. The purpose of the alliance was to offer City National's customers who banked in China a larger platform from which to invest. By the close of 2006 e-checks were offered to City National's business clients. This allowed customers to scan checks and transmit them to the bank with the click of a computer button.

In 2008 City National partnered with the U.S. Commercial Service, an arm of the U.S. Department of Commerce, in an effort to increase U.S. exports. A special focus was placed on improving international trade between small and mid-sized U.S. businesses with those in other countries. Programs that helped City National to strengthen America's exports included their Working Capital Guarantee, the International Buyer Credit Program, the Transportation Security Exports Program, and the medical equipment initiative. Financing for the medical equipment initiative helped to fund medical supplies to other countries in an effort to improve the standard of living in those countries.

## ECONOMIC CHALLENGES

As reported in a 2009 *Dow Jones* article by Matthias Rieker, the fact that City National continued to manage sizable entertainment industry accounts helped the company remain profitable during the global financial meltdown that began in 2008. In 2009 15 percent of the bank's accounts were in the entertainment industry.

However, default personal and commercial real estate loans did not leave City National unscathed during the 2008 mortgage crisis; the company received $600 million in Troubled Asset Relief Program (TARP) money from the U.S. Treasury Department. By December 2009 City National had paid back $400 million of the TARP funds it had received from the federal government.

While much of the national and international financial markets and other business industries, regardless of size, struggled to remain solvent from 2007 through 2009, City National marked its 17th year of profitability. At year end 2009, the bank posted a profit of $51.3 million. (This amount was down by about 50 percent from 2008, however, which was itself much lower than the 2007 profit of $231.6 million.) The bank also acquired Imperial Capital Bank, a deal that was assisted by the Federal Deposit Insurance Corporation (FDIC) and added an additional $3.3 billion in assets to City National's financial sheet. When asked if he had plans to entertain selling City National, Russell Goldsmith told the *Los Angeles Business Journal,* "We have enjoyed great success as an independent company and we run this company on the belief that, as an independent company … we can continue to build shareholder value."

*Rhonda Campbell*

## PRINCIPAL SUBSIDIARIES

City National Bank

## PRINCIPAL DIVISIONS

Commercial Banking; Private Client Services; Business Trust and Investments; International Banking Services; Entertainment Industry Banking; Online; Treasury Management Services.

## PRINCIPAL COMPETITORS

Bank of America Corporation; Cathay General Bancorp; Comerica Incorporated; Downey Financial Corporation; FirstFed Financial Corporation; SVB Financial Group; Wells Fargo & Company.

## FURTHER READING

Berry, Kate. "City National Grows into L.A.'s Largest Independent," *Los Angeles Business Journal,* May 12, 2003.

"Bram Goldsmith: Maverick Banker to Stars,"*Los Angeles Times,* July 21, 1985.

"City National Bank Awards 64 Literacy Grants Totaling $70,000 to Teachers," *Wall Street Journal,* March 15, 2010.

"City National Bank Names Cloyde Executive Vice President and Director of Banking Services," *Business Wire,* October 9, 1998.

"City National Creates Banking and Administrative Center with Lease of up to 310,000 Square Feet." *Business Wire,* November 20, 2003.

Rieker, Matthias, "Business Banking Helps City National Through Crisis," *Dow Jones Newswires,* December 31, 2009.

"Russell Goldsmith to Take Over as City National's CEO," *Los Angeles Times,* September 29, 1995.

"Top Wealth Managers" *Wall Street Journal,* September 28, 2009.

# Clear Channel Communications, Inc.

200 East Basse Road
San Antonio, Texas 78216
U.S.A.
Telephone: (210) 822-2828
Fax: (210) 822-2299
Web site: http://www.clearchannel.com

*Wholly Owned Subsidiary of CC Media Holdings, Inc.*
*Founded:* 1972
*Employees:* 19,295 (2009)
*Sales:* $5.551 billion (2009)
*NAICS:* 515112 Radio Stations; 515120 Television
    Broadcasting; 541850 Display Advertising; 541870
    Advertising Material Distribution Services

■ ■ ■

Clear Channel Communications, Inc. (Clear Channel), is a U.S.-based media conglomerate that operates in the business areas of radio broadcasting and outdoor advertising or displays. In the United States, Clear Channel is the number one radio company, owning 894 domestic radio stations, with 149 stations operating in the 25 largest U.S. markets. These stations offer an assortment of programming formats, including adult contemporary, country, contemporary hit radio, rock, urban, and oldies. Overall, the company's radio stations have a total weekly listening base of more then 113 million people, based on Arbitron National Regional Database figures for the spring 2009 ratings period. In addition to its broadcasting business, Clear Channel operates Premiere Radio Networks, a national radio network that, produces, distributes, or represents approximately 90 syndicated radio programs and services for approximately 5,000 radio stations. The company also owns various sports, news, and agriculture networks. The company, along with joint venture partners, operates more than 140 radio stations in Australia and New Zealand.

Clear Channel's Americas Outdoor Advertising segment includes operations in the United States, Canada, and Latin America and focuses on urban markets with dense populations. In the United States the company owns or operates approximately 195,000 displays and conducts operations in 49 of the 50 largest U.S. markets. The company's outdoor assets consist of billboards, street furniture and transit displays, airport displays, mall displays, and wallscapes. The company's international outdoor advertising business segments include operations in Asia, Australia, and Europe, with approximately 639,000 displays in 32 countries. Clear Channel is owned by CC Media Holdings, Inc., an investment group led by Thomas H. Lee Partners and Bain Capital.

## EARLY 1970S: ORIGINS

For L. Lowry Mays, everything changed in 1972. A graduate of Texas A&M University, Mays left Texas with a degree in petroleum engineering and entered Harvard University, where he earned a graduate degree in business. From there, it was back to Texas, where Mays settled in as an investment banker. It was a natural progression from his years at Harvard, but when two businessmen walked into his office at the small invest-

## COMPANY PERSPECTIVES

We believe in providing superior value to customers through high quality, technologically advanced, fairly priced services designed to meet customer needs better than all the possible alternatives. We believe the ultimate measure of our success is to provide a superior value to our stockholders.

ment banking concern he was running in San Antonio, Mays' life took a defining turn. The two men, both San Antonio professionals, asked the 36-year-old Mays for help in raising $175,000 to buy a struggling FM radio station named KEEZ. Mays agreed and delved into researching the details of the radio business, demonstrating a thoroughness that would become one of his trademarks in later years. As preparations for the project were underway, the two businessmen backed out of the deal, leaving Mays with a head full of information about the radio industry. Mays pursued the investment opportunity on his own, enlisting the help of a local car dealer named B. J. (Red) McCombs, borrowing $175,000 from a bank, and purchasing KEEZ strictly as an investment. "I had no intention of getting into the broadcast business," Mays recalled years later.

Nevertheless, he soon began to demonstrate the assiduous, hands-on type of management that would become one of his defining trademarks. He and McCombs (whose later business achievements included acquiring the San Antonio Spurs professional basketball team) poured more cash into the station and changed its format to country music. At the same time, the partners expanded the station's sales force and increased its promotion budget, with a focus on maximizing advertising revenue. Making money in broadcasting, Mays reasoned, required forging a close and profitable relationship with the advertisers whose dollars drove a radio station's financial growth. Music format changes and programming adjustments were made, to be sure, but increasing cash flow by attracting advertisers was the chief concern. "Our whole philosophy, whether it's radio or television," Mays later remarked, "is that our business is selling automobiles, or tamales, or toothpaste. That's our business: helping people sell Fords."

Under Mays's scrutiny, the floundering KEEZ was transformed into a profitable business within a year, and this success encouraged May to delve deeper into the broadcasting business. With the cash flow generated by

KEEZ, Mays and McCombs purchased two radio stations located in Tulsa, Oklahoma, over the next two years. By this point, in 1974, Mays had already established the blueprint for Clear Channel's future expansion. In the years to follow, he would acquire distressed stations in such mid-sized, second-tier markets as El Paso (Texas), Memphis (Tennessee), Louisville (Kentucky), and New Orleans (Louisiana), and bring them to profitability. Each acquisition candidate had to meet strict criteria before joining the Clear Channel fold, and, once added to the company's portfolio of broadcasting properties, each acquisition was transformed by the same principles. This transformation included doubling the company's sales force, increasing marketing activities, and placing greater emphasis on attracting new advertisers. Mays rarely tinkered with a station's programming format. Instead, all efforts were directed at the acquisition's financial performance. "We want to be able to have both an immediate impact on the revenues," Mays explained, "and an immediate impact on the expenses."

### PUBLIC OFFERING IN 1984 SPAWNS LITTLE GROWTH: 1984–91

Moving cautiously in the decade that followed the acquisition of the two Tulsa stations, Mays gradually added to his stable of radio stations as he learned the business. Developments in 1984, however, promised to usher in a new era of animated growth. In that year, the Federal Communications Commission (FCC) loosened ownership restrictions for radio and television properties, decreeing that companies could own up to 12 AM stations, 12 FM stations, and 12 television stations. Prior to 1984, the FCC barred companies from owning more than seven properties in each category. Mays and the rest of the broadcasting industry celebrated the news. "We knew this was going to be a trend, that these laws would continue to change," remembered Mays. Preparing for a period of energetic expansion, he took Clear Channel public in 1984, raising $7.5 million in an initial public offering (IPO). As expected, companies began acquiring broadcasting properties in earnest, swallowing up one after another to take advantage of the relaxed ownership restrictions. Clear Channel, however, did not participate. Conspicuous by his absence from the acquisition frenzy, Mays was criticized by industry observers as a former investment banker who analyzed deals and then decided not to get involved. Mays later explained that Clear Channel's inactivity was not due to a lack of effort or interest. "We looked at radio properties every day," he said. "They just didn't meet the investment criteria we set up. If you stick by your

## KEY DATES

**1974:** L. Lowry Mays constructs the blueprint for Clear Channel expansion.

**1984:** Mays takes Clear Channel public, raising $7.5 million in an initial public offering.

**1988:** Mays jumps into the television market, acquiring a station in Mobile, Alabama.

**1991:** The company's 18 radio stations and six television stations generate revenues of $74 million and earnings of more than $1 million.

**1994:** Clear Channel merges with Metroplex Communications, a Tampa, Florida, competitor.

**1996:** Clear Channel owns 121 radio stations and 11 television stations, making it the second-largest radio group in the country behind Westinghouse/CBS.

**2000:** Clear Channel acquires AMFM, Inc., and SFX Entertainment, Inc., a worldwide promoter, producer, and presenter of live entertainment events.

**2001:** Radio division reorganizes management structure by geographic regions.

**2005:** Clear Channel offers 10 percent of Clear Channel Outdoor in initial public offering and spins off Clear Channel Entertainment to shareholders.

**2008:** Clear Channel announces the completion of a merger with an indirect wholly owned subsidiary of CC Media Holdings, Inc.

targets for return on investment, it will take you out of the market."

In the wake of the 1984 FCC ruling, Mays made several acquisitions, but by 1987 his company was effectively out of the radio acquisition market. In 1988, when all radio acquisitions had been put on hold, Mays jumped into the television market, acquiring a station in Mobile, Alabama, that was an affiliate of the Fox TV network, which was just beginning its bid to become the fourth major network in the country. After acquiring the station in Mobile, Mays went on to purchase television stations in Tucson (Arizona), Jacksonville (Florida), Tulsa, Wichita (Kansas), and Memphis, each a Fox affiliate except for the Tucson property.

The foray into television broadcasting proved to be a financial boon for Clear Channel, particularly because

of the success enjoyed by the Fox TV network as it developed into the country's fourth major television network. Clear Channel issued a second stock offering in mid-1991, raising $25 million to pay for debt incurred in its late 1980s acquisition campaign, which had significantly strengthened the company's financial stature. By the end of 1991, the company's 18 radio stations and six television stations generated revenues of $74 million and earnings of more than $1 million.

### EXPANSION: 1992–97

Beginning in mid-1992, Mays changed course and began to acquire radio stations at a voracious rate, motivated by changing conditions in the radio industry. Companies that had acquired radio stations during the 1980s had paid high prices, and during the economic recession of the early 1990s many of those companies were saddled with debt and forced to sell. Consequently, the price of radio properties dropped dramatically, creating numerous opportunities for Mays. For the financial resources to wage an acquisition campaign, Mays relied on the guarantees of nine major banks, which totaled a hefty $150 million. By mid-1993, $110 million of the total had been used to acquire 31 radio stations and seven television stations in mid-sized Sunbelt markets, and Clear Channel had catapulted to the top of its industry.

In 1994 Clear Channel merged with a Tampa, Florida, competitor named Metroplex Communications. In 1995 the company leaped well beyond its established operating territory when it acquired a 50 percent interest in the Australian Radio Network. By the end of that year, Clear Channel owned 36 radio stations and 10 television stations, which represented a modest increase over the total number of properties it owned in 1993. The figures were deceptive, however, because they did not accurately convey the financial progress the company had made during the two-year period. Annual revenues between 1993 and 1995 exploded from $135 million to $244 million, while the company's net income swelled from $9 million to $32 million.

As a result of the strategy employed by Mays, Clear Channel exited 1995 in enviable financial shape and ready to take advantage of a momentous announcement by the FCC. The Telecommunications Act of 1996 lifted national radio ownership restrictions and eased local limitations, touching off a spate of acquisitions for those with the financial wherewithal to acquire broadcasting properties. Clear Channel was one of those companies in a financial position that permitted aggressive expansion and, in fact, was leading the pack. The Telecommunications Act of 1996 took effect in February 1996, and by June, Clear Channel had acquired or was in the process of acquiring $581 million worth of radio and television stations. "They're very savvy and they're very focused," one analyst remarked as Clear Channel grew rapidly during the first half of 1996. "All their acquisitions are great, and they have yet to trip up." With 70 radio stations (43 FM, 27 AM) and 16 television stations under its control by June 1996, and 34 more acquisitions pending, the company had ample opportunities to make a mistake, but under the guiding eye of Mays, Clear Channel had moved resolutely forward and emerged from the mid-1990s stronger than ever. The company's history of robust cash-flow growth and its discipline in acquiring stations for bargain prices had investors clamoring for more. Between 1990 and 1996, the company's stock soared from $2.72 a share to a remarkable $73 a share, piquing Wall Street's interest in what the company would do during the late 1990s.

By October 1996 clear Channel owned 121 radio stations and 11 television stations, making it the second-largest radio group in the country behind Westinghouse/CBS. As the company prepared plans for the late 1990s and the beginning of the 21st century, more acquisitions were in the offing. At the beginning of 1997, Mays had more than $1 billion at his disposal for future acquisitions and expressed no desire to slow down in the years ahead. "We're the fastest-growing media company in the country," Mays told *Fortune* magazine. "We're going to be the acquirer, not the acquiree," he promised.

Clear Channel's progress in 1997 set the tone for the company's course of development in the future. In April the company acquired Eller Media Company, the oldest and largest billboard operator in the United States with more than 50,000 outdoor display faces in 15 major metropolitan markets. In June the company acquired a 32 percent interest in Spanish-language broadcaster Heftel Broadcasting Corp., which carried Clear Channel into major metropolitan markets for the first time. "We're trying to consolidate the Spanish broadcasting industry itself," Mays explained, as he formulated plans for developing clusters of Spanish-language stations. In October the company made its next definitive move, signing an agreement to purchase Universal Outdoor Inc., which added 88,000 outdoor display faces to Clear Channel's billboard holdings and made the company the second-largest outdoor advertiser in the country.

## GROWING INTO A MEDIA GIANT: 1998–2002

In 1998 the company continued to expand its radio division via the addition of 38 stations, bringing the total number of stations owned or programmed by Clear Channel to 204. The company also acquired the

More Group Plc, an outdoor advertising company operating in 25 countries around the world. The company acquired Universal Outdoor in 1998 for its outdoor advertising division and a 40 percent interest in Grupo Acir, the largest operator of radio stations in Mexico.

Clear Channel substantially enhanced its radio presence with its acquisition of Jacor Communications in 1999, bringing the company's total number of radio stations owned or programmed to 625. That same year, the company acquired Dauphin, a European outdoor advertising agency. Noting the company's outstanding performance over the past decade, the *Wall Street Journal* ranked Clear Channel as the fifth-best-performing stock of the nineties.

The company continued to expand in 2000 with the acquisition of AMFM, Inc., which created a national radio platform for the company. Clear Channel also purchased SFX Entertainment, Inc., a worldwide promoter, producer, and presenter of live entertainment events. Other acquisitions included the outdoor assets of Donrey Media, Taxi Tops, and Ackerley Media. Clear Channel's efforts in expansion led to the company's total number of worldwide radio stations owned or programmed to more than 1,100 and total outdoor advertising displays to approximately 700,000. The company's entertainment division also produced and marketed the three top grossing concert tours in 2001.

By 2002 Clear Channel was operating in 65 countries worldwide. The company also consummated its merger with the Ackerley Group, Inc. (Ackerley), on June 14, 2002, for $497 million in stock. The acquisition of the outdoor advertising company with more than 6,000 displays in Massachusetts, New Jersey, New York, Oregon, and Washington was made to boost Clear Channel's media presence in key United States cities. The purchase of Ackerley also included a portfolio of 18 television and four radio stations in Alaska, California, New York, Oregon, and Washington.

## MAJOR CHANGES: 2003 ON

Over the three decades since its founding, Clear Channel's growth gained widespread recognition. "Wall Street admires the nation's largest radio broadcasting conglomerate ... as a fast-growing, profitable multimedia empire," wrote Lynnley Browning in an article for the *New York Times*. However, Clear Channel's competitors, particularly smaller radio stations and media outlets, did not look kindly on the company's domination of the industry. Accusations were made that Clear Channel resembled a monopoly in the radio broadcasting business. Nevertheless, as Browning pointed out in the *New York Times* article, other broadcasting companies were "adopting many strategies pioneered by Clear Channel, including million-dollar contests for listeners and attractive package deals for advertisers that cover many stations."

Although it was a recognized media giant that far outpaced most of its competitors, Clear Channel was not about to rest on its laurels. In 2005 the company offered 10 percent of Clear Channel Outdoor in an initial public offering and spun off its Clear Channel Entertainment subdivision to stockholders under the name Live Nation. The following year, the company hired Goldman, Sachs & Co. as a financial advisor to help evaluate various strategic alternatives to enhance shareholder value.

In November 2006 the company announced that it had entered into a merger agreement with a private equity group led by Bain Capital Partners, LLC and Thomas H. Lee Partners, L.P. The agreement would lead to the group acquiring Clear Channel. Clear Channel announced the completion of the merger on July 30, 2008. The merger was with an indirect, wholly owned subsidiary of CC Media Holdings, Inc. (CCMH), formed by Bain Capital Partners, LLC and Thomas H. Lee Partners, L.P (THL). The transaction was valued at approximately $24 billion. "Clear Channel can offer advertisers access to the largest radio platform in the US," Scott Sperling, co-president of THL told Kelly Holman in an interview for *Investment Dealers' Digest*. "It's a company that's been a leader in providing unique and superior programming at the local and national level, and we believe Clear Channel will be the strongest player in this industry."

The worldwide economic downturn that began in 2008 ultimately affected Clear Channel. In 2008 the company sold its TV stations to Newport Television. Clear Channel's parent company CCMH went on to initiate a restructuring program in the fourth quarter of 2008. Clear Channel announced in January of the following year that it was eliminating 1,850 positions, or about 9 percent of its staff. Despite the tough economic environment, which played a large role in reduced revenues for the company, Mark Mays, Clear Channel's president and chief executive officer, remained optimistic, telling Stephanie Clifford of the *New York Times*: "Everyone in our investor group, on the board and in the executive leadership team remains bullish about the long-term growth prospects for Clear Channel."

As of December 31, 2009, the company estimated that the benefit of its restructuring program was approximately $441.3 million in aggregate reductions to fixed operating and corporate expenses. The company believed the benefit of these initiatives would be fully realized in the early 2010s.

*Jeffrey L. Covell*
*Updated, David Petechuk*

## PRINCIPAL DIVISIONS

International Outdoor Advertising; Outdoor Advertising (United States); Radio Broadcasting.

## PRINCIPAL COMPETITORS

CBS Corporation; Citadel Broadcasting Corporation; Cumulus Media Inc.; JCDecaux S.A.; Lamar Advertising Company.

## FURTHER READING

Brockinton, Langdon, "Clear Channel Tunes in Billboard Business," *MEDIAWEEK*, October 27, 1997, p. 20.

Browning, Lynnley, "Making Waves on Air: Big Radio's Bad Boy," *New York Times*, June 19, 2002, p. C1.

"Clear Channel Communications, Inc. Completes Merger with Private Investor Group," *Business Wire*, July 30, 2008.

Clifford, Stephanie, "Clear Channel Plans to Trim 1,850 Jobs," *New York Times*, January 21, 2009, p. B2.

Holman, Kelly, "Bain, THL Tune $24B Clear Channel Buy," *Investment Dealers' Digest*, January 19, 2009, p. 23.

Poole, Claire, "The Accidental Broadcaster," *Forbes*, June 8, 1992, p. 58.

"Radio Giant, Live Acts Promoter Join Forces," *Variety*, March 6, 2000, p. 4.

Rathbun, Elizabeth, "Texas Size: Clear Channel Builds a Broadcast Dynasty," *Broadcasting & Cable*, October 7, 1996, p. 56.

Roman, Leigh Ann, "Clear Channel's Presence in Memphis Mirrors Nationwide Trend of Station Consolidation," *Memphis Business Journal*, March 24, 1997, p. 49.

Serwer, Andrew E., "The Best Li'l Broadcaster in Texas," *Fortune*, August 19, 1996, p. 26.

Viles, Peter, "Clear Channel: Sunbelt Success Story," *Broadcasting & Cable*, July 5, 1993, p. 19.

# Cloud Peak Energy Inc.

505 South Gillette Avenue
Gillette, Wyoming 82717
U.S.A.
Telephone: (307) 687-6000
Fax: (307) 687-6015
Web site: http://www.cloudpeakenergy.com

*Public Company*
*Founded:* 1901 as Kennecott Mines Company.
*Employees:* 1,529 (2009)
*Sales:* $1.398 billion (2009)
*Stock Exchanges:* New York
*Ticker Symbol:* CLD
*NAICS:* 212111 Bituminous Coal and Lignite Surface
  Mining

■ ■ ■

Cloud Peak Energy Inc. (Cloud Peak) is the third-largest coal producer in the United States, specializing in the production of low-sulfur, high-quality, subbituminous coal. This type of coal is commonly used for electricity generation, which is why electrical utilities are Cloud Peak's primary customers. In 2009 Cloud Peak produced over 93 million metric tons of coal.

In 2010 Cloud Peak Energy owned three surface coal mines in Montana and Wyoming: The Antelope Mine and the Cordero Rojo Mine, located in Wyoming, and the Spring Creek Mine, located near Decker, Montana. In addition, the company owned a 50 percent nonoperating interest in the Decker Coal Company, which operated another mine in Decker.

In November 2009 Cloud Peak Energy Inc. went public with an initial public offering (IPO) on the New York Stock Exchange (NYSE). Previously, the company was a wholly owned subsidiary of Rio Tinto Energy America (RTEA), the U.S. coal-producing arm of Rio Tinto plc, a large international mining company.

## KENNECOTT ANCESTRY: 1901

Cloud Energy's origins are most closely tied with the Kennecott Energy Company, founded in 1901 as the Kennecott Mines Company. A mining engineer named Stephen Birch acquired the rights to a property near Kennicott Glacier in Alaska. A clerical mistake named the company "Kennecott" instead of that of its namesake. Birch received funding from J.P. Morgan and the Guggenheims, both powerful parties in the mining industry.

In 1933, following Kennecott's first unprofitable year, Birch was succeeded as president and chairman by E. T. Stannard, a director of J.P. Morgan and Company. Around that time, the market was beginning to show the effects of a new flood of copper from Rhodesia (now Zambia and Zimbabwe). Since Kennecott was set up as a high-production outfit, cutting back production was not a practical strategy. Stannard instead sought out new markets. Although this policy made no significant gains, Kennecott was bailed out in the late 1930s, as was the copper industry in general, by greatly increased demand for copper in preparation for entry into World War II.

Stephen Birch died in 1940, leaving management of the company firmly in Stannard's hands. Through the first half of the 1940s, the war kept production moving at a healthy pace, and Kennecott's operating revenues reached a peak of $265 million in 1943. When the war ended, however, Stannard saw that Kennecott's continued growth would depend upon its willingness to diversify and explore new geographical and geological arenas. In 1945 Stannard allotted half a million dollars for exploration, a figure comparable to that spent by its main competitors, Phelps Dodge and Anaconda.

Oil, gold, and titanium were the principal commodities on which Kennecott began to focus. In 1945 the company teamed up with Continental Oil for a joint prospecting and drilling venture. By this time, Kennecott was a major U.S. gold producer, since that metal is often a natural byproduct of copper mining. It was not until 1947, however, that the company went looking for gold directly. That year, Kennecott's exploration chief, Anton Gray, was sent gold-hunting in South Africa. This action resulted in the creation of the Kennecott-Anglovaal Exploration Co., Ltd., a joint gold-exploration firm.

More important was the company's entry into the titanium business. Titanium is found in ilemite, one of the most abundant minerals in the earth's surface. Ilemite had been discovered in parts of Quebec in the early 1940s, and Kennecott began its search in the region in 1944. Two years later, Kennecott's explorers, led by Gray, discovered the largest ilemite deposit in the world, over 100 million metric tons, at Lake Tio in eastern Quebec. Kennecott spent a half million dollars finding, claiming, and measuring the mine. In 1948 Quebec Iron and Titanium Corp. (Q.I.T.) was formed, with Kennecott controlling two-thirds interest, and New Jersey Zinc Co., which had been exploring the area as well, owning the remaining share.

Expansion continued in the 1950s and 1960s. In 1953 Kennecott purchased the Kaiser Aluminum and Chemical Corp. In the 1960s, the company expanded into lead, zinc, and silver under new CEO Frank Milliken. Under pressure to find expansion avenues, Milliken undertook international expansion by investing in a Chilean copper mine. The mine was later nationalized and Kennecott took a large loss, albeit a mitigated

one, as Milliken was aware of the possibility of losing the investment.

In 1968 Kennecott acquired Peabody Coal Co., the largest producer of coal in the United States, for $622 million. However, after a prolonged legal battle, the Federal Trade Commission (FTC) forced Kennecott to divest the subsidiary in 1977. Many years would pass before Kennecott reentered the coal industry.

## PROXY FIGHTS, BUYOUTS AND EXPANSION: 1981–97

In the 1970s, the copper market was sluggish due to increased supply as other companies entered the market. In 1976 Kennecott suffered a loss of $10.9 million. In 1977 Kennecott acquired Carborundum Co., a manufacturer of industrial products. This acquisition angered some stockholders who believed that the $568 million Kennecott paid was too much. A group of stockholders filed a suit to block the acquisition. The failed suit led to a proxy fight, launched in 1978, led by Roland Berner, chief executive of Curtiss-Wright Corporation, a maker of aircraft engines. By March 1978, Curtiss-Wright owned 9.9 percent of Kennecott's stock. The proxy fight was also ultimately unsuccessful, but resulted in a management team consisting of Carborundum executives and a board of directors consisting of disgruntled stockholders. The beleaguered CEO, Frank Milliken, retired, replaced by Thomas D. Barrow, who had been an executive at Exxon. In 1981, cash-strapped by the proxy battle and falling copper prices, Barrow negotiated the acquisition of Kennecott by Standard Oil Co. of Ohio (SOHIO).

In 1987, as SOHIO's stock price fell, British Petroleum offered to buy the remaining 45 percent of shares that it did not already own in SOHIO. Kennecott became a subsidiary of BP Minerals. This allowed Kennecott to pursue upgrades to its flagship copper mine, Bingham Canyon.

In 1989 Rio Tinto Zinc (RTZ) purchased the mining assets of BP to become the world's largest producer of gold outside South Africa. The inclusion of Kennecott, now one of the most well-known names in mining, was also a boost to RTZ. Under RTZ, Kennecott became Kennecott Utah Corporation. RTZ would later merge with Australia's CRA Limited and rename the company RTZ-CRA Group. This was the largest mining company in the world. In 1997 RTZ-CRA would rename itself Rio Tinto PLC.

With its parent's deep pockets, Kennecott once again pursued expansion into the coal industry by purchasing smaller coal companies throughout the United States. In 1993 Kennecott purchased Nerco, be renamed Rio Tinto Energy America (RTEA), as the name Kennecott was more recognizable as a copper mining company. At the time, Kennecott Copper faced decreasing copper prices and considerable cleanup costs at its Utah copper operation. The name change would associate the coal operations with the global recognition of Rio Tinto as a minerals and mining company.

Despite a challenging economy, KEC enjoyed increased production and earnings between 2001 and 2003. In 2001 KEC invested $379.5 million in Jacobs Ranch for an additional northern tract. The North Jacobs Ranch tract contained 515 million metric tons of recoverable coal reserves, increasing the life of the mine from 5 to 23 years.

## ACQUISITIONS AND DIVESTITURE: 2004–07

Between 2004 and 2006, Kennecott expanded its mines while enjoying strong demand for its low-cost, low-sulphur coal. Low-sulphur coal delivers competitive cost per delivered energy unit. In addition, U.S. customers, mostly utilities, faced restricted sulphur emissions, making Kennecott's coal attractive. In 2004 Kennecott expanded the Antelope mine by acquiring land to the west of the mine, increasing reserves from 195 million metric tons to 400 million tons. During this time, the Colowyo plant was found to have higher operating and development costs than previously estimated, resulting in a $160 million write-off of its assets.

The year 2007 came with increased input prices and decreased demand. Diesel, labor, and heavy-equipment tire prices increased along with the effective tax rate. Demand curtailed due to customers having stockpiled coal reserves in the previous year. However, RTEA continued its expansion. The Spring Creek mine was expanded by approximately 107 million metric tons, and the Colowyo mine was expanded by 83 million tons.

In 2007 Rio Tinto acquired Alcan, a global materials supplier of high-quality bauxite, alumina, and aluminium. The acquisition required Rio Tinto to take on $40 billion in additional debt.

To add to its growing difficulty, Rio Tinto faced two hostile takeover attempts. Competitor BHP Billiton had long expressed an interest in acquiring Rio Tinto, but a bid was never accepted, as Rio Tinto believed the offer of three BHP shares for every Rio Tinto share was underpriced. In 2008 BHP pursued but later dropped a $62 billion hostile takeover attempt, citing deteriorating global economic conditions. Chinese aluminium

Inc., from the struggling PacifiCorp. Nerco owned mines in Spring Creek, Wyoming, and Antelope, Montana, plus a 50 percent nonoperating interest in the Decker Coal Company. A week later, the company acquired the Codero Mining Company from Sun Co. In 1994 Kennecott purchased Colowyo Coal Company, located south of Craig, Colorado, from specialty chemicals company W.R. Grace. In 1998 Kennecott purchased the assets of Jacobs Ranch from the Kerr-McGee Corp. and the Caballo Rojo mine from Marigold Land Company, an affiliate of Drummond Company, Inc.

These acquisitions would complete the coal-producing assets of Rio Tinto Energy America (RTEA), totaling seven mines. The Codero Mine, Caballo Rojo, and Antelope mines are located in Wyoming, the Jacobs Ranch, Spring Creek, and Decker mines are located in Montana, while the Colowyo mine is located in Colorado. In 1997, the Codero and Caballo Rojo mine operations were merged and named the Codero Rojo mine.

In 1997 Kennecott Corporation was divided into three separate subsidiaries: Kennecott Utah Copper Corporation, Kennecott Minerals Company, and Kennecott Energy Company (KEC). A new subsidiary called Kennecott Exploration Company was created to support the three subsidiaries in seeking new mining resources. KEC held the U.S. coal mines. In May 2006 Rio Tinto announced that the Kennecott Energy Company would corporation Chinalco worked to prevent this acquisition, believing that the two companies commanded too much power over prices in the industry. Chinalco teamed up with the U.S.-based Alcoa Inc. to purchase 9 percent of Rio Tinto.

Heavily indebted and trying to avoid a hostile takeover, Rio Tinto decided to streamline its assets, at which point it announced its intention to sell its U.S. coal assets. The Colowyo mine was separated from RTEA, as it was not a part of the divestiture plans, due to its "complex financial arrangements," according to a Rio representative.

## CLOUD PEAK ENERGY: 2009 AND BEYOND

In November 2009 Cloud Peak Energy completed an IPO for $741 million. In 2009 Rio Tinto still owned 48.3 percent interest in Cloud Peak Energy. The new company would own the Antelope, Spring Creek, and Cordero Rojo mines with a nonoperating interest in the Decker Mine in Montana. The Jacobs Ranch was sold to Arch Coal for $764 million, while the Colowyo Mine was retained by Rio Tinto, due to its financial ties with Rio Tinto.

The year 2009 was a healthy financial year for Cloud Peak, with revenues up and operting income nearly doubling from the previous year. In the early 2010s, economic recovery was expected to lead an increased demand for electricity, as indicated by a forecast by the Energy Information Administration, which estimated a 2 percent increase in demand during 2010. It was also likely that reduced production from

competing companies in the Central Appalachian mines and metallurgical coal would increase demand. CEO Colin Marshall stated to analysts, "We believe the first quarter of 2010 saw the transition from an oversupplied coal market to one where utilities are seeing increased demand for electricity and are raising their expectations for coal burn."

*Sara K. Huter*

## PRINCIPAL SUBSIDIARIES

Antelope Coal LLC; Caballo Rojo LLC; Cloud Peak Energy Finance Corp.; Cloud Peak Energy Resources LLC (51.7%); Cloud Peak Energy Services Company; Codero Mining LLC; Decker Coal Company (50%); Spring Creek Coal LLC.

## PRINCIPAL COMPETITORS

Arch Coal, Inc.; Chevron Mining, Inc.; CONSOL Energy, Inc.; Massey Energy Company; Peabody Energy Corporation.

## FURTHER READING

"Cloud Peak Energy Inc. Announces Results for First Quarter 2010," *Business Wire,* May 12, 2010.
"Kennecott Completes Acquisition of Colowyo Coal Mine from W.R. Grace," *Business Wire,* December 7, 1994.
MacNamara, William, "Rio to Spin off US Coal Mines," *Financial Times,* August 14, 2009.
"RTZ-CRA Group's Kennecott to Buy Caballo Rojo Coal Mine from an Affiliate of Drummond Company Inc.," *Business Wire,* January 21, 1997.
Worden, Edward, "Kennecott to Buy More Coal Mines in Wyoming," *American Metal Market* 101, no. 36 (1993): 6. February 24, 1993.

# CNP Assurances

4, place Raoul Dautry
Paris, Cedex 15 75015
France
Telephone: (+33-1-42) 18-88-88
Fax: (+33-1-42) 18-86-55
Web site: http://www.cnp.fr

*Public Company*
*Founded:* 1959 as Caisse Nationale de Prévoyance
*Employees:* 4,630 (2009)
*Sales:* €47.88 billion ($64.8 billion) (2009)
*Stock Exchanges:* Euronext
*Ticker Symbol:* CNP
*NAICS:* 523999 Miscellaneous Financial Investment Activities; 524113 Direct Life Insurance Carriers; 524224 Direct Health and Medical Insurance Carriers; 525110 Pension Funds

■ ■ ■

CNP Assurances, a *Fortune* Global 500 company, has been the leading personal life insurer in France since 1991, and one of the top five providers of life insurance in all of Europe. The company is based in Paris, France, and also has operations in 15 countries, including Italy, Spain, Argentina, Brazil, and China. CNP Assurances offers products in the areas of savings, pensions, and personal risk to meet the needs of individuals and groups. Its range of products includes life, health, death, property, accident, and disability insurance, as well as savings products, financial services, asset management, personal risk coverage, and pensions. The company's range of services addresses the needs of the elderly and disabled, and financial services are offered with payments low enough that the services are accessible to customers in even the lowest income brackets. Of CNP Assurance's 22 million policy holders, 14 million reside in France.

CNP Assurances's products are distributed through 20,000 locations of the French postal service La Poste and the state savings banks La Caisse Nationale des Caisses d'Epargne (Groupe Caisses d'Epargne). Approximately three-fourths of the company's total product sales are made through these outlets. Not only do these locations sell CNP's products, but they are also company shareholders who own a total of about 35 percent of the company. CNP has also established loan insurance partnerships for group insurance policies with more than 250 financial institutions. Its pension and personal risk products are distributed through mutual insurers, local authorities, and other companies.

## INSURANCE WITH 19TH-CENTURY ROOTS

Although CNP Assurances was founded in 1959, its roots in the insurance industry date back more than 150 years, and its roots in savings began nearly 200 years ago. It originated from three state-owned insurance companies. The first, Caisse nationale d'assurance en cas d'accident, dates back to 1868 and specialized in accident insurance. The second, the Caisse nationale d'assurance en cas de deéceés, was established in 1848, with a specialization in death and disability insurance. The third, the Caisse de retraite pour la vieillesse, was

# COMPANY PERSPECTIVES

With 150 years' experience of designing and managing insurance products and operations in 15 countries, CNP Assurances's mission is to partner clients throughout their life, by providing them with protection against the risks of everyday life.

established in 1949, with a specialization in retirement pensions.

In 1949 the government of France formed the Caisse nationale d'assurance sur la vie by combining its death and disability insurance company with its retirement insurance company. Ten years later, in 1959, the government merged this company with its accident insurance company, creating the Caisse nationale de Preévoyance, which later became CNP Assurances. The government also made Caisse nationale de Preévoyance a part of the Caisse des Deépoôts et Consignations (CDC). CDC is a French financial organization under the control of the Parliament, and it owns almost 40 percent (39.99%) of CNP. Being created by the mergers of such long-established companies, CNP's origins date back to 1850, which was when the life insurance market was in its infancy.

## OPERATING IN THE 20TH CENTURY

The Caisse Nationale de Prévoyance became a public sector company in 1987. Public sector companies are owned by the government and the taxpayers. In 1992 it became CNP Assurances, a public limited company governed by the French Insurance code. A public limited company is like a limited liability company (LLC), which protects shareholders by limiting their financial risk to what they contribute into the business. Unlike an (LLC), a public limited company may offer shares to the public as well.

CNP Assurances has employed several strategies to make its products accessible to all. It has worked to develop insurance programs for underprivileged entrepreneurs through the Fondation Entrepreneurs de le Cité. Working with some of its partners, CNP has also donated large sums of money to help develop companies in underprivileged areas in order to benefit disadvantaged community members financially and to give them the opportunity to access credit and risk protection. The company has also established policies

which take into account the availability of new medical treatments, which allow loan insurance to be available to those suffering from health risk. This policy alone has lowered the company's rejection rate of such policies by two-thirds since 2001, making CNP's rejection rate one of the lowest of any insurance company.

## ESTABLISHING THE CNP HEALTH FOUNDATION IN 1993

In 1993 the CNP Health Foundation was established to support CNP Assurances's commitment to the community in the areas of health care improvements, disease prevention, better patient care, medical research, and more accessible health care. The foundation has received €534,000 in funding each year from CNP Assurances. This foundation focuses on fighting and managing pain.

Between 1994 and 1997, the CNP Health Foundation provided money to establish 10 facilities to provide dental care free of charge to the needy and has contributed to the cost of training 1,800 volunteers to work at the facilities. Also in 1994, the CNP Foundation partnered with the French Cystic Fibrosis Association to provide home schooling for approximately 15,000 children who are unable to attend classes due to illness or accidents. The CNP Foundation has also supported the connection between health care and education by giving financial support to the production of a film to help those who work with children to detect dyslexia in preschool-aged children so they can receive the help they need. Dyslexia affects approximately 10 percent of French residents.

## CHANGING OWNERSHIP: 1998–2000

In 1998, CNP Assurances was first quoted on the Paris Stock Exchange by offering 22 percent of its capital to the public. Before this, the majority of the French government's holding in the company was transferred to three of CNP's largest holders. These were the Caisse des Dépôts, La Poste, and Caisses d'Epargne. To this point, the government's holding of the company had been 42.38 percent. The flotation raised FRF 5.54 billion ($1.01 billion) and lowered the government's holding of the company to about 1 percent. Although the country lowered its holdings of the company significantly, the shares were sold to mostly state-run institutions, leaving CNP in a unique position in the insurance market.

Two years later, in 2000, a pact was signed by the founding shareholders of CNP, which strengthened the stable ownership structure of the company. The pact was

## KEY DATES

**1959:** Caisse Nationale de Prévoyance is created by the merger of two French companies within the Caisse des Dépôts group.

**1987:** Caisse Nationale de Prévoyance becomes a public sector company.

**1992:** Caisse Nationale de Prévoyance becomes CNP Assurances, a public limited company governed by the French Insurance Code.

**1998:** CNP Assurances is first quoted on the Paris Stock Exchange by offering 22 percent of its capital to the public.

**2009:** A long-term partnership between CNP Assurances and Barclays is created.

in place through the end of 2008. It outlined that the largest portion of the company was owned by Caisse des Dépôts, which held 39.99 percent. The next largest portion of CNP Assurances, 35.48 percent, was owned by the holding company Sopassure. Sopassure was 50.1 percent owned by La Poste and 49.9 percent owned by a holding company associated with Groupe Caisses d'Epargne. The public owned 23.44 percent of CNP Assurances, with the French State owning the remaining 1.09 percent.

## OFFERING PERSONAL SERVICES: 2001

In 2001 CNP Assurances developed Filassistance, or "the living facilitator." Its creation was in response to the Barloo plan, which was sponsored by France's minister of employment, social cohesion and housing, to increase the personal services available to France's aging population. Filassistance offers programs to help with the transition into retirement as well as services that allow the elderly or those with disabilities to remain in their own homes. Transportation, support services, legal information, aid in arranging in-home assistance, and counseling services are available around the clock. Over three million clients have taken advantage of the services offered by this organization.

Similar to the services provided by Filassistance, CNP Services é la Personne uscs a network of 10,000 service providers to meet the personal needs of its clients. The long list of available services include housekeeping, childcare, tutoring, computer lessons, personal care, legal advice, home maintenance and repair, and delivery of meals, groceries, and medication.

## CHANGES WITHIN THE COMPANY: 2003–09

CNP Assurances entered into an agreement with Matmut, France's sixth-largest motor insurer, in 2003. The equal partnership between the two companies will be in place until 2013. The purpose was to offer high-quality personal risk insurance to Matmut's 2.4 million customers.

Also in 2003, CNP made a commitment to support the UN Global Compact. Principle 10 of the compact required that businesses work against all forms of corruption. CNP has established policies to fight money laundering and prevent the funding of terrorist organizations. Updated procedures and specialized personnel are used to identify transactions that could be suspected of being used for these purposes.

In 2005 CNP Capitalia Vita was introduced when CNP Assurances acquired 57.5 percent of Fineco Vita. Although it was renamed CNP Capitalia Vita, 38.8 percent of the company was retained by the Capitalia Group. In 2008 Capitalia was merged into UniCredit. As a result, CNP Assurances and UniCredit came to an agreement regarding CNP Capitalia Vita, their joint venture company. Under this agreement, CNP Capitalia Vita continued offering its loan and personal insurance products. The company's sales would be exclusively distributed through the Banca di Roman and the Banco di Sicilia.

In 2009 CNP Assurances and Barclays Bank PLC entered a 25-year agreement to develop life insurance through Barclays international networks. This would expand CNP's presence in Spain, Portugal, and Italy. Through this agreement, CNP acquired 50 percent of Barclays' Viday Pensiones, the existing life insurance company in Spain and Portugal. Also, under this agreement, Barclays would begin new insurance dealings in Italy.

According to a September 10, 2009, article on the *Insurance Business Review* Web site, Gilles Benoise, CNP Assurances's group chief officer, said, "We are delighted to launch this partnership with such a highly regarded bank as Barclays. CNP's long standing experience and expertise in life insurance, particularly in Southern Europe, combined with the growth capacity of Barclays in this region will create long term value for all parties. Moreover, this partnership refocuses and strengthens CNP's footprint in the region."

## LOOKING TO THE FUTURE

In the company's March 2009 investors report, CNP viewed its strengths as including the vitality of its distribution networks, the offering of loan and personal risk insurance, the company's low policy administration costs, and its high quality asset/liability management. Challenges the company believed it faced included slower growth of the life insurance market in France and adapting to changes in the market of Italy. CNP Assurances ranked 196 on *Fortune* magazine's Global 500 list during 2009, down from a ranking of 112 the previous year. Although Standard & Poors downgraded the company's rating from AA to AA-, the organization believes CNP Assurances has a stable outlook and views the fact that a "government-related entity is the largest shareholder of CNP" as having a positive impact on the company.

As of 2010, CNP continued to expand internationally, with a focus on gaining a greater presence in Europe and South America. This plan of expansion was based on building in markets that offered strong growth potential for personal insurance and finding well-established partners that were able to offer strong networks for selling life insurance.

*Diane Milne*

## PRINCIPAL SUBSIDIARIES

CNP IAM; CNP International; CNP Seguros de Videa (76.47%, Argentina); Investissement Trésor-Vie (ITV); LaBanque Postale Prévoyance (50%); Préviposte.

## PRINCIPAL DIVISIONS

Savings; Personal Risk; Pensions; Property & Casualty; Health Insurance; Loan Insurance.

## PRINCIPAL COMPETITORS

Assurances Générales de France; AXA Group; Groupama S.A.

## FURTHER READING

"Barclays, CNP Form Life Insurance JV in Spain, Portugal, Italy," *Insurance Business Review,* insurance-business-review. com, September 10, 2009.

"France Sells CNP but Delays France Telecom," *Privitisation International,* November 1, 1998.

Hoovers. "CNP Assurances," hoovers.com.

"CNP Assurances: France's Leading Personal Insurer," Investors Report Presentation, March 2009.

"CNP Assurances Press Release," thefreelibrary.com, December 18, 2003.

Crepy, Virginie, and Paola Del Curatolo, "CNP Assurances Lowered to 'AA–' from 'AA' Because of Weakened Capital Adequacy; Outlook Stable," *Standard & Poors Rating Direct,* 2009.

The United Nations Global Compact, "The Ten Principles," unglobalcompact.org.

Wankel, Charles, ed., "CNP Assurances," *Encyclopedia of Business in Today's World,* Thousand Oaks, CA: Sage, 2009, p. 285.

*The Coca-Cola Company*

# Coca-Cola Enterprises, Inc.

■

**2500 Windy Ridge Parkway**
**Atlanta, Georgia 30339**
**U.S.A.**
**Telephone: (770) 989-3000**
**Fax: (770) 989-3790**
**Web site: http://www.cokecce.com**

*Public Company*
*Incorporated:* 1986
*Employees:* 70,000 (est., 2009)
*Sales:* $21.64 billion (2009)
*Stock Exchanges:* New York
*Ticker Symbol:* CCE
*NAICS:* 312111 Soft Drink Manufacturing

■ ■ ■

In 1986 the Coca-Cola Company combined company-owned bottlers and formed Coca-Cola Enterprises, Inc. (CCE). In 2009 the Coca-Cola Company owned approximately 34 percent of CCE's outstanding common stock. As the world's largest Coca-Cola bottler, CCE draws its revenues from marketing, producing, and distributing nonalcoholic beverages that represent approximately 16 percent of total Coca-Cola volume worldwide. The company serves approximately 419 million consumers throughout the United States, Canada, the U.S. Virgin Islands and other Caribbean islands, Belgium, France, Great Britain, Luxembourg, Monaco, and the Netherlands.

North American bottling territories are located in 46 states, the District of Columbia, the U.S. Virgin

Islands, and other Caribbean islands, and all 10 provinces of Canada. The company's five top brands in North America are Coca-Cola, Diet Coke, Sprite, Dasani, and Dr. Pepper. European bottling territories include Belgium, France, Great Britain, Luxembourg, Monaco, and the Netherlands. The company's top five brands in Europe are Coca-Cola, Diet Coke, Coca-Cola/Light, Coca-Cola Zero, Fanta, and Capri-Sun. In 2010 the Coca-Cola Company bought CCE's North American bottling business.

## EARLY HISTORY: 1899

Among the collection of bottling operations composing CCE during the 1990s, the oldest traced its roots back to 1899, when one of the most incredible and profitable transactions in U.S. business history occurred. That year, thirteen years after the first Coca-Cola drink mixture was concocted, two lawyers from Chattanooga, Tennessee, bought the exclusive rights to sell America's newest beverage, Coca-Cola, in bottles. For what retrospectively ranks as one of the biggest bargains in the annals of business history, the two lawyers together paid $1 for Coca-Cola's exclusive bottling rights, giving the investors what would a century later evolve into a multibillion dollar enterprise for having paid two quarters apiece.

Based on the actions the two entrepreneurs took immediately after investing their $1, they did have some idea of the fortune they had just acquired. With the help of financier John T. Lupton, the two lawyers divided the country into small territories and sold regional rights of the sale of Coca-Cola to other entrepreneurs, thus beginning the development of an intricate and massive network of Coca-Cola bottlers.

# COMPANY PERSPECTIVES

Working with The Coca-Cola Company, we turn their secret syrup into our sweet success. We're the world's largest bottler, marketer and distributor of some of the planet's favorite beverages. While you won't find our dedication, commitment, and passion on the label, you can definitely taste the pride in everything we do.

The franchising of Coca-Cola bottling operations, superintended by John T. Lupton, made fortunes for many independent bottlers, most notably for Lupton himself and his heirs, as the web of bottling operations spread across the country, embracing every corner of the nation. For The Coca-Cola Company, the relationship with its bottlers was also a profitable one. The company marketed its product, then sold Coca-Cola concentrate to bottlers who performed the less profitable task of sweetening and carbonating the syrup, packaging it, then distributing it to retailers. Working as such, the process of making and selling Coca-Cola grew into an enormous business, profiting The Coca-Cola Company and, to a lesser extent, the independent, regionally-based Coca-Cola bottlers. The Coca-Cola empire functioned in this manner for nearly the next century.

## COMPANY FOUNDED: 1944

Although The Coca-Cola Company maintained some ownership of the bottling of its product, an overwhelming majority of the bottling of Coca-Cola was performed by the independent bottlers who were first ceded bottling rights by Lupton and the two Chattanooga lawyers. In 1944 the predecessor to the Coca-Cola Enterprises company that operated during the 1990s was formed as a wholly owned subsidiary of The Coca-Cola Company to manage the small portion of bottling operations directly owned by its parent company. This company was deactivated in 1970, then reactivated 16 years later, in 1986, when almost coincidental developments forced The Coca-Cola Company to jump into the bottling business in an aggressive manner. The result was Coca-Cola Enterprises, Inc., a nearly $3 billion bottling operation comprising a majority of the independent bottling companies that had packaged and distributed Coca-Cola in cans and bottles for more than the previous half century.

Truly a modern creation despite its links to 1944 and 1899, Coca-Cola Enterprises was formed as more of a solution to developments in the soft drink industry that begged a response than as a strategic maneuver effected by The Coca-Cola Company. The origins of Coca-Cola Enterprises may be traced to when the descendants of John T. Lupton, led by a man of the same name, initiated negotiations with The Coca-Cola Company about selling their bottling operations, which were the largest of the soft drink company's sundry independent bottlers.

The company, headed by the latest John T. Lupton, and aptly named JTL Corporation, began negotiating with The Coca-Cola Company in January 1986. The Coca-Cola Company at this point owned bottling operations that constituted roughly 11 percent of its domestic sales volume, to which the addition of JTL's bottling operations, located in Texas, Florida, Colorado, and Arizona, would add another 14 percent, giving the Coca-Cola Company direct control over one quarter of its domestic sales volume. JTL, with $1 billion in estimated 1985 sales, represented a significant acquisition for The Coca-Cola Company for it would bring the company's bottling ownership more in line with rival PepsiCo Inc., which had always owned a sizeable portion of its bottling operations.

Negotiations between JTL and The Coca-Cola Company continued throughout January 1986, with an agreement to merge reached before the end of the month. As negotiations to complete the merger carried into February, another large Coca-Cola bottling operation became available when Beatrice Companies, Inc., a Chicago-based food concern and owner of the second-largest collection of Coca-Cola bottling operations, began looking to sell its stake in bottling Coca-Cola. Beatrice was in the process of being acquired by Kohlberg Kravis Roberts & Company in a $6.2 billion leveraged buyout that forced Beatrice to divest a wealth of assets before mid-1987. Slated for divestiture was the company's most profitable major segment, specifically Coca-Cola bottling facilities stretching across nine states, including one of the country's most lucrative regions, California.

## CCE REESTABLISHED

Faced with either letting the two largest bottling operations in the country fall into potentially hostile hands or acquiring them, the Coca-Cola Company's management opted for the latter, quickly finding themselves in the midst of purchasing two companies with combined annual revenues of more than $2 billion. The potential consolidation of these two enormous bottling organizations was reflective of an industry-wide pattern that had developed during the previous 10 years, as small independent bottlers merged and became large independent bottlers, winnowing the ranks of the bot-

## KEY DATES

**1886:** John Pemberton creates Coca-Cola syrup.
**1900:** First bottling firm and franchise formed, and plants open in Chattanooga and Atlanta.
**1914:** Coca-Cola Bottlers Association is formed.
**1916:** The contour bottle is developed and enters the market.
**1955:** New bottles in 10-, 12-, and 26-ounce sizes successfully introduced.
**1982:** Diet Coke introduced.
**1986:** Coca-Cola Enterprises Inc. formed.
**2002:** Vanilla Coke and Diet Vanilla Coke introduced; Lowry F. Kline is elected chairman of the board and chief executive officer.
**2006:** John F. Brock named president and CEO.
**2010:** Coca-Cola Company buys North American bottling business.

tling industry to compete more effectively in the new era of the "cola wars." In 1975 there were an estimated 2,400 soft drink bottling plants in the United States. Ten years later, when JTL's and Beatrice's bottling groups were up for sale, the number of plants had dropped to 1,400, and by 1990 the number was down to 730.

As The Coca-Cola Company's negotiations with JTL and Beatrice dragged on through the spring and into the summer of 1986, speculation abounded that The Coca-Cola Company would form a separate bottling entity with the two acquisitions and the bottling operations it already owned. Although purchasing JTL's and Beatrice's bottling operations would give the soft drink company more control over its bottlers than it had in the past, the addition of the two heavyweight bottlers would also give the soft drink company considerable debt. A solution to this problem would come later, but as the summer wore on, the agreement to acquire the largest of the two companies, JTL Corp., fell apart, making The Coca-Cola Company's worries about assuming debilitating debt appear moot.

Some members of the Lupton family had decided in late June against selling the source of their family's fortune, wishing instead to remain independent, as they had for nearly a century. At about the same time JTL withdrew from negotiations with The Coca-Cola Company, however, an agreement between The Coca-Cola Company and Beatrice was reached, stipulating that the soft drink company would purchase Beatrice's

bottling group for $1 billion. Two weeks later, the directors of JTL made an about-face, deciding again to sell their bottling operations to the Coca-Cola Company for $1.4 billion.

The two transactions were completed in the fall, forming the foundation for a new prodigious force in the soft drink bottling industry, Coca-Cola Enterprises, Inc., a company that would become known throughout the industry as CCE. The Coca-Cola Company borrowed $2.4 billion to buy JTL and Beatrice's bottling group, incurring enough debt to dilute its earnings. To avoid this drain on its finances, the soft drink company's management decided to sell 51 percent of CCE's ownership to the public. By doing so, the debt accumulated from its bottling acquisitions was wiped off The Coca-Cola Company's financial books, while the stock-buying public was relied upon to invest $1.5 billion to get CCE up and running.

### EARLY YEARS: 1980S

Several days after filing the prospectus for its CCE public offering, The Coca-Cola Company signed an agreement to buy Coca-Cola Bottling Company of Southern Florida with the intention of turning around and selling the bottling group to CCE. This was a maneuver the soft drink company did and would continue to do, as it allowed The Coca-Cola Company to build up its control over its domestic bottlers located in regions contiguous to the bottling operations it already owned through its 49 percent stake in CCE. Donald Keough, chief operating officer of The Coca-Cola Company and CCE's chairman, superintended this expansion of CCE's operating territory, but the bottling company was essentially stewarded during its first years by Brian Dyson, who was described by the *Wall Street Journal* as a "professorial Argentine who runs marathons." Dyson was selected as CCE's chief executive officer after earning much praise as the president of Coca-Cola USA, the domestic soft drink arm of The Coca-Cola Company. In that capacity, Dyson had spearheaded the soft drink company's marketing forays into the sale of Diet Coke and the company's reformulated "new" Coke.

In his new position, Dyson faced the formidable task of satisfying CCE's shareholders in a business essentially foreign to The Coca-Cola Company. In contrast to the company he left to lead CCE, Dyson found himself in the less profitable, more capital-intensive business of carbonating Coca-Cola concentrate, bottling it, and selling it to stores, where the contentious pricing battle between The Coca-Cola Company and PepsiCo reached its most palpable point. Ironically, in this battle, The Coca-Cola Company and

CCE fought for divergent goals. The Coca-Cola Company was concerned primarily with the volume of concentrate it sold, which generally increased when the retail price of Coke dropped, while CCE was concerned primarily with keeping its production and distribution costs as far below the retail price of Coke as possible. Thrust into this new, somewhat alien segment of the soft drink industry, Dyson went about bottling and selling a very familiar product, increasing the scope of CCE operations throughout the late 1980s.

In July 1987 CCE acquired the group of bottling companies The Coca-Cola Company had acquired in the fall of 1986, paying its 49 percent owners $173 million for bottling properties in Florida, Alabama, and Texas. Six months later, in January 1988, CCE agreed to pay $500 million to acquire additional bottlers from The Coca-Cola Company, this time for operations serving Florida (Miami, specifically), Tennessee (Memphis), Delaware, and Maryland. This set of acquisitions gave The Coca-Cola Company control over 45 percent of its domestic volume.

## GROWTH THROUGH ACQUISITIONS

Other minor acquisitions followed, including the absorption of West Georgia Coca-Cola Bottlers, Inc., Coca-Cola Bottling Co. of West Point-LaGrange, Palestine Coca-Cola Bottling Co., and Coca-Cola Bottling Co. of Greenville, Inc., all purchased in 1989. As CCE entered the 1990s, it purchased another large bottler from The Coca-Cola Company, Coca-Cola Bottling Company of Arkansas, for an estimated $250 million, leading the way to an acquisition the following year that signaled significant changes at CCE. Available for acquisition was Johnston Coca-Cola Bottling Company of Chattanooga, of which The Coca-Cola Company already owned 20 percent. Johnston represented roughly 11 percent of national Coca-Cola volume, second in size only to CCE itself.

Serving a population base of 27.5 million spread across 15 states, Johnston's operations would place 55 percent of total domestic Coca-Cola bottling volume under one operational and financial structure, CCE. Perhaps as equally beneficial for CCE was the managerial expertise the company would obtain through its purchase of Johnston. This infusion of new management was needed because CCE, in the four years since its formation, had demonstrated lackluster performance by executing its role as a Coca-Cola bottler in 26 states with disappointing results.

During CCE's first four years of existence, much of Coca-Cola's domestic volume growth was derived not from CCE's bottling operations but from The Coca-Cola Company's independent franchised bottlers. Much of the blame for CCE's woes, which in addition to flat sales included low employee morale, was placed on the shoulders of the company's chief executive, Dyson. Critics charged that Dyson lacked the "street smarts" and the proper personality to deal with retailers. Whatever the cause of CCE's ailments, it was clear that CCE needed to substantially ameliorate its performance. Johnston's president and chief operating officer, Henry Schimberg, and its 45 percent owner, Summerfield K. Johnston, were perceived as the managers able to effect such a turnaround.

Summerfield Johnston, whose grandfather purchased the first Coca-Cola bottling franchise in 1901, and Schimberg, who was slated to occupy the same positions at CCE as he did at Johnston, were respected as skilled bottling managers. Under Schimberg's leadership, Johnston Bottling had recorded 8 percent annual growth in sales volume (twice the industry rate) and nearly quintupled its operating profit during the same span that Dyson had overseen CCE's flat growth. Dyson, it readily became apparent, was on his way out, a prediction made by the business press when it was learned that Dyson was not even informed of the pending Johnston acquisition until a deal had been struck.

## STRATEGIC MANEUVERS: 1991–2000

In December 1991 CCE acquired Johnston and with it, the talents of Schimberg, who took over the day-to-day operations of CCE. In his new post, Schimberg successfully achieved a profitable balance between the opposing goals of price and volume. Between 1991 and 1993, operating profit rose from $538 million to $804 million, while bottle-and-can case growth jumped from 0 percent to 4 percent. More important to CCE's shareholders, who held a 51 percent stake in the company, CCE's stock price climbed from $12.25 to $19.00 by 1994, giving both CCE shareholders and CCE management hope that the company would continue to record encouraging growth in the future.

As CCE entered the mid-1990s, Schimberg's strategic maneuvers continued to work their magic. By reorganizing the company, Schimberg decentralized CCE's management to drive decision making down as close to the point of retail sale as possible.

## NEW MANAGEMENT INITIATIVES: 2000–05

On July 10, 2001, the company completed its acquisition of Herb Coca-Cola, the country's third-largest

Coca-Cola bottler in the United States. With this acquisition, CCE was responsible for selling approximately 80 percent of the Coca-Cola Company's bottle-and-can volume in North America. That same year, the company announce that it was cutting 2,000 jobs, or about 3 percent of its worldwide workforce, in an effort to streamline its North American operations and save $80 to $100 million in the process.

Vanilla Coke was introduced in 2002 and became the company's most successful new product in 20 years. That same year, Lowry F. Kline was elected chairman of the board and CEO of CCE. The following year, the company unveiled a new revenue management initiative in its North American division. The plan called for a change of focus from primarily being concerned with volume to a more disciplined, company-wide approach to pricing. Michael Branca, an analyst with Lehman Brothers, told *Business World* contributor Andrew Kaplan, "Importantly, CCE's revenue management initiatives are designed to increase pricing ahead of cost inflation. That's new."

In December 2003 CCE announced that the company's president and chief operating officer, John R. Alm, had been elected president and CEO. Kline remained executive chairman of the board and retained active management duties. Over the course of the year, the company continued to improve operational efficiency and marketplace execution while bringing to the market innovations in new beverages and packaging. Financial highlights for 2003 included strong earnings per share growth with an increase of 28 percent over comparable 2002 results, increasing levels of free cash flow, and reduced net debt levels.

## MAJOR CHANGES: 2006–10

John F. Brock, formerly chief operating officer of Cadbury Schweppes and chairman of Dr Pepper/Seven Up Bottling Group Inc., was named president and CEO of CCE in 2006. That year the company also completed a distribution agreement with Hornell Brewing Co. Inc., maker of AriZona Iced Tea, a top-selling ready-to-drink tea brand in the United States. Under Brock's leadership, the company went on to take several steps to improve financial performance and shareholder value, including establishing a new Global Operating Framework. In 2008 Brock was named chairman of the board and CEO.

The company's 2008 net sales earned it a number one ranking among U.S. bottlers. According to a contributor to *Beverage World*, the company "ended the year with some momentum and signs of progress." In addition, CCE was commended in the *Beverage World*

article for making progress in its corporate responsibility and sustainability efforts, such as expanding its hybrid electric vehicle fleet. That year also saw CCE and Coca-Cola Company complete agreements with Hansen Natural Corporation to distribute Hansen's category-leading Monster Energy drinks line in six Western European countries, Canada, and selected areas of the United States.

The economic downturn in the United States that began in 2008 resulted in a drop in volume of 5 percent for the company in 2009. Nevertheless, the company recorded an increase in profits to $731 million for the year compared to a loss of $4.39 billion in 2008. However, the company's European results were much better overall as it achieved a third consecutive year of growth through a balance of both volume and pricing growth.

In early 2010, the company announced that The Coca-Cola Company was buying its North American bottling business, a deal that was expected to be completed by the end of the fourth quarter. Overall, the deal included The Coca-Cola Company selling its Norwegian and Swedish bottling business to CCE and an option for CCE to buy The Coca-Cola Company's 83 percent stake in its German bottling business. CCE chairman and CEO Brock told *Beverage World* contributor Heather Landi that the company "remains the preeminent Western European bottler and a key strategic partner with the Coca-Cola Company." Brock noted that the company planned to "continue to improve … our expanded presence in Europe."

*Jeffrey L. Covell*
*Updated, David Petechuk*

## PRINCIPAL SUBSIDIARIES

BHI Finance LLC; Bottling Holdings (International) Inc.; Bottling Holdings (Luxembourg) SARL; Coca-Cola Enterprises Inc.; Coca-Cola Enterprises Ltd. (Great Britain); Coca-Cola Entreprise SAS (France).

## PRINCIPAL COMPETITORS

Dr Pepper Snapple Group, Inc.; Groupe Danone S.A.; Kraft Foods Inc.; Nestlé S.A.; PepsiCo, Inc.

## FURTHER READING

"Coca-Cola Enterprises Maintains a Little Sparkle," just-drinks. com, February 10, 2010.

Kaplan, Andrew, "Price Point: An Up-Close Look at Coca-Cola Enterprises' More Disciplined Approach to Revenue

Management and What It May Mean for the US Bottling Industry," *Business World*, December 15, 2003, p. 20.

Landi, Heather, "Coke to Buy CCE North American Ops,"

*Beverage World*, March, 2010, p. 8.

"Top 25 U.S. Bottlers Report 2009: Ranked by 2008 Net Sales," *Business World*, August 15, 2009, p. 30.

# Commerce Bancshares, Inc.

1000 Walnut
Kansas City, Missouri 64106
U.S.A.
Telephone: (816) 234-2000
Toll Free: (800) 453-2265
Fax: (816) 234-2019
Web site: https://www.commercebank.com

*Public Company*
*Founded:* 1865 as Kansas City Savings Association
*Employees:* 5,239 (2009)
*Net Income:* $169.1 million (2009)
*Assets:* $18.1 billion (2009)
*Stock Exchanges:* NASDAQ
*Ticker Symbol:* CBSH
*NAICS:* 522110 Commercial Banking; 522292 Mortgage Banking

■ ■ ■

Commerce Bancshares, Inc., is a regional bank holding company. Its largest holding, Commerce Bank, has established more than 350 locations across Missouri, Kansas, Illinois, Oklahoma, and Colorado. Commerce Bancshares also holds subsidiaries engaged in mortgage banking, leasing, credit-related insurance, venture capital and real estate activities.

## CIVIL WAR BEGINNINGS

In 1865, the same year the American Civil War ended with the Union's defeat of the Confederacy, Abraham Lincoln was assassinated, and the Thirteenth Amendment to the U.S. Consitution ended slavery, Francis Reid Long founded the Kansas City Savings Association in Kansas City, Missouri. Long was born in Woodford County, Kentucky. He moved to Kansas City and with Nathaniel Grant and A. S. Branham founded Long, Grant & Company, which would become the Kansas City Savings Association. Long became mayor of Kansas City in 1869. Under Long's tenure as mayor, the city built the Hannibal Bridge, which was the first bridge to cross the Missouri River, and established Kansas City as a major Midwestern city and rail center.

In 1881 William Stone Woods acquired controlling interest in the savings association. The institution's priorities shifted to funding regional growth in Kansas City and the surrounding areas. Loans were directed mainly at developing railroad transportation and distribution. Woods renamed the institution as the National Bank of Commerce, which was more in line with the bank's new direction.

The National Bank of Commerce became the principal correspondent bank for bank clearings in the area southwest of Chicago and St. Louis. Prior to 1913 businesses in the United States depended on a network of private banks, which in turn needed correspondent banks to provide credit and liquidity. A correspondent bank accepted the deposits of, and performed services for, banks which were called respondent banks. After 1913 the U.S. government established the Federal Reserve Bank to take over this function. However, before the creation of the Federal Reserve Bank, the National Bank of Commerce became one of the largest

## COMPANY PERSPECTIVES

Commerce Bank will be the preferred provider of targeted financial service in our communities based on strong customer relationships. We will strengthen these relationships by providing the right solutions that combine our technology, expertise, and financial strength. Our goal is to create customer loyalty, shareholder value, and employee satisfaction.

banks in the country and was the largest bank west of Chicago.

## MISSOURI BANKING DYNASTY

From April 1903 to May 1905, the bank employed the future U.S. president Harry S. Truman. Truman worked in various capacities. According to his supervisor, Truman was "a willing worker, almost always here and tries hard to please everybody. We never had a boy in the vault like him before. He watches everything very closely and by his watchfulness, detects many errors which a careless boy would let slip through. His appearance is good and his habits and character are of the best." Truman left the bank to go to work for the Union National Bank. At the time, the National Bank of Commerce was located in the Journal Building at 10th and Walnut Streets. The building burned down in 1906 and was replaced with a building called the Commerce Tower.

Truman's job with the National Bank of Commerce may have been due to his father's close relationship with William Thorton Kemper (William T. Kemper), who became president of the National Bank of Commerce in 1903, the same year Truman started working at the bank. Truman's father, John Anderson Truman, traded grain commodity futures alongside William T. Kemper until John Anderson Truman lost his fortune. Little did the board know that by hiring Kemper they were launching a Missouri banking dynasty. William T. Kemper became the patriarch of a major banking family that developed, in addition to Commerce Bankshares, the United Missouri Bank (UMB).

William T. Kemper led the National Bank of Commerce through difficult times. In 1907 the United States was in a deep economic recession. The New York Stock Exchange plummeted almost 50 percent and a panic ensued. This came to be known as the Panic of 1907 or the 1907 Bankers' Panic, and it resulted in numerous runs on banks and trust companies. During the panic many customers feared the banks would become insolvent and they would lose their savings, so they demanded their savings en masse. The banks, as a matter of practice, made loans and investments and kept only a small percentage of its total savings funds on hand. This meant that the banks were not able to release all the funds demanded by customers, so a run destabilized the banks. Many banks went into bankruptcy.

The National Bank of Commerce experienced a six-week period of runs before the Office of Comptroller of the Currency (part of the U.S. Treasury Department) placed the bank in receivership. Under receivership the comptroller acted as the "receiver," taking custodial responsibility for the bank's assets and liabilities. The comptroller managed the repayment of depositors and the recapitalization of the bank before returning the bank to its owners.

In 1906 William Stone Woods founded another banking institution, the Commerce Trust Company (Commerce Trust). The purpose of Commerce Trust was to offer private banking and comprehensive trust services for individuals, families, corporate executives, and business owners. Woods named William T. Kemper as president of Commerce Trust.

In 1917, after returning from the brink of bankruptcy, the National Bank of Commerce merged with the Commerce Trust Company. The new entity was named Commerce Bank of Kansas City (Commerce Bank) and William T. Kemper became president of the new bank with $80 million in deposits.

## A FRIENDLY RIVALRY

In 1919 William T. Kemper appointed his son James M. Kemper as president of City Center Bank, but he would resign a month later and James's older brother Rufus Crosby Kemper, Jr., (R. Crosby) took over. William T. Kemper died in 1938 but not before naming his son James "Big Jim" Kemper as his successor as president of Commerce Bank. With R. Crosby Kemper and James Kemper at the helms of their respective banks, a friendly rivalry was launched between the two brothers. This rivalry would define Missouri's financial and philanthropic history for years to come. City Center Bank would later be renamed United Missouri Bank (UMB). Crosby's descendants became known as the UMB Kempers, and James's descendants became known as the Commerce Kempers. The rivalry continued when cousins James Kemper, Jr., and R. Crosby, Jr., took over for their fathers in the early 1960s.

The family control of Commerce Bank kept the bank on an even keel through the remainder of the

## KEY DATES

**1865:** Francis Reid Long founds Kansas City Savings Association.
**1881:** W. S. Woods acquires controlling interest in Kansas City Savings Association.
**1903:** William T. Kemper becomes president of Bank of Commerce.
**1906:** W. S. Woods founds Commerce Trust Company.
**1917:** Bank of Commerce and Commerce Trust Company merge.
**1995:** Company honored as "Best Bank in Missouri" by *Money* magazine.
**2009:** Company's net income falls for fourth consecutive year.

century. The rivalry between the Kemper cousins took on the characteristics of their participants. James Kemper, Jr., was more reserved and self-effacing than his cousin, a more flamboyant presence. During the 1980s, the Kemper family titans of banking engaged in a bit of one-upmanship, building up their banks into two of the Midwest's strongest regional banking companies and growing their own fortunes as well. The banks engaged in several transactions that enabled the companies to leap frog back and forth in terms of total assets. The companies even built new corporate headquarters directly across from each other.

### CONSERVATIVE WAY TO SUCCESS

James Kemper, Jr.'s conservative personality carried over to his bank, which gained a reputation for its conservative management. When mergers and acquisitions consumed independent banks across the state, Commerce took advantage and established an aggressive community focus. It allowed its branches to operate as independent community banks as much as possible. Market managers responded not only to directives from the corporate headquarters but also to the individual bank presidents. Each market was autonomous with regard to pricing and deal structuring, and there was even some autonomy in determining product offerings and delivery systems. In effect, the bank created a more entrepreneurial structure, giving the community bank presidents the freedom to make decisions that were appropriate for their particular community.

Another example of Commerce Bank's conservative approach was that it was a little slower than other banks

to get into the branch expansion game of the 1990s. Whereas the number of branches in the St. Louis market grew 39 percent between 1995 and 2005, Commerce Bank's branch network grew only 29 percent. The advantage was that the bank kept expenses under control. The bank preferred this sort of organic growth to the less conservative mergers and acquisitions approach to corporate growth. When the bank did choose to acquire a bank it tended to go for smaller deals that filled a specific need or extended a specific market. These sort of deals were easier and less costly to integrate into their current operations than the larger, more costly, transformational types of acquisitions.

Throughout its history Commerce Bank has made some strong moves in banking technology. In 1928 the bank started the first 24-hour transit department in the country. This facility sped up the transit of checks between participating banks. In the 1960s the bank introduced a full-scale international department, the first of its kind. In 1984 the bank created Special Connections, a card with the combined features of a credit card and ATM card. In the 1990s the bank established a browser-based intranet and leapt past the mainframe-to-client server technology that most other companies instituted. This foresight saved the company millions of dollars in capital investment. The bank also developed a highly advanced customer relations management (CRM) system to help market to and manage customers. The system tracked not only the bank's contacts with its customers but also their relationships with other banks and changes in their business.

### THE FOURTH KEMPER

Commerce Bank entered the 21st century under the leadership of a fourth generation of Kempers. David Kemper, who took over as president in the mid-1980s, had an unusual educational background, holding a master's degree in English literature from Oxford University and a bachelor's degree in history from Harvard University. He also earned a master of business administration degree from the Stanford Graduate School of Business.

Under the bank's parent company, Commerce Bancshares, David Kemper moved the company into other services that complemented Commerce Bank's banking services. Commerce Bancshares ventured into asset management, credit insurance, mortgage banking, venture capital, and equipment leasing. In the process, the company gained recognition for both its technological leadership and its rock-solid balance sheet. *Money* magazine named the bank the "Best Bank in Missouri" in 1995. In 1997 a Dean Witter report named Commerce Bank as one of the top 10 banks in the nation for technology. In 2008 Commerce Bancshares, Commerce Bank's holding company, was ranked seventh among the top 150 publicly traded bank companies in *Bank Director* magazine's Bank Performance Scorecard.

However, while Commerce has enjoyed a long history of profitability, not all was entirely healthy with the company's balance sheet. In 2009 net income was $169.1 million, marking another year since 2005 in which profit was less than the previous year. In 2005 net income was $223 million, dropping to $220 million in 2006, $207 million in 2007, and $189 million in 2008. During the same time period, Commerce's provisions for loan losses steadily increased, from $29 million in 2005 to $161 million in 2009. While the company remained in the black, a continued surge in loan losses would dampen Commerce's profitability through the early 2010s.

*Aaron Hauser*

## PRINCIPAL SUBSIDIARIES

Capital for Business, Inc.; CBI Insurance Company; CBI-Kansas, Inc.; CFB Partners, LLC; CFB Partners II, LLC; CFB Venture Fund I, Inc.; CFB Venture Fund II, L.P.

## PRINCIPAL COMPETITORS

Bank of America Corporation; Fifth Third Bancorp; Marshal & Ilsley Corp.; National City Corp.; UMB Financial Corporation; U.S. Bancorp.

## FURTHER READING

Curley, John, "Who's News: One-upmanship of the Kemper Cousins Is the Best Show in Missouri Banking," *Wall Street Journal,* May 28, 1985.

Lahey, Susan, "Slow and Steady in Kansas City," *Bank Director,* 12, no. 1, January 1, 2002, p. 46.

Margolies, Dan, "Restored Commerce Trust Building in Kansas City, Mo., Will Reopen Today," *Kansas City Star,* October 9, 2002.

Milligan, Jack, "A Banker's Tale," *Bank Director,* 16, no. 4, p. 26.

"Truman Places: National Bank of Commerce," trumanlibrary. org.

"What's in a Name?" *Ingram's,* 23, no. 12, December 1, 1997, p. 56.

# Computer Sciences Corporation

3170 Fairview Park Drive
Falls Church, Virginia 22042
U.S.A.
Telephone: (703) 876-1000
Web site: http://www.csc.com

*Public Company*
*Incorporated:* 1959
*Employees:* 92,000 (est., 2009)
*Sales:* $16.74 billion (2009)
*Stock Exchanges:* New York
*Ticker Symbol:* CSC
*NAICS:* 541512 Computer Systems Design Services;
    334419 Other Electronic Component Manufactur-
    ing; 511210 Software Publishers; 541330 Engineer-
    ing Services; 541513 Computer Facilities Manage-
    ment Services

■ ■ ■

A *Fortune* 200 company, Computer Sciences Corporation (CSC) is one of the world's largest providers of
information technology (IT). The company has three
main lines of business. CSC's Business Solutions &
Services sector provides industry-specific, technology-
enabled business solutions, industry-specific business
process outsourcing solutions, consulting and systems
integration, and software and systems development. The
Global Outsourcing Sector includes secure IT management for applications and infrastructure, applications
portfolio management, testing services, remote
infrastructure services, mobility and end-user services.

This sector also provides networks, computing, and storage services. The company's North American Public Sector features program management services, systems
integration services, infrastructure services, and specialized engineers solutions and services. CSC provides
these services to a wide range of industries throughout
the world, including the United States, Canada, Brazil,
Chile, most of Europe, Australia, and several countries
in Asia, such as China, Japan, India, Korea, and
Vietnam. In addition to providing services to chemical,
energy, and natural resources industries, the company
also has clients in financial services, health services,
manufacturing, and consumer technology. CSC is a
major government and defense contractor and generates
approximately one-third of its revenues from U.S.
federal agencies.

## COMPANY FOUNDING AND EARLY YEARS: 1959–68

CSC was formed in Los Angeles in 1959 by Fletcher
Jones and Roy Nutt with only $100 in capital. Jones
entered the infant computer industry by chance. He had
taken a job as a mathematical analyst in the data
processing section of Chance Vought Aircraft Company
because it was the best job offer he received after
graduating from college. From there Jones became director of the Columbus division computer center for North
American Aviation. His acquaintance, Roy Nutt, a top
member of United Aircraft Corporation's data processing staff, shared Jones's opinion that large amounts of
new software would soon prove a crucial need for the
growing computer industry. A number of computer
manufacturers were coming out with new models, and

the two felt the manufacturers would never be able to write the necessary software in-house.

Computer Sciences Corporation stepped in to offer its software writing services to major computer manufacturers, among them International Business Machines (IBM). One of the firm's early jobs was to design a large software system for Honeywell. It later wrote a complete package of programs for Univac. From the start, however, Jones felt that the biggest profits in software lay in creating proprietary software (software to which they would hold exclusive rights) that could be sold to a large number of users, not in custom-written programs for specific customers. More than a decade later, firms like Microsoft Corporation, Lotus Development Corporation, and Computer Associates proved the validity of Jones's assessment.

The firm's first major proprietary software was Computax, a large, complex set of programs used to calculate individual income taxes and prepare a tax return. It was used chiefly by accountants doing corporate and personal tax returns. Computax proved popular and was turned into an independent company, with CSC holding a 38 percent interest. By 1965, with company profits at $2.7 million, the 34-year-old Jones was worth $20 million and appeared in *Time* magazine as part of a cover article on young millionaires.

Government contracts have been an important source of CSC revenue, and the firm started signing

them early in its history. In June of 1966, for example, CSC signed a $5.5 million contract with the National Aeronautics and Space Administration (NASA) to support a computation laboratory in Huntsville, Alabama. Annual sales reached $53.5 million by 1968, and the firm became the first software company to go public. Software development had become the fastest-growing segment of the flourishing computer industry, and CSC dominated the market.

## NEW VENTURES AND TECHNOLOGIES

The firm moved into new ventures, introducing Computicket, which made it possible for consumers to buy computerized tickets to entertainment events through non-box-office vendors. In 1968 only about 1 percent of U.S. computers were linked to each other, so the plan was an ambitious and formidable task for a small, young company to realize alone. CSC had been working with Western Union for four years to develop methods for transmitting computerized information over telegraph wires. Jones and Russell W. McFall, president of Western Union, agreed in principle to merge their companies in 1968.

Although it was only one-sixth of the size of Western Union, CSC was to be the dominant partner. The 117-year-old Western Union was growing very slowly, while the nine-year-old CSC was soaring. The merger fell through, but CSC decided to continue with Computicket anyway. It also continued to grow, reaching $6.8 million in profits on $80 million in sales in 1968. William R. Hoover, who had been with CSC since 1964, took over daily operations in 1969, leaving Jones free to concentrate on long-term strategy.

Jones forged ahead with an even more challenging plan. Dubbed the Infonet system, the goal was to create a nationwide computer network offering customers computer power and software via communications lines. Jones planned 20 centers to be opened by mid-1970. CSC was forced to expand its services by the beginning of the 1970s because computer makers had added to their in-house programming staffs and no longer required much work from outside companies. As a result, CSC's profit growth fell, and it searched for new markets, particularly time-sharing (leasing computer time to companies that did not own their own units).

Meanwhile CSC continued to make its money developing software packages for customers and received $118 million in revenue in this area in 1972 out of a total of $127.5 million for the firm. This included a broadened relationship with various U.S. government agencies. The firm also developed a computerized air

## KEY DATES

**1959:** Computer Sciences Corporation is founded.
**1968:** CSC is the first software company to go public.
**1979:** CSC loses $1.9 million after the Iranian Revolution when its operations there cease.
**1988:** CSC becomes the fifth-largest supplier of information technology to the U.S. federal government.
**1999:** CSC fights off hostile takeover bid by Computer Associates International.
**2001:** CSC wins U.S. State Department contracts worth approximately $100 million to implement e-government solutions to improve visa processing and issuance services worldwide.
**2007:** Mike Laphen is appointed CSC's CEO.
**2008:** Company moves its corporate headquarters from El Segundo, California, to Falls Church, Virginia.
**2010:** CSC forms a joint partnership with Intec, a global provider of business support systems.

cargo handling system for Heathrow Airport in London and did work for large corporations like General Electric and Travelers Insurance.

## FACING CRISES

CSC was the largest computer software and services company in the United States, but not all of its customers were happy. The firm signed a contract with New York City's Off-Track Betting Corporation in 1970 to develop a system that would enable wagers on horse races to be placed by telephone and at branch offices. CSC took several months to get the system off the ground, however, allowing competitors like Control Data to get into the race. By 1972 CSC operated 462 betting terminals, only about half of Off-Track Betting's total, and soon thereafter, Off-Track Betting canceled CSC's contract.

The capital-intensive development of Computicket and Infonet posed far worse problems for CSC. Without the resources of a company like Western Union to help it, the costs of developing these network-based services were devastating. Computicket ran into stiff competition from Control Data's Ticketron, and CSC wrote off $12.7 million in Computicket development costs in 1970 and scrapped the project. At that point

the firm's long-term debt was $82 million, while its equity was only $42 million.

Largely because of this cash crunch, CSC sold Computax in 1971. The firm took a $62.8 million write-off on product development costs in 1972, mostly for the expensive Infonet venture. By mid-1972 only six Infonet centers were in operation, and they were running at less than 50 percent of capacity. CSC was forced to pay a penalty to Sperry Rand because it had to cancel an order for $13 million worth of Sperry computers. Takeover rumors circulated, but the firm remained the leading independent software company in contract services, with 90 percent of revenue coming from services rather than proprietary software, which had not sold nearly as well as expected.

CSC was overextended and facing another cash crisis in late 1972. That same year, Jones died when his single-engine plane crashed into a California hillside. Hoover, then 42, was named his successor, although some analysts thought the firm might go bankrupt. A well-timed government contract probably saved the company, however. The 51-month contract to supply computer services to the General Services Administration was highly profitable, bringing needed cash and an infusion of credibility to the beleaguered CSC. The contract was for remote computing services, and CSC used Infonet to fulfill it. Although the contract was renewed in February 1976, the firm remained only moderately profitable, making $7 million on sales of $220 million in 1975. The software market had grown from $997 million in 1967 to about $5.5 billion in 1976, but competition had increased dramatically and CSC's market share had shrunk.

## SHIFTING FOCUS

About half of the firm's revenue was coming from the U.S. government by the mid-1970s, prompting industry analysts to warn that CSC was overly dependent on government contracts. Critics pointed out that government contracts were usually short-term and that bureaucrats faced constant pressure to diversify their sources of computer services. The critics were proven at least partially right in 1977 when the General Services Administration contract expired and was put up for bids, making it a far less profitable deal.

CSC lost $1.9 million after the 1979 Iranian Revolution when its operations there ceased. It also lost millions of dollars after it bought the troubled computer services businesses of Itel Incorporated. CSC was forced to spend an additional several million dollars in legal fees defending itself against Justice Department charges of fraud. The margin of the firm's data services division declined to about 15 percent by 1981, from a high of 22 percent. Despite these difficulties, CSC remained the largest independent computer services company in volume, with sales of $600 million in 1980.

The company did well, if not spectacularly, by selling time-sharing. Infonet, the primary component of this system, accounted for 50 percent of sales in 1980, but this niche disappeared quickly, buried under the rapid spread of desktop computer networks that took over many of the functions of mainframe computers. As a result, Hoover shifted CSC's focus again, this time towards systems integration. (System integration typically implied the use of computers as the base for a communications networks, usually for government agencies like the Navy or NASA).

## DEFENSE, SPACE, AND THE PUBLIC SECTOR

CSC was NASA's fourth-largest customer and benefited from the defense buildup that took place in the early 1980s under President Ronald Reagan, winning a $45.6 million contract in 1981 for work at Cape Canaveral. It also signed a $221 million contract to computerize the Saudi Arabian ministry of the interior. CSC soon got into hospital information systems as well, after winning a large contract to take care of California's Medicaid computer services. In late 1981 it landed a $20 million, five-year contract for processing Medicaid claims in Tennessee. Although CSC was doing well in this niche, other firms, including Ross Perot's quickly growing Electronic Data Systems, were aggressively aiming for many of the same markets.

After a surge in business in the early 1970s, CSC's growth remained flat until about 1986, when revenue approached $1 billion. Then, when government contracts began moving toward large, fixed-price deals, CSC benefitted, winning 60 percent of the large contracts that it bid on. In early 1986 it signed a $278 million agreement to develop a secure data network for the U.S. Customs Service. New contracts for 1986 added up to $1.3 billion, about as much as the previous three years combined.

Growth in the commercial segment of the systems integration market, standing at 38 percent a year, was by far outstripping the federal segment's 17 percent annual growth. Large corporations like Eastman Kodak, Kmart, and Exxon were using systems integrators to choose their hardware and develop their software, but their contracts were generally much smaller than government deals, making marketing and selling that much more important. Government contracts, with their safe but

low-margin work, accounted for about 70 percent of revenues, but CSC was diversifying and aimed to increase commercial work significantly.

To move toward that goal, the firm began an acquisition spree, hoping to quickly build its technical staff and marketing ability. Targeting companies in the health care and systems integration fields, CSC built upon areas in which it was already active. One of the first acquisitions was Computer Partners Incorporated. In 1986 CSC paid $20 million for this small Boston company, which specialized in designing systems for corporations and had strength in the retail and distribution market. Two years later, CSC bought a consulting firm, Index Group Inc., hoping to compete with large accounting firms that advised corporate management on what computer systems and software to buy.

## DEFENSE REMAINS SOLID

Hoover also spruced up CSC management, appointing six new managers to important positions and focusing on large contracts. One of those contracts was a $186 million office automation deal it signed with the U.S. Air Force that included linking 13,000 telephones with computers. By 1988 CSC had become the fifth-largest supplier of information technology to the federal government, with sales for the year reaching $1.2 billion.

To better compete in the commercial arena, the firm formed a new commercial-systems group in 1989 to offer systems integration in the United States and Europe. Despite this move, most of CSC's important contracts continued to be government-related. It negotiated a $170 million contract with NASA to provide software for the Ames Research Center in 1989. In 1990 CSC renewed a $65.7 million deal with NASA for engineering services at an experimental center at Wallops Island, Virginia. It also won a four-year contract worth up to $70 million with the U.S. Army Communications and Electronics Command and signed a five-year data-processing and telecommunications services contract with the Environmental Protection Agency worth around $350 million.

In 1991 CSC won a five-year contract worth up to $68 million from the Defense Information Systems Agency to maintain and operate systems supporting the command and control of U.S. forces worldwide, and the firm beat out Xerox Corp. for a U.S. Army contract to develop a computer information system for weapons parts. That contract was worth an estimated $744.2 million. Riding this wave of large contracts, the firm's sales reached $1.5 billion in 1990 and $1.74 billion in 1991.

## CORPORATE BUSINESS AND ACQUISITIONS

Helped by a resurgence in corporate outsourcing in the early 1990s, CSC did sign some large corporate contracts, including a 10-year deal with General Dynamics valued at about $3 billion. General Dynamics contracted its entire information systems division to CSC, which acquired 2,600 General Dynamics employees. CSC also paid $200 million for General Dynamics' nationwide data center infrastructure. In 1992 the firm signed a $64 million, 10-year contract with WCI Steel Inc. to do data processing. Nonetheless, revenues from the U.S. government were $1.07 billion in 1991, compared with revenues of $423 million from commercial sources. Operating income reached $130 million in 1991, up from $107 million in 1989, and CSC used its cash to continue acquiring information companies.

## TAKEOVER BID: 1999

From 1993 to 1998, CSC's stock appreciated nearly 400 percent, far outpacing the S&P 500. The company's success made it attractive to other companies as a business partner. However, in 1999, what began as friendly merger talks between CSC and Computer Associates International (CA) turned into a hostile takeover bid as CA offered $108 per share of common CSC stock. CSC formally rejected the takeover bid and then, through its chairman Van Honeycutt, the company filed a bribery suit against CA's founder and CEO Charles Wang. A countersuit was eventually filed by CA.

CA eventually backed off from its takeover bid, and in October 1999 both companies called off the pending lawsuits against each other. In addition, the companies announced an expansion of their global software licensing agreement. In a *Computerworld* article, industry analyst and consultant Jonathan Eunice noted that, following the end of the litigation proceedings, the companies "came together and did some really good work" together in fostering certain CA management and application development software.

## ACQUISITIONS AND NEW CONTRACTS: 2001–03

Even as the battle with CA festered, CSC made several moves to improve and expand the company, including buying and merging Nichols Research Corp., another information technology firm. Like CSC, Nichols

Research conducted significant business with space and terrestrial communications firms and government agencies. The company also won a 10-year U.S. Army logistics modernization contract that led to the world's largest enterprise resource planning (ERP) system installation. Other acquisitions soon followed, including acquiring the assets of BHP IT, a wholly owned subsidiary of the Australia-based firm BHP (a global natural resources company). CSC also acquired the Mynd Corporation, a financial services company focusing primarily on insurance-related products and service offerings.

The company continued to excel in gaining government contracts. In 2001 CSC won State Department contracts to implement e-government solutions to improve visa processing and issuance services in countries around the world. The contract was valued at $100 million. CSC was also chosen by the U.S. Navy as one of 21 vendors for a $14.5 billion contract to provide professional support services for the Naval Sea Systems Command (NAVSEA) and its affiliated directorates, program executive offices, and field activities. Another contract, valued at $107.5 million, was awarded to CSC by the Federal Systems Integration and Management Center (FEDSIM) to support the U.S. Department of State's Diplomatic Telecommunications Services Program Office.

In April 2001 the company announced that its annual revenues exceeded $10 billion. CSC continued to garner major government contracts, including a subcontract from General Dynamics to work on the U.S. Army's Land Warrior program, an ensemble for soldiers that contains weapon-mounted sensors, wireless communications, and GPS-based navigation and computers. Despite its success gaining government contracts, CSC sought to further bolster its government services capabilities by acquiring DynCorp, which ranked among the largest U.S.-based, employee-owned technology and outsourcing firms, in March 2003.

## A GLOBAL OUTLOOK

Following the appointment of Mike Laphen as CSC's president and chief operating officer in 2003, the company garnered several important contracts to bolster its international business. The company-led Prism Alliance, which included BT and Xansa, signed an IT outsourcing contract with Royal Mail Group, a U.K. government-owned public limited company providing mail, parcels, and express services. The contract was valued at $2.4 billion. In addition, CSC won the largest application outsourcing contract in the insurance industry from Zurich Financial Services, a seven-year agreement that was estimated at approximately $1.3 billion.

The company, which had developed into the world's largest IT services provider, named Mike Laphen CEO in 2007. That same year Laphen initiated the Project Accelerate initiative to further growth. Among its goals was to target a 10 percent annual increase in its government business, especially within the areas of health services, logistics, training and simulation, command and control, identity management credentialing, and infrastructure services. At the same time, the company looked to expand its commercial clients, which accounted for 60 percent of CSC's business. A *Washington Technology* article quoted Bob Welch, group vice president and general manager at research firm IDC Global Services, as saying: "What they're trying to do is build as consistent a business on the commercial side as they have in the federal sector."

The company moved its corporate headquarters from El Segundo, California, to Falls Church, Virginia, in 2008. It also announced that its annual revenues surpassed $15 billion, a figure that rose to $16.7 billion the following year. Despite the company's success, it pointed to the economically difficult times as an incentive to maintain its focus on cost and operational efficiencies. Nevertheless, the company planned to continue to invest in the future through globalizing operations while aggressively pursuing public sector and commercial markets. In line with its global goals, the company announced in April 2010 that it was forming a joint partnership with Intec, a global provider of business support systems (BSS) solutions, to provide a comprehensive suite of BSS solutions to communications service providers.

*Scott M. Lewis*
*Updated, David Petechuk*

## PRINCIPAL SUBSIDIARIES

AdvanceMed Corporation; CSC Enterprises (partnership); CBSI Financial Services Corporation; Century Corporation; Dekru B.V. (Netherlands); DynCorp.; Fortune Infoscribe Ltd. (India); Mynd Partners; Welkin Associates, Ltd.

## PRINCIPAL DIVISIONS

Business Solutions and Services; Government Outsourcing Services; North American Public Sector.

## PRINCIPAL COMPETITORS

Accenture Inc.; HP Enterprise Services, LLC; IBM Global Services; Tata Consultancy Services Limited; Wipro Technologies.

## FURTHER READING

"Aggressive Moves: Health, Logistics, IC Management among CSC Targets," *Washington Technology,* December 10, 2007, p. 22.

"CA and CSC Sign Truce, Renew Ties," *Computerworld,* October 11, 1999, p. 4.

"CAS, Intec Ink Global Partnership," *Total Telecom Online,* April 19, 2010.

"CSC Continues Support of Army's Land Warrior Program," *EDP Weekly's IT Monitor,* March 31, 2003, p. 8.

# Constellation Energy Group, Inc.

■

100 Constellation Way
Baltimore, Maryland 21202
U.S.A.
Telephone: (410) 470-2800
Toll Free: (800) 258-0499
Fax: (410) 783-3629
Web site: http://www.constellation.com

*Public Company*
*Incorporated:* 1906 as Consolidated Gas Electric Light
    and Power Company of Baltimore
*Employees:* 7,200 (2009)
*Revenues:* $15.6 billion (2009)
*Stock Exchanges:* New York
*Ticker Symbol:* CEG
*NAICS:* 221112 Fossil Fuel Electric Power Generation;
    221122 Electric Power Distribution

■ ■ ■

Constellation Energy Group, Inc. (CEG), is a utility holding company with diversified operations in energy and environmental projects. Power generation and distribution are the company's two primary areas of business, and the Baltimore Gas and Electric Company (BGE) is the firm's largest revenue-generating subsidiary. BGE provides electricity and gas to business and residential customers in Baltimore and 10 central Maryland counties. CEG provides electrical and services to over one million customers.

## COMPANY ORIGINS

Baltimore Gas and Electric Company dates back to 1816, when Rembrandt Peale, William Gwynn, and three other partners formed the Gas Light Company of Baltimore. Peale was the son of the painter Charles Willson Peale and was himself a well-known painter of portraits and historical scenes. Gwynn was a local businessman. Another of the partners was a wealthy merchant, William Lorman. Within a week of a successful demonstration of gas lighting in a location that later became the Peale Museum, the new company secured a franchise to light the streets and homes of Baltimore, Maryland, with gas. Lorman was the company's first president, serving from 1816 to 1832. The Gas Light Company set to work laying pipes throughout Baltimore, bringing the new method of lighting to more neighborhoods. The company's first seven years were hard, producing no profit. The new company faced several problems of a technical nature. The method of gas manufacturing it had adopted proved inadequate for large-scale production, and there were no means of measuring the quality of the gas produced. In addition, although gas meters existed in England, they were not available in the United States. Since there was no method for measurement of gas used, the company had to charge a flat annual rate.

The Gas Light Company continued to lose money, and by 1818 the company had exhausted its capital. To raise the money necessary to continue operating, the company made an initial public stock offering in 1818. The capital raised by the offering was used to buy equipment to expand the number of customers Gas Light Company served. By increasing its customer base, the company could sell more gas and thus increase profit. Between 1818 and 1821, Baltimore, in common with other U.S. cities, was rocked by financial panic. The company's new influx of capital saw it through this period. In 1822, using a process already established in England, the company began manufacturing gas from coal. (Previously tar was the raw material used.) Coke, a byproduct of this process, was a salable commodity. The company paid its first dividends in 1826.

By 1830 the company was again running low on capital and was unable to continue to grow as quickly as the city of Baltimore. Much of the capital raised in 1818 had been spent on experimentation and on pipes and equipment of unsatisfactory quality. In 1833 the company issued new stock to raise capital.

The use of gas meters was underway in some homes by 1834, despite widespread opposition by members of the public, who did not trust the accuracy of gas meters. In reality, the meters lowered rates for most consumers.

Meanwhile, the city was still inadequately lit due to the cost of laying pipes, and by 1850 critics of the company, including Baltimore's mayor, voiced complaints. In 1860 Gas Light's first local competitor, Peoples' Gas Light Company, was formed. The organizers of Peoples' capitalized on Gas Light Company's unpopularity in persuading members of the Maryland state legislature to charter their company. Peoples' did not begin to operate until 1871, however, due first to internal disagreements among its founders, then to the Civil War.

## POST-CIVIL WAR COMPETITION

In 1861 the Civil War broke out, imposing difficulties and setbacks, especially in railroad traffic. The war ended in 1865, but the higher cost of living, and thus of doing business, that it produced continued. Peoples' Gas Light Company began to operate in 1871, after reaching an agreement with Gas Light Company to divide the city. In 1876 Consumers Mutual Gas Light Company of Baltimore, another contender in the increasingly profitable industry, was formed. Fierce price wars between the three gas companies were waged until 1880 when the

companies merged to become the Consolidated Gas Company of Baltimore City.

In 1881 two electric light companies, Brush Electric Light Company and the United States Electric Light and Power Company, appeared in the city. Consolidated Gas was not yet involved in electric light, which was still fairly experimental at this time. When Thomas Edison's incandescent light bulb came into common use during the late 19th century, however, electric light became the standard. Electricity became the new competitor to gas.

In 1904 the city was devastated by the Great Baltimore Fire. Company employees labored to protect exposed mains from exploding. Despite the loss of property and the disruption of commerce, the company emerged prosperous and on solid ground and began to attract New York financiers.

By 1906 it had become clear to the leaders of Consolidated Gas that most homes and businesses favored electricity over gas for lighting. It was also clear that both gas and electric companies could operate more inexpensively and efficiently if they did not duplicate services. In 1906, therefore, Consolidated Gas Company of Baltimore City merged with Consolidated Gas Electric Light and Power Company to form Consolidated Gas Electric Light and Power Company of Baltimore. The new company provided fully integrated gas and electric service in Baltimore. Its capital shortages behind it, Consolidated grew at a healthy pace. During the financial panic and depression of 1907 and 1908, the new company managed a small increase in sales.

The Public Service Commission of Maryland was created in 1910 to regulate utilities. Also during this time, natural gas was becoming a popular substitute for manufactured gas. In 1910 J. E. Aldred became chairman and embarked upon vigorous expansion. Much of the company's electricity was supplied by hydroelectric plants on the Susquehanna River, and Consolidated owned several gas generating plants.

With production in place, the company could offer more competitive rates. The domestic economy, especially manufacturing, was boosted when World War I started in Europe. After the United States entered the war in 1917, demand for fuel rose. Soon a coal shortage developed, coincident with a severe cold wave. This period of strain and high prices did not end after the war. Two rate increases were granted and cost-cutting measures enforced to make up for the increased cost of labor and of coal, oil, and gas manufacture. In 1921 a contract was signed between Consolidated, United Railways & Electric Company, and Pennsylvania Water & Power Company, under which all of Baltimore's electric power was organized under one management. It

```
┌─────────────────────────────────────────┐
│                                          │
│           KEY DATES                      │
│              ─■─                         │
│  ┌────────────────────────────────────┐ │
│  │ 1906: Baltimore Gas and Electric   │ │
│  │       Company is incorporated.     │ │
│  │ 1946: William Schmidt, Jr., is     │ │
│  │       named president and          │ │
│  │       chairman.                    │ │
│  │ 1999: Constellation Energy Group   │ │
│  │       Incorporated becomes the     │ │
│  │       holding company for          │ │
│  │       Baltimore Gas and Electric   │ │
│  │       Company.                     │ │
│  │ 2005: Company partners with AREVA  │ │
│  │       to create UniStar.           │ │
│  │ 2009: Company reports $15.6        │ │
│  │       billion in revenues.         │ │
│  └────────────────────────────────────┘ │
└─────────────────────────────────────────┘
```

was another year of depressed earnings, but Consolidated began to recover in 1922 and 1923.

Due to several years of low water levels in the Susquehanna, the company began relying more heavily on its Baltimore steam plants in 1923, and Consolidated ordered two large turbine generators. By 1924 electric refrigerators and other appliances had become increasingly popular. The company was expanding to the north for power supplies. It entered an entirely new field in 1925 with the establishment of WBAL, a radio station that was sold to the American Radio News Corporation in 1935. In 1926 the use of gas continued to grow. The company's Gould Street generating station began service in 1927 and was the first of the city's power plants to burn pulverized coal. In 1928 the company further diversified with the purchase of the Terminal Freezing & Heating Company. Steam heating was related to Consolidated's gas and electric interests, but the purchased system still had to be overhauled.

## LEAN YEARS DURING THE DEPRESSION

In 1928, to simplify its corporate structure, a number of companies held by Consolidated were dissolved and absorbed. The company contracted to buy two-thirds of the energy generated by the Safe Harbor Water Power Company in 1931. Safe Harbor produced hydroelectricity at a plant on the Susquehanna River. In the early 1930s there was a boom in air conditioning, and population and industry increased in Baltimore as well. However, these factors did not entirely offset the effects of the Depression.

By 1936 the company's lean years were abating. That year it signed a long-term contract for electricity supply with Bethlehem Steel Company. In 1939 Consolidated benefited from a number of newly established large industrial plants in Baltimore. Within two years, World War II began to have an impact on the U.S. economy. War and the defense industry stimulated production, and Consolidated was called upon to meet higher demands. During the war, the company had to use lower quality fuels to meet the demands of increased production. Electric and gas sales soared.

In 1946, the year after the war's end, William Schmidt, Jr., was elected president and chairman. At this time, gas use was in steady decline nationwide, while the cost of manufacturing gas had risen nearly 300 percent in two decades. Consolidated was still expanding its capacity to provide service to new customers. In 1948 its third 60,000-kilowatt generating unit was completed, and a fourth was ordered. Another, larger plant was under way at the company's Westport, Maryland, site.

The company had been working to discontinue the production and sale of manufactured gas and to convert to natural gas, and the conversion was completed in 1950. It was an enormous undertaking that involved changes in equipment from pipelines to appliances, and the total cost of the conversion to the company was $9 million. The lower cost of natural gas led to increased consumption. In 1951 a 20-year effort to convert Baltimore's electric system from direct current (DC) to alternating current (AC) was completed.

In 1955 the company's name was changed to Baltimore Gas and Electric Company (BGE). The following year, BGE formed one of the world's largest fully integrated power pools when it signed a contract with seven other electricity distributors to inaugurate the Pennsylvania-New Jersey-Maryland Interconnection.

## STEADY GROWTH: 1960S–80S

The 1960s saw more steady growth, marked by construction of a new BGE headquarters in 1964 and the announcement in 1967 that BGE would build Maryland's first nuclear-powered generating plant. The two-unit facility was built at Calvert Cliffs, about 60 miles south of Baltimore, and represented an enormous investment. The first of these units was in operation by 1975. In its first year, it produced more than a third of the company's generation and reduced customer fuel rate adjustment charges by more than $50 million. The second unit began operation in 1977.

Demand had continued to grow, and in 1981 the Safe Harbor Hydroelectric Project started a four-year expansion project. In an effort to improve profitability, BGE trimmed its operating budget in 1982 and 1983 and sought diversification into other businesses. In 1983 however, the Maryland Public Service Commission turned down BGE's application to form a holding company, stating that Maryland law forbade such a structure for utilities. The holding company reorganization would have enabled BGE to diversify freely. In 1986 BGE formed Constellation Holdings, Inc., a subsidiary through which it planned to expand its non-utility interests, despite being denied the right to form a holding company.

By the mid-1980s, problems with the Calvert Cliffs nuclear power plant began to emerge. The Nuclear Regulatory Commission (NRC) fined the company for procedural and equipment violations at the plant in 1985. The NRC proposed further fines for alleged violations at the Calvert Cliffs plant in 1988. By year's end, the NRC placed Calvert Cliffs on its watch list of plants "warranting close agency monitoring" because of "declining performance." In 1988 these units were providing 40 percent of BGE's fuel mix and were the company's lowest-cost producers of power.

Calvert Cliffs' second unit was shut down in 1989 after stress and erosion cracks were discovered. The NRC identified a number of equipment and managerial problems at the plant, and the first unit was also closed for inspection.

The shutdown of Calvert Cliffs forced BGE to purchase more expensive electricity from other utilities. The cost incurred by the idled plant ran to $300,000 a day, and BGE sought numerous rate increases that were held up by debate. In addition, the NRC fined BGE for safety-related violations, one of which involved a worker's death. The restart of Calvert Cliffs' first unit eased the expense of purchased electricity somewhat, but the facility's second unit was closed until May 1991.

With the start-up of Calvert Cliffs' second unit in 1991, BGE's prospects improved. A second coal-fired unit at Brandon Shores also went into operation early in 1991. Debate was ongoing among regulatory officials regarding how much of the cost of the Calvert Cliffs failure could be passed on to customers. Company-estimated total replacement power costs ran to $415 million.

## DEREGULATION: 1992–98

In 1992 the company faced a dramatic shift in the way it did business when Congress passed the Federal Energy Policy Act. The act permitted competition in the wholesale power market and, by allowing retail competition, signaled the end of regulated, regional monopolies. Although its relatively small size and regional coverage would work against it in a competitive market, analysts felt BGE's customer mix could be a benefit. Since it had few industrial customers, BGE would not be so much at the mercy of large manufacturers who would set one

supplier against another in a bidding war. However, BGE apparently felt the disadvantage of its size and responded to the act's passage by looking for a partner that would help cut costs through economies of scale.

BGE forged an agreement to merge with Washington, D.C.-based Potomac Electric Power Co. (PEPCO) in 1995. Stockholders approved the deal in 1996, and the Federal Energy Regulatory Commission gave its permission in 1997. Maryland followed suit with conditional approval, but the process was held up by conditions placed on the merger by the District of Columbia. BGE and PEPCO had proposed splitting the expected savings from the merger evenly between customers and shareholders. D.C. regulators, however, wanted customers to get a larger share and made that a condition of the merger. BGE and PEPCO would not agree to that condition, and the two companies called off the merger in December 1997. The companies had invested more than two years and $100 million in arranging the merger.

In 1998 BGE began a major organizational restructuring that split the company into three discrete units: utility operations, power generation, and unregulated subsidiaries. Part of the reorganization entailed the creation of Constellation Enterprises Inc., a holding company for the utility's unregulated subsidiaries.

## BGE BECOMES CONSTELLATION ENERGY GROUP INCORPORATED

In early 1999 the Maryland legislature passed the Electric Customer Choice and Competition Act, legislation which further deregulated the industry. In April 1999 Constellation Energy Group (CEG) became the holding company for BGE and its subsidiaries. BGE was the largest of the acquisitions by far, as the regulated electric company serviced more than 1.1 million customers. BGE's residential, industrial, and retail customers helped CEG realize $3.9 billion in revenues in 2000. However, the following year proved trying for CEG and the energy sector at large.

As noted in CEG's 2001 annual report, declining energy prices, the demise of the Houston, Texas, energy company Enron, and changes in the California energy markets placed sizable strain on public and private energy sectors. To meet the challenges, CEG focused on cutting costs and repositioning itself so that it could compete more effectively in the open market.

To accomplish these goals, CEG discontinued a four-year relationship with Goldman Sachs effective October 26, 2001. It also sold operations it had in Guatemala. It cost CEG approximately $355 million to end its deal with Goldman. Separation of CEG's retail services and merchant energy businesses drove the deal closure. Even while CEG ended its relationship with Goldman, it hired Stu Rubenstein (a former Goldman Sachs employee) to head up its energy commodities group.

Despite leadership changes, 2001 proved challenging. In response to energy struggles and corporate scandals of 2001, management had this to say in the company's annual report: "We have created a new staff role of Chief Risk Officer (John R. Collins), who is focused on defining and managing all key risks across the company. It was particularly gratifying that our prudent business practices allowed us to avoid any material Enron-related losses."

A year later, Constellation Energy Group (CEG) reported total revenues of $4.7 billion. The company serviced more than 3,000 major businesses and owned more than 11,300 megawatts of energy-generating power.

## FOCUS ON NUCLEAR ENERGY

In November 2003 CEG announced plans to acquire the R. E. Ginna Nuclear Power Plant from the Rochester (New York) Gas & Electric Corporation. It cost CEG $401 million to acquire the 495-megawatt nuclear power plant. Located about 50 miles southwest of CEG's Nine Mile Point Nuclear Power Station, the purchase was expected to maximize service to the company's clients in upstate New York. Combined with the company's other power plants, the Rochester, New York, addition helped CEG to generate 28,000 megawatts of energy by July 2004.

Late in 2005, the company filed a motion to receive a combined construction and operating license through the U.S. Nuclear Regulatory Commission. CEG contracted with AREVA Incorporated, an international energy manufacturer, to form UniStar Nuclear. Michael J. Wallace, executive vice president at CEG, was named co-chief executive at the newly formed company. As of 2010, CEG and UniStar awaited approval from the U.S. Nuclear Regulatory Commission to build its first EPR Reactor. The company hoped to build the reactor next to its southern Maryland Calvert Cliffs Nuclear Power Plant.

On December 19, 2005, CEG and Florida Power & Light Group Incorporated (FPL) announced their plans to merge. The deal was expected to generate approximately $27 billion in annual revenue and $57 billion in total assets. It would also make the combined firm (slated to be called Constellation Energy) the largest competitive energy supplier in the United States.

Together the companies would have over 21,000 employees. FPL would remain headquartered in Juno Beach, Florida, while CEG's headquarters would remain in Baltimore, Maryland. Lewis Hay, chairman of FPL, was slated to become CEG's new CEO.

However, late in 2006 the $12.5 billion deal fell through. According to a *New York Times* article, regulatory and judicial uncertainties (which had increased since the collapse of Enron) caused both companies to step away from the business marriage. However, failure to close the deal did not prevent CEG from seeking another partner with which to build nuclear power plants in the United States. The next likely partner, Électricité de France (EDF), committed $350 million toward the partnership. The French electric company was 87 percent government-owned and had 58 reactors. In addition to funding, EDF was to invest as much as 9.9 percent in CEG's common share stock. A year later, in 2007, the deal remained on the table. Incomplete nuclear reactor designs and lack of approval to build new reactors in the United States stalled the deal, but in 2008 EDF agreed to pay $4.5 billion for a 49.99 percent interest in Constellation Energy Nuclear Group, LLC.

## A CHALLENGING ECONOMIC MARKET

Economic turmoil in the financial investment and banking industries did not leave CEG untouched. By September 18, 2008, CEG's shares had dropped 50 percent over their previous price less than a week earlier. To offset losses, the company sold interest in its Oklahoma gas and oil wells. One company subsidiary, Fellon-McCord & Associates, was also put up for sale. In 2008 the company reported a net loss of $1.3 billion.

Although CEG started to rebound during the first quarter of 2010, challenges remained. The company reported $15.6 billion in revenues in 2009. To shore up its liquidity and increase its ability to generate energy, on April 8, 2010, the company closed its deal to purchase a $140 million wind energy project in Garrett County, Maryland.

*Carol I Keeley*
*Updated, Susan Windisch Brown and Rhonda Campbell*

## PRINCIPAL SUBSIDIARIES

Baltimore Gas and Electric Company; Constellation Enterprises Inc.; Constellation Power, Inc.

## PRINCIPAL COMPETITORS

Allegheny Energy, Inc.; American Electric Power Company, Inc.; Duke Energy Corporation; Pepco Holdings, Inc.; Progress Energy, Inc.

## FURTHER READING

"Areva, Constellation Energy Announces Plans to Submit for Combined Construction and Operating License," areva.com, November 15, 2005.

"Edwin F. Hale Sr. Sues Maryland-based Constellation Energy for $65M," AllBusiness.com, August 10, 2009.

Hamilton, Martha M., "PEPCO, Baltimore Gas Cancel Two-Year-Old Plan to Merge," *Washington Post,* December 23, 1993, p. 1.

King, Thomson, *Consolidated of Baltimore: 1816–1950.* Baltimore, MD: Consolidated Gas Electric Light and Power Company of Baltimore.

McQuaid, Kevin L., "BGE to Split Itself into Three Parts," *Baltimore Sun,* March 7, 1998, p. 16C.

Romero, Simon, "Two Electricity Giants to Combine, With Focus on Coal and Nuclear," *New York Times,* December 20, 2005.

Sparks, Debra, "Baltimore Gas & Electric: Time to Unplug," *Financial World,* August 1, 1995, p. 20–21.

"Utilities Call Off a Merger Deal," *New York Times,* October 26, 2006.

# Copperbelt Energy Corporation PLC

■

37B Cheetah Road
**Private Bag E835**
**Kabulonga,**
**Lusaka,**
**Zambia**
**Telephone: (260) 01 261647**
**Fax: (260) 01 261640**
**Web site: http://www.cecinvestor.com**

*Public Company*
*Founded:* 1954
*Employees:* 351 (2009)
*Sales:* $154.2 million (2009)
*Stock Exchanges:* Lusaka Stock Exchange
*NAICS:* 221111 Electric Power Generation, Transmission, and Distribution

■ ■ ■

Copperbelt Energy Corporation PLC (CEC) is the leading power production company in Zambia, accounting for about 50 percent of the total power supply in the country. CEC operates and maintains roughly 550 miles of power lines, 38 substations, and a host of gas turbine generators. The location of CEC's control center in Zambia's mineral-rich Copperbelt province enables the company to achieve reliability, efficiency, and effectiveness in the supply of power to many companies that run mining activities in that region.

Over the years, CEC has successfully been providing mining companies in the Copperbelt region with unique power supply products and services designed to address emergency power back-up needs in the companies. The other core activities of CEC include marketing power for its customers in areas within and without the Copperbelt region, as well as selling electricity internationally to countries such as the Democratic Republic of Congo (DRC).

## COMPANY FOUNDING AND EARLY YEARS: 1954–64

The formation of the Rhodesia-Congo Border Company in 1954 was a joint initiative of several mining companies in Zambia's Copperbelt region. These companies were interested in harnessing the advantages of economies of scale by importing hydroelectric power from the DRC for distribution among the mining companies in the Copperbelt region. As such, the joint venture saw the mining companies from the Rhodesia-Congo Border Company establish a power line in 1956 that connected Zambia's Kitwe to DRC's Katanga. This power line carried approximately 220 kilovolts of hydroelectric-generated electricity from the DRC to Zambia.

The incorporation of the Rhodesia-Congo Border Company in the mid-20th century marked a new beginning for electric energy production and distribution in Zambia. The company was founded with the principal objectives of transmitting geothermal and hydroelectric power to a host of mining companies and organizations that were undergoing an accelerated rate of growth. The discovery of enormous amounts of deposits and reserves of copper, iron, and other metal minerals in the Copperbelt region greatly increased mining and industrial activities in the region, and this increased the demand for electric energy to run heavy mining machinery and related equipment. This meant that the Rhodesia-Congo Border Company entered the energy production, supply, and distribution industry at a time when the demand for industrial energy and power greatly outstripped the available supply.

The ready market for Rhodesia-Congo Border Company's energy products and services enabled the company to build a firm foundation for its power production and distribution infrastructure in a favorable business environment, and this early advantage helped the company dominate the energy industry in Zambia for many years. The company remained a key revenue and foreign exchange earner for Zambia's colonial government until 1964 when the country attained independence. As Zambia ushered in a new era of self-rule, the Rhodesia-Congo Border Company was renamed Copperbelt Power Company.

## ECONOMIC REFORMS IN ZAMBIA: 1968–82

In the late 1960s economic reforms took place in Zambia in which the state began to acquire the majority ownership stake in all foreign-owned companies. The nationalization process was spearheaded through the 1968 Mulungushi Reforms under which the Industrial Development Corporation (INDECO) was incorporated to oversee the transformation of the privately owned mining companies into state-owned corporations. The government-initiated economic reforms of 1968 were more or less gradual takeover programs of foreign-owned companies in Zambia in which the state sought to empower the indigenous populations economically.

The economic reforms in Zambia began taking shape in 1970 when the Zambian government formed an additional umbrella body, the Mining Development Corporation (MINDECO), to propagate the majority shareholding interests of the government in all the key copper mining companies in the country. MINDECO

started performing its statutory responsibilities with the acquisition of the majority shareholding stake in the Zambia Anglo American Corporation and subsequently renamed it Nchanga Consolidated Copper Mines (NCCM) in January 1970. MINDECO also acquired the majority shareholding stake in Rhodesia Selection Trust and subsequently changed its name to Roan Consolidated Mines (RCM).

However, the daily operational activities in RCM and NCCM remained under the original management structures of Rhodesia Selection Trust and Zambia Anglo American Corporation respectively until 1973, when the government assumed the leading operational management roles in the two companies. Copper mining companies in Zambia underwent gradual nationalization transformations through the 1970s and culminated in the merger of RCM and ZCCM to form one large, government-owned state corporation, Zambia Consolidated Copper Mines (ZCCM).

The formation of ZCCM in 1982 subsequently led to the conversion of Copperbelt Power Company from an independent corporate entity into a government-run corporation. This change in the corporate status of the Copperbelt Power Company granted the government of Zambia greater leverage in influencing the operational and strategic directions of the company.

## WAVE OF PRIVATIZATION IN ZAMBIA

The state majority ownership of Copper Mining Companies in Zambia lasted until the first part of the 1990s. In 1991 Zambia held its first multiparty elections since independence, and Fredrick Chiluba of the Movement for Multiparty Democracy (MMD) won decisively against the incumbent president, Kenneth Kaunda of the United National Independence Party (UNIP). The defeat of the incumbent government by the opposition party in the country's first multiparty elections ushered in a new political era and a subsequent shift in the economic policies of the country.

In the 1990s a privatization wave swept through the entire African continent, and Zambia was not left behind. President Fredrick Chiluba's new government moved to promulgate economic privatization policies with the objective of reigniting growth in the country's stagnant economy. As such, Zambia experienced a shift of economic policies from nationalization of private-owned and foreign-owned companies to privatization of state-owned corporations.

ZCCM was one of the first state corporations in Zambia to be transformed into private corporate entities in a privatization process that began in 1996. The

## KEY DATES

**1954:** Group of mining companies form Rhodesia-Congo Border Company to help meet their electrical power needs.
**1964:** Independence for Zamiba; company renamed Copperbelt Power Company.
**1982:** Copperbelt Power becomes state-run entity under control of Zambia Consolidated Copper Mines (ZCCM).
**1997:** Copperbelt is privatized and incorporated.
**2008:** Company lists stock on the Lusaka Stock Exchange.

Zambian government gradually surrendered its majority stake of the various energy and mining divisions in ZCCM to the private sectors through the sale of shares to local and international mining companies and to private investors as well. According to information contained in the CEC Web site, the first successful bid for ZCCM's power energy division was made in 1997 by a joint venture of the consortium formed by the National Grid Zambia BV, Cinergy Corporation, and the Zambia-based Technical Power Division Team. This privatization deal between the Zambian government and the private sector consortium paved the way for the incorporation of CEC on September 9, 1997. The ownership structure of the company was transformed, with the National Grid Zambia BV and Cinergy Corporation acquiring 38.5 percent shareholding each, the Zambia-based Technical Power Division Team acquiring 3 percent shareholding, and ZCCM retaining 20 percent shareholding.

In 2003 CEC registered a major milestone in its international growth and expansion when the Environmental Council of Zambia (ECZ) awarded the company an approval for meeting the benchmarks for environmental regulations. This enabled the company to execute one of the preliminary phases of the Second Zambia-DRC Cross Border Power project. The initial phase of relocating and resettling the communities affected by the project was completed in 2006, effectively paving the way for the mainstream project activities.

## SHAREHOLDING STRUCTURE CHANGES: 2006–08

The private sector consortium consisting of National Grid Zambia BV, Cinergy Corporation, and the Zambia-based Technical Power Division Team jointly managed the short-term activities and long-term objectives of CEC until 2006 when the shareholding structure of the company was changed again. The transfer of CEC's majority shareholding took place in February 2006 when the National Grid Zambia BV and Cinergy Corporation agreed to the indirect sale and purchase of 77 percent of CEC's shareholding to Zambian Energy Corporation through its Zambian Energy Corporation (Netherlands) BV subsidiary. The transfer of the majority shareholding of CEC materialized in October 2006 when the Zambian government sanctioned the transaction.

The Zambian Energy Corporation successfully introduced new strategic measures in the management of CEC's power production, transmission, and distribution processes and enhanced the growth of the company's profits. The Zambian Energy Corporation particularly concentrated on the establishment of long-term business opportunities with its key customers and partners in the Copperbelt region. Some of the long-term energy supply agreements made by the company included agreements to supply power to Mopani Copper Mines, Luanshya Copper Mines Plc, and Konkola Copper Mines. These agreements were scheduled to expire in March 2015, March 2016, and March 2020, respectively.

In 2008, 25 percent of Zambia Energy Corporation's stake in CEC was floated at the Lusaka Stock Exchange (LSE) following the company's desire to expand its capital base. Indeed, the strong structural, operational, and prospective fundamentals of the company for most of the first decade of the 21st century had sparked increasing investor interest in the company. Twenty percent of the share floatation was offered to the public, corporate institutions, and fund management organizations, while 5 percent was reserved for Zambia Energy Corporation's employees through an established employee share ownership plan of the company. The 2008 share floatation saw the ownership structure of the company change, with Zambia Energy Corporation's majority shareholding reduced to 52 percent. Individual shareholders totaled 15.8 percent while 7.2 percent of the floated shares were purchased by a funds management company, the African Life Financial Services Zambia Limited. The Zambian government, through the ZCCM, retained its 20 percent shareholding.

## GROWTH PROSPECTS

In 2010 CEC had dual core plans to expand its energy production and transmission capacity as well as enhance its power supply output to its key customers. The company projected to experience growth in its operations and revenues with the completion of the 80-megawatt expansion to the Frontier Mine of First Quantum Minerals Limited. The $11 million Frontier Mine project contract was awarded to CEC in 2006.

The growth prospects of CEC were boosted further by the expected expansion of power supply to the Konkola Copper Mines Plc by a range of between 100 and 170 megawatts. CEC was also set to expand its customer base when Luanshya Copper Mines opened its Muliashi Mine project. In addition, CEC's operations were ready to grow with the increase of power supply to customers of Mopani Copper Mines and TEAL Exploration and Mining Incorporated.

CEC and its Congo (DRC) cross-border power supply partner, the DRC-based Société Nationale d'Électricité (SNEL), projected to expand power supply to DRC through the construction of a second transmission power line across the border, which would almost double capacity to 500 megawatts from the 2010 figure of 260 megawatts. Although the cross-border project experienced delays after 2003 due to international regulatory restrictions, CEC set 2010 as the completion date for the project. All these developments posed positive future growth in the company's scope of operations and revenue.

*Paul Ingati*

## PRINCIPAL COMPETITORS

Chibuluma Mines PLC; Luanshya Copper Mines PLC; Mopani Copper Mines PLC.

## FURTHER READING

"CEC Corporate Milestones," Copperbelt Energy Corporation, 2010.

"Copperbelt Coup Hits CAMAC," *Investors Chronicle,* September 4, 2007.

Kachingwe, Kelvin, "Zambia: Hard Times on the Copperbelt," *Inter Press Service English Newswire,* June 23, 2009.

Silweya, John O., and Immanuel Sampa Ketapa, "Copperbelt Energy Corporation Experiences on Two Failures of Merlin Gerin Type SB 6-72 Circuit Breakers," Copperbelt Energy Corporation.

"Zambia: Construction Plans for Proposed $600,000,000 Hydro Power Station, Ministry of Energy and Water Development," *WWP-Business Opportunities in Africa & the Middle East,* February 1, 2000.

# Corn Products
# International, Inc.

5 Westbrook Corporate Center
Westchester, Illinois 60154
U.S.A.
Telephone: (708) 551-2600
Toll Free: (800) 443-2746
Fax: (708) 551-2700
Web site: http://www.cornproducts.com

*Public Company*
*Founded:* 1906 as Corn Products Refining Company
*Employees:* 8,100 (2009)
*Sales:* $3.67 billion (2009)
*Stock Exchanges:* New York
*Ticker Symbol:* CPO
*NAICS:* 311221 Wet Corn Milling; 424490 Other Grocery and Related Products Merchant Wholesalers.

■■■

Over the past century Corn Products International, Inc., (CPI) has developed from a regional refining company to become a global corporation, one of the largest corn refining and ingredient companies in the world. Growing from a single refining plant in Illinois, in 2010 CPI operated in 15 countries through its own plants as well as joint ventures and alliances. The company remains focused on its status as the leading supplier of starches and sweeteners such as dextrose, syrups, and glucose. CPI customers range across 60 countries and hail from a wide spectrum, from the food and beverage industry to pharmaceuticals, paper, and textile concerns.

## MARKET DOMINANCE: 1906–12

The origins of CPI lie back in the nineteenth century and a process invented by Thomas Kingsford in 1842. An English immigrant to the United States, Kingsford developed wet milling, whereby starch could be separated from corn. This process in turn led to the development of cornstarch and corn syrup as food additives. A whole new industry sprang up, and by the beginning of the twentieth century a variety of regional companies had been created. A period of rapid consolidation followed. In the 1900s, three leading corn refining companies merged to form the Corn Products Company, producer of Karo syrup. The new company was soon producing 84 percent of U.S. corn starch.

Enter Edward T. Bedford, president of the New York Glucose Company, a competitor of the Corn Products Company. In 1906 Bedford orchestrated a merger of his own company with the Corn Products Company and Warner Sugar Refining Company, and the Corn Products Refining Company, direct antecedent of CPI, was born.

Within two years, construction began on a new refining plant in central Illinois. In 2010 the Argo refining plant remained the company's largest facility, although a century after its construction it only employed 400 workers, down from an all-time high of 3,000. At one time, there were so many workers that the company built the nearby community of Bedford Park just to house its employees.

Also in 1908, the company made its first business deals in the European market, opening sales offices in Germany and the United Kingdom. These initial

## COMPANY PERSPECTIVES

Corn Products International has a simple but ambitious mission: to become the premier regional provider of agriculturally based products and ingredients worldwide.

ventures would establish CPI's presence throughout Europe for many decades.

In 1911 Karo syrup comprised 80 percent of the company's sales. That year, CPI began marketing Mazola corn oil as well as syrups, jams, and starches (both edible and laundry). Many of these products were marketed as generics destined for relabeling by regional distributors, thus giving CPI an even larger market presence than the casual consumer might have presumed.

### EXPANSION AND TRUST ISSUES: 1913–33

By 1920 CPI had established a near monopoly in certain sectors, with up to 90 percent market share for some refined corn products. All this activity brought the attention of the federal government, which charged CPI in 1913 with violating the Sherman Antitrust Act. By 1919, after several rounds of litigation, the Supreme Court decided against dissolving the company, although it did order CPI to divest itself of several holdings.

Undeterred by all the litigation, in 1919 the company established its first international joint venture when it acquired controlling interest in a Canadian company, the Canada Starch Company. That same year, CPI put down manufacturing roots in Europe by purchasing a plant in Germany.

With its first international purchase complete, CPI began an aggressive expansion abroad in the 1920s and 1930s. Several more German plants were purchased in 1921. Argentina was the site of CPI's first Latin American business in 1928. A year later, wet-milling facilities were established in Brazil. A year after that, CPI further consolidated its Latin American ventures with an expansion into Mexico, and in 1933, the company established a corn-refining outfit in Colombia. The Colombian venture would prove particularly successful. By the end of the twentieth century, the CPI plant in Colombia had become that country's top corn wet-miller in terms of grind capacity.

By the 1930s CPI's owned or licensed international assets could be found in North America (Canada,

Mexico, and the Dominican Republic); Europe (Czechoslovakia, England, France, Italy, the Netherlands, Switzerland, and Yugoslavia); South America (Argentina and Brazil); and Asia (Korea and Japan).

### WAR AND PROSPERITY: 1934–57

The food market was relatively secure during the Great Depression of the 1930s. Founder Edward Bedford had died in 1931 leaving a strong and prosperous company. With the entry of the United States into World War II, CPI faced its first serious challenge.

In a much better position financially and logistically than its British and Russian allies, the United States had committed to an ambitious aid program called Lend-Lease. Part of the Lend-Lease plan involved supplying food to allied armies; this, in addition to the demands of feeding its own armies, placed a huge strain on the U.S. food industry. Strict civilian rationing was imposed by the U.S. government along with price controls.

The government prices on corn were so low that many corn farmers turned to pig farming, using their corn as feed for their hogs rather than selling to refineries. CPI was forced to close two refineries, and it nearly closed its main plant at Argo. Fortunately, a little over a year after these closures World War II came to an end, and the government rationing and price controls were lifted. CPI got back to regular business and was soon expanding again, enjoying the benefits of the general postwar economic boom.

By 1958 CPI had engaged in a series of acquisitions that culminated that year with the purchase of West Germany's C. H. Knorr Company. Long a staple on European grocery shelves, Knorr's bullion cubes and dehydrated soups would quickly become a familiar sight in the United States as well. Other postwar expansions had led CPI to involvement not just in corn and chemical refining, but also in the production of feed grains, rail and shipping lines, construction, and even banking.

### BEST FOODS: 1959–69

In May 1959 the Corn Products Refining Company merged with Best Foods, Inc., finalizing a process that had begun in September 1958. The resulting company, which was now well placed to develop into grocery products as well as manufacturing, was dubbed the Corn Products Company. With access to the products of its overseas interests and now Best Foods, CPI put out an impressive line of commercial and industrial products. Its factories produced such familiar brand names as Mazola corn oil (and margarine, introduced in

## KEY DATES

**1906:** Corn Products Refining Company founded through a merger of leading U.S. corn refiners.

**1958:** Corn Products Refining Company merges with The Best Foods, Inc., to become the Corn Products Company.

**1969:** Corn Products Company becomes CPC International.

**1997:** Corn Products International, Inc., is spun off from CPC to form an independent company.

**2008:** A tribunal finds Mexico liable to Corn Products for violating NAFTA trade agreements.

1961), Hellmann's mayonnaise and salad dressings, Karo syrup, Skippy peanut butter, Thomas' English Muffins (in 1970), Rit dyes, and Shinola shoe polish.

In 1966 the company passed $1 billion in sales for the first time. With its expanded product base, CPI was able to resume an aggressive program of international expansion. The same year as the merger with Best Foods, CPI began to expand its South American operations, moving into Uruguay and Venezuela. Two years later, in 1961, the company expanded into Chile also.

Expansion in Asian markets resumed as well. In 1959 new businesses were opened up in the Philippines, and in 1962 the company acquired the largest corn-refining plant in Pakistan. The following year, a Knorr manufacturing plant was opened up in Japan. In 1967 CPI established a presence in Malaysia, becoming that country's only supplier of dextrose and glucose syrup solids.

As the company expanded, it began to shift towards production of packaged foods. A reflection of its shift in focus can be seen in the company's 1969 name change, when it officially became known as CPC International. This move was intended to disassociate it from its agricultural manufacturing origins.

### MILESTONES AND SETBACKS: 1970–87

The 1970s were, for the most part, a time of continued steady growth for CPI. In 1973 the company extended its South American presence into Ecuador and established itself in Africa when it opened a plant in Kenya, becoming the only wet-milling operation in

Central or East Africa. The following year, in 1974, the company began entering into a series of agreements that opened up South Africa as well. That same year saw CPI's sales pass $2.5 billion.

The 1970s were also the first decade where CPI encountered serious opposition to its long-held market dominance. When both the Coca-Cola and PepsiCo companies decided to make the switch from using cane sugar to high fructose corn syrup for their soft drink sweetening agents, CPI found itself unprepared for the intense competition that move would bring to the corn-milling industry. Agri-business firms like the Archer Daniels Midland Co. (ADM) and Cargill Inc. began aggressively moving into wet-milling corn, and CPI saw its market share decrease significantly.

Nevertheless, three new corn refining plants located in Stockton, California; Winston-Salem, North Carolina; and Port Colborne, Ontario, were constructed in 1981, a year after CPI's sales had passed the $4 billion mark. In 1983 a partnership between CPI subsidiary Canada Starch Company and a corn refiner in London, Ontario, resulted in the formation of Casco Inc., Canada's only in-country corn refiner.

It was not all expansion, however. In 1987 the company sold its South African interests and, after six decades of manufacturing involvement in European markets, CPI divested itself of its $600 million European corn-milling operations. This move came largely in response to an attempted corporate takeover by Revlon chairman Ronald O. Perelman.

### RESTRUCTURING: 1988–96

Although the CPI board was able to block the takeover by buying back 20 percent of its shares at a cost of $836.9 million and subsequently buying out Perelman to the tune of $88.5 million, the money came largely from selling off assets. In the wake of the takeover attempt and sale of assets, significant company restructuring followed. In 1988 CPI cut its workforce by 17 percent and consolidated its many international holdings into a single group, ending its practice of allowing a fair amount of independence to its overseas ventures.

In the wake of the takeover attempt, the company refocused its attention on foodservice and consumer food operations. From 1986 to 1990, CPI acquired 17 consumer food businesses in North America, Latin America, and Europe. As the new decade began, CPI concentrated on purchasing small operations in countries such as the Czech Republic, Hungary, Poland, Israel, and Indonesia. Using these newly acquired local brands as beachheads, CPI would then funnel its own overseas products into the new markets.

Antitrust litigation reared its head once more as well. A civil antitrust lawsuit accused several corn-refining companies, including CPI, ADM, and Cargill, of collusion and price-fixing. In 1996 CPI agreed to pay a $7 million settlement.

## SPIN-OFF: 1997–2007

Although CPI established operations in Thailand and expanded its business in Brazil in 1997, that year was chiefly notable for what came at the end. On December 31 Corn Products International, Inc., was officially spun off from the Corn Products Corporation (CPC), becoming its own publicly traded entity. The move came at a time when CPI, overshadowed by larger competitors, was selling its corn syrup at a lower price than ever before. As a newly independent company, CPI ranked fourth in the $10-billion corn-refining industry.

By the end of the first decade of the twenty-first century, Corn Products International, through its own properties, subsidiaries, and joint ventures, maintained operations in 42 plants spread across 22 countries. Since its spin-off from CPC, CPI acquired controlling interest in its Korean business from Doosan Corp in a $65 million deal in 2005. It also acquired a majority interest in its Mexican venture Arcania, a move that would involve CPI in an ongoing battle between Mexican sugar growers and U.S. corn syrup producers.

At stake in this conflict was the Mexican soda market, one of the largest in the world. Starting around the beginning of the century, Mexican soft drink manufacturers decided to make the switch from sugar to corn syrup, and CPI, with its long presence in the country, was well-placed to take advantage of the switch, giving it a head start over competitors like ADM. CPI was aided in its endeavors by the ruling of an international tribunal, which found that steep tariffs and financial incentives granted to domestic fructose suppliers by the Mexican government were in violation of the NAFTA trade agreement.

When CPI was spun off from CPC, industry analysts like Christine McCracken, writing in *Crain's Chicago Business* predicted that CPI was ripe for a takeover and would "get taken out eventually."

The predicted takeover attempt did not emerge until 2008, when the agri-business company Bunge Ltd., a giant in the field of fertilizer, milled product, and edible oil production, struck a deal to acquire CPI for $4.8 billion. According to the July 2008 issue of *Candy Industry*, the deal was aimed at "establish[ing] an integrated, global presence in the corn value chain." However, investors did not think the deal was sweet enough, and by November the deal had collapsed as both companies' stock prices plummeted.

## 21ST CENTURY CHALLENGES

CPI increased its net sales in 2008 by 16 percent to $3.94 billion, and in 2009 it was ranked fifth by *Forbes* magazine in its list of America's Best Managed Companies. However, even with these accolades, as the company entered the 2010s the future of the corn-milling industry had never been more uncertain.

Reports from groups like the American Heart Association on corn syrup's ubiquity and potential negative health risks began to appear with some frequency. Various reports linked widespread consumption of corn syrup to a rise in everything from autism to diabetes to obesity. As a result, consumer pressure began leading major manufacturers to switch back to sugar in some or all of their products. Even First Lady Michelle Obama weighed in against corn syrup, typifying a new breed of American consumer looking for fewer calories and more ingredients perceived to be more "natural."

"There's not a shred of evidence that these products are different biologically," said David Ludwig, director of the Optimal Weight for Life Program at Children's Hospital in Boston, quoted in *Crain's Chicago Business*. But despite such counter-claims, the surge in popular opinion ("100% marketing and 0% science," as Ludwig put it) had led to predictions of flat corn syrup prices.

An upside of the reaction against corn syrup for CPI is that it may be looking at a chance to increase its market share. Other corn-milling outfits have been increasingly looking towards corn-derived biofuels like ethanol as an alternative to the sweetener market. This increased interest in ethanol has increased demand for corn, doubling the price per bushel over 10 years, and CPI, which had resisted moving into biofuels, was able to raise its prices as it had fewer competitors.

CPI had also been exploring diversification into non-corn-syrup sweeteners. In 2007 the company acquired two manufacturers, Getec Guanabara Quirnica Industrial S.A. in Brazil and SPI Polyoils of Delaware. Both companies manufactured a type of sugar-free, low-calorie sweetener called polyol. It would seem that after a century, CPI was looking toward a time when corn-milled sweeteners would no longer be its stock in trade.

*David Larkins*

## PRINCIPAL SUBSIDIARIES

Canada Starch Company Inc. (Canada); The Chicago, Peoria, and Western Railway Company; Corn Products Kenya Limited (Kenya); CP Ingredients Limited (England); Feed Products Limited; GTC Oats, Inc.

## PRINCIPAL COMPETITORS

Almex S.A. de C.V.; Archer Daniels Midland Company; Cargill, Incorporated; National Starch andChemical Company; Tate and Lyle Ingredients Americas, Inc.

## FURTHER READING

Merrion, Paul, "Public Sours on Illinois' Sweet Spot," *Crain's Chicago Business* 32, no. 32 (2009): 3.

Murphy, H. Lee. "Global Reach Sweetens Syrup Maker' Outlook," *Crain's Chicago Business* 22, no. 5 (1999): 4.

Stainburn, Samantha, "Corn Products: How Sweet It Is," *Crain's Chicago Business* 30, no. 53 (2007): 35.

"Sweet Deal as Bunge Purchases Corn Products," *Candy Industry* 173, no. 7 (2008): 9.

Tita, Bob, "Mexico Lifts Corn Products," *Crain's Chicago Business* 28, no. 11 (2005): 4.

# CPC Corporation, Taiwan

No. 3 Sungren Rd., 12th Fl.
Shinyi Chiu, Taipei 11010
Taiwan
Telephone: (+886) 2-8789-8989
Fax: (+886) 2-8789-9021
Web site: http://www.cpc.com.tw

*State-Owned Company*
*Founded:* 1946 as Chinese Petroleum Corporation
*Employees:* 14,843 (2008)
*Sales:* NWD 945.2 billion ($28.84 billion) (2008)
*NAICS:* 22121 Natural Gas Distribution; 48621
   Pipeline Transportation of Natural Gas; 211111
   Crude Petroleum and Natural Gas Extraction;
   324110 Petroleum Refineries; 324121 Asphalt Pav-
   ing Mixture and Block Manufacturing; 324122
   Asphalt Shingle and Coating Materials Manufactur-
   ing; 324191 Petroleum Lubricating Oil and Grease
   Manufacturing; 324199 All Other Petroleum and
   Coal Products Manufacturing.

■ ■ ■

The CPC Corporation, Taiwan (CPC), is the state-run
petroleum company of Taiwan. In this capacity, CPC
engages in all aspects of petroleum manufacture and
sale, from exploration to production to refining to storage and transportation and finally to sales. The
company's stakes in oil and gas exploration ventures
range across the globe, from the Americas to the Asian
Pacific Rim to Africa. It was not until the first decade of
the twenty-first century that CPC faced its first major
competition, first from domestic, then international,
corporations.

By the end of 2008, CPC operated 645 filling stations directly and franchised a further 1,387 stations. All
told, CPC filling stations accounted for 70 percent of
Taiwan's service stations. In addition to its market share
in retail filling stations, in 2008 CPC also held more
than 72 percent of the Taiwanese solvent and chemical
market along with 29 to 45 percent of the toluene and
35 to 42 percent of the xylene markets. Since the 1980s
CPC has also been involved in importing liquid natural
gas (LNG) to supplement Taiwan's low natural reserves.

## A STATE-OWNED ENTERPRISE: 1946–57

The origins of CPC Corporation are bound up with the
twentieth-century history of China and Taiwan. In the
wake of the fall of the Chinese Empire in 1912, the
Republic of China was established and eventually
stabilized under the Kuomintang government.

Its leader, Chiang Kai-shek, was soon engaged in a
civil war against Mao Zedong and his Chinese Communist Party. The infighting was put on hold between
1937 and 1945 as China fought for its very survival
against the invading Japanese, but once the Second
Sino-Japanese War and World War II came to an end,
the civil war picked up again. By 1949 the Chinese
Communists were declaring victory and the Kuomintang faction was in full retreat.

Chiang Kai-shek's supporters, numbering 1.5 million people, left mainland China bound for the nearby

island of Taiwan, formerly known as Formosa. There they joined the island's six million residents and formed a new country, the last stronghold of the Republic of China.

The CPC followed its government across the Straits of Formosa in 1949, having been founded on mainland China in 1946. Moving from its headquarters in Shanghai to Taiwan's new capital, Taipei, by 1952 CPC had been officially tasked with supplying the island nation its energy as well as directing development of new petrochemical and oil refining ventures. As a state-owned company under the direction of the Ministry of Economic Affairs, CPC was part of a larger centralized economic plan to keep 56.6 percent of industrial production under government control.

## INDUSTRIAL PRODUCTION: 1958–69

Taiwan's government had a vested interest in keeping tight control on vital industrial companies like CPC. Taiwan in the 1950s was a largely agrarian economy with few petrochemical resources. Over the next three decades, CPC would play a significant role in transforming Taiwan into a modern industrialized country with a robust and well-developed petrochemical industry.

The first steps were taken in 1958, when CPC's Kaohsiung Refinery began producing sulfur and sulfuric acid. Charged with supplying basic and intermediate petrochemical raw materials primarily using Taiwan's scarce and hard-to-find natural resources, CPC used its refinery at Kaohsiung, Taiwan's largest and most industrialized port, to its fullest potential.

Following quickly on the beginnings of sulfur production, CPC plants were soon turning out benzene, toluene, and xylene by 1960. With these raw materials, CPC was able to manufacture naphtha and rubber solvents, which were then supplied to hundreds of

burgeoning Taiwanese industries. By 1968 CPC built its first naphtha cracking plant for the production of ethylene gas from naphtha, making the Kaohsiung port a petrochemical center and future site of numerous plastics and chemical firms.

## ENERGY CRISIS AND EXPLORATION: 1970–81

Taiwan's explosive economic growth of the 1960s and 1970s, known as the "Taiwan Miracle," established the Republic of China as a major player in Asia. Yet the tiny island's rapid industrialization only served to put greater strain on CPC's ability to meet increasing demand. The fact that Taiwan and mainland China remained in an open state of war until 1979 made the Taiwanese government that much more anxious to protect its petrochemical assets, as vital as they were to national defense.

To that end, in 1970 CPC's existing petroleum exploration division was given a much wider mandate. Previously limited to Taiwan and its immediate offshore environs, a series of joint ventures sent CPC exploratory teams around the world to Southeast Asia, the Middle East, Africa, Australia, and South America.

Even as CPC was finding success in joint ventures working under the name OPIC (Overseas Petroleum and Investment) with Conoco in Indonesia and the Ecuadorian Amazon, the worldwide energy crisis struck in 1973. The timing was particularly challenging for CPC as the crisis came at a time when Taiwan was becoming ever more dependent on foreign oil imports: between 1973 and 1980, the total import value of oil jumped from 2.6 percent to 20.6 percent. In response to the rising prices and petrochemical shortages brought about by the crisis, CPC adopted a strategy of increased focus on conservation, diversification of suppliers, and insistence on long-term supply contracts.

The latter strategy paid off particularly well. By 1979 CPC was actually enjoying an increase in deliveries from major suppliers even as other countries were dealing with cancellations or nondeliveries of their spot market purchases. That same year, in light of Taiwan's rapidly depleting natural reserves, the decision was made to begin importing liquid natural gas (LNG). (Between 1971 and 1983, Taiwan's indigenous energy dropped from 37 percent of the total supply to a mere 12 percent.) To accomplish this task, ground was broken on an $800 million project to construct an LNG receiving station near Kaohsiung.

## CHEN YAOSHENG: 1982–90

The long-term contract strategy and decision to import LNG were both the product of a man named Chen

# KEY DATES

**1946:** The Chinese Petroleum Corporation is founded in Shanghai under the direction of the Resources Committee.

**1949:** The CPC relocates with the Kuomintang government to Taiwan, where its headquarters is established in Taipei under the direction of the Ministry of Economic Affairs.

**1970:** Under joint ventures with international companies and host countries, the CPC begins expanding exploration activities into Southeast Asia, the Middle East, Africa, Australia, and South America.

**1979:** The decision is made to import liquid natural gas (LNG); construction begins on an $800 million receiving terminal.

**2001:** The Taiwanese government begins to privatize CPC.

**2007:** The company's board of directors approves a change of name to CPC Corporation.

Yaosheng, one of the most important figures in CPC history. A chemist by trade, Chen had started out in the early 1970s as CPC's director in the Chinese Government Procurement and Service Mission in New York before becoming vice president of the company in 1978, then president in 1982.

It was Chen's policies that led to the construction of the LNG receiving station at Yung An Hsiang near Kaohsiung, and the subsequent construction of a 350-mile long pipeline to carry the LNG inland, where it was slated to be used for everything from household to commercial to industrial uses. CPC under Chen, who had been named chairman of the board in 1985, signed a 20-year long-term contract with Indonesia's state-run Pertamina company. Starting in 1990, the year the LNG receiving plant was completed, the contract called for 1.5 million tons of LNG to be imported from Indonesia every year, which, along with several new offshore natural gas wells that began operating in 1986, greatly alleviated market strain.

Chen's long-term contract policies were also instrumental in CPC's continued prosperity amidst the second oil shortage in 1979 and the resulting global recession. This approach required discipline and foresight. Even when predicted import supply levels fell short of demand, CPC maintained a policy of incremental adjustments to existing contracts rather than adding new spot market purchases.

Under Chen Yaosheng CPC's top priority was shoring up Taiwan against oil shortages. A government policy was enacted to keep a 90-day reserve of oil on hand at all times, and oil exporting only took place in order to balance issues of supply and demand. Perhaps the most dramatic instance of CPC's focus on securing its international oil supply came in 1990, when the company elected to drastically reduce its oil imports from Saudi Arabia and Kuwait.

This decision was made after Saudi Arabia, which supplied Taiwan with fully a third of its imported oil, announced it was cutting its supplies to Taiwan by 40 percent. This move confirmed a concern for CPC, that Middle Eastern countries like Kuwait, which accounted for an addition 19 percent of Taiwan's imports, and Saudi Arabia were too susceptible to political pressure from mainland China. The decision was therefore made to drastically reduce Middle Eastern imports and focus increasingly on exports from politically stable countries outside Beijing's sphere of influence. OPIC launched new exploratory missions in the Philippines, Indonesia, Malaysia, Ecuador, Papua New Guinea, and Australia, and CPC strengthened ventures with the United States, Namibia, and Malaysia.

## ENVIRONMENTAL ISSUES

Aside from worries over Taiwan's dependence on foreign energy suppliers, another major challenge facing CPC at the dawn of the 1990s was the growing concern over the petrochemical industry's environmental impact. Taiwan was only just emerging from its long postwar authoritarian period into a new democratic era, and the populace was increasingly making its voice heard. A series of massive protests about the petrochemical industry's environmental impact underscored the importance of the issue to Taiwan's citizenry. A 1989 opinion poll placed the issue second only in importance to "social order" and well ahead of increased democratization. The protests even managed to halt construction on CPC's fifth naphtha cracking plant.

In response, CPC offered a short-term concession of building a swimming pool and hospital along with the naphtha plant and, as a more long-term solution, that year set up an environmental protection division. The new division enacted a series of policy changes, the most important of which was that each new CPC plant was required to undergo an environmental impact assessment and would not get the go-ahead without governmental approval of these reports. CPC also initiated a scenic landscaping program for its industrial facilities, looked into methods to reduce emissions and pollutants, installed automatic detection and alarm systems to warn against dangerous toxic gases, and improved its refinery waste and solid waste disposal methods.

CPC also took steps to make environmentally conscious changes in its oil imports. In February 1996 the company signed an agreement with British Petroleum to purchase low-sulfur North Slope oil from Alaska. Although more expensive, the new oil would result in lower emissions to meet new governmental standards. In 1999, CPC also began selling a low-emission 98-octane fuel at 300 of its service stations.

## MOVING TOWARDS PRIVATIZATION: 1991–2003

Although the government of Taiwan had started out playing a heavy role in its developing industries, between 1952 and 1989 state-controlled industrial output dropped a dramatic 36 percentage points, from 46.2 percent to just 10 percent. This transition had been a result in part of the government's practice of offering low interest and tax rebates to developing industries. These policies had led to an explosion of factory construction between 1950 and 1980, a three-decade period that saw the number of industrial operations in Taiwan increase 1,200 percent.

By the early 1990s even an industrial giant like CPC, which at the time was Taiwan's largest enterprise and was solely responsible for the entire country's petroleum industry, was beginning to feel the pressure to privatize and compete on an open market. Economic policies were becoming increasingly liberalized and Taiwan was competing more and more on a global market scale. On July 12, 1991, CPC publicly issued 20 percent of its shares for sale on the Taipei Stock Exchange. Five years later, the Fair Trading Law opened up Taiwan's domestic petroleum market to competition and slated CPC for privatization by 2001.

The scheduled privatization did not work out as planned. In 2002, the Taiwanese government announced plans to sell two-thirds of CPC's shares to the public, but this move was met with intense opposition from CPC's nearly 15,000 employees, many of whom were members of politically powerful labor unions. Furthermore, the opening of Taiwan's petroleum market had brought intense competition, particularly from rival domestic company Formosa Plastics Group (FPG). FPG, which had been around since the 1950s, was Taiwan's largest plastics and petrochemical manufacturer, and it opened an oil refinery in 1999. It then began selling its gas through Taiwan's second-largest chain of service stations to compete directly with

CPC. CPC's attentions became increasingly focused on merely fending off FPG's aggressive expansion.

CPC was also faced with internal problems in the late 1990s and first decade of the 21st century. In December 1996 Chairman Chang Tzu-yaun was asked to step down from his post amid allegations of corruption and nepotism. As the first decade of the new millennium came to a close, CPC posted a $10.67 million deficit due to a combination of government-fixed gas prices and soaring cost of oil. To correct the deficit, CPC was forced to raise its gas prices 10 percent right at a time when it was facing some of its stiffest commercial competition. Lastly, CPC found itself the center of some controversy when it changed its name in 2007 from Chinese Petroleum to CPC Corporation.

The name change was the result of an official "desinicizing" program in which the Taiwanese government aimed to remove the words "China" or "Chinese" from all official organizations. The move was widely criticized by both mainland Chinese and Taiwanese opposition-party politicians.

## DIVERSIFICATION AND INVESTMENTS: 2004–10

Faced with increased competition, loss of governmental support and its long-held monopoly, record deficits, and damage to its brand name, CPC implemented an aggressive strategy of diversification on a global scale. The new priority was on new joint venture opportunities, acquisitions, and mergers. Starting back in the 1990s, CPC struck deals with foreign corporations, jointly building a refining complex in Brunei with Japan's Kanematsu company in 1997, and even entered into a joint venture with the China National Offshore Oil Corp., the first such deal between oil producers from mainland China and Taiwan.

In 2006 CPC invested $30 million into a joint venture with the African country of Chad to explore oil reserves. The same year, a similar oil exploration deal was struck with Malaysia's state-run Petronas. The following year, the company acquired Browse LNG from Woodside Petroleum Ltd. CPC also received permission from the government in 2007 to embark on a five-year, $487-million overseas oil and gas exploration project. Finally, in 2010, CPC signed another long-term contract for the supply of LNG, this time with the Exxon Mobil Corporation. This contract supplemented a 20-year long-term contract CPC finalized with Qatar-based RasGas II in 2005.

Domestic improvements continued at a rapid pace as well. A six-year, $1.25-billion project got under way in 2004 to build an ethylene expansion plant. The following year, plans were announced for an ambitious project in which CPC would partner with two financial services firms and ten domestic petrochemical companies to build an $11.6 billion petrochemicals complex.

Despite the increased competition, CPC held on to a strong market position thanks in large part to its name recognition and long presence as Taiwan's premiere oil and gas company. The company commanded a large tanker fleet capable of shipping 1.2 million tons of oil, and three refineries with a combined capacity of 720,000 barrels per day. On the other hand, CPC's refineries were starting to show their age, and were unable to process the less expensive high sulfur crude oil that FPG's more modern facilities could.

Entering the second decade of the 21st century, CPC was faced with losing its position as top oil products supplier. FPG, already producing 524,000 barrels per day in 2007, announced plans for a $3 billion refining complex which, when completed, would put it well ahead of CPC's refining capabilities. A law passed in April 2007 significantly lowered the entry barrier for foreign oil companies, and CPC was soon facing direct competition from oil giants Shell and Exxon Mobil. Whether CPC will be able to compete on its own after five decades of government protection remains to be seen.

*Joanne E. Cross*
*Updated, Mariko Fujinaka; David Larkins*

## PRINICIPAL SUBSIDIARIES

China American Petrochemical Co. Ltd. (38.57%); Chun Pin Enterprise Co. Ltd. (49%); CPC-Shell Lubricant Co. Ltd. (49%); Dai Hai Petrol Corp. (35%); Faraway Maritimes Shipping Co. (40%); KuoKuang Power Co. Ltd. (45%); Kuokuang Petrochemical Technology Co. (43%); NiMiC Ship Holding Co., Ltd. (45%); NiMiC Ship Management Co., Ltd. (45%); Qatar Fuel Additives Company Limited (20%); Ras Laffan Liquefied Natural Gas Company Limited II (5%).

## PRINCIPAL COMPETITORS

Formosa Plastics Group; Royal Dutch Shell; Exxon Mobil.

## FURTHER READING

Alperowicz, Natasha, "Taiwan's CPC Proceeds with Scrap-and-Build Cracker," *Chemical Week* 171, no. 20 (2009): 19.

"Chinese Petroleum Corporation SWOT Analysis," *SWOT Analysis*, Nov. 2008:1.

"CPC Corporation," *International Directory of Company Histories*. Farmington Hills, MI; The Gale Group, Inc, 2006.

"Chinese Petroleum Corp," *Notable Corporate Chronologies*. Online Edition. Gale, 2008.

Haldis, Peter, and Joanna Franco, "Taiwan's CPC Raises Gasoline, Diesel Prices," *Global Refining & Fuels Today* 1, no. 5 (2009): 10.

"Scholars Slam 'De-sinicizing' Moves by Taiwan Authorities," *Xinhua News Agency*, February 13, 2007.

# Crédit Industriel et Commercial S.A.

—■—

6, avenue de Provence
Paris, 75009
France
Telephone: (+33 1) 45 96 96 96
Fax: (+33 1) 45 96 96 66
Web site: https://www.cic.fr

*Public Company*
*Founded:* 1859 as Société Générale de Crédit Industriel
et Commercial
*Employees:* 22,656 (2008)
*Net Banking Income:* EUR 3.206 billion ($4.34 billion,
2008)
*Stock Exchanges:* Paris
*Ticker Symbol:* CIC
*NAICS:* 522110 Commercial Banking; 522120 Savings
Institutions; 522291 Consumer Lending; 522310
Mortgage and Nonmortgage Loan Brokers; 523110
Investment Banking and Securities Dealing; 524128
Other Direct Insurance (except Life, Health, and
Medical) Carriers.

■ ■ ■

Crédit Industriel et Commercial S.A. (CIC), a *Fortune*
Global 500 company, is France's fourth-largest banking
group. CIC had 3.46 million retail clients in 2008, and
almost one-third of the companies operating in France
used the services of CIC. The company is based in Paris,
included five regional banks throughout France, and
operated 2,122 branches in 2008. That year CIC had

operations in more than 35 countries spanning five
continents.

CIC offers a range of products and services for
individuals and corporate customers, including bank
and savings accounts, mortgages, loans, portfolio
management, capital development, consumer credit, car
insurance, and home insurance. The main focuses of
CIC are retail banking and providing financial services
for businesses and self-employed professionals. The largest subsidiaries of CIC include CIC Lyonnaise de
Banque, Adepi, CIC Banque BSD-CIN, and CIC Est.
As of 2008, the French banking company Crédit Mutuel Centre Est Europe owned 91.76 percent of CIC,
and 1.35 percent was owned by the public.

## NINETEENTH-CENTURY BEGINNINGS

CIC was established in 1859 and was the first of
France's enduring corporate banks. This was a very
prosperous time in French history. Industry was growing
rapidly, and finances were desperately needed to fund
the building of railroads. At the time, the only money
available to French bankers was their own fortunes and
a small amount of private capital. With such limited
funds, the bankers were not able to solve the financial
problems created by the railroads. In CIC's 2008 annual
report, Michel Lucas, president of the CIC Executive
Board, explained the the company's origins when he
stated, "On May 7, 1859, a decree signed by Emperor
Napoleon III authorized the establishment, in accordance with the law of the time, of 'the limited liability company formed in Paris under the name Société

Générale de Crédit Industriel et Commercial' and approved its bylaws as contained in deeds executed on April 30 and May 6 before Mr. Dufour, public notary, Paris."

Lucas went on to explain, "This first deposit-taking bank represented a complete break with the past, in that it sought to capture the savings of the public at large, with a view to siphoning off temporarily idle and unproductive funds and using them to finance the working requirements of business." CIC was basically introduced to be an international investment bank. The directors of the bank included not only French bankers but also an English director, Prussia's former minister of finance, and Russia's Prince Soltykoff. At first, the founders planned to use the company to introduce France to a form of English depositing and banking and the use of checks. However, during the first few years of its operation, the company established a pattern of corporate investment banking. The importance of investment banking soon declined with the depression of the French economy that occurred in the 1870s.

Between 1864 and 1881, several new regional and local banks were founded in France's leading cities, and their creation was endorsed by CIC. However, CIC was not directly involved with these banks, as they operated independently of the company. In 1895 CIC began its expansion into other countries. CIC's London branch was the company's first venture outside of France.

### ESTABLISHING THE CIC GROUP

By 1913 the stability of the regional banks endorsed by CIC was in jeopardy due to the quick expansion of other agencies that had been created by larger institutions. In order to access the large amounts of capital needed to meet the needs of their own growing business, the regional banks resumed their relationship with CIC and later became a part of the group. These institutions included Banque Scalbert, Banque Dupont, Société Normande, Crédit Havrais, Crédit Nantais, Credit de l'Ouest, Banque Régionale de l'Ouest, and Banque d'Alsace et de Lorraine.

The banking crisis of 1930 through 1935 caused most of the regional banks to turn to CIC for financial support. CIC decided to limit the amount of intervention in these banks, where representatives of the company sat on the board of directors. In 1931 the CIC Group was created. Since that time, several other institutions have joined the group, including Banque Transatlantique, Banque Journel, and Banque Regionale de l'Ain. The group later became a member of the Suez-Union des Mines group in 1968.

The Banque de Suez et de l'Union des Mines was originally the Compagnie universelle du canal maritime de Suez, a company created in 1858 to manage and develop the Suez Canal. This maritime passage, which links the Mediterranean Sea with the Red Sea, was built to shorten the trade route between Europe and India. The company eventually became one of the richest corporations in France. The 160-kilometer canal was nationalized in 1956, causing the Compagnie universelle du canal maritime de Suez to lose its investment, so it reinvented itself in the world of finance as Campagnie Financière de Suez in 1958. In its new role, the company managed financial assets. The following year, a bank subsidiary was created, which was eventually renamed Banque de Suez et de l'Union des Mines. The majority of CIC's capital, approximately 72 percent, was held by the Suez group from 1971 through 1982.

### CHANGES DURING THE 1980S

In 1982 a law was passed that changed the nature of the CIC Group's shareholders. As a result, most of the banks in the CIC and Suez Groups were nationalized, including CIC and its regional banks. The CIC Group was reorganized, and several changes were made. The Compagnie Financière du CIC was created as the group's holding company, and the CIC was transformed into a Parisian bank called CIC de Paris. The CIC Union Européenne International et Cie was created as a specialized bank to reorganize all international activities. The Groupe des Assurances Nationales (GAN), a state-owned insurer, became a new shareholder with the purpose of reinforcing the group's equity base. Following this, the Banque de l'Union Européenne also joined the group.

By 1984 the government of France had given CIC complete ownership of Banque de l'Union Européenne as well as enough shares in the regional banks to hold controlling interest in their share capital. CIC Paris was created as a subsidiary for these banking businesses. CIC became the parent company of the group and was renamed Compagnie Financière de Crédit Industriel et Commercial. The following year, GAN acquired an interest in the company, which grew as the government's and the Suez group's interests decreased.

## KEY DATES

**1859:** Société Générale de Crédit Industriel et Commercial is established as the first deposit-taking bank in France.
**1864:** The company begins endorsing the creation of several regional and local banks.
**1913:** The company's first international branch is opened in London.
**1982:** The CIC Group nationalizes CIC and its regional banks; the state-owned insurer Groupe des Assurances Nationales (GAN) becomes a new shareholder in the company.
**1998:** CIC is listed on the Paris Stock Exchange.
**2008:** CIC acquires Citibank's banking operations in Germany.

By 1987 Campagnie Financière de CIC owned all of the capital of its banking subsidiaries. The French government then transferred all of its remaining shares in the regional banks to the company. In 1990 the company merged with Banque de l'Union Européenne. This merger formed Compagnie Financière de CIC et de l'Union Européenne, which used the name Union Européenne de CIC.

### PRIVATIZATION

In 1996 the French government announced plans to privatize CIC. The sale ended up being postponed by three months because although two offers for the company had been made, neither offer was high enough. This would have caused a serious capital loss for Européenne de CIC's parent company, GAN. According to the *New York Times,* Jean Arthuis, France's finance minister, "was determined that the bank would be sold eventually."

In 1997 the French government continued its privatization plans by selling GAN and CIC. This sale followed GAN's FRF 7.5 billion ($1.2 billion) losses over a period of the previous two years, and its government assistance bailout of FRF 24 billion ($3.84 billion). As a result of the bailout, the European Commission set a June 1998 deadline for the privatization of both GAN and CIC.

In 1998 the CIC group was reorganized, transforming the bank into a public company, which was then listed on the Paris Stock Exchange. The government of France sold a 67 percent stake in Européenne de CIC to Banque Fédérative du Crédit Mutuel (BFCM). At the time of the sale, Crédit Mutuel stated that it planned to slightly increase the number of CIC employees over a period of five years. The sale sparked some controversy. Some critics believed that the government chose Crédit Mutuel as CIC's new owner in order to avoid trouble from CIC's unions and politicians. On the other hand, according to a 1998 article in the *Banker,* Dominique Strauss-Kahn, the economics, finance, and industry commissioner, "argued simply that Crédit Mutuel's offer—at FRF 13.3 billion ($2.2 billion) for two-thirds of the shares—was financially in line with the two alternative bids, and it matched or was better than the alternatives on all other criteria."

### INTERNATIONAL EXPANSION

CIC made a number of changes during the early part of the 21st century, many of which helped solidify the company's presence around the globe. In 2001 CIC bought Ubitrade Capital Markets from Ubitrade to manage the company's credit bond activities. Prior to this purchase, Ubitrade Capital Markets was already managing CIC's derivatives trading activities. During this same year GAN sold its 23 percent share in CIC to a subsidiary of Crédit Mutuel, Ventadour Investissement.

In 2004 CIC signed a Business Cooperation Agreement with the Bank of East Asia, Limited, (BEA) outlining plans for cooperation between the banks in Greater China. At the time, BEA was the largest independent bank in Hong Kong. This agreement allowed CIC to increase its international presence and meet increasing demands for corporate banking and services in China. During the same year, a cooperation agreement was also signed with Europe's banca Popolare di Milano, further strengthening CIC's international presence.

In November 2008 CIC entered an agreement to take control of the Cofidis, a consumer credit subsidiary of 3 Suisses International, which operated in nine countries throughout Europe. In December of the same year, CIC spent EUR 4.7 billion to purchase Citibank's banking operations in Germany, which had 339 branches and specialized in consumer credit. This acquisition added 3.4 million customers to CIC, as well as adding to its international operations.

Despite these opportunities for growth, CIC faced serious financial challenges during 2008. In the company's annual report, Lucas stated, "After the troubled financial context of 2007 came the year 2008, which was characterized by a financial and economic crisis without precedent. CIC and its majority shareholder Crédit Mutuel were not spared, but, thanks to the streamlining policy pursued over the last several years, it did not suffer the violent shocks that some of its counterparts did in France, Europe, and elsewhere." Although CIC may have fared better than some other companies, the negative financial impact was considerable. In addition to the company's net income dropping from EUR 1,204 million ($1,598.95 million) in 2007 to EUR 206 million ($273.57 million) in 2008, the company also suffered loan losses totaling EUR 630 million ($836.66 million).

According to an August 2009 press release, during this year CIC was "pursuing its strategy of growth, modernizations, quality improvement and extension of its branch network, to better serve its member-customers and its clientele of private individuals, professionals, and businesses." As part of the company's plan for growth, CIC announced its decision to issue 20 million new bonds. During this same year, CIC increased its holdings of Banque Marocaine du Commerce Exterieur (BMCE) from 15 percent to 19.9 percent. CIC had been working with this private bank since 2004 in the areas of retail and investment banking, focusing on markets in Africa. Also in 2009, CIC acquired the Spanish Banco Popular network in France. It was renamed CIC Iberbanco.

With its priority given to development in 2009, CIC's branch networks in France showed growth during the year. By August the company reported that within the span of one year, it had gained more than 5.5 million customers. Of those, over 5.2 million were via acquisitions. As a result of acquiring these new companies, outstanding customer loans and deposits increased as well. The company received a ranking of 431 on the *Fortune* Global 500 list for 2009, down from a ranking of 421 the previous year. However, the ranking was an improvement from a ranking of 461 in 2007.

As it looked to the future in a difficult economic context, CIC stated in a press release that it planned to pursue the commercial development of its branch network. It also hoped to enrich its range of products and services in all markets.

*Diane Milne*

## PRINCIPAL SUBSIDIARIES

CIC Banque BSD-CIN; CIC Banque CIO-BRO; CIC Banque Transatlantique; CIC Est; CIC Finance; CIC Lyonnaise de Banque; CIC Société Bordelaise; CM-CIC Securities; Groupe des Assurances du Crédit Mutuel (20.5%).

## PRINCIPAL DIVISIONS

Banking; Private Banking; Private Equity; Specialized Businesses; Insurance; Shared Services Companies.

## PRINCIPAL COMPETITORS

BNP Paribas S.A.; Crédit Agricole S.A.; Groupe BPCE; Natixis; Société Générale.

## FURTHER READING

"Banks and Banking," in *Encyclopedia of Modern Europe: Europe 1789–1914: Encyclopedia of the Age of Industry and Empire,* eds. John Merriman and Jay Winter, p. 170–76.

"CIC Privatization Is Called Off," *New York Times,* November 15, 1996.

Jack, Andrew, "CIC Sale to Mutualist Surprises," *Banker* 148, no. 867 (1998): 9.

Monegar, Francois, and Thiellet, Aurelie, "My Credit Profile: Banque Federative du Credit Mutuel 'A+/Stable/A–'," *Standard & Poor's,* March 17, 2010.

Moody's Investors Service. "Credit Opinion: Banque Fédérative du Crédit Mutuel," March 12, 2010.

Shearlock, Peter, "Foreign Legion Head French Privatisation," *Banker* 147 no. 859 (1997): 17–18.

# Crimson Exploration Inc.

**717 Texas Avenue**
**Suite 2900**
**Houston, Texas 77002**
**U.S.A.**
**Telephone: (713) 236-7400**
**Fax: (713) 236-4424**
**Web site: http://www.crimsonexploration.com**

*Public Company*
*Founded:* 1987 as Gallup Acquisitions Inc.
*Employees:* 74 (2009)
*Sales:* $112.4 million (2009)
*Stock Exchanges:* NASDAQ
*Ticker Symbol:* CXPO
*NAICS:* 211111 Crude Petroleum and Natural Gas
    Extraction

■ ■ ■

Crimson Exploration Inc. (Crimson) is an independent energy company. Its purpose is to acquire, exploit, explore, and develop natural gas and crude oil properties. The company operates in Texas, Colorado, and Mississippi. Generally, properties have proved reserves (demonstrating a reasonable geological certainty of recoverable product) of oil or natural gas, and include both developed and undeveloped properties. In 2010 the majority of the company's productive wells (88 out of 134) were in East Texas.

Crimson's operations consist of four geographic areas. The East Texas region includes 1,600 million cubic feet equivalent (MMcfe) of proved reserves and 17,300 acres in San Augustine and Sabine counties. This region was acquired in 2008 and 2009. The Southeast Texas region includes 27,100 MMcfe of proved reserves and 27,100 acres in Liberty, Madison, and Grimes counties. The South Texas region includes 49,200 MMcfe of proved reserves and 90,200 acres in Bee, Brooks, Lavaca, DeWitt, Zapata, Webb, and Matagorda counties. The Colorado and Other region includes 5,200 MMcfe of proved reserves and 16,900 acres in Adams County, Colorado, and a minor crude oil property in Mississippi.

## A COMPANY OF MANY NAMES

Crimson Exploration was incorporated in 1987 as Gallup Acquisitions Inc. The company was first headquartered in Baton Rouge, Louisiana. In 1992 the company changed its name to First Preference Fund, Inc., and that same year to Gulfwest Oil Company (Gulfwest), incorporating in Texas. Name changes aside, it was not until 1993 that the company began acquiring properties for the exploration and development of oil and natural gas. The company's business plan consisted of four items. The first goal was to establish a base of producing properties to provide cash flow. Once that was done, the company hoped to enhance the value and accelerate the rate of return on producing properties. If these first two steps were successful, Gulfwest would then acquire additional producing properties and work to expand the daily operation of properties for effective and profitable management.

In June 1993 Gulfwest completed its first initial public offering (IPO), generating $2.2 million. The company was listed on the NASDAQ SmallCap Market and the Boston Stock Exchange. Using the net proceeds, Gulfwest purchased interests in 57 oil fields in East Texas and a 37.5 percent ownership of a natural gas pipeline system.

Soon after its IPO, Gulfwest embarked on an aggressive growth strategy. In 1994 Gulfwest doubled its holdings, buying interests in undeveloped land, pipeline, and oil and gas properties. In 1995 Gulfwest acquired Petrolinn Oil and Gas, adding proved oil and gas reserves estimated at 1.6 billion barrels of oil and 2.7 billion cubic feet of natural gas. By the end of 1996, Gulfwest had working interests in 450 wells with proved reserves of 3.6 million barrels of oil and 8.0 million MMcfe of natural gas.

Gulfwest's growth strategy carried substantial risk. Except for the first acquisition in 1993, all purchases were financed with long-term debt, which increased from $2 million to $13 million between 1996 and 1997. Gulfwest's CEO, Marshall A. Smith III, intensified efforts to increase daily production to earn enough to continue operations. However, in 1997, long-term debt was refinanced to extend due dates to 2000. Arthur Andersen, the company's auditor, resigned its services due to a disagreement in which Arthur Andersen cited the company as a "going concern." This indicated that there was substantial doubt that the company would be able to continue for a reasonable period of time.

## DELISTING AND PRIVATIZATION: 1998–99

By 1998 Gulfwest had yet to record a profitable year due mostly to the high cost of interest on its long-term debt. Also in 1998 one of Gulfwest's properties was determined to be overvalued, and the company recorded a $2.3 million impairment charge, an amount that exceeded that year's sales. Gulfwest sold off two subsidiaries, and management determined to focus on exploration and exploitation of natural gas instead of crude oil, reducing the risk of price fluctuations. At the

time, Gulfwest's reserves consisted of 51 percent natural gas and 49 percent crude oil. Management also decided to expand exploration and exploitation capabilities rather than going the traditional route of acquiring properties with proved reserves. Finally, the company announced its decision to discontinue distributing dividends on its common stock.

Marshall determined that Gulfwest's indebtedness would hinder its future, and so he sought outside capital. Gulfwest was delisted from the NASDAQ SmallCap market and the Boston Stock Exchange due to its failure to maintain minimum financial standards. In response, major stockholder J. Virgil Waggoner converted his promissory notes from the company to common stock, an action that gained Waggoner a 78.2 percent share of the total company, as well as primary ownership rights and sole voting rights.

Although Gulfwest's indebtedness had been identified as a hindrance, the company pursued another major acquisition, purchasing all of Pozo Resources Inc. (Pozo) interests in oil and gas leases and related wells and equipment in Colorado and north Texas. The purchase price of $10.5 million was financed by long-term debt and preferred stock.

## BRIEF PROFITABILITY: 2000–01

Increased production from the previous year's acquisitions and higher commodity prices contributed to a 233 percent increase in revenue in 2000 from the previous year. This increase in revenue resulted in a positive net income of $353,000.

Gulfwest continued its focus on increasing its natural gas reserves. By the end of 2001, reserves constituted 53 percent natural gas and 47 percent crude oil. In order to more accurately describe the company's activities, the name Gulfwest Oil was changed to Gulfwest Energy Inc.

The year 2001 again saw increased revenue and profitability, primarily from new properties and gas production from developed properties. Two acquisitions in Texas and Louisiana added proved reserves of 1.2 million barrels of oil and 9.5 billion cubic feet of natural gas. The purchase price of $15 million was arranged with a combination of notes payable, preferred stock, cash, warrants, and common stock. By the end of 2001, the company had $26 million in long-term debt.

## NEW OWNERSHIP, NEW NAME: 2002–06

Increased interest costs on debt and hedging activities caused the company to return to the red in 2002 and

## KEY DATES

**1987:** Gallup Acquisitions Inc. formed.
**1993:** Company changes name to Gulfwest Oil Company and completes initial public offering on the NASDAQ Smallcap Market and Boston Stock Exchange.
**1998:** Gulfwest is privatized and relocated to Houston, Texas.
**1999:** NASDAQ and Boston Stock Exchange delist Gulfwest's stock.
**2004:** Private equity affiliate of Oaktree Capital Management (OCMGW) buys controlling interest in Gulfwest and renames the company Crimson Exploration, Inc.
**2009:** Crimson generates $94 million in public offering.

2003. The company cited the inability to obtain new capital as the reason for the lack of new development. Debt totaled $43 million and came due within the year, resulting in a penalty fee in 2003. Hedging activities, the practice of selling gas and oil in the future at fixed prices, resulted in a loss of $1.6 million in 2002.

Gulfwest's inability to generate new capital was apparently the cause of an unfinished merger in 2003. In July 2003 Gulfwest and Starlight Corporation of Denver signed a letter of agreement to merge. The merger would have resulted in a company with combined resources of 95 billion cubic feet equivalent (Bcfe) of oil and gas reserves. The merger was subject to the approval of Gulfwest's debt holders agreeing to financing. Instead of pursuing the merger, Gulfwest worked to recapitalize the company for future growth.

In 2004 Gulfwest renegotiated its largest loan of $26 million, paying off $15.7 million, and the rest was forgiven. At that time, the company also negotiated with an affiliate of the private equity firm Oaktree Capital Management, OCMGW Capital (OCMGW), to purchase 45 million shares, representing a controlling interest of Gulfwest. Waggoner still held a large portion of the company and remained an executive, owning 38 percent of outstanding common stock. In 2005 OCMGW purchased 81,000 preferred shares for $40.5 million, and the proceeds were used to retire the remaining debt. (Preferred stock, although somewhat more flexible, carries similar obligations to long-term debt.) Instead of making interest payments, Gulfwest was now obligated to pay dividends on preferred stock.

In conjunction with the recapitalization, Gulfwest changed its name to Crimson Exploration. The company reincorporated from Texas to Delaware so that OCMGW could take advantage of favorable antitakeover laws in that state. Wells Fargo approved a credit line of $100 million for Crimson, subject to the company meeting financial criteria (covenants). Management was largely replaced. Waggonner, Marshall, and other shareholders were issued promissory notes or preferred stock in exchange for their ownership of the company. The new CEO and chairman of the board was Allan D. Keel.

While Crimson attempted to acquire properties in 2005 and 2006, all bids ultimately failed to close. Hurricane Rita, which caused over $11 billion in damage to the U.S. Gulf Coast in late September 2005, somewhat offset production in 2005, but higher prices brought increased revenue. However, obligations on preferred stock resulted in net losses for 2005 and 2006.

## ACQUISITIONS, RESTRUCTURING, AND PUBLIC OFFERING: 2007 AND BEYOND

In 2007 and 2008, Crimson purchased a package of properties located in South Texas and South Louisiana from EXCO Resources, producing a sixfold increase in the asset base. Revenues increased eightfold, from $22 million to $187 million. However, the company also took on $260 million of debt to finance the acquisition, producing a thirtyfold increase in long-term obligations. Interest expense was once again the reason for a net loss of $4.9 million in 2007. The full benefit of the EXCO acquisition was not realized until 2008. Despite its obligations for preferred stock and interest charges, Crimson recorded a 2008 profit of $42 million.

Crimson restructured the company by geographical location. The new structure consisted of operations located in South Texas, Southeast Texas, East Texas, and Colorado and Other. South Texas and Southeast Texas contained 92 percent of Crimson's proved reserves, with 97,800 acres and 76.3 Bcfe proved reserves. The company sold its interests in Louisiana to a private company for $7.3 million.

On December 22, 2009, Crimson began trading on the NASDAQ Global Market with the ticker symbol CXPO. The offering generated $94 million, making a dent in long-term debt. While the proceeds were quite a bit lower than the $165 million the company had expected to earn, investors were somewhat bullish on Crimson's stock. Crimson's major stockholder, OCMGW, no longer owned a controlling interest, with 40 percent of the company's common stock. While prices on gas and crude oil were lower, resulting in decreased revenues, Crimson paid off some debt and reduced costs. Interest charges, preferred dividends, and hedging activities totaling $52 million contributed to a 2009 net loss of $39 million.

The future for Crimson Exploration depended on its conservative growth combined with disciplined hedging activities. In early 2010, Crimson's earnings were lower than 2009 due to decreased productivity after the sale of noncore assets in Louisiana. However, Crimson had built an enviable asset base of properties that could banked on. Gulfwest/Crimson has had access to capital and financial markets over the years due to this, but found itself unable to grow and capitalize these assets because of its high leverage and lack of cash flow. Commodity prices for crude oil and natural gas are also volatile, leading to large variations in hedging gains and losses. Crimson's successful future depended on reducing its leverage to gain flexibility in developing its resources and using those resources to drill its wells and sell its products.

*Sara K. Huter*

## PRINCIPAL DIVISIONS

Colorado and Other; East Texas; South Texas; Southeast Texas.

## PRINCIPAL COMPETITORS

Anadarko Petroleum Corporation; Cabot Oil & Gas Corporation; Delta Petroleum Corporation; GMX Resources Inc.; Parallel Petroleum Corporation.

## FURTHER READING

"Arthur Andersen Disagrees with Client on 'Going Concern' Qualification," *Accounting Today* 10, no. 11 (1996): 14.

"Crimson Exploration Announces Addition to Management Team," *Business Wire,* May 24, 2010.

"Crimson Exploration Inc. Acquires South Texas Assets from EXCO Resources, Inc. for $289 Million and Refinances Existing Debt," *Business Wire,* May 8, 2007.

"Crimson Exploration Inc. Announces Agreement to Sell Non-Core South Louisiana Assets," *Business Wire,* January 11, 2010.

"Crimson Exploration Inc. Announces Effects of Hurricane Rita," *Business Wire,* September 27, 2005.

"GulfWest and Starlight Sign Letter of Agreement for Merger," *Business Wire,* July 25, 2003.

# CSN Stores LLC

—■—

**800 Boylston Street, Suite 1600**
**Boston, Massachusetts 02199**
**U.S.A.**
**Telephone: (617) 880-8593**
**Toll Free: (800) 593-5251**
**Fax: (617) 880-8594**
**Web site: http://www.csnstores.com**

*Private Company*
*Founded:* 2002
*Employees:* 600 (est. 2010)
*Sales:* $250 million (est. 2010)
*NAICS:* 442110 Furniture Stores; 442210 Floor Covering Stores; 442299 All Other Home Furnishings Stores; 444130 Hardware Stores; 448210 Shoe Stores; 448320 Luggage and Leather Goods Stores; 453210 Office Supplies and Stationery Stores; 453910 Pet and Pet Supplies Stores; 453920 Art Dealers; 453998 All Other Miscellaneous Store Retailers (except Tobacco Stores); 454111 Electronic Shopping

■ ■ ■

CSN Stores LLC is a privately held online retailer focusing on home and office goods. Within a period of a few short years, the Boston-based company has grown to become a top online U.S. retailer of home and office goods, with more than 200 online boutiques under the umbrella of CSN. Products from CSN Stores range from furniture and appliances to baby products and greenhouses, and they are available online to customers in the United States, Canada, the United Kingdom, and Germany. New niche stores are being added continuously, increasing the product range of CSN. All products are drop-shipped to the customer, and the company's entire supply chain is outsourced, with the exception of a warehouse which accepts returns. These products are then resold at a deep discount or are donated to charity.

CSN offers more than 1.5 million product choices from over 4,000 leading brands at competitive prices, and boasts more than seven million visitors to its sites each month. CSN believes that its winning combination of selection, service, and savings is what sets the company apart from other online retailers. The company's tagline, "Shop Easy," sums up the type of retail experience it strives to offer each customer.

In 2010 CSN Stores had grown into a $250 million company with over 200 shopping sites and more than 600 employees. Most of the sites are named by the main product or styles they sell, such as Luggage.com, AllModern.com, WritingDesksAndMore.com, Cookware.com, and BedroomFurniture.com.

## BUILDING A NEW COMPANY: 2002–07

When the company began in 2002, there were only two employees and one online store. These employees, Cornell classmates Niraj Shah and Steve Conine, were the founders of the company and as of 2010 were CSN's CEO and chairman, respectively.

## COMPANY PERSPECTIVES

The mission of CSN Stores is to build a lasting organization that succeeds and grows by making online shopping rewarding for its customers, partners, and employees.

When they co-founded CSN Stores, Shah and Conine were not new to the idea of establishing a company. Previously, they cofounded Spinners Incorporated, an information technology (IT) services firm that offered services to a number of *Fortune* 500 companies. They sold the company to iXL, a publicly traded global technology consulting firm, in 1998, and remained as senior executives there. Shah served as chief operating officer (COO) of iXL, and Conine was COO of the company's London office. While Shah was COO iXL's revenue tripled to $480 million. Later, Shah and Conine worked together to found Simplify Mobile, a software company that provided mobile phone management solutions. They sold the company in 2001.

When Shah and Conine decided to launch another new company, their research revealed that many small e-commerce companies were growing at rates of 20 to 30 percent each year, without using sophisticated technology or marketing. Shah and Conine therefore decided to take advantage of the Internet marketing boom. While many items were already being sold through well-established online stores, furniture and housewares were mostly being sold through very small or ineffective outlets that did not obtain prime space in search engine results. The partners determined that as people became more comfortable with shopping online, they would begin making larger purchases, such as furniture. By establishing an effective way to sell such items, and putting their background in the IT field to use, they believed they could set themselves apart from the smaller, ineffective existing online stores.

Using their own finances, Shah and Conine launched CSN Stores with a single online boutique, RacksandStands.com. The two partners ran the company themselves, without any employees. During its first year, CSN reported $425,000 in sales. In the company's second year, three additional Web-based stores were added to CSN, and an additional nine stores were added in the third year.

Over the next several years, the company continued to add online niche stores to its collection. Based on its growth between 2004 and 2007, CSN Stores was

ranked the fourth fastest-growing private company in the state of Massachusetts by *Boston Business Journal.* In 2007 CSN's annual growth rate reached 83 percent and company sales exceeded $202 million. These sales figures were an 87 percent increase over the previous year and an increase of 638 percent over sales in 2004.

## REACHING INTERNATIONAL MARKETS: 2008

In May 2008 *Internet Retailer*'s Top 500 guide to the largest retail Web sites named CSN Stores as the third-largest housewares and home furnishings e-retailer in the United States. The company also ranked in the top 20 in the categories of fastest-growing online retailer and online retailers with the largest increase in sales. J. P. Werline, a consultant with *Downtown e-Commerce* in Westchester, Pennsylvania, specializing in market and search-engine optimization, told the magazine regarding CSN, "I look at their list of stores and I'm floored. They're the sleeping giant that a lot of people don't know about."

During that same year, CSN began offering access to its online stores to Canadian customers in response to demand from consumers in that country. According to an August 21, 2008, article in the *Boston Globe,* Shah stated, "We believe Canadian consumers have been underserved by their online shopping options. But now we can give Canadians the same wide selection of products, well-trained customer service counselors and savings opportunities that our US customers enjoy."

Reaching into Canada was just the beginning of CSN's international expansion. In December 2008 the company announced the availability of its goods in the United Kingdom. CookwareEssentials.co.uk was the company's first Web site to offer products to customers outside the United States and Canada. At the time of the announcement, CSN stated that it planned to continue its expansion into the United Kingdom and other European countries, such as Germany, over the coming year, including the launch of CSN Stores' headquarters in Galway, Ireland, which opened in January 2009.

The customer support center in Ireland provided 200 new jobs to the people of Galway. Conine noted, "Eventually, we hope to become a one-stop shop for U.K. consumers, as we are in the U.S. As we continue to build relationships with more U.K. suppliers, we hope to expand into new categories and launch site after site, as we did in the U.S. when we started our operations in 2002." The site's advanced navigation capabili-

## KEY DATES

**2002:** CSN Stores begins with two employees and one online store.

**2007:** CSN Stores' annual growth rate reaches 83 percent; company sales exceed $202 million.

**2008:** CSN Stores is named the third-largest housewares and home furnishings e-retailer in the United States in *Internet Retailer*'s Top 500 guide of the largest retail Web sites.

**2009:** CSN Stores opens its first overseas headquarters in Galway, Ireland.

**2010:** CSN Stores shows 60 percent increase in sales during the first quarter as compared to the same period of the previous year; company sales exceed $250 million.

ties were intended to make it easier to use than many other sites available to customers in this region.

## CHANGING WITH THE TIMES: 2009

In April 2009 CSN Stores launched www.Fitness EquipmentAndMore.com as a way for people to reduce stress and cut down on gym memberships during a period of economic uncertainty. The purpose of the site was to introduce healthier lifestyles at home and to contribute to consumers' overall wellness. The site included fitness and exercise equipment, as well as a blog updating visitors to the site on fitness trends. Other sites introduced during the year included CSNOffice. com, FlooringSelect.com, WheelchairSelect.com, and KuecneundHaushalt.de.

Also in response to changing economic times, CSN recognized that many consumers were limiting their use of credit cards. In response, the company introduced payment option that allowed secure cash purchases to be made using online banking, as is used to pay other household bills. The secure bank-to-bank transactions eliminated the need for a credit card to make purchases and avoided personal information being transmitted over the Internet.

In September 2009 Walmart.com introduced "Walmart Marketplace," which included products from other online retailers, including CSN Stores. This added the availability of approximately one million new products to Wal-Mart's online customers, who were able to purchase items from CSN and other companies through Wal-Mart's checkout process.

## INCREASING AVENUES OF ADVERTISEMENT: 2010

As is true with any company operating during times of financial crisis, CSN Stores looked into new avenues for revenue. In January 2010 CSN Stores partnered with Google AdSense, which placed text ads on Web pages, as an additional source of revenue. Many online stores had not used this strategy, as it was seen as advertising for the competition. However, this service was gaining popularity in the world of e-commerce as a way to earn revenue from those visiting the Web sites. During the initial trial, CSN Stores's marketing research analyst, Sean Anderson, said the company was encouraged by the potential revenue stream the ads would provide.

Also in 2010, the company introduced CSN Local, "an online advertising program designed to point shoppers on the various CSN online stores to local retailers if they are not buying from CSN." CSN Local's vice president of strategic initiatives, John Mulliken, said in the April 17, 2010, issue of *Furniture-Today*, "The best way we can serve our consumers is to work with local retailers to drive all of CSN's visitors who don't want to purchase something online into the right local showroom." He explained that this would cause customers to return to CSN as a trusted source in the future when they are looking for furniture or decor.

## LOOKING TO THE FUTURE

Increasing sales of bedroom and dining furniture between the summer of 2009 and the spring of 2010 were encouraging to CSN as an indication of improving consumer confidence. High first quarter sales for 2010 showed a 64 percent increase in CSN's sales for the same period of the previous year. Despite the slow economic recovery around the world, CSN had an excellent six-month period. Growth in several of the store's categories had increased by more than 200 percent during the previous 12 months, which allowed the company to hire 80 new employees during the first three months of 2010, bringing the total number of staffers to more than 600.

"This growth follows more than 18 months of investment by the company, focused on expanding CSN's North American business, establishing its European headquarters in Galway, Ireland, and launching several sites for customers in the U.K. and Germany," according to a *PR Newswire* article in April 2010. Categories that had the greatest impact on the company's growth during the beginning of 2010 were fitness equipment, which increased by 1,200 percent, recreation room gear (350% increase), bedding/mattresses (250% increase), upholstery (150% increase), and youth/toys (110% increase). Most of the company's other categories exceeded sales expectations, including accents, cookware, luggage, rugs, and office furniture.

Shah and Conine's original vision for CSN Stores was to have hundreds (or thousands) of niche sites. This strategy worked well for the company, and the future held more of the same. In order to stay relevant in the world of online retailing, CSN endeavored to continually offer customers greater selection, faster shipping, more available pictures of the product lines, and any other factor that would make shopping with the company easier and more interesting. According to a *PR Newswire* article in March 2010, Shah stated, "We have invested significantly in our expansion during the recession and the recovery to maximize our growth in 2010 and beyond."

*Diane Milne*

## PRINCIPAL DIVISIONS

Baby & Kids; Furniture; Health & Fitness; Home Decor; Home Improvement; Housewares; International; Outdoor Living; Pet; School & Office Supplies; Shoes, Bags, & Luggage.

## PRINCIPAL COMPETITORS

Cost Plus, Inc.; Cymax Stores, Inc.; Hayneedle, Inc.; IVG Stores; Pier 1 Imports, Inc.; Williams-Sonoma, Inc.

## FURTHER READING

"CSN Stores' 2010 Sales Up 60% Over 2009," *PR Newswire,* March 12, 2010.

"CSN Stores Enjoys Its Best Q1 Ever," *PR Newswire,* April 14, 2010.

"CSN Stores Ranked in Top Tier of Massachusetts' Fastest-Growing Businesses," *News Blaze,* April 18, 2008.

Gardener, Elizabeth, "One Size Fits All: CSN's Recipe for Success: Niche the Sites, Unify the Back-End," *Internet Retailer,* June 2008.

"Mulliken Joins CSN Stores as Strategic Initiatives VP," *Furniture-Today,* April 17, 2010, p. 34.

Reidy, Chris, "CSN Stores Courts Canadian Customers," *Boston Globe,* August 21, 2008.

Zmuda, Natalie, "E-tailers Seek Revenue Boost from Ads That May Even Tout Rivals; Target, CSN Stores, Walmart Turn Their Sites into Media with Sponsored Links," *Advertising Age* 81, no. 10 (2010): 2.

# CVR Energy Corporation

2277 Plaza Drive
Suite 500
Sugar Land, Texas 77479
U.S.A.
Telephone: (281) 207-3200
Web site: http://www.cvrenergy.com

*Public Company*
*Founded:* 1906 as The National Refining Company
*Employees:* 667
*Sales:* $3.14 billion (2009)
*Stock Exchanges:* New York
*Ticker Symbol:* CVI
*NAICS:* 324110 Crude petroleum refineries; 325311
    Nitrogenous fertilizer materials manufacturing

■ ■ ■

CVR Energy Corporation is a publicly traded holding company for subsidiaries Coffeyville Resources Refining & Marketing, LLC and Coffeyville Resources Nitrogen Fertilizers, LLC. Coffeyville Resources Refining & Marketing refines crude oil into transportation products such as gasoline, diesel fuels, and propane. Coffeyville Resources Nitrogen Fertilizers produces ammonia and urea ammonium nitrate (UAN), both used as fertilizers to promote plant growth. While the company's headquarters are located in Sugar Land, Texas, all of the company's physical plant operations are located in Coffeyville, Kansas.

## THE NATIONAL REFINING COMPANY EXPANDS

CVR Energy's history dates back to 1906 when the National Refining Company built a refinery in Coffeyville, Kansas. The refinery was part of the company's effort to expand operations westward. At the time the National Refining Company was the second-largest oil company in the United States (Standard Oil was the largest). Headquartered in Cleveland, Ohio, the National Refining Company refined crude oil into kerosene, which was used by most households and cities to power lamps for lighting.

J. I. Lamprecht, a former banker, founded the National Oil Company in 1880. When he incorporated in 1884 he renamed the company the National Refining Company. Lamprecht's goal was to offer his customers a higher-quality product than what was offered by his competitors and command a higher price as well. In its early years, the company expanded mostly in the Cleveland area. In 1897 the company bought a refining plan in Findlay, Ohio. The Coffeyville refinery was its first venture outside Ohio. The National Refining Company chose the Kansas site because of protections afforded independent oil producers by laws passed in 1905 by the Kansas legislature.

The National Refining Company built the Coffeyville refinery on 75 acres donated by the Citizens Commercial Club. The company invested $250,000 in the construction of the plant. In its first year the refinery employed 75 people and processed 2,500 barrels of crude oil. While this might seem like much by modern standards, it was the largest independent

## COMPANY PERSPECTIVES

At CVR Energy, we strive to safely optimize quality output, enhance the value of customers' operations based upon their specific needs, increase shareholder value, and recognize and reward the creativity and initiative of our employees who help us reach these goals.

Our employees take personal responsibility for making success happen and they do it with pride. We have an entrepreneurial environment, where leadership and new ideas are recognized and rewarded 24 hours a day, seven days a week. With this kind of environment, you will not find our people waiting for instruction. Instead, they take the initiative, decide what needs to be done, and then find a way to do it even better.

and pursued an ambitious industrial policy at home to support its military abroad. As part of those efforts the government built an aviation gasoline plant at the National Refining Company's Coffeyville refinery. The new plant brought with it the latest in refining technology. The upgrades included a catalytic cracking unit, a feed preparation unit, a hydrofluoric acid alkylation unit, and an isomerization unit. A catalytic cracking unit uses a catalyst or chemical agent to aid in the process of breaking down the heavier molecules of crude oil into lighter products. A hydrofluoric acid alkylation unit produces the high-octane elements of gasoline. The isomerization unit reforms a chemical substance into a similar substance with different chemical properties so that it can be used for other purposes. The upgrades enabled the company to produce quality high-octane fuel for both automobiles and airplanes employed in the war effort. The upgrades also allowed the National Refining Company to significantly increase yield while lessening the hazards endemic to thermal cracking. Also, as part of its continued capacity growth, the refinery connected to the Great Lakes Pipeline. Capacity grew to 20,000 barrels a day.

refinery in Kansas at that time. In addition to kerosene, the refinery produced gasoline, lubricating oils, fuel oil wax, and machine oils. Over the next few years capacity quickly grew to 5,000 barrels a day. The development of thermal cracking enabled the company to increase production significantly. Cracking is a chemical process of breaking up (cracking) the complex organic molecules of crude oil and its by-products into less complex or lighter molecules. This cracking process allows refineries to derive or distill (from crude oi) lighter petroleum products such as gasoline and gases such as methane, ethane, ethylene, propane, and propylene. Thermal cracking uses extreme heat or steam to distill the end products.

### TECHNOLOGY BRINGS GROWTH

During World War I, the National Refining Company, including the Coffeyville refinery, joined the war effort by supplying lubricating oils to the military. In 1920 J. I. Lamprecht died after an operation for appendicitis, and his son, W. H. Lamprecht, took over the company. Later that decade, the company developed a patent for refining crude oil into bright stock lubricating oils. Bright stock lubricating oils are blended with neutral oils to produce automotive engine lubricating oils. The company also moved into the octane-enhanced leaded gasoline market. The capacity of the refinery rose to 9,000 barrels a day.

The company took a major leap in technology in the 1940s. The United States had joined World War II

### THE COOPERATIVE WAY

In 1944 The National Refining Company sold the Coffeyville refinery to the Cooperative Refinery Association (CRA). The CRA was founded in 1943 by five regional farm supply cooperatives who had joined together to help their members solve wartime shortages of petroleum products. The CRA started by acquiring and managing the Globe Oil Refinery and Pipeline, and it made its first steps toward expansion by purchasing the Coffeyville refinery of the National Refining Company.

By the 1950s the Coffeyville refinery's capacity had grown to 24,000 barrels a day. The increase in capacity was mostly due to new facilities and expanded old ones. The CRA added a platformer unit, which was used to boost the octane rating of gasoline. The CRA also added a unifiner unit, which was used to produce jet fuel.

Over the next few decades CRA made several more efforts to modernize and improve operations. The company modernized the alkylation units. It also built an additional vacuum unit to aid in distillation and expanded the coking unit (part of the cracking process). CRA also built a wastewater treatment facility to aid with operations and reduce the refinery's environmental negative impact. By the end of the 1970s capacity at the refinery had grown to 45,000 barrels a day.

In 1982 CRA merged with Farmland Industries to become its Farmland Petroleum Division. Like the CRA, Farmland Industries was formed as a cooperative

## KEY DATES

**1906:** National Refinery Company builds refinery in Coffeyville, Kansas.

**1940:** Government builds aviation gasoline facility at Coffeyville plant to support war effort.

**1944:** National Refining Company sells refinery to the Cooperative Refinery Association (CRA).

**1982:** Farmland Industries merges CRA into petroleum operations.

**2004:** Coffeyville Resources, LLC purchases refinery and adjacent nitrogen plant.

**2005:** Goldman Sachs & Co. and Kelso & Company purchase Coffeyville Group Holdings, LLC.

**2007:** CVR Energy consummates successful IPO.

to help small farmers join together and increase their economic power in the marketplace. Farmland Industries began as the Union Oil Company, a cooperative of smaller oil companies. Howard A. Cowden founded the Union Oil Company in Kansas City, Missouri. Cowden was an experienced hand in the cooperative movement having been the secretary for the Missouri Farmers Association (MFA). Under Cowden's leadership the Union Oil Company expanded into a wide range of products, including automobile accessories, paint, and twine. It sold all its products under the CO-OP brand. After its product line had diversified, the company changed its name to the Consumers Cooperative Association (CCA) in 1935. Even with the many different lines of products, the company was still predominantly an oil company, and CCA realized that it needed a refinery. In 1939 CCA built a refinery in Phillipsburg, Kansas, and by the end of the 1940s CCA had become a significant independent oil company.

One of CCA's most profitable ventures was fertilizer. To meet the post-World War II demand for fertilizer, CCA built a nitrogen plan in 1954. The substantial cost of the plant brought the company to the edge of bankruptcy, but CCA managed to make it through the financial crisis, and by 1958 CCA's revenues were over $100 million. The cooperative ranked 327th among the *Fortune* 500. While petroleum products had dominated the business in the past, accounting for 70 percent of revenues, fertilizer soon took over. The fertilizer business pushed petroleum down to below 50 percent of CCA's revenues. As a result, the cooperative increasingly became more focused on farm

supply and services. In 1961 Cowden retired as CCA's chief executive and handed the reigns over to Homer Young, who had been with the cooperative since 1931. Soon after Young took over, CCA changed its name to Farmland Industries, Inc.

While the 1970s were good years for farmers, the economic slump of the early 1980s brought difficulties. In 1982, the same year it merged CRA into its operations, Farmland Industries posted a loss for the first time in its history. The company managed to return to fiscal health in the latter half of the decade. Under Farmland's guardianship, the Coffeyville refinery discontinued production of lubricating oil and expanded production in other areas. Farmland started producing diesel fuel after adding a hydrodesulfurization unit to its facility. The company also expanded operations with a new catalytic cracking unit, a second crude unit, and a third vacuum unit. By the end of the 1990s the capacity of the refinery increased to 100,000 barrels a day.

The new millennium brought another time of economic difficulties. Farmland showed a loss of $29.5 million for fiscal year 2000. Robert Honse took over as CEO of Farmland Industries that year, and Honse instituted cost-cutting measures, including eliminating hundreds of jobs and shedding assets. Honse's efforts, while somewhat effective, could not prevent Farmland from having to file for Chapter 11 bankruptcy in 2002. Even before bankruptcy Farmland had been trying to unload the Coffeyville refinery. The cooperative was unwilling to invest the funds necessary to upgrade the plant to meet new specifications instituted by the Environmental Protection Agency (EPA).

## BIG DEAL MAKING BRINGS REBIRTH

In 2003, Pegasus Capital Advisors, LP, a private equity fund in Greenwich, Connecticut, created an affiliate named Coffeyville Resources, LLC (Coffeyville Resources). Pegasus created Coffeyville Resources as part of its leverage buyout process to purchase assets from Farmland and manage them. Coffeyville Resources offered $281 million for the Coffeyville refinery and an adjacent fertilizer plant, which Farmland built in 2000. The offer was part of a bankruptcy auction, but Coffeyville Resources faced no opposition. The bankruptcy court quickly approved the purchase plan. Coffeyville Resources paid $22 million in cash, $85 million in working capital, and $174 million in assumed liabilities for the complex. During bankruptcy proceedings, the EPA and the Kansas Department of Health and Environment (KDHE) claimed that the refinery has been in violation of the federal Clean Air Act and state air pollution control regulations since the 1990s.

Farmland had failed to install the appropriate emissions controls or best available control technology (BACT) when it increased the refinery's capacity from 71,000 to 125,000 barrels per day. As part of the purchase, Coffeyville Resources had to agree to bring two refining facilities formerly owned by Farmland Industries into compliance with federal and state environmental laws.

In early 2005 Coffeyville Resources registered for an initial public offering (IPO), but the company quickly withdrew its IPO registration when Goldman Sachs & Co. (Goldman Sachs Funds) and Kelso & Company (Kelso Funds) stepped forward with an offer for the company. Goldman Sachs Funds and Kelso Funds formed a partnership under the name Coffeyville Acquisition, LLC (Coffeyville Acquisition) in order to completed the purchase.

In September 2006 Coffeyville Acquisition formed CVR Energy, Inc. Coffeyville Acquisition transferred all its businesses to CVR Energy in exchange for CVR Energy's common stock.

Kansas experienced massive flooding in June 2007. The flood submerged the Coffeyville refinery and caused a spill of over 1,000 barrels or about 40,000 gallons. The company also shut down its nitrogen plant temporarily until the flooding subsided. The spill and shutdown caused a spike in the price of unleaded gasoline on the wholesale market.

In October 2007 CVR Energy consummated its IPO. As of December 2009, approximately 64 percent of CVR's outstanding shares were owned by Goldman Sachs Funds (28%) and Kelso Funds (36%). The remainder of shares were publicly traded on the New York Stock Exchange. CVR moved its headquarters to Sugar Land, Texas, but kept its operations in Coffeyville, Kansas. By the end of 2007 the refinery reached a capacity of 108,000 barrels a day. In 2009 petroleum and fertilizer represented 94 percent and 6 percent of revenues respectively. The formation of CVR Energy was a return to the company's roots, focusing mainly on refining oil and using the latest technology to offer high-quality petroleum products to its customers. With U.S. residents continuing to use large amounts of oil and related products for their energy and transportation needs, CVR Energy was well poised to meet supply with demand.

*Aaron Hauser*

## PRINCIPAL SUBSIDIARIES

CL JV Holdings, LLC; Coffeyville Nitrogen Fertilizers, Inc.; Coffeyville Pipeline, Inc.; Coffeyville Refining & Marketing, Inc.; Coffeyville Resources, LLC; Coffeyville Resources Crude Transportation, Inc.; Coffeyville Terminal, Inc.; CVR Partners, LP; CVR Special GP, LLC.

## PRINCIPAL COMPETITORS

Conoco Phillips; Frontier El Dorado Refining Company; Gary-Williams Energy Corporation; Koch Industries, Inc.; National Cooperative Refinery Association; Valero Energy Corporation.

## FURTHER READING

Eckart, Ben, "The National Refining Company," enarco.com.

"Farmland Completes Sale of Refinery and Plant," *New York Times*, March 5, 2004, p 3.

Fite, Gilbert Courtland, *Beyond the Fence Rows: A History of Farmland Industries, Inc., 1929–1978*. Columbia: University of Missouri Press, 1978.

Piotrowski, Matt, "In Latest Foray, Goldman Sachs Takes Chance With Kansas Refinery," *Oil Daily*, July 15, 2005.

Vardi, Nathan, "Slick; Goldman Sachs Had It Made After It Bought a Refinery in Small-town Kansas. Then Came the Flood," *Forbes*, September 17, 2007, p. 50A.

# Dai-Ichi Life Insurance Company, Limited

———■———

13-1, Yurakucho 1-chome, Chiyoda-ku
Tokyo, 100-8411
Japan
Telephone: (81) 3-3216-1211
Fax: (81) 3-5221-3971
Web site: http://www.dai-ichi-life.co.jp

*Public Company*
*Founded:* 1902
*Employees:* 54,276 (2009)
*Sales:* ¥2,904,336 million ($29.57 billion, 2009)
*Stock Exchanges:* Tokyo
*Ticker Symbol:* JP: 8750
*NAICS:* 524113 Direct Life Insurance Carriers

■ ■ ■

Dai-Ichi Life Insurance Company, Limited (Dai-Ichi), meaning "The First" Life Insurance Company, is based in Tokyo, Japan. Dai-Ichi offers life insurance, pension plans, asset management, and other insurance products. Serving over eight million policy holders, Dai-Ichi is over 100 years old and operates internationally in Europe, Asia, and North America.

On April 1, 2010, Dai-Ichi demutualized and offered shares of ownership on the Tokyo Stock Exchange, ending the company's long history as a mutual company. Dai-Ichi Mutual Life Insurance Company was renamed to Dai-Ichi Life Insurance Company, Limited.

## PIONEERING MUTUAL INSURANCE: 1902

In 1902 36-year-old Tsuneta Yano issued a pamphlet titled "Characteristics of My Company." These characteristics became the foundation for Japan's first mutual insurance company, the Dai-Ichi Mutual Life Insurance Company (Dai-Ichi).

Although there were insurance companies already in existence in Japan, Yano's concept of a mutual insurance company was the first of its kind. A mutual company is owned by its policyholders instead of shareholders. In the case of Dai-Ichi, this business model embraced the primary principle, "The Policyholder is Number One."

Yano remained as president of Dai-Ichi until 1938, when he began to relinquish his daily responsibilities in order to pursue his passion for statistics. He became a prominent actuarial expert in Japan, publishing mathematical tables ranging from multiplication tables to cologarithms (logarithms of reciprocal numbers) tables. Most notable were tables that converted British, Japanese, and American measures. Yano compiled one of the earliest mortality tables in Japan. Perhaps his most enduring contribution is as the original author of *Nippon, a Chartered Survey of Japan,* which is still updated and published today. In addition to his publications, Yano founded a number of institutions associated with insurance and served the Japanese government in the areas of education, public health, and welfare. Yano died in 1951 and was inducted into the Insurance Hall of Fame in 1970.

# COMPANY PERSPECTIVES

To maintain the management philosophy of "Customer First" that we have practiced since 1902, Dai-Ichi Life and Dai-Ichi Life Group will continue to reform in line with the times, aiming to create new value for people and achieve sustainable growth.

## NATURAL DISASTER AND WAR: 1920–55

The market for life insurance grew in Japan in the 1920s. On September 1, 1923, the Great Kanto Earthquake hit the southern regions of Tokyo and Yokohama. The disaster killed over 100,000 and destroyed 460,000 dwellings. This disaster created a demand for life insurance, as people grew more wary of unforeseen calamity. As Japan began preparing for war in the 1930s, the market for life insurance grew even more. By 1932 Dai-Ichi had become the second-largest life insurance company in Japan.

In 1938 Dai-Ichi moved its location to downtown Tokyo, famously the headquarters of General Douglas MacArthur during the occupation after World War II. General MacArthur's office has been preserved for public viewing. Reconstruction after World War II consisted not only of demilitarizing and restructuring the government but also reforming the country's market structure.

Prior to World War II, Japanese companies operated under the umbrella of the *zaibatsu,* combinations of cooperating companies led by banks. In 1937 the four leading *zaibatsu* controlled one-third of deposits, foreign trade, and heavy industries. Deemed as monopolies by the allied forces, the structures were dismantled. In addition, the *zaibatsu* were largely responsible for the buildup of the Japanese military, as alliances between government and company officials set the foundation for the *zaibatsu* to provide the capital, managerial skills, and raw materials.

Dai-Ichi Mutual was founded under the umbrella of Dai-Ichi Bank, Ltd., without *zaibatsu* ties until 1943, when it merged with Mitsui Bank, one of the most powerful banks in Japan. However, the merger was separated in 1948, after World War II. When allied forces dismantled the Japanese market structure, Dai-Ichi Mutual, without the strong historical foundation of the *zaibatsu,* was in a beneficial position by not having to make painful infrastructure changes. Both Dai-Ichi Bank and Dai-Ichi Mutual later became a part of one of

the six largest *keiretsu,* a structure similar to the *zaibatsu* but without the massive market power.

The market for life insurance was strong during the decades after the war as the nation's economy rebounded. Many life insurance companies modeled Dai-Ichi's structure as a mutual company, reinforcing Yano's first principle, "The Policyholder is Number One."

In 1950 Dai-Ichi's management demonstrated its principle of Social Trust by introducing the Public Health Award, established to honor organizations or individuals that contribute to public health and sanitation. Recipients were companies or individuals operating in areas ranging from medical treatment, environmental improvement, or welfare for the physically disabled. The award was regarded as very prestigious. In addition to recognition, recipients were awarded an audience with the Emperor and Empress.

## INTERNATIONAL EXPANSION

By 1960 Dai-Ichi Mutual was ready to expand internationally. However, Dai-Ichi found resistance, particularly in Asia, as tensions were strained in areas Japan had occupied during the war. In 1970 Dai-Ichi established the Foundation for the Advancement of Life Insurance in Asia (FALIA). FALIA offered education about insurance products through seminars and publications, with the ultimate goal of establishing international relationships.

Dai-Ichi expanded into the United States by first buying real estate. In 1975 Dai-Ichi established an office in New York City to study the U.S. insurance market, setting the stage for expanding into the U.S. market. In 1987 Dai-Ichi bought two-thirds of the Manhattan Citi-Corp Center. In 1990 Dai-Ichi capitalized the Lincoln Life Insurance Company, buying $312 million worth of preferred stock in the company, marking the first investment in a U.S. company for Dai-Ichi. In 2000 Dai-Ichi took advantage of the deregulated environment that no longer separated life and nonlife insurance and formed a joint venture with American Family Life Assurance Company of Columbus (AFLAC) to market certain AFLAC products in Japan.

Expansion into Europe followed a similar pattern. In 1982 Dai-Ichi established an office in London in order to establish a presence in Europe. Eight years later, Dai-Ichi Mutual established a joint venture with British investment banking firm NatWest Investment Management. This was a strategic move to strengthen investment in Japanese securities, and it utilized NatWest's expertise in quantitative analysis of financial instruments. Dai-Ichi also hoped to gain entrance into the pension fund markets overseas.

```
┌─────────────────────────────────────────────┐
│                                               │
│              KEY DATES                        │
│                    ■                          │
│  ┌─────────────────────────────────────────┐ │
│                                               │
│  1902: Tsuneta Yano issues "Characteristics of My │
│        Company," establishing the Dai-Ichi Mutual │
│        Life Insurance Company, Japan's first mutual │
│        insurance company.                     │
│  1975: Dai-Ichi's first overseas representative office is │
│        established in New York.               │
│  1997: Dai-Ichi introduces the "Lifelong Plan." │
│  2001: Dai-Ichi wins the "Japan Quality Award." │
│  2007: Dai-Ichi expands operations to Vietnam. │
│  2010: Dai-Ichi Mutual Life demutualizes and starts │
│        trading on the Tokyo Stock Exchange.   │
│                                               │
└─────────────────────────────────────────────┘
```

While Dai-Ichi established a representative office in Hong Kong similar to the European and U.S. offices, expansion in the Asia-Pacific area was slow. Eventually, relationships were developed through FALIA, with participants of Thailand, China, Indonesia, Malaysia, and Korea attending FALIA seminars. In 1988 Dai-Ichi participated in a loan to a Chinese bank, but it was not until 2003 that Dai-Ichi was able to buy a portion of a Chinese company. Dai-Ichi bought 1 percent of the shares of China's second-largest insurer, Ping An Insurance. In 2007 Dai-Ichi acquired Vietnam's fifth-largest insurance company, Bao Minh CMG, making Dai-Ichi Mutual the first Japanese life insurance company in Vietnam.

In the 1990s the decline of the Japanese stock market and Japanese companies' efforts to compete internationally caused the gradual dissolution of the *keiretsu* structure. While the structure was beneficial to core companies in the *keiretsu* groups, subcontracting companies often had to compete with each other for patronage of the core companies without the ability to search for business elsewhere. These smaller companies eventually found ways to become more market-oriented and moved away from *keiretsu* relationships, causing core companies to follow suit. In 1999 Dai-Ichi formed a business alliance with the Industrial Bank of Japan (IBJ), a long-time competitor of the lead bank in its own *keiretsu,* Dai-Ichi Kangyo. (Dai-Ichi Kangyo would later merge with IBJ to become the Mizuho Financial Group.)

Dai-Ichi's growth was slowed in the late 1990s because of the Great Hanshin Earthquake of 1995, which was one of the costliest natural disasters ever to hit Japan. Life insurance claims were so numerous that Dai-Ichi Mutual was forced to simplify its lengthy claims process. However, the disaster also resulted in the creation of the subsidiary Dai-Ichi Property and Casualty Insurance in 1996. While life insurers were kept busy, very few Japanese citizens were insured for damages caused by earthquakes. In 2002 the subsidiary would merge with Yasuda Fire and Marine Insurance Co., which would later become Sompo Japan Insurance, Inc.

## AN AWARD-WINNING CONCEPT

In 1998 Japan's Diet (parliament) enacted the Financial System Reform Act, deregulating the insurance, banking, and securities industries. This sweeping reform was known as the "Big Bang." Specifically, the rating system for insurance approval was simplified, and rate restrictions by the Japanese government were relaxed. Also, the legislation opened the way for foreign competition for certain types of specialty health insurance products, such as cancer and nursing care.

With the imminent regulatory changes, Dai-Ichi introduced the "Lifelong Plan" concept in 1997, responding to customers' concerns and the economic shifts at the time. Falling birthrates, the aging population, and a saturated life insurance market prompted Dai-Ichi to offer products for its customers through every stage of life. Products included medical, long-term nursing, cancer, and life insurance through its alliances with AFLAC, Sompo Japan, and others.

In November 2001 Dai-Ichi Mutual was awarded the Japan Quality Award in recognition of the Lifelong Plan concept. The Japan Quality Award is modeled after the Malcolm Baldrige National Quality Award in the United States. Recipients are judged to have the highest regard for the needs of customers and to have created new value for society.

## THE 21ST CENTURY: DEMOGRAPHICS AND DEMUTUALIZATION

The early years of the 21st century presented many challenges for Dai-Ichi that led to its decision to end its ownership structure and offer its shares on the Tokyo Stock Exchange.

In 2002 the stagnant Japanese economy caused a decrease in new insurance policies along with increased cancellations as household income declined. In addition, Japan's demographics, including an aging population and a decreasing birth rate, further shrunk the market for Dai-Ichi's products. Liquid reserves were strained by low interest rates and stock prices, as investments are a major source of capital for insurance companies. Over the next seven years, Dai-Ichi would raise over ¥385 billion in order to secure its financial base. In annual reports 2003 through 2007, Dai-Ichi informed its policyholders that dividends would be ceased until the company could achieve an internal reserve of ¥2 trillion for payment of claims.

In addition to demographic and economic setbacks, Dai-Ichi also experienced an investigation that tarnished its public image. The Japanese insurance industry was investigated when the insurance company Meiji Yasuda Life was revealed to have refused to pay insurance benefits that were due. This discovery led to a probe of all Japanese insurers, and the top four insurers, including Dai-Ichi, were found to have failed to pay ¥59.3 billion ($538 million) for over 725,000 policyholders. Overall, the industry was ordered to pay 1.2 million policy claims, totaling ¥91 billion ($821 million).

In 2007 Dai-Ichi adopted a plan to demutualize, or sell, the company's shares to the public. In 2009 policyholders approved the plan. Dai-Ichi attributed this decision to go public to the necessity of public financing for continued growth. On April 1, 2010, Dai-Ichi raised over ¥1 trillion ($11 billion) on the Tokyo Stock Exchange. The Initial Public Offering (IPO) was the largest in the world since Visa's IPO of $19.7 billion in 2008. With the offering, Dai-Ichi changed its name and became Dai-Ichi Life Insurance Company, Limited.

The new structure as a public company released Dai-Ichi from some insurance regulations, such as selling nonparticipating products. It also offered more flexibility for mergers and acquisitions through the exchange of shares, rather than cash transactions. With a sluggish national economy and saturated home insurance market, Dai-Ichi's ability to acquire companies and expand internationally would be the key to the company's fortunes in the 2010s.

*Sara K. Huter*

## PRINCIPAL SUBSIDIARIES

Dai-Ichi Frontier Life Insurance Co., Ltd.; The Dai-Ichi Life Information Systems Co., Ltd.; Dai-Ichi Life Insurance Company of Vietnam, Ltd.

## PRINCIPAL DIVISIONS

Group Life Insurance; Individual Life Insurance; International Life Insurance Business; Internal Control and Overall Risk Management; Investment.

## PRINCIPAL COMPETITORS

Meiji Yasuda Life Insurance Company; Nippon Life Insurance Company; Sumitomo Life Insurance Company.

## FURTHER READING

Banham, Russ, "Japan's New Insurance Frontier," *Risk Management,* March 1995.
———, "History of the Dai-Ichi Kangyo Bank Ltd.," referenceforbusiness.com.
Kwok, Vivian Wai-yin, "Dai-Ichi Mutual Life Sees IPO As A Life Preserver," forbes.com, December 6, 2007.
Tajima, Keigo, "*KEIRETSU*," in *Encyclopedia of Business Ethics and Society,* Thousand Oaks, CA: Sage Publications, 2008.
Tilley, Kate, "Kobe Fails to Shake Japanese Renewals," *Business Insurance,* March 6, 1995.
———, "Tsuneta Yano," insurancehalloffame.org.

# DigitalGlobe, Inc.

1601 Dry Creek Drive
Suite 260
Longmont, Colorado 80503
U.S.A.
Telephone: (303) 684-4000
Toll Free: (800) 655-7929
Fax: (303) 682-3848
Web site: http://www.digitalglobe.com

*Public Company*
*Founded:* 1992 as Worldview Imaging Corporation
*Employees:* 507 (2009)
*Sales:* $281.9 million
*Stock Exchanges:* New York
*Ticker Symbol:* DGI
*NAICS:* 334220 Space satellites, communications, manufacturing

∎∎∎

DigitalGlobe, Inc., (DigitalGlobe) offers high-resolution Earth imagery products and services through the use of its three remote sensing satellites. The company also offers a range of value-added products that take advantage of its satellite imagery such as three-dimensional (3D) terrain models, elevation datasets, and crisis event services. Its products and services support a wide variety of applications including defense, intelligence, mapping and analysis, environmental monitoring, energy exploration, and infrastructure management. DigitalGlobe's customers include government, defense and intelligence organizations, private individuals, and corporations. The company sells its solutions directly and through various resellers.

DigitalGlobe offers both standard imagery, which is readily available in its existing image library, and custom imagery, which requires tasking the company's satellites to satisfy the customer's requirements. The company also has its Direct Access Program (DAP), which enables customers, who must be approved by the U.S. government, to task and downlink data directly from DigitalGlobe's satellites. DigitalGlobe was one of the first private commercial providers of detailed imagery using satellites. Previously, such satellites and their imagery were the province of governments and their military and intelligence organizations.

## NEW LAW BRINGS NEW OPPORTUNITIES

In 1992 the Land Remote Sensing Policy Act became law. This legislation permitted private companies to enter the satellite imaging business. For security reasons, the U.S. government still exerted a certain amount of control. Federal regulations said that licensed companies could photograph anything from space and sell the imagery on the open market, but companies must allow the government "shutter control," which meant the government could shut off the cameras in times of war or international tensions and deny access to strategic areas if it deemed that the imagery might compromise national security. Another restriction was that companies must allow the federal government to screen foreign customers.

## COMPANY PERSPECTIVES

DigitalGlobe is the clear leader in the global commercial Earth imagery and geospatial information market. The company's technical superiority and innovation, unparalleled commitment to customer service, extensive business partner network, and open systems philosophy make DigitalGlobe the preferred supplier of imagery products to government and commercial markets.

Even before the Land Remote Sensing Policy Act went into effect, Walter Scott and Doug Gerull moved early to take advantage of the opportunities created by the new law. Scott was a computer scientist who until the end of 1991 was the head of the "Brilliant Pebbles" and "Brilliant Eyes" projects for the Lawrence Livermore Laboratories. Both projects were part of the controversial U.S. Strategic Defense Initiative (SDI), more commonly referred to as the "Star Wars" program. Politicians hoped that the SDI would use advanced satellite technology to protect the United States and its allies from attack by ballistic nuclear missiles. Gerull was an executive at the Intergraph Corporation, a leading company in geographic information systems. Scott and Gerull came together to found the Worldview Imaging Corporation (Worldview).

Scott and Gerull started Worldview with mostly Silicon Valley financing. One of the company's backers was Edward Teller, the architect of the hydrogen bomb. They located the company's headquarters in Longmont, Colorado. In January 1992 Worldview received approval from the National Oceanic and Atmospheric Administration (NOAA) to move forward with plans to develop remote sensing satellites and sell the images of the Earth commercially. At the time, the United States' satellite system was known to produce imagery so accurate that it could represent objects as small as a football. The governments of the United States, France, and the Soviet Union did sell satellite images commercially through private companies, but the images were of significantly lower resolution. There were some publicly available systems but the resolution was also very low. The French SPOT system offered resolution to 10 meters and the U.S. Landsat satellites offered images but with resolution of only 30 meters. These resolutions were only good enough to see large objects such as large vehicles and buildings. The NOAA licensed the Earth Observation Satellite Company (EOSAT) in Lanham,

Massachussetts, to sell these lower-resolution images on the commercial market. EOSAT was a partnership between Hughes Aircraft and RCA.

In 1993 the U.S. Department of Commerce followed up on NOAA's actions and granted Worldview a license to build and operate a satellite system to gather high-resolution digital imagery of the Earth for commercial sale. Worldview's efforts, as well as its competitors, drew great interest from potential customers, who saw the potential practical uses for high-resolution imagery. These companies also generated some controversy among politicians, military experts, and civil liberties advocates, who saw perils inherent to such high-resolution imagery. The politicians and military experts said that smaller nations or rebel armies around the world could use the imagery for strategic information in fighting their enemies, including the United States. Civil liberties advocates saw such surveillance as an intrusion upon a citizen's right to privacy. As Worldview and other U.S. companies moved forward with government approval, nations such as France, Russia, South Africa, India, and Israel started their own efforts to develop satellite geographic information systems (GIS) using remote sensing satellites.

## EARLYBIRD AND QUICKBIRD LOST

In 1995 Worldview merged with the remote sensing subsidiary of another Colorado-based satellite company, Ball Aerospace Corporation (Ball Aerospace). They formed a new entity named Earthwatch, Inc. The intent behind the merger was to create economies of scale to better handle the high cost of developing satellites. On December 24, 1997, a Russian commercial Start-1 rocket launched from Svobodny Cosmodrome and carried the Earthwatch's Earlybird I satellite into space. The satellite featured a panchromatic camera with a 3-meter (9.8-foot) resolution and a multispectral camera with a 15-meter (49-foot) resolution. A panchromatic camera is a camera that senses all levels of light including radiation beyond the visible wavelength (infrared). A multispectral camera allows for multiple photographs at specific wavebands (e.g., red, blue, green, infrared), so the viewer can separate out a particular wavelength and analyze aspects of the terrain that might not be visible to the human eye. Both cameras were able to convert images into digital form to be transmitted to controllers on the ground. The satellite was to provide pictures from space as small as 3 meters across in black in white and 15 meters across in color. Shortly after launch, the satellite communicated to the ground controllers that it had reached its circular orbit of 473 kilometers above the Earth.

## KEY DATES

**1992:** Walter Scott and Doug Gerull found World-view Imaging Corporation.

**1995:** Worldview merges with remote sensing subsidiary of Ball Aerospace Corporation; changes name to Earthwatch, Inc.

**1997:** Earlybird I satellite launched into orbit; communication with Earlybird I lost four days after launch.

**2000:** Quickbird I satellite launched into space; Quickbird I never makes orbit and is lost.

**2001:** Earthwatch changes name to DigitalGlobe.

**2007:** Worldview I satellite launched into orbit and communication is successful.

**2009:** Worldview II satellite launched into orbit and communication is successful.

On December 28th, four days after launch, the Earlybird I stopped communicating with Earthwatch's ground control center. The satellite was still undergoing calibration, a six- to eight-week process, when communication stopped. Controllers never regained communication with the satellite. However briefly it lasted, the Earlybird I was Earthwatch's first imaging satellite and represented the first civilian "spy" satellite in history.

Two months later, Earthwatch laid off 44 employees. The company underwent reorganization, and Doug Gerull resigned his position as executive vice president. The Earlybird I failure sent tremors across the nascent industry. Earthwatch and other players worried that the mishap would send venture capital looking for less risky projects.

The company was forced to accelerate its efforts to launch its next family of satellites, the Quickbird I and II. Earthwatch found investors to fund Quickbird I, and in May 1996 the company completed a private equity placement of $70 million in stock to help fund the Quickbird II. Ball Aerospace developed and manufactured the Quickbird I satellite. Earthwatch also brought in Kodak and Fokker Space B.V. to supply components of the projects.

In September 1999 competitor Space Imaging Corporation successfully launched its Ikonos satellite, making it the only commercial viable remote sensing satellite in operation. On November 20, 2000, Earthwatch had its turn. A Russian Kosmos-3 rocket carried Earthwatch's Quickbird I into space. The rocket took off from the Plesetsk Cosmodrome. The rocket ascended without trouble, but once in orbit, the controllers almost immediately lost contact with the Quickbird I satellite. The Russians reported that the second stage of the rocket shut down too early and left the satellite in a shallow orbit, possibly making it a ballistic object that would fall to earth.

The satellite was lost. Earthwatch had insured the satellite for $265 million on a $55 million investment. The loss of a second satellite was a difficult setback, but Earthwatch was not alone in facing such failures. Two other companies had lost satellites. Space Imaging lost its first Ikonos satellite in 1999, and Orbital Imaging lost its OrbView-4 satellite in 2001.

In September 2001 Earthwatch changed its name to DigitalGlobe. By this point, the company had operated for almost nine years without any revenues, and it had assembled several new investors to keep operations afloat. New investors included ITT Industries, Morgan Stanley, Hitachi Ltd., and Telespazio SpA.

## THIRD ATTEMPT BRINGS SUCCESS

On October 18, 2001, a Boeing Delta II rocket launched from Vandenberg Air Force Base, California, carrying the Quickbird II satellite. The rocket successfully put the satellite in its correct orbit at a 450-kilometer, 98-degree sun-synchronous orbit. Communications were successful, and the company had its first successful remote sensing satellite in space. At the time, the Quickbird II delivered the highest-resolution, commercially available imagery of Earth. The satellite featured a 60-centimeter (24 inch) panchromatic camera and a 2.5-meter (7 feet, 10 inches) multispectral camera. This meant that the satellite could capture the image of an object as small as 60 centimeters. It was also fast, capable of capturing a 16.5 kilometer by 16.5 kilometer image in approximately 4.5 seconds.

The successful launch of Quickbird II also launched the company into a frenzy of activity. Even before the company finished the two month calibration period it demonstrated Quickbird II's capabililties by publishing imagery of Antarctica, Bangkok, and Washington D.C. The company also started to form several strategic partnerships to help deliver its imagery to customers across the world. The company secured distributors for its imagery, including Eurimage for the European market and its funding partner Hitachi for the Asian market. DigitalGlobe also began leveraging its technology to generate revenue. DigitalGlobe partnered with VARGIS to deliver Quickbird II's data to customers.

The company had begun transitioning from a satellite engineering company into a company focused on sales, marketing, and customer service. The company made a big leap in that effort when in January 2002 it signed a six-year channel partnership agreement with SPOT Image Corporation, its French competitor. Under the agreement DigitalGlobe agreed to act as the single-point distributor for SPOT's products and services in U.S. agricultural and defense markets. DigitalGlobe hired 80 people between October 2001 and March 2002.

## CREATING A CONSTELLATION

By 2002 the United States had lost its edge in the satellite imagery market. Nations across the globe had remote sensing satellites in space. Even though other nation's satellites did not offer the same level of resolution as those employed in the United States, they were good enough for the needs of most customers. In 2003 the National Imagery and Mapping Agency (NIMA) initiated the NextView program intended to guarantee that the United States retained its leadership position in developing satellite technology. NIMA, later renamed the National Geospatial-Intelligence Agency (NGA), was part of the U.S. Department of Defense and was responsible for providing satellite imagery, mapping, and similar geospatial intelligence to support national security efforts. NIMA awarded DigitalGlobe a $72 million contract under the NextView program. (At the same time, NIMA awarded a similar contract for $120 million to Space Imaging Corporation.) The NIMA contract had a ceiling of $500 million and would fund DigitalGlobe's next effort, the Worldview satellite program, particularly the Worldview I and Worldview II satellites.

In the meantime, Quickbird II was still DigitalGlobe's main source of revenue. In January 2004 DigitalGlobe and Keyhole Corporation agreed to combine Quickbird II's imagery with Keyhole's Internet-based, 3D mapping software to form an integrated service for customers. Ten months later, Google Inc., the Internet search engine company, bought Keyhole, and the joint venture became the basis for Google Earth and adding satellite images to Google Maps.

Google Earth was Google's mapping software and service, which allowed customers to move quickly around the world, zoom into areas, and even take 3-D virtual tours of some buildings. Google Maps was the Google search engine's mapping component. This put DigitalGlobe's imagery in front of the millions of Internet users across the world. When they searched for directions using Google's search engine they could

choose to see the terrain of their journey as a satellite image instead of a normal map.

By mid-2004 the satellite imagery industry still consisted of only a few players, so when the NGA opened bidding on another $500 million NextView contract, it barred DigitalGlobe from making a bid. NGA wanted to grow the fledgling industry and encourage more competition. Also, the U.S. government did not want to be in the position of depending on only one company for all its imagery. Regardless, the company was well on its way toward developing the Worldview satellites with the most advanced imaging technology available.

In September 2007 a Boeing Delta II 7920 rocket lifted off from Vandenberg Air Force Base and successfully carried the Worldview I satellite into orbit. The panchromatic camera on Worldview I was designed to collect black-and-white images with a resolution of 50 centimeters (20 inches), which was only slightly higher in resolution than Quickbird II, but the satellite also included a much higher storage capacity, allowing it to cover more area and cover it faster. Controllers established successful communications with the satellite and the Worldview I became the first successful satellite under the NGA's NextView program.

On May 14, 2008, the company completed its initial public offering and began trading on the New York Stock Exchange under the ticker symbol DGI. In June 2009 the NGA awarded an extension to DigitalGlobe's contract through to March 2010 and accompanied the extension with $100 million to complete the project.

In October 2009 a Boeing Delta II rocket lifted off from Vandenberg Air Force Base and successfully carried the Worldview II satellite to its orbit. Worldview II carried a panchromatic camera with a 46-centimeter (18-inch) resolution and an eight-band multispectral camera with a 184-centimeter (72-inch) resolution. The panchromatic camera offered another small step toward better resolution, and the eight-band multispectral camera offered better feature identification, extraction, and a more accurate reflection of the world's natural color. Under the NextView contract the NGA would be the largest customer of Worldview I and the Worldview II imagery, but DigitalGlobe could sell imagery from these satellites to its commercial customers as well.

By the end of 2009 DigitalGlobe's prospects looked good. The company had a constellation of three remote sensing satellites orbiting the Earth. Together, the satellites had a capacity to capture two million kilometers a day. As of May 2010 DigitalGlobe's digital library consisted of over one billion square kilometers of imagery, to which the company added on an ongoing basis.

*Aaron Hauser*

## PRINCIPAL DIVISIONS

Commercial; Defense and Intelligence.

## PRINCIPAL COMPETITORS

Department of Space (Government of India); GeoEye Inc.; Google, Inc.; ImageSat International N.V.; Microsoft Corp.; National Remote Sensing Agency; Orbital Sciences Corporation; SPOT Image S.A.; Trimble Navigation Limited.

## FURTHER READING

Anselmo, Joseph C., "New Satellite Uses Spur Space Boom," *Aviation Week & Space Technology,* June 3, 1996, p. 87.

"Ball Aerospace, WorldView Combine Remote Sensing Ventures," *Aerospace Daily,* January 27, 1995, p. 133.

Barnes, Scottie, "Quickbird On Target," *Geospatial Solutions,* January 1, 2002, p. 12.

Barnes-Svarney, Patricia, "Eyes in the Sky," *Popular Science,* August 1, 1995, p. 24.

Beauprez, Jennifer, "Third Time's the Charm; DigitalGlobe's Satellite-photo Strategy Clicks," *Denver Post,* March 18, 2002, p. C.01.

Broad, William J., "First Civilian Spy Satellite Soars into Space, Launched in Russia by a U.S. Company," *New York Times,* December 25, 1997, p. 16.

————. "Satellites for Hire Have Eyes for You, First Commercial Spy Craft Launches This Spring Amid Predictions of Hope, Horror," *Austin American-Statesman,* February 10, 1997, p. A1.

Cantwell, Rebecca, "Earthwatch's Earlybird Satellite Stops Talking; Silence Not Uncommon, Say Longmont Scientists Who Launched Spacecraft," *Rocky Mountain News,* January 3, 1998, p. 1B.

————. "Earthwatch Lays Off 44 after Satellite Fails, Setback Could Start Ripple Effect through Remote Sensing World," *Rocky Mountain News,* February 3, 1998, p. 1B.

"Contact Lost With Quickbird Satellite; Commercial Imagery Market Suffers Setback," *Space Business News,* November 22, 2000.

Gupta, Vipin, "New Satellite Images for Sale," *International Security,* June 22, 1995, p. 94.

Markoff, John, "Company News: A Plan for Close-Up Images of Earth From Space," *New York Times,* February 12, 1993.

"Worldview Merger Seen as Harbinger for Field Formed by Ball Aerospace and WorldView Imaging Corp. to Launch Remote-sensing Satellites," *Space News,* January 30, 1995, p.4.

# Discover Financial Services

——■——

**2500 Lake Cook Road**
**Riverwoods, Illinois 60015**
**U.S.A.**
**Telephone: (224) 405-0900**
**Toll Free: (800) 347-2683**
**Fax: (224) 405-3555**
**Web site: http://www.discoverfinancial.com**

*Public Company*
*Founded:* 1986
*Employees:* 10,500 (2010)
*Sales:* $3.1 billion (2009)
*Stock Exchanges:* New York
*Ticker Symbol:* DFS
*NAICS:* 522210 Credit Card Issuing

■ ■ ■

Although Discover Financial Services is most recognized as a credit card issuer, it is also a banking and electronic payment services company.

Discover divides its products into two business segments: Direct Banking and Payment Services. Direct Banking includes credit cards, loans, and deposits. Payment Services operates the PULSE network, an ATM/debit network that links more than 4,400 financial institutions with automated teller machines (ATMs) and point-of-sale (POS) terminals. Diners Club and third-party credit, debit, and prepaid cards are also included in the Payment Services segment.

## A SUPER BEGINNING: 1985–86

Dean Witter Financial Services Group, a subsidiary of Sears, Roebuck and Co., developed and marketed the Discover card. It was notable for being a card with no annual fee. The first purchase made by a Discover card occurred on September 17, 1985, when a Sears employee bought $26.77 of merchandise. Discover continued to test-market the card in San Diego and Atlanta.

On January 26, 1986, the Discover card was introduced with a commercial advertisement during the Super Bowl XX. In addition to no annual fee, the Discover card also pioneered a cash-back rewards program.

## AN IMPERFECT MARRIAGE: 1987–97

The Discover card received a warm reception from both cardmembers and merchants. By 1988 it had signed 20 million new customers and thousands of new merchants. It also reported a profit of $80 million. However, as a stand-alone product, the Discover card found difficulty gaining acceptance at large retailers, as it was deemed a competing product for their own charge cards. Parent company Sears also struggled to overcome lost sales by not accepting Visa and MasterCard credit cards. In 1993, in an effort to refocus its efforts on its core retail business, the struggling retailer spun off Dean Witter, making it a publicly traded company. In 1997 Dean Witter merged with Morgan Stanley.

## COMPANY PERSPECTIVES

We have continuously been a leading innovator and driver of change in the credit card industry. From the outset, Discover has worked to expand the network, which connects millions of merchant and cash access locations, as well as markets, and supports a full range of credit, debit, and prepaid cards, including the Discover Card.

As the Discover card gained acceptance, a natural synergy for the company was to offer expanding network functions linking ATMs and POS terminals to Discover cardmembers. With this in mind, in 1995 Discover changed its name to NOVUS Services, Inc. The change was made to distinguish the company as one that offered more products than just the Discover card. The company would later change its name to Discover Financial Services, Inc., in 1999.

## COMPETING WITH A MONOPOLY: 2001–04

Since its inception, the Discover card was at a disadvantage when competing with the already entrenched Visa and MasterCard brands. Visa and MasterCard had formed a joint venture to issue cards through banking institutions. When Discover approached banks to offer the same licensing structure, it found that Visa and MasterCard bylaws prevented issuing banks from offering competing credit cards. In 2001 this practice was ruled a violation of antitrust laws, a decision that was upheld by the Supreme Court in 2004.

The 2004 ruling allowed Discover to form partnerships with GE Consumer Finance, HSBC, and Metris, three of the largest credit card issuers in the world. In addition, Discover teamed with Wal-Mart to issue a Wal-Mart Discover credit card. Wal-Mart was a vocal proponent of the antitrust suit against Visa and MasterCard, believing that Discover's merchant network provided a less expensive platform for accepting credit cards.

## TEAMING UP TO PREVENT FRAUD

In 2003 Discover retained Frank Abagnale as an advisor and consultant to prevent credit card fraud. Abagnale was best known as the author of *Catch Me If You Can*, a story based on his life and the inspiration for the movie of the same name.

## MERGER WITH PULSE: 2004

In 2004 Discover announced an agreement to merge with PULSE EFT Association. PULSE was an ATM/debit network that linked approximately 90 million cardmembers with over 250,000 ATMS and 3.3 million POS terminals. The merger created a strategic alignment to further expand brand acceptance of the Discover card. "We believe the combination of the PULSE and Discover networks will create a leading electronic payments company offering a full range of products and services that will represent an attractive choice for financial institutions, merchants and consumers, " said David W. Nelms, chairman and chief executive officer of Discover Financial Services. "Together, we intend to be a robust competitor in the important and rapidly growing debit market."

While both sides spoke enthusiastically about the merger, the impact of adding PULSE to Discover was positive but not hugely significant. Income from PULSE-based operations was $673,000 in 2005 and almost tripled to $1.8 million in 2006, but these amounts paled in comparison to the earnings gained from Discover's credit card business in the same years. Those amounts were $5.41 billion and $5.75 billion, respectively, demonstrating that while the acquisition of PULSE aided Discover's bottom line, it did not substantially impact the company's overall business position.

## GROWTH AND DIVESTITURE: 2004–08

By 2004 Discover had positioned itself as a leading technology company by introducing and supporting innovative products in the credit card industry, such as its introduction of the industry's first keychain credit card in 2002. Between 2004 and 2008, Discover pursued alliances with companies such as Pay By Touch, ViVOtech, On Track Innovations, Motorola, and Apple. These partnerships enabled Discover to offer and support payment options such as fingerprinting, mobile phone POS, and microchips. For advances and innovations such as these, Discover was listed among the top 100 tech companies by *Computerworld* in 2007.

Other new products offered enhanced customer service. The Discover Motiva Card encouraged responsible credit use by rewarding on-time payments with cash back. DebitProtect was a neural network fraud notification system that alerted cardmembers and financial institutions of possible fraudulent use of debit

## KEY DATES

**1986:** Discover Card is unveiled at the Super Bowl.
**1993:** Sears divests Dean Witter and Discover.
**1997:** Dean Witter and Discover merges with Morgan Stanley.
**2004:** U.S. Department of Justice antitrust lawsuit against Visa and MasterCard is resolved.
**2007:** Morgan Stanley divests Discover; Discover Financial begins trading on the NYSE.
**2008:** Discover acquires Diners Club International.

cards. Credit ScoreTracker was a service that educated cardmembers about credit scores and how to improve them. It also alerted cardmembers of changes in their credit scores.

In December 2006 Morgan Stanley announced that it would spin off the company. An investment bank, Morgan Stanley had not done well in the consumer finance market, and diveting itself of Discover was a way to appease disgruntled shareholders and allow the company to focus on its core operations. On July 2, 2007, Discover Financial Services began trading on the New York Stock Exchange (NYSE). "We believe this will maximize value for Morgan Stanley and Discover shareholders, " said CEO John Mack. "We are confident that Discover will be a strong stand-alone company."

The divestiture followed the ousting of CEO Phillip Purcell, who had proposed the spinoff in 2005. Purcell had been the original CEO of Dean Witter, the creator of the Discover card. The divestiture seemed to be a welcome change to shareholders. Upon the announcement at day's end, Morgan Stanley's stock reached a 52-week high, up 3 percent.

### GOING INTERNATIONAL

As the company expanded its product line, it also expanded its geographical reach. On December 5, 2005, Liu Tinghuan, chairman of UnionPay, purchased a necktie at Macy's Herald Square in New York City with a card issued by UnionPay. This purchase marked the first resulting from a strategic alliance between Union-Pay, China's only bankcard payment network, and Discover. UnionPay's cards were integrated onto the PULSE network, allowing Chinese travelers in the United States to use their Chinese-issued credit cards.

In February 2006 Discover acquired Goldfish from Lloyds TSB Bank in the United Kingdom. Goldfish was

a credit card issuer with two million cardmembers. At the time, the United Kingdom was experiencing severe credit deterioration. Discover took an estimated $422 million write-off, making up the majority of the company's $637 million reduction in pre-tax income in 2007. In March 2008 Discover sold the portfolio to Barclays Bank PLC.

In August 2006 Discover entered into an agreement with JCB, the largest card issuer in Japan. JCB integrated its ATM and merchant base to accept PULSE and Discover Network platforms. In turn, Discover integrated its networks to accept JCB cards.

In July 2008 Discover acquired Diners Club from Citigroup, strategically aligning itself to further expand its international presence. Diners Club was established in 1950 and was the first charge card in the world. At the time of the acquisition it generated more than $30 billion of annual card volume outside North America, and was accepted at more than eight million locations in 185 countries. Integrating the Diners Club network with PULSE allowed U.S. companies to use Discover cards internationally, while allowing international Diners Club cardmembers to use their cards in North America.

In January 2010 Discover entered into an agreement to allow Korean payment network BC Card to utilize the PULSE and Diners Club networks for purchases outside Korea. Korean cardmembers spend approximately $12.6 billion per year on international expenditures.

### WINDFALL

In 2008 Discover received $2.75 billion in damages from Visa and MasterCard resulting from Discover's 2004 antitrust suit against the credit card issuers. At the time, this was the third-largest reported antitrust settlement in U.S. history. The settlement came after Discover's split with Morgan Stanley, which resulted in disagreement over the distribution of the proceeds. Discover settled with Morgan Stanley for $775 million on February 5, 2010.

### CARD ACT

On February 22, 2010, the Credit Card Accountability, Responsibility and Disclosure (CARD) Act went into effect. This legislation was intended to prohibit predatory practices by credit card companies. The act required more disclosures, interest rate simplification, and fewer fees.

Discover expected CARD Act restrictions to result in reduced interest income, which typically accounted for over half of the company's revenues. While Discover has not predicted the estimated reduction amount, credit card advisory firm R. K. Hammer predicted that the CARD Act would result in $5.5 billion in lost revenue this year and more than $50 billion through 2015 for the industry.

## ECONOMIC RECESSION AND RECOVERY

Unemployment rates, limited liquidity, and consumer spending and indebtedness affected Discover's consumer portfolios. Delinquencies increased to 4.92 percent in 2009. Charge-offs increased from 5.01 percent in 2008 to 7.45 percent in 2009. In addition, reduced consumer spending resulted in a 5 percent reduction in credit card sales. Early 2010 figures showed delinquencies increasing to 5.50 percent, and the charge-off rate jumping to 9.11 percent.

Industry experts expected credit card delinquencies and charge-offs to level out in the early 2010s as consumers reduce credit card usage. However, the regulatory changes might present unprecedented challenges for Discover and other traditional card issuers during this decade. As the credit card industry struggled, subprime credit outlets, such as payday loan companies, were experiencing growth. While these subprime lenders charged high interest rates and fees, credit card companies were prohibited from doing the same for customers with high-risk profiles. In response, Discover and other credit card companies changed pricing models to cushion future losses of interest and fee revenue. Even so, the impact of the CARD Act and the growing competition from other credit avenues made it difficult to ascertain Discover's future growth opportunities, although its core credit card business should keep the company in business for years to come.

*Sara K. Huter*

## PRINCIPAL SUBSIDIARIES

Bank of New Castle; Diners Club International Ltd; Discover Bank; Discover Card Limited; Discover Financial Services (Canada), Inc.; Discover Financial Services (Cayman) Limited; Discover Financial Services (Hong Kong) Limited; Discover Financial Services (UK) Limited; Discover Financial Services Insurance Agency, Inc.; Discover Information Technology (Shanghai) Limited; Discover Products Inc.; Discover Properties LLC; Discover Receivables Financing Corporation; Discover Services Corporation; DFS International Inc; DFS Services LLC; Goldfish Bank Limited; GTC Insurance Agency, Inc.; PULSE Network LLC.

## PRINCIPAL DIVISIONS

Direct Banking; Discover Bank; Payment Services.

## PRINCIPAL COMPETITORS

American Express Company; MasterCard Incorporated; Visa Inc.

## FURTHER READING

Berg, Eric N., "For Sears's Discover, Next Step Is Harder," *New York Times,* February 7, 1990.

"Discover Will Sell a Card Unit in Britain at a Big Loss," *New York Times,* February 8, 2008.

Federal Reserve. "What You Need to Know: New Credit Card Rules," federalreserve.gov, February 22, 2010.

"Pulse EFT Association to Merge With Discover Financial Services," discoverfinancial.com, November 15, 2004.

Spicer, Jonathan, "WRAPUP 4-Credit Card Data Hints at U.S. Consumer Rebound," reuters.com, March 15, 2010.

Thomas Jr., Landon, "Spinoff Set by Summer for Discover," *New York Times,* December 20, 2006.

# DynaVox, Inc.

**2100 Wharton Street**
**Suite 400**
**Pittsburgh, Pennsylvania 15203**
**U.S.A.**
**Telephone: (412) 381-4883**
**Fax: (412) 381-5241**
**Web site: http://www.DynaVoxtech.com**

*Public Company*
*Incorporated:* 1983
*Employees:* 364 (2009)
*Sales:* $91.16 million (2009)
*Stock Exchanges:* NASDAQ
*Ticker Symbol:* DVOX
*NAICS:* 33429 Other Communications Equipment Manufacturing; 33911 Medical Equipment and Supplies Manufacturing

■ ■ ■

DynaVox, Inc. (also known as DynaVox Mayer-Johnson), is the leading provider of speech-generating devices and symbol-adapted special education software. These tools aid individuals with significant speech, language, and learning difficulties due to amyotrophic lateral sclerosis (ALS, or Lou Gehrig's disease), stroke, traumatic brain injury, cerebral palsy, autism, intellectual disabilities. or other conditions. In 2009 DynaVox offered six portable communication devices, including the V and Vmax, Eyemax System, Xpress, Tango, M3, and DynaWrite to meet the needs of individuals with varying degrees of mobility and dexterity. DynaVox also of-fered the BoardMaker software suite developed for individuals with speech or learning difficulties. The company offered both online and in-person training on its products.

## BEGINNINGS: 1983–89

In 1983 Gary Killiany created a device to help a young woman with cerebral palsy "speak" for the first time. Killiany was an undergraduate engineering student at Carnegie-Mellon University and a volunteer at the Rehabilitation Institute of Pittsburgh. He teamed up with his professor, Mark Friedman, to create the EyeTyper. The Eyetyper enabled people with com-munication disabilities to create and compose messages by moving their eyes.

Killiany, Friedman, and their business partner, Til-den Bennett, formed Sentient Systems Technology, Inc., in the same year. The Eyetyper evolved through three generations in the first few years. Sentient eventually sold the patent to the U.S. Navy. Proceeds from the sale gave the company the capital it needed to expand and develop more advanced augmentative communication (AAC) solutions. Sentient Systems Technology began with one product and three employees in 1983 and would grow to employ more than 364 people by 2010.

## MANY TECHNOLOGICAL ADVANCES: 1990–2000

Sentient moved past the Eyetyper and began to develop more extensive hardware and software solutions to benefit people with a wide range of communication disabilities. Sentient's proprietary voice augmentation technology, with its "predictive language" capability, helped users with speech difficulty to formulate sentences and communicate through a voice synthesizer. These DynaVox-branded products began shipping to customers in 1991. (Although the devices featured the brand name Dynavox, the company did not change its name for some years.) They featured touch screens with dynamic displays that changed according to user selection.

In 1993 Sentient introduced word and grammar prediction, helping users compose messages more quickly. At the same time, Sentient also distributed DigiVox, an AAC tool combining recorded speech with changeable paper overlays.

The last part of the decade saw technological advances in many industries, including AAC tools. Sentient engineers produced many new, innovative products during this period. In 1996 Sentient introduced the DynaVox 2 and DynaVox 2c, portable tools that were designed for wheelchair users and came with hardware so they could be mounted. The DynaVox 2c had a color screen. In the same year, Sentient rolled out DynaVox software for Mac and DOS computers.

In early 1998 Sentient Systems Technology was acquired by Sunrise Medical. One year later it changed its name to DynaVox Systems LLC. DynaVox continued to operate as a subsidiary of Sunrise and remained in Pittsburgh, Pennsylvania. Sunrise manufactured and marketed assistive technology devices and rehabilitation products for people with disabilities and developed patient care products used in hospitals, nursing homes and homecare settings. The two companies offered

complementary products that in many cases worked together. For example, the DynaVox 2 device could easily be mounted to the Sunrise Quickie 2 manual and power wheelchairs.

By May 1999 DynaVox sales had reached $5 million, a 23 percent increase over the previous year. DynaVox reported a high number of orders for their new products, the DynaVox and Dynamyte devices and software. U.S. sales jumped and, using Sunrise's distribution channels, DynaVox saw increasing sales in Canada and the United Kingdom. DynaVox also released the Dynamo in the fall of 1999. This product integrated digitized speech with a dynamic display.

Although the Dynamo's display was black and white, it eliminated the need for paper overlays which were previously required for most digitized speech devices. The Dynamo promoted faster communication by accessing messages faster than earlier devices. It introduced intricate page organization capabilities and offered flexible selection methods (touch screen, single switch scanning, or serial mouse pause) and 30 minutes of record time. Users could also back up their devices to their computers.

## RAPID GROWTH: 2001–05

Beginning on January 1, 2001, Medicare began covering AAC devices. Medicare beneficiaries with Part B coverage were entitled to receive "speech generating devices" (SGDs), categorized as durable medical equipment, under the new guideline. By 2010 all DynaVox devices were covered, along with switches, switch mounts, device rental and repair.

In 2002 Dyanvox introduced the Dynawrite. It was the first type-and-talk device in the DynaVox family designed for users with a wide range of motor skills. Also in 2002, DynaVox struck a deal with Cepstral, a leading developer of text-to-speech software, under which Cepstral would lend its natural-sounding synthetic voices to the DynaVox devices. Cepstral created adult male, adult female, and child's voices for DynaVox so users had a choice of whether to use the mechanical voice or a voice closer to natural speech. In 2003 Cepstral and DynaVox extended their partnership and established Cepstral as the preferred provider of voices for DynaVox. Cepstral subsequently offered voices in a larger variety of U.S. English, as well as male and female voices in Canadian French, American Spanish, German, and U.K. English, so that users could express themselves using voices closer to their individuality and culture.

In 2004 private equity firm Vestar Capital Partners purchased Sunrise Medical. This led to DynaVox parting ways with Sunrise Medical. As an independent company, Dynavox acquired Mayer-Johnson and Enkidu Research, Inc. Mayer-Johnson developed symbol-based products, training, and services to enhance learning and expression for people with special needs. Special educators, speech and language pathologists, parents, and caregivers had used Mayer-Johnson's Picture Communication Symbols (PCS) in personal and clinical settings for more than 20 years.

The MightyMo and MiniMo, a new line of portable digitized devices with color screens were introduced the same year. The MiniMo and MightyMo featured preloaded symbol sets, prerecorded page sets, customization, screens easily readable inside and outside, 100 minutes of storage space, file backup, and the ability to run household appliances. It afforded individuals a new measure of independence.

## CONTINUING TO HELP PEOPLE: 2006–08

In 2006 DynaVox donated $116,000 in equipment and systems to the Department of Communicative Disorders and Sciences in the University at Buffalo's College of Arts and Sciences to help train speech-language pathologists. Later the same year, Joe Swenson, CEO of DynaVox since 2002, was named CEO of the Year by the Pittsburgh Technology Council. DynaVox was also named the number one life sciences company in the council's Tech 50 awards program, the first time in its 10-year history that the same company had taken top honors in both categories. Less than a year later, Swenson left DynaVox abruptly. Statements released by DynaVox and Swenson wished each other well, but no reason was given for Swenson's departure. Ed Donnelly, a DynaVox board member since 2004, replaced Swenson as CEO.

In 2007 the company launched the fifth generation of speech communication solutions, the V and Vmax. Featuring a fully functional integrated computer, the devices enabled users to communicate in person, by phone, and via text message and e-mail. DynaVox incorporated the AT&T Natural Voices text-to-speech (TTS) software in the V and Vmax. The M3, the updated version of the MiniMo and MightyMo, was released later in the year, as well as the portable devices Palmtop3 and iChat 3, significantly expanding DynaVox's handheld offerings.

The EyeMax, the newest version of the EyeTyper, was released in 2008. Users were able to activate this combination of the Vmax and the EyeMax accessory by blinking or staring at a section of the screen. The device enabled individuals living with ALS, cerebral palsy, stroke, traumatic brain injury or spinal cord injury to communicate faster and easier.

DynaVox introduced two more initiatives before the end of 2008. The company launched AdaptedLearning.com (later to become BoardmakerShare.com), a free online community used to share adapted curricula created with Boardmaker Software Family products developed by Mayer-Johnson. DynaVox also unveiled a solution created specifically to support veterans with traumatic brain injury (TBI). The Co-Pilot was a mechanism that assisted individuals with TBI by stimulating the functions that influence organizational skills, memory, emotional responses, and social skills. The small, handheld device combined several tools into one system, including a GPS unit, picture and audio cues, audible alerts, and other components that helped users navigate daily tasks and become more independent, lessening the weight on caregivers.

## CONTINUING TO GROW: 2009 AND BEYOND

In July 2009 DynaVox acquired Blink Twice, the developer of Tango, a device for children and teens with speech and language difficulties. Subsequently, DynaVox moved production from Blink Twice's Baltimore plant to Pittsburgh. As of 2010, Tango was the only DynaVox device aimed specifically at children, using characters that grow with the child and Phrase-First language structure.

In August 2009 DynaVox introduced the Xpress. Eurotech Group, a company that developed small, fast components for handheld devices, supplied the Eurotech Catalyst Module that made the Xpress a portable, powerful, wireless communications device. DynaVox offered products in all sizes, from devices that were larger and had capabilities closer to a laptop, to small, handheld devices that individuals could carry in their pockets.

Also in August 2009 Augie Nieto joined the DynaVox board of directors. Nieto was the founder and former CEO of Life Fitness, a large manufacturer of health fitness machines including exercise bikes, treadmills, and rowing machines. In 2005, Nieto was diagnosed with ALS and subsequently began communicating using the EyeMax device. Nieto added both business acumen and personal product experience to his board service.

Later that year, in November, DynaVox released a portable activity player called Mobile Activity Player. It offered wireless connectivity and the ability to run activities created in the BoardMaker Plus! software developed by Mayer-Johnson. The Mobile Activity Player allowed teachers to assign individual activities to students whether they were in or out of the classroom.

DynaVox acquired Eye Response Technologies, a technology company in the field of eye tracking, in early 2010. At the same time, DynaVox filed the paperwork for an initial public offering (IPO). The stock was offered in April 2010. DynaVox was considered to be a strong stock, but came up for sale midway through the day after investors had shown little interest in previous stocks. Despite this handicap, DynaVox raised $140.6 million, only a little short of the $150 million it expected to raise. Two weeks after its IPO, DynaVox posted its third quarter results, showing that its quarterly profit was double that of the second quarter, and sales had jumped during the previous year.

During the three fiscal years up to July 2009 DynaVox's sales increased 50 percent, from $66.2 million to $91.2 million. Its profits increased almost 80 percent, from $4.9 million to $8.8 million. Given this success, it seemed likely that Dynavox's products would continue to be well received in the 2010s. Since Medicare covered AAC devices, either partially or in their entirety, more and more individuals would be able to use DynaVox's speech devices to communicate.

*Andrea Newell*

## PRINCIPAL DIVISIONS

DynaVox Systems, LLC; Mayer-Johnson, LLC.

## PRINCIPAL COMPETITORS

Active Voice, LLC; Fonix Corporation; Nuance Communications, Inc.; Simulations Plus, Inc.

## FURTHER READING

"DynaVox Supports Speech Language, Hearing Clinic," *US Fed News Service, Including US State News,* March 6, 2006.

"DynaVox Systems LLC Merges with Blink Twice," *PR Newswire,* July 6, 2009.

"Sunrise Medical Announces Acquisition of Sentient Systems Technology, Inc.," *Business Wire,* February 13, 1998.

# East Africa Breweries Limited

**Thika Road**
**P.O. Box 30161-00100**
**Nairobi**
**Kenya**
**Telephone: (254) 020 864 4000**
**Fax: (254) 020 856 1090**
**Web site: http://www.eabl.com**

*Public Company*
*Incorporated:* 1922
*Employees:* 1000
*Sales:* KES 34.4 billion ($420 million)
*Stock Exchanges:* Nairobi
*NAICS:* 312120 Breweries

■ ■ ■

East African Breweries Limited (EABL) is a leading brewer and distiller of a wide range of alcoholic beverages in East Africa. The company's beer and spirit brands dominate the Kenyan and Ugandan markets and are also recognized worldwide. In addition to the famous Tusker Lager beer brand, EABL also brews Tusker Malt, White Cap Lager, Pilsner Lager, Pilsner Ice, Allsops, and Citizen Special Lager. Some of the company's spirits brands include Ritchot Brandy and Kenya Kane. Alvaro, a soft drink that competes against various soft drink brands, is the other major brand of EABL.

EABL has vested interests in brewing, distilling, and supplementary industries, and it operates a well-knit regional and international distribution network for its alcohol and beverage products. Some of the company's key export markets include the United States, the United Kingdom, Japan, Canada, and Djibouti.

## COMPANY FOUNDING AND EARLY YEARS: 1922–30

The formal incorporation of Kenya Breweries Limited occurred in 1922 when it was registered to operate as a private company. The company was originally founded by George Hurst, H. A. Darling, Charles Hurst, and a group of other friends and associates who set up a brewery plant in the Ruaraka area of Nairobi. The successful incorporation of Kenya Breweries Limited in 1922 was followed by a series of minor successes, including the brewing of the first beer, delivery of the first batch of beer to the Stanley Hotel (Nairobi), holding the first annual general meeting, and appointing the first brewer.

Kenya Breweries Limited experienced a major setback in 1923 when one of the founders of the company, George Hurst, died following an accident that occurred during an elephant hunting expedition. In addition, the company had to contend with low production capacity because of the infrastructural constraints and technological limitations that were characteristic of Kenya in the early 1920s. For example, it was not until 1924 that a power line was connected to the company's brewing plant in Ruaraka. The arrival of an electric power line in the company paved way for the expansion of its production capacity to 20,000 gallons a day and the eventual installation of a pasteurization plant.

The increased operation in the production activities of Kenya Breweries steered the company into a profit-making path as was demonstrated by the declaration of its first dividends in 1926. The company continued to experience accelerated growth in the second half of the 1920s, and in 1929 malted barley was used in its beer production processes for the first time. The company launched its first lager beer in 1930.

## GROWTH AND EXPANSION: 1930S–1940S

Kenya Breweries continued to experience astronomical growth in its beer production and distribution capacity in the 1930s through well-executed operational and strategic goals. In 1934 the company changed its status to that of a public limited company and made subsequent changes in its management structures. These developments enhanced the capital structure of Kenya Breweries Limited, and by 1935 the company made its first acquisition through a buyout of the Tanganyika Breweries.

The expanded and dominant presence of the company in Kenya and Tanganyika (now mainland Tanzania) prompted a change of its name to East Africa Breweries Limited in 1936. However, the company faced its first major test on its hold of the majority market share in 1937 when a new competitor, Taylor Breweries, entered the beer brewing and malting industry. The entry of a competitor was a new phenomenon for the East African Breweries Limited at the time. As such, the company's management adopted appropriate measures designed to protect its dominating presence in the East African market. These strategies included price cuts, new product development, and diversification into the production of spirits brands.

EABL devoted much of its surplus capital to expansion activities throughout the 1940s as the company focused on diversifying as well as increasing production of its core beer products. As the company was operating in a politically restricted environment that was characteristic of the colonial era in Kenya, the company's products were targeted at particular demographic markets that mainly consisted of the settler communities (Europeans, primarily British). The company sought to expand its market share by meeting the tastes and preferences of different demographic groups as much as possible.

## FURTHER EXPANSION: 1950S–1960S

EABL continued to pursue its expansion strategies in Kenya and the East African region through acquisitions, buyouts, and the setting up of new subsidiaries. The company successfully established the Mombasa Brewery in 1951. Sir Everlyn Baring, then governor of Kenya, graced the official opening of the Mombasa Brewery in February 1952. However, the biggest event of the company in the 1950s was its listing on the Nairobi Stock Exchange in 1954. The company utilized its new-found financial strength to expand its presence in Uganda through the acquisition of a financial holding in Uganda Breweries in 1959. EABL company's board opened its doors to its first African directors, J. M. Muchura and J. Thuo, in 1960.

EABL continued to experience favorable business prospects during the sunset years of colonial rule in Kenya in the early 1960s. The completion of a merger between EABL and Allsopp (East Africa) Limited in 1962 paved the way for the conversion of EABL into a holding company and the eventual reestablishment of Kenya Breweries as the trading arm of the company. The operating assets and liabilities of the company's units in Nairobi and Mombasa were also placed under the control of Kenya Breweries once again.

The smooth transition of Kenya from a colony to an independent state enhanced the business environment in the country as more investment opportunities opened up for the indigenous populations in the country. In 1964 EABL asserted its presence in Tanzania by acquiring significant equity interests in Tanzania's Kilimanjaro Breweries. The incorporation of Guinness East Africa Limited in Kenya in 1965 and the buyout of City Breweries Limited in 1969 were the company's main successful expansion strategies of the 1960s.

## SETBACKS AND STRATEGY CHANGES: 1970S–1980S

EABL shored up its financial capital through a public share issue in 1972. The company's dominance in the beer production industry elicited much interest from local and international investors and led to oversubscription of the share issue. However, the company experienced a major setback in 1972 when Idi Amin

## KEY DATES

**1922:** George Hurst, H. A. Darling, Charles Hurst, and a group of other friends set up a brewery plant in the Ruaraka area of Nairobi.
**1935:** Company acquires Tanganyika Breweries.
**1972:** Uganda Breweries nationalized following coup led by Idi Amin.
**1986:** New distribution agreement introduces company's products to North American markets.
**2008:** Company launches Alvaro, its first soft drink.

took over the reins of power in Uganda through a military coup and nationalized Uganda Breweries. As a consequence of this action, EABL had to forfeit its shareholding interests in the Uganda Breweries. In 1976 EABL endured yet another investment setback when the Tanzanian government nationalized its brewing interests in the country.

The harsh political and legal environments that were characteristic of the brewing industry in Uganda and Tanzania prompted a change of strategy by EABL in the 1980s. The company shifted its strategies towards expanding its presence and product range in the Kenyan market. As such, the company executed its strategy shift with the laying of the foundation stone for the Kisumu Brewery during an event that was led by the president of Kenya at the time, Daniel Moi, in 1982. The launch of Tusker Premium beer and the decision to diversify into bottle and glass manufacturing followed in the same year. The Kisumu Brewery was later commissioned in 1982 while the construction of the Central Glass Industry, the company's bottle and glass manufacturing unit, began in 1985.

The second half of the 1980s was extremely eventful as the company registered consistent progress on its diversification and market expansion strategies. In particular, the company achieved tremendous success in its export markets in 1986 when its trading unit, Kenya Breweries, signed a landmark beer distribution agreement with a U.S.-based company. This was the first time that the company exported its beer to the distant North American market.

Major structural changes were introduced at EABL in 1988 in a process that culminated in the return of the company's previous name, Kenya Breweries Limited. Subsequently, the status of EABL as the group's holdings

unit was suspended and merged with those of the group's trading unit, Kenya Breweries.

The newly named company's board of directors started implementing strategic plans designed to achieve lean and efficient production by cutting down on the number of employees through voluntary retirement programs. Kenya Breweries further shored up its brand portfolio with the introduction of the Tusker Malt Export Lager and Citizen Lager into the Kenyan market in 1995 and 1996, respectively. Citizen lager was the company's first beer brewed from exclusively nonmalted barley. The company marked its 75th anniversary with the installation of a technologically advanced bottling line at the Ruaraka brewing plant in 1997.

### CONTINUING DOMINANCE: 21ST CENTURY

After switching from Kenya Breweries Limited to East African Breweries Limited once again, the company entered the 21st century with enhanced operational and financial fundamentals. The company was named "The Most Respected Company in the East African Region" in a joint PricewaterhouseCoopers and Nation Media Group survey in 2001, the same year that it appointed a woman, Wanjiku Mugane, to its board of directors for the first time. The company's license agreement with South African Breweries International (SABI) in 2002 saw the company enhance its hold and dominance in the Kenya Brewing industry.

EABL almost gained a monopoly status in Kenya in an agreement that saw it close its Moshi-based Kibo Brewery in Tanzania but retain a 20 percent share in the company. In turn, SABI closed its Thika-based Castle Breweries in Kenya but retained a shareholding of 20 percent in East African Breweries Limited. The implementation of the license agreement saw EABL remain the sole beer producer and distributor for several years before the entry of Keroche Breweries Limited into the beer market.

In 2002 EABL compensated for its withdrawal from the Tanzanian market when the company purchased International Distillers Uganda Limited from Selviac Nederland B. V. for approximately KES 300 million. The company also acquired 46.32 percent of Kenya Wines Agencies (KWA) Holdings in 2002. East African Breweries Limited entered the records in 2005 when it became East Africa's first company to accumulate asset valuation in excess of $1 billion.

The company also posted a 26 percent increase in its annual sales from KES 29.5 billion in 2007 to KES 32.5 billion in 2008. The company's 2009 net sales revenues increased by 6 percent to reach KES 34.4 billion. The positive growth trend in the company's business activities was attributed to the consistent expansion into regional and other international markets globally.

## DIVERSIFYING INTO SOFT DRINKS: 2008

EABL ventured into the production and distribution of soft drinks in 2008 when it launched its first-ever soft drink, Alvaro. The entry of EABL into the soft drink production placed the company on a collision course with The Coca Cola Company, the world's leading soft drink manufacturer, which had dominated the Kenyan market for many years. The two companies got engaged in accusations and counter accusations through proxies over the chemical composition of the Alvaro brand.

EABL's main competitors charged that Alvaro was more of an alcoholic drink than a soft drink because it was produced from raw materials that contained alcoholic substances. As such, there were concerns that an unsuspecting public would be exposed to an alcoholic drink sold in the market as a soft drink. The controversy surrounding Alvaro spilled over to the Kenyan parliament and the Kenyan government, which had to intervene through its quality assurance agency to ascertain the chemical composition of the drink. The Alvaro brand survived the controversy when the Kenya Bureau of Standards allayed any fears, stating that the drink did not contain any alcoholic content.

As it looked to the future, East African Breweries Limited consistently pursued expansion strategies to widen its presence in the Eastern Africa region and globally. In addition to opening offices in different cities around the world, the company also sought strategic partnerships with beer distributors in all parts of the world. The company has also been diversifying its product range in accordance with its market-led strategic pursuits.

*Paul Ingati*

## PRINCIPAL SUBSIDIARIES

Kenya Breweries Ltd.; Uganda Breweries Ltd.; International Distillers Uganda Ltd.; East African Maltings Ltd.; Central Glass Industries Ltd.; UDV Kenya Inc.; Kenya Wines Agencies Limited.

## PRINCIPAL COMPETITORS

Anheuser-Busch InBev S.A./N.V.; The Coca-Cola Company; Heineken N.V.; Keroche Industries Limited; SABMiller plc.

## FURTHER READING

"About EABL," East African Breweries Limited, 2010.

"EABL's End Year Profits Soar by 22 Percent: Gross Profit Grows to Kshs. 17.4 Billion up from 12.2 Billion," East African Breweries Limited, 2008.

"EABL Expands to Rwanda," East African Breweries News Archive, 2010.

"EABL Full-Year Results Impressive Despite Tough Trading Environment," East African Breweries Limited, August 28, 2009.

"East African Breweries Limited Improves Plant Cap," East African Breweries Limited, June 8, 2007.

"EABL Out Sources Machicha Business," East African Breweries Limited, November 14, 2006.

"Gerald Mahinda Heads for Brandhouse as Seni Adetu Joins EABL," East African Breweries Limited, June 5, 2009.

# Eastman Chemical Company

———— ■ ————

**200 South Wilcox Drive**
**P. O. Box 511**
**Kingsport, Tennessee 37660**
**U.S.A.**
**Telephone: (423) 229-2000**
**Fax: (423) 229-2145**
**Web site: http://www.eastman.com**

*Public Company*
*Founded:* 1920 as subsidiary of Eastman Kodak
    Company
*Employees:* 10,000 (approx., 2009)
*Sales:* $5.047 billion (2009)
*Stock Exchanges:* New York
*Ticker Symbol:* EMN
*NAICS:* 325131 Inorganic Dye and Pigment
    Manufacturing; 325188 All Other Basic Inorganic
    Chemical Manufacturing; 325199 All Other Basic
    Organic Chemical Manufacturing; 325211 Plastics
    Material and Resin Manufacturing; 325221 Cel-
    lulosic Organic Fiber Manufacturing; 325910 Print-
    ing Ink Manufacturing; 325998 All Other Miscel-
    laneous Chemical Product and Preparation
    Manufacturing; 541712 Research and Development
    in the Physical, Engineering, and Life Sciences
    (except Biotechnology).

■ ■ ■

Founded in 1920 as a subsidiary of the Eastman Kodak
Company, Eastman Chemical Company was spun off as
an independent company by Kodak in 1994. Eastman

Chemical produces a wide range of plastics, chemicals,
and fibers and is a world leader in the production and
recycling of polyester plastics.

## U.S. CHEMICAL PRODUCTION IN THE WAKE OF WORLD WAR I

When World War I broke out in 1914, George Eastman
watched the supply of essential materials arriving from
European producers to his company, the Eastman
Kodak Company, slow to a trickle. The ramifications
were nearly disastrous. The company had grown
dependent on European manufacturers for many of the
raw materials required to sustain its operations,
particularly photographic paper, optical glass, and
gelatin, without which Eastman's photography empire
would shrivel into insolvency. Also of great importance
and in short supply during the war years were the
numerous chemicals crucial to the photography
company's production processes, including methanol,
acetic acid, and acetone. As the war dragged on, Eastman's predicament grew increasingly severe, and film
production at Eastman Kodak's manufacturing facilities
in Rochester, New York, nearly ground to a halt.

Determined to ensure Kodak's future self-reliance,
Eastman decided the most prudent solution was to
develop an independent supply of chemicals. Accordingly, after the conclusion of the war, Eastman and
other Kodak delegates began searching for a suitable
location for a Kodak-owned and operated chemical
production facility. As Kodak employees were scouting
the country, a resident of Kingsport, Tennessee, named
J. Fred Johnson was conducting a nationwide search of

his own, hoping to sell a half-built wood distillation plant to an interested party. Johnson, an employee of the Kingsport Improvement Company, was attempting to revitalize Kingsport's economy, which had thrived during the war but was limping along at the war's conclusion, bereft of the business generated by the manufacturing industries that had temporarily established operations in Kingsport for war-related work.

One company that had come to Kingsport during the war was the American Wood Reduction Company, which had contracted with the federal government to construct a wood distillation plant for making methanol and other related chemicals. Before the plant was finished, however, the war ended and American Wood Reduction cut its ties to Kingsport, leaving a lone watchman to stand guard over the partly constructed facility. After the retreat of American Wood Reduction, Johnson began his search for an industrial concern that could use the idle wood distillation plant.

By 1920 Kodak and Johnson had found each other, and a group of Kodak representatives led by Perley S. Wilcox, a future chairman of Kodak and an employee since 1898, arrived in Kingsport to examine the half-built wood distillation facility Johnson was eager to sell. Finding it to their liking, the Kodak group pushed for its acquisition, and later that year George Eastman authorized the purchase of the plant and surrounding acreage for $205,000. Wilcox was named director and general manager of the new company, becoming the first leader of Tennessee Eastman Corporation, a Kodak subsidiary.

Shortly after the construction of the wood distillation plant was finished, the solitary watchman who had guarded an architectural skeleton was replaced by more than 300 Tennessee Eastman employees, who were given the task of meeting Kodak's substantial chemical needs. Kodak's Rochester facilities required 40,000 gallons of methanol per month, in addition to other necessary chemicals such as acetic acid and acetone.

Tennessee Eastman delivered its first shipment of methanol to Rochester in July 1921. The company generated $35,000 in sales after its first year, but its total production fell short of Kodak's chemical needs for the next several years. In addition, the Kingsport plant was unprofitable and would remain so long after its production volume was raised to a sufficient level.

## PRODUCT DIVERSIFICATION IN THE 1920S AND 1930S

By the mid-1920s Tennessee Eastman was satisfying Rochester's monthly methanol needs, but weak profits continued to hound Tennessee Eastman for another decade. To improve profitability, the company began marketing the byproducts created from the Kingsport plant's distillation processes, including charcoal, tars, wood preservatives, and other process wastes. Charcoal powder and wood tar were combined to form a charcoal briquette that the company sold as cooking and household fuel, transforming the 300 railroad cars of charcoal dust the company produced each month into a money-making sideline business. Other byproducts from the Kingsport plant also were marketed, including coal tars and various derivatives of acetone (which were sold to sugar refineries), as well as lumber.

Process economy started Tennessee Eastman down the road toward profitability and provided a springboard for diversification into segments of the chemical industry exclusive of Kodak's needs. Sales in 1930 were $1.95 million, with acetic anhydride and lumber ranking as the company's two major products. During the 1930s, Tennessee Eastman began to make pivotal contributions to its parent company's Rochester facilities, beginning with its manufacture of cellulose acetate in 1930. Kodak had experimented with using cellulose acetate as a film base back in 1907, striving to replace flammable nitrocellulose with a nonflammable alternative. The company's innovation quickly became the industry standard.

Perhaps more important, Tennessee Eastman distinguished itself as a leader and pioneer in the chemical industry through its production of acetate yarn. An experimental acetate yarn plant had been constructed in 1928, and by 1931 the Kingsport-based facility had begun large-scale production, churning out 287,000 pounds of yarn that year alone. Within a decade, Tennessee Eastman's acetate yarn was recognized throughout the textile industry as the best quality yarn on the market, securing the company's economic stability for the next two decades and paving the way for the development of other mainstay products.

One year after large-scale production of acetate yarn had begun, Tennessee Eastman began producing Tenite

## KEY DATES

**1920:** Tennessee Eastman Corporation is created as a subsidiary of Eastman Kodak Company.
**1931:** Tennessee Eastman begins large-scale production of acetate yarn.
**1950:** Texas Eastman Company is formed.
**1951:** Tennessee Eastman Corporation becomes Tennessee Eastman Company.
**1954:** Eastman begins producing polyethylene.
**1968:** Eastman Chemicals Division is formed.
**1990:** Eastman Chemicals Division is reorganized as Eastman Chemical Company.
**1994:** Eastman Chemical Company is incorporated.
**2000:** Eastman announces that it will begin online marketing of its chemicals and polymers.
**2005:** Eastman breaks ground on plan with new technology for producing PET resin.
**2007:** Eastman introduces a new BPA-free copolyester.

cellulosic plastics, which were used for radio parts, toys, telephones, and automobile steering wheels. That year, 1932, also was the first year Tennessee Eastman's trade sales exceeded its sales to Kodak.

## REORGANIZATION: 1950–68

By 1940 Tennessee Eastman was recording nearly $30 million in annual sales, an exponential increase from the $1.95 million generated ten years earlier. The increase had been fueled primarily by the company's production of acetate yarn, which by this point was Tennessee Eastman's single major product, as it would be a decade later, when annual sales stood at $130 million. Kodak organized an additional chemical subsidiary in 1950, Texas Eastman Company, then formed Eastman Chemical Products, Inc., in 1953 to serve as the marketing arm for both Texas Eastman and Tennessee Eastman. Tennessee Eastman, meanwhile, had undergone a name change, switching its corporate title from Tennessee Eastman Corporation to Tennessee Eastman Company in 1951. Although the name change was minor, a significant development occurred contemporaneously that dramatically altered the company's future. During the early 1950s, Tennessee Eastman developed cellulose acetate filter tow, which was used in cigarette filters, giving the company a product that drove sales upward for the next half century and supplanted acetate yarn as its mainstay product.

With filter tow sales leading the way, Tennessee Eastman registered $244 million in annual sales in 1960, continuing to record exponential leaps in annual revenues decade by decade. In 1968 the Eastman Chemicals Division of Eastman Kodak Company was formed, bringing together the various chemical concerns within Kodak's corporate structure and unifying them as a division. When it was organized, the chemicals division included Tennessee Eastman, Texas Eastman Company, Carolina Eastman Company, Eastman Chemicals Products, Inc., and related marketing organizations.

With this collection of companies banded together, annual sales generated by the division shot upward, swelling to $588 million in 1970, a revenue total derived in large part from the production of filter tow and polyester fibers. Late in the decade, the Eastman Chemicals Division introduced polyethylene terephthalate (PET) resin, used to make plastic containers. The addition of PET to the division's product line helped annual sales exceed $2 billion by the beginning of the 1980s.

In 1990 Kodak reorganized its chemicals division, renaming it Eastman Chemical Company. Annual sales by this point exceeded $3.5 billion, ranking the company among the largest chemical concerns in the world. With large market shares in PET and cellulosics, Eastman Chemical entered the 1990s as the jewel of the Kodak empire. Kodak, on the other hand, was not faring as well. As the decade progressed, debt began to mount, and Eastman Chemical was put in the awkward position of supplying cash to its debt-heavy parent, a reversal of roles for the former captive chemical supplier that complicated its corporate priorities and hobbled its investments in chemical operations.

As a result, Kodak spun off its chemical subsidiary to Kodak shareholders on the first day of 1994, creating the tenth-largest chemical company in the country. As part of the spin-off, Eastman Chemical was saddled with $1.8 billion in long-term debt. By the end of its first year as an independent company, however, Eastman Chemical had whittled its debt down by $600 million, reducing its ratio of debt to total capital from 63 percent to 48 percent during a 12-month span. Sales also continued to grow into the mid-1990s, surpassing the $5 billion mark for the first time in 1995.

## GLOBALIZATION: 1991–2000

Eastman Chemical moved toward its future as an independent chemical supplier supported by the four core product groups of container plastics, specialty polyester packaging plastics, coatings materials for paints and solvents, and filter tow. Like other major chemical companies, Eastman realized that international expansion was the only way to maintain a competitive edge into the next century. Overall, the U.S. chemical industry saw significant growth in exports in the first half of the 1990s, from $43 billion in 1991 to $64.7 billion in 1996, and Eastman was no exception. In 1994 approximately one-third of Eastman's $4.3 billion in total sales came from international markets, but by 1997 foreign sales exceeded $1.8 billion and accounted for 39 percent of the company's total sales. Much of the increase was the result of increased production capacity, both at home and abroad. In 1996 and 1997, Eastman opened new container plastics manufacturing operations in Mexico and Spain. In 1998 it began production at plants in Argentina and Malaysia, and at two new plants in The Netherlands. Also in 1997, Eastman Chemical Ltd., Singapore took steps toward establishing a niche in the burgeoning Chinese market, investing several hundred million dollars into new facilities in the Special Economic Zone of Shenzhen, China.

Eastman's expansion plans ultimately got ahead of economic reality, however, and by 1997 the company found itself burdened with significant production overcapacity. This reversal of fortune was in part the result of decreased demand for the company's specialty and performance products, particularly in the United States and China. Increased competition, brought on by globalization and the struggle over emerging marketplaces, also contributed to the excess capacity. The subsequent lower prices and decreased volume were accompanied by rising raw material costs, and Eastman suffered steadily decreasing earnings from 1996 to 1998.

The company responded to this sudden downturn with an aggressive restructuring plan. It implemented a drastic cost-reduction program, pledging to cut $500 million in expenses between 1997 and 2000, and in 1999 it reorganized itself into two business segments, polymers and chemicals. In addition, by the end of 2000 the company divested itself of the propylene glycol segment of its fine chemicals division, to focus its attention on potentially more lucrative adhesives, inks, and coatings markets.

In the late 1990s Eastman also made strides toward establishing Internet capability. The commodity nature of chemicals made them a logical fit for e-commerce, since they were subject to fairly regular international standards, which made the selling process relatively straightforward. Eastman was determined to take advantage of the new technology, and in October 2000 it announced a plan to make its chemicals and polymers available through online business-to-business relation-

ships with existing customers, as well as through its Web site and a number of virtual marketplaces.

This reorganization, along with the shift to e-commerce, made some downsizing inevitable, and Eastman's workforce was reduced by almost 2,000 employees between 1996 and 1999. By 1999, however, Eastman saw a slight increase in business for the first time in four years, and in 2000 it was able to announce a plan to increase its PET manufacturing capacity by 110,000 metric tons a year. Optimism continued as the company announced plans to split Eastman into two separate publicly traded entities. Eastman was to concentrate on specialty chemicals including polymers, paints, coatings, adhesives, and resins for everything from inks to diapers to signs with revenues of more than $3 billion, and the spin-off, named Voridian, would take Eastman's PET recyclable business and acetate tow operation with a total revenues of $2 billion.

## NEW CHALLENGES: THE 21ST CENTURY

By November 2001, the company faced a tougher marketplace. World demand, especially for PET, plummeted. Also, oil and other raw materials prices continued to rise. The company's third quarter earnings dropped by 76 percent compared to the previous year. As a result, the company delayed the proposed de-merger. In February 2002, amid further signs of poor world demand and several plant closings, the company resolved to cancel the de-merger. Instead, Eastman maintained the split and operated the entities as two separate divisions. Also, the company continued to reduce capacity by closing down 360 million pounds of PET capacity across its Toronto, Canada, and Kingsport, Tennessee, facilities.

Eastman and other chemical companies had come to realize that significant growth would not come from innovative products or increases in capacity. Instead, a company needed to leverage its know-how to innovate in other ways, either by making processes more efficient or creating more effective methods of distribution. As the difficult recession took its toll on Eastman's profitability its e-commerce distribution efforts became increasingly more critical to its future. In January 2001, Eastman announced that it had established fifteen system-to-system connections with its trading partners, including Colgate-Palmolive, ExxonMobil, and PPG. Eastman also formed a 50-50 joint venture with Henderson China Holdings to create chemical e-business Web sites in China and surrounding regions. The joint venture, named Asia BizNet, would use its Web sites to help companies manage procurement and develop customer relationships. The company also made efforts to integrate the Internet into every aspect of its supply chain.

Despite such efforts, difficult times persisted through much of 2003. The company announced plans to sell off parts of its underperforming coatings, adhesives, speciality polymers, and inks (CASPI) division. Eastman targeted $100 million in cost savings and slashed salaries in an effort to counter the increase in raw materials costs and avoid layoffs. Despite such efforts, in September 2003, the company announced a layoff of 2,400 workers, about 15 percent of its workforce. A month later, the company announced another layoff of 600 workers. Most of the layoffs came from the CASPI division.

The company also began a strategy of outsourcing certain processes but unlike other companies, Eastman did not outsource to other companies. Instead, it formed specialized divisions and spun off the divisions as separate entities. One such entity was Cendian, which specialized in logistics for chemical and plastics companies. Another was Ariel Research Corp., a provider of international chemical and regulatory compliance solutions for environmental, health, and safety operations. Eastman remained the largest customer for these companies, but they could offer their services to other companies as well.

The year 2004 brought slightly better results for most chemical companies, including Eastman, but the chemicals industry still remained underwater. The company sold Ariel Research to 3E Company. In 2005 Eastman broke ground on a new production facility in Columbia, South Carolina. The new facility promised to use the company's latest production technology for making PET resin more effectively, using fewer steps and with a smaller plant footprint. As another sign of the company's financial woes it closed down its subsidiary, Cendian, due to poor performance, and reintegrated the subsidiary's logistical functions into the company' main operations. In 2006 the company reorganized its businesses into two major groups. The first group, chemicals and fibers, included performance chemicals and intermediates, fibers and coatings, and CASPI. The second group, polyesters, included polymers and plastics. The company's intention was to group together units that shared assets and technologies. As part of this reorganization, Voridian, the division that was created to be a spin-off in 2003, was dismantled and integrated into the new corporate structure. This new plan and corporate structure was very much in line with an industry trend to improve growth and profitability although reduced inefficiencies and better distribution.

In late 2007, Eastman introduced a new heat resistant copolyester for kitchen applications. The new polyester offered more design flexibility and better durability than similar products. Most importantly, it was free of bisphenol-A (BPA). Several governments raised health concerns about BPA in 2008, and many retailers removed plastic products from their shelves because they contained BPA. Eastman offered its new copolyester as an alternative and reaped the benefits. The company began moving capital from its poorly performing PET operations to its quickly growing copolyester business. Nonetheless, 2009 brought a continued downturn in the market, particularly in the plastics-related businesses. Plastics-related sales fell more than 25 percent. The company's PET sales fell 33 percent, and sales of its specialty plastics, including its new copolyester, fell 19 percent. Chemical companies, including Eastman, continued laying off workers and pursuing cost-cutting measures. During the early part of 2009, Eastman announced that it was considering selling its PET unit, but it was uncertain what price the company would receive in an already financially strapped industry. While the company had a positive outlook entering 2010, it was uncertain how the worldwide recession would effect the company's prospects for recovery over the coming year.

*Jeffrey L. Covell*
*Updated, Stephen Meyer; Aaron Hauser*

## PRINCIPAL SUBSIDIARIES

Eastman Chemical Asia Pacific Private Limited (Singapore); Eastman Chemical Europoort B.V. (Netherlands); McWhorter Holdings Ltd. (UK); TX Energy, LLC.

## PRINCIPAL DIVISIONS

Coatings, Adhesives, Specialty Polymers, and Inks; Fibers; Performance Chemicals and Intermediates; Performance Polymers; Specialty Plastics.

## PRINCIPAL COMPETITORS

BASF Aktiengesellschaft; Celanese Corporation; Daicel Chemical Industries Ltd.; The Dow Chemical Company; Mitsubishi Rayon Co. Ltd.; Rhodia S.A.; UAB Korelita; Wellman, Inc.

## FURTHER READING

"Eastman Realigning Chemical Business into Two Major Groups," *Platts Commodity News,* March 6, 2006.
Esposito, Frank, "Eastman Chemical Seeing the Early Stages of

Recovery," *Plastics News,* February, 8, 2010, p.13.

Mullin, Rick, "Innovative Growth," *Chemical Week,* March 13, 2002, p. 17–22.

———, "Eastman Installs its Engine from the Top Down,"

*Chemical Week,* May 22, 2002, p. 23.

Nolan, Amy, "Eastman to Delay Company Split Due to Poor Economy," *Knoxville News-Sentinel,* November 21, 2001, p. C1.

# Echo Global Logistics Inc.

—■—

**600 West Chicago Avenue**
**Suite 725**
**Chicago, Illinois 60610**
**U.S.A.**
**Telephone: (800) 354-7993**
**Fax: (888) 796-4445**
**Web site: http://www.echo.com**

*Public Company*
*Founded:* 2005
*Employees:* 663
*Sales:* $259.6 million (2009)
*Stock Exchanges:* NASDAQ
*Ticker Symbol:* ECHO
*NAICS:* 488510 Freight Transportation Arrangement

■ ■ ■

Echo Global Logistics Inc. (Echo) is a leading provider of transportation management services. Utilizing Web-based software applications and a database of 24,000 transportation providers, the company seeks to identify excess transportation capacity and obtain competitive shipping rates for its clients. Echo arranges transportation across all major modes including truckload, less than a truckload, intermodal, domestic air, expedited, and international transportation services. The company's core logistic services includes rate negotiation, shipment execution and tracking, carrier management, routing compliance, freight bill audit and payment, and performance management and reporting.

## COMPANY FOUNDING: 2005

Echo Global Logistics was founded in January 2005 by three Chicago-area entrepreneurs, Richard A. Heise Jr., Eric P. Lefkofshy, and Bradley A. Keywell, as a privately held limited liability company in the freight and logistics business. Their goal was to apply Web-based technology to transportation, logistics, and supply chain management. Internally, Echo referred to itself as a technology company in the transportation and logistics business.

The function of the freight and logistics industry is in bringing products to market via the supply chain. A rudimentary supply chain begins with a manufacturer who needs a constant supply of raw materials to produce manufactured goods. These goods are then shipped to distribution facilities, which distribute the products to stores and then to the consumer.

The industry is dependent on and responsive to economic factors which influence commercial trade. As globalization began to spread, trade and tariff restriction eased, and world trade dramatically increased. In 1980 the total value of two-way merchandise trade in the United States stood at $467 billion, but by 2006 the value had grown to $2,942 billion. According to the World Trade Organization, the total value of world merchandise trade would grow from $8,907 billion in 2004 to $11,783 billion in 2006 and $13,619 billion by 2007.

With global economic trends favorable to the freight and logistics sector, Echo looked to carve out a niche in this burgeoning industry sector.

## ACQUIRING RESOURCES

When Echo Global Logistics opened its doors for business in March 2005, the company had two glaring deficiencies. The first was its very structure. Privately held companies tend to have problems raising capital. With no shares to sell, raising money in the capital markets is a non-issue, and investment bankers may shy away from lending large sums of money to companies with limited liability.

The second glaring deficiency was that the founders of Echo had little to no experience in freight, logistics, or supply chain management. Richard A Heise Jr. was primarily a private investor. Bradley A. Keywell, who was a driving force behind Echo, and Eric P. Lefkofsky were both lawyers by training.

The most prominent feature that these three individuals shared was that they were all entrepreneurs. As entrepreneurs, they started, organized, and developed businesses. They were willing to assume the financial risk to take an idea and turn it into a business that would become a going concern. In fact, Keywell has sometimes been referred to as a serial entrepreneur.

## SERIAL ENTREPRENEUR

In 1991 Bradley A. Keywell received his bachelor of business administration degree from the University of Michigan. In the same year, he was named one of the top 10 collegiate entrepreneurs by the Association of Collegiate Entrepreneurs. Keywell would go on to graduate cum laude with a law degree two years later.

Fresh out of law school in 1993, Keywell and his university friend Eric Lefkofsky purchased Wisconsin-based Brandon Apparel Company. While neither man appeared to have any experience in the apparel business, they combined some cash of their own and a loan from the city of Columbus, Wisconsin, which was desperate to keep jobs in the community, to fund the venture. Further financing was secured through Wisconsin's Johnson Bank.

This venture by Keywell and Lefkofsky did not go as planned, however. An initial loan of $5 million from

Johnson Bank was increased to $6.4 million, but then Johnson Bank sued Keywell and Lefkofsky, claiming the men had defaulted on the loan. Other suits were filed, summary judgments were appealed, and the entire affair descended into a legal morass. (All lawsuits were resolved many years later.)

While still embroiled in the Brandon Apparel affair, in 1999 Keywell cofounded an Internet company named Starbelly, which modernized the promotional merchandising industry. The industry, which produces company promotional material such logos for clothing, briefcases, and coffee cups, is a $75 billon per year industry. Keywell estimated correctly that by using the Internet, he could cut prices by 30 to 40 percent and reduce delivery times by 75 percent. He collaborated with Corel Corporation, a Canadian software company that specialized in graphic design, to develop software which allowed customers to design their own merchandise. Starbelly would also create online stores that allowed customers and employees to shop and order via the Internet, with all products being shipped within seven days.

Within a year of its creation, Starbelly caught the eye of Ha-Lo Industries, one of the market leaders in the supply of promotional material. In January 2000 Ha-Lo had embarked on a strategy to use its substantial customer base as leverage and evolve into an online marketer. Ha-Lo acquired Starbelly for $240 million to provide what Ha-Lo CEO John Kelly called the cornerstone of Ha-Lo's e-transformation strategy. By using Internet technology, Ha-Lo could bring the market closer to the consumer and improve operating efficiencies and communications.

In 2000 Keywell noted that the *Fortune* 1000 companies of the world were increasingly demanding Internet-based procurement methods. It was a lesson he would apply to Echo Global Logistics.

## ECHO OPERATIONS

Despite these deficiencies, Echo Global Logistics earned revenues of $7.3 million in its first year of operations. In large part, the effects of globalization were forcing a rapid transformation in business. Companies were forced to be more nimble in response to the changing environment. Many had to refocus on their core business to maintain a competitive edge and find ways to outsource peripheral functions. While trade barriers were falling, the complexity of international trade and the ensuing difficulties of communications and information were increasing.

By the first half of 2006, Echo had attracted the attention of potential investors. New Enterprise Associates, one of the largest technology investors in the United States, had shown an interest in the company and its attempts to apply Web technology to the freight and logistics business. With investors now willing to back the company, in June 2006 Echo Global Logistics converted from a limited liability company to a corporation under the laws of the State of Delaware.

Its new status enabled the company to begin the search for the human talent which could grow the business into a world-class competitor. Two key appointments would be made, one in late 2006 and one in early 2007, which would transform the organization.

In December 2006 Echo appointed Douglas R. Waggoner as its chief executive officer. Waggoner had more that twenty years experience in the transportation industry. He had been the CEO of USF Bestway, a major American freight-handling corporation. He had also founded SelecTrans LLC, a company that developed freight management software.

In February 2007, Samuel K. Skinner was appointed chairman of the board of directors of Echo Global Logistics. Skinner was another transportation veteran but with a political pedigree. He had served as the secretary of transportation and was later chief of staff at the White House under President George H.W. Bush.

The two men would transform Echo Global Logistics from a small freight company into a large and profitable third-party logistics provider, or 3PL, to use the industry term.

## EXPANDING THE BRAND

Echo is non-asset-based in the sense that it does not own the physical assets of a transportation company. It has no trucks or warehouses, and it owns no rail cars or delivery centers.

What the company does do is use proprietary technology to provide customized solutions to the transportation and logistic requirements of its clients. The technology platform is called Evolved Transportation Manager (ETM). EMT software allows Echo to analyze a client's transportation requirements and match them to availability in the market place. It tracks available capacity and pricing from market sources. It can find an appropriate service level, track shipments, and provide historical transaction information. It can transfer shipment data directly into the customer's financial management system. This allows the client greater visibility and analysis of freight expenditures that result in cost savings.

The development of third-party logistics providers grew out of the deregulation of the transport industry in the 1980s. With regulation gone, the transportation industry lacked the cohesiveness of an organized marketplace. Lack of information on availability and capacity resulted in inefficiencies. It has been estimated that as much as 30 percent of U.S. transportation capacity could be idle due to poor organization. The development of information technology in the 1990s would bring buyer and seller together. Third-party logistics companies driven by information technology would fill the niche.

According to an industry survey taken in 2004 of *Fortune* 500 companies, more than 80 percent of them were using 3PLs for all or part of their shipping needs, up from 38 percent in 1991. Of the businesses that took part in the survey, more than 70 percent reported that using a 3PL had a positive or very positive impact on logistic costs.

Waggoner knew the route that Echo needed to follow to position itself as a key third-party logistics provider. In April 2007 Echo acquired SelecTrans LLC and its freight management software. Waggoner had been a founder of SelecTrans. Equipped with modern information technology, Echo needed to establish itself provider of freight and logistics services.

Waggoner also embarked upon a strategy to gain a presence for Echo throughout the United States. In May 2007 Echo acquired Mountain Logistic of Park City, Utah. This company had headquarters in Utah and offices in Los Angeles. By acquiring it, Echo gained a presence in the west and particularly on the West Coast. In October of the same year, Bestway Solutions, an established 3PL in Portland, Oregon, was purchased, giving Waggoner and Echo a door to the northwestern United States.

Sticking to its core of being a non-asset-based provider, Echo needed a resource with which it could access transportation providers. In June 2009 it acquired

Raytrans Distribution Services, a transportation broker-age firm. Raytrans specialized in flatbed, over sized, and auto haul services.

As Echo kept expanding, its business and revenues were also climbing. By 2007 its revenues topped $95 million and would soar to $202.8 million in 2008 and $259.6 million in 2009. In October 2009 Echo Global Logistics became a publicly traded company with an IPO on the NASDAQ.

In 2010 Waggoner and the Echo team focused on expanding into key metropolitan areas to capture market share. In March, a new sales office was opened in Atlanta, Georgia, to develop the market in the southeastern United States and in April, a new office was opened in Dallas, Texas, to cover the southern region. These offices would develop sales organizations in previously untapped markets.

*Ian MacDonald*

## PRINCIPAL COMPETITORS

C.H. Robinson Worldwide Inc.; Expeditors International of Washington Inc.; FedEx Corp.; Freightquote.com Inc.; JB Hunt Transport Inc.; Ozburn-Hessey Logistics LLC; Total Quality Logistics Inc.; Transplace texas L.P.

## FURTHER READING

Adler, Matthew, and Gary Hufbauer, "Policy Liberalization and US Merchandise Trade Growth, 1980–2006," Peterson Institute for International Economics, Working Paper No. 09-2, May 11, 2009.

Bounds, Gwendolyn, Kelly Spors, and Raymund Flandes, "The Secrets of Serial Success," *Wall Street Journal,* August 20, 2007.

Johnson, Paul, "Brandon Apparel Fails to Repay All of Wisconsin State Loan," *Wisconsin State Journal,* August 21, 1997.

Lieb, Robert, and Brooks Bentz, "The Use of Third Party Logistics Services by Large American Manufacturers – The 2004 Survey," *Transportation Journal* 44 no. 2 (2005): 5–15.

MacDonald, Andrea, "How Companies Choose and Manage 3PLS," *World Trade,* February 1, 2007.

Vasiliauskas, Aidas, and Gražzvydas Jakubauskas, "Principle Benefits of Third Party Logistics Approach When Managing Logistics Supply Chain," *Transport,* 22, no. 2 (2007): 68–72.

# Emdeon Inc.

3055 Lebanon Pike
Suite 1000
Nashville, Tennessee 37214
U.S.A.
Telephone: (615) 932-3000
Fax: (615) 231-7972
Web site: http://www.emdeon.com

*Public Company*
*Founded:* 1996 as Healtheon
*Employees:* 2,100 (2010)
*Revenues:* $918.4 million (2009)
*Stock Exchanges:* New York
*Ticker Symbol:* EM
*NAICS:* 54199 All Other Professional, Scientific, and Technical Services

∎ ∎ ∎

Emdeon Inc. provides revenue and payment cycle solutions for its customers, connecting payers, providers, and patients to integrate and automate crucial business and administrative functions throughout the patient process. Emdeon concentrates on the three customer segments of providers, payers, and pharmacy services. Emdeon helps health care professionals (providers) reduce administrative costs and increase profits. Emdeon helps payers and preferred provider organizations (PPOs) improve their processes and lower administrative costs. Emdeon Pharmacy Services helps streamline the prescription process, enabling both national pharmacy chains and independent pharmacies to benefit from increased accuracy, efficiency, and higher profitability.

## THE BEGINNINGS OF HEALTHEON AND WEBMD: 1996–99

Jim Clark, founder of Silicon Graphics and Netscape Communications, Inc., founded Healtheon in January 1996. Its original aim was to provide information services to help employers and employees manage health plan benefits programs, not compete with other sites offering health content to end users. Healtheon's target customers were insurers and health-maintenance organizations.

In 1999 Healtheon partnered with IBM to expand its offerings and enable physicians and consumers to use the Internet to connect to their hospitals, health plans, managed care organizations, labs and pharmaceutical companies. The same year Healtheon also struck a deal with Drugstore.com to offer users a portal to purchase health and wellness products. In May 1999 Healtheon and WebMD, a Web site offering health care information to end users, announced plans to merge and create a new cradle-to-grave Internet health care and e-commerce company called Healtheon/WebMD. In addition to the two companies merging, other companies invested in the new venture, including a $250 million stake by the Microsoft Corporation. Other investors, including Excite, Intel, Covad, Softbank, and Superior Consulting combined to chip in another $360 million in capital. The new board was made up of four representatives from Healtheon, four from WebMD, and one from Microsoft.

WebMD launched on October 5, 1998. The Web site was filled with medical information available to health care professionals and the general public. WebMD grew rapidly, inking deals with Physician Sales and Services, a medical supply distributor, and Internet service provider CompuServe. The company also acquired Sapient Health Network and partnered with Lycos, a large online community, all within its first six months. WebMD continued its momentum by forming a strategic alliance with the DuPont Digital Consumer Health group, the first partnership the pharmaceutical giant formed with its new digital consumer health business. By May 1999, when it merged with Healtheon, WebMD had achieved extremely high brand visibility in just eight months.

### THE RISE OF HEALTHEON/WEBMD: 1999

In June 1999 Dell made an undisclosed investment in Healtheon/WebMD, and in July, Healtheon/WebMD announced another deal with Dell, Inc. The partnership linked the two companies' Web sites. Dell added a link to WebMD on its health care site and created a co-branded WebMD Web page that allowed WebMD subscribers to price, order, and track Dell systems via a private, secure site. Dell also placed a WebMD link on its new Dellnet.com consumer site. Dellnet.com provided consumers with direct links to products and services through a branded portal that began shipping on Dell Dimension desktops in July 1999.

Beginning in September, Healtheon/WebMD became the exclusive sponsor and content provider for CBS SportsLine's Health & Wellness arena, bringing users the latest health and medical news, information, and updates from WebMD experts. CBS and WebMD also created daily interactive health-related events and online support communities to encourage communication. WebMD was the official sponsor of all injury reports on CBS SportsLine for both collegiate and professional sports.

WebMD continued to grow and expand. In October 1999, Breast Cancer Awareness Month, Healtheon/WebMD spearheaded a national breast cancer awareness program along with HealthSouth Corporation and Tenet Healthcare Corporation, providing free mammograms to women, regardless of insurance coverage. During the next year, WebMD/Healtheon struck deals with several more partners and moved into many other aspects of the health care industry by fostering various relationships with Electronic Data Systems, Eli Lilly and Company, Humana Health Insurance, Medic Computer Systems, the American College of Sports Medicine, and the American College of Surgeons.

### STARTING DOWN A ROCKY ROAD: 2000

In January 2000 Healtheon/WebMD acquired Envoy Corporation, the electronic data interchange (EDI) unit of Quintiles Transnational Corporation. Envoy was a large provider of EDI products and services to the health care industry. In addition, Healtheon/WebMD and Quintiles announced their intention to jointly develop a Web-based suite of products and services for the health care industry. Healtheon/WebMD gave Quintiles exclusive rights to de-identified Envoy transaction data and named Quintiles the exclusive licensee of de-identified Healtheon/WebMD data. Healtheon/WebMD pledged to ensure that no personally identifiable patient data was disclosed.

A little more than a year later, in April 2001, WebMD initiated legal proceedings to sever its alliance with Quintiles. WebMD had become aware that supplying patient data gathered from billing forms to Quintiles for market research violated state privacy laws, so it halted the data flow. In response, Quintiles obtained a restraining order to force WebMD to continue to supply the data. When the state restraining order expired, WebMD stopped the data flow once again. A federal restraining order again forced WebMD to supply the data as legal proceedings continued.

As the case gained prominence in the news, patients became aware that their medical billing information was not private and was being used for market research. In December 2001 the legal battle ended. Healtheon/WebMD agreed to pay $185 million to purchase Healtheon/WebMD stock from Quintiles, and Quintiles gave up its data rights after March 2002.

In September 2000 Healtheon/WebMD announced the completion of its merger with Medical Manager Corporation and its subsidiary, CareInsite, Inc., as well as the completion of its acquisition of OnHealth Company. Medical Manager developed and distributed a

## KEY DATES

**1996:** Jim Clark founds Healtheon.
**1999:** Healtheon merges with WebMD.
**2003:** Federal authorities launch investigation into WebMD's Medical Manager division for fraudulent accounting practices.
**2005:** WebMD Corporation spins off WebMD into its own entity.
**2007:** Parent Emdeon renamed HLTH Corporation, while Emdeon Business Services keeps the Emdeon name.
**2010:** Emdeon forges partnerships with Medicity and Enclarity.

popular physician practice management system, while CareInsite provided network and clinical communications services to the health care sector. At the same time, it changed its name from Healtheon/WebMD to WebMD Corporation but continued to trade under the symbol HLTH. Between its initial public offering (IPO) in 1999 and November 2000, WebMD had merged with or acquired 17 other companies.

### DIFFICULT YEARS: 2000–01

As WebMD continued to form new partnerships, some old partnerships were ending. In December 2000, DuPont and WebMD terminated their alliance, more than three years before its original end date of March 2004. In January 2001 WebMD and News Corp dissolved the $1 billion partnership they formed in December 1999. In April 2001 the Microsoft Corporation, which had initially pledged to invest $250 million over five years and underwrite $150 million in physician subscriptions, revised its 1999 deal with WebMD. Soon after, WebMD announced that it was moving away from subscription-based sponsorship as a revenue stream. In October 2001 the two companies terminated another agreement where Microsoft was to provide technology for WebMD software for physicians.

In October 2000 Healtheon founder Jim Clark resigned, followed by Jeffrey Arnold, co-CEO and founder of WebMD. Between October 2000 and May 2001, the chief technology officer, chief operating officer, chief marketing officer, and executive vice president of strategic relationships also all resigned. The restructuring of the company led not only to personnel changes but also to job cuts, beginning in the fall of 2000 when WebMD moved its headquarters from Atlanta to New Jersey. In May 2001 WebMD announced that it would cut 350 more jobs, bringing the total to 1,450 by the end of the year.

In September 2001 Janus Capital Corporation sold 11 million shares of WebMD stock at a large loss. Janus originally bought the stock for $930 million ($62 a share), but at the time it sold, WebMD stock was trading for between $4.50 and $9.44 a share, resulting in Janus receiving only between $49.5 million and $103.8 million for the sale. One year earlier, four Janus funds sold 15 million shares of WebMD stock, and Smith-Kline Beecham, a founding investor, sold 900,000 shares. Between September 2000 and September 2001 WebMD stock value plummeted. WebMD reported a $3.1 billion loss for 2000, and, in March 2002, WebMD posted a net loss of $6.7 billion for 2001. Despite these losses, analysts believed that WebMD still had enough capital to continue operating.

### FEDERAL INVESTIGATION: 2002–05

WebMD formed some new partnerships in 2002 and early 2003. In April 2002 WebMD partnered with AOL to reach its more than 32 million AOL and CompuServe subscribers, and it also acquired Medscape Portals. In April 2003 WebMD added dentists to its target audience when PracticeWorks selected WebMD Envoy as its clearinghouse for dental transactions.

On September 4, 2003, agents of the Federal Bureau of Investigation (FBI) and and Internal Revenue Service (IRS) executed search warrants on three WebMD offices in Elmwood Park, New Jersey, and Tampa and Alachua, Florida. The federal investigation centered on WebMD's Medical Manager division. Earlier in 2003, WebMD fired two employees for embezzlement and initiated a lawsuit against them. The federal authorities were investigating WebMD's Medical Manager dealer acquisition program and Medical Manager's financial reports for 1999.

By January 2005 three Medical Manager employees had pled guilty to fraudulent accounting practices by confessing to falsely inflating the company's financial results from 1997 (prior to its acquisition by WebMD) and continuing through five fiscal quarters after WebMD assumed ownership. In April 2005 Michael Singer, founder of Medical Manager, resigned. In December 2005 the United States Attorney announced indictments against 10 former officers and employees of Medical Manager, including Singer. One defendant died, four were dismissed, and two were transferred to Florida for trial. Singer entered into a plea agreement. In March 2010 two other defendants were found guilty after a trial.

## BECOMING EMDEON: 2005

In September 2005 WebMD Corporation spun off WebMD Health Corporation as a separate company. It commenced trading under the symbol WBMD. The parent company then renamed itself Emdeon Inc. but continued to trade under the symbol HLTH until 2009, when it began trading under the symbol EM. Emdeon Corporation's businesses included Emdeon Business Services, Emdeon Practice Services, WebMD Health, and Porex.

The end of 2005 was a financially shaky time for Emdeon Inc. Share prices fell and earnings did not meet analyst projections, and the company's losses were compounded by its legal trouble and dented public image. Emdeon's woes continued when its CEO had to step down due to serious illness.

Although Emdeon sold its two largest business units in 2006, *Health Data Management* reported that it was still a major player in the health care industry. Emdeon sold the Emdeon Practice Services division to Sage Software, Inc., and sold a majority interest in its Business Services unit to General Atlantic Partners, yet all three companies forged future beneficial relationships. Emdeon continued to operate the Emdeon Business Services claims clearinghouse after it was sold to General Atlantic Partners and retained 50 percent control on the board of directors. When Sage Software bought Emdeon Practice Services, Sage contracted Emdeon to serve its physicians until 2013.

In May 2007 Emdeon announced another name change. Emdeon Business Services, sold to General Atlantic in 2006, retained the Emdeon name while Emdeon, Inc., changed its name to HLTH Corporation and continued to trade under the HLTH symbol.

## HEALTH CARE EVOLUTION: 2009 AND BEYOND

In 2009 Emdeon prepared and launched a successful IPO, after which it was listed on the New York Stock Exchange under the symbol EM. Analysts claimed that electronic processors were in a good position to benefit from health care reform, especially since the administration of President Barack Obama planned to focus on efficiency by using technology. This premise fueled higher stock prices, resulting in $367 million in gross proceeds.

The health care industry was poised to undergo large-scale, long-awaited changes as the result of public pressure and politics. To help people navigate the complicated health care waters, Emdeon launched a user-friendly Health Insurance Portability and Accountability Act of 1996 (HIPAA) Web site in early 2010. In March 2010 Emdeon also rolled out a mobile phone application for its Emdeon Vision platform. With it, health care providers could see a snapshot of their claims and related cash flow.

In March 2010 Emdeon and Medicity partnered to create a national health information exchange, leveraging Emdeon's national network of payers, providers, and pharmacies and Medicity's clinical network. At the same time, Emdeon announced an agreement to buy Healthcare Technology Management Services (HTMS), a management consulting company. In May 2010, Emdeon announced another partnership with Enclarity, a health care information solutions company that delivered accurate, timely, and comprehensive data on health care providers. The partnership aimed to improve data quality, eliminate unnecessary claims, and streamline the process. Both partnerships illustrated Emdeon' goal to continue to provide business outsourcing services to the health care industry throughout the 2010s.

*Andrea Newell*

## PRINCIPAL SUBSIDIARIES

CareInsite LLC; Dakota Imaging LLC; Envoy LLC; eRx Network, LLC; ExpressBill LLC; Medi-Fax, Inc.

## PRINCIPAL DIVISIONS

Payer Services; Pharmacy Services; Provider Services.

## PRINCIPAL COMPETITORS

Affiliated Computer Services, Inc.; Anacomp, Inc.; Auxilio, Inc.; DocuData Solutions, L.C.; SOURCECORP, Incorporated.

## FURTHER READING

"Emdeon Earns Honors for Innovation and Business Intelligence Strategies," *PR Newswire,* October 22, 2008.

"Questions Swirling Around WebMD," *Cincinnati Post,* October 11, 2005.

"Sage to Acquire Emdeon Practice Services, a Provider of Software and Services to Doctors and Small Clinics in the U.S.," *M2 Presswire,* August 9, 2006.

"Slimmed-down Emdeon Still a Player," *Health Data Management,* January 1, 2007.

# Equity Bank Limited

**Ragati Road**
**NHIF Building, 14th Floor**
**P.O. Box 75104-00200**
**Nairobi**
**Kenya**
**Telephone: (020) 274-4000**
**Fax: (020) 273-7276**
**Web site: http://www.equitybank.co.ke**

*Public Company*
*Founded:* 1984
*Employees:* 1,395 (2009)
*Income:* KES 15.68 billion ($192 million, 2009)
*Stock Exchanges:* Nairobi
*NAICS:* 522110 Commercial Banking

■ ■ ■

Equity Bank Limited runs operation in Kenya, Uganda, and Southern Sudan. The bank offers a diversified range of banking services that include business banking with emphasis on retail and corporate banking, personal banking, Internet banking, and mobile banking. The company is also well known for its extensive microfinance operations. Equity Bank had 155 branches, 512 Automatic Teller Machines (ATMs), and more than 4,000 points of sale as of December 2009. Most of the bank's operations are in Kenya, with the bank boasting more than 4.2 million customer deposit accounts in the country.

Equity Bank has evolved over the years to become one of the most prolific banks in Kenya, boasting over half of the total number of customer bank accounts in Kenya. The bank recorded tremendous success in the first decade of the 21st century as evidenced by the high number of recognitions and achievements awarded to it by high-profile international organizations. For instance, in 2009 Equity Bank was considered Africa's leading company in business performance by the Africa Investor Index, and it was also lauded as the Microfinance Bank of the Year at the African Banker Awards. In 2010 Equity Bank Limited's chief executive officer, Dr. James Mwangi, was recognized by the *Financial Times* of London as one of the top 50 business leaders in emerging markets.

## EQUITY BUILDING SOCIETY: 1984–93

Equity Bank has been one of Kenya's most inspiring success stories in the banking sector, having started off as a building society and having become the leading bank in Kenya and the East African region as a whole. Peter Kahara Munga and his close associates founded Equity Building Society in what was largely a family-run small business enterprise. The first board of directors of the building society consisted of five close associates and included Munga and John Mwangi, two men who were later to play prominent roles in the management of Equity Bank. The board of directors maintained influence over all aspects of the building society's business activities and they were hardly distinguishable from the executive team.

Equity Building Society started operations in 1984 and operated as a regionally based mortgage finance company in the central region of Kenya. Registered under the provisions of the Building and Society Act, Equity Building Society was legally mandated to extend mortgage finance and low-interest loans in addition to receiving deposits from customers. John Mwangi replaced the founding CEO of the Equity Building Society in 1986, a year during which the company's core long-term lending opportunities started stagnating. In the same year, the building society registered losses amounting to KES 5 million when it was unable to grow its deposits and loans beyond KES 23 million and KES 7 million, respectively.

The company's pursuit of optimized business opportunities was based on a strategic focus in the central region of Kenya, but this proved difficult as more established competitors in the industry had garnered a competitive edge in the market. Despite concerted efforts by the management of Equity Building Society to increase its market share in the mortgage financing industry, the bank's prospects kept on diminishing.

## TECHNICALLY INSOLVENT: 1993

The poor business prospects of Equity Building Society became evident in 1993 when an audit by the Central Bank of Kenya confirmed that the building society had become technically insolvent. At this point, the amount of the building society's loan book that faced the nonpayment risks exceeded 50 percent. In an article titled "Equity Bank's Market-Led Revolution," Graham Wright and David Cracknell noted that losses accumulated by the building society exceeded KES 33 million relative to a paid up capital base of about KES 3 million. The building society also operated on a reduced liquidity ratio of 5.8 percent, contrary to the 20 percent regulatory limits recommended by the Central Bank of Kenya.

The unfortunate state of affairs had left the management of the building society with no option but to use the deposits of customers to settle operational expenses of the company. This was a very critical moment for Equity Building Society because news of the bank's technical insolvency sent jitters among its creditors, debtors, individual customers, corporate customers,

suppliers, and employees. As might be expected, the building society suffered from eroding customer confidence.

## CORE OPERATIONAL AND STRUCTURAL TRANSFORMATIONS: 1994–2004

The challenges that exposed Equity Building Society to imminent insolvency paved the way for a change of strategy towards diversification of the bank's range of financial services. The building society's management particularly focused on the introduction of a microfinancing product in a bid that was targeted at bringing on board low-income earners, small-scale businesses, grassroots self-help groups, and cooperative institutions. The microfinance banking product enabled Equity Building Society to regain its footing in the financial sector by gaining a competitive edge over the key players in the industry.

The strategic shift of the bank's focus paid off mainly because many commercial banks in Kenya hardly paid any attention to the microfinance range of financial products. The provision of microfinance services had remained a preserve of local and international nongovernmental organizations, but these institutions often lacked adequate financial resources to meet the ever-increasing demand for low-interest loans.

The microfinance banking product is credited for having enabled Equity Building Society to penetrate all parts of the country to the grassroots level. The Building Society experienced tremendous growth in customer numbers in a quick turnaround that saw it become the largest and most dominant microfinance institution in Kenya at the beginning of the 21st century. The standing of Equity Building Society in Kenya's financial industry was further boosted by the introduction of new financial and banking legislation in 2000 that paved the way for mortgage banks and building societies to fully extend services offered by commercial banking with only a few exceptions.

Equity Building Society registered a major legal and operational transformation on December 31, 2004, when it was finally converted into a full commercial bank, operating as Equity Bank Limited. The conversion of the increasingly successful building society into a full commercial bank was necessitated by voluminous financial business opportunities, a wide national network, and the unrivalled grassroots appeal that the bank had achieved. Notably, the bank retained its strategy of targeting the low-income segment of Kenyan

```
┌─────────────────────────────────────────────┐
│                                               │
│              KEY DATES                        │
│                  ■                            │
│  ─────────────────────────────────────       │
│  1984:  Equity Building Society begins as a   │
│         regional mortgage finance company.    │
│  1993:  Equity Building Society becomes       │
│         technically insolvent.                │
│  2000:  New banking legislation allows        │
│         building societies to operate more    │
│         like commercial banks.                │
│  2004:  Company converts to a full commercial │
│         bank.                                 │
│  2009:  Equity Bank accounts for more than 50 │
│         percent of Kenya's total bank         │
│         accounts.                             │
│                                               │
└─────────────────────────────────────────────┘
```

society of which the majority lacked access to affordable loans and financial service due to resource limitations.

## FAST PACE OF GROWTH: 2005–08

The full entry of Equity Bank Limited into the business of commercial banking in January 2005 marked a new chapter in Kenya's banking history, as the bank went on to become the largest bank in the country, accounting for more than 54 percent of the total bank accounts as of December 2009.

The shares of Equity Bank Limited were floated in the Nairobi Stock Exchange (NSE) market in August 2006. During the first day of trading at the NSE, the bank's shares were initially valued at KES 6.3 billion, a valuation that grew over the years to hit the KES 21 billion mark by the end of 2009. During the listing of Equity Bank's shares at the NSE in August 2006, a total of 90 million shares were listed privately. The successful initial public offering (IPO) of Equity Bank Limited's shares at the NSE saw the company become the world's second microfinance institution ever to be listed with its IPO.

Equity Bank Limited also ventured to provide a mobile banking service that targeted remote and rural parts of the country. Equity Mobile Banking was a concept through which secure and armored vehicles were used as mobile bank branches to extend banking services in rural towns and market centers to enable locals to transact business through their bank accounts. According to statistics contained in Wright and Cracknell's article, by December 2006 the bank had established 28 branches operating as mobile units which served more than 45,000 clients. According to Wright and Cracknell, the bank's staff in the mobile services units totaled 132, its mobile loan portfolio was in excess of KES 230 million, and the savings balance for the

mobile banking units was in excess of KES 340 million in 2006.

The ownership structure of Equity Bank underwent a major transformation in 2007 when Helios Investment Partners acquired a 24.99 percent stake, worth KES 11.2 billion, of the bank's total shareholding. The deal granted Helios Investment Partners an automatic seat on the bank's board of directors, which was awarded to Babatunde Soyoye.

In May 2008 Equity Bank Shares had become the most valuable shares in the NSE, trading at an average price of KES 279. These developments prompted the bank's management and NSE to consider a share split of the bank's stocks because the high stock prices had made the shares unaffordable to the majority of the ordinary or individual investors. In 2008 Equity Bank Limited also successfully completed a major regional expansion venture when it acquired the Uganda Microfinance Limited at a cost of KES 2 billion and converted it into Equity Bank Uganda.

## EQUITY GROUP FOUNDATION

Equity Bank has established a formidable network of corporate social responsibility (CSR) programs in Kenya, Uganda, and Southern Sudan in accordance with the bank's social development goals. The bank advanced its CSR programs through the Equity Group Foundation, which worked to provide education and social welfare benefits to needy people in areas in which the bank operated. The Equity Bank's scholarship program operated in partnership with the MasterCard Foundation and was one of the notable educational and social welfare activities advanced by the bank. In 2009 alone, the partnership between Equity Group Foundation and MasterCard Foundation enabled more than 600 orphaned and bright students from poor family backgrounds to gain access to education. Previous scholarship programs were largely targeted at secondary school students in all parts of the countries where the bank had established branches.

## MORE GROWTH: 2009 AND BEYOND

Equity Bank reported tremendous financial results in the 2009 financial year. The asset base for the Group grew despite the effects of the global financial crisis and high inflation rates in the domestic market. According to a news article published on Equity Bank's Web site titled "Equity Bank Grows to Exceed Kshs 100 Billion in Asset Base," bank CEO James Mwangi acknowledged that the "bank's good performance was the outcome of consistent execution of strategic growth objectives coupled with performance efficiency and enhanced risk management internal control systems." The bank's fast pace of capital growth was largely boosted by its expansion exploits regionally and the diversification of its financial products range.

Equity Bank's 2009 strategic plan was aimed at the expansion of the bank's branch networks nationally and regionally so as to secure a sustainable platform for future revenue growth, a move that saw the bank increase its overall branch network by 27 units during the year. At the release of the Group's 2009 financial results, Mwangi reaffirmed the bank's commitment to domestic and regional expansion strategies while striving to achieve efficient and effective delivery of banking services through the adoption of innovative information and e-commerce technologies.

*Paul Ingati*

## PRINCIPAL SUBSIDIARIES

Equity Bank Uganda; Equity Bank Southern Sudan.

## PRINCIPAL COMPETITORS

Barclays Bank of Kenya Limited; Co-operative Bank of Kenya; KCB Bank Group; Standard Chartered Bank Group.

## FURTHER READING

"Are the Equity Bank and Safaricom Engines Running out of Steam?" consumerinsightafrica.com.

"Equity Bank Annual Report 2009," Equity Bank, 2010.

"Equity Bank Group Grows to Exceed Kshs 100 Billion in Asset Base: Groups Posts Kshs 5.27 Billion Profit before Tax Reflecting a Growth of 5% over Last Years Results," Equity Bank Press Release, February 18, 2010.

"Equity Bank Limited Profile and Analysis," wazua.com.ke, 2010.

"Equity Bank: Mobile Banking," financialdeepening.org.

"Equity's Quest for Control Sparks War at Mortgage Firm," businessdailyafrica.com, April 9, 2010.

"Exceeding Expectations for Microfinance Investment: Share Price Soars in Equity Bank's First Official Listing at Nairobi Stock Exchange," microcapitalmonitor.com, August 9, 2006.

Irungu, Geoffrey, "Analysts See Equity Bank Share Headed for a Split," *Business Daily (Nairobi)*, May 8, 2008.

Wright, Graham A. N., and David Cracknell, "Equity Bank's Market-led Revolution," microsave.org, 2007.

# First Citizens Bancshares Incorporated

---

4300 Six Forks Road
Raleigh, North Carolina 27609
U.S.A.
Telephone: (919) 716-7000
Toll Free: (888) 323-4732
Fax: (919) 716-2844
Web site: http://www.firstcitizens.com

*Public Company*
*Founded:* 1898
*Employees:* 5,006 (2009)
*Net Income:* $116.3 million (2009)
*NAICS:* 522110 Commercial Banking

■ ■ ■

Operating under its parent company, First Citizens Bancshares Incorporated, First Citizens Bank and Trust Company offers its clients commercial banking, wealth management, and insurance products and services. In 2010 the bank operated 370 branches in North Carolina, Virginia, Tennessee, West Virginia, Maryland, Washington, and California. In December 2008, during the heart of the global recession that wreaked havoc on financial institutions, First Citizens Bank and Trust Company was named Greenwich Associate's National Winner for Business Banking.

## FOUNDING FAMILY INFLUENCE

First Citizens Bank and Trust Company (originally named The Bank of Smithfield) was founded on March

1, 1898, in Smithfield, North Carolina. First Citizens was the first bank to open in the city of Smithfield. Tobacco, and later, cotton, were two leading industries in Smithfield at the time when First Citizens Bank was started. Early customers of the bank were largely individuals and small-business owners who worked in the agriculture industry. Twenty years after it was established, Robert Powell Holding was hired to work at the bank as a teller. Colleagues affectionately referred to Robert as "R. P." Passion for banking coupled with a strong work ethic propelled Holding upward through the company ranks. In 1935 he became president and chairman at First Citizens Bank and Trust Company. The coming years would see additional Holding family members take on leadership roles at the bank.

When Robert Holding died suddenly in 1957, First Citizens Bank was operating more than 45 branch offices. The bank's assets totaled $220 million. Robert's three sons, Robert, Jr., Frank, and Lewis, got more involved in the day-to-day operations of the bank after their father died. The oldest son, Robert, Jr., was 31 years old at the time while Lewis was 29 and Frank, the youngest, was 27. The middle son, Lewis, was named president and chief executive officer of the bank in 1957. He first began working at the bank in 1953. Frank was named company vice president and Robert, Jr., became bank chairman.

In 1979 Lewis Holding was named chairman of First Citizens Bank after his older brother, Robert Jr., died. Under Lewis Holding's leadership, First Citizens Bank operations expanded to more than 400 branches. About his brother Lewis's leadership skills, Frank Holding told the *Triangle Business Journal* in its "Businessper-

COMPANY PERSPECTIVES

■

The bank strives to help our customers achieve a lifetime of success.

son of the Year: The Holding Family" article, "First came liquidity, then capital, then asset quality, all in front of profits. Lewis never, never chased profits by taking undue risks."

Akin to his father, Lewis Holding learned the value of exercising prudent business and financial management skills. After all, those skills had helped his father to steer First Citizens Bank through the Great Depression. Years later these same business and financial management skills would help Lewis steer the company through the crisis that rocked the financial industry, particularly savings and loan companies, from 1984 through 1995.

First Citizens Bank worked with the government organization, Resolution Trust Corporation (founded in 1989 by President George H.W. Bush), to acquire several firms throughout the 1980s and 1990s. These businesses included the Commercial and Farmers Bank of Rural Hall, Peoples Bank of North Carolina, and First State Bank. Other acquisitions that First Citizens Bank made during this period were Caldwell Savings Bank of Lenoir, North Carolina; Surety Federal Savings and Loan Association of Morganton, North Carolina; Pioneer Savings Bank of Rocky Mount, North Carolina; Heritage Federal Savings and Loan Association of Monroe, North Carolina; and North Carolina Savings and Loan Association of Charlotte, North Carolina.

The purpose of the Resolution Trust Corporation was to oversee the disposal of assets of savings and loans firms that failed during the crisis. Before the Resolution Trust Corporation closed in December 1995, it oversaw approximately 747 savings and loan failings. Twenty-five million American bank accounts (worth $460 billion in assets) were impacted by the savings and loan failings. Acquisitions that First Citizens Bank made during the savings and loan crisis were amongst the most numerous in the bank's history. (In the 21st century, when another financial crisis sent many instititutions into insolvency, First Citizens Bank would pick up additional banks during this crisis as well.)

Another change at First Citizens Bank took place in 1980. James B. Hyler, Jr., came aboard as chief financial officer. He served as bank president from 1988 through 1994, when he was named vice chairman and chief

operating officer. Before he was hired to work at the bank, Hyler spent 10 years working as an auditor at Ernst and Young. Hyler would spend 28 years at First Citizens Bank and would later be credited for grooming Lewis Holding's successor.

## COMMUNITY FOCUS AND CONTINUED GROWTH

In addition to acquiring distressed banks, Lewis Holding grew First Citizens Bank's customer base. He courted professionals like dentists, attorneys, physicians, and small-business owners who worked in industries outside agriculture. First Citizens Bank reported $71 million in earnings for 1999. That same year First Citizens Bank rolled out its eBanking platform. The service allowed the bank's customers to access their accounts on the Internet, where they could apply for credit and loans, transfer funds, pay vendor expenses, and request a stop payment be made on a previously written check, and order bank statements, copies of personal and business checks as well as order new checks. The eBanking platform also let customers of the bank export and download data from their banking accounts to personal spreadsheets and accounting software at home.

On September 22, 1999, First Citizens Bank created relief funds to aid victims of Hurricane Floyd, which had hit North Carolina and the mid-Atlantic region earlier that month, causing extensive damage. The bank also donated $100,000 toward hurricane relief efforts. Six-month-long emergency consumer loans, payment deferrals on accounts that were in good standing, and a waiver of early withdrawal penalties for certificates of deposits used to meet emergency expenses associated with Hurricane Floyd were among the relief efforts that the bank undertook. These and other efforts led *American Banker* magazine to choose First Citizens Bank as one of the top 50 small business lenders in the United States.

In 2000 First Citizens acquired Greensboro Insurance Services, a general property, casualty, and group insurance firm headquartered in Greensboro, North Carolina. The goal of this acquisition was to grow the bank's insurance services division. First Citizens Bank aimed to keep Greensboro Insurance Services intact while it moved the company alongside its existing insurance services division, which represented regional and national companies.

The fourth quarter of 2000 saw First Citizens Bank move to expand its insurance services division further when it announced its intention to acquire Wimbish Insurance Agency. Also headquartered in Greensboro, North Carolina, Wimbish Insurance Agency had been

## KEY DATES

**1898:** Bank of Smithfield, later known as First Citizens, is founded in Smithfield, North Carolina.

**1935:** Robert Powell Holding is named president and chairman of First Citizens Bank and Trust Company.

**1957:** Lewis Holding is named president and chief executive officer of First Citizens Bank and Trust Company.

**1999:** First Citizens Bank and Trust Company introduces its eBanking service.

**2001:** First Citizens Bank and Trust Company acquires Wimbish Insurance Agency.

**2008:** Frank Holding, Jr., is named the chairman of First Citizens Bank and Trust Company.

in existence since 1933. Personal and commercial insurance lines, including medical malpractice and automobile and home insurance, were key products offered by the agency. The deal closed in 2001.

The year 2001 was one of physical growth for First Citizens Bank as the company opened six new branch offices. First Citizens Bank also opened a new 24,000-square-foot office in Raleigh, North Carolina. Members of the bank's executive management and administration teams relocated to the new facility.

Tennessee was the next state in which First Citizens Bank established a presence. In 2005 the bank opened its first branch office in downtown Nashville, Tennessee. John Bennett, a local Nashville banker with 10 years of commercial, retail, and private banking experience, was hired to lead the Nashville market. The following year First Citizens Bank opened an office in Knoxville, Tennessee in the Parkside Business Center. In 2008 the bank expanded its physical presence to Washington, D.C.

## LOOKING TO THE FUTURE

In January 2008 octogenarian Lewis Holding, the man who took the helm at First Citizens Bank in 1957 after his father, Robert Holding, died suddenly, decided to retire. His nephew, Frank Holding, Jr., was named as his successor. In their February 1, 2008, article, "Hyler Laid Groundwork for Holding Family Succession," *Triangle Business Journal* reported that James Hyler fulfilled his role not only in aiding the bank in generating increased

revenue but also in laying the groundwork for the power shift at the bank within the Holding family. "You know, when he was starting out at the bank, Frank Jr. worked for Hyler," Mike Patterson, a former First Citizens Bank executive, is quoted in the article as saying. "Jim was Frank's mentor."

First Citizens Bank had $16.7 billion in assets in 2008, the year that Lewis Holding resigned as chairman. When he took over in 1957, the bank had $220 million in assets. About the management shift, Frank Jr. told *Triangle Business Journal*, "Mr. Lewis Holding's pioneering spirit and leadership—combined with his personal devotion and professional commitment to First Citizens BancShares [parent company of First Citizen Bank]—have positioned us for a strong future. It is a tribute to his 52-year leadership that BancShares is the stable, successful corporation it is today. I'm excited about this new era for our company and the five-member executive management team, with 150 years of First Citizens banking experience, that will lead us." Edward L. Willingham was named president of First Citizens Bank in February 2009. The 55-year-old Willingham was first hired at the bank in 1987.

In 2009, while global financial and economic markets continued to be volatile, First Citizens Bank was one of the banks that chose not to receive federal Troubled Asset Relief Program (TARP) funds. In his March 10, 2010, letter to shareholders, Frank Holding, Jr., stated, "What began as a lackluster financial year ended with our reporting earnings that were 27.8 percent higher than 2008." That same year, First Citizens Bank acquired California-based Temecula Valley Bank. The purchase added 11 branch offices to First Citizens Bank, expanding its presence into Southern California. It also gave First Citizens Bank access to Temecula Valley's $1.5 billion in total assets. Also in 2009 First Citizens Bank purchased Venture Bank of Washington, an acquisition that further strengthened First Citizens Bank's West Coast presence.

After a brief illness, in September 2009, Lewis Holding, First Citizens' former long-serving chairman, died. In 2010 the Holding family continued to have leadership roles at the bank through Lewis's brother, Frank, and his son, Frank Holding, Jr., as well as Hope Holding Connell (Lewis Holding's niece) and Carmen Holding Ames (Lewis Holding's daughter).

In March 2010 First Citizens Bank purchased assets and assumed liabilities in Sun American Bank, a financial institution headquartered in Boca Raton, Florida. Sun American Bank had 12 branch offices in Florida, particularly in Miami-Dade, Palm Beach, and Broward counties. At the time of the deal, Sun American was reported to have $536 million in total assets. About the purchase, Frank Holding, Jr., was quoted at the bank's official Web site as stating, "This agreement will allow us to extend our presence in Florida and focus on building long-term relationships with our new customers. Our bank is recognized for its strength, stability and exceptional service, and we look forward to a smooth transition."

*Rhonda Campbell*

## PRINCIPAL SUBSIDIARIES

First Citizen Bank and Trust Company; IronStone Bank; Neuse, Inc.

## PRINCIPAL COMPETITORS

Bank of America Corp.; BB&T Corporation; Regions Financial Corp.; SunTrust Banks Inc.; Wells Fargo and Company.

## FURTHER READING

Campbell, Dakin, "First Citizens Expands in U.S. West as Six More Banks Collapse," Bloomberg.com, January 30, 2010.

"First-Citizens Bank & Trust Company," *Bloomberg Business Week,* bloomberg.com.

"First Citizens Bank Selects NCR For Exclusive ATM, Services and APTRA(TM) Deal; Five-Year Contract," allbusiness. com, March 1, 2006.

"First Citizens Reports Earnings for First Quarter 2010," *Wall Street Journal,* April 26, 2010.

"Lewis Holding Hands Chairman's Job at First Citizens to Nephew Frank," *Triangle Business Journal,* February 25, 2009.

"Longtime First Citizens CEO Lewis Holding Dies," *The Herald Sun,* September 2009.

Weisbecker, Lee, "The Holding Family," *Triangle Business Journal,* December 25, 2009.

———, "Hyler Laid Groundwork for Holding Family Succession," *Triangle Business Journal,* February 1, 2008.

# First Data Corporation

5565 Glenridge Connector, N.E.
Suite 2000
Atlanta, Georgia 30342
U.S.A.
Telephone: (303) 967-8000
Toll Free: (800) 735-3362
Fax: (303) 967-7000
Web site: http://www.firstdata.com

*Private Company*
*Incorporated:* 1971 as First Financial Management
    Corporation
*Employees:* 24,900 (2009)
*Sales:* $9.31 billion (2009)
*NAICS:* 522320 Financial Transactions Processing,
    Reserve, and Clearinghouse Activities

■ ■ ■

First Data Corporation is one of the world's largest providers of electronic commerce and payment services to merchants, financial institutions, and card issuers. (These include debit cards, credit cards, ATM cards, and the like.) The company handles a transaction volume of $1.4 trillion and serves more than five million merchant locations and 2,000 card issuers all over the world. *Fortune* ranked First Data Corporation 295th on its 500 list in 2009.

## BIRTH OF TWO DATA PROCESSING COMPANIES: 1970S

First Data Resources was incorporated in 1971, and by 1976 had become the data processor for both Visa and MasterCard bank-issued credit cards. American Express, which was attempting to build a financial services operation, bought First Data Resources in 1980 to perform processing functions. First Data Resources flourished in this new environment and became the largest bank-processing company in the United States. However, it proved to be an awkward fit with its parent company, and in 1992 American Express spun off the profitable division.

First Financial Management, which was also founded in 1971 and which merged with First Data Resources in 1995, was created as the data processing unit of the First Railroad and Banking Company of Georgia. First Financial was established to process checks by electronically following them through the banking system. By 1983 the operation was reaping $24 million in revenues and had become the largest banking data processor in the Southeast. When First Financial was spun off from its corporate parent in 1983, the company's president promised investors that he would raise First Financial's revenues to $100 million a year within four years. To achieve this stunning rate of growth, First Financial would have to acquire companies rather than develop new ventures from scratch. Thus in 1984 First Financial embarked on a decade-long buying streak.

## FIRST FINANCIAL'S ACQUISITIONS IN THE 1980S

In March 1984 First Financial paid $2 million for Marion, Illinois-based United Computer Services, Inc., and one month later purchased Financial Systems, Inc. First Financial offered $200,000 for certain assets of First American National Bank-Eastern in May 1984, and in August the company rounded out its first year of acquisitions with the purchase of Financial Computer Services, Inc., for $750,000.

The impetus fueling First Financial's string of acquisitions was the company's agenda to become a major player in the commercial transaction industry. First Financial believed that the future of banking and commerce would be driven by electronic and computerized information, not by cumbersome paper slips and forms. The company's goal was to become the middleman for a wide variety of exchanges in which electronic data was manipulated, acting as a support system for the financial industry of the future.

To attain this status, First Financial continued its rapid pace of acquisitions in 1985, buying four computer data services during the year. In February it paid $135,000 for the assets of the Data One Corporation and in June acquired an interest in Financial Data Services, Inc., for $2.75 million. In the following month Decimus Data Services joined the First Financial family, and in December the company paid $229,000 for Bob White Computing Services.

In making acquisitions, First Financial sought out relatively small entrepreneurial firms that would help the company increase its list of clients. Since it was cumbersome and time-consuming to win new customers in the financial services field, First Financial found it more economical to buy a small company than to individually recruit each of its customers. When First Financial purchased a small firm, the company did not, however, insist that the smaller company's operations be broken down and merged with those of First Financial. Instead, the company left them intact in the same location and with the same management, culture, and individual style. First Financial had a decentralized management philosophy, and although there was ample overlap in its operations, the company did not attempt to institute central marketing or sales operations. Former owners of properties that had been bought were encouraged through stock deals to stay and to work for First Financial, because their ownership in First Financial could be liquidated only over time.

After a brief pause First Financial resumed its acquisitions at the end of 1986, buying the customer base of American Information Services, Inc., for $2.5 million in August. In the following month the company bought American Data Technology, Inc., for $2.2 million, and in October 1986 it acquired Mid-Continent Computer Services for $23 million. These purchases were designed to strengthen First Financial by building up its revenues. In March of the following year First Financial bought Tel-A-Data Limited for $8.2 million and the Confidata Corporation for $500,000. Four months later First Financial also purchased American Automated and its On-Line Terminal Services for $4.3 million.

In the last four months of 1987, First Financial made three purchases that moved it strongly into a new field and nearly tripled the size of its operations. In October 1987 the company bought the National Bancard Corporation (NaBanco) of Fort Lauderdale, Florida, for $48 million. With the acquisition of this company, First Financial moved aggressively into the market for credit card transaction processing. Later that month First Financial added to its holdings in this area when it purchased Endata, Inc., of Nashville, Tennessee. With these moves First Financial became one of the three largest merchant credit card processors in the United States. The company decided to enter this field after its examination of why banks were unable to make money on their credit card operations. First Financial found that banks lost money when they had to collect and manipulate paper credit card receipts from merchants. By installing electronic terminals at cash registers, the company was able to eliminate this step and make credit card transaction processing much more lucrative.

In addition to its credit card operations, First Financial also purchased the First Data Management

## KEY DATES

**1976:** First Data becomes the first processor of Visa and MasterCard bank-issued credit cards.

**1980:** American Express buys 80 percent of First Data Resources.

**1992:** First Data spins off from American Express and holds an initial public offering. Company names Henry "Ric" Duques as CEO.

**1995:** First Data merges with First Financial Management Corporation, owner of Western Union Financial Services, Inc.

**1996:** First Data Merchant Services forms as a result of the merger between Card Establishment Services and National Bancard Corp.

**2002:** Charlie Fote becomes CEO.

**2004:** First Data merges with Concord EFS.

**2005:** Ric Duques returns as CEO and chairman.

**2006:** First Data Corporation spins off Western Union into an independent, publicly traded company.

**2007:** Kohlberg Kravis Roberts & Co. (KKR) acquires First Data Corporation, which becomes a private equity company. Michael D. Capellas is named CEO and chairman.

Company of Oklahoma City at the end of 1987 and Midwest Com of Indiana, Inc., for which it paid $400,000. At the end of the year First Financial reported revenues of $175 million, which yielded profits of $11.6 million. The president had met and nearly doubled his goal of three years earlier.

First Financial built on these strong returns by embarking on further acquisitions in 1988. In February the company continued its expansion into the credit card business by purchasing the processing contracts between retail merchants and Manufacturers Hanover Trust Company. In December First Financial enhanced its computer operations when it bought Appalachian Computer Services, a company based in Kentucky, for $46.5 million. "We're continuing on our path to be a significant financial-transaction company, and this rounds out one of our services," First Financial's chief financial officer told the *Atlanta Business Chronicle.*

By this time First Financial had accumulated more than 25,000 customers, including over 1,500 financial institutions. The total had been achieved through the company's 27 acquisitions, which came, on average, once every three months. First Financial ended 1988

with revenues of $423.7 million, an increase of more than 100 percent over the previous year. Profits reached $29.3 million. Nearly half, by far the largest part, of this income was contributed by First Financial's credit card processing operations.

Early in 1989 First Financial announced that it would branch out beyond its core transaction processing businesses to acquire a Georgia savings and loan association, despite the fact that this industry had been in a severe and protracted slump. The company took the step in order to protect its lucrative credit card processing operations. Concerned that the major credit card companies might one day issue rules that would prevent third-party companies such as First Financial from processing transactions, it decided to buy into the credit card industry in order to gain some say over how the accounts were handled. In order to become a credit card issuer, it was necessary to own a financial institution. By buying Georgia Federal Bank in May 1989 for $234 million, First Financial became the issuer of more than 100,000 credit cards. In addition, Georgia Federal had 11 percent of its deposits in the Atlanta market, where it was the largest thrift institution. Despite its size and strategic importance, Georgia Federal's acquisition by First Financial left the financial community worried about the company's prospects, and First Financial's stock price began to fall.

### REORGANIZATION AND MORE ACQUISITIONS: 1990–94

At the beginning of 1990 First Financial announced that it would switch its stock listing from the over-the-counter market to the New York Stock Exchange. In this way the company hoped to shore up its financial reputation and increase its attractiveness to foreign investors. Just a few days later First Financial also announced that it had reorganized its Financial Services Group into a subsidiary and changed its name to BASIS Information Technologies, Inc. This new entity comprised First Financial's original business operations, which provided check-clearing services to independent local banks, as well as 16 acquisitions that the company had made. With this restructuring along functional lines, the company hoped that BASIS would be better equipped to compete for the business of small financial institutions through its 24 data processing centers around the United States. By the end of its first quarter in business as a separate entity, however, BASIS was reporting only a 10 percent profit margin, half of what First Financial executives had predicted.

This news, combined with an announcement that the federal government would investigate the real estate holdings of First Financial's thrift institution and with general jitteriness about the savings and loan industry, forced First Financial's stock price into a steep decline in the spring of 1990. As the company used its stock to finance acquisitions, the drop in the value of its stock curtailed the number of purchases it could make.

By the start of the summer First Financial's stock price had begun to recover, and the company announced in August that it had finalized its purchase of two Atlanta businesses, Nationwide Credit and Online Financial Communication Systems. With its purchase of the first company, First Financial entered the debt collection business. With the purchase of the Zytron Corporation in the same month, First Financial enhanced its Endata operations. The company also bought the Electro Data Corporation of Denver and the Bank of Boston's credit card contracts. In December 1990 First Financial announced that it had also acquired the credit card contracts of the Southeast Bank of Florida, which had one of the ten largest merchant contract portfolios. Shortly before this the company had completed its acquisition of the same operations from the Bank of New York, bringing a total of 12,000 new merchant customers to the company's credit card subsidiary. NaBanco, First Financial's credit card subsidiary, had become the nation's largest credit card processing company, with an annual growth rate of 40 percent.

Although First Financial's pace of acquisitions slowed in 1991, its revenues climbed to $1.2 billion. In the following year First Financial made a number of key purchases. In July 1992 the company augmented its credit verification operations by buying TeleCheck Services, Inc., and its subsidiary, the Payment Services Company, for $156 million. Shortly afterward First Financial expanded its ownership of TeleCheck franchises to 97 percent.

As part of this shift in corporate direction, First Financial divested itself of its savings and loan subsidiary, selling the Georgia Federal Bank and its subsidiary, First Family Financial Services. After a planned sale of this property in the summer of 1992 fell through, First Financial petitioned the Georgia state banking regulators for permission to form a credit card bank, called the First Financial Bank. After transferring Georgia Federal's data processing business to the new subsidiary, the sale of the thrift was completed when First Union Corporation paid $153 million for the property.

At the end of 1992 First Financial also announced that it would sell its BASIS Information Technologies subsidiary, the company's original business, which now contributed only 10 percent of First Financial's revenues. The move came on the heels of a $150 million lawsuit filed in October 1992 against International Business Machines Corporation (IBM), alleging that IBM had failed to implement a new computer system properly, thereby damaging the company's operations. After receiving a cash settlement from IBM, First Financial completed the sale of BASIS to FIServe, Inc., for $96 million in February 1993.

In July 1993 First Financial activated the First Financial Bank as a credit card issuer, making it the sponsoring bank on customer contracts for the NaBanco processing operation. In addition, the company moved more aggressively into the health care field, purchasing Hospital Cost Consultants and VIPS, which marketed a Medicare claims processing system. First Financial also took a step into a new industry in 1993 when it purchased International Banking Technologies, Inc., for $47 million. This company had helped extend banking operations to supermarkets by negotiating agreements between grocers and financial institutions. With the move First Financial hoped to introduce its own services to a wider market. By the end of 1993 First Financial's revenues had grown to $1.67 billion.

The paths of First Financial and First Data first crossed in 1994, when each attempted to acquire Western Union Financial Services, the world's leading money transfer company. Western Union was an attractive target for both of these financial services powerhouses. First Financial wanted to acquire Western Union in order to branch out into a new market segment. Although the company had not previously ventured into consumer-oriented operations, Western Union's business was not outside the sphere of First Financial's expertise. After all, First Financial was already experienced in conducting money transactions for commercial customers. "Western Union is one of the most recognized trademarks in the world, with decades of experience in providing reliable services to consumers not currently targeted by our existing businesses," First Financial's president told the *Atlanta Journal-Constitution* on August 30, 1994. First Data, on the other hand, wanted Western Union in order to expand its presence in the consumer transaction market. (First Data had previously entered this market with its MoneyGram business, which it operated in conjunction with American Express.) First Financial ultimately won the rivals' protracted bidding war, paying $1.9 billion to take control of Western Union.

## MERGER OF FIRST FINANCIAL AND FIRST DATA IN 1995

The firms were soon to meet on a less contentious field. In June 1995 they shocked the financial services industry by announcing merger plans, which they intended to accomplish through a stock swap. The information services field was growing more crowded, as computer and telecommunications companies began to offer the same sorts of services First Data and First Financial provided. Merchant processing was "a very concentrated industry and [was] getting even more so," an industry analyst explained to *American Banker.* "There is a lot of logic in the merger." According to the *San Diego Union-Tribune,* First Data and First Financial would be "better able to compete" by joining forces against their competitors in the crowded segment. As Ric Duques, the chairman and CEO of First Data stated in a press release, "our merged companies will have the required resources to meet new demands."

Due to antitrust concerns, First Data was required to divest itself of its MoneyGram operation before the merger could be completed. The resulting company, which bore the name First Data Corporation, had net revenues of more than $4 billion and maintained a 30 percent share of the diverse credit card processing market. To streamline itself further, the nascent corporation began to rid itself of divisions that operated outside its core of financial support services. First Data Corporation concentrated instead on the three key sectors of payment instruments, merchant processing, and card issuing.

The company continued to grow, but it did so less through acquisitions (as First Financial and the old First Data had done in the past) and more through strategic alliances that bolstered First Data Corporation's market position. In 1996 First Data signed an agreement to perform credit card processing for the entity that came out of the merger of Chemical Bank and Chase Manhattan, which was one of the ten largest credit card issuers in the country. That same year, First Data won a ten-year contract from retail behemoth Wal-Mart Stores, Inc., to provide comprehensive payment and electronic commerce services to all of its outlets.

In 1997 First Data forcefully entered the realm of Internet commerce. Internet purchasing was expected to increase at astronomical rates, and First Data Corporation's partnership with Microsoft in 1997 was intended to keep First Data Corporation firmly at the center of this new commercial realm. The company formed a joint venture with Microsoft called MSFDC, which was an electronic bill payment company. At the same time, First Data Corporation continued to develop its traditional operations. The company joined with Chase Manhattan Bank to create a merchant bank alliance named Chase Merchant Service, LLC, which offered data processing and related services to merchants for credit, debit, and stored-value card transactions. First

Data Corporation's 1997 sales soared to more than $5 billion.

The company continued to pursue online merchants in 1998 and 1999, forging more alliances with leading Web businesses. In November 1998 First Data Corporation announced a ten-year marketing deal with iMall, a designer and host of Web sites for retail merchants that was acquired by ExciteHome in 1999. First Data Corporation also teamed up with Yahoo! Store's 4,000 merchants, as well as barnesandnoble.com, for which it contracted to perform credit card processing for all transactions.

## SPINNING OFF WESTERN UNION: THE 21ST CENTURY

In the aftermath of the September 11, 2001, terrorist attacks against the United States, First Data Corporation was concerned that it would not be able to sustain the growth it has enjoyed in the past. The company, particularly its Western Union unit, came under intense scrutiny of regulators for compliance with anti-money-laundering rules. The central concern of regulators was the movement of funds to terrorist organizations. First Data Corporation did not admit guilt but settled several of these complaints by paying large fines ($3 million and $8 million) for its supposed compliance failures. Also, the company faced an increase in competition from Travelers Express/MoneyGram, which signed a significant deal with Wal-Mart Stores, Inc., to increase its presence. Other competitors such as Citigroup Inc. and Bank of America Corp. made inroads into the wire transfer business, particularly in Mexico and other Latin American countries.

In 2002 Charlie Fote became CEO of the company. First Data Corporation soon returned its old ways, taking on further acquisitions to drive growth. In 2003 First Data acquired TeleCash Kommunikations-Service GmbH, a Germany-based provider of point of sale (POS) terminals, and in 2004 the company made a bid to purchase Concord EFS Inc. for $7 billion. Concord EFS operated Star, which was the nation's largest debit transaction network. In October 2003 U.S. regulators sued to stop the merger. Regulators feared that the deal would reduce competition among financial-transaction networks and ultimately result in higher prices for customers. First Data Corporation reached a settlement with the regulators that required them to sell its 64 percent stake in NYCE, its debit transaction routing unit. NYCE would operate as a separate entity unit until First Data Corporation could find a buyer. In 2004 First Data Corporation and Concord EFS completed their merger. While the loss of NYCE was difficult, the gain of Star, with its 1.26 million automated teller machines and merchant debit-card pads, was a much more valuable acquisition.

Earnings at First Data Corporation's Western Union unit were increasingly disappointing. At the time, the industry was enjoying a surge in demand, but prices were falling precipitously. The price of a $500 transfer had dropped from $25 in 2000 to $13 in 2005. The Internet and ATM machines made access to funds easier and cheaper. Such alternate routes made Western Union's distribution network a costly liability rather than a benefit.

As with other threats to its business, First Data Corporation responded by buying the competition. In October 2005 the company acquired Vigo, a niche player that handled cash transfers from the United States to Latin America. Vigo's network included 4,000 U.S. agents and almost 40,000 locations in Latin America. In November 2005, in what was viewed as an odd move, CEO Charlie Fote retired and was succeeded by his predecessor, Henry "Ric" Duques. Duques had served as CEO for a ten-year term before Fote took the job.

In January 2006 First Data Corporation announced it would spin off Western Union into an independent, publicly traded company. The announcement came as a surprise since the unit still contributed 40 percent to First Data Corporation's revenues and about 60 percent of its operating profit. First Data Corporation made a strategic decision to make the credit card business its core operation. Soon after First Data Corporation's announcement, Western Union announced that it would stop sending telegrams after 150 years in the business, leaving money transactions as its sole source of revenue. The de-merger of Western Union from First Data Corporation was completed in late 2006.

Also during 2006, the company made further moves to increase its worldwide reach. First Data and Standard Chartered Bank teamed up to launch Merchant Services, a merchant alliance serving markets throughout Asia Pacific. The company also acquired GZS, expanding its position in the German market, and Argencard, a leading payment processor in Argentina and Uruguay.

## KKR TAKES THE COMPANY PRIVATE IN 2007

In April 2007 the private-equity firm Kohlberg Kravis Roberts & Co. (KKR) approached First Data Corporation and offered to buy the company for $24 billion. First Data Corporation may have appealed as a leveraged buyout target for several reasons. The spin-off of Western Union and some inconsistencies in leadership (Duques to Fote and back to Duques) showed a

company struggling for focus and organization. At the same time, First Data Corporation exhibited good cash flow, something private-equity firms strongly desired. In 2006 the company earned $7.08 billion with a net income of $1.5 billion. After negotiations, the final deal came to $26 billion, and the company named Michael Capellas as CEO. Capellas had been CEO of MCI Inc. from 2002 to 2006. In September 2007 First Data Corporation became a private equity company.

First Data Corporation continued to expand its international operations, opening an office in Pakistan, forming AIB Merchant Services with Allied Irish, and entering the Polish market by making an agreement with Allianz Bank. In 2009 the company worked with WestLB to launch First Merchant Solutions to provide card acceptance for retailers in Germany and across Europe. As the company moved forward it seemed well positioned to focus on merchant and consumer financial processing services and continue as a dominant worldwide player in these markets.

*Elizabeth Rourke*
*Updated, Rebecca Stanfel; Aaron Hauser*

## PRINCIPAL DIVISIONS

Financial Institutions; Government and Education; Merchants.

## PRINCIPAL COMPETITORS

Elavon; Fidelity National Information Services, Inc.; Fiserv, Inc.; Total System Services, Inc.

## FURTHER READING

Bauerlein, Valerie, "Western Union's Last Telegram Marks the Conclusion of an Era," *Wall Street Journal,* February 3, 2006, p. B3.

Bauerlein, Valerie, Dennis K. Berman, and Robin Sidel, "KKR Is in Talks to Acquire First Data," *Wall Street Journal,* April 2, 2007, p. A3.

Bauerlein, Valerie, and Joann S. Lublin, "First Data Hires Tech-Industry Veteran as New Chief," *New York Times,* July 11, 2007, p. B10.

Beckett, Paul, and Carrick Mollenkamp, "Western Union's Parent, First Data, Is on a High Wire," *Wall Street Journal,* February 7, 2003, p. C1.

"Business Brief — First Data Corp.: Treasury Department Action Results in $3 Million Fine," *Wall Street Journal,* March 7, 2003, p. B7.

"Financial Services Brief — First Data Corp.: Accord with U.S. Appears Near to Allow Purchase of Concord," *Wall Street*

*Journal,* December 15, 2003, p. A8.

McKay, Betsy, "Western Union to Be Spun Off from First Data," *Wall Street Journal,* January 27, 2006, p. B4.

Millman, Joel, and Robin Sidel, "First Data Changes CEOs — Will It Be Enough?" *Wall Street Journal,* November 29, 2005, p. C1.

Sapsford, Jathon, and Robin Sidel, "U.S. Sues to Block First Data Merger —Justice Department Says Acquisition of Concord Would Reduce Competition," *Wall Street Journal,* October 24, 2003, p. A3.

# Flextronics International Ltd.

———— ■ ————

**2 Changi South Lane**
**Singapore, Singapore 486123**
**Singapore**
**Telephone: (65) 6890 7188**
**Toll Free: (877) 825-8971**
**Fax: (65) 448 6040**
**Web site: http://www.flextronics.com**

*Public Company*
*Incorporated:* 1969 as Flextronics Inc.
*Employees:* 165,000 (approx., 2010)
*Sales:* $24.11 billion (2010)
*Stock Exchanges:* NASDAQ
*Ticker Symbol:* FLEX
*NAICS:* 334413 Semiconductor and Related Device
     Manufacturing; 334418 Printed Circuit Assembly
     Manufacturing; 541420 Industrial Design Services

■ ■ ■

Flextronics International Ltd. is one of the largest electronic manufacturing services (EMS) providers in the world in terms of production and distribution. In 2010 the company had more than 26.6 million square feet of facility space. Flextronics expanded significantly by acquiring other manufacturers while taking advantage of the desire of original equipment manufacturers (OEMs) to outsource manufacturing and sell off their manufacturing facilities. Flextronics' ten largest customers, which included such global technology giants as Hewlett-Packard, Dell, Ericsson, and Xerox, accounted for just under half of all sales in 2009.

In addition to manufacturing, Flextronics offers a full range of design services that enable it to create, test, and manufacture a product based on a customer's concept. Flextronics serves the manufacturing needs of customers in telecommunications, networking, computers, consumer electronics, and related industries.

## FROM "BOARD STUFFER" TO CONTRACT MANUFACTURER: 1969–92

Flextronics Inc. was founded in 1969 by Joe McKenzie to provide overflow manufacturing services to Silicon Valley companies that needed more printed circuit boards than they could produce in-house. The companies sent their overflow work to Flextronics, where McKenzie and his wife hand-soldered all the parts onto the boards and then returned the finished goods. This type of work was known as "board stuffing."

The business did well in the 1970s, and in 1980 Flextronics was sold to Bob Todd, Joe Sullivan, and Jack Watts. Todd became CEO and transformed the company from a board stuffer to a contract manufacturing firm. The company pioneered automated manufacturing techniques to reduce labor costs associated with board assembly. It introduced board-level testing to insure quality and in 1981 became the first U.S. manufacturer to go offshore, setting up a manufacturing facility in Singapore.

Flextronics expanded its services in the 1980s and began delivering turnkey solutions in the middle of the decade. Based on customer specifications, Flextronics would handle everything from buying parts to manufacturing. The company also began offering computer-aided design (CAD) services, designing and blueprinting an entire printed circuit board based on a customer's idea. In 1987 the company was able to go public, but it was just three weeks before the stock market crashed.

Flextronics expanded to produce working, shippable products in the late 1980s. Its disk and tape subsystems were used in Sun Microsystems workstations. The Hayes modem was also a product that Flextronics helped assemble. The company built a global manufacturing base with factories located throughout Asia. Unfortunately for the company, these factories relied on a high-volume U.S. market that virtually crashed during the economic recession of the early 1990s. As profits disappeared and losses mounted, survival of the company became paramount.

Since the Asian operations were still profitable, one option would have been to scale back or close the company's U.S. facilities. The high cost of closing a manufacturing facility, however, would have bankrupted the company. Instead, the Asian plants were spun off as a separate company and taken private in 1990 with the help of outside funding. The U.S. plants were subsequently closed.

## GROWTH THROUGH ACQUISITIONS: 1993–98

The new, private company, renamed Flextronics International Ltd., had its headquarters in Singapore. Michael Marks became chairman in July 1993 and CEO in January 1994. The company had another initial public offering (IPO, or more accurately in this case, 2PO) in 1994, becoming a publicly traded company for the second time. Marks's strategy was to rebuild the company's U.S. presence. This worked, and from 1992 to 1995 revenues nearly tripled to $237 million.

From 1993 to 1998, when Flextronics' revenues surpassed $1 billion (later restated to $2.3 billion to reflect acquisitions), the company completed more than 12 acquisitions. It built a global infrastructure for high-volume manufacturing, expanded its purchasing and engineering capabilities, and increased its workforce from 3,000 to more than 13,000. At the core of Flex-

tronics' international growth was its industrial park model. Located in low-cost regions (including Mexico, Brazil, Hungary, China, and later in Poland and the Czech Republic) Flextronics' industrial parks brought suppliers on-site to decrease logistics costs, increase time-to-market, decrease shipping costs, and improve communication and quality. The co-location of manufacturing operations and suppliers in the industrial parks gave Flextronics greater operational flexibility and responsiveness to customer needs.

In 1994 Flextronics acquired nChip, which specialized in semiconductor packaging and multichip modules. In 1995 Microsoft picked Flextronics as its new turnkey contract manufacturer for its mouse.

In December 1996 Flextronics closed its contract electronic manufacturing plant in Richardson, Texas. The closure was part of the company's strategy to shutter its smaller plants in order to create larger campuses, or industrial parks, at other locations. Workers at the plant were offered jobs at Flextronics' San Jose, California, facility. During the same year Flextronics acquired two companies in Hong Kong (the Astron Group and FICO Plastics Ltd.) and the Ericsson Business Networks production facility in Karlskrona, Sweden. The latter deal was finalized in April 1997.

In 1997 Flextronics completed a 150,000-square-foot expansion of its manufacturing and research and development facilities in San Jose, California, where its U.S. headquarters was located, giving it a total of 280,000 square feet in two buildings. The company also expanded its global facilities, including an expansion of its plant in China from 210,000 square feet to 450,000 square feet, and built a new plant in Guadalajara, Mexico. By the end of 1997 Flextronics was ranked as the fifth-largest contract manufacturer in the United States, up from tenth in 1995.

Between March 1997 and mid-1998 Flextronics acquired seven manufacturing-related operations in Brazil, Hungary, Italy, Sweden, and the United States. As a result of these acquisitions, Flextronics' revenue more than doubled.

## MORE ACQUISITIONS, PARTNERSHIPS: 1998–2000

In 1998 Flextronics introduced a worldwide network of Product Introduction Centers (PICs), which were facilities that designed, prototyped, tested, and launched new products, thereby shortening critical time-to-market. Among the products designed and built by Flextronics were 3Com's Palm Pilot and the Microsoft mouse.

Hewlett-Packard selected Flextronics to be a primary manufacturer in Europe for its inkjet printers.

## KEY DATES

**1969:** Company is founded in Silicon Valley as Flextronics Inc. by husband and wife team.

**1980:** Flextronics sold to Bob Todd, Joe Sullivan, and Jack Watts.

**1981:** Flextronics becomes the first U.S manufacturer to go offshore, setting up a manufacturing facility in Singapore.

**1987:** Flextronics goes public.

**1990:** The company goes private in a leveraged buyout and is reorganized as Flextronics International Ltd. with Singapore as its new base.

**1994:** Flextronics goes public for the second time.

**1997:** Company acquires Ericcson production facility in Sweden.

**1998:** Flextronic begins forming its global network of Product Introduction Centers.

**2007:** Flextronics acquires Solectron Inc.

**2008:** New tax increases in China affect Company and its subsidiaries.

Flextronics would supply printed circuit board assemblies and complete box assembly for the printers, which would be manufactured at the company's industrial park in Hungary.

By mid-1998 Flextronics had 2.6 million square feet of manufacturing space in 26 operation centers in Europe, the Americas, and Asia. Acquisitions around this time included contract manufacturers Neutronics Holdings A.G., Conexao Informatica Ltd. of Brazil, and Altatron Inc. It also acquired DTM Products Inc., which produced injection molded plastics, and Energipilot A.B., which provided cables and engineering services.

Flextronics had aggressively gained manufacturing contracts among telecommunications and networking OEMs, including Ericsson, Motorola, Alcatel Alsthom, Bay Networks, and Cisco Systems. Telecommunications and networking products accounted for 46 percent of the company's revenue, followed by consumer goods (29%), computer products (12%), medical products (4%), and other (9%).

In April 1999 Flextronics announced that it would purchase a second manufacturing facility from Ericsson, this one located in Visby, Sweden. The purchase was part of a trend among contract manufacturers to acquire the manufacturing facilities of OEMs. Upon completion of the purchase Flextronics also announced a new global

supply agreement with Ericsson. In June Flextronics strengthened its presence in Western Europe by acquiring Finnish telecommunications contract manufacturer Kyrel EMS Oyj for approximately $100 million in stock. Flextronics strengthened its relationship with Compaq when it won a new order to supply Compaq with printed circuit board assemblies for PC servers.

In January 2000 Flextronics was ranked third on *Industry Week*'s list of "100 Best-Managed Companies." The company continued to acquire manufacturing facilities from OEMs, who were willing to divest them to concentrate on their core competencies.

In a move to increase its design capabilities, Flextronics appointed Nicholas Brathwaite to the new post of senior vice president and chief technology officer. Brathwaite came to Flextronics in 1996 when the company acquired nChip, and he led the development of Flextronics' Product Introduction Centers (PICs).

In March 2000 Flextronics added more than 600,000 square feet of manufacturing space on the East Coast with the acquisition of four companies based in North Carolina's Research Triangle: Circuit Board Assemblers, Newport Technology Inc., EMC International, and Summit Manufacturing.

Flextronics made several more acquisitions during 2000, with no end in sight. The largest was The Dii Group, completed in April 2000 for $2.4 billion, which gave Flextronics a manufacturing presence in Ireland, Germany, and the Czech Republic as well as additional assembly capacity in China, Malaysia, Mexico, Austria, and the United States. Other acquisitions included Uniskor Ltd., the largest and fastest-growing EMS in Israel, for $20 million, and enclosure maker Palo Alto Products International.

Flextronics' aggressive acquisitions strategy began to affect the company's bottom line in fiscal 2001. For the first quarter ending June 30, 2000, the company reported a $368.9 million loss. Without amortization and one-time charges, the company would have reported a $71.7 million profit.

### CONTINUED PURCHASES: 2001–07

In the early years of the 21st century, Flextronics International continued to enter long-term pacts and engage in acquisition sprees. In 2004 Flextronics was selected by Gizmondo Europe Ltd. to manufacture *Gizmondo,* a multientertainment device with cutting edge capabilities. Gizmondo Europe Ltd. was a subsidiary of Tiger Telematics, a leading designer of gaming consoles.

Flextronics International registered a major expansion in October 2007 when it completed the 100 percent acquisition of Solectron at a cost of $3.6 billion. Solectron was a leading manufacturer of electronics and provider of supply chain services to EOMs. Flextronics International acquired all Solectron's common stock that were outstanding in a process that led to a massive expansion of the company's financial base and operating activities.

Flextronics International experienced a major legal setback in its China market in 2007 when the country's tax law was reviewed to lift tax holidays and incentives that were previously provided to business organizations to encourage investment. The new law that took effect in January 2008 was designed to increase taxation rates by 25 percent within a five-year period. The new tax measures in China affected all the company's subsidiaries and corporate customers in the country.

## WEATHERING THE ECONOMIC CRISIS: 2008–09

FLextronics International Ltd experienced a 12.3 percent increase of revenues during its 2009 fiscal year when it posted total sales of $30.9 billion compared to $27.6 billion in the 2008 fiscal year. The increase in the company's sales was attributed to the acquisition of Solectron and an increase in the number of new customers in the company's multiple target market segments. However, the positive trends in the company's growth of revenue persisted only during the first half of the 2009 fiscal year as the company's sales took a gradual downward turn in the second half of the year.

The economic recession that began at the end of 2007 changed operational and strategic dynamics in many corporate institutions and manufacturing business organizations, and Flextronics was no exception. The economic crisis particularly affected the company's key customers and destination markets in the United States, Europe, and Asia. Flextronics International also had to bear the consequences of increased restructuring charges following bankruptcy or insolvency of a number of its key customers that included Nortel.

Flextronics International experienced reduced business performance in the 2010 fiscal year ($6.83 billion less in annual sales) as a result of a diminished number of OEM customers as well as reduced manufacturing and supply chain outsourcing activities. The company further experienced reduced sales in all its key markets consisting of computing, mobile, infrastructure, consumer digital, and industrial markets.

Nonetheless, the company started experiencing indications of positive turnaround during the second half of the 2010 fiscal year. The $24.1 billion revenue

posted by Flextronics International Ltd during the 2010 fiscal year represented a 22 percent reduction compared to the 2009 fiscal year, a clear indication of the adverse effects of the global economic crisis. The company's activities in Asia accounted for the majority of its total sales at 48 percent, while its interests in the United States and Europe contributed 33 percent and 19 percent of total sales, respectively.

## FUTURE PROSPECTS

The long-term growth prospects of Flextronics International Ltd were targeted towards the dominance of the technological outsourcing industry. The EMS outsourcing market is defined by great growth potential with average penetration rates that are yet to exceed 25 percent of the available opportunities. The company was also pursuing cost reduction strategies and shorter production life cycles for its diversified range of EMS products so as to pass the benefits of competitive advantage to its OEMs and manufacturing outsourcing partners.

*David P. Biancoa*
*Updated, Paul Ingati*

## PRINCIPAL SUBSIDIARIES

Astron Group Limited (Hong Kong); Chatham International Holdings B.V. (Netherlands); Irish Express Cargo Limited (Ireland); Multek China Limited (China); Power Systems technologies Ltd. (Mauritius); Solectron Network Systems Limited (UK); Vista Point Technologies, Inc.

## PRINCIPAL COMPETITORS

Celestica Inc.; Hon Hai Precision Industry Co., Ltd.; Jabil Circuit, Inc.; Sanmina-SCI Corp.

## FURTHER READING

Davis, Jack, "Flextronics Plans Cutbacks as It Tries to Rationalize Current Structure," SiliconBeat.com, March 10, 2009.
———, "Ex-CEO at Seagate Joining Flextronics Board," SiliconBeat.com, April 15, 2009.
"Flextronics Makes Bid for Parts Maker," *New York Times,* May 21, 2002.
"Form 10-K: Flextronics International Ltd.—Flex," flextronics.com, May 24, 2010.
Markoff, John, "High-Tech Manufacturing Enjoys a Boom: Flextronics Has Microsoft, Ericsson Pacts," *San-Diego Union Tribune,* February 25, 2001.

McCormack, Karyn, "Flextronics Adds Key Part: The Electronic Manufacturing Services Outfit Buys Rival Solectron to Bolster Its Position in a Tough Industry," BusinessWeek.com, June 2007.

"Tiger Telemaatics Selects Flextronics," emsnow.com September 1, 2004.

# Franklin Resources, Inc.

One Franklin Parkway
Building 920
San Mateo, California 94403
U.S.A.
Telephone: (650) 312-3000
Toll Free: (800) 632-2301
Fax: (650) 312-5606
Web site: http://franklintempleton.com

*Public Company*
*Founded:* 1947
*Employees:* 7,700 (2009)
*Sales:* $4.194 billion (2009)
*Stock Exchanges:* New York
*Ticker Symbol:* BEN
*NAICS:* 523920 Portfolio Management; 523930 Investment Advice.

∎∎∎

Franklin Resources, Inc. (Franklin), is one of the largest investment management companies in the United States. The company's central line of business is managing a large pool of mutual funds, which includes equity, fixed-income, and cash management portfolios. In 2009 Franklin managed about $520 billion in assets with over 21 million shareholder accounts worldwide. As the company's Templeton subsidiary is an integral part of the overall organization, the firm is commonly known as Franklin Templeton.

FOUNDED: 1947

Rupert H. Johnson, Sr., founded Franklin in 1947 in New York. He started the company out of his brokerage office on Wall Street and named the company after Benjamin Franklin. To Johnson, Franklin represented the idea of prudent financial management. His first line of mutual funds, the Franklin Custodian Funds, were a mix of managed equity and bond funds. Charles B. Johnson took over from his father in 1957. At the time, the company managed assets of $2.5 million. With a staff consisting of Johnson and one other employee, the company slowly began to grow. Much of Franklin's success has been attributed to Charles Johnson's shrewd recognition that even the world of investment services could benefit from proper marketing. Some industry insiders suggested that Franklin was more important for its marketing success than its investment success.

In 1965 Charlie Johnson's brother, Rupert Johnson, Jr., joined the company. The Johnson brothers faced a volatile time as the 1960s brought wide swings between bull and bear markets. Franklin went public in 1971, and in 1973 the company acquired Winfield & Company, a San Mateo-based investment firm. Soon after, the company moved its headquarters from New York to California. The newly formed company had about $250 million in assets under management and 60 employees. A stock market crash in 1973 to 1974 nearly wiped out the company, but the Johnsons managed to bring the company back from the brink and bounce back stronger than before. The company started one of the first funds specializing in gold stocks, and this fund gained momentum in the late 1970s as inflation rose. Franklin offered a succession of new fund products during the 1980s, a decade in which the percentage of families investing in mutual funds grew from 6 percent to about 25 percent. By the end of the decade, Franklin was running 73 funds and Franklin Money Fund became the company's first billion-dollar fund.

## NOVEL FUNDS

In the early 1980s, while other fund companies anticipated a rush for equity funds, Franklin maintained that the real action would be with fixed income funds. Franklin pioneered mortgage-backed securities and single-state municipal bonds. Franklin's $14.2 billion Franklin U.S. Government Securities Fund was the nation's first fund to invest in Government National Mortgage Association bonds. Then the company introduced the $14.3 billion California Tax-Free Income Fund, the first tax-free state bond fund in the United States. Income from this fund earned by California residents was not subject to state or federal income tax. With high state income taxes and falling interest rates, the timing on this new product could not have been better. Investors were taking their money out of money funds and looking to invest in tax-free yields instead. By 1984 the state fund had grown to $825 million, doubling the assets that Franklin managed to $2 billion. By 1990 these two funds would account for half of Franklin's $49 billion in mutual fund assets.

During the mid-1980s, while other companies were starting overseas funds, Franklin continued to offer U.S.-based funds to U.S. buyers. Like many other investment companies, Franklin also planned to offer credit cards, consumer loans, and insured certificates of deposit. Furthermore, Franklin bought a real estate syndicate for $11 million. By this time, the company had become a real family business. Charles and Rupert owned 40 to 50 percent of company stock. Four other family members also worked at Franklin, including Charles's son, Charles E. Johnson, a Harvard MBA, and two of Charles's other children.

In 1987, while stocks were rising, Franklin stocks slipped, but when the market crashed in the fall, Franklin barely dropped, and its low-risk funds became a popular place to protect savings. The following year, Franklin announced that it would open an Adjustable-Rate Mortgage Securities Fund, which would still protect the investor's principal but would also pay higher returns on investment. Franklin funds remained conservative investments.

While most funds did little advertising directly to consumers, Johnson believed strongly in the power of advertising Franklin's funds. During the 1980s, Johnson dramatically increased the advertising for his fast-growing company and its funds. Unlike Fidelity Investments, the nation's largest mutual fund company, Franklin sold its funds through broker-dealers rather than directly to investors. In 1990 Franklin began a print ad campaign to make sure its name was familiar to investors and potential investors. Johnson told *Forbes* magazine, "Our feeling was that name recognition was important." Johnson even hired quarterback Joe Montana to peddle funds on television ads. Johnson noted that a celebrity such as Montana would reach people who ordinarily might not even pay attention to an ad for financial services.

In 1988 the company purchased the L.F. Rothschild Fund Management Company. From 1982 to 1989 the company's assets under management grew from $2 billion to $40 billion.

## ACQUISITION OF TEMPLETON

In the 1990s, Franklin was looking for opportunities abroad. In 1992 it was able to gain an immediate presence abroad through acquisition of another major player in the mutual funds market, Templeton, Galbraith & Hansberger Ltd., a mutual funds management company. Franklin acquired Templeton for $913 million and was thereby elevated from fifth to fourth place on the mutual-funds companies list in the United States. The only larger mutual funds companies were Fidelity Investments, Merrill Lynch, and Vanguard Group. Franklin alone controlled $69 billion in assets, and the purchase of Templeton gave Franklin management combined assets of almost $90 billion. The sale also meant that Franklin could sell Templeton's overseas funds to U.S. shareholders and sell its own funds in the foreign market Templeton had established. The sale of Templeton to Franklin was the largest transaction ever involving an independent mutual fund company.

Franklin decided to operate Templeton as a separate subsidiary. Although Franklin and Templeton funds had little in common, they were excellent complements to one another. Templeton's 80-year-old founder John

## KEY DATES

**1947:** Rupert H. Johnson, Sr., founds Franklin Resources as a small fund company.

**1957:** Charles B. Johnson, Rupert's son, takes over control of the company.

**1971:** Franklin Resources becomes a public company.

**1984:** Company's California Tax-Free Income Fund almost doubles Franklin's assets.

**1992:** Franklin Resources acquires Templeton, Galbraith, and Hansberger Ltd.

**1996:** Franklin Resources acquires Heine Securities Corporation.

**2000:** Franklin Resources acquires Bisset & Associates.

**2004:** Franklin settles a lawsuit regarding market-timing by agreeing to pay several fines.

**2005:** Gregory Johnson, grandson of founder, becomes CEO.

**2009:** Company begins to rebound after prolonged bear market.

Templeton, renowned in investment circles for his ability to pick stocks, told the *Wall Street Journal,* "The two organizations fit like a hand in a glove." For one thing, they both sold their funds through brokers and financial planners and charged an up-front sales fee. Templeton emphasized equities, while Franklin stressed fixed-income funds, and Templeton mostly managed global funds while Franklin generally managed U.S. funds. Officials predicted that shareholders soon would be able to move funds between the two without penalty to diversify their holdings. At the time of the transaction, John Templeton's stock in his company was valued at $440 million, and he was expected to continue as an adviser to Franklin Templeton.

Although the price for acquiring Templeton was high, Franklin was well positioned to handle it, having almost no debt at the time, $370 million in cash and other liquid assets, and financial backing from Chemical Bank and Hellman & Friedman. John Templeton and other Templeton shareholders were also willing to invest $75 million in the merger by buying restricted Franklin stock. The Templeton company also had the advantage of being based in the Bahamas where the tax rate on profits was far lower than that in the United States.

Franklin's negotiating team was headed by Charles E. Johnson, oldest son of Franklin's president and chairman, Charles B. Johnson. The younger Johnson saw the acquisition as a key move, since he believed that any company that wanted to remain an important player in the fund market had to "go global." Johnson, senior vice-president and head of corporate development, was expected to lead the company when his father retired.

## PROFITS AND LAWSUITS

According to a 1992 *Business Week* article, the fund industry had grown 500 percent in the previous 10 years. During that time, Franklin's total assets under management grew 3,000 percent, and its stock price skyrocketed by more than 42,000 percent, with much of this growth on a diet of fixed-income funds. These were U.S. government securities and municipal bonds. Franklin's staff also grew from 26 to more than 3,000 employees.

The immense profits of the 1980s had also prompted an excessive fee lawsuit against Franklin. Two shareholders, filing their suit in 1987, accused Franklin of charging excessive fees for managing its Franklin U.S. Government Securities Fund. This was the first excessive fee suit involving a bond mutual fund to go to trial, although five other suits had been filed (and dismissed) for excessive fees involved in management of money market mutual funds. In 1990 a judge dismissed the complaint against Franklin after a six-day trial, noting that the only main arguments presented by the plaintiffs was that Franklin "simply made too much money managing that fund." The judge ruled that Franklin's after-tax profit was "reasonable," and that the plaintiffs "failed to prove that Franklin realized economies of scale as the fund increased in size, or that economies of scale, if realized, were not shared with investors."

Fiscal problems in California caused some concern for mutual fund companies in the early 1990s. Franklin managed the $12 billion California Tax Free Income Fund, the nation's largest tax-exempt bond mutual fund, and the company was confident that few if any of the riskier bonds (known as Mello-Roos bonds) would default. However, Franklin remained the largest holder of Mello-Roos bonds, which were sold to finance infrastructure development in new communities in the state. According to the *Wall Street Journal,* Mello-Roos bonds did not trade often and were not rated by credit-rating companies; a default could send holders hurrying to sell. Franklin therefore remained cautious in its California investments.

In June 1996 Franklin agreed to purchase Heine Securities Corporation for $610 million. Heine was owned by Michael Price, a value investor heralded on Wall Street. This was one of three large acquisitions by mutual fund management companies at the time. Both Morgan Stanley Group and Merrill Lynch & Company agreed to purchase smaller fund companies. All three acquisitions, including Franklin's, married a larger company with substantial sales capabilities with smaller companies that offered strong products. In the case of Heine, its Mutual Series Funds were considered to be a highly valuable addition to Franklin's offerings. However, some analysts shook their heads at this purchase since the price was so out of proportion to Heine's revenues, which hovered around $100 million on $17 billion in assets. Nonetheless, Heine was a highly profitable operation with very low overhead and a marketing budget of zero. The hope was that Heine with Franklin's marketing resources would bring in more than enough assets to make up for any deficiencies in the deal.

## THE 21ST CENTURY

During the early part of the new century, Franklin engaged in series of acquisitions to boost its domestic business. In 2000 Franklin's Templeton subsidiary purchased Bisset & Associates Investment Management, Ltd., for $95 million. In 2001 Franklin made an aggressive move into the personal wealth management business by purchasing Fiduciary Trust International, one of the biggest players in that industry, for $825 million. Then, in August 2003, the company acquired Darby Overseas Investments, Ltd., an emerging markets private equity firm, for $75.88 million in cash.

The mergers and their resulting added revenues helped Franklin cover up what would have been disappointing performance during the first few years of the decade. The company was facing the same difficulties as other mutual fund companies during that difficult financial period. Stock values plummeted and some firms experienced a substantial exodus of funds. In July 2002 firms experienced a record outflow from mutual funds of around $52.6 billion. Franklin moved forward with its strategic acquisitions, but it also exacted a string of cost-cutting measures to stem the flow of red ink. For the most part, Franklin succeeded in avoiding the dismal results that other firms experienced but its performance was far short of previous years. In March 2003 the market began a rally that would continue until late 2008, when the country was experiencing a major recession.

In late 2003, Franklin became embroiled in a trading scandal. The state of Massachusetts and the Securities and Exchange Commission (SEC) investigated Franklin and other mutual fund companies for helping investors market-time their mutual fund trades. Market-timing was a rapid trading of mutual fund shares. This practice benefited short-term traders, but it skimmed profits from investors who held shares on a longer-term basis. Even though the practice was technically legal, firms specified in their prospectus that this sort of activity would not be done. However, they did it anyway at the behest of wealthy clients. In February 2004 Massachusetts regulators brought civil fraud charges against Franklin. The regulators claimed that Franklin executives had approved a deal with a wealthy Las Vegas investor that enabled him to market-time his trades in one of the Franklin funds at the expense of other investors in the same fund. Franklin claimed that while the trades took place, they had little or no effect on the returns of their investors. In late 2004, after a lengthy public relations debacle, Franklin settled the case out of court. Franklin reached a settlement with federal regulators, agreeing to pay a $50 million fine, and a month later, the company settled with the Massachusetts regulators, paying a $5 million fine.

The following year, Gregory E. Johnson, Charles Johnson's son, became chief executive officer of Franklin. Charles stayed on as chairman, helping comply with a new regulation put upon mutual fund companies that they have a separate independent chairman as part of their corporate structure. This regulation was a response to the recent trading scandals. Greg led the company during a period of substantial growth, mainly due to a favorable market. The bull market took hold and Franklin's assets under management rose dramatically. The market took a downward turn in 2007 as the country began its slip into recession. This was the beginning of a deep and painfully long bear market, lasting into 2009. Franklin and other firms faced steep drops in values. However, the conservative nature of Franklin's holdings seemed to help it avoid worse returns than it might have faced otherwise.

The stock market began to rebound toward the end of 2009, and investors saw Franklin Resources as a solid pick for moving funds in the future. By early 2010 the market had rebounded, and Franklin enjoyed a successful rebound as well. While it was uncertain whether the company would be able to continue on this positive track in the 2010s, Franklin's conservative style of management and the guidance of its founding family, the Johnsons, would serve its investors well over the long-term.

*Wendy J. Stein*
*Updated, Aaron Hauser*

## PRINCIPAL SUBSIDIARIES

Darby Holdings, Inc.; Fiduciary International, Inc.; Franklin Templeton Services, LLC; Templeton Worldwide, Inc.

## PRINCIPAL COMPETITORS

BlackRock, Inc.; FMR LLC; Northern Trust Corporation; State Street Corporation; The Vanguard Group.

## FURTHER READING

"Franklin to Pay $5 Million," *New York Times,* September 21, 2004, p. 17.

Gilpin, Kenneth N., "Franklin Set To Buy Heine in Another Big Fund Accord," *New York Times,* June 26, 1996, p. 1.

Hechinger, John, and Tom Lauricella, "Franklin Named in State Charges in Fund Scandal," *Wall Street Journal,* February 5, 2004, p. C1.

Hechinger, John, Tom Lauricella, and Gregory Zuckerman, "Former Fred Alger Official Pleads Guilty — SEC Brings Its Own Charges; In Massachusetts, Regulators Probe a Trio of Fund Firms," *Wall Street Journal,* October 17, 2003, p. C1.

Korn, Melissa, and Aparajita Saha-Bubna, "Franklin Resources' Net Income Soars — Money Manager Sees Record Intake," *Wall Street Journal,* April 29, 2010, p. C11.

Lowenstein, Roger, "Both Franklin and Price Get Their Value," *Wall Street Journal,* June 27, 1996, p. C1.

Mamudi, Sam, "Franklin Makes List of Most-improved — Profit Declines Taper at Asset Manager," *Wall Street Journal,* April 29, 2009, p. C13.

————, "Analysts Take Shine To Money Managers — As Markets Rise, So does Potential Upside," *Wall Street Journal,* September 29, 2009, p. C11.

Shipman, John, "View Is Mixed for Franklin Resources Inc. — Financial-Services Concern Is Taking Closer Look at Revenue and Costs," *Wall Street Journal,* December 31, 2001.

————, "Continued Weakness Raises Anxiety," *Wall Street Journal,* October 7, 2002, p. C17.

# Frontier Oil Corporation

**10000 Memorial Drive, Suite 600**
**Houston, Texas 77024-3411**
**U.S.A.**
**Telephone: (713) 688-9600**
**Fax: (713) 688-0616**
**Web site: http://www.frontieroil.com**

*Public Company*
*Incorporated:* 1977 as Wainoco Oil Corporation
*Employees:* 843 (2009)
*Sales:* $4.237 billion (2009)
*Stock Exchanges:* New York
*Ticker Symbol:* FTO
*NAICS:* 324110 Petroleum Refineries; 211111 Crude
    Petroleum and Natural Gas Extraction; 213112
    Support Activities for Oil and Gas Field Explora-
    tion; 424720 Petroleum and Petroleum Products
    Merchant Wholesalers (except Bulk Stations and
    Terminals).

■ ■ ■

Frontier Oil Corporation, an S&P 400 company and
the *Houston Chronicle*'s 2006 Company of the Year,
came up from modest origins. Located far away from
the giant Gulf Coast refineries and Texas oil country,
Frontier Oil is an oil refining operation that has carved
out a niche for itself in the Midwest and Rocky
Mountain regions. The company has two refineries
(Cheyenne, Wyoming, and El Dorado, Kansas) with a
combined average annual capacity of almost 200,000
barrels a day.

## EARLY YEARS: 1949–82

Founded in 1949 as Wainoco Oil Corporation, the
company originally dealt in oil and natural gas
production. Initially incorporated in Calgary, Alberta,
Canada, Wainoco relocated and reincorporated in the
state of Wyoming in 1976. Prior to 1968, Wainoco was
a publicly held shell corporation trading on the Toronto
Stock Exchange. That year, John Ashmun and three
business partners purchased the company with an aim
toward making it a profitable venture in its own right.

Under Ashmun's guidance, Wainoco expanded into
the U.S. market. In 1972 a new company office was
opened in Houston. Within 10 years, the company was
listed on the New York Stock Exchange.

## JAMES GIBBS, PRESIDENT: 1982–97

In 1982, a year after going public on the New York
Stock Exchange, Wainoco hired a young Texan by the
name of James R. Gibbs as its vice president of finance.
By this time, Wainoco owned a smattering of oil and
natural gas fields across the United States, Canada,
Indonesia, and Colombia. However, things were not
looking well for Wainoco's future.

The energy industry in the early 1980s was in a
depression, coming out of the second big energy crisis in
a decade. Crude oil was going for a mere $8.50 a barrel.
In 1984 Wainoco's very existence was threatened by a
hostile takeover attempt by shareholders bent on
liquidating the company's assets. James Gibbs first made
a name for himself in fending off the liquidation when

## COMPANY PERSPECTIVES

Frontier's mission is to sustain long-term prosperity for our employees, communities, and shareholders.

he put together a "poison pill" deterrence strategy, a fairly new concept at the time that paid off. (The poison pill approach refers to several different ways an existing company makes itself unpalatable to a party interested in acquiring the business.)

In 1987 Gibbs was elevated to company president on the merits of his actions during the attempted merger and also for helping to engineer the purchase of an oil well under Beverly Hills High School. The school had started bringing in considerable income by allowing oil companies to drill for reserves beneath the campus. Although the new well would produce 1,000 barrels per day over the next 10 years for Wainoco, the move would come back to haunt Gibbs and his company further down the road.

### A NEW FRONTIER: 1998–2002

By far the most lasting legacy of James Gibbs' tenure at Wainoco was his decision to lead the company into refining. Gibbs had a bold strategy. He wanted to buy refineries in a sagging market, with an eye toward the day when the market would turn around, and to purchase only refineries capable of handling cheaper kinds of oil in addition to the more expensive grades.

Not all oils are created equal, and the "sour heavy" oils, which are less pure and higher in sulfur content, require considerably more refining and more specialized equipment than the purer, less sulfurous "sweet light" oils. In an interview with *Forbes* magazine in 2008, Gibbs explained his strategy: "We knew from our Canada operations that heavy oil was easy to find. Whenever the price of light crudes spiked, we'd see a lot of different heavies come on the market." Gibbs wanted to be in a position to exploit those fluctuations.

On September 17, 1991, Wainoco paved the way for its strategic shift when it purchased Wyoming company Frontier Holdings, Inc., for approximately $50 million in cash and one million shares of common stock. Along with the acquisition came Frontier's single 38,000-barrel-per-day (bpd) Cheyenne facility, a refinery equipped for handling heavy crude oil as per Gibbs's plan.

In 1995 the company sold off all of its increasingly unprofitable U.S. oil and gas production operations.

This move left oil production facilities in Canada and, more importantly, the Frontier refinery in Wyoming, which by 1993 was bringing in fully 85 percent of the company's profits. By 1998 Wainoco had divested itself of all of its oil and natural gas production operations, choosing to focus exclusively on refining. That same year, the company officially changed its name to reflect its new direction. Frontier Oil Corporation was born.

### REFINING THE NEW DIRECTION

The sale of its Canadian Oil and Gas division brought an influx of money that Frontier used to pay down debt accrued from years of unprofitable oil exploration and production and, in 1999, purchase a second refinery at El Dorado, Kansas.

The new refinery, one of the Midwest's largest at 110,000 barrels per day (bpd), quadrupled Frontier's refining capacity. Like its Cheyenne cousin, the El Dorado plant was a "complex refinery" able to handle heavy crude as well as produce more refined petroleum products. Lastly, but of no less importance, was the fact that the new refinery was plugged into a pipeline in Cushing, Oklahoma, which gave it access to oil from west Texas, Canada, and the Gulf Coast. The move cost the company dearly, coming in at $170 million when the company at the time was valued at less than half that amount.

With the El Dorado refinery, Frontier opened itself up to new markets along the "eastern slope" of the Rocky Mountains, expanding from their base around Denver, Colorado; western Nebraska; and eastern Wyoming. Together, the two plants produced a mix of gasoline, diesel and jet fuels, asphalt, and petroleum coke. Gibbs was able to keep the company focused exclusively on refining by negotiating a deal to retail Frontier gasoline through Shell and Texaco stations.

The purchase of complex refineries was soon paying off as supplies of Canadian sweet light crude began to drop off and heavy crude increasingly became Canada's top petroleum export. "We bought good plants at the right place, cheap," Gibbs said in a 2006 interview with the *Houston Chronicle*. "We got lucky and had a good idea."

### ERIN AND HOLLY: 2003–06

As Frontier Oil moved into the new millennium, not everything was breaking their way, however. The period between 2003 and 2006 would find Frontier involved in high-profile lawsuits and countersuits, as well as witness the collapse of a promising merger that would have doubled the company's size.

## KEY DATES

**1949:** Wainoco Oil Corporation is founded in Calgary, Alberta, Canada, as an oil and gas exploration company.

**1972:** Wainoco opens a U.S. office in Houston, Texas.

**1987:** James R. Gibbs becomes company president and CEO, inaugurating the company's shift towards refining.

**1998:** Wainoco officially changes its name to Frontier Oil Corporation and begins focusing exclusively on refining operations.

**2003:** Frontier Oil becomes part of a massive lawsuit over Beverly Hills High School oil drilling operations in the 1980s and 1990s.

The root cause of all these problems lay in the oil well Wainoco had purchased under Beverly Hills High School (BHHS). In April 2003 Frontier was named in a mass toxic tort class-action lawsuit brought by a group of law firms under the collective direction of legal celebrity Erin Brockovich. The suit alleged emissions caused by the drilling beneath the high school by a variety of oil companies (including Wainoco) had led to a "cancer cluster" among BHHS students and neighbors. In all, 450 plaintiffs in seven lawsuits named Frontier as a defendant. Claims ranged from personal injury and wrongful death to loss of consortium and/or fear of contracting diseases, and also included claims for punitive damages.

Gibbs told *Forbes* the lawsuit was "a load of bull." Although denying any wrongdoing or negligence, Frontier purchased a $100-million insurance policy to protect itself against possible court rulings. At the same time, the company was attempting to engineer its largest merger to date, with Dallas refiner Holly Corporation. Holly's Utah and New Mexico plants would have doubled Frontier's size, and talks were in the works to acquire the company for $450 million.

Unfortunately, the negative publicity and uncertainty brought on by Frontier's involvement with the Beverly Hills lawsuit led to Holly backing out of the deal. Frontier responded with a lawsuit against Holly for breach of contract, to which Holly responded with a countersuit. By 2005 a judge had ruled in Holly's favor, ordering that neither company owed the other any dam-

ages and bringing the matter to a close. The merger opportunity was lost amidst litigation and "bad blood," as Gibbs put it to *Forbes*.

As for the Beverly Hills lawsuit, a judge dismissed some of the plaintiffs' claims in 2006 on the grounds of insufficient evidence, and in 2008 Frontier settled with the remaining plaintiffs for $6.3 million.

## OUTLOOK

Oppenheimer analyst Fadel Gheit described Frontier Oil as a "small fish in a very small pond" in reference to its market share and regional penetration. In 2009 Valero Energy, Frontier's primary competitor, maintained a presence in 44 states as well as abroad in Canada, Latin America, and the Caribbean. Contrasted to this was Frontier Oil's distribution network in Colorado, Wyoming, Montana, Utah, Kansas, Oklahoma, eastern Nebraska, Iowa, Missouri, North Dakota, and South Dakota.

However, Frontier made its niche status work. James Gibbs summed things up by saying "Crack spreads and crude oil differential are the story for Frontier Oil." In layman's terms, he was speaking of the wide gap between the low cost of the crude oil Frontier bought and the high-priced, quality product it produced; in other words, simple economics.

In addition to being able to buy and refine low-priced oil, transportation costs were kept low due to the refineries' strategic locations, sales were concentrated exclusively on the more stable wholesale market, and the company's versatile refineries kept it safe from the usual volatile market fluctuations of crude oil prices. Frontier Oil consistently boasted some of the most robust balance sheets in the industry, with low debt and money left over to reinvest into its refineries.

Small fish it may be, but by 2003 Frontier Oil had risen to become the fourth-largest private sector employer in Cheyenne and one of Wyoming's largest publicly traded companies. Frontier consistently outperformed its competitors like Holly Corporation and Sunoco Inc. Between 2003 and 2007, capitalizing on refinery outages among some of the industry's giants, Frontier Oil's net profit rose from $4.2 million to $499 million.

In February 2007 Frontier added Ethanol Management Company to its assets. Acquiring the Denver-based ethanol processing plant gave the company a products terminal and blending facility capable of handling 25,000 barrels per day, giving Frontier the ability to produce finished gasoline-ethanol blends, and even bio-diesel, deliverable directly to the growing Denver market.

## FORGING AHEAD WITHOUT GIBBS

On December 31, 2008, James Gibbs retired from his position as president and chief executive officer of Frontier Oil. He left behind a company utterly transformed from the one he joined 26 years earlier. Once a shell company, then a middling oil and gas producer, at the close of the first decade of the twenty-first century Frontier Oil stood as one of the most successful regional oil refiners in the United States.

There can be little doubt that Frontier has benefited from the general boom in oil prices over the first decade of the 21st century. Analysts were predicting a market downturn starting in 2012. Before he left his position at Frontier, Gibbs spoke to his company's strategy in the face of an uncertain future: "We're going to keep right on expanding. We will consistently be profitable when others aren't."

*David Larkins*

## PRINCIPAL COMPETITORS

Holly Corporation; Sinclair Oil Company; Suncor Energy, Inc.; Valero Energy Corporation.

## FURTHER READING

*Frontier Oil SWOT Analysis,* Datamonitor, August 2009, p. 1–9.

Helman, Christopher, "Wild Frontier," *Forbes,* March 10, 2008.

Hensel Jr., Bill, "Heavy Crude Helped Lift Frontier to the Top," *Houston Chronicle,* May 21, 2006, p. 4.

Horowitz, Joy, *Parts Per Million: The Poisoning of Beverly Hills High School.* New York: Penguin, 2007.

*National Petroleum News,* 97, no. 6 (June 2005).

"Wainoco Announces Retirement of Its Chairman and Appointment of New CEO," *PR Newswire,* February 25, 1992.

# Genworth Financial Inc.

6620 West Broad Street
Richmond, Virginia 23230
U.S.A.
Telephone: (804) 281-6000
Toll Free: (888) 436-9678
Fax: (804) 662-2414
Web site: http://www.genworth.com

*Public Company*
*Founded:* 1871 as The Life Insurance Company of Virginia
*Employees:* 6,000 (2009 est.)
*Total Revenue:* $9.069 billion (2009)
*Stock Exchanges:* New York
*Ticker Symbol:* GNW
*NAICS:* 524113 Direct Life Insurance Carriers; 524128 Other Direct Insurance (except Life, Health, and Medical) Carriers.

■ ■ ■

Genworth Financial Inc. (Genworth) offers financial securities in the segments of retirement income and wealth management, mortgage insurance, life insurance, long-term care insurance, and Medicare supplement insurance. It is one of the leading providers of mortgage insurance in Australia, Canada, Mexico, New Zealand, and parts of Europe. These products are sold through a distributor network of independent financial agents.

## LIFE BEFORE GENERAL ELECTRIC

Genworth is a result of a lengthy and complex series of mergers and acquisitions played out over the span of

130 years. Over that time, names and subsidiaries have changed, often multiple times. The subsidiary Genworth Life Insurance Company, for example, started its corporate life as the United Pacific Life Insurance Company in 1956 on the other side of the United States from its eventual Virginia-based owner.

Genworth Financial itself is directly descended from the Life Insurance Company of Virginia, headquartered in that state's capital of Richmond. Genworth's corporate headquarters remained in that historic city as of 2010, although the scope of its operations had expanded considerably since the 1870s.

The Life Insurance Company of Virginia remained a regional insurance outfit for nearly the first century of its existence, providing coverage for residents of Virginia and not much farther beyond. Its fortunes began to change in April 1967, when an agreement was reached with another regional Richmond-based insurer, Lawyers Title Insurance Corporation, to combine forces under the banner of a holding company to be called the Richmond Corporation.

## MERGERS AND ACQUISITIONS

Ten years later, the Richmond Corporation merged with The Continental Group, and the Life Insurance Company of Virginia found itself operating on a much larger scale for the first time. The Continental Group was an international company with a wide and diverse range of services.

Tapping into the resources brought about by the merger with Continental, the Life Insurance Company of Virginia was able to branch out into international markets, offering payment protection plans to European markets. In 1978 the company also started offering long-term care insurance, still one of Genworth's strongest and most important segments.

In 1984 the Life Insurance Company of Virginia began offering universal life insurance and products. That same year, in June, it found itself again part of a new merger, this time as The Continental Group's board voted to accept a deal from an organization called KMI Continental, Inc. KMI was jointly owned by Peter Kiewit Sons, Inc., and Murdock Investments. This new merger deal proved to be short-lived for the Life Insurance Company of Virginia (Life of Virginia), however. In April 1986, a holding company known as the Combined International Corporation, which controlled the Combined Insurance Company of America, bought Life of Virginia for $557 million.

## GENERAL ELECTRIC: 1995–2003

By the time Combined (renamed Aon Corporation in 1987) entered the picture, the Life Insurance Company of Virginia had long since established itself as an insurance provider for upscale markets. Life of Virginia continued to operate in this capacity under the aegis of Aon until it was swept up, one more time, in a new acquisition deal.

This time the corporation that came calling was a true corporate giant. General Electric (GE) in the mid-1990s was engaged in an aggressive expansion into life insurance, part of a general trend of consolidation that was sweeping the industry at that time. In 1996, for example, GE paid $1.8 billion to acquire the First Colony Corporation.

Slightly more modest was GE's acquisition the previous year of the Life Insurance Company of Virginia, which was bought from Aon Corporation for

the tidy sum of $960 million. In a related deal, GE also bought the Union Fidelity Life Insurance Company from Aon. Both companies joined an ever-growing stable of life and mortgage insurance companies under the GE umbrella.

## THE CREATION OF GELAAC

With an ever-growing and diverse collection of companies, GE shortly began a reorganization. The Life Insurance Company of Virginia officially ceased to exist, merging with the Harvest Life Insurance Company and coming out with the name GE Life and Annuity Assurance Company, or GELAAC for short.

GELAAC was Life of Virginia in all but name, but now greatly expanded in scope. Still headquartered in Richmond, GELAAC took in as subsidiaries a wide range of the other insurance companies GE had acquired. Many of these subsidiaries are still operated by Genworth, although any reference to General Electric in the companies' names was expunged in the years following Genworth's initial public offering.

Although GELAAC was performing well, by 2003 General Electric was looking to get out of the insurance business. In November of that year, GE announced that it would be divesting itself of GELAAC and its various subsidiaries, ridding the company of almost all its life and mortgage insurance assets. GELAAC would become an independent company in its own right, Genworth Financial. The company was incorporated in Delaware in anticipation of going public the next year.

## ENTER GENWORTH: 2004–07

Interest in Genworth's initial public offering (IPO) was running high as May 2004 approached. Michael D. Fraizer, a GE employee with 24 years with the company who had held the positions of chairman, president, and CEO of GE Financial Assurance Holdings, was tapped to continue in the same capacities with Genworth.

When the IPO finally came, it was overshadowed somewhat by Google's IPO in August, but nevertheless Genworth immediately became what *Forbes* magazine in 2006 called "a stealth financial giant" in the insurance industry thanks to the large number of subsidiaries it inherited from GE and the 130-year tradition of the Life Insurance Company of Virginia.

For example, prior to its acquistion by GE, Life of Virginia had been established for two decades as a premier provider of long-term care insurance, a type of insurance that picks up where traditional health insurance and Medicare leave off. This provides coverage for policyholders unable to perform basic activities, such as those suffering from Alzheimer's or Parkinson's disease. Thanks to this precedent set by Life of Virginia, and expansions undertaken during its tenure as a GE subsidiary, Genworth entered the market as the largest long-term care insurance seller in the United States.

Genworth also inherited and built upon a network of distribution consisting of sales specialists and independent agents, establishing an immediate presence and market share in the segments of Retirement and Protection, International, and U.S. Mortgage. The Retirement and Protection division accounted for the company's greatest share of revenue, nearly two-thirds in 2008. The International segment was well-established in Canada, Mexico, Australia, New Zealand, and Europe, and had an ever-increasing presence in the emerging markets of China, India, and the Middle East.

Genworth was ranked first in the United States in variable annuities, again a legacy of Life of Virginia's largely affluent clientele. It was the number four provider of term life insurance, and fifth-largest mortgage insurance provider in the United States. The latter category would prove momentous for the company in coming years.

## WEATHERING THE STORM: 2008–10

By 2006 General Electric sold the last of its shares in Genworth, severing the final ties to its former subsidiary. That same year, *Forbes* magazine predicted a good long-term outlook for the company, quoting a Deutsche Bank analyst who predicted Genworth would hit its goal of a 12 percent equity return by 2008. Global events would intervene to prove otherwise.

In 2007 a combination of fraudulent lending practices and inflated house prices began to snowball into the greatest financial crisis the United States had faced since the Great Depression. By 2008, as thousands of homeowners began defaulting on their mortgages, companies like Genworth that provided mortgage insurance were faced with their worst-case scenario. Genworth CEO Fraizer spoke of those dark days of economic free fall with *Forbes* magazine in 2010.

"The first thing you had to do was face reality and assume reality was far worse than anything you've ever dreamed of," Fraizer said. "You had to say, 'This could be permanent. Now what do I do?'" What Fraizer did was tell his employees, "We will do everything we need to keep our promises." He said that although "in some cases" the company had to nullify mortgage insurance policies that did not meet underwriting standards, ultimately Genworth was able to keep over 17,000 mortgages intact with restructured loans.

Genworth would most likely not have been able to meet its U.S. obligations without the support of its diversified, international client base, including, perhaps ironically, its strong presence in mortgage insurance in Canada and Australia. Total revenue of Genworth's international business actually increased from 2007 to 2008 by a total of 8.1 percent. Even so, net income fell from $1.154 billion in 2007 to a net loss of $572 million in 2008.

In a 2010 article for *BusinessWeek Online,* Standard & Poor's analyst Bret Howlett told of how in 2009 Genworth was at the "top of [the] list" of companies that were suspected to be insolvent due to the heavy losses it had incurred in its investments during the financial crisis. Net income in 2009 was again a loss, although the amount this time ($399 million) was less than the previous year.

## LOOKING AHEAD

"Genworth's earnings picture is still very uncertain," Citigroup analyst Colin Devine told *BusinessWeek Online* in March 2010. Predictions differed as to when Genworth could look forward to a time of profitability in its mortgage insurance division. CEO Fraizer pegged 2011 as the comeback year, but industry analysts said a return to profitability would occur in 2013 at the earliest.

Fraizer remained cautiously optimistic. Genworth's chief commercial officer, Rohit Gupta, shared that optimism and as early as September 2009 the company was offering two mortgage products that other insurers, even the major companies, were not willing to touch: second homes and cash-out refinancings.

It was a bold move for a company long considered the most conservative in the mortgage insurance industry, and a sign of the lengths Genworth was willing to go to get back on its feet. However, in his interview with *Forbes*, Fraizer took pains to emphasize that Genworth's main focus was on core growth. "We have capital available for targeted, and I underline targeted, acquisitions that could complement one of our [core] areas," he stressed.

One core area Genworth would likely focus on was international growth. With the worth of its international investments borne out during the financial crisis, and the vulnerability of having 71 percent of its net sales concentrated in the United States, it seemed likely that Genworth would continue to benefit from expanding into the emerging and untapped markets of Asia and the Middle East.

*David Larkins*

## PRINCIPAL SUBSIDIARIES

American Agriculturist Services, Inc.; Centurion Financial Advisers, Inc.; Financial Insurance Company Limited (UK); Genworth Financial Asia Limited (Hong Kong); Genworth Mortgage Insurance Corporation; Genworth Seguros Vida S.A. de C.V. (Mexico); River Lake Insurance Company.

## PRINCIPAL COMPETITORS

CMG Mortgage Insurance Company; MetLife Inc.; Mortgage Guaranty Insurance Corporation; Northwestern Mutual Life Insurance Company; Prudential Life Insurance Company; Radian Guaranty Inc; Republic Mortgage Insurance Company.

## FURTHER READING

Augstums, Ieva M., "Genworth Financial CEO Says 'Reinvent Everything'" *Forbes.com,* April 22, 2010.

Light, Larry. "Demographics and Density." *Forbes.com,* November 22, 2006.

"Genworth Financial, Inc. SWOT Analysis," *Global Markets Direct,* 2008: 1–6.

Muolo, Paul, "Genworth Adds 'Risky' Products," *National Mortgage News* 34 no. 1 (2009): 10.

Steverman, Ben. "Comeback of the Year: Behind Genworth's 700% Rebound," *BusinessWeek Online,* March 26, 2010: 3.

# Global Partners L.P.

**800 South Street**
**Suite 200**
**P.O. Box 9161**
**Waltham, Massachusetts 02454**
**U.S.A.**
**Telephone: (781) 894-8800**
**Toll Free: (800) 685-7222**
**Fax: (781) 398-4160**
**Web site: http://www.globalp.com**

*Public Company*
*Founded:* 1933 as Slifky's Reliable Oil Delivery Service
*Employees:* 250 (2009)
*Sales:* $5.818 billion (2009)
*Stock Exchanges:* New York
*Ticker Symbol:* GLP
*NAICS:* 424710 Petroleum Bulk Stations and Terminals;
   454311 Heating Oil Dealers

■ ■ ■

Global Partners L.P. (Global), a leading regional wholesale distributor of gasoline, kerosene, heating oil, and residual oil, comes from roots stretching back to the 1930s. The company is publicly traded on the New York Stock Exchange and supplies products to a wide range of wholesalers and retailers in every state in the northeastern United States, from Maine to Pennsylvania. With 22 storage facilities owned, leased, or maintained throughout the Northeast as of 2009, Global boasted a storage capacity of 9.30 million barrels.

A *Fortune* 500 company, Global also sells gasoline and diesel, both unbranded and under the brand name of Diesel One, to about 975 wholesalers and gas stations. The company's roots lie in heating oil, which it continues to sell under the brand name of Heating Oil Plus to 1,100 wholesalers and retailers. Overall, wholesale sales accounted for 94 percent of Global's business in 2009.

## SLIFKY'S: 1933–59

Global comes from humble roots and typifies the American entrepreneurial dream. Founded in 1933 by two Polish immigrant brothers, Abraham and Bernard Slifka, the company was then known as Slifky's Reliable Oil Delivery Service. (Slifka and Slifky are variant spellings of the same last name.) True to its name, Slifky's delivered home heating oil from a 275-gallon truck that serviced Dorchester, Massachusetts, and neighboring Boston-area communities. For those not familiar with heating oil, it is a substance that, despite its name, bears more of a resemblance to diesel gasoline rather than crude oil. Even into the 21st century heating oil is still delivered in large trucks to residential locations where natural gas and propane are scarce or too expensive. (In the United States, these residences are primarily in the Northeast.)

The heating oil delivery business has always been competitive, but Slifky's carved out sufficient market share to thrive and survive on the local level. Slifky's averaged just under a million retail gallons delivered each year, and it quickly became a family business. In 1948 young Fred Slifka (Abraham's son) started working

## COMPANY PERSPECTIVES

Customers benefit from our vast experience in energy markets and our dedication to meeting their needs. Global Partners has a proven record of supplying product under difficult market conditions. Our expertise in traditional and emerging fuel markets enables us to be at the forefront of competitive, reliable energy supply.

for the company, driving delivery trucks. In 1955 he took over the business from Abraham and Bernard.

That same year, Fred began to change the direction of Slifky's after a chance encounter led to the company's first acquisition, a one-man oil trucking company. Fred had gotten to chatting with the truck driver, who soon revealed that he loathed his job. Fred offered to ease the man's burden by buying his truck and route from him, and the course of the company was forever altered. Fred and his brother Richard set their sights on expanding Slifky's beyond mere home delivery and into the realms of wholesale and retail oil sales.

### ATLAS OIL: 1960–82

The plan was to grow the company by buying other firms. The first major acquisition came with the purchase of Atlas Oil in 1963. Fred and Richard Slifka formed a partnership in the wake of the Atlas acquisition, and Slikfy's was no more. In its place was Atlas Oil Company. Under the name of Atlas, the Slifkas gradually expanded by buying out local competitors, incrementally expanding their geographic range as they increased their revenue. All told, during the Atlas years over 30 companies were acquired in this fashion.

By 1971 Atlas was enjoying sales of eight million gallons. This total more than doubled that year with the acquisition of Lipson Oil, which brought Atlas's yearly sales to a grand total of 20 million gallons. This record expansion came right on the verge of the 1973 oil crisis, in which an embargo on oil exports from Arab countries resulted in an unprecedented spike in oil prices. The oil crisis turned into an opportunity for Atlas. As the big petroleum companies frantically began cutting costs and liabilities, Fred Slifka was able to step in and get a good deal from Chevron, who offered the company one of its 500,000 gallon storage tanks that it would soon be vacating. Atlas was therefore able to transition into terminal storage, making it a major wholesale distributor in one stroke.

That initial terminal storage deal was soon dwarfed by another that brought eight million gallons of storage in South Boston, this time acquired from Texaco. Atlas moved further into wholesaling when Fred Slifka bid for and won a contract to deliver fuel to Pease Air Force Base, located in New Hampshire. With government fuel allocations, Atlas was able to compete in the same wholesale price range as international oil companies. Even as another energy crisis loomed at the end of the 1970s, Atlas continued expanding. The acquisition of Glendale Oil in 1978 was the company's second-largest after Lipson.

In order to manage all this new wholesale distribution activity, a subsidiary company called Global Petroleum Trading Company was set up in 1982. This was accomplished through the sale of the old retail heating oil side of the company. The money from the sale, along with a Small Business Administration (SBA) loan, was reinvested into the company's first scaled waterborne terminal facility, purchased from ARCO. In a September 2007 interview with *Oil & Energy* magazine, Fred Slifka recalled that the ARCO terminal, Atlas's first big acquisition of the 1980s, "put us in a different ballgame."

### A DIFFERENT BALLGAME: 1983–2004

The Arco terminal was located near Revere, Massachusetts, and boasted a 500,000 barrel capacity. With the ARCO terminal under its belt, Atlas had become a solidly established regional supplier. The company continued expanding. More terminals were bought, along with big Exxon and BP regional retail chains. In 1985 Global Petroleum, as the company was now called, purchased Washington, D.C.'s Griffith Consumers and returned to the retail game with its acquisition of Griffith subsidiary Carl King, Inc. Griffith and Carl King were both retail distributors of gasoline and other petroleum products.

With the exception of a brief period at the end of the 1990s, however, Global maintained its wholesale focus for the remainder of the century. The exception came in the form of the purchase of Atlantic Fuels Marketing (renamed Alliance after its acquisition), a retailer of heating oil. By 2000, however, Global had again sold off its retail assets and returned to an exclusively wholesale distribution business model.

Throughout the 1990s, Global continued expanding. It continued to boost storage capacity when possible, and in 1998 the company began to expand its New England presence in earnest, purchasing a terminal located in Portland, Maine, and leasing a million-barrel terminal in Rhode Island. In 1998 the company partnered with Repsol YPF, a major oil company. For the first time, the Slifka family lost controlling interest in their own company. By way of compensation, between 1998 and 2004, Global's owners would enjoy over $84 million in payouts. Yet the money did not do enough to satisfy the desire of the Slifkas to renew ownership. (By this time Fred Slifka had been joined by his son Eric in the company ranks.) This was accomplished in 2003, when the Slifka family was able to reacquire controlling interest in the company from Repsol. Plans were soon under way to take Global public.

### INCORPORATION: 2005–10

On October 17, 2005, brothers Fred and Richard Slifka, acting as chairman and vice chairman, respectively, rang the opening bell at the New York Stock Exchange, celebrating the October 4 initial public offering (IPO) of stock in Global Partners LP. Incorporated in Delaware but still headquartered in Waltham, Massachusetts, the new incarnation of Global was a master limited partnership in which the Slifka family retained majority interest in the company.

The master limited partnership was an ideal way for Global to incorporate. Capital costs were kept low, and because every stockholder is considered a partner in the business, taxes are more efficient. The downside of the master limited partnership is that investor distributions are paid out in contractually defined quarterly installments. However, this is offset by Global's relatively stable income earned from wholesale distribution and transport.

In the wake of its successful IPO, Global continued to expand into terminal storage, a keystone of its wholesale distribution strategy. In 2006 the company added a 170,000-barrel terminal in Macungie,

Pennsylvania, and a 100,000-barrel site at Bridgeport, Connecticut. Another 2006 milestone was that, for the first time in company history, the volume of sale of heating oil, the cornerstone product going back to Slifky's Reliable Oil Delivery Service, was eclipsed by volume sales of gasoline and diesel.

In 2007 Global moved aggressively into the New York market, purchasing three terminals from Exxon-Mobil in Albany and Newburgh, New York, and in nearby Bridgeport, Connecticut. The crowning purchase for that year was two Long Island ExxonMobil terminals that boasted a combined storage capacity of 430,000 barrels. Although Global had maintained throughput and supply in New York, the terminal acquisitions signaled the company's entry as a serious presence in New York wholesale distribution.

### GLOBAL STRATEGIES

Terminal acquisition was a key to Global's business plan because of the multiple uses Global made of its terminals. First and foremost, the terminals were used for local storage. With over 20 terminals peppered across the Northeast, Global was able to benefit from efficient logistics and save on transportation costs. This led into the second use Global made of its terminal sites, as they were in effect "warehouses" for its direct wholesale inventory. Lastly, any terminal space not being utilized by the company was licensed to third parties for throughputs and marketing.

Global's business strategy emphasized efficiency and vertical integration in nearly every aspect of its operation. One of the keys to the company's acquisition strategy had been the practice of purchasing not just a physical property but also the marketing business tied in to the acquired asset. Eric Slifka, who became president and CEO in 2005, summed up Global's key to success in his interview with *Oil & Energy*. It was due, he said, to "our ability to optimize our assets by vertically integrating supply, terminalling and marketing."

Three years after its IPO, Global's strategy seemed to be paying off. In 2008 the company was ranked fifth among Massachusetts companies with highest dividend yield, 291st out of the top 500 companies with largest business revenue (and eighth in Massachusetts), and ninth overall in *Fortune* 500 energy companies. In 2008 the company also opened up a deepwater marine terminal at the port of Providence, Rhode Island, and expanded into new territory with a 160,000-barrel lease on terminal capacity in Philadelphia, contributing to a company record of 86 million barrels of refined petroleum products supplied to customers that year.

## LOOKING TO THE FUTURE

Eric Slifka noted in 2007 that he believed "the heating oil business is at a critical time in its lifecycle." His words proved prescient. The global economic crisis of 2008 and 2009, coupled with unprecedented high oil prices during the same time, hit Global hard, just as it did every other petroleum company, wholesale and retail alike.

To offset the financial difficulties imposed by this recession, Global continued to expand its asset base and pursue its proven strategy of terminal acquisition in key markets in the Northeast. The company also began to branch out into ethanol, beginning with a tank refurbishment project intended to add 180,000 barrels of ethanol storage in 2010. The project, located in Albany, New York, was an international joint venture with Canadian Pacific Railway Limited.

Looking to the future, Global's strategy was to continue with its terminal investments and focus on transportation fuels while expanding into new fuels such as natural gas and biofuels. Global's latest terminal acquisition, announced in April 2010, was of three facilities in Newburgh, New York, purchased from Warex Terminals Corporation for $47.5 million. The new facilities boosted Global's gasoline and distillate storage capacities in southern New York by 900,000 barrels.

As Global entered the second decade of the 21st century, it set its sights on expanding beyond its regional core. The strategy remained the same: to acquire terminal storage and associated marketing infrastructures. The company realized that this goal might prove difficult, as it had built up debt of over a half-billion dollars in the course of its previous acquisitions. In order to help offset this debt, in March 2010 Global offered 3.4 million common shares priced at $22.75 each, a reduction of 5 percent off the most recent stock value.

In 2010 the Slifka tradition carried on at Global. Although the family were no longer majority stock holders, Eric Slifka retained his position as chief executive officer and president of the company. He was the third generation of the family to run the company since the days when a single truck made the rounds in Dorchester, Massachusetts, delivering heating oil. Despite the uncertain economic climate and a receding petroleum market, Slifka and his company seemed determined to continue that long legacy of growth and success.

*David Larkins*

## PRINCIPAL SUBSIDIARIES

Chelsea Sandwich LLC; Glen Hes Corp.; Global Companies LLC; Global Energy Marketing LLC; Global Montello Group Corp.

## PRINCIPAL COMPETITORS

Getty Petroleum Marketing; Hess Corporation; Irving Oil Corporation; The Rice Companies; Sprague Energy Corp.

## FURTHER READING

"Global Partners LP to Ring Opening Bell at New York Stock Exchange," *PR Newswire,* October 14, 2005.

Global Partners LP, "Form 10-K," *Morningstar Document Research,* March 12, 2010.

"GLP," *Company Profile,* Hoover's, Inc., 2010.

"Growth Is a Way of Life at Global," *Oil & Energy,* September 2007.

# Greylock Partners

2929 Campus Drive
Suite 400
San Mateo, California 94403
U.S.A.
Telephone: (650) 493-5525
Fax: (650) 493-5575
Web site: http://www.greylock.com

*Private Company*
*Founded:* 1965
*Employees:* 40
*NAICS:* 523910 Venture Capital Companies

■ ■ ■

Greylock Partners (Greylock) is a venture capital investment firm that focuses primarily on information technology and communication start-ups. Although this is the company's focus, it invests across the board in ventures in every phase of development. Its primary areas of investment include services, especially Internet-based; enterprise infrastructure (such as network security); software; and semiconductor companies. Greylock has also invested in the health care and biotech arenas when opportunities have presented themselves.

Although most of its business is centered in the United States, Greylock maintains offices in India and Israel and has also invested in European and Chinese companies. All told, Greylock has invested in hundreds of companies over the course of its history. Of these investments, 150 have had successful initial public offerings and 100 more have turned a profit through mergers and acquisitions.

## A PRIVATE FIRM

Greylock is a private company, and it shows in its public presence. Performance numbers are not available to the public, and the company keeps a low profile for the most part. In a 2001 interview with *Venture Capital Journal* one of the top partners in the firm, Bill Kaiser, noted, "We are really trying not to emphasize the individual partners so much as we are trying to emphasize the firm and its collective strengths."

Those "collective strengths" are built on a solid foundation stretching back nearly a half-century. Greylock Partners was founded in 1965 by two men, Bill Elfers and Dan Gregory. They were joined shortly thereafter by Charlie Waite. All three of the company's initial partners had experience in finance and venture capital. Elfers and Gregory, in fact, founded Greylock after meeting at American Research and Development Corporation (ARDC), one of the first modern venture capital firms.

ARDC was the first private investment firm to look for capital outside of the traditional source of wealthy families and individuals. Its founder, Charles Doriot, has been called "the father of venture capitalism," and his goal was to cultivate small business investments among the upwardly mobile middle class in the post-World War II U.S. economy.

## COMPANY PERSPECTIVES

Greylock Partners' role is to support a company's management team in building a world-class enterprise by acting as a responsible and constructive member of the company's board of directors. This takes on many shapes and forms but includes working to build a management team, facilitating relationships with other companies, helping to set a company's strategic direction, and raising additional capital.

## VENTURE SOFTWARE CAPITAL: 1965–2002

These values and strategies were carried forward by Elfers and Gregory to Greylock in 1965. Greylock's foundation would not have been possible without the emergence of the private equity fund and the passage of the 1958 Small Business Investment Act. The latter was a first step in creating a formal, professional venture capital industry licensed through the Small Business Administration. Private equity funds were an emerging form of limited partnership that set up the members of a venture capital firm as general partners and the investors as limited partners. In addition to putting up the capital, the limited partners paid a small annual fee. In exchange, when the returns on the investment were realized, the investors would realize a return on their money plus a certain percentage of the final profits.

As of 2010, Greylock had organized 13 limited partnerships to raise capital for its investments. (Limited partnerships were organized in 1965, 1973, 1979, 1983, 1985, 1987, 1990, 1994, 1997, 2000, 2001, 2005, and 2009.) Remarkably, many of the investors who were on board with the early limited partnerships continued to invest for over 40 years in Greylock. Part of this loyalty can be attributed to Greylock's treatment of its investors, which goes above and beyond industry standards. For example, most venture capital firms have an annual meeting with their limited partners, but Greylock has biannual meetings.

After Greylock's 2009 limited partnership was announced, one long-time investor, Andrew K. Golden of the Princeton University Investment Co., told *Wireless News*, "In this difficult environment, all investors need to be particularly selective about the funds in which they invest....Our investment in Greylock...represents the lion's share of the commitments we plan to make to venture capital funds this year." As can be seen by the organization Golden is affiliated with, Greylock has

maintained the direction established by the American Research and Development Company, reaching out beyond traditional sources of investment capital to work with university endowments and nonprofit foundations.

Although most of the venture capital companies founded in the 1960s and 1970s were located in California's Silicon Valley, particularly along a particular stretch of Sand Hill Road that made the street synonymous with information technology investments, Greylock started up in Cambridge, Massachusetts. The Boston area was the East Coast locus of emerging information technology, and Greylock was there to fund many emerging enterprises. Greylock's first venture into software investment was with Boston-based Cullinane Corp., founded in 1968, which in 1978 would go on to become the first independent software company to go public.

When Cullinane was acquired by Computer Associates in 1989 for $300 million, Greylock witnessed a handsome return on its investments. By that point the firm was well on its way to carving out a niche of backing small, start-up computer and information technology companies. As Kaiser put it, "We are not hesitant to get involved in something that isn't all baked and is really just an idea." Other notable companies supported by capital from Greylock in the 1980s and 1990s included Trilogy (a software services company), Legato Systems and Decru Inc. (both computer software storage companies), and Ascend Communications (one of the big suppliers of Internet hardware in the 1990s).

## INVESTING IN SOCIAL NETWORKING: 2003–10

In April 2006 Greylock was part of a $27.5 million round of fundraising by the emerging social networking web site Facebook. Launched in February 2004, Facebook was part of a new breed of Web site, one that focused on connecting people through the Internet and allowing them to socialize with each other online. Facebook was following closely on the heels of social networking pioneers like LinkedIn and MySpace, and from its humble origins in the Harvard dorm room of founders Mark Zuckerberg, Dustin Moskovitz, and Chris Hughes, it had relocated to Palo Alto, California, and began building a following. Four months after Greylock's capital investment, Facebook reached nine million users. Eight months later, it had 20 million users and by October 2007 had topped 50 million. A deal made with Microsoft for a 1.6 percent stake in the company indicated Facebook's total value was approximately $15 billion.

Although getting in early on an investment in what by 2010 had become the leading social networking site

## EXPANSION AND RELOCATION

In 1994 three-quarters of Greylock's investments were headquartered on the East Coast of the United States with the remaining quarter on the West Coast. Fifteen years later, that ratio was exactly reversed. The focus of software and information technology business had shifted to the other side of the country, centered in the so-called Silicon Valley in California. In actuality the Santa Clara Valley at the southern end of the San Francisco Bay Area, the region had become the hub of high-tech industry since the 1970s. In the 21st century, the new face of Silicon Valley was Internet-based companies like Google, and the decision was made at Greylock to officially decamp from Boston after 45 years and move west. As Greylock partner Bill Helman told the *New York Times* when the move was announced, "Silicon Valley is the most important market for what we do. It's important we can say we're Silicon Valley-based."

The company had maintained an office in the Bay Area city of San Mateo but with the move came big plans to shift to new offices in the heart of Silicon Valley. Greylock did not abandon Boston entirely, leaving behind a small office in Waltham, Massachusetts, and two full-time partners, but the focus of the company had clearly shifted.

During the first decade of the 21st century, Greylock's focus also began to expand beyond the United States in earnest. Beginning in 2001, the company had been doing business in Israel, but in 2006 the company took the next step by opening a regional office in Herzliya, Israel. The new Greylock Israel was a dedicated $150 million fund specifically for investments in Israeli high-tech companies. The following year, Greylock opened regional offices in India, another emerging center of high-tech industry. Greylock has also expanded farther into Asia by associating with the Northern Light fund of China.

Despite its low public profile, Greylock had a demonstrated ability to add well-known names to its portfolio of partners. Two notable examples were Reid Hoffman of LinkedIn, who came aboard in 2009, and Mozilla's CEO John Lilly, who joined in 2010. Greylock partner David Sze explained to *Wireless News,* "At Greylock we place a high value on hiring partners with deep operating experience at companies with explosive growth." Bringing in Hoffman and Lilly dramatically exemplified Sze's statement. Hoffman had cofounded LinkedIn, one of the first social networking sites and the Internet's largest professional networking site, in 2003, and Lilly was at the helm of Mozilla, maker of the Fire-

on the Internet might seem like an obvious move in hindsight, in the first years of the 21st century there was considerable doubt among venture capital investors regarding social networking and other elements of Web 2.0, as it was called. The dot-com crash of 2000 and 2001 had left many skeptical of putting money into Internet firms with big dreams and little market share. However, Greylock's long-standing policies paid off for it, not just in the case of Facebook, but also with several other Internet start-ups such as Digg (a "meta-news" service that allows users to rate and promote articles), Constant Contact (a business e-mail management Web site), and Pandora (an Internet-based radio station that plays music according to each listener's individual tastes).

Although Greylock funded companies at any stage, it preferred to get in early, as it did with social networking and Web 2.0 companies. More than merely a venture capital company, Greylock's strategy and philosophy included active participation in board meetings of the companies it invested in. It was not unusual for Greylock partners to serve as lead director, in fact. This was because all of Greylock's partners came to the company with extensive knowledge gained from senior-level corporate positions in technology companies like Apple, IBM, and Yahoo!. Greylock literature referred to this approach as "the company building process."

The company's approach could be seen as having three basic elements. First, the firm focused on early-stage investments in high-value sectors. Next, it applied a business philosophy based on the values of integrity, honesty, and teamwork and thought of the investment as a long-term partnership. In addition, the firm attempted to make the company or entrepreneur the central focus while Greylock remained the "invited guest."

fox Internet browsing software. The first serious challenger to Microsoft's Internet Explorer, Firefox went from 20 million to 400 million users during Lilly's five-year tenure.

As the importance of social networking and new Internet technologies continued to grow, so too did Greylock's future prospects. The success of Greylock's strategy could be seen in the fact that its 2009 limited partnership raised $75 million more than the initial half-billion-dollar target.

*David Larkins*

## PRINCIPAL COMPETITORS

Accel Partners; Bessemer Venture Partners; Highland Capital Partners; Lightspeed Venture Partners; Polaris Venture Partners.

## FURTHER READING

Christopher, Alistair, "Greylock's Bill Kaiser: Learning Opportunities," *Venture Capital Journal,* June 1, 2001.

Garland, Russell, "Greylock Loses No Steam as It Hits Middle Age," *Wall Street Journal,* December 10, 2009.

"Greylock Partners Finalizes $575 Million Venture Fund," *Wireless News,* November 16, 2009.

Miller, Claire Cain, "Boston as Fading Venture Hot Spot," *New York Times,* May 25, 2009.

# Guardian Life Insurance Company of America

---

7 Hanover Square
New York, New York 10004-4025
U.S.A.
Telephone: (212) 598-8000
Toll Free: (866) 425-4542
Fax: (212) 919-2170
Web site: http://www.guardianlife.com

*Private Company*
*Founded:* 1860 as Germania Life Insurance Company of
New York
*Employees:* 5,400
*Sales:* $7.693 billion (2009)
*NAICS:* 524113 Direct Life Insurance Carriers
(Primary); 523930 Investment Advice; 525910
Open-End Investment Funds; 524114 Direct
Health & Medical Insurance Carriers; 525110 Pen-
sion Funds

■ ■ ■

The Guardian Life Insurance Company of America
(Guardian) is a mutual insurance company that offers
life, long-term care, disability income, medical and
dental insurance products. The company's dental
network covers more than six million people across the
United States. The company also offers 401(k) plans,
annuities, and other financial products and trust
services.

## A REVOLUTIONARY COMPANY:
### 1860–1914

The foundation of Guardian Life Insurance Company
of America lies far back in the 19th century in Germany. In 1848 popular unrest and open revolution
swept through Europe. Every country save the United
Kingdom, the Netherlands, and Russia experienced
some kind of uprising that year and the year following,
but few regions were as affected as Germany.

Germany was not a unified country at that time,
but rather a patchwork conglomerate of independent
cities and states. The impetus to unify and make
Germany a major European power founded on
principles of social justice and democracy led to the
March Revolution. During that month, uprisings broke
out in Prussia, Austria, Bavaria, Saxony, and other parts
of Germany. By the end of the year, however, whatever
small victories these uprisings had achieved had been
suppressed by the autocratic powers.

In the wake of the failure of the March Revolution
and its fallout, there was a mass exodus of disillusioned
Germans to countries such as the United Kingdom,
Canada, Australia, and the United States that promised
a chance to start over. For a significant number of these
"Forty-Eighters," it was not a simple matter of ideology.
Many were wanted in their home country for treason
against the government for their activities in the
uprisings.

## HUGO WESENDONCK AND GERMANIA

One of the Forty-Eighters who arrived in New York
City in 1849 was Hugo Wesendonck. Back home in
western Germany, Hugo had been a civil rights lawyer
and political ideologue. His beliefs led him to help draft
a pro-unification provisional German constitution at the

Frankfurt National Assembly. This action led to eventual treason charges from the authorities.

After making a comfortable living for himself as an importer in Philadelphia, Wesendonck returned to New York City. By the late 1850s he was heavily involved in the antislavery movement and the nascent Republican Party, as well as with German-American immigration issues. At the time, Germans comprised one of the fastest-growing immigrant groups in the United States, numbering about one million strong.

Wesendonck was ready to get out of the importing business and start giving back to his community. He envisioned a life insurance company that would provide for the ever-expanding German-American community of New York. To that end, in 1860 the charismatic Wesendonck (who was once described as possessing "an air of indisputable gravity and authority" by an underling) gathered 21 like-minded fellows together at Delmonico's restaurant. All prosperous German immigrants like himself, they met with the intention of forming a new company, and over the course of lunch they laid out plans for what would soon become the Germania Life Insurance Company of New York.

Founded as the company was with explicit goals to help the German immigrant community, Wesendonck would have chosen to make Germania a fully mutual company if he could have. By New York state law, however, Germania had to form as, at best, a mixed company, one founded on mutual principles but offering public stocks as well.

## A MIXED BEGINNING

Germania officially started business operations on July 16, 1860, with Wesendonck as president and 14 agents to issue policies. Eight years later, despite some tough times struggling through the years of the American Civil War, the company's stable of agents had expanded to 279.

By that point, Germania had expanded well beyond its initial sphere of the New York City metropolitan area, acquiring new policyholders in cities like Boston, Chicago, Cincinnati, Detroit, Philadelphia, and even

San Francisco and the New Mexico Territory. International expansion into Canada, Mexico, and Europe would soon follow.

By this time the company had also encountered the limits of its mutual, cash-only philosophy, a philosophy that clashed with the common practice of the day in which life insurance companies issued promissory notes in lieu of cash dividends. Although this policy made sure Germania's policyholders were well-protected and could expect cash payments for their policies rather than IOUs, it also required Germania to create enough business to be able to keep the cash flowing. Wesendonck himself was responsible for much of the company's resulting growth, traveling the country to give talks on his experience as a "famous Forty-Eighter" and, incidentally, sell hundreds of new insurance policies. All the hard work paid off, for between 1863 and 1869, Germania's expense ratio, a measure of the company's cash expenses versus cash receipts, dropped from 37.83 to 18.77 percent.

## THROUGH DEPRESSION AND PROSPERITY

The solid foundation built during Germania's first 10 years were to prove crucial during the economically volatile latter half of the 19th century. Between 1874 and 1878, the United States suffered through a severe economic depression, and life insurance companies suffered along with everyone else. At the beginning of the 1870s there were 129 life insurance companies operating in the United States. By decade's end, that number had plummeted to 55.

## FROM GERMANIA TO GUARDIAN: 1915–40

The sober, hardworking example set by Hugo Wesendonck and his contemporaries at Germania assured a solidly successful first half-century. In 1905 the company faced its first major test in the form of the Armstrong Committee. It was also the first major test of the insurance industry as a whole.

At the beginning of the 20th century in the United States, the public's ire, as at the beginning of the 21st century, was largely focused on big business, wealthy capitalists, and their excesses. When Equitable Life Insurance Company founder Henry J. Hyde died in 1891, he left most of his stock to his 23-year-old wastrel of a son, James. So scandalous were the younger Hyde's ostentatious displays of wealth that he was forced to resign from his own company, bought out for $2.5 million.

## KEY DATES

**1860:** After being charged with treason in Germany and fleeing to the United States, Hugo Wesendonck founds the Germania Life Insurance Company in New York to provide coverage for the swelling ranks of German immigrants arriving in the United States.

**1917:** Germania changes its name to Guardian Life Insurance Company.

**1925:** Guardian becomes a wholly mutual company.

**1940:** Guardian begins moving beyond life insurance and into health and accident insurance.

**2001:** Guardian merges with Berkshire Life Insurance Company.

In light of the fact that James had been collecting a mere $3,514 in annual dividends, this buyout total alone was enough to raise eyebrows. The ensuing public outcry led to the formation of a committee in the New York legislature under Senator William Armstrong. Soon, what began as an investigation of Equitable Life Insurance turned into an investigation of the entire life insurance industry.

The aftermath of the Armstrong investigation would change the face of the industry. In the wake of its findings of shady accounting practices, corruption, fraud, forgery, and corporate excess, life insurance came under heavy legislation in states across the country. Companies were humbled, corporate heads rolled, and drastic changes were implemented in investment regulation, dividend distribution, and agent commissions. Germania, however, carried along as always, for it was one of the few life insurance companies to be completely exonerated of any wrongdoing.

### GERMANIA AND LIBERTY CABBAGE

If the Armstrong investigation had been a test of Germania's worth, the entry of the United States into World War I in 1917 would prove a public relations crucible in the form of the company's very name.

Thanks to successful propaganda efforts from the Allied powers in Europe, Germany had from the start of the war in 1914 been depicted as the sole aggressor, the "savage brute" who brought war to the world. Actions such as the submarine sinking of the passenger liner *Lusitania* only reinforced this image in the minds of many Americans, and when the United States went to war, Germany and all things German overnight became Public Enemy Number One.

Sauerkraut was re-dubbed Liberty Cabbage. Many public school districts banned the teaching of German. Not a few German-Americans emulated the British royal family and changed their last names to something less Germanic-sounding. In such a highly charged atmosphere, Germania had little choice but to make a similar maneuver. Therefore, it shed its old name and became the Guardian Life Insurance Company of America. To further cement its status as a patriotic company, Guardian bought a half-million dollars' worth of Liberty Bonds on the first day they were offered.

### DOMESTIC REFOCUSING

Guardian made another big change during the war years besides just a name switch. It began to retrench, getting out of European markets it had steadily been expanding into ever since opening its first Berlin office in the late 1860s. As two-thirds of Guardian's European policies were in Germany and another one-fifth in Austria-Hungary (the two main contenders on the losing side of World War I), this only made good business sense. As might be expected, the Central European political and economic situation was in utter chaos in the wake of the war.

Although Guardian was divesting itself of European policies, the company still maintained strong ties to Germany. By 1921, for example, when the German Reichsmark was essentially worthless, Guardian took to sending over shipments of U.S. currency and food in an effort to provide what help it could.

Furthermore, the company was determined that its exit from Europe would not harm its U.S. policyholders, and efforts were redoubled in the United States to drum up enough new business to offset the losses incurred from liquidating European policies. (By the end of the 1950s, Guardian had even pulled out of Canada and Mexico, focusing exclusively on the United States.)

### GOING MUTUAL

Losses incurred by Guardian's policyholders in Germany coupled with the worldwide flu pandemic of 1918 spelled potentially disastrous losses after World War I. However, the company had enough surplus to absorb the losses and move forward, and it was soon aiming to making a move toward full mutualization. This long-held goal was finally achieved in 1925. By 1946 Guardian had acquired all remaining outstanding stock and its conversion to a wholly mutual company was complete.

The key difference between a mutual company and one that offers stocks is that in a mutual company, every policyholder is also a shareholder. That is to say, there are no private owners of a mutual company, and profits are paid directly to the policyholders through annual dividends. There are downsides to the mutual approach. For one thing, there is little incentive for growth, and profits tend to not be as high as for privately owned companies. Furthermore, payment of dividends is contingent on profit and not guaranteed.

## RECORD GROWTH, STELLAR RETURNS: 1941–89

Over a century after its founding, Guardian was still sticking to the core principles laid down by Hugo Wesendonck. Those principles were reiterated by Daniel J. Lyons, company president for much of the 1960s, who stated "Don't do any deals…unless they are good for the policyholder, the agent, and the company. It has got to be good for each of the three parties to the deal."

By the time Lyons spoke those words, however, Guardian had branched out beyond just offering life insurance. Under the leadership of the dynamic James A McLain, who served as company president from 1940 to 1956 and as board chairman from 1957 to 1963, Guardian first expanded into offering health and accident insurance, then group insurance.

McLain was followed in his role as president by his protégés Daniel J. Lyons (1964–68) and George Conklin (1969–76). This trio collectively steered Guardian toward record growth. By the 1970s the company was bringing in unprecedented returns and had exceeded $1 billion in assets. By 1980 the company had also exceeded $1 billion in premium income, and a direct recognition program, in which policyholders agreed not to borrow against the cash values of their policies, was resulting in higher dividends.

By the time Conklin stepped down from his position as board chairman and retired from Guardian in 1980, he had also played a role in putting Guardian on the cutting edge of emerging computer technology and introduced a new strategy of decentralization. Throughout the 1980s, Guardian regionalized by moving back-office locations out of New York to neighboring states like Pennsylvania.

## STAYING MUTUAL: 1990–2001

Guardian's regionalization program was undertaken in part due to the uncertain economic situation of the 1980s. The end of the decade brought the greatest crisis yet for the insurance industry in the form of the savings and loan crisis.

For the life insurance industry, the early 1990s was a time of widespread bankruptcy, consolidation, and demutualization. The latter, in particular, swept the life insurance industry from the mid-1990s onward. Large mutual companies, such as Prudential, MetLife, and John Hancock all demutualized and paid policyholders accumulated profits in excess of $100 billion. Guardian ultimately elected to stay the course, maintaining the mutual approach that had worked so well for decades.

As Guardian moved into a new century, it continued to look toward proven strategies across the board. In an interview with *National Underwriter: Life and Health* magazine in February 2010, Guardian CEO Dennis Manning outlined the company's new refocusing strategy aimed at small businesses. Guardian would no longer try to be "all things to all people." In the same interview, Manning admitted that Guardian had looked at demutualizing in the past and periodically revisited the issue, but "nothing I see would cause me to recommend to the board to demutualize."

## MERGERS AND LOOKING FORWARD: 2002–10

Nevertheless, Guardian did not remain stagnant. In 2001 Guardian finalized a merger with another venerable life insurance company, Berkshire Life Insurance. Like Guardian, Berkshire's roots stretched back to the 19th century, but its focus had been mainly in disability insurance. With the two companies coming together, Guardian became the second-largest disability insurance company in the United States.

Despite high ratings and a strong reputation in the industry, Guardian did experience its share of controversy in the wake of the merger. In 2009, as part of a cost-cutting move, the company canceled policies that covered unlimited in-home care for disabled policyholders. When the plight of one such policyholder, a wheelchair-bound man stricken with muscular dystrophy and million-dollar annual medical bills, made the front page of the *Washington Times*, a public outcry arose. Within a month, Guardian reversed its decision.

By 2010 Guardian could boast life, disability, accident, and health (including HMO, PPO, and dental) insurance policies as well as retirement plans and annuities offered through its main offices and several subsidiaries. These policies were distributed through a agency system of about 80 agencies, 3,000 representatives, and 80,000 licensed brokers.

Despite declining trends in sales of variable annuities and life insurance during the economic downturn of 2008 to 2010, Guardian's 2009 annual report reported the fact that "[e]ven as many financial institutions seek and receive federal assistance under the U.S. government's Troubled Asset Relief Program, Guardian has no need to" and that a record dividend had been paid out that year. Guardian appeared on track to weather the economic crisis just as it had countless others over the course of its 150-year history.

*David Larkins*

## PRINCIPAL SUBSIDIARIES

American Financial Systems, Inc.; Berkshire Life Insurance Company of America (BLICOA); e-Money Advisor Holdings, LLC; First Commonwealth, Inc.; Guardian Baillie Gifford Limited; The Guardian Insurance & Annuity Company, Inc. (GIAC); Guardian Investor Services LLC (GIS); Guardian Trust Company, FSB; Innovative Underwriters, Inc.; Managed Dental Care (California); Managed DentalGuard, Inc. (New Jersey); Managed DentalGuard, Inc. (Texas); Park Avenue Life Insurance Company; Park Avenue Securities LLC; RS Investment Management Co. LLC.

## PRINCIPAL COMPETITORS

Massachusetts Mutual Life Insurance Company; MetLife, Inc.; Nationwide Mutual Insurance Company; New York Life Insurance Company; Northwestern Mutual Life Insurance Company.

## FURTHER READING

Cisse, Rokhaya, and Weigang Bo, "Company Profile: Guardian Life Insurance Company of America," *Moody's Insurance,* May 2009, p. 1–7.

Ehart, William, "Health Insurer Restores Man's Coverage after Public Uproar," *Washington Times,* October 23, 2009, p. 1.

*Guardian Life Ins. Co. of America SWOT Analysis,* July 2009, p. 1–8.

Piotnik, Steve, "From Where He Sits, Guardian's CEO Likes the View," *National Underwriter: Life and Health,* February 1, 2010, p. 1.

Wipperfurth, Heike, "Guardian Finds Mutual Ground in Berkshire Merger," *Crain's New York Business* 16 no. 38 2000; p. 10.

Wright, Robert E., and George David Smith, *Mutually Beneficial: The Guardian and Life Insurance in America.* New York: New York University Press, 2004.

# Hartford Financial Services Group, Inc.

---

**One Hartford Plaza**
**Hartford, Connecticut 06115**
**U.S.A.**
**Telephone: (860) 547-5000**
**Web site: http://www.thehartford.com**

*Public Company*
*Founded:* 1810 as Hartford Fire Insurance Company
*Employees:* 28,000 (2009 est.)
*Revenues:* $24.70 billion (2009)
*Stock Exchanges:* New York
*Ticker Symbol:* HIG
*NAICS:* 524126 Direct Property and Casualty Insurance Carriers; 524113 Direct Life Insurance Carriers; 524126 Direct Property and Casualty Insurance Carriers; 524210 Insurance Agencies and Brokerages; 524291 Claims Adjusting; 551112 Offices of Other Holding Companies

■ ■ ■

The Hartford Financial Services Group, Inc., commonly known as "The Hartford," is one of the largest insurance and investment companies in the United States. It also has offices in Japan, Brazil, the United Kingdom, Canada, and Ireland. A *Fortune* 100 company with revenues in excess of $24 billion in 2009, The Hartford is a top provider of life insurance, automobile and homeowners' insurance, group and employee benefits, and business insurance. In addition, the company is a leader in the field of investment, offering such products as mutual funds, annuities, and college savings plans.

Headquartered in Hartford, Connecticut, The Hartford operates through various subsidiaries, independent agents and brokers, financial institutions, and online services. The group prides itself on its customer service and its mission to help millions of customers worldwide create a secure and prosperous future. Having been in business for 200 years, The Hartford is the nation's oldest insurance company.

## EARLY YEARS: 1794–1835

Hartford, Connecticut, located on the Connecticut River, was settled in 1623 as a Dutch trading post. In 1636 a colony was formed there by English settlers, and due to its advantageous location the town gradually transformed from an agricultural settlement into a thriving merchant trade center. Coffee, rum, spices, and molasses were shipped to England, the West Indies, and the Far East. Of significant concern for Hartford merchants was the ever-present risk of fires, storms, accidents, and pirate attacks. As groups of merchants sought to minimize the damaging effects of these dangers, the insurance industry in the United States was born. In the early 21st century, Hartford is the home of many of the nation's largest insurance companies and is known as the "Insurance Capital of the World."

As early as 1794, prominent citizens of Hartford had joined in an underwriting venture known as Hartford Fire Insurance, which was not incorporated at the time. Before then, insurance offered in the Hartford area had focused on the shipping trade. On March 10, 1794, businessmen Jeremiah Wadsworth, Daniel Wadsworth, John Caldwell, John Morgan, and Peleg Sanford

## COMPANY PERSPECTIVES

We help our customers pursue a financially secure future by anticipating their needs and providing competitive financial products.

opened the Hartford Fire Insurance Office "for the purpose of insuring Houses, Household Furniture, Goods, Wares, Merchandise etc against Fire," read an advertisement in the local newspaper that was reprinted in a 100-year history written by Charles W. Burpee. Although the partnership ended in 1798, many of the men involved in the Hartford Fire Insurance company continued to pursue their interests in underwriting.

On June 27, 1810, Daniel Wadsworth and John Morgan, well-known and influential capitalists in Hartford, directed the official incorporation of the Hartford Fire Insurance Company. Nathaniel Terry was elected its first president and Walter Mitchell its secretary. Because Mitchell's law office also served as headquarters for what quickly became known simply as "The Hartford," he received $30 per year to cover the cost of firewood. The first agent was appointed in December of that year, followed by the company's first out-of-state agent in 1811. Early on, agents did not receive a commission for the policies they wrote, only 50 cents on each policy over $1,000.

In 1822 The Hartford reinsured the New Haven Fire Insurance Company, one of the first instances of reinsurance in the country. Three years later, The Hartford wrote a fire insurance policy for Yale University in New Haven, Connecticut, the first of its kind for a U.S. institution of higher learning. The Hartford had established itself as the country's leading insurance provider and paid claims quickly when losses occurred. On December 16, 1835, newly elected president Eliphalet Terry faced The Hartford's first major catastrophe when New York City's business district was devastated by a huge fire. Traveling to New York in a horse-drawn sleigh during a blizzard, Terry paid all the company's damage claims, the sum of which was $64,974, with personal funds. Impressed by Terry's act, people who had once been skeptical of the value of fire insurance turned to The Hartford for coverage.

### EXPANSION: 1850–70

While The Hartford's main business was conducted directly from the home office, the company was expanding its reach beyond Connecticut. The United States was quickly developing, and enterprise kept pace with this rapid growth, prompting The Hartford to open offices in other states. The Hartford headquarters became part of what evolved into the Eastern Department, which eventually covered Maine, New Hampshire, Vermont, Massachusetts, Rhode Island, New York, New Jersey, Maryland, Pennsylvania, Delaware, Arkansas, the District of Columbia, and parts of Canada.

A widening customer base encouraged The Hartford to seek further expansion. In May 1852 the board of directors established the company's Western Department, with Columbus, Ohio, a major center of the livestock business, as its headquarters. Originally, the territory covered by this department comprised eight states: Ohio, Indiana, Michigan, Illinois, Wisconsin, Iowa, Missouri, and Kentucky. However, it included 11 more (West Virginia, Kansas, Nebraska, Minnesota, North Dakota, South Dakota, Wyoming, Colorado, New Mexico, Oklahoma, and Tennessee) by 1910. The Western Department was so prosperous that it had to employ special agents and traveling supervisors to manage business. As the city of Chicago proved to be the commercial and financial center of the Mississippi Valley, the department headquarters were moved from Columbus to Chicago in 1863.

During this expansion period, The Hartford was gaining influential customers. In 1859, Robert E. Lee, future general of Confederate forces during the Civil War, obtained an insurance policy for "Arlington," the Lee family home that would become part of Arlington National Cemetery. Two years later, President Abraham Lincoln purchased a fire insurance policy from The Hartford to protect his home and property in Springfield, Illinois. He paid a premium of $24 for a $3,200 policy.

The success of the Western Department encouraged further westward expansion. In 1870 The Hartford organized its Pacific Department, which included California, Oregon, Washington , Montana, Idaho, Utah, Nevada, Arizona, Alaska, British Columbia, and the Hawaiian Islands. Headquartered in San Francisco, the Pacific Department allowed The Hartford to conduct business coast to coast.

### CLAIMS AND COVERAGE: 1871 TO 1913

Throughout its history, The Hartford had paid policyholders thousands of dollars for damage caused by fires. Shortly after The Hartford opened its Pacific Department, one of the worst disasters of the nineteenth century struck Chicago. Started on October 8, 1871, the Great Chicago Fire destroyed almost 17,500 build-

## KEY DATES

**1825:** The Hartford writes a fire insurance policy for Yale University, the first of its kind for a U.S. institution of higher learning.

**1861:** President Abraham Lincoln purchases a fire insurance policy for his Springfield, Illinois, home.

**1906:** The Hartford pays $11.6 million in claims after a massive earthquake devastates San Francisco.

**1931:** The Hartford writes contract bonds for the construction of the Hoover Dam.

**1970:** ITT Corporation acquires The Hartford for $1.4 billion.

**1995:** The Hartford becomes an independent entity after being released by ITT Corporation.

**2010:** The Hartford celebrates its 200th anniversary.

ings and killed over 300 people. The Hartford paid almost $2 million in claims, its largest loss to that time. A Boston fire one year later cost the insurance company almost $500,000. On April 18, 1906, a massive earthquake hit San Francisco, devastating almost 500 city blocks. The Hartford paid $11.6 million in damage claims.

Despite these catastrophes, The Hartford continued to grow. A Texas Department was formed in the summer of 1906, with headquarters in Dallas. Back at the home office in Hartford, plans were made to open a Marine and Transportation Department in 1909. The contracts issued under this department reflected the wide scope of insurance that The Hartford had been developing since its conception. Policies offered by the Marine and Transportation Department included auto, motor boat, and horse and wagon insurance. In addition, coverage was offered for personal effects while traveling, samples carried by traveling salesmen, mail, and merchandise in transit.

With the Marine and Transportation Department as its guide, The Hartford Accident and Indemnity Company was formed in 1913 to provide a variety of insurance coverage. Among the types of policies available were accident, automobile liability, personal damage, and business interruption. Even as they offered business interruption insurance, The Hartford took steps after World War I to help wounded veterans who were unable to return to the jobs they held before the war

find employment. Many of these men were given jobs with The Hartford family.

### A MAJOR PLAYER: 1920S TO 1990S

For decades, The Hartford insured or contracted many of the United States' greatest icons. In 1920, for instance, a "sickness policy" was purchased by baseball great Babe Ruth. The terms of Ruth's policy stated that The Hartford would protect his earnings if illness were to prevent him from playing during the season. In 1931 The Hartford wrote contract bonds for the construction of the Hoover Dam. In 1933 the company wrote the first bond contract in connection with the construction of San Francisco's Golden Gate Bridge, which was opened in 1937. In 1952 President Dwight D. Eisenhower purchased a comprehensive liability policy for his 190-acre farm. The Hartford attained international status when it provided comprehensive liability insurance for the first meeting of the United Nations in October 1945.

Throughout the years, The Hartford demonstrated consistent growth and strength in the insurance industry. Expanding its operations into the life insurance business, The Hartford acquired the Columbian National Life Insurance Company in Boston, Massachusetts, in 1959. In 1970 The Hartford itself was acquired by the ITT Corporation, a conglomerate that spent the 1960s and 1970s taking over such businesses as the Sheraton hotel chain, Avis Rent-A-Car, and Continental Baking, the maker of Wonder Bread. The takeover cost ITT $1.4 billion, the largest in U.S. history to that date. The combined company was renamed ITT-Hartford Group, Inc.

Under the ITT umbrella in the 1980s, The Hartford became the first major insurance company to introduce universal life insurance coverage, a division that flourished quickly. In 1984 The Hartford won an important contract to provide auto and homeowners' insurance to members of the American Association of Retired Persons (AARP), the nation's leading lobbying group for people age 50 and over. This contract was still in effect over 25 years later. As The Hartford offered new products, including its famous Director variable annuity, it outgrew its existing building. In 1986 The Hartford moved to its new 173-acre headquarters in Simsbury, Connecticut.

On December 20, 1995, The Hartford regained its independence when ITT Corporation ended its 25-year ownership of the company due to shifts in ITT operations. Being its own entity allowed The Hartford to be traded publicly on the New York Stock Exchange under the ticker symbol HIG. The next year, The

Hartford began to offer mutual funds and received its first DALBAR Life Insurance Service Award, which represents achievement of the highest level in the financial services industry. Before the end of the decade, The Hartford changed its name from ITT Hartford Group, Inc., to The Hartford Financial Services Group, Inc.

## THE 21ST CENTURY

The first decade of the twenty-first century proved to be another period of change. In the aftermath of the terrorist attacks against the United States on September 11, 2001, The Hartford donated money to the United Way and other charities, in addition to paying out more than $850 million in losses. Other opportunities for community outreach resulted in a partnership between The Hartford and the U.S. Paralympics, as well as a corporate sponsorship of the National Collegiate Athletic Association (NCAA).

After three years of successfully selling variable annuities in Japan via a joint venture with Nikko Securities, The Hartford began offering fixed annuities as well. The Hartford further branched out into foreign business by entering the U.K. investment market. In 2005 the company was named a *Fortune* 100 company.

As the decade came to a close, The Hartford garnered accolades from various organizations. In 2009 alone, it was recognized by G.I. Jobs as a "Top 100 Military Friendly Employer" for its corporate recruiting programs for veterans; by *InformationWeek* as number 15 on the 2009 *InformationWeek* 500 for its innovative use of grid technology; and by Corporate Insight's Annual Monitor Awards as the "Best of Breed" for its Web services in the banking, brokerage, credit card, annuity, mutual fund, and mutual fund advisor industries. The Hartford was also named one of the "World's Most Ethical Companies" by the Ethisphere Institute, an international think-tank dedicated to promoting business ethics, corporate social responsibility, anticorruption, and sustainability. An *Enhanced Online News* article reported that Alex Brigham, executive director of the Ethisphere Institute, commented, "The Hartford's promotion of a sound ethical environment shines within its industry and shows a clear understanding that operating under the highest standards for business behavior goes beyond goodwill and 'lip-service' and is intimately linked to performance and profitability."

While The Hartford prepared to celebrate its bicentennial on May 10, 2010, the company was also busy taking steps to repay a $3.4 billion bailout loan it accepted from the Federal Reserve's Trouble Asset Relief Program (TARP) in June 2009. In March 2010 The Hartford announced that it would conduct a public offering of equity and debt securities in order to secure funds to reimburse the government. In an *insurancejournal.com* article, Liam E. McGee, chairman, president, and CEO of The Hartford, thanked the American public for their support: "We appreciate the critical role the government and the American taxpayers have played in stabilizing the financial markets...The Hartford always viewed this investment as temporary capital and intended to return it as soon as it was prudent."

*Alicia Elley*

## PRINCIPAL DIVISIONS

Life; Property and Casualty.

## PRINCIPAL COMPETITORS

Allstate Insurance Company; American Family Insurance Group; American International Group, Inc.; Liberty Mutual Insurance Group; Metlife, Inc.; Nationwide Mutual Insurance Company; Progressive Corp.; Travelers Companies, Inc.; United Services Automobile Association.

## FURTHER READING

Asher & Adams, *(The Hartford Fire Insurance Company) The Company's History.* New York: Asher & Adams, 1875.

Burpee, Charles W., *One Hundred Years of Service, Being the History of the Hartford Fire Insurance Company.* New York: Matthews-Northrop Works, 1910.

Greenwald, Judy, "May Turn to Sale of P/C Operations: Struggling Life Units Seen As Drag on Results of Combined Company," *Business Insurance,* April 27, 2009, p. 1.

"The Hartford Named as One of the 'World's Most Ethical Companies' Again in 2010," eon.businesswire.com, March 22, 2010.

"The Hartford to Repay TARP Money," insurancejournal.com, March 17, 2010.

Hechler, David, "They Aced the Stress Test: The Financial Meltdown Gave The Hartford's Lawyers a Chance to Prove Their Worth," *Corporate Counsel,* June 2009, p. 62.

"A Veneer of Stability: The Hartford Wears Its Age Proudly in a New Campaign," *Financial Services Marketing,* January–February 2001, p. 22.

# Hayneedle Incorporated

12720 I Street
Suite 200
Omaha, Nebraska 68137
U.S.A.
Telephone: (402) 884-3134
Toll Free: (800) 216-2616
Fax: (402) 505-5330
Web site: http://www.hayneedleinc.com

*Private Company*
*Founded:* 2002
*Employees:* 300+ (est. 2009)
*Sales:* $200 million
*NAICS:* 454111 Electronic Shopping

■ ■ ■

Hayneedle Incorporated comprises 220 online stores. As a privately owned firm, Hayneedle Incorporated is funded by Insight Venture Partners and Sequoia Capital. Operating under the slogan "Variety, sweet variety," Hayneedle sells a broad range of niche market specialty products including household furniture, pet supplies, games, sporting gear, and office equipment.

## A SINGLE STORE

NetShops started out in 2002 as one online retail store. Although the dot-com bubble had burst two years earlier, and the opportunity to create massive wealth by building and operating an online retail business did not loom as large as it once did, three Omaha residents

(Doug Nielsen, Julie Mahloch, and Mark Hasebroock) decided to give online retail a shot. Intent on creating a niche market on the Internet, the three founders looked for a specialty store that focused on selling and distributing a single product line.

Prior to cofounding NetShops, Doug Nielsen created three other start-ups, one of which was GiftPoint. com. Before serving as chief executive officer at GiftPoint.com, Nielsen earned his bachelor's degree from the University of Nebraska in 1990. The other professional who helped to found GiftPoint.com was Julie Mahloch, who also graduated from the University of Nebraska. Mahloch earned a bachelor's degree in business administration from the university.

Hayneedle Incorporated's third founder, Mark Hasebroock, worked as the chief operating officer at GiftCertificates.com, a company that acquired GiftPoint.com on March 6, 2000. Prior to joining GiftCertificates.com, Hasebroock worked at a financial investment firm, McCarthy and Company. Also a University of Nebraska graduate, during his early years in business as an independent Hasebroock owned a string of Vic's Corn Popper stores. He received his master's of business administration degree from Creighton University.

GiftCertificates.com was founded in 1997. The same year that the company acquired GiftPoint.com, it also purchased GiftSpot.com (April 17, 2000). GiftCertificates.com was a privately held firm that had offices in New York City, New York, and Omaha, Nebraska. Target markets for GiftCertificates.com included countries that had high Internet credit card

## COMPANY PERSPECTIVES

By providing a rewarding shopping experience, exceptional service, true product variety, and the right content to buy with confidence, hayneedle.com helps customers find what they love and love what they find.

and gift certificate usage. Overlap in job functions at the three companies was minimal. GiftCertificates.com integrated the GiftPoint.com Web site into its own. As reported in its 2000 Edgar filing, GiftCertificates.com granted, "former executive officers and members of senior management of Giftpoint.com bonuses in the form of common stock and options to acquire [GiftCertificates.com] common stock in connection with the merger."

To fund NetShops, Nielsen, Mahloch, and Hasebroock used monies that they received from the GiftCertificates.com buyout. The trio also contacted Insight Venture Partners and Sequoia Capital. Venture Partners was created in 1995, seven years before Hayneedle was founded. Based in New York City, the venture capital firm provided seed money to entrepreneurs seeking to launch new Internet, software, and technology companies. The other lead investor, Sequoia Capital, had been in existence for 40 years. Other companies that Sequoia had worked with include Apple Computer, Cisco Systems, Google, Oracle, Yahoo!, and YouTube.

With adequate financing, Nielsen, Mahloch, and Hasebroock focused on acquiring their first online store. Hammocks.com was the company that the trio chose. As its name implied, the online store sold hammocks and products related to the outdoor recliner, such as stands, chairs, and pillows.

## GROWTH AND EXPANSION

This initial Web site did well, so the founders decided to add more. From 2002 through 2004, the fledgling company, known as NetShops, Inc., grew to include more than a dozen online stores. AdirondackChairs.com, Patio-FurnitureUSA.com, PorchSwings.com, and Benches.com were among the new stores that NetShops purchased or launched. The next two years would see the company grow explosively, adding over 100 stores that offered more than 120,000 products across various categories such as patio and garden, home accessories,

furniture, infants and children, pets and animals, athletics, and seasonal. Funding for the additional stores came through direct customer sales and from Insight Venture Partners and Sequoia Capital. About the growth, Doug Nielsen, the CEO of Netshops, told *Practical Ecommerce* in a 2007 article, "Netshops.com Finds Its Niche," "After our initial success of Hammocks.com, we began to research other niche outdoor and indoor home categories. It has really evolved into a wide breadth of products outside of the home category." When asked how NetShops set itself apart from other large online retailers, Nielsen told *Practical Ecommerce*, "Our distinguishing factors are superior customer service, product selection and competitive pricing. We also are extremely focused on making the shopping experience as user centric as possible. We are constantly evaluating new technologies, etc."

To help increase traffic at its many Web sites, NetShops rolled out an affiliate program. Affiliates could earn up to 8 percent commission each time visitors to their Web sites clicked over to one of the NetShops online retail stores to purchase a product. To receive the commission, the purchases had to be made within the first 30 days that the customers visited a NetShops online store. Average commissions ranged from 3 to 8 percent, and there was no cost to join the program.

In 2006 NetShops acquired several companies including Thralow, Incorporated, which was based out of Proctor, Minnesota. Thralow started operating on the Internet in 1996. Niche online markets was its forte as well, and Peppers.com (a sunglass retail store) was Thralow's first retail site. Thralow consisted of 30 online retail stores such as Binoculars.com, Pans.com, and Telescopes.com when NetShops acquired it. Prior to the close of the deal, Thralow reported $26 million in annual sales. Post acquisition, Thralow was expected to continue to operate out of Minnesota. In an *Internet Retailer* article, NetShops CEO Doug Nielsen had this to say about the purchase: "Thralow's family of stores is perfectly suited to NetShops' commitment to operating tightly focused stores that offer specialty products at prices within almost any budget."

On November 27, 2006 (the day known as Cyber Monday, the first Monday after Black Friday, the first shopping day after Thanksgiving), NetShops grossed $1 million in sales, a 65 percent increase over the previous year. The company's new Google checkout service, its recently acquired companies (i.e., Thralow), and its newly developed retail sites (i.e., Sleds.com, eMetal Detectors.com, WorldGlobes.com) accounted for much of the growth. Twenty percent of Telescopes.com and Binoculars.com sales were processed through the Google checkout service. At the end of 2006, NetShops

## KEY DATES

**2002:** NetShops is founded by Doug Nielsen, Julie Mahloch, and Mark Hasebroock.
**2006:** NetShops generates $114.5 million in total revenue.
**2007:** Carter Cast, former Walmart.com CEO, is named CEO of NetShops.
**2009:** Company changes name to Hayneedle Incorporated.
**2010:** Hayneedle Incorporated moves primary distribution center to Monroe, Ohio.

Inc. reported $114.5 million in total revenue. The next year marked the third year that NetShops made the *Inc.* magazine Top 500 online company ranking. NetShops ranked 104th on the list, moving up 16 spots from its 120th ranking in 2006.

In 2007 *Inc.* magazine added a category to its annual listings in order to rank the fastest-growing companies in the United States. NetShops made the list the first year it was created. As reported at its official Web site, CEO Doug Nielsen noted, "We're very proud to receive such validation of our growth and promise for the future." Nielsen went on to say that, "It's satisfying to see how far we've come, but the real excitement is in what lies ahead." At the time NetShops Inc. owned 150 online specialty stores.

After being in business for five years, NetShops had sold products to more than one million customers. As if to measure the company's ability to connect with its returning customers, PowerReviews, an online customer review service, worked with the University of Nebraska at Omaha College of Information Science and Technology to analyze response rates to customer reviews. The study found that customer reviews posted at online stores owned by NetShops had a direct correlation to 26 percent of NetShops's sales. New and returning customers were significantly impacted by what other NetShops customers thought about a product or service.

### COPING WITH THE RECESSION OF 2008 AND 2009

As NetShops sought to lower its e-mail direct marketing costs and increase sales, it partnered with Strong Mail Systems, Incorporated in 2008. Prior to the deal, NetShops's cost per thousand (CPM) pricing model proved economically counterproductive. Delivery and customer click through rates did not justify CPM pricing rates.

After NetShops contracted with Strong Mail, however, the company saw its e-mail marketing delivery rates increase from 93.5 percent in 2008 to 97.5 percent in 2009, and its sales rise 168 percent from 2008 through May 2010.

This showed how strongly NetShops was rebounding from the global recession of 2008 and 2009, which had left its mark on the company. Economic distress began to loom in 2007, and to counter eroding consumer confidence in the market, NetShops hired Carter Cast late in 2007 as chief executive officer. Doug Nielsen remained as chairman. As the former CEO of Walmart.com, Cast brought two decades of marketing, e-commerce, and executive management experience to NetShops.

However, even a change in upper management could not prevent a drop in sales at NetShops. In February 2009 the company laid off 42 employees. As reported on Omaha's KETV-7, cuts were "across the board." Cast told KETV-7 that NetShops reported "high sales" from January through August 2008, but that the recession had impacted sales starting late in the third quarter of 2008. Hayneedle paid its laid off workers two weeks of severance for each year that they were employed at the firm.

The company also decided to rename itself Hayneedle as part of an overall rebranding effort. When Cast was asked about Hayneedle's rebranding efforts in the *Omaha World-Herald*, he stated, "Hayneedle is a consumer brand that connects all of these stores." Ash ElDifrawi, the chief marketing officer at Hayneedle Incorporated, told the newspaper that, "Company research showed that consumers like to buy more than one item at a time and that many consumers didn't realize that Hayneedle (formerly NetShops) operated the different sites." Both Carter and Ash told the *Herald* that, "The company started its rebranding before the recession, and it remained a priority."

In February 2010 Hayneedle inked a deal with Industrial Developments International, a privately held real estate company, to lease a 501,357-square-foot building. Located in the Monroe, Ohio, Logistics Center, the building was to be used by Hayneedle as an additional distribution facility. The facility, about a 20-minute drive from downtown Cincinnati, Ohio, allowed Hayneedle to increase its distribution center capacity by 50 percent. For the deal Hayneedle received a $97,837 tax credit from the state of Ohio. The company expected to inhabit the facility starting June 1, 2010. (The length of the tax credit is six years, but to realize the full tax savings Hayneedle must lease the facility for a minimum of nine years.) The Monroe, Ohio, facility has been tagged to become the company's primary distribution center.

While the recession caused some short-term financial problems for Hayneedle, Internet commerce remained a growing sector of the global economy as more and more people shopped online. This trend boded well for Hayneedle and its barn full of retail Web sites.

*Rhonda Campbell*

## PRINCIPAL DIVISIONS

Baby and Kids; Furniture; Home Accessories; Patio and Garden; Pets and Animals; Seasonal and Gifts; Sports and Games.

## PRINCIPAL COMPETITORS

Amazon.com Inc.; Buy.com Inc.; CSN Stores LLC; eBay Inc.; Overstock.com Inc.; SmartBargains.com L.P.

## FURTHER READING

"42 NetShops Workers Lose Jobs," KETV 7.com, February 5, 2009.

Greater Omaha Chamber, "Competition Determines Top Ten Omaha Employers," March 27, 2006.

Laue, Christine, "NetShops Rebounds with Rebrand," *Omaha World Herald,* August 12, 2009.

"NetShops Acquires Online Niche Retailer Thralow Inc.," *Internet Retailer,* November 16, 2006.

"Netshops.com Finds Its Niche," *Practical eCommerce,* July 29, 2007.

"StrongMail Enables Hayneedle.com to Dramatically Increase Sales and Reduce Costs," *InfoTech,* May 25, 2010.

# HCC Insurance Holdings Inc.

13403 Northwest Freeway
Houston, Texas 77040-6094
U.S.A.
Telephone: (713) 690-7300
Fax: (713) 462-2401
Web site: http://www.hcc.com

*Public Company*
*Founded:* 1974
*Employees:* 1,864 (2009)
*Sales:* $2.374 billion
*Stock Exchanges:* New York
*Ticker Symbol:* HCC
*NAICS:* 524126 Direct Property and Casualty Insurance
Carriers; 524130 Reinsurance Carriers; 524210
Insurance Agencies and Brokerages

■ ■ ■

HCC Insurance Holdings, Inc., (HCC) is an international specialty insurance group that sells specialized property/casualty insurance, underwrites for its own and other insurance companies, and offers related services for commercial and individual customers. Headquartered in Houston, Texas, the company has offices across the United States and in the United Kingdom, Spain, Ireland, and Bermuda. HCC markets its products both directly to customers and via a network of independent and affiliated agents, brokers, producers, and third-party administrators. In addition to direct and reinsurance policies for the aviation, marine, and offshore energy industries, the company's wide range of products includes property/casualty and health

policies; medical stop-loss; directors' and officers' liability coverage; and workers' compensation and occupational accident insurance. The company's many subsidiaries also offer surety and life coverage. HCC operates in five business areas: diversified financial products; group life, accident, and health; aviation; London market account; and other specialty lines.

## COMPANY FOUNDING AND EARLY YEARS: 1974–90

In 1969 Stephen L. Way, who was born in Great Britain, was 20 years old and had been in the insurance business five years. He began his career in 1964 at the age of 15, working for the insurance company Willis Faber in London. Following a trip to the United States, Way suggested that his then employer, the London-based insurance broker the Bradstock Group, establish an office in New York City. Although the company's board ultimately rejected the plan, Way, who resigned from his post as managing director of the company's aviation division, went to New York anyway. "I had no job or money but it worked out OK," Way noted in an interview for *Reactions*.

Way's first entrepreneurial effort was to establish Westminster Insurance Managers, which he eventually sold to Aviation Office of America (later known as American Eagle). With $800,000 in capital, Way relocated to Houston, Texas, in 1973 and in 1974 set up his own insurance brokerage company called Stephen L. Way International (SWI), the precursor to HCC. The company began as a managing general agent (MGA) in the insurance industry focusing on serving as a surplus lines and reinsurance broker.

In 1980 SWI encountered a difficult market because MGAs had developed a bad reputation, as Way told *Business Insurance* contributor Stacy Shapiro. Way remarked that, "if you were one [an MGA], then you had to be bad." SWI was losing business and, in 1981, Way converted his company of 10 employees into an insurance company initially called International Indemnity Co. The name was soon changed to the Houston Casualty Company, which has remained HCC's principal insurance company subsidiary.

The business struggled for the next five years, but Way and his company received a significant boost in 1987 when banker J. P. Morgan & Co Inc. decided to make a $10 million investment in the company upon the condition that the investment would be repaid when HCC went public. "The name [recognition of J. P. Morgan] on the balance sheet was probably more important than the money," Way told Shapiro for a 1997 *Business Insurance* article, noting that the well-known banking company's support indicated to many industry observers that the company was sound.

### EXPANSION: 1990–2005

Over the years, HCC focused on disciplined underwriting as the key to the organization's success. "In our formative years, we wrote short-term business and we didn't try to grow in a soft market," Way noted in his interview for *Reactions* magazine. "Other players did but they should have been shrinking not growing. We kept our powder dry and our capital is still there."

In 1992 HCC went public and raised its capitalization to $100 million via two offerings. From the company's beginning as SWI in 1974 on through to 1997, HCC expanded its business via 10 acquisitions. Among the most strategic of these acquisitions was IMG Insurance Co. of Amman, Jordan, in 1988, giving HCC an international presence focusing on the non-U.S.

marine and energy business. Another major purchase was LDG Management Co. of Wakefield, Massachusetts. HCC acquired the managing general agency in 1995 for four million shares, which were valued at the time at about $70 million.

HCC made a third major acquisition in 1997. Over a period of several months, Way had directed the company's acquisitions of several aviation insurance firms, including Southern Aviation Insurance Underwriters in Alton, Alaska, and Signal Aviation Underwriters Inc. in Dallas, Texas. The largest of the various acquisitions, however, was a merger with Avemco Corp., in a 8.5 million share, stock-for-stock transaction. Avemco was an underwriter of general aviation risks and would continue to operate as a subsidiary of HCC. The various acquisitions led HCC to become one of four major aviation insurance firms in the United States.

HCC kept on growing through its disciplined underwriting and strategic acquisitions strategy. In 1999 the company acquired Rattner Mackenzie, Ltd., which was originally established as a Lloyd's of London reinsurance broker, and the Centris Group Inc., an HCC competitor based in Costa Mesa, California. The company's acquisitions in 2001 included the purchase of ASU International LLC (ASU). An underwriting agency focusing on specialty lines of insurance, ASU was recognized for pioneering nontraditional disability products for professional athletes, entertainers, and high-profile people in the business world. Other purchases included the 2002 acquisitions of Mag Global Financial Products, which became HCC Global, and St. Paul Espana, which became HCC Europe.

In a 2004 interview with *Rough Notes* magazine contributor Sandra Carcione, HCC's executive vice president in charge of agency operation, Craig Kelbel, commented on the company's success, noting that since the company's founding "we've grown through consistently profitable underwriting results and numerous targeted acquisitions, where today we have more than $1 billion in equity."

### STOCK OPTION SCANDAL

Widespread and growing probes into U.S. companies' stock options practices in 2006 eventually led to HCC. An independent probe of HCC's option-granting practices from 1995 to 2006 was authorized by HCC's audit committee. The probe uncovered improper stock option granting practices by HCC. The probe also led to the resignation of HCC's founder and chief executive when it was determined that some of Way's option grants were incorrectly priced. As part of his resignation,

# KEY DATES

**1974:** Stephen L. Way establishes insurance broker-age company called Stephen L. Way International (SWI), the precursor to HCC Insurance Holdings.

**1981:** SWI is converted to an insurance company named Houston Casualty Company.

**1987:** J. P. Morgan & Co. Inc. invests $10 million into HCC and gives the company name recognition.

**1992:** HCC makes its initial public offering.

**1997:** HCC acquires AVEMCO Corp., making the company one of the top four aviation insurance firms in the United States.

**2008:** HCC receives approval from Lloyd's of London to set up a syndicate and offer the international products of HCC's recently acquired Multinational Underwriters LLC.

Way would end his employment without receiving any further compensation, including bonus pay. The company's founder also agreed to pay the company for the difference of the incorrectly priced options he had exercised.

HCC also became one of several hundred U.S. companies to be investigated by the U.S. Securities and Exchange Commission (SEC) for its option-granting practices. "At issue is whether company executives illegally backdated the grants, increasing the value of the options by timing them at low points and thereby increasing executives' payouts," wrote Raymond J. Lehmann for *A.M. Best Newswire.*

The company agreed to restate its 10-K annual report for 2005 to reflect new financial results from 2003 to 2005. The company also announced that, because its accounting practices were being investigation over a 10-year period, its annual statements from 1997 to 2005 were not to be relied upon. In late December 2006, the company completed its own stock option practices review. The review had no impact on the company's net revenue, cash, or cash flow for the period but did lead to a net after-tax decrease in shareholders' equity of $3.3 million. The company, however, soon faced a class action suit, which it settled in 2008 with the company agreeing to pay $10 million into a settlement fund. Terms of the settlement included no admission of liability or wrongdoing by HCC.

## MAINTAINING ITS GAME PLAN: 2006–09

In 2004 *Rough Notes* magazine contributor Sandra Carcione described HCC as having a unique business mix that included a diverse group of affiliates involving specialty insurers, MGAs, and a reinsurer intermediaries. "Describing this organization is a bit like deciding what an elephant looks like by feel, rather than sight—it depends on where you're touching it," wrote Carcione.

The company continued expanding its specialty insurance lines by acquiring Indianapolis-based Nova Underwriters Inc. in 2006. That company specialized in medical stop-loss insurance and became part of HCC's Perico Life unit. In that same year, HCC closed its acquisition of the assets of Allianz Life of North America's health products division for $240 million. The division provided excess medical insurance for self-insured corporations. Then, in 2008, HCC purchased the Indianapolis-based life, accident, and health insurer MultiNational Underwriters LLC. In the process, the company received approval from Lloyd's of London to set up Syndicate 4141 to offer MultiNational's products internationally. Another 2008 acquisition was the Surety Company of the Pacific, a writer of license and permit bonds in Encino, California.

HCC ended 2008 by purchasing another company, Arrowhead Public Risk, a division of Virginia's Arrowhead General Insurance Agency, Inc., that specialized in risk management for the public entity sector. The company began 2009 by acquiring VMGU Insurance Agency, a leading underwriter of the lumber, building materials, forest products, and woodworking industries.

Despite the economic downturn and severe recession that began in 2008, HCC produced good results. Revenues decreased slightly to $2.279 billion in 2008, down from $2.388 billion the year before. However, earnings began moving upward again in 2009.

## LOOKING TO THE FUTURE

In its 2009 annual report, the company stated that, with assets valued at $8.8 billion and shareholders' equity of $3.0 billion as of December 31, 2009, it was well capitalized and well positioned to continue its success. In addition, HCC maintained high financial ratings within the insurance industry. HCC's major domestic insurance companies received financial strength ratings of "AA (Very Strong)" from Fitch Ratings, "A1 (Good Security)" from Moody's Investors Service, Inc., and "A+ (Superior)" by A.M. Best Company, Inc. It was also rated "AA" by Standard & Poor's.

The company's major moves in 2009 did not involve acquisitions but rather several strategic decisions to further focus on its specialty market, including the sale of Rattner Mackenzie Limited (RML) to Guy Carpenter & Company, LLC. "This transaction will enable HCC to focus on its core businesses while enabling RML to develop its business proposition in conjunction with Guy Carpenter," HCC president and chief executive officer John N. Molbeck, Jr., noted in a *GlobeNewswire* article. The company also combined its two Lloyd's syndicates for more streamlined operation and planned to continue to use Lloyd's of London as their primary access to international business.

HCC stated its plans to continue to make opportunistic acquisitions in the future based on the company's requirement for return for investment and cultural fit. Although it found most opportunities for mergers and acquisitions disappointing for 2009, HCC hoped to see a more productive future in the acquisition arena in the early 2010s.

*David Petechuk*

## PRINCIPAL SUBSIDIARIES

Avemco Insurance Company; G.B. Kenrick & Associates, Inc.; HCC International Insurance Company PLC (UK); HCC Life Insurance Company; HCC Specialty Underwriters, Inc.; Houston Casualty Company; Illium, Inc.; Professional Indemnity Agency, Inc.; U.S. Specialty Insurance Company.

## PRINCIPAL DIVISIONS

Diversified Financial Products; Group Life, Accident & Health; Aviation; London Market Account; Other Specialty Lines.

## PRINCIPAL COMPETITORS

ACD Limited; American International Group; Chubb Corp.; Lloyd's of London; The Travelers Companies, Inc.; XL Capital Ltd.; U.S. Aviation Insurance Group.

## FURTHER READING

Carcione, Sandra, "HCC's Specialty Line-Up Serves Variety of Agents' Needs," *Rough Notes,* March, 2004.

"HCC Insurance Holdings Announces Sale of Rattner Mackenzie Limited to Guy Carpenter," *GlobeNewswire,* October 5, 2009.

Lehmann, Raymond J., "Options Probe Prompts HCC to Restate Earnings," *A.M. Best Newswire,* December 20, 2006.

"No Skeletons in HCC's Closet," *Reactions,* December, 2002, p. 35.

Shapiro, Stacy, "HCC Executive Turning Heads in Aviation Market," *Business Insurance,* May 26, 1997, p. 3.

# Heartland Payment Sytems, Inc.

—■—

90 Nassau Street
Princeton, New Jersey 08542
U.S.A.
Telephone: (609) 683-3831
Toll Free: (888) 798-3131
Fax: (609) 683-3815
Web site: http://www.heartlandpaymentsystems.com

*Public Company*
*Founded:* 1997
*Employees:* 3,055 (2009)
*Sales:* $1.652 billion (2009)
*Stock Exchanges:* New York
*Ticker Symbol:* HPY
*NAICS:* 522320 Financial Transactions Processing, Reserve, and Clearinghouse Activities; 518210 Data Processing, Hosting, and Related Services.

■ ■ ■

Heartland Payment Systems, Inc., (Heartland) provides credit and debit card, payroll, and related processing services to retailers, hotels, and restaurant merchants. Headquartered in Princeton, New Jersey, the company processes more than 11 million transactions a day and more than $80 billion in transactions a year, facilitating the exchange of information and funds between merchants and cardholders' financial institutions. The company also provides electronic payment processing to merchants, which includes services such as merchant setup and training, transaction authorization and electronic draft capture, clearing and settlement,

merchant accounting, merchant assistance, and support and risk management. Additional services supplied to the company's merchants include gift and loyalty programs, prepaid and store-valued solutions, and paper check processing. Heartland also sells and rents point-of-sale devices and supplies. One of the largest privately owned payment processors, Heartland provides bank-card payment processing services to approximately 173,400 active small to mid-sized merchants throughout the United States. The company also owns a majority interest in Canada's Collective Point of Sale Solutions Ltd. (CPOS), which serves 6,600 merchants in Canada offering payment processing services and point-of-sale solutions.

## COMPANY FOUNDING AND DEVELOPMENT: 1997–2001

Robert O. Carr, who worked in the payments and software development industries for 25 years, joined with Heartland Bank in March 1997 to establish Heartland Payments Systems, LLC, as a subsidiary of the St. Louis, Missouri, bank. The company, which began with three employees, processed its first card transaction on July 15, 1997. In its first year of operation, the company acquired 2,350 clients.

In 1999 Heartland joined forces with CyberSource to provide wireless carriers with an e-commerce service that offered merchant account setup combined with secure real-time credit-card payment processing and other e-commerce transactions. The company incorporated in Delaware in June of 2000 but soon found itself running a cash-flow deficit, posting a $9.7

## COMPANY PERSPECTIVES

Heartland's success is the result of a superior long-term customer relationship sales model and a commitment to technological innovation, which inspired an internally developed, client server-based transaction processing platform for brick-and-mortar merchants. Heartland prides itself on a concentrated and dedicated merchant focus and is the founder of The Merchant Bill of Rights, a public advocacy initiative that educates merchants about fair credit and debit card processing practices. For Heartland, remaining true to its original vision—while also understanding and harnessing technological innovation—will mean continued growth for its business as well as new services that will help merchants improve and grow their own businesses.

million loss for 2000. As a result, the company had to sell some card-processing contracts even as it was seeking to assemble a strong contract portfolio. "It was a somewhat self-defeating situation," Robert H. B. Baldwin, Jr., Heartland's CFO, told David Carey for an article in the *Daily Deal.*

Heartland announced in October 2001 that Greenhill Capital Partners (Greenhill) was investing $25 million for a minority stake in the company. Greenhill noted that it chose to invest in Heartland because the company had been clearly outpacing the card-processing sector's overall 7 to 10 percent annual growth. At the time of the investment, Heartland had just slightly more than a 1 percent share of the market.

Following Greenhill's investment, the company received a $40 million infusion of new capital via private equity investment from LLR Partners Inc. and their affiliated investment funds. In addition to retiring the company's debt, Heartland planned to use the investment capital to execute long-range strategic business plans, including building its national sales and service organization and developing its transaction processing platform. At the time of the investment, Hitchel L. Hollin, a partner in LLR, was quoted in a *Business Wire* article as saying: "As a leading player in a fragmented industry, Heartland offers the scale and sophistication to leverage the trend toward alternative forms of electronic payments across its large and diverse merchant base."

### LOOKING TO GROW: 2002–06

With strong financial support, Heartland soon established itself as a fast-rising company. In 2002 *Inc.* magazine ranked the company number 57 in its list of the fastest-growing private companies in the United States. It was also ranked 13th in the 2002 Billion-Dollar Bankcard Acquiring Report. Evidence of the company's success was reflected by the company's growth from a $1 billion processing year in 1998 to $5 billion in 2000. In July 2003 the company announced that June had represented the first month in its history when it processed $1 billion in card volume (out of a total of $1.6 billion) through a single card association, namely VISA U.S.A.

In May 2004 Heartland, which had grown to become the eighth-largest merchant processor in the United States, announced that it was planning an Initial Public Offering of common stock to raise up to $75 million. The company's stock began trading on the New York Stock Exchange (NYSE) on August 12, 2005, at an initial price of $18 per share. Overall, Heartland sold 2.621 million shares for $457.2 million, with private shareholders selling 4.13 million shares.

Following its impressive early performance on the NYSE, the company began making plans to expand. A primary focus of Heartland was to make new business deals. "We're not only looking at buying other payroll companies and (their) products, but tech companies as well to help us compete," Mark Strippy, president of the company's Payment Services division, told Shawn A. Turner in an article in *Crain's Cleveland Business.* Following up on its expansion and acquisition plans, the company purchased Debitek in February 2006. Based in Chatanooga, Tennessee, Debitek made readers and other devices that enabled prepaid debit card payments. The following year, Heartland acquired the assets of eSecure Peripherals Inc., a provider of card readers for vending machines.

In a 2006 article in *Sales & Marketing Management,* Robert O. Carr, the company's chairman and chief executive, associated much of Heartland's growth to various compensation approaches designed to spur on his sales force. As a result, in 2006 about 50 percent of Heartland's gross margin went toward spending on the company's sales force, including compensation. "We knew that our company's future was in the hands of the leaders of our sales organization, so we wanted them to participate in the wealth created as we built a large, successful enterprise," Carr told Julia Chang in a *Sales & Marketing Management* article. The next year, Heartland was named "Financial Services Sales Organization of the Year" in the "Best Run Sales Organization" category by *Selling Power* magazine.

## KEY DATES

**1997:** Company begins as Heartland Payments Systems LLC.

**2003:** Company processes first $1 billion in card volume through a single card association.

**2005:** Heartland makes initial public offering (IPO) on New York Stock Exchange (NYSE).

**2006:** Heartland purchases Debitek Inc.; launches major public advocacy initiative called the Merchant Bill of Rights.

**2009:** Heartland experiences data breach crisis; introduces new technology to secure customer data.

## THE MERCHANT BILL OF RIGHTS

By the end of 2006, Heartland had launched a major public advocacy intiative titled "The Merchant Bill of Rights." Designed to help the owners of small and mid-sized businesses manage the cost and complexity of credit and debit card acceptance, the initiative established a playing field where owners of businesses would have access to the same card processing resources and cost structures as larger merchants. The goal was to help the company's merchant clients who did not have the resources of purchasing organizations to effectively manage their costs. Through the initiative the merchants could determine which processor best met their needs and, as a result, realize significant savings.

A centerpiece of the initiative was the establishment of the Merchant Bill of Rights Web site at merchantbillofrights.org. The Web site served as an information clearinghouse that business owners could use to learn more about the mechanics of card processing. They could receive industry tips, share best practices, and ask questions about the industry. Noting that "most business owners and entrepreneurs do not fully understand the factors that drive card processing costs or how to manage them," Carr told Joseph Crivelli of *Business Credit* that the initiative and the Web site would empower "business owners to learn how card acceptance works and take an active role in controlling these growing costs."

The Merchant Bill of Rights proposed 10 fundamental rights to protect businesses. Examples of these rights include: "the right to know the fee for every transaction—and who's charging it," "the right to know all transaction middleman," and "the right to know all surcharges and bill-backs." Carr told Crivelli: "By

promoting fair credit and debit card processing practices, The Merchant Bill of Rights will be a driving force for industry change."

## FACING A DATA BREACH

Heartland continued to perform well in 2007 and 2008. It achieved record earnings of $35.9 million in 2007, up 26 percent from fiscal year 2006. In 2008, despite a faltering economy, Heartland reported a net income of $41.8 million, a 17 percent increase over 2007.

In January 2009 however, the company announced that it had been hit with a malware attack and that a large cache of financial data may have been compromised. Among the data were card numbers, expiration dates, and, in some cases, cardholder names. "We have industry-leading encryption, but the data has to be unencrypted to request information," Robert H. B. Baldwin, Jr., the company's president and chief financial officer, told *New York Times* contributors Eric Dash and Brad Stone. "The sniffer was able to grab that authorization at that point."

The company immediately contacted federal authorities, who began investigating the breach. The fallout from the data breach presented one of Heartland's biggest challenges in years. In addition to regulatory investigations, Heartland faced numerous lawsuits. Company representatives, however, stated that they were in compliance with payment card industry data security standards and, as a result, should not be held responsible for the incident. In the meantime, the company notified retailers about the breach and created a Web site, 2008breach.com, to provide merchants and cardholders with information about the breach and tips for protecting data.

## DEALING WITH THE AFTERMATH

The fallout from the data breach, as well as the turbulent economy, caused Heartland to go into the red in the first quarter of fiscal year 2009. The company reported a loss of $2.5 million compared with net income of $8.9 million for the same quarter the previous year. In May 2009 the company announced that it had set aside more than $12.6 million to cover costs related to the major data breach.

On August 17, 2009, the Department of Justice announced the indictment of a suspect in the breach. The suspect, Albert Gonzalez, was a former informant for the U.S. Secret Service who helped hunt hackers. Despite facing 19 lawsuits that were eventually consolidated into one, Heartland and Carr, its chairman and chief executive, received kudos from many industry observers for their response to the breach, which may have been the largest of its kind ever as the breach involved data from more than 100 million cards. The company's efforts included accelerating an end-to-end encryption project for protecting card data.

"Generally when something like this happens, the CEOs hide," Avivah Litan, an analyst at Gartner Inc. told *Computerworld* contributor Jaikumar Vijayan. "Some might question his real motives. But the bottom line [is], he is elevating the debate around card security and even got card companies to speak about end-to-end encryption."

## LOOKING TOWARD THE FUTURE: THE 2010S

Heartland's performance in 2009 reflected an unstable economy and was also impacted by the costs and publicity associated with the data breach it had suffered near the end of 2008. Although small and mid-sized merchant (SME) transaction processing volume was $59 billion, up 1.7 percent from 2008, Heartland recorded a net loss of $51.8 million, or $1.38 per share. The company's operating income also contracted to $49.9 million in 2009, from $70.6 million in 2008. The contraction was primarily due to the impact economic conditions had on revenues and an increase in general and administrative expenses.

The costs associated with the breach continued into 2010 when the company announced in January of that year that they had agreed to a settlement with Visa Issuers. Heartland would provide up to $60 million for claims associated with the data security breach. According to an article in *American Banker*, Robert Dodd, an analyst with Morgan Keegan & Co., noted that the potential settlement costs of the breach to Heartland could total up to $100 million.

Looking to the future, Heartland introduced a new encryption process. It also unveiled a new payments portal called ConfirmPay that enables health care providers to confirm patient insurance eligibility and payment responsibility at the point of care. Another technology introduced by the company, called Smart-Link, consolidates multiple in-store communication lines into one broadband that carries encrypted transaction data. Although the company found opportunities for mergers and acquisitions disappointing for 2009, Heartland planned to continue to make future acquisitions based on the company's requirement for return for investment and cultural fit.

*David Petechuk*

## PRINCIPAL SUBSIDIARIES

Debitek Inc.; Heartland Acquisition, LLC; The Heartland Payroll Company, LLC.

## PRINCIPAL COMPETITORS

Banc of America Merchant Services, LLC; Chase Paymentech Solutions, LLC; Elavon, Inc.; Fiserv, Inc.; Global Payments Inc.

## FURTHER READING

Carey, David, "Greenhill Capital Closes Its Largest Deal," *Daily Deal,* October 11, 2001.

Chang, Julia, "Spread the Wealth: Letting Your Salespeople Profit when Your Company Does," *Sales & Marketing Management,* June 2006, p. 18.

Crivelli, Joseph, "The Merchant Bill of Rights," *Business Credit,* November-December, 2006, p. 20.

Daseh, Eric, and Brad Stone, "Cred Card Processor Says Some Data Was Stolen," *New York Times,* January 21, 2009.

"Heartland Payment Systems Secures $40 Million Private Equity Financing from Greenhill Capital Partners and LLR Partners," *Business Wire,* October 12, 2001.

"Heartland to Pay Issuers up to $60M in Visa Settlement," *American Banker,* January 11, 2010, p. 7.

Turner, Shawn A., "Heartland Heading for Growth after Strong IPO Performance," *Crain's Cleveland Business,* September 12, 2005, p. 7.

Specialty Chemicals

# Hexion Specialty
# Chemicals, Inc.

180 East Broad Street
Columbus, Ohio 43215
U.S.A.
Telephone: (614) 225-4000
Fax: (614) 225-4127
Web site: http://www.hexion.com

*Public Company*
*Founded:* 2005
*Employees:* 6,200 (2009)
*Sales:* $4.03 billion (2009)
*NAICS:* 325211 Plastics Material and Resin
    Manufacturing; 325199 All Other Basic Organic
    Chemical Manufacturing; 325998 All Other
    Miscellaneous Chemical Product and Preparation
    Manufacturing; 32552 Adhesive Manufacturing

■ ■ ■

Hexion Specialty Chemicals, Inc., a *Fortune* 500 company, is the world's largest producer of thermosetting resins, or thermosets, which are a key ingredient in a variety of paints, glues, preservatives, adhesives, and ink sold in both the industrial and consumer markets. Hexion operates 94 production sites located in North America, Latin America, Europe, and the Asia-Pacific region. Serving 8,300 industrial customers in more than 100 countries, Hexion provides a wide range of resin technologies, specialty products, and technical support that helps industrial companies bind, bond, and coat thousands of products sold in diverse markets. These markets include forest products, architectural and industrial paints, packaging, consumer products, and automotive coatings, as well as higher growth markets such as electrical laminates, composites, and UV cured coatings.

## ESTABLISHING A NEW COMPANY: 2005

Hexion, which is owned by affiliates of the investment firm Apollo Management LP, was established in 2005 via the combination of Borden Chemical, Resolution Performance Products (RPP), and Resolution Specialty Materials (RSM). Hexion's various component companies have a rich history and background. Borden Chemical, for example, dates back to a company founded by Gail Borden in 1857 and named the New York Condensed Milk Company. Eventually renamed Borden, Inc., the company was widely known for its various food products.

Borden branched out into glue and other chemical products in 1929 with the purchase of Casein Co. of America, located in Bainbridge, New York. In 1958 the chemical segments of the company were renamed Borden Chemical. At the time of the merger forming Hexion, Borden Chemical was a leading global producer of binding and bonding resins, performance adhesives, and the building-block chemical formaldehyde. Borden had 48 manufacturing facilities in nine countries and reported 2004 sales of $1.7 billion. In April 2005, prior to the completion of the merger to create Hexion, Borden also acquired Bakelite, a leading European producer of phenolic and epoxy composite reins and molding compounds.

Apollo had previously acquired the Houston-based RPP from the Shell Oil Company in November 2000. In 2004 RPP was a worldwide manufacturer and developer of epoxy resins and the leading global maker of Versatic acids and derivatives. The company had 950 employees and reported 2004 sales of $996 million. Apollo Management formed RSM in 2004 by accumulating various CASPI (coatings adhesives, specialty polymers, and ink raw materials) businesses acquired from the Eastman Chemical Company. Also based in Houston, RSM had 2004 annual sales of $768 million with 2,100 employees working in facilities in the United States, Europe, and China.

The combination of these companies to form Hexion resulted in the company becoming the largest producer of thermosetting resins in the world. Borden Chemical CEO and president, Craig O. Morrison, who had become president and CEO of Borden Chemical in 2002, was named CEO and president of the new company. "This merger is an exciting development," Morrison was quoted as saying in a *Business Wire* article. He went on to note that the combined companies have "complementary businesses with outstanding technologies and products, and excellent synergies."

Morrison was not the only one that saw many opportunities for the newly formed Hexion. In an article for the *Chemical Market Reporter*, Howard Blum, director of the New Jersey-based consultancy Kline & Company noted: "Coupled with the need to consolidate a mature industry—or at least a group of products under one family or name—Hexion's creation can add zest to what has been otherwise a fairly mature market." Blum added: "The formation of Hexion enables it to position itself deeper in the value chain: they have been able to consolidate some of the applications and some of their resins across a broader performance spectrum."

## FACING CHALLENGES

With its formation, Hexion entered a worldwide market for thermoset resins estimated at $34 billion annually with the various sectors of Hexion generating about $19 billion in sales per year. Despite the opportunities

Apollo and many industry experts saw with Hexion's formation, the company also faced challenges. Borden Chemical had recorded a net loss of $179 million in 2004. Furthermore, the CASPI units acquired from Eastman by Apollo had posted a 2003 loss of $358 million.

As a result of these losses and other factors, Hexion came with a heavy debt that some observers noted could become heavier, resulting in obstacles to future expansion. On June 30, 2005, Hexion's debt amounted to $2.4 billion, and the company was warning that it could take on more debt. In addition, numerous competitors' chemical plants were being relocated to regions in Asia where they could operate at lower cost. Scott Reeves, in an article for the *Forbes.com* Web site, noted: "Hexion will face sharp price pressure and could be stuck with uncompetitive plants in the U.S. and Western Europe." Reeves also noted that a downturn in any number of sectors, including construction, electronics, oil and gas production, and cars, could "erode revenue and profitability."

The company's second quarter results were announced in August 2005 with reported sales of $1.2 billion, an increase of 16 percent over the three merging companies' sales on a *pro forma* basis for the previous year's period. Nevertheless, the company reported a net loss of $57 million. This loss included the impact of $71 million in costs associated with the formation of the company, as well as a loss from discontinued operations.

When Apollo announced its intention to form Hexion, the parent company stated that it expected to raise a potential $800 million when it launched its initial public offering (IPO). In September 2005, Hexion sets its proposed IPO of 20 million shares at an expected price of $21–24 per share and expected to receive $245 million in net proceeds. However, in June 2006, the company announced that it was suspending its IPO of common stock because of adverse market conditions, specifically downturns in the overall equities markets and the specialty chemical sector.

## EXPANSION PLANS

Despite its debt, Hexion set out to expand its specialty chemical business starting in February 2007 with the purchase of the Australian company Orica Limited, a manufacturer of formaldehyde and formaldehyde-based binding resins primarily used in the forest products industry. The company's goal was to strengthen its position in European wood products market. The Orica acquisition included three manufacturing facilities in Australia and New Zealand. In November 2007 Hexion

## KEY DATES

**2005:** Company is formed via a merger of Borden Chemical, Resolution Performance Products, and Resolution Specialty Materials.

**2007:** Hexion purchases the German company Arkema GmbH and the Australian company Orica Limited, the latter purchase including three manufacturing facilities in Australia and New Zealand.

**2008:** Hexion and the Huntsman Corporation agree to settlement to end merger; Hexion wins presitigious R&D 100 Award.

**2010:** Hexion and Shanxi Sanwei Group Co. Ltd. form a joint venture company to build and operate a new plant in Shanxi Province, China.

acquired Arkema GmbH. A German-based company, Arkema manufactured formaldehyde and formaldehyde-based resins. The company generated revenues of approximately $127 million in 2006.

Not all of Hexion's expansion plans came to fruition, however. In mid-July 2007, Hexion signed a $10.6-billion deal to purchase Huntsman Corporation, a corporation that manufactured chemical products for a global market. Huntsman had previously made a merger agreement with French company Basell S.A. but terminated the transaction after Hexion made a higher bid.

When Huntsman announced disappointing first-quarter results in April 2008, Hexion began seeking recourse to terminate the transaction with no or limited liability. In June 2008 Hexion filed suit in Delaware stating that it had no obligation to complete the transaction because Huntsman's declining performance constituted a "material adverse effect" (MAE) under the merger agreement. The suit also stated that Hexion's liability to Huntsman should be capped at $325 million. In response, Hunstman claimed that Hexion had knowingly and intentionally breached the merger agreement and that Huntsman had not suffered an MAE, meaning that Hexion had no right to terminate the merger agreement. Huntsman also argued that Hexion's liability was not limited to the $325-million reverse termination fee.

A Delaware court rejected Hexion's claims for relief from the merger and ordered the company to perform its covenants under the merger agreement, including making a reasonable best effort to complete the transaction. The court also enjoined Hexion from taking any action that would impair, delay, or prevent the financing of the transaction or the merger's completion. Nevertheless, the merger never took place as Huntsman terminated the proposed merger between the two companies in December 2008. The settlement agreement with Huntsman and other parties resulted in Hexion paying Hunstman the $325-dollar million merger agreement termination fee.

## FORGING AHEAD

As of 2010, deteriorating global economic and financial market conditions had continued to impact Hexion, which had a decrease in net sales of 34 percent in 2009 as compared to 2008. Overall, in 2009 the company had revenues of $4.0 billion, compared to $6.1 billion in 2008. The company cited lower volumes as accounting for $1.1 billion of the decline.

Hexion experienced decreased demand for its products due to several factors. A major issue was the decrease in sales to the construction industry due to a precipitous drop in the building and housing markets, including commercial and residential construction and residential repair and remodeling. Furthermore, weakened levels of production in both the U.S. and European automobile markets had adversely affected company sales. Hexion was also highly leveraged with outstanding indebtedness over $3 billion as of December 31, 2009.

Nevertheless, at the end of 2009, Hexion operated 35 domestic and production and manufacturing facilities in 19 states and 56 foreign production and manufacturing facilities primarily in Australia, Canada, Brazil, China, the Czech Republic, France, Germany, Italy, Korea, Malaysia, the Netherlands, New Zealand, Spain, and the United Kingdom. The company's major customers included 3M, Ashland Chemical, BASF, Bayer, Dupont, GE, Halliburton, Honeywell, Owens Corning, and PPG Industries.

Despite the economic downturn, the company maintained its position as a strong competitor in the chemical industry and a leading producer of adhesive and structural resins and coatings. The company's strategy for growth included efforts to develop and market new products via joint research and development efforts with customers and research partnership formation. Hexion also looked to expand its global reach in faster growing regions of the world, especially the Asian-Pacific, Eastern European, and Latin American markets, where use of the company's products had been increasing.

Another stated area of interest for the company's future is the development of "green products." The company intended to continue to develop products that are environmentally advanced and support various customers' overall sustainability initiatives. As an example, in July 2008 the company won a prestigious R&D 100 Award for making one of the 100 most significant proven technological advances of the year, according to *R&D* magazine. Referred to as the "Oscars of Invention," the award recognized Hexion for its leadership in developing a commercially viable technology for a bio-based powder coating based on renewable resource feedstocks, such as soybeans and corn.

The company also offered a new resin platform in 2009 for offset inks under its Eco-Rez brand name. The inks contained up to 12 percent higher renewable content than prior products. In addition, the new family of resins and varnishes did not contain phenol, also known as carbolic acid. Research has shown that skin exposure to high amounts of phenol can produce skin burns, liver damage, dark urine, irregular heartbeat, and even death.

Hexion also built a new production facility in Esslingen, Germany. Opened in April 2010, the facility replaced a smaller facility in Stuttgart, Germany. The facility manufactured specialty epoxy resin and bonding pastes used in manufacturing large-dimension composite wind turbine blades for the wind energy market. Epoxy resins manufactured at the plant were also used for marine, automotive, mass transit, and other applications.

On March 29, 2010, Hexion announced that it was forming a joint venture company with the Shanxi Sanwei Group Co., Ltd. The venture would include a new plant in Shanxi Province, China, to produce VeoVA monomer, a key building ingredient used in water-based decorative coatings, redispersible powers, and adhesives. Named Sanwei Hexion Chemicals Limited, the joint venture respresented the first manufacturing capacity for VeoVA monomer in Asia. The company announced that once the new manufacturing facility was complete, the global capacity for this specialty material would increase by 30 percent. The company planed to continue to expand in various global markets where it anticipated growth.

*David Petechuk*

## PRINCIPAL SUBSIDIARIES

Borden Chemical International, Inc.; Hexion Specialty Chemicals Australia Pty.; Hexion Specialty Chemicals Holding B.V. (Netherlands); Hexion Specialty Chemicals Management (Shanghai) Co., Ltd. (China); Hexion Química Indústria e Comércio Ltda. (Brazil); Hexion U.S. Finance Corp.; Resolution Specialty Materials Rotterdam B.V. (Netherlands).

## PRINCIPAL DIVISIONS

Coatings and Inks; Epoxy and Phenolic Resins; Formaldehyde and Forest Product Resins; Performance Products.

## PRINCIPAL COMPETITORS

BASF; Dow Chemical Company; Dynea Indria PT; Formosa Plastics Coproration; Georgia-Pacific LLC; Huntsman Corporation; Nan Ya Electronics Inc.

## FURTHER READING

"Borden Chemical, Inc., Resolution Performance Products LLC and Resolution Specialty Materials LLC to Merge," *Business Wire,* April 25, 2005.

"Hexion Specialty Chemicals Inc and Shanxi Sanwei Group Co Ltd Form Joint Venture Company, Will Build Plant in Shanxi Province, China to Produce VeoVa Monomer," *Chemical Business Newsbase,* March 29, 2010.

Lerner, Ivan, "Hexion: The New Themoset Leader," *Chemical Market Reporter,* May 9, 2005, p. 9.

Reeves, Scott, "Hexion IPO Could Be Toxic," *Forbes.com,* February 23, 2006.

Seewald, Nancy, "Ferro and Hexion Report Losses, Workforce Reductions," *Chemical Week,* March 9, 2009, p. 9.

# Hindustan Petroleum Corporation Ltd.

Petroleum House
17 Jamshedji Tata
Mumbai, 400 020
India
Telephone: (+91-22) 2286-3900
Fax: (+91-22) 2287-2992
Web site: http://hindustanpetroleum.com

*Public Company*
*Founded:* 1952
*Employees:* 11,246 (2009)
*Sales:* INR 1.318 trillion ($25.62 billion) (2009)
*Stock Exchanges:* India; Bombay
*Ticker Symbol:* HPCL
*NAICS:* 324110 Petroleum Refining; 424710 Petroleum
Bulk Stations and Terminals; 424720 Petroleum
and Petroleum Products Merchant Wholesalers
(except Bulk Stations and Terminals)

■■■

Hindustan Petroleum Corporation Ltd. (HPCL), a *Fortune* Global 500 corporation, is India's second-largest oil refiner, accounting for more than 16 percent of the country's total oil refining needs. HPCL's two major refineries, which are located in the Indian cities of Mumbai and Visakhapatnam, produce a wide variety of petroleum fuels and specialty products. These specialty products include lubricants, with HPCL owning and operating the largest lube refinery in India with a 40 percent share of the lube oil market. In 2009 the company had 8,330 gas stations throughout India and

held a 16.95 percent equity in Mangalore Refinery & Petrochemicals Ltd., which operated a state-of-the-art refinery. The company's marketing network is facilitated by a supply and distribution infrastructure comprising terminals, aviation service stations, liquid petroleum gas (LPG) bottling plants, inland relay depots and retail outlets, and lube and LPG distributorships. The Indian government owns 51 percent of the company.

## THE INDIAN OIL INDUSTRY: 1867–1950

The oil industry in India began in 1867 when oil was discovered at Makum near Margherita in the state of Assam. Despite having a long history with the oil industry, very few indigenous Indian businesspeople were in the industry. The only notable Indian oil industry had been run primarily in the 1930s by a small number of Indian oil traders. These traders circumvented the foreign companies' cartel to conduct a small trade in areas such as diesel and kerosene, selling primarily to the Soviet Union at less than market prices. Supplies, however, were hard to obtain regularly, and the Indian entrepreneurs also lacked a good marketing network and were unable to compete with the multinational oil companies.

When India gained its independence from Great Britain in 1947, the new government recognized that oil and gas was an important resource, so it targeted these resources for rapid industrial development. Nevertheless, foreign companies initially controlled the country's oil and gas industry, with all of the country's domestic oil production at the time still coming only from Assam.

## COMPANY PERSPECTIVES

Hindustan Petroleum's goal is to be a world-class energy company known for caring and delighting the customers with high-quality products and innovative services across domestic and international markets with aggressive growth and delivering superior financial performance. The company will be a model of excellence in meeting social commitment, environment, health and safety norms and in employee welfare and relations.

That state is also home to the world's oldest operating oil refinery, which was built in Digboi in 1901.

The Indian government soon found itself in conflict with foreign-owned oil companies following the country's independence. India's new leaders began to assess the country's oil industry. They were specifically interested in changing the fact that most of the country's oil industry was essentially controlled by a private monopoly led by a combination of European and U.S. oil companies composed of such major companies as Burma, Shell, and Standard Oil.

In 1949 India requested advice from British and U.S. oil companies concerning India's desire to become more self-sufficient in oil by building a refinery. A joint technical committee was formed that eventually advised against the project because it would not be profitable. Foreign oil companies offered to build two refineries but only if they were able to sell the resulting products at 10 percent above world parity price. The government initially refused but would relent two years later as India's oil industry continued to sputter. After building the two refineries, the foreign companies found themselves in increasing conflict with the Indian government.

### BEGINNINGS: 1952–80

HPCL's origins date back to 1952 with the establishment of the Standard Vacuum Refining Company of India Limited under the Indian Companies Act of 1913. Two years later, the Oil and Natural Gas Commission (ONGC) was established as a department of the Geological Survey of India. India's Industrial Policy Resolution of 1956 led to the Indian government having sole and exclusive control of petroleum exploration and production. In 1959 the Indian Parliament made ONGC the country's first national oil company.

On March 31, 1963, the Standard Vacuum Refining Company of India became ESSO Standard Refining Company of India Limited. Eleven years later, on July 15, 1974, the company's name was changed to the Hindustan Petroleum Corporation Limited. S. Krishnaswami was named the company's first chairman and managing director.

In 1976, during Prime Minister Indira Ghandi's emphasis on nationalism, the government decided to nationalize the country's remaining independent refineries. Caltex Oil Refining Ltd. was subsequently merged with Hindustan Petroleum. HPCL was further expanded in 1979 when Kosangas Company Ltd. was merged with HPCL. At this time, the government owned a 60.31 percent share of HPCL.

### INCREASED ENERGY NEEDS

During the 1970s, India's oil consumption grew at 8 percent per year, and HPCL embarked on a number of projects. In 1983 it increased the capacity of its lube plant by an additional 74,000 tons per annum of high viscosity index lube base stocks. Two years later the corporation started a project to expand its crude distillation capacity at Mumbai by 2 million tons per annum. In 1995 the company entered into a memorandum of understanding with Saudi Arabian Oil Co. (Saudi Aramco) to set up a 1-million-ton refinery in Punjab. Another joint venture the following year with Colas S.A. of France led the company to form the Hindustan Colas Ltd. and begin its first state-of-the-art bitumen emulsion plant at Vashi.

The Indian government approved the New Exploration Licensing Policy (NELP) in March 1997. This policy sought to increase exploration activity and to ensure a level playing field in the upstream sector between private and public sector companies. The following year, HPCL set up a joint venture with domestic financial institutions for oil and gas exploration both in India and abroad.

HPCL also experienced a severe setback in operations in 1997 when an explosion at its refinery at Visakhapatnam killed 56 people within a 500-meter radius of the explosion and critically injured many others. Caused by a leak in an LPG pipeline, the explosion first ignited six storage tanks. This was followed by a fire that swept through the refinery, destroying numerous buildings and tanks. The explosion also caused 100,000 people to flee the area. The refinery reopened on January 15, 1998, after four months of repair at a cost of roughly $25 million.

## KEY DATES

**1952:** The Company is incorporated as Standard Vacuum Refining Company of India Limited.
**1962:** Company changes name to ESSO Standard Refining Company of India Limited.
**1974:** Hindustan Petroleum Corporation Limited comes into being after the takeover and merger of Esso and Lube India Undertaking.
**1979:** Kosan Gas Company, the concessionaries of Hindustan Petroleum in the domestic liquid petroleum gas (LPG) market, are taken over and merged with Hindustan Petroleum.
**2008:** Company creates joint venture CREDA-HPCL Biofuel Ltd to conduct biofuel research on jatropha plants.

## THE 21ST CENTURY: GROWTH AND EXPANSION

In 2003 HPCL became the second-largest oil company in India and was listed eighth among the "Top 10" in *Asiamoney*'s corporate governance poll, which recognized companies with superior corporate governance. Nevertheless, in March of that year, the Indian government announced plans to privatize two key petroleum refining and marketing companies, including HPCL. Rajeev Gupta, who was head of investment banking at DSP Merrill Lynch, told *Euromoney* contributor Kala Rao that the company would be attractive to investors because its origins as a foreign company made it better managed than many other public sector companies. He also noted: "There is little doubt about the quality of [the] asset on offer." Nevertheless, the planned sale of 34 percent of the state's shares of HPCL never went through due to regulation and legal obstacles.

The company's 2003–04 fiscal year report showed that HPCL was a "quality asset." HPCL had gross sales of more than $12 billion as well as a healthy after-tax income. The fiscal year saw the company's refineries achieve the highest ever combined crude output of 13.7 million metric tons (MMT) compared to the previous year's best of 12.9 MMT. The company also achieved high sales growth in India with a growth of 2.9 percent compared to a 2.4 percent sales growth for the overall industry.

The new millennium also saw HPCL proceed on a number of projects, including upgrading its two refineries at Mumbai and Visakhapatnam and plans to build a new pipeline between Mundra and Delhi. In 2005

HPCL announced that it was teaming up with BP to build a new refinery in Bhatinda, India, in the northern Indian state of Punjab. HPCL purchased the property in 1999, and the company had been looking for a major partner to complete the project. However, BP pulled out of the project the following year because the investment climate was unattractive. In 2007 HPCL teamed up with the Luxembourg-based Mittal Investments, which was able to take a 49 percent stake in the refinery project. Mittal's stake in the project was made possible by the Indian government's ruling in 1997 to allow an increase in the foreign direct investment limit in state-owned refineries. The refinery, when completed, will produce 180 billion barrels per day.

## CHALLENGES

Despite its ongoing expansion plans, HPCL and other Indian oil companies suffered a drop in profits in 2008, with retained earnings falling about two-thirds at HPCL. The culprit was a volatile economy and losses on the sale of diesel, petrol, LPG, and kerosene within India. In the fall of 2008, the subprime mortgage crisis that began in the United States led to the worst economic contractions throughout the world since the Great Depression. Oil prices fell drastically to $34 a standard barrel by December 2008.

Although the company faced difficult economic times, HPCL went on in its 2008–09 fiscal year report to post an all-time high in sales of petroleum products. The company's profits were aided by government compensation for selling fuel below market prices. The company also experienced several business milestones for the fiscal year. The Bathinda refinery project was going smoothly with a projected completion set for 2011. In addition, the LPG Cavern Storage Facility, a joint venture with Total France, handled a total volume of 578 thousand tons in its first full year of operation.

India's economy was growing, especially in terms of increasing demand for energy. During the first decade of the twenty-first century, India's energy consumption increased at an average annual rate of about 5 percent. At this rate, energy demands in India would double every 14 years. As a result, HPCL expected the demand for oil in India to increase for the foreseeable future. The company invested in areas such as city gas distribution and renewable energy to diversify its revenue stream while poising itself to take advantage of emerging opportunities. With participating interests in 26 exploration blocks, HPCL was looking for prospective fields both domestically and internationally.

While the greatest part of the company's efforts focused on oil and natural gas, the company recognized that India's growing energy consumption resulted in a larger carbon footprint that would affect the environment. As a result, HPCL began developing several alternative energy projects based on the thrust for renewable energy based on concerns about energy security and climate change. The company invested in wind energy projects in the state of Maharashtra and Rajasthan. The company created a new subsidiary, CREDA-HPCL Biofuel, to explore the potential for cultivating and transforming certain nonedible oil yielding plants (such as jatropha) into viable biofuels.

HPCL's overall strategy was to ensure steady capital investment for long-term growth while reducing the impact volatility through rigorous scrutiny of costs. The company began setting up modern, state-of-the-art infrastructure in various Indian states that had been largely left out of the development boom. The company, which had only a marginal presence in many of these states, was planning to aggressively tap the rural market in India through special format retail outlets for its gas and diesel. Approximately 2,000 new rural outlets were being planned.

*David Petechuk*

## PRINCIPAL SUBSIDIARIES

CREDA-HPCL Biofuel Ltd. (74%); Hindustan Colas Ltd.; HPCL-Mittal Energy Ltd. (49%).

## PRINCIPAL DIVISIONS

Aviation; Bulk Fuel; Liquid Petroleum Gas (LPG); Lubes; and Refineries.

## PRINCIPAL COMPETITORS

BP plc; Chevron Corporation; Exxon Mobil Corporation; Royal Dutch Shell plc.

## FURTHER READING

"Hindustan Petroleum Q4 Profits Surge," *Global Refining & Fuels Report,* June 3, 2009.

"HPCL Plans to Expand Its Rural Presence," *Accord Fintech,* February 19, 2010.

"India's Best Public Sector Enterprises – Hindustan Petroleum Corporation LTD (Records 19 Percent CAGR in Income for 2003–2008)," *India Business Insight,* December 31, 2009.

Kala, Rao, "Oil Firm Privatization Looks Set to Take a Winding Road," *Euromoney,* March, 2003, p. 22.

# HomeAway, Inc.

1011 West Fifth Street
Suite 300
Austin, Texas 78703
U.S.A.
Telephone: (512) 493-0382
Web site: http://www.homeaway.com

*Private Company*
*Founded:* 2005 as WVR Group, Inc.
*Employees:* 540 (2009)
*Sales:* $120 million (est. 2009)
*NAICS:* 531390 Real estate listing services

■ ■ ■

HomeAway, Inc., is a Web site that helps match home-owners or property managers with vacationers. Owners who rent their homes or additional homes for short periods during the year pay to advertise their property on one of the company's Web sites. Vacationers search the sites for properties that fit their needs, contact the owner, and arrange the dates and payment for their vacation. HomeAway also lists vacation rental properties for sale to those interested in purchasing and managing vacation rental homes.

## FIVE TO START

In April 2004 Brian Sharples joined with Austin Ventures, a venture capital company, to form an investment company. The company's general purpose was information services, and Sharples began looking for a more specific business idea to fuel investment and create revenues. Sharples was a former Bain and Company employee with an MBA from Stanford University, and the former CEO of IntelliQuest Information Group. IntelliQuest was an Austin-based high-tech market research firm that was sold to the WPP Group in 2000. Soon after Sharples formed the investment company, Carl Shepherd joined the company. Shepherd was former chief operating officer of Hoovers, Inc., an Austin-based business information company. Sharples and Shepherd came up with the idea of entering the vacation rental business and named their company WVR Group (WVR). Unofficially, WVR stood for World Vacation Rentals. The two founders raised $38 million to get their idea off the ground. Within five months, they had purchased five established Web sites that listed vacation rentals. These first sites were CyberRentals.com, GreatRentals.com, A1Vacations.com, Holiday-Rentals.co.uk, and Rent101.com.

The largest and most successful of the sites was the Vermont-based company CyberRentals, a site founded in 1995 by Hunter Melville and Dave Bollinger. Melville and Bollinger have been credited with being the first to bring the vacation rentals business to the Internet. At the time WVR purchased CyberRentals the site had more than 15,000 properties and served more than 12,000 owners. In spring 2005 *Forbes* magazine named the site the "Best of the Web."

The next largest site in WVR's portfolio was GreatRentals. The company was founded in 1996 by Jan and Pat Voorhis. The couple had purchased a Florida condo in 1996, and the management company they hired failed to keep the condo rented, so they

## COMPANY PERSPECTIVES

We inspire each other to push the limits. We operate at Internet speed. We deliver extraordinary results. We are one global team. Walk the halls and you will see cross-functional teams working to deliver new benefits to our customers. Listen in and you will hear colleagues from four different time zones planning a new product rollout. Ask a question about performance and you will get data and analysis that demonstrates extraordinary results. Send an e-mail and you will find five volunteers eager to move your project forward. Every day at HomeAway is different, and we like it that way.

turned to the Internet for a solution. The Michigan couple started with a modest Web site that posted a handful of vacation rental properties for themselves and a few friends. What began as a family business grew into one of the few Web sites to survive the dot-com collapse of the late 1990s. By the time WVR purchased Great-Rentals the site listed 10,000 properties around the world, and about 900,000 people searched its listings each month. Both Jan and Pat Voorhis became investors in WVR and joined the company's advisory board.

Vacation rental sites like CyberRentals and Great-Rentals used the Internet to make what was once available only to elite vacationers into a widely available option for mainstream travelers. While the Internet made rental homes more available, the number of couples that traveled with children had grown significantly. As a result, the need for family-friendly living facilities also grew. For many vacationing families, the privacy, the availability of a kitchen, and the flexibility in living spaces made vacation homes more appealing than traditional hotels. In addition, vacationers had become much more Internet-savvy. All these factors helped online vacation rental sites grow significantly from the late 1990s through the early years of the 21st century.

After purchasing its initial five sites, WVR invested in upgrading each site's technology to give both owners and vacationers a better all-around experience. This included more powerful search capabilities and better site design for easier navigation.

In July 2005 Christine Karpinski joined the company. Karpinski was a vacation rental expert and author who had written extensively about the vacation rental market, especially concerning the issues faced by rental property owners. She took the position of director, owner advocacy, later to become director of owner community.

## WORLDWIDE ACQUISITIONS

In December 2005 WVR acquired Vacation Villas International GmbH (VVI), which operated the German-language site FeWo-direkt.de and the English-language site vacationvillas.net. VVI was founded in 1997 by Kerstin Fuehrer. VVI had over 9,600 property listings in Europe and around the world, and its site served more than seven million travelers each year. With the addition of VVI's sites, WVR brought its listings up to 65,000 properties in the United States and Europe. In May 2006 WVR renamed Rent101.com as TripHomes.com and relaunched the site with a new design and more than 15,000 condos, villas, and homes listed on the site for rental.

In June 2006 WVR became HomeAway, Inc. With the renaming of the company came the launch of its flagship Web site, HomeAway.com. The company also announced an infusion of $7 million of new venture capital investment from its current funders. The new U.S.-based Web site consolidated the listings from its other sites, including CyberRentals, GreatRentals, A1Vacations, Holiday-Rentals, FeWo-direkt and TripHomes. The consolidated Web site boasted more than 60,000 homes, condos, guest houses, cottages, and cabins in 90 countries. In order to retain site loyalty, the two largest U.S. Web sites, CyberRentals and GreatRentals, retained their separate identities. Their logos identified them as "A HomeAway Company" while the other Web sites were completely replaced by the new HomeAway.com Web domain. The German site, FeWo-direkt, kept both names, with HomeAway the most prominent, in a split branding effort.

HomeAway's success in online travel sites drew other companies into the market. LeisureLink.com linked small rental companies with hundreds of thousands of travel agents across North America. Escapia developed a Web-based software program that helped rental owners manage every aspect of their business, including reservations, accounting, and maintenance. While these companies were dwarfed in size by HomeAway, HomeAway made additional moves to bolster its share of the market.

In October 2006 HomeAway.com announced a partnership with USAToday.com to create an affiliate site, usatoday.homeaway.com. This was a common method of increasing site traffic. Less-trafficked sites built up their own traffic by creating partner or affiliate sites for companies with an already established customer

## KEY DATES

**2004:** Brian Sharples and Carl Shepherd found WVR Group; company purchases five vacation rental Web sites.

**2005:** Company acquires Vacation Villas International GmBH.

**2006:** Company becomes HomeAway, Inc., and secures $160 million financing; company acquires VRBO.com, reaches 130,000 vacation home listings in 130 countries.

**2007:** HomeAway acquires Abritel.fr, VacationRentals.com, and OwnersDirect.co.uk.

**2009:** Company acquires Homelidays.com and starts reservation management system.

**2010:** Company launches nationwide advertising campaign and launches HomeAway Real Estate.

base. The more traffic HomeAway boasted, the more attractive its site became to potential vacation homeowners looking to advertise their property to the most visitors.

### BUYING THE COMPETITION

In November 2006 HomeAway secured $160 million in debt and equity financing to purchase VRBO.com, the company's biggest competitor and the largest vacation rental Web site in the United States. VRBO, which stands for Vacation Rentals by Owner, was founded in 1995 by David Clouse. The merger raised HomeAway's listings to 130,000 in nearly 100 countries. The deal was financed by Austin Ventures, Redpoint Ventures, American Capital (ACAS), Institutional Venture Partners (IVP), and Trident Capital. Under the deal, VRBO would continue to operate under its own brand and with the same management team.

The years 2007 and 2008 brought further acquisitions. HomeAway added French-based Abritel.fr, U.S.-based VacationRentals.com, and U.K.-based Owners Direct.co.uk to its portfolio in 2007. The VacationRentals merger added 30,000 properties to the company's listings. In 2008 HomeAway purchased EscapeHomes.com, a vacation real estate Web site. EscapeHomes became HomeAway's first venture into the buying and selling of vacation real estate. In September 2008 HomeAway unveiled a redesign of its HomeAway.com site, and a month later the company broke ground for

its new corporate headquarters on West Fifth Street in Austin, Texas. The new building would be Gold-level, LEED-certified, which is a very high environmental building rating (Platinum is highest).

HomeAway's aggressive deal-making continued in late 2008 when the company secured $250 million in private financing. The funds were provided by new investors Technology Crossover Ventures and two of its previous partners, IVP and Redpoint Ventures. The funds were quickly put to work in 2009 with a site redesign of Holiday-Rentals and VacationRentals. The company also acquired Paris-based Homelidays.com, which added more than 40,000 listings to HomeAway's site.

### BROADENING FOCUS WITH NEW DIRECTIONS

In an effort to broaden its reach the company launched a Web-based reservation management system for property owners. This represented the company's first venture into the actual professional aspects of property management and customer service. For an annual subscription payment, the HomeAway system let owners who were listed on HomeAway customize payment schedules, invoices, securely collect rental fees, manage customer transactions, and instantly deposit payments. After building up a significant database of properties and rental transactions, the company leveraged its data to produce market research and published its first Vacation Rental Marketplace Report. In June 2009 the company announced a deal with the *New York Times* to provide vacation rental listings on the *Times*'s Real Estate and Great Homes as Destinations Web sites. Toward the end of 2009, the company moved into its new headquarters.

The world was in deep recession in 2009, and in 2010, even though the U.S. economy was beginning to show signs of recovery, the effects of the recession were still prevalent. However, despite the difficult economy HomeAway continued to grow and appeared rather recession-proof. Many homeowners, facing a poor housing market, resorted to renting their homes to make extra cash, and HomeAway was in a good position to take advantage. In February 2010 HomeAway launched a nationwide advertising campaign, beginning with a Super Bowl commercial. A month later, the company acquired BedandBreakfast.com, moving beyond vacation home rentals and widening its scope to encompass other hotel alternatives. HomeAway also acquired Alugue-Temporada.br, a leading Brazilian vacation rental site. The company launched a five-star rating system on VBRO, allowing vacationers to review and rate their experiences with the properties. In April 2010 HomeAway launched HomeAway Real Estate, an online marketplace for buying and selling vacations homes. The venture into real estate sales listings signaled Home-Away's continued movement into areas beyond its original core business of vacation home rental listings.

*Aaron Hauser*

## PRINCIPAL DIVISIONS

Abritel.fr; AlugueTemporada.com.br; BedandBreakfast.com; HomeAway.com; HomeAway.co.uk; HomeAway.es; HomeAwayRealEstate.com; Homelidays.com; Owners Direct.co.uk; VacationRentals.com; HomeAway.de; VRBO.com.

## PRINCIPAL COMPETITORS

Expedia, Inc.; Orbitz Worldwide, Inc.; Priceline.com Inc.; Travelocity.com L.P.; TripAdvisor LLC.

## FURTHER READING

Ante, Spencer E., "HomeAway: A Find in Online Vacation Rentals," *Bloomberg Businessweek,* November 11, 2008.

Frater, Stephen, "No Longer Just a Cottage Industry; The Consolidation of Vacation Rental Web Sites Is Under Way," *Saratota Herald-Tribune,* June 19, 2006, p. 10.

Hawkins, Lori, "Austin Firm Laying Claim to Vacations Home Rental; WVR Group Raises $38 million in Venture Capital to Build Web Site," *Austin American-Statesman,* July 18, 2005, p. D1.

————, "Want to Get Away from It All? Web Site Aims to Help," *Austin American-Statesman,* June 7, 2006, p. D1.

"HomeAway.com Selected by USAToday.com to Power Its Online Vacation Rental Classifieds," *Business Wire,* October 3, 2006.

"HomeAway Secures Record $160 Million in Financing," *Business Wire,* November 13, 2006.

Miller, Claire Cain, "Bits: Vacation Rental Site Raises $250 Million," *New York Times,* November 11, 2008.

Nolan, Clancy, "New Travel Sites Seek to Carve Niches – Venture Capital Is Betting on Start-Ups to Tap Luxury Vacation Market," *Wall Street Journal,* August 23, 2006, p. D5.

"Noted Travel Authority Joins WVR Group," *Business Wire,* July, 18, 2005.

Schlegel, Erich, "Some Companies (Like Wal-Mart) Thrive Despite Recession," *USAToday.com,* December 5, 2008.

"Vacation Rental Novices Forge Online Success; Self-Taught Retirees Turn Experiment into Industry Force," *PR Newswire,* July 18, 2005.

"WVR Group Acquires Operator of European Vacation Rentals Web Site, Vacation Villas International; WVR Grows Listings to 65,000 U.S. and European Rental Properties," *Business Wire,* December 6, 2005.

# Hudson City Bancorp, Inc.

—■—

West 80 Century Road
Paramus, New Jersey 07652
U.S.A.
Telephone: (201) 967-1900
Toll Free: (866) 448-9498
Fax: (201) 967-0559
Web site: http://www.hcsbonline.com

*Public Company*
*Founded:* March 27,1868
*Assets:* $60.3 billion (2009)
*Employees:* 1,552 (2009)
*Stock Exchanges:* NASDAQ
*Ticker Symbol:* HCBK
*NAICS:* 521110 Monetary Authorities-Central Bank;
    522110 Commercial Banking; 522292 Real Estate
    Credit; 523110 Investment Banking and Securities
    Dealing

■ ■ ■

Hudson City Bancorp, Inc., a New Jersey-based savings
and loan holding company, is ranked among the top 25
banks in the United States. Operating through its
subsidiary, Hudson City Savings Bank (Hudson City
Savings), the company performs savings bank operations
and other related financial activities. In addition to retail
savings banking services that feature traditional deposit
products, such as certificates of deposit (CDs) and
individual retirement accounts (IRAs), Hudson City
Bancorp engages in residential real estate mortgage loans
and consumer loans. Based in Paramus, New Jersey, the

company purchases mortgages, mortgage-backed securities, and other securities issued via enterprises sponsored
by the U.S. government. Over the years, Hudson City
Bancorp has continued to thrive, opening branches in
New York, New Jersey, and Connecticut. In 2008 the
bank began receiving deposits from customers
throughout the United States via its online banking
service.

## EARLY YEARS: 1868–1920

On March 27, 1868, the State of New Jersey Legislature
granted a special charter to 29 individuals. The charter
allowed them to start a savings bank in what was then
the small City of Hudson. The city's first mayor, Garrett
D. Van Reipen, a descendent of Dutch settlers, became
the first president of the newly formed Hudson City
Savings Bank.

Following the Civil War, small independent communities such as Hudson found that their resources
were under strain due to demands for efficient government and services. As a result, in 1870 the City of Hudson merged with Bergen City and Jersey City to create
the modern Jersey City, making it the second-largest city
in the state of New Jersey. Hudson City Savings Bank
proceeded to grow with the new city and the entire state
of New Jersey. By the end of the nineteenth century,
New Jersey had a population of more than one million
people, and Hudson City Savings had garnered more
than $1 million in assets and deposits. The next decade,
the bank had accumulated $2 million in assets.

The U.S. Congress declared war on Germany in
1917, thus entering the carnage of World War I that

## COMPANY PERSPECTIVES

At Hudson City, our goal has always been simple. We will continue to succeed in the marketplace by providing better value, while remaining focused, efficient, loyal, and trustworthy. To some, this may sound simplistic or even naive, but time and time again, we've found that it's a business model that is easier to describe than to replicate.

had been going on in Europe since 1914. Hudson City Savings Bank joined in the war effort, selling Liberty Loan bonds and Victory Loan bonds. In addition to selling its allotment of bonds, the bank purchased a half million dollars of war bonds. In January 1918 Robert J. Rendall was named the bank's president, a position he held until his death in 1950. This was one of the longest tenures as bank president in the company's history.

### BRANCHING OUT: 1920–80

Hudson City Savings opened its second office in the 1920s. The bank also moved its main office from its old headquarters on Newark Avenue to 587 Summit Avenue in Jersey City. The bank, like many other financial institutions in the United States, was thriving until the stock market crashed in 1929. The Great Depression followed and many banks were forced to close. Hudson City Savings Bank, however, remained solvent and in full operation. The company achieved this feat, in part, by being very cautious and deliberate in its loan and mortgage business, a trait that would serve Hudson City well throughout other troubled periods in banking. By the end of the 1930s, the bank boasted total assets exceeding $11 million and reserves of $800,000.

On December 7, 1941, the Japanese bombed Pearl Harbor, and the United States once again found itself entering a worldwide conflict overseas. To support the war effort, Hudson City Savings Bank sold millions of dollars' worth of U.S. War Bonds. The years following the end of World War II saw the bank continue to prosper. By 1950 Hudson City Savings had opened three Jersey City branches with total assets of more than $26 million.

Like much of the U.S. economic sector, the bank prospered in the 1950s as the baby boom marked the beginning of significant growth in the U.S. population. New Jersey's growth rate was twice the national average, and the state increased its population by 1.2 million by the end of the decade. This population surge benefited the bank as it continued to grow, accumulating more than $50 million in assets by 1959 as the bank made more than $25 million in Veterans Administration (VA) and Federal Housing Authority (FHA) mortgage loans.

Throughout its growth, the Hudson City Savings Bank was confined by state laws that made it illegal for banks to operate across county lines. In the late 1960s, however, new laws were passed making cross-county operations legal. Hudson City Savings Bank proceeded to open its fifth branch and its first branch across the county line in the city of Waldwick. By this time, the bank had $175 million in assets.

Kenneth L. Birchby joined the bank in 1966 and was named president and CEO in 1968. He went on to head a period of rapid expansion in the 1970s as the bank established 37 branches in 12 New Jersey counties despite the extended bear market and economic malaise. Bank headquarters were relocated from Jersey City to neighboring Bergen County, New Jersey, in 1978. As the company moved into its new crescent-shaped building, it reported total assets and deposits of more than $1.1 billion.

### NAVIGATING CRISIS: 1980–99

The 1980s and early 1990s saw new pressures and problems for the banking industry in the form of skyrocketing inflation and interest rates. Nevertheless, just as it had survived and even prospered during the Great Depression while other banks failed, once again Hudson City Savings Bank used a cautious, measured approach to navigate the financial storm and maintain its financial stability.

Leonard S. Gudelski was named the bank's president in 1981. He oversaw the bank's continued growth and expansion. Under his leadership and the guidance of Ronald E. Hermance, Jr., who was hired as senior executive vice president and chief operating officer in 1988, the bank survived the late 1980s savings and loan crisis. Commonly referred to as the S&L crisis, the failure of more than 700 saving and loan associations resulted in an ultimate cost of more than $160 billion, with the U.S. government covering approximately $124 billon of these costs. Hudson City Savings Bank remained on stable ground as the 1990s began with total assets of $3.2 billion and 69 branches.

As the United States suffered through a recession from 1990 to 1992, New Jersey banking industry laws underwent significant changes. Many banks disappeared, many merging into larger national banking concerns. Hudson City Savings, however, remained focused on

## KEY DATES

**1868:** The State of New Jersey Legislature grants a special charter to the Hudson City Savings Bank.

**1900:** Hudson City's assets and deposits grow to more than $1 million.

**1978:** Bank relocates headquarters to Bergen County.

**1990:** Hudson City has 69 branches and total assets of $3.2 billion.

**1999:** Hudson City Savings becomes a wholly owned subsidiary of Hudson City Bancorp, Inc.

steady growth while maintaining its independence. In 1992 Hudson City Savings became the largest savings bank in New Jersey. Furthermore, *Money* magazine named Hudson City Savings one of the safest banks in New Jersey, followed by a 1995 designation as the "Best Bank in New Jersey." Ronald E. Hermance, Jr., was named the 11th president of Hudson City Savings Bank in January 1997.

### HUDSON CITY BANCORP FORMED: 1999

As the new century approached, Hudson Savings began a plan of reorganization. In February 1999 the bank became a wholly owned subsidiary of Hudson City Bancorp, Inc. For the first time in its history, it made a public offering of 54.35 million shares of common stock priced at $10 per share. The IPO raised $540 million in new capital as a 47 percent ownership stake was sold to the public. At that time, the bank's assets exceeded $8 billion. On July 13, 1999, the United States Federal Reserve formally recognized Hudson City Bancorp as the mutual holding company for Hudson City Savings Bank.

Despite the reorganization, Hudson City Bancorp continued its business plan of focusing primarily on one-to-four-family mortgage loans as the foundation of its business. "We are not flashy," Leonard S. Gudelski, the bank's chairman and chief executive officer told John Reosti in an interview for an *American Banker* article published in 2000. "We do not trade securities, our fee income is nominal, and we do not have a venture capital arm. With us, day in and day out it is interest received minus interest expense."

### BUSINESS AS USUAL: 2002–05

On January 1, 2002, the bank's president, Ronald E. Hermance, Jr., was promoted from COO to CEO of the new holding company. Although falling interest rates and an unprecedented refinance boom was taking place, Hudson City Bancorp remained dedicated to its business model of focusing primarily on fixed-rate home loans. "Hudson City is about the purest thrift out there," Rick Weiss, an analyst at Janney Montgomery Scott LLC in Philadelphia, told *American Banker* contributor John Reosti.

By October 2003 Hudson City had begun the process of converting to a federal thrift charter as it sought to expand its business opportunities beyond New Jersey while lessening its tax and regulatory burdens. In terms of expanding beyond New Jersey, the federal thrift charter made it easier for Hudson City Savings to open branches in neighboring states, where acquisitions and mergers were reducing the number of traditional savings banks.

On January 1, 2004, the company changed from a Bank Holding Company to a Domestic Entity Other according to the Federal Reserve System categorization. This designation is generally defined as a domestic institution that takes part in banking business in the United States. The move was part of the company's plan to provide a significant stock offering, which would be the company's second step toward mutual-to-stock conversion.

### STOCK OFFERING: 2005

On January 1, 2005, Ronald Hermance, Jr., was named the company's chairman while retaining his appointments as president and CEO. In July 2005 Hudson City raised $3.9 billion in new capital as it completed the largest stock offering ever by a U.S. bank and the seventh-largest public offering in history at the time. This second-step conversion involved selling the 53 percent ownership stake that the company held as a mutual holding company. The company had become a fully publicly held entity, and the new Hudson City Bancorp common stock traded on the NASDAQ National Market under the ticker symbol HCBK.

By this time the company had opened its first out-of-state branch in Southold, New York, on New York's Long Island, as well as two branches in the New York City borough of Staten Island. Although the company was continuing with its plans to expand throughout the Northeast corridor, the company planned no drastic changes in its business plan. "We're going to continue to focus on our game plan," Ronald E. Hermance, Jr., told *American Banker* contributor John Reosti. "We asked for this money to continue doing the things and producing the results the market has become accustomed to over the past six years."

By 2007 Hudson City Savings Bank had more than 100 branches in New Jersey, New York, and Connecticut. With more than $35 billion in assets, the bank had become the largest savings bank in New Jersey and the third-largest savings and loan association in the United States. On February 14, 2007, Hudson City Bancorp was added to the S&P 500 Index by Standard & Poor's.

## THE RECESSION: 2007

A financial crisis began in 2007 as the U.S. banking system faced a liquidity shortfall. As a result, large financial institutions collapsed, and in 2008 numerous banks were "bailed out" with money from the federal government. Furthermore, the housing market also suffered, and numerous homeowners faced eviction and foreclosure. As prolonged vacancies seemed inevitable in the housing market and unemployment rates rose, many economic observers stated that the United States was facing its worst financial crisis since the Great Depression of the 1930s.

As the banking and financial worlds faced extraordinary challenges and changes, Hudson City Bancorp marked its 10th consecutive year of record earnings in 2008. Eric Dash, writing for the *New York Times*, noted: "Hudson City is one of the few bright spots in an industry beset with gloom and doom." According to Dash, unlike much of the banking industry that decided to widen their loan offers, Hudson City continued to emphasize "collecting deposits and issuing mortgages, preferring to operate as a mom-and-pop boutique instead of a financial department store." Dash added: "It continued to screen borrowers carefully, since it planned to hold their loans instead of selling them to outside investors. And it steered clear of complex investments its executives could not value, the kind that would later turn toxic as the housing market collapsed."

In December 2008 editors at *Forbes* magazine picked the New Jersey company as "The best-managed company in the banking industry" and "one of the best recession stocks." In the article on the *Forbes.com* Web site, the editors noted: "One theory that has not held up, especially in 2008, is that financial services are a safe place to invest during a downturn. We have only identified one Platinum 400 bank, Hudson City Bancorp ... that met our screening criteria." The Platinum 400 are chosen based on factors such as sales and earnings growth, earnings outlook, debt to total capital, and stock market returns.

By 2010 the company had more than 130 branches in the New York City metropolitan area, including Long Island, New Jersey, and Fairfield County, New Jersey. Despite the recession, from 2000 to 2010, the company's growth rate in assets has exceeded 20 percent. In January 2010 the company reported record annual earnings of $527.2 million in 2009 as compared to $445.6 million in 2008, marking the company's 11th consecutive year of earnings growth since its 1999 public offering.

On March 4 2010, Hudson City Bancorp announced that it was submitting an application to the Office of Comptroller of the Currency (OCC) to convert from a federally chartered stock savings bank to a national bank. The company also announced its intention to file an application with the Federal Reserve to become a bank holding company. An article on the *TradingMarkets.com* Web site quoted the company's president and chief executive officer, Ronald E. Hermance, Jr., as saying: "Our decision to convert to a national bank charter results from, among other things, our resolve to continue our solid level of performance and growth in the banking industry and to maintain the trust and confidence of our customer base during these uncertain financial times."

Hermance went on to note that part of the move was to "stay ahead" of potential changes in laws and regulations concerning oversight by the federal government. "In order to accomplish this, we believe that it is necessary to take affirmative action by converting to a national bank charter now," Hermance noted in the *TradingMarkets.com* Web site article. Nevertheless, Hermance pointed out that the company had no plans to drastically alter its basic business model. Instead, Hudson City Bancorp will continue to focus on originating and buying first mortgage loans on residential properties.

*David Petechuk*

## PRINCIPAL SUBSIDIARIES
Hudson City Savings Bank.

## PRINCIPAL COMPETITORS
Bank of America Corporation; BB&T Corporation; M&T Bank Corporation; PNC Financial Services Group; Wells Fargo & Company.

## FURTHER READING
Dash, Eric, "Caution Pays for a Lender in New Jersey," *New York Times*, August 13, 2008.

"Hudson City Applies to Convert to National Bank," TradingMarkets.com, March 5, 2010.

"Hudson City, Lakeland Post Strong Fourth-quarter Earnings" NorthJersey.com, January 21, 2010.

Linder, Craig, "N.J.'s Hudson City Seeks Switch to OTS," *American Banker,* October 22, 2003, p. 4.

Newman, Richard. "Hudson City Sees Take Over Targets," NorthJersey.com, February 3, 2010.

Reosti, John, "At Hudson City of N.J., Simplicity is Prosperity: Vanilla Works as other Thrifts Change Flavor," *American Banker,* August 2, 2000, p. 1.

————, "A Plain-Vanilla Strategy Still First Choice at Hudson City," *American Banker,* November 7, 2002, p. 1.

————, "Cash-Flush Hudson City Eyes Multistate Expansion," *American Banker,* June 17, 2005, p. 1.

Zajac, Brian, "America's Best Big Companies; Best Recession Stocks," Forbes.com, December 22, 2008.

# ITOCHU Corporation

—■—

5-1, Kita-Aoyama 2-chome
Minato-ku, Tokyo, 107-8077
Japan
Telephone: (81) 3 3497-2121
Toll Free: (866) 545-5878
Fax: (81) 3 3497-4141
Web site: http://www.itochu.co.jp

*Public Company*
*Founded:* 1858
*Employees:* 60,000 (est. 2009)
*Sales:* ¥3.42 trillion ($34.80 billion, 2009)
*Stock Exchanges:* Tokyo; Frankfurt
*Ticker Symbol:* 8001; IOC
*NAICS:* 551112 Offices of Other Holding Companies; 424410 General Line Grocery Merchant Wholesalers; 212111 Bituminous Coal and Lignite Surface Mining; 213111 Drilling Oil and Gas Wells; 313210 Broadwoven Fabric Mills; 315225 Men's and Boys' Cut and Sew Work Clothing Manufacturing; 315228 Men's and Boys' Cut and Sew Other Outerwear Manufacturing; 315234 Women's and Girls' Cut and Sew Suit, Coat, Tailored Jacket, and Skirt Manufacturing; 331312 Primary Aluminum Production; 333120 Construction Machinery Manufacturing; 333319 Other Commercial and Service Industry Machinery Manufacturing; 333518 Other Metalworking Machinery Manufacturing; 522298 All Other Non-Depository Credit Intermediation; 531210 Offices of Real Estate Agents and Brokers; 532412 Construction, Mining and Forestry Machinery and

Equipment Rental and Leasing; 561510 Travel Agencies

■ ■ ■

ITOCHU Corporation is involved in domestic trading, import/export, and overseas trading of various products such as textiles, machinery, information and communications technology, aerospace, electronics, energy, metals, minerals, chemicals, forest products, general merchandise, food, finance, insurance, and logistics services, as well as business investment in Japan and overseas.

ITOCHU Corporation is the third-largest of Japan's general trading companies (which are known as *sogo shosha*) behind only Mitsui & Co., Ltd., and Mitsubishi Corporation. These companies are general in nature, handling a wide range of products and services in nearly every industry. General trading companies specialize in bringing together buyers and sellers of a variety of products and services on a global level and then handling finance and transport of the resulting transaction. The companies derive most of their revenues from commissions earned through these short-term transactions.

ITOCHU has a global network of more than 1,000 subsidiaries and affiliated companies in approximately 74 countries.

## EARLY HISTORY

ITOCHU's founder, Chubei Itoh, was born in 1842, the son of a dry goods merchant. In 1853, the year

The ITOCHU group respects the individual, society, and the future in its Commitment to the Global Good. At the heart of ITOCHU Corporation's basic management policy is a commitment to becoming a highly attractive global enterprise by constantly reexamining its foundation and continuing to take on new challenges and pursuing innovation, while always taking into account the significant changes taking place in the global economy. Our vision of a *truly global enterprise* is a company that is recognized as being truly global by every stakeholder (including shareholders, creditors, business partners, and society) around the world and supported by a corps of "global talent" who embrace a diverse set of global values regardless of such factors as age, gender, or national origin.

Admiral Matthew Perry from the United States "opened" Japan to international trade, Itoh began to accompany his older brother on sales trips to Osaka and Kyoto. By 1858 the younger Itoh was making his own sales trips, selling cloth to merchants in Okayama and Hiroshima. Two years later, at the age of 18, he established his own wholesale business and worked diligently to expand his small operation.

The 1860s were a time of upheaval and change in Japan. The 264-year-old government of the Tokugawa Shogun was overthrown in 1868 by loyalists of the Meiji Emperor. Itoh's business, however, continued to prosper in spite of the civil war. In 1872 he opened a small shop in Osaka and within five years was one of the largest textile wholesaler/retailers in the city. A branch was opened in Kyoto in 1883, and the Osaka shop was designated the Itoh *Honten,* or "head office."

Chubei Itoh and his nephew Tetsujiro Sotoumi opened a third shop in Kobe in 1885. The Itoh-Sotoumi Company was primarily involved in the exportation of textile goods through *shokan,* or foreign trading agents. The export trade was very profitable, in spite of the *shokan,* who collected large commissions. Profits from export sales were reinvested in the company's domestic operations. Itoh opened a foreign office in Shanghai in an effort to bypass the *shokan* and their commissions. It was a difficult market to enter, however, and the company's representatives lacked the proper skills needed to deal effectively with Chinese

merchants. As a result, the Shanghai office consistently lost money. In 1893 Itoh established Itoh Itomise (Thread and Yarn Store), from which C. Itoh & Company and ITOCHU were directly descended.

## SON TAKES OVER BUSINESS

Itoh died in 1903 and his second son, also named Chubei, inherited the business. The younger Itoh was well trained and proved to be every bit as adept in business affairs as his father.

A few years before, Japan had asserted its political dominance in northeast Asia when it defeated Russia in a war for influence in the region. In particular, Chosen (Korea) became a neocolonial possession of Japan. In 1898 a new *shokan* called Chosenya was established to handle trade between Japan and the Korean peninsula. It was a lucrative and developing market in which Chosenya had a monopoly. In 1905, however, the younger Itoh once again attempted to bypass the middlemen. He posted two company representatives in Korea and later opened a full branch office in Seoul.

Itoh's business ventures on the Asian mainland deteriorated during 1907. In Chosen there was increasing dissatisfaction with the "low quality of Japanese products." On the other hand, representatives in Shanghai found it increasingly difficult to manage exchange rate fluctuations between the gold-based yen and the silver-based Chinese currency. Mismanagement at the Shanghai office became so acute that by 1908 it was sold to its employees and severed from the Itoh company.

The company recovered quickly, due mainly to a rapid increase in domestic trading activity. In March 1910 Chubei Itoh, aged 23, went to London reportedly to study business administration. It is more likely, however, that he spent his time negotiating arrangements with English merchants. He discovered that the *shokan,* who presented themselves as powerful international figures in Japan, were actually small agencies with relatively little influence overseas. Itoh purchased large quantities of high-grade wool and other products directly from wholesalers in London and sent them to his company in Japan. Itoh also discovered that bank loans in London were commonly set at around 2 percent to 3 percent, substantially less than the 11 percent to 13 percent charged by the Yokohama Specie Bank in Japan. Taking advantage of these two factors enhanced Itoh's ability to undersell competitors in Japan and reinvest a larger portion of the company's profits. In 1914, meantime, Itoh reorganized Itoh Itomise under the name C. Itoh & Company. Four years later the company became a public stock company and changed its name to C. Itoh & Company, Ltd.

## KEY DATES

**1858:** Chubei Itoh, company founder, begins linen trading operations.

**1872:** Itoh opens a shop in Osaka.

**1903:** Itoh dies and his second son, also named Chubei, inherits the business.

**1918:** Company becomes a public stock company and changes its name to C. Itoh & Company, Ltd.

**1921:** Serious recession leads C. Itoh deeply into debt; it is forced to restructure and is renamed the Marubeni Company; Daido Trading is created from a division of C. Itoh Trading.

**1944:** Japanese government orders Sanko, Daido Trading, and a subsidiary of Itoh called Kureha Textiles to merge and form a new company, Daiken Manufacturing.

**1949:** SCAP, the military occupation authority, orders Daiken divided into several separate companies, including C. Itoh & Company, Ltd.

**1977:** The Japanese government arranges for the acquisition of Ataka & Co., Ltd., by Itoh.

**1985:** Company takes 40 percent stake in new joint venture, Japan Communications Satellite Co.

**1992:** Company changes its name to ITOCHU Corporation.

**1994:** Company writes off $662 million in nonperforming assets in aftermath of the bursting of the Japanese bubble economy.

**2001:** Marubeni-Itochu Steel Inc. is established.

**2008:** Company acquires a stake in a Brazilian iron ore mining business.

**2010:** Company acquires SolarNet LLC, and, collectively, becomes the largest solar distribution network in the United States.

### WORLD WAR I TO WORLD WAR II

Japan was a victorious nation in World War I and as a result was awarded substantial commercial and military rights in the Pacific. It was a period of tremendous growth for large Japanese companies, particularly the large conglomerates which had become known as *zaibatsu,* or "money cliques." C. Itoh & Company was not considered a *zaibatsu* like Mitsui, Mitsubishi, or Sumitomo. It was, however, a substantial company, engaged in commercial trading at a time when trade had become extremely important to the continued growth of the Japanese economy.

The strong economy and rising demand for textile products transformed the import trading division of C. Itoh virtually overnight. Demand for Itoh's products continued to grow faster than supply, causing prices (and therefore, profit margins) to rise with them. By 1919 the trading division had grown to twice the size of its parent company, and foreign offices had been established in New York, Calcutta, Manila, and four cities in China. As Itoh's volume of trade grew, so did its variety of products. In addition to textile and agricultural products, the company handled machinery, iron and steel products, and automobiles.

Like most economies that experience strong economic reversals during periods of rapid expansion, Japan entered a serious recession in 1920 which adversely affected consumer demand. Due to the fact that C. Itoh was still a relatively small company without the full backing of a *zaibatsu* bank, it was forced to borrow heavily in order to cover its obligations and went deeply into debt. The following year the company reorganized. C. Itoh & Company was restructured and named the Marubeni Company. Another new company called Daido Trading was created from a division of C. Itoh Trading. It had previously been responsible for trade with Southeast Asia and the United States but was ruined when demand for imports disappeared.

All three Itoh companies were forced to lay off hundreds of workers and suspend stock dividends for several years. Their recovery was slow, but gained momentum later in the 1920s. Ironically, these companies experienced their strongest postrecession growth during the worldwide depression of the 1930s. The Calcutta branch, which was closed in 1921, reopened in 1931. In the following years new offices were opened in Australia, Thailand, and Indonesia. It was during this period that the benevolent one-man-rule of Chubei Itoh II was replaced by a more consensus-oriented presidential form of management.

The decade of the 1930s was a difficult period for Japanese business and politics. Right-wing militarists had terrorized their way to power and threatened not only to nationalize the nation's industries but to dominate all of East Asia and the western Pacific. In the short term, the *zaibatsu* and other large companies stood to benefit greatly because they were the primary suppliers of machinery, weapons, and provisions to the growing Japanese military. In the long term, however, these same militarists had pledged to nationalize the *zaibatsu* and other companies. The Itoh companies were only three of hundreds that were placed in the difficult position of collaborating with the military government.

The militarists led Japan into a war against China in 1937 and later against Britain in 1940 and the United States in 1941. That year Itoh merged with Marubeni & Company and Kishimoto & Company to form a new company called Sanko K.K. The concentration of resources was intended to facilitate greater efficiency and conserve limited resources.

Despite the position of Japanese industry and the military, neither had the ability to mobilize or develop new technologies quickly enough to prevent the Allies from turning the war in their favor. Matters became particularly desperate when the Japanese mainland (and its factories) came within range of U.S. bombers. In 1944, as part of an effort to rationalize Japanese industry, the government ordered Sanko, Daido Trading, and a subsidiary of Itoh called Kureha Textiles to merge. The new company, called Daiken Manufacturing, existed for about a year before Japan surrendered.

## POSTWAR REORGANIZATION

After the war, the military occupation authority, Supreme Commander of Allied Powers (SCAP), implemented a complete reorganization of Japanese industry. Many U.S.-style commercial laws were enacted, including an antimonopoly law which outlawed the *zaibatsu*. Although Daiken (Itoh) was not as large as the *zaibatsu*, SCAP ordered it divided into several companies.

When the reorganization was completed in 1949, C. Itoh & Company, Ltd., Kureha Cotton Spinning Co., Ltd., Marubeni Co., Ltd., and a small manufacturer of nails called Amagasaki Nail Works, Ltd., were made independent companies under separate management groups. Both Itoh and Marubeni were given the authority to conduct both domestic and international business. Itoh exported Japanese textile products on a barter basis in return for foreign grain. The trade was stable and profitable, and it enabled the company to establish itself quickly.

In 1950 Itoh trade representatives were dispatched to India, Pakistan, and the United States. The United Nations war effort in Korea necessitated a change in commercial policies in Japan. On short notice Japanese companies, including Itoh, were contracted to supply food, clothing, and other provisions to U.N. forces in Korea. Itoh, which had already established an international network of suppliers, was quickly prepared to meet the sudden increase in business. The company product line, long dominated by textile products, was diversified to include petroleum, machinery, aircraft, and automobiles.

When the Korean War ended in 1952 many of Itoh's military contracts were canceled. The demobilization in Korea caused a serious recession during 1953 and 1954. Hundreds of smaller trading companies were forced into bankruptcy. C. Itoh, however, was larger and better able to endure the poor economic conditions. It later took over the business of the smaller bankrupt companies and continued to expand its product line.

Unlike the former *zaibatsu* groups, the postwar Itoh companies (C. Itoh, Marubeni, and Kureha) did not merge back together. During this period *zaibatsu* groups circumvented many antimonopoly laws by coordinating their individual company strategies through banking groups (called *keiretsu*). C. Itoh was neither a prewar *zaibatsu* nor a member of a postwar *keiretsu* group. During the later 1950s, however, the company accumulated enough capital to begin large-scale lending operations.

## EVOLVING FROM *SOGO SHOSHA* TO HOLDING COMPANY: 1960S–90S

C. Itoh & Company and *keiretsu* group leaders such as Mitsui Bussan, Mitsubishi, and Sumitomo were engaged primarily in trading. They became known as *sogo shosha*, or "general trading companies." C. Itoh experienced strong growth during the 1960s, particularly on the strength of its trading activities. An international information network was created which made the company more responsive to business opportunities around the world.

In the late 1960s Itoh identified an opportunity to develop a nickel and cobalt mine at Greenvale in northeastern Australia. Itoh, in partnership with Australian interests, Mitsubishi, and Nissho Iwai, started the project in 1971. Raw materials from the mine were to be sold to Kawasaki Steel and Nisshin Steel, among others, and used to produce stainless steel.

When the Organization of Petroleum Exporting Countries (OPEC) forced a dramatic increase in the price of oil in 1973, oil-dependent countries such as Japan found themselves seriously vulnerable to inflation and interruptions of supply. C. Itoh recognized this as an area of great opportunity. In coordination with C. Itoh Fuel Company, Itoh invested heavily in the development of new technologies for petroleum production.

In the mid-1970s the Japanese government became concerned about another trading company called Ataka & Co., Ltd., which was nearly bankrupt. Ataka had gained a reputation for mismanagement and inefficiency. It was repeatedly warned by banks and the government to practice greater discipline. When it appeared that Ataka's demise was inevitable, the Japanese government stepped in. In order to prevent the failure of such a large company (Ataka was Japan's tenth-largest trading firm), the government hastily arranged for a major portion of it to be absorbed by Itoh. When the merger was affected on October 1, 1977, C. Itoh & Company moved from being the fourth to the third-largest Japanese trading firm. The merger greatly increased Itoh's interests in steel and chemicals and further reduced textiles to about 20 percent of total sales volume.

In addition to its trading activities, C. Itoh was involved in a number of large industrial projects in the 1980s, acting as a coordinator and providing financial support. Itoh's largest foreign projects were the Hassi-R'Mel natural gas plant in Algeria, a cashmere factory in Mongolia, the Baoshan steel complex near Shanghai (led by Nippon Steel), and the Kaduna oil refinery in Nigeria (with Chiyoda Chemical). Early in 1987, however, Itoh backed out of the Greenvale Mine project when it appeared that demand for nonferrous metals would not recover. The company was also involved in the development of natural resources, including petroleum products and uranium, and metals (despite ending its involvement with Greenvale).

The late 20th century was marked by the steady decline of the traditional *sogo shosha* activities of providing marketing, financial, and distribution services to other companies. Their customers grew more powerful thanks to the help of the trading companies, but as their customers grew in size they increasingly decided to bring in-house the services they had once paid the *sogo shosha* to perform. As noted in a 1988 *Financial World* article, the trading companies were putting themselves out of business.

Under the leadership of president Isao Yonekura, Itoh responded to this fundamental shift by adding to its trading activities longer-term equity investments in joint ventures and affiliates actually producing products and services, thereby shifting from a pure trader to more of an investment holding company. Two of the main areas for the company's investments were the related fields of telecommunications and multimedia. In 1985 Japan Communications Satellite Co. (JCSAT) was formed as a joint venture of C. Itoh (40 percent), Hughes Communications (30 percent), and Mitsui (30 percent). Four years later JCSAT became the first company in Japan to launch and operate a private communications satellite.

In 1991 Itoh and Toshiba Corporation each contributed $500 million to gain a combined 12.5 percent stake in Time Warner Inc.'s movie, television, and cable TV businesses. The partners also formed a joint venture, Time Warner Entertainment Japan Corp., to operate Time Warner's operations in Japan, including home video, movie, and TV program distribution. Itoh and Toshiba each held 25 percent of this venture, with the U.S. firm holding the remaining half. In 1992 C. Itoh & Co. changed its name to ITOCHU Corporation, adopting a transliteration of its Japanese name. At the time of the name change, ITOCHU had held the position as the largest of the *sogo shosha* for several years.

The bursting of the late 1980s Japanese economic bubble led to prolonged difficulties for most of the *sogo shosha*. As a byproduct of the stagnation of their core trading activities, nearly all of the *sogo shosha* had diversified aggressively into financial investments during the speculative bubble, which reached its peak in 1988 and 1989. The trading companies built up large stock portfolios and became hooked on the revenues they could gain through arbitrage (*zaiteku*).

Once the bubble burst, the *sogo shosha* were left with huge portfolios whose worth had plummeted. The companies were forced to eventually liquidate much of their stock holdings. ITOCHU's troubles were even greater because the company had made large investments in the hot Japanese real estate market during the bubble. In fiscal 1994 ITOCHU recorded about $662 million in extraordinary losses to write off insolvent financial and real estate subsidiaries and other nonperforming assets. This led the company to post a net loss of ¥14.13 billion ($137.5 million) for the year.

## CONTINUED DIFFICULTIES LEAD TO NEW STRATEGIC PLAN

The entire decade of the 1990s was a challenging one for the *sogo shosha* not only because of the lingering effects of their overzealous 1980s investments but also due to the stagnant Japanese economy of the early and mid-1990s, the Asian economic crisis that began in 1997, and the Japanese recession that followed the latter. ITOCHU was heavily involved in such troubled nations as Thailand and Indonesia. In late 1997, then, ITOCHU continued to restructure with the disposal or writing off of ¥230 billion ($1.8 billion) in bad loans and nonperforming assets. This led to an even larger loss of ¥91.93 billion ($713.9 million) for fiscal 1998.

Still reeling from its financial difficulties, the company raised additional cash ($1.17 billion) through the sale of its Time Warner stake in three separate transactions in 1998 and 1999. Losses for fiscal 1999 were reduced to ¥34.09 billion ($283 million), but the company did not pay a dividend for the first time in 50 years. By this time, ITOCHU had fallen to the number three position among *sogo shosha*, having been surpassed by Mitsui and Mitsubishi.

Under the leadership of President and CEO Uichiro Niwa, ITOCHU in April 1999 initiated a two-year strategic plan called Global-2000. A key aspect of the plan was the shifting of the company to a holding company structure, with ITOCHU's seven division companies gaining greater management autonomy. Headquarters staff would be slashed from 280 to about 100 and would be responsible only for corporate planning and auditing. In another streamlining move, the company's board of directors would be reduced from 45 members to between 10 and 15. In addition, consolidated subsidiaries would be reduced by about one-third by March 2001, with a goal of increasing the portion of profitable subsidiaries from about 60 percent to 80 percent.

The increased emphasis on profitability was a major shift for a trading company as the *sogo shosha* had traditionally valued market share and sales growth ahead of returns on investments. The newfound pursuit of profits was also evident in the industries ITOCHU targeted for future growth, which included such potentially lucrative fields as information, multimedia, and financial services.

## A NEW MILLENNIUM: FORGING AHEAD

As expected, the company recorded a net loss of ¥88.3 billion for fiscal year 2000. The Japanese economy continued to struggle through the next year. Although the economies of other countries in which ITOCHU operated remained relatively stable, the company reported its overall consolidated results in 2001 remained the same as the previous year for total trading transactions and gross trading profit. Nevertheless, the company's strategic plan showed positive results with significant increases in trading income and net income.

In 2001 ITOCHU joined forces with Automated Power Exchange Inc. to launch Japan's first private Internet-based electric power exchange. That same year, ITOCHU made a deal with the Marubeni Corp. to integrate their steel businesses. The new company was named Marubeni-Itochu Steel Inc. The following year, two U.S. companies, Clark Steel Framing and Western Metal Lath, became part of the newly formed Marubeni Itochu Steel America Inc., which was then renamed MISA. As a result, MISA became one of only two national steel framing and lath manufacturing companies in the United States.

By the end of fiscal year 2003, the company was still facing difficult economic times. Its fiscal earnings declined 26 percent to $167 million on revenues of $4.7 billion. One of the causes, as cited by the company, was

a drop off in sales for the Aerospace, Electronics & Multimedia Company division due to a slump in Japan's IT industry. Stagnant markets and the company's efforts to reduce less profitable transactions also resulted in decreased sales in other divisions, most notably the Plant, Automobile & Industrial Machinery Company, the Energy, Metals & Minerals Company, and the Construction & Realty Division. The company's overall total trading transactions were also adversely affected by the transfer of the company's steel business in the previous fiscal year to the company's affiliate Marubeni-Itochu.

## A NEW PRESIDENT REINFORCES GLOBAL FOCUS

In 2004 the company named a new president, Eizo Kobayashi, who succeeded Uichiro Niew, who was named ITOCHU's chairman. In a profile of Kobayashi for *Japan Inc.,* Jessie Wilson noted: "The impression we received is of a man who has the leadership skills and commitment to lead the $100-billion Itochu forward." Wilson noted later in the article that "talking to both Itochu employees and CEOs of other companies, we heard repeatedly a message of a well-developed business acumen, great people skills, and an element of luck—all key virtues for the CEO of such a massive company in the cut-throat business of international trading."

In 2004 the company also acquired a 4.8 percent stake in a Western Australia ore mine from BHP Billiton and paid $94.4 million for bankrupt men's casual wear manufacturer Raika Co. In addition, the company agreed to market the warehouse management and shipping systems of U.S.-based Manhattan Associates Inc. to businesses in Japan. Although the company had revenues in 2004 that exceeded the $5 billion mark for the first time, the firm still posted a loss of approximately $300 million.

Despite the declines in several key economic indicators over the previous four years, the company's various management reforms helped the company rebound in fiscal year 2005. ITOCHU showed a profit of $723 million on revenues of $5.8 billion. In addition, the company reported a reduction in its net interest-bearing debts by half. As a result, the company began preparing to shift its focus for a more offensive approach to business, including increasing its total assets.

As the company pursued its new approach it announced that the Chinese government had granted permission for ITOCHU, Mitsubishi Corp., and Misubishi Chemical Corp. to jointly produce terephthalic acid (used primarily as a precursor to a polyester compound used in making clothing and plastic bottles) at a new facility in Ningbo, Zhejiang Province. Furthermore, the company began efforts to accelerate investments to develop Indonesia's natural resources and social infrastructure. ITOCHU's president Kobayashi met with Indonesian vice president Jusuf Kalla to present him with a five-year investment plan that included ITOCHU joining forces with Sumitomo Corporationa and others to build Jakarta's first subway system. Other projects included three large power plants, an oil refinery upgrade, and development of coal and liquefied petroleum gas resources.

In 2006 the company formed an agriculture-related production business in the eastern Chinese province of Shandong in conjunction with Sumitomo Chemical and Asahi Breweries. It also became part of a joint venture named Fuel DME Production Co. to produce a potential next-generation fuel called dimethyl ether. The next major move occurred in 2007 with the acquisition of 15 Gulf of Mexico gas fields in a $155 million deal with Range Resources.

A worldwide economic recession that began in 2007 contributed to the company's decline in net income. Much of this loss was attributed to a reduction in the automobile and construction machinery trading transactions. However, the beginning of the next fiscal year saw the company move ahead with its strategic global solar energy strategy. Since 2006, the company had made a number of strategic investments in the area, including acquiring Solar Depot, a California-based wholesale distributor and systems integrator. ITOCHU's next major move in the United States was to acquire SolarNet LLC, making ITOCHU collectively the largest solar distribution network in the United States. This business transaction highlighted the company's continued focus on developing its reputation as a major global enterprise.

*Updated, David E. Salamie; David Petechuk*

## PRINCIPAL SUBSIDIARIES

ITOCHU International Inc. (USA); ITOCHU Latin America S.A. (Panama); ITOCHU Brasil S.A. (Brazil); ITOCHU Europe PLC (UK); ITOCHU Deutschland GmbH (Germany); ITOCHU France S.A.; ITOCHU Italiana S.p.A. (Italy); ITOCHU Middle East F.Z.E. (Bahrain); ITOCHU Australia Ltd.; ITOCHU Singapore Pte. Ltd.; ITOCHU Textile Materials (Asia) Ltd. (Hong Kong); ITOCHU (China) Holding Co., Ltd.; ITOCHU Taiwan Corporation.

## PRINCIPAL DIVISIONS

Textile Company; Machinery Company; ICT, Aerospace, & Electronics Company; Energy, Metals & Minerals Company; Chemicals, Forest Products & General Merchandise Company; Food Company; Finance, Realty, Insurance & Logistics Services Company.

## PRINCIPAL COMPETITORS

Archer-Daniels-Midland Company; Daewoo Group; Hutchison Whampoa Limited; Hyundai Group; Inchcape pic; Jardine Matheson Holdings Limited; Kanematsu Corporation; LG Group; Marubeni Corporation; Mitsubishi Corporation; Mitsui & Co., Ltd.; Nichimen Corporation; Nissho Iwai Corporation; Samsung Group; Sumitomo Corporation; Swire Pacific Limited; TOMEN Corporation.

## FURTHER READING

"Acquisition Gives Itochu Largest Solar Power Distribution Network In US.," *Space Daily*, April 14, 2009.

"ITOCHU to Step up Investment in Indonesia," *AsiaPulse News*, December 12, 2005.

Wilson, Jessie, "The Rise of Eizo Kobayashi: And How Investing Is Becoming Itochu's New Business Line," *Japan Inc.*, January 2005, p. 13.

# ITT Corporation

1133 Westchester Avenue
White Plains, New York 10604
U.S.A.
Telephone: (914) 641-2000
Fax: (914) 696-2950
Web site: http://www.itt.com

*Public Company*
*Founded:* 1920 as International Telephone & Telegraph
*Employees:* 40,200 (est. 2009)
*Sales:* $10.90 billion (2009)
*Stock Exchanges:* New York
*Ticker Symbol:* ITT
*NAICS:* 333911 Pump and Pumping Equipment Manufacturing; 333995 Fluid Power Cylinder and Actuator Manufacturing; 334417 Electronic Connector Manufacturing; 334419 Other Electronic Component Manufacturing; 334515 Instrument Manufacturing for Measuring and Testing Electricity and Electrical Signals; 336399 All Other Motor Vehicle Parts Manufacturing

■ ■ ■

Once known primarily as a telecommunications company, ITT Corporation maintains interests in military technology, fluid technology such as industrial pumping and waste treatment devices, and motion and flow control devices. Since its foundation, the corporation has been lauded as one of the largest and most profitable in the United States and reviled as an emblem of runaway corporate greed. In the 21st century, having passed through a sustained three-decade period of divestments, splits, and mergers, ITT maintains a much lower public profile, primarily focused on its defense and information technology divisions.

## INTERNATIONAL TELEPHONE: 1920–28

When Lt. Col. Louis Richard Sosthenes Behn and his brother Hernand founded the International Telephone & Telegraph Company in 1920, they expected to take advantage of an industry market that barely existed outside of the United States. In 1920 the United States boasted 64 phones per 1,000 inhabitants, while Germany was estimated to have 9 phones per 1,000 inhabitants, Britain 5 per 1,000, and France a mere 3 per 1,000. At that time, three companies, Siemens, Ericsson, and AT&T, dominated what there was of the world market.

Although theirs was a small company, the Behns were well-positioned to compete in the growing international market. They had operated South Puerto Rico Telephone Company since 1905 and Cuban Telephone Company since 1916, and in both cases they used ingenuity and skill to transform inefficient companies into well-run, profitable operations with good service records. Sosthenes Behn's tour of duty with the American Expeditionary Force in World War I (where he gained the rank of lieutenant colonel) set in motion his vision for an international telephone system. Behn intended to achieve this international system via IT&T, which he and his brother Hernand formed in 1920 as the holding company for their existing companies and for those they would acquire.

The way IT&T expanded into the European market provided an example of the way it would conduct business during most of the Behn era. The combined effects of good timing, well-placed connections, and Sosthenes' charm brought IT&T the concession for telephone service in Spain in 1924. Timing was crucial due to the fact that before 1924 IT&T's securities were a questionable issue on Wall Street. However, the company's consistent growth and steadily expanding earnings, coupled with the support of National City Bank, provided Wall Street analysts with a good reason to support IT&T's venture into the Spanish telephone market. Behn provided the rest by placing influential Spaniards on the board of IT&T's new company, CTNE, and charming the appropriate members of the Spanish government.

The Spanish concession, operated by CTNE, furnished IT&T with an entrance into the European market, one that Behn wasted no time in expanding. Upset with the quality of equipment available to him, he began to search for an equipment manufacturing company to purchase. Timing and connections again helped IT&T. In 1925 the U.S. government was pressuring AT&T to divest its overseas operations, which included International Western Electric Company, a European-based manufacturer of telephonic equipment. A National City banker arranged a meeting between Walter Gifford, chairman of bank customers at AT&T, and Sosthenes Behn, which resulted in the sale of the company to IT&T on September 30, 1925, along with temporary use of some of AT&T's patents.

After ITT acquired the Spanish concession and the International Western Electric Company, it entered a period of rapid growth. ITT became one of the most highly valued stocks in the bull market of the period, enabling it to acquire numerous companies, mostly in the telecommunications field. Behn's dream for the international telephone system came closer to reality, and his reputation as a cosmopolitan and shrewd businessman increased.

### DISASTER STRIKES: 1929–45

IT&T had become an international company holding manufacturing companies and operating concessions in France, Germany, Britain, and much of Latin America.

National citizens ran IT&T's subsidiaries in every country with a facility, while corporate headquarters in New York played a passive management role.

The search for additional companies continued, although Behn's acquisition program placed IT&T heavily in debt. The debt seemed manageable in the thriving world economy of the late 1920s, and IT&T continued to be a popular stock despite the fact that a recession would hurt the company. Yet if a recession would hurt IT&T, the Great Depression nearly put it out of business. The debt accumulated during the 1920s was only part of IT&T's problems, as the very nature of the company's business exacerbated its financial difficulties.

In the restrictive trade atmosphere of the early part of the Depression, many foreign nations refused to allow U.S.-based IT&T to repatriate earnings from its subsidiaries. IT&T was therefore deprived of significant revenues and threatened with bankruptcy through much of the Depression, despite eliminating dividends to shareholders. To make matters worse, IT&T lost a good manager when Hernand Behn died in 1933.

At the beginning of World War II, in Argentina, Spain, and elsewhere, IT&T's holdings were in danger of being taken from the company by governments sympathetic to Germany. Profits again became impossible to repatriate. Behn's business acumen enabled him to sell some of IT&T's holdings (in Romania, for instance) and helped avoid having others (particularly SEG and Lorenz in Germany) taken from the company at a time when foreign operations of other major U.S. manufacturers were not treated as well. As much a factor in these matters was Behn's penchant for employing mostly nationals, of whom the head of SEL had some influence with Adolf Hitler. Still, these events earned IT&T the ire of many Americans, and after the war it was one of several companies accused of collusion with Hitler and the Nazi regime, an accusation that would linger long afterwards.

### POSTWAR RESTRUCTURING: 1946–58

IT&T's difficulties in the Depression and World War II made Behn determined to reduce its dependence on its non-U.S. companies. Behn abandoned the focus on the international telephone system and established IT&T's new goal of deriving two-thirds of its revenues from U.S. companies.

However, this goal was difficult to achieve. IT&T had consolidated some operations within the United States in response to the war, centered around a company called Federal Electric, an earlier acquisition.

## KEY DATES

**1920:** Louis Sosthenes Behn founds International Telephone & Telegraph (IT&T) with his brother.

**1924:** IT&T begins telephone service in Spain, its first international market.

**1945:** In the wake of World War II, IT&T is implicated in colluding with the Nazi government.

**1959:** A new era is initiated with the appointment of Harold Geneen as chairman. The company drops the ampersand from its name, becoming simply ITT.

**1963:** Under Geneen's direction, ITT begins an aggressive campaign of acquisitions, averaging one company a month.

**1971:** ITT sees its public image plummet after several run-ins with the U.S. Justice Department over its acquisitions and accusations of political bribery and manipulation at home and abroad.

**1980:** Rand Vincent Araskog becomes ITT chairman and initiates a decade-long program of shedding ITT's many subsidiary companies.

**1992:** The last of ITT's international telecommunication interests are sold off.

**1995:** ITT splits into three companies; ITT Industries carries forward the core company interests of electronics, automotive, and defense products.

**1998:** After a series of mergers and acquisitions, ITT Industries is the sole remaining company with the ITT name.

**2006:** ITT Industries changes its name to ITT Corporation.

**2007:** ITT pleads guilty to violating international arms trafficking laws and forfeits profits from selling night-vision technology.

Federal's electronics and military contracts made it a significant revenue earner during the war, and Behn hoped the company could gain a portion of the postwar market for consumer electronics and durables. Such efforts were mixed at best and, as a result, Behn looked to merge IT&T with one of several large U.S. companies, including Sylvania, Raytheon, the American Broadcasting Co. (ABC), and RCA in order to realize his postwar goal of a company earnings distribution. None of the larger mergers materialized, but those that did, such as Coolerator and Capehart-Farnsworth, drained capital and performed poorly, keeping IT&T's stock low in a bull market.

Such domestic difficulties weakened IT&T and Behn's position as leader. Although IT&T was once again profitable, the dividend was not restored, and stockholders began to challenge Behn's decisions. A boardroom battle for power occurred, which Behn eventually lost, despite having reinstated the dividend in 1951. He remained chairman until he died in 1956, although his power was largely symbolic after 1953.

During this time, the company's emphasis was on overseas operations, although even the European subsidiaries were posting smaller than expected profits. Some observers commented that the three years spanning Behn's death and Harold Geneen's accession at IT&T saw nothing more significant than a change of logo from IT&T to ITT.

## GENEEN'S ACQUISITIONS: 1959–78

If there was a lull in company growth and productivity, it ended in 1959 when Harold Sydney Geneen took over as head of ITT. Geneen's management abilities had been showcased at such firms as American Can, Bell & Howell, Jones & Laughlin, and Raytheon, and at ITT he became almost a synonym for excellence in management. The Geneen method of "Management by Meetings" was popularized and widely imitated.

Geneen had drive, ambition, and seemingly endless energy. He also believed firmly that companies should aim at both short- and long-term growth, not stability. He first reorganized ITT with a management shakeup and thorough cost-cutting measures. In his first five years, over 30 percent of the company's executives were replaced, although in keeping with ITT tradition few were fired. Instead, executives regarded as lacking the necessary skills were worked to the point where they would quit. As one executive remarked, "Nothing matters to him but the job—not the clock, not your personal life, nothing." So many executives would come and go during the Geneen era that ITT was compared to a revolving door, and a *Forbes* magazine reporter even jokingly dubbed the company Geneen University.

Geneen instituted changes he saw as absolutely essential. As he put it, without his changes he wondered "how long it would have gone on before it cracked wide open." This was not an entirely accurate perception for ITT was a growing company, even if it fell short of its earnings potential. Part of the problem stemmed from the Behn legacy, including the almost complete lack of cohesion among subsidiaries. Geneen worked to correct this and increased headquarters' role in the affairs of subsidiaries through yearly meetings and required reports.

In 1963 ITT began to make a significant number of acquisitions. Geneen promoted the notion of a diversified company as a strong company, one able to weather downturns in a particular sector of the economy through its holdings in other sectors. Such strength made a diversified company the best vehicle for corporate growth. In theory, assets could be transferred to the appropriate divisions, and the company would be less dependent on individual clients as well as cyclical markets.

Geneen's purchases emphasized U.S. operations over European ones, with an aspiration that 55 percent of ITT's revenues come from U.S. subsidiaries. When he set out, the ratio was 60/40 in favor of international operations. Several factors influenced his decision, including French and British advocacy of nationalization of certain ITT subsidiaries, Cuban leader Fidel Castro's expropriation of ITT's Cuban Telephone, and intensifying competition in the European telecommunications market.

Geneen achieved his objective through the frenetic acquisition of 350 companies from 1959 to 1979. In the early 1960s, acquisitions averaged one per month. Purchases included Avis, Inc. (car rentals), Continental Baking Co. (Wonder bread, Twinkies), Sheraton Corp. of America (hotels), Grinnell Corp. (vending machines, foodservice), Bobbs-Merrill (publishing), Levitt Homes (suburban residential construction), Eason Oil Company (heating oil), W. Atlee Burpee Co. (seeds), Pennsylvania Glass Sand Co., and many others. Geneen's cost-cutting measures and his complementary acquisition program helped ITT meet his first five-year goal, namely, to double earnings and income. In this way, ITT became a billion-dollar corporation in 1962, and by 1969 it had quadrupled in size. Under Geneen, ITT's revenues increased from $800 million to $22 billion, and the conglomerate became the fourth-largest employer in the United States with 368,000 employees on its payrolls.

## A CRACKED PUBLIC IMAGE

ITT made its move into the U.S. market at the same time as a number of other companies, part of a merger trend that due to its size and complexity caused a large amount of consumer distrust. In a decade, the 1960s, that would become increasingly anti-big business, multinationals and especially conglomerates became targets of frequent attacks in the nation's press, fueled by

books such as *Up the Corporation*. Some people thought that ITT symbolized what was wrong with big business.

Questionable actions in the United States and abroad did nothing to allay those perceptions. The first of a stunning series of setbacks for ITT came in 1968, when the conglomerate lost its bid to acquire the American Broadcasting Company when the U.S. Justice Department challenged the takeover on antitrust grounds. The Justice Department made several more moves against ITT, including litigation attempting to prevent its takeover of Hartford Fire Insurance in 1970. ITT agreed to divest assets equal to those of Hartford's, including Avis, Levitt, Canteen, and Grinnell, and pledged not to acquire any companies with assets over $100 million until 1981. Much negative publicity arose from these confrontations with the Justice Department.

ITT's image with the U.S. public was further damaged in 1971. That year, ITT was accused of bribing Republican officials into locating the 1968 Republican National Convention at the Harbor Beach Sheraton in San Diego. At the same time, Chilean officials accused ITT of interfering in that country's elections. The corporation allegedly hoped to prevent election of a leftist president who threatened to nationalize ITT's business interests there.

These incidents alone would have cast a shadow over Geneen's final years as head of ITT. But to make matters worse, of his hundreds of acquisitions, only the Pennsylvania Glass Sand Company was an immediate source of profits for ITT. Additionally, the purchase of Levitt Homes would eventually prove a disaster. Writing in 1992 for *Business Horizons,* Danny Miller compared Geneen's managerial style to Icarus of Greek mythology, for both characters' greatest assets led to their demise.

## THE GREAT WINNOWING: 1979–94

In 1978 Geneen, aged 67, stepped down from the chair of ITT, although he remained on the board until 1983. His immediate successor did not remain long and was soon replaced with the little-known Rand Vincent Araskog. Araskog was a West Point graduate who had worked at Honeywell before joining ITT in 1968. The new leader was promoted from within ITT and was expected to be Geneen's pawn, but this proved a misconception. At first, Araskog boldly declared that ITT would return to its telecommunications roots and compete directly with AT&T in the domestic market. However, economic realities, including the massive debt racked up during Geneen's tenure, soon thwarted that plan. In 1979 ITT had over $4 billion in debt, an amount more than 40 percent of its capitalization. In response, Araskog embarked on what *Financial World* later called "a gigantic corporate garage sale the likes of which the world will probably never see again."

From 1979 to 1983, Araskog sold off businesses worth $200 million each year and used the proceeds to pay down ITT's debt. By the end of 1984, the company had divested 69 subsidiaries totaling nearly $2 billion. Araskog did his job so well, in fact, that his slimmed-down, cash-rich corporation became one of the first high-stakes takeover targets of the 1980s. While fighting off hostile overtures from corporate raiders, Araskog continued to liquidate ITT's holdings, selling more than 100 subsidiaries by 1986. The CEO's focus on retaining a profitable core of market leaders in insurance, finance, and automotive and industrial engineering conspicuously left out ITT's historical base of telecommunications. In 1986, after long negotiations, Araskog sold a majority stake in ITT's overseas telecommunications business to Cie Générale d' Electricité (which later became Alcatel Alsthom Compagnie Générale d' Electricité) for $2 billion to form a joint venture, Alcatel N.V. Abandoning the U.S. portion of the business precluded a $105 million write-off that year.

By the end of the decade, ITT's debt was below 30 percent of capital, and Araskog was credited with paring the company down to a profitable core. The CEO was paid generously ("lavishly," in *Business Week*'s 1994 estimation) for his achievements, receiving more than $5 million in salary alone in 1989. However, Wall Street seemed not to appreciate the changes at ITT. The corporation's stock trailed Standard & Poor's 500 index by 36 percent from 1979 to the end of 1991. Institutional investors, especially the California Public Employees' Retirement System (Cal-PERS) revolted against ITT when, in 1990, Araskog's salary doubled to $11.4 million in spite of a 20 percent decline in the corporation's stock price and a 30 percent drop in income from operations. Under fire from Cal-PERS, Araskog and ITT's board agreed to tie executive compensation to stock performance.

From 1992 to 1994, ITT's stock price rose 46 percent, to nearly 85 cents a share, driven in part by new asset sales. In 1992 the company sold off its 37 percent interest in Alcatel to its partner for $3.6 billion. However, even after over a decade of pruning, ITT was still one of the most diversified companies in the world.

It was clear that if ITT was ever going to truly focus on core industries, it would have to continue its process of cutting back. But the era of divestments was over. By 1995 the final phase of Araskog's plan was ready to go into effect. In June of that year, ITT split into three companies. These were ITT Corp., ITT Hartford, and ITT Industries. Each new company took a select slice of the old company's earning pie. ITT Corp. comprised the entertainment branch, absorbing the hotels, casinos, and information services subsidiaries. ITT Hartford took the company's insurance assets. ITT Industries took the electronics, industrial, and defense technology branches.

## AND THEN THERE WAS ONE: 1995–2005

An appreciation of the sheer size of ITT prior to its three-way split can be gained by the fact that when *Business Week* magazine ranked the Top 1000 companies of 1996, all three ITT spin-offs were in the upper 400 of the list. Each company had a market value in excess of $3 billion. If ITT had not split up, the combined worth of all three companies would have been $15.5 billion.

Over the next two years, however, two of the three ITT spinoffs would cease to exist in the forms they were spun off in. ITT Hartford was the first to go, changing its name to Hartford Financial Services Group Inc. in May 1997. ITT Corp. seemed to be on a winning trajectory initially. As owner of the international hotel chain Sheraton, it was well placed to remain competitive in the hospitality industry. In 1996 ITT Sheraton formed a joint venture with an Israeli tourism agency, and the same year ITT Sheraton's Park Tower opened in Buenos Aires. At 181 rooms, it was the largest luxury hotel in Latin America. In 1997, however, ITT Corp. was the target of a hostile takeover attempt by Hilton Hotels Corp. To prevent the takeover, ITT Corp. split again into three new companies. In February 1998, a severely weakened ITT Corp. was purchased by Starwood Hotels & Resorts for $10.2 billion.

The acquisition of ITT Corp. left ITT Industries the sole holder of the ITT name a mere three years after the big split. However, the company did not go the way of its brethren and set about carving a niche for itself in its three industries of defense/military technology, fluid management, and motion and flow control. The latter category covered everything from beverage machines to shock absorbers to aircraft. In 1996, for example, ITT finalized a contract with Mercedes Benz to produce systems such as antilock brakes and traction control devices for a line of their mid-priced sport utility vehicles.

The jewel in ITT's crown, however, was its Defense division, which supplied the U.S. government with high-tech devices for use in its armed forces. For example, in July 1999 ITT beat out defense contractor Raytheon and won a lucrative $46.5 million government contract to develop an experimental communication system for use by infantry soldiers. The following March, the company inked another government deal, this one worth $7.5 million, to produce 31 remote transmitters for use on board special operations helicopters. In 2001 the company landed a $13.4 million contract to upgrade the Air Force's fleet of B-52 bombers.

By 2002 the company's sales had grown by 6.6 percent over the previous year to nearly $5 billion. Net income was up a whopping 37.3 percent that year. With the money flowing in, ITT looked towards getting back into the acquisitions game. The company acquired PCI Membrane Systems, Wedeco AG Water Technology, and Shanghai Hengtong Purified Water Development Co. Ltd. in 2003 and 2004. In 2004 the company's largest acquisition in some time took place with the $725 million purchase of Eastman Kodak's remote sensor technology division. Profits and revenue continued to grow by leaps and bounds, and in 2005 ITT landed its biggest government contract yet, as it was awarded $681 million for the maintenance of the U.S. military's communications networks in Africa and Asia.

## NIGHT VISION AND BEYOND: 2006–10

In 2007 ITT's forward progress stumbled over its Night Vision division. The origins of the debacle stretched back two decades to the original ITT Corporation, which had won a lucrative government contract to manufacture night vision goggles for the military. Unfortunately for ITT, little distinction was apparently made regarding precisely which nation's military was to receive the goggles, or so the U.S. government alleged. In April 2007 ITT pled guilty to charges of violating International Traffic in Arms Regulations.

The gravity of the charges was reflected in a statement by Julie Meyers, assistant secretary of Homeland Security, to *Business Week* magazine: "No other major defense contractor has pleaded guilty to a violation of laws restricting the export of arms and military technology." ITT was slapped with a $100 million fine for selling night vision technology to China. ITT agreed to allocate half of the amount of the fine to develop new night vision technology to offset the technological secrets given away to foreign militaries. ITT CEO Steven Loranger issued a statement reiterating that although the "settlement relate[d] to the actions of a few individuals in one of our 15 business units, we regret very much that these serious violations occurred." As a further penalty, ITT was required by the government to provide tracking information for every package that left its warehouses.

The potential fall-out from the night vision case could have cost ITT dearly. As of 2010, roughly half its business was coming from government contracts. That year, however, ITT won yet another night vision contract, this time valued at nearly $20 million. With global defense spending on the rise, ITT looked secure in its dominant market niche position as high-technology defense supplier. Likewise, its fluid management division was strongly positioned to take advantage of predicted water shortages and increased waste management across the developing world. Having weathered the recession of 2008 and 2009 with relatively few problems, ITT appeared poised to carry the legacy of its namesake forward into the 21st century.

*April Dougal Gasbarre*
*Updated, David Larkins*

## PRINCIPAL SUBSIDIARIES

Astro-Optics Labs; Carbon Fuel Company; Darlington, Inc.; EDO Artisan, Inc.; Gilcron Corporation; Goulds Pumps, Inc.; ITT Cannon International, Inc.; ITT Fluid Technology International, Inc.; ITT Waste & Wastewater U.S.A. Inc.; ITT Water Technology, Inc.

## PRINCIPAL DIVISIONS

Defense & Information Solutions; Fluid Technology; Motion & Flow Control.

## PRINCIPAL COMPETITORS

Ebara Corporation; Lockheed Martin Corporation; Northrop Grumman Corporation; Raytheon Company; United Technologies.

## FURTHER READING

Araskog, Rand, *The ITT Wars: An Insider's View of Hostile Takeovers.* New York: Beard Books, 2000.

Burns, Thomas S., *Tales of ITT: An Insider's Report.* Boston: Houghton Mifflin, 1974.

Epstein, Keith, "ITT to Plead Guilty in Export Case; The Defense Contractor Will Forfeit $100 Million for Selling Night-vision Technology to China," *Business Week Online,* March 28, 2007.

Hammonds, Keith H., "Carving ITT into Three Slices," *Business Week,* June 26, 1995.

"ITT Industries Wins Contract Worth Up to 681 Mln Usd from US Army," *AFX International Focus,* December 15, 2005.

Sampson, Anthony, *The Sovereign State of ITT.* New York: Stein and Day, 1973.

Sobel, Robert, *ITT: The Management of Opportunity.* New York: Truman Talley, 1982.

# KBC Group N.V.

**Havenlaan 2**
**Brussels, B-1080**
**Belgium**
**Telephone: (+32) 2 429 85 45**
**Telephone: (+32) 2 429 65 01**
**Fax: (+32) 2 429 81 60**
**Web site: https://www.kbc.com**

*Public Company*
*Founded:* 1935 as Kredietbank
*Employees:* 54,185 (2009)
*Total Assets:* €5.310 billion ($7.222 billion, 2009)
*Stock Exchanges:* New York; Euronext; Brussels; Luxembourg
*Ticker Symbol:* KBC
*NAICS:* 522110 Commercial Banking; 522291 Consumer Lending; 523920 Portfolio Management; 524114 Insurance Carriers

∎∎∎

One of Europe's foremost financial groups, KBC Group N.V. (KBC) offers a wide range of bank, insurance, and asset management services to over 12 million customers in Europe, Asia, and the United States. KBC controls three underlying companies: KBC Bank, KBC Insurance, and KBL European Private Bankers, all of which comprise numerous branches and specialized subsidiaries. As one of the top three financial institutions in Belgium, KBC provides services and products to retail customers, private banking clients, and small and medium-sized companies. It is the country's leading brokerage firm and boasts its flexibility in responding to market trends due to its ability to switch between classic deposit, life insurance, and bank-related investment products according to demands in the market.

Since its creation in 2005, KBC has functioned as an integrated bancassurance group. Bancassurance, also known as the Bank Insurance Model, refers to the sale of insurance products and financial services through one organization. Typically, an insurance company sells its products through bank sales channels. For instance, a bank that gives a mortgage loan to a customer usually requires that the borrower purchase homeowners' insurance. If the financial institution is a bancassurance group, then the borrower can buy that policy directly from the bank. Insurance companies write and administer their own policies, and the commission from insurance sales is shared between the insurance company and the bank.

KBC operates primarily in the sectors of traditional banking, European private banking, insurance, and holding company activities. Traditional banking functions include loans, deposits, savings certificates, leasing, payments, and securities within Belgium, while European private banking manages banking and insurance activities outside of the country. Insurance deals in personal and group life insurance, nonlife insurance, and reinsurance. Holding company activities handles marketing, logistics, and communication services.

## COMPANY PERSPECTIVES

Through our customer-friendliness, efficiency, enterprising spirit, and capacity for innovation, we will provide the best solutions for our customers, earn the loyalty of our employees, guarantee a high return to our shareholders, and contribute towards the economic, social, and cultural development of the community to which we belong.

In all our endeavors, we will distinguish ourselves from other institutions by the professionalism, determination, and unity we demonstrate in pursuing our goals.

## GROWTH: 1930S–70S

Officially formed on March 5, 2005, the history of KBC Group N.V. begins long before then, as it had been associated with the Kredietbank of Belgium. Kredietbank, established in 1935, was the only Belgian financial institution under Flemish control to survive the worldwide Great Depression of the 1930s. The bank specialized in short-term loans to small and medium-sized companies in northern and central Belgium for several years before expanding its operations. Post-World War II development in the 1940s enabled the bank to increase its number of branches throughout Belgium, as well as look for opportunities to develop a strong business network outside of the country. Enjoying the steady growth of Belgium's economy during the postwar years, Kredietbank became the first Belgian bank to offer medium-term fixed interest bonds. In addition, the bank debuted a passbook savings account, a type of account well-suited for customers who had infrequent transactions, in order to compete with rural banks.

In the 1960s Kredietbank's business strategy was centered on extending its network of branches, along with introducing such popular customer services as international traveler's checks, bank cards that replaced checks, and credit cards. Kredietbank was the first Belgian bank to install an automated teller machine (ATM) and, working with two other banks, developed a number of ATM banking services. Beginning in 1966, Kredietbank concentrated on building a more visible international presence by opening offices in New York and Mexico City. The bank would go on to establish branch offices in many other areas, including South Africa, the Cayman Islands, the United Kingdom, Spain

(Madrid), Australia (Melbourne), Iran (Tehran), and Japan (Tokyo).

## IMPLEMENTATION OF CHANGES: 1970S–2005

A decade of global expansion and an increase in domestic dealings initiated a change in Kredietbank's organizational structure. In 1978 Kredietbank implemented a management system comprising three separate divisions. One of these divisions focused on the bank's commercial business, while the second division provided special financial services. This second division was controlled by Almanij, a holding company considered to be Kredietbank's parent company because it had been Kredietbank's majority shareholder since the bank's creation. The third division used the Kredietbank S.A. Luxembourgeoise as a center for international merchant and investment banking, offering customized financial services through a network of subsidiaries.

During the 1980s, a worldwide economic downturn slowed Kredietbank's international growth. Nevertheless, the bank continued to offer customers new products and services, including investment options in mutual funds and gold. Kredietbank also introduced the Tele-KB, a technology that allowed commercial customers to conduct their banking business remotely. Via a telecommunications system, the TELE-KB gave clients the capability to access the bank's computers both to make electronic transactions and to receive up-to-date personal account information, as well as general economic and financial data.

In 1998 Kredietbank merged with CERA bank and ABB-insurance, Belgian companies whose origins could be traced back to the 1890s. The result of the merger was the KBC Bank and Insurance Holding Company. That same year, KBC made headlines when it launched its integrated bancassurance model, which was a relatively new approach to financial and insurance services at the time. From 1999 to 2005, KBC renewed its efforts to build its business presence in Central and Eastern Europe. Its first acquisition under the name KBC was of ČSOB, a bank serving the Czech Republic and Slovakia, in 1999. KBC continued to extend its position as an international bancassurance organization over the next six years by acquiring banks and insurance companies in Hungary, Poland, Slovakia, and the Czech Republic. By 2005 KBC had become one of the top three forces in Belgium's finance industry.

On March 2, 2005, KBC Bank and Insurance Holding Company merged with Almanij to form the KBC Group N.V. At the time of the merger, the new KBC Group announced that its principle entities would

## KEY DATES

**1935:** The Kredietbank of Belgium is formed.

**1988:** Kreidietbank CERA, a Belgian agricultural co-operative bank, merges with a Belgian insurance company (ABB) to form the KBC Bank and Insurance Holding Company.

**1999:** KBC expands its presence in Central and Eastern Europe by acquiring ČSOB, the bank of the Czech Republic and Slovakia.

**2005:** KBC Bank and Insurance Holding Company merges with its parent company, Almanij, to form KBC Group N.V.

**2006:** KBC sets up KBC-Goldstate Fund Management in a joint venture between KBC Asset Management and Goldstate Securities, a Chinese company.

**2007:** KBC acquires ING's shares of International Factors Belgium, which is renamed KBC Commercial Finance.

**2009:** The Belgian government gives a loan guarantee of €22.5 billion ($30.6 billion) to help KBC offset losses on collateralized debt obligations (CDOs).

be KBC Bank, KBC Insurance, Kredietbank S.A. Luxembourgeoise, KBC Asset Management, and Gevaert, an imaging technologies company. According to a press release issued at the time, the merger was expected "on the one hand, to achieve complete unity of strategy, capital and management, enhance visibility and increase the ... liquidity of the KBC, and, on the other, to streamline the organizational structure, harness synergies between Group companies, and ensure management continuity." KBC executives believed that the merger would boost the group's profile both domestically and globally "by joining private banking, private equity and real estate expertise more closely into the already successful retail bancassurance and corporate banking models."

### EXPANSION: 2005–08

In the months following the merger, KBC added a network of European banks to its group, signing agreements governing cross-border payment processing and acquiring companies in regions in Germany, the Netherlands, and France, among others. In July 2005 KBC's subsidiaries Gevaert and KBC Investco joined to form KBC Private Equity, which became the group's

sole provider of private equity capital. KBC Group was named Belgium's "Bank of the Year" in 2005 by the *Banker,* a monthly international financial affairs publication.

In 2006 KBC instituted a new management structure, one that created the five business units that would carry the company into the next decade: Belgium, Central & Eastern Europe and Russia (CEER), Merchant Banking, European Private Banking, and Shared Services & Operations. Each of these units had its own management strategies and objectives. Except for KBC Bank N.V., which was divided between the Belgium Business and the Merchant Banking Business Units, all of KBC's branches and subsidiaries were assigned to one specific business unit. The Belgium Business Unit oversaw the retail and private banking and insurance activities of KBC Bank N.V. and KBC Insurance, as well as the activities of various subsidiaries located in Belgium. The CEER Business Unit managed of all retail bancassurance and merchant banking in Central and Eastern Europe and in Russia, while KBC's Merchant Banking Unit encompassed companies that provided services to corporate customers worldwide, with the exception of those managed by CEER. The European Private Banking Business Unit controlled the activities of both the KBL European Private Bankers Group and the life insurance company VITIS Life. All four of these business units received products, support, and services from divisions that comprised the Shared Services & Operations Business Unit.

KBC's business dealings in 2006 continued to focus on the international market. The company signed a cooperation agreement with China Export & Credit Insurance Corporation (SINOSURE), which enabled both entities to offer a wide range of finance options to customers exporting goods from China. In November of that year, KBC further involved itself in the Chinese financial market when it helped establish KBC-Goldstate Fund Management, a joint management firm venture between KBC Asset Management and the Chinese company Goldstate Securities. KBC strengthened its position in France with the acquisition of Aballea Finance, a wealth management firm. To simplify its legal structure amidst all the acquisitions, mergers, and selling of investments, KBC Group N.V. merged with Gevaert so that the group's structure consisted of a holding company (KBC Group N.V.) and three operating companies: KBC Bank, KBC Insurance, and KBL European Private Bankers.

In keeping with its policy of expansion, KBC spent much of 2007 conducting business in foreign markets. In March KBC entered the Romanian market when it agreed to purchase a majority stake in Romstal Leasing and Swiss Capital, a brokerage firm. In addition to taking control of Equitas, an online securities brokerage in Hungary, KBC assumed full ownership of A Banka, a Serbian bank, and Hipobroker, a Serbian securities broker. KBC Commercial Finance was created after KBC acquired ING's shares of International Factors Belgium. Companies in Russia, Bulgaria, and Latvia were also bought in full or in part by KBC in 2007.

## EFFECTS OF WORLDWIDE RECESSION

As it celebrated its 10th anniversary in 2008, KBC was honored with several industry recognitions. In July it received a *Euromoney* Award for Excellence as the best bank in Belgium. *Euromoney* awards are the most prestigious in the global banking industry. KBC was also nominated by the *Banker* as the "Best Bank" in both Belgium and Hungary and shared the prize for "Best Corporate Social Responsibility Report" with Umicore, a materials technology group headquartered in Belgium. The company was also proud to launch its new corporate Web site in 2008, which would be named the "Best Corporate Web site in Belgium" by the Belgian Association of Financial Analysts in 2009.

Despite these accomplishments, however, KBC experienced setbacks directly related to the worldwide recession of 2008. The group posted its first-ever quarterly loss in October after Moody's lowered the ratings of the company's collateralized debt obligations (CDOs), high-risk securities backed by bonds, loans, and other assets. KBC's group ratings were downgraded first by Standard & Poor's and then by Fitch. In December, Moody's once again substantially lowered the ratings of CDOs, and the interest rate on traditional savings accounts and mortgages was lowered in response to European Central Bank rate cuts. Facing such economic difficulties, KBC announced that it would take steps to save costs internally. At the end of the year, the company had a 2008 income of €4.827 billion, almost €5 billion less than its 2007 revenue of €9.802 billion.

In 2009 KBC, reeling from the repercussions of the recession, reached an agreement with the Flemish Regional Government concerning government funding to increase the group's capital. The company spent the year undergoing major changes in its operations, taking measures to reduce the group's risk profile, to review risk management, and to further increase its capital. In November, the European Commission approved the strategic plan proposed by KBC and the Belgian government, which allowed the company to receive a loan guarantee of €22.5 billion ($30.6 billion) from the Flemish Regional Government to help the company offset its losses on CDOs.

In 2010 KBC began to implement its new strategic plan for the upcoming years. One of the biggest changes was in the company's expansion and acquisition policies. Replacing purchasing activities would be the scaling down or sale of noncore activities, which analysts predicted would reduce KBC's risk-weighted assets by around 25 percent. Although the group's primary business would still involve providing bancassurance services to small and medium-sized companies, individual banking and insurance operations would be responsible for meeting minimum profitability requirements. Also, KBC would concentrate its efforts in its "core countries" of Belgium, the Czech Republic, Slovakia, Hungary, Poland, and Bulgaria. KBC believed that the overall plan would give the company the flexibility to handle potential financial downturns without a devastating impact on its capital.

*Alicia Elley*

## PRINCIPAL SUBSIDIARIES

Antwerp Diamond Bank N.V.; ČSOB a.s. (Czech Republic, Slovakia); KBC Bank; KBS Financial Products; KBC Insurance; KBL European Private Bankers (99.9%): Merck Finck & Co. (Denmark).

## PRINCIPAL DIVISIONS

Belgium; Central & Eastern Europe and Russia (CEER); Merchant Banking; European Private Banking; Shared Services & Operations.

## PRINCIPAL COMPETITORS

BNP Paribas; Deutsche Bank AG; Dexia SA; HSBC Holdings plc; ING Groep N.V.

## FURTHER READING

"Belgium's KBC Quits Reverses," *American Banker,* February 26, 2010, p. 9.

"Company Spotlight: KBC Group," *MarketWatch: Financial Services,* March 2007, p. 29–34.

"Destroy, Rebuild," *Business Europe,* November 16, 2009, p. 2.

Dombey, Daniel, "Vermeiren to Step Down at KBC," *Financial Times,* November 27, 2002, p. 16.

Inter-Alpha Group of Banks, "KBC Group," inter-alpha.com, April 21, 2010.

Jolly, David, "Belgium to Aid KBC Once Again," *International Herald Tribune,* May 15, 2009, p. 16.

Legrand, Corinne, *New Trends in World Bancassurance.* Seattle: Milliman, Inc., 2004.

# KfW Bankengruppe

Palmengartenstrasse 5-9
Frankfurt am Main, D-60325
Germany
Telephone: (49 69) 7431-0
Toll Free: (866) 654-7564
Fax: (49 69) 74 31-2944
Web site: http://www.kfw.de

*Government-Owned Company*
*Founded:* 1948
*Employees:* 4,265 (2009)
*Sales:* EUR 1.127 billion ($1.4 billion 2009)
*NAICS:* 52111 Monetary Authorities-Central Bank

■ ■ ■

KfW Bankengruppe (KfW) is a promotional bank serving the German domestic economy and a development bank for various developing countries. Some 80 percent of its equity capital is owned by the German federal government, with the remainder owned by the German Lander (individual German states) governments. On behalf of the Federal Republic of Germany, the KfW finances investments for numerous projects to develop social and economic infrastructure, industry, and environmental protection in more than 100 countries. The KfW raises the funds for its programs in the domestic capital market, and in foreign capital markets through its wholly owned subsidiary KfW International Finance Inc. in the United States. Governed by the German Banking Act, loans taken out and bonds and notes issued by KfW, as well as loans to third parties guaranteed by KfW, are considered equivalent to obligations of the Federal Republic of Germany itself. KfW

ranks among Germany's largest banks. Headquartered in Frankfurt am Main, the bank also has a branch office in Berlin.

As a bank with economic-policy objectives, KfW has three primary areas of interest. First, it provides purpose-tied, long-term loans that finance projects at favorable fixed interest rates for German small and medium-sized enterprises, for the protection of the environment, structural adjustment of certain economic sectors, regional development purposes, or other government policy objectives. Second, the company provides long-term loans to German firms mainly for export to developing countries, transportation projects, and international project finance loans for securing raw materials for German industry. The company's third focus is to help launch projects at home and abroad in which Germany has considerable interest, primarily in developing and newly industrialized countries as well as in Central and Eastern Europe. This assistance is made through loans and grants within the framework of the Federal Republic of Germany's Policy of Financial Cooperation with developing countries.

## FINANCING GERMANY'S RECONSTRUCTION: 1948–53

As KfW's original name, Kreditanstalt für Wiederaufbau (reconstruction loan corporation), suggests, the KfW was founded to finance urgent reconstruction projects after World War II. It became well known as the financial institution which allocated Marshall Plan funds in Germany. After World War II had ended, the U.S. and British military governments discussed the possible structure of a new banking and monetary system in

## COMPANY PERSPECTIVES

As a bank, KfW Bankengruppe (KfW) has a public mission. Although it is not an institution with political responsibilities, its mission is to serve the public interest through banking means. Its public mandate cannot be rigidly defined. In the course of its sixty-plus-year history, the KfW repeatedly had to—and did—adapt rapidly and flexibly to the frequently changing political and economic requirements with an efficient decision-making procedure not subject to a long, bureaucratic chain of command.

Germany. While the U.S. military government preferred the idea of decentralizing the German banking system by creating a "Bank of German States" with central banks on the state level, the British military government insisted on establishing a central financial institution for the German reconstruction.

Finally in the summer of 1947, after almost a year of negotiations, the Allies agreed on a compromise which included the establishment of a central "Loan Corporation" to finance reconstruction projects. In June 1948 all the parties agreed on the main principles for this institution, and the Anglo-American military government assigned the German authorities the task of setting it up. In October 1948 the "KfW Law" was passed by the German Economic Council and went into effect on November 18, 1948. In 1949, the year in which two separate German states were founded, the KfW started its business operations as a corporation under public law directly answerable to the federal government.

It took the young Federal Republic of Germany about five years to rebuild the country after World War II. The German economy grew at about 8 percent per year. The KfW contributed to this effort significantly, mainly by channeling funds from the Allied forces into industries that were key in attracting economic growth and by long-term export financing.

KfW's first chairman, Marshall Aid advisor Dr. Otto Schniewind, calculated in 1948 that about DEM 8.3 billion was needed to fund urgent reconstruction projects, but finding sources of funding proved extremely difficult. Foreign capital markets were out of reach, the new German Deutschmark had lost 14 percent of its value in only six months, and it was feared that massive government deficit spending would weaken trust in the new currency. KfW's first attempt, in the fall of 1949, to raise money on the limited German capital market by issuing long-term bonds failed miserably. In the end, the KfW was left with the counterpart funds from the Allies, including Government and Relief in Occupied Areas (GARIOA) and the Marshall Fund money. GARIOA counterparts were food and commodity imports financed by the U.S. defense budget before the Marshall Aid program, announced by U.S. Secretary of State George C. Marshall in June 1947, was actually carried out. However, those sources were usually connected with far-reaching ideas on the part of the givers about how they were to be used.

In the reconstruction years, the KfW allocated about half of its credit volume directly to companies, while the other half was issued through the borrower's "house bank." Tens of thousands of individual farmers received individual loans as blanket credit lines from two specially designated banks for farmers. However, upon request of the Allies, counterpart funds were granted only by the German federal government, which also evaluated the applicants and even scheduled individual loans.

Between 1949 and 1953, the KfW concentrated on providing financing for sectors crucial to economic reconstruction which needed a large amount of financing and industries with limited access to funds, such as the highly regulated energy and housing sectors. More than half of the KfW's credit volume in those years went into coal mining, power generation, and steel, which helped manage the rising demand for energy and raw material by other industries. A total of DEM 1.1 billion was provided mainly for larger manufacturing companies in the chemical, cement, and other raw materials industries and for export-intensive machinery building and mechanical and electrical engineering firms. About DEM 286 million went into the shipbuilding industry. By 1953 the KfW had channeled DEM 623 million into residential construction. Another DEM 500 million, about 20 percent of KfW's total credit volume in those years, was directed into the farming and food industries.

## SECURING SUSTAINABLE GROWTH: 1954–60

By 1954 the KfW had basically fulfilled its mission to allocate financial aid for German reconstruction. However, the German government did not want to dissolve an organization that had gained a great deal of expertise on the support of economic development that was politically desirable. KfW board member Dr. Herbert Martini, who had assisted Schniewind in carrying out Marshall Aid programs and authored a big part of the KfW Law, showed brilliant strategic foresight and

## KEY DATES

**1949:** KfW starts its business operations as a corporation under public law directly answerable to the federal government.

**1950s:** KfW concentrates on providing financing for sectors crucial to economic reconstruction such as the highly regulated energy and housing sectors.

**1961:** KfW becomes involved in a cofinancing project with the World Bank and the International Development Organization.

**1971:** Company introduces the ERP equity participation program to help strengthen the equity capital base of small and medium-sized businesses.

**1992:** KfW starts coordinating Germany's economic consultation activities for Central and Eastern European countries.

**2001:** KfW acquires DEG-Deutsche Investitions- und Entwicklungsgesellschaft mbH from the Federal Republic; company issues first €5 billion bond under its new € Benchmark Programme.

**2003:** Deutsche Ausgleichsbank, based in Bonn, is merged into KfW.

**2006:** KFW launches "Housing Environment, Growth" initiative to fund measures that save energy in building rehabilitation and new construction.

**2008:** Company posts EUR 2.743 billion loss as a result of global financial crisis.

initiative in opening new sources of funding and new tasks for the KfW. He convinced older, skeptical KfW board members (as well as politicians in Bonn) that the KfW could be developed into a multipurpose financial institution that acted in the public interest of Germany.

After the London Debt Agreement of February 27, 1953, had established the amount of international debt owed by Germany to the United States, the European Recovery Program (ERP) special fund was set up by the German government. Administered by the former Ministry for the Marshall Plan, which was now called Ministry for Economic Cooperation, the ERP special fund soon became KFW's foremost source of capital, totaling over DEM 4.6 billion between 1954 and 1960. Between 1958 and 1960 the KfW also raised almost

DEM 1 billion by establishing long-term bonds and new medium-term fixed-rate notes shortly called Kos (the abbreviation for "Kassenobligationen") on the German capital market.

Most of the funds provided through the KfW in the second half of the 1950s were aimed at supporting structurally weak regions such as the Saarland (which joined the Federal Republic after French occupation ended in 1957), the regions bordering East Germany, and isolated West Berlin. Beginning in 1954, the KfW administered the "Berlin Contract Financing" program fueled by the ERP special fund which offered investment loans for West German companies who contracted with suppliers in West Berlin. Beginning in 1960 the KfW offered liquidity assistance to commercial banks in West Berlin. The KfW opened its Berlin office in 1960 to carry out those programs, and by the end of the year the loans issued reached a total of DEM 728 million. Almost DEM 500 million was earmarked by the KfW for environmental protection projects, primarily sewage disposal and water purification. Another DEM 664 million was channeled through the KfW by the European Coal and Steel Community (ECSC), granted to promote the German coal, iron, and steel industries between 1954 and 1960.

Export financing was another important field of activity which the KfW had begun in the early 1950s. At that time, commercial banks only offered short-term loans to German exporters. The federal government ordered the KfW to finance middle- and long-term German export risks for up to 24 months. To secure its own share of this risky but potentially promising business, the private banking sector formed the Ausfuhrkredit Aktiengesellschaft (AKA) in spring 1952. The AKA took over the DEM 600 million rediscount facility, 14 specialists, and all the contracts previously managed by the KfW. However, it soon became clear that the AKA was refusing to back exports to politically unstable countries such as Turkey and Yugoslavia, and that it was not interested in financing export risks for more than four years. Realizing the need for longer-term export financing, the KfW offered AKA-follow-up loans with practically no risk to exporters. The so-called Hermes credit programs were backed financially by the German government and managed by the Hermes Kreditversicherungs AG, one of the world's leading export credit agencies. In the following years, the KfW was able to raise significant funds for export financing to developing countries, mainly from public insurance companies and also, after the Deutschmark became freely convertible in 1958, from free capital markets. Up until 1959, export financing was granted to German suppliers. From 1959 the German government also offered credits to foreign buyers tied to German exports through the KfW, the

"Hermes guarantees." In 1960 KfW's DEM 265 million for export financing was granted for exports of power stations and industrial plant to such countries as Pakistan, Mexico, Chile, Spain, and Greece, with 58 percent of the total issued as buyer loans.

By the end of the 1950s, the KfW had transformed itself from an interim distribution agency for postwar reconstruction funds into a financial institution supporting the German economy in gaining and sustaining a leading position in the world markets. Owned jointly by the federal and Lander governments, its new long-term funding basis was established through the ERP special fund as well as through KfW bonds in the capital market. While the KfW operated with some 50 employees in 1949, that number increased to about 150 in 1951 and reached about 180 in 1960. At the same time, KfW's balance sheet total rose from under DEM 1 billion in 1949 to about DEM 5 billion in 1954.

## NEW TASKS AS A DEVELOPMENT BANK: 1961–70

On August 16, 1961, when the Wall was being erected in Berlin, the KfW Law was amended to add a new task to the bank's agenda in addition to investment and export financing. This new task was financing projects in foreign countries, development aid projects in particular. At the same time the KfW's capital structure was altered. The federal government took over 80 percent of KfW's equity capital which was increased from DEM 1 million to DEM 1 billion, while the Lander, now including the Saarland and Berlin, held 20 percent.

In the 1960s the KfW made a massive entrance into the international arena. As early as in 1958 the KfW had granted loans to foreign countries such as Iceland, Sudan, and India to enable them to pay German exporters quickly. A legendary program was the secret "Operation Business Partner" under which the KfW channeled about DEM 630 million in covert loans to Israel between 1961 and 1965 on behalf of the German government. The program arose after the Israeli prime minister, David Ben Gurion, met German chancellor Konrad Adenauer at the Waldorf Astoria Hotel in New York City in March 1960 and requested financial help. Following German official diplomatic recognition of Israel in 1965, Israel was given official capital aid.

One of KfW's international credit programs was aimed at securing raw material supplies for the German economy, which was traditionally highly dependent on imports. In 1960 the KfW granted its first financing loan of DEM 208 million to the Lamco iron ore project in Liberia. Other loans were given to mining companies

in South Africa. A special five-year mineral oil promotion program was launched in 1964. For larger international projects in which more than one party had a stake, the KfW worked with other financial institutions, pooling resources and distributing the risk. In 1961 the KfW became involved for the first time in a cofinancing project with the World Bank and the International Development Organization in the Roseires dam project in Sudan, organizing a mixed financing loan amounting to DEM 175 million. In another cofinancing project in Bolivia, KfW became partners with the Inter-American Development Bank and the United States Agency for International Development in 1962. Four years later the bank cofinanced textile projects in Cameron and Chad with the Deutsche Gesellschaft fur wirtschaftliche Zusammenarbeit (DEG), a German economic development organization, and the European Investment Bank (EIB). Two particularly noteworthy commercial German mixed financing projects were the UNINSA steelworks in Spain and the Atucha I nuclear power station in Argentina, to which the KfW contributed DEM 450 million and DEM 175 million, respectively.

The change of ministers in Bonn under four chancellors in the space of a decade resulted in a high turnover rate on the KfW's board of directors. However, new tasks meant growth. Its staff rose from over 200 in 1961 to more than 400 in 1966, and reached over 500 in 1970. The balance sheet total grew steadily during that decade, from about DEM 11 billion in 1961 to approximately DEM 23 billion in 1970. In 1961 the KfW granted about DEM 2.6 billion to domestic and international organizations. At the end of the decade KfW's financial commitments totaled more than DEM 3.5 billion. The bank's financial resources during the 1960s were composed of DEM 6.5 billion from the German government, with about three-quarters of that coming from the ERP special funds, and DEM 4.9 billion raised on the capital market from the issue of long-term bonds and bearer debt securities.

## FUNDING GERMAN BUSINESS AND FUND-RAISING ON WALL STREET: 1971–89

The KfW started the 1970s with a fundamental restructuring program. First of all, its main focus was redirected towards the domestic economy. The collapse of the Bretton Woods international monetary system based on fixed interest rates in the early 1970s, as well as extensively increasing oil prices caused by the newly formed OPEC cartel, created difficult domestic and international market conditions for the German economy. To serve German industry better, new departments were set up which specialized in promotional programs for particular industry sectors which also included the proven export financing and commodity loan programs. KfW's international activities, including development aid and other financial cooperation projects, were served by departments organized by country or geographical region. In 1974 Helmut Schmidt, then German finance minister and later German chancellor, became chairman of the board of directors at KfW.

In order to promote domestic investment the KfW developed its own low-interest loan programs which were not funded by the German government as in the reconstruction years but by funds raised on the capital market. The share of the ERP special fund in KfW's total financial funding for the promotion of domestic projects dropped from 32 percent in 1971 to 15 percent in 1989. The new programs were targeted at small and mid-sized businesses which, because of their size, did not traditionally have access to the international capital markets to satisfy their financial needs. The KfW offered long-term investment loans with favorable interest rates to this clientele through its so-called "M-programs" by refinancing the other bank loans that borrowers had to apply and be approved for. The M-programs encouraged investments aimed at energy saving, environmental protection, and innovation, and their annual volume grew from DEM 500 million in 1971 to DEM 6 billion in 1989. Another program introduced in 1971, the ERP equity participation program, helped strengthen the equity capital base of small and medium-sized businesses. It was supported by the German economics ministry, as was a cyclical stimulation program launched jointly with the federal government in 1981 to encourage the development of new energy technologies with a budget of DEM 5.4 billion. In 1978 the KfW granted its first loan in a foreign currency. In succeeding years a growing part of its business was conducted in foreign currencies.

Besides KfW's activities for small and mid-sized businesses, the bank also supported large German companies by cofinancing certain projects of high importance. These included a conveyor belt built by Krupp for the transportation of phosphates stretching over 100 kilometers through the Spanish Sahara, as well as the Bosporus bridge in Istanbul which connected Asia with Europe. Other projects included the Atucha II nuclear power station in Argentina, to which KfW contributed loans worth DEM 1 billion, and the Channel Tunnel connecting Great Britain with continental Europe. International capital aid and financial cooperation projects were increasingly directed towards social infrastructure.

A particularly noteworthy international aid project received financial support from the KfW in fall 1975 when Poland was granted a loan of DEM 1 billion to facilitate the migration of ethnic Germans to the Federal Republic. A major project which served commercial goals was the Airbus project. The Airbus, a civilian jumbo jet developed in the 1960s by a consortium of European aircraft manufacturers, had to break into the competitive world market dominated by North American firms such as Boeing, Douglas, and Lockheed. In 1976 the KfW granted Airbus loans to airlines in Korea, India, and South Africa. Two years later the KfW cofinanced a major deal with Eastern Airlines, the first Airbus order from a U.S. airline.

In order to sustain its ambitious programs, the KfW was constantly looking for new sources of funding. One of those new sources came in the form of partners from Saudi Arabia who had been able to accumulate significant wealth in oil. In 1975 the KfW raised its first loans against borrowers' notes from the Saudi Arabian Monetary Agency (SAMA), mainly due to the personal effort of management board member Alfred Becker. In the mid-1980s the KfW took another crucial step towards new fund-raising opportunities when it applied for an international credit rating. For its domestic 6 percent DEM bond, backed by the institutional liability of the Federal Republic of Germany, KfW was rated "Triple-A," the highest rating possible, by the agencies Moody's and Standard & Poor's in 1986. Two years later the KfW was admitted by the U.S. Securities and Exchange Commission as the first German financial institution to issue bonds on the U.S. capital market. KfW International Finance Inc., headquartered in Wilmington, Delaware, started doing business in 1988 by issuing its first bonds, worth $500 million, on Wall Street. As a result of these efforts, the KfW raised funds worth DEM 17.4 billion on the capital markets in 1989, compared with DEM 2.4 billion in 1971.

## REUNIFICATION AND GLOBAL CHALLENGES: 1990–99

In the 1990s the KfW, a child of World War II, had to deal with the war's ultimate aftermath. After the fall of the Berlin Wall in 1989, a large portion of the financing offers were directed at projects aimed at rebuilding the East German economy. As early as March 1990 the KfW opened an office in Berlin for the first time since its previous one closed at the end of 1974. During 1990 the bank launched various programs, such as a start-up program for companies owned nationally by the soon to be dissolved German Democratic Republic (GDR, known informally as East Germany), a program for mid-sized East German firms, a municipal loan program for the new East German Lander, and a housing modernization program. German reunification took place on October 3, 1990, and by the end of that year the KfW's financial commitments to the new East German Lander reached DEM 4.2 billion, and over two-thirds of all investment loans channeled into the domestic economy went there.

However, the biggest deal to that time in the history of the KfW was made when the German government agreed to spend DEM 7.8 billion in subsidies on the construction of new homes in the Soviet Union for officers of the USSR army leaving the former East Germany. Over half a million Soviet soldiers and civilians stationed in the GDR in 1989 had to be transferred back to the Soviet Union by the end of 1994. In December 1992 German chancellor Helmut Kohl agreed to spend additional DEM 550 million to cofinance this ambitious project. More than 45,000 dwellings, together with the necessary technical and social infrastructure (from power stations to playgrounds), were built in the Soviet Union in only four years. Other KfW programs were launched to give former members of the Soviet army a civilian professional training, and to enhance living conditions for ethnic Germans in the former USSR. In 1992 the KfW also started coordinating Germany's economic consultation activities for Central and Eastern European countries. In the following years coordination agencies were opened in Moscow, Kiev, and Minsk. In 1996 the KfW granted a DEM 1 billion loan to the Russian foreign trade bank for financing projects of mutual interest.

In 1994 the KfW merged with Staatsbank Berlin, the central bank of the former GDR. Effective October 1, 1994, the federal finance minister transferred the assets and liabilities of the Staatsbank Berlin to the KfW. After the merger the bank's equity capital was raised to DEM 7.23 billion and its staff grew to 1,615. KfW's sectoral business was reorganized and an advisory council for promotional measures in the new Lander set up. With the year 1998 two amendments of the German Banking Act went into effect which placed the KfW on a level with the federal government as a borrower, and the government became legally liable for funds raised by the KfW and for associated derivatives business.

## INCREASING EUROPEAN AND WORLDWIDE EFFORTS: 2000–03

As KfW moved into the 21st century, it focused on fulfilling one of its newer missions, namely to provide more support within the context of the European Union (EU). By 2001 the bank was offering financing to small and medium-sized enterprises in eight European countries. Furthermore, the company supported almost all EU candidate countries in establishing their own promotional banks. The company also started its new EUR Benchmark Programme with the market introduction of the first EUR 5 billion bond issued under the program.

KfW issued a second EUR 5 billion bond in 2001. The company started 2002 with a EUR 5 billion five-year benchmark bond issue followed by two three-year, EUR 5 billion bond issuances. For the second year running, KfW was named borrower of the year by *EuroWeek*. In addition to its long-term funding volume increasing from EUR 39 billion in 2001 to EUR 52 billion in 2002, the company also began to rely on the dollar as its most important source of funds instead of the Euro.

"KfW has continued to be one of the true strategic global borrowers," Stuart McGregor, head of the frequent borrower syndicate at Merrill Lynch in London, told Anousha Sakoui and Seb Boyd in an article for *EuroWeek*. "Following on from its amazing success in 2001, it was not only able to widen its investor base but has truly broken into the underlying government investor base in Europe and the domestic dollar bid in the U.S."

In 2003 KfW established the wholly owned, independent banking subsidiary KfW IPEX-Bank to offer project, structured, and export finance services. In addition to existing locations in Sao Paulo, Bangkok, Ankara, and Beijing, the move included new representative offices in London, New York, and Paris. Worldwide, the bank came to conduct all market activities of KfW done on commercial terms. For example, in 2005, the bank granted a long-term investment load of $133 million to Volkswagen Mexico S.A. in Puebla to revamp the existing plant for production of the company's new Jetta model. By 2008, however, the European Commission expressed concerns about unfair competition due to KfW's benefit of having federal loan guarantees. As a result, KfW ended up making IPEX Bank legally and financially independent.

## NEW INITIATIVE, ECONOMIC CRISIS, AND REORGANIZATION: 2006–09

In 2006 KfW, on behalf of the German government, launched the "Housing Environment, Growth," initiative. The initiative primarily funded building rehabilitation measures that lead to energy savings and the construction of new, low-energy homes. The highly popular initiative resulted in promotional loans totaling EUR 32.9 billion for modernization measures over the years 2006 and 2007. KfW would go on to invest 20 percent of its entire financing volume in national and international environmental projects. In 2008 the company's Housing and Environment group committed EUR 33.8 billion for housing and environmental protection projects in Germany.

The subprime mortgage crisis in the United States that led to a worldwide economic downturn beginning in 2008 also had repercussions for KfW. The company led the rescue of one of the first European banks to be hit by the crisis, the industrial lender IKB. However, German prosecutors opened an investigation into bank executives who may have acted criminally in allowing KfW to transfer EUR 319 million to the U.S. investment bank Lehman Brothers on the very day it declared bankruptcy. "The investigation has been set up to establish whether executives breached their fiduciary duties—the legal relationship of trust—by failing to prevent the transfer when knowledge of Lehman's liquidity problems were already in the public domain," wrote David Gow in an interview for the *Guardian Online* Web site.

No charges were formally filed, but 2008 was still a rough year for the company. KfW posted EUR 2.743 billion loss as a result of the global financial crisis. In response, in early 2009 KfW began reorganizing its business areas. Under the new structure, the company conducted its business in six major areas. KfW Mittelstandsbank (KfW SME Bank) focused on small and medium-sized enterprises and other commercial clients. KfW Privatkundenbank (KfW Private Client Bank) focused on private clients, and KfW Kommunalbank (KfW Municipal Bank) was responsible for public clients, such as municipalities. Export and project finance remained in the hands of KfW Ipex Bank while KfW Entwicklungsbank and Deutsche Investitions- und Entwicklungsgesellschaft mbH oversaw promotion of developing and transition countries. The final area of business focus emphasized the financial markets, which comprised KfW's treasury, funding, securitization, and other capital markets-related activities.

In 2009 total commitments of export and project finance amounted to EUR 8.9 billion compared with EUR 17.6 billion in 2008. This significant decrease was principally due to investment plans being postponed by companies in Germany and abroad, which resulted in reduced demand for loans. In addition, due to the generally increased market risks resulting from the global economic and financial crisis, KfW IPEX Bank's lending policy became more selective.

## DOMESTIC MARKET BOOMS

In terms of the German domestic market, 2009 saw KfW provide EUR 50.9 billion for industry, the environment, housing, and education in Germany, up from the previous year sum of EUR 45.4 billion. Furthermore, in the areas of trade and industry, KfW made EUR 23.8 billion available, primarily targeting small and medium-sized enterprises. Environmental investments for the year were also up 12.5 percent from the previous year to EUR 19.8 billion.

The company's future plans focused primarily on following through on the company's missions to offer support to encourage sustainable improvement in economic, social, and business conditions. KfW was also chosen in 2010 to be the arm through which Germany would provide its share of the European Union's rescue package for the economic crisis in Greece, primarily in the form of loans.

*Evelyn Hauser*
*Updated, David Petechuk*

## PRINCIPAL SUBSIDIARIES

KfW International Finance Inc. (USA); KfW IPEX-Bank GmbH; Deutsche Investitions- und Entwicklungsgesellschaft mbH; Technologie-Beteiligungs-Gesellschaft mbH; Finanzierungs- und Beratungsgesellschaft mbH; Deutsche Energie-Agentur GmbH (26 %).

## PRINCIPAL COMPETITORS

Bayerische Landesbank; Deutsche Bank Aktiengesellschaft; WestLB AG.

## FURTHER READING

Gow, David, "Kfw in Frankfurt: Police Raid German's 'Dumbest Bank,'" guardian.co.uk, October 22, 2008.

Sakoui, Anousha, and Seb Boyd, "E.On and KfW Buck Market Trend," *Euroweek*, February 14, 2003, p. S6.

"The World's Safest Banks 2009," *Global Finance,* October 2009, p. 80.

# Kiewit Corporation

**3555 Farnam Street**
**Omaha, Nebraska 68131**
**U.S.A.**
**Telephone: (402) 342-2052**
**Toll Free: (866) 206-4220**
**Fax: (402) 271-2939**
**Web site: http://www.kiewit.com**

*Private Company*
*Founded:* 1884 as Kiewit Brothers
*Employees:* 15,000 (2009 est.)
*Revenues:* $9.985 billion (2009)
*NAICS:* 212111 Bituminous Coal and Lignite Surface
Mining; 236210 Industrial Building Construction;
236220 Commercial and Institutional Building
Construction; 237310 Highway, Street, and Bridge
Construction; 237110 Water and Sewer Line and
Related Structures Construction

■ ■ ■

Once called Peter Kiewit Sons' Inc., Kiewit Corporation
is one of the largest construction and mining companies
in the world. Although considered to be one of the
major producers of coal in the United States, Kiewit's
primary source of revenue comes from its general
contracting business. Construction accounts for over 80
percent of its sales, followed by mining and
telecommunications. A closely held, employee-owned
company that has eschewed publicity throughout its
existence, Kiewit nevertheless has gained notoriety and
enjoyed considerable success by constructing many of

the country's highways, bridges, dams, tunnels, public
utility facilities, and defense installations.

## THE EARLY YEARS: 1884–1931

The roots of Kiewit stretch back to 1884 when Peter
Kiewit, the son of Dutch immigrants who had settled in
Iowa, struck out on his own and opened a masonry
business in Omaha, Nebraska. By 1912 two of Kiewit's
six children, George and Ralph, had joined the business,
and the company became Peter Kiewit & Sons. Having
added general contracting to its business, Peter Kiewit &
Sons completed small construction projects for Omaha
residences and businesses. After the death of the elder
Kiewit in 1914, George and Ralph took control of the
company. The company was renamed Peter Kiewit's
Sons.

By 1920 the youngest of the Kiewit children, also
named Peter, left Dartmouth College in his freshman
year and joined the company as a foreman. After several
years the young Kiewit, who would eventually run one
of the largest construction companies in the nation,
began estimating, bidding, and supervising entire
projects. He landed the first million-dollar contract for
the company, the construction of Omaha's Livestock
Exchange Building.

In 1930 Peter Kiewit suffered the obstruction of a
blood vessel resulting from the chronic inflammation of
his veins, a condition called phlebitis. His doctors
informed him that he would be a semi-invalid for the
rest of his life. Meanwhile family members began to pull
out of the company, a move begun by George Kiewit in
the mid-1920s. It appeared that the Kiewit legacy,

## COMPANY PERSPECTIVES

Innovation, hard work, and integrity. These are the keys to Kiewi's success. Kiewit is one of North America's largest and most respected construction and mining organizations, as well as one of the largest employee-owned firms in the country. For over 125 years, we have delivered world-class solutions to projects of every size, in every market. No project is too challenging or unique, too big or small. Our goal for every project is the same. Build it safely, on time, on budget and with no surprises.

Kiewit is successful because our people have the ability and desire to build exciting and challenging projects. Kiewit people possess a drive to excel and a willingness to take on new and unique responsibilities. We have initiative. We explore innovative ideas. We seek better solutions. We are enthusiastic, hardworking, and committed to quality and excellence.

nearly 50 years old, was at an end as Peter Kiewit remained confined to a hospital bed for nine months. The next year, however, only a few months after leaving the hospital, Peter Kiewit formed a company, named in honor of his father, called Peter Kiewit Sons' Company.

## BUILDING A CONSTRUCTION COMPANY: 1930S–50S

With total assets of roughly $100,000, Kiewit decided to expand into heavy construction, hoping to win contracts for the construction of highways, bridges, dams, and tunnels. The first of Kiewit's many gambles, the decision proved to be fortuitous. By moving in the direction of heavy construction, Kiewit placed the company in a position to win many of the large construction projects that characterized the construction industry of the 1930s.

Kiewit's first project in this arena, a Texas road-building contract, was not a tremendous success. He was unable to complete the work on schedule and had spent half of his working capital by the time the job was completed. The project was a valuable learning experience, however. By the time President Franklin D. Roosevelt's New Deal public works program began soliciting bids for Public Works Administration projects, Kiewit had honed his bidding and scheduling abilities. During this era of increased, federally supported construction, Kiewit's projects included a canal and

reservoir for the Loup River Public Power and Irrigation District in Nebraska and a similar project near the North Platte river. The budget for these two contracts exceeded $3 million.

The profits gained through Public Works Administration projects during the 1930s provided a stable foundation for the company, although by 1940, with crews working in seven or eight states, Kiewit was still considered a small contracting company. It had, however, assembled a cadre of young men with the ability to undertake projects of formidable scope. This pool of talent proved valuable during the construction boom ignited by World War II, which provided the economic stimulus to dramatically increase Kiewit's size. Its first large defense project was the construction of the cantonments at Fort Lewis, Washington, for $8 million. This initial foray into defense contracts, the first of many to be awarded to Kiewit, was followed by the construction of Camp Carson in Colorado for $43 million and military installations in Alaska for $35 million. In all, Kiewit completed nearly $500 million worth of World War II projects, placing the company among the nation's biggest builders.

The end of the war did not signal the end of Kiewit's involvement in military contracts. In 1950 the U.S. Corps of Army Engineers approached Kiewit for assistance in a joint venture to construct bomber airplane and housing installations in Greenland. Known as "Operation Blue Jay," the project required the importation of 5,000 workers to build the facilities that later became Thule Air Force Base. In 1952 Kiewit was awarded a $1.2 billion Atomic Energy Commission contract to build a uranium plant in Portsmouth, Ohio. The project, which at that time represented the largest construction contract the government had ever given a single builder, demonstrated the strides Kiewit had made since its first experience with heavy construction in Texas 20 years earlier. The plant was completed six months ahead of schedule for $268 million below the original estimate. By the end of the decade, Kiewit had gained a reputation as the contractor able to build large facilities, no matter where they might be located. In 1958 the U.S. Army awarded Kiewit a $5 million contract to build Alaska's first nuclear facility. A year later Kiewit crews began the construction of two radar stations on the Greenland ice cap for a $13 million U.S. Defense Department contract.

## BECOMING AN INDUSTRY GIANT: THE 1960S

Multimillion-dollar contracts had quickly become the norm for Kiewit, but the company still continued to

# KEY DATES

**1884:** Peter Kiewit opens a masonry business in Omaha, Nebraska.

**1912:** Company becomes Peter Kiewit & Sons.

**1930s:** Company, now Peter Kiewit's Sons, successfully bids on several Public Works Administration projects.

**1950:** The U.S. Corps of Army Engineers approaches Kiewit for assistance in a joint venture to construct bomber airplane and housing installations in Greenland.

**1958:** The U.S. Army awards Kiewit a $5 million contract to build Alaska's first nuclear facility.

**1970:** Kiewit's coal mining operations experience a boom in production.

**1971:** The company is awarded a $50 million contract by the U.S. Army to begin preliminary work on building facilities at Malmstrom Air Force Base in Montana for the Safeguard anti-ballistic missile program.

**2001:** Kiewit is recognized as the largest federal highway contractor for the year; the company receives the same recognition again in 2002.

**2004:** The company is awarded one of the largest highway contracts in U.S. history; the $1.35 billion joint venture project involves rebuilding 17 miles of interstate highway in Salt Lake City, Utah.

**2008:** The ownership structure of the company changes when stock is held in a company employee ownership plan; Kiewit is no longer required to file financial reports with the SEC.

take on smaller jobs. While the massive uranium plant in Ohio was being constructed, another Kiewit crew worked in Wyoming to complete a $2,000 paving contract. It was Peter Kiewit's reasoning that the smaller projects provided excellent training for his project supervisors. A mistake made on a small project could prove costly, but a mistake made on a multimillion-dollar project could prove disastrous. Accordingly, young supervisors were initially given smaller contracts to oversee. If they demonstrated the ability to complete a project on schedule successfully and, preferably, under the estimated budget, they were then given the opportunity to undertake larger contracts.

Kiewit believed in giving his project mangers almost full control over their projects, but by no means did he allow the reins of the company to be taken completely out of his hands. To ensure that Kiewit projects were progressing on schedule, he would often travel to job sites and supervise the proceedings from a distance through binoculars. A competitive atmosphere was created in which employees could quickly rise to the upper echelon of Kiewit management, and especially productive employees were rewarded with Kiewit stock. Peter Kiewit's approach to the construction business and to his employees, aside from striking some as overbearing, produced remarkable results. Under his watchful eye, the company had evolved from a small, family-operated business into a giant in the construction industry.

By the 1960s, the company had developed into an almost self-subsistent organization. Kiewit owned over 40 corporations involved in nearly every facet of enterprise related to construction and day-to-day operations. Global Surety & Insurance Co. handled the medical and health policies for Kiewit employees, while another company provided them with life insurance. Other subsidiaries leased earth-moving equipment and quarried rock and gravel, while still others mined coal to supply public utility facilities. By subcontracting and supplying much of its own construction operations, Kiewit was able to schedule different phases of a project and limit cost overruns. Consequently, the bidding for contracts could be done much more precisely and, as a result, profits were increased.

Unlike the early 1930s, when few companies were capable of fulfilling the large-scale Public Works Administration contracts, by the mid-1960s, the competition for large construction contracts had become fierce. Although many cities required the construction of urban transportation systems, highways, bridges, tunnels, and public utility facilities, the volume of work was outpaced by the number of heavy construction companies vying for the contracts. This increased competition placed even more importance on the ability of a construction company to bid a price that would win and still earn a profit. Often construction companies were forced to bid at cost then hope that the price of materials would drop sufficiently to realize a profit.

Kiewit, however, had learned through trial and error how to make the gamble of estimating a project less risky. Groups of Kiewit engineers were known to occupy entire floors of hotels near possible job sites while they astutely figured costs. Kiewit had suffered serious losses in some of its ventures, as evidenced by the company's construction of a dam and power facilities in California's Sierra Nevada mountains for the

Sacramento Municipal Utility District. A miscalculation in the amount of soil needed to be excavated from the site eventually caused the project to be completed nearly a year behind schedule and millions of dollars over budget. However, such experiences served as lessons for future projects, and the wisdom built up over the past 30 years allowed Kiewit to remain in the black during a time when many big construction companies lost money.

Construction projects during the 1960s continued to focus on areas in which Kiewit had expertise. The U.S. Air Force awarded the company a $68 million contract in 1961 for the construction of Minuteman intercontinental ballistic missile launch bases near Minot Air Force Base in North Dakota. The same year Kiewit, along with four other general contracting companies, won a $40 million contract to construct a 300-mile paved highway in Afghanistan for the U.S. Army Corps of Engineers. Two years later Kiewit shared, in another joint venture, a $51 million contract for the construction of the Wells hydroelectric dam on the Columbia River in Washington State. Among other projects, Kiewit crews completed an $80 million contract for the Portage Mountain Dam in Vancouver, British Columbia, and a section of Toronto's subway system. In addition, Kiewit also undertook extensive construction of federal highways during the 1960s, winning contracts for more than half a billion dollars over a five-year period, an amount twice as much as any other contractor.

In 1962 Peter Kiewit, who normally shied away from publicity, surprised many observers by purchasing the World Publishing Co., publisher of the *Omaha World-Herald,* Omaha's daily newspaper. Vying with newspaper magnate Samuel I. Newhouse, Kiewit sought to keep ownership of the newspaper in Omaha. In a last-minute bid, Kiewit offered $400,000 more than Newhouse and purchased the newspaper, its production plant, KETV television station, and a medical building, for $40.5 million.

## GROWTH AND CHANGE: THE 1970S

In 1970 Kiewit's coal mining operations experienced a boom in production. Growing public concern over air pollution had persuaded utility and manufacturing companies to seek cleaner burning types of coal. The low sulphur content of the coal mined by Big Horn Mining Co, a Kiewit subsidiary located in a small Wyoming town aptly named Kleenburn, generated less pollution and became a highly sought-after variety of coal. Before air pollution became a general concern, Big Horn had shipped a few carloads at a time, but by the early 1970s three trains were shipping 60 to 65 cars of coal each week to such utility companies as Chicago's Commonwealth Edison Co. and Kansas City Power & Light Co. Kiewit's rate of coal production was further augmented when another of its subsidiaries, Rosebud Coal Sales Co., signed a joint agreement to mine low-sulphur coal in Montana. Producing over five million metric tons of coal annually, Rosebud Coal supplied steam-electric generating plants in the Rocky Mountain and Midwest areas. The company gained an even greater share of the coal market in 1976, when Black Butte Coal Co., a joint venture with Rocky Mountain Energy, landed contracts to supply three million tons of coal annually to Idaho Power & Light Co. for 25 years and to Commonwealth Edison Co. for 20 years.

In addition to experiencing dramatic growth in its coal mining concerns, Kiewit's construction operations continued to garner business. In 1971 the company was awarded a $50 million contract by the U.S. Army to begin preliminary work on building facilities at Malmstrom Air Force Base in Montana for the Safeguard antiballistic missile program. A year later, the army awarded an additional $110.9 million for the project, which entailed the construction of a wide array of facilities, including roads, fences, buildings, and a complex of underground concrete and steel missile silos. In 1978 Kiewit won yet another contract from the army for $245.3 million to build a power plant at the Bonneville lock and dam in Washington State.

In 1979, after nearly half a century of presiding over the operations of Peter Kiewit Sons', Peter Kiewit died. His immediate successor, Robert Wilson, died soon after of heart surgery complications, and Walter Scott, Jr., was named chairman, president, and chief executive that same year. The son of Kiewit's first chief engineer, Scott had joined Kiewit as an engineer after he graduated from Colorado State University.

Scott quickly took over where Peter Kiewit had left off by landing two giant contracts. The first was for the $426 million Ft. McHenry tunnel under Baltimore's harbor, while the second involved the construction of $400 million worth of facilities for the Washington Public Power Supply System. After this initial success, Scott directed the company toward several other large contracts during the early 1980s, including a $208 million dam and hydroelectric plant for Canada's Saskatchewan Power Corp. and a $129 million hydroelectric plant for the Alaska Power Authority.

## A DECADE OF DIVERSIFICATION: THE 1980S

By 1983, however, high interest rates had begun to severely limit the number of large public building projects. The U.S. Army Corps of Engineers, a major customer of Kiewit's throughout its existence, had not initiated any civil projects in the previous four years. Sensing the growing trend away from giant construction projects, Scott began to lead Kiewit toward further diversification and the pursuit of smaller construction jobs. That year the company acquired Empire Savings, Building & Loan Association, the largest state-chartered savings and loan in Colorado, for $65 million. The following year Kiewit and financier David H. Murdock purchased Continental Group Inc., a packaging, forest products, insurance, and energy concern, for $2.75 billion. Kiewit initially owned 80 percent of Continental, but fully acquired the company in 1985 after purchasing Murdock's stake. Continuing to diversify, Kiewit invested in MFS Communications, a local phone service provider, and purchased Life Insurance Co. of Virginia the following year for $557 million, augmenting the insurance holdings of the former Continental Group, now renamed KMI Continental Inc.

After enlarging the breadth of its investments, the company was reorganized in 1986 to better reflect the more diverse nature of its businesses. Peter Kiewit Sons' Inc., as the parent company, would provide management, administrative, and financial services to its three business groups, which were the Kiewit Construction Group, Kiewit Mining Group, and Kiewit Holdings Group.

By the end of the decade, roughly two-thirds of Kiewit's sales came from Continental Can Co., the major packaging component of the Continental Group acquisition. Nonetheless, Kiewit had sold off many of Continental's subsidiaries for a considerable profit, and as the company entered the 1990s it searched for a purchaser of its remaining unrelated holdings. Kiewit found a buyer for Continental Can in 1991, and the company returned to a more concentrated pursuit of its specialty, construction. By 1993 the average construction contract was for $5.3 million, with a typical year bringing in 200 to 300 contracts.

## COMMUNICATIONS, CONTRACTS, AND CONTROVERSY: 1991–2005

During the mid-1990s, the company sold one communications company and started up another. In 1995 Kiewit spun off its 40 million shares of MFS Communications to company employees. These employees enjoyed a $3.3 million windfall in 1996 when World-Com purchased MFS Communications for approximately $12.4 billion in stock. Scott, who owned 16 million shares of MFS, enjoyed the largest piece of the

pie, bringing in about $750 million for his holdings. Two years later, Kiewit invested $3 billion to develop Level 3 Communications, a new IP-based fiber optic network for both local and long-distance calls. Level 3 then awarded Kiewit the $2 billion contract to build its 15,000-mile long-distance network.

Large projects and highway contracts marked the beginning of the 21st century for Kiewit. During the first years of the new century, the company was involved in several megaprojects, including the "Big Dig" in Boston, the "T-Rex" Interstate expansion project in Denver, and the "Big Pipe" project in Portland. The Boston and Denver contracts were valued at more than $1 billion each. The Portland project involved a $500 million contract to build a 22-foot-wide, six-mile-long sewage collection tunnel system along the Willamette River. As far as highways were concerned, the company was awarded $527.5 million in federal highway contracts in 2001, $490 million in 2002, and $393.5 million in 2003, making Kiewit the largest federal highway contractor during 2001 and 2002, and the second largest in 2003. During 2004, Kiewit had 34 contracts totaling more than $100 million. These projects included a $1.35 billion joint venture project in Salt Lake City, rebuilding approximately 17 miles of interstate highway, making it one of the largest highway contracts in the history of the United States.

After working with the company for more than 20 years, Bruce Grewcock, whose father had been in charge of Kiewit's construction and mining operations in the past, became president and CEO of the company in 2004. He replaced Ken Stinson, who had held the position since 1992. Stinson continued to serve as chairman of the board. During his years at the helm, Kiewit's construction and mining revenues doubled to $3.4 billion, and shareholder equity nearly tripled.

The company's workmanship was put under the microscope in 2005 when allegations arose that a Kiewit-led joint venture produced faulty welds on the Skyway section of the Bay Bridge in San Francisco, California. Following several investigations, including examinations by the Federal Highway Administration, it was found that the construction of the structure met or exceeded safety requirements set by the state of California. In fact, one report stated that the welds were 30 percent stronger than required.

Despite the negative publicity surrounding these allegations, Kiewit showed continued financial success. Sales in 2005 increased by 23.7 percent over the previous year to reach $4.14 billion, nearly half of which was from transportation contracts, such as bridges, railroads, mass transit systems, and highways. At the time, more than 75 percent of the company's jobs were government contracts, and 92 percent of company revenues resulted from construction operations, with the remaining 8 percent coming from the mining division.Net income for the company reached $228 million, an increase of 13 percent from the previous year.

## BUILDING A FUTURE: 2008 AND BEYOND

A major change occurred in January 2008 regarding the ownership structure of the company, when 99 percent of the outstanding stockholders voted to hold the stock in a company employee ownership plan. Each of the approximately 1,800 stockholders received one unit of ownership for each of their shares of stock, and the company was no longer required to file financial reports with the Securities and Exchange Commission, saving the company $1 million each year. Another change for the company took place when Kiewit acquired TIC Holdings as a wholly owned subsidiary. The two companies had worked together on a number of projects in the past and shared similar businesses philosophies and structures. TIC continued to run as a stand-alone company with three strategic business units, TIC Industrial, TIC Infrastructure, and TIC Diversified. Overall Kiewit had a financially successful year. Revenues in 2008 reached more than $8 billion.

Kiewit became involved in a number of large projects during the last few years of the new decade. Cloudworks Energy, a company based in Vancouver, awarded Kiewit a $392 million contract in October 2008 for the construction of six hydroelectric generating facilities in British Columbia. During 2009 Kiewit Pacific Co., a subsidiary of Kiewit, began working on a $211 million project to expand and upgrade Bakersfield, California's wastewater treatment plant. Revenues in 2009 increased by 24.6 percent to $9.985 billion, although profits actually decreased by 2.2 percent.

During 2010 the company began working on several hydroelectric projects in Canada, which were scheduled to take several years to complete. In May, an agreement was reached between Brookfield Renewable Power in Toronto, and several partners, including Kiewit, to launch the feasibility stage of SaskPower's Pehonan Hydroelectric Project on the Saskatchewan River. Following this assessment stage, which could last as long as four years, Kiewit could be involved in the construction phase of the project, which would "increase Saskatchwan's installed renewable generation capacity by approximately 250 megawatts," according to the Internet Wire. In June the company partnered with Aecon Group Inc., a Canadian construction company, to design and build the $1.7 billion Lower Mattagami Hydroelectric Complex for Ontario Power Generation.

The project was expected to take approximately five years to complete.

In 2010 Kiewit ranked number 238 on the *Fortune* 500 list, up from a ranking of 312 the previous year. While the company could be proud of the fact that it was one of the few able to compete for billion-dollar projects, it continued to complete smaller projects as well. As of 2010, the average company project was under $15 million. As the builder of billions of dollars worth of U.S. highways, in addition to the many dams, tunnels, public utility facilities, and military installations that dot the country, Kiewit had left an indelible mark on the North American landscape. While contracting for construction projects entails considerable risk, especially for larger projects, Kiewit, one of the country's oldest and most experienced heavy construction companies, could draw upon its past to build toward the future.

*Jeffrey L. Covell*
*Updated, Diane Milne*

## PRINCIPAL SUBSIDIARIES

Kiewit Construction Group Inc.; Kiewit Corporation; Kiewit Diversified Group Inc.; Kiewit Mining Group Inc.; TIC Holdings.

## PRINCIPAL DIVISIONS

Buildings; Electrical; Federal; Marine; Mining; Oil and Gas; Power; Transportation; Underground; Water Resources.

## PRINCIPAL COMPETITORS

Bechtel Group, Inc.; Fluor Corporation; Foster Wheeler A.G.; Granite Construction Incorporated; Jacobs Engineering Group, Inc..

## FURTHER READING

"BRIEF: Kiewit Shareholders Approve Change," *Omaha World-Herald (Omaha, NE)*, January 3, 2008.

"Brookfield and Its First Nations Partners Proceed with Feasibility Stage of the Pehonan Hydroelectric Project," *Internet Wire*, May 13, 2010.

"Canada: Peter Kiewit Sons Co. Wins Contract for Six Run-of-River Hydroelectric Projects," *TendersInfo*, October 13, 2008.

"Contractor Hired for Project," *Omaha World-Herald (Omaha, NE)*, February 7, 2005.

"Kiewit 2005 Revenue Rose to $4.15 Billion," *Omaha World-Herald (Omaha, NE)*, March 2, 2006.

"Kiewit/Aecon Joint Venture Awarded $1.7 Billion Contract for Lower Mattagami Hydroelectric Complex," *CNW Group*, June 7, 2010.

"Kiewit Pacific Co.—Bakersfield Wastewater Treatment Plant," *Building and Construction Southwest*, September 2, 2009.

"Omaha, Neb.-based Construction Firm Names New CEO," *Omaha World-Herald (Omaha, NE)*, December 28, 2004.

"Top Contractor," *International Construction* 43, no. 1 (2004): 10.

"U.S. Agency Says Kiewit Bridge Work Is All Right," *Omaha World-Herald (Omaha, NE)*, October 24, 2005.

# Markel Corporation

—■—

**4521 Highwoods Parkway**
**Glen Allen, Virginia 23060**
**U.S.A.**
**Telephone: (804) 747-0136**
**Toll Free: (800) 446-6671**
**Fax: (804) 965-1600**
**Web site: http://www.markelcorp.com**

*Public Company*
*Founded:* 1920s
*Employees:* 2,800 (est. 2009)
*Sales:* $2.07 billion
*Stock Exchanges:* New York
*Ticker Symbol:* MKL
*NAICS:* 524126 Direct Property and Casualty Insurance
Carriers

■ ■ ■

Markel Corporation is a specialty insurance provider, underwriting and marketing products to a variety of niche markets. The company operates in three primary areas: excess and surplus (E&S) lines, specialty admitted, and the London insurance market. In general, E&S insurance lines are provided for atypical or hard-to-place risks that the standard insurance market does not cover (and that the state guaranty fund does not protect). Examples covered by Markel range from earthquake policies for office buildings to accident insurance for yachts. Specialty admitted insurance is another niche that provides coverage for unique activities that again have atypical or hard-to-place risks associated with

them. Through its subsidiary Markel International, the company offers specialized insurance to Europe and other world markets.

## FOUNDER SAMUEL MARKEL

In the early 1920s, Samuel A. Markel was an insurance agent in Norfolk, Virginia, when that city passed a law requiring that all buses be insured. At the time, motor transportation was relatively new, and "jitney buses" were unregulated. (Jitneys were large cars that charged a "jitney," or nickel, for a ride.) If a person owned a jitney bus, he could be a jitney bus operator.

When Sam Markel attempted to get coverage for the jitney operators he represented, no insurance agency would accept the policy. In response, Markel and the jitney bus operators created the Mutual Casualty Association, providing a way for the operators to insure themselves. When Richmond, Virginia, created a law similar to Norfolk's, the Mutual Casualty Association expanded to that city, and since Richmond was larger than Norfolk, the association moved as well.

As high insurance costs threatened to drive many jitney operators out of business (taking the Mutual Casualty Association with them), Markel worked to make the buses safer so that there would be fewer accidents. When accidents did occur, Markel established an all-hours service to provide rapid settlements.

In 1926 the Mutual Casualty Association became the American Fidelity and Casualty Company, a stock company. Around this time Markel expanded his coverage from buses to motor freight carriers, another fledgling industry that was largely unregulated. Once again, Markel took actions to regulate the industry and make it safer for clients, operators, and the company that insured the operators. By organizing bus and truck associations in various states, Markel helped build the motor transportation industry into a viable alternative to rail transportation.

## THE MARKEL TWINS

In 1930 Markel formed Markel Service, Incorporated, to provide direct and reinsurance coverage for American Fidelity and Casualty. During this decade the company became the nation's largest insurer of buses and trucks, and Samuel kept the company in the family by having both sets of twin sons work for him. Older twins Lewis and Irvin joined first, and they were followed by Stanley and Milton. When Samuel Markel died in 1954, the company passed smoothly to the next generation of Markels.

The company continued operating in its specialized transportation niche, crossing the border north with its 1951 creation of Markel Service Canada, Ltd. Markel was now international but still focused on its original specialized markets.

In the early 1960s, Lewis and Irvin Markel wanted to build a unique office building to house the company's headquarters. They contacted Haigh Jamgochian, a Richmond-born architect who had gained notoriety by creating a treehouse-like design for a Richmond building. That building was never built, but in 1962 Jamgochian started designing the new Markel building. This structure was reportedly influenced by the recently completed Guggenheim Museum in New York City, a structure famous for its modern design, as well as an aluminum-wrapped baked potato served to Jamgochian at a dinner. In 1966 the new Markel headquarters, a bowl-shaped structure bound by three concentric bands of hammered, crinkled aluminum, was completed, and the building remained a distinctive landmark of the Richmond landscape into the 21st century.

## THE TRIUMVIRATE

In the decades following World War II, the U.S. insurance industry changed dramatically. Lines of coverage were needed to cover new and nonstandard risks, and with many large insurance companies focused only on providing standard forms and rates, specialty insurance markets came into being. Initially, these new niches were of little interest to Markel, but as the excess and surplus market continued to grow, the company began to consider branching out.

Pondering aside, Markel did not make substantial moves into the broader specialty insurance market until 1978, when a trio of new leaders took control of the company: cousins Anthony and Steve Markel, and Alan Kirshner, who was married at the time to Flo Markel, one of Samuel Markel's granddaughters. Kirshner assumed presidency of the company, which in 1978 had a value of around $8 million. Under the guidance of these three men, in 1980 Markel formed the Essex Insurance Company, an excess and surplus insurance business. This company continued as part of Markel's E&S business segment, providing coverage for catastrophe-exposed property, motor truck cargo, marinas, and restaurants.

Realizing that a move into more markets would require capital, Markel went public in 1986. (The initial share price was $8.33, but since the company never issued a stock split, the price in 2009 was around $320.) After the public offering, in 1987 Markel purchased a 50 percent interest in Shand, Morahan and Company, an Illinois-based company with knowledge of professional liability and medical malpractice coverages. Shand, Morahan also operated its own E&S subsidiary, the Evanston Insurance Company. Purchase of Shand boosted Markel's presence in the E&S field, and Shand's underwriting ability was also notably helpful, as Markel tried to focus its operations more on underwriting. To

## KEY DATES

**1920:** (approx.) Sam Markel creates Mutual Casualty Association to provide insurance coverage for bus operators in Norfolk, Virginia.

**1926:** Mutual Casualty Association becomes American Fidelity & Casualty Company (AF&C).

**1930:** Markel Service Company formed to handle all activities of AF&C.

**1951:** First international venture, Markel Service Canada, begins.

**1980:** Essex Insurance Company created to underwrite excess and surplus insurance lines.

**1990:** Markel increases ownership of underwriter Shand, Morahan from 50 to 100 percent.

**2000:** Terra Nova Holdings purchased, giving company access to international markets.

**2009:** Company acquires Agri-Risk Services.

accomplish this, Markel began to divest itself of its Canadian subsidiary as well as its brokerage and claims operations. Markel purchased the remaining half of Shand in 1990.

This preference for underwriting over brokering could be seen in another Markel purchase, that of the Rhulen Agency in 1989. Although this agency was primarily a brokerage, Markel gradually changed the focus of the agency to underwriting and moved the company from Monticello, New York, to Richmond. The Rhulen purchase was just one of several acquisitions made by Markel from the late 1980s through the 1990s. Others included American Underwriting Managers, a company that was part of the Shand acquisition and which specialized in personal motorcycle and watercraft insurance, and Investors Underwriting Managers, which focused on difficult general liability and product liability work.

Throughout the first two decades under Kirshner, Markel grew dramatically. A company valued at $8 million in 1978 was valued over one hundred times that amount by 1997, the year it switched from the NASDAQ to the New York Stock Exchange. With a higher company profile, Markel made two additional acquisitions in 2000. By purchasing the book of property and casualty insurance held by the Scottsdale branch of the Acceptance Insurance Company, Markel was able to create Markel Southwest Underwriters. This expanded

Markel's presence in this E&S arena, and it also gave Markel an expanded presence in the western and southwestern United States. While Markel Southwest Underwriters has written coverages nationwide, its focus has been on commercial property in the region west of the Mississippi River.

The second significant purchase in 2000 was Markel's acquisition of Terra Nova Holdings, Ltd. This Bermuda-based company had operations in both France (Corifrance) and the United Kingdom (Terra Nova Insurance Company, Terra Nova Capital Limited, and Octavian Syndicate Management). Through this purchase, Markel gained access to specialty insurance markets worldwide. By 2008 the London segment of Markel's business would account for about 31 percent of the company's gross written premiums (GWP), a sizable portion for a business acquired only eight years earlier. (The company's E&S segment would still provide the bulk of GWP in 2008, accounting for just over half.)

## THE 21ST CENTURY

In any niche market, the paucity of market size is counteracted by the lower number of competitors. From 2000 to 2003 Markel continued to thrive, with gross written premiums surging from $1.13 billion in 2000 to $2.57 billion in 2003. However, increased competition caused this number to drop in 2004, as more firms wrote specialty insurance policies. This was in part due to excess capital, which allowed insurance companies to write more claims than they typically would and in areas they might normally avoid. Whatever the reason, the ultimate effect of this increased competition drove prices down and made overall market conditions less favorable. Markel's GWP in 2004 was $2.52 billion, a figure that dropped the following year to $2.4 billion due in part to losses stemming from Hurricane Katrina, a devastating storm that struck the U.S. Gulf Coast in August 2005.

Increased competition continued to slow earnings in 2006 and 2007. The company opened its Markel Global Marine and Energy in Houston in 2007 but shuttered the operation one year later. Also closing in 2008 was the company's Markel Re unit, an E&S underwriting subsidiary. In part, these actions were due to a tumultuous 2008 which saw the company's earnings buffeted by hurricanes Ike and Gustav as well as the global financial crisis. Markel's GWP in 2008 plunged to $2.13 billion, a level slightly below its 2002 mark, and the company realized a net investment income loss of $407.6 million on its portfolio.

While 2008 was bleak, Markel entered 2009 looking to expand certain niche markets and enter new ones, if possible. The company acquired Agri-Risk Services that year, making it part of the company agricultural division. Agri-Risk insures horses, farms, and trainers, and while Markel has had an agricultural division for some time, the purchase of Agri-Risk marked a determination to gain a larger presence in the livestock/bloodstock specialty insurance market, which is estimated to be worth around $100 million annually.

Markel showed a profit in 2009 with net income at $201 million, one year after posting a net loss of $59 million. However, premiums decreased once more, and the company's investment portfolio continued to post a net loss ($96 million), albeit a much smaller one than in 2008. Markel entered the 2010s with its primary business lines continuing to face increased competition and tougher overall economic conditions.

*Drew D. Johnson*

## PRINCIPAL SUBSIDIARIES

Excess and Surplus subsidiaries: Markel Brokered Excess and Surplus Lines; Markel Essex Excess and Surplus Lines; Markel Shand Professional/Products Liability; Markel Southwest Underwriters. Specialty Admitted subsidiaries: Markel American Specialty Personal and Commercial Lines; Markel Specialty Program Insurance. London Market: Markel International.

## PRINCIPAL COMPETITORS

Alliant Insurance Services; Allied Specialty Insurance; American Specialty Insurance and Risk Services; Great American Insurance Group; Lexington Insurance; Praetorian Specialty Insurance.

## FURTHER READING

"CEO Alan I. Kirshner Epitomizes 'Markel Style'," *Richmond Times-Dispatch,* October 27, 2009.

"A Guide to the Haigh Jamgochian Papers, circa 1930–2006," ead.lib.virginia.edu.

"The History of Markel," markelcorp.com, October 28, 2009.

"Markel Acquires Agri-Risk Services, Inc.," theHorse.com, October 13, 2009.

Markel Corporation Annual Report, 2008, October 28, 2009.

Markel Corporation Form 10-K, December 2008.

Markel Corporation Proxy Statement, December 2008.

"Markel Global Marine and Energy Opens Ocean Marine Unit," *Insurance Journal,* October 2007.

"Markel's GWP Hopes are Scuppered by Competition," *Europe Intelligence Wire,* August 13, 2009.

"New Entrant in Insurance," *Farmer's Guardian,* October 9, 2009.

Slipek, Jr., Edward, "Space Aged," *Style Weekly,* styleweekly.com, June 9, 2009.

# Medco Health Solutions, Inc.

———— ■ ————

**100 Parsons Pond Drive**
**Franklin Lakes, New Jersey 07417**
**U.S.A.**
**Telephone: (201) 269-3400**
**Toll Free: (800) 251-7690**
**Fax: (201) 269-1109**
**Web site: http://www.medcohealth.com**

*Public Company*
*Founded:* 1992 as Medco Containment Services
*Employees:* 22,850 (2009)
*Net Revenues:* $59.8 billion (2009)
*Stock Exchanges:* New York
*Ticker Symbol:* MHS
*NAICS:* 446110 Pharmacies and Drug Stores; 454113 Mail-Order Houses

■ ■ ■

Serving some 65 million members, Medco Health Solutions, Inc., (Medco) is the country's largest prescription benefits manager (PBM). Medco manages pharmacy benefits for private and public employers, health plans, labor unions, and government agencies, as well as for individuals covered by Medicare Part D Prescription Drug Plans. In addition to operating both mail-order and call center pharmacies, the company has partnerships with a nationwide network made up of approximately 60,000 retail pharmacies. In 2009 alone, Medco managed 695 million prescriptions, including 103 million prescriptions through its mail-order pharmacies. Touting itself to be "the world's most

advanced pharmacy," Medco holds almost 30 U.S. patents for patient data management, automated pharmacy technology, and front-end pharmacy technology.

## COMPANY BEGINNINGS: 1983–90

Medco Health Solutions, Inc., had its beginnings as Medco Containment Services, which was formed as a holding company in 1983 by financier Martin Wygod. With a controlling interest in Porex Technologies, a company that manufactured surgical and filtration products, and $10 million from the sale of another one of his investments, Wygod sought a new venture. He found an opportunity in National Pharmacies, a small mail-order prescription drug company and vitamin distributor that posted annual revenues of around $25 million. Under the name Medco Containment Services Incorporated, Wygod purchased National Pharmacies for $30 million in cash and Porex stock shares. The vitamin division was dropped so that the company could concentrate on the mail-order drug business.

Although the mail-order prescription business had been in existence long before the founding of Medco, only 2 percent of all prescriptions filled in the United States in 1984 were done through mail-order services, most of these through the Veterans Administration. Wygod saw a virtually untapped market in large corporations that were seeking ways to reduce their costs for employee prescriptions. He focused on selling maintenance medication through the funded benefit drug plans of HMOs, corporations, state retirement systems, and unions. Within six months, Medco had acquired accounts with such major U.S. companies as General Motors, Alcoa, and Georgia-Pacific.

In 1985 Medco acquired Paid Prescriptions from Computer Sciences Corporation. Paid Prescriptions was a small company that provided its customers with a prescription drug card that could be used at approximately 40,000 pharmacies across the country. This move allowed Medco to launch a national, integrated retail and mail pharmacy network service in 1989. Medco offered subscribers the option of filling prescriptions at participating drugstores or using the mail-order service for lower copays. Customers continued to buy some medications, such as antibiotics, at local pharmacies, while medications for such chronic illnesses such as high blood pressure and diabetes were purchased through Medco's mail-order service. Medco, through its integrated network, could also collect information about how much customers spent on prescriptions and then sell that information to sponsors of health plans.

By the early 1990s, nearly 40 percent of the U.S. population was covered by some kind of funded drug benefit plan, up from about 5 percent in 1983. Medco specialized in maintenance medication for chronic conditions and provided mail-order drugs through 900 different coverage plans offered by various corporations and organizations. According to *Forbes* journalist Howard Rudnitsky, Medco reported that it saved customers 20 percent or more over retail pharmacy prices, primarily because it encouraged the use of generic drugs that cost less. In addition, Medco's automated network allowed pharmacists and technicians to process well over 60 orders per hour, all of them reviewed for accuracy by two pharmacists.

### SPECIAL PROGRAMS: 1990–92

In late 1990 Medco created controversy when, through its Prescribers Choice Program, it actively negotiated

significant discounts from major drug manufacturers for its formulary, or a list of the preferred prescription medications covered by a health plan. In return for a volume discount from a pharmaceutical company, Medco would promote that company's medication (a "preferred" drug) over the same type of drug from another provider. Medco pharmacists were specially trained to evaluate a patient's condition, along with any other medications taken. If a Medco pharmacist determined that a physician had prescribed an expensive drug when a preferred drug could be safely substituted, the pharmacist contacted the physician and told him or her about the less expensive, equally effective drug. According to the *Wall Street Journal*, over 40 percent of doctors agreed to rewrite their prescriptions, with Medco being given permission to change some 50,000 prescriptions each month.

Members of the medical community argued that the Prescribers Choice Program limited prescription options and virtually eliminated a patient's freedom of choice. Physicians contended that Medco was taking control of their patients' treatment plans. Retail pharmacies complained that they could not receive the same deep discounts as Medco, which by then was able to offer medications to millions of customers. Drug companies accused Medco of monopolizing the pharmaceutical market. Nevertheless, most major U.S. pharmaceutical companies, fearful of alienating the nation's largest pharmacy benefits provider, had signed with Medco by 1993.

In 1992 Medco introduced its Diabetic Patient Support Program, the first health management program ever offered by a pharmacy benefits provider. The program emphasized patient education designed to promote self-management. In addition, pharmacists were available via telephone to talk with patients about the disease, including symptoms or complications, and to offer information about lifestyle modifications. One of the important features of the Diabetic Patient Support Program was that pharmacists helped monitor patients' compliance with the treatment plans prescribed by their doctors. The success of this program set a precedent for many other health management programs that were developed throughout the industry during the 1990s and the first decade of the 21st century.

### PHARMACY AUTOMATION: 1993–2001

Medco was acquired as a wholly owned subsidiary of Merck & Co., Inc., a global pharmaceutical company, in 1993. One year later, Medco Containment Services changed its name to Merck-Medco Managed Care. In 1995 Merck-Medco introduced Partners for Healthy Ag-

# KEY DATES

**1993:** Financier Martin Wygod establishes Medco Containment Services as a holding company.

**1993:** Medco is acquired by U.S. pharmaceutical manufacturer Merck.

**1994:** Medco Containment Services changes its name to Merck-Medco Managed Care.

**1996:** Merck-Medco opens its first fully automated dispensing pharmacy in Las Vegas, Nevada.

**2003:** Merck spins off Medco as an independent publicly traded company on the NYSE.

**2005:** Medco acquires Accredo Health Group, Inc., a specialty pharmacy for patients with complex chronic conditions.

**2008:** Medco expands internationally with the acquisition of Netherlands-based Sweden Apoteket and Europa Apotheek Venlo B.V.

**2010:** Medco acquires DNA Direct, Inc.

ing, a health management program to protect senior citizens against age-related drug complications. At the time, Merck-Medco served around 10 million members over the age of 65, a population with six times the risk of being hospitalized due to inappropriate drugs or dosages. The purpose of the program was to reduce the number of adverse reactions caused by inappropriate, ineffective, or otherwise potentially dangerous medications prescribed for elderly patients. Using an online computerized drug utilization review (DUR), Merck-Medco provided patient-specific messages to both pharmacists and physicians before medications were dispensed. A study published in the October 14, 1998, issue of the *Journal of the American Medical Association* showed that doctors who were counseled by Merck-Medco pharmacists changed their patients' prescriptions 24 percent of the time.

Throughout the 1990s, Merck-Medco continued to use technology to facilitate relations between patients, physicians, and pharmacists. It pioneered technological advances in mail-order drug dispensing when it opened its first fully automated mail-service pharmacy in Las Vegas in 1996. In 1998 Merck-Medco unveiled merckmedco.com, a Web site that gave members online access to their pharmacy benefit information, as well as the option to order prescription refills online.

Merck-Medco made headlines in 2001 when it opened its second automated mail-service pharmacy. Located in Willingboro, New Jersey, the facility was

quite large and technologically advanced, with the capability of dispensing 800,000 prescriptions per week. That same year, Merck-Medco formed a partnership to create RxHub, LLC, in order to develop an electronic exchange that would enable physicians who used electronic prescribing technology to link with pharmacies, pharmacy benefit managers, and health plans. As a result of the company's progressive approach, merckmedco.com became the first Internet pharmacy to achieve $1 billion in prescription sales.

## AN INDEPENDENT ENTITY

In 2003 Merck spun off Medco as an independent publicly traded entity named Medco Health Solutions, Inc. In an official press release issued in August 2003, Merck chairman, president, and chief executive officer Raymond V. Gilmartin explained, "With the spin-off, the market now has the ability to value each entity as 'pure plays' in their respective industries. We believe that by establishing Merck and Medco Health as two separate companies, we will enhance the potential for success of both businesses and, as a result, increase shareholder value."

Soon after the spin-off, however, Medco faced a lawsuit brought forth by 20 states alleging that Medco violated laws against unfair trade practices. The lawsuit charged that Medco pressured doctors to switch medications for its own financial gain rather than for the well-being of patients. Pennsylvania attorney general Jerry Pappert was quoted by the *Seattle Times* as saying, "Consumers and their doctors should make the decision of switching from one medication to another based on the best interests of the patient, not because a PBM has found a way to make money." Although Medco agreed to pay $29 million to settle the case, that agreement did not include an admission of guilt or a finding of inappropriate business conduct by the company. A portion of the settlement, $2.5 million, was to reimburse patients for medical tests that were required after their prescriptions had been changed. Medco was also required to provide new disclosures to both prescribers and patients, which included the company's financial incentives for advocating drug changes.

In 2005 Medco acquired Accredo Health Group, Inc., a company that provided specialty pharmacy and related services for patients with certain complex, chronic diseases. Medco then incorporated Critical Care Systems, a company that provided pharmaceutical products and infusion services to patients with such disorders as hemophilia. In 2007 Medco paid $1.5 billion for PolyMedica Corp., a prominent supplier of diabetes treatment products in the United States. At the time, Medco served an estimated 2.8 million customers with diabetes, a healthcare sector worth more than $25 billion per year. In its merger with PolyMedica, which included the Liberty Healthcare brand, Medco gained almost 1 million additional diabetes customers.

The year 2007 saw Medco introduce what was considered at the time its key clinical achievement, Therapeutic Resource Centers (TRCs). Guided by clinical procedures, teams of TRC pharmacists focused on the care of patients with chronic and complex conditions, including diabetes, cancer, asthma, high cholesterol, and high blood pressure. By accessing integrated health information, TRC pharmacists could help reduce health care costs and better serve patients. Almost half of Medco's 2,600 pharmacists worked in TRCs across the nation, providing disease-specific therapy management for chronically ill patients, a group that accounted for 96 percent of pharmacy spending and 75 percent of all health care spending in the United States.

Also in 2007, Medco announced a joint study with Mayo Collaborative Services, Inc., to evaluate the clinical, medical, and cost-saving potential of genetic testing using blood thinners. One year later, Medco released findings that demonstrated an increase in major cardiovascular risks in patients taking the blood thinner found in the drug Plavix and a common heartburn medication together. These findings led the U.S. Food and Drug Administration to order a label change for Plavix, one of the top-selling drugs in the United States.

## EXPANSION: 2008 AND BEYOND

Medco expanded internationally in 2008 when it acquired a majority stake in Europa Apotheek Venlo B.V., a privately owned company based in the Netherlands that provided clinical health care and mail-order pharmacy services in Germany and the Netherlands. Also that year, Medco entered into a partnership with Sweden Apoteket, Sweden's government-owned retail pharmacy. Looking to improve clinical and financial outcomes for the country's health care system, the Swedish government enlisted the help of Medco in designing and testing an automated electronic prescription review system based on the one used in Medco's U.S. locations. In January 2010 the Apoteket-Medco team announced that it had developed Elektroniskt ExpeditionsStod, one of the first national centralized DUR programs outside of the United States. Customized to incorporate Sweden's drug and clinical guidelines, the system would help Apoteket improve quality control, thereby reducing incidents involving adverse drug reactions.

Even as it branched out into foreign markets, Medco continued its expansion in the United States. In

2009 Medco began construction on an automated dispensing pharmacy in Whitestown, Indiana, a facility that would house the Medco Therapeutic Resource Center for oncology patients. During this time, Medco also launched its Medco Research Institute. According to medcoresearch.com: "Medco Research is the intersection of high tech and high touch—efficient and effective. Medco is dedicated to furthering the cause of evidence-based, protocol-driven medicine… [by] collaborating with some of the world's most prestigious institutions on what we call precision medicine—a commitment to safe and effective prescribing based on comparative effectiveness and evidence-based protocols. Medco Research is committed to regularly publishing and sharing these peer-reviewed research efforts to elevate and accelerate important clinical discussions to help improve the quality of healthcare."

Medco's commitment to being a leader in linking cutting-edge science to daily health care needs was evident once again when it acquired DNA Direct, Inc., in February 2010. DNA Direct was founded in 2005 to educate health care professionals and patients alike about the growing field of genomic medicine. As genetic testing became more prevalent in the 21st century, pretest consultation was mandatory in many areas, such as breast and ovarian cancer risk. Integrating DNA Direct's existing physician and patient support tools with Medco's clinical expertise was expected to provide the health care industry with a comprehensive service in genetic medicine. The acquisition of DNA Direct illustrates Medco's continued strategy of employing technology to create and improve modern health care products and services.

*Alicia Elley*

## PRINCIPAL SUBSIDIARIES

Accredo Health Group, Inc.; Infinity Infusion, LLC; Liberty Healthcare Group, Inc.; Medco Health Solutions GmbH (Germany); Systemed, LLC.

## PRINCIPAL DIVISIONS

Benefit Design and Management; Diabetes Management; Home Healthcare; My RX Choices; Products; Medicare Prescription Plan; Optimal Health; Personalized Medicine Program; Pharmacy Network Management; Therapeutic Resource Centers; RationalMed; Specialty Pharmacy Solutions.

## PRINCIPAL COMPETITORS

Aetna, Inc.; CIGNA Corporation; CVS Caremark Corporation; Express Scripts, Inc.; Humana Inc.; United

Health Group Incorporated; Walgreen Co.; Wal-Mart Stores, Inc.

## FURTHER READING

"About Medco Research," medcoresearch.com.

Business Wire Editors, "Merck & Co., Inc. Completes Spin-Off of Medco Health Solutions, Inc.," allbusiness.com, August 20, 2003.

Johnson, Linda A., "Medco to Settle Benefits Lawsuit for $29 Million," *Seattle Times,* April 27, 2004.

————, "$1.5B Medco Health Deal for PolyMedica," *USA Today,* August 28, 2007.

Monane, Mark, Dipika M. Matthias, Becky A. Nagle, and Miriam A. Kelly, "Improving Prescribing Patterns for the Elderly Through an Online Drug Utilization Review Intervention," *Journal of the American Medical Association,* October 14, 1998, p. 1249–52.

Rudnitsky, Howard, "Drugs by Mail," *Forbes,* April 15, 1991.

Taulli, Tom, "Medco's Purchase of DNA Direct Could Yield a Big Payoff," dailyfinance.com, February 4, 2010.

Tiersten, Sylvia, Marion Webb, and Marty Graham, "San Diego's Wealthiest 2009," *San Diego Business Journal,* December 14, 2009, p. 20.

WebMD Corporation, "Wygod, Martin," novelguide.com, March 29, 2010.

Werthemeimer, Albert I., and James E. Knoben, "The Mail-Order Prescription Drug Industry," *Health Services Report,* November 1973, p. 852–56.

# Micron Technology, Inc.

8000 South Federal Way
P.O. Box 6
Boise, Idaho 83707
U.S.A.
Telephone: (208) 368-4000
Fax: (208) 368-4435
Web site: http://www.micron.com

*Public Company*
*Founded:* 1978
*Employees:* 18,200 (est. 2009)
*Sales:* $4.803 billion (2009)
*Stock Exchanges:* NASDAQ
*Ticker Symbol:* MU
*NAICS:* 334413 Semiconductor and Related Device Manufacturing; 334111 Electronic Computer Manufacturing; 334119 Other Computer Peripheral Equipment Manufacturing; 334412 Printed Circuit Board Manufacturing

■ ■ ■

Micron Technology, Inc. (Micron), engages in the design and production of memory chips and related products. Having grown from a small operation in the basement of a dentist's office in Boise, Idaho, into an internationally recognized and respected manufacturer of memory chips, Micron continues to manufacture DRAM (dynamic random access memory) memory chips and has also moved into NAND Flash memory. Micron's chips are used in technologies ranging from personal computers to MP3 players to USB and Flash storage devices. Micron also operates a digital imaging segment for webcams, cell phones, and cameras under the Aptina brand name.

## EARLY STRUGGLES: 1978–81

During the summer months of 1978, three design engineers left their jobs at Mostek Corporation, a pioneer in the design and production of semiconductors, to join Inmos Ltd., a British-financed competitor. On the surface, this may have appeared an unremarkable switch of employers by a small number of employees, but at Mostek tempers flared. These three engineers, Ward Parkinson, Dennis Wilson, and Douglas Pittman, were not the first employees to leave Mostek for better offers from Inmos. One former Mostek employee, in fact, had cofounded Inmos, and Mustek's management wanted to stanch the flow of additional employee departures, particularly if those employees were moving to Inmos. A legal battle ensued, with Mostek filing a suit against Inmos that called for a permanent injunction to stop further raids on its personnel. Mostek also attempted to enjoin Inmos from starting operations, but both of these demands were dismissed, including charges that the three engineers took trade secrets from Mostek to Inmos.

Caught in the middle of these accusations, the three engineers made the summer's squabble moot in October, when, led by Ward Parkinson, they decided to leave Inmos and start their own design and consulting company, Micron Technology. Incorporated that month, five days after Parkinson left Inmos, the company established modest operations in the basement of a dentist's office

## COMPANY PERSPECTIVES

Micron is one of the world's leading semiconductor companies. We're an innovator and industry leader, developing groundbreaking technologies that transform what's possible. We're also a partner with other manufacturers and enablers, making it easier for our customers to try new things and gain competitive advantages in their markets.

in Boise, Idaho, performing essentially the same work for the same people as they had before the summer began. All three had been working on a 64-kilobit (K) random access memory (RAM) program while at Mostek, and after the dispute between Inmos and Mostek, the three contracted to design a 64K chip for Mostek, Micron's first and, it appeared, only customer.

The company had been formed with the intent of serving only Mostek. Parkinson told *Electronic News,* a trade publication, "We are not looking for other customers." However, the idea of working for Mostek on an exclusive basis was short-lived, falling apart the following year when United Technologies acquired Mostek. United Technologies canceled the contract with Micron, leaving the fledgling company without any customers. The three design engineers, later joined by Parkinson's twin brother, Joseph L. Parkinson, a Wall Street lawyer and eventual leader of Micron, decided to continue designing the 64K chip on their own and began looking for investors to finance their endeavor.

The first of Micron's many struggles, the loss of the contract with Mostek, tested the company's commitment to manufacture semiconductor chips in a market dominated by giant Japanese electronic companies. Success in the memory chip market was essentially determined by size issues. To wit, the smaller the size of the chip and the greater the size of its memory capabilities, the greater the manufacturer's profits and market share. In this race for smaller chips and greater memory, the Japanese were well ahead, rivaled only by large U.S. companies based typically in California's Silicon Valley, the U.S. hub of semiconductor research and production. Industry pundits and, more important, loan officers and venture capitalists strongly believed no new U.S. memory chip manufacturer could enter the market as late as 1979 and hope to succeed, and certainly not a tiny company based in Boise, Idaho. Micron's search for financing met with nothing but failure. As Ward Parkin-

son later related to *Forbes,* his typical response from investors "wasn't 'no,' it was 'Hell, no'."

## TURNING WEAKNESS INTO STRENGTH

However, as was often true throughout its history, Micron's weaknesses were its strengths, or, more precisely, the company drew from characteristics regarded as weaknesses and used them to its advantage. With its decision to enter the memory chip manufacturing arena, Micron immediately inherited the three weaknesses of its size, its location, and the late date of its entry into the memory chip market. To overcome these problems, Micron drew upon one of its weaknesses, its location, and canvassed wealthy Idaho residents for an interest in Micron. There, at home, the company found success, enlisting the support of a machine shop operator, Ron Yanke, a wealthy sheep rancher, Tom Nicholson, and Allen Noble, a wealthy potato farmer, all Boise residents. Next came Micron's wealthiest supporter, John R. Simplot, a billionaire potato farmer and the largest supplier of potatoes to McDonalds. McDonalds in turn invested $1 million in Micron in 1980 and later poured tens of millions of dollars into Micron. With this distinctly Idahoan cadre of investors, Micron began operations, starting with $9 million in an industry that conventionally required at least a $100 million start-up investment.

Micron's location also served it well in other important areas that gave the company a much-needed boost in its transformation from a design and consulting firm to a manufacturer of memory chips. Land in Idaho was considerably cheaper than in Japan or in the Silicon Valley, which helped to reduce start-up costs. Labor was cheaper, and Idaho's hydroelectric power rates were roughly one-third of the rates paid by California memory chip manufacturers. With these advantages, Micron required less initial capital investment. In addition, its small size forced the company to examine the production methods employed by other manufacturers closely with the hope of identifying inefficiencies in conventional processes. This bare-bones approach to all aspects of the memory chip business enabled Micron to operate in an industry dominated by much larger and perhaps more complacent competitors. Its cost-cutting approach enabled the company to construct its first factory for $20 million, roughly one-quarter of the typical cost for a semiconductor manufacturing facility.

However, Micron could not control all aspects of the memory chip business. As Micron was making its transformation, Japanese electronic companies such as Hitachi, NEC, and Fujitsu had gained an early lead in the market for 64K DRAM chips, a key component of

## KEY DATES

**1978:** Ward Parkinson, Dennis Wilson, and Douglas Pittman found Micron Technology.

**1982:** Micron ships over one million chips.

**1984:** Micron becomes a publicly held corporation.

**1985:** The price of 64K chips plummets from approximately $4 to 25 cents, and the price of 256K chips falls from $20 at the beginning of the year to $2.50 by its conclusion.

**1987:** Micron loses $22.9 million.

**1991:** Micron enters the personal computer market with the establishment of a new subsidiary, Edge Technology, Inc.

**1996:** Chip prices fall 75 percent, shaving $250 million off the company's record profits of the previous year. Micron suspends construction on its Utah fabrication plant.

**1999:** Sales of computer systems drop off, making up only 36 percent of total sales. Sales of memory chips make up more than 60 percent of total revenue.

**2004:** After three years of losses, Micron's sales grow by 42 percent.

**2009:** Sales decrease from previous year by slightly more than $1 billion.

**2010:** Micron acquires Swiss memory chip company Numonyx B.V. for $1.2 billion.

computers, video games, and telecommunications systems. By 1981 Japanese companies had secured 70 percent of the global market for 64K DRAM chips, without having to contend with any serious challenge from U.S. manufacturers. Finally, two U.S. companies, Texas Instruments and Motorola, began volume production of 64K chips the following year, whereas other U.S. contenders like Intel, National Semiconductor, and Mostek did not begin production until late 1982. Worse, the U.S. chips were received poorly by the market. For Micron, these developments were unfavorable because they strengthened Japan's grip on the market and kept worldwide attention, the attention of potential Micron customers, focused on Asia.

### SIZE MATTERS: 1982–84

As it turned out, what Micron lacked in financial backing and timeliness of product entry, it made up for in product quality and innovation. Micron shipped over one million chips in 1982, alone a noteworthy achieve-ment when compared to the production totals of its competitors but also notable in the quality and size of its chips. With bigger, easier-to-read memory cells than competing chips, Micron's chips were more reliable and were also remarkably small, 40 percent smaller than Motorola's chip and 15 percent smaller than Hitachi's chip.

In early 1983, Micron achieved a dramatic breakthrough when it further reduced the size of its chips, thus garnering the attention of semiconductor engineers and customers worldwide. Micron's 1982 chip measured 33,000 square mils (one mil equals one-thousandth of an inch), whereas the new chip measured 22,000 square mils, roughly half the size of Japan's leading chips and one-third smaller than Texas Instruments' chip. As the size of Micron's chips decreased, so did the company's manufacturing costs, giving the company a significant advantage over its competitors and a springboard toward viability in the global semiconductor market.

The financial rewards of this innovation in memory chip production arrived the following year, in 1984, the same year Micron became a publicly held corporation. For the year, Micron earned $29 million in after-tax profit on revenues of $84 million, a profit-to-revenue ratio that ranked among the highest recorded by electronics companies worldwide. Micron used part of the proceeds from its success with its 64K chip to begin development of the industry's next benchmark semiconductor chip, the 256K chip, which the company began shipping in small quantities by the end of the year.

### UNFAIR TRADE: 1985–86

However, earlier in the year, significant developments in the semiconductor industry had occurred that promised to radically change the industry's future and Micron's position in it. In September of that year, when worldwide demand for chips exceeded supply, Micron drastically reduced the price of its chips, selling each for $1.95, well below the international list price of $3.40. It was a move to strengthen the company's position in the memory chip market at the expense of profit margins, a temporary maneuver to increase its customer base and undercut its competitors. At the same time, several major U.S. manufacturers, such as Intel and AMD, retreated from the fierce competition of the Japanese companies and into the high-performance, specialty chip market, where competition was less intense. Micron had decided to stay in the conventional chip market, and its price reduction was an indication of its intent. However, it was also a strategy the Japanese had been employing for a year.

For Micron, its price reduction was a way of increasing business, but the ploy was only temporary because undercutting competitors' prices hurt profits, leaving Micron without money it sorely needed. For the Japanese companies, however, price reductions could be adopted as a long-term strategy because their large reservoirs of cash could withstand significant reductions in profits. As the Japanese companies continued lowering prices, U.S. competitors began to exit the market for memory chips. National Semiconductor suspended plans to market a 256K chip in 1985, Intel announced it was closing all of its RAM production during the fall, and United Technologies closed Mostek's operations the same year.

The effect of this aggressive pricing strategy was disastrous for Micron. In 1985 the price of 64K chips plummeted from approximately $4 to 25 cents, and the price of 256K chips fell from $20 at the beginning of the year to $2.50 by its conclusion. Micron's earnings followed this pattern, falling from $28.9 million in 1984 to $154,000 in 1985. For Micron the worst was yet to come. The company had to cope without half of its workforce, which was laid off in the spring of 1985, and without one of its two production lines, which also fell victim to the downward swing of memory chip prices. In 1986 the company lost $33.9 million and generated $48.8 million in revenue, significantly less than 1985's total of $75.8 million.

Micron responded by formally accusing the Japanese semiconductor industry in 1985 of creating the collapse of the U.S. industry by illegally flooding the U.S. market with products sold below manufacturing costs, a practice commonly known as "dumping." Several months later, in the fall, Micron filed a $300 million antitrust lawsuit against six Japanese electronics companies. The result of these and other, repeated dumping charges against the Japanese led to the signing of the Semiconductor Trade Agreement between the United States and Japan in 1986, which established fair prices for Japanese memory chips and, according to Micron's management, enabled the company to start a recovery.

## MARKET FLUCTUATIONS: 1987–95

Before the recovery, Micron recorded another dismal year, equally poor as 1986. The company lost $22.9 million in 1987, although total sales climbed to $91.1 million, but in 1988 both revenues and earnings recorded substantial leaps as revenues soared to $300.5 million and earnings jumped to $97.9 million. Once again recording profits, Micron moved forward, still operating in a highly competitive market dominated by Japanese companies, something the Semiconductor

Trade Agreement had not altered. Sales climbed to $446.4 million in 1989 and earnings increased modestly to $106.1 million. The following year demonstrated the volatility of the semiconductor market when the arrival of a nationwide recession caused sales to fall to $333 million and earnings to plummet to $4.9 million.

In 1991 Micron entered the personal computer market with the establishment of a new subsidiary, Edge Technology, Inc. Edge was created to manufacture personal computers at competitive prices. It was hoped that steady revenues from the PC division would help lessen the effect of fluctuation in the memory chip market. A year later, Edge Technology changed its name to Micron Computer, Inc.

During the recession years of the early 1990s, revenues recorded modest gains, rising to $425.3 million in 1991, then reaching $506.3 million the following year, but earnings still remained too low, rising to only $6.6 million by 1992. That year, Micron canceled its plans to develop microprocessors and decentralized its operations, dividing the company into five subsidiary companies with Micron Technology, Inc., serving as the parent company and Micron Semiconductor, Inc., as the core operating unit.

In 1993 the semiconductor market once again demonstrated its volatility, but this time in a positive direction, particularly for Micron shareholders. Revenues increased 63 percent, bringing the year's total to $828.3 million, but the most remarkable increase was recorded in Micron's profits, which soared to $104.1 million, nearly reaching the total generated before the recession in 1989. With profits on the upswing and global demand for semiconductors outstripping supply, Micron initiated a phase of rapid growth. The semiconductor division began a $60 million expansion, projected to increase output by 20 to 25 percent. Micron Computer likewise kicked off an expansion project, which would add a 100,000-square-foot manufacturing facility in Idaho and 1,200 new employees. The company's stock rose sharply, achieving a 200 percent increase during 1993.

The semiconductor market was booming. In response to growing demand for memory chips, in 1994 Micron announced plans to build a new $1.3 billion manufacturing complex in Utah. That same year, the company acquired PC manufacturer ZEOS, merging it with its Micron Computer and Micron Custom Manufacturing subsidiaries to become Micron Electronics. Within two years, Micron Electronics had doubled the capacity of its Idaho operation and added two new facilities in North Carolina and Malaysia.

## OVERSUPPLY AND SHRINKING PROFITS: 1996–99

After three highly profitable years, Micron again fell victim to market fluctuations. Beginning in late 1995, a glut of memory chips started a price spiral that was to severely damage Micron's profits. During the company's fiscal 1996, chip prices fell 75 percent, shaving $250 million off the company's record profits of the previous year. Faced with thinning margins and resulting shareholder unease, Micron suspended construction on its Utah fabrication plant.

The next two years proved to be no better. Chip prices dropped another 40 percent in 1997 and 60 percent again the following year, leaving Micron with a 1998 year-end loss of $233.7 million. Despite financial woes, the company expanded its operations in late 1998 with the acquisition of Texas Instruments's memory division. Management was banking on the belief that memory chip prices would rebound, and that when they did, the newly bulked-up Micron would be prepared. "The additional wafer fabs, joint-venture relationships, Singapore assembly and test operation, royalty-free patent cross-license, and favorable TI financing create an opportunity to further reduce our cost of manufacturing and position us as one of the world's largest DRAM producers," Micron president and CEO Steve Appleton said in the company's 1998 annual report.

In 1998 Micron attributed 46 percent of its revenues to memory chip sales and 48 percent to its Micron Electronics division's sales of PC systems. In 1999 Micron began to enter the digital imaging sector when it acquired a one-third stake in the company Pix-Tech Inc. That same year, it also inked lucrative deals with computer manufacturing giants Compaq and Gateway for inclusion of its DRAM chips in their computers.

## MORE BOOM, MORE BUST: 2000–04

The Gateway and Compaq deals helped break Micron out of its revenue slump, and by 2000 the company was posting record earnings of $727 million. Micron followed up the bumper year by making its first major international expansion. Fittingly, it was in Japan, the source of so many of the company's woes in its early days, that Micron triumphantly landed, acquiring KMT Semiconductor Ltd. from Kobe Steel Ltd. The company was immediately renamed Micron Japan and quickly became Micron's face in the Japanese market. Further Asian expansion occurred the same year with the opening of a regional office in China to handle sales, assembly, and processing in that country.

After such a dynamic year for its computer chip division, and in the face of flagging sales from its MicronPC division, Micron decided to get out of the personal computer manufacturing industry completely. It would focus on what it had always done well, which was build newer and better computer chips. Accordingly, MicronPC was sold off in 2001 to Gores Technology Group. Although PC sales were not anywhere near the level they had been in the mid-1990s, the loss of MicronPC impacted the bottom line for some years to come.

Despite expanding domestically, acquiring Virginia-based Dominion Semiconductor from Toshiba Corp. and renaming it Micron Virginia in 2002, by 2003 the company was again struggling. That year saw the third consecutive year in which the company reported operating at a loss. In order to cut further losses, Micron sold off its SRAM (static RAM) inventory to Cypress Semiconductor Corp. and elected to concentrate on DRAM manufacturing exclusively. The cuts, along with robust returns coming in from expanding overseas markets, did the trick and by 2004 Micron was again posting profits. In fact, that year sales grew a whopping 42 percent to $4.4 billion.

## NEW DIRECTIONS: 2005–2010

The emerging new computer chip technology of the first decade of the 21st century was Flash drives, data storage chips that could carry their information from device to device. Used in portable "Flash drives," digital cameras, MP3 players, and other devices, Flash chips were the wave of the future, and Micron characteristically was on the cutting edge of development.

In November 2005 Micron entered into a joint venture with Intel Corp. known as IM Flash Technologies LLC. Both companies invested $1.2 billion into developing and marketing NAND Flash memory chips, cutting edge memory storage chips that accessed and wrote data at higher rates than other Flash chips. IM Flash Technologies quickly caught the attention of major manufacturers, not the least of which was Apple Computers, which placed a $500 million order with the company shortly after it opened for business.

The year 2005 was a turning point for Micron. With earnings continuing to spike upwards, the company launched a strategy of expansion and acquisition. In 2006 Micron acquired Idaho-based manufacturer ZiLOG's Nampa for $5 million, California-based Lexar Media for $850 million, and the image division of Avago Technologies for $53 million. In 2007 a $250-million manufacturing facility was established in Xi'an, China, Micron's first such facility in that country. Micron launched a new joint venture in 2008, this time with Taiwan's Nanya Technology Corp. to manufacture DRAM.

In May 2009 Micron acquired Displaytech Inc., further strengthening its imaging division and formally expanding it beyond the memory chip industry. On December 30, 2009, Micron voluntarily switched its stock from trading on the New York Stock Exchange to the NASDAQ Global Select Market. In 2010 Micron completed its largest acquisition to date, purchasing the two-year-old Swiss memory chip company Numonyx B.V. for $1.2 billion in stock trade. As the company Web site put it, "Micron's acquisition of Numonyx brings together two memory leaders to offer one of the most comprehensive, competitive, and innovative product portfolios in the industry."

It is perhaps ironic, considering Micron's early trials at the hands of Japanese companies, that by 2010 fully two-thirds of the company's sales originated on the Asian side of the Pacific Rim. In 2010 Micron continued to target original equipment manufacturers and retailers. Both Intel and Hewlett-Packard could be counted among Micron's steady customers in the United States, and the company maintained international manufacturing plants from the Americas (the United States and Puerto Rico) to Europe (Italy) to Asia (China, Japan, and Singapore). All in all, Micron's 2010 operations were a far cry from the three-man operation opened up in the basement of a dentist's office in Boise, Idaho.

*Jeffrey L. Covell*
*Updated, Shawna Brynildssen; David Larkins*

## PRINCIPAL SUBSIDIARIES

Lexar Media Inc.; Micron Europe Limited (United Kingdom); Micron Japan, Ltd.

## PRINCIPAL COMPETITORS

Elpida Memory, Inc.; Hynix Semiconductor, Inc.; Samsung Electronics Co.; SanDisk Corporation; Toshiba Corporation.

## FURTHER READING

Chakravarty, Subrata N., "We've Heard All That Before," *Forbes*, December 31, 1984, p. 34.

Davis, Dwight B., "Micron's Formula: Be the First to Make Money," *Electronic Business*, March 1993, p. 59.

Fisher, Lawrence M., "The Rescue of a U.S. Chip Company," *New York Times*, April 6, 1988, p. D1.

Gianturco, Michael, "The Semiconductor Double Take," *Forbes*, April 2, 1990, p. 170.

Gilder, George, "Idaho's New Breed of RAMs," *Forbes*, March 14, 1983, p. 130.

Hershberger, Steven, "3 Engineers Exit Inmos, Form Firm," *Electronic News*, October 23, 1978, p. 1.

"Micron Launches $450 Million Offering of Common Stock and Convertible Senior Notes," *Investment Weekly News*, April 25, 2009.

"Micron to Acquire Lexar for $688 Million," *New York Times*, March 9, 2006.

Miller, Michael W., "Fallen Star: Precipitous Decline of Memory Chip Firm Shakes the Industry," *Wall Street Journal*, January 17, 1986, p. 1.

# Mitsubishi Corporation

**3-1, Marunouchi 2-chome**
**Chiyoda-ku, Tokyo 100-8086**
**Japan**
**Telephone: (81) 3-3210-2121**
**Fax: (81) 3-3210-8583**
**Web site: http://www.mitsubishi.com**

*Public Company*
*Founded:* 1870 as Tsukumo Shokai
*Employees:* 60,039 (2010)
*Sales:* ¥ 369.9 billion ($4 billion) (2009)
*Stock Exchanges:* Tokyo; London
*Ticker Symbol:* 8058; MBC
*NAICS:* 424710 Petroleum Bulk Stations and Terminals; 324110 Petroleum Refineries; 423130 Tire and Tube Merchant Wholesalers; 423310 Lumber, Plywood, Millwork, and Wood Panel Merchant Wholesalers; 423410 Photographic Equipment and Supplies Merchant Wholesalers; 423430 Computer and Computer Peripheral Equipment and Software Merchant Wholesalers; 423510 Metals Service Centers and Other Metal Merchant Wholesalers; 423610 Electrical Apparatus and Equipment, Wiring Supplies, and Related Equipment Merchant Wholesalers; 423620 Electrical and Electronic Appliance, Television, and Radio Set Merchant Wholesalers; 423690 Other Electronic Parts and Equipment Merchant Wholesalers; 424130 Industrial and Personal Service Paper Merchant Wholesalers; 424310 Piece Goods, Notions, and Other Dry Goods Merchant Wholesalers; 424410 General Line Grocery Merchant Wholesalers; 424420 Packaged Frozen Food Merchant Wholesalers; 424490 Other Grocery and Related Product Merchant Wholesalers; 424610 Plastics Materials and Basic Forms and Shapes Merchant Wholesalers; 424690 Other Chemical and Allied Products Merchant Wholesalers; 424720 Petroleum and Petroleum Products Merchant Wholesalers (except Bulk Stations and Terminals); 424910 Farm Supplies Merchant Wholesalers; 424940 Tobacco and Tobacco Product Merchant Wholesalers; 441110 New Car Dealers; 541611 Administrative Management and General Management Consulting Services

■ ■ ■

Appearing on everything from automobiles to agricultural goods, the Mitsubishi Corporation's (Mitsubishi) three diamond logo has become one of the most familiar symbols in the world. Mitsubishi companies are represented in virtually every country in the world, and the company has had a dominant presence in the development of eastern Asia since the 1870s. The Mitsubishi Group is characterized as a *keiretsu* (banking conglomerate), a family of businesses linked through Japanese history and tradition, as well as cross-shareholdings, interlocking directorates, and personal contacts. This scheme provides Mitsubishi affiliates with common and well-known brand names, access to credit, and protection from hostile takeover.

Mitsubishi Corporation is Japan's largest *soga shosha* (general trading house). Mitsubishi has more than 200 bases of operations in approximately 80 countries worldwide. Mitsubishi, which has more than

## COMPANY PERSPECTIVES

For Mitsubishi Corporation, our origins lie in the Three Corporate Principles that have constituted our corporate philosophy since our foundation: Corporate Responsibility to Society, Integrity and Fairness, and International Understanding through Trade. The Three Corporate Principles espouse the cultivation of a business that contributes to the future of the world and humanity. They commit us to conduct business with fairness and integrity at all times, while seeking to balance social and environmental needs. The "Corporate Standards of Conduct" and the "Environmental Charter" have been formulated in accordance with the Three Corporate Principles. Striving to raise corporate value as a global business enterprise, the company aims to contribute to the continual advancement of society.

500 group companies, engages in business with customers in virtually every industry, including energy, metals, machinery, chemicals, food, and general merchandise. Overall, the company is organized into six business groups: Industrial Finance, Logistics & Development; Energy; Metals; Machinery; Chemicals; and Living Essentials.

### COMPANY FOUNDED: 1834

Mitsubishi is the family business of the House of Iwasaki. Its founder, Yataro Iwasaki, was born in 1834, a peasant who purchased samurai status with the help of relatives. Despite his rural heritage, Iwasaki developed contacts with a number of urban administrators in the Tosa prefecture (or fiefdom). Later, as a Tosa official and member of the administrative class, Iwasaki established a number of personal relationships with influential politicians whose assistance and favoritism would later prove indispensable.

After the restoration of the Meiji emperor in 1868, the new government initiated a national program of industrial modernization. It established and operated several model corporations which were later sold to private investors. At this time, however, the only private interests with enough money to purchase these corporations were established companies run by Japan's richest families. Family companies such as Mitsui, Sumitomo, and Yasuda greatly expanded their financial interests when they took control of the government companies.

Yataro Iwasaki, however, was not from a rich family. Nevertheless, in 1870, during the first years of the Meiji government, he was able to purchase Tsukumo Shokai, the official Tosa shipping company. In 1873 he changed its name to Mitsubishi, which is Japanese for "three diamonds." Iwasaki was dedicated to an occupation as a merchant and to making Japanese shipping companies competitive with the large foreign lines.

Mitsubishi's greatest supporter in government, Finance Minister Shigenobu Okuma, was a close friend of Iwasaki. He lobbied on behalf of Mitsubishi, designating the company for numerous subsidies and privileges. When the Japanese government launched a punitive military expedition against the island of Formosa (Taiwan) in 1874, Okuma saw to it that Mitsubishi was chosen to provide the ships. The government later offered direct subsidies to Mitsubishi Shokai (company) to ensure that Japan remained competitive in world shipping. With the active support and protection of the government, Mitsubishi, like Mitsui, Sumitomo and Yasuda, evolved into a *zaibatsu* (money clique).

### ENTERING THE MARITIME TRADE: 1877–85

By 1877 80 percent of Japanese maritime traffic was controlled by the Mitsubishi Shokai. Iwasaki, however, had incurred some political and professional disfavor as a result of his privileged influence in government and trading practices. On numerous occasions Iwasaki was personally attacked in newspapers for his unscrupulous business practices. The other *zaibatsu*, particularly Mitsui, relied heavily on Mitsubishi for shipping and suffered greatly from its monopoly prices. Customers shipping freight on Shokai boats were obliged to use Mitsubishi warehouses and insure their goods with the Mitsubishi Maritime Insurance Company.

In 1880 Mitsui supported the creation of a rival shipping company called Tokyo Fuhansen. Within a year Mitsubishi had succeeded in driving Fuhansen out of business. However, after Okuma died in 1881, his political opponents joined Iwasaki's competitors with the common goal of breaking the Mitsubishi shipping monopoly. The following year Fuhansen was reorganized, merged with several other smaller shipping companies, and renamed Kyodo Unyu (United Transport). Kaoru Inoue, a political enemy of Okuma and close friend of Mitsui's Takashi Masuda, convinced the government to invest heavily in Kyodo Unyu. Thereafter, Mitsubishi and Kyodo Unyu engaged in an extremely costly and intense competition which drained both companies of virtually all their resources.

During the battle with Kyodo Unyu, Mitsubishi attempted to consolidate its operations by securing a guaranteed source of fuel. In 1881 the company purchased the Takashima coal mine. Iwasaki also sent representatives to the northern island of Hokkaido to investigate its potential for coal mining. After gaining control of coal resources, Iwasaki turned his attention to gaining control of a ship supplier. Iwasaki reminded the government that the Russians had just completed a naval base at Vladivostok, while Japan's major shipyard at Nagasaki was barely able to handle minor repairs. Mitsubishi won a contract to lease and later purchase the bankrupt Nagasaki Shipyard from the government.

By 1885 the battle for supremacy in Japanese shipping was deadlocked. That year the director of Kyodo Unyu, Eiichi Shibusawa, invited the government to impose a regulatory monopoly on shipping. Suddenly it was learned that Yataro Iwasaki had acquired a controlling interest in Kyodo Unyu. In what may have been the world's first hostile takeover, Iwasaki secretly purchased a majority of his competitor's stock. He consolidated both companies into the Nihon Yusen Kaisha (NYK), or Japan Shipping Company, and denied managerial roles to both Masuda and Shibusawa who were stunned by their defeat. However, Iwasaki was unable to savor his victory, as he died shortly afterward.

## BROADENING SCOPE AND DIVERSIFICATION: 1886–1921

Iwasaki's associates, all of whom were samurai, were unable to assert themselves as independent managers until after Iwasaki died. Despite the fact that Mitsubishi was organized as a company, Iwasaki operated it as a family concern and exercised authoritarian control. His younger brother, Yanosuki Iwasaki, assumed the leadership of Mitsubishi Shokai and NYK in 1886.

The following year the Mitsubishi Shipbuilding Company became the first Japanese concern to manufacture a ship made of steel and equipped with a boiler. Japanese production of "black ships" for transportation and the military propelled Japan into a higher class of naval power. The major shipping companies, NYK and OSK (Osaka Shosen Kaisha), expanded their routes to China and Korea, and by 1899 to Europe, North America, India, and Australia.

NYK was a major beneficiary of the Sino-Japanese War (1894–95), which opened several ports in continental Asia to increased Japanese trade. Like many of the other *zaibatsu*, Mitsubishi participated in Japan's colonization of Korea, Manchuria, and Taiwan. Mitsubishi, however, was primarily involved in establishing shipping links and developing an infrastructure in the colonial territories.

In 1893 Yanosuke Iwasaki initiated a reorganization of Mitsubishi and changed its name to Mitsubishi Goshi Kaisha. Three years later he diversified the company's operations by purchasing the Sado gold mine and Ikuno silver mine. He also purchased and developed a 110-acre swamp which later became some of the most expensive property in the Tokyo business district.

Koyata Iwasaki (who replaced Yanosuke as head of the company in 1916) continued the diversification program. Between 1917 and 1919 Mitsubishi established internal divisions for banking, mining, real estate, shipbuilding, and trading. As a victor in World War I, Japan was legitimized as a major world power with great influence in the Pacific. However, this legitimization was owed to the *zaibatsu* (and not least Mitsubishi), which had built Japan into what it was.

In 1918 Mitsubishi was incorporated as a joint-stock company (totally owned by the Iwasaki family). At that time Mitsubishi Shoji Kaisha (Trading Company) was established as a separate business entity. Between 1917 and 1921 several more of the company's divisions were made independent public companies in order to attract investor capital. Mitsubishi Shipbuilding (later Mitsubishi Heavy Industries) was created in 1917, Mitsubishi Bank in 1919, and Mitsubishi Electric in 1921.

## DEALING WITH POLITICAL TURMOIL AND WAR: 1921–44

In the ensuing decade, nationalist political terrorists gained influence in the military and government. Political assassinations claimed the lives of many moderate and leftist figures. In 1932 terrorists murdered Takuma Dan, head of Mitsubishi's chief rival, Mitsui. Many of the *zaibatsu* tempered their growth during this period to avoid becoming targets of the militarists, who had seized power in Japan.

The militarists envisioned a regional economic regime for eastern Asia called the Greater East Asia Co-Prosperity Sphere. As part of this scheme, Japan would be responsible for industry and management, China for agriculture, Manchuria and Korea for mining and forestry, Indonesia for oil, and the Philippines for fishing. For this reason, the *zaibatsu* were essential partners to the militarists. They alone had the resources and expertise to implement such an ambitious development strategy. Mitsubishi, in particular, was involved in the most important fields of shipping, shipbuilding, mining, heavy manufacturing, electrical generation, warehousing, and trading.

After the Japanese invasion of China in 1937, Mitsubishi was required to provide the military and occupation forces with warships, aircraft, vehicles, weapons, and provisions. When Japan invaded the rest of eastern Asia and bombed Pearl Harbor in 1941, the uneasy partnership between the *zaibatsu* and the militarists became more important. Companies such as Mitsubishi continued to search for profit. They also comprised the military/industrial complex which perpetuated Japan's ability to make war.

While Mitsubishi Shipbuilding turned out warships, the aircraft division of Mitsubishi Heavy Industries manufactured over 18,000 warplanes, the most important of which was the "Zero." The simple technology of the Zero made it possible for thousands to be built quickly. Its vast numbers and ability to climb and accelerate made it one of the most formidable weapons of the war.

In 1945 Japan surrendered to U.S. forces, which during the previous year had destroyed Japan's major cities, and with them Japan's major factories. What remained of Mitsubishi was left in ruins. The U.S. oc-cupation forces under General Douglas MacArthur formulated an industrial plan for the reconstruction of Japan which included the implementation of American-style antimonopoly laws. As a result of the legislation, the *zaibatsus* were outlawed and use of their prewar logos was banned. Mitsubishi was divided into 139 independent companies. In addition, severe restrictions prevented the companies from coordinating business strategies and setting up cross ownership of stock.

## COMPANY REASSEMBLES: 1949–70

The communist revolution in China during 1949 and the Korean War (1950–53) significantly increased the strategic value of Japan as an industrial power and U.S. ally. Many of the punitive laws imposed on Japan by the occupation authority were lifted. Subsequent legislation in Japan weakened the effect of the antimonopoly laws. Starting in 1950 several of the former Mitsubishi *zaibatsu* companies had been allowed to reassemble. The surviving core of company interests readapted the Mitsubishi Shoji Kaisha name and the triple diamond logo. In 1953 the Mitsubishi Bank (called the Chiyoda Bank during the occupation) started to use its old name and began to coordinate the various former Mitsubishi companies. In 1954 Mitsubishi Shoji merged with three of its former component companies and started to reestablish its worldwide trading network.

A number of associated companies were created during the 1950s, including the Mitsubishi Gas Chemical Company and the Mitsubishi Petrochemical Company. The company's most important foreign associate, the Mitsubishi International Corporation (MIC), was established in the United States in 1954. MIC carefully observed industrial and consumer trends in the United States and played an important part in the formation of Mitsubishi's long-term international planning. MIC also served as a training ground for international representatives of Mitsubishi.

Japan's Ministry of International Trade and Industry (MITI) played an active role in maintaining a healthy balance of monopolistic competition between the new *zaibatsu* of Mitsui, Mitsubishi, Sumitomo and others. MITI was responsible for the excellent coordination of resources, planning, and development which allowed Japanese companies to grow and perform successfully in the postwar period. With the new *zaibatsu* as its instrument, MITI prepared Japan for several decades of export-led growth.

As a result of the direction provided by MITI, Mitsubishi anticipated Japan's increasing demand for various mineral commodities. In the 1960s Royal Dutch Shell discovered a large deposit of natural gas in the sultanate of Brunei. At the time, demand for natural gas was increasing rapidly in Japan. Mitsubishi participated with the government of Brunei and Royal Dutch Shell in developing a system whereby natural gas could be compressed into a refrigerated liquid and shipped in specially designed tankers.

## LOOKING TO FURTHER SHORES: 1971–84

Next Mitsubishi turned its attention to the untapped mineral potential of Australia and Papua New Guinea. The company formed a subsidiary called Mitsubishi Australia to participate in a large coal mining project at Bowen Basin in Queensland. Beginning in 1971 raw materials were shipped from Australia to Japan where they were used to produce iron and steel.

In 1969 Mitsubishi helped to create a forestry company called Balikpapan Forest Industries at Sotek, Indonesia. In 1973 Mitsubishi formed a joint venture with the Mexican government to produce salt in Baja California, and with the Kenyan government to develop the tourist industry in that country. In the late 1970s Mitsubishi established a joint marketing agreement with the Chrysler Corporation to sell cars in the United States built by the Mitsubishi Motor Company.

In 1971 Mitsubishi Shoji Kaisha changed its name to Mitsubishi Corporation, an Anglicized name intended to reflect the company's growing internationalization. By this time, however, the amalgamation of the prewar Mitsubishi combine had ceased. Top level managers in the associated Mitsubishi companies were reluctant to give up their independence (and possibly their jobs) by placing themselves under the direction of other managers.

The *keiretsu* organizational scheme emerged from Mitsubishi's growth (and that of other Japanese conglomerates), which was accompanied by an accumulation of debt. Majority holdings of virtually all affiliates were maintained within the *keiretsu,* thereby preventing hostile takeover when share prices of a given member slipped dangerously low. For example, when affiliate Akai Electric Co. encountered financial problems in the early 1980s, Mitsubishi Bank bailed it out. When Mitsubishi Heavy Industries' shipbuilding business slowed mid-decade, some of its employees were placed with other "three diamond" affiliates. The *keiretsu* also prevented Kuwait Petroleum Corp.'s threatened takeover of Mitsubishi Oil in 1984.

## CHANGING FORTUNES: 1986–98

Takeo Kondo was named president of Mitsubishi in June of 1986. That year, after 18 years as Japan's leading trading firm, Mitsubishi fell to fifth place. A few months after assuming the corporation's leadership, Kondo presented a plan for reorganizing and reviewing its operations. In November, however, Kondo suddenly died. He was replaced by Shinroku Morohashi, a vice president whom Kondo had charged to implement the restructuring plan. The "K-plan," as it became known, involved the divestiture of unprofitable operations, reorganization of staff, entry into newer, more promising fields such as high technology, and the introduction of more efficient administrative techniques.

Aggressive international acquisitions by Mitsubishi affiliates grabbed headlines in the late 1980s and helped it expand from its base in heavy industry. In 1985, for example, Mitsubishi Motors increased its cooperation with Chrysler Corp. through the creation of Diamond-Star Motors. In 1989 and 1990, Mitsubishi Estate Co. acquired a controlling interest in Rockefeller Center at a cost of nearly $1 billion. Around the same time, Mitsubishi Corp. boosted its chemicals interests with a controlling stake in Aristech Chemical Corp. of Pittsburgh. Other high-profile purchases included Eastman Kodak's Verbatim and California's Pebble Beach golf course. In 1990 the company's Mitsubishi Motors moved to form a joint venture with German automaker Daimler-Benz and acquired one-third of Netherlands-based Volvo the following year.

The group's fortunes, as well as the Japanese economy, declined in the late 1980s and early 1990s. Falling demand in Mitsubishi Corporation's vital fuels segment combined with a strong-yen recession. In addition, many Japanese companies ceased to rely on the trading services provided by *sogo shosha* (general trading companies) like Mitsubishi Corp. In many cases they found it more cost effective to develop their own international networks. These factors combined to effect a steady revenue decline, from ¥19.73 trillion in 1991 to ¥17.28 trillion in 1994.

The 1992 appointment of British-born and Harvard-educated Minoru "Ben" Makihara as president of Mitsubishi Corp. was viewed by some observers as an attempt to improve the Japanese business's poor reputation in the United States. Perhaps not coincidentally, however, Makihara's father worked for Mitsubishi in London, and his wife was a great-granddaughter of the company founder.

## INTO THE 21ST CENTURY

With the uncertainty of the Japanese economy lingering, Mitsubishi established the "MC2000" management plan in 1998 focusing on "self-reform for the 21st century." The ultimate goal was to shore up the company's foundations for the future. In 2001 Mitsubishi updated its management plan as an aggressive new blueprint for growth to coincide with an ever-increasing global economy. That same year, the company introduced the Business Unit System to its Business Groups, which clarified the strategic mission of each of the Business Units, the smallest units for organizational control and earnings management.

However, that same year the U.S. regulatory officials found Mitsubishi guilty of collaborating with UCAR International in a price-fixing scheme involving graphite electrodes. From February 1991 until January 1995, Mitsubishi Corporation owned 50 percent of UCAR, the world's largest producer of graphite electrodes. The indictment charged that Mitsubishi knowingly counseled and arranged efforts at price fixing. In addition, the U.S. Justice Department charged that Mitsubishi also helped in the sale of graphite electrodes and then sought to conceal the conspiracy's existence from customers. For its role in the scheme, Mitsubishi was fined $134 million.

Over the next few years, the company continued with its plans for growth. In 2002, with Mitsui & Col, Daicel Chemical Industries Ltd., and Lino Kaiun Kaisha Ltd., Mitsubishi agreed to establish the International Methanol Co., a joint venture to create a natural gas methanol plant in Saudi Arabia. In November 2004 the company acquired 11.75 million shares of Isuzu Motor Ltd. for $9.4 billion. Yorihiko Kojima was also named the new president of Mitsubishi, keeping in line with the company's tradition of replacing presidents after they served two three-year terms. Kojima was credited with helping create the company's first specialized risk-management department in 1999.

In February 2005 the company received an agreement from Indonesia-based Pertamina to allow Mitsubishi to import 20,000 barrels per day of crude oil for the next six years. Also in 2005, DaimlerChrysler divested its ownership stake (approximately 12 percent) in Mitsubishi but remained the company's business partner in several areas. These projects included joint development and production of engines, the shared use of vehicle architecture, and the joint production of passenger vehicles with Mitsubishi Motors North America.

### RECORD GROWTH: 2005–08

Another major move in 2005 was the company's new partnership with the Development Bank of Japan to manage the country's first private equity fund. Both Mitsubishi and the bank contributed $37 million to the fund. For fiscal year 2005, the company did well due to a large increase in the gross profit at the Metal One

Corporation subsidiary. High earnings also stemmed from the consolidation of food-related subsidiaries and the acquisition of new food-related subsidiaries.

As both the Japanese and worldwide economy continued to expand, Mitsubishi once again reported strong results for fiscal year 2006–07. This increase resulted primarily from the firm growth in the company's coking coal subsidiary in Australia and in steel products, as well as higher earnings in the Machinery, Chemicals, and Living Essentials business groups.

By the end of fiscal year 2008, the company had recorded double digit earnings growth for five years in a row. Always interested in improving the company's internal operations, Kojima and the company introduced two new business groups: the Business Innovation Group and the Industrial Finance, Logistics & Development Group. Among the company's major initiatives was a strategy to ramp up the sale of industrial machinery in Brazil, China, India, and Russia. In addition, the company formed a joined venture with Mitsubishi Motors Corp. to create Mitsubishi Motor Sales (China) Inc. to import and sell vehicles of Mitsubishi. In 2008 Mitsubishi ranked as the largest general trading company in Japan.

The economic downturn that began in late 2007 impacted Mitsubishi as it did many other large corporations. As result, over the 2008–09 fiscal year, the company's various group businesses were negatively impacted by a sharp decline in market prices in many sectors. The downturn ultimately resulted in the company reporting a drop in earnings, resulting primarily from lower profits from fund investments and real estate businesses. Nevertheless, the company continued to build up its operating base for finance-related businesses, including establishing the Marunouchi Capital Company, Ltd., as an investment fund management company.

### EMERGING BUSINESSES FOR THE FUTURE

As Mitsubishi entered the second decade of the 21st century, two areas of focus concerning energy and the environment included the company's ongoing efforts to further develop electric cars with large-capacity lithium-ion batteries, as well as an increased focus on solar power and biomass fuels. For example, the company agreed to participate in a solar photovoltaic power generation project in Portugal developed by Spain-based ACCIONA, S.A., one of the world's largest integrated renewable energy companies. Mitsubishi also established Forest Energy Hita Co., Ltd., and Forest Energy Kadogawa Co., Ltd. as the first companies in Japan to produce biopellets as a substitute for coal.

As president and CEO of the company, Kojima continually emphasized the company's need to focus on emerging businesses. As a result, efforts in the emerging business sector came under Kojima's direct control. In an interview with Jonathan Sobel for *Business Day* of South Africa, Kojima remarked that, if there were ever a consensus that "we can't spend money because times are tough," the company would cease to think about the future.

*Updated, April Dougal Gasbarre; David Petechuk*

## PRINCIPAL SUBSIDIARIES

AGREX, Inc. (USA); Bewith, Inc. (Japan); Diamond Realty Investments, Inc. (USA); Frontier Carbon Company (50%, Japan); MC Capital Inc, (USA); Metal One Specialty Steel Corp. (Japan); Petro-Diamond Singapore (Pte.) Ltd.

## PRINCIPAL DIVISIONS

Chemicals; Energy; Industrial Finance, Logistics, & Development; Living Essentials; Machinery; Metals.

## PRINCIPAL COMPETITORS

ITOCHU Corporation; Marubeni Corporation; Mitsui & Co., Ltd.; Sojitz Corp.; Sumitomo Corporation; Toyota Tsusho Corp.

## FURTHER READING

"DaimlerChrysler Pulls Stake in Mitsubishi," *AdWeek Western Edition,* November 11, 2005.

"Mitsubishi Corporation Acquires 34% Stake in World's Largest Solar Photovoltaic Project, Owned by ACCIONA," *ChemicalBusiness Newsbase,* March 5, 2009.

"Mitsubishi Socked with $134 Million Fine for Role in International Price-Fixing Cartel," *FTC: Watch,* May 14, 2001, p. 12.

Sobel, Jonathan, "Breaking the Oriental Silence in a Global Market," *Business Day* (South Africa), February 24, 2009.

# Molina Healthcare, Inc.

---

**200 Oceangate**
**Suite 100**
**Long Beach, California 90802-4317**
**U.S.A.**
**Telephone: (562) 435-3666**
**Toll Free: (888) 562-5442**
**Fax: (562) 437-1335**
**Web site: http://www.molinahealthcare.com**

*Public Company*
*Founded:* 1980
*Employees:* 2,800 (est., 2009)
*Sales:* $3.669 billion (2009)
*Stock Exchanges:* New York
*Ticker Symbol:* MOH
*NAICS:* 524114 Direct Health and Medical Insurance
   Carriers

■ ■ ■

Molina Healthcare, Inc., is a multistate managed healthcare organization that serves patients who have traditionally faced barriers to quality health care. The company's clients are primarily people covered under Medicare, Medicaid, the Children's Health Insurance Program (CHIP), and other government-sponsored health insurance programs for low-income families and individuals. The company's various health plans are locally operated by its wholly owned subsidiaries in the states of California, Florida, Michigan, Missouri, New Mexico, Ohio, Texas, Utah, and Washington. Molina Healthcare also has 17 primary care clinics in California.

Revenues are derived primarily from premium revenues paid to the company's health plans by the relevant state Medicaid authority, with revenues jointly financed by the federal and state governments. The company also derives revenues from the federal Centers for Medicare and Medicaid Services (CMS). As of December 2009, Molina had approximately 1.45 million members enrolled in its health care plans.

## COMPANY FOUNDED: 1980

Molina Healthcare grew out of the medical experience of C. David Molina, M.D., who opened the first intensive care unit at Pacific Hospital in Long Beach, California, in 1962. Molina would run the emergency room (ER) at Pacific Hospital for more than two decades. During that time, Molina recognized that he was seeing many patients in the ER whose medical problems did not require a visit to the ER. Molina suggested that the hospital should open clinics to address the needs of this patient population in a more cost-effective manner. When the hospital administrators failed to show interest in his plan, Molina decided that he would open his own clinic.

The ER problem stemmed primarily from underprivileged patients relying too much on ER care to access the medical system. Writing in the book *One Nation, Underprivileged: Why American Poverty Affects Us All,* Mark Robert Rank noted various reasons why the underprivileged rely on ER services. "Due to limited access to medical care, coupled with lower levels of education, the poor are more likely to let health problems fester until they become extremely problematic, requir-

## COMPANY PERSPECTIVES

Molina Healthcare's top priority is to provide the communities that we serve with access to high-quality care. By reaching out to members in the community, including seniors, parents, children, and families, we are able to teach them how to live healthier. Our mission—providing care in an efficient and caring manner— is more important than ever.

ing emergency measures," wrote Rank, who added that, "because of restricted access to conventional health care, the poor tend to use emergency room visits as a way of accessing the medical care system for situations that would normally be considered routine."

Molina opened his first clinic to serve the underprivileged in California in 1980 and soon after opened two more, thus establishing Molina Medical Centers. According to Molina's son, who approximately 15 years later would become CEO of the company, his father initially focused on immigrants on Medicaid. These individuals typically could not access medical care because many physicians would not treat them due to limits in government program fees. "While most other health-care plans focused on large employer groups, we [focused] on low-income immigrants with language issues," J. Mario Molina, M.D., the founder's son, told *Time* magazine contributor Jeffrey Ressner.

## OPPORTUNITY TO GROW: 1985–90

Initially, Molina Healthcare served people in Medi-Cal, California's Medicaid system. A few years after establishing the company, Molina found his company facing an early crisis. The California state government had made the decision to contract only with health maintenance organizations (HMOs) for its Medi-Cal patients and not directly with medical groups such as Molina Medical Centers. Molina realize that to continue to serve his patient population, his company would have to become an HMO. "You had to have $1 million in reserves to become licensed, and fortunately for us my father had always taken the money he had generated from the business and plowed it back in," J. Mario Molina remarked to *Los Angeles Business Journal* contributor Deborah Crowe. The company obtained an HMO license in California in 1985.

Eventually, other health care plans in California began to no longer serve Medicaid patients in an effort

to improve profits. Molina quickly recognized an opportunity to grow. At about the same time in the 1990s, a consultant friend of the company's founder noted that company's great success in California raised the issue of whether it was due specifically to California and its programs or rather was associated with something about the Medicaid patients themselves. If the company's success was due to the latter, the consultant noted, then the business model for the company should work well in other states.

After C. David Molina died in 1996, his son J. Mario was named chairman of the board and took over the chief executive role at Molina Healthcare. At some point, all five of David Molina's children had worked for the company, and John C. Molina was the company's chief financial officer in 2010. Two other daughters also worked at the company before leaving to start families.

In an interview with *Los Angeles Business Journal* contributor Laurence Darmiento, John Molina pointed out that his father had unquestionably been the boss, but the children felt well prepared to take over the company. Molina also told Darmiento: "The other thing (his death) really brought into focus was the long-term goals. Whenever we would ask him what he wanted to do, his guiding principal was to build the business."

In 1997 the company began its expansion outside of the state of California by starting a new health plan in Utah. Two years later it acquired a plan in Michigan and then one in the state of Washington in 2000. That same year, the company was renamed Molina Healthcare, Inc., a California corporation.

## GOING PUBLIC: 2000–05

As the company entered the 21st century, Molina Healthcare saw its net income more than double, up from $15 million in 2000 to $30.1 million in 2001. Revenues also increased from $329.4 million to $503 million. In 2002 the company was sixth on the *Business Journal*'s list of fastest-growing private companies.

In June 2003 the company reincorporated from California to Delaware. Molina went public the following month, raising $115.5 million in its initial public offering of 6.6 million shares. At the time, the company covered 511,000 Medicaid beneficiaries.

In his interview with *Los Angeles Business Journal* contributor Deborah Crowe, Molina explained the company's decision to go public, noting that as a family-owned company that had no debt, profits were traditionally put back into the company. When enough cash or assets had been acquired, the company would go

## KEY DATES

**1980:** Molina Medical Centers opens three primary care clinics.

**1985:** Company obtains an HMO license in California.

**2000:** Company renamed Molina Healthcare, Inc.

**2003:** Company reincorporates in Delaware and makes initial public offering.

**2008:** Molina Healthcare acquires Mercy CarePlus.

**2010:** Molina buys health information management business run by Unisys Corp. for $135 million.

out and make an acquisition. Admittting that this approach is a "very slow way to grow" for an HMO because of needed cash reserves, Molina also told Crowe that bankruptcy proceedings involving other plans had made it difficult for Molina to get a bank loan for expansion.

After the company went public, it looked to expand into other states. "We are definitely in an acquisition mode," David Erickson, the company's vice president and CIO, told Richard R. Rogoski in an article for *Health Management Technology.* In 2004 the Molina Healthcare entered the market in New Mexico when it acquired the managed care company Health Care Horizons for $69 million in cash. The company went on to announce plans to expand to Texas and Ohio.

## CONTINUING EXPANSION:
## 2005–08

Many industry observers were skeptical of Molina Healthcare's decision to go public, and in 2005 the company faced a crisis in stock investor confidence when its stock, which had doubled to over $50 a share, tumbled to $25 per share following a profit warning issued by the company in July 2005. Other issues that shook investor confidence included the loss of a lucrative Medi-Cal contract in Riverside and San Bernardino counties in California following a clerical error that occurred in the company's proposals. Earlier in 2003, the company's Utah subsidiary also experienced cash flow problems as the state delayed making Medicaid payments.

Nevertheless, in his 2007 interview with Deborah Crowe of the *Los Angeles Business Journal,* Molina said he did not second-guess the company's decision to go public, noting that Molina Healthcare's membership

had risen from 511,000 in 2003 to one million in 2007. Part of this growth was due to the company entering the Missouri market with the purchase of the St. Louis-based MercyCare Plus in November 2007, firmly establishing itself in the Midwest market. As for keeping Wall Street observers happy, Molina told Crowe: "My father used to say, this is the business of nickels. You have to watch the small things—little nickels add up to dollars."

Despite some questions about the company expanding too rapidly, the company repeatedly appeared in the *U.S. News and World Report* listing of "America's Best Health Plans." The company's overall financial results also improved in 2007. The company's consolidated earnings for the fiscal year were $58 million, a 28 percent increase over the previous year. Revenues from premiums also increased by nearly 25 percent from $2 billion in 2006 to $2.5 billion in 2007.

In 2008 the company announced its plans to enter the Florida market by acquiring Florida NetPASS, LLC, a provider of care management and administrative services to approximately 58,000 Florida MediPass members in south and central Florida. The company operated in nine states: California, Florida, Michigan, Missouri, New Mexico, Ohio, Texas, Utah, and Washington.

## DIVERSIFYING FOR THE FUTURE:
## 2009 ON

Several factors contributed to making 2009 a disappointing year overall. Amidst the deep recession experienced throughout the United States that year, both federal and state governments faced budget cuts that negatively impacted Molina Healthcare as the local governments reduced premium rates or benefits for programs run by the company. High unemployment also led to program enrollment increases, leading to higher short-term medical costs. Another factor was the H1N1 flu epidemic, which especially affected the portion of the population that primarily makes up the company's health plan membership.

Despite the setbacks, the company continued to look toward the future and plan for new business opportunities. The company sought to maintain its goal of diversifying revenue sources, not only geographically but also in terms of services offered. In January 2010 Molina Healthcare made its largest acquisition in the company's history. The company agreed to buy the health information management business run by Unisys Corp. for $135 million. The Virginia company helps state governments keep track of treatment of low-income Medicaid patients.

Writing for the *Los Angeles Business Journal,* Deborah Crowe noted that the acquisition of Unisys would provide the company with opportunities to foster new relationships with various state governments and their Medicaid services programs that employed the traditional fee-for-service approach. Some industry analysts were wary of the company branching out into new ancillary markets, with Matt Perry, an analyst at Well Fargo Securities, telling Crowe that the move "adds execution risk to Molina's operations." Molina told Crowe he understood peoples' concerns and that the company had challenges to face in the future. He noted: "We're now asking analysts to start covering a type of company that none of them have covered before."

*David Petechuk*

## PRINCIPAL SUBSIDIARIES

Alliance for Community Health, LLC; Molina Healthcare Insurance Company; Molina Healthcare of California; Molina Healthcare of California Partner Plan, Inc.; Molina Healthcare of Florida, Inc.; Molina Healthcare of Michigan, Inc.; Molina Healthcare of Nevada, Inc.; Molina Healthcare of New Mexico, Inc.; Molina Healthcare of Ohio, Inc.; Molina Healthcare of Texas, Inc; Molina Healthcare of Utah, Inc.; Molina Healthcare of Virginia, Inc.; Molina Healthcare of Washington, Inc.; Molina Information Systems, LLC.

## PRINCIPAL COMPETITORS

Aetna, Inc.; AmeriChoice Corporation; Centene Corporation; CIGNA Corporation; United Health Group, Inc.; WellPoint, Inc.

## FURTHER READING

Crowe, Deborah, "Man with a Plan," *Los Angeles Business Journal,* April 30, 2007, p. 20.

———, "Long Beach Firm Hopes Investors Endorse Pickup: Molina Expands into Information Management with Deal," *Los Angeles Business Journal,* January 25, 2010, p. 5.

Darmiento, Laurence, "Family Business Is Healthy but Molina Faces Choices," *Los Angeles Business Journal,* Ocotber 13, 2005, p. 10.

Rank, Mark Robert, *One Nation, Underpivileged: Why American Poverty Affects Us All,* New York: Oxford University Press, 2004.

Ressner, Jeffrey, "The Expert Caregiver: Mario Molina," *Time,* August 22, 2005, p. 54.

Rogoski, Richard R., "Bases Covered: Multistate Managed Care Organization Uses Information Technology to Meet Regulatory Requirements and Save More than $1 Million in Labor Costs," *Management Technology,* April, 2004, p. 12.

# Nation Media Group

Nation Centre
Kimathi Street
P.O. Box 49010-00100
Nairobi
Kenya
Telephone: (254) 20 2221222
Fax: (254) 20 2213946
Web site: http://www.nationmedia.com

*Public Company*
*Founded:* 1959
*Employees:* 470 (2009)
*Sales:* KES 8.7 billion ($106 million, 2009)
*Stock Exchanges:* Nairobi
*NAICS:* 511110 Newspaper Publishers; 515120 Television Broadasting

■ ■ ■

Nation Media Group is Kenya's leading publishing and broadcasting company with a market share of more than 75 percent in the newspaper publishing industry. Founded during the colonial era in Kenya, Nation Media Group has undergone tremendous transformations over the years to become the undisputed market leader in the newspaper publishing and broadcasting industry. A public company, the majority of its shares are held by the Aga Khan Fund for Economic Development.

Over the years, Nation Media Group has diversified into various forms of publishing and broadcasting products that include newspapers, magazines, television broadcasting, online news sites, and radio entertainment. Some of the notable newspaper and magazine publications of the company include the *Daily Nation, Sunday Nation,* the *East African, Weekly Advertiser, Business Daily,* and *What's On* magazine. Nation Media also operates NTV Kenya, a television station, and the 96.4 Easy FM radio station.

## COMPANY FOUNDING AND EARLY YEARS: 1959–69

Nation Media Group was founded in 1959 by His Highness the Aga Khan, a young prince who had assumed the worldwide leadership of the Shia Imami Ismaili Muslim community at the height of the independence struggle in Kenya and Africa as a whole. Although he assumed the leadership mantle of his community at the mere age of 20, the young Aga Khan had already developed a keen interest in the political processes in the country, and he frequently consulted with the leading Kenya African nationalists, such as Tom Mboya, James Gichuru, Julius Kiano, and Jomo Kenyatta, to discuss the future path of the country. The young prince's attachment and commitment to Kenya's preindependence political processes was attributable to his residence in one of the Nairobi suburbs for most of his childhood.

His Highness the Aga Khan's decision to open a newspaper organization was particularly motivated by the lack of a mouthpiece for African freedom fighters, for most newspapers of the time favored the colonial establishment. Therefore, His Highness the Aga Khan brought on board Michael Curtis, his media aide who had formerly served as an editor with London's *News Chronicle,* to start an independent and unbiased newspaper and press organization. Curtis quickly moved into action and rented a building that had previously been used as a bakery along Victoria Street (now Moi Avenue), and set up the first premises for the *Taifa Leo* newspapers. The newly formed newspaper and press organization hired John Bierman to the position of editor and recruited the production staff as well who were tasked with the responsibility of laying the foundation for a newspaper organization that would address the plight of Africans.

*Taifa Leo,* a daily newspaper published in the local Swahili language, was the first publication of the Nation Media Group. The readership of *Taifa Leo* mainly consisted of ordinary Kenyans, and it hit the stands at the height of the struggle for independence from colonialism in Kenya. The founder of *Taifa Leo,* His Highness the Aga Khan, had at the core of his objectives the intention to use the local Swahili daily newspaper to sway public opinion towards African nationalism so as to bring to an end colonial rule in Kenya. As such, *Taifa Leo* became synonymous with the struggle for independence in Kenya.

Infrastructure challenges notwithstanding, *Taifa Leo* penetrated many parts of Nairobi city and its environs as well as major towns in the country, effectively providing the founder the much-needed fundamental resources and opportunities for establishing a strong foundation and distribution network for the media house.

The *Sunday Nation* and the *Daily Nation* were launched, in English, as sister publications to *Taifa Leo*

in 1960. The *Sunday Nation* came into existence as the *Nation* newspaper in March 1960 and was published on a weekly basis until seven months later when a sister daily newspaper, the *Daily Nation,* was launched. The *Nation* title was changed to the *Sunday Nation* a few months before the launch of the *Daily Nation.* The first *Daily Nation* newspaper hit the stands in October 1960 and since then, Nation Media Group has never looked back. The *Daily Nation* and *Sunday Nation* went on to become the dominant daily and weekly newspapers in Kenya, commanding the majority market share in the newspaper publishing industry.

Because the *Sunday Nation* and the *Daily Nation* newspapers were founded during the sunset years of colonial rule, the publishing company was deeply embroiled in the freedom struggle in Kenya and the entire East Africa region. In his series of articles about the Nation Media Group's history, Gerry Loughran stated that the *Nation* newspaper publications were founded on the solid principles of rule of law, dignity in human life, justice, peace, and liberty across all communities in east Africa irrespective of color, religion, race, or creed. Moreover, the *Nation* was committed to the desire to influence the adoption of a democratic system based on African majority rule in the East African territories. Notably though, the newspaper's radical political stance in the colonial era portended negative implications in its commercial pursuits. This was because the African audience that the company's newspaper publications targeted was largely illiterate, while the majority of the communities which held the consumer power shunned its publications.

In the early 1960s Nation Media Group demonstrated its business prowess in the print production area by pioneering the adoption of modern and cutting-edge printing technologies and also by being the first media house in East Africa to use phototypesetting. By the mid-1960s, the weekly and daily newspapers of the *Nation* media house were based on quality printing and production standards.

Nation Media's technological advancements transformed the company's weeklies and dailies into the most preferred sources of news in the country among both the settler and indigenous communities in a trend that saw the company gain market leadership in the publishing industry in the late 1960s. In fact, according to Loughran, the *Nation* registered its first real profits in 1968 and gained circulation leadership in 1969 after a long journey in which it had to overcome commercial difficulties related to the company's radical political stance during the preindependence period.

## KEY DATES

**1959:** His Highness the Aga Khan forms a proindependence newspaper organization.
**1960:** *Daily Nation* and *Sunday Nation* start to be published.
**1970:** Nation Media Group lists on the Nairobi Stock Exchange.
**1999:** Nation Media Group branches out into television and radio broadcasting.
**2008:** Company forms a digital division.

## PUBLIC LIMITED COMPANY: 1970

In 1970 the media house marked its 10th anniversary with the installation of one of Africa's most advanced rotary presses which enabled the company to include fully colored press photograph coverage and advertisements. His Highness the Aga Khan also used the 10th anniversary celebrations to turn his strategic vision into a reality by transformating the Nation Media Group into a public limited entity. The Aga Khan had owned 100 percent of Nation Media Group shares until 1970 because he had single-handedly financed the founding of the media organization following the lack of adequate venture and investor capital opportunities in the early 1960s.

As such, the Aga Khan offered the shares of the media organization to the public for sale with the motivation of safeguarding the company against possible takeover by the Kenyan government through nationalization programs. Nation Media Group was finally listed in the Nairobi Stock Exchange in 1970 following the successful growth of the company's publishing activities and an increase in its annual revenue earnings. The company offered 40 percent of its three million shares at a share price of KES 5 per share in an initial public offering (IPO) that was magnanimously oversubscribed.

## TREMENDOUS GROWTH: 1982–98

In 1982 Kenya experienced turbulent times when renegade Kenya Army soldiers staged a failed coup attempt against the government. However, the delicate political situation did not deter the management of Nation Media Group from pursuing optimized business opportunities through local and international partnerships. That same year Nation Media recorded KES 13.4 million in pretax profits, the second-highest profit in the company's history up to then. Nation

Media also entered into a "twinning agreement" with the *St. Petersburg Times,* a U.S. paper based in Florida. The twinning agreement was a partnership that provided training and professional exchange program opportunities for the staff of the two media organizations.

By 1983 the countrywide outlets for Nation Media's newspapers had increased to more than 5,000 outlets from less than 500 outlets in the 1960s. As the media organization marked its 25th anniversary in March 1985, its daily circulation had reached 150,000 and its annual before tax profit was in excess of $1 million.

In the 1990s, Kenya's political landscape underwent major transformations with the establishment of multiparty politics. The country held its first multiparty elections in 1992, which were won by the incumbent president, Daniel Toroitich Arap Moi. Despite the tense environment that characterized the first multiparty elections in Kenya, the *Nation* continued to inspire Kenyans with balanced reporting of the unfolding events. By the second half of the 1990s, the daily circulation of Nation Media newspapers had grown to more than 200,000 newspapers.

## TELEVISION AND RADIO BROADCASTING: 1999 AND BEYOND

Nation Media Group expanded into the broadcasting industry in 1999 with the launch of the Nation TV station and Nation FM radio station. The electronic broadcasting channel enabled the company to enhance the delivery of news and information and influence public opinion as well. The radio and TV broadcasting introduced a new dimension to the company's information communication strategy by bringing on board entertainment in the form of music, comedy, soaps, and movies to complement the delivery of news and information.

The frequencies of Channel 42 Nation TV and 96.4 Nation FM radio were licensed to cover the Nairobi area only until 2003, when the Communication Commission of Kenya granted the company the licenses for countrywide frequencies for radio and TV broadcasting. Following the success in the acquisition of national broadcasting rights, Nation Media Group put up numerous transmitters in all the major towns and broadcasting transmission points in Kenya in a move that earned the two electronic broadcasting channels of the company instant countrywide audience and following. Whereas Nation TV broadcasted in English and Swahili, 96.4 Nation FM radio broadcasted only in the English language.

Nation TV and Nation FM Radio underwent numerous transformations in the following years as the company sought to respond to the ever-changing demands of TV and radio audiences. The management of Nation Media Group particularly focused on the branding aspect of the two electronic broadcasting channels in order to identify more with the target audiences and ward off threats from its key competitors. To this end, Nation TV was rebranded as NTV Kenya in May 2005, the same year during which the company upgraded its TV broadcasting division with state-of-the-art studio and transmission equipment.

Nation Media Group expanded its TV broadcasting interests to the East Africa region when it launched NTV Uganda. The regional and global presence of NTV Kenya was further enhanced in 2007 when Nation Media Group's digital broadcasting channel joined YouTube to relay real-time Internet video and voice broadcasting. The entry of NTV Kenya to the YouTube channel was an instant success as the TV station recorded more than 320,000 views within the first month of its YouTube subscription. Statistics contained in the YouTube Web site in April 2010 indicated that NTV Kenya's YouTube channel had registered a total of 7,374 subscribers in addition to receiving channel views and total upload views in excess of 4.5 million and 41.9 million, respectively.

The rebranding mission of 96.4 Nation FM Radio was delayed until 2007 when its name was changed to Easy FM. The presence of stiff competition in the FM broadcasting segment in Kenya prompted the company to undertake thorough public relations and advertising campaigns to promote the new Easy FM brand to the public.

The success of the Easy FM radio station led to the launch of Nation Media Group's second radio station, QFM, in 2008. This radio station hosted 24-hour highly interactive and entertaining talk shows broadcast in the Swahili language. QFM was an instant success, becoming one of the most popular Swahili radio stations in Kenya within the first four months of its launch. QFM went on to become the leading Swahili talk show radio station in Kenya.

Nation Media Group diversified its advertising revenue sources with the entry of its broadcasting channels. The company's advertising revenue rose significantly after the incorporation of the broadcasting division. Nation Media Group's strategy of investing in a chain of FM radio stations particularly paid off in term of revenue growth. In a *Business Daily* article titled, "NMG Defies Harsh Economy to Post Sh588m Profit," Immanuel Were acknowledged that Nation Media Group's investments in various FM radio stations bore fruit by contributing 13 percent of the revenue growth in the company in the first half of 2009.

## GOING DIGITAL: 2008

Nation Media Group ventured into the digital world in 2008 when the company created the Nation Digital Division (NDD). The establishment of the NDD was targeted at enhancing the company's presence in digital media through the adoption of advanced information communication technology applications. The adoption of innovative and synergistic digital applications by the NDD paid dividends as the company successfully established a conspicuous presence on various Internet communications platforms as well as in the mobile telecommunications segment.

The Nation Media Group hosted its 50th anniversary celebrations on March 20, 2009, in a one-week event that also doubled as the Africa Media Conference. The celebrations were graced by His Highness the Aga Khan and were attended by Kenya's president Mwai Kibaki, Rwandan president Paul Kagame, and Kenya's prime minister Raila Odinga. Other dignitaries included Benjamin William Mkapa and Joachim Chissano, retired presidents of Tanzania and Mozambique respectively. The event provided an opportunity for participants to reminisce about the steady growth of the *Nation* and journalism from the humble beginnings in the late 1950s through to the 21st century.

*Paul Ingati*

## PRINCIPAL SUBSIDIARIES

Monitor Publications Limited (Uganda); Mwananchi Telecommunications Limited (Tanzania); NTV Uganda.

## PRINCIPAL COMPETITORS

K24 Television Corporation; Kenya Broadcasting Corporation; Royal Media Group Limited; The Standard Group Limited.

## FURTHER READING

"About *Daily Nation*," Nation Media Group, 2010.
"About Us," Nation Media Group, 2010.
"*Daily Nation* Kenya Newspaper," Kenya-Advisor.com, 2010.
"Equity Market Research: Nation Media Group," Faida Investment Bank, February 2010.
Loughran, Gerry, "The Journey of the Nation: 1960–1969: From Conception to Maturity," Nation Media, 2010.

————, "The Journey of the Nation: 1970–1979: Challenge to the Constitution," Nation Media, 2010.

————, "The Journey of the Nation: 1980–1989: Kenya Suffers an Attempted Coup," Nation Media, 2010.

Were, Emmanuel, "NMG Defies Harsh Economy to Post Sh588m Profit," *Business Daily*, August 27, 2009.

# NetApp, Inc.

495 East Java Drive
Sunnyvale, California 94089-1125
U.S.A.
Telephone: (408) 822-6000
Toll Free: (877) 263-8277
Fax: (408) 822-4501
Web site: http://www.netapp.com/us

*Public Company*
*Founded:* 1992
*Employees:* 7,976 (2009)
*Sales:* $3.406 billion (2009)
*Stock Exchanges:* NASDAQ
*Ticker Symbol:* NTAP
*NAICS:* 334112 Computer Storage Device Manufacturing; 511210 Software Publishers

■ ■ ■

NetApp, Inc., is one of the largest companies in the world specializing in computer storage and data management solutions. The company's data storage products attach to networks and enable companies to store and share data among employees. With sales in more than 130 countries, the company provides a wide range of services, from assessment and consulting to implementation and management of data and storage needs. Featuring a wide range of data storage solutions, NetApp is a leading seller of network-attached storage (NAS) systems for mid-sized to large enterprises. The company provides a wide range of data management software and also offers data protection systems and software designed to deliver nondisruptive, comprehensive protection for sensitive data. NetApp also offers data retention and archiving products. The company collaborates with key industry leaders, such as the IBM Corporation and Microsoft Corporation, to develop integrated solutions that optimize the performance of these companies' applications to NetApp systems. The company has subsidiaries around the world, including France, Germany, Italy, Japan, Australia, South Africa, India, Malaysia, and Bermuda. NetApp outsources its manufacturing operations to companies in the United States, Scotland, China, Singapore, and the Netherlands. Among NetApp's many customers are Citicorp Securities, Lockheed, Merrill Lynch, Oracle, Yahoo!, and Texas Instruments.

## COMPANY FOUNDED: 1992

David Hitz, James Lau, and Michael Malcolm founded NetApp in 1992 as Network Appliance, Inc. The company's founders believed that existing methods of data storage were too complex and came up with the idea of creating dedicated devices for storage called "appliances," thus the "appliance" in the company's original name. The trio acquired private and venture capital funding in the amount of $12.8 million to develop a dedicated, nonprogrammable server.

Prior to cofounding Network Appliance with Malcom, Hitz and Lau both worked at Auspex Corporation, a computer data storage solution manufacturer. Lau, who earned a master's degree in computer engineering from Stanford University, was a senior engineer responsible for file systems and microkernel design. (A kernel represents the bridge between computer applications and the data process performed at the hardware level, while a microkernel is a kernel that provides the various mechanisms required to implement an operating system.)

Before becoming a computer scientist and electrical engineer, Hitz worked as a cowboy, which, according to the company's Web site, gave him "valuable management experience by herding, branding, and castrating cattle." Although equating business management with experience as a cowboy may seem farfetched, Hitz explained the connection in an interview with Deni Connor for the *Network World* Web site. "In situations when you are with twenty other guys on a ranch in the middle of the desert for instance, you probably don't know how to do the task and the expert in it is nowhere near, so you just dive in [and] do your best" said Hitz, who also authored the 2009 business book *How to Castrate a Bull: Unexpected Lessons on Risk, Growth, and Success in Business.* Hitz told Connor that he chose "How to Castrate a Bull" as part of the title "because one of the book's themes is taking risks."

The company's first network appliance product line was released in June 1993. NetApp's "filers" were unique because they were dedicated to the one task of storing data. (Filers are disk storage devices that own and control a file system and present directories and files to hosts over the network.) In addition, the devices did not need specialized hardware. Instead, the founders developed a proprietary software architecture that integrated their products with industry standard hardware. As a result, NetApp's founders had found a way to provide a uniquely versatile and universal solution to data storage and retrieval.

## OVERCOMING THE DOUBTERS: 1995–2001

Despite bringing to the market a data storage and retrieval device that operated faster than a general purpose server, the company faced difficulties in its initial years. A major problem was convincing larger companies to set aside their skepticism over the founders' novel idea. One reason for such widespread

reluctance was because the integration of the Internet and networking as a way to share information had not yet been well established. As a result, over the initial years of operation, sales were slow and expenses were high, resulting in annual losses that peaked at $4.7 million in 1995, despite substantially increasing revenues in the 1995 fiscal year to $14.7 million as opposed to the $2.2 million the company registered in sales in fiscal year 1994.

In 1994 Daniel Warmenhoven replaced Michael Malcolm as chief executive officer of NetApp. The change in guard resulted partly because the company was seeking to complete a second round of financing that stipulated that Malcolm step down. After spending 13 years working for IBM, Warmenhoven had held several management positions at Hewlett-Packard Co. and been president of Network Equipment Technologies (NET) in 1989, where he also served as chief executive officer and chairman before joining NetApp.

Following Warmenhoven's installation as CEO, NetApp received much-needed venture capital funding from Sequoia Capital. The following year, Warmenhoven took the company public after developing a direct sales network instead of relying solely on indirect sales channels. Under Warmenhoven's supervision, the company went on to establish a sales force and small sales outlets across the United States. Indirect sales in London and Paris remained as the company's primary sales strategy overseas.

NetApp thrived during the rapid growth of the Internet in the mid-1990s. The company posted its first annual profit in 1996 with $6.6 million in net income as companies began to realize the potential value of networking and sharing data via the Internet. For example, the Internet service provider Yahoo! began using NetApp systems to store its customer's voluminous e-mail messages. As a result, in the latter half of the 1990s, NetApp became one of the fastest-growing computer-based companies in the United States, with its annual revenue growing to $1 billion by 2001.

## THE BUBBLE BURSTS: 2001–02

During the rapid growth of the Internet and computer technologies in the 1990s, new Internet companies, or "dot-com" companies, proliferated. As many investors sought to get in on the action, numerous bad investments were made in companies that would either take years to make a profit or would ultimately fail because of insubstantial business plans. In 1999 457 initial public offerings (IPOs) took place, with most of the IPOs being offered by companies involved in the Internet and new technology. As a reflection of the dot-com

## KEY DATES

**1992:** Company founded and incorporated as Network Appliance, Inc.
**1993:** Company releases its first products.
**1996:** NetApp introduces the industry's first multi-protocol storage appliance.
**1999:** NetApp is added to the NASDAQ-100 and S&P 500.
**2003:** NetApp enters the Chinese market through an agreement with Digital China.
**2008:** Company officially changes its name from Network Appliance to NetApp, Inc.

craze, 117 of these IPOs doubled in price during the first day of trading. By the end of 2001, however, the Internet bubble had burst. In that year only 76 IPOs took place without a single one doubling on the first day of trading.

Despite inking a $1 billion technology and business deal with the world's largest chip maker, Intel, NetApp cut its staff by 200 people in August of that year after coming up short on sales. The first layoff in the company's history represented approximately 8 percent of its 2,400-person workforce. In fiscal year 2002 NetApp's revenues declined to $798 million from the previous year's revenues of $1 billion.

Despite the setback, NetApp would make a rapid recovery as the company continued to introduce new technology and make new alliances. As a result, the company's revenues climbed steadily over the following years. In March 2003 NetApp announced a new deal with Digital China to introduce its technologies and products to that country. For fiscal year 2003 the company announced $892.06 million in revenue and a profit of $76.47 million, up from just $3.03 million in the prior fiscal year.

## NEW PRODUCTS AND ALLIANCES: 2003–09

The company continued to think strategically about storage infrastructure needed to store, manage, protect, and distribute information as the explosive growth of data became a more monumental challenge for many companies. In December 2003 the company unveiled a series of new products that featured high-end capabilities designed to make these products a one-stop source for storage and NetApp the only storage vendor some customers would need. In an interview with Cordelia

Lee for the *Asia Africa Intelligence Wire,* company cofounder Lau remarked "All of the big companies are talking about grid computing."

Grid computing involves the combination of computer resources from various administrative domains all designed to work for a common objective. Lau told *Asia Africa Intelligence Wire* contributor Lee, "I think the industry will see more adoption of grid computing probably in the next two to three years." At the time, NetApp was already collaborating with Oracle, a database giant, to develop infrastructure components that would help companies design and deploy grid architectures.

By October 2006, NetApp had sold more than 10,000 units of its latest line of corporate data storage devices. The company also departed somewhat from focusing primarily on its standard clientele of small and mid-size companies and began to aim for more business from corporate data centers, which link and exchange huge amounts of information between computer networks. In the process, the company not only bundled its products into Oracle and Microsoft databases that form the foundation for most corporate data centers, NetApp also convinced IBM to get rid of its data storage devices and incorporate NetApp's products instead. "This is incredibly important for us from a strategic standpoint because IBM has such a huge footprint in the marketplace," Patrick Rogers, vice president of NetApp's Products and Alliances division, told *Investor's Business Daily* contributor Daniel Del'Re.

Despite the worldwide economic downturn, NetApp continued to perform well, increasing its revenues by 3 percent in 2009 for a total of $3.4 billion compared to $3.3 billion for fiscal year 2008. In an *Entertainment Close-up* article, company chairman and CEO Dan Warmenhoven noted that the company's "team performed admirably to close a challenging fiscal year." Warmenhoven added later in the same article: "Customers are increasingly turning to NetApp for help solving their storage and data management challenges in the face of shrinking budgets."

## THE GOOD, THE BAD, AND THE FUTURE

NetApp did face one major setback in 2009, however. The company agreed to pay the U.S. government $128 million plus interest to settle a contract fraud case involving the company's contracts with the government to sell hardware, software, and data storage management services to various government entities. The settlement resolved all allegations concerning the government's claim that NetApp knowingly failed to meets its contractual obligations by providing the General Services Administration (GSA) with current, accurate, and complete information about the company's commercial sales practices, such as discounts offered to other commercial customers.

On the positive side, in 2009 NetApp was named "The Best Place to Work in the U.S." by *Fortune* magazine. The company was also listed on the magazine's "100 Best Companies to Work For" list for the previous six years.

In August 2009 the company announced that its future would lie in the hands of Tom Georgens, who was appointed by the company's board of directors to replace Warmenhoven as CEO after 15 years of Warmenhoven heading up the company. Warmenhoven stayed on as chairman of NetApp's board of directors. Georgens had been serving as president and chief operating officer for the company.

In the 2010s NetApp planned to further nurture strategic partnerships with companies such as IBM and Fujitsu. In addition, the company continued to focus on its primary goal of expanding its long-term market share via strategic investments and accelerated growth.

*David Petechuk*

## PRINCIPAL COMPETITORS

EMC Corporation; Hewlett-Packard Company; Hitachi Data Systems Corporation; International Business Machines Corporation; Sun Microsystems Inc.

## FURTHER READING

Connor, Deni, "NetApp Founder: Creating a Start-Up Is like Castrating Bulls," networkworld.com, January 27, 2009.

Del're, Daniel, "New Work Appliance Inc. Sunnyvale, California; NetApp Works on Supplying Data Storage to the Biggest Firms," *Investor's Business Daily,* October 16, 2006.

Lee, Cordelia, "NetApp Redefines Storage," *Asia Africa Intelligence Wire,* April 8, 2004.

"NetApp Reports 4Q Results," *Entertainment Close-up,* May 23, 2009.

# New Enterprise Associates

5425 Wisconsin Avenue
Suite 800
Chevy Chase, Maryland 20815
U.S.A.
Telephone: (301) 272-2300
Fax: (301) 272-1700
Web site: http://www.nea.com

*Private Company*
*Founded:* 1977
*Employees:* 120 (est., 2010)
*Capital Under Management:* $11 billion (2010)
*NAICS:* 523999 Miscellaneous Financial Investment
    Activities

■ ■ ■

New Enterprise Associates (NEA) is a leading global venture capital firm. As of 2010, the company had in excess of $11 billion of capital under management across 13 funds and had provided funds for more than 650 new businesses, including many familiar names such as TiVo, Macromedia, and CareerBuilder. Of the companies that have been funded by NEA, more than 160 have eventually gone public, and more than 245 have been acquired by other companies.

NEA focuses on building businesses in the fields of information technology, health care, and energy technology, with a special interest in firms that are working on major changes in technology, minimally invasive surgical procedures, or how a certain process works. The

company has investing activities in four continents, as well as affiliate offices in both India and China.

NEA's strong reputation is recognized throughout the venture capital field. Smaller firms know that NEA makes informed decisions regarding its investments and often follow suit. Wenli Yu, CEO of Seneca Networks, was quoted in *Washington Techway* as stating, "It is absolutely an advantage for NEA to lead the first round" of investments. He continued, "People know they [NEA] do their homework, so a lot of smaller VCs become interested in jumping in on the investment." Other investors have been known to make their funds available to companies with the contingency that NEA be involved as well.

Historically, about 10 percent of NEA's investments produce a return of about 10 times the amount of the investment. About 30 percent provide a return of about 5 percent, and on another 30 percent the company basically breaks even. In about 30 percent of its ventures, NEA loses most or all of the money it has invested.

## BEGINNING THE DREAM: THE 1970S

When C. Richard Kramlich graduated from Harvard Business School, he said he was "disappointed that there was very little awareness or interest in the entrepreneurial spirit," according to the *Business Journal*. After working with several other companies, Kramlich approached a guru in the field of venture capital, Arthur Rock, and together they founded Arthur Rock & Associates in 1969. Two of the companies they funded were Intel Corp. and Apple Computer Inc. After nine years, Kramlich left the company.

Soon after, in 1977, Kramlich, Frank Bonsai (an investment banker), and Charles Newhall (an analyst from T. Rowe Price) founded New Enterprise Associates with the backing of T. Rowe Price. The Baltimore-based company also had a presence on the West Coast, allowing the company to identify the best opportunities across the United States and to create a wide network of resources and experience. The founders of NEA believed that successful long-term investors must be able to select best deals and provide the necessary funds at the right time. Their dream was to assist entrepreneurs in building successful companies.

At the time of the company's founding, there were only about three venture firms in the Baltimore area, one of which was actually a real estate firm, and another had not made any investments in over 25 years. For the first year, the company's three cofounders worked without any pay until they closed their first fund in 1978. The fund totaled $16.4 million, which was invested by the Deere family of John Deere tractors and T. Rowe Price.

## BUILDING SUCCESSES: THE 1980S

By the time another venture capital company was formed in the same region in 1984, NEA was closing its third fund, valued at $126 million. The new company, Grotech Capital, which raised $12 million that year, was influenced by NEA in two ways. Not only was the company Newhall's idea, Bonsai actually introduced the two cofounders of Grotech.

During 1984 NEA invested in a total of 30 companies, including 15 start-ups. Two of these ventures included Telebit Corp. and Healthsouth Rehabilitation Corp. At the time, Telebit had developed

a computer modem that was two to three times faster than other modems. Healthsouth operated several outpatient centers for those recovering from serious injuries, heart attacks, and strokes. The company also coinvested with Grotech for the first time during 1984. The firms invested in Joshua Slocum, a women's clothing company.

During that year, NEA 3, a $126 million fund, was closed. *Washington Techway* reported in 2002 that Newhall considered this NEA's least successful fund, "mainly because the initial public offering and merger-and-acquisition markets had slowed down considerably in the mid-to-late '80s, leaving portfolio companies without an exit strategy for a long period." This fund had an internal rate of return of approximately 6 percent, compared to the common 20 percent to 25 percent return.

In 1985 an article in *Fortune* magazine explained that NEA had $187 million "committed to three funds of its own and half interest in another fund." At the time, the firm was looking outside the field of high technology for new ventures in which to invest. By 1985 the company's first fund reported a compound annual rate of return of 47 percent, despite a slight decline the previous year. The second fund's return was 65 percent at the time. As of the same year, a group of high-tech companies were NEA's greatest investment successes, but it had also invested in a California-based chain of home improvement warehouse retailers called homeClub, as well Dimensional Credit Corp., a company based in San Francisco which issued commercial paper (unsecured debt) to small companies at attractive interest rates.

By 1989 companies funded by NEA employed 25,000 people and had annual sales totaling $3.2 billion. A September 3, 1990, article in the *Business Journal* stated that NEA was "a portrait of success in an otherwise uncertain economic period in the United States. More than 130 companies nationwide have counted on New Enterprise for funding." At that time, the firm had 53 partners with offices in eight locations including San Francisco, Boston, Baltimore, New York, Cleveland, and Dallas.

## A PROSPEROUS DECADE: 1990–99

The 1990s proved to be a prosperous decade for venture capitalists because of the Internet boom, and NEA profited from this leap in technology. At the height of this period, NEA usually earned a minimum of 10 times its investment, with 40 to 50 times return on the investment also occurring. One of NEA's most financially successful investments was in Juniper Networks, which

```
┌─────────────────────────────────────────────┐
│                                               │
│              KEY DATES                        │
│                   ─■─                          │
│                                               │
│  1977:  New Enterprise Associates (NEA) is founded │
│         by Frank Bonsai, C. Richard Kramlich, and  │
│         Charles Newhall in Baltimore, Maryland.    │
│  1990:  The *Business Journal* calls NEA "a portrait of │
│         success in an otherwise uncertain economic │
│         period."                              │
│  2000:  NEA ranks second only to J.P. Morgan  │
│         Partners for the total amount of venture │
│         capital invested during the year.     │
│  2003:  NEA is the first venture capital firm to raise a │
│         $1 billion fund since 2001.           │
│  2006:  The company's NEA 12 fund raises more │
│         than $2.5 billion, which at the time is the │
│         largest in the history of the company, and the │
│         second-largest fund in the history of the │
│         industry.                             │
│                                               │
└─────────────────────────────────────────────┘
```

was a top 25 initial public offering (IPO) during 1999. The firm invested $3 million in the information technology (IT) and computer networking products company in 1996 and enjoyed a return exceeding 500 times that amount within three short years.

Another extremely successful venture in 1999 was NEA's investment in Xros, a pioneer in all optical networks for switching data in the form of light. NEA was part of an investment of $20 million. Seven months later, Xros was purchased by Nortel for $3.2 billion, giving NEA a profit of approximately $700 million.

However, not all of NEA's investments during the final decade of the 20th century were successful. While the company avoided dot-coms for the most part, it did invest in an Internet greeting card company, Egreetings. NEA executives admitted they did not believe in the company's business model but did expect that the management team would be able to make the plan work. Eventually, Egreetings was acquired, but NEA lost approximately three-fourths of the $6 million invested.

## BREAKING INVESTMENT
## RECORDS: 2000–05

In 2000 NEA ranked second only to J.P. Morgan Partners for the total of venture capital invested during the year. However, according to a January 2002 article in *Washington Techway*, "NEA was no exception to the venture capital fallout in 2001. Twenty-one of its portfolio companies, or 10 percent of its active invest-

ments, didn't survive the year. Although it largely avoided dot-coms, the firm invested heavily in telecom equipment companies, a sector that has taken a heavy beating." However, the company continued to invest in the down market during that year, unlike many struggling venture firms at the time. During 2001 NEA invested $260 million in a total of 27 new companies. It also readied itself to pounce on new opportunities in the future by adding more partners. The group prepared to invest NEA 10, which was the largest start-up fund in U.S. history at that time. The fund closed at $2.3 billion, of which nearly 70 percent was from the investors who participated in NEA 10 and organizations that these investors had created.

During the late 1990s, NEA invested approximately 90 percent of its money in information technology companies. During the early years of the 21st century, the company increased its investments in the field of life sciences and planned to use about one-third of NEA 10 to finance health care companies. The other two-thirds of NEA 10 was planned for IT companies, focusing on enterprise and security software ventures, with less emphasis on the communications sector.

The amount of money invested by venture capital firms during 2002 was at its lowest since 1997. However, NEA was the second most active firm, second only to Intel Capital that year. NEA closed 100 deals and invested a total of $490 million. Although the majority of the deals were in the field of IT, its deals in the area of health care required a greater financial stake.

In 2003 NEA was the only venture capital firm to invest in Vonage, a company offering hardware and services to allow users to utilize the Internet to make unlimited phones calls for $40 each month. NEA's investment was $12 million, with the remainder of Vonage's $65 million in funding coming from company management as well as strategic and individual investors. Company founders and management of Vonage had provided the initial $30 million over the previous two years and continued to hold more than half of the company.

Near the end of 2003, NEA became the first venture capital only firm to raise a $1 billion fund since 2001. Not only was the amount of the fund itself significant, it was also encouraging to the venture capital industry as a whole. According to a January 2004 article in *Private Equity Week*, "This is an arena that has been stagnant for years, and only occasionally brightened by the promise of a massive influx of new offering memorandums from veteran firms." At the time, most funds were $400 million or less.

While NEA had invested in medical device and drug companies in the past, during 2005 it invested in a type of company that was different than its previous ventures. NEA, along with Woodbrook Capital Investors, provided more than $12 million to launce Bariatric Partners, Inc., a chain of medical centers providing bariatric surgeries such as laparoscopic gastric banding and gastric bypass. The idea was presented by the chairman of NEA's portfolio company, Hospital Partners of America. At the time, the number of these medical procedures being performed was increasing. However, only two companies had health centers dedicated to such surgeries.

## A COMPANY ON THE MOVE:
## 2006–07

During 2006 the NEA 12 fund raised in excess of $2.5 billion, which at that time was the largest in the company's history, and the second-largest in the history of the industry. Approximately 65 percent of this money was invested into expansion or growth stage companies, with the remaining 35 percent invested into seed or early-stage companies. More than 60 percent of the companies invested in by this fund were IT firms. Approximately 25 percent of the money supported companies in the field of health care and biotechnology, and about 10.5 percent supported industrial and energy companies. Raising such a large fund during the trying economic conditions of that period would normally have raised concerns, but NEA's reputation quieted many critics. Mark Heesen, head of the National Venture Capital Association told *Business Week Online*, "I'd be concerned it if weren't NEA."

Also during 2006, NEA made a significant global move when it partnered with the Boston-based firm, Greylock Partners, to cofound Northern Light Venture Fund, a venture capital firm based in Beijing and focused on China. NEA and Greylock remained special limited partners. Northern Light later closed its first fund with $120 million.

In February 2007 NEA opened an office in India, stating that this region "offers an attractive environment for our venture investing," according to *Private Equity Week*. Early-stage investing was relegated to Indo US Ventures, a Bangalore-based independent firm of which NEA owned 20 percent. Prior to this, NEA had only made a single direct investment in a company based in India when it contributed $9 million to Sasken Communication Technologies, a telecommunications software service company, in 2005, although NEA had backed other companies with operations in the country.

During 2007 the company also moved its headquarters from Baltimore to Chevy Chase, Maryland. While the operational staff remained in Baltimore, NEA's group of East Coast partners were then based in the new offices. The move gave the company room for growth and was chosen due to its centralized location.

## FUNDING THE FUTURE: 2008
## AND BEYOND

During 2008 NEA invested $574 million into a total of 93 different deals. By October 2009, NEA had invested a total of $350 million into 61 companies during the year. In early 2010, the funds were raised for NEA 13, which at $2.48 billion was 20 times larger than the average venture fund raised during 2009. It was also the largest fund raised since the global financial crisis began in 2008. Originally, when the company started collecting the funds in November 2008, it planned to collect $3 billion. The company's focus for the fund was health care, energy, and tech companies, including both start-ups and more mature companies that needed financial backing in order to grow. The biggest investment was in Clovis Oncology, which planned to focus on new cancer treatments.

Critics expressed concern that it would be difficult for NEA to generate a large enough return on its latest fund because selling start-ups through IPOs was nearly impossible at the time, and a large fund such as NEA 13 would need a large IPO. In the wake of the economic crisis of the previous years, many believed that venture businesses should be smaller. However, Kramlich and his investors believed that "startups need serious money if they're going to tackle the kinds of issues that boost the economy and raise living standards," according to *Business Week*. This was the fourth time that NEA had raised funds of $1 billion or more. Not only were all three of the previous funds successful, they each ranked in the top 30 percent of all funds that were raised during those same years.

In March 2010 the *Wall Street Journal* included seven of NEA's portfolio companies on its list of "Top 50 Venture-Backed Companies." These companies included Fusion-io, NuroPace, Suniva, Workday, CVRx, Force10 Networks, and SmartDrive Systems. These companies represented firms doing business in information technology, health care, and energy technology, all three of NEA's core investment areas.

*Diane Milne*

## PRINCIPAL SUBSIDIARIES

New Enterprise Associates (Beijing), Ltd. (China); New Enterprise Associates (India) Pvt. Ltd.

## PRINCIPAL DIVISIONS

Energy Technology; Healthcare; Information Technology.

## PRINCIPAL COMPETITORS

Hummer Winblad Venture Partners; Internet Capital Group, Inc.; Kleiner Perkins Caufield & Byers; Mayfield Fund; Sequoia Capital.

## FURTHER READING

Barrett, Brendan, "NEA: Old Monkey, New Technology; With a $2.3 Billion War Chest, New Enterprise Associates, One of the Nation's Venture Capital Firms, Is Gearing up for a Busy Future," *Washington Techway,* 2002, p. 28.

Goldman, James S., "Richard Kramlich: He Got His First Bright Idea at 11, Illuminating an Enterprising Spirit,"*Business Journal* 8, no. 20 (2002): 12.

Haslip, Alexander, "NEA Closes on $2.45 B",*Private Equity Week* 16, no. 41 (2009): 11.

————, "NEA to Invest up to $200M in India: The Firm Joins a Crowded Market of PE Firms Focusing on the South Asian Country," *Private Equity Week* 14, no. 8 (2007): 1.

Hector, Gary, "A Tough Slog for Venture Capitalists," *Fortune,* June 10, 1985, p. 110.

Mullaney, Tim, "The Last Hurrah of a Venture Capitalist," *Business Week,* February 1, 2010, p. 61.

"NEA Bellies up to Gastric Deal," *Private Equity Week* 12, no. 42 (2005): 5.

"NEA's Even Bigger Thinking; The Venture Capital Firm Has Raised $2.5 Billion to Invest in Life Sciences and Emerging Markets. Can It Wisely Spend That Much Money?" *Business Week Online,* July 10, 2006.

Primack, Dan, "The Next Generation of Funds Has Arrived,"*Private Equity Week* 11, no. 1 (2004): 1.

"Vonage Dials up $35m Round," *Private Equity Week* 10, no. 46 (2003): 3.

# NewMarket Corporation

—■—

330 South Fourth Street
Richmond, Virginia 23219
U.S.A.
Telephone: (804) 788-5000
Fax: (804) 788-5688
Web site: http://www.newmarket.com

*Public Company*
*Founded:* 1887 as Albemarle Paper Manufacturing
Company
*Employees:* approx., 1,100 (2009)
*Sales:* $1.53 billion (2009)
*Stock Exchanges:* New York
*Ticker Symbol:* NEU

■ ■ ■

NewMarket Corporation (NewMarket) is a holding
company and the parent company of Afton Chemical
Corporation, Ethyl Corporation, NewMarket Development Corporation, and NewMarket Services Corporation. NewMarket is one of the world's leading suppliers
of petroleum additives for lubricating oils and fuels.
Lubricant additives are used mainly with metal-to-metal
parts and include engine oils, transmission fluids, gear
oils, and hydraulic oils. They are designed to reduce friction and extend the life of machinery. Fuel additives are
designed to improve the performance of gasoline, diesel,
and biofuels. They improve ignition, reduce emissions,
assist in combustion efficiency, and improve fuel
economy.

NewMarket has research facilities in both the
United States and the United Kingdom, with
manufacturing facilities in Europe and North and South
America. The company sells its products globally, with
foreign markets accounting for roughly three-fifths of all
sales in 2009.

## EARLY HISTORY

The origins of the NewMarket Corporation extend back
to the latter half of the 19th century in the United
States. It is the story of how a small paper company,
harvesting the resources at its disposal, adapted to
change and adopted new technologies to survive and
prosper. In many respects, it mirrors the industrial
development of the United States itself.

In 1887 a group of business interests in Richmond,
Virginia, formed the Albemarle Paper Manufacturing
Company. The bitter and protracted American Civil
War had been over for more than two decades, and the
country was transforming itself from a rural agrarian
society into an industrial power.

Expansion, growth, and industrialization would be
the hallmarks of the transformation. The population of
the United States, which numbered less than 40 million
in 1865, would surpass 62 million by 1890 and
continue to increase. Immigration, which had
contributed 10 million new citizens by 1890, would add
15 million more by 1914.

Industrial production, based on the nation's vast
natural resources, would increase to meet the demands
of the growing population. In 1860 the United States

was ranked fourth in output amongst manufacturing nations. By 1894 it was first, doubling the output of Great Britain, the previous world leader.

The raw materials that the Albemarle Paper Company required were nearby. The state of Virginia is located in what is known as the U.S. Southern Forest Region. Often referred to as "America's wood basket," the area provided an abundance of softwoods ideal for Albemarle's two main products of kraft paper (used in packaging) and blotter paper, an absorbent.

Throughout this period and into the first half of the 20th century, the company would continue a steady, if unspectacular, production of paper products. Technology and change, however, would start to catch up with the company after World War II. It would face the challenge of adopting new technology and adapting to change or going out of business. Fortunately for the company, when change did come, Albemarle had an innovator at the helm.

Floyd Dewey Gottwald was 20 years old when he joined the Albemarle Paper Company as a clerk in 1918. By all accounts, the Richmond native was industrious, hardworking, and forward thinking. He had studied chemistry at the College of William and Mary, and once employed he used his savings to buy shares in the company. Gottwald rose through the ranks, eventually becoming president of Albemarle in 1941. He would be instrumental in adapting the company, sometimes begrudgingly, to new technology and business opportunities. He laid the foundation that would see the organization through the 20th century and beyond.

## CREATION OF A CONGLOMERATE

By the 1950s the Albemarle Paper Manufacturing Company had all the appearances of a static corporation. New technologies and practices were beginning to render its products obsolete and erode its profits. The fountain pen was being replaced by the widespread acceptance of the ballpoint pen as a writing instrument of choice. As the demand for fountain pens decreased, so did the demand for blotting paper. In addition, the company's production of kraft paper, used to make paper bags and other packaging materials, was jeopardized by the increasing use of plastic bags and plastic packing material.

Unable to influence the decline in sales of blotting paper, Albemarle was faced with the choice of adapting to the new world of plastic or going out business. However, it lacked both the facilities and the technology to produce polyethylene film, a key process in the manufacturing of plastic, which its competitors were already using. Albemarle needed to find a chemical supplier if it was to survive. The opportunity would arise in the form of a chemical company called the Ethyl Corporation.

The Ethyl Corporation was a joint venture of General Motors Corporation and Standard Oil of New Jersey. Its primary product was tetraethyl lead (TEL), which it produced in association with the DuPont Chemical Corporation. Tetraethyl lead is a chemical compound used originally as a gasoline additive. It was invented in 1921 by the American industrial researcher and mechanical engineer Thomas Midgley. Midgley had discovered that adding tetraethyl lead to gasoline eliminated "knock" in internal combustion engines. Engine knock, or "pinging" as it is sometimes referred to, occurs when fuel is detonated outside of the normal combustion process. It can lead to waste of fuel, increased pressure on the motor, and premature wear on mechanical parts.

Under Gottwald's leadership, Albemarle approached Ethyl Corporation to enlist it as a chemical supplier. The highly profitable Ethyl Corporation showed little interest in the tiny paper company. Undaunted, Gottwald continued to pursue Ethyl as a partner. In addition, there were rumors that Ethyl might be put up for sale. The patent that it held on tetraethyl lead had expired in 1947 and concerns had already been raised on the harmful effects of lead on human health. The three major players within Ethyl Corporation were General Motors, Standard Oil of New Jersey, and DuPont Chemical. Each of these large businesses were wary of U.S. antitrust laws, which virtually eliminated them as potential sole owners.

Gottwald put together a consortium of investors, which included banks, insurance companies, and investment houses, and in 1962, he purchased the Ethyl Corporation for $200 million. The news stunned the business world. A tiny paper company from Richmond, Virginia, with earnings in 1961 of $1.8 million had just absorbed a company more than 10 times its size and financed the entire deal with debt. It was believed to the

# KEY DATES

**1887:** Albemarle Paper Manufacturing Company is formed in Richmond, Virginia.
**1921:** Tetraethyl lead, an antiknocking agent in gasoline, is invented.
**1941:** Floyd D. Gottwald becomes president of Albemarle Paper Manufacturing.
**1962:** Albemarle acquires Ethyl Corporation.
**2004:** NewMarket Corp. created as holding company for Ethyl Corporation and Afton Chemical Corporation.

largest leveraged buyout in history.

As might be expected, the new entity required reorganization. The company adopted the Ethyl name and moved Ethyl's headquarters to Richmond. Although the new company had a huge debt, it also had a much larger income, for Ethyl had earned $24.0 million in 1961.

The company embarked on a series of acquisitions, purchasing VisQueen, a major producer of polyethylene film, in 1963. In 1966 it absorbed the William Bonnel Company, an aluminum producer, and the following year it acquired the Oxford Paper Company, a manufacturer of bleached paper used in printing and publishing. It expanded its plastics business by producing plastic bottles, and it became a leader in the production of polyvinyl chloride (PVC) for piping. The company also continued to produce tetraethyl lead and expanded to Europe, where it found new markets for its additives.

By 1971 the tiny paper company known as Albemarle had been transformed into a conglomerate called the Ethyl Corporation with sales of $577 million. The next decade, however, would bring new challenges to Ethyl, which would almost drive it out of business.

## ADAPTION AND DIVERSIFICATION

Concerns about the environmental and health effects of lead began to gain public attention in the late 1960s. The potential adverse effects of lead were not new. Almost from the discovery of tetraethyl lead, controversy had surrounded the impact of lead on human health. In 1924 some 50 workers at three separate petroleum refineries became ill from lead contamination, and five would eventually die of their illness. Even Thomas Midgley, who had invented the product, had contracted lead poisoning and was forced into an extended leave to recuperate.

While working on a project to determine the age of planet Earth, an American scholar and geophysicist named Clair Patterson had identified increasing lead levels in the atmosphere. From core ice samples he had taken in Greenland, Patterson was able to demonstrate that lead levels had increased dramatically since the introduction of tetraethyl lead as a gasoline additive. The campaign to eliminate leaded fuel had begun.

By 1972 concerns about the effects of lead on human health and the environment had reached the government of the United States. Through the Environmental Protection Agency, the government announced plans to move towards the elimination of lead as a fuel additive.

The announcement was a potential disaster for the Ethyl Corporation. Despite its expansion into plastics and aluminum, tetraethyl lead was still its flagship product. The additive accounted for only 36 percent of company sales but contributed 60 percent of company profit.

Gottwald and his management team were under no illusions about the long-term prospects for leaded gasoline additives, but they elected to fight back. They formed a committee named the Ethyl Air Conservation Group, made up of company executives and lawyers, in an attempt to counter the claims of environmentalists and to represent the leaded fuel industry in the United States. In the face of overwhelming scientific evidence on the harmful effects of lead, the effort was doomed to failure. It did, however, perhaps serve one useful purpose, for it bought the Ethyl Corporation time. The phasing out of leaded fuel, announced in 1972, would not begin until 1976, and it would be 1986 before it was completed. This gave Ethyl time to adapt.

The company began to refocus itself in many ways. It placed greater emphasis on its chemical and plastic products. It became a major producer of plastic bottle caps and a major supplier of the plastic linings for disposable infant diapers.

In addition, Ethyl Corporation produced chemicals for the semiconductor business as well as bromides and herbicides. It also became a bulk supplier of ibuprofen, an over-the-counter pain medicine.

While these changes were being made, Ethyl Corporation continued to buy and sell assets as part of its growth strategy. In 1975 it sold the Oxford Paper Company. In 1981 it purchased the First Colony Life Insurance Company, which specialized in selling coverage to high-risk individuals. It sold off the company in 1993.

Finally, Ethyl established an energy group, which leased mineral rights and explored for oil and gas in the United States. In 1989 it created Tredegar Industries from its aluminum, plastic, and energy products and then sold the company off. The firm also resurrected the Albemarle name and sold off its specialty chemical business as the Albemarle Corporation.

While all this was underway, Ethyl remained interested in the petroleum additives business. Despite the decline in lead sales, there were other petroleum additives, such as oil additives, diesel additives, and non-leaded gasoline additives. In 1992 Ethyl acquired Amoco Petroleum Additives in the United States and Nippon Cooper in Japan. Texaco Additives was added in 1996.

As the 21st century approached, Ethyl Corporation was still focused on the petroleum additives industry, and a new generation of the Gottwald family was in control.

## NEWMARKET CORPORATION

By 2004 Ethyl Corporation was a much narrower and more focused organisation. Under the guidance of Thomas E. Gottwald, Floyd's grandson and a company director since 1994, and with the approval of the shareholders, the company was reorganized and restructured as the NewMarket Corporation.

NewMarket was structured as a holding company, to own and control various subsidiary companies. Subsidiary Afton Chemical Corporation is a specialty chemical company, which develops, manufactures, and blends fuel and lubricant additives. Its brands include Hitec Performance additives, Biotec Performance Additive Solutions, Greenburn Combustion Technologies, MMT, Axcel, and Tecgard Metalworking Additives.

Subsidiary Ethyl Corporation manufactures and distributes gasoline and diesel performance additives and diesel cetane improvers. Two other subsidiaries assist these primary business ventures. NewMarket Development Corporation owns and operates all of NewMarket property holdings in Richmond, Virginia, while NewMarket Services provides administrative services and support to all NewMarket companies.

The early years of NewMarket went well. The company topped $1 billion in sales in 2005, and the company has stayed well above the $1 billion mark ever since, although sales did take a slight dip in 2009. Net income was healthy between 2005 and 2009 as well. Although leaded gasoline has become a distant memory, NewMarket entered the 2010s as a world leader in petroleum additives.

*Ian MacDonald*

## PRINCIPAL SUBSIDIARIES

Afton Chemical Corporation; Ethyl Corporation; NewMarket Development Corporation; NewMarket Services.

## PRINCIPAL COMPETITORS

BASF AG; InFineum France; Chevron Oronite; Innospec Inc.; Lubrizol Corporation; SNPE S.A.

## FURTHER READING

Blackwell, John Reid, "NewMarket Corp.—The New Ethyl." *Richmond Times Dispatch,* June 12, 2006.

Friedman, Milton, *A Monetary History of the United States, 1867–1960.* National Bureau of Economic Research, 1963.

"The Gottwald Jinx," *Time,* April 17, 1972.

Needleman, Herbert L., "The Removal of Lead from Gasoline: Historical and Personal Reflections," *Environmental Research* 84 no. 1 (September 2000): 20–35.

Virginia Department of Agriculture and Consumer Services, "Virginia Woods."

# ONEOK Inc.

---

100 West Fifth Street
Tulsa, Oklahoma 74103
U.S.A.
Telephone: (918) 588-7000
Fax: (918) 588-7960
Web site: http://www.oneok.com

*Public Company*
*Founded:* 1906 as Oklahoma Natural Gas Company
*Employees:* 4,758 (2009)
*Revenue:* $11.11 billion (2009)
*Stock Exchanges:* New York
*Ticker Symbol:* OKE
*NAICS:* 221210 Natural Gas Distribution

■ ■ ■

ONEOK Inc. (pronounced "one oak") is one of the largest distributors of natural gas in the United States, servicing more than two million customers in Oklahoma, Kansas, and Texas. ONEOK's energy services operation focuses on marketing natural gas and related services to local distribution companies, industrial customers, and power generators. ONEOK is the sole general partner and 42.8 percent owner of ONEOK Partners L.P., a large, publicly traded master limited partnership.

A *Fortune* 500 company, ONEOK has been recognized by that magazine as one of the "World's Most Admired Companies," and as one of "America's Most Reputable Companies."

## THE EARLY YEARS: 1906–20

ONEOK began as Oklahoma Natural Gas (ONG) and was formed in an era when natural gas was treated as a nuisance in the oil fields. In 1906 Territorial Congressman Dennis T. Flynn and businessman C. B. Ames decided to pipe gas from northeastern Oklahoma to Oklahoma City, which at the time was served by a manufactured gas facility. To do this, on October 12, 1906, they formed the Oklahoma Natural Gas Company with backers Theodore N. Barnsdall of the Barnsdall Oil Company and former Standard Oil officer Glen T. Braden.

Flynn, who was ONG's first president, signed contracts to supply local distributors, and on December 28, 1907, a month after Oklahoma was admitted to the union as the 46th state, a 100-mile pipeline, costing $1.7 million, was completed from Tulsa to Oklahoma City.

Braden replaced Flynn after the pipeline's completion, and he managed the nascent company in an Oklahoma that had no highways and few schools but more than its share of "high noon" law that was enforced by the fastest gun. This was the period when state legislators were expected to check their sidearms with the sergeant-at-arms in each legislative body. During World War I, Braden increased the company's capitalization to $10 million and reduced the price of its stock from $100 to $25 per share.

In 1921 Harry Heasley replaced an ill Braden as president. Heasley soon created two oil companies to exploit the extensive oil-bearing properties ONG had found while seeking natural gas. The second of these,

Oklahoma Eastern, was later merged with Devonian Oil through an exchange of stock.

## A DECADE OF CHANGE: THE 1920S

In the mid-1920s, the U.S. economy boomed, and the oil and gas business boomed with it. With such increased economic activity, ONG became a takeover target. On July 31, 1926, the company was sold to New York investment bankers White, Weld, and Company.

White, Weld, and Company promptly renamed the company Oklahoma Natural Gas Corporation and sold it to Phillips Petroleum, which wanted it as an outlet for its vast Texas Panhandle gas holdings. Phillips elected a new board, named R. C. Sharp as president, and moved the company's headquarters to Tulsa, which was rapidly becoming a focal point of the nation's oil and gas industry. In Tulsa, Phillips also arranged for the building of a new 10-story, $600,000 headquarters.

Phillips used ONG until it could complete its own pipeline to the Midwest and then, on October 15, 1927, sold it to the American Natural Gas Corporation, a holding company subsidiary of utility company financiers G. L. Ohrstrom and Company, Inc.

Ohrstrom's aim, like that of many utility holding companies, was to extract cash from its holdings. It used a variety of methods to do this, including taking a profit from brokered acquisitions. For instance, it purchased and then sold to ONG the Southern Kansas Gas Company, the Western Gas Service Company of Texas, and the gas properties of Oklahoma Gas and Electric Company.

At this point, ONG's shares were moving up sharply because of the large dividends it was paying in the form of preferred stock. As was common, ONG's dividends bore no relation to its true rate of growth. What revenue increases the company did experience came from stock sales rather than productivity. In fact, during this period, employees sold stock house to house. It was inevitable that the situation would correct itself

and it did. On October 29, 1929, the stock market crashed, plunging ONG and Ohrstrom into turmoil along with the rest of U.S. industry.

## UNDER NEW MANAGEMENT: THE 1930S

At ONG, management changed rapidly. In June 1930 Oklahoma Natural Gas Corporation president Thomas R. Weymouth resigned and was replaced by E. C. Deal, who traded the company's Texas properties for the Oklahoma Natural Gas Corporation in eastern Oklahoma. Then, through arrangements with Tri-Utilities, which was an Ohrstrom holding company, Deal constructed a pipeline from the Quinton field in eastern Oklahoma to Sand Springs, just west of Tulsa.

In October 1931 Deal resigned as president and was elected chair of the board of directors. To meet obligations, his successor, retired army colonel E. A. Olsen, interrupted dividends on common stock, paid little or no dividends on preferred stock, cut salaries, canceled vacations, and laid off employees.

In 1932 Olsen resigned and was replaced by Robert W. Hendee. Within a year, the company brought in A. E. Bradshaw, executive vice president of the First National Bank and Trust Company of Tulsa, to reorganize its finances. Bradshaw dissolved the Oklahoma Natural Gas Corporation and reincorporated it in Delaware as the Oklahoma Natural Gas Company. He exchanged stock, extended short-term debt, and honored current bonds. After the company completed Bradshaw's $30 million refinancing program in 1936, it shed its holding company and contracted Stone and Webster Service Corporation for management advisory services previously provided by the holding company.

Service had suffered during the Ohrstrom years, and the public was so dissatisfied that it almost built a municipal gas plant in Oklahoma City. To make matters worse, the Oklahoma legislature, responding to the demands of retailers, prohibited ONG from merchandising appliances. A return to normalcy began on June 1, 1936, when Joseph "Jos" Bowes gained the ONG presidency. Smart and tough, Bowes improved customer relations and emphasized that as an Oklahoma company, ONG owed allegiance to its customers and shareholders only.

Bowes fostered ONG's financial health through the late 1930s, and by 1940, when a sustained cold spell froze wells and threatened to interrupt service, he was able to initiate a heavy construction program to upgrade major lines and build additional ones. That year ONG also paid $4.7 million for Central States Power and Light Corporation, a gas utility that served Stillwater,

## KEY DATES

**1906:** Oklahoma Natural Gas Company is formed to pipe gas from northeastern Oklahoma to Oklahoma City.

**1926:** Company is sold to New York investment bankers White, Weld, and Company, who rename the company Oklahoma Natural Gas Corporation.

**1936:** Joseph Bowes becomes company president and emphasizes company allegiance is to Oklahoma customers.

**1950s:** Company acquires interest in a natural gas gathering system.

**1968:** Thermal Systems, Inc., a subsidiary, is created to build central cooling and heating plants.

**1971:** ONG serves 500,000 customers and generates more than $100 million in revenues.

**1982:** Company hurt by onerous take-or-pay contracts, which force company to buy gas even when there are no customers to purchase it.

**1997:** Agreement with Western Resources gives company access to customers in Kansas and Oklahoma.

**2004:** ONEOK becomes a majority general partner in Northern Border Partners, L.P., one of the largest publicly traded master limited partnerships.

**2005:** ONEOK acquires natural gas liquids businesses owned by Koch and uses the business to create its Natural Gas Liquids operating segment.

**2006:** ONEOK acquires 45.7 percent of Northern Border Partners (NBP) and 17.5 percent general partner interest in the partnership. NBP is renamed ONEOK Partners.

Henryetta, Holdenville, and what was to become the Clinton area of western Oklahoma.

## MEETING STORAGE AND DISTRIBUTION NEEDS: THE 1940S

World War II drew many employees into the military and increased demands on ONG's distribution system. In fact, the necessity of supplying eight major military installations in Tulsa, Oklahoma City, Enid, Norman,

and Muskogee led the company to build a 96-mile high-pressure pipeline from the Cement and Chickasha fields to the Stroud junction, halfway between Tulsa and Oklahoma City.

During the war, ONG also began storing gas in depleted gas formations. In the late 1930s, the company pioneered research and development of what became a widely used technology in which gas was injected into formations that effectively became underground storages. The injections would take place principally in the summer months when there was low customer demand. The gas was withdrawn later, usually in the winter, to meet high demand. The process subsequently alleviated the demands on the transmission system to transport large amounts of gas long distances if underground storages could be located near population centers. The company continued to develop underground storages and created five of them strategically located throughout the system.

Following the war, ONG acquired distribution operations in the Oklahoma communities of Sand Springs, Crescent, Dover, Guthrie, Hennessey, and Kingfisher, bringing its 1950 customer total to 270,000. That year it also renovated its Tulsa office building and purchased the five-story Key Building in Oklahoma City. Both buildings were provided with gas air-conditioning, which was a relatively new innovation.

## GROWTH AND EXPANSION: THE 1950S–1960S

In the early 1950s the company acquired an interest in a natural gas gathering system and in three gasoline plants in Oklahoma's Garvin and McClain counties. It spent $10 million annually on capital improvements as it linked its Depew underground gas storage facility with Oklahoma City and Tulsa, constructed service centers in Oklahoma City and Tulsa, built a gas processing plant in the Ringwood Field of Major County, and installed an advanced microwave and VHF radio communications system.

Bowes reported to shareholders that 1954 had been the company's best financial year. Earnings rose to $1.62 a share from $0.94 a year earlier, and for the first time gas-fired central heating installations in homes edged out floor furnaces as a means of residential heating.

The company grew internally through the mid-1950s, and in the late 1950s and early 1960s returned to acquisition and expansion. It expanded its Garvin County gasoline plant, and in 1959 it bought an interest in the Laverne gas processing plant in northwestern Oklahoma. In 1960 it acquired the Northern Oklahoma

Gas Company, the Standard Gas Company, and the State Fuel Supply Company, gaining distribution operations in the Oklahoma cities of Ponca City, Newkirk, Perry, Madill, Tishomingo, Anadarko, Wewoka, and Lindsey.

In 1964 H. A. "Tex" Eddins replaced Bowes as chairman of the board. Eddins, who had become president in 1955, had already made his mark on ONG, creating, in June 1962, the company's first wholly owned subsidiary, Oklahoma Natural Gas Gathering Company (ONGGC). ONGGC gathered gas from around the state and sold it in interstate commerce. Unlike its parent, ONGGC operated interstate and was therefore subject to federal regulation.

Eddins was concerned with ensuring an adequate long-term gas supply. He began a program of securing reserves in the Red Oak Field of southeastern Oklahoma. In 1965 he acquired Zenith Natural Gas Company and converted Zenith's Kansas properties into a second subsidiary. In 1966 he formed Oklahoma Natural Gas Transmission Company, which built and operated a 93-mile transmission pipe from Red Oak in eastern Oklahoma to Sapulpa, southwest of Tulsa.

## ECONOMIC AND TECHNOLOGICAL CHANGES: THE MID-1960S

Tragically, Eddins died suddenly on April 26, 1966, while attending an employee service awards meeting. He was replaced by executive vice president C. C. "Charlie" Ingram, an engineer who had joined the company in 1940 as an engineer trainee following his graduation from the University of Oklahoma.

Ingram emphasized exploration and gas purchases and reacted quickly to changing economic conditions and technologies. In his first two years as CEO, he began the process of computerization, adopted plastic pipe for distribution systems, embraced less expensive techniques of laying pipe, and launched a major sales campaign to combat the electric industry's "total electric home" promotional program. In 1968 he formed Thermal Systems, Inc., which built central cooling and heating plants in Tulsa and Oklahoma City and, eventually, a cold storage warehouse.

## SHORTAGES IN THE GAS SUPPLY: THE 1970S

In 1970, with gas supply as a primary concern, Ingram reorganized ONG's operating department, established a gas supply department, and formed Oklahoma Natural Development Corporation.

Gas supply was a problem everywhere, but while oil was encountering foreign interruptions, in the natural gas industry the federal government itself was the cause of shortages. Wellhead prices for gas transported across state lines was set at politically attractive but economically unrealistic levels, and interstate gas companies found it increasingly difficult to compete for new supplies. Being an intrastate gas utility and not subject to federal regulation of what price it could pay, ONG was able to acquire adequate gas supplies in the midst of shortages throughout the rest of the industry.

In 1971 ONG served 500,000 customers and generated more than $100 million in revenues. Ingram and newly named president Wayman E. Humphrey remained focused on supply. In 1972 they formed ONG Exploration Company and encouraged customers to conserve. In 1973 the company's intrastate status allowed it to remain competitive for new gas supplies even as the Arab oil embargo tightened energy supplies and many companies within the U.S. energy industry were caught short.

To insure access to new supplies, Ingram in 1973 created ONG Western Inc. to build a 200-mile, $20 million pipeline into the gas-rich Anadarko basin of western Oklahoma. He incorporated ONG of Norway, Inc., to bid on oil and gas leases in the North Sea and by 1974 was spending a yearly $9 million for exploration and production, including a $3 million wildcat program.

## INDUSTRY CHANGES: THE MID-1970S–1980

The mid-1970s was a time of customer growth for ONG, despite real and threatened shortages. In 1974 it began making large deliveries to the first of five large new fertilizer plants. Its 1976 earnings increased by 51 percent, and in 1977 it extended pipelines 500 miles and installed a computerized customer information system.

Nevertheless, an overall solution to the continuing shortages in the interstate market was needed. Although Oklahoma Natural survived without interruption in service to its customers and sold emergency deliveries to interstate companies, pressure was building on Congress to act.

Congress provided a solution when it passed the Natural Gas Policy Act of 1978. The NGPA deregulated wellhead prices for newly found gas and therefore provided incentive for exploration. However, the act, which eventually released vast supplies, caused price fluctuation during the 1980s, which resulted in major changes in the industry.

In December 1980 ONG changed its corporate name to ONEOK Inc. Pronounced "one oak," the new name was meant to change perceptions. The company had indeed grown and diversified. Oklahoma Natural Gas had become a major player in the industry. It distributed gas to 215 communities, wholesaled it to distributors serving 47 states, and had some 600,000 residential customers. Within ONEOK's nonutility division, the ONEOK Energy Companies, ONEOK Exploration Company explored for oil and natural gas, while Smart Drilling Company, acquired in 1979, was a contract-drilling operation.

## A DIFFICULT PERIOD: THE EARLY TO MID-1980S

In 1981 and 1982, sales reached record $1 billion levels. Revenues were also reaching record heights, as was capital spending, which topped $181 million in 1982. This spending included subsidiary TransTex Pipeline Company's share of the new Red River Pipeline, and Caney River Transmission Company's share of the new Ozark Gas Transmission System, which crossed the Arkoma Basin from Oklahoma to Arkansas.

Despite these records, by 1982 the company was feeling the pinch of recession-caused weaknesses in the industrial market. This market was especially important because ONEOK had signed take-or-pay contracts with its own suppliers and was therefore obliged to pay for gas even when it had no customers. Since 1982 take-or-pay claims amounted to some $108 million, Ingram and newly named CEO J. E. Tyree were faced with the necessity to economize. They cut costs, reduced ONG's capital budget, and fought these claims in court. Nevertheless, a weak economy, sparse contract-drilling demand, lower investment tax credits, increased interest costs, and a $12.8 million drilling write-off in Malta all cut 1983 earnings per share to $2.51 from 1982's $4.88.

To make matters worse, even though executives did what they could to keep industrial deliveries high by cutting prices to ONG's five fertilizer plant customers to keep them in business, deliveries continued to fall from 1982's 281 billion cubic feet (bcf) to 242 bcf. The erosion of deliveries exposed ONEOK to heavy take-or-pay claims.

Weather and rate increases helped the company recover to a degree in 1984. While ONEOK tried to look optimistic as it opened a new 17-story company headquarters in downtown Tulsa, it cut capital expenditures, moved away from natural gas exploration, and reduced the number of rigs in its contract-drilling operation.

Events of 1985 continued to be sobering. Earnings per share continued to fall, as did demand. New federal regulations allowed industrial users to purchase gas from the wellhead and transport it through pipeline-capacity leases. On the energy side, ONEOK drilling company reported a net loss of $5 million, about half of which was attributable to a three-rig write-down.

## TURNING THINGS AROUND: 1986–96

On the positive side, executives instituted a long-range planning strategy, moving strongly into oil production by acquiring Imperial Oil for $9.4 million and forming ONG Transmission Company to handle opportunities in pipeline capacity leases. These opportunities were made more lucrative by the fact that Oklahoma was the nation's third most prolific gas-producing state.

In 1986 a sluggish economy, warm weather, and unrecoverable take-or-pay settlements of almost $6.2 million forced ONEOK into drastic economies. It consolidated offices, cut down on drilling, and through early retirement policies, reduced its work force by 380, or nearly 15 percent. Things continued to deteriorate in 1987. After a jury awarded Forest Oil $50 million in a take-or-pay suit, banks withdrew an $85 million line of credit, and ratings services downgraded ONEOK's debt.

To get ONEOK back on its financial feet, J. D. Scott, who had become president and CEO in 1986, interrupted regular dividends, appealed the Forest Oil verdict, and established reserves of $112.3 million for unresolved take-or-pay disputes. In 1988 he continued downsizing by providing an early retirement package and incentives for 113 employees to resign or retire. He also sold slightly more than 50 percent of the company's exploration leases. A light at the end of the tunnel began to appear in 1989, when earnings per share rose 71 percent, dividends were restored, and exploration and production activities became profitable for the first time in five years. In 1990 Standard and Poors and Duff and Phelps upgraded ONEOK's debt to A- from BBB+.

Scott displayed his own confidence through acquisitions and expansions. He committed to a major expansion of the Ozark Gas Transmission System, announced a ONEOK Exploration strategy committed to riskier plays with bigger payoffs, acquired the Lone Star Gas Company in central Oklahoma, and continued a research, development, and demonstration project, begun in 1980, that used natural gas as an alternative fuel for vehicles.

In 1992 ONEOK remained optimistic despite a significantly warmer than normal winter and unprofitable spot market prices. The company formed ONEOK

Gas Marketing to pool and market the products of Oklahoma's independent producers, and it created ONEOK Technology Company to develop and market a new meter-setting device.

## GROWTH AND EXPANSION: 1997–2003

During the late 1990s, the company entered into several transactions focused on growth and expansion. In 1997 ONEOK entered an agreement with Western Resources in which ONEOK paid $660 million for the right to serve Western's gas customers in Kansas and Oklahoma, and Western gained 45 percent of ONEOK's equity stock. ONEOK almost doubled its number of customers and was able to purchase and distribute gas more efficiently and at a lower cost. As a result of the alliance, ONEOK formed Kansas Gas Services, which, by 2010, was the largest distribution company of natural gas in Kansas, with more than 643,000 customers and nearly 13,000 miles of distribution mains and services.

Two years later, in 1999, ONEOK acquired Koch Midstream Enterprise's Oklahoma natural gas gathering and processing assets, including eight processing plants and about 3,250 miles of gathering pipeline. The acquisition cost ONEOK $285 million but helped the company work towards its goal of maximizing values in its nonregulated assets. These include natural gas reserves and processing plants, as well as gathering, transportation, and marketing operations.

The following year, ONEOK made two significant purchases to support the company's plan of expansion in the mid-continent area. First, the company acquired $307.7 million in midstream gas assets when it purchased Dynegy, Inc., including eight gas processing plants as well as interests in two others, as well as approximately 7,000 miles of gathering and intrastate transmissions systems. Following this, ONEOK bought Kinder Morgan's natural gas gathering and processing businesses in Kansas, Oklahoma, and West Texas, as well as the company's gas marketing and trading business, several storage and pipeline properties, six processing plants, and 12,000 miles of pipeline. This transaction made ONEOK a top-20 gas marketer.

Between 1998 and 2003, the company invested more than $2.8 billion in capital improvement and expansion projects, which supported its strategic growth plan. In 2003 the company acquired Wagner & Brown's Cotton Valley reserves in East Texas for $240 million, which expanded the company's footprint in Texas and provided access to nearly 600 additional wells. The company also acquired Texas Gas Service during 2003, which also included a natural gas distribution system

and the related business in Mexico. However, ONEOK sold its interest in Mexico for about $2 million the following year.

## MORE ACQUISITIONS: 2004–05

Over the next several years, several significant events took place within the company that would impact the future operations of ONEOK. The first occurred during 2004 when ONEOK became a majority general partner in Northern Border Partners, L.P., one of the largest publicly traded master limited partnerships, through the purchase of Northern Plains Natural Gas Company for $175 million. The Northern Border Pipeline carried about 22 percent of all natural gas imported from Canada into the United States during that year. The growth of Northern Border Partners (NBP) would allow ONEOK to compete more effectively by using the tax advantages and lower cost of capital that were available to master limited partnerships.

The following year, the company acquired Koch Industries' natural gas liquids business, an entity ONEOK had its eye on for years, for $1.35 billion. The company used the businesses to create its Natural Gas Liquids operating segment, which also included ONEOK's existing NGL marketing business. The acquisition gave ONEOK a NGL system that connected much of the supply in Oklahoma, parts of Texas, and Kansas with key market centers in Kansas and Texas. Since more than 80 percent of the revenue from the system was fee-based, the acquisition also lowered ONEOK's risk profile significantly.

## THE INTRODUCTION OF ONEOK PARTNERS: 2006–08

ONEOK's centennial year was marked by a 62 percent increase in the company's stock price, no short-term debt, and about $1 billion in cash or cash equivalents. In February 2006, ONEOK agreed to transfer all of its gathering and processing, natural gas liquids, and pipeline and storage businesses to Northern Border Partners, with the belief that NBP would be able to compete more effectively with these assets. In return, NBP paid ONEOK $1.35 billion in cash, an amount equal to what ONEOK paid for the natural gas liquids business the previous year. Including stock, the deal was worth about $3 billion. Following the transaction, ONEOK owned 45.7 percent of NBP. ONEOK also purchased TransCanada Corporation's 17.5 percent general partner interest in NBP for $40 million, giving ONEOK 100 percent general partner interest in NBP. In May of that year, NBP was renamed ONEOK Partners, and the partnership began trading under the symbol OKS. ONEOK Partners reported an operating income of $510 million by the end of the year.

During its second year of operation, ONEOK Partners acquired NGL Pipeline, an interstate natural gas liquids and refined petroleum products pipeline system and the related assets for about $300 million. The system spanned 1,624 miles from Bushton and Conway, Kansas, to Chicago. The acquisition also included storage capacity, eight NGL terminals, and a 50 percent coownership of Heartland with ConocoPhillips, which was the managing partner of the joint venture.

ONEOK Partners enjoyed record-setting performance during 2008, with all of the businesses in the partnership performing well. The operating income rose to $644.8 million, an increase of 44 percent over the previous year. The partnership gave ONEOK about two-thirds of each dollar generated, and distributed $251.7 million in cash to ONEOK during the year. Operating income of the natural gas distribution segment of the company reached $188.8 million, an increase of more than 8 percent over the previous year, and 66 percent over 2005. The energy services segment's operating income decreased by 63 percent to $75.7 million, due in part to volatile markets and a decline in natural gas prices during the winter months. ONEOK Partners invested approximately $1.2 billion in several growth projects, the majority of which were focused on the NGL business. ONEOK Partners placed six projects in service during the year, including several extension and expansion pipelines.

## CONTINUING TO GROW: 2009 AND BEYOND

During 2009, ONEOK Partners completed a more than $2 billion internal growth program, which readied the partnership for a second major growth phase which was set to begin in 2010. In April of that year, the company announced plans to invest as much as $470 million to construct a new natural gas processing plant in North Dakota. This plant was being built to meet the needs of producers in the Bakken Shale in the Williston Basin in North Dakota and the Woodford Shale in Oklahoma. An additional $200 million investment for expansion and upgrades in the Bakken Shale, and $55 million for

new well connections in the Woodford Shale, were also planned. Capital expenditures in these areas were forecasted to be as high as $500 million per year through 2015, depending on market needs.

*Jordan Wankoff*
*Updated, Diane Milne*

## PRINCIPAL SUBSIDIARIES

Kansas Gas Marketing Company; ONEOK Energy Marketing Company; ONEOK Energy Services Canada, Ltd.; ONEOK Partners, L.P. (45.1%).

## PRINCIPAL DIVISIONS

Kansas Gas Service Company; Oklahoma Natural Company; ONEOK Gas Transportation Company; Texas Gas Service Company.

## PRINCIPAL COMPETITORS

Atmos Energy Corporation; Dynegy Inc.; El Paso Corporation; OGE Energy Corp.; The Williams Companies, Inc.

## FURTHER READING

"ONEOK Buys Koch Natural Gas Liquids Biz for $1.3 Billion," *Journal Record (Oklahoma City)*, July 5, 2005.

"ONEOK Closes $285 Million Koch Midstream Asset Acquisition," *PR Newswire*, May 2, 1999.

"ONEOK Completes Purchase of Dynegy's Mid-Continent Assets," *Pipe Line & Gas Industry*, May 2000, p. 9.

"ONEOK Completes Purchase of Koch NGL Businesses," *Pipeline & Gas Journal* 232, no. 8 (2005): 4.

"ONEOK Partners Beat Earnings," *Zacks*, February 25, 2010.

Roth, Stephen, "Kansas Gas Service Marks Quiet Start for Partnership," *Kansas City Business Journal*, December 12, 1997, p. 7.

Shook, Barbara, "Acquisitions from KML, Dynegy Boost ONEOK Midstream Assets," *Natural Gas Week* 16, no. 34 (2000): 18.

"Westar Sells Rest of ONEOK Stock; Cantor Fitzgerald to Resell Shares," *Daily Oklahoman (Oklahoma City)*, November 22, 2003.

# Pepco Holdings, Inc.

**701 Ninth Street, N.W.**
**Washington, D.C. 20068**
**U.S.A.**
**Telephone: (202) 872-2000**
**Fax: (202) 331-6750**
**Web site: http://www.pepcoholdings.com**

*Public Company*
*Founded:* 2001 as New RC, Inc.
*Employees:* 5,110 (2009)
*Revenues:* $9.26 billion (2009)
*Stock Exchanges:* New York
*Ticker Symbol:* POM
*NAICS:* 221122 Electric Power Distribution; 551112 Offices of Other Holding Companies

■ ■ ■

Pepco Holdings, Inc. (PHI), a diversified holding company, is one of the largest energy delivery companies in the mid-Atlantic region, serving approximately 1.9 million customers in Delaware, the District of Columbia, Maryland, and New Jersey. Headquartered in Washington, D.C., PHI is engaged in both regulated and competitive energy sectors. It supplies the regulated transmission and distribution of electricity service through its subsidiaries, Pepco, Delmarva Power, and Atlantic City Electric, as well as natural gas service through Delmarva Power. PHI competes in the deregulated energy industry through Conectiv Energy, which manages power plant assets and sells energy and fuel on the wholesale market. PHI also includes Pepco Energy Services, a leading supplier of energy and energy-related services for residential, small business, and large commercial customers.

## BEGINNINGS: 2000–02

Pepco Holdings, Inc., was formed by the Potomac Electric Power Company (Pepco) to acquire Conectiv Energy. Seeking to expand their presence in the utility industry, business executives at Pepco and Conectiv Energy initiated steps in 2000 to form a publicly traded holding company that would control the assets and merchant activities of Pepco and Conectiv. The resulting entity would be Pepco Holdings, Inc., which was incorporated under the name New RC, Inc., on February 9, 2001. That same month, Pepco and Conectiv Energy publicly announced plans for a merger that would make each utility a subsidiary of New RC, Inc., and each company began a corporate restructuring process. On January 22, 2002, the name of New RC, Inc., was officially changed to Pepco Holdings, Inc.

Having been approved by stockholders of both companies and federal regulatory agencies, the merger between Pepco and Conectiv Energy was completed on August 1, 2002, with PHI garnering combined assets in excess of $12 billion and combined revenues of $8 billion (2001). Under the terms of the merger, PHI acquired Conectiv for a combination in cash and stock valued at approximately $2.2 billion. For each share of Pepco stock owned, shareholders received one share of PHI stock, while shares of Conectiv stock were exchanged for 50 percent cash and 50 percent PHI stock.

The vision for Pepco Holdings, Inc., is to be the premier energy delivery and services company in the mid-Atlantic region through employees focused on customer service, reliability, and profitability. PHI engages in a flexible business strategy centered on opportunities in our field of expertise: energy.

At the time PHI was formed, Pepco, which had been incorporated in Virginia in 1896, served over 700,000 customers in a 640-square-mile area, including the District of Columbia and portions of Prince George's and Montgomery counties in Maryland. Conectiv, formed in 1996, delivered electricity to more than 1 million customers in a 7,500-square-mile area across Delaware, Maryland, Virginia, and New Jersey. Combined, Pepco and Conectiv delivered some 50,000 gigawatt hours of power each year. Although customers would deal with the same local utility company, the merger had the potential to offer important benefits on a larger scale. According to an August 1, 2002, PHI press release, "PHI, by virtue of its size and scope, will be better positioned to enhance delivery services and improve system reliability while keeping costs down by spreading such costs over a larger customer base." In addition, the proximity of Pepco and Conectiv was expected to help speed up repairs during weather emergencies because the two companies would be able to share resources.

## MAJOR SUBSIDIARIES

As the umbrella company of Pepco and Conectiv, PHI assumed control of various operating units within both companies. Besides Pepco and Conectiv, these subsidiaries included Atlantic City Electric, Delmarva Power, and Pepco Energy Services. Conectiv Energy had been formed in 1998 to serve as a holding company for Atlantic City Electric and Delmarva Power. Both Atlantic City Electric and Delmarva Power operated under the brand name Conectiv Power Delivery until 2005, when they resumed their former brand names in a public relations move by PHI to strengthen its connections to the regions served by the two utilities. In a March 31, 2005, press release, Dennis Wraase, chairman, president, and CEO of Pepco Holdings, Inc., at the time commented, "We believe the traditional utility names better reflect our ties to the local communities we serve and more clearly communicate who we are. The

Conectiv name was introduced at a time when the company was expanding into non-utility lines of business. This is no longer the case; going forward, the utility business, which makes up 70% of our revenues, will be our major focus."

Both Atlantic City Electric and Delmarva Power were well-established companies when they were acquired by PHI in 2002. Atlantic City Electric had roots that reached back to 1886, when the Electric Light Company of Atlantic City was founded in response to the city's development as a resort area. By the end of the first decade of the 21st century, the company, a regulated utility, provided electric service to more than 500,000 customers in southern New Jersey. Delmarva Power & Light Company was incorporated in Delaware in 1909 and in Virginia in 1979. Delmarva Power, also a regulated utility, provided electric and gas service to over 500,000 customers in Delaware and the Delmarva Peninsula.

Established in 1995, Pepco Energy Services evolved under the guidance of PHI to become a leader in energy-saving and sustainable energy products and services in North Carolina, Massachusetts, New York, Illinois, and Tennessee. Pepco Energy Services provided customers (utilities and municipalities, for instance) with products and services that helped them control energy use, limit energy expenditures, and harness alternative sources of energy in their facilities. A deregulated company, Pepco Energy Services was free to bid on contracts with commercial, institutional, industrial, and government entities. In December 2009 the company announced that it would no longer actively market retail electricity and natural gas in order to focus on energy performance contracting, renewable energy, and combined heat and power generation.

## UTILITY CHALLENGES

Within eight years of its inception, PHI had attained revenues of roughly $10.7 million. From 2003 on, PHI ranked in the top 300 on the *Fortune* 500 list, and in 2004, it was named to that magazine's Top 50 List of Best Companies for Minorities. The company's selection was based on its diversity in hiring methods, employee programs, and purchasing practices. Despite these accomplishments, PHI experienced significant setbacks in its utility service.

As the population in the mid-Atlantic states continued to grow, customers were impacted by the effects of a congested power transmission system, one that could not keep up with increasing demands of power, especially during times of inclement weather. Among the major storms that struck the East Coast during the

21st century, was Hurricane Isabel, which cost PHI around $70 million in storm restoration efforts. Hitting land in September 2003, Isabel disrupted PHI power services to around 55 million people. This was 75 percent of Pepco's customer base and 43 percent of Conectiv's service area, and some outages lasted more than 10 days. People all over the region were outraged at what they considered PHI's lack of emergency preparedness. In response, PHI hired James Lee Witt Associates (JLWA) to conduct a review of its emergency response procedures. Although JLWA's overall findings indicated that PHI had performed within industry standards, the power company took major steps toward improving its electricity restoration performance, including working more closely with state departments of transportation and local water, cable, and telephone companies.

Continued power outages in the region prompted the U.S. Department of Energy to consult with PJM Interconnection about building a new transmission system. (PJM is a regional transmission organization that coordinates the movement of wholesale electricity in many areas of the eastern United States.) No transmission line had been built in the mid-Atlantic region since the early 1980s, when power usage was on average 21 percent lower in most households. PJM estimated that congestion in its eastern transmission corridor cost customers over $1 billion in 2005 alone. The result of the collaboration between PJM and the Department of Energy was the design for a Mid-Atlantic Power Pathway (MAPP), a 230-mile electric transmission system that would provide a boost in both system capacity and electric reliability to customers. PHI was to have primary responsibility for the construction of the power line. In a February 2009 press release, Wil-

liam M. Gausman, Pepco Holdings, Inc., vice president for asset management and planning commented, "the [existing] system is stressed. Without MAPP, the region will be exposed to increased risk of experiencing brownouts and blackouts in the future." In October 2007, PJM approved PHI's proposal to build the 230-mile interstate power line.

PHI filed applications with the Public Service Commission of Maryland for authorization to build the MAPP in February 2009, as well as a joint federal-state permit application to the Maryland Department of the Environment and the U.S. Army Corps of Engineers to build the power line in wetlands and waterways. In late 2009 PHI began work on the $1.2 billion MAPP project, which was slated for completion in 2014. However, on January 11, 2010, PHI filed a request with the Maryland Public Service Commission to suspend construction until June pending a reassessment of the region's overall transmission needs. The postponement was the result of a decision made by members of the Potomac-Appalachian Transmission Highline project (PATH) to delay the construction of a large power line that would feed into PHI's MAPP project.

## ENERGY SUSTAINABILITY

Many of PHI's initiatives in the latter half of the decade focused on energy sustainability and alternative forms of energy. In 2007, for example, PHI reaffirmed its commitment to convert its fleet of 2,000 vehicles to more environmentally friendly technologies, such as electric hybrids. By May of that year, PHI had over 80 hybrid vehicles, including a 42-foot hybrid electric bucket truck. In addition to adding 30 hybrid cars and SUVs to its fleet, PHI was preparing to convert its vehicles to use such alternative fuels as biodiesel, natural gas, and E85, a mix of 85 percent ethanol and 15 percent gasoline.

In June 2009 PHI's Edison Place, its corporate headquarters building, received U.S. Green Building Council LEED certification for "Existing Buildings: Operations & Maintenance," the first such certification in Washington, D.C., at the time. In September PHI was recognized as a leader among U.S. corporations in addressing issues of climate change by the 2009 S&P Carbon Disclosure Project. In a press release following the announcement, Joseph M. Rigby, chairman and CEO of Pepco Holdings, Inc., stated, "We regard PHI's ranking in this year's Carbon Disclosure Project survey results as validation of our ongoing commitment to environmental protection and resource conservation, a long-held core value that is fundamental to PHI's identity as a good corporate citizen."

PHI's environmentally conscious ventures included partnering with automobile giant General Motors to power Chevrolet's new plug-in vehicle, the Volt. According to a January 2010 article in *Transmission & Distribution World*, Rigby holds that "PHI is committed to working with the auto industry, the Department of Energy, local governments and the utility industry to overcome numerous challenges, including support for both a public and commercial charging infrastructure, affordable vehicle-charging rates and supportive permitting and codes for vehicle charging stations." PHI purchased 10 Volts to use in a study of the impact of vehicle charging on the electrical grid. At the onset of the project, two charging stations were installed at PHI's headquarters in Washington, D.C., with plans for eight additional charging stations to be installed within PHI's service area by 2011. Employees in Maryland, southern New Jersey, Delaware, and the District of Columbia were scheduled to drive the Volts as part of the company's fleet of vehicles for two years. At the end of that trial period, PHI officials planned to evaluate not only the feasibility of adding electric vehicles to their fleet, but also the effects of these vehicles on the electrical power grid. "Smart meters and smart grid technologies will be incorporated with the charging stations to collect information about energy consumption and enable customers to recharge at the most economical time of day, such as during off-peak hours when electric demand is lowest," reported *Transmission & Distribution World*.

In 2009, when President Barack Obama called for federal agencies to cut greenhouse emissions by 28 percent by 2020, the Department of Defense began exploring options for energy improvements at 2,100 buildings on its five military installations in its Military District of Washington. With input from the Department of Energy's National Renewable Energy Lap, the Department of Defense selected Pepco Energy Services from a competitive field, awarding the company the largest ever energy savings performance contract. As of March 2010, Pepco Energy Services had upgraded the energy performance of 688 buildings through such changes as retrofitting existing plumbing fixtures with ultra-low-flow units, which would reduced annual water consumption by 30.1 million gallons.

It seemd that in the 2010s PHI was likely to devote a significant percentage of its resources to sustainability projects, believing that these "green" projects, along with the development of the MAPP, are the keys to its continued success.

*Alicia Elley*

## PRINCIPAL SUBSIDIARIES

Atlantic City Electric Company; Delmarva Power & Light Company; Conectiv; Potomac Electric Power Company.

## PRINCIPAL COMPETITORS

American Electric Power; CenterPoint Energy; Dominion Resources Inc.; Duke Energy; Edison International; Entergy Corporation; Exelon Corporation; FirstEnergy Corp.; Public Service Enterprise Group; Southern Co.

## FURTHER READING

"Blizzard Conditions Lift, Enable Pepco to Resume Power Restoration," *New York Times,* February 11, 2010.

"Citing PATH Delay, Pepco Slows Its Power Line, Too," *Energy Daily,* January 11, 2010, p. 5.

"FERC Approves Incentives for Pepco's Mid-Atlantic Grid Expansion," www.ferc.gov, November 3, 2008.

"Pepco Energizes First Plug-In Vehicle Charging Stations," *Transmission & Distribution World,* January 27, 2010.

"Pepco Holdings, Inc., Review in Process," m2.com, March 17, 2008.

Sinha, Vandana, "Pepco Holdings Puts a Hold on Transmission Line Plans," *Washington Business Journal,* January 11, 2010.

# PG&E Corporation

**One Market Spear Tower**
**Suite 2400**
**San Francisco, California 94105**
**U.S.A.**
**Telephone: (415) 267-7000**
**Toll Free: (800) 743-5000**
**Fax: (415) 267-7268**
**Web site: http://www.pge.com**

*Public Company*
*Incorporated:* 1905
*Employees:* 19,425 (2009)
*Sales:* $13.40 billion (2009)
*Stock Exchanges:* New York
*Ticker Symbol:* PCG
*NAICS:* 221122 Electric Power Distribution

∎ ∎ ∎

PG&E Corporation is a holding company for the Pacific Gas and Electric Company (Pacific), one of the largest gas and electric utilities in the United States. Pacific has a service area covering about 70,000 square miles, covering most of northern and central California. In 2009 Pacific had over five million electrical customers and approximately 4.3 million natural gas customers. The company is regulated by one of the toughest state regulatory bodies in the United States, the California Public Utility Commission (CPUC).

## BEGINNING OF THE UTILITY

Pacific Gas and Electric Company (PG&E) was formed in 1905 by John Martin and Eugene de Sabla, Jr., to acquire and merge power companies in central California. Martin and de Sabla, who had earlier been involved with gold mines in the Yuba River region north of Sacramento, California, began in the 1890s to use hydroelectric power to operate their mines. De Sabla located customers and raised the capital for their first hydroelectric plant in Nevada City, California, in 1895. Martin handled the engineering with help from William Stanley, developer of the Westinghouse alternating-current electrical system. The plant proved successful and convinced them there was a market for electrical power in Sacramento and San Francisco. They built another plant in 1898 and in 1899 formed Yuba Power Company to build a third, more powerful facility.

In 1900 the three plants were consolidated into Bay Counties Power Company, with de Sabla as president and general manager. In 1901 the company built a 140-mile transmission line, the world's longest at that time, to power an electric railway in Oakland, California. The line, suspended across the San Francisco Bay, carried 60,000 volt, quite a high voltage for the time, and attracted great publicity. The company then joined its three plants into a single power grid, although it remained primarily a power-generating company not a distribution-based utility.

In 1903 de Sabla and Martin formed California Gas & Electric Company (CG&E) to buy power companies and merge them into a large electric grid that could use economies of scale to its advantage. In the next few years CG&E bought many power companies, backed by capital from New York financiers. CG&E's acquisitions included long-established utilities like Oakland Gas Light & Heat Company, serving Oakland and Berkeley, and United Gas & Electric Company, serving communities south of San Francisco. In 1905 de Sabla and Martin bought San Francisco Gas & Electric Company (SFG&E), the dominant utility in San Francisco, giving the company a power grid in the most important city in central California. They merged SFG&E with CG&E to form Pacific Gas and Electric Company, capitalized at about $45 million. The San Francisco company had steam power plants, which complemented PG&E's hydroelectric plants by carrying peak loads when demand was high or when freezes or droughts cut hydroelectric output.

## GROWTH THROUGH ACQUISITIONS

PG&E continued buying power companies and merging electric grids. By 1914 it owned the largest integrated regional system on the Pacific Coast and was one of the five largest utilities in the United States. It supplied 1.3 million people in a 37,000-square-mile area and had 36 percent of California's electric and gas business. During most of this period the company's steam-power capacity was growing faster than its hydroelectric capacity, partly because of the falling price of California crude oil. In 1912 PG&E began to increase its hydroelectric capacity. Using water from the South Yuba and Bear Rivers, it built a series of six plants with a projected capacity of 190,750 horsepower. A 110-mile transmission line strung across steel towers carried 100,000 volts to PG&E's switching station at Cordelia, California.

PG&E also continued to grow through mergers. In 1927 it bought the Sierra and San Francisco Power Company, and in 1930 it bought its only major competitor, the Great Western Power Company. In 1935 PG&E consolidated the operations of the companies it had bought.

PG&E and most other electric utilities were not greatly affected by the Great Depression because of their status as monopolies. Most sales that were lost to declin-

ing industry were made up by increasing residential rates.

In 1948 Pacific signed an interchange agreement with Southern California Edison Company that stated that either company would sell the other excess electricity when needed until 1962. PG&E continued to expand, buying Vallejo Electric Light & Power Company in 1949 and Pacific Public Service Company in 1954. By 1955 PG&E's network extended into 46 counties in northern and central California. It supplied electricity to 168 cities and towns and gas to 146 cities and towns. Pacific operated 57 hydroelectric plants and 12 steam plants generating about 84 percent of its total electric output, but bought 68 percent of its gas from El Paso Natural Gas Company. The company had 18,000 employees. Total revenue for 1954 was $386 million.

In 1957 PG&E and the General Electric Company constructed the small Vallecitos atomic power plant. Plans for a large nuclear power plant at Bodega Bay, north of San Francisco, were scrapped in the early 1960s because of public opposition. Instead, the company constructed a 63,000-kilowatt nuclear power plant at Humboldt Bay near Eureka, California, in 1963. From 1968 to 1970, Pacific participated in a design study of a 350,000-kilowatt sodium-cooled nuclear power plant. The company contributed $10 million over the following 10 years to a joint U.S. government-industry project to build the first large sodium-cooled reactor. It also began construction of two pressurized-water nuclear power plants at Diablo Canyon, expected to total one million kilowatts. The plants were scheduled to be finished in 1975 and 1976.

By 1973 PG&E was the second-largest utility in the United States, with 65 hydroelectric plants and 12 steam electric plants and total revenue of $494 million. The Diablo Canyon nuclear power plants, however, were running years behind schedule. PG&E entered the 1970s expecting demand to increase by 6 percent to 7 percent annually, as it had for years. Instead, California was growing rapidly, and demand grew faster than PG&E had projected. In addition, natural gas, which fueled the steam electric plants, was in short supply in California. The energy crisis of the early 1970s sent the price of gas skyrocketing, and the company's natural gas business shriveled. Between 1975 and 1984 PG&E lost 60 percent of its industrial gas sales.

PG&E announced the urgent need to convert its plants to oil, which was also in short supply. At a cost of $100 million, the conversion involved building moorings for oil supertankers at seven of PG&E's 12 steam electric plants. To pay for the conversion, the company asked for a $233 million rate increase by 1975, the largest in California history.

## KEY DATES

**1905:** Pacific Gas and Electric Company is formed.

**1930:** PG&E acquires competitor Great Western Power Company.

**1955:** PG&E's network extends into 46 counties in northern and central California.

**1957:** PG&E and the General Electric Company construct the small Vallecitos atomic power plant.

**1973:** PG&E is the second-largest utility in the United States, with 65 hydroelectric plants and 12 steam electric plants and total revenue of $494 million.

**1981:** The California Public Utility Commission (CPUC) authorizes the company to begin a six-year, interest-free home loan program for customers who install insulation or energy-saving devices.

**1988:** PG&E takes a $576 million charge to pay for cost overruns during the construction of the Diablo Canyon nuclear plant.

**1995:** PG&E becomes the subsidiary of incorporated holding company PG&E Corporation.

**1996:** The company agrees to pay $333 million to plaintiffs in the town of Hinkley, California.

**2001:** PG&E Corporation files for Chapter 11 bankruptcy on April 6.

**2004:** PG&E Corporation emerges from bankruptcy on April 12.

**2010:** PG&E Corporation receives approval from the CPUC to develop up to 500 megawatts of solar power over the following five years.

## RATE HIKES AND THE ENERGY CRISIS

The California Public Utilities Commission (CPUC), the state body that regulates PG&E, traditionally had been one of the toughest in the United States. From 1966 to 1974, however, when Ronald Reagan was governor of California, the CPUC became more sympathetic to utilities. One decision by the Reagan-appointed commission allowed utilities to increase rates without public hearings as the price of oil increased. By early 1974, with the price of oil soaring, rate increases were enacted almost monthly. As a result, PG&E's $233 million rate increase received wide news coverage and

was opposed vigorously by consumer groups, which used public outrage to push for utility reform. Jerry Brown, Reagan's successor, appointed reform-oriented commissioners to the CPUC. In 1975 the CPUC ordered PG&E to offer a minimal amount of electricity at subsidized rates to all residential customers. The move was opposed by PG&E and its largest customers, whose electric rates would pay for the subsidy.

PG&E also faced opposition from environmentalists. The Environmental Defense Fund (EDF) confronted the utility, claiming PG&E would not need to build more power plants if it used its existing capacity more wisely. Both sides ran television commercials to push their viewpoints. The EDF eventually helped pressure PG&E into using alternative energy suppliers (such as windmill farms) and use strategies (such as redirecting customer demand) to stretch generating capacity further. By the late 1970s PG&E was offering incentives to customers who fulfilled their energy requirements at nonpeak hours.

In 1979 the CPUC granted PG&E a $269 million annual rate increase, but it also pushed the company to buy more power from alternative energy sources. In 1980 the CPUC granted a $530 million gas- and electric-rate increase, but over the next few years it ordered the company to give several refunds. Net income for 1980 was $525 million. In 1981 the CPUC authorized the company to begin a six-year, interest-free home loan program for customers who installed insulation or energy-saving devices.

One of the two Diablo Canyon nuclear plants was finished in 1981, but PG&E did not receive permission to begin testing because of concerns that the plant, located just two miles from an earthquake fault, was not safe. Questions were also raised about quality control during the plant's construction. Protesters blockaded the plant for two days while the U.S. Nuclear Regulatory Commission considered approving its start-up. Permission was granted in late 1981, and in 1982 the company hired Bechtel Power Corporation to manage the project while it was completed and licensed. In late 1983 uranium fuel was finally loaded into the Diablo Canyon reactor, and testing began in 1984. The company then requested rate increases to pay for the plant, which cost $5.8 billion, 18 times initial projections.

At the same time the company continued buying electricity from alternative sources. Under the 1978 Public Utility Regulatory Policies Act, U.S. electric utilities were required to buy power offered by independent producers at prices set by state utility commissions. In 1982 PG&E signed a contract to buy most of the wind-generated power from a wind farm in Solano County,

California. In 1983 it agreed to buy all the electricity from a solar-energy power plant being built by a subsidiary of Atlantic Richfield Company. By mid-1986 PG&E had signed 695 contracts to buy 20 percent of alternative capacity planned for the United States, more than half of PG&E's own capacity. The company had so many alternative generating contracts that it had excess capacity.

In 1982 PG&E appointed Richard Clarke as head of utility operations. Clarke won CPUC approval to overhaul the structure of natural gas rates for PG&E's industrial customers. That move helped reverse a long decline in gas sales and doubled the utility's net income to $1 billion during the next four years. Also in 1982 the CPUC ordered PG&E to suspend its large fuel-oil contract with Chevron USA Inc. PG&E had signed a long-term contract with Chevron during the early 1970s, when natural gas prices and power-demand projections were high. In 1981, however, capacity increased due to alternative electric sources, and natural gas prices dropped. In part because PG&E had contracted to buy more expensive fuel oil, residential electric rates rose 6 percent in 1981. The CPUC used contingency provisions in PG&E's oil contract that allowed for suspension of deliveries if a government agency ordered it.

In 1984 the CPUC granted the company $697 million in rate increases, a 1.7 percent hike. Net income for 1984 was $975 million. In 1985 the CPUC ordered PG&E to lower its natural gas rates by $316.9 million per year. The following year the company acquired the 48.9 percent of Pacific Gas Transmission Company that it did not already own in a stock swap valued at $164 million, and in 1986 Pacific Gas Transmission became a wholly owned subsidiary of PG&E.

In 1986 Richard Clarke became chairman and chief executive officer of PG&E, and George Maneatis became president. While PG&E's managers had traditionally begun as engineers, Clarke was an attorney-turned-manager, and his experience as an attorney served his company's interest in the ensuing years.

California had become the most competitive power market in the United States, partly because of high rates the CPUC had mandated for independent power generators. Since PG&E had to buy relatively high-priced power from independents, the company's electricity rates were forced up. To protect residential customers from the rising costs, the CPUC raised industrial power rates and used them to subsidize residential rates. As a result, many large industrial customers devised plans to build their own power stations or to import power from other states where electricity was 15 percent to 30 percent cheaper. To be more competitive, Clarke pressed

the CPUC to make changes that would allow his company to offer better rates to large customers and to set up a major accounts program that would give individual attention to PG&E's biggest customers.

## UTILTY REORGANIZES

In 1988 PG&E reorganized into five new business divisions. Four of the divisions focused on primary markets such as electric supply, gas supply, distribution, and nonutility business. The electric supply division generated, transported, bought, and sold electricity for the distribution division and for other wholesale customers throughout the western United States. The gas supply division acquired natural gas for the distribution and electric supply divisions and for large customers outside PG&E's service area. To help accomplish this, it operated about 5,000 miles of pipeline from Southern California to Alberta, Canada, as well as underground storage tanks. The distribution division provided gas, electric, and steam service to customers and was responsible for maintaining the customer base. The nonutility operations included natural gas exploration and production, enhanced oil recovery, real estate development, and power plant operations. The company formed a subsidiary, PG&E Enterprises, to manage the nonutility businesses. The fifth division, engineering and construction, provided services to the other divisions and was responsible for designing and building most of the company's dams, power plants, and other transmission and distribution systems. The new structure was designed to help managers identify costs, know their customers, understand their competition, and respond quickly to technological and regulatory changes.

In 1988 the company took a $576 million charge to pay for cost overruns during the construction of the Diablo Canyon nuclear plant. The charge reduced net income for 1988 to $62.1 million.

Also in 1988 PG&E-Bechtel Generating Company, a joint venture of PG&E and Bechtel Power, began construction of its first power plant, in Montana. The joint venture was formed to build and operate plants outside of PG&E's territory. By 1990 the venture had completed the Montana plant, had one under way in Pennsylvania, and was planning another in New Jersey.

PG&E was well prepared for the major earthquake that hit the San Francisco area in 1989. Although power was cut off from 1.4 million customers, it was restored to one million of them within 12 hours. The company sustained $100 million in damage, mostly to transmission and generating equipment, with distribution and communications barely disrupted.

In 1990 the company added a sixth division, nuclear power generation, which was responsible for the

Diablo Canyon nuclear power plants and the support services they required. Earnings were strong in 1990, with an increase of 10.5 percent from 1989. PG&E had held the operating costs of its utility business at 1986 levels, while utility revenues had increased 20 percent during the years 1986 to 1990. The utility business accounted for about 70 percent of PG&E's earnings in 1990, but the company, through PG&E Enterprises, continued to pursue nonutility ventures that offered a potentially higher return than the strictly regulated utility operations.

In 1996 PG&E reached a settlement with about 600 plaintiffs in the town of Hinkley, California, who asserted that PG&E contaminated groundwater with chromium. Plaintiffs in the $333 million settlement claimed that PG&E was aware of the contamination for 25 years but did nothing about it. Prior to the settlement, 39 cases went to trial, resulting in damages of $131 million. The case was the basis for the Hollywood movie *Erin Brockovich* in 2000. A $295 million settlement followed with additional plaintiffs in 2006.

## DEREGULATION

PG&E Corporation incorporated in 1995 to hold interests in energy businesses, becoming the holding company for the PG&E utilities and its subsidiaries in 1997. The move anticipated California's 1998 deregulation of public utilities, which required that existing investor-owned utilities purchase power at market rates and sell power to customers at fixed, preregulation prices. As part of the deregulation process, PG&E sold a substantial portion of its energy-generating assets, including six fossil-fuel plants and a geothermal plant, and was no longer able to generate enough power to supply its customers.

However, the deregulation of the industry did not go as well as hoped. During the California energy crisis of 2000 to 2001, energy speculators drove up the cost of power, forcing PG&E to purchase electricity at much higher rates than it could sell to customers. The corporation went from a net profit of $719 million in 1998 to a net loss of $73 million in 1999 and $3.36 billion net loss in 2000. The corporation declared bankruptcy on April 6, 2001. The company remained in Chapter 11 bankruptcy for three years. It was eventually bailed out by the money from the state. PG&E emerged from bankruptcy on April 12, 2004.

Under California law, utility companies had to source at least 20 percent of their power from renewable resources by 2010. As it worked to comply, PG&E became a leader in the construction and purchase of clean energy. In April 2010, it received approval from the CPUC to develop up to 500 megawatts of solar power over the following five years.

In 2009 the company began installing gas and electric smart meters, which monitor use multiple times per day and provide the utility company information about peak and off-peak power use. With that information, utilities planned to charge more for peak power, shifting customer demand to nonpeak times and reducing the need to fire out the more expensive and less environmentally friendly ways of producing power during peak times. PG&E planned to installed 10 million smart meters by 2012, though not without controversy. The CPUC received complaints from about 600 customers in early 2010 that their electricity bills rose significantly after smart meters were installed.

*Scott M. Lewis*
*Updated, Catherine Meyrat*

## PRINCIPAL SUBSIDIARIES

Pacific Gas and Electric Company.

## PRINCIPAL COMPETITORS

Edison International; PacifiCorp; Sempra Energy.

## FURTHER READING

"CPUC OK's PG&E Solar Photovoltaic Program," *San Francisco Business Times,* April 22, 2010.

Riddell, Lindsay, "PG&E Laying Off 500 People, " *San Francisco Business Times,* November 13, 2009.

———, "CPUC Picks Firm to Investigate PG&E Smart Meters," *San Francisco Business Times,* March 30, 2010.

———, "PG&E Gets $25M from Stimulus for Compressed Air Energy Storage," *San Francisco Business Times,* May 6, 2010.

Shaw, Michael, "PG&E to Pay $14.75M for Pendola Fire Damage," *Sacramento Business Journal,* July 28, 2009.

# PJM Interconnection L.L.C.

Valley Forge Corporate Center
955 Jefferson Avenue
Norristown, Pennsylvania 19403
U.S.A.
Telephone: (610) 666-8980
Toll Free: (866) 400-8980
Fax: (610) 666-4379
Web site: http://www.pjm.com

*Regional Transmission Organization (RTO)*
*Founded:* 1927 as P.A.-N.J. Interconnection
*Membership:* 564 (2009)
*Revenues:* $215 million (2009)
*NAICS:* 221122 Electric Power Distribution

■ ■ ■

PJM Interconnection L.L.C. is a regional transmission organization (RTO) that manages the generation and transmission of wholesale electric power in all or part of the states of Delaware, Illinois, Indiana, Kentucky, Maryland, Michigan, New Jersey, North Carolina, Ohio, Pennsylvania, Tennessee, Virginia, West Virginia, and the District of Columbia. Managing electricity movement services for approximately 51 million customers, the company helps ensure the reliability of North America's largest centrally dispatched electrical power grid, or an interconnected network for delivering electricity from suppliers to consumers. PJM coordinates around 164,000 megawatts of generating capacity over a grid consisting of 56,350 miles of transmission lines. Its 564 members include power generators, transmission owners, electricity distributors, power marketers, and large consumers.

PJM administers the largest competitive wholesale electric market in the world, managing the buying and selling of wholesale electricity through its Energy Market. As a federally regulated RTO, the company is a neutral controlling party that is responsible for overseeing fair competition among electric power buyers and sellers. In addition to promoting itself as an energy company, PJM emphasizes its role as an information technology company that provides a continuous flow of real-time information, as well as a finance company that extends credit for energy transactions.

## POWER POOL: 1927–89

The beginnings of PJM can be traced to 1927, when two utilities in Pennsylvania, Philadelphia Electric Company and Pennsylvania Power & Electric, joined the Public Service Electric & Gas Company of New Jersey to form P.A.-N.J., one of the world's first continuing power pools. The U.S. Energy Information Administration defines a power pool as "two or more interconnected utilities that plan and operate to supply electricity in the most reliable, economical way to meet their combined load." The primary benefits of a power pool are that major electric outages are less likely to occur and power costs are reduced. Utility companies, power generators, and power marketers coordinate their operations through an interconnection power pool, which is recognized as an independent operating body. As such, it does not own the equipment it directs, including power lines and power plants.

Recognizing the advantages of sharing their generating resources, the three companies signed an agreement that anticipated estimated savings of $45 million over the next eight years. Two additional utilities, Baltimore Gas & Electric Company and General Public Utilities, signed on as members in 1956, and the pool became known as PJM Interconnection. (The P is from Pennsylvania, the J from Jersey, and the M from Maryland.) With the addition of these two entities, the function of the power pool expanded to include the use of a numerical formula to forecast energy demands. Under the terms of the 1956 PJM arrangement, each of the five member companies agreed to meet predicted capacity requirements by providing sufficient capacity and related transmission facilities. The utilities had the option of using their own resources, installing new ones, or purchasing sufficient capacity in order to fulfill their obligations. This idea of buying and selling power capacity formed the basis of the modern wholesale electricity market.

Throughout the years, PJM added new services for its members, which required the company to keep pace with new developments in technology. In 1962, for example, PJM installed its first online computer to control generation. Maintaining system reliability was of utmost importance because the PJM Agreement mandated that its utilities meet an established capacity requirement, along with a daily operating reserve requirement. By the time power giant Pepco (Potomac Electric Power Company) had joined PJM in the mid-1960s, PJM was effectively using computer programs to monitor those reserve requirements. In 1968 the company implemented its first Energy Management System, an information technology system that made it possible to watch transmission grid operations in real time. This continuous flow of real-time information would eventually allow members to make informed, timely decisions about pricing, demand, and system conditions. Ultimately, data gathered through the Energy Management System enabled the PJM control center to balance electricity supply and demand.

By 1973 PJM had the ability to dispatch generation within the power pool from a central location due to the organization of its Office of Interconnection and its technological advantages. Central dispatch quickly proved economically sound because it took into account such factors as fuel availability and resource reliability. So significant were the savings that central dispatch soon became referred to "economic dispatch." PJM continued to grow as more and more utilities in the Mid-Atlantic region joined the power pool, which was shown in a 1990 study to provide over $1 billion in value to its members each year.

## ENERGY MARKET

The 1990s were marked by many important milestones that would define the future of PJM. In 1993 the PJM Interconnection Association was formed for the purpose of administering the power pool. After becoming a fully independent entity in 1997, PJM opened its bid-based Energy Market. Membership was opened to nonutilities, and an independent Board of Managers was elected. Later that year, the Federal Energy Regulatory Commission (FERC) approved PJM as the nation's first fully functioning independent system operator (ISO) accountable for the reliable operation of the power transmission system as well as the administration of the competitive wholesale electricity market. (ISOs operate, but do not own, transmission systems, providing open access to the grid for nonutility users.)

From the time it opened in 1997, PJM's wholesale electricity market worked much like a stock exchange in that it established a price for large blocks of electricity by matching supply with demand. PJM coordinated the continuous buying, selling, and delivery of wholesale electricity through competitive spot markets, or markets in which energy is bought and sold on an immediate, short-term basis. Functioning as a market operator, PJM balanced the needs of suppliers, wholesale customers, and other market participants and monitored market activities in order to ensure open and equitable access.

PJM's transformation into an ISO facilitated locational marginal pricing (LMP), which in turn increased price transparency, allowing the least expensive product to be better identified. LMP enables members to identify supply shortages or congestion, a condition that occurs when there is not enough transmission capacity to carry out all needed power transactions at the same time. Through LMP, PJM was able to use transparent, readily available information to communicate simultaneously with market participants. As a result, each of PJM's member utilities could determine the best approach to congestion or supply shortages for it own operations. PJM's Energy Market relied on LMP to reflect the value of an energy block at the specific location and time it was delivered. If the lowest-priced

## KEY DATES

**1927:** The Pennsylvania-New Jersey (P.A.-N.J.) Interconnection is formed by three utilities, creating the world's first continuing power pool.

**1956:** The pool is renamed PJM after two more utility companies join P.A.-N.J. Interconnection.

**1962:** PJM installs its first online computer to control generation.

**1968:** The company completes its first Energy Management System.

**1993:** The PJM Interconnection Association is formed to administer the power pool.

**2001:** PJM becomes the first fully functioning RTO in the United States.

**2010:** PJM launches PJM EnviroTrade.

electricity could reach all locations, prices were the same across the region. If a location experienced transmission congestion, then the electricity provided to meet demand in that area would cost more. PJM offered financial incentives to members for developing and implementing ways to keep the electrical grid free of congestion, a strategy that would help regulate pricing in the long run.

By the end of the first decade of the 21st century, PJM's Energy Market consisted of day-ahead and real-time markets. In a day-ahead market, hourly LMPs were calculated for the next operating day, as opposed to a real-time market in which LMPs were calculated at five-minute intervals based on actual grid operating conditions. PJM members and customers could follow market fluctuations as they happened and submit bids based on real-time data using PJM's online eTools. Included in these market exchanges were alternative power supplies, such as wind, hydro, and solid waste sources of generation. As of 2010, PJM had administered over $103 billion in energy and energy-service trades. It also extended and managed credit for market transactions, conducting a business similar that of a finance company.

### EXPANSION AS AN RTO

In the early 21st century, the FERC encouraged the formation of RTOs to oversee transmission grids in multistate areas. The an RTO was required to have four characteristics. Independence—An RTO must be independent of any market participant. Scope and regional configuration—An RTO must serve an appropriate region. Operational authority—An RTO must have operational authority for all transmission under its control. Short-term reliability—An RTO must have exclusive authority for maintaining the short-term reliability of the grid it operates.

The FERC determined that PJM met all four of these requirements in 2001, and PJM received full RTO status in December 2002, making the company the nation's first fully functioning RTO at the time. In order to uphold the responsibilities of an RTO, PJM was responsible, for example, for determining transmission prices that would promote efficient use and expansion of transmission and generation, developing market mechanisms for managing transmission congestion, and ensuring reliability practices among members.

From 2002 to 2005, numerous utilities became part of PJM. Among these companies were such major utilities as Allegheny Power (2002), which operated a five-state transmission system; Commonwealth Edison (2004); American Electric Power (2004); and Duquesne Light and Dominion (2005). The integration of additional power companies expanded the resources available to meet consumer demands for electricity, thereby increasing the benefits of PJM's wholesale electricity market for power suppliers.

PJM Environmental Information Services, Inc., (PJM EIS) was formed in early 2005 to launch an environmental and emissions tracking system for the region covered by PJM. Known as the Generation Attributes Tracking System (GATS), the system was a collaborative effort, developed by state utility regulators, consumer advocates, state environmental protection agencies and energy offices, electric market participants, and environmental activists. GATS tracked generation attributes and the ownership of those attributes as they were traded or used to satisfy government standards. GATS data was utilized to produce electronic certificates that identified what generation attributes were required by specific power suppliers in order to meet state policies and to document green, or sustainable, energy. Members accessed GATS through a paid subscription. According to a press release issued by PJM EIS on April 15, 2005, Jeanne M. Fox, president of the New Jersey Board of Public Utilities, said, "New Jerseyans are serious about the environment, and they want clean energy. GATS gives us, as regulators, the effective measure we need to ensure compliance with New Jersey's renewable portfolio standards."

In December 2005 PJM authorized the addition of $464 million to the $2 billion already approved for upgrades to the electrical grid in the 13-state PJM region. The improvements were part of the Regional Transmission Expansion Plan (RTEP), which would enhance transmission reliability, support competitive electricity markets, and make certain that the grid continued to deliver an adequate electricity supply. Although the RTEP process determined the needs for a transmission project, it did not review or approve the site for a transmission line. That responsibility belonged to the states affected by the project. An important goal of the RTEP was to keep the grid in compliance with reliability standards. In addition to providing reliability system upgrades, funding for the RTEP would cover upgrades to interconnect new generation sources, as PJM expected to integrate more members in the subsequent years.

## INDUSTRY INFLUENCE: 21ST CENTURY

PJM received Platts's Global Energy Award of "Energy Transporter of the Year" in 2006, the first year the award was given. The award recognized excellence in the transport of energy, whether electricity, natural gas, coal, or oil. Platts based its decision on PJM's ability in 2005 to deliver record amounts of electricity and its completion of a series of integrations that doubled its size. In June 2005 PJM had become the first central grid operator in the world to manage an electric load of more than 100,000 megawatts (MW). Only one month later it surpassed that record when it handled a world-record 134,017 MW during a heat wave.

The year 2006 also marked the beginning of projects that fell under the RTEP process. Called "transmission backbone" projects because of their essential importance to the PJM transmission system, these projects provided a boost in both system capacity and electric reliability to customers throughout the PJM region. For instance, the Potomac-Appalachian Transmission Highline (PATH) would travel approximately 300 miles from the Amos Substation in West Virginia to the Kemptown Substation in Maryland upon completion. Another one, the Susquehanna-Roseland Project, involved the construction of a line extending from the Susquehanna Substation in Pennsylvania to the Roseland Substation in New Jersey. One of the largest undertakings was the Mid-Atlantic Power Pathway (MAPP) project, a 230-mile electric transmission system running from the Possum Point station in Virginia through the Delmarva Peninsula to the Salem Station in New Jersey. By the end of 2009, PJM had received around $794 million in economic stimulus funds from the Department of Energy under the American Reinvestment and Recovery Act. These funds

were allocated so that PJM could complete its grid projects and begin other ones the company deemed necessary.

As renewable energy and green energy sources continued to play a huge role in the governance of industry all over the world, PJM launched PJM EnviroTrade in 2010. This subsidiary offered a monthly auction for the purchase and trade of solar renewable energy certificates (RECs). According to the Environmental Protection Agency, an REC "represents the property rights to the environmental, social, and other nonpower qualities of renewable electricity generation." RECs give buyers flexibility "in procuring green power across a diverse geographical area… [and] applying the renewable attributes to the electricity use at a facility of choice." PJM EnviroTrade initially provided services to buyers and sellers in New Jersey, Pennsylvania, Ohio, Delaware, Maryland, and the District of Columbia, with plans to extend the solar RECs to PJM's entire region.

The influence of PJM as a leading RTO reached well beyond the United States. As of 2010, over 70 nations had sent delegates to visit PJM in order to learn about its market model and its operation of the power grid. In addition, PJM had cooperative agreements with several large international grid operators, including Tokyo Electric Power Company, North China Grid Company, and Electricité de France.

*Alicia Elley*

## PRINCIPAL SUBSIDIARIES

PJM EIS; PJM EnviroTrade; PJM Technologies.

## FURTHER READING

"ATSI Signs Agreement to Join PJM," thestreet.com, December 18, 2009.

Bowring, Joseph E., and Robert E. Gramlich, "The Role of Capacity Obligations in a Restructured Pennsylvania-New Jersey-Maryland Electricity Market," *Electricity Journal,* November 2000, p. 57–67.

Kerecman, Joe, "Creating A Tracking System for Renewable Energy," *North American Wind Power,* May 2006.

Morris, Margaret, "First Energy Block Grant Received," *NJ.org Green Pages 2009,* June 23, 2009.

"Renewable Energy Certificates," epa.org, September 3, 2009.

Smith, Rebecca, "States Challenge Utility Costs," *Wall Street Journal—Eastern Edition,* June 3, 2008, p. A6.

U.S. Department of Energy. U.S. Energy Information Administration, "Glossary: P," eia.doe.gov, April 2008.

# Principal Financial Group Inc.

—■—

711 High Street
Des Moines, Iowa 50392
U.S.A.
Telephone: (515) 247-5111
Toll Free: (800) 986-3343
Fax: (515) 246-5475
Web site: http://www.principal.com

*Public Company*
*Founded:* 1879 as Bankers Life Association
*Employees:* 14,487 (2009)
*Revenue:* $8.85 billion (2009)
*Stock Exchanges:* New York
*Ticker Symbol:* PFG
*NAICS:* 524114 Direct Health and Medical Insurance
Carriers; 524113 Direct Life Insurance Carriers;
524210 Insurance Agencies and Brokerages; 525110
Pension Funds; 551112 Offices of Other Holding
Companies

■ ■ ■

Serving approximately 18.6 million customers around
the world, Principal Financial Group Inc. (The
Principle) is a financial company that offers a wide range
of products and services to businesses, individuals, and
institutions. These offerings include retirement and
investment services, life and health insurance, and banking through an extensive network of subsidiaries. In addition to being a leading provider of 401(k) plans in the
United States, The Principal has offices in 12 countries

located throughout Asia, Australia, Europe, and Latin
America.

## MEMBERSHIP

The Principal traces its origins to the founding of the
Bankers Life Association in 1879 by Edward Temple, a
banker from Chariton, Iowa. For several years before
Bankers Life was established, Temple and other
members of the Bankers Association of Iowa had
discussed a life insurance system based on a plan that
had been set up by a local group of ministers. Temple
suggested a guarantee fund system in which each
member would pay the association $1 for each year of
his age at the time he became a member for each
$2,000 insurance policy, or certificate, he wanted to
procure. This initial deposit, the bankers believed, was a
guarantee that a member would not abandon the
organization.

Temple secured a charter on July 1, 1879, thus officially establishing Bankers Life Association. Bankers
Life, headquartered in Des Moines, was one of the earliest life insurance companies in Iowa at the time. The
first policy written by the new organization was for
Temple himself, who served as Bankers Life's president
from 1879 until his death in 1909. As previously
discussed by Temple and his colleagues, fees to join were
based on the age of the insured at the time he joined
the association. The premiums, collected quarterly, were
based on a certain percentage of the total guarantee
fund. Early on, the amounts collected from members
fluctuated from five to ten cents annually.

To Temple, honor and integrity formed the basis of any business operation, and, in his opinion, many existing insurance companies charged excessive premiums or were otherwise unscrupulous, especially in paying benefit claims. Just as Temple expected the insurance field to uphold high principles, he and his colleagues insisted that the certificate holders of Bankers Life to adhere to strict standards as well. Membership was open only to healthy men between the ages of 25 and 55, while women were excluded from membership because childbirth was considered too risky. All applicants were required to have a full medical examination before they would be considered for membership.

Certificate holders were continuously monitored for unacceptable behaviors, such as smoking or recklessness, and were even encouraged to report other members' bad habits to the Bankers Life office. In addition, the company denied membership based on occupations or geographic regions deemed hazardous. Temple and his colleagues justified Bankers Life's code of conduct by reasoning that the company was promoting low mortality rates. Simply put, fewer deaths meant fewer claims that Bankers Life had to pay. If someone's death could be attributed to alcohol or drug use, Bankers Life did not award death benefits to the family of the deceased.

Despite such restrictions, Bankers Life quickly grew after its first year of operation, when a mere 58 men joined. Initially, the company offered memberships exclusively to bankers and their employees. Soon, however, memberships, which were sold through banks, were extended to men who had "the approval of an officer of, or employee occupying a position of trust in some banking institution." By its 10-year anniversary, Bankers Life had more than $29 million in life insurance premiums. The company had also moved six times because it had outgrown its office space.

## AN ASSESSMENT ASSOCIATION

Bankers Life was organized as an assessment association. This meant that members simply paid premiums that were sufficient to meet the company's mortality and managing expenses. If the Bankers Life's reserve fund was exhausted, the company had the right to call for increased assessments adequate to pay all expenses. As a result, its certificate holders paid much smaller premiums than those collected by reserve life insurance companies, which required policy holders to pay sufficient money not only to cover current expenses but also to create a reserve fund equal to the face value of the policy at the time of the insured's death. In contrast, Bankers Life built its reserve, or guaranteed, fund from the payments forfeited by lapsed members and from the interest earned on the guaranteed fund.

Since it was an assessment association, Bankers Life was consistently managed as a business with an exacting budget. Temple drew no salary for many years after the company began doing business. At the time of his death in 1909, his salary as president of the company was well below what other heads of insurance companies, particularly those in the eastern United States, received. For instance, when the company had over $4.56 million of insurance in force, Temple had an annual salary of $7,000, while executives in comparable positions made up to $50,000 a year. Even office supplies were closely accounted for, as employees who needed a new pencil had to trade in an old one less than two inches long.

## COMPANY CONVERSION

In 1905 the American insurance industry faced charges of corruption, spurred on by the *New York World*. The newspaper accused insurance companies of speculating with policy funds, a financial action that does not guarantee the safety of the initial investment, for their own financial gain. An investigation led by attorney Charles Evans Hughes revealed that insurance companies had misappropriated funds and paid off political figures who were supposed to regulate the industry. The majority of the companies called into question were reserve insurance organizations, a fact that reinforced Temple's belief in the strength of Bankers Life as an assessment insurance company. Nevertheless, members of the association began to debate the possibility of transforming Bankers Life into a mutual fund reserve company.

No action was taken to change Bankers Life until Temple died in 1909. New president Ernest E. Clark then led the board in converting the association to a mutual life insurance company. Supporters argued that Bankers Life could not continue as an assessment company because it would not be able to pay its future death claims with the premiums it was currently collecting. Board members loyal to Temple's plan

## KEY DATES

**1879:** Edward Temple establishes the Bankers Life Association.
**1909:** After Temple dies, the board of directors votes to change the association to a mutual life insurance company.
**1941:** The company begins to write life, health, accident, annuity, and hospital group insurance policies.
**1962:** Bankers Life recruits women by introducing a "9–3" plan that allows them to work during the time their children are in school.
**1985:** Bankers Life changes its name to The Principal Financial Group.
**1990:** The Principal forms its first foreign company and soon has operations in Argentina, Brazil, China, Chile, Hong Kong, India, and Mexico.
**2001:** The Principal becomes a publicly traded company.

pointed out that the switch to a mutual reserve plan would require members to pay two to five times higher premiums, thereby alienating a large percentage of Bankers Life customers. Furthermore, they contended, the move was motivated by greed and was a betrayal of the principles upon which Bankers Life had been founded.

Amidst such objections, Bankers Life was officially changed from an association to a mutual legal reserve company known as the Bankers Life Company in 1911. The first several years after the conversion showed significant losses. At the end of 1911, Bankers Life had $4.90 million of insurance in force. On December 31, 1912, it had $4.57 million. One year later, that figure had dropped to $4.30 million, followed by another decrease in 1915 to $4.06 million of insurance in force.

Elected president of Bankers Life in 1916, George Kuhns was a progressive businessman who was intent on reviving the company. Bankers Life decided to drop some of its membership restrictions, including those on travel, occupation, and residency. Within the first six months of Kuhns's leadership, Bankers Life financial figures showed $4.15 million of insurance in force. With the end of World War I in 1918 came an explosion in the public's demand for life insurance, and Bankers Life's insurance in force reached $8.44 million by 1925.

## EFFECTS OF THE GREAT DEPRESSION

The stock market crash of October 1929 and the subsequent Great Depression had the potential to devastate Bankers Life. Faced with this reality, Gerard Nollen, who had become president after Kuhn's death in 1926, was still intent on celebrating both the company's 50th anniversary and its reaching $1 billion of life insurance in force. Nollen held a banquet for employees and their wives in January 1930, giving each person in attendance a 10-dollar gold piece to show his optimism for the future of Bankers Life.

Throughout the 1930s many Bankers Life customers were unable to pay their premiums and were forced to let their policies lapse. Others borrowed against their policies so that by 1934, Bankers Life had more money being given out in loans than coming in from premium payments. The company's insurance in force dropped to $7.23 million. Undaunted, Bankers Life offered new policies that proved popular despite the economy. One of these was the Family Protection Plan, which paid higher benefits for dependent children. Another program was the Grant of Possession Policy. This plan allowed farmers who were not able to make payments to lease the farm to Bankers Life, while still living and working there for free.

## NEW VENTURES

By 1938 Bankers Life had suffered the worst of the Great Depression's effects. After building a new corporate headquarters in 1940, the company expanded its offerings in 1941 and began to write life, health, accident, annuity, and hospital group insurance policies. This last area of insurance, group, had historically been dominated by a select few large companies, such as Aetna, Prudential, and Travelers. Bankers Life made its mark in the field by introducing group permanent life insurance. Traditional group life insurance was terminated when a person's employment ended. Most state laws allowed the former employee to convert the group policy to an individual policy at his own expense. Bankers Life, however, provided group life insurance that remained in effect on a permanent basis. Bankers Life group insurance in force accounted for one-third of the company's in force total in 1954.

Bankers Life continued to expand its operations in the 1950s and 1960s. Branching out into other sectors of the insurance industry in 1957, it began giving those customers who already owned life insurance policies the option of buying additional coverage without taking a medical examination. In 1962 Bankers Life offered a life insurance policy that paid dividends but had lower premiums than other mutual companies' policies. A revolutionary program called the "9 to 3 Plan" was also introduced in 1962. Prior to that year, Bankers Life had followed a standard industry practice of terminating female employees once they got married. The 9 to 3 Plan ended that practice and allowed women to work during the time their children were in school.

In 1968 Bankers Life entered the mutual fund business, forming Bankers Life Equity Services Corporation (which became known as Princor Financial Services Corporation) as a broker-dealer to market the funds and Bankers Life Equity Management Company (later known as Principal Management Corporation) to serve as an investment advisor to the funds.

In the 1970s Bankers Life once again distinguished itself in the insurance world when it offered automobile and homeowners insurance through employers rather than directly to individuals. The City of Des Moines was one of its earliest customers. In 1977 Bankers Life introduced adjustable life insurance, which could be adapted by customers in response to changing needs in their lives. Customers could adjust their coverage and premium costs using a computerized system. Within two years of its debut, adjustable life insurance accounted for almost 40 percent of all new insurance sales. Toward the end of the decade, Bankers Life assets had grown from $8 billion in 1968 to $26 billion in 1978, and the business was one of the fastest-growing established life insurance companies in the United States.

### EXPANSION

As Bankers Life continued to expand, there arose a need for a name that reflected a common identity for all of its subsidiaries that tied back to the original company. Government regulators had denied applications of the name Bankers Life in the company's new financial endeavors. To solve this problem, Bankers Life changed its name to The Principal Financial Group in 1985.

The 1980s reflected further growth and diversification under The Principal umbrella. In addition to acquiring Eppler, Guerin & Turner, the Southwest's largest independent stock brokerage firm, in 1986, The Principal assumed control of the Delaware Charter Guarantee & Trust Company. This latter company administered individual and group retirement plans for mutual fund distributors, as well as clients of brokerage firms. In 1987 The Principal formed Principal Health Care, a subsidiary that handled health-maintenance and preferred-provider organizations, both of which were popular in the 1980s.

Entering the 1990s, The Principal, predicting that the insurance industry would develop in other countries

as it had in the United States, seized the opportunity to expand operations internationally. With the vision of giving people around the world their first chance to plan for retirement, The Principal opened an office in Madrid, Spain, in 1990. Companies in Argentina, Brazil, China, Chile, Hong Kong, and Mexico were established by the end of the decade. By 2010 The Principal had added Australia, Malaysia, Singapore, and the United Kingdom to its list of foreign operations.

### PUBLIC COMPANY

The Principal filed its Initial Public Offering (IPO) and became a public company traded on the New York Stock Exchange in October 2001. It became a member of the S&P 500 in July 2002 and was named one of the "100 Best Companies to Work For" by *Fortune* magazine for seven consecutive years (2003–09). The Principal garnered numerous awards for its industry leadership, workplace excellence, community and ethical leadership, and technology innovation.

Having secured its position as a major player in finance and insurance, The Principal continued to introduce new products and services. In January 2007, for example, The Principal debuted the Principal Survivorship Universal Life Protector, a universal life insurance policy that helped pay estate and settlement transfer costs after a policyholder's death. When the United States suffered a deep economic downturn that began in 2008, The Principal published *Navigating Your Way through Market Turbulence*. One in a series of educational resources about surviving the financial slump, this guide provided an in-depth look at how market conditions could affect four common types of retirement plans. As the economy appeared to stabilize in 2010, The Principal encouraged people to reevaluate their retirement plans to make certain that they were putting enough into retirement accounts to compensate for what had been lost. Although long past its early days as an assessment association, The Principal continues to seek methods to expand its business while following the beliefs and ideals of founder Edward Temple.

*Alicia Elley*

### PRINCIPAL SUBSIDIARIES

Columbus Circle Investors; Edge Asset Management; Post Advisory Group, LLC; Principal Bank; Principal Commercial Acceptance, LLC; Principal Commercial Funding, LLC; Principal Development Investors, LLC; Principal Enterprise Capital, LLC; Principal Financial Advisors, Inc.; Principal Funds Distributor, Inc.;

Principal Global Investors, LLC; Principal Life Insurance Company; Principal Management Corporation; Principal Real Estate Investors, LLC; Principal Trust Company (Asia) Limited (HongKong); Princor Financial Services Corporation; Spectrum Asset Management, Inc.

## PRINCIPAL DIVISIONS

International Operations; Global Asset Management; Retirement & Investments; Insurance; Health & Wellness; Banking.

## PRINCIPAL COMPETITORS

AXA S.A.; Black Rock Inc.; CIGNA Corp.; ING Groep N.V.; John Hancock and Associates; Lincoln Financial Group; MetLife Inc.

## FURTHER READING

Hempel, Jessi, "In the Land of Women," *Fortune,* February 4, 2008, p. 68–69.

"Hughes, Charles Evans 1862–1948," *American Decades.* 2001.

Lee, Barney, "JP Morgan, PNC, Principal Financial Take Top Fund Awards Honors," *Money Management Executive,* October 27, 2008, p. 1–14.

National Association of Life Insurance Policy Holders, *History of the Bankers Life Association of Des Moines, Iowa.* Chicago: National Association of Life Insurance Policy Holders, 1915.

"Principal Launches Flex Product," *Benefits Selling,* September 2009, p. 26.

Schwieder, Dorothy, *Iowa: The Middle Land.* Ames: Iowa State University Press, 1996.

Wall, Joseph Frazier, *Policies and People, The First Hundred Years of the Bankers Life, Des Moines, Iowa.* Englewood Cliffs, NJ: Prentice-Hall, 1979.

# Qwest Communications
# International, Inc.

■

1801 California Street
Denver, Colorado 80202
U.S.A.
Telephone: (303) 992-1400
Toll Free: (800) 899-7780
Fax: (303) 992-1724
Web site: http://www.qwest.com

*Public Company*
*Incorporated:* 1988 as SP Telecom
*Employees:* 30,138 (2009)
*Sales:* $12.31 billion (2009)
*Stock Exchanges:* New York
*Ticker Symbol:* Q
*NAICS:* 517110 Wired Telecommunications Carriers;
517212 Cellular and Other Wireless Telecommunications; 518111 Internet Service Providers

■ ■ ■

From its origins as the fiber-optic network-building subsidiary of Southern Pacific Transportation Co., Qwest Communications International, Inc., has grown through acquisitions to offer local and long-distance telephone services, as well as a range of Internet, multimedia, data, and voice services that are sold to business, consumer, and government customers.

Qwest operates primarily in the states of Arizona, Colorado, Idaho, Iowa, Minnesota, Montana, Nebraska, New Mexico, North Dakota, Oregon, South Dakota, Utah, Washington, and Wyoming. This is the region where its fiber-optic network exists. In 2009 the

company had almost three million broadband customers, and close to one million subscribers each for its video and wireless services. The company also offers digital satellite services through a partnership with DIRECTV, and wireless services through a partnership with Verizon Wireless. In 2010 telecom firm CenturyTel announced plans to acquire Qwest.

## SP TELECOM BUILDS TELECOMMUNICATIONS LINES: 1988–95

Qwest Communications International originated as a subsidiary of the giant railroad company Southern Pacific Transportation Co. In 1988, reclusive Denver billionaire Philip Anschutz acquired Southern Pacific from Sante Fe Industries after the Interstate Commerce Commission ruled that the 1983 merger of the Atchison, Topeka & Santa Fe Railroad with Southern Pacific was anticompetitive. Anschutz, who had gained much of his wealth in the oil industry, first entered the railroad industry with the 1984 purchase of the Rio Grande Railroad for $500 million. His company, Anschutz Corp., paid about $1.8 billion for Southern Pacific, with much of it being leveraged debt.

SP Telecom was established in San Francisco in 1988 as a subsidiary of Southern Pacific Transportation Co. It was founded to construct telecommunications lines along Southern Pacific's 15,000 miles of railroad right-of-way. It was part of the company when Anschutz acquired it, but he later reorganized it as a subsidiary of Anschutz Corp. In 1992 Anschutz negotiated an easement agreement with Southern Pacific to lay fiber-optic cable along 11,700 miles of its tracks.

It should be noted that SP Telecom was not the first successful telecommunications spin-off from Southern Pacific. Earlier, the railroad giant had created and sold another subsidiary that later became Sprint Corp. (The first two letters in Sprint were taken from its parent's name.)

By 1993 the privately held SP Telecom had annual revenue of more than $50 million and employed 410 people. During the early 1990s SP Telecom built fiber-optic linkups for other carriers, sold space on its fiber-optic network, and introduced commercial products including a video teleconferencing system. In mid-1993 it began offering commercial services such as long-distance, 800-number, calling-card, and debit-card products.

## BECOMING QWEST AND GOING PUBLIC

In 1995 SP Telecom moved to Denver after acquiring the Dallas-based firm Qwest Communications Corp. and taking over its name and facilities. Anschutz also expanded his telecommunications holdings in 1995 with the purchase of Interwest Communications C.S. Corp. Around this time he also agreed to sell his interest in Southern Pacific to the Union Pacific Corp. for about $1.6 billion worth of stock, which made him Union Pacific's largest shareholder.

In May of that year, Qwest reached an agreement with CSX Transportation Inc. to use its rail corridors to install a high-speed, high-volume fiber-optic network. CSX owned 19,000 miles of track in 20 eastern states. Qwest already had a strong presence in the West through agreements with Southern Pacific Rail Corp. and Santa Fe Railway. The agreement with CSX would enable Qwest to build a fiber-optic network from coast to coast.

In laying its fiber-optic cables, Qwest would bury four to six high-density polyethylene pipes at a time, each capable of carrying a separate system. It used a $1 million, 76-ton rail-mounted plow that laid the pipe next to the rail line at a depth of four to five feet. The machine was capable of laying about eight miles per day.

That year, Qwest completed a fiber-optic link between Sacramento and Los Angeles. The company had plans to build a national fiber-optic network. Other companies, such as AT&T and Sprint, were in the process of doing the same. Later in 1995, Qwest gained permission to link several Mexican cities, including Mexico City, Monterrey, and Guadalajara, with about 5,000 miles of fiber-optic cable. This network was later linked to U.S. long distance carriers at the U.S.-Mexican border.

The company initiated an initial public offering (IPO) on June 23, 1997, renaming itself Qwest Communications International, Inc. The offering raised $297 million on the sale of 13.5 million shares. Only 14 percent of the company was offered to the public, however, with the rest being held by Philip Anschutz. The IPO gave the company a market capitalization of $2.1 billion. Joseph Nacchio became Qwest's new president and CEO in 1997, after leaving the number three post at AT&T, where he had been head of AT&T's consumer services until late 1996.

Qwest's strategy in building its nationwide fiber-optic network was that a ground-based network would be more reliable for the transmission of data than satellite-based networks. Demand for high-speed networks that could transmit data as well as audio and video were set to explode over the next five years, and this demand would be led by banks and other financial institutions. In addition, deregulation would bring other companies, including the regional Bell operating companies (RBOCs), into the long-distance market. Also, costs for fiber and equipment were expected to drop dramatically.

At the time it went public, Qwest had already negotiated for nearly 90 percent of the right-of-ways it needed to complete its 13,000-mile network. Qwest had reached agreements with Frontier Corp. (the fifth-largest long-distance carrier in the United States), WorldCom Inc. (the fourth-largest long-distance carrier and the largest Internet access provider with its acquisition of UUNet), and GTE Corp. (the largest non-Bell local telephone company). Those three companies would together lease about half of the capacity of Qwest's network for an investment of about $1 billion. Qwest also received $90 million in vendor financing from Nortel. Other potential revenue streams were expected to come from the RBOCs and from Internet service providers (ISPs), for whom Qwest planned to install sophisticated switching equipment.

Later in 1997, Qwest acquired Colorado's largest ISP, SuperNet Inc., for $20 million. SuperNet was also the state's oldest ISP, having been originally founded by

## KEY DATES
■

**1988:** SP Telecom is established as a subsidiary of Southern Pacific Transportation Co.

**1995:** SP Telecom assumes the name of Qwest Communications Corp. and goes public later in the year as Qwest Communications International, Inc.

**1998:** Qwest acquires long-distance carrier LCI International for $4.4 billion.

**1999:** Qwest receives a $3.5 billion investment from BellSouth and initiates takeover bids for US West and Frontier Communications.

**2000:** Qwest completes acquisition of US West.

**2001:** Qwests posts a $4 billion net loss and prepares for billion-dollar write-down from the US West merger. Qwest refuses to hand over customer call records to the U.S. National Security Agency.

**2002:** Qwest stock drops to about $2 a share, from more than $60 share in 2000.

**2007:** Former CEO Joe Nacchio is sentenced to six years in prison for insider trading.

**2010:** Communications company CenturyTel announces the acquisition of Qwest on April 22 in a $10.6 billion stock-swap.

the Colorado Advanced Institute of Technology and other local universities as a nonprofit venture. Qwest also introduced the first advertising campaign for its fiber-optic telecommunications network. The print campaign, estimated to cost between $5 million and $10 million, employed the tagline, "Ride the light." Qwest's network was now projected to reach 125 U.S. cities and several cities in Mexico, have 16,000 miles of fiber-optic cable, and be completed in mid-1999. For 1997, Qwest reported revenue of $697 million.

### ACQUISITIONS AND EXPANSION: 1997–99

With Internet usage increasing dramatically in 1997, Qwest made plans to take advantage of the expansion of voice-over-Internet protocol (VoIP) services. In December 1997 Qwest announced it would offer IP-based services to users in nine western cities. The service was expected to resolve voice-quality problems associated with IP-based telephone services. It was initially offered as a consumer long-distance package at 7.5 cents per minute, with business customers to follow.

In March 1998 Qwest announced it would acquire the McLean, Virginia-based long-distance carrier LCI International Inc. for $4.4 billion. The deal would create the fourth-largest long-distance carrier in the United States behind AT&T, MCI Worldcom, and Sprint Corp. The combined companies would have about 5,800 employees and revenue of $2.3 billion. The acquisition gave Qwest two million long-distance customers and a well-established sales force. In the same month, Qwest also announced that it would purchase EUNet, a European ISP based in Amsterdam with about 60,000 customers and 1997 revenue of $55 million, for $154 million.

A month later, Qwest activated the portion of its fiber network that connected Los Angeles, San Francisco, and New York, giving the company more than 5,400 route-miles of its network in service.

Soon thereafter, RBOC Ameritech (which was in the process of being acquired by SBC Communications Inc., formerly Southwestern Bell) announced that it would begin offering long-distance service through an alliance with Qwest. The plan was challenged by other long-distance carriers, however, who pointed out that the Telecommunication Act of 1996 required the RBOCs, which had virtual monopolies on local phone markets, to prove their local market was open to competition before they could offer long-distance services. Qwest and US West had reached a similar agreement earlier in 1998 that was also challenged. Later in the year the Federal Communications Commission (FCC) ruled against the agreements.

In mid-1998 Qwest announced it would offer long-distance service in Europe. While the acquisition of ISP EUNet gave Qwest data services, it planned to offer voice services by making deals with established carriers in Europe. Meanwhile, back in the United States Qwest sold bandwidth on its fiber network to competitive local exchange carrier (CLEC) Electric Lightwave for $122 million. Qwest also sold $60 million worth of bandwidth to Digital Broadcast Network Corp. for IP-based ATM services.

In September 1998 Qwest acquired Icon CMT of Weehawken, New Jersey, for $185 million in stock. Icon CMT provided Internet-based services, such as web hosting, intranets, online stock trading, and online publications for larger corporations. Qwest also formed a three-year alliance with Netscape Communications to provide Netscape's web portal, NetCenter, with a range of telecommunications services including Internet access.

In December 1998 Qwest and Microsoft Corp. announced an agreement whereby Microsoft would invest $200 million in Qwest, taking a 1.3 percent minority interest in the company. Qwest, in turn, would use the

Microsoft Windows NT Server OS as the basis of its electronic commerce, Web hosting, streaming media, managed software, and virtual private networking services to be introduced in 1999. Qwest's 1998 revenue was reported at $2.2 billion.

As part of its national fiber network, Qwest had completed local fiber-optic rings in 10 cities in 1998. The company's Seattle ring ran through Microsoft's Redmond, Washington, campus, giving Qwest the ability to provide broadband connectivity directly to Microsoft.

At the beginning of 1999, Qwest invested $1.5 million in CLEC Covad Communications Group Inc. In exchange, Covad provided Qwest customers with high-speed digital subscriber line (DSL) service in 22 markets. Covad also agreed to purchase network capacity from Qwest to interconnect its high-speed local networks. It was Qwest's first investment in DSL local networks.

Also in January of that year, Qwest introduced its first Internet services for consumers and small businesses, offering flat-rate service for $19.95 a month. Qwest's long-distance customers, however, would only pay $14.95 a month for the service, which was called Q.home. Qwest also announced it would offer paging, conferencing, and faxing services from its Web site. In a move to increase its bandwidth, America Online Inc. selected Qwest to provide it with national Internet connectivity services in a deal valued at $13 million.

Also in 1999, Qwest announced it would be able to expand its high-speed DSL services into more markets through a $15 million agreement with Rhythms Net-Connections Inc., a local DSL provider. The agreement involved 31 cities, with some overlap with the 22 cities serviced under Qwest's agreement with Covad Communications.

A consortium of banks and financial institutions, led by Bank of America, agreed to provide Qwest with a $1 billion revolving credit facility starting in April 1999. Also in April, Bell South Corp. agreed to purchase a 10 percent interest in Qwest for $3.5 billion. The investment would enable BellSouth to bolster its digital data services and use Qwest as its wholesale provider, while Qwest would use BellSouth for local service where possible. The funds also enabled Qwest to reduce the debt it took on for overseas expansion, and it helped the company finance construction on the rest of its fiber-optic network.

In May Qwest president and CEO Joseph Nacchio gave up his title of president to Afshin Mohebbi, who also became Qwest's chief operating officer in charge of day-to-day operations. Nacchio would remain as CEO and focus on overall corporate performance, develop-

ment, and long-term strategies. Prior to the change, Mohebbi had most recently been the president and managing director of U.K. markets for British Telecom.

## ACQUISITION OF US WEST

Rumors soon surfaced that Qwest might be a long-term acquisition target for BellSouth, which had a 10 percent interest in the company. Those rumors, however, were quickly overshadowed when Qwest announced hostile takeover bids for US West, a RBOC with local phone customers in 14 western states, and Frontier Communications, the fifth-largest U.S. long-distance carrier. At the time, US West was the subject of a $52 billion takeover proposal from Global Crossing Ltd., a Bermuda-based company that was building an undersea fiber-optic network. Wall Street reacted to the announcement by driving Qwest's stock down more than 20 percent.

At first, US West rejected Qwest's bid and reaffirmed its commitment to Global Crossing. Qwest responded by increasing its offer to $68 a share for Frontier and $69 a share for US West, or about $48 billion in all. Global Crossing's offer amounted to about $11 billion for Frontier and $30 billion for US West. Following the new offer, both Frontier and US West agreed to discuss the proposal with Qwest. Qwest and US West quickly reached an agreement whereby Qwest would acquire US West for an amount estimated between $35 billion and $50 billion, according to various sources. As part of the purchase, Qwest agreed to forego providing long-distance service in US West's territory. Qwest's acquisition of US West also had the effect of diluting BellSouth's interest in the new company from 10 percent to about 3.5 percent. Qwest subsequently withdrew its offer for Frontier, and Frontier agreed to be acquired by Global Crossing for $10.9 billion.

By the summer of 1999, Qwest had about 8,700 employees, while US West had 55,000 employees. The acquisition not only gave Qwest a huge workforce, but also 25 million US West local phone customers in 14 western states. Before the acquisition was finalized in 2000, US West CEO Solomon Trujillo announced he would not remain with the new company, leaving Joseph Nacchio in charge.

Qwest's acquisition of US West had to pass several regulatory hurdles, including approval from the U.S. Department of Justice (DOJ), the Federal Trade Commission (FTC), the Federal Communications Commission, and public service commissions in seven of the 14 states served by US West.

The US West acquisition received approval from the DOJ and the FTC in September. Shareholders of both companies approved the merger in November.

Qwest completed its national fiber-optic network with 18,500 route miles in September 1999. In December it added 4,300 route miles in Canada and Mexico. In the first two months of 2000 the company experienced service problems due to the rapid expansion of its customer base, including frame relay service slowdowns and circuit outages lasting up to 11 days. Qwest's 1999 revenue was $3.92 billion, with net income of $458 million.

The FCC gave its approval of the US West acquisition in March 2000, but six state public service commissions had yet to rule on the merger following Colorado's approval in 1999. Rumors surfaced that Deutsche Telekom AG, Europe's largest telecommunications company, had made a $100 billion bid for both companies. Qwest announced that talks with Deutsche Telekom would not continue, however, following objections from US West.

In addition, Qwest was in the process of selling part of its long-distance business to Touch America, a subsidiary of the Montana Power Co. Under federal rules Qwest would not be able to offer long-distance service within states served by US West. In July 2000 the FCC approved the sale of Qwest's long-distance assets in US West territory to Touch America for $193 million. About 250,000 Qwest subscribers, 1,800 miles of fiber-optic network, and 170 Qwest sales agents were involved in the transaction. The operations that were sold represented about 6 percent of Qwest's customers and accounted for about $300 million in annual revenue.

By July, the merger with US West had received approval from the state public service commissions and was a "done" deal. In many cases, state approval was gained by agreeing to negotiate new service quality standards. Estimates of the price of the merger ranged from $35 billion to $80 billion. The new company would lose the US West name and continue using the Qwest name. Qwest immediately held a meeting for about 10,000 employees at the Pepsi Center in Denver, where it announced that it was dropping some 17 lawsuits US West had brought against various state public utility commissions. Altogether, the merged companies had about 70,000 employees worldwide. Later in the year Qwest announced it would streamline its workforce by cutting about 11,000 employee positions and 1,800 contractor positions by the end of 2001.

In the two years after the merger went through in July 2000, Qwest cut about 25,000 jobs from the combined company. The merger weighed heavily on Qwest, which posted a $4 billion net loss in 2001, and in 2002 Qwest took a $34.8 billion write-down of goodwill and other intangibles from the US West merger.

## SAYING NO TO THE NATIONAL SECURITY ADMINISTRATION

On May 11, 2006, *USA Today* broke the story that the National Security Administration (NSA) had been secretly collecting the phone call records of tens of millions of Americans, using data provided by AT&T, Verizon, and BellSouth. The NSA said it was using the data to analyze call patterns in order to deter terrorist activity. The only big telecom company the NSA approached for phone records that refused to cooperate was Qwest, over concerns about the legal implications of handing over customer information without government warrants. The news contributed to a furor over the George W. Bush administration's domestic surveillance program and caused an upswell of public goodwill toward Qwest.

However, not all the press about Qwest was positive. In 2007 a judge sentenced former Qwest CEO Joe Nacchio to six years in prison for making $52 million on insider trading in 2001. (Nacchio had resigned from Qwest in 2002.) Nacchio was ordered to forfeit the $52 million and pay a $19 million fine. Prosecutors alleged that Nacchio made the trades while keeping quiet that the company would perform below investor expectations later in the year. Qwest stock dropped from more than $60 a share in 2000 to about $2 in 2002.

In his fight against insider trading charges, Nacchio said that he had refused a request for phone records by the NSA in February 2001, nearly eight months before the terrorist attacks against the United States on September 11, 2001. He claimed that the NSA retaliated by denying Qwest lucrative governmental contracts. As part of his defense, Nacchio claimed that his knowledge of future secret contracts with the NSA and other governmental agencies made Qwest's financials better than was publicly known and their loss contributed to Qwest's poor performance after he had sold stock. Nacchio successfully appealed the six-year sentence due to a court error in calculating how much he profited from his crime. A new trial was scheduled for late 2010.

## QWEST IS ACQUIRED

Communications company CenturyLink announced on April 22, 2010, that it would acquire Qwest for $10.6

billion in stock and the assumption of nearly $12 billion in debt. The move would create the third-largest provider of local phone and Internet service in the United States. As of December 2009, the two companies operated in 37 states and served about five million broadband customers, 1.4 million video subscribers, 850,000 wireless clients, and had 17 million access lines. At the time of the acquisition, Qwest posted revenue for 2009 of $12.31 billion and a net profit of $662 million.

CenturyLink was the fifth-largest telecommunications company in the United States at the time of the acquisition, with more than seven million phone lines in 33 states and about 20,000 employees. It had 7.5 million access lines, 2.1 million broadband customers, 450,000 video subscribers, and almost 17,000 miles of core fiber network. CenturyLink reported profit of $647.2 million in 2009, from revenue of $4.97 billion. It was agreed that the merged company's headquarters would be in Monroe, Louisiana, the location of CenturyLink, which changed its name from CenturyTel in May 2010. The former headquarters of Qwest in Denver would retain a reduced staff. Savings from the merger were estimated at $625 million within three to five years.

*David P. Bianco*
*Updated, Catherine Meyrat*

## PRINCIPAL SUBSIDIARIES

Qwest Broadband Services, Inc; Qwest Capital Funding, Inc; Qwest Communications Company, LLC; Qwest Services Corporation.

## PRINCIPAL COMPETITORS

AT&T Corporation; Sprint Nextel Corporation; T-MobileUSA Inc.; Verizon Communications Inc.

## FURTHER READING

Cauley, Leslie, "NSA Has Massive Database of Americans' Phone Calls," *USA Today,* May 11, 2006.

Harden, Mark, "Judge Sentences Nacchio to Six years, Orders Him to Forfeit $52M, Pay $19M Fine," *Denver Business Journal,* July 27, 2007.

———, "For 80 years, Qwest Buyer CenturyTel Has Grown through Acquisition into National Giant," *Denver Business Journal,* April 22, 2010.

———, "Qwest to Be Sold to CenturyTel," *Denver Business Journal,* April 22, 2010.

———, "Qwest's Future Owner CenturyTel Changes Its Name," *Denver Business Journal,* May 21, 2010.

"Qwest's Latest Annual Report Paints Bleak Picture," *Portland Business Journal,* April 8, 2002.

Shane, Scott, "Former Phone Chief Says Spy Agency Sought Surveillance Help Before 9/11," *New York Times,* October 14, 2007.

# Rabobank Group

—■—

**Croeselaan 18**
**P. O. Box 17100**
**Utrecht, 3500 HG**
**The Netherlands**
**Telephone: (31) 30 216-0000**
**Toll Free: (800) 942-6222**
**Web site: http://www.rabobank.com**

*Cooperative*
*Founded:* 1864
*Employees:* 59,311 (2009)
*Revenue:* EUR 11.87 billion ($14.7 billion, 2009)
*NAICS:* 522110 Commercial Banking

■ ■ ■

Rabobank Group is one of the leading banks in the the Netherlands. Unlike its chief domestic rivals, Rabobank has clung steadfastly to its status as a private cooperative, composed of numerous independent member banks with a worldwide branch network under the Rabobank name. In 2009 the bank had 147 local banks with 1,010 branches spread throughout the country. With a cooperative membership of roughly 1.8 million, Rabobank supplies financial products in one form or another to some 9.5 million customers in 48 countries. Formed in order to provide financial support to the Netherlands' farming community, Rabobank remains true to its roots and accounted for 85 percent of the country's food and agriculture-related financial services business in 2009.

## FARMERS COOPERATIVE MOVEMENT IN THE 19TH CENTURY

Rabobank's origins lay in the cooperative banking movement of the 19th century. In 1864 Friedrich Wilhelm Raiffeisen, of Heddesdorf in Germany, started up a local banking cooperative that was to inspire similar cooperatives worldwide. Raiffeisen's model was based on providing mutual assistance to its members, especially in the form of loans and other financial assistance, providing a sense of commitment to community that has remained a hallmark of the cooperative banking movement into the 21st century. The Raiffeisen banks operated on a local basis as part of a larger cooperative network. Administration was frugal, and all profits were reinvested in the bank. The Raiffeisen form of cooperative banking soon spread across the German border into the Netherlands, where it held a strong appeal for the country's farmers.

The first Dutch financial organization to meet the full criteria of the Raiffeisen model was the Coöperatieve Landbouwersbank en Handelsvereeniging, in Lonneker, near Enschede. Established in 1896, this bank remained in operation for nearly 70 years. The establishment of the Lonneker bank, and its emphasis on the agricultural community, inspired the start-up of other farming-focused banking cooperatives.

Hard hit by the economic climate, and finding little assistance from the traditional financial community, the Netherlands' farmers turned to the Raiffeisen cooperative model of mutual aid. The first of these farmer-owned cooperative banks appeared in 1897, called the

Sustained autonomous growth is a leading factor in the strategic course that Rabobank Group aims to steer in the coming years. This strategy centers around our company's core competence in the Food & Agri-business sector.

Boerenleenbank (or "farmers loan bank"), in the town of Geldorp, quickly followed by similar Boerenleenbanks in Leene, Heeze, and Heeswijk. By the following year, the Boerenleenbank concept had spread through much of the Netherlands.

In 1898 the first initiatives were taken to group together the many independently operating Boerenleenbanks under a central administration. In June of that year, a group of southern farmers' banks formed the Coöperatieve Vereeniging van Raiffeisen-Banken en Landbouwvereenigingen in Utrecht. This was followed soon after in the north by the creation of the Coöperatieve Centrale Boerenleenbank in Eindhoven. Member banks of both the northern and southern cooperatives remained independently operated, yet benefitted from a central administration. The Dutch farmers' union, the Nederlandsche Boerenbond, which had been behind the formation of the banking cooperatives, had initially intended to form a single, nationally operating central organization. Efforts were made to merge the two groups together in that same year. The two organizations, echoing traditional north-south tensions, were unable to agree on a merger, however.

By the 1920s, the farmers' banking cooperative movement had spread throughout the Netherlands, comprising more than 1,200 locally operating member banks. The combined assets of these banks gave the cooperatives a position as one of the Netherlands' largest savings and loan institutions. These farmers' cooperatives retained a near-monopoly on the agricultural community savings and loan market until the 1950s, when the Dutch banking industry began to restructure. Where banks had typically focused on single-product activities, more and more banks were beginning to offer multiple products. In 1957, for example, the country's commercial banks began offering savings accounts for the first time.

The farmers banking cooperatives quickly responded to the changing banking climate by expanding their services. In the early 1960s, the cooperatives began offering insurance services. In 1965 the coopera-

tives added commercial accounts and other services. In that year, the Centrale Boerenleenbank acquired Amsterdam-based private broker and bank Schretlen & Co. Two years later, the two cooperatives joined together to form the Bankgirocentrale. By the end of the decade, both cooperatives were also operating travel agency services.

At the start of the 1970s, the two cooperatives announced their intention to join forces. The actual merger took place in December 1972, forming the Coöperatieve Centrale Raiffeisen-Boerenleenbank. The new organization quickly became known as Rabobank. Comprising more than 1,500 independent banks, which took on the Rabobank name, the new financial institution became one of the country's top three providers of banking and other financial services.

## DIVERSIFICATION: 1960-2000

Despite diversifying its portfolio of financial products since the early 1960s, Rabobank remained focused on providing traditional retail banking products to an exclusively Dutch, and especially agricultural market. In the late 1970s, faced with increasing competition from traditional banks, the farmers' cooperative began to open outwards. In the 1970s, Rabobank joined with a number of other European banking cooperatives to form the Unico Banking Group. Two years later, Rabobank dropped the membership requirement for its private depositors, and only customers arranging business and professional loans were required to become Rabobank members. This change enabled Rabobank to find wider appeal among the general Netherlands population, and by the 1990s the bank was able to claim that roughly half of the country's 14 million citizens were customers of one or more of its financial products. Nevertheless, Rabobank succeeded in retaining a large membership base, which neared some 600,000 by the end of the century. At the same time, Rabobank had successfully maintained its low operating costs and strong profits, enabling the bank to achieve the coveted Triple-A rating from both Moody's and Standard & Poor.

Rabobank's future growth opportunities in the Netherlands remained limited, however. Increasing pressure from its capital-rich, publicly listed competitors, at a time when financial barriers among European Community member states had begun to fall, forced Rabobank to look beyond the Netherlands' borders. The bank took its first international steps in 1983, when it acquired 84 percent of ADC A Bank in Germany. Also during that year, Rabobank opened its first overseas office, in London, heralding the launch of the company's global operations, Rabobank International.

## KEY DATES

**1864:** A cooperative bank is founded by Friedrich Wilhelm Raiffeisen in Heddesdorf, Germany.

**1897:** Boerenleenbank ("farmer's loan bank") is founded in Geldorp, Netherlands, with Raiffeisen's bank as a model.

**1898:** Grouping of the many bank co-ops occurs, under Coöperatieve Vereeniging van Raiffeisen-Banken en Landbouwvereenigingen in the south, and Coöperatieve Centrale Boerenleenbank in the north.

**1925:** Dutch farmers bank cooperative achieves national penetration.

**1957:** Dutch banking is deregulated.

**1961:** Co-ops introduce insurance services.

**1965:** Co-ops introduce commercial banking services.

**1967:** The two major co-ops form a joint venture, Bankgirocentrale.

**1972:** Rabobank emerges from the merging of the two major co-ops.

**1986:** Rabobank begins offering mutual funds.

**2010:** Rabobank Group and Agricultural Bank of China sign a memorandum of understanding.

Rabobank also began stepping up diversification of its product portfolio. In 1986 the bank began offering mutual funds and shareholder products, including the Rabobank Obligatiefonds and the Rabobank Andelenfonds. The bank also stepped up its activities beyond the agricultural sphere, to the extent that, by 1987, loans to the business community outpaced loans to the agricultural market for the first time. In that year, also, the bank's leadership was given to Herman Wijffels. As head of Rabobank until the late 1990s, Wijffels was given much of the credit for developing Rabobank's international business and transforming it into one of the world's top financial institutions. By the beginning of the 1990s, Rabobank determined to diversify its activities in order to become a full-service financial services provider offering banking, investment, and insurance products.

While Rabobank's publicly traded counterparts were able to finance aggressive expansion and acquisition programs, Rabobank, guarding its private, cooperative status, had to look elsewhere for growth. The cooperative took a two-pronged approach. The first part

involved extending its financial expertise, particularly in the high-growth food and agricultural sector, to a worldwide scale. For this the company pursued an internal growth strategy, opening new branches and entering new country markets, while also seeking local partnerships and acquisitions in the agricultural banking sector, such as the 1989 purchase of Primary Industry Bank of Australia. By the middle of the decade, Rabobank International was present in more than 30 countries; by the beginning of the new century, nearly 160 Rabobank International and other subsidiary branches operated in more than 40 countries.

The second prong to Rabobank's 1990s growth strategy came through a series of strategic mergers. The first occurred in 1990, when Rabobank merged with insurance cooperative Interpolis, bringing the latter's portfolio of insurance products to Rabobank's customers. Rabobank also entered the sales promotions products category (leasing, wholesale financing, and other debt financing) for the international durable equipment manufacturing market with De Lage Landen. Both Interpolis and De Lage Landen operated primarily in the Netherlands, but with worldwide interests as well. In the early 1990s, Rabobank, which had developed a modest assets management business, began to approach Robeco, one of the world's leading assets management companies, based in Rotterdam. The cooperation between Rabobank and Robeco became a partnership when Rabobank acquired 50 percent of Robeco in 1996, with an option to acquire full ownership, and completed the acquisition in 1998. The total purchase price of around NLG 1 billion gave the privately held Robeco the much-needed capital to fund its own worldwide expansion and added Robeco's strong assets portfolio to Rabobank's list of products.

By the late 1990s, Rabobank's transformation into a diversified financial products provider had largely been completed. Yet the bank remained a relatively small player in a market set to see explosive growth with the launch of the Euro in 1999. As its publicly listed competitors moved towards an aggressive consolidation of the European financial market, mirroring a continuing worldwide consolidation, Rabobank was forced to look beyond the Netherlands borders in order to secure its position in Europe. Analysts saw the inevitability of alliances among Rabobank and its European cooperative counterparts, such as Credit Agricole of France. Instead, Rabobank turned first to Dutch insurance broker Achmea Holding NV, with the intention to form a 50-50 joint venture offering asset management, pension, life insurance and other insurance products. That deal, however, fell through.

## RABOBANK IN THE 21ST CENTURY

The year 2002 saw Rabobank enhance its expansion strategies at the international level through the acquisition of Ireland's ACC Bank and U.S.-based Valley Independence Bank. That year major changes were introduced in the management structure of the Rabobank Group in a move that was largely intended to simplify the bank's overall management structures. As such, the board of directors was abolished and substantive powers transferred to the Central Delegates Assembly. The allocation of greater authority to the Central Delegates Assembly strengthened the influence of its local member banks. The Central Delegates Assembly was placed under the leadership of an executive board with the responsibility of managing the day-to-day business of the bank in addition to advancing the interests of the Group's local member banks.

Rabobank Group ventured into the cyber world in 2003 when it acquired Alex, an Internet broker for banking and financial services. The acquisition of Alex bolstered the bank's strategic initiatives of using information technology to enhance its services locally while simultaneously gaining more presence in international cooperative and banking sectors. The bank also went on to add commercial real estate financing to its product portfolio through the acquisition of FGH Bank in 2003.

The Rabobank Group experienced a minor setback in its corporate social responsibility initiatives in July 2007 when a leading International Cycling Union (UCI) rider, Michael Rasmussen, was dismissed from the Rabo Cycling Team. The dismissal of Rasmussen occurred after the UCI failed to establish his whereabouts. The UCI stated that Rasmussen had given wrong information about where he was staying. The dismissal of Rasmussen generated a lot of controversy for the bank's sponsoring unit as well as across the UCI sporting fraternity. As such, the Rabobank Group had to adopt appropriate damage control measures to protect its image and corporate sponsorship track record.

The Rabobank Group reported reduced net income in 2009, down from EUR 2.7 billion in 2008 to EUR 2.2 billion in 2009. The downward shift of the Group's business prospects in 2009 saw its interest income reduced to EUR 19.7 billion from 27.2 billion in 2008.

## MEMORANDUM OF UNDERSTANDING WITH AGRICULTURAL BANK OF CHINA: 2010

In April 2010 Rabobank Group strengthened its position in China by signing a memorandum of understanding (MOU) with the Agricultural Bank of China (ABC). The MOU enabled the two financial institutions to share technical expertise and experiences in their core business areas of wholesale banking, business financing, leasing, and asset management. The MOU represented a significant strategic success as it provided Rabobank Group with the opportunity to enhance its presence in China through ABC's enviable branch network in the country.

*M. L. Cohen*
*Updated, Paul Ingati*

### PRINCIPAL SUBSIDIARIES

ACC Bank; De Lage Landen; Eureko (39%); Interpolis; Robeco; Sarasin, Schretlen & Co.;

### PRINCIPAL COMPETITORS

ABN Amro Bank N.V.; Crédit Agricole Group; Deutsche Bank AG; HSBC Holdings plc; ING Groep N.V.

### FURTHER READING

"The History of Rabobank," rabobank.com, November 2006.

"Rabobank Group and Agricultural Bank of China Sign Strategic Co-operation Memorandum of Understanding," Rabobank Group, Press Release, April 6, 2010.

"Rasmussen Dismissed from Rabo Cycling Team: Statement from Rabobank about Rasmussen's Dismissal," *New York Times*, July 26, 2007.

"Sheldon Sussman Named Head of Global Financial Markets for Rabobank International," *PR Newswire*, July 12, 2006.

# RailAmerica, Inc.

7411 Fullerton Street
Suite 300
Jacksonville, Florida 32256
U.S.A.
Telephone: (904) 538-6100
Toll Free: (800) 342-1131
Web site: http://www.railamerica.com

*Public Company*
*Founded:* 1986
*Employees:* 1,553 (2009)
*Sales:* $410.6 million (2009)
*Stock Exchanges:* New York
*Ticker Symbol:* RA
*NAICS:* 482111 Line-Haul Railroads

■ ■ ■

RailAmerica, Inc., is a leading owner and operator of short-line and regional freight railroads in North America. In 2010 the company operated 40 individual railroads with 7,400 miles of track in 27 U.S. states and three Canadian provinces. An important component of the North American transportation infrastructure, RailAmerica carries freight such as farm and food products, lumber and forest products, paper and paper products, metals, chemical, and coal for a diverse group of customers. It also provides non-freight services such as railcar storage, railcar repair, and land leasing for advertising or cellular communication towers.

## COMPANY FOUNDED: 1986

RailAmerica grew out of the global deregulation and privatization of the railroad industry that took place in the 1980s. As governments began to divest themselves of state-owned railroads, and competition began to replace regulation as an operating principle, the opportunities for private investors began to grow.

In 1986 Gary Marino was the CEO of Boca Raton Capital Corporation, a Florida-based venture capital company. A former U.S. army officer with a master of business administration degree from Fordham University, Marino realized that a small-line railroad, with lower costs, could profit from the remnants being discarded by both governments and the large Class I railroad companies. He formed RailAmerica to fill the void.

With $125,000 in equity and an additional $1.4 million raised from institutional investors, RailAmerica purchased its first small-line railroad in 1986. The Huron and Eastern Railway owned 83 miles of track in Michigan and was being sold by CSX Corp., a large Class I railroad.

From its austere beginnings, RailAmerica would grow to become a company international in scope, with operations not just in North America but also in South America and Australia. It would acquire railroads, miles of tracks, locomotives, railcars, and over 1,500 employees.

COMPANY PERSPECTIVES

RailAmerica's objective is to provide local rail freight customers with services that facilitate the prompt pick-up and delivery of goods.

## GROWTH OF RAILROADS AND GOVERNMENT REGULATION

North America is largely composed of two land mass leviathans. The United States, combined with its northern neighbor Canada, occupy approximately 7.6 million square miles of land, nearly five times the size of western Europe. Both countries shared similar patterns of development and growth and both were dependent on the railroad industry to open their respective territories for settlement. In the United States, the first transcontinental railway was completed in 1869, whereas Canada completed its transcontinental rail line in 1871.

Realizing the significance of the railroads to national development, both countries were heavy regulators of the industry. The cautious Canadians went so far as to form a state-owned, government-run transcontinental railway. This regulation served both public policy and the industry for almost a century. It nurtured the new industry and allowed the development of state and provincial route systems that connected to transcontinental main trunk rail lines.

## DECLINE IN RAILROADS AND DEREGULATION: POST-WORLD WAR II

The decades following World War II would see significant changes in the rail industry, particularly in North America. The United States would complete the interstate highway system, and Canada built the Trans-Canada highway from Newfoundland in the east to British Columbia in the west. Rail traffic began a slow but steady decline, starting with passenger traffic, which began to slip away first to the private automobile and later to the developing airline industry.

With new paved highways, the trucking industry began to expand and siphoned off freight shipments, particularly in the area of general freight shipments. By 1975 railways carried only 37 percent of intercity freight shipments, compared to 70 percent prior to World War II.

Major railroads were finding it increasing difficult to survive. Railroad track was expensive to maintain, but

under regulation, abandonment was an arduous process. Low-density, low-yield routes were a financial drag on railroad companies. Compounding the problem was the high cost of labor across the industry. The workforce was largely represented by powerful unions that kept labor costs high, and selling track meant selling it with union rules in place.

The United States and Canada made several attempts at deregulation, but it was the Staggers Rail Act of 1980, passed in the U.S. Congress, which was the most significant. The act greatly reduced the regulatory powers of the U.S. government. It gave the railroads the freedom to set freight rates and made rail track abandonment of unprofitable routes an easier process. It allowed railroads to consolidate with other carriers and permitted the sale of routes to nonunionized companies. Canada would pass its own, very similar, deregulatory laws some time thereafter.

The effects on the industry were immediate. Mergers and consolidation saw the number of Class I railroads decline from 56 in 1975 to just seven by 2005. As large railroads needed to downsize to remain competitive, thousands of miles of surplus track were slated for abandonment. The transcontinental railroads were shifting from the carriage of general freight to becoming bulk commodity carriers, leaving the freight business to the trucking industry.

This environment created an opportunity for the short-line and regional railroads that had developed alongside the Class I railroads. With lower cost structures, they could provide competition for the trucking industry and help alleviate the problems of rail line abandonment.

## RAILROAD CLASSIFICATIONS

The classification of railroads is largely a product of the revenues they produce. Generally speaking, a Class I railroad is a line that has revenues in excess of $267 million per year. A regional railroad has revenues between $21 and $267 million and is categorized as a Class II. The small-line railroads generally fit into Class III and have revenues of $21 million or less. While short-line and regional railroads are an important and integral part of the rail transportation system, they are tiny compared to the Class I railroads. In 1998 Class I railroads in North America earned $32 billion in revenues, while the combined short-line and regional lines earned less than $3 billion. Every mile of track owned by a Class I generated revenues of approximately $269,000. In comparison, short lines generated $60,000 per mile of track.

Short-line railroads act as feeder lines to the large transcontinental railroads. The average domestic short-line railway contains about 100 to 150 miles of track. They cater largely to small shippers located along their tracks.

Short-line railroads are attractive to small shippers because they can enhance a small shipper's logistics and ability to manage inventory, giving the small shipper a competitive advantage. They are also advantageous to Class I railroads, allowing the large lines to maintain contact with small shippers and to provide services which otherwise might be uneconomical to the large lines.

## STRATEGY AND GROWTH: 1986–95

RailAmerica set out to become an industry leader by acquiring and integrating short-line or regional railroads. Marino positioned RailAmerica to take advantage of the changes that deregulation had on the industry. The company would acquire track and equipment that the major railroads deemed as either surplus to their needs or too expensive to operate profitably. The company would also reduce expenses and cut costs by consolidating back office functions and clustering field operations. In addition, it would acquire companies which would complement its core functions.

The company's main competitors would be the trucking industry. Most small shippers perceived the trucking industry, often locally owned, to be more customer-orientated that the large railways. Rail line abandonment would place truckers in a monopoly position.

RailAmerica enjoyed limited success in the first few years of operations but with the capital-intensive nature of the railroad industry, it felt the need to raise money, and in 1992 went to the market with its first initial public offering (IPO). While the offering was termed premature and raised only $3 million, it did get RailAmerica's name into the public realm. In 1993 the company had revenues of $4 million and carried 15,000 carloads of freight.

In the following years, the company would make two complementary investments. In 1994 it acquired KalynSiebert Incorporated, a manufacturer of heavy-duty trailers for industrial and commercial users, and in 1995 it acquired Steel City Truck Lines, a regional freight carrier in Sault Ste. Marie, Ontario.

Three other significant events would occur before the end of 1995. RailAmerica acquired Dakota Rail Inc., which owned five short-line railroads and a significant railcar repair facility. In October it entered into the first of several credit facility arrangements with the National Bank of Canada, which would finance future growth, and in November, it established Rail-America Equipment Corporation to build a portfolio of transportation equipment to meet the needs of its own subsidiaries.

## EXPANSION: 1997–2001

Having established a solid base in North America and with funding in place, RailAmerica began to search out new opportunities outside of the continent.

Canada and the United States were not the only nations deregulating and privatizing their transportation sectors. Governments around the globe were shedding state-owned industries. In 1997 RailAmerica acquired a railroad with 1,400 miles of track, 31 locomotives, and 963 railcars in the South American nation of Chile and formed it into a company called Ferronor. The main commodities carried by the railroad were minerals from the north to Chile's export ports along the west coast. Within a year, the company was moving 69,000 carloads of freight and had revenues of $48.0 million.

In 1999 an opportunity arose in Australia, when a former government-owned railroad was put up for sale. RailAmerica purchased the line for $103.0 million and took possession of 3,150 miles of track, 106 locomotives, and 2,644 railcars. The company named the new venture Freight Australia.

In 2000 RailAmerica made one of its most significant and expensive acquisitions when it acquired the assets of RailTex, a major competitor in the small-line railroad industry in the United States. For $325 million, RailAmerica vaulted into the position of largest small-line railroad company in the world. It owned 39 short-line and regional railroads, moved 1.15 million carloads of freight, operated 11,000 miles of track, and had revenues of $357.9 million.

The company continued domestic expansion through 2001 by acquiring ParkSierra Corp., with three railroads on the west coast, and StatesRail, with its eight small-line railroads.

## RATIONALIZATION: 2003–04

By 2003 the heady days of mergers and acquisitions in the railroad industry were ending, and RailAmerica, which had expanded rapidly, began to reexamine its priorities. The company had an impressive record of expansion since its founding in 1986 with 83 miles of track. A good deal of its growth had been financed through debt, and by 2003 its net debt-to-capitalization was in excess of 60 percent.

To counteract this high debt load, the company embarked on a rationalization plan with a goal of shedding $100 million in nonstrategic, noncore assets. By returning to core business functions, RailAmerica hoped to reduce debt, improve earnings, and bring more efficiency to its operations. Therefore, the company sold off Freight Australia in 2004 for $204 million, nearly double what it had paid for it just five years before. It would also shed its operations in Chile.

In 2004 Gary Marino, the CEO of RailAmerica since the company was formed, retired. He was succeeded by Charles Swinburn, a RailAmerica board member. Swinburn had more than 30 years' experience in the industry, having held several positions with the U.S. Department of Transportation. Swinburn set out to refocus the company on its North American operations. He listed his primary goals as controlling costs, increasing shareholder value, and focusing on the customer.

Swinburn also needed to cultivate and grow the relationships between his short-line and regional railroads and the large Class I railroads. The two groups were mutually dependent.

## REORGANIZATION: 2005–07

By 2005 RailAmerica was beginning to realize some of the advantages of its rationalization process. Revenues increased in 2005 to $423.7 million and income from operations produced a profit of $30.8 million compared to a loss of $23.1 million in 2004.

In 2006 Swinburn reorganized the entire company. Operating areas were cut to three business units. Certain corporate functions were moved to a shared services model. The goal was to create a leaner corporate structure with fewer layers of management. To make the company more responsive to customer needs, business decisions would be left up to local managers.

The 2006 financial results, which were affected by the reorganization, were also negatively impacted by events outside of the company. A decline in housing starts resulted in a drop in lumber shipments, and a native land dispute in Canada disrupted traffic for most of the year.

However, despite the temporary financial setbacks, the reorganized RailAmerica, with its focus on North America, was still a viable entity with good prospects. It attracted the attention of Fortress Investment Group, a leading alternative asset management group with more than $30 billion under management. According to Wesley Edens, the CEO of Fortress, the company had been searching for an investment vehicle in the North American rail industry. Fortress viewed RailAmerica as a well-diversified railroad company that would fit well into its portfolio of assets.

In the fall of 2006, Fortress announced its plan to purchase the shares of RailAmerica and to take the company private. To ensure that it achieved that goal, Fortress offered RailAmerica shareholders a premium of 32 percent above the market-trading price of their shares. The deal was completed in 2007 and RailAmerica became a privately held company.

## NEW CEO AND AN IPO: 2008 AND BEYOND

Shortly after the deal, Charles Swinburn retired as CEO of RailAmerica and was replaced by John E. Giles, another veteran of the transportation and railroad industries with more than 35 years of experience. Giles was to put his own stamp on RailAmerica by reorganizing the company once again. The company replaced the three business units created under Swinburn with five operation regions, each with a regional vice president. Giles also relocated RailAmerica's headquarters from Boca Raton to Jacksonville, Florida. Fortress Investment Group had acquired the assets of Florida East Coast Railroad in 2008 and had applied to merge the two companies, which would be operated from Jacksonville.

In 2009 RailAmerica returned to the market with a new IPO as Fortress Investment sought to pay down debt and provide funds for further expansion. On October 16, 2009, the company sold 22 million shares of stock. All told, this generated $143.1 million in capital for the company. It seemed likely that this would allow RailAmerica to acquire additional short-line

*RailAmerica, Inc.*

railroads in the 2010s if the company deemed them a good fit to its ongoing operations.

*Ian MacDonald*

## PRINCIPAL SUBSIDIARIES

Alabama & Gulf Coast Railroad; Arizona & California Railroad; California Northern Railroad; Cape Breton Central Nova Scotia Railway; Cascade & Columbia River Railroad; Central Oregon & Pacific Railroad; Central Railroad of Indiana; Chicago, Ft. Wayne, & Eastern Railroad; Connecticut Southern Railroad; Consolidated Virginia Railroads; Dallas, Garland, & Northeastern Railroad; Huron Eastern Saginaw Valley Railway; Indiana & Ohio Railway; Missouri & Northern Railroad; New England Central Railroad; Ottawa Valley Railway; Otter Trail Valley Railroad; Point Comfort & Northern Railroad; Puget Sound & Pacific Railroad; San Diego Valley Railroad; San Joaquin Valley Railroad; Southern Carolina Central Railroad; Southern Ontario Railway; Toledo, Peoria, & Western Railway; Ventura County Railroad.

## PRINCIPAL COMPETITORS

Genesee & Wyoming, Inc.; New Prime, Inc.; Omni-TRAX, Inc.; TransAm Trucking, Inc.; Watco Companies, Inc.

## FURTHER READING

Hemphill, Mark W., "The Plight of Short Line Railroads," *Trains,* March 2004.

Jacobs, Daniel G., "Back on Track," *Smart Business,* July 2006.

"A Long View on Short-Line Rails," *Barrons,* November 2009.

Luczak, Marybeth, "With RailAmercia CEO Charles Swinburn," *Railway Age,* August 2004.

McCormick, Carroll, "Canada's Other Railways," *Canadian Transportation Logistics,* October 2007.

"RailAmerica Chairman, President, & CEO Interview," *Wall Street Corporate Reporter,* June 1998.

Winston, Clifford, "The Success of the Staggers Rail Act of 1980," AEI-Brookings Joint Center for Regulatory Studies, October 2005.

# Redflex Holdings Limited

**31 Market Street**
**South Melbourne, Victoria 3205**
**Australia**
**Telephone: (+61) 3 9674 1715**
**Fax: (+61) 3 9699 3566**
**Web site: http://www.redflex.com**

*Public Company*
*Founded:* 1995
*Sales:* AUD 130.9 million (2009)
*Stock Exchanges:* Australia
*Ticker Symbol:* RDF
*NAICS:* 334290 Other Communications Equipment
   Manufacturing; 541330 Engineering Services

■■■

Redflex Holdings Limited (Redflex) is a leader in providing traffic enforcement services and products worldwide, owning the largest network of red-light and speed cameras globally. As such, the company provides an array of products and technologies to help reduce traffic violations (and increase traffic fines).

Redflex has operations across the globe, with traffic cameras and related services in Qatar, the United Kingdom, Poland, New Zealand, the United States, and its home nation of Australia. Business in the United States is its largest sector, as Redflex's operations in 241 cities across 21 states accounted for almost 90 percent of revenue in 2009. While the company continues to expand its operation in the United States and elsewhere, it also faces continued legal challenges and adverse legislation from groups opposed to remote traffic camera laws and fines.

## COMPANY ORIGINS

Established in 1995, Redflex was listed on the Australian Stock Exchange in 1997. However, some of the company's holdings precede these dates. For instance, Redflex Traffic Systems Inc., owned by Redflex and registered in Delaware, has had a business presence in the United States since 1985. Creating Redflex Holdings was a way to combine many smaller companies into an entity able to expand globally.

## IMPACT OF TERRORIST ATTACKS

The terrorist attacks against the United States on September 11, 2001, impacted surveillance industries. As a result of the attacks, many U.S. cities grew increasingly concerned with security. At the same time, new legislation gave governments greater powers of surveillance while making citizens more concerned about the so-called surveillance state. Law enforcement and government bodies grew increasingly interested in surveillance technologies, paving the way for Automatic Number Plate Recognition (ANPR) and other enforcement systems. At the same time, citizen groups began to worry about what they perceived as eroding personal rights. This dual tension created an increase in business for Redflex but also increased the amount of litigation and criticism directed at the company.

## COMPANY PERSPECTIVES

Redflex is committed to reducing traffic violations and accidents, a fact reflected in the company motto: "Making a Safer World." By helping local governments automate traffic enforcement, Redflex believes it can help discover more traffic violations and can also help discourage those who speed or run red lights. It is the only company in the world that designs, develops, manufactures, tests, and maintains traffic enforcement cameras. Redflex is also unique in relying heavily on digital camera technology rather than film cameras.

## RAPID GROWTH

In early 2003 Redflex continued to expand into the U.S. market. By the end of the year, Redflex had contracts with 20 cities across five U.S. states. The company also had contracts in three Australian states as well as contracts for red-light cameras in five countries, including Saudi Arabia and Bahrain. In May 2003 the company combined and consolidated its Australian operations by relocating to a new facility in South Melbourne. The new location provided offices, a laboratory, and camera assembly and product testing facilities.

By December 2003 Redflex had acquired Locktronic Pty Ltd, a competitor based in Victoria. Earlier in the year, Redflex and Locktronic Pty Ltd had settled a lawsuit over patent issues, although details of the settlement were not released. This did not end all litigation, however, for around the same time the Locktronic deal was finalized Redflex was accused of patent infringement by another competitor, Nestor Inc. Nestor filed a lawsuit against Redflex and another competitor, Transol, for allegedly using a similar video-based monitoring system which Nestor had patented and sold since 1998.

## LITIGATION AND CHANGES: 2004–05

By early 2004 Redflex was in a strong market position. The company had contracts with 53 cities, including 43 American cities across nine U.S. states. As in 2003, the company led the market in number of installed systems, market share, and installation rate. Adding to the positive news for the company was the fact that Nestor voluntarily withdrew its patent infringement claim against Redflex in 2004. Throughout 2004 Redflex continued to expand into new cities.

However, during 2005, Redflex started to have different legal troubles as a result of legislation passed in the United States. In 2005, Ohio passed Bill 56 in the Ohio House of Representatives. This bill required a law enforcement officer to be present when any enforcement, including the automated enforcement Redflex offered, took place. This bill was the first of many proposed laws over the years which would challenge the legal status of Redflex services and products in the United States.

Despite the brewing legal complications, more cities continued to sign up for Redflex's services. The company expanded into Texas and continued to sign new contracts with U.S. cities. Redflex also received new contracts in Australia, Greece, Spain, Taiwan, and the UK.

## CONTINUED GROWTH AND LITIGATION: 2006

In 2006 legal and legislative action stemming from challenges to Redflex's legal authority in the United States continued. In March of that year, a resident of Minneapolis successfully challenged in district court a citation issued by a Redflex system. On March 14, Minnesota Hennepin County District Judge Mark S. Wernick deemed traffic enforcement cameras unconstitutional after the American Civil Liberties Union of Minnesota launched a suit alleging the cameras were violating constitutional rights. After the decision, Minneapolis halted its Redflex camera program. In March 2006, Ohio Court of Common Pleas Judge David E. Henderson also deemed traffic enforcement cameras in Steubenville to be a violation of rights and ordered the city to refund the tickets which had already been paid by motorists.

At the heart of the legal challenges against Redflex and other red-light camera providers were concerns about how tickets were issued. In order to allow red-light cameras, some cities had to pass ordinances. However, some citizens were able to successfully challenge these ordinances in court, alleging that they violated state rules. For instance, in Minnesota, the state traffic code required a uniformity of traffic laws to allow drivers to be reasonably sure of rules as they traveled through the state, without confusion. Also, all states had rules of criminal procedure and most of these rules relied heavily on due process. Judges ruled in various court cases that cities did not have the authority to change city ordinances to permit traffic cameras. They also decided that in many cases, red-light cameras violated state rules regarding due process.

By September 2006 Redflex reported that about 10 percent of its installed base of cameras in the United

## KEY DATES

**1995:** Redflex is established.
**1997:** Redflex is listed on the Australian Stock Exchange.
**2003:** Redflex's Australian holdings combined in one facility in South Melbourne.
**2007:** 1000th Redflex traffic enforcement camera installed.
**2008:** Redflex pays its first dividend.

States were not producing revenue. In some cases, this was due to road work. However, a significant part of this profit loss was due to legal and legislative problems.

Despite legal difficulties, Redflex continued to expand. By July 2006 the company had 667 installed systems in the United States, a 44 percent increase over the previous year. The company was present in 16 states and signed new contracts each year. In 2006 Redflex posted a 55 percent revenue growth over the previous fiscal year.

In the same year Redflex released its new ticket processing software, Redflex Traffic Systems Image and Infringement Processing System (IIPS), operational in Western Australia. The system automated the enforcement and citation of traffic violations, issuing tickets that included photo evidence of the offence. While the communications division had posted more modest profits than the traffic enforcement division of Redflex, this new development raised hopes for the communications operations. By late 2006, however, Redflex chose to focus on its more profitable traffic enforcement projects, selling its U.S.-based Redflex Communications Systems Pty Ltd and its subsidiaries (Redflex Communications Pty Ltd and Redflex Communications Systems Inc.) to Allied Technologies Group Limited for $8.2 million.

### EXPANSION AND INCREASING MARKET SHARE: 2007

In 2007 Redflex expanded into Missouri, Louisiana, Mississippi, and Massachusetts. The state of Arizona expressed interest in introducing Redflex solutions on state freeways on a broader basis. This program would be one of the most ambitious U.S. Redflex projects as it would introduce cameras over a broad road system rather than placing cameras strategically at specific intersections.

In 2007 Redflex continued to face lawsuits from irate drivers who claimed their tickets were inaccurate or a violation of rights. However, Bill 56 in Ohio was vetoed. That bill would have made it more difficult for Redflex to operate in Ohio because it would have required an officer to be present at each citation. Connecticut, South Carolina, and Virginia all passed legislation which would make it easier for traffic enforcement cameras to operate legally.

### IMPROVED TECHNOLOGY: 2008

In early 2008 Reflex signed a major contract with Qatar. The company also developed a pilot project in New Zealand, continuing to expand business beyond its focus on the United States and Australia. On the technological front Redflex worked to develop real-time video which would allow for instant confirmation of speeding violations, an independent secondary speed check system, and in-road sensors which allowed for greater speed detection accuracy.

Opposition to traffic enforcement cameras still continued, however, and events turned tragic in 2008 when a Redflex employee was shot and killed while working in Phoenix, Arizona. Douglas Georgianni's killer was eventually apprehended and while Redflex's Arizona operations were temporarily suspended, mobile photo enforcement vehicles were once again introduced into the community after the crime.

In 2009 the company added REDFLEXplatescan to its list of products. The technology allowed for automatic license plate recognition and monitoring. As in previous years, the law played a major role in the company's U.S. operations. Mississippi, Montana, and Maine passed legislation which tightened rules regarding camera enforcement. Maryland and New York, however, passed legislation which strengthened the role of traffic violation enforcement cameras and technology in these states. FCC violation suits brought against Redflex in Texas, Ohio, Arizona, New Mexico, and Louisiana were dismissed. Redflex appointed Andrejs Bunkse as general counsel to deal with an increasingly large number of legal cases.

### CHALLENGES TO THE U.S. PROGRAM: 2010

At the start of 2010 profits slipped, due in part to economic troubles around the world as well as continuing legal challenges to the company's services and products. The company faced increasing difficulties due to collection problems and an unfavorable exchange rate.

Redflex was further plagued with problems with its project in Arizona. According to a 2010 article in the *Times* (London), people learned simply to ignore the tickets sent by Redflex, resulting in roughly $90 million unpaid tickets. The tickets become void in Arizona after three months if they were not served by an individual. Rather than going to court to fight tickets, many drivers were ignoring the citations.

The *Times* article further announced that the lucrative widespread Arizona project to bring 76 cameras across the state was "on the verge of bankruptcy." The Arizona project initially received considerable support from then Arizona governor Janet Napolitano, but according to the article, only about $37 million of about $127 million fines were collected between 2009 and 2010. According to the *Times* article, Redflex had invested $16 million in the project, creating considerable pressure on the company. The new Arizona governor, Jan Brewer, proved less supportive of the camera traffic enforcement project.

Some motorists took out their frustrations on the company's cameras, damaging them, setting them off on purpose, or covering them up. In addition, groups such Arizona Citizens Against Photo Radar formed. A group known as CameraFRAUD organized in Virginia, Maryland, Louisiana, Washington, D.C., and elsewhere. In fact, lobby groups were cited by a number of media outlets as another possible reason for the slump in Redflex profits.

At the beginning of the 2010s, it seemed likely that Redflex's future would continue to be influenced by two primary, opposing forces. On one side, governments, local and otherwise, would continue to enlist the company's services in order to tighten traffic enforcement laws and boost fees earned through traffic fines. On the other hand, groups opposed to remote traffic enforcement would continue to undercut the company's profitability through legal challenges and other means.

*A. Antonow*

## PRINCIPAL SUBSIDIARIES

Aerospace Systems Pty. Ltd.; Redflex Enforcement Services Pty Ltd (Australia); Redflex Pty Ltd Australia; Redflex Traffic Systems (California) Inc; Redflex Traffic Systems Limited UK; Redflex Traffic Systems Australia Pty Ltd Australia; Redflex Traffic Systems (Canada) Ltd; RTS R & D Pty Ltd.

## PRINCIPAL COMPETITORS

Affiliated Computer Services (ACS); American Traffic Solutions Inc (ATS); Argus Solutions Limited; Mikoh Corporation Limited; Nestor Inc.; Transol Corp.

## FURTHER READING

Ayres, Chris, "Where Speed Cameras May Be Just a Flash in The Pan," *Times*, January 11, 2010, p. N11.

Beveridge, John, "Cameras Catch Candid Culprits," *Herald Sun*, January 13, 2010, p. B36.

Boreham, Tim, "Redflex Highlights Hurdles On Road," *Australian*, December 24, 2009, p. F22.

Hawthorne, Mark, "Thorney Battle for Control of Redflex Board," *Age*, November 12, 2009, p. B2.

"More Towns Install Red Light Cameras, but at What Price?" *Daily Herald*, October 12, 2008, p. 1.

"Red-light Cameras Get Green Light in Geneva," *Daily Herald*, January 8, 2008, p. 1.

"Safety or Money Red-light Cameras Snag Right-hand Turners, but Are They Making Suburban Roads Safer?" *Daily Herald*, July 12, 2009, p. 1.

Stoff, Rick, "Red-light Cameras Not about the Money; Raking It in Nonetheless," *St. Louis Journalism Review*, December 2007, p.11–12.

# rue21, Inc.

800 Commonwealth Drive
Suite 100
Warrendale, Pennsylvania 15086
U.S.A.
Telephone: (724) 776-9780
Fax: (724) 776-4111
Web site: http://www.rue21.com

*Public Company*
*Founded:* 1976 as Pennsylvania Fashions
*Employees:* 5,765 (2010)
*Net Sales:* $525.6 million (2010)
*Stock Exchanges:* NASDAQ
*Ticker Symbol:* RUE
*NAICS:* 448110 Men's Clothing Stores; 448120 Women's Clothing Stores; 448130 Children's and Infants' Clothing Stores; 448140 Family Clothing Stores; 448150 Clothing Accessories Stores; 448210 Shoe Stores

■ ■ ■

Rue21, Inc., is a specialty retailer offering casual apparel for young men and women, accessories, footwear, jewelry, and fragrances. The company operates only in the United States and offers a variety of fashions at value prices, while regularly updating inventory. The merchandise available typically targets teenagers, and this demographic is reflected in the company name, which represents the French word *rue,* meaning "street," and the age (21) that, according to the company, "everyone wants to be."

Many of the stores' employees are high school and college students. With Top 40 in-store music and a presence on social networking sites that appeal to a young crowd, the store aims to be a destination for customers to gather and socialize with friends. The company even consults a panel of teenagers to gather feedback on products and fashion trends. The majority of rue21's marketing and advertising is through e-mail, Web site promotions and contests, and fashion blogs on Facebook, MySpace, Twitter, and YouTube, although products are not sold online.

Third-party brands as well as the company's own rue21 etc!, Carbon, rueKicks, and tarea by rue21 are available in the stores. Rue21 etc! is the company's line of girls' jewelry and accessories, rueKicks is one of the company's lines of footwear and fragrances, tarea by rue21 is the line of intimate apparel, and Carbon is the line of male apparel and accessories. The company's business model maintains low inventory levels for faster turnaround of products. Also, no single vendor accounts for more than 8 percent of the store's merchandise, which minimizes product risk and limits the company's dependence on any single product provider. The company has one wholly owned subsidiary, r services llc, which was established to administer the company's gift card program.

## PENNSYLVANIA FASHIONS:1976–2001

Rue21 was founded by Gene Klein in 1976 as Pennsylvania Fashions. The company sold clothing for men, women, and children under several banners, including Rue 21 and Stock Room. Originally, most of the company's merchandise "was packed into crowded aisles filled with oversized signs touting the low prices," according to *Chain Store Age*. However, the company later introduced its own Rue 21 brand, "in an effort to take control of its merchandise and expand its customer base."

In 1989 Cary Klein acquired the company from his father. Within three years, sales grew from $50 million to $130 million. The younger Klein explained that the company was able to sell items at value prices as a result of buying directly from manufacturers and purchasing items at bargain prices, such as when a manufacturer ran behind schedule on an order and companies had the opportunity to cancel the order. Pennsylvania Fashions also depended on a high volume of sales to make up for the company's profit margins being less than the 50 percent often charged by retailers.

By 1998 the company operated 250 stores. Cary Klein sold a 50 percent interest in the company in a private recapitalization, which provided a cash infusion into the business while allowing him to maintain control of the operations. Saunders, Karp and Megrue (SKM), a private equity firm in Connecticut, purchased a half-stake in the company, with long-term plans of working toward an initial public offering. SKM's other investments included popular clothing stores Charlotte Russe and The Children's Place. (Saunders, Karp and Megrue later merged with Apax Partners Worldwide, a private equity firm, in February 2005.)

In 2001 Klein stepped down as CEO while retaining his half-stake ownership in the company, and Bob Fisch took his place. (As of 2010, Fisch was still CEO and also president of the company.) Klein's reasons for relinquishing the reigns included a slowing economy and the company's need for a new leader. According to the *Pittsburgh Business Times* Klein said, "I thought the business was ready for some fresh ideas." Klein, who remained chairman of the board, further commented, "I would only do it if I found somebody who could do it

better than I could. And I think we've found that gentleman." After taking control of Pennsylvania Fashions, Fisch said he "began repositioning our company by aligning our stores under one brand name, strengthening our management team, honing our fashion value merchandise approach and refocusing our store growth strategy." At the time Fisch took over, the company's annual sales were between $180 million and $200 million.

## THE INTRODUCTION AND GROWTH OF RUE21: 2002–08

In February 2002 rue21's parent company, Pennsylvania Fashions Inc., filed for voluntary Chapter 11 bankruptcy protection "to address the financial challenges resulting primarily from a tough retail environment," according to the *Daily Deal*. The company stated its intention to reevaluate its real estate holdings, remodel some stores, and close others as part of the restructuring. During this time, the company closed 75 stores while continuing to operate the remainder of the locations, the distribution center, and the company headquarters as usual.

Fifteen months later, in May 2003, the company emerged from the bankruptcy under the brand name of rue21, with plans to build the rue21 brand and implement an aggressive plan for new store expansion over the following five-year period. At the time, the company had 170 stores, 35 of which had opened within the previous year.

In the late part of 2006, the company introduced a new, larger store layout, containing a rue21 etc! store-in-store, which sold the company's line of jewelry and accessories for girls. The new layout model boasted a total of more than 4,700 square feet, with rue21 etc! accounting for about 1,000 square feet of that space. By the end of that year, the company had a total of 229 stores, supporting the company's postbankruptcy intentions of expansion. Net sales for the fiscal year ending January 28, 2006, were $192.8 million. By the following year, the company had a total of 278 stores, and net sales had increased to $225.6 million.

Over the next year, the company continued its growth. Net sales for the fiscal year ending February 2, 2008, were $296.9 million, and the company had a total of 352 stores. In April 2008 the company established a five-year, $60 million senior secured revolving credit facility, which was later amended in November 2009. The company initially borrowed approximately $27.2 million to satisfy all outstanding long-term debts. By the end of 2008, the company had grown to include a total of 449 stores, and net sales for the fiscal year were $391.4 million, representing a 31.8 percent increase over the previous year.

## BECOMING A PUBLIC COMPANY: 2009

During November 2009, rue21 became a public company when its stock was offered for the first time on the NASDAQ. The initial public offering gave the company $29.2 million in net proceeds, which were used to repay $25.8 million that was outstanding from the senior secured credit facilities.

At the end of 2009, the company had a total of 534 stores in 43 states, with the greatest concentration of store locations being in the South. During 2009 88 new stores were opened, and 26 stores were converted to the larger layout plan. Net sales for 2009 were $525.6 million, which was a 34.3 percent increase over the previous year. The company's net income was $22 million, a 74.2 percent increase over 2008.

In February 2010 rue21 completed an offering of nearly seven million shares of common stock. The stock was sold by funds advised by Apax Partners L.P., the principal stockholder of the company, and some of the company's management team members. Following this, Apax owned approximately 29 percent of rue21's outstanding common stock. Rue21 did not receive any of the proceeds from the offering.

## PLANS FOR FUTURE GROWTH AND EXPANSION

As a company, rue21 focused on diversification and growth through diversified products, flexible real estate, and balanced growth. The majority of the company's net sales were from the girls' apparel category, although the company was hopeful that the expansion of the line of mens' apparel and accessories would provide significant revenue as well.

As of January 2010, 52 percent of rue21 stores were located in strip centers, 27 percent were in regional malls, and 21 percent were in outlet centers. Most of the company's locations were in small and middle-market communities of 25,000 to 200,000 residents with income levels that did not usually support higher-end retailers. These locations were often overlooked by traditional specialty apparel stores, making rue21 the primary junior and young people's specialty store in the community, which limited the amount of competition from other large value apparel retailers and department stores. According to an article in *WWD*, Fisch said that the company was focused on underserved markets. "He explained that Rue21 is carving a niche in those underserved markets, stating, 'We do well in markets where people have not heard of us, [where consumers] are starved for fashion. We're in the sweet spot of fashion and business,' he said. 'Value is here to stay.'"

During 2010 rue21 planned to open 100 new stores, as well as convert 30 existing stores to the larger layout plan. As of January 30 of that year, more than 55 percent of the stores were already in the new layout. New stores generally achieve sales of $900,000 to $1.1 million during their first year of operation.

Challenges that faced rue21 as it looked to the future included the very population that the company served. *Investors Business Daily* pointed out, "Teen clothing retailers serve a notoriously fickle customer base. If Rue21 doesn't keep up with current fashion trends, its shoppers could readily defect to any of a number of vendors, including Aeropostale, American Eagle and even big-box stores like Target."

According to rue21's 2009 Annual Report, the company viewed its competitive strengths as its compelling "fashion meets value proposition," presence in locations with limited direct competition, distinct company and customer culture, and its strong and experienced management team. Rue21's growth strategy is based on the company's belief that it is "positioned to take advantage of significant opportunities to increase net sales and net income." The company invested considerable funds to upgrade its distribution facility and systems during the end of 2009, which allowed for the support of 1,300 stores.

One of the most important elements of the company's growth strategy was to convert existing stores to the larger store layout. The company also planned to increase square footage by opening enough new stores to nearly double the number of locations to a total of more than 1,000 stores by 2015. While opening new stores can be an expensive venture, rue21 had little debt following the IPO, putting the company in a stronger financial position for expansion. Another growth *rue21, Inc.*

strategy included driving comparable store sales. One way the company planned to make this happen was by growing the apparel and accessory line for men, an area in which there was limited competition at value prices.

*Diane Milne*

## PRINCIPAL SUBSIDIARIES

r services llc.

## PRINCIPAL DIVISIONS

Girls' Accessories; Girls' Apparel; Guys' Apparel and Accessories.

## PRINCIPAL COMPETITORS

Aéropostale, Inc.; American Eagle Outfitters Inc.; Forever 21, Inc.; Gap Inc.; J. Crew Inc.; Target Corp.; Wal-Mart Stores, Inc.

## FURTHER READING

*2009 Annual Report,* rue21inc.com.

Oddi, David, "Take on the World in Your Own Way — with an UN-IPO," *Discount Store News,* November 22, 1999, p. 12.

"Pennsylvania Fashion Goes Under," *Daily Deal,* February 4, 2002.

"Resurrected Teen Apparel Retailer Tries To Buck Industry Trends," *Investor's Business Daily,* November 10, 2009, p. A05.

"rue21 Announces Its Emergence from Reorganization under Chapter 11," *PR Newswire,* May 19, 2003.

Schooley, Tim, "Cary Klein Quits CEO Post at Pennsylvania Fashions," *Pittsburgh Business Times,* July 13 2001, p. 1.

Wilson, Marianne, "Rue 21 Rolls Out the Barrel," *Chain Store Age,* October 1999, p.128.

Young, Vicki M., "Rue 21 Registers for IPO," *WWD,* September 21, 2009, p. 5.

———, "Sales Help Rue21 Double Income," *WWD,* December 9, 2009, p. 14.

Young, Vicki M., and Alexandra Steigrad, "Rue21 Launches on NASDAQ," *WWD,* November 16, 2009, p. 12.

# Safaricom Limited

Safaricom House, Waiyaki Way,
Westlands P.O. Box 46350-00100
Nairobi
Kenya
Telephone: (254) 20 427 2100
Web site: http://www.safaricom.co.ke

*Public Company*
*Founded:* 1993
*Employees:* 2,387 (2009)
*Sales:* KES 40.66 billion ($500 million, 2009)
*Stock Exchanges:* Nairobi
*NAICS:* 517212 Cellular and Other Wireless Communications

■ ■ ■

Safaricom Limited is a mobile telecommunications service provider operating a national network in Kenya. The company provides a diversified range of communication services that include voice, data, money transfer, fixed broadband, and messaging services.

Safaricom Limited's prepay, postpay, international roaming, and dialing voice services have gained preferential status in the Kenyan telecommunications market. The integration and convergence of the company's voice and data services enhanced the quality and standards of its communication services and solutions. Indeed, Safaricom Limited's ranking quality of data services combines WiMax wireless, 3G network, and advanced fiberoptic technologies to deliver top-notch video and voice data to its customers through high-speed broadband channels.

Safaricom Limited had achieved a market share of 84 percent and a customer subscription base of 41.51 million by September 2009. The impressive results confirmed the company's status as the largest and most successful mobile telecommunications service provider in the country. The company has further asserted its position as the leading mobile telephony service provider in Kenya by introducing value-added service categories aimed at winning increased service subscription and customer loyalty. Safaricom Limited commands the majority market share in the mobile telecommunications services industry and was Kenya's most profitable company for the entire first decade of the 21st century.

In 2009 mobile communications company Vodafone owned 40 percent of Safaricom Limited, the Kenyan government owned 35 percent, and the remaining 25 percent was publicly owned.

## COMPANY FOUNDING AND CHANGING OWNERSHIP STRUCTURE: 1993–2000

The Kenya Posts and Telecommunications Corporation (KPTC) launched the Safaricom mobile telephony in 1993 as a monopoly mobile telephone network provider. According to information contained in Safaricom Limited's Web site, the Safaricom mobile telephone service was run as an operational unit (department) of KPTC and relied on networking technology that is commonly referred to as analogue ETACS. The use of analogue ETACS lasted until 1996 when KPTC adopted GSM network technology as a result of market demands for a more effective and reliable mobile communications network.

Notably, mobile voice and data services were hardly visible in the Kenyan telecommunications market for most of the 1990s. The high costs of operations and the subsequent high prices made the mobile telephony industry less attractive to investors and customers alike. The use of mobile telecommunications services was therefore limited to corporate organizations, security agencies, and wealthy individuals. It was not until Safaricom transformed from a department of KPTC into a full state corporation that a new wave of investor and customer interest in mobile telecommunications industry emerged. The elevation of the Safaricom mobile telecommunications services into a full state corporation paved the way for the incorporation of Safaricom Limited in April 1997 in accordance with the provisions of the Companies Act of Kenya.

The ownership structure of Safaricom changed again in May 2000 when Vodafone, a leading cellular communications service provider based in the United Kingdom, purchased a 40 percent stake in the company, leaving the government of Kenya with a 60 percent ownership. However, the company remained a state corporation as per the provisions of Kenya's State Corporations Act. Safaricom Limited ceased to be a state corporation in 2008 when the government of Kenya offered a public share issue of 25 percent of its ownership stake in the company.

## MOBILE MONEY TRANSFER: 2005–07

Safaricom Limited's cellular money transfer and payment service, M-PESA, was launched as a pilot project in October 2005. M-PESA was an innovative e-commerce application that enabled Safaricom Limited's service subscribers to send money, receive money, pay bills, or purchase airtime through their mobile phones. The M-PESA service was a product of cooperative efforts between Safaricom Limited and Vodafone, and its tremendous success has seen it emerge

as a viable model for mobile money transfers and payments across the world. In fact, the M-PESA project was Vodafone's brainchild, as the company is credited for developing the M-PESA concept before entering a partnership deal that saw Safaricom Limited participate in the role of running the pilot project of the concept in Kenya. According to information contained in the Vodafone Web site, the funding of the pilot phase of the M-PESA money transfer and payment service was achieved through the joint initiative of Vodafone and the U.K.'s Department for International Development (DFID).

Safaricom Limited officially launched M-PESA service in February 2007, effectively ushering in a new era in the financial and money transfer industries. The development and eventual implementation of the M-PESA platform by Safaricom Limited made Kenya the first country in the world to adopt such a service. Safaricom Limited limited the sending of money through M-PESA to Safaricom network subscribers only but allowed cross-network money transfer, such that subscribers of other mobile service networks could receive money through their short messaging service (SMS). The company successfully established a countrywide M-PESA system that included individual M-PESA agents, restaurants, microfinance institutions, cooperative societies, supermarkets, hardware shops, and banks. These places allowed customers to deposit money or withdraw money from their cellular M-PESA accounts.

Initially, the M-PESA concept targeted individuals lacking adequate access to bank accounts and individuals whose incomes were insufficient to operate bank accounts. However, the M-PESA experience generated so much interest among the Kenyan population that it penetrated all class levels in society and was no longer perceived to be merely a financial transactions channel for low-income people. The M-PESA money transfer and payment service gained widespread recognition and preference among populations across the spectrum because of the speed, ease, and convenience it provided in financial transfers and transactions across the country. According to statistics contained in the Qrevisions Web site, the subscriber base for Safaricom M-PESA service had exceeded four million customers and had transacted cash transfers in excess of KES 3 billion as of January 2009.

## STEADY RISE TO SUCCESS: 2007–08

Safaricom Limited's business performance has been marked by a steady rise since the beginning of the 21st century, as demonstrated by its impressive profits. In

## KEY DATES

**1993:** Kenya Posts and Telecommunications Corporation starts Safaricom mobile phone service.

**1997:** Safaricom Limited spun off from parent as its own company.

**2000:** Vodafone purchases 40 percent stake in company.

**2005:** M-PESA, cellular money and payment transfer system, debuts.

**2007:** Safaricom Limited stock offered on Nairobi Stock Exchange for the first time.

2007, for example, the company registered profits of KES 12 billion, a margin which increased by about 13 percent to KES 13.8 billion in 2008. Safaricom Limited further registered a growth of approximately 40 percent in its operation cash flows from KES 21 billion in 2007 to about KES 30 billion in 2008. However, it should be noted that the company's operating expenses also increased as a result of its network maintenance and expansion strategies, strategic initiatives for acquiring and retaining customers, and costs associated with computer licensing.

Another major development in Safaricom Limited's strategic push was the company's 2008 acquisition of a majority stake in One Communications Limited, a Kenyan-based information technology company that operated countrywide high-speed data communication services powered by fixed WiMAX technology. Safaricom Limited purchased 51 percent of the company's shareholding at a cost of KES 180 million. The acquisition of One Communications Limited effectively supplemented Safaricom Limited's 3G broadband communications network with a powerful fixed broadband network designed particularly for corporate clients.

### THE SAFARICOM FOUNDATION

Safaricom Limited has actively been involved in major corporate social responsibility (CSR) programs throughout the country ever since the company was founded. The company took its CSR initiatives a notch higher through the establishment of the Safaricom Foundation in August 2003. The Safaricom Foundation is a charity organization registered under the Non-Governmental Organizations Act of 1990 and primarily draws its funding from the Vodafone Group Foundation and Safaricom Limited.

The launch of the Safaricom Foundation formed an appropriate channel through which the company promoted its CSR initiatives throughout the country by supporting socioeconomic development. The period between 2003 and 2010 saw the foundation enter successful partnerships with other like-minded charitable organizations in Kenya to eradicate poverty, promote health, enhance children's access to education opportunities, and participate in the conservation of the environment.

The foundation has indeed been steadfast in its social and economic development programs aimed at improving the quality of life among the poor and destitute families in Kenya. For example, in the year 2009 alone, the foundation awarded grants amounting to hundreds of millions of shillings to various grassroots, regional, and national charity organizations in the country. The foundation's commitment to support sports activities in Kenya has been best demonstrated by the consistency of its annual events such as the Lewa Marathon which has been held at the Lewa Wildlife Conservancy since 2005.

### INITIAL PUBLIC OFFERING: 2008

Safaricom Limited registered tremendous success in the first years of the 21st century. and by 2002 the company had become a success story in Kenya. Evidently, the part privatization of Safaricom mobile telecommunication services in 2000 transformed the company into a superbrand and one of the most respected companies in Kenya and Africa as a whole. The good financial performance and positive market fundamentals that characterized Safaricom Limited ignited investor interest both locally and internationally. In 2008 the company floated 40 billion shares in what became one of the biggest initial public offerings (IPO) ever in Sub-Saharan Africa. The offering of 25 percent of the company's stock to the public reduced the government's ownership of the company from 60 to 35 percent.

However, Safaricom Limited's IPO came with some controversy following revelations that 5 percent of Vodafone's 40 percent stake in the company was held by Mobitelea, a company whose legal status, identity, and ownership could not be ascertained. Mobitelea sparked so much political and financial controversy in 2007 that the matter had to be referred to Kenya's Parliamentary Select Committee on Finance for investigations. The controversy notwithstanding, the investor interest in Safaricom Limited's shares remained as high as ever, as was demonstrated by the IPO's oversubscription.

For a few weeks after the IPO, Safaricom Limited's stocks registered a consistently poor performance at the

Nairobi Stock Exchange (NSE), sometimes hitting the lowest share prices ever witnessed in that stock market. Whereas the floating of too many shares for the Safaricom IPO was widely blamed for the company's stagnant and declining stock price, a cheap IPO share price also seemed to have been a key contributing factor. The Safaricom IPO price was valued at KES 5 ($0.06) per share.

The global economic crisis also contributed to the low price levels of the Safaricom shares because many foreign and local investors offloaded their shares out of panic, resulting in excess Safaricom shares relative to the demand for the shares at the time. As such, the Safaricom shares remained undervalued for a long time as individual, organizational, and corporate financial investors sought to sell their shares for alternative investments. Indeed, the global financial crisis hit the world's leading economic powerhouses just a few months after the Safaricom shares opened for trading for the first time at the NSE.

The low dividend earnings for the Safaricom shares prompted many short-term investors and speculators to sell their shares. For example, in the 2009 financial year, the company's board of directors declared a final dividend of KES 4 billion, a figure that translated to a paltry KES 0.10 for each share held. However, Safaricom's chief executive officer, Michael Joseph, was keen to assure investors that the company's share price at the stock market was not related to the company's stocks or fundamentals at all. Indeed, Safaricom Limited enjoyed strong operational fundamentals and market performance as demonstrated by the fact that it was the most profitable company in Kenya for most of the first decade of the 21st century.

## M-PESA GOES INTERNATIONAL: 2010

During the launch of the M-PESA money transfer service, the CEO of Vodafone's Non-European Affiliates, Gavin Darby, hinted that Safaricom and Vodafone intended to use the M-PESA application platform to spread the cellular money transfer and payment system to the international level. According to Darby, Vodafone successfully pursued the expansion of the mobile transfer service through partnership efforts with Citigroup in a deal that was designed to facilitate the remittance of money internationally using mobile phones.

The concept of an international mobile transfer and payment system was motivated by the immense success of Safaricom's M-PESA service and was particularly targeted at people working, pursuing education, or doing business abroad. The success of Vodafone's and Citi-

group's joint venture was credited to the success of M-PESA pilot project in Kenya. The United Kingdom was the first country where a prototype of the M-PESA service application platform was directly applied through which Safaricom customers in the two countries could send or receive money.

For the 2010s, the board of directors and management of Safaricom Limited put in place well-defined strategic goals aimed at sustaining and enhancing the company's market leadership in communications and data services. The company committed more than KES 23 billion in the expansion of its national infrastructure to extend to the rural parts of the country not covered by the Safaricom service network. The company also developed plans to spread the M-PESA service to more countries across the globe so as to enhance its mobile commerce strategies.

*Paul Ingati*

## PRINCIPAL SUBSIDIARIES

One Communications Limited.

## PRINCIPAL COMPETITORS

Essar Telecom Kenya; Telkom Kenya; Zain Kenya Ltd.

## FURTHER READING

"About Us," Safaricom Limited, 2010.

"About Vodafone," Vodafone, 2010.

Mason, Paul, "Newsnight Correspondent Paul Mason Travels through Kenya Using a Map of the Country's Mobile Phone Networks as His Guide," *BBC News,* January 8, 2007.

Mayaka, Charles, "Safaricom Limited: Crafting a Business and Marketing Strategy for a New Market," CasePlace.org, 2005.

"Mobile Payments," *Economist,* June 28, 2007.

Nyongesa, George, "Safaricom IPO: Kenya's Commercial Success Story," *African Executive,* April 9, 2008.

"Safaricom: A Floating Hope for Africa," HTRF-Africa.com, June 10, 2008.

"Safaricom and Vodafone Launch M-PESA, a New Mobile Payment Service," vodafone.com, February 13, 2007.

"Safaricom: Largest IPO in Sub-Saharan Africa's History," *Kenyan Entrepreneur,* June 9, 2008.

"Safaricom Limited: A Brief History, Core Business and Other Business Segments," *Quantitative Revisions,* April 12, 2010.

"Safaricom Market Share Surpasses 80% as Rivals Look to Emulate M-PESA Success," wirelessintelligence.com, 2010.

"Safaricom Owns 51% Stake in One Communications (Kenya)," wirelessfederation.com, August 22, 2008.

Schwartz, Michael, "Vodafone, Safaricom, Western Union Partner for International Money Transfers," developingtelecoms.com, January 5, 2009.

# Sahara Bank

10 First of September Street
P.O. Box 270
Tripoli 218
Libya
Telephone: (021) 333-2771
Fax: (021) 444-2920
Web site: http://saharabank.com.ly

*Public Company*
*Founded:* 1964
*Employees:* 1,500 (est., 2009)
*Sales:* LYD 126 million ($95 million, 2009)
*NAICS:* 522110 Commercial Banking

∎∎∎

In addition to providing diversified financing and trading products, the Sahara Bank operates with a capital base of LYD 126 million and is Libya's second-largest bank, behind only the Jamahiriya Bank of Libya. Over the years, the bank's key strategic inputs have been targeting expansion of both its domestic and international financial markets.

Sahara Bank has a countrywide presence in Libya. The bank provides a wide range of corporate, retail, and Islamic banking products to its customers. (All Islamic products and investments are vetted by the company's Sharia Supervisory Committee.) The bank's wide product portfolio stands out as one of its main sources of competitive advantage with respect to its special banking services that include trade financing, institutional financing, and Islamic banking.

The bank's approach to the provision and innovation of its financial services portfolio are focused on the three key product lines of institutional banking, corporate banking, and retail banking. Indeed, the bank endeavors to provide exceptional institutional banking services through the development of valuable business relationships with state organizations and financial institutions such as banks, microfinance institutions, and insurance companies. The bank's corporate banking service line focuses on offering specialized and dedicated services to organizations while its retail banking service line focuses on creation of new products.

Sahara Bank is part of the BNP Paribas Group, an international banking conglomerate based in France. The company's alliance with this group aids Sahara Bank's international presence.

## FROM BANCO DI SICILIA TO SAHARA BANK: 1964–69

Sahara Bank was founded in 1964 as Banco di Sicilia and was modeled along the lines of an Italian commercial bank. The bank's first customers were business organizations, entrepreneurs, and professionals of Italian origins. In 1969 the government of Libya embarked on a nationalization process through which the government acquired the controlling stakes in multinational companies and privately owned business enterprises. The nationalization movement in Libya was triggered by a military coup that drove Colonel Muammar Qaddafi into power. It was through the nationalization process that most commercial banks in the country were converted into government institutions.

The Libyan government passed a decree that required the multinational companies and privately owned institutions to sell 51 percent of the value of their total shareholding capital to the government. Subsequently, the Libyan government bought 51 percent shareholding of the Banco di Sicilia and changed its name to Sahara Bank. The government went on to take over all the foreign shareholding of the bank, leaving only 17 percent of its total shareholding to private investors of Libyan origins. Other banks that were affected by the nationalization process included Barclays Bank, which was renamed the Jamahiriya Bank, and the Banco di Roma, which was renamed Umma Bank.

In 1972 the Libyan government instituted further banking reforms that led to its total takeover of the Jamahiriya Bank and the Umma Bank. However, the government retained its joint ownership of the Sahara Bank with private investment institutions. Even with this split ownership, the influence of the Libyan government in Sahara Bank's operational and corporate affairs was heavy throughout the 1970s as the government enhanced its nationalization programs. The situation worsened for the bank's private investors in 1978 when the government lifted all property rights enshrined in the country's constitution. The effect of government policies in this period was the suffocation of most of the private investment opportunities in Libya.

The woes facing Sahara Bank's operational capacity intensified in 1986 when a financial crisis hit the global financial markets. Banks could no longer lend money to customers and corporate institutions following a slump in economic growth. Interbank lending opportunities also diminished as the lending rates of banks doubled. Therefore, Sahara Bank operated in a harsh economic environment that was characteristic of domestic and international financial difficulties at the time.

Nonetheless, the government of Libya started pursuing political and economic reforms that were targeted at transforming the economic structures in the country in order to promote the growth of private business enterprises. The economic and political reforms particularly targeted the privatization of various state enterprises that had been taken over through the nationalization process.

## LOCKERBIE AND LIBYA'S ECONOMY: 1988–99

The Lockerbie bombing of 1988 resulted in Libya becoming embroiled in a diplomatic row with the United States and most countries of Western Europe. (A Libyan national was convicted of blowing up Pan Am Flight 103, killing all passengers. Large sections of the plane fell around Lockerbie, Scotland.) The gradual isolation of the country in diplomatic circles worsened the investment environment in the country as international business and financial opportunities were significantly diminished. The world's leading economies, including the United States, Britain, Italy, and France, imposed economic sanctions and trade embargos against Libya in a well-orchestrated move that was designed to deny the country export opportunities for its vast oil resources.

The Sahara Bank was one of the key financial institutions badly hit by the diplomatic and economic isolation of Libya by most of the world's developed nations. The bank's international transactions collapsed and its local financial transactions recorded the lowest levels ever. Unlike the fully nationalized banks which were cushioned by the government of Libya from the effects of the retarded economic growth, Sahara Bank bore the full brunt of the economic impasse.

Economic development in Libya suffered yet another setback in 1992 when the United Nations imposed economic and political sanctions against the country following Libya's refusal to hand over for trial two Libyan nationals who had been indicted in connection with the Lockerbie bombing. The UN-imposed economic sanctions significantly affected the potential international business opportunities in Libya. The Sahara Bank was one of the financial institutions that had to cope as business opportunities were largely reduced to trading transactions as Libya gradually gravitated toward a cash economy. Lack of adequate international funding for development projects also affected the progress of financial institutions as borrowing and lending continued to diminish.

The economic stagnation had a far-reaching impact on the Sahara Bank because it was partly owned by private investors whose interests were primarily motivated by profits. The bank had to contend with the provision of mainly trade financing as the country reverted to a cash economy. Moreover, the bank's credit and lending capacity was decimated because it could not access loans from the leading global financial institutions

## KEY DATES

**1964:** Banco di Silicia is formed along the lines of an Italian commercial bank.

**1969:** Nationalization process begins, leading to state control and change of name to Sahara Bank.

**1988:** Lockerbie bombing and subsequent embargoes and trade sanctions weaken Libyan economy.

**2003:** United Nations and other sanctions lifted.

**2007:** Sahara Bank forms strategic partnership with BNP Paribas Group.

such as the World Bank and the International Monetary Fund. Indeed, the bank was badly hit by the retardation of economic growth in Libya, as was evidenced by the collapse of the country's key economic development indexes. Libyan banks operated in this difficult economic environment throughout the 1990s.

Economic development in Libya was granted a major reprieve in 1999 when the United Nations suspended the economic and political sanctions imposed in 1992. The country's political class also instituted numerous reforms that opened up business and investment opportunities in Libya. As such, the country's financial sector became active as both local and foreign investment activities took root in the country. The Sahara Bank started posting improved profit volumes as it reviewed its business strategy to suit the improved business environment in the country.

### ECONOMIC REFORMS: 2003–05

The government of Libya started warming up to the countries of the West at the onset of the 21st century. In 2003 Libya initiated its first steps towards healing its diplomatic wounds when the country's leadership accepted responsibility for the 1988 Lockerbie bombing. The country further struck a conciliatory tone with the United Nations and the United States when it renounced its pursuit of nuclear weapons. The United Nations finally lifted economic and political sanctions imposed against Libya in 2003 following a series of political reforms in the country. The United States also warmed up towards Libya in 2004 when it partially lifted its economic, military, and financial aid sanctions against the country.

The end of the diplomatic row between Libya and countries of the West (as well as the United Nations)

opened new doors for economic reforms in the country. Libyan leader Colonel Muammar Qaddafi appointed a new prime minister, Shukri Ghanem, to revolutionize the country's key economic, political, and social sectors. The finance and banking sectors were some of the key economic sectors in Libya that were placed under gradual transformation programs. Appropriate measures and legislations were adopted to reverse the nationalization of the 1970s to pave the way for the privatization of the nationalized banks and registration of foreign-owned banks and other financial institutions. All these developments rekindled business prospects at Sahara Bank.

The reforms in Libya's banking and financial sector were fast-tracked with the introduction of a new banking law in 2005. All commercial banks in the country were required by the Central Bank of Libya to raise their minimum capital to LYD 100 million. The Sahara Bank met the new regulatory requirements by raising its minimum capital to LYD 126 million.

### STRATEGIC PARTNERSHIP WITH BNP PARIBAS GROUP: 2007

Sahara Bank made a major strategic move in 2007 through a partnership deal with BNP Paribas Group. The bank entered the partnership with the BNP Paribas Group with the objective of gaining competitive advantage through expanded market outreach, efficiency in process orientation, and enhanced operational capacity. The strategic intent of the partnership between the Sahara Bank and the BNP Paribas Group was premised on the development of a formidable domestic, regional, and international operational infrastructure for Sahara Bank.

In 2010 the BNP Paribas Group was an international financial services and global banking institution that enjoyed a worldwide presence and advanced resource and networking capacity. BNP Paribas Group was based primarily in Europe and ran operations in a total of 84 countries throughout Europe, North America, Asia, the Middle East, and North Africa. The other competitive advantages associated with BNP Paribas Group's operational and strategic infrastructure included its sharia-law-compliant Islamic banking products, investment and institutional banking services, as well as enhanced international financing capacity.

The international profile of Sahara Bank was enhanced significantly through the integrative pursuit of its expansion strategies with BNP Paribas Group. Sahara Bank has since been able to extend unique banking and Islamic-oriented financial products to its domestic and international customers through the well-established network channels of the BNP Paribas Group.

## LANDMARK CORPORATE ACHIEVEMENTS: 2009

In 2009 the Sahara Bank launched the Young Graduate Program, a training opportunity targeted at providing a launching pad for career development to Libyan university graduates. The program, which targeted students of Libyan nationality, was aimed at attracting graduates with outstanding qualifications, providing training on international standards of banking, and developing the potential of young Libyans. The program was managed by the bank's human resources department and involved structured training and orientation programs followed by integration of the young graduates into the organization's work structure. Twelve young graduates were selected during the first selection process in June 2009. The Sahara Bank Young Graduate program was a well-designed strategic plan that enabled the bank to assemble teams of knowledgeable employees for its nationwide branch network.

In April 2009 Sahara Bank launched the Flash Libya newsletter. Flash Libya, which was published in both English and Arabic, was the bank's first internal newsletter. The newsletter was introduced to publish news and information about the ongoing activities and transformations of the bank, and it formed an appropriate link between the employees and the management of the bank. The title of the newsletter was later changed to Flash Sahariya in a move designed to ensure that the newsletter met the bank's corporate communication objectives. Flash Sahariya provided the employees of the Sahara Bank with regular updates concerning training, human resources management, progress of different projects, and communication from the bank's management.

For the future, Sahara Bank has developed concrete strategic plans targeted at enhancing its strategic partnership with the BNP Paribas Group. The bank's strategic measures have been designed to ensure that its customers in Libya gain access to a wide range of international banking and financial services. Indeed, there seemed reason to believe that the diversification of Sahara Bank's services would transform the bank's focus on trade financing and enhance its corporate banking, project financing, and retail banking products in response to Libya's fast-transforming economy.

*Paul Ingati*

## PRINCIPAL COMPETITORS

The Agricultural Bank; Jamahiriya Bank; Libyan Arab Foreign Bank; National Commercial Bank; Umma Bank.

## FURTHER READING

"2010 Index of Economic Freedom – Libya," heritage.org, 2010.

"Bertelsmann Stiftung, BTI 2010 – Libya Country Report," Gütersloh: Bertelsmann Stiftung, 2009.

"BNP Paribas, a Pioneer in Islamic Banking," Sahara Bank, 2007.

"BNP Paribas Wins Race for Stake in Sahara Bank, Libya," *Middle East Economic Digest*, July 20, 2010.

Layas, Mohammed, "Libya Foreign Investment: The Six Key Figures in Libyan Investment," *Middle East Economic Digest*, October 3, 2010.

Luxford, Kate, "Libya Beats a Path to Foreign Bankers: Slow-Paced Reform and Privatization Look Set to Provide Opportunities for Foreign Investment in the Libyan Banking Sector, but with a Lot of Provisos," *Euromoney*, September 1, 2005.

"Safaricom Market Share Surpasses 80% as Rivals Look to Emulate M-PESA Success," wirelessintelligence.com, 2010.

"Sahara Bank First Young Graduate Programme," Sahara Bank, October 11, 2010.

"Sahara Bank Launches Its First Internal Newsletter 'Flash Libya'," Sahara Bank, April 1, 2009.

Williams, Stephen, "Ghaddafi Conquers Rome," *African Business*, 2009.

# Sempra Energy

101 Ash Street
San Diego, California 92101
U.S.A.
Telephone: (619) 696-2000
Web site: http://www.sempra.com

*Public Company*
*Founded:* 1886
*Employees:* 13,839 (2009)
*Sales:* $1.119 billion (2009)
*Stock Exchanges:* New York
*Ticker Symbol:* SRE
*NAICS:* 221122 Electric Power Distribution; 486210 Pipeline Transportation of Natural Gas; 221210 Natural Gas Distribution; 221122 Electric Power Distribution

■ ■ ■

Sempra Energy (Sempra) is a *Fortune* 500 energy services holding company which was formed by the 1998 merger of Pacific Enterprises and Enova Corporation. Sempra Energy's subsidiaries provide electricity, natural gas, and value-added products and services. Sempra possesses a large regulated utility customer base in the United States, serving 29 million customers, mostly in California. The company operates around the globe, maintaining a presence in North and Central America, Europe, and Asia. The Sempra name is derived from the Latin word for "always."

## PACIFIC LIGHTING: 1886–1905

Pacific Lighting Corporation was founded in San Francisco in 1886 as Pacific Lighting Company by C. O. G. Miller and Walter B. Cline. Both men, who had worked for Pacific Gas Improvement Company, a company owned by Miller's father, saw an opportunity to start their own business when their employer decided not to use the newly invented Siemens gas lamp. Miller and Cline began buying Siemens lamps in San Francisco and soon expanded into the southern California utility business, buying a one-half interest in a gas manufacturing plant in San Bernardino, California. Their business flourished, and in 1889 Pacific Lighting Company bought three Los Angeles-area gas and electric firms with combined assets of more than $1 million. Miller and Cline created a subsidiary, called the Los Angeles Lighting Company, to consolidate the three formerly competing firms. Pacific Lighting's attention remained focused on the Los Angeles area for most of the next century.

Pacific Lighting supplied the gas and lighting for the small but rapidly growing city of Los Angeles. Los Angeles Lighting immediately began to make needed improvements in the Los Angeles gas system, which subsequently led to a decrease in prices. The company faced stiff competition from numerous small utilities during the 1890s, however, that retarded its growth. To help increase profits, Los Angeles Lighting began importing and selling coal and gas-powered appliances, hoping to stimulate the demand for gas. Pacific Lighting then bought a controlling interest in Los Angeles Electric Company in 1890, and in 1904 it combined all of its Los Angeles lighting and electric operations to form Los Angeles Gas and Electric Company (LAG&E). In 1907 Pacific Lighting Company was incorporated and changed its name to Pacific Lighting Corporation.

## GROWING GAS PAINS: 1906–24

Pacific Lighting's gas sales increased tenfold between 1896 and 1906 as Los Angeles expanded. Sales grew further after the San Francisco earthquake of 1906 caused many to move from northern California to Los Angeles. The city grew so fast that Pacific Lighting could not meet demand, and some parts of the city went without gas for days during cold spells in the winter of 1906 to 1907. Seeing an opportunity, a group of Los Angeles businessmen created the City Gas Company in an effort to win Pacific Lighting's dissatisfied customers. The City Gas Company could not match the resources of the older Pacific Lighting, however, and in 1910 it sold out to Pacific Light and Power, which owned Southern California Gas Company, one of Pacific Lighting's largest competitors. A conservatively run company, Pacific Lighting concentrated on supplying its service area and collecting its rates while rivals Southern Gas and Southern Counties Gas Company of California worked on new gas technology.

By 1915 the Los Angeles utility industry was dominated by Pacific Lighting Corporation and three other firms. These utilities were extremely unpopular with the public and had to continually fight off the threat of municipal ownership and government regulation. Pacific Lighting and the other utilities fought Los Angeles's attempts to build a municipal electric system by trying to block the financing and by launching time-consuming lawsuits. In 1917 the utilities came under the jurisdiction of the newly formed California Public Utilities Commission (CPUC).

Since Pacific Lighting supplied its services to Los Angeles's densely populated downtown area, where operating costs were low, another municipal utility would not be able to match its rates. This situation

slowed the momentum of the municipal ownership movement, and the battle remained stalemated throughout the 1920s. Meanwhile, southern California continued to grow rapidly, and Pacific Lighting put its resources into expanding its services, spending $10 million to build a new electric plant and to enlarge its substations. To fight off municipal ownership, Pacific Lighting began a public relations campaign and sold stock.

## THE MUNICIPAL MOVEMENT: 1925–40

After the Great Depression began in 1929, the tide shifted toward municipal ownership of utilities, partly because cash-starved citizens hoped municipal ownership would lower their bills, and partly due to the anticorporate political climate. In 1929 the city of Los Angeles announced it was going to buy Pacific Lighting's electrical properties. The city had contracted to buy a share of the hydroelectric power produced by the new Hoover Dam and wanted to use Pacific Lighting's power grid to deliver it. The company's electric properties provided one-sixth of its revenue, so it fought the move as long as it could. Pacific Lighting, however, needed to renew its gas franchise, and the city would do that only if the company agreed to sell its electric properties. The properties were sold to the city in 1937 for $46 million.

Although stung by the loss of its electric operations, Pacific Lighting continued to grow as a gas utility. It ran its operations conservatively, initially expanding its services only to regions that could be served by existing gas generating plants. As natural gas became more widely available in California, Pacific Lighting's gas operations expanded.

Pacific Lighting had acquired control of the gas distribution systems of Southern Counties Gas in 1925, Santa Maria Gas Company in 1928, and Southern California Gas in 1929. These companies had expanded more aggressively than Pacific Lighting, particularly around Los Angeles, in some cases quadrupling output during the 1920s. Part of this expansion came from the rapid growth of Los Angeles, and part from new uses for gas, such as space heating and water heating. By 1930 Los Angeles led the United States in natural gas consumption, and Pacific provided gas to half the population of California. It was the largest gas utility in the United States, serving nearly two million people. Pacific Lighting made broad policy decisions for its new subsidiaries, but left the day-to-day operating decisions to the management of the individual firms.

Natural gas was a more efficient and less expensive fuel than manufactured gas. As Pacific Lighting and its

## KEY DATES

**1886:** Pacific Lighting Company formed.

**1933:** An earthquake causes extensive damage to Pacific Lighting's gas pipeline system.

**1947:** Pacific Lighting spends $25 million to build the Biggest Inch pipeline, which brings large amounts of natural gas to California from southern Texas.

**1965:** Pacific Lighting restructures its pipeline subsidiary, Pacific Lighting Gas Supply Company, and changes its name to Pacific Lighting Service and Supply.

**1967:** The firm moves its headquarters from San Francisco to Los Angeles.

**1998:** Pacific Enterprises and Enova Corporation merge under the name Sempra Energy.

**1999:** Sempra announces $1.9 billion merger deal with Colorado's KN Energy Inc., then calls the deal off four months later.

**2001:** Sempra reaps record profits during California energy crisis.

**2002:** The state of California files a complaint against Sempra, asking to renegotiate deals cut during the energy crisis, claiming they were negotiated under duress.

**2010:** Sempra agrees to pay the state of California $410 million to settle the last of the lawsuits stemming from the 2001 energy crisis.

subsidiaries had switched to natural gas during the 1920s, both gas rates and gas consumption had dropped. To compensate for the loss in volume, Pacific Lighting successfully promoted gas for industrial use. Industrial customers were attracted to the low rates and ease of handling associated with natural gas, as well as to the fact that natural gas did not require storage facilities. Industries used natural gas primarily during the summer to absorb Pacific Lighting's excess capacity, while during the winter Pacific Lighting required industries to use more energy from other sources. To maintain natural gas sources as the fuel became more scarce in the Los Angeles area, Pacific Lighting built longer pipelines, aided by improvements in technology.

Pacific Lighting worked on advertising campaigns with other gas utilities during the Great Depression to counter the belief that gas supplies would soon run out and to promote the sales of gas-fueled appliances. This successful campaign helped the company weather the Depression, despite decreased use of its gas by industry.

In 1933 an earthquake caused extensive damage to Pacific Lighting's gas pipeline system, as did torrential rains in 1938. In an attempt to help recoup some of the losses suffered during the 1930s, Pacific attempted to combine Southern Counties Gas and Southern California Gas. The request was denied by California regulators, however, on the grounds that two companies, even if owned by the same holding company, would produce more competition than would one company.

### RISING SUPPLY COSTS: 1941–52

During World War II Pacific Lighting diverted energy to defense manufacturers and converted an old gas plant to the manufacture of war-related chemicals. The demand for natural gas increased dramatically during and after the war, and Pacific Lighting sought new means of keeping pace. New defense industries drew even more people to southern California, so conditions for the company during the late 1940s and 1950s were similar to those during the 1920s, requiring large capital outlays for new construction.

In 1947 Pacific Lighting spent $25 million to build the Biggest Inch pipeline, which brought large amounts of natural gas to California from southern Texas. Demand grew so quickly that an extension to the large gas fields of the Texas panhandle was built in 1949. The company also built vast underground storage areas in southern California. Over the next ten years, Pacific Lighting greatly increased the volume of its interstate delivery system, and out-of-state gas made up 90 percent of the company's supply. In addition, the company had promoted gas-powered appliances so effectively that 90 percent of all cooking ranges and 98 percent of water heaters and home-heating systems in southern California used natural gas. To meet demand, Pacific Lighting offered industries low rates in exchange for using other energy sources when demand peaked on cold winter days.

By 1950 the cost of bringing gas to customers had doubled since the years before World War II, but rates had risen only 15 percent. Pacific Lighting repeatedly sought unpopular rate hikes during the 1950s, and it increased its public relations efforts to help improve its image. Prices stabilized in the early 1960s as a result of regulatory changes that gave Pacific Lighting and its suppliers greater pricing flexibility. By the mid-1960s Pacific Lighting had become the largest gas supplier in the world, and its prices were among the lowest in the United States. Company head and founder C. O. G.

Miller died in 1952, and his son Robert Miller became chairman.

## RESTRUCTURING AND THE ENERGY CRISIS: 1953–79

In 1965 Pacific Lighting restructured its pipeline subsidiary, Pacific Lighting Gas Supply Company, and changed its name to Pacific Lighting Service and Supply. In 1967 the firm moved its headquarters from San Francisco to Los Angeles. Three years later, Pacific Lighting received regulatory permission to merge Southern California and Southern Gas into one company, called Southern California Gas Company. Pacific Lighting created another subsidiary in 1972, Pacific Lighting Coal Gasification Company, to build a coal gasification plant.

Meanwhile, despite the new pipelines, by the late 1960s gas supplies were dwindling again. Paul Miller, who became president of Pacific Lighting in 1968, sought additional supplies across an increasingly wider area, including Alaska, the Canadian Arctic, and the Rocky Mountains. In 1970 the company created another subsidiary called Pacific Lighting Gas Development Company, to find new gas sources. It soon signed a contract with Gulf Oil Canada to purchase large amounts of gas from a new pipeline that the company was building in Canada's Northwest Territories. Pacific Lighting also got involved in the Alaska Natural Gas Transportation System approved by the U.S. government in 1976, although more than a decade passed before any gas from the project was transported to southern California.

The energy crisis in the 1970s presented grave problems. Energy needs were increasing while Pacific Lighting's gas suppliers began cutting back the company's supplies. Pacific Lighting considered bringing in liquid gas from overseas, while working with Pacific Gas & Electric, another California utility. The two firms began construction of a liquid natural gas plant at Little Cojo Bay, California, in 1979, although construction was halted in 1984 because the natural gas shortage had eased. The shortage ended because of conservation efforts and a federal law passed in 1978 that partially deregulated prices for new gas finds. The deregulation led to higher prices, which in turn caused widespread complaints. The company launched another public relations campaign on radio and television to explain why prices were rising.

The price increases, fuel shortages, and slowing population growth in southern California convinced Pacific Lighting executives to begin diversifying. At first Pacific Lighting's new affiliates were gas-related, but soon the company branched into real estate, air conditioning, agriculture, alternative energy, and retailing. In the early 1970s, Southern California Gas began two major solar energy research projects. More importantly, the company moved into gas and oil exploration and development. In 1975 Pacific Lighting Exploration Company invested in drilling in the Dutch sector of the North Sea. The ventures into agriculture and air conditioning were sold off in the late 1970s and early 1980s. In 1987 the firm sold its real estate operations for $325 million, believing the money could be more profitably invested elsewhere.

## BEYOND NATURAL GAS: 1980–90

In 1983 Pacific Lighting bought Terra Resources, which owned oil and gas property in 18 states. Five years later it bought Sabine Corporation, a Dallas, Texas-based exploration firm. By the late 1980s, oil and gas exploration provided 11 percent of Pacific Lighting's revenue. Pacific Lighting still wanted to move into areas unrelated to the utility business, however, and in 1986 it bought Thrifty Corporation, a chain of Los Angeles-based retail stores. The purchase gave Pacific Lighting ownership of 500 Thrifty Drug Stores, 27 Thrifty Jr. Drug Stores, and 89 Big 5 sporting goods stores. Pacific acquired Thrifty in a stock swap valued at $886 million, or 25 times Thrifty's annual earnings.

Thrifty had been founded in 1919 by two brothers, Harry and Robert Borun, and their brother-in-law, Norman Levin. Initially the firm sold drugs and sundries wholesale. After the stock market crash in 1929, the firm opened its own cut-rate drugstores. By World War II the firm operated 17 stores in the Los Angeles area. In the 1950s, with strip malls appearing and Thrifty's sales dropping, the firm switched to larger stores with a broader selection. In the 1970s, with competition increasing, Thrifty adopted a more aggressive marketing strategy, switching from low-end promotions to a policy of total discounts. By the mid-1980s the firm feared a hostile takeover. When Pacific Lighting offered to buy Thrifty, the company reluctantly accepted, partly because Pacific Lighting had a reputation for allowing its subsidiaries great freedom.

Pacific Lighting moved further into retailing in the next two years, buying more sporting-goods retailers in the Midwest and in Colorado, more than 100 Pay'n Save drugstores, and 37 Bi-Mart general merchandise stores. These purchases made Pacific Lighting the second-largest sporting-goods retailer in the United States and the largest drugstore chain in the western United States. To reflect its increasing diversity, Pacific Lighting changed its name to Pacific Enterprises in 1988. Paul Miller retired in 1989, and James R. Ukropina became chairman and CEO, ending 103 years of leadership by the Miller family.

In buying Thrifty, Pacific Enterprises had decided to trade short-term profits for long-term growth. The purchase left Pacific Enterprises short of funds, while its retail operations suffered from price wars, shoplifting, increased competition from supermarkets, and changing economics. The company also failed to find any large oil or gas deposits, and its core business suffered. To pay its stock dividends, Pacific Enterprises borrowed money and raised it by issuing stock, a move which worried some Wall Street analysts. To deal with the situation, Ukropina restructured management and temporarily cut back on oil and gas drilling. Revenue for 1990 was $6.92 billion, although the firm suffered a net loss of $43 million due to write-offs incurred by both its retail and gas and oil exploring operations.

## THE BIRTH OF SEMPRA ENERGY: 1991–98

Willis B. Wood Jr. was named CEO in 1991 and led the company through restructuring that refocused on the core utility business and restored the parent company to a sound financial footing. Wood was succeeded by Richard D. Farman near the end of the decade, shortly before Pacific Enterprises' announced a merger with Enova Corporation.

Having announced the merger plans in October 1996, Pacific Enterprises and Enova Corporation awaited approvals by the California Public Utilities Commission, the Federal Energy Regulatory Commission, and the Securities and Exchange Commission. The merger was completed in June 1998, and the entity that resulted from the combined operations of both companies was named Sempra Energy. The new board of directors consisted of 16 members, with eight representatives from each of the merging companies.

Enova Corporation, a leading energy management company providing electricity, gas, and value-added products and services in the United States and Mexico, joined Pacific Enterprises to form the largest public company headquartered in San Diego. Prior to the merger, Enova boasted the ownership of San Diego Gas & Electric Company, which had 1.2 million electric meters and 715,000 natural gas meters, serving three million consumers. Pacific Enterprises' contribution to the deal included its interstate and offshore natural gas pipelines, centralized heating and cooling facilities, and natural gas distribution operations in Latin America.

After reorganizations, the new corporation was the parent company of eight subsidiaries based in the United States, including Sempra Energy Solutions.

Former Pacific Enterprises shareholders received 1.5038 shares of Sempra Energy common stock for each share of Pacific that they had owned prior to the merger deal. Sempra Energy's market value was deemed to be $6.2 billion on the day of its founding.

## EXPANSION AND ANOTHER ENERGY CRISIS: 1999–2005

With such a strong foundation, it was natural that Sempra quickly began looking into growth opportunities. The same year as its formation, it purchased CNG Energy Services from Consolidated Natural Gas Co. for $48 million. The following year, in February 1999, Sempra announced it had reached agreement to merge with Colorado's KN Energy Inc. for the tidy sum $1.9 billion. KN Energy was the sixth-largest natural gas pipeline company in the United States, and the second-largest pipeline operator. Sempra looked poised to continue its growth on a national scale, but by June the company had called off the deal, citing below-average earnings on KN Energy's part. Nevertheless, Sempra pushed ahead with expansion in 1999, opening European offices in England, Germany, and Norway.

Between 2000 and 2001, Sempra's already strong performance saw a major boost in the form of the California energy crisis. As was later revealed, some utility companies such as Enron, Inc., caused the crisis by manipulating supply of electricity, causing shortages and "rolling brownouts" throughout the state. Energy companies, including Sempra, reaped major profits off the skewed supply and demand, and in the midst of the crisis the state, desperate to restore normalcy, signed contracts highly favorable to the energy companies. Although Sempra benefited in the short-term from the crisis, the fallout and repercussions of the event would dog the company for the remainder of the decade.

In 2002, as the cause behind the crisis came to light, California filed a complaint against Sempra with the Federal Energy Regulatory Commission. This was only the beginning of the litigation, most of it alleging that Sempra acted knowingly in manipulating the market and squeezing lopsided contracts out of a panicked customer base. The last suits were not settled until 2010, when Sempra cut a deal with the state of California. In exchange for a $410 million settlement, Sempra would admit to no wrongdoing and any ongoing lawsuits and legal proceedings would be considered closed.

The threat of lawsuits was not enough to put Sempra off making good on its record profits. The influx of money was turned towards expansion, namely solidifying the company's reach beyond its traditional base of

California and moving into the traditional heart of the natural gas industry, the Gulf Coast. To that end, in 2003 Sempra purchased a liquid natural gas terminal in Louisiana. In April of 2004, Sempra set into motion over a billion dollars' worth of expansion plans. First, the company revealed plans to construct a $600 million liquefied natural gas receiving terminal located in Port Arthur, Texas. It also announced an ambitious, $430-million acquisition deal to purchase 10 Texas power plants. The following year, Sempra Commodities formed a joint venture with Pennsylvania's New Hope Partners to produce ethanol.

## STRENGTHS AND WEAKNESSES: 2006–10

Despite its increasing reach, expansion, and acquisitions, the heart of Sempra remained in Southern California. Of the copmany's 29 million customers, the Southern California Gas Co., in an operating range that stretched out over 20,000 square miles, serviced 20 million. A further 3.4 million customers were claimed by the San Diego Gas & Electric company, which covered a service area stretching from the southern reaches of the greater Los Angeles area all the way to the Mexican border.

Some analysts believed that Sempra's continuing geographic focus would prove to be a weakness. Over 90 percent of its revenues were generated in the United States in 2009, a very high percentage for an international company. Moreover, only a tenth of 1 percent of its revenues originated in Asia, far and away the best and fastest-growing market for energy companies. Market analysts suggested that Sempra risked missing out on emerging opportunities for growth in Asia through its continued focus on North America.

However, in 2010 Sempra's position remained strong. Sempra's focus on cleaner-burning natural gas, for example, positioned it as a strong competitor in a market increasingly sensitive to environmental concerns. Already an industry giant, Sempra looked poised to continue expanding throughout the 2010s.

*Scott M. Lewis*
*Updated, Allison A. Jones; David Larkins*

## PRINCIPAL SUBSIDIARIES

Pacific Enterprises; San Diego Gas & Electric; Sempra Commodities; Sempra Pipelines & Storage; Sempra Generation; Sempra LNG; Southern California Gas Company.

## PRINCIPAL COMPETITORS

Edison International; PacifiCorp; PG&E Corporation.

## FURTHER READING

Calbreath, Dean, "Sempra Energy Loses a Round to California Officials over Power Contract," *San Diego Union-Tribune,* December 24, 2002.

Engstrand, Iris, and Kathleen Crawford, *Reflections: A History of the San Diego Gas & Electric Company, 1881–1991.* San Diego Historical Society, 1991.

"Enova and Pacific Complete Merger; New Firm Largest U.S. Customer Base," *Electric Utility Week,* July 6, 1998.

Littlefield, Douglas R., and Thanis C. Thorne, *The Spirit of Enterprise.* Los Angeles: Pacific Enterprises, 1990.

"National Energy Marketers Tap Top Power Companies for New Leadership," *Business Wire,* August 7, 1998.

Pechdimaldji, Stephan, "Amex to Trade Options on Sempra Energy," *PR Newswire,* June 29, 1998.

Rose, Craig, "Power Crisis Catches Up to Sempra," *San Diego Union-Tribune,* November 26, 2005.

"Sempra Energy," *Notable Corporate Chronologies..* Thomson Gale, 2007.

Wolff, Eric, "Sempra to Pay $410M in Energy Crisis Settlement: Deal with State Closes Book on Sempra and Crisis," *North County Times,* April 29, 2010.

# Shanghai Baosteel Group Corporation

—■—

**Baosteel Tower**
**Pu Dian Road 370**
**Pudong New District**
**Shanghai, 200122**
**China**
**Telephone: (86) 21-5835 0000**
**Telephone: (86) 21-5835 8888**
**Fax: (86) 21-6840 4832**
**Web site: http://www.baosteel.com**

*State-Owned Company*
*Founded:* 1978 as Baoshan Iron & Steel
*Employees:* 108,914
*Sales:* CNY 246.84 billion ($36.12 billion) (2008)
*Stock Exchanges:* Shanghai
*Ticker Symbol:* 08 Boasteel Bond
*NAICS:* 331111 Iron and Steel Mills; 331210 Iron and Steel Pipe and Tube Manufacturing from Purchased Steel; 331221 Rolled Steel Shape Manufacturing

■ ■ ■

A state-owned conglomerate, Shanghai Baosteel Group Corporation (Baosteel) is China's leading steel enterprise and the third-largest steel producer in the world. With an annual steel production of approximately 30 million tons, Baosteel dominates the Chinese steel industry, controlling more than 10 percent of the total market. Baosteel's focus is the manufacture of superior-quality iron and steel products using the most advanced technology available in the industry. Its main products are high-grade carbon, stainless, and specialty alloyed

steels formed into plates and tubing widely used for household appliances, aerospace engineering projects, oil exploration, nuclear power facilities, shipbuilding, electronic instrumentation, building construction, and a variety of other manufacturing needs. A leader on the domestic front, Baosteel is also a force in the worldwide metallurgical market and exports products to over 40 countries and regions, including the United States, Japan, Korea, and Germany.

## CHINA'S STEEL INDUSTRY: PRE–1978

China's steel industry was largely undeveloped when the People's Republic of China was formed in 1949. Most steel used by the country was manufactured by Anshan Iron and Steel, which had been established in Northeast China under Japanese rule in 1916. In an effort to develop the nation's iron and steel industry, the People's Republic of China began to invest in the construction of new steel facilities during the 1950s. Wuhan Iron and Steel opened for production in 1958, while a number of other smaller steel plants were built around the country. China's steel output increased dramatically throughout the 1950s.

In the 1960s, however, China's steel industry took a downturn; production had decreased by half in the early years of the decade. Many plants had to shut down furnaces because the equipment had been used beyond their capacity in a short time. The Chinese government decided to take steps to centralize control of the steel industry by shutting down many of the smaller plants

COMPANY PERSPECTIVES

Baosteel is, first and foremost, people. Exacting is our spirit; study and innovation is our road; pursuit of the first class is our goal. Baosteel is full of vigor and opportunity, and we look with confidence towards the future.

and borrowing new technology from other countries. Because of such intervention, the success of the steel industry was closely tied to the stability of the political climate in China.

Baosteel came into being at a time of momentous change in the history of China. At a meeting of the Third Plenary Session of the Eleventh Central Committee of the Communist Party of China in Beijing from December 18 to 22, 1978, government leaders embarked on a major policy of economic reform known as *gaige kaifang*. Meaning "reform and opening up" or "open door," *gaige kaifang* was intended to make China a global economic power by allowing the formation of rural ventures and private enterprises. Prior to the *gaige kaifang* policy, the state had held total control of all productive assets in keeping with the country's socialist and communist political organization. China's new economic plan called for the relaxation of state control over the industrial sector, along with opening up the nation to non-Chinese trade and investment. With the goal of producing 80 million tons of steel per year within the next 10 years, the government began renovating and modernizing its existing steel-production facilities.

## BUSINESS ESTABLISHING PERIOD: 1978–85

Baosteel, founded as Baoshan Iron & Steel, was China's first key industrial investment project. The site, which had been selected in December 1977, was in the Baoshan District of Shanghai, a location on the coast of the East China Sea that would facilitate the import and export of goods. Construction began on the facility on December 23, 1978, just one day after the close of the Third Plenary Session. The plant was to be modeled after what was then considered to be the world's most modern steel facility, a Japanese complex operated by Nippon Steel Corporation. In addition to providing substantial financial resources for the Baoshan site, the Chinese government made certain that the people working on the project were the best engineers and managers

in the country and had access to the most advanced technology available at the time.

The building of the plant continued from 1978 to 1985, a time the corporation still refers to as its "Business Establishing Period." During this time, Baoshan leaders worked fervently to establish a business culture that would reflect the company's main values of good faith and synergy. Integral to this culture was a commitment to quality, efficiency, and profit. From executives to field workers, employees would be expected to conduct themselves with a sense of honor and hold themselves to high standards of responsibility and strict workplace discipline. Baoshan consulted with the Nippon Steel Corporation in the development of a centralized, consistent management model. Having a clearly defined organization and culture, it was agreed, would show Baoshan's dedication to being a first-class world enterprise.

As the plant's opening day neared, Baoshan promoted the "Spirit of 1985," a campaign centered around both pride and safety. This strategy served to heighten levels of anticipation and boost morale, even as it reminded people not to become lax in their performance as the project drew to an end. When the No. 1 Blast Furnace was ignited in September 1985, Baosteel celebrated its standing as one of the most modern integrated steel production facilities of the day.

## AN INDUSTRY GIANT: 1985–2000

Baoshan profited from its position as China's steel industry flagship at the onset of operations. The company received a number of important contracts as a result of the nation's burgeoning economic expansion. In 1989 alone, Baoshan was selected to be the principal supplier to Shanghai Automotive Industry Group, another government flagship corporation. With two more blast furnaces ignited in 1991 and 1994, Baoshan increased production, allowing it to win valuable contracts throughout the 1990s.

As China's economy continued to flourish, the steel industry found its resources being consumed at a rate that exceeded production. Forced to rely on foreign suppliers for a large percentage of its iron and steel needs, the government began to back the construction of more steel plants throughout the country. In 1994 Baoshan, facing a level of competition unlike anything it had ever experienced, formed the Shanghai No. 5 Steel Works International Trading Co., Ltd., to assist its parent company in export trade operations.

At home Baoshan concentrated its efforts on strengthening its position as a leader in steel

## KEY DATES

**1978:** Construction on the Baoshan Iron & Steel plant/site begins in Shanghai.

**1985:** The No. 1 Blast Furnace is ignited.

**1989:** The company wins a contract to be the major steel supplier to the Shanghai Automotive Industry Group.

**1994:** The Shanghai No. 5 Steel Works International Trading Co., Ltd., is formed to handle export trade marketing operations.

**1998:** Baoshan merges with Shanghai Metallurgical Holding Group and Meishan Iron & Steel Co., Ltd., to become Shanghai Baosteel Group Corporation (Baosteel).

**2001:** Baosteel becomes the world's third-largest steel company when it partners with the Shougang Group and the Wuhan Iron and Steel Group Corporation.

**2010:** The Baosteel Stage opens at the World Expo 2010 in Shanghai.

manufacturing through a variety of industry-specific services and strategic alliances. For example, the company founded the Shanghai Baosteel Industry Inspection Corporation, an entity that provided quality-control inspections and equipment diagnostic service for Baosteel steel facilities and other clients. By the end of the decade, Baoshan's business dealings reached into the areas of finance, trade, real estate, transportation, information technology, and construction.

According to Nam Young-Sook et al in *Reforming China's Enterprises,* Baoshan "had 37 wholly owned subsidiaries and 18 holding subsidiary companies, including four joint ventures with foreign enterprises in China and 15 joint ventures overseas" by 1998. The company's success spurred the Chinese government to initiate a merger between Baoshan and the Shanghai Metallurgical Holding Group and Meishan Iron & Steel, two state-owned enterprises that had been losing money. In 1998 the three companies merged under the name of Shanghai Baosteel Group Corporation. Once the restructuring of the conglomerate had taken place, Baosteel's sales revenue increased from CNY 68.4 billion ($10.1 billion) in 1999 to CNY 161.8 billion ($23.7 billion) within five years. The return on equity grew from 0.69 percent in 1999 to 12.77 percent in 2004.

## GLOBAL PRESENCE: 2000–10

China was one of the last major trading nations to join the World Trade Organization in 2001. In doing so, China sent a message to the world that it was prepared to be a key force in the global economy. As one of China's preeminent corporations, Baosteel was listed on the Shanghai Stock Exchange, becoming China's largest offering on the public market at the time. Shares in the company were restricted to Chinese investors only. The Baosteel Group reorganized the Shanghai No. 5 Steel Works International Trading Co., Ltd., into the Fortune Trust & Investment Co., Ltd., a company which was responsible for optimizing Baosteel's financial investments, and announced an intention to list Baosteel on the New York Stock Exchange at some future date.

Baosteel actively continued to participate in the restructuring of the domestic steel industry throughout the first decade of the 21st century. Partnering with the Shougang Group and the Wuhan Iron and Steel Group Corporation in 2001, Baosteel moved into place as the world's third-largest steel company. In that same year, Baosteel formed an important alliance on the technology front with Germany's ThyssenKrupp. Also at this time, Baosteel began exploring new steel production technologies in a move toward being more competitive in the international automobile market. Its efforts were rewarded when it was selected to be the primary supplier to the Italian automaker Fiat. In 2003 Baosteel paid around $270 million to acquire the Baogang Yichang Steel Sheets Corporation and Lubao Steel Pipe Corporation, thereby incorporating two of its industry competitors. A few years later, Baosteel also partnered with household appliance company Haier to develop new technologies in appliance steel products.

In addition to acquisitions, partnerships, and mergers, other business ventures have brought recognition to the Baosteel corporation. In April 2000, the Baosteel Group founded Shanghai Baosight Co., Ltd. (Baosight), a software enterprise. Since its inception, Baosight has established 150 patents, 143 registered software products, 261 registered software copyrights, and 110 identified technological trade secrets. The company undertook many notable projects with the Republic of China's National Development and Reform Commission, the Ministry of Science and Technology, and the Ministry of Industry and Information Technology. In both 2007 and 2008, Baosight was recognized as one of China's Top 10 Innovation Software Enterprises by the China Software Industry Association.

The Baosteel Group spent the latter half of the decade focusing not only on retaining its status as a global steel giant but also on being a leader in environmental sustainability. Baosteel created the Environmental Protection and Resource Utilization Department to strengthen how the company managed environmental issues, including keeping abreast of current laws, regulations, and policies. In 2006 Baosteel became the second business in China to join the World Business Council for Sustainable Development (WBCSD), a CEO-led, global association of approximately 200 companies that dealt exclusively with business and sustainable development. January 1, 2008, saw the founding of Baosteel Development Co., Ltd., an enterprise which comprised the Industrial Property, Factory Operation, and Resource Recycling business units. Using cutting-edge technology, Baosteel implemented various procedures for reducing factory emissions, recycling wastewater, and recovering residual energy and heat from manufacturing processes. In 2008 Baosteel was honored as the "Model Enterprise for Clean and Environmentally Friendly Production" by the China Iron & Steel Association.

Since its beginnings, Baosteel has been highly visible in the Shanghai community. In 1990 the Baosteel Education Fund was set up to reward teachers for excellence in the classroom and to provide students funding for higher education. Other educational outreach programs donated supplies to disadvantaged schools in underdeveloped provinces. Baosteel also sponsored the Everlasting Love, Eyesight Restoring Project, which provided free cataract surgery for the poor. In 2008 alone, 1,707 patients received operations that restored their vision. When an earthquake devastated Wenchuan County, Sichuan Province, on May 12, 2008, Baosteel organized a disaster response team that delivered tents, blankets, food, and water to the area. Within a month, Baosteel built steel-plate barracks for six villages to house people whose homes had been destroyed by the earthquake. From 2007 to 2009, Baosteel's Shanghai Pudong Iron & Steel Co., Ltd., provided resources for the World Expo 2010 held in Shanghai. The venue's "Baosteel Stage", a 1.29 million-square-foot pavilion, was slated to become a permanent part of a new commercial district in Shanghai. In the early 2010s, Baosteel looked well positioned to maintain its standing as a leading steel enterprise, both in China and across the globe.

*Alicia Elley*

## PRINCIPAL SUBSIDIARIES

Baoshan Iron & Steel Co., Ltd.; Baosteel Developing Co., Ltd.; Baosteel Resources Co., Ltd.; Baosteel Talent Development Institute; Fortune Trust Co., Ltd.; Guangzhou Iron & Steel Enterprises Group; Ningbo Iron & Steel Co., Ltd.; Shanghai Baosteel Engineering Equipment Co., Ltd.; Shanghai Baosteel Industry Inspection Corporation.

## PRINCIPAL DIVISIONS

Resource Development; Steel Processing; Technology Service; Finance; Production Services.

## PRINCIPAL COMPETITORS

Alcoa Inc.; ArcelorMittal; China Minmetals Corporation; China Steel Corporation; Hebei Iron & Steel Group; JFE Holdings; Lyban Iron and Steel Co.; Nippon Steel Corporation; POSCO; Sinosteel Corporation; Tata Steel Ltd.; ThyssenKrupp AG; United States Steel Corporation.

## FURTHER READING

"Baosteel Clarifies Rumor of Acquiring European Mills," mysteel.net, February 27, 2010.

"Baosteel Engineering Bags SMS Project from Hubei Xinyegang," steelguru.com, March 1, 2010.

"Baosteel Group Ranks No. 3 'World-class Steel Companies,'" news.alibaba.com, August 5, 2009.

Hong, Xu, "Baosteel Group Ponders Stake in European Stainless Steel Mill," interfax.cn, February 25, 2010.

Hu, Zuliu, and Moshin S. Khan, "Why Is China Growing So Fast?" imf.org, June 1997.

Liu, Kang, *Globalization and Cultural Trends in China*. Honolulu: University of Hawaii Press, 2003.

Sirkin, Harold L., James W. Hemerling, and Arindam K. Bhattacharya, *GLOBALITY: Competing with Everyone from Everywhere for Everything*. New York: Business Plus, 2008.

"The Third Plenary Session of the 11th Central Committee of the Communist Party of China," bjreview.com, December 22, 1978.

Williams, Felicity, "Baosteel May Be Replaced," *Melbourne Herald Sun*, August 2, 2008, p. 87.

Young-Sook, Nam, Qiumai Yang, and Charles Pigott, *Reforming China's Enterprises: China in the Global Economy*. Paris: OECD Publishing, 2000.

# SLM Corp.

■

12061 Bluemont Way
Reston, Virginia 20190
U.S.A.
Telephone: (703) 810-3000
Toll Free: (888) 272-5543
Fax: (800) 848-1949
Web site: http://www.salliemae.com

*Public Company*
*Founded:* 1972
*Employees:* 8,000 (2009 est.)
*Net Income:* $324 million (2009)
*Stock Exchanges:* New York
*Ticker Symbol:* SLM
*NAICS:* 522291 Consumer Lending

■ ■ ■

Better known by the name of one its subsidiary companies, Sallie Mae, SLM Corp. (SLM) traces its origins to a government-funded program aimed at making it easier for students to get loans for college. Sallie Mae's mission was to provide a secondary market for the exchange of federally insured, guaranteed student loans. Over the course of its history, SLM has grown from a wholesale, government-funded supplier of loans to a private company that funds more than half its own loans and dabbles in debt management, collections, and other financial services. A leader in the student loan industry, Sallie Mae serves about 10 million students and their families through its loan programs.

## SALLIE MAE'S MISSION

The United States Congress created Sallie Mae to make student loans more liquid, and therefore give lenders a greater incentive to participate in the Guaranteed Student Loan Program (GSLP). Sallie Mae began by offering two basic services, which were loan purchases and warehousing advances (secured loans and lines of credit). By purchasing student loans, Sallie Mae offered lenders liquidity. The knowledge that they could sell the loans and were not required to use the money to make new student loans made lenders less nervous about tying up money in student loans in the first place. Under its warehousing program Sallie Mae lent financial institutions money to make new student loans by accepting existing loans or other government securities as collateral.

Guaranteed student loans were a special market for several reasons. The Guaranteed Student Loan Program (GSLP), created in 1965 by the Higher Education Act, was established to supplement the government's grant and work-study programs, which helped students finance higher education. Under the GSLP, the federal government assumed the risk for defaulted student loans. Originally, the government guaranteed the loans directly, but state and nonprofit agencies later directly insured the loans, backed up by federal reinsurance.

The GSLP allowed qualified students to borrow a certain amount at a special fixed interest rate each year they were in school. While students were in school, and for a short grace period after they left, the federal government paid the interest on their loans, so that a student had to pay back only the principal plus the interest accrued after graduation. In addition, the government paid a special allowance to lenders to make up the difference between the low rate of interest students paid and the market rate of return. It was typically set a few percentage points above the 90-day treasury bill rate. Thus, if the borrowing rate for students was 8 percent, and the treasury bill rate was 10 percent, lenders got the 2 percent difference between that rate and the 8 percent students paid, plus 3.25 percent on top of that, adjusted quarterly according to the treasury bill rate.

Since collection procedures made carrying student loans costly once they reached the repayment phase, many lenders sold student loans to Sallie Mae when the student graduated. Student loans were costly not because student default rates were high (defaults were guaranteed by the government anyway), but because they were relatively small loans that required a lot of work. In addition to the federal collection and reporting requirements that had to be followed to qualify for the government guarantee in the case of default, student loans were often complicated to keep track of. For example, students had to be granted deferments for unemployment, a return to school, or any of a host of other reasons.

Sallie Mae's high volume meant that the company could administer the collection of loans with greater cost effectiveness. By 1988 Sallie Mae held 24 percent of all outstanding student loans. Thus, Sallie Mae insured an adequate supply of credit for educational needs by enabling lenders to hold onto their loans during the lucrative in-school phase, sell the loans when they began to require more attention, and use the money to make new loans.

## OPEN FOR BUSINESS: 1973–79

As a federally chartered corporation, Sallie Mae's history was shaped by legislation. After adjusting the interest rates and special allowances for GSLP borrowers and lenders for several years, in its efforts to make enough educational credit available, Congress chartered Sallie Mae in 1972 to create a secondary market for student loans. The company opened for business in 1973 with financing from Washington, D.C. banks, repaying these loans through the sale of federally guaranteed securities the same year. After that, Sallie Mae depended on financing from the Federal Financing Bank (an arm of the Treasury Department) from which it could borrow money at very attractive rates. However, Congress never intended for Sallie Mae to be government-supported, and in 1981 Sallie Mae started raising the money it needed on public capital markets. After that, it became known for its inventive financing schemes, which were designed to lock in floating-rate liabilities to match its floating-rate assets.

In 1974 Sallie Mae made its first issue of common stock, raising $24 million in capital. The sale of this stock was restricted to banks or educational institutions, who were required to buy 100 shares in order to participate in Sallie Mae's programs. This requirement was later lowered to 50 shares, and small institutions were exempt.

In 1976 the lender allowance was tied to the 90-day treasury bill rate, and its ceiling was raised from 3 percent to 5 percent. That year, in an effort to reduce the red tape and inefficiencies that often accompany federal programs, the government transferred responsibility for the GSLP to the states and encouraged them to set up their own guaranteeing agencies. It also authorized Sallie Mae to buy loans originated under a newly created Health Education Assistance Loan (HEAL) Program to help graduate students in the health professions finance their educations.

By 1977 Sallie Mae was able to issue its first dividend. The next year, the Middle Income Assistance Act removed all income restrictions for student borrowers in response to complaints from middle-income families that they were too rich to get assistance but too poor to pay rising education costs, especially if they had more than one child in college at a time. Since students were no longer required to demonstrate financial need to qualify for loans, the program expanded rapidly from $2 billion in new loans in 1978, to $3 billion in 1979, to $8 billion in 1980.

In 1978 Congress also removed the ceiling on the special allowance to lenders, setting the allowance simply at 3.5 percent above the 90-day treasury bill rate, so that lenders were guaranteed a market rate of return. That, and the elimination of the paperwork involved in determining eligibility, made student loans more attractive to lenders. Sallie Mae grew accordingly, from assets of $1.6 billion in 1979 to $7.5 billion in 1982.

<table>
<tr><td colspan="2">

## KEY DATES

■

</td></tr>
<tr><td>**1972:**</td><td>The Student Loan Marketing Association (SLMA), also called Sallie Mae, is created by the U.S. Congress as a publicly owned, for-profit company.</td></tr>
<tr><td>**1973:**</td><td>The company opens for business with financing from Washington, D.C. banks, repaying these loans through the sale of federally guaranteed securities the same year.</td></tr>
<tr><td>**1974:**</td><td>Sallie Mae makes its first issue of common stock, raising $24 million in capital.</td></tr>
<tr><td>**1977:**</td><td>Sallie Mae issues its first dividend.</td></tr>
<tr><td>**1981:**</td><td>Congress reinstates a needs test for borrowers with a family income above $30,000. Congress also pushes Sallie Mae to lessen its reliance on federal funds more quickly.</td></tr>
<tr><td>**1991:**</td><td>Sallie Mae owns a third of the $49 billion market in outstanding guaranteed student loans.</td></tr>
<tr><td>**1996:**</td><td>Congress passes legislation requiring the privatization of Sallie Mae. To appease shareholders against the move, the company moves forward with a plan to repurchase 20 million shares.</td></tr>
<tr><td>**1997:**</td><td>SLM Corp. becomes the parent company of SLMA as dissenting shareholders push through an alternate privatization plan.</td></tr>
<tr><td>**2004:**</td><td>Four years ahead of schedule, the privatization of Sallie Mae is completed and the company's federal charter returned to Congress.</td></tr>
<tr><td>**2007:**</td><td>An anticipated $25 billion buyout of Sallie Mae by J.C. Flowers & Co. falls through.</td></tr>
<tr><td>**2010:**</td><td>Sallie Mae announces its plans to lay off 2,500 employees in the wake of the Obama administration's federal student loan overhauls.</td></tr>
</table>

## CASHING IN: 1980–86

In 1980, as a prime rate near 20 percent pushed the cost of the GSLP sky-high, Congress made further amendments to the Higher Education Act. For the first time since 1968, the interest rate charged to student borrowers was raised. More important to Sallie Mae, however, were changes that increased the company's range of operations and gave it new ways of raising capital, to begin weaning it from federal support.

Congress set the expiration of Sallie Mae's authority to issue federally guaranteed obligations at 1984, but gave the secretary of the treasury power to buy as much as $1 billion of nonguaranteed Sallie Mae securities, and authorized Sallie Mae to issue nonvoting common stock.

Congress also broadened the services Sallie Mae could offer, giving the company much greater flexibility in making warehousing advances by loosening the restrictions on what Sallie Mae could accept as collateral for them and by liberalizing the requirement that warehousing advances go directly back into student loans. Sallie Mae was also permitted to consolidate or refinance loans for highly indebted students, to make advances to state and other nonprofit agencies for their student loan operations, and to make loans directly to students in areas of the country where there was insufficient credit available.

In 1981, under the Ronald Reagan administration, Congress reinstated a needs test for borrowers with a family income above $30,000. Congress also pushed Sallie Mae to lessen its reliance on federal funds more quickly. Accordingly, expiration of Sallie Mae's authority to issue federally guaranteed obligations was moved up to 1982, and in mid-1981 Sallie Mae made its first public offering of short-term discount notes. Congress also continued to broaden Sallie Mae's activities, authorizing the company to deal with educational loans not insured by the GSLP and to buy and sell the obligations of state and nonprofit educational-loan agencies.

During the remainder of the 1980s, Sallie Mae experimented with ways of raising funds at as low a cost as possible. Since all of its assets (the student loans it had bought and the warehousing advances it had made) earned a floating rate of interest tied to the 90-day treasury bill rate, Sallie Mae preferred to borrow money at a floating rate tied to the same indicator. The company was very successful at doing this. With both assets and liabilities tied to the treasury bill rate, Sallie Mae was insensitive to changes in the interest rate. As a quasi-governmental agency whose assets (those same student loans) were guaranteed by the federal government, Sallie Mae was able to raise money easily, and fairly inexpensively.

As the cost of education continued to outdistance inflation, student loans continued to be in heavy demand. Thus, Sallie Mae's assets grew at a breakneck pace in the 1980s, going from $1.6 billion in 1979 to $28.63 billion in 1988, an increase of nearly 1,700 percent. To Sallie Mae, which made its money on the fixed spread between its floating-rate assets and floating-rate liabilities, increased assets meant increased profits. In April 1983 Sallie Mae made its first offering of preferred stock, and in September of that year it made its initial offering of nonvoting common stock, thus becoming a publicly owned company.

## CHANGES BREWING: 1986–93

In 1986, when Congress reauthorized the Higher Education Act of 1965, it again broadened Sallie Mae's range of operations. It also required a needs test for all loan applicants, even those with family incomes of less than $30,000, and lowered the allowance to lenders to 3.25 percent above the treasury bill rate. Sallie Mae was given the latitude to deal loans to educational institutions for physical improvements. Congress also authorized the establishment of the College Construction Loan Insurance Association (Connie Lee) to provide insurance for loans to academic institutions for facilities. Sallie Mae helped set up Connie Lee, which opened for business in 1988.

By the early 1990s, Sallie Mae was known as one of the most innovative borrowers around. It experimented with exotic deals such as New Zealand-dollar-denominated notes, and securities tied to the dollar-yen exchange rate. It was a consistent moneymaker, and its stock flew high on Wall Street. Institutions owned three-quarters of its shares by 1991. Sallie Mae was perceived as a champion moneymaker because it was the Department of Education, not Sallie Mae, which would be responsible for defaulted loans. The only way Sallie Mae could falter was if it bought loans that did not comply with federal regulations.

To avert this, the company kept very close tabs on the banks it bought loans from. It also began servicing more of its own loans. In 1990 it serviced about 40 percent of its loans in-house, and by the next year this figure had grown to almost 50 percent. This kept operational costs down, while assets continued to rise. By 1991 Sallie Mae owned a third of the $49 billion market in outstanding guaranteed student loans.

In spite of Sallie Mae's evident health and vitality, various government figures began to suggest ways of changing the company. In April 1991 the Congressional Budget Office recommended closer government scrutiny of Sallie Mae and her government-sponsored siblings Fannie Mae (Federal National Mortgage Association) and Freddie Mac (Federal Home Loan Mortgage Corporation). Although all three of these companies were not only financially sound but also actually quite profitable, the costly federal bailout of the Savings and Loan Association made the government more cautious about entities it guaranteed. President George H. W. Bush suggested that the government might make loans directly to students, as a cost-saving measure. Sallie

Mae's chief executive, Lawrence Hough, had been given a salary package worth over $2 million, and this apparently seemed wasteful to the Bush administration. However, quick criticism from many quarters brought an end to Bush's plan, and Sallie Mae seemed destined to go along its way as merrily as ever.

Unexpectedly, Sallie Mae's bubble burst soon after. In 1993, its stock was selling at a high of $74.50, but then began a slide, landing at almost half that price two years later. Profits fell as well, as President Bill Clinton revived Bush's idea to have the government lend directly to students. The government program started up in 1994, landing about 5 percent of student loans. By the 1995–96 school year, however, the government handled about 40 percent. Clinton also asked Sallie Mae to pay new fees on loans it handled, eroding profits. The company was divided on how to proceed, precipitating a shareholder revolt.

## SHAREHOLDER REVOLT: 1994–99

Sallie Mae's chief operating officer, Albert Lord, resigned from his post in January 1994 over differences with CEO Hough. However, in 1995 Lord organized a slate of dissidents to run for seats on Sallie Mae's board. Although both sides favored the inevitable privatization of the company, Lord's faction wanted to move faster and more aggressively and to expand into new business areas. Hough and Lord had once been friends, but the proxy fight became bitter. Finally Hough announced that he would resign his post if his side won the board elections, hoping to appease shareholders who were critical of him personally. But Lord's side won the crucial board seats, and his Committee to Restore Value at Sallie Mae had their way.

Lord and his new management quickly implemented a reorganization plan. They set up a Delaware-chartered holding company, SLM Holding Corp., as a publicly traded company that held the Student Loan Marketing Association. Lord also moved to cut costs, both in loan acquisition and in overhead. His plan was to cut the cost of buying student loans by 50 percent over the next five years. Lord's new management also raised cash by "securitizing" a large portion of its loans. This meant that loans were sold to trusts, which then issued securities to back the loans.

The new corporation wanted to be able to invest in new products and services and get out from under the instability caused by government oversight. For example, the Higher Education Act of July 1998 asked for changes in the way student loan rates were set, but it was not clear how the changes would be implemented and what the effect on Sallie Mae would be. The uncertainty of this legislation, and other legislation that might follow, made it difficult for Sallie Mae to predict its finances. Sallie Mae's new management emphasized working with Congress and the president to find ways to hold costs down for students, without making student loans completely unprofitable for financial institutions. The new company hoped to have more flexibility to respond to changes, and to pursue new business as opportunities presented themselves.

## PRIVATIZING AND OPPORTUNITIES LOST: 2000–07

Legislation passed by Congress in 1995 had provided for Sallie Mae privatizing no later than 2009, but the new corporation was determined to beat that goal handily as it entered the 21st century. In 2002 SLM Holding Corp. shortened its name to SLM Corp. and announced that it had voluntarily shifted its target for privatization from 2008 to 2006. It managed to beat even this goal, finding itself by 2004 on track to complete privatization by the end of the following year. In December 2004 the company returned its federal charter to Congress, marking the official end of an era.

By this point the company had seen profits climbing ever higher, surging to $1.5 billion in 2003. The company invested some of the capital gained from its rapid growth into acquisitions. In August 2004 SLM agreed to a $4.5 billion acquisition of Southwest Student Services Corp., the student loan subsidiary of Arizona-based Helios Education Foundation. Exactly two years later, Sallie Mae acquired Upromise, a company that focused on college savings plans called Section 529 plans. A statement released by Sallie Mae touted the natural fit between the "No. 1 paying-for-college company in the country" and the "No. 1 saving-for-college company in the country."

Around the same time it was undergoing expansion, SLM was also dealing with internal controversies. An investigation launched by the Securities and Exchange Commission (SEC) had found accounting irregularities in the company's books. Once a model of corporate oversight, the company was scandalized by the SEC's findings, which reported three executives shifting earnings figures around in order to meet monthly goals and so earn bonuses for themselves. One executive lost his job in the wake of the scandal, and another was demoted.

However, such events were quickly forgotten amidst increased profits and rising stock value. The company was performing far above industry analysts' predictions, and by 2007 it had attracted the attention of a certain Mustang Holdings Corp., an entity that represented af-

filiates of such heavy financial hitters as J.C. Flowers & Co., Bank of America, and JPMorgan. Mustang approached SLM with a tremendous initial offer of $25 billion in cash for a majority share in the company. Were the merger to go through, Sallie Mae would become a privately held company. It was not to be, however.

Around the same time as the merger deal was being worked out, the first rumblings of the major changes that would come to vex Sallie Mae and the entire student loan industry were beginning to be felt. First came the initial shockwaves of the impending global recession in the form of the 2007 subprime mortgage crisis. Already skittish in an increasingly unstable financial environment and the squeeze that was being put on the credit market, SLM's prospective buyers backed out of the deal when in the same year new student loan legislation was passed and signed into law. SLM filed a lawsuit, rejected a smaller counteroffer, then dropped the suit in January 2008 in exchange for resettling $30 billion in debt held with Bank of America and JPMorgan.

## A SHIFTING MARKETPLACE: 2008–10

The 2007 subprime crisis heralded the onset of global recession and panic in 2008. By March 2009 SLM's stock, which had been trading at nearly $60 a share not two years earlier, plummeted to a mere $3 a share. Such dramatic shifts were not unheard of for financial companies weathering the recession, but by 2010 SLM's stock had barely recovered, trading at $10 a share a year after bottoming out. The reason for this paltry recovery lay in the shifting and uncertain future that faced the student loan industry with the election of Barack Obama as president of the United States in 2008.

Like Bill Clinton and George H. W. Bush before him, President Obama set his sights early on reforming the business of providing loans to college students. From its inception, Sallie Mae had drawn on the Federal Family Education Loan Program (FFELP) to subsidize its loans. Sallie Mae was the largest manager of FFELP loans in the industry, and the program had been a cornerstone of the company's loan strategy since its inception. The FFELP would not only provide some of the funds for private lenders to secure loans, but would guarantee the loans against default. Four out of every five loans held by Sallie Mae were federally insured in 2008, and that percentage had been on the rise prior to the new federal legislation. Calling FFELP wasteful, President Obama pushed legislation through Congress, against the considerable opposition of Sallie Mae and other private student loan companies, and eliminated the program effective June 30, 2010. In the wake of the bill's passage in March of that year, Sallie Mae immediately announced that it would be cutting its workforce by 2,500 "soon."

With the announcement of the latest round of layoffs in 2010, SLM was looking at cutting its workforce nearly in half from its high of 12,000 employees in 2006. There could be little doubt that the company, which had been flying so high just a few years before, was facing an uncertain future. As of 2010, Sallie Mae was faced with the task of orchestrating a major shift in its focus, moving from being an originator of loans to a servicer of loans while completely restructuring and overhauling its portfolio.

*A. Woodward*
*Updated, David Larkins*

## PRINCIPAL SUBSIDIARIES

AFS US, Inc.; Arrow Financial Services, LLC; Cavalier Funding LLC; Mustang Funding I, LLC; Sallie Mae Bank; Southwest Student Services Corporation.

## PRINCIPAL COMPETITORS

Bank of America Corp.; KeyCorp; Student Loan Corp.

## FURTHER READING

Chernenkof, Kelly, "Sallie Mae Blames 2,500 Layoffs on Obama's Student Loan Overhaul," FOXNews.com.

de Senerpont Domis, Olaf, "Dissidents Are Elected to Lead Sallie as Private Direct-to-Student Lender," *American Banker,* August 1, 1997: 1.

"House Votes Measure to Privatize Sallie Mae," *Wall Street Journal,* September 21, 1995.

Mollison, Caitlin, "Sallie Mae Can't Wait to Rid Itself of Govt Shackles," *Dow Jones News Service,* June 27, 1996.

Ramstack, Tom, "Sallie Mae Looks to College Savings," *Washington Times,* June 6, 2006.

"Sallie Mae Completes Acquisition of Southwest Student Services Corporation," *PR Newswire,* October 15, 2004.

"Sallie Mae, Flowers Settle Lawsuit," *Private Equity Week,* February 4, 2008, p. 7.

"Sallie Suitors Scared Off? 'Wild West of the College Loan Business?'." *Investment Dealers' Digest,* July 23, 2007.

"SLM Corporation Completes Privatization of Student Loan Marketing Association," *PR Newswire,* December 29, 2004.

"Student Loan Marketing Association Prepares for Early Privatization," *PR Newswire,* January 24, 2002.

"Violations Alleged at Student Loan Firm," *Boston Globe,* December 13, 1991.

# SolarWinds, Inc.

3711 South MoPac Expressway
**Building Two**
**Austin, Texas 78746**
**U.S.A.**
**Telephone: (512) 682-9500**
**Toll Free: (866) 530-8100**
**Fax: (512) 682-9301**
**Web site: http://www.solarwinds.com**

*Public Company*
*Founded:* 1998
*Employees:* 354 (2009)
*Sales:* $116.4 million (2009)
*Stock Exchanges:* New York
*Ticker Symbol:* SWI
*NAICS:* 511210 Software Publishers; 541511 Custom computer program or software development

■ ■ ■

SolarWinds, Inc. (SolarWinds), oddly enough, has little to do with the sun or the wind. Instead, the company develops and sells software and services that help information technology (IT) professionals manage computer networks. The company's software products, some of which can be downloaded by customers for free, help IT managers monitor the activity on their networks. Their target market is mid-market organizations managing from 100 to 5,000 employees that need a scalable solution for 250 to 10,000 elements connected to the network. Customers use the software to institute solutions that keep the network operating smoothly, especially during high-traffic spikes that can cause significant data bottlenecks and network slowdowns. SolarWinds also manages thwack.com, an online forum for IT professionals. The forum allows members to submit problems or questions concerning computers and computer networks and receive comments and download software "fixes" from other members of the forum. While thwack.com was initially a customer service venue for SolarWinds' products and services, the Web site has become much more, growing a life of its own with over 49,000 members in 2010 who discuss a wide variety of network management topics and solutions.

## WATCHING THE NETWORK

In 1998 the potential Y2K computer glitch was already making headlines. Computer programmers, software company executives, and network managers, not to mention the public at large, feared the advent of the new millennium would bring widespread computer crashes. Networks were considered especially vulnerable since network servers run a multitude of programs to keep them stable and protect them from external attack. Many companies were busily developing and commanding big fees for fixes to the programming code, but Dave and Don Yonce, two brothers from Tulsa, Oklahoma, focused on more mundane aspects of the problem. They were concerned that if something were to go wrong on a computer network, like a Y2K crash, the network manager would not know where and when it happened in real time so would not be able to fix it

## COMPANY PERSPECTIVES

One of the key elements of our success is our connection to the IT management community and we work to understand the challenges they face on a daily basis. Through SolarWinds' growing online community, thwack.com, we offer users a forum for problem solving, peer support, and sharing technology for all of our products. This active user-community input is combined with decades of network management experience to deliver a wide range of solutions and tools to address the real-world needs of IT professionals. Our reputation in the market has been defined and maintained by both the quality of our solutions, as well as our dedicated employees.

quickly. He or she would not be able to discover what part of the network caused the problem or what areas were affected. Some companies had from 100 to 10,000 devices attached to a network, and any number of them could be sending or receiving data over the Internet.

This situation arose over the years as networks became progressively more and more complex. Early on, networks were easier to monitor because all the devices on the network shared the same data highway along a single Ethernet wire. Networks grew more complex as people demanded more data-intensive applications, including those that could move a wide variety of files across the network and upload and download files via the Internet. Data moving though networks increasingly faced bottlenecks, and networks experienced significant slowdowns. Network managers had to redesign their networks to distribute the labor of handling data traffic. To accomplish this, network managers often segmented the network into nodes to split up the traffic. These nodes were smaller neighborhoods of computers, each with a hub or router to manage the data transfer within the neighborhood, between neighborhoods, and with the central network servers. This added complexity made earlier monitoring applications and hardware obsolete.

The Yonces and other developers created network management tools to handle the new complexity network managers faced. They used a data-transmission protocol called Simple Network Management Protocol (SNMP) which is an Internet protocol built to handle the multitude of nodes designed into newer networks.

## FREE TOOLS AND "TRY AND BUY"

The Yonce's software tool, which could be purchased and downloaded from an Internet Web site, analyzed traffic across all the segments of the network, regardless of how many segments or devices. Their software also presented monitoring data in real time and in graphical form. Although they were little more than a couple of guys throwing their code onto the Web, the Yonce brothers were able to deliver a quality product while maintaining low overhead. They were also able to deliver their software and updates to their customers more quickly and at lower cost. This gave them a competitive edge over larger competitors in the market.

The Yonces' online store was modest and offered some tools for free and other tools for a licensing fee. In addition to the monitoring software, they offered their TFTP Server for free. This practice of offering basic or entry-level tools for free while charging for its more advanced tools set a pattern for how SolarWinds would do business going forward. In addition, its priced items could be downloaded on a trial basis. This "try and buy" method has become common among the smaller software developers who sell via the Internet.

The Yonces were not overly ambitious in marketing their Web site and products. They had an "if we build it they will come" strategy, which most marketers consider unlikely to succeed, but the Yonces' efforts proved the exception to the rule. They received their first purchase just 10 minutes after launching the Web site, and over next few years, they attracted several partners who integrated the Yonce's tools into their network management packages.

The Yonces bet their future on a modular approach to network management software. They kept their software in small modules that performed a specific function. These modules could be run independently or in conjunction with other modules. This modularity allowed their software to be integrated with other software packages that enabled the network manager to debug, or correct, network problems.

## MONITORING FROM A DISTANCE

What fueled the company's biggest wave of growth was the rise of managed service providers (MSPs). MSPs were companies or contractors hired by other companies to manage their networks and provide network services under a service contract. MSPs wanted to monitor their clients' networks from a distance and reduce the number of costly on-site visits. If slowdowns or other problems occurred, the MSP needed to assess the network from wherever they could access the Internet. In 2005 the MSP business was booming, and companies offering

## KEY DATES

**1998:** Dave and Don Yonce found SolarWinds in Tulsa, Oklahoma.
**2006:** Company moves headquarters to Austin, Texas.
**2007:** Company launches thwack.com and purchases Neon Software and ipMonitor.
**2008:** Company introduces Orion Application Performance Manager.
**2009:** Company has successful initial public offering and purchases Dallas-based Tek-Tools, Inc.

software platforms to support the MSP business benefited as well. Companies like N-able Technologies, LPI Level Platforms, Kaseya, and Silverback Technologies drew attention from the major MSPs, and as a result, these companies were able to grow significantly. Even with such a crowded field, many MSPs were dissatisfied with the available alternatives. They wanted something different.

Around this time SolarWinds' name made its way into discussion groups on the Internet, and a network of people began mentioning SolarWinds to their colleagues. MSPs began looking closely at the company's software as a potential MSP software platform. For MSPs, SolarWinds' software offered an excellent graphical interface and visual representation of the network. It was also well integrated with the Internet, making it easy to monitor from a distance. Also, with the low price of $2,500, well below competitors, SolarWinds looked even more attractive than what was currently available on the market. The company quietly attracted an ever larger and more loyal following, and its business grew significantly. Sales increased by 40 percent and its business expanded to reach 30 countries. The staff grew from 2 to 60 by the end of 2005. The company branded its monitoring software under the name Orion Network Performance Monitor.

In 2006 the company's staff doubled, and it moved its offices to a larger facility on South Yorktown Avenue in Tulsa. The new facility was more than five times the size of its previous offices. Clients such as AOL Time Warner and Cisco Systems signed on as customers. SolarWinds also received a significant infusion of cash from venture capital firms Austin Ventures, Bain Capital, and Insight Venture Partners. Michael Bennett became president and CEO of SolarWinds. Bennett was a former partner in Austin Ventures and the founder of

Alterpoint, Inc., another network management technology company. In late 2006 SolarWinds moved its headquarters to Austin, Texas, but the company maintained its offices in Tulsa.

## A NEW KIND OF MARKETING

By early 2007 the company had about 40,000 copies of its Orion Network Performance Monitor (Orion NPM) software installed without having spent one dollar on marketing. In that same year, the company would make a move into a new method of marketing that would prove to have a major impact. Back in 2005, the company formed an online customer service forum instead of the typical customer service call center. The site allowed customers to post their problems on the site and either the company or other customers would respond with solutions or comments. The content of this Web site also helped SolarWinds make improvements to its software for future releases. The site quickly grew to over 7,000 registered members.

In 2007 the company assembled 17 of SolarWinds' largest customers as a Community Site Advisory Board. The purpose of the board was to help the company develop the customer service site into a more significant resource for the board members and other network professionals. The software engineers at the companies helped develop a new and more substantial site under the name thwack.com. The site added blogs and a content exchange where members downloaded other members' templates, scripts, reports, and how-to documents.

The thwack.com Web site was in line with a new marketing trend. Companies used online forums and blogs to attract professionals in their industry regardless of whether they used their products or not. The strategy was to create a site as a valuable resource, where members came together "electronically" and shared problems, concerns, and ideas. The site required members to register, so the company gained useful information about their customers. This information could be leveraged to fuel other marketing efforts such as marketing e-mails and Webinars (online seminars). Also, the company could monitor site traffic and observe what areas were of the most concern to their customers. SolarWinds' thwack.com became a good argument for this new marketing method's effectiveness. By 2008 the site had more than doubled its membership to around 16,000 registered users, who had contributed over 30,000 posts to the site. The site also featured over 200 member-contributed downloads, which had been accessed more than 10,000 times. The site grew to over 49,000 members in 2010.

SolarWinds, Inc.

## STAYING AHEAD OF TECHNOLOGY

In early 2007 SolarWinds purchased Neon Software, a competitor in Lafayette, California. Neon's LANsurveyor had received praise from industry experts for its ability to discover, map, and visualize the topology of a network to its manager. Later that year, SolarWinds bought ipMonitor Corporation, another competitor based in Ottawa, Canada. This firm brought with it over 5,000 new customers as well as technologies that SolarWinds incorporated into its own software. At the end of 2007, SolarWinds increased its customer base to 50,000, including 350 of the *Fortune* 500 companies. The company also boasted that over one million network managers were using its free tools.

In 2008 SolarWinds launched its Orion Application Performance Manager, later renamed the Orion Network Configuration Management (Orion NCM). Orion NCM marked the company's first move into software that did more than just monitor networks. Orion NCM could operate as a stand-alone application or be integrated with the Orion NPM. Revenues grew from $61.7 million in 2007 to 93.1 million in 2008. The company's profit rose 64 percent, and its customer base grew to 80,000, including 400 of the *Fortune* 500 companies. The company also opened a sales and support center in Singapore and a development facility in the Czech Republic.

In May 2009 SolarWinds successfully executed a public offering and raised $112.5 million. At the time, the stock market was experiencing a dearth of initial public offerings (IPOs), and SolarWinds represented the first venture-backed IPO in nine months. In early 2010 SolarWinds acquired Tek-Tools, Inc., a Dallas-based network management software company, for $42 million in cash and stock. Tek-Tools brought to SolarWinds its expertise in storage management and virtual systems management. This move put SolarWinds in a position to offer products to help monitor and manager virtualization or virtual machines, a growing area of network design. Virtual machines are simulations of real machines. A process virtual machine supports one task or function, and a system virtual machine supports a complete operating system to achieve all the normal tasks of a fully functional computer. Whichever the case, the virtual machine exists only on the server and not as a physical machine (like a personal computer). Tek-Tools was founded in 1996 and at the time of the merger had employees in both Dallas and Chennai, India. The Tek-Tools engineers in India became part of SolarWinds' initial move to build a development team in that country.

At the end of 2009, the company had 88,000 customers, including 425 of the *Fortune* 500 companies. In February 2010 Michael Bennett stepped down as CEO of the company for health reasons, and the company's chief financial officer, Kevin Thompson, stepped into the position. SolarWinds entered 2010 still offering what it called products created by (software) engineers for engineers. It retained its successful model of offering free tools and trial-to-purchase versions of its flagship software packages. The company continued to grow its customer base without the use of conventional marketing methods, involving nothing beyond word-of-mouth and traffic from its online forum site thwack. com.

*Aaron Hauser*

## PRINCIPAL COMPETITORS

CA, Inc.; Cisco Systems, Inc.; EMC Corporation; Hewlett-Packard Company; International Business Machines Corporation; NetApp, Inc.

## FURTHER READING

Cauthron, Matt, "Tulsa Software Company Moves to Larger Facility: Officials Cite Growing Work Force as Cause for Expansion," *Journal Record*, May 26, 2006.

Hawkins, Lori, "SolarWinds Expands with $42 Million Purchase," *Austin American-Statesman*, January 28, 2010, p. B05.

———, "Executive Shake-up at SolarWinds as CEO Exits Top Post," *Austin American-Statesman*, February 11, 2010, p. B07.

Miller, Clair Cain, and Ashlee Vance, "Bits: SolarWinds Beats Odds with Public Offering," *New York Times*, May 20, 2009.

Neel, Dan, "Solar Power – From Online Storefront to Red-hot MSP Platform," *Computer Reseller News*, January 22, 2007, p. 30.

Ohlhorst, Frank, "SolarWinds Brings Order to Network Confusion," *eWeek*, April 5, 2010, p. 20–23.

Schuyler, Michael, "Measuring Network Traffic," *Computers in Libraries*, September 2001, p. 55.

"SolarWinds Acquires ipMonitor," *Tulsa Business Journal*, April 24, 2007.

"SolarWinds Acquires TekTools Storage Management Suite 398389," *eWeek*, January 27, 2010.

"SolarWinds Makes Waves in Network Management," *eWeek*, May 18, 2007.

"SolarWinds Surpasses 1 Million User Milestone; Company Continues to Give Back to the Network Community; Three New Tools Available," *M2PressWIRE*, October, 8, 2007.

# Spectra Energy
# Corporation

5400 Westheimer Court
Houston, Texas 77056
U.S.A.
Telephone: (713) 627-5400
Toll Free: (888) 293-7867
Fax: (713) 627-4691
Web site: http://www.spectraenergy.com

*Public Company*
*Incorporated:* 2007
*Employees:* 5,400 (2009)
*Sales:* $4.55 billion (2009)
*Stock Exchanges:* New York
*Ticker Symbol:* SE
*NAICS:* 221210 Companies in Natural Gas Distribution; 211111 Companies in Crude Petroleum and Natural Gas Extraction; 486210 Companies in Pipeline Transportation of Natural Gas

∎∎∎

Spectra Energy Corporation, a publicly owned *Fortune* 500 company, functions as a liaison between natural gas sources and premium markets throughout the United States and Canada. A leading natural gas infrastructure company, its three main functions in the industry are natural gas gathering and processing, transmission, and storage and distribution. Spectra Energy owns one of the largest natural gas transportation systems in North America, consisting of over 19,000 miles of transmission pipelines and 285 billion cubic feet of storage capacity. Headquartered in Houston, Texas, Spectra Energy also

has U.S. offices in Colorado, Massachusetts, Oklahoma, and Tennessee, and Canadian offices in Alberta, Ontario, Vancouver, and Nova Scotia.

## EMERGENCE

Although it was a new company incorporated in 2007, Spectra Energy leaders emphasized an industry connection that dated back to the late 1920s, when the Panhandle Eastern Pipeline Company, a natural gas services company, was established in Houston, Texas. Another important entity in the history of the development of Spectra Energy was Texas Eastern Transmission, which was founded in 1947 following the purchase of two crude oil pipelines from the U.S. government. This transaction allowed for natural gas transmission services to reach from the fields of east Texas to the northeastern part of the United States. In 1989, Texas Eastern became a wholly owned subsidiary of Panhandle Eastern in a $3.32 billion deal. The two companies together became known as PanEnergy and operated four major pipelines: Panhandle Eastern Pipe Line, Trunkline Gas, Texas Eastern Transmission, and Algonquin Gas Transmission.

In 1997 Duke Energy gained national attention when it announced the merger of Duke Power, a leading electric utility headquartered in Charlotte, North Carolina, with PanEnergy. In 2002 Duke Energy purchased East Tennessee Natural Gas from El Paso Energy and Market Hub Partners LP, a natural gas salt cavern storage business. Two years later, Duke Energy acquired Westcoast Energy. This move significantly strengthened the company's natural gas transmission and

## COMPANY PERSPECTIVES

We will create superior and sustainable value for our investors, customers, employees, and communities by providing natural gas gathering, processing, transmission, storage, and distribution services

storage capacity by adding 6,000 miles of transmission pipeline, 155 billion cubic feet of storage, and 16,500 miles of distribution pipeline. Duke Energy had established itself as a premier diversified energy corporation.

By the beginning of 2006, the energy industry was experiencing changes that had not been fully anticipated. For instance, the stock market was unsteady, which meant that trade in the merchant power plant business (companies that produce power as a commodity) was volatile. In addition, affiliate rules had become more restrictive than ever, and industry experts debated whether the power industry should be disaggregated, or separated. All of these factors prompted Duke Energy's board of directors to begin evaluating the advantages and disadvantages of operating a combined electric power and gas company. They found that the interaction of the diverse business groups within Duke Energy had become complicated. Furthermore, the investment community showed an inclination not to value the combined unit. "It became clear," said Duke energy's chairman and CEO Paul M. Anderson, "that today's market awards a higher value to pure-play companies than to energy superstores."

In June 2006 Duke Energy's board of directors voted to spin off its natural gas business in a move that would create a publicly traded, pure-play company devoted to only one line of business. The result was Spectra Energy. From June to December, Duke Energy's executives separated the gas assets from the electric, created a management team, and named a board of directors for Spectra Energy. A strategy for growth was developed, along with a financial plan to support that strategy. When the market opened on January 2, 2007, Duke Energy shareholders received one share of Spectra Energy for every two shares of Duke Energy they owned.

### COMPANY DYNAMICS

Spectra Energy executives were excited about the potential of Spectra Energy as an independent company in the natural gas services business. In a Letter from the Chairman titled "Why Spectra Energy? Why Now?" available on the company's Web site, chairman of the board Paul M. Anderson called Spectra Energy a "'designer company' formed to aggressively pursue myriad opportunities that are emerging in the rapidly evolving North America natural gas industry."

In 2006 financial experts in the natural gas energy sector had predicted that the demand for natural gas would increase by more than 75 percent by 2030, in relation to a 60 percent rise in global energy demand during the same time frame. As a result, many companies were preparing for significant infrastructure growth and development. Since it had been separated from Duke Energy, the organization of Spectra Energy had a solid foundation of experience, assets, and customer relationships, giving it an edge over similar start-up enterprises. The president and CEO of Spectra Energy at the time of its formation until December 2008 was Fred J. Fowler, former president of Duke Energy Gas Transmission. Analyzing market forecasts, Fowler realized the potential Spectra Energy had to capitalize on the shifting dynamics in the natural gas industry and the vast opportunities for expansion.

According to the letter "Where Is Spectra Energy Going? How Will We Get There?" on the company's Web site, Fowler believed that Spectra Energy was created at "the right time—and for all the right reasons." Spectra Energy would be a powerhouse in the natural gas market because, he stated, "We know the business of natural gas infrastructure. We know our markets—and the shifting dynamics of our sector. We know how to grow—and how to finance growth and deliver lasting value. We know our customers—and they know us." The confidence of both Fowler and Anderson helped show the business community that Spectra Energy would be held to high expectations from within to meet the high expectations of investors and the general public.

### MIDSTREAM OPERATIONS

The natural gas industry is typically divided into upstream, downstream, and midstream sectors. Often described as the exploration and production area, the upstream segment focuses on finding and producing natural gas. The downstream sector handles the sales and distribution of natural gas and products derived from or associated with natural gas. From the start, Spectra Energy was classified a midstream business because it specialized in natural gas gathering and processing, transmission, and storage and distribution services. As such, Spectra Energy conducted its midstream business through four segments: U.S. Transmission, Western Canada Transmission and

## KEY DATES

**2007:** Spectra Energy separates from Duke Energy and becomes an independent publicly traded company.
**2007:** Spectra Energy forms Spectra Energy Partners, LP, a master limited partnership (MLP).
**2008:** The company is named to the Dow Jones Sustainability Index for North America.
**2008:** Fred J. Fowler retires as president and CEO and is replaced by Greg Ebel.
**2009:** Spectra Energy Partners, LP, acquires Ozark Gas Transmission and Ozark Gas Gathering.

Processing, Union Gas Distribution, and DCP Midstream Field Services. Each of the company's multiple subsidiaries fulfills its various functions as part of a midstream conglomerate. Each major business is described as follows:

The U.S. Transmission segment, which included the storage of natural gas as well as its transmission, provided pipeline infrastructure and storage services for the conveyance of gas from various supply sources to key markets in the Mid-Atlantic and northeastern United States. Received from producing areas in Canada and along the Gulf Coast, natural gas was transported using one of the largest natural gas systems in the United States, consisting of close to 19,100 miles and 285 billion cubic feet of storage capacity. In 2010 Spectra Energy utilized five primary U.S. transmissions systems for its standard daily operations: Texas Eastern, Algonquin, East Tennessee, Maritimes & Northeast Pipeline, and Gulfstream. All of these pipelines were capable of delivering vast amounts of natural gas to markets all over the United States and Canada.

The Western Canada Transmission and Processing segment of Spectra Energy's operations included the divisions of BC Pipeline, BC Field Services, Midstream, and an Empress System for natural gas liquids (NGLs). Fully regulated by Canada's National Energy Board, in 2009 BC Pipeline controlled about 1,800 miles of natural gas transmission pipeline. The purpose of BC Field Services was to gather raw natural gas from such diverse supply sources as the Yukon and Alberta and transport them to one of five natural gas processing facilities. To compete in the NGL field, Spectra Energy established the Empress System to extract, transport, store, and market natural liquid gasses.

Union Gas Limited, an integrated natural gas storage, transmission, and distribution company, joined Spectra Energy in the split from Duke Energy in 2007. First incorporated in 1922, Union Gas had assets of $5 billion and approximately 2,200 employees at the end of 2009. Through this Canadian subsidiary, Spectra Energy provided retail distribution services to some 1.3 million residential, commercial, and industrial customers in over 400 Ontario communities. Union Gas operated the Dawn Hub, the largest underground natural gas storage facility in Canada and one of the largest in North America. The Dawn Hub averaged more than 7.5 billion cubic feet per day of natural gas trading activity in 2009 alone. In addition to serving Ontario, Union Gas provided storage and transportation services to other utilities and customers in Quebec and the United States. (In 2010 Union Gas introduced several new programs for power-producing customers, giving them more flexibility in requesting changes to their service and more options for delivery services.)

As a result of Duke Energy's January 2007 spin-off, Duke Energy Field Services changed its name to DCP Midstream. Soon after, through a joint venture with ConocoPhillips, Spectra Energy extended its midstream business interests to include DCP Midstream, one of the largest NGL marketers in the United States. With plants in 17 states, the company gathered and transported over 6.6 billion cubic feet of raw natural gas, produced around 360,000 barrels of NGL, and marketed and traded an average of 450,000 barrels of NGL each day in 2009.

## EXPANSION

In 2007 Spectra Energy formed Spectra Energy Partners, LP, a master limited partnership based in Delaware that owned and operated natural gas pipeline and storage businesses. With a management team experienced in commercial operations, regulatory and ratemaking policies, and strategic analysis, Spectra Energy Partners facilitated investment opportunities. In 2009 Spectra Energy Partners, LP, purchased Ozark Gas Transmission and Ozark Gas Gathering. By the spring of 2010 its major operations included East Tennessee Natural Gas, Ozark Gas Transmission, Saltville Gas Storage Company, Gulfstream Natural Gas (24.5 percent ownership), and Market Hub Partners (50 percent ownership).

From the time it became its own entity, Spectra Energy embarked on a number of pipeline extension projects. In 2007 it initiated 13 projects at a capital cost of $650 million. The year 2008 saw 19 ventures, while 10 jobs were begun in 2009. The development was planned at sites throughout Spectra Energy's North American region. In Fort Nelson, British Columbia, for example, Spectra Energy kicked off a multiphase expansion program that included reactivating an existing processing facility to increase capacities for gathering and processing natural gas from the Horn River. Also begun in 2009 was the development of a new salt dome storage cavern in Acadia Parish in Louisiana. By mid-December 2009, 9 out of 10 of its expansion projects scheduled for the year had been completed.

According to an article by Fred Nieto, Spectra Energy's "capital spending for 2010 included 11 projects (valued at $1 billion total) with expansion focused on the Northeast, specifically opportunities in the Marcellus shale, an area in the Appalachian Range." Florida is also a specific target, reported Nieto, "due to the state increasing the amount of its natural gas-fired power generation." Completion dates for Spectra Energy's 2010 expansion projects ranged from spring 2010 to November 2013. One of these, the Texas Eastern Appalachia to Market Expansion Program (TEAM), drew a great deal of industry attention. TEAM was designed add to the security, reliability, and diversity of supply options for moving natural gas supplies from the Appalachian region to markets in the Northeast. Unique to the natural gas industry, TEAM would allow shippers the opportunity to develop custom transportation services using multiple existing and proposed new receipt points.

In 2009 Spectra Energy's total revenues dipped slightly, but the young company continued to post a healthy profit. This financial well-being emboldened the company to continue its strategy of undertaking substantial projects like TEAM. Said Greg Ebel, who became Spectra Energy's president and CEO in 2008, "Our assets are fully built and with both the combination of good luck and good foresight, we're in a great

position to be able to take advantage of these large plays."

*Alicia Elley*

## PRINCIPAL SUBSIDIARIES

Algonquin Gas Transmission L.L.C.; DCP Midstream LLC (50%); East Tennessee Natural Gas L.L.C.; Maritimes & Northeast Pipeline LLC (78%); Market Hub Partners Canada L.P.; Saltville Gas Storage Company L.L.C.; Spectra Energy Transmission L.L.C.; Texas Eastern Transmission L.P.; Union Gas Limited (Canada); Western Transmission Company Limited (Canada).

## PRINCIPAL COMPETITORS

Crosstex Energy Inc.; Enbridge Energy Management L.L.C.; Energy Transfer Equity L.P.; Enterprise GP Holdings L.P.; NuStar Energy L.P.; ONEOK Inc.; Plains All American Pipeline L.P.; Targa Resources Partners L.P.

## FURTHER READING

Hitchings, Monique, and Frank Nieto, "Spectra Energy Focuses on Western Canada for Growth," *Global Refining & Fuels Report,* October 7, 2009, p. 14.

Nieto, Frank, "Spectra Energy: Consistent Growth through Cost Reductions, Strong Projects," *Gas Processors Report,* December 10, 2009, p. 3.

Peters, Josh, and Avi Feinberg, "Spectra Energy SE," *Morningstar Dividend Investor,* January 2010, p. 19.

Schroeter, Jeffrey W., "The Merchant Revolution," *Mechanical Engineering Power,* May 2000.

Tubb, Rita, "Natural Gas Demand Continues to Drive Worldwide Pipeline Construction Activity," *Pipeline & Gas Journal,* January 1, 2008.

# Vitacost.com Inc.

**5400 Broken Sound Blvd, NW**
**Suite 500**
**Boca Raton, Florida 33487**
**U.S.A.**
**Telephone: (561) 982-4180**
**Toll Free: (800) 381-0759**
**Web site: http://www.vitacost.com**

*Public Company*
*Founded:*1994 as Nature's Wealth Company
*Employees:* 292 (2009)
*Net Sales:* $191.8 million (2009)
*Stock Exchanges:* NASDAQ
*Ticker Symbol:* VTC
*NAICS:* 325411 Medicinal and Botanical Manufacturing; 454111 Electronic Shopping.

∎∎∎

Vitacost.com Inc. is a leading online retail and direct marketing company of products and services to promote health and wellness. The company's product line is designed to meet the needs of a range of demographic groups, including adults, children, and pets, and includes items from four main categories: vitamins, minerals, herbs, and supplements; bodybuilding and sport products; natural care products; and natural and organic food products. Consumers can find a wide range of goods to meet a variety of needs, from acne to anti-aging products, weight loss to muscle building, and shampoo to salad dressing. Products are available to address a number of medical conditions including high blood pressure, diabetes, and allergies. These products can be purchased through the company Web site or print catalog.

The inventory available through Vitacost.com includes more than 30,000 products offered by more than 1,600 brands, including the company's own Nutraceutical Sciences Institute (NSI), Cosmeceutical Sciences Institute (CSI), Best of All, Smart Basics, and Walker Diet brands. These proprietary products accounted for approximately 30 percent of the company's sales in 2009. Third-party products offered represent most major domestic brands of vitamins and supplements, in addition to products from many smaller specialty brands. Available product lines include Atkins, Burt's Bees, Carson, Jarrow, Kashi, Nature's Way, New Chapter, Rainbow Light, and Twinlab.

Vitacost.com's operations include the company's call centers, manufacturing plants, and two distribution centers. Products can be shipped to Canada, Hong Kong, and Taiwan, in addition to the United States. The company does not charge membership fees. At the end of 2009, Vitacost.com reported approximately 1.1 million customers over the previous 12-month period, which was a 35 percent increase over the previous year. Since its beginning, the company has completed more than 10 million customer orders. In 2009 about 80 percent of orders were from repeat customers.

## NATURE'S WEALTH COMPANY: 1994

Vitacost.com was founded in 1994 as Nature's Wealth Company, a catalog retailer of vitamins and supplements. The company began in Springfield, Illinois, although two years after its beginning, the operation was relocated to Boynton Beach, Florida, to gain significantly more warehouse space. Nature's Wealth was founded by Dr. Allen Josephs, a neurologist, and Wayne Gorsek, an entrepreneur, and it was backed by approximately 200 investors.

Since the company's founding, Josephs served in several positions, including president, director of research, CEO, and chairman of the board, while continuing to practice medicine. He also authored the company's weekly "For Your Health" online newsletter. Gorsek, who is self-taught in the field of natural health alternatives, convinced Josephs of the benefits of vitamins prior to their cofounding of the company. He served as the company's CEO until the beginning of 2007, at which time he resigned, serving as a consultant until July 2008. From that point, he served as chief operations architect, a nonexecutive position, until his retirement in December 2009.

### NEW BEGINNINGS: 1999–2000

Five years after the company's beginning, several changes took place. In July 1999 Nature's Wealth raised $1.5 million of working capital through the private placement of some of the company's common stock. The required investment was a minimum of $300,000 from each potential stock holder. Also in 1999, the e-commerce Web site Vitacost.com was introduced, allowing customers to purchase products online as well as from the catalog. Although the company continued to offer its products through its print catalogue, by 2007 90 percent of sales were made via the Internet. At the same time as the launch of the online retailing aspect of Nature's Wealth, the company introduced its own line of vitamins and supplements, offered under its proprietary NSI brand.

Nature's Wealth began operating under the name Vitacost.com, Inc., the following year. During 2000 Vitacost.com was recognized for its unique, conservative

business practices. While other companies sold similar goods, Vitacost.com required that all products be strictly overseen by a group of highly qualified physicians and considered to be safe for consumers. In February 2000 an article in *Newsweek* promoted the fact that Vitacost.com refused to sell products it believed to be dangerous or useless. According to the article, "Vitacost sends products to an independent lab for testing. A recent look at popular arthritis remedies, for example, found that one contained only one fifteenth the recommended dose of its active ingredient." Another example of the company's strict monitoring of the product lines it sells was the fact that Vitacost refused to sell products that contained ephedra, an ingredient commonly found in weight loss supplements but considered to be potentially dangerous. Josephs told *Knight Ridder/Tribune Business News,* "We're a business, but we also want to help consumers make safe and educated decisions about the products they buy." During 2000 the company's annual revenues reached $3.6 million, which was a 1,000 percent increase over its revenues from 1996.

### INCREASING ONLINE PRESENCE: 2001–02

During 2001 Vitacost.com acquired four health Web sites, which increased the company's customer base by 700 percent, as well as increasing the company's revenues considerably. The acquisition added Healthshop.com, Healthzone.com, Smartbasics.com, and Vitamindiscount.com to Vitacost's family. Healthshop.com, also an online health and wellness site, had recently added a natural and organic foods component, which included more than 1,800 specialty grocery items, the majority of which were organic. HealthZone.com offered more than 16,000 products related to health and wellness, and it owned Healthshop.com and Smartbasics.com. With the addition of these sites, Vitacost.com anticipated a 100 percent increase in annual revenues as compared to the previous year.

In July 2002 Vitacost.com paid $186,000 to purchase the assets of DrKoop.com, a company which had previously filed bankruptcy. Originally, DrKoop.com was cofounded by U.S. surgeon general Dr. C. Everett Koop to "provide online health information to consumers in areas such as chronic illness, food and nutrition, fitness, and medical breakthroughs. Early on, this Web site was an overwhelming success, receiving a million hits per month after 2 years of operation, and about 4 million unique visitors per month at its peak," according to the *Encyclopedia of E-Commerce, E-Government and Mobile Commerce.* At one time, DrKoop.com had been valued at more than $1 billion. However, when the dot-com bubble burst around the

## KEY DATES

**1994:** Nature's Wealth Company founded in Springfield, Illinois, as a catalog-based retailer of vitamins and supplements.
**1999:** Vitacost.com is introduced as the company's e-commerce Web site; the company launches its own line of vitamins and supplements.
**2000:** Nature's Wealth Company changes its name to Vitacost.com, Inc.
**2006:** Vitacost.com is inducted into *Inc.* magazine's "Inc. 500 Lifetime Hall of Fame" as a result of being one of the 500 fastest-growing privately held companies in the United States during the previous five consecutive years.
**2009:** Vitacost.com becomes a public company.

beginning of the 21st century, DrKoop.com crashed as its investors fled in droves. Vitacost.com bought the company with the belief that online medical information was still a potential growth area. The purchase included the names, trademarks, Web site, and the e-mail addresses of those registered with the site.

### CONTINUED GROWTH: 2004–08

Two years after purchasing DrKoop.com, Vitacost.com, Inc., sold Vitacost Holdings, Inc., to Choice Media, Inc., an Internet health care information network that specialized in marketing and advertising for health care businesses. The acquisition gave DrKoop.com to Choice Media and opened the door for Choice Media to offer pharmaceutical manufacturers a larger advertising network.

In 2006 Vitacost.com was honored by *Inc.* magazine when it was inducted into the "Inc. 500 Lifetime Hall of Fame." This recognition came as a result of being one of the 500 fastest-growing privately held companies in the United States during five consecutive years, from 2001 through 2005.

In June 2007 Vitacost.com filed for an initial public offering (IPO) of its stock with the Securities and Exchange Commission. At the time, the company hoped to raise as much as $57 million through the IPO. However, by the beginning of 2008, the stock market decline caused concern that there would not be sufficient demand for the stock, so financial advisors recommended waiting for conditions to improve before offering the stock to the public.

In April 2008 the company's manufacturing facility in Lexington, North Carolina, was built and began producing the majority of the company's proprietary products in-house. This gave Vitacost.com the capability to produce more than one billion tablets and capsules each year. The transition from using third-party manufacturers to using the company's own manufacturing facility resulted in short-term losses of about $3.2 million. However, this change was expected to add to the company's profit in the months following the transition.

Annual sales for the company continued to climb, aided in part by consumers' increased attention to issues of health and nutrition. A survey conducted by Ipsos-Public Affairs for the Council for Responsible Nutrition (CRN) in 2008 reported that 64 percent of adults in the United States used dietary supplements at some point during that year. Vitacost.com's net sales for 2008 reached $143.6 million.

### A PUBLIC COMPANY: 2009

Although leaders at Vitacost.com had been planning to take the company public for approximately three years, the time had not been right. However, this changed during 2009. The market showed improvement during March, and in September Vitacost's representatives began presenting the company to potential investors. On September 24, 2009, Vitacost.com common stock was first traded on the NASDAQ Global Market under the symbol VTC.

Net proceeds from the initial public offering were approximately $47.1 million, which was intended to retrofit the company's manufacturing equipment and pay down some outstanding debts. Following the IPO, the company's 11 officers and directors owned about 17.5 percent of Vitacost's stock.

In 2009 the *Nutrition Business Journal's* 2009 U.S. Nutrition Industry Overview projected that sales of dietary supplements would grow at a rate of about 5 percent each year over the following five-year period. This indicated continued growth for the health and wellness industry. Vitacost.com's net sales for 2009 totaled $191.8 million, which was an increase of approximately $48 million over the previous year.

On March 3, 2010, Great Hill Partners, an investment firm based in Boston, Massachusetts, invested more than $60 million to acquire 19.7 percent of the common stock of Vitacost.com, making the investment company the majority stock holder.

According to the company's annual report filed in March 2010, Vitacost.com expected an increased demand for dietary supplements and health and wellness products in the future as a result of an increased focus on healthy living, a shift from health care to prevention, an increased acceptance of dietary supplements, and the aging population in the United States. A 2008 study by the Natural Marketing Institute reported that nearly 60 percent of consumers in the United States were interested in health and wellness. In addition, about 80 percent of doctors and nurses in the country recommended the use of dietary supplements. As a result of the rising costs of health care, the U.S. government and citizens have turned their focus to preventive care measures. Vitacost.com expected this trend to result in increased sales of vitamins, supplements, and health and wellness products to improve health, while reducing expenditures for health care.

Despite the aforementioned trend, in April 2010 the company announced that it had decreased its revenue estimates for first quarter and full year profits. Reasons for the cut included disappointing sales, manufacturing problems at the North Carolina facility which delayed more than $1 million in shipments, and increased sales of third-party products, which were less profitable to the company.

As it looked to the future, Vitacost.com planned to expand internationally. As of 2010, about 98 percent of the company's sales were to customers in the United States. However, the company planned to translate the Vitacost.com Web site into several languages that would allow products to be marketed in countries throughout Asia, Europe, and Latin America. It seemed likely that this international expansion, as well as current health care trends among consumers, would show continued growth for Vitacost.com.

*Diane Milne*

## PRINCIPAL SUBSIDIARIES

Vitacost Limited (Ireland).

## PRINCIPAL DIVISIONS

Bodybuilding and Sport Products; Natural and Organic Food Products; Natural Care Products; Vitamins, Minerals, Herbs, and Supplements.

## PRINCIPAL COMPETITORS

Amazon.com Inc.; CVS Pharmacy Inc.; Drugstore.com Inc.; General Nutrition Centers Inc.; Herbalife Ltd.; Puritan's Pride; Rite Aid Corp.; USANA Health Sciences Inc.; Vitamin Shoppe Inc.; Vitamin World Inc.; Walgreen Co; Wal-Mart Stores Inc.; Whole Foods Market Inc.

## FURTHER READING

"Boynton's Vitacost.com Acquires Four Health Care Sites," *Miami Daily Business Review* 75, no. 172, 2001.

Fakler, John T., "David Meets Goliath of Nutritional Supplements," *South Florida Business Journal,* May 25, 2000, p. 60A.

Fisher, Margie, "586% Sales Growth: Lessons from Vitacost. com," philippine-imarketing.com.

Hawkins, James, "DrKoop Hits the Skids," *Physician Executive* 28, no. 5 (September-October 2002): 5.

"HealthZone.com Closes Acquisition with Industry's Premier E-Commerce Site, HealthShop.com,"*PR Newswire,* May 25, 2000.

O'Buyonge, A. Abrams, and Leida Chen, "E-Health Dot-Coms' Critical Success Factors,"*Encyclopedia of E-Commerce, E-Government and Mobile Commerce.* Vol. 1. Hershey, PA: Idea Group Reference, 2006, p. 370–84.

Singer, Glenn, "Boynton Beach, Fla.-Based Internet Store Takes Conservative Approach for Site," *Knight Ridder/Tribune Business News,* December 18, 2000.

"Vitacost CEO Kerker Helped Take Boca Supplement Firm Public," *Palm Beach Daily Business Review,* January 13, 2010.

Williams, Stephen, "A Flag for the Dregs," *Newsweek,* February 28, 2000, p. 74.

# WESCO International, Inc.

225 West Station Square Drive
Suite 700
Pittsburgh, Pennsylvania 15219
U.S.A.
Telephone: (412) 454-2200
Fax: (412) 454-2505
Web site: http://www.wesco.com

*Public Company*
*Founded:* 1922
*Employees:* 6,100 (2009)
*Sales:* $4.624 billion (2009)
*Stock Exchanges:* New York
*Ticker Symbol:* WCC
*NAICS:* 423610 Companies in Electrical Apparatus and Equipment, Wiring Supplies, and Related Equipment Merchant Wholesalers; 423830 Companies in Industrial Machinery and Equipment Merchant Wholesalers; 423840 Companies in Industrial Supplies Merchant Wholesalers

∎ ∎ ∎

WESCO International, Inc., is a publicly traded holding company for WESCO Distribution, Inc. Headquartered in Pittsburgh, Pennsylvania, the company has an international presence in Australia, Canada, China, Mexico, Nigeria, the United Kingdom, United Arab Emirates, and Singapore. Through seven highly automated distribution centers and approximately 400 branch locations, WESCO provides electrical and lighting products, wire and conduit materials, and automa-

tion and data communication equipment to over 115,000 customers of all sizes worldwide. WESCO's biggest customers range from Boeing to PepsiCo to Dow Chemical. Offering more than one million products from some 23,000 different suppliers, WESCO is one of the largest providers of industrial maintenance, repair, and operating (MRO) supplies in the United States. The company serves a wide range of markets, including electrical contractors, municipal power authorities, public power cooperatives, government agencies, telecommunications businesses, and educational institutions, among others.

## WESTINGHOUSE SUBSIDIARY: 1922–94

The history of WESCO dates back to 1886, when inventor and entrepreneur George Westinghouse founded the Westinghouse Electric Corporation in Pittsburgh. The company was one of the nation's first commercial alternating current power generating stations, lighting the city of Great Barrington, Massachusetts. In 1893, Westinghouse provided lighting for the World's Fair held in Chicago. The company introduced the first U.S. public utility steam turbine generator, followed by the first main-line, alternating-current-powered train in 1905, and the first all-electric kitchen range in 1917. Five years later, Westinghouse formed the Westinghouse Electric Supply Company (WESCO) as its distribution arm.

WESCO, which sold electrical products manufactured by Westinghouse, supplied customers across the country for over 70 years. During that time,

## COMPANY PERSPECTIVES

Our mission is to be a high-performance organization delivering a competitive advantage to our customers through innovative product solutions and value-added services.

Our vision is to become the recognized distribution leader in the industrial, construction, and utility supply chains for electrical and industrial products and services that provide superior customer value and shareholder returns.

WESCO's business strategy was centered around meeting industry needs by providing inventory, technical expertise, and products quickly, striving to meet its goal of consistent accuracy. In 1974 WESCO entered the international market when it opened an office in Saudi Arabia, as well as a domestic export operations office in Pittsburgh. From 1922 to 1994, the company recorded around $1.5 billion in sales, with approximately 85 percent of its transactions in the area of nonresidential construction. WESCO conducted business through some 175 branches in the United States and Canada and gradually expanded its operations to include limited supply relationships with companies other than Westinghouse.

## INTERNATIONAL GROWTH: 1994–2001

In 1994 the private investment company of Clayton, Dubilier, & Rice (CD&R), which had been serving as WESCO's management team, purchased WESCO from Westinghouse. CD&R, known for its success in creating new growth-centered corporate environments led by strong management teams, turned WESCO's focal point onto acquisitions. In its first six years under the leadership of CD&R, WESCO acquired 25 companies, which represented annual sales in 2000 of $1.3 billion. Such transactions expanded WESCO's geographic footprint, as well as diversified its end-markets and supplier base. Businesses taken over by WESCO included Control Corporation of America (2000), Liberty Electrical Supply Co., Inc. (1999), WR Control Panels, Inc. (1998), Diversified Electric Supply Company (1997), Nevada Electrical Supply (1996), and Manufactured Housing Supply (1995).

In April 1998 a leveraged recapitalization was initiated by WESCO management. Receiving sponsorship from an investment group led by The Cyprus Group, the management of WESCO attained the company from CD&R in a buyout exceeding $1.1 billion. WESCO International, Inc., a new holding company, was formed as a result of the recapitalization. WESCO International, Inc., made its initial public offering of common stock on the New York Stock Exchange on May 12, 1999. Shares offered when trading began numbered 9.72 million, costing $18.00 per share.

The growth WESCO enjoyed from 1994 to 2001 included more than company takeovers. Sales from 1994 to 2001 grew to $3.7 billion. In addition, WESCO launched two programs that would prove instrumental to the company's business strategy: the National Accounts Program and the Integrated Supply Program. According to the company's Web site, "WESCO's National Accounts Program offers customer savings through inventory and transaction cost reduction, SKU consolidation, price and productivity improvements, application engineering, and energy savings." National Account Managers worked alongside experts in implementation and cost improvement, contract administrators, and pricing analysts to develop service and supply programs specific to individual clients.

Integrated Supply is an industry term describing the result of a company's consolidating its supplier base for the purpose of increasing efficiency in purchasing and pricing. WESCO's Integrated Supply Program was operated primarily through the Bruckner Supply Company, which it had acquired in 1998. Both the National Accounts Program and the Integrate Supply Program would continue to be key business functions into the 2010s.

## INDUSTRY DOWNTURN: 2001–03

Beginning in 2001 and lasting through 2003, WESCO was affected by a severe downturn in the electrical supply industry. In response, WESCO suspended its acquisition program and concentrated on investing in sales and marketing, as well as generating a strong cash flow. WESCO was one of 87 U.S. companies that drew criticism from such consumer groups as Citizens for Tax Justice and the Institute on Taxation and Economic Policy for being exempt from paying federal income taxes at least one year between 2001 and 2003. Some companies received tax breaks even if they did not pay taxes, with many companies requesting refunds of taxes paid in years past. According to the report *Corporate Income Taxes in the Bush Years,* Internal Revenue Service tax settlements reduced WESCO's federal income tax by $5 million in 2002 and $3 million in 2003. Amortization of intangibles, which is a method of writing off the

## KEY DATES

**1922:** Westinghouse Electric Corporation forms WESCO to sell Westinghouse-manufactured products.

**1994:** WESCO is purchased from Westinghouse by Clayton, Dubilier & Rice.

**1999:** WESCO International, Inc., goes public on the New York Stock Exchange.

**2003:** WESCO's LEAN program is launched.

**2006:** WESCO enters the voice-data-video market with its takeover of Communications Supply Corporation.

**2007:** WESCO acquires J-Mark Inc., Monti Electric Supply, and Deutsch Engineered Connecting Devices.

capital costs of assets over a fixed period of time, allowed WESCO to claim tax savings of $3 million in 2001, $6 million in 2002, and $7 million in 2003.

In the spring of 2003 WESCO introduced its LEAN project, which the company broadly referred to at the time as "the process of continuously eliminating waste across the business and value chain." Its initial application was in sales and warehousing. As the program proved to be highly successful, WESCO expanded the scope of LEAN through the years so that it became recognized as a company-wide strategic program to increase productivity in administration, sales, and operations. LEAN initiatives eventually focused largely on nine target areas: warehouse operations, sales, pricing, transportation, purchasing, inventory, accounts receivable, administrative procedures, and accounts payable.

### ECONOMIC RECOVERY: 2004–07

The next few years reflected economic recovery for WESCO. The company resumed its acquisition program, in addition to expanding its product categories. By investing in its marketing programs, WESCO was able to improve both its capital structure and its sales growth. From 2004 through 2007, for instance, the company posted sales of $6.1 billion, with $1.1 billion of that amount coming from seven new acquisitions. WESCO announced on July 29, 2005, that The Cypress Group LLC and its affiliate stockholders had agreed to sell their remaining 9,075,536 shares of WESCO common stock. Since all net proceeds from the sale would go to the selling stockholders, WESCO

would not receive any money from the transaction. That same year, WESCO Distribution entered into an agreement to sell $150 million of its Senior Subordinated Notes due in 2017. (A subordinated note is a bond that may be converted into common stock. If the issuer goes bankrupt and is forced to liquidate its assets, other debt must be repaid before the subordinate note is repaid.) WESCO planned to use net proceeds from the sale to help finance its acquisition of the Carlton-Bates Company.

In August 2005, WESCO announced an agreement to purchase the Carlton-Bates Company, located in Little Rock, Arkansas. The all-cash transaction gave WESCO a stronger presence in the original equipment manufacturer (OEM) market. Carlton-Bates specialized in the production of such electrical components as switches, diodes, motor starters, relays, fuses, and cable. The company also offered a line of programmable industrial workstations, logic controllers, and input/output systems. At the time WESCO acquired the company, Carlton-Bates served approximately 20,000 customers with an inventory in excess of 80,000 units and posted sales of around $300 million. Quoted in *Electrical Wholesaling*'s article, "WESCO agrees to Purchase Carlton-Bates," WESCO chairman and chief executive officer Ron Haley commented, "This important acquisition provides a unique opportunity to more deeply penetrate the original equipment manufacturer market segment with specialty products, applications and value-added services."

On November 6, 2006, WESCO announced the completion of its acquisition of Communications Supply Corporation (CSC), a company that distributed low-voltage network infrastructure products, as well as wire and cable products. CSC had been founded in 1972 as an independent distributor of telecommunications supplies and technology in the New England region. In the years before its buyout by WESCO, CSC had steadily acquired wire and cable suppliers in such areas as New York, New Jersey, Washington D.C., and Seattle and was the 14th largest distributor on *Electrical Wholesaling*'s "2006 Top 200 Distributors." WESCO's takeover of CSC marked its expansion into the voice-data-video market, as CSC, through a network of 32 branches, distributed a range of products to support voice and data communications, building automation, and security surveillance. The merger of WESCO and CSC resulted in the largest electrical and data communications distributions network in North America. By 2010 CSC, headquartered in Carol Stream, Illinois, had over 900 employees, 33 warehouses, and $90 million in inventory.

Along with the 2007 acquisitions of J-Mark Inc., a leading U.S. provider of interior products for the manufactured housing industry, and Monti Electric Supply, an electrical components distributor for construction projects, WESCO entered into a strategic venture with Deutsch Engineered Connecting Devices, Inc. WESCO and Deutsch intended to work together to increase business with existing customers in the specialized heavy-duty connector market.

## CONTINUED GROWTH

Besides continuing to accelerate its LEAN initiatives within the company in 2008 and 2009, WESCO concentrated on extending LEAN services directly to customers through a LEAN Customer Value Creation (LCVC) program. The LCVC process consisted of four steps. It began with WESCO representatives meeting with customers in order to establish the customers' goals in cost reduction and improvements in quality, productivity, and safety. Next, WESCO's team of solution experts reviewed the customers' goals, aligning them with LCVC solutions. After consulting with the client to prioritize solution options, WESCO representatives and customers teamed up for a Search for Savings event, in which opportunities to meet the goals and requirements of the customers were identified within the market. Finally, WESCO experts customized a solution plan that would maximize productivity and profit for the customer. LCVC centered around the solution categories of construction, engineering services, energy, sustainability, integrated supply, maintenance and production support, safety and security, supply chain optimization, training, and working capital.

In 2009 WESCO showed a disappointing performance margin due to the worldwide economic downturn that began in 2008. Factors contributing to WESCO's low numbers were less demand in construction markets, increased prices in such commodities as oil, and an ongoing decline in industrial demands for power. Revenue for 2009 was down 24 percent as compared to 2008. In response, management implemented a series of strategic cuts. These moves included closing some WESCO branches, laying off 16 percent of their workforce, and enforcing various discretionary spending freezes. The company also began to pursue economic stimulus funds offered by the federal government.

Despite financial difficulty, however, WESCO executives invested in its front end business, increasing its sales force by 5 percent in the fourth quarter of 2009. It expanded international operations, forming subsidiaries in China, Australia, and Africa. WESCO management expected capital expenditures for growth initiatives in 2010 to be around $20 million. Additionally, the company planned to explore opportunities for acquisitions, although management emphasized the importance of ensuring that any potential takeovers meet profit expectations. Overall, WESCO executives were optimistic about the company's financial performance and growth opportunities in 2010 and beyond.

*Alicia Elley*

## PRINCIPAL SUBSIDIARIES

Bruckner Supply Company, Inc.; Carlton-Bates Company; CDW Holdco, LLC; Communications Supply Company; WDC Holding, Inc.; WESCO Distribution, Inc.; WESCO Distribution Canada Company.

## PRINCIPAL DIVISIONS

Industrial; Construction; Utility; Commercial, Institutional, and Governmental.

## PRINCIPAL COMPETITORS

Airgas, Inc.; Anixter International, Inc.; Applied Industrial Technologies; BlueLinx Holdings; Genuine Parts Company; Graybar Electric Company, Inc.; Reliance Steel & Aluminum Company; W. W. Grainger, Inc.

## FURTHER READING

"Big Corporations Pay No Taxes Get Rewarded with Rebates," ibew.org, September 27, 2004.

Duvall, Mel, "The Path Less Taken: Wesco International Didn't Want to Pony Up Big Bucks for a Traditional Enterprise Resource Planning System," *Baseline* May 14, 2007.

Funk, Dale, "WESCO Agrees to Purchase Carlton-Bates," *Electrical Wholesaling,* September 1, 2005.

———, "WESCO Expands into VDV Market with Purchase of Csc," *Electrical Wholesaling,* November 1, 2006.

———, "WESCO Drops Out of Bidding War for IDG," *Electrical Wholesaling,* May 1, 2008.

McIntyre, Robert S., and T. D. Coo Nguyen, *Corporate Income Taxes in the Bush Years,* ctj.org, September 2004.

"WESCO Financial Corp.," in *Mergent's Handbook of NASDAQ Stocks.* New York: Mergent Inc., Fall 2008, p. 304.

"WESCO Sustainability Summits Energize Purchasing to Go Green," *Purchasing,* November 2009, p. 20–21.

# Westinghouse Air Brake Technologies Corporation

1001 Air Brake Avenue
Wilmerding, Pennsylvania 15148
U.S.A.
Telephone: (412) 825-1000
Fax: (412) 825-1019
Web site: http://www.wabtec.com

*Public Company*
*Founded:* 1869 as Westinghouse Air Brake Company
*Employees:* 5,812 (2009)
*Sales:* $1.4 billion
*Stock Exchange* New York
*Ticker Symbol:* WAB
*NAICS:* 336510 Railroad Rolling Stock Manufacturing

∎ ∎ ∎

Westinghouse Air Brake Technologies Corporation (Wabtec) came into being in November 1999, the result of a merger between Westinghouse Air Brake Company and Motive Power Industries. It is a world leader in the supply of equipment and aftermarket services to railroads and mass transit companies. Wabtec produces brake systems, electronic train control systems, switches, couplings, door control, and air conditioning systems. It also produces heat exchange equipment for rail, marine, power generation, industrial, and off road equipment. Sale of aftermarket parts and services accounts for about half of all revenue.

## THE WESTINGHOUSE YEARS

George Westinghouse (1846–1914) was one of the most prolific American inventors, industrialists, and entrepreneurs of the late eighteenth century. With little formal training in mechanical engineering, his knowledge was garnered first at his father's agricultural manufacturing business and later as an engineer on a U.S. naval vessel during the American Civil War.

Westinghouse's interest in railroad technology was sparked when in 1866 he learned of a train wreck in New York State. This accident was caused by a head-on collision of two freight trains. Despite good weather conditions and a level track, the trains were unable to stop in time. Part of the reason for this was that the breaking system in use at that time was a manually operated hand brake. In order to stop a train the engineer in the locomotive would sound the train's whistle. At the signal, brakemen would move from car to car to adjust the brakes. Each car was equipped with a brake wheel, which when turned would apply pressure to the brakes on the car's wheels. (The brakes were made of either wood or cast iron.)

The inherent drawbacks of this system were numerous. Often brakemen were forced to move from car to car by climbing onto the roof of the train, a precarious practice at best and often injurious or fatal. In addition, it was almost impossible to apply equal pressure to all brakes simultaneously. The amount of pressure depended on how well the brakemen understood the signals from the locomotive. Uneven pressure or worse, no pressure at all, could cause the cars to collide, thereby resulting in derailment. Emergency stopping was impossible.

Westinghouse had learned of a technique in Europe where compressed air was being used to power drills at a tunnel construction site. He began to work on the idea of using the force of compressed air as a method to activate the brakes on a train.

In the spring of 1869, Westinghouse patented his air brake system for trains. The system used compressed air from the locomotive to feed auxiliary tanks on each car. By raising or lowering the amount of air in the system, the engineer could control braking from the locomotive. This unified braking system provided for even pressure to be applied throughout the length of the train, greatly reducing the incidents of cars colliding and causing derailments. In September 1869, Westinghouse formed the Westinghouse Air Brake Company.

The development of the Westinghouse air brake was to have a profound effect on the railroad industry. It greatly increased the safety of rail travel and reduced the length of time required to plan a stop. In addition, it permitted heavier and longer trains to travel at higher speeds and still make safe and efficient stops. With shorter travel times trains reduced the amount of coal and water consumed by the locomotive. Last but not least, the air brake also made emergency stopping possible.

With so many inherent benefits, there was great demand for the new system. By 1874 the Westinghouse Air Brake Company had equipped 2,281 locomotives and 7,254 railroad cars with air brakes. Other nations soon realized the value of the new technology, and Westinghouse Air Brake entered a period of rapid international expansion starting with France (1878), England (1881), Germany (1884), and Russia (1899).

Demand soon outstripped the capacity of the company's original facility in Pittsburgh, Pennsylvania, so a larger facility was secured in Allegheny, Pennsyl-

vania. Within a decade, the company outgrew this facility as well. In need of a permanent home, the company purchased land at Wilmerding, Pennsylvania, and built both a plant and a town for its employees.

The Westinghouse Air Brake Company established itself as one of the most progressive employers of its time. It established Saturday as a half workday. It created a pension plan and provided group life insurance, disability payments, and medical services. It also allowed lengthy vacations for employees who had wokred with the company for a long period of time. These labor policies were put in place well before they became the norm in other industries.

## THE NEW CENTURY

By 1911 George Westinghouse had relinquished control of the Westinghouse Air Brake Company. He died three years later.

Operations at the company passed through a series of veteran employees, some having more than 40 years of service with the organization. The company continued to expand its business by adapting its technology to other forms of transportation. Growing urban populations led to increase demand for transit. Streetcars, subways, and buses provided new opportunities for the company's products. In 1921 Westinghouse Air Brake began to develop pneumatic breaking systems for automobiles and trucks.

During both world wars, the company produced munitions and electronic equipment for the military. During World War II, Westinghouse Air Brake developed pneumatic systems for the U.S. Navy and later adapted the same compressed air systems for the commercial marine industry.

With the end of World War II in 1945, the demand for railroad transportation began to decline. The development of the interstate highway system resulted in the automobile becoming the choice of consumers for short- to medium-length travel. The burgeoning airline business started to become the choice of business and long haul travelers. Passenger traffic by rail began to fall rapidly.

Freight traffic was similarly affected. With modern paved highways, the trucking industry was able to provide real competition to the railroads. In 1920 approximately 75 percent of all intercity freight was moved by rail. However, by 1975, it was only 35 percent.

Despite its efforts to adapt and improve its technology, Westinghouse Air Brake was still heavily dependent on the railroad industry. When railroad demand diminished, so did the demand for Westinghouse Air

## KEY DATES

**1869:** George Westinghouse patents air brake; Westinghouse Air Brake Company incorporated.
**1878:** First international facility opens in France.
**1968:** American Standard absorbs Westinghouse Air Brake Company and renames organization WABCO Railroad.
**1984:** William E. Kassling appointed head of WABCO Railroad.
**1990:** Kassling leads management buyout of WABCO Railroad Establishes Westinghouse Air Brake Co.
**1995:** Westinghouse Air Brake Co. begins trading on the NYSE.
**1999:** Westinghouse Air Brake Co. merges with MotivePower Industries and forms Westinghouse Air Brake Technologies Corporation.

Brake products. In 1968 the company was taken over by American Standard Companies Inc. American Standard was an established provider of air conditioning, plumbing, and transportation products. It placed the Westinghouse Air Brake Company into its railway products group as a division it named WABCO Railway.

In 1988 American Standard became the target of a hostile takeover bid by Black & Decker Corporation. In order to thwart the hostile bid American Standard succumbed to a bid by the California investment bank, Kelso & Company, a firm with ties to American Standard. In a leveraged buyout, Kelso & Company purchased American Standard for $3.2 billion in April 1988.

Although the buyout by Kelso & Company saved American Standard from Black & Decker, the new privately held company had a serious debt problem. Its long-term debt obligations were almost 90 percent of the firms's total capital, and its $250 million per year interest payments were an onerous burden on the struggling business.

With a serious debt problem and in need of cash, American Standard began to sell assets. In 1990 William E. Kassling, who had been in charge of WABCO Railway at American Standard since 1984, led a management buyout of the North American operations of the railway braking products group. The European operations were sold to a Swedish investment firm. The new company was renamed the Westinghouse Air Brake Co.

### WABTEC

Back on its own again, Westinghouse Air Brake Co. quickly established three goals. The first was to focus on international growth, the second to expand aftermarket services, and the third was to acquire companies with an entrepreneurial spirit. These goals guided the company's strategy during the 1990s and helped return it to health and increased profitability.

In 1995 Westinghouse Air Brake went public and began trading on the New York Stock Exchange. This provided capital to allow it to acquire companies. One year later, Westinghouse Air Brake purchased Australian Futuris Industrial Products and subway door maker Vapor Corp. In 1997 the company added Stone Safety Service Corporation and Stone UK Limited, a manufacturer of passenger train air conditioners. It also acquired an Italian door control company and the heavy rail air condition business of Thermos King.

In 1998, to augment its aftermarket product line, it bought the rail service centers of Comet Industries, the railway electronic division of Rockwell International, and the coupler company Lokring Corporation. Westinghouse Air Brake also purchased RFS (E) Limited, a British railway overhaul and maintenance provider.

Westinghouse Air Brake also entered into two joint ventures. One, in India, was created to sell railway brake shoes. The second was with MotivePower Industries, a U.S. company that manufactured components for locomotives and the marine, power, and industrial markets. The joint venture was to manufacture components for locomotives and railcars in Mexico. The joint venture with MotivePower was to prove significant. The two companies, sensitive to the business environment and with products and services that complemented each other, merged as equal partners in 1999 to form Westinghouse Air Brake Technologies.

### 21ST CENTURY: CONTINUED GROWTH

Operating under the name of Wabtec, the company continued the strategy of growth through acquisitions and international investment. Wabtec began to rationalize its operations by closing some facilities, moving some product lines offshore, and trimming its workforce.

In 2008 the company purchased Standard Car Truck Company, a manufacturer of railcar stabilization equipment. It also acquired a majority shareholding in Beijing Wabtec Huaxia Technology Company, a supplier of railroad friction products in China. In 2009 Wabtec entered into a 50-50 joint venture with Shenyang Locomotive and Rolling Stock Railway Brake Company.

Shenyang is China's largest manufacturer of locomotive and train car braking systems.

Westinghouse Air Brake Technology Company reported sales of $1.4 billion in 2009. This was a slight drop from the previous year, when sales were $1.57 billion. However, in 2009 legislation was passed by the U.S. Congress with billions earmarked to upgrade the nation's transportation infrastructure. Money was designated for proejcts such as high-speed rail ($8 billion), public transportation ($8.4 billion), and AMTRAK ($1.3 billion). Increased government spending on transportation infrastructure bodes well for Wabtec's fiscal future.

*Ian MacDonald*

## PRINCIPAL SUBSIDIARIES

Allied Friction Products Australia Pty. Ltd.; Becorit GmbH (Germany); Cardinal Pumps and Exchangers, Inc.; Durox Company; MotivePower, Inc.; Pioneer Friction Limited (India); Railroad Friction Products Corporation; Standard Car Truck Company; Unifin International LP (Canada); Vapor Europe S.r.L. (Italy); Vastbond Limited (Cyprus); Wabtec Corporation.

## PRINCIPAL COMPETITORS

Alstom S.A.; Electro-Motive Diesel, Inc.; GE Transportation Systems; New York Air Brake Company (Knorr Bremse GmbH).

## FURTHER READING

Babcock, Michael W., *Efficiency and Adjustment: The Impact of Railroad Deregulation.* Washington, DC: Cato Institute, January 31, 1984.

"Class 1s, The Industry Standards," American-rails.com, April 8, 2010.

Hambleton, Ronald, *The Branding of America.* Dublin, NH: Yankee Publishing, 1987

Rodrigue, J-P, C. Comtois, and B. Slack, *The Geography of Transport Systems.* 2nd ed. New York: Routledge, 2009.

New Zealand Government Railways Department, "The Westinghouse Air Brake," *Railway Magazine,* December 15, 1926.

# Cumulative Index to Companies

Listings in this index are arranged in alphabetical order under the company name. Company names beginning with a letter or proper name such as Eli Lilly & Co. will be found under the first letter of the company name. Definite articles (The, Le, La) are ignored for alphabetical purposes as are forms of incorporation that precede the company name (AB, NV). Company names printed in **bold** type have full, historical essays on the page numbers appearing in bold. Updates to entries that appeared in earlier volumes are signified by the notation (**upd.**). This index is cumulative with volume numbers printed in bold type.

Borland International, Inc., 9 80–82
Boron, LePore & Associates, Inc., 45 43–45
Borrego Solar Systems, Inc., 111 43–46
Borroughs Corporation, 110 59–63
BorsodChem Zrt., 113 58–61
Bosch *see* Robert Bosch GmbH.
Boscov's Department Store, Inc., 31 68–70
Bose Corporation, 13 108–10; 36 98–101 (upd.)
Boss Holdings, Inc., 97 78–81
Boston Acoustics, Inc., 22 97–99
Boston Apparel Group, 112 61–66 (upd.)
Boston Basketball Partners L.L.C., 115 69–74 (upd.)
The Boston Beer Company, Inc., 18 70–73; 50 111–15 (upd.); 108 111–18 (upd.)
Boston Celtics Limited Partnership, 14 67–69 *see also* Boston Basketball Partners L.L.C.
Boston Chicken, Inc., 12 42–44 *see also* Boston Market Corp.
The Boston Consulting Group, 58 32–35
Boston Edison Company, 12 45–47
*Boston Globe see* Globe Newspaper Company Inc.
Boston Market Corporation, 48 64–67 (upd.)
Boston Pizza International Inc., 88 33–38
Boston Professional Hockey Association Inc., 39 61–63
Boston Properties, Inc., 22 100–02
Boston Scientific Corporation, 37 37–40; 77 58–63 (upd.)
The Boston Symphony Orchestra Inc., 93 95–99
Botswana Life Insurance Limited, 116 83–86
Bou-Matic, 62 42–44
Boulanger S.A., 102 57–60
Bourbon *see* Groupe Bourbon S.A.
Bourbon Corporation, 82 49–52
Bouygues S.A., I 562–64; 24 77–80 (upd.); 97 82–87 (upd.)
Bovis *see* Peninsular and Oriental Steam Navigation Company (Bovis Division)
Bowater PLC, IV 257–59
Bowen Engineering Corporation, 105 39–42
Bowlin Travel Centers, Inc., 99 71–75
Bowman Distillery *see* A. Smith Bowman Distillery, Inc.
Bowne & Co., Inc., 23 61–64; 79 74–80 (upd.)
Bowthorpe plc, 33 70–72
The Boy Scouts of America, 34 66–69
Boyd Bros. Transportation Inc., 39 64–66
Boyd Coffee Company, 53 73–75
Boyd Gaming Corporation, 43 80–82
The Boyds Collection, Ltd., 29 71–73
Boyne USA Resorts, 71 65–68

Boys & Girls Clubs of America, 69 73–75
Bozell Worldwide Inc., 25 89–91
Bozzuto's, Inc., 13 111–12
BP p.l.c., 45 46–56 (upd.); 103 60–74 (upd.)
BPB plc, 83 46–49
Braathens ASA, 47 60–62
Brach's Confections, Inc., 15 63–65; 74 43–46 (upd.)
Bradford & Bingley PLC, 65 77–80
Bradlees Discount Department Store Company, 12 48–50
Bradley Air Services Ltd., 56 38–40
Brady Corporation, 78 50–55 (upd.)
Brake Bros plc, 45 57–59
Bramalea Ltd., 9 83–85
Brambles Industries Limited, 42 47–50
Brammer PLC, 77 64–67
The Branch Group, Inc., 72 43–45
BrandPartners Group, Inc., 58 36–38
Brannock Device Company, 48 68–70
Brascan Corporation, 67 71–73
Brasfield & Gorrie LLC, 87 72–75
Brasil Telecom Participaçoes S.A., 57 67–70
Braskem S.A., 108 119–22
Brass Eagle Inc., 34 70–72
Brauerei Beck & Co., 9 86–87; 33 73–76 (upd.)
Braun GmbH, 51 55–58; 109 76–81 (upd.)
Bravo Company, 114 81–84
Bravo Health Insurance Company, Inc., 107 53–56
Brazil Fast Food Corporation, 74 47–49
Brazos Sportswear, Inc., 23 65–67
Bread Loaf Corporation, 107 57–60
Breeze-Eastern Corporation, 95 67–70
Bremer Financial Corporation, 45 60–63; 105 43–49 (upd.)
Brenco, Inc., 104 39–42
Brenntag Holding GmbH & Co. KG, 8 68–69; 23 68–70 (upd.); 101 85–90 (upd.)
Brescia Group *see* Grupo Brescia.
Briazz, Inc., 53 76–79
The Brickman Group, Ltd., 87 76–79
Bricorama S.A., 68 62–64
Bridgelux, Inc., 112 67–69
Bridgepoint Education, Inc., 108 123–27
Bridgeport Machines, Inc., 17 52–54
Bridgestone Corporation, V 234–35; 21 72–75 (upd.); 59 87–92 (upd.)
Bridgford Foods Corporation, 27 71–73
Briggs & Stratton Corporation, 8 70–73; 27 74–78 (upd.)
Brigham Exploration Company, 75 72–74
Brigham's Inc., 72 46–48
Bright Horizons Family Solutions, Inc., 31 71–73
Brightpoint Inc., 18 74–77; 106 68–74 (upd.)
Brightstar Corp., 114 85–88
Brillstein-Grey Entertainment, 80 41–45

Brinker International, Inc., 10 176–78; 38 100–03 (upd.); 75 75–79 (upd.)
The Brink's Company, 58 39–43 (upd.)
BRIO AB, 24 81–83; 103 75–79 (upd.)
Brioche Pasquier S.A., 58 44–46
Brioni Roman Style S.p.A., 67 74–76
BRISA Auto-estradas de Portugal S.A., 64 55–58
Briscoe Group Ltd., 110 64–67
Bristol Farms, 101 91–95
Bristol Hotel Company, 23 71–73
Bristol-Myers Squibb Company, III 17–19; 9 88–91 (upd.); 37 41–45 (upd.); 111 47–54 (upd.)
Bristow Helicopters Ltd., 70 26–28
BRITA GmbH, 112 70–72
Britannia Soft Drinks Ltd. (Britvic), 71 69–71
Britannica.com *see* Encyclopaedia Britannica, Inc.
Brite Voice Systems, Inc., 20 75–78
British Aerospace plc, I 50–53; 24 84–90 (upd.) *see also* BAE Systems plc.
British Airways PLC, I 92–95; 14 70–74 (upd.); 43 83–88 (upd.); 105 50–59 (upd.)
British American Tobacco PLC, 50 116–19 (upd.); 114 89–95 (upd.)
British-Borneo Oil & Gas PLC, 34 73–75
British Broadcasting Corporation Ltd., 7 52–55; 21 76–79 (upd.); 89 111–17 (upd.)
British Coal Corporation, IV 38–40
British Columbia Telephone Company, 6 309–11
British Energy Plc, 49 65–68 *see also* British Nuclear Fuels PLC.
The British Film Institute, 80 46–50
British Gas plc, V 559–63 *see also* Centrica plc.
British Land Plc, 54 38–41
British Midland plc, 38 104–06
The British Museum, 71 72–74
British Nuclear Fuels PLC, 6 451–54
British Oxygen Co *see* BOC Group.
The British Petroleum Company plc, IV 378–80; 7 56–59 (upd.); 21 80–84 (upd.) *see also* BP p.l.c.
British Railways Board, V 421–24
British Sky Broadcasting Group plc, 20 79–81; 60 66–69 (upd.)
British Steel plc, IV 41–43; 19 62–65 (upd.)
British Sugar plc, 84 25–29
British Telecommunications plc, V 279–82; 15 66–70 (upd.) *see also* BT Group plc.
The British United Provident Association Limited, 79 81–84
British Vita plc, 9 92–93; 33 77–79 (upd.)
British World Airlines Ltd., 18 78–80
Britvic Soft Drinks Limited *see* Britannia Soft Drinks Ltd. (Britvic)
Broadcast Music Inc., 23 74–77; 90 74–79 (upd.)

Clear Channel Communications, Inc., 23 130–32; 116 121–25 (upd.)
Clearly Canadian Beverage Corporation, 48 94–97
Clearwire, Inc., 69 95–97
Cleary, Gottlieb, Steen & Hamilton, 35 106–09
Cleco Corporation, 37 88–91
The Clemens Family Corporation, 93 156–59
Clement Pappas & Company, Inc., 92 52–55
Cleveland-Cliffs Inc., 13 156–58; 62 71–75 (upd.)
The Cleveland Clinic Foundation, 112 91–95
Cleveland Indians Baseball Company, Inc., 37 92–94; 115 126–31 (upd.)
Click Wine Group, 68 86–88
Clif Bar Inc., 50 141–43
Clifford Chance LLP, 38 136–39
Clinton Cards plc, 39 86–88
Cloetta Fazer AB, 70 58–60
Clopay Corporation, 100 106–10
The Clorox Company, III 20–22; 22 145–48 (upd.); 81 83–90 (upd.)
Close Brothers Group plc, 39 89–92
The Clothestime, Inc., 20 141–44
Cloud Peak Energy Inc., 116 126–29
Clougherty Packing Company, 72 72–74
Cloverdale Paint Inc., 115 132–34
Club Méditerranée S.A., 6 206–08; 21 125–28 (upd.); 91 121–27 (upd.)
ClubCorp, Inc., 33 101–04
CMC see Commercial Metals Co.
CME see Campbell-Mithun-Esty, Inc.; Central European Media Enterprises Ltd.; Chicago Mercantile Exchange Inc.
CMG Worldwide, Inc., 89 157–60
CMGI, Inc., 76 99–101
CMIH see China Merchants International Holdings Co., Ltd.
CML Group, Inc., 10 215–18
CMO see Chi Mei Optoelectronics Corp.
CMP Media Inc., 26 76–80
CMS Energy Corporation, V 577–79; 14 114–16 (upd.); 100 111–16 (upd.)
CN see Canadian National Railway Co.
CNA Financial Corporation, III 228–32; 38 140–46 (upd.)
CNET Networks, Inc., 47 77–80
CNG see Consolidated Natural Gas Co.
CNH Global N.V., 38 147–56 (upd.); 99 100–112 (upd.)
CNP see Compagnie Nationale à Portefeuille.
CNP Assurances, 116 130–33
CNPC see China National Petroleum Corp.
CNS, Inc., 20 145–47 see also GlaxoSmithKline plc.
Co-operative Group (CWS) Ltd., 51 86–89
Coach, Inc., 10 219–21; 45 111–15 (upd.); 99 113–120 (upd.)
Coach USA, Inc., 24 117–19; 55 103–06 (upd.)

Coachmen Industries, Inc., 77 104–07
Coal India Limited, IV 48–50; 44 100–03 (upd.)115 135–40 (upd.)
Coalition America Inc., 113 87–90
Coastal Corporation, IV 394–95; 31 118–21 (upd.)
Coats plc, V 356–58; 44 104–07 (upd.)
COBE Cardiovascular, Inc., 61 68–72
COBE Laboratories, Inc., 13 159–61
Coberco see Friesland Coberco Dairy Foods Holding N.V.
Cobham plc, 30 129–32
Coborn's, Inc., 30 133–35
Cobra Electronics Corporation, 14 117–19
Cobra Golf Inc., 16 108–10
Coca-Cola Bottling Co. Consolidated, 10 222–24
The Coca-Cola Company, I 232–35; 10 225–28 (upd.); 32 111–16 (upd.); 67 111–17 (upd.)
Coca-Cola Enterprises, Inc., 13 162–64; 116 134–39 (upd.)
Cochlear Ltd., 77 108–11
Cockerill Sambre Group, IV 51–53; 26 81–84 (upd.) see also Arcelor Gent.
Codelco see Corporacion Nacional del Cobre de Chile.
Codere S.A., 110 88–92
Coeur d'Alene Mines Corporation, 20 148–51
COFCO see China National Cereals, Oils and Foodstuffs Import and Export Corp.
The Coffee Beanery, Ltd., 95 100–05
Coffee Holding Co., Inc., 95 106–09
Coflexip S.A., 25 103–05 see also Technip.
Cogent Communications Group, Inc., 55 107–10
Cogentrix Energy, Inc., 10 229–31
Cognex Corporation, 76 102–06
Cognizant Technology Solutions Corporation, 59 128–30
Cognos Inc., 44 108–11
Coherent, Inc., 31 122–25
Cohu, Inc., 32 117–19
Coinmach Laundry Corporation, 20 152–54
Coinstar, Inc., 44 112–14
Colas S.A., 31 126–29
Cold Spring Granite Company, 16 111–14; 67 118–22 (upd.)
Cold Stone Creamery, 69 98–100
Coldwater Creek Inc., 21 129–31; 74 88–91 (upd.)
Coldwell Banker Real Estate LLC, 109 132–37
Cole National Corporation, 13 165–67; 76 107–10 (upd.)
Cole Taylor Bank, 107 74–77
The Coleman Company, Inc., 9 127–29; 30 136–39 (upd.); 108 171–77 (upd.)
Coleman Natural Products, Inc., 68 89–91
Coles Express Inc., 15 109–11
Coles Group Limited, V 33–35; 20 155–58 (upd.); 85 49–56 (upd.)

Cole's Quality Foods, Inc., 68 92–94
Colfax Corporation, 58 65–67
Colgate-Palmolive Company, III 23–26; 14 120–23 (upd.); 35 110–15 (upd.); 71 105–10 (upd.)
Colle+McVoy, 110 93–96
Collectors Universe, Inc., 48 98–100
College Hunks Hauling Junk see CHHJ Franchising LLC.
Colliers International Property Consultants Inc., 92 56–59
Collins & Aikman Corporation, 13 168–70; 41 91–95 (upd.)
The Collins Companies Inc., 102 88–92
Collins Industries, Inc., 33 105–07
Colonial Properties Trust, 65 115–17
Colonial Williamsburg Foundation, 53 105–07
Color Kinetics Incorporated, 85 57–60
Colorado Baseball Management, Inc., 72 75–78
Colorado Boxed Beef Company, 100 117–20
Colorado Group Ltd., 107 78–81
Colorado MEDtech, Inc., 48 101–05
Colt Industries Inc., I 434–36
COLT Telecom Group plc, 41 96–99
Colt's Manufacturing Company, Inc., 12 70–72
Columbia Forest Products Inc., 78 74–77
The Columbia Gas System, Inc., V 580–82; 16 115–18 (upd.)
Columbia House Company, 69 101–03
Columbia Manufacturing, Inc., 114 138–41
Columbia Sportswear Company, 19 94–96; 41 100–03 (upd.)
Columbia TriStar Motion Pictures Companies, II 135–37; 12 73–76 (upd.)
Columbia/HCA Healthcare Corporation, 15 112–14
Columbus McKinnon Corporation, 37 95–98
Com Ed see Commonwealth Edison.
Comair Holdings Inc., 13 171–73; 34 116–20 (upd.)
Combe Inc., 72 79–82
Comcast Corporation, 7 90–92; 24 120–24 (upd.); 112 96–101 (upd.)
Comdial Corporation, 21 132–35
Comdisco, Inc., 9 130–32
Comerci see Controladora Comercial Mexicana, S.A. de C.V.
Comerica Incorporated, 40 115–17; 101 120–25 (upd.)
Comex Group see Grupo Comex.
COMFORCE Corporation, 40 118–20
Comfort Systems USA, Inc., 101 126–29
Cominco Ltd., 37 99–102
Comisión Federal de Electricidad, 108 178–81
Command Security Corporation, 57 71–73
Commerce Bancshares, Inc., 116 140–43

First Nationwide Bank, 14 191–93 *see also* Citigroup Inc.

First Niagara Financial Group Inc., 107 131–35

First of America Bank Corporation, 8 187–89

First Pacific Company Limited, 18 180–82

First Security Corporation, 11 117–19 *see also* Wells Fargo & Co.

First Solar, Inc., 95 146–50

First Team Sports, Inc., 22 202–04

First Tennessee National Corporation, 11 120–21; 48 176–79 (upd.)

First Union Corporation, 10 298–300 *see also* Wachovia Corp.

First USA, Inc., 11 122–24

First Virginia Banks, Inc., 11 125–26 *see also* BB&T Corp.

The First Years Inc., 46 191–94

Firstar Corporation, 11 127–29; 33 152–55 (upd.)

FirstEnergy Corp., 112 170–75 (upd.)

FirstGroup plc, 89 216–19

FirstMerit Corporation, 105 176–79

Fiserv, Inc., 11 130–32; 33 156–60 (upd.); 106 186–90 (upd.)

Fish & Neave, 54 109–12

Fisher Auto Parts, Inc., 104 152–55

Fisher Communications, Inc., 99 164–168

Fisher Companies, Inc., 15 164–66

Fisher Controls International, LLC, 13 224–26; 61 96–99 (upd.)

Fisher-Price Inc., 12 167–69; 32 190–94 (upd.)

Fisher Scientific International Inc., 24 162–66 *see also* Thermo Fisher Scientific Inc.

Fishman & Tobin Inc., 102 124–27

Fisk Corporation, 72 132–34

Fiskars Corporation, 33 161–64; 105 180–86 (upd.)

Fisons plc, 9 224–27; 23 194–97 (upd.)

5 & Diner Franchise Corporation, 72 135–37

Five Guys Enterprises, LLC, 99 169–172

Fives S.A., 107 136–40

FKI Plc, 57 141–44

Flagstar Companies, Inc., 10 301–03 *see also* Advantica Restaurant Group, Inc.

Flanders Corporation, 65 149–51

Flanigan's Enterprises, Inc., 60 128–30

Flatiron Construction Corporation, 92 119–22

Fleer Corporation, 15 167–69

FleetBoston Financial Corporation, 9 228–30; 36 206–14 (upd.)

Fleetwood Enterprises, Inc., III 484–85; 22 205–08 (upd.); 81 159–64 (upd.)

Fleming Companies, Inc., II 624–25; 17 178–81 (upd.)

Fletcher Challenge Ltd., IV 278–80; 19 153–57 (upd.)

Fleury Michon S.A., 39 159–61

Flexsteel Industries Inc., 15 170–72; 41 159–62 (upd.)

Flextronics International Ltd., 38 186–89; 116 236–240 (upd.)

Flight Options, LLC, 75 144–46

FlightSafety International, Inc., 9 231–33; 29 189–92 (upd.)

Flint Ink Corporation, 13 227–29; 41 163–66 (upd.)

FLIR Systems, Inc., 69 170–73

Flo *see* Groupe Flo S.A.

Floc'h & Marchand, 80 119–21

Florida Crystals Inc., 35 176–78

Florida East Coast Industries, Inc., 59 184–86

Florida Gaming Corporation, 47 130–33

Florida Power & Light Company *see* FPL Group, Inc.

Florida Progress Corp., V 621–22; 23 198–200 (upd.) *see also* Progress Energy, Inc.

Florida Public Utilities Company, 69 174–76

Florida Rock Industries, Inc., 46 195–97 *see also* Patriot Transportation Holding, Inc.

Florida's Natural Growers, 45 160–62

Florists' Transworld Delivery, Inc., 28 136–38 *see also* FTD Group, Inc.

Florsheim Shoe Group Inc., 9 234–36; 31 209–12 (upd.)

Flotek Industries Inc., 93 217–20

Flour City International, Inc., 44 181–83

Flow International Corporation, 56 132–34

Flowers Industries, Inc., 12 170–71; 35 179–82 (upd.) *see also* Keebler Foods Co.

Flowserve Corporation, 33 165–68; 77 146–51 (upd.)

FLSmidth & Co. A/S, 72 138–40

Fluke Corporation, 15 173–75

Fluor Corporation, I 569–71; 8 190–93 (upd.); 34 164–69 (upd.); 112 176–82 (upd.)

Fluxys SA, 101 188–91

FlyBE *see* Jersey European Airways (UK) Ltd.

Flying Boat, Inc. (Chalk's Ocean Airways), 56 135–37

Flying J Inc., 19 158–60

Flying Pigeon Bicycle Co. *see* Tianjin Flying Pigeon Bicycle Co., Ltd.

FMC Corp., I 442–44; 11 133–35 (upd.); 89 220–27 (upd.)

FMR Corp., 8 194–96; 32 195–200 (upd.)

FN Manufacturing LLC, 110 155–59

FNAC, 21 224–26

FNMA *see* Federal National Mortgage Association.

Foamex International Inc., 17 182–85

Focus Features, 78 118–22

Fokker *see* N.V. Koninklijke Nederlandse Vliegtuigenfabriek Fokker.

Foley & Lardner, 28 139–42

Follett Corporation, 12 172–74; 39 162–65 (upd.)

Foncière Euris, 111 136–40

Fonterra Co-Operative Group Ltd., 58 125–27

Food Circus Super Markets, Inc., 88 92–96

The Food Emporium, 64 125–27

Food For The Poor, Inc., 77 152–55

Food Lion LLC, II 626–27; 15 176–78 (upd.); 66 112–15 (upd.)

Foodarama Supermarkets, Inc., 28 143–45 *see also* Wakefern Food Corp.

FoodBrands America, Inc., 23 201–04 *see also* Doskocil Companies, Inc.; Tyson Foods, Inc.

Foodmaker, Inc., 14 194–96 *see also* Jack in the Box Inc.

Foot-Joy Inc., 113 146–49

Foot Locker, Inc., 68 157–62 (upd.)

Foot Petals L.L.C., 95 151–54

Foote, Cone & Belding Worldwide, I 12–15; 66 116–20 (upd.)

Footstar, Incorporated, 24 167–69 *see also* Foot Locker, Inc.

Forbes Inc., 30 199–201; 82 115–20 (upd.)

Force Protection Inc., 95 155–58

The Ford Foundation, 34 170–72

Ford Gum & Machine Company, Inc., 102 128–31

Ford Motor Company, I 164–68; 11 136–40 (upd.); 36 215–21 (upd.); 64 128–34 (upd.)

Ford Motor Company, S.A. de C.V., 20 219–21

FORE Systems, Inc., 25 161–63 *see also* Telefonaktiebolaget LM Ericsson.

Foremost Farms USA Cooperative, 98 116–20

FöreningsSparbanken AB, 69 177–80

Forest City Enterprises, Inc., 16 209–11; 52 128–31 (upd.); 112 183–87 (upd.)

Forest Laboratories, Inc., 11 141–43; 52 132–36 (upd.); 114 195–200 (upd.)

Forest Oil Corporation, 19 161–63; 91 182–87 (upd.)

Forever 21, Inc., 84 127–129

Forever Living Products International Inc., 17 186–88

FormFactor, Inc., 85 128–31

Formica Corporation, 13 230–32

Formosa Plastics Corporation, 14 197–99; 58 128–31 (upd.)

Forrester Research, Inc., 54 113–15

Forstmann Little & Co., 38 190–92

Fort Howard Corporation, 8 197–99 *see also* Fort James Corp.

Fort James Corporation, 22 209–12 (upd.) *see also* Georgia-Pacific Corp.

Fortis, Inc., 15 179–82; 47 134–37 (upd.); 50 4–6

Fortum Corporation, 30 202–07 (upd.) *see also* Neste Oil Corp.

Fortune Brands, Inc., 29 193–97 (upd.); 68 163–67 (upd.)

Fortunoff Fine Jewelry and Silverware Inc., 26 144–46

Forward Air Corporation, 75 147–49

HSBC Holdings plc, 12 256–58; 26 199–204 (upd.); 80 155–63 (upd.)

HSN, 64 181–85 (upd.)

Huawei Technologies Company Ltd., 87 228–231

Hub Group, Inc., 38 233–35

Hub International Limited, 89 260–64

Hubbard Broadcasting Inc., 24 226–28; 79 207–12 (upd.)

Hubbell Inc., 9 286–87; 31 257–59 (upd.); 76 183–86 (upd.)

Huddle House, Inc., 105 226–29

The Hudson Bay Mining and Smelting Company, Limited, 12 259–61

Hudson City Bancorp, Inc., 116 295–99

Hudson Foods Inc., 13 270–72 *see also* Tyson Foods, Inc.

Hudson River Bancorp, Inc., 41 210–13

Hudson's Bay Company, V 79–81; 25 219–22 (upd.); 83 187–194 (upd.)

HuffingtonPost.com, Inc., 111 227–30

Huffy Corporation, 7 225–27; 30 239–42 (upd.)

Hughes Electronics Corporation, 25 223–25

Hughes Hubbard & Reed LLP, 44 230–32

Hughes Markets, Inc., 22 271–73 *see also* Kroger Co.

Hughes Supply, Inc., 14 246–47

Hugo Boss AG, 48 206–09

Huhtamäki Oyj, 64 186–88

HUK-Coburg, 58 169–73

Hulman & Company, 44 233–36

Hüls A.G., I 349–50 *see also* Degussa-Hüls AG.

Human Factors International Inc., 100 229–32

Humana Inc., III 81–83; 24 229–32 (upd.); 101 250–56 (upd.)

The Humane Society of the United States, 54 170–73

Hummel International A/S, 68 199–201

Hummer Winblad Venture Partners, 97 218–21

Humphrey Products Company, 110 221–25

Hungarian Telephone and Cable Corp., 75 193–95

Hungry Howie's Pizza and Subs, Inc., 25 226–28

Hunt Consolidated, Inc., 7 228–30; 27 215–18 (upd.)

Hunt Manufacturing Company, 12 262–64

Hunt-Wesson, Inc., 17 240–42 *see also* ConAgra Foods, Inc.

Hunter Fan Company, 13 273–75; 98 208–12 (upd.)

Hunting plc, 78 163–16

Huntingdon Life Sciences Group plc, 42 182–85

Huntington Bancshares Incorporated, 11 180–82; 87 232–238 (upd.)

Huntington Learning Centers, Inc., 55 212–14

Huntleigh Technology PLC, 77 199–202

Hunton & Williams, 35 223–26

Huntsman Corporation, 8 261–63; 98 213–17 (upd.)

Huron Consulting Group Inc., 87 239–243

Hurricane Hydrocarbons Ltd., 54 174–77

Husky Energy Inc., 47 179–82

Hussey Seating Company, 114 235–38

Hutchinson Technology Incorporated, 18 248–51; 63 190–94 (upd.)

Hutchison Whampoa Limited, 18 252–55; 49 199–204 (upd.); 111 231–38 (upd.)

Huttig Building Products, Inc., 73 180–83

Huy Fong Foods, Inc., 107 206–09

HVB Group, 59 237–44 (upd.)

Hvide Marine Incorporated, 22 274–76

Hy-Vee, Inc., 36 275–78

Hyatt Corporation, III 96–97; 16 273–75 (upd.) *see* Global Hyatt Corp.

Hyde Athletic Industries, Inc., 17 243–45 *see also* Saucony Inc.

Hyder plc, 34 219–21

Hydril Company, 46 237–39

Hydro-Quebéc, 6 501–03; 32 266–69 (upd.)

Hylsamex, S.A. de C.V., 39 225–27

Hynix Semiconductor Company Ltd., 111 239–43

Hypercom Corporation, 27 219–21

Hyperion Software Corporation, 22 277–79

Hyperion Solutions Corporation, 76 187–91

Hypo Real Estate Holding AG, 112 214–19

Hyster Company, 17 246–48

Hyundai Group, III 515–17; 7 231–34 (upd.); 56 169–73 (upd.)

# I

I Grandi Viaggi S.p.A., 105 230–33

I.C. Isaacs & Company, 31 260–62

I.M. Pei & Associates *see* Pei Cobb Freed & Partners Architects LLP.

i2 Technologies, Inc., 87 252–257

IAC Group, 96 194–98

Iams Company, 26 205–07

IASIS Healthcare Corporation, 112 220–23

IAWS Group plc, 49 205–08

Iberdrola, S.A., 49 209–12

Iberia Líneas Aéreas De España S.A., 6 95–97; 36 279–83 (upd.); 91 247–54 (upd.)

IBERIABANK Corporation, 37 200–02

IBJ *see* The Industrial Bank of Japan Ltd.

IBM *see* International Business Machines Corp.

IBP, Inc., II 515–17; 21 287–90 (upd.)

Ibstock Brick Ltd., 37 203–06 (upd.)

Ibstock plc, 14 248–50

IC Industries Inc., I 456–58 *see also* Whitman Corp.

ICA AB, II 639–40

Icahn Enterprises L.P., 110 226–29

ICEE-USA *see* J & J Snack Foods Corp.

Iceland Group plc, 33 205–07 *see also* The Big Food Group plc.

Icelandair, 52 166–69

Icelandic Group hf, 81 182–85

ICF International, Inc., 28 200–04; 94 240–47 (upd.)

ICI *see* Imperial Chemical Industries plc.

ICL plc, 6 240–42

ICN Pharmaceuticals, Inc., 52 170–73

ICON Health & Fitness, Inc., 38 236–39; 102 175–79 (upd.)

ICU Medical, Inc., 106 237–42

Idaho Power Company, 12 265–67

IDB Communications Group, Inc., 11 183–85

IDB Holding Corporation Ltd., 97 222–25

Ideal Mortgage Bankers, Ltd., 105 234–37

Idealab, 105 238–42

Idearc Inc., 90 241–44

Idemitsu Kosan Co., Ltd., IV 434–36; 49 213–16 (upd.)

Identix Inc., 44 237–40

IDEO Inc., 65 171–73

IDEX Corp., 103 222–26

IDEXX Laboratories, Inc., 23 282–84; 107 210–14 (upd.)

IDG Books Worldwide, Inc., 27 222–24 *see also* International Data Group, Inc.

IDG Communications, Inc *see* International Data Group, Inc.

IdraPrince, Inc., 76 192–94

IDT Corporation, 34 222–24; 99 214–219 (upd.)

IDX Systems Corporation, 64 189–92

IEC Electronics Corp., 42 186–88

IFF *see* International Flavors & Fragrances Inc.

IFP *see* Irish Food Processors Ltd.

IG Group Holdings plc, 97 226–29

IGA, Inc., 99 220–224

Igloo Products Corp., 21 291–93; 105 243–47 (upd.)

IGT *see* International Game Technology.

IHC Caland N.V., 71 178–80

IHI *see* Ishikawajima-Harima Heavy Industries Co., Ltd.

IHOP Corporation, 17 249–51; 58 174–77 (upd.)

Ihr Platz GmbH + Company KG, 77 203–06

IHS Inc., 78 167–70

II-VI Incorporated, 69 353–55

IKEA Group, V 82–84; 26 208–11 (upd.); 94 248–53 (upd.)

IKON Office Solutions, Inc., 50 236–39

Ikonics Corporation, 99 225–228

Il Fornaio (America) Corporation, 27 225–28

ILFC *see* International Lease Finance Corp.

Ilitch Holdings Inc., 37 207–210; 86 195–200 (upd.)

Illinois Bell Telephone Company, 14 251–53

Illinois Central Corporation, 11 186–89

International Brotherhood of Teamsters, 37 211–14; 115 253–58 (upd.)
International Business Machines Corporation, III 147–49; 6 250–53 (upd.); 30 247–51 (upd.); 63 195–201 (upd.)
International Controls Corporation, 10 368–70
International Creative Management, Inc., 43 235–37
International Dairy Queen, Inc., 10 371–74; 39 232–36 (upd.); 105 248–54 (upd.)
International Data Group, Inc., 7 238–40; 25 237–40 (upd.)
International Electric Supply Corp., 113 171–75
International Family Entertainment Inc., 13 279–81 *see also* Disney/ABC Television Group
International Flavors & Fragrances Inc., 9 290–92; 38 244–48 (upd.)
International Game Technology, 10 375–76; 41 214–16 (upd.)
International House of Pancakes *see* IHOP Corp.
International Lease Finance Corporation, 48 218–20
International Management Group, 18 262–65 *see also* IMG.
International Multifoods Corporation, 7 241–43; 25 241–44 (upd.) *see also* The J. M. Smucker Co.
International Olympic Committee, 44 244–47
International Paper Company, IV 286–88; 15 227–30 (upd.); 47 187–92 (upd.); 97 234–43 (upd.)
International Power PLC, 50 280–85 (upd.)
International Profit Associates, Inc., 87 248–251
International Rectifier Corporation, 31 263–66; 71 181–84 (upd.)
International Shipbreaking Ltd. L.L.C., 67 213–15
International Shipholding Corporation, Inc., 27 241–44
International Speedway Corporation, 19 221–23; 74 157–60 (upd.)
International Telephone & Telegraph Corporation, I 462–64; 11 196–99 (upd.)
International Total Services, Inc., 37 215–18
Internationale Nederlanden Groep *see* ING Groep N.V.
Interpool, Inc., 92 176–79
The Interpublic Group of Companies, Inc., I 16–18; 22 294–97 (upd.); 75 202–05 (upd.)
Interscope Music Group, 31 267–69
Intersil Corporation, 93 250–54
Interstate Bakeries Corporation, 12 274–76; 38 249–52 (upd.)
Interstate Batteries, 110 238–41
Interstate Hotels & Resorts Inc., 58 192–94

Intertek Group plc, 95 208–11
InterVideo, Inc., 85 179–82
Intevac, Inc., 92 180–83
Intimate Brands, Inc., 24 237–39
Intrado Inc., 63 202–04
Intrawest Corporation, 15 234–36; 84 192–196 (upd.)
Intres B.V., 82 178–81
Intuit Inc., 14 262–64; 33 208–11 (upd.); 73 188–92 (upd.)
Intuitive Surgical, Inc., 79 217–20
Invacare Corporation, 11 200–02; 47 193–98 (upd.)
Invensys PLC, 50 286–90 (upd.)
Inventec Corp., 113 176–79
inVentiv Health, Inc., 81 205–08
The Inventure Group, Inc., 96 199–202 (upd.)
Inverness Medical Innovations, Inc., 63 205–07
Inversiones Nacional de Chocolates S.A., 88 199–202
Investcorp SA, 57 179–82
Investor AB, 63 208–11
Invitrogen Corporation, 52 182–84
Invivo Corporation, 52 185–87
Iogen Corporation, 81 209–13
IOI Corporation Bhd, 107 220–24
Iomega Corporation, 21 294–97
IONA Technologies plc, 43 238–41
Ionatron, Inc., 85 183–86
Ionics, Incorporated, 52 188–90
Iowa Beef Processors *see* IBP, Inc.
Iowa Telecommunications Services, Inc., 85 187–90
Ipalco Enterprises, Inc., 6 508–09
IPC Magazines Limited, 7 244–47
Ipiranga S.A., 67 216–18
Ipsen International Inc., 72 192–95
Ipsos SA, 48 221–24
IranAir, 81 214–17
Irex Contracting Group, 90 245–48
IRIS International, Inc., 101 261–64
Irish Distillers Group, 96 203–07
Irish Food Processors Ltd., 111 248–51
Irish Life & Permanent Plc, 59 245–47
Irkut Corporation, 68 202–04
iRobot Corporation, 83 212–215
Iron Mountain, Inc., 33 212–14; 104 209–12 (upd.)
IRSA Inversiones y Representaciones S.A., 63 212–15
Irvin Feld & Kenneth Feld Productions, Inc., 15 237–39 *see also* Feld Entertainment, Inc.
Irwin Financial Corporation, 77 213–16
Irwin Toy Limited, 14 265–67
Isbank *see* Turkiye Is Bankasi A.S.
Iscor Limited, 57 183–86
Isetan Mitsukoshi Holdings Ltd., V 85–87; 36 289–93 (upd.); 114 239–48 (upd.)
Ishikawajima-Harima Heavy Industries Company, Ltd., III 532–33; 86 211–15 (upd.)
The Island ECN, Inc., 48 225–29
Isle of Capri Casinos, Inc., 41 217–19

Ispat Inland Inc., 30 252–54; 40 267–72 (upd.)
Israel Aircraft Industries Ltd., 69 215–17
Israel Chemicals Ltd., 55 226–29
Israel Corporation Ltd., 108 276–80
ISS A/S, 49 221–23
Istituto per la Ricostruzione Industriale S.p.A., I 465–67; 11 203–06 (upd.)
Isuzu Motors, Ltd., 9 293–95; 23 288–91 (upd.); 57 187–91 (upd.)
Itaú *see* Banco Itaú S.A.
ITC Holdings Corp., 75 206–08
Itel Corporation, 9 296–99
Items International Airwalk Inc., 17 259–61
ITM Entreprises SA, 36 294–97
Ito En Ltd., 101 265–68
Ito-Yokado Co., Ltd., V 88–89; 42 189–92 (upd.)
ITOCHU Corporation, 32 283–87 (upd.); 116 300–306 (upd.)
Itoh *see* C. Itoh & Co.
Itoham Foods Inc., II 518–19; 61 138–40 (upd.)
Itron, Inc., 64 202–05
ITT Corporation, III 98–101; 116 307–12 (upd.)
ITT Educational Services, Inc., 33 215–17; 76 200–03 (upd.)
ITT Sheraton Corporation, III 98–101 *see also* Starwood Hotels & Resorts Worldwide, Inc.
ITV plc, 104 213–20 (upd.)
ITW *see* Illinois Tool Works Inc.
Ivan Allen Workspace L.L.C., 113 180–83
Ivar's, Inc., 86 216–19
IVAX Corporation, 11 207–09; 55 230–33 (upd.)
IVC Industries, Inc., 45 208–11
iVillage Inc., 46 253–56
Iwerks Entertainment, Inc., 34 228–30
IXC Communications, Inc., 29 250–52

## J

J & J Snack Foods Corporation, 24 240–42
J&R Electronics Inc., 26 224–26
The J. Paul Getty Trust, 105 255–59
J. & W. Seligman & Co. Inc., 61 141–43
J.A. Jones, Inc., 16 284–86
J. Alexander's Corporation, 65 177–79
J.B. Hunt Transport Services Inc., 12 277–79
J. Baker, Inc., 31 270–73
J C Bamford Excavators Ltd., 83 216–222
J. C. Penney Company, Inc., V 90–92; 18 269–73 (upd.); 43 245–50 (upd.); 91 263–72 (upd.)
J. Crew Group, Inc., 12 280–82; 34 231–34 (upd.); 88 203–08
J.D. Edwards & Company, 14 268–70 *see also* Oracle Corp.
J.D. Power and Associates, 32 297–301

Providian Financial Corporation, 52 284–90 (upd.)

Provigo Inc., II 651–53; 51 301–04 (upd.)

Provimi S.A., 80 292–95

PRS *see* Paul Reed Smith Guitar Co.

Prudential Financial Inc., III 337–41; 30 360–64 (upd.); 82 292–98 (upd.)

Prudential plc, III 334–36; 48 325–29 (upd.)

PSA Peugeot Citroen S.A., 28 370–74 (upd.); 54 126

PSF *see* Premium Standard Farms, Inc.

PSI Resources, 6 555–57

Psion PLC, 45 346–49

PSS World Medical, Inc., 115 397–402 (upd.)

Psychemedics Corporation, 89 358–61

Psychiatric Solutions, Inc., 68 297–300

PT Astra International Tbk, 56 283–86

PT Bank Buana Indonesia Tbk, 60 240–42

PT Gudang Garam Tbk, 103 339–42

PT Indosat Tbk, 93 354–57

PT Semen Gresik Tbk, 103 343–46

PTT Public Company Ltd., 56 287–90

Pubco Corporation, 17 383–85

Public Service Company of Colorado, 6 558–60

Public Service Company of New Hampshire, 21 408–12; 55 313–18 (upd.)

Public Service Company of New Mexico, 6 561–64 *see also* PNM Resources Inc.

Public Service Enterprise Group Inc., V 701–03; 44 360–63 (upd.)

Public Storage, Inc., 21 52 291–93

Publicis Groupe, 19 329–32; 77 346–50 (upd.)

Publishers Clearing House, 23 393–95; 64 313–16 (upd.)

Publishers Group, Inc., 35 357–59

Publishing and Broadcasting Limited, 54 299–302

Publix Super Markets, Inc., 7 440–42; 31 371–74 (upd.); 105 345–51 (upd.)

Puck Lazaroff Inc. *see* The Wolfgang Puck Food Company, Inc.

Pueblo Xtra International, Inc., 47 311–13

Puerto Rico Electric Power Authority, 47 314–16

Puget Sound Energy Inc., 6 565–67; 50 365–68 (upd.)

Puig Beauty and Fashion Group S.L., 60 243–46

Pulaski Furniture Corporation, 33 349–52; 80 296–99 (upd.)

Pulitzer Inc., 15 375–77; 58 280–83 (upd.)

Pulsar Internacional S.A., 21 413–15

Pulte Homes, Inc., 8 436–38; 42 291–94 (upd.); 113 310–15 (upd.)

Puma AG Rudolf Dassler Sport, 35 360–63

Pumpkin Masters, Inc., 48 330–32

Punch International N.V., 66 258–60

Punch Taverns plc, 70 240–42

Puratos S.A./NV, 92 315–18

Pure World, Inc., 72 285–87

Purina Mills, Inc., 32 376–79

Puritan-Bennett Corporation, 13 419–21

Purolator Products Company, 21 416–18; 74 253–56 (upd.)

Putt-Putt Golf Courses of America, Inc., 23 396–98

PVC Container Corporation, 67 312–14

PW Eagle, Inc., 48 333–36

PWA Group, IV 323–25 *see also* Svenska Cellulosa.

Pyramid Breweries Inc., 33 353–55; 102 343–47 (upd.)

Pyramid Companies, 54 303–05

PZ Cussons plc, 72 288–90

# Q

Q.E.P. Co., Inc., 65 292–94

Qantas Airways Ltd., 6 109–13; 24 396–401 (upd.); 68 301–07 (upd.)

Qatar Airways Company Q.C.S.C., 87 404–407

Qatar National Bank SAQ, 87 408–411

Qatar Petroleum, IV 524–26; 98 324–28 (upd.)

Qatar Telecom QSA, 87 412–415

Qdoba Restaurant Corporation, 93 358–62

Qiagen N.V., 39 333–35

QLT Inc., 71 291–94

QRS Music Technologies, Inc., 95 349–53

QSC Audio Products, Inc., 56 291–93

QSS Group, Inc., 100 358–61

Quad/Graphics, Inc., 19 333–36

Quaker Chemical Corp., 91 388–91

Quaker Fabric Corp., 19 337–39

Quaker Foods North America, II 558–60; 12 409–12 (upd.); 34 363–67 (upd.); 73 268–73 (upd.)

Quaker State Corporation, 7 443–45; 21 419–22 (upd.) *see also* Pennzoil-Quaker State Co.

QUALCOMM Incorporated, 20 438–41; 47 317–21 (upd.); 114 337–43 (upd.)

Quality Chekd Dairies, Inc., 48 337–39

Quality Dining, Inc., 18 437–40

Quality Food Centers, Inc., 17 386–88 *see also* Kroger Co.

Quality King Distributors, Inc., 114 344–47

Quality Systems, Inc., 81 328–31

Quanex Corporation, 13 422–24; 62 286–89 (upd.)

Quanta Computer Inc., 47 322–24; 110 385–89 (upd.)

Quanta Services, Inc., 79 338–41

Quantum Chemical Corporation, 8 439–41

Quantum Corporation, 10 458–59; 62 290–93 (upd.)

Quark, Inc., 36 375–79

Quebéc Hydro-Electric Commission *see* Hydro-Quebéc.

Quebecor Inc., 12 412–14; 47 325–28 (upd.)

Quelle Group, V 165–67 *see also* Karstadt Quelle AG.

Quest Diagnostics Inc., 26 390–92; 106 383–87 (upd.)

Questar Corporation, 6 568–70; 26 386–89 (upd.)

The Quick & Reilly Group, Inc., 20 442–44

Quick Restaurants S.A., 94 357–60

Quicken Loans, Inc., 93 363–67

Quidel Corporation, 80 300–03

The Quigley Corporation, 62 294–97

Quiksilver, Inc., 18 441–43; 79 342–47 (upd.)

QuikTrip Corporation, 36 380–83

Quill Corporation, 28 375–77; 115 403–06 (upd.)

Quilmes Industrial (QUINSA) S.A., 67 315–17

Quinn Emanuel Urquhart Oliver & Hedges, LLP, 99 350–353

Quintiles Transnational Corporation, 21 423–25; 68 308–12 (upd.)

Quixote Corporation, 15 378–80

The Quizno's Corporation, 42 295–98

Quovadx Inc., 70 243–46

QVC Inc., 9 428–29; 58 284–87 (upd.)

Qwest Communications International, Inc., 37 312–17; 116 400–05 (upd.)

# R

R&B, Inc., 51 305–07

R&R Partners Inc., 108 407–10

R.B. Pamplin Corp., 45 350–52

R.C. Bigelow, Inc., 49 334–36

R.C. Willey Home Furnishings, 72 291–93

R.G. Barry Corp., 17 389–91; 44 364–67 (upd.)

R. Griggs Group Limited, 23 399–402; 31 413–14

R.H. Macy & Co., Inc., V 168–70; 8 442–45 (upd.); 30 379–83 (upd.) *see also* Macy's, Inc.

R.J. Reynolds Tobacco Holdings, Inc., 30 384–87 (upd.)

R. M. Palmer Co., 89 362–64

R.P. Scherer Corporation, I 678–80 *see also* Cardinal Health, Inc.

R.R. Bowker LLC, 100 362–66

R.R. Donnelley & Sons Company, IV 660–62; 38 368–71 (upd.); 113 316–21 (upd.)

Rabobank Group, 26 419; 33 356–58; 116 406–09 (upd.)

RAC *see* Roy Anderson Corp.

Racal-Datacom Inc., 11 408–10

Racal Electronics PLC, II 83–84 *see also* Thales S.A.

RaceTrac Petroleum, Inc., 111 415–18

Racing Champions Corporation, 37 318–20

Rack Room Shoes, Inc., 84 314–317

Radeberger Gruppe AG, 75 332–35

Radian Group Inc., 42 299–301 *see also* Onex Corp.

Remington Arms Company, Inc., 12
415–17; 40 368–71 (upd.)
Remington Products Company, L.L.C.,
42 307–10
Remington Rand *see* Unisys Corp.
Rémy Cointreau Group, 20 451–53; 80
308–12 (upd.)
Renaissance Learning, Inc., 39 341–43;
100 367–72 (upd.)
Renal Care Group, Inc., 72 297–99
Renault Argentina S.A., 67 325–27
Renault S.A., 26 401–04 (upd.); 74
264–68 (upd.)
The Renco Group, Inc., 114 353–56
Renfro Corporation, 99 362–365
Rengo Co., Ltd., IV 326
Renishaw plc, 46 358–60
RENK AG, 37 325–28
Renner Herrmann S.A., 79 353–56
Reno Air Inc., 23 409–11
Reno de Medici S.p.A., 41 325–27
Rent-A-Center, Inc., 45 365–67
Rent-Way, Inc., 33 366–68; 75 336–39
(upd.)
Rental Service Corporation, 28 386–88
Rentech, Inc., 110 395–98
Rentokil Initial Plc, 47 332–35
Rentrak Corporation, 35 371–74
Repco Corporation Ltd., 74 269–72
Replacements, Ltd., 110 399–402
REpower Systems AG, 101 424–27
Repsol-YPF S.A., IV 527–29; 16 423–26
(upd.); 40 372–76 (upd.)
Republic Engineered Products Inc., 7
446–47; 26 405–08 (upd.); 106
408–14 (upd.)
Republic Industries, Inc., 26 409–11 *see
also* AutoNation, Inc.
Republic New York Corporation, 11
415–19 *see also* HSBC Holdings plc.
The Republic of Tea, Inc., 105 365–68
Republic Services, Inc., 92 323–26
Res-Care, Inc., 29 399–402
Research in Motion Limited, 54
310–14; 106 415–22 (upd.)
Research Triangle Institute, 83 322–325
Réseau Ferré de France, 66 266–68
Reser's Fine Foods, Inc., 81 337–40
Resorts International, Inc., 12 418–20
Resource America, Inc., 42 311–14
Resources Connection, Inc., 81 341–44
Response Oncology, Inc., 27 385–87
Restaurant Associates Corporation, 66
269–72
Restaurants Unlimited, Inc., 13 435–37
Restoration Hardware, Inc., 30 376–78;
96 347–51 (upd.)
Retail Ventures, Inc., 82 299–03 (upd.)
Retractable Technologies, Inc., 99
366–369
Reuters Group PLC, IV 668–70; 22
450–53 (upd.); 63 323–27 (upd.)
Revco D.S., Inc., V 171–73 *see also* CVS
Corp.
Revell-Monogram Inc., 16 427–29
Revere Electric Supply Company, 96
352–55
Revere Ware Corporation, 22 454–56

Revlon Inc., III 54–57; 17 400–04
(upd.); 64 330–35 (upd.)
Rewards Network Inc., 70 271–75
(upd.)
Rewe International AG, 113 327–31
REWE-Zentral AG, 103 355–59
REX Stores Corp., 10 468–69
Rexam PLC, 32 380–85 (upd.); 85
353–61 (upd.)
Rexel, Inc., 15 384–87
Rexnord Corporation, 21 429–32; 76
315–19 (upd.)
The Reynolds and Reynolds Company,
50 376–79
Reynolds Metals Company, IV 186–88;
19 346–48 (upd.) *see also* Alcoa Inc.
RF Micro Devices, Inc., 43 311–13
RFC Franchising LLC, 68 317–19
RFF *see* Réseau Ferré de France.
RGI *see* Rockefeller Group International.
Rheem Manufacturing Company, 113
332–35
Rheinmetall AG, 9 443–46; 97 343–49
(upd.)
RHI AG, 53 283–86
Rhino Entertainment Company, 18
457–60; 70 276–80 (upd.)
RHM *see* Ranks Hovis McDougall.
Rhodes Inc., 23 412–14
Rhodia SA, 38 378–80; 115 411–15
(upd.)
Rhône-Poulenc S.A., I 388–90; 10
470–72 (upd.)
Rhythm & Hues Studios, Inc., 103
360–63
Rica Foods, Inc., 41 328–30
Ricardo plc, 90 352–56
Rich Products Corporation, 7 448–49;
38 381–84 (upd.); 93 368–74 (upd.)
The Richards Group, Inc., 58 300–02
Richardson Electronics, Ltd., 17 405–07
Richardson Industries, Inc., 62 298–301
Richfood Holdings, Inc., 7 450–51; *see
also* Supervalu Inc.
Richton International Corporation, 39
344–46
Richtree Inc., 63 328–30
Richwood Building Products, Inc. *see* Ply
Gem Industries Inc.
Rickenbacker International Corp., 91
408–12
Rick's Cabaret International, Inc., 112
329–33
Ricoh Company, Ltd., III 159–61; 36
389–93 (upd.); 108 411–17 (upd.)
Ricola Ltd., 62 302–04
Riddell Sports Inc., 22 457–59; 23 449
Ride, Inc., 22 460–63
Ridley Corporation Ltd., 62 305–07
Riedel Tiroler Glashuette GmbH, 99
370–373
The Riese Organization, 38 385–88
Rieter Holding AG, 42 315–17
Riggs National Corporation, 13 438–40
Right Management Consultants, Inc.,
42 318–21
Riklis Family Corp., 9 447–50
Rimage Corp., 89 369–72

Rinascente S.p.A., 71 308–10
Rinker Group Ltd., 65 298–301
Rio Tinto plc, 19 349–53 (upd.) 50
380–85 (upd.)
Ripley Corp S.A., 102 353–56
Ripley Entertainment, Inc., 74 273–76
Riser Foods, Inc., 9 451–54 *see also*
Giant Eagle, Inc.
Ritchie Bros. Auctioneers Inc., 41
331–34
Rite Aid Corporation, V 174–76; 19
354–57 (upd.); 63 331–37 (upd.)
Ritter Sport *see* Alfred Ritter GmbH &
Co. KG.
Ritter's Frozen Custard *see* RFC
Franchising LLC.
Ritz Camera Centers, 34 375–77
The Ritz-Carlton Hotel Company,
L.L.C., 9 455–57; 29 403–06 (upd.);
71 311–16 (upd.)
Ritz-Craft Corporation of Pennsylvania
Inc., 94 365–68
Riunione Adriatica di Sicurtà SpA, III
345–48
Riva Fire *see* Gruppo Riva Fire SpA.
The Rival Company, 19 358–60
River Oaks Furniture, Inc., 43 314–16
River Ranch Fresh Foods LLC, 88
322–25
Riverbed Technology, Inc., 101 428–31
Riverwood International Corporation,
11 420–23; 48 340–44 (upd.) *see also*
Graphic Packaging Holding Co.
Riviana Foods, 27 388–91; 107 373–78
(upd.)
Riviera Holdings Corporation, 75
340–43
Riviera Tool Company, 89 373–76
RJR Nabisco Holdings Corp., V 408–10
*see also* R.J Reynolds Tobacco Holdings
Inc., Nabisco Brands, Inc.; R.J.
Reynolds Industries, Inc.
RM Auctions, Inc., 88 326–29
RMC Group p.l.c., III 737–40; 34
378–83 (upd.)
RMH Teleservices, Inc., 42 322–24
Roadhouse Grill, Inc., 22 464–66
Roadmaster Industries, Inc., 16 430–33
Roadway Express, Inc., V 502–03; 25
395–98 (upd.)
Roanoke Electric Steel Corporation, 45
368–70
Robbins & Myers Inc., 15 388–90
Roberds Inc., 19 361–63
Robert Bosch GmbH, I 392–93; 16
434–37 (upd.); 43 317–21 (upd.);
108 418–25 (upd.)
Robert Half International Inc., 18
461–63; 70 281–84 (upd.)
Robert Mondavi Corporation, 15
391–94; 50 386–90 (upd.)
Robert Talbott Inc., 88 330–33
Robert W. Baird & Co. Incorporated,
67 328–30
Robert Wood Johnson Foundation, 35
375–78
Robertet SA, 39 347–49
Roberts *see* F.L. Roberts & Company, Inc.

RSC *see* Rental Service Corp.
**RSH Ltd.,** 110 407–11
**RSM McGladrey Business Services Inc.,** 98 333–36
**RTI Biologics, Inc.,** 96 362–65
**RTI International Metals Inc.,** 114 361–65
**RTL Group SA,** 44 374–78
**RTM Restaurant Group,** 58 322–24
**RTZ Corporation PLC,** IV 189–92 *see also* Rio Tinto plc.
**Rubbermaid Incorporated,** III 613–15; 20 454–57 (upd.) *see also* Newell Rubbermaid Inc.
**Rubio's Restaurants, Inc.,** 35 379–81; 107 379–83 (upd.)
**Ruby Tuesday, Inc.,** 18 464–66; 71 317–20 (upd.)
**Rudolph Technologies Inc.,** 94 375–78
**rue21, Inc.,** 116 419–22
**The Rugby Group plc,** 31 398–400
Ruger Corporation *see* Sturm, Ruger & Co., Inc.
**Ruhrgas AG,** V 704–06; 38 405–09 (upd.)
**Ruhrkohle AG,** IV 193–95 *see also* RAG AG.
**Ruiz Food Products, Inc.,** 53 287–89
**Rumpke Consolidated Companies Inc.,** 113 344–47
**Rural Cellular Corporation,** 43 340–42
**Rural Press Ltd.,** 74 282–85
**Rural/Metro Corporation,** 28 396–98
**Rush Communications,** 33 373–75 *see also* Phat Fashions LLC.
**Rush Enterprises, Inc.,** 64 336–38
**Russ Berrie and Company, Inc.,** 12 424–26; 82 304–08 (upd.)
**Russell Corporation,** 8 458–59; 30 399–401 (upd.); 82 309–13 (upd.)
**Russell Reynolds Associates Inc.,** 38 410–12
**Russell Stover Candies Inc.,** 12 427–29; 91 426–32 (upd.)
**Russian Aircraft Corporation (MiG),** 86 343–46
**Russian Railways Joint Stock Co.,** 93 380–83
**Rust International Inc.,** 11 435–36
**Rusty, Inc.,** 95 358–61
**Ruth's Chris Steak House,** 28 399–401; 88 338–42 (upd.)
**RWD Technologies, Inc.,** 76 320–22
**RWE Group,** V 707–10; 50 396–400 (upd.)
**Ryan Beck & Co., Inc.,** 66 273–75
**Ryan Companies US, Inc.,** 99 382–385
**Ryanair Holdings plc,** 35 382–85
**Ryan's Restaurant Group, Inc.,** 15 419–21; 68 327–30 (upd.)
**Ryder System Inc.,** V 504–06; 24 408–11 (upd.); 113 348–53 (upd.)
**Ryerson Tull, Inc.,** 40 381–84 (upd.)
**Ryko Corporation,** 83 329–333
**The Ryland Group, Inc.,** 8 460–61; 37 343–45 (upd.); 107 384–88 (upd.)
**Ryoshoku Ltd.,** 72 300–02

RZB *see* Raiffeisen Zentralbank Österreich AG.
RZD *see* Russian Railways Joint Stock Co.

# S

**S&C Electric Company,** 15 422–24
**S&D Coffee, Inc.,** 84 339–341
**S&K Famous Brands, Inc.,** 23 421–23
S&P *see* Standard & Poor's Corp.
**S-K-I Limited,** 15 457–59
**S.A.C.I. Falabella,** 69 311–13
S.A. Cockerill Sambre *see* Cockerill Sambre Group.
s.a. GB-Inno-BM *see* GIB Group.
**S.C. Johnson & Son, Inc.,** III 58–59; 28 409–12 (upd.); 89 382–89 (upd.)
**S4C International,** 115 416–19
**SAA (Pty) Ltd.,** 28 402–04
**Saab Automobile AB,** 32 386–89 (upd.); 83 334–339 (upd.)
**Saab-Scania A.B.,** I 197–98; 11 437–39 (upd.)
**Saarberg-Konzern,** IV 196–99 *see also* RAG AG.
**Saatchi & Saatchi plc,** I 33–35; 33 328–31 (upd.)
SAB *see* South African Breweries Ltd.
Sabanci Holdings *see* Haci Omer Sabanci Holdings A.S.
**Sabaté Diosos SA,** 48 348–50 *see also* OENEO S.A.
**Sabena S.A./N.V.,** 33 376–79
SABIC *see* Saudi Basic Industries Corp.
**SABMiller plc,** 59 352–58 (upd.)
**Sabratek Corporation,** 29 410–12
**Sabre Holdings Corporation,** 26 427–30; 74 286–90 (upd.)
**Sadia S.A.,** 59 359–62
**Safaricom Limited,** 116 423–26
**Safe Flight Instrument Corporation,** 71 321–23
**SAFECO Corporation,** III 352–54
**Safeguard Scientifics, Inc.,** 10 473–75
**Safelite Glass Corp.,** 19 371–73
**SafeNet Inc.,** 101 438–42
**Safeskin Corporation,** 18 467–70 *see also* Kimberly-Clark Corp.
**Safety 1st, Inc.,** 24 412–15
**Safety Components International, Inc.,** 63 342–44
**Safety-Kleen Systems Inc.,** 8 462–65; 82 314–20 (upd.)
**Safeway Inc.,** II 654–56; 24 416–19 (upd.); 85 362–69 (upd.)
**Safeway PLC,** 50 401–06 (upd.)
**Saffery Champness,** 80 324–27
**Safilo SpA,** 40 155–56; 54 319–21
**SAFRAN,** 102 363–71 (upd.)
**Saft Groupe S.A.,** 113 354–58
**Saga Communications, Inc.,** 27 392–94
**The Sage Group,** 43 343–46
**Sage Products Inc.,** 105 369–72
**SAGEM S.A.,** 37 346–48 *see also* SAFRAN.
**Sagicor Life Inc.,** 98 337–40
**Sahara Bank,** 116 427–30
**Saia, Inc.,** 98 341–44

SAIC *see* Science Applications International Corp.
Sainsbury's *see* J Sainsbury PLC.
Saint-Gobain *see* Compagnie de Saint Gobain S.A.
**St. Jude Children's Research Hospital, Inc.,** 114 366–71
**Saks Incorporated,** 24 420–23; 41 342–45 (upd.); 114 372–77 (upd.)
**Salant Corporation,** 12 430–32; 51 318–21 (upd.)
**Salem Communications Corporation,** 97 359–63
**salesforce.com, Inc.,** 79 370–73
**Salick Health Care, Inc.,** 53 290–92
**Salix Pharmaceuticals, Ltd.,** 93 384–87
Sallie Mae *see* SLM Holding Corp.
**Sally Beauty Company, Inc.,** 60 258–60
**Sally Industries, Inc.,** 103 377–81
**Salomon Inc.,** II 447–49; 13 447–50 (upd.) *see also* Citigroup Inc.
**Salomon Worldwide,** 20 458–60 *see also* adidas-Salomon AG.
**Salt River Project,** 19 374–76
**Salton, Inc.,** 30 402–04; 88 343–48 (upd.)
**The Salvation Army USA,** 32 390–93
**Salvatore Ferragamo Italia S.p.A.,** 62 311–13
**Salzgitter AG,** IV 200–01; 101 443–49 (upd.)
**Sam Ash Music Corporation,** 30 405–07
**Sam Levin Inc.,** 80 328–31
**Samick Musical Instruments Co., Ltd.,** 56 297–300
**Sam's Club,** 40 385–87; 115 420–24 (upd.)
**Sam's Wine & Spirits,** 96 366–69
**Samsonite Corporation,** 13 451–53; 43 353–57 (upd.)
**Samsung Electronics Co., Ltd.,** 14 416–18; 41 346–49 (upd.); 108 433–40 (upd.)
**Samsung Group,** I 515–17
**Samuel Cabot Inc.,** 53 293–95
**Samuels Jewelers Incorporated,** 30 408–10
**San Diego Gas & Electric Company,** V 711–14; 107 389–95 (upd.)
**San Diego Padres Baseball Club L.P.,** 78 324–27
**San Francisco Baseball Associates, L.P.,** 55 340–43
**San Francisco Opera Association,** 112 337–39
**San Miguel Corporation,** 15 428–30; 57 303–08 (upd.)
**Sanborn Hermanos, S.A.,** 20 461–63 *see also* Grupo Sanborns, S.A. de C.V.
**Sanborn Map Company Inc.,** 82 321–24
**SanCor Cooperativas Unidas Ltda.,** 101 450–53
**The Sanctuary Group PLC,** 69 314–17
**Sandals Resorts International,** 65 302–05
**Sanders Morris Harris Group Inc.,** 70 285–87

Scott Fetzer Company, 12 435–37; 80 339–43 (upd.)

Scott Paper Company, IV 329–31; 31 409–12 (upd.)

Scottish & Newcastle plc, 15 441–44; 35 394–97 (upd.)

Scottish and Southern Energy plc, 13 457–59; 66 279–84 (upd.)

Scottish Media Group plc, 32 404–06; 41 350–52

Scottish Power plc, 49 363–66 (upd.)

Scottish Radio Holding plc, 41 350–52

ScottishPower plc, 19 389–91

Scottrade, Inc., 85 374–77

The Scotts Company, 22 474–76

Scotty's, Inc., 22 477–80

The Scoular Company, 77 379–82

Scovill Fasteners Inc., 24 433–36

SCP Pool Corporation, 39 358–60

Screen Actors Guild, 72 310–13

The Scripps Research Institute, 76 323–25

SDGE *see* San Diego Gas & Electric Co.

SDL PLC, 67 340–42

Sea Containers Ltd., 29 428–31

Seaboard Corporation, 36 414–16; 85 378–82 (upd.)

SeaChange International, Inc., 79 374–78

SEACOR Holdings Inc., 83 347–350

Seagate Technology, 8 466–68; 34 400–04 (upd.); 105 382–90 (upd.)

The Seagram Company Ltd., I 284–86; 25 408–12 (upd.)

Seagull Energy Corporation, 11 440–42

Sealaska Corporation, 60 261–64

Sealed Air Corporation, 14 429–31; 57 313–17 (upd.)

Sealed Power Corporation, I 199–200 *see also* SPX Corp.

Sealright Co., Inc., 17 420–23

Sealy Corporation, 12 438–40; 112 353–57 (upd.)

Seaman Furniture Company, Inc., 32 407–09

Sean John Clothing, Inc., 70 288–90

SeaRay Boats Inc., 96 374–77

Sears plc, V 177–79

Sears Roebuck de México, S.A. de C.V., 20 470–72

Sears, Roebuck and Co., V 180–83; 18 475–79 (upd.); 56 309–14 (upd.)

Seat Pagine Gialle S.p.A., 47 345–47

Seattle City Light, 50 423–26

Seattle FilmWorks, Inc., 20 473–75

Seattle First National Bank Inc., 8 469–71 *see also* Bank of America Corp.

Seattle Lighting Fixture Company, 92 331–34

Seattle Pacific Industries, Inc., 92 335–38

Seattle Seahawks, Inc., 92 339–43

Seattle Times Company, 15 445–47

Seaway Food Town, Inc., 15 448–50 *see also* Spartan Stores Inc.

SEB Group *see* Skandinaviska Enskilda Banken AB.

SEB S.A. *see* Groupe SEB.

Sebastiani Vineyards, Inc., 28 413–15

The Second City, Inc., 88 354–58

Second Harvest, 29 432–34

Securicor Plc, 45 376–79

Securitas AB, 42 336–39; 112 358–63 (upd.)

Security Capital Corporation, 17 424–27

Security Pacific Corporation, II 349–50

SED International Holdings, Inc., 43 367–69

La Seda de Barcelona S.A., 100 260–63

Seddon Group Ltd., 67 343–45

SEGA Corporation, 73 290–93

Sega of America, Inc., 10 482–85

Segway LLC, 48 355–57

SEI Investments Company, 96 378–82

Seibu Department Stores, Ltd., V 184–86; 42 340–43 (upd.)

Seibu Railway Company Ltd., V 510–11; 74 299–301 (upd.)

Seigle's Home and Building Centers, Inc., 41 353–55

Seiko Corporation, III 619–21; 17 428–31 (upd.); 72 314–18 (upd.)

Seino Transportation Company, Ltd., 6 427–29

Seita, 23 424–27 *see also* Altadis S.A.

Seitel, Inc., 47 348–50

The Seiyu, Ltd., V 187–89; 36 417–21 (upd.)

Sekisui Chemical Co., Ltd., III 741–43; 72 319–22 (upd.)

Select Comfort Corporation, 34 405–08

Select Medical Corporation, 65 306–08

Selecta AG, 97 370–73

Selectour SA, 53 299–301

Selee Corporation, 88 359–62

Selfridges Retail Ltd., 34 409–11; 107 401–05 (upd.)

The Selmer Company, Inc., 19 392–94

SEMCO Energy, Inc., 44 379–82

Semen Gresik *see* PT Semen Gresik Tbk

Seminis, Inc., 29 435–37

Semitool, Inc., 18 480–82; 79 379–82 (upd.)

Sempra Energy, 25 413–16 (upd.); 116 431–36 (upd.)

Semtech Corporation, 32 410–13

Seneca Foods Corporation, 17 432–34; 60 265–68 (upd.)

Sennheiser Electronic GmbH & Co. KG, 66 285–89

Senomyx, Inc., 83 351–354

Sensient Technologies Corporation, 52 303–08 (upd.)

Sensormatic Electronics Corp., 11 443–45

Sensory Science Corporation, 37 353–56

SENTEL Corporation, 106 432–34

La Senza Corporation, 66 205–07

Sephora Holdings S.A., 82 335–39

Seppälä Oy, 113 359–62

Sepracor Inc., 45 380–83

Sequa Corporation, 13 460–63; 54 328–32 (upd.)

Sequana Capital, 78 338–42 (upd.)

Serco Group plc, 47 351–53

Serologicals Corporation, 63 351–53

Serono S.A., 47 354–57

Serta, Inc., 28 416–18

Servco Pacific Inc., 96 383–86

Service America Corp., 7 471–73

Service Corporation International, 6 293–95; 51 329–33 (upd.)

Service Merchandise Company, Inc., V 190–92; 19 395–99 (upd.)

The ServiceMaster Company, 6 44–46; 23 428–31 (upd.); 68 338–42 (upd.)

Servidyne Inc., 100 388–92 (upd.)

Servpro Industries, Inc., 85 383–86

Seton Company, Inc., 110 418–21

7-Eleven, Inc., 32 414–18 (upd.); 112 364–71 (upd.)

Sevenson Environmental Services, Inc., 42 344–46

Seventh Generation, Inc., 73 294–96

Severn Trent PLC, 12 441–43; 38 425–29 (upd.)

Severstal Joint Stock Company, 65 309–12

Seyfarth Shaw LLP, 93 388–91

SFI Group plc, 51 334–36

SFX Entertainment, Inc., 36 422–25

SGI, 29 438–41 (upd.)

Shakespeare Company, 22 481–84

Shaklee Corporation, 12 444–46; 39 361–64 (upd.)

Shamrock Foods Company, 105 391–96

Shanghai Baosteel Group Corporation, 71 327–30; 116 437–40 (upd.)

Shanghai Petrochemical Co., Ltd., 18 483–85

Shangri-La Asia Ltd., 71 331–33

Shanks Group plc, 45 384–87

Shannon Aerospace Ltd., 36 426–28

Shared Medical Systems Corporation, 14 432–34 *see also* Siemens AG.

Sharp Corporation, II 95–96; 12 447–49 (upd.); 40 391–95 (upd.); 114 378–83 (upd.)

The Sharper Image Corporation, 10 486–88; 62 321–24 (upd.)

The Shaw Group, Inc., 50 427–30

Shaw Industries, Inc., 9 465–67; 40 396–99 (upd.)

Shaw's Supermarkets, Inc., 56 315–18

Shea Homes *see* J.F. Shea Co., Inc.

Sheaffer Pen Corporation, 82 340–43

Shearer's Foods, Inc., 72 323–25

Shearman & Sterling, 32 419–22

Shearson Lehman Brothers Holdings Inc., II 450–52; 9 468–70 (upd.) *see also* Lehman Brothers Holdings Inc.

Shed Media plc, 104 414–17

Shedd Aquarium Society, 73 297–99

Sheetz, Inc., 85 387–90

Sheffield Forgemasters International Ltd., 115 425–28

Shelby Williams Industries, Inc., 14 435–37

Sheldahl Inc., 23 432–35

Shell Oil Company, IV 540–41; 14 438–40 (upd.); 41 356–60 (upd.) *see also* Royal Dutch/Shell Group.

SLM Corp., 25 425–28 (upd.); 116 441–46 (upd.)

Slough Estates PLC, IV 722–25; 50 435–40 (upd.)

Small Planet Foods, Inc., 89 410–14

Small World Toys, 115 429–32

Smart & Final LLC, 16 451–53; 94 392–96 (upd.)

Smart Balance, Inc., 100 398–401

SMART Modular Technologies, Inc., 86 361–64

SmartForce PLC, 43 377–80

Smarties see Ce De Candy Inc.

SMBC see Sumitomo Mitsui Banking Corp.

Smead Manufacturing Co., 17 445–48

SMG see Scottish Media Group.

SMH see Sanders Morris Harris Group Inc.; The Swatch Group SA.

Smith & Hawken, Ltd., 68 343–45

Smith & Nephew plc, 17 449–52; 41 374–78 (upd.)

Smith & Wesson Corp., 30 424–27; 73 306–11 (upd.)

The Smith & Wollensky Restaurant Group, Inc., 105 418–22

Smith Barney Inc., 15 463–65 see also Citigroup Inc.

Smith Corona Corp., 13 477–80

Smith International, Inc., 15 466–68; 59 376–80 (upd.)

Smith Micro Software, Inc., 112 384–87

Smith-Midland Corporation, 56 330–32

Smithfield Foods, Inc., 7 477–78; 43 381–84 (upd.); 114 384–89 (upd.)

SmithKline Beckman Corporation, I 692–94 see also GlaxoSmithKline plc.

SmithKline Beecham plc, III 65–67; 32 429–34 (upd.) see also GlaxoSmithKline plc.

Smith's Food & Drug Centers, Inc., 8 472–74; 57 324–27 (upd.)

Smiths Group plc, 25 429–31; 107 406–10 (upd.)

Smithsonian Institution, 27 410–13

Smithway Motor Xpress Corporation, 39 376–79

Smoby International SA, 56 333–35

Smorgon Steel Group Ltd., 62 329–32

Smucker's see The J.M. Smucker Co.

Smurfit Kappa Group plc, 26 442–46 (upd.) ; 83 360–368 (upd.)112 388–95 (upd.)

Snap-On, Incorporated, 7 479–80; 27 414–16 (upd.); 105 423–28 (upd.)

Snapfish, 83 369–372

Snapple Beverage Corporation, 11 449–51

SNC-Lavalin Group Inc., 72 330–33

SNCF see Société Nationale des Chemins de Fer Français.

SNEA see Société Nationale Elf Aquitaine.

Snecma Group, 46 369–72 see also SAFRAN.

Snell & Wilmer L.L.P., 28 425–28

SNET see Southern New England Telecommunications Corp.

Snow Brand Milk Products Company, Ltd., II 574–75; 48 362–65 (upd.)

Soap Opera Magazine see American Media, Inc.

Sobeys Inc., 80 348–51

Socata see EADS SOCATA.

Sociedad Química y Minera de Chile S.A.,103 382–85

Sociedade de Jogos de Macau, S.A.see SJM Holdings Ltd.

Società Finanziaria Telefonica per Azioni, V 325–27

Società Sportiva Lazio SpA, 44 386–88

Société Air France, 27 417–20 (upd.) see also Air France–KLM.

Société BIC S.A., 73 312–15

Societe des Produits Marnier-Lapostolle S.A., 88 373–76

Société d'Exploitation AOM Air Liberté SA (AirLib), 53 305–07

Société du Figaro S.A., 60 281–84

Société du Louvre, 27 421–23

Société Générale, II 354–56; 42 347–51 (upd.)

Société Industrielle Lesaffre, 84 356–359

Société Luxembourgeoise de Navigation Aérienne S.A., 64 357–59

Société Nationale des Chemins de Fer Français, V 512–15; 57 328–32 (upd.)

Société Nationale Elf Aquitaine, IV 544–47; 7 481–85 (upd.)

Société Norbert Dentressangle S.A., 67 352–54

Société Tunisienne de l'Air-Tunisair, 49 371–73

Society Corporation, 9 474–77

Sodexho SA, 29 442–44; 91 433–36 (upd.)

Sodiaal S.A., 19 50; 36 437–39 (upd.)

SODIMA, II 576–77 see also Sodiaal S.A.

Soft Pretzel Franchise Systems, Inc., 108 456–59

Soft Sheen Products, Inc., 31 416–18

Softbank Corporation, 13 481–83; 38 439–44 (upd.); 77 387–95 (upd.)

Sojitz Corporation, 96 395–403 (upd.)

Sol Meliá S.A., 71 337–39

Sola International Inc., 71 340–42

Solar Turbines Inc., 100 402–06

Solarfun Power Holdings Co., Ltd., 105 429–33

SolarWinds, Inc., 116 447–50

Sole Technology Inc., 93 405–09

Solectron Corporation, 12 450–52; 48 366–70 (upd.)

Solo Cup Company, 104 424–27

Solo Serve Corporation, 28 429–31

Solutia Inc., 52 312–15

Solvay & Cie S.A., I 394–96; 21 464–67 (upd.)

Solvay S.A., 61 329–34 (upd.)

Somerfield plc, 47 365–69 (upd.)

Sommer-Allibert S.A., 19 406–09 see also Tarkett Sommer AG.

Sompo Japan Insurance, Inc., 98 359–63 (upd.)

Sonae SGPS, S.A., 97 378–81

Sonat, Inc., 6 577–78 see also El Paso Corp.

Sonatrach, 65 313–17 (upd.)

Sonera Corporation, 50 441–44 see also TeliaSonera AB.

Sonesta International Hotels Corporation, 44 389–91

Sonic Automotive, Inc., 77 396–99

Sonic Corp., 14 451–53; 37 360–63 (upd.); 103 386–91 (upd.)

Sonic Innovations Inc., 56 336–38

Sonic Solutions, Inc., 81 375–79

SonicWALL, Inc., 87 421–424

Sonnenschein Nath and Rosenthal LLP, 102 384–87

Sonoco Products Company, 8 475–77; 89 415–22 (upd.)

SonoSite, Inc., 56 339–41

Sony Corporation, II 101–03; 12 453–56 (upd.); 40 404–10 (upd.); 108 460–69 (upd.)

Sophus Berendsen A/S, 49 374–77

Sorbee International Ltd., 74 309–11

Soriana see Organización Soriana S.A.B. de C.V.

Soros Fund Management LLC, 28 432–34

Sorrento, Inc., 19 51; 24 444–46

SOS Staffing Services, 25 432–35

Sotheby's Holdings, Inc., 11 452–54; 29 445–48 (upd.); 84 360–365 (upd.)

Soufflet SA see Groupe Soufflet SA.

Sound Advice, Inc., 41 379–82

Souper Salad, Inc., 98 364–67

The Source Enterprises, Inc., 65 318–21

Source Interlink Companies, Inc., 75 350–53

The South African Breweries Limited, I 287–89; 24 447–51 (upd.) see also SABMiller plc.

South Beach Beverage Company, Inc., 73 316–19

South Dakota Wheat Growers Association, 94 397–401

South Jersey Industries, Inc., 42 352–55

Southam Inc., 7 486–89 see also CanWest Global Communications Corp.

Southcorp Limited, 54 341–44

Southdown, Inc., 14 454–56 see also CEMEX S.A. de C.V.

Southeast Frozen Foods Company, L.P., 99 423–426

The Southern Company, V 721–23; 38 445–49 (upd.)

Southern Connecticut Gas Company, 84 366–370

Southern Electric PLC, 13 484–86 see also Scottish and Southern Energy plc.

Southern Financial Bancorp, Inc., 56 342–44

Southern Indiana Gas and Electric Company, 13 487–89 see also Vectren Corp.

Southern New England Telecommunications Corporation, 6 338–40

Standex International Corporation, 17 456–59; 44 403–06 (upd.)

Stanhome Inc., 15 475–78

Stanley Furniture Company, Inc., 34 412–14

Stanley Leisure plc, 66 310–12

The Stanley Works, III 626–29; 20 476–80 (upd.); 79 383–91 (upd.)

Staple Cotton Cooperative Association (Staplcotn), 86 373–77

Staples, Inc., 10 496–98; 55 351–56 (upd.)

Star Banc Corporation, 11 465–67 *see also* Firstar Corp.

Star of the West Milling Co., 95 386–89

Starbucks Corporation, 13 493–94; 34 415–19 (upd.); 77 404–10 (upd.)

Starcraft Corporation, 30 434–36; 66 313–16 (upd.)

Starent Networks Corp., 106 446–50

StarHub Ltd., 77 411–14

Starkey Laboratories, Inc., 52 323–25

StarKist Company, 113 368–72

Starrett *see* L.S. Starrett Co.

Starrett Corporation, 21 471–74

StarTek, Inc., 79 392–95

Starter Corp., 12 457–458

Starwood Hotels & Resorts Worldwide, Inc., 54 345–48

Starz LLC, 91 445–50

The Stash Tea Company, 50 449–52

State Auto Financial Corporation, 77 415–19

State Bank of India, 63 354–57

State Farm Mutual Automobile Insurance Company, III 362–64; 51 341–45 (upd.)

State Financial Services Corporation, 51 346–48

State Grid Corporation of China, 108 470–74

State Street Corporation, 8 491–93; 57 340–44 (upd.)

Staten Island Bancorp, Inc., 39 380–82

Stater Bros. Holdings Inc., 64 364–67

Station Casinos, Inc., 25 452–54; 90 390–95 (upd.)

Statnett SF, 110 439–42

Statoil ASA, 61 344–48 (upd.)

The Staubach Company, 62 338–41

STC PLC, III 162–64 *see also* Nortel Networks Corp.

Ste. Michelle Wine Estates Ltd., 96 408–11

The Steak n Shake Company, 41 387–90; 96 412–17 (upd.)

Steamships Trading Company Ltd., 82 353–56

Stearns, Inc., 43 389–91

Steel Authority of India Ltd., IV 205–07; 66 317–21 (upd.)

Steel Dynamics, Inc., 52 326–28

Steel Technologies Inc., 63 358–60

Steelcase Inc., 7 493–95; 27 432–35 (upd.); 110 443–50 (upd.)

Stefanel SpA, 63 361–63

Steiff *see* Margarete Steiff GmbH.

Steilmann Group *see* Klaus Steilmann GmbH & Co. KG.

Stein Mart Inc., 19 423–25; 72 337–39 (upd.)

Steinberg Incorporated, II 662–65

Steiner Corporation (Alsco), 53 308–11

Steinway Musical Instruments, Inc., 19 426–29; 111 446–51 (upd.)

Stelco Inc., IV 208–10; 51 349–52 (upd.)

Stelmar Shipping Ltd., 52 329–31

Stemilt Growers Inc., 94 407–10

Stepan Company, 30 437–39; 105 438–42 (upd.)

The Stephan Company, 60 285–88

Stephens Inc., 92 344–48

Stephens Media, LLC, 91 451–54

Steria SA, 49 382–85

Stericycle, Inc., 33 380–82; 74 316–18 (upd.)

Sterilite Corporation, 97 382–85

STERIS Corporation, 29 449–52

Sterling Chemicals, Inc., 16 460–63; 78 356–61 (upd.)

Sterling Drug Inc., I 698–700

Sterling Electronics Corp., 18 496–98

Sterling European Airlines A/S, 70 300–02

Sterling Financial Corporation, 106 451–55

Sterling Software, Inc., 11 468–70 *see also* Computer Associates International, Inc.

STET *see* Società Finanziaria Telefonica per Azioni.

Steuben Glass *see* Corning Inc.

Steve & Barry's LLC, 88 377–80

Stevedoring Services of America Inc., 28 435–37

Steven Madden, Ltd., 37 371–73

Stew Leonard's, 56 349–51

Stewart & Stevenson Services Inc., 11 471–73

Stewart Enterprises, Inc., 20 481–83

Stewart Information Services Corporation, 78 362–65

Stewart's Beverages, 39 383–86

Stewart's Shops Corporation, 80 360–63

Stickley *see* L. and J.G. Stickley, Inc.

Stiebel Eltron Group, 107 411–16

Stiefel Laboratories, Inc., 90 396–99

Stihl *see* Andreas Stihl AG & Co. KG.

Stillwater Mining Company, 47 380–82

Stimson Lumber Company Inc., 78 366–69

Stinnes AG, 8 494–97; 23 451–54 (upd.); 59 387–92 (upd.)

Stirling Group plc, 62 342–44

STMicroelectronics NV, 52 332–35

Stock Yards Packing Co., Inc., 37 374–76

Stoddard International plc, 72 340–43

Stoll-Moss Theatres Ltd., 34 420–22

Stollwerck AG, 53 312–15

Stolt-Nielsen S.A., 42 356–59; 54 349–50

Stolt Sea Farm Holdings PLC, 54 349–51

Stone & Webster, Inc., 13 495–98; 64 368–72 (upd.)

Stone Container Corporation, IV 332–34 *see also* Smurfit Kappa Group plc

Stone Manufacturing Company, 14 469–71; 43 392–96 (upd.)

Stonyfield Farm, Inc., 55 357–60

The Stop & Shop Supermarket Company, II 666–67; 24 460–62 (upd.); 68 350–53 (upd.)

Stora Enso Oyj, IV 335–37; 36 447–55 (upd.); 85 396–408 (upd.)

Storage Technology Corporation, 6 275–77

Storage USA, Inc., 21 475–77

Storehouse PLC, 16 464–66 *see also* Mothercare plc.

Stouffer Corp., 8 498–501 *see also* Nestlé S.A.

Strabag SE, 113 373–79

Strand Book Store Inc., 114 390–93

StrataCom, Inc., 16 467–69

Stratagene Corporation, 70 303–06

Stratasys, Inc., 67 361–63

Strattec Security Corporation, 73 324–27

Stratus Computer, Inc., 10 499–501

Straumann Holding AG, 79 396–99

Strauss Discount Auto, 56 352–54

Strauss-Elite Group, 68 354–57

Strayer Education, Inc., 53 316–19

StreamServe Inc., 113 380–83

Stride Rite Corporation, 8 502–04; 37 377–80 (upd.); 86 378–84 (upd.)

Strine Printing Company Inc., 88 381–84

Strix Ltd., 51 353–55

The Strober Organization, Inc., 82 357–60 *see also* Pro-Build Holdings Inc.

The Stroh Brewery Company, I 290–92; 18 499–502 (upd.)

Strombecker Corporation, 60 289–91

Strongwell Corporation, 110 451–54

Stroock & Stroock & Lavan LLP, 40 418–21

Strouds, Inc., 33 383–86

The Structure Tone Organization, 99 427–430

Stryker Corporation, 11 474–76; 29 453–55 (upd.); 79 400–05 (upd.)

Stuart C. Irby Company, 58 333–35

Stuart Entertainment Inc., 16 470–72

Student Loan Marketing Association, II 453–55 *see also* SLM Holding Corp.

Stuller Settings, Inc., 35 405–07

Sturm, Ruger & Company, Inc., 19 430–32

Stussy, Inc., 55 361–63

Sub Pop Ltd., 97 386–89

Sub-Zero Freezer Co., Inc., 31 426–28

Suburban Propane Partners, L.P., 30 440–42

Subway, 32 442–44 *see also* Doctor's Associates Inc.

Vornado Realty Trust, 20 508–10; 112 469–74 (upd.)

Vorwerk & Co. KG, 27 502–04; 112 475–79 (upd.)

Vosper Thornycroft Holding plc, 41 410–12

Vossloh AG, 53 348–52

Votorantim Participaçoes S.A., 76 375–78

Vought Aircraft Industries, Inc., 49 442–45

Vranken Pommery Monopole S.A., 114 501–05

VSE Corporation, 108 533–36

VSM *see* Village Super Market, Inc.

VTech Holdings Ltd., 77 481–84

Vueling Airlines S.A., 97 445–48

Vulcabras S.A., 103 500–04

Vulcan Materials Company, 7 572–75; 52 392–96 (upd.)

# W

W + K *see* Wieden + Kennedy.

W.A. Whitney Company, 53 353–56

W. Atlee Burpee & Co., 27 505–08

W.B Doner & Co., 56 369–72

W.B. Mason Company, 98 456–59

W.C. Bradley Co., 69 363–65

W.H. Brady Co., 16 518–21 *see also* Brady Corp.

W. H. Braum, Inc., 80 407–10

W H Smith Group PLC, V 211–13

W Jordan (Cereals) Ltd., 74 382–84

W.L. Gore & Associates, Inc., 14 538–40; 60 321–24 (upd.)

W.P. Carey & Co. LLC, 49 446–48

W.R. Berkley Corporation, 15 525–27; 74 385–88 (upd.)

W.R. Grace & Company, I 547–50; 50 522–29 (upd.)

W.S. Badcock Corporation, 107 461–64

W.W. Grainger, Inc., V 214–15; 26 537–39 (upd.); 68 392–95 (upd.)

W.W. Norton & Company, Inc., 28 518–20

Waban Inc., 13 547–49 *see also* HomeBase, Inc.

Wabash National Corp., 13 550–52

Wabtec Corporation, 40 451–54

Wachovia Bank of Georgia, N.A., 16 521–23

Wachovia Bank of South Carolina, N.A., 16 524–26

Wachovia Corporation, 12 516–20; 46 442–49 (upd.)

Wachtell, Lipton, Rosen & Katz, 47 435–38

The Wackenhut Corporation, 14 541–43; 63 423–26 (upd.)

Wacker-Chemie AG, 35 454–58; 112 480–85 (upd.)

Wacker Construction Equipment AG, 95 438–41

Wacoal Corp., 25 520–24

Waddell & Reed, Inc., 22 540–43

Waffle House Inc., 14 544–45; 60 325–27 (upd.)

Wagers Inc. (Idaho Candy Company), 86 416–19

Waggener Edstrom, 42 424–26

Wagon plc, 92 407–10

Wah Chang, 82 415–18

Wahl Clipper Corporation, 86 420–23

Wahoo's Fish Taco, 96 454–57

Wakefern Food Corporation, 33 434–37; 107 465–69 (upd.)

Wal-Mart de Mexico, S.A. de C.V., 35 459–61 (upd.)

Wal-Mart Stores, Inc., V 216–17; 8 555–57 (upd.); 26 522–26 (upd.); 63 427–32 (upd.)

Walbridge Aldinger Co., 38 480–82

Walbro Corporation, 13 553–55

Waldbaum, Inc., 19 479–81

Waldenbooks, 17 522–24; 86 424–28 (upd.)

Walgreen Co., V 218–20; 20 511–13 (upd.); 65 352–56 (upd.)

Walker Manufacturing Company, 19 482–84

Walkers Shortbread Ltd., 79 464–67

Walkers Snack Foods Ltd., 70 350–52

Wall Drug Store, Inc., 40 455–57

Wall Street Deli, Inc., 33 438–41

Wallace Computer Services, Inc., 36 507–10

Walsworth Publishing Company, Inc., 78 445–48

The Walt Disney Company, II 172–74; 6 174–77 (upd.); 30 487–91 (upd.); 63 433–38 (upd.)

Walter E. Smithe Furniture, Inc., 105 484–87

Walter Industries, Inc., III 765–67; 22 544–47 (upd.); 72 368–73 (upd.)

Walton Monroe Mills, Inc., 8 558–60 *see also* Avondale Industries.

WaMu *see* Washington Mutual, Inc.

Wanadoo S.A., 75 400–02

Wang Laboratories, Inc., III 168–70; 6 284–87 (upd.) *see also* Getronics NV.

Warburtons Ltd., 89 487–90

WARF *see* Wisconsin Alumni Research Foundation.

The Warnaco Group Inc., 12 521–23; 46 450–54 (upd.) *see also* Authentic Fitness Corp.

Warner Chilcott Limited, 85 446–49

Warner Communications Inc., II 175–77 *see also* AOL Time Warner Inc.

Warner-Lambert Co., I 710–12; 10 549–52 (upd.) *see also* Pfizer Inc.

Warner Music Group Corporation, 90 432–37 (upd.)

Warners' Stellian Inc., 67 384–87

Warrantech Corporation, 53 357–59

Warrell Corporation, 68 396–98

Warsteiner Group, 113 460–64

Wärtsilä Corporation, 100 442–46

Warwick Valley Telephone Company, 55 382–84

Wascana Energy Inc., 13 556–58

The Washington Companies, 33 442–45

Washington Federal, Inc., 17 525–27

Washington Football, Inc., 35 462–65

Washington Gas Light Company, 19 485–88

Washington H. Soul Pattinson and Company Limited, 112 486–91

Washington Mutual, Inc., 17 528–31; 93 483–89 (upd.)

Washington National Corporation, 12 524–26

Washington Natural Gas Company, 9 539–41 *see also* Puget Sound Energy Inc.

The Washington Post Company, IV 688–90; 20 515–18 (upd.); 109 577–83 (upd.)

Washington Scientific Industries, Inc., 17 532–34

Washington Water Power Company, 6 595–98 *see also* Avista Corp.

Wassall Plc, 18 548–50

Waste Connections, Inc., 46 455–57

Waste Holdings, Inc., 41 413–15

Waste Management Inc., V 752–54; 109 584–90 (upd.)

Water Pik Technologies, Inc., 34 498–501; 83 450–453 (upd.)

Waterford Wedgwood plc, 12 527–29; 34 493–97 (upd.) *see also* WWRD Holdings Ltd.

Waterhouse Investor Services, Inc., 18 551–53

Waters Corporation, 43 453–57

Watkins-Johnson Company, 15 528–30

Watsco Inc., 52 397–400

Watson Pharmaceuticals Inc., 16 527–29; 56 373–76 (upd.)

Watson Wyatt Worldwide, 42 427–30

Wattie's Ltd., 7 576–78

Watts of Lydney Group Ltd., 71 391–93

Watts Water Technologies, Inc., 19 489–91; 115 479–83 (upd.)

Wausau-Mosinee Paper Corporation, 60 328–31 (upd.)

Waverly, Inc., 16 530–32

Wawa Inc., 17 535–37; 78 449–52 (upd.)

The Wawanesa Mutual Insurance Company, 68 399–401

WAXIE Sanitary Supply, 100 447–51

Waxman Industries, Inc., 9 542–44

WAZ Media Group, 82 419–24

WB *see* Warner Communications Inc.

WD-40 Company, 18 554–57; 87 455–460 (upd.)

We-No-Nah Canoe, Inc., 98 460–63

WE: Women's Entertainment LLC, 114 506–10

Weather Central Inc., 100 452–55

The Weather Channel Companies, 52 401–04 *see also* Landmark Communications, Inc.

Weather Shield Manufacturing, Inc., 102 444–47

Weatherford International, Inc., 39 416–18

Weaver Popcorn Company, Inc., 89 491–93

Webasto Roof Systems Inc., 97 449–52

Webber Oil Company, 61 384–86

# Index to Industries

## Aerospace

Finmeccanica S.p.A., 84
First Aviation Services Inc., 49
G.I.E. Airbus Industrie, I; 12 (upd.)
GE Aircraft Engines, 9
GenCorp Inc., 8; 9 (upd.)
General Dynamics Corporation, I; 10
    (upd.); 40 (upd.); 88 (upd.
GKN plc, III; 38 (upd.); 89 (upd.)
Goodrich Corporation, 46 (upd.); 109
    (upd.)
Groupe Dassault Aviation SA, 26 (upd.)
Grumman Corporation, I; 11 (upd.)
Grupo Aeropuerto del Sureste, S.A. de
    C.V., 48
Gulfstream Aerospace Corporation, 7; 28
    (upd.)
HEICO Corporation, 30
Héroux-Devtek Inc., 69
International Lease Finance Corporation,
    48
Irkut Corporation, 68
Israel Aircraft Industries Ltd., 69
Kolbenschmidt Pierburg AG, 97
Kreisler Manufacturing Corporation, 97
Lancair International, Inc., 67
Latécoère S.A., 100
Learjet Inc., 8; 27 (upd.)
Lockheed Martin Corporation, I; 11
    (upd.); 15 (upd.); 89 (upd.)
Loral Space & Communications Ltd., 54
    (upd.)
Magellan Aerospace Corporation, 48
Martin Marietta Corporation, I
Martin-Baker Aircraft Company Limited,
    61
McDonnell Douglas Corporation, I; 11
    (upd.)
Meggitt PLC, 34
Messerschmitt-Bölkow-Blohm GmbH., I
Moog Inc., 13
Mooney Aerospace Group Ltd., 52
N.V. Koninklijke Nederlandse
    Vliegtuigenfabriek Fokker, I; 28 (upd.)
New Piper Aircraft, Inc., The, 44
Northrop Grumman Corporation, I; 11
    (upd.); 45 (upd.); 111 (upd.)
Orbital Sciences Corporation, 22; 107
    (upd.)
Pemco Aviation Group Inc., 54
Pratt & Whitney, 9
Raytheon Aircraft Holdings Inc., 46
Raytheon Company, II; 11 (upd.); 38
    (upd.); 105 (upd.)
Robinson Helicopter Company, 51
Rockwell Collins, 106
Rockwell International Corporation, I; 11
    (upd.)
Rohr Incorporated, 9
Rolls-Royce Allison, 29 (upd.)
Rolls-Royce plc, I; 7 (upd.); 21 (upd.)
Rostvertol plc, 62
Russian Aircraft Corporation (MiG), 86
Safe Flight Instrument Corporation, 71
Sequa Corporation, 13; 54 (upd.)
Shannon Aerospace Ltd., 36
Sikorsky Aircraft Corporation, 24; 104
    (upd.)
Smiths Industries PLC, 25

Snecma Group, 46
Société Air France, 27 (upd.)
Spacehab, Inc., 37
Spar Aerospace Limited, 32
Sukhoi Design Bureau Aviation
    Scientific-Industrial Complex, 24
Sundstrand Corporation, 7; 21 (upd.)
Surrey Satellite Technology Limited, 83
Swales & Associates, Inc., 69
Teledyne Technologies Inc., 62 (upd.)
Textron Lycoming Turbine Engine, 9
Thales S.A., 42
Thiokol Corporation, 9; 22 (upd.)
Umeco plc, 114
United Technologies Corporation, I; 10
    (upd.); 34 (upd.); 105 (upd.)
Van's Aircraft, Inc., 65
Vector Aerospace Corporation, 97
Vought Aircraft Industries, Inc., 49
Whittaker Corporation, 48 (upd.)
Woodward Governor Company, 13; 49
    (upd.); 105 (upd.)
Zodiac S.A., 36

# Agribusiness & Farming

AeroGrow International, Inc., 95
Ag-Chem Equipment Company, Inc., 17
AGCO Corporation, 13; 67 (upd.)
Agland, Inc., 110
Agrium Inc., 73
Alamo Group Inc., 32
Andersons, Inc., The, 31
BayWa AG, 112
Bou-Matic, 62
Corn Products International, Inc., 116
CTB International Corporation, 43 (upd.)
DeBruce Grain, Inc., 112
Garst Seed Company, Inc., 86
George W. Park Seed Company, Inc., 98
Kubota Corporation, III; 26 (upd.)
Pennington Seed Inc., 98
SLC Participaçoes S.A., 111
Staple Cotton Cooperative Association
    (Staplcotn), 86
W. Atlee Burpee & Co., 27
Wilbur-Ellis Company, 114

# Airlines

A/S Air Baltic Corporation, 71
AAR Corp., 28
Aer Lingus Group plc, 34; 89 (upd.)
Aeroflot - Russian Airlines JSC, 6; 29
    (upd.); 89 (upd.)
Aerolíneas Argentinas S.A., 33; 69 (upd.)
Air Berlin GmbH & Co. Luftverkehrs
    KG, 71
Air Canada, 6; 23 (upd.); 59 (upd.)
Air China Limited, 46; 108 (upd.)
Air France–KLM, 108 (upd.)
Air Jamaica Limited, 54
Air Mauritius Ltd., 63
Air New Zealand Limited, 14; 38 (upd.)
Air Pacific Ltd., 70
Air Partner PLC, 93
Air Sahara Limited, 65
Air Wisconsin Airlines Corporation, 55
Air Zimbabwe (Private) Limited, 91

AirAsia Berhad, 93
Air-India Limited, 6; 27 (upd.)
AirTran Holdings, Inc., 22
Alaska Air Group, Inc., 6; 29 (upd.)
Alitalia-Linee Aeree Italiana, S.p.A., 6; 29
    (upd.); 97 (upd.)
All Nippon Airways Co., Ltd., 6; 38
    (upd.); 91 (upd.)
Allegiant Travel Company, 97
Aloha Airlines, Incorporated, 24
America West Holdings Corporation, 6;
    34 (upd.)
American Airlines, I; 6 (upd.)
AMR Corporation, 28 (upd.); 52 (upd.)
Amtran, Inc., 34
Arrow Air Holdings Corporation, 55
AS Estonian Air, 71
Asiana Airlines, Inc., 46
ATA Holdings Corporation, 82
Atlantic Coast Airlines Holdings, Inc., 55
Atlantic Southeast Airlines, Inc., 47
Atlas Air, Inc., 39
Austrian Airlines AG (Österreichische
    Luftverkehrs AG), 33
Aviacionny Nauchno-Tehnicheskii
    Komplex im. A.N. Tupoleva, 24
Avianca Aerovías Nacionales de Colombia
    SA, 36
Azerbaijan Airlines, 77
Bahamas Air Holdings Ltd., 66
Banner Aerospace, Inc., 37 (upd.)
Braathens ASA, 47
Bradley Air Services Ltd., 56
Bristow Helicopters Ltd., 70
British Airways PLC, I; 14 (upd.); 43
    (upd.); 105 (upd.)
British Midland plc, 38
British World Airlines Ltd., 18
Cargolux Airlines International S.A., 49
Cathay Pacific Airways Limited, 6; 34
    (upd.); 111 (upd.)
Ceské aerolinie, a.s., 66
Chautauqua Airlines, Inc., 38
China Airlines, 34
China Eastern Airlines Corporation
    Limited, 31; 108 (upd.)
China Southern Airlines Company
    Limited, 33; 108 (upd.)
Comair Holdings Inc., 13; 34 (upd.)
Consorcio Aviacsa, S.A. de C.V., 85
Continental Airlines, Inc., I; 21 (upd.); 52
    (upd.); 110 (upd.)
Copa Holdings, S.A., 93
Corporación Internacional de Aviación,
    S.A. de C.V. (Cintra), 20
Cyprus Airways Public Limited, 81
dba Luftfahrtgesellschaft mbH, 76
Delta Air Lines, Inc., I; 6 (upd.); 39
    (upd.); 92 (upd.)
Deutsche Lufthansa AG, I; 26 (upd.); 68
    (upd.)
Eastern Airlines, I
easyJet Airline Company Limited, 39
EgyptAir, 6; 27 (upd.)
EL AL Israel Airlines Ltd., 23; 107 (upd.)
Emirates Group, The, 39; 81 (upd.)
Ethiopian Airlines, 81
Etihad Airways PJSC, 89

## Automotive

## Beverages

## Bio-Technology

Invitrogen Corporation, 52
Judge Group, Inc., The, 51
Kendle International Inc., 87
Landec Corporation, 95
Life Technologies, Inc., 17
LifeCell Corporation, 77
Lonza Group Ltd., 73
Martek Biosciences Corporation, 65
Medarex, Inc., 85
Medtronic, Inc., 8; 30 (upd.); 67 (upd.)
Meridian Bioscience, Inc., 115
Millipore Corporation, 25; 84 (upd.)
Minntech Corporation, 22
Mycogen Corporation, 21
Nektar Therapeutics, 91
New Brunswick Scientific Co., Inc., 45
Omrix Biopharmaceuticals, Inc., 95
Pacific Ethanol, Inc., 81
Pharmion Corporation, 91
Qiagen N.V., 39
Quintiles Transnational Corporation, 21
RTI Biologics, Inc., 96
Seminis, Inc., 29
Senomyx, Inc., 83
Serologicals Corporation, 63
Sigma-Aldrich Corporation, I; 36 (upd.);
   93 (upd.)
Starkey Laboratories, Inc., 52
STERIS Corporation, 29
Stratagene Corporation, 70
Talecris Biotherapeutics Holdings Corp.,
   114
Tanox, Inc., 77
TECHNE Corporation, 52
TriPath Imaging, Inc., 77
Viterra Inc., 105
Waters Corporation, 43
Whatman plc, 46
Wilmar International Ltd., 108
Wisconsin Alumni Research Foundation,
   65
Wyeth, 50 (upd.)

## Chemicals

A. Schulman, Inc., 8; 49 (upd.)
Aceto Corp., 38
Air Products and Chemicals, Inc., I; 10
   (upd.); 74 (upd.)
Airgas, Inc., 54
Akzo Nobel N.V., 13; 41 (upd.); 112
   (upd.)
Albaugh, Inc., 105
Albemarle Corporation, 59
AlliedSignal Inc., 9; 22 (upd.)
ALTANA AG, 87
American Cyanamid, I; 8 (upd.)
American Vanguard Corporation, 47
Arab Potash Company, 85
Arch Chemicals Inc., 78
ARCO Chemical Company, 10
Arkema S.A., 100
Asahi Denka Kogyo KK, 64
Atanor S.A., 62
Atochem S.A., I
Avantium Technologies BV, 79
Avecia Group PLC, 63
Azelis Group, 100

Baker Hughes Incorporated, III; 22
   (upd.); 57 (upd.)
Balchem Corporation, 42
BASF SE, I; 18 (upd.); 50 (upd.); 108
   (upd.)
Bayer A.G., I; 13 (upd.); 41 (upd.)
Betz Laboratories, Inc., I; 10 (upd.)
BFGoodrich Company, The, 19 (upd.)
BOC Group plc, I; 25 (upd.); 78 (upd.)
BorsodChem Zrt., 113
Braskem S.A., 108
Brenntag Holding GmbH & Co. KG, 8;
   23 (upd.); 101 (upd.)
Burmah Castrol PLC, 30 (upd.)
Cabot Corporation, 8; 29 (upd.); 91
   (upd.)
Calgon Carbon Corporation, 73
Caliper Life Sciences, Inc., 70
Calumet Specialty Products Partners, L.P.,
   106
Cambrex Corporation, 16
Campbell Brothers Limited, 115
Catalytica Energy Systems, Inc., 44
Celanese Corporation, I; 109 (upd.)
Celanese Mexicana, S.A. de C.V., 54
CF Industries Holdings, Inc., 99
Chemcentral Corporation, 8
Chemi-Trol Chemical Co., 16
Chemtura Corporation, 91 (upd.)
China Petroleum & Chemical
   Corporation (Sinopec Corp.), 109
Church & Dwight Co., Inc., 29
Ciba-Geigy Ltd., I; 8 (upd.)
Clorox Company, The, III; 22 (upd.); 81
   (upd.)
Croda International Plc, 45
Crompton Corporation, 9; 36 (upd.)
CVR Energy Corporation, 116
Cytec Industries Inc., 27
Degussa-Hüls AG, 32 (upd.)
DeKalb Genetics Corporation, 17
Dexter Corporation, The, I; 12 (upd.)
Dionex Corporation, 46
Dow Chemical Company, The, I; 8
   (upd.); 50 (upd.); 114 (upd.)
DSM N.V., I; 56 (upd.)
Dynaction S.A., 67
E.I. du Pont de Nemours & Company, I;
   8 (upd.); 26 (upd.); 73 (upd.)
Eastman Chemical Company, 14; 38
   (upd.); 116 (upd.)
Ecolab Inc., I; 13 (upd.); 34 (upd.); 85
   (upd.)
Eka Chemicals AB, 92
Elementis plc, 40 (upd.)
Engelhard Corporation, 72 (upd.)
English China Clays Ltd., 15 (upd.); 40
   (upd.)
Enterprise Rent-A-Car Company, 69
   (upd.)
Equistar Chemicals, LP, 71
Ercros S.A., 80
ERLY Industries Inc., 17
Ethyl Corporation, I; 10 (upd.)
Evonik Industries AG, 111 (upd.)
Ferro Corporation, 8; 56 (upd.)
Firmenich International S.A., 60
First Mississippi Corporation, 8

FMC Corporation, 89 (upd.)
Formosa Plastics Corporation, 14; 58
   (upd.)
Fort James Corporation, 22 (upd.)
Fuchs Petrolub AG, 102
G.A.F., I
General Chemical Group Inc., The, 37
Georgia Gulf Corporation, 9; 61 (upd.)
Givaudan SA, 43
Great Lakes Chemical Corporation, I; 14
   (upd.)
GROWMARK, Inc., 88
Grupo Comex, 115
Guerbet Group, 46
H.B. Fuller Company, 8; 32 (upd.); 75
   (upd.)
Hauser, Inc., 46
Hawkins Chemical, Inc., 16
Henkel KGaA, III; 34 (upd.); 95 (upd.)
Hercules Inc., I; 22 (upd.); 66 (upd.)
Hexion Specialty Chemicals, Inc., 116
Hillyard, Inc., 114
Hoechst A.G., I; 18 (upd.)
Hoechst Celanese Corporation, 13
Huls A.G., I
Huntsman Corporation, 8; 98 (upd.)
Ikonics Corporation, 99
IMC Fertilizer Group, Inc., 8
Imperial Chemical Industries PLC, I; 50
   (upd.)
Inergy L.P., 110
International Flavors & Fragrances Inc., 9;
   38 (upd.)
Israel Chemicals Ltd., 55
KBR Inc., 106 (upd.)
Kemira Oyj, 70
KMG Chemicals, Inc., 101
Koppers Industries, Inc., I; 26 (upd.)
Kwizda Holding GmbH, 102 (upd.)
L'Air Liquide SA, I; 47 (upd.)
Lawter International Inc., 14
LeaRonal, Inc., 23
Loctite Corporation, 30 (upd.)
Lonza Group Ltd., 73
Loos & Dilworth, Inc., 100
Lubrizol Corporation, The, I; 30 (upd.);
   83 (upd.)
LyondellBasell Industries Holdings N.V.,
   45 (upd.); 109 (upd.)
M.A. Hanna Company, 8
MacDermid Incorporated, 32
Makhteshim-Agan Industries Ltd., 85
Mallinckrodt Group Inc., 19
MBC Holding Company, 40
Melamine Chemicals, Inc., 27
Methanex Corporation, 40
Mexichem, S.A.B. de C.V., 99
Minerals Technologies Inc., 52 (upd.)
Mississippi Chemical Corporation, 39
Mitsubishi Chemical Corporation, I; 56
   (upd.)
Mitsui Petrochemical Industries, Ltd., 9
Monsanto Company, I; 9 (upd.); 29
   (upd.)
Montedison SpA, I
Morton International Inc., I; 9 (upd.); 80
   (upd.)
Mosaic Company, The, 91

Foncière Euris, 111
Fortune Brands, Inc., 29 (upd.); 68 (upd.)
Fraser & Neave Ltd., 54
Fuqua Industries, Inc., I
General Electric Company, 34 (upd.); 63 (upd.)
Genting Bhd., 65
GIB Group, 26 (upd.)
Gillett Holdings, Inc., 7
Gillette Company, The, III; 20 (upd.); 68 (upd.)
Granaria Holdings B.V., 66
Grand Metropolitan PLC, 14 (upd.)
Great American Management and Investment, Inc., 8
Greyhound Corporation, I
Groupe Bolloré, 67
Groupe Dubreuil S.A., 102
Groupe Louis Dreyfus S.A., 60
Grupo Brescia, 99
Grupo Carso, S.A. de C.V., 21; 107 (upd.)
Grupo Clarín S.A., 67
Grupo Industrial Bimbo, 19
Grupo Industrial Saltillo, S.A. de C.V., 54
Gulf & Western Inc., I
Haci Omer Sabanci Holdings A.S., 55
Hagemeyer N.V., 39
Hankyu Corporation, 23 (upd.)
Hanson PLC, III; 7 (upd.); 30 (upd.)
Hanwha Group, 62
Harbour Group Industries, Inc., 90
Hawk Corporation, 59
Henry Crown and Company, 91
Hitachi Zosen Corporation, III; 53 (upd.)
Ho-Chunk Inc., 61
Hutchison Whampoa Limited, 18; 49 (upd.); 111 (upd.)
Hyundai Group, III; 7 (upd.); 56 (upd.)
IC Industries, Inc., I
IDB Holding Corporation Ltd., 97
Idealab, 105
Ilitch Holdings Inc., 37; 86 (upd.)
Inchcape PLC, III; 16 (upd.); 50 (upd.)
Industria de Diseño Textil S.A. (Inditex), 64
Industrie Zignago Santa Margherita S.p.A., 67
Ingersoll-Rand PLC, III; 15 (upd.); 55 (upd.); 115 (upd.)
Ingram Industries, Inc., 11; 49 (upd.)
Instituto Nacional de Industria, I
International Controls Corporation, 10
International Telephone & Telegraph Corporation, I; 11 (upd.)
Investor AB, 63
Ishikawajima-Harima Heavy Industries Company, Ltd., III; 86 (upd.)
Israel Corporation Ltd., 108
Istituto per la Ricostruzione Industriale, I
ITOCHU Corporation, 32 (upd.)
J.R. Simplot Company, 60 (upd.)
Japan Tobacco Inc., 113 (upd.)
Jardine Matheson Holdings Limited, I; 20 (upd.); 93 (upd.)
Jason Incorporated, 23
Jefferson Smurfit Group plc, 19 (upd.)
Jim Pattison Group, The, 37

Jordan Industries, Inc., 36
José de Mello SGPS S.A., 96
Justin Industries, Inc., 19
Kanematsu Corporation, IV; 24 (upd.); 102 (upd.)
Kao Corporation, 20 (upd.)
Katy Industries, Inc., I; 51 (upd.)
Keppel Corporation Ltd., 73
Kesko Ltd. (Kesko Oy), 8; 27 (upd.)
Kidde plc, I; 44 (upd.)
King Ranch, Inc., 60 (upd.)
Knowledge Universe, Inc., 54
Koç Holding A.S., I; 54 (upd.)
Koch Industries, Inc., 77 (upd.)
Koninklijke Nedlloyd N.V., 26 (upd.)
Koor Industries Ltd., 25 (upd.); 68 (upd.)
Körber AG, 60
K2 Inc., 16; 84 (upd.)
L.L. Knickerbocker Co., Inc., The, 25
Lancaster Colony Corporation, 8; 61 (upd.)
Larry H. Miller Group of Companies, 29; 104 (upd.)
LDI Ltd., LLC, 76
Lear Siegler, Inc., I
Lefrak Organization Inc., 26
Leucadia National Corporation, 11; 71 (upd.)
Linde AG, 67 (upd.)
Litton Industries, Inc., I; 11 (upd.)
Loews Corporation, I; 12 (upd.); 36 (upd.); 93 (upd.)
Loral Corporation, 8
LTV Corporation, I; 24 (upd.)
LVMH Moët Hennessy Louis Vuitton S.A., 33 (upd.); 113 (upd.)
M&F Worldwide Corp., 38
Marmon Group, Inc., The, IV; 16 (upd.); 70 (upd.)
Marubeni Corporation, I; 24 (upd.); 104 (upd.)
MAXXAM Inc., 8
McKesson Corporation, I
McPherson's Ltd., 66
Melitta Unternehmensgruppe Bentz KG, 53
Menasha Corporation, 8; 59 (upd.)
Metallgesellschaft AG, 16 (upd.)
Metromedia Company, 7; 61 (upd.)
Minnesota Mining & Manufacturing Company (3M), I; 8 (upd.); 26 (upd.)
Mitsubishi Corporation, I; 12 (upd.); 116 (upd.)
Mitsubishi Heavy Industries, Ltd., III; 7 (upd.); 40 (upd.)
Mitsui & Co., Ltd., I; 28 (upd.); 110 (upd.)
Molson Companies Limited, The, I; 26 (upd.)
Mondragón Corporación Cooperativa, 101
Montedison S.p.A., 24 (upd.)
Munir Sukhtian Group, 104
NACCO Industries, Inc., 7; 78 (upd.)
Nagase & Co., Ltd., 61 (upd.)
National Service Industries, Inc., 11; 54 (upd.)
New Clicks Holdings Ltd., 86

New World Development Company Limited, 38 (upd.)
Nichimen Corporation, 24 (upd.)
Nichirei Corporation, 70
Nissho Iwai K.K., I
Noble Group Ltd., 111
Novar plc, 49 (upd.)
Ogden Corporation, I
Onex Corporation, 16; 65 (upd.)
Orkla ASA, 18; 82 (upd.)
Park-Ohio Holdings Corp., 17; 85 (upd.)
Pentair, Inc., 7; 26 (upd.); 81 (upd.)
Petrobras Energia Participaciones S.A., 72
Philip Morris Companies Inc., 44 (upd.)
Poliet S.A., 33
Powell Duffryn plc, 31
Power Corporation of Canada, 36 (upd.); 85 (upd.)
PPB Group Berhad, 57
Preussag AG, 17
Procter & Gamble Company, The, III; 8 (upd.); 26 (upd.); 67 (upd.)
Proeza S.A. de C.V., 82
PT Astra International Tbk, 56
Pubco Corporation, 17
Pulsar Internacional S.A., 21
R.B. Pamplin Corp., 45
Rank Organisation Plc, The, 14 (upd.)
Raymond Ltd., 77
Red Apple Group, Inc., 23
Roll International Corporation, 37
Rubbermaid Incorporated, 20 (upd.)
S.C. Johnson & Son, Inc., III; 28 (upd.); 89 (upd.)
Samsung Group, I
San Miguel Corporation, 15
Sara Lee Corporation, II; 15 (upd.); 54 (upd.); 99 (upd.)
Schindler Holding AG, 29
Scott Fetzer Company, 12; 80 (upd.)
Sea Containers Ltd., 29
Seaboard Corporation, 36; 85 (upd.)
Sealaska Corporation, 60
Sequa Corporation, 13; 54 (upd.)
Sequana Capital, 78 (upd.)
SHV Holdings N.V., 55
Sideco Americana S.A., 67
Sime Darby Berhad, 14; 36 (upd.)
Sistema JSFC, 73
SK Group, 88
Société du Louvre, 27
Sojitz Corporation, 96 (upd.)
Sonae SGPS, S.A., 97
Spectrum Brands, Inc., 109 (upd.)
Standex International Corporation, 17; 44 (upd.)
Steamships Trading Company Ltd., 82
Stinnes AG, 23 (upd.)
Sudbury Inc., 16
Sumitomo Corporation, I; 11 (upd.); 102 (upd.)
Swire Pacific Limited, I; 16 (upd.); 57 (upd.)
Talley Industries, Inc., 16
Tandycrafts, Inc., 31
TaurusHolding GmbH & Co. KG, 46
Teijin Limited, 61 (upd.)
Teledyne, Inc., I; 10 (upd.)

## Construction

Kraus-Anderson Companies, Inc., 36; 83 (upd.)
Kuhlman Corporation, 20
Kumagai Gumi Company, Ltd., I
Laing O'Rourke PLC, 93 (upd.)
Land and Houses PCL, 104
Ledcor Industries Limited, 46
Lennar Corporation, 11
L'Entreprise Jean Lefebvre, 23
Lincoln Property Company, 8
Lindal Cedar Homes, Inc., 29
Linde A.G., I
M. A. Mortenson Company, 115
Manitowoc Company, Inc., The, 18; 59 (upd.)
MasTec, Inc., 55
Matrix Service Company, 65
May Gurney Integrated Services PLC, 95
McCarthy Building Companies, Inc., 48
MDU Resources Group, Inc., 114 (upd.)
Mellon-Stuart Company, I
Michael Baker Corp., 14
Modtech Holdings, Inc., 77
Morrison Knudsen Corporation, 7; 28 (upd.)
Morrow Equipment Co. L.L.C., 87
Mota-Engil, SGPS, S.A., 97
New Holland N.V., 22
Newpark Resources, Inc., 63
Nortek, Inc., 34
NVR Inc., 8; 70 (upd.)
Obayashi Corporation, 78
Obrascon Huarte Lain S.A., 76
O'Connell Companies Inc., The, 100
Ohbayashi Corporation, I
Opus Corporation, 34; 101 (upd.)
Orascom Construction Industries S.A.E., 87
Orleans Homebuilders, Inc., 62
Panattoni Development Company, Inc., 99
Parsons Brinckerhoff Inc., 34; 104 (upd.)
Parsons Corporation, The, 8; 56 (upd.)
PCL Construction Group Inc., 50
Peninsular & Oriental Steam Navigation Company (Bovis Division), The, I
Pepper Construction Group, LLC, The, 111
Perini Corporation, 8; 82 (upd.)
Peter Kiewit Sons' Inc., 8
Philipp Holzmann AG, 17
Pinguely-Haulotte SA, 51
Post Properties, Inc., 26
Pulte Homes, Inc., 8; 42 (upd.); 113 (upd.)
Pyramid Companies, 54
Redrow Group plc, 31
Rinker Group Ltd., 65
RMC Group p.l.c., III; 34 (upd.)
Robertson-Ceco Corporation, 19
Rooney Brothers Co., 25
Rottlund Company, Inc., The, 28
Roy Anderson Corporation, 75
Ryan Companies US, Inc., 99
Ryland Group, Inc., The, 8; 37 (upd.); 107 (upd.)
Sandvik AB, IV; 32 (upd.); 77 (upd.)
Schuff Steel Company, 26

Seddon Group Ltd., 67
Servidyne Inc., 100 (upd.)
Shimizu Corporation, 109
Shorewood Packaging Corporation, 28
Simon Property Group Inc., 27; 84 (upd.)
Skanska AB, 38; 110 (upd.)
Skidmore, Owings & Merrill LLP, 69 (upd.)
SNC-Lavalin Group Inc., 72
Speedy Hire plc, 84
Stabler Companies Inc., 78
Standard Pacific Corporation, 52
Stone & Webster, Inc., 64 (upd.)
Strabag SE, 113
Structure Tone Organization, The, 99
Suffolk Construction Company, Inc., 114
Sundt Corp., 24
Swinerton Inc., 43
Tarmac Limited, III, 28 (upd.); 95 (upd.)
Taylor Wimpey PLC, I; 38 (upd.); 115 (upd.)
Technical Olympic USA, Inc., 75
Terex Corporation, 7; 40 (upd.); 91 (upd.)
ThyssenKrupp AG, IV; 28 (upd.); 87 (upd.)
TIC Holdings Inc., 92
Tishman Construction Company, 112
Toll Brothers Inc., 15; 70 (upd.)
Trammell Crow Company, 8
Tridel Enterprises Inc., 9
Tully Construction Co. Inc., 114
Turner Construction Company, 66
Turner Corporation, The, 8; 23 (upd.)
U.S. Aggregates, Inc., 42
U.S. Home Corporation, 8; 78 (upd.)
Urban Engineers, Inc., 102
Urbi Desarrollos Urbanos, S.A. de C.V., 81
VA TECH ELIN EBG GmbH, 49
Vecellio Group, Inc., 113
Veidekke ASA, 98
Veit Companies, 43; 92 (upd.)
Vinci S.A., 113 (upd.)
Wacker Construction Equipment AG, 95
Walbridge Aldinger Co., 38
Walter Industries, Inc., III; 22 (upd.); 72 (upd.)
Weitz Company, Inc., The, 42
Whiting-Turner Contracting Company, 95
Willbros Group, Inc., 56
William Lyon Homes, 59
Wilson Bowden Plc, 45
Wood Hall Trust PLC, I
WorleyParsons Ltd., 115
Yates Companies, Inc., The, 62
Zachry Group, Inc., 95

## Containers

Ball Corporation, I; 10 (upd.); 78 (upd.)
BWAY Corporation, 24
Chesapeake Corporation, 8; 30 (upd.); 93 (upd.)
CLARCOR Inc., 17; 61 (upd.)
Constar International Inc., 64
Continental Can Co., Inc., 15
Continental Group Company, I

Crown Cork & Seal Company, Inc., I; 13 (upd.); 32 (upd.)
Crown Holdings, Inc., 83 (upd.)
DIC Corporation, 115
Gaylord Container Corporation, 8
Golden Belt Manufacturing Co., 16
Graham Packaging Holdings Company, 87
Greif Inc., 15; 66 (upd.)
Grupo Industrial Durango, S.A. de C.V., 37
Hanjin Shipping Co., Ltd., 50
Heekin Can Inc., 13
Inland Container Corporation, 8
Interpool, Inc., 92
Kerr Group Inc., 24
Keyes Fibre Company, 9
Libbey Inc., 49
Liqui-Box Corporation, 16
Longaberger Company, The, 12
Longview Fibre Company, 8
Mead Corporation, The, 19 (upd.)
Metal Box PLC, I
Mobile Mini, Inc., 58
Molins plc, 51
National Can Corporation, I
Owens-Illinois, Inc., I; 26 (upd.); 85 (upd.)
Packaging Corporation of America, 51 (upd.)
Pochet SA, 55
Primerica Corporation, I
Printpack, Inc., 68
PVC Container Corporation, 67
Rexam PLC, 32 (upd.); 85 (upd.)
Reynolds Metals Company, 19 (upd.)
Royal Packaging Industries Van Leer N.V., 30
RPC Group PLC, 81
Sealright Co., Inc., 17
Shurgard Storage Centers, Inc., 52
Smurfit Kappa Group plc, 112 (upd.)
Smurfit-Stone Container Corporation, 26 (upd.); 83 (upd.)
Sonoco Products Company, 8; 89 (upd.)
Thermos Company, 16
Tim-Bar Corporation, 110
Toyo Seikan Kaisha, Ltd., I
U.S. Can Corporation, 30
Ultra Pac, Inc., 24
Viatech Continental Can Company, Inc., 25 (upd.)
Vidrala S.A., 67
Vitro Corporativo S.A. de C.V., 34

## Drugs & Pharmaceuticals

A.L. Pharma Inc., 12
A. Nelson & Co. Ltd., 75
Abbott Laboratories, I; 11 (upd.); 40 (upd.); 93 (upd.)
Aché Laboratórios Farmacéuticas S.A., 105
Actavis Group hf., 103
Actelion Ltd., 83
Adolor Corporation, 101
Akorn, Inc., 32
Albany Molecular Research, Inc., 77
Alfresa Holdings Corporation, 108
Allergan, Inc., 77 (upd.)

## Education & Training

ChartHouse International Learning
   Corporation, 49
Childtime Learning Centers, Inc., 34
Computer Learning Centers, Inc., 26
Corinthian Colleges, Inc., 39; 92 (upd.)
Cornell Companies, Inc., 112
Council on International Educational
   Exchange Inc., 81
DeVry Inc., 29; 82 (upd.)
ECC International Corp., 42
Edison Schools Inc., 37
Educate Inc., 86 (upd.)
Education Management Corporation, 35
Educational Testing Service, 12; 62 (upd.)
GP Strategies Corporation, 64 (upd.)
Green Dot Public Schools, 99
Grupo Positivo, 105
Huntington Learning Centers, Inc., 55
ITT Educational Services, Inc., 39; 76
   (upd.)
Jones Knowledge Group, Inc., 97
Kaplan, Inc., 42; 90 (upd.)
KinderCare Learning Centers, Inc., 13
Knowledge Learning Corporation, 51; 115
   (upd.)
Kumon Institute of Education Co., Ltd.,
   72
LeapFrog Enterprises, Inc., 54
Learning Care Group, Inc., 76 (upd.)
Learning Company Inc., The, 24
Learning Tree International Inc., 24
Lincoln Educational Services Corporation,
   111
LPA Holding Corporation, 81
Management and Training Corporation,
   28
Mount Sinai Medical Center, 112
National Heritage Academies, Inc., 60
New School, The, 103
Noah Education Holdings Ltd., 97
Nobel Learning Communities, Inc., 37;
   76 (upd.)
Plato Learning, Inc., 44
Renaissance Learning, Inc., 39; 100 (upd.)
Rosetta Stone Inc., 93
Scientific Learning Corporation, 95
Strayer Education, Inc., 53
Sylvan Learning Systems, Inc., 35
Whitman Education Group, Inc., 41
Youth Services International, Inc., 21

## Electrical & Electronics

ABB ASEA Brown Boveri Ltd., II; 22
   (upd.)
ABB Ltd., 65 (upd.)
Acer Incorporated, 16; 73 (upd.)
Acuson Corporation, 10; 36 (upd.)
ADC Telecommunications, Inc., 30 (upd.)
Adtran Inc., 22
Advanced Circuits Inc., 67
Advanced Micro Devices, Inc., 6; 30
   (upd.); 99 (upd.)
Advanced Technology Laboratories, Inc., 9
Agere Systems Inc., 61
Agilent Technologies Inc., 38; 93 (upd.)
Agilysys Inc., 76 (upd.)
Aiwa Co., Ltd., 30
AKG Acoustics GmbH, 62

Akzo Nobel N.V., 13; 41 (upd.)
Alienware Corporation, 81
Alliant Techsystems Inc., 30 (upd.); 77
   (upd.)
AlliedSignal Inc., 9; 22 (upd.)
Alpine Electronics, Inc., 13
Alps Electric Co., Ltd., II; 44 (upd.)
Altera Corporation, 18; 43 (upd.); 115
   (upd.)
Altron Incorporated, 20
Amdahl Corporation, 40 (upd.)
American Power Conversion Corporation,
   24; 67 (upd.)
American Superconductor Corporation,
   97
American Technical Ceramics Corp., 67
American Technology Corporation, 103
Amerigon Incorporated, 97
Amkor Technology, Inc., 69
AMP Incorporated, II; 14 (upd.)
Amphenol Corporation, 40
Amstrad plc, 48 (upd.)
Analog Devices, Inc., 10
Analogic Corporation, 23
Anam Group, 23
Anaren Microwave, Inc., 33
Andrew Corporation, 10; 32 (upd.)
Anixter International Inc., 88
Anritsu Corporation, 68
Anthem Electronics, Inc., 13
Apex Digital, Inc., 63
Apple Computer, Inc., 36 (upd.); 77
   (upd.)
Applied Materials, Inc., 114 (upd.)
Applied Micro Circuits Corporation, 38
Applied Power Inc., 9; 32 (upd.)
Applied Signal Technology, Inc., 87
Argon ST, Inc., 81
Arotech Corporation, 93
ARRIS Group, Inc., 89
Arrow Electronics, Inc., 10; 50 (upd.);
   110 (upd.)
Artesyn Technologies Inc., 46 (upd.)
Ascend Communications, Inc., 24
Astronics Corporation, 35
ASUSTeK Computer Inc., 107
Atari Corporation, 9; 23 (upd.); 66 (upd.)
ATI Technologies Inc., 79
Atmel Corporation, 17
ATMI, Inc., 93
AU Optronics Corporation, 67
Audiovox Corporation, 34; 90 (upd.)
Ault Incorporated, 34
Autodesk, Inc., 10; 89 (upd.)
Avnet Inc., 9; 111 (upd.)
AVX Corporation, 67
Axcelis Technologies, Inc., 95
Axsys Technologies, Inc., 93
Ballard Power Systems Inc., 73
Bang & Olufsen Holding A/S, 37; 86
   (upd.)
Barco NV, 44
Bel Fuse, Inc., 53
Belden CDT Inc., 19; 76 (upd.)
Bell Microproducts Inc., 69
Benchmark Electronics, Inc., 40
Bharat Electronics Limited, 113
Bicoastal Corporation, II

Black Box Corporation, 20; 96 (upd.)
Blonder Tongue Laboratories, Inc., 48
Blue Coat Systems, Inc., 83
BMC Industries, Inc., 17; 59 (upd.)
Bogen Communications International,
   Inc., 62
Borrego Solar Systems, Inc., 111
Bose Corporation, 13; 36 (upd.)
Boston Acoustics, Inc., 22
Bowthorpe plc, 33
Braun GmbH, 51; 109 (upd.)
Bridgelux, Inc., 112
Brightpoint Inc., 18; 106 (upd.)
Brightstar Corp., 114
Broadcom Corporation, 34; 90 (upd.)
Bull S.A., 43 (upd.)
Burr-Brown Corporation, 19
BVR Systems (1998) Ltd., 93
Cabletron Systems, Inc., 10
Cadence Design Systems, Inc., 48 (upd.)
Cambridge SoundWorks, Inc., 48
Campbell Hausfeld, 115
Canadian Solar Inc., 105
Canon Inc., III; 18 (upd.); 79 (upd.)
Carbone Lorraine S.A., 33
Cardtronics, Inc., 93
Carl Zeiss AG, III; 34 (upd.); 91 (upd.)
Cash Systems, Inc., 93
CASIO Computer Co., Ltd., III; 16
   (upd.); 40 (upd.)
C-COR.net Corp., 38
CDW Computer Centers, Inc., 52 (upd.)
Celestica Inc., 80
Checkpoint Systems, Inc., 39
Chi Mei Optoelectronics Corporation, 75
Christie Digital Systems, Inc., 103
Chubb, PLC, 50
Chunghwa Picture Tubes, Ltd., 75
Cirrus Logic, Inc., 48 (upd.)
Cisco Systems, Inc., 34 (upd.); 77 (upd.)
Citizen Watch Co., Ltd., III; 21 (upd.);
   81 (upd.)
Clarion Company Ltd., 64
Cobham plc, 30
Cobra Electronics Corporation, 14
Coherent, Inc., 31
Cohu, Inc., 32
Color Kinetics Incorporated, 85
Comfort Systems USA, Inc., 101
Compagnie Générale d'Électricité, II
Concurrent Computer Corporation, 75
Conexant Systems Inc., 36; 106 (upd.)
Continental Graphics Corporation, 110
Cooper Industries, Inc., II; 44 (upd.)
Cray Inc., 75 (upd.)
Cray Research, Inc., 16 (upd.)
Creative Technology Ltd., 57
Cree Inc., 53
CTS Corporation, 39
Cubic Corporation, 19; 98 (upd.)
Cypress Semiconductor Corporation, 20;
   48 (upd.)
D&H Distributing Co., 95
Dai Nippon Printing Co., Ltd., 57 (upd.)
Daiichikosho Company Ltd., 86
Daktronics, Inc., 32; 107 (upd.)
Dallas Semiconductor Corporation, 13; 31
   (upd.)

National Instruments Corporation, 22
National Presto Industries, Inc., 16; 43 (upd.)
National Semiconductor Corporation, II; 26 (upd.); 69 (upd.)
NEC Corporation, II; 21 (upd.); 57 (upd.)
Network Equipment Technologies Inc., 92
Nexans SA, 54
Nintendo Company, Ltd., III; 7 (upd.); 28 (upd.); 67 (upd.)
Nokia Corporation, II; 17 (upd.); 38 (upd.); 77 (upd.)
Nortel Networks Corporation, 36 (upd.)
Northrop Grumman Corporation, 45 (upd.); 111 (upd.)
Oak Technology, Inc., 22
Océ N.V., 24; 91 (upd.)
Oki Electric Industry Company, Limited, II
Omnicell, Inc., 89
OMRON Corporation, II; 28 (upd.); 115 (upd.)
Oplink Communications, Inc., 106
OPTEK Technology Inc., 98
Orbit International Corp., 105
Orbotech Ltd., 75
Otari Inc., 89
Otter Tail Power Company, 18
Palm, Inc., 36; 75 (upd.)
Palomar Medical Technologies, Inc., 22
Parlex Corporation, 61
Peak Technologies Group, Inc., The, 14
Peavey Electronics Corporation, 16
Philips Electronics N.V., II; 13 (upd.)
Philips Electronics North America Corp., 13
Pioneer Electronic Corporation, III; 28 (upd.)
Pioneer-Standard Electronics Inc., 19
Pitney Bowes Inc., III; 19 (upd.); 47 (upd.)
Pittway Corporation, 9; 33 (upd.)
Pixelworks, Inc., 69
Planar Systems, Inc., 61
Plantronics, Inc., 106
Plessey Company, PLC, The, II
Plexus Corporation, 35; 80 (upd.)
Polaroid Corporation, III; 7 (upd.); 28 (upd.); 93 (upd.)
Polk Audio, Inc., 34
Potter & Brumfield Inc., 11
Premier Industrial Corporation, 9
Protection One, Inc., 32
QUALCOMM Incorporated, 114 (upd.)
Quanta Computer Inc., 47; 79 (upd.); 110 (upd.)
Racal Electronics PLC, II
RadioShack Corporation, 36 (upd.); 101 (upd.)
Radius Inc., 16
RAE Systems Inc., 83
Ramtron International Corporation, 89
Raychem Corporation, 8
Raymarine plc, 104
Rayovac Corporation, 13; 39 (upd.)
Raytheon Company, II; 11 (upd.); 38 (upd.); 105 (upd.)

RCA Corporation, II
Read-Rite Corp., 10
Redback Networks, Inc., 92
Reliance Electric Company, 9
Research in Motion Ltd., 54
Rexel, Inc., 15
Richardson Electronics, Ltd., 17
Ricoh Company, Ltd., III; 36 (upd.); 108 (upd.)
Rimage Corp., 89
Rival Company, The, 19
Rockford Corporation, 43
Rogers Corporation, 61; 80 (upd.)
S&C Electric Company, 15
SAGEM S.A., 37
St. Louis Music, Inc., 48
Sam Ash Music Corporation, 30
Samsung Electronics Co., Ltd., 14; 41 (upd.); 108 (upd.)
Sanmina-SCI Corporation, 109 (upd.)
SANYO Electric Co., Ltd., II; 36 (upd.); 95 (upd.)
Sarnoff Corporation, 57
ScanSource, Inc., 29; 74 (upd.)
Schneider Electric SA, II; 18 (upd.); 108 (upd.)
SCI Systems, Inc., 9
Scientific-Atlanta, Inc., 45 (upd.)
Scitex Corporation Ltd., 24
Seagate Technology, 8; 34 (upd.); 105 (upd.)
SEGA Corporation, 73
Semitool, Inc., 79 (upd.)
Semtech Corporation, 32
Sennheiser Electronic GmbH & Co. KG, 66
Sensormatic Electronics Corp., 11
Sensory Science Corporation, 37
SGI, 29 (upd.)
Sharp Corporation, II; 12 (upd.); 40 (upd.); 114 (upd.)
Sheldahl Inc., 23
Shure Inc., 60
Siemens AG, II; 14 (upd.); 57 (upd.)
Sierra Nevada Corporation, 108
Silicon Graphics Incorporated, 9
Siltronic AG, 90
SL Industries, Inc., 77
Sling Media, Inc., 112
SMART Modular Technologies, Inc., 86
Smiths Industries PLC, 25
Solectron Corporation, 12; 48 (upd.)
Sony Corporation, II; 12 (upd.); 40 (upd.); 108 (upd.)
Spansion Inc., 80
Spectrum Control, Inc., 67
SPX Corporation, 10; 47 (upd.); 103 (upd.)
Square D, 90
Sterling Electronics Corp., 18
STMicroelectronics NV, 52
Strix Ltd., 51
Stuart C. Irby Company, 58
Sumitomo Electric Industries, Ltd., II
Sun Microsystems, Inc., 7; 30 (upd.); 91 (upd.)
Sunbeam-Oster Co., Inc., 9
SunPower Corporation, 91

Suntech Power Holdings Company Ltd., 89
Suntron Corporation, 107
SunWize Technologies, Inc., 114
Synaptics Incorporated, 95
Syneron Medical Ltd., 91
SYNNEX Corporation, 73
Synopsys, Inc., 11; 69 (upd.)
Syntax-Brillian Corporation, 102
Sypris Solutions, Inc., 85
SyQuest Technology, Inc., 18
Taiwan Semiconductor Manufacturing Company Ltd., 47
Tandy Corporation, II; 12 (upd.)
Tatung Co., 23
TDK Corporation, II; 17 (upd.); 49 (upd.); 114 (upd.)
TEAC Corporation, 78
Technitrol, Inc., 29
Tech-Sym Corporation, 18
Tektronix, Inc., 8
Teledyne Technologies Inc., 62 (upd.)
Telxon Corporation, 10
Teradyne, Inc., 11; 98 (upd.)
Texas Instruments Inc., II; 11 (upd.); 46 (upd.)
Thales S.A., 42
Thomas & Betts Corporation, 11; 54 (upd.); 114 (upd.)
THOMSON multimedia S.A., II; 42 (upd.)
THQ, Inc., 92 (upd.)
Titan Corporation, The, 36
TiVo Inc., 75
TomTom N.V., 81
Tops Appliance City, Inc., 17
Toromont Industries, Ltd., 21
Trans-Lux Corporation, 51
Trimble Navigation Limited, 40
TriQuint Semiconductor, Inc., 63
TT electronics plc, 111
Tweeter Home Entertainment Group, Inc., 30
Ultimate Electronics, Inc., 69 (upd.)
Ultrak Inc., 24
Uniden Corporation, 98
Unisys Corporation, 112 (upd.)
United Microelectronics Corporation, 98
Universal Electronics Inc., 39
Universal Security Instruments, Inc., 96
Varian, Inc., 12; 48 (upd.)
Veeco Instruments Inc., 32
VIASYS Healthcare, Inc., 52
Viasystems Group, Inc., 67
Vicon Industries, Inc., 44
Victor Company of Japan, Limited, II; 26 (upd.); 83 (upd.)
Vishay Intertechnology, Inc., 21; 80 (upd.)
Vitesse Semiconductor Corporation, 32
Vitro Corp., 10
Vizio, Inc., 100
VLSI Technology, Inc., 16
Vorwerk & Co. KG, 112 (upd.)
VTech Holdings Ltd., 77
Wells-Gardner Electronics Corporation, 43
WESCO International, Inc., 116

Westinghouse Electric Corporation, II; 12 (upd.)
Winbond Electronics Corporation, 74
Wincor Nixdorf Holding GmbH, 69 (upd.)
WuXi AppTec Company Ltd., 103
Wyle Electronics, 14
Xantrex Technology Inc., 97
Xerox Corporation, III; 6 (upd.); 26 (upd.); 69 (upd.)
Yageo Corporation, 16; 98 (upd.)
York Research Corporation, 35
Zenith Data Systems, Inc., 10
Zenith Electronics Corporation, II; 13 (upd.); 34 (upd.); 89 (upd.)
Zoom Telephonics, Inc., 18
Zoran Corporation, 77
Zumtobel AG, 50
Zytec Corporation, 19

## Engineering & Management Services

AAON, Inc., 22
Aavid Thermal Technologies, Inc., 29
Acergy SA, 97
AECOM Technology Corporation, 79
Alliant Techsystems Inc., 30 (upd.)
Altran Technologies, 51
AMEC plc, 112
American Science & Engineering, Inc., 81
Amey Plc, 47
Analytic Sciences Corporation, 10
Arcadis NV, 26
Arthur D. Little, Inc., 35
Austin Company, The, 8; 72 (upd.)
Autostrada Torino-Milano S.p.A., 101
Babcock International Group PLC, 69
Balfour Beatty plc, 36 (upd.)
BE&K, Inc., 73
Bechtel Corporation, I; 24 (upd.); 99 (upd.)
Birse Group PLC, 77
Bowen Engineering Corporation, 105
Brock Group of Companies, The, 114
Brown & Root, Inc., 13
Bufete Industrial, S.A. de C.V., 34
C.H. Heist Corporation, 24
Camp Dresser & McKee Inc., 104
CDI Corporation, 6; 54 (upd.)
CH2M HILL Companies Ltd., 22; 96 (upd.)
Charles Stark Draper Laboratory, Inc., The, 35
Coflexip S.A., 25
CompuDyne Corporation, 51
Cornell Companies, Inc., 112
Corrections Corporation of America, 23
CRSS Inc., 6
Dames & Moore, Inc., 25
DAW Technologies, Inc., 25
Day & Zimmermann Inc., 9; 31 (upd.)
Donaldson Company, Inc., 16; 49 (upd.); 108 (upd.)
Doosan Heavy Industries and Construction Company Ltd., 108
Dycom Industries, Inc., 57
Edwards and Kelcey, 70
EG&G Incorporated, 8; 29 (upd.)

Eiffage, 27
Elliott-Lewis Corporation, 100
Essef Corporation, 18
Exponent, Inc., 95
FKI Plc, 57
Fluor Corporation, 34 (upd.); 112 (upd.)
Forest City Enterprises, Inc., 52 (upd.)
Foster Wheeler Ltd., 6; 23 (upd.); 76 (upd.)
Framatome SA, 19
Fraport AG Frankfurt Airport Services Worldwide, 90
Freese and Nichols, Inc., 107
Fugro N.V., 98
Gale International Llc, 93
Georg Fischer AG Schaffhausen, 61
Gilbane, Inc., 34
Great Lakes Dredge & Dock Company, 69
Grontmij N.V., 110
Grupo Dragados SA, 55
Halliburton Company, III; 25 (upd.); 55 (upd.)
Halma plc, 104
Harding Lawson Associates Group, Inc., 16
Harley Ellis Devereaux Corporation, 101
Harza Engineering Company, 14
HDR Inc., 48
Hittite Microwave Corporation, 106
HOK Group, Inc., 59
ICF Kaiser International, Inc., 28
IHC Caland N.V., 71
Invensys PLC, 50 (upd.)
Jacobs Engineering Group Inc., 6; 26 (upd.); 106 (upd.)
Jacques Whitford, 92
Jaiprakash Associates Limited, 101
Judge Group, Inc., The, 51
JWP Inc., 9
KBR Inc., 106 (upd.)
Keith Companies Inc., The, 54
Keller Group PLC, 95
Klöckner-Werke AG, 58 (upd.)
Kvaerner ASA, 36
Layne Christensen Company, 19
Louis Berger Group, Inc., The, 104
MacNeal-Schwendler Corporation, The, 25
Malcolm Pirnie, Inc., 42
Mason & Hanger Group Inc., 110
McDermott International, Inc., III; 37 (upd.)
McKinsey & Company, Inc., 9
Mead & Hunt Inc., 113
Michael Baker Corporation, 51 (upd.)
Mota-Engil, SGPS, S.A., 97
MSE, Inc., 113
National Technical Systems, Inc., 111
NBBJ, 111
Nooter Corporation, 61
NTD Architecture, 101
Oceaneering International, Inc., 63
Odebrecht S.A., 73
Ogden Corporation, 6
Opus Corporation, 34; 101 (upd.)
PAREXEL International Corporation, 84
Parsons Brinckerhoff Inc., 34; 104 (upd.)

Parsons Corporation, The, 8; 56 (upd.)
PBSJ Corporation, The, 82
Petrofac Ltd., 95
Quanta Services, Inc., 79
RCM Technologies, Inc., 34
Renishaw plc, 46
Ricardo plc, 90
Rosemount Inc., 15
Roy F. Weston, Inc., 33
Royal Vopak NV, 41
Rust International Inc., 11
Sandia National Laboratories, 49
Sandvik AB, IV; 32 (upd.); 77 (upd.)
Sarnoff Corporation, 57
Science Applications International Corporation, 15; 109 (upd.)
SENTEL Corporation, 106
Serco Group plc, 47
Siegel & Gale, 64
Siemens AG, 57 (upd.)
SRI International, Inc., 57
SSOE Inc., 76
Stone & Webster, Inc., 13; 64 (upd.)
Sulzer Ltd., III; 68 (upd.)
Susquehanna Pfaltzgraff Company, 8
Sverdrup Corporation, 14
Technip, 78
Tech-Sym Corporation, 44 (upd.)
Teledyne Brown Engineering, Inc., 110
Tetra Tech, Inc., 29
ThyssenKrupp AG, IV; 28 (upd.); 87 (upd.)
Towers Perrin, 32
Tracor Inc., 17
TRC Companies, Inc., 32
U.S. Army Corps of Engineers, 91
Underwriters Laboratories, Inc., 30
United Dominion Industries Limited, 8; 16 (upd.)
URS Corporation, 45; 80 (upd.)
VA TECH ELIN EBG GmbH, 49
VECO International, Inc., 7
Vinci, 43
Volkert and Associates, Inc., 98
VSE Corporation, 108
Weir Group PLC, The, 85
Willbros Group, Inc., 56
WS Atkins Plc, 45

## Entertainment & Leisure

A&E Television Networks, 32
Aardman Animations Ltd., 61
ABC Family Worldwide, Inc., 52
Academy of Television Arts & Sciences, Inc., 55
Acclaim Entertainment Inc., 24
Activision, Inc., 32; 89 (upd.)
Acushnet Company, 64
Adams Golf, Inc., 37
Adelman Travel Group, 105
AEI Music Network Inc., 35
Affinity Group Holding Inc., 56
Airtours Plc, 27
Alaska Railroad Corporation, 60
Aldila, Inc., 46
All American Communications Inc., 20
All England Lawn Tennis & Croquet Club, The, 54

## Financial Services: Banks

## Financial Services: Excluding Banks

## Food Products

## Food Services, Retailers, & Restaurants

## Health, Personal & Medical Care Products

## Hotels

## Information Technology

## Insurance

## Legal Services

Holme Roberts & Owen LLP, 28
Hughes Hubbard & Reed LLP, 44
Hunton & Williams, 35
Jenkens & Gilchrist, P.C., 65
Jones, Day, Reavis & Pogue, 33
Kelley Drye & Warren LLP, 40
King & Spalding, 23; 115 (upd.)
Kirkland & Ellis LLP, 65
Lambda Legal Defense and Education
    Fund, Inc., 106
Latham & Watkins, 33
LeBoeuf, Lamb, Greene & MacRae,
    L.L.P., 29
LECG Corporation, 93
Legal Aid Society, The, 48
Mayer, Brown, Rowe & Maw, 47
Milbank, Tweed, Hadley & McCloy, 27
Morgan, Lewis & Bockius LLP, 29
Morrison & Foerster LLP, 78
O'Melveny & Myers, 37
Oppenheimer Wolff & Donnelly LLP, 71
Orrick, Herrington and Sutcliffe LLP, 76
Patton Boggs LLP, 71
Paul, Hastings, Janofsky & Walker LLP,
    27
Paul, Weiss, Rifkind, Wharton &
    Garrison, 47
Pepper Hamilton LLP, 43
Perkins Coie LLP, 56
Phillips Lytle LLP, 102
Pillsbury Madison & Sutro LLP, 29
Pre-Paid Legal Services, Inc., 20
Proskauer Rose LLP, 47
Quinn Emanuel Urquhart Oliver &
    Hedges, LLP, 99
Robins, Kaplan, Miller & Ciresi L.L.P., 89
Ropes & Gray, 40
Saul Ewing LLP, 74
Seyfarth Shaw LLP, 93
Shearman & Sterling, 32
Sidley Austin Brown & Wood, 40
Simpson Thacher & Bartlett, 39
Skadden, Arps, Slate, Meagher & Flom,
    18
Slaughter and May, 112
Snell & Wilmer L.L.P., 28
Sonnenschein Nath and Rosenthal LLP,
    102
Southern Poverty Law Center, Inc., 74
Stroock & Stroock & Lavan LLP, 40
Sullivan & Cromwell, 26
Troutman Sanders L.L.P., 79
Vinson & Elkins L.L.P., 30
Wachtell, Lipton, Rosen & Katz, 47
Weil, Gotshal & Manges LLP, 55
White & Case LLP, 35
Williams & Connolly LLP, 47
Willkie Farr & Gallagher LLP, 95
Wilmer Cutler Pickering Hale and Dorr
    L.L.P., 109
Wilson Sonsini Goodrich & Rosati, 34
Winston & Strawn, 35
Womble Carlyle Sandridge & Rice, PLLC,
    52

## Manufacturing

A.O. Smith Corporation, 11; 40 (upd.);
    93 (upd.)

A.T. Cross Company, 17; 49 (upd.)
A.W. Faber-Castell
    Unternehmensverwaltung GmbH &
    Co., 51
AAF-McQuay Incorporated, 26
Aalborg Industries A/S, 90
ACCO World Corporation, 7; 51 (upd.)
Acme United Corporation, 70
Acme-Cleveland Corp., 13
Acuity Brands, Inc., 90
Adolf Würth GmbH & Co. KG, 49
AEP Industries, Inc., 36
Aga Foodservice Group PLC, 73
Agfa Gevaert Group N.V., 59
Ahlstrom Corporation, 53
Aktiebolaget Electrolux, 22 (upd.)
Albert Trostel and Sons Company, 113
Alfa Laval AB, III; 64 (upd.)
Alliance Laundry Holdings LLC, 102
Allied Defense Group, Inc., The, 65
Allied Products Corporation, 21
Alltrista Corporation, 30
ALSTOM, 108
Alvis Plc, 47
American Cast Iron Pipe Company, 50
American Equipment Company, Inc., 104
American Homestar Corporation, 18; 41
    (upd.)
American Locker Group Incorporated, 34
American Seating Company, 78
American Tourister, Inc., 16
American Woodmark Corporation, 31
Amerock Corporation, 53
Ameron International Corporation, 67
AMETEK, Inc., 9; 114 (upd.)
Ampacet Corporation, 67
Anchor Hocking Glassware, 13
Andreas Stihl AG & Co. KG, 16; 59
    (upd.)
Andritz AG, 51
Applica Incorporated, 43 (upd.)
Applied Films Corporation, 48
Applied Materials, Inc., 10; 46 (upd.)
AptarGroup, Inc., 69
Arc International, 76
Arçelik A.S., 100
Arctic Cat Inc., 16; 40 (upd.); 96 (upd.)
AREVA NP, 90 (upd.)
Ariens Company, 48
Aristotle Corporation, The, 62
Armor All Products Corp., 16
Armstrong Holdings, Inc., III; 22 (upd.);
    81 (upd.)
Art's Way Manufacturing Co., Inc., 101
Ashley Furniture Industries, Inc., 35
Assa Abloy AB, 112
Atlantis Plastics, Inc., 85
Atlas Copco AB, III; 28 (upd.); 85 (upd.)
Atwood Mobil Products, 53
Austin Powder Company, 76
AZZ Incorporated, 93
B.J. Alan Co., Inc., 67
Babcock & Wilcox Company, The, 82
Badger Meter, Inc., 22
Baldor Electric Company, 21; 97 (upd.)
Baldwin Technology Company, Inc., 25;
    107 (upd.)
Ballantyne of Omaha, Inc., 27

Bally Manufacturing Corporation, III
Baltimore Aircoil Company, Inc., 66
Bandai Co., Ltd., 55
Barmag AG, 39
Barnes Group Inc., 13; 69 (upd.)
Barry-Wehmiller Companies, Inc., 90
Bassett Furniture Industries, Inc., 18; 95
    (upd.)
Bath Iron Works, 12; 36 (upd.)
Baxi Group Ltd., 96
Beckman Coulter, Inc., 22
Beckman Instruments, Inc., 14
Behr Process Corporation, 115
BEI Technologies, Inc., 65
Bekaert S.A./N.V., 90
Belleek Pottery Ltd., 71
Benjamin Moore & Co., 13; 38 (upd.);
    115 (upd.)
Benninger AG, 107
Berger Bros Company, 62
Bernina Holding AG, 47
Berwick Offray, LLC, 70
Bianchi International (d/b/a Gregory
    Mountain Products), 76
BIC Corporation, 8; 23 (upd.)
Bing Group, The, 60
Binks Sames Corporation, 21
Binney & Smith Inc., 25
BISSELL Inc., 9; 30 (upd.)
Black & Decker Corporation, The, III; 20
    (upd.); 67 (upd.)
Blodgett Holdings, Inc., 61 (upd.)
Blount International, Inc., 12; 48 (upd.)
Blyth, Inc., 18; 74 (upd.)
Bodum Design Group AG, 47
Bombril S.A., 111
Borrego Solar Systems, Inc., 111
Borroughs Corporation, 110
Boston Scientific Corporation, 37; 77
    (upd.)
Boyds Collection, Ltd., The, 29
BPB plc, 83
Brady Corporation 78 (upd.)
Brammer PLC, 77
Breeze-Eastern Corporation, 95
Brenco, Inc., 104
Bridgeport Machines, Inc., 17
Briggs & Stratton Corporation, 8; 27
    (upd.)
BRIO AB, 24; 103 (upd.)
BRITA GmbH, 112
Broan-NuTone LLC, 104
Brother Industries, Ltd., 14
Brown & Sharpe Manufacturing Co., 23
Brown Jordan International Inc., 74
    (upd.)
Broyhill Furniture Industries, Inc., 10
Bruker Corporation, 113
BSH Bosch und Siemens Hausgeräte
    GmbH, 67
BTR Siebe plc, 27
Buck Knives Inc., 48
Buckeye Technologies, Inc., 42
Bulgari S.p.A., 20; 106 (upd.)
Bulova Corporation, 13; 41 (upd.)
Bundy Corporation, 17
Burelle S.A., 23
Bush Industries, Inc., 20

Butler Manufacturing Company, 12; 62 (upd.)
California Cedar Products Company, 58
Cameron International Corporation, 110
Campbell Scientific, Inc., 51
Canam Group Inc., 114
Cannondale Corporation, 21
Capstone Turbine Corporation, 75
Caradon plc, 20 (upd.)
Carbide/Graphite Group, Inc., The, 40
Carbo PLC, 67 (upd.)
Cardo AB, 53
Carrier Corporation, 7; 69 (upd.)
Cascade Corporation, 65
Catalina Lighting, Inc., 43 (upd.)
Central Sprinkler Corporation, 29
Centuri Corporation, 54
Cepheid, 77
Champion Enterprises, Inc., 17
Charisma Brands LLC, 74
Charles Machine Works, Inc., The, 64
Chart Industries, Inc., 21; 96 (upd.)
Chemring Group plc, 113
Chittenden & Eastman Company, 58
Christian Dalloz SA, 40
Christofle SA, 40
Chromcraft Revington, Inc., 15
Cincinnati Lamb Inc., 72
Cincinnati Milacron Inc., 12
Cinemeccanica SpA, 78
Circon Corporation, 21
CIRCOR International, Inc., 115
Citizen Watch Co., Ltd., III; 21 (upd.); 81 (upd.)
Clark Equipment Company, 8
Clopay Corporation, 100
Cloverdale Paint Inc., 115
Cognex Corporation, 76
Colfax Corporation, 58
Colt's Manufacturing Company, Inc., 12
Columbia Manufacturing, Inc., 114
Columbus McKinnon Corporation, 37
Compass Minerals International, Inc., 79
Concord Camera Corporation, 41
Congoleum Corporation, 18; 98 (upd.)
Controladora Mabe, S.A. de C.V., 82
Corrpro Companies, Inc., 20
Corticeira Amorim, Sociedade Gestora de Participaço es Sociais, S.A., 48
CPAC, Inc., 86
Crane Co., 8; 30 (upd.); 101 (upd.)
C-Tech Industries Inc., 90
Cuisinart Corporation, 24
Culligan Water Technologies, Inc., 12; 38 (upd.)
CUNO Incorporated, 57
Curtiss-Wright Corporation, 10; 35 (upd.)
Cutera, Inc., 84
Cymer, Inc., 77
D. Swarovski & Co., 112 (upd.)
Daikin Industries, Ltd., III
Dalian Shide Group, 91
Danfoss A/S, 113
DCN S.A., 75
De Rigo S.p.A., 104
Dearborn Mid-West Conveyor Company, 56
Deceuninck N.V., 84

Decora Industries, Inc., 31
Decorator Industries Inc., 68
Deere & Company, 113 (upd.)
Delachaux S.A., 76
De'Longhi S.p.A., 66
DEMCO, Inc., 60
Denby Group plc, 44
Denison International plc, 46
Department 56, Inc., 14
Detroit Diesel Corporation, 10; 74 (upd.)
Deutsche Babcock A.G., III
Deutsche Steinzeug Cremer & Breuer Aktiengesellschaft, 91
Deutz AG, 39
Dial-A-Mattress Operating Corporation, 46
Diebold, Incorporated, 7; 22 (upd.)
Dixon Industries, Inc., 26
Dixon Ticonderoga Company, 12; 69 (upd.)
Djarum PT, 62
DMI Furniture, Inc., 46
Dorel Industries Inc., 59
Dover Corporation, III; 28 (upd.); 90 (upd.)
Dresser Industries, Inc., III
Drew Industries Inc., 28
Drexel Heritage Furnishings Inc., 12
Duncan Toys Company, 55
Dunn-Edwards Corporation, 56
Duracell International Inc., 9; 71 (upd.)
Durametallic, 21
Duriron Company Inc., 17
Dürkopp Adler AG, 65
Dynea, 68
Eagle-Picher Industries, Inc., 8; 23 (upd.)
East Penn Manufacturing Co., Inc., 79
Eastern Company, The, 48
Eastman Kodak Company, III; 7 (upd.); 36 (upd.); 91 (upd.)
Ebara Corporation, 83
EDO Corporation, 46
Edwards Group Limited, 115
Ekco Group, Inc., 16
Ekornes ASA, 110
Elamex, S.A. de C.V., 51
Electrolux AB, III; 53 (upd.)
Eljer Industries, Inc., 24
Elkay Manufacturing Company, 73
EMCO Enterprises, Inc., 102
Encore Wire Corporation, 81
Endress+Hauser Holding AG, 102
Energizer Holdings Inc., 32; 109 (upd.)
Energy Conversion Devices, Inc., 75
Energy Recovery, Inc., 108
EnerSys Inc., 99
Enesco Corporation, 11
Engineered Support Systems, Inc., 59
English China Clays Ltd., 40 (upd.)
EnPro Industries, Inc., 93
Escalade, Incorporated, 19
ESCO Technologies Inc., 87
Essel Propack Limited, 115
Esterline Technologies Corp., 15
Ethan Allen Interiors, Inc., 12; 39 (upd.)
Eureka Company, The, 12
Excel Technology, Inc., 65
EXX Inc., 65

Fabbrica D' Armi Pietro Beretta S.p.A., 39
Facom S.A., 32
FAG—Kugelfischer Georg Schäfer AG, 62
Faiveley S.A., 39
Falcon Products, Inc., 33
Fanuc Ltd., III; 17 (upd.); 75 (upd.)
FARO Technologies, Inc., 87
Faultless Starch/Bon Ami Company, 55
Featherlite Inc., 28
Fedders Corporation, 18; 43 (upd.)
Federal Prison Industries, Inc., 34
Federal Signal Corp., 10
FEI Company, 79
Figgie International Inc., 7
Firearms Training Systems, Inc., 27
First Alert, Inc., 28
First Brands Corporation, 8
First Years Inc., The, 46
Fisher Controls International, LLC, 13; 61 (upd.)
Fisher Scientific International Inc., 24
Fisher-Price Inc., 12; 32 (upd.)
Fiskars Corporation, 33; 105 (upd.)
Flanders Corporation, 65
Flexsteel Industries Inc., 15; 41 (upd.)
FLIR Systems, Inc., 69
Flour City International, Inc., 44
Flow International Corporation, 56
Flowserve Corporation, 33; 77 (upd.)
FN Manufacturing LLC, 110
Forward Industries, Inc., 86
FosterGrant, Inc., 60
Francotyp-Postalia Holding AG, 92
Frank J. Zamboni & Co., Inc., 34
Franke Holding AG, 76
Franklin Electric Company, Inc., 43
Franklin Mint, The, 69
Freudenberg & Co., 41
Friedrich Grohe AG & Co. KG, 53
Frigidaire Home Products, 22
FSI International, Inc., 17
Fuel Systems Solutions, Inc., 97
Fuel Tech, Inc., 85
Fuji Photo Film Co., Ltd., III; 18 (upd.); 79 (upd.)
Fuqua Enterprises, Inc., 17
Furniture Brands International, Inc., 39 (upd.)
Furon Company, 28
Furukawa Electric Co., Ltd., The, III
G.S. Blodgett Corporation, 15
Gaming Partners International Corporation, 93
Ganz, 98
Gardner Denver, Inc., 49
Gates Corporation, The, 9
Gaylord Bros., Inc., 100
GEA AG, 27
Geberit AG, 49
Gehl Company, 19
Gelita AG, 74
Gemplus International S.A., 64
General Bearing Corporation, 45
General Cable Corporation, 40; 111 (upd.)
General Housewares Corporation, 16
geobra Brandstätter GmbH & Co. KG, 48

Viskase Companies, Inc., 55
Vita Plus Corporation, 60
Vosper Thornycroft Holding plc, 41
Vossloh AG, 53
W.A. Whitney Company, 53
W.C. Bradley Co., 69
W.H. Brady Co., 17
W.L. Gore & Associates, Inc., 14; 60
   (upd.)
Wabash National Corp., 13
Wabtec Corporation, 40
Walbro Corporation, 13
Wärtsilä Corporation, 100
Washington Scientific Industries, Inc., 17
Wassall Plc, 18
Waterford Wedgwood plc, 12; 34 (upd.)
Watts of Lydney Group Ltd., 71
Watts Water Technologies, Inc., 19; 115
   (upd.)
Weather Shield Manufacturing, Inc., 102
Weber-Stephen Products Co., 40
Weeres Industries Corporation, 52
Weg S.A., 78
Welbilt Corp., 19
Weru Aktiengesellschaft, 18
West Bend Co., 14
Westell Technologies, Inc., 57
Westerbeke Corporation, 60
Wheaton Science Products, 60 (upd.)
Whirlpool Corporation, III; 12 (upd.); 59
   (upd.)
White Consolidated Industries Inc., 13
Wilbert, Inc., 56
Wilkinson Sword Ltd., 60
William L. Bonnell Company, Inc., 66
William Zinsser & Company, Inc., 58
Windmere Corporation, 16
Winegard Company, 56
WinsLoew Furniture, Inc., 21
Wiremold Company, The, 81
Wolverine Tube Inc., 23
Woodcraft Industries Inc., 61
Wood-Mode, Inc., 23
World Kitchen, LLC, 104
Württembergische Metallwarenfabrik AG
   (WMF), 60
WWRD Holdings Limited, 106 (upd.)
Wyant Corporation, 30
Wyman-Gordon Company, 14
Wynn's International, Inc., 33
X-Rite, Inc., 48
York International Corp., 13
Young Chang Co. Ltd., 107
Young Innovations, Inc., 44
Zapf Creation AG, 95
Zep Inc., 113
Zindart Ltd., 60
Zippo Manufacturing Company, 18; 71
   (upd.)
Zygo Corporation, 42

## Materials

AK Steel Holding Corporation, 19; 41
   (upd.)
American Biltrite Inc., 16; 43 (upd.)
American Colloid Co., 13
American Standard Inc., III; 30 (upd.)

Ameriwood Industries International Corp.,
   17
Andersen Corporation, 10
Anhui Conch Cement Company Limited,
   99
Apasco S.A. de C.V., 51
Apogee Enterprises, Inc., 8
Asahi Glass Company, Ltd., III; 48 (upd.)
Asbury Carbons, Inc., 68
Bairnco Corporation, 28
Bayou Steel Corporation, 31
Berry Plastics Group Inc., 21; 98 (upd.)
Blessings Corp., 19
Blue Circle Industries PLC, III
Bodycote International PLC, 63
Boral Limited, III; 43 (upd.); 103 (upd.)
British Vita plc, 9; 33 (upd.)
Brush Engineered Materials Inc., 67
Bryce Corporation, 100
California Steel Industries, Inc., 67
Callanan Industries, Inc., 60
Cameron & Barkley Company, 28
CARBO Ceramics, Inc., 108
Carborundum Company, 15
Carl Zeiss AG, III; 34 (upd.); 91 (upd.)
Carlisle Companies Inc., 8; 82 (upd.)
Carpenter Co., 109
Carter Holt Harvey Ltd., 70
Cementos Argos S.A., 91
CEMEX S.A. de C.V., 20; 59 (upd.)
Century Aluminum Company, 52
Ceradyne, Inc., 65
CertainTeed Corporation, 35
Chargeurs International, 6; 21 (upd.)
Chemfab Corporation, 35
Cimentos de Portugal SGPS S.A.
   (Cimpor), 76
Ciments Français, 40
Cold Spring Granite Company Inc., 16;
   67 (upd.)
Columbia Forest Products Inc., 78
Compagnie de Saint-Gobain, III; 16
   (upd.); 64 (upd.)
Cookson Group plc, III; 44 (upd.)
Corning Inc., III; 44 (upd.); 90 (upd.)
CRH plc, 64
CSR Limited, III; 28 (upd.); 85 (upd.)
Dal-Tile International Inc., 22
David J. Joseph Company, The, 14; 76
   (upd.)
Dexter Corporation, The, 12 (upd.)
Dicken Masch Plastics LLC, 90
Dyckerhoff AG, 35
Dynamic Materials Corporation, 81
Dyson Group PLC, 71
ECC Group plc, III
Edw. C. Levy Co., 42
84 Lumber Company, 9; 39 (upd.)
ElkCorp, 52
Empire Resources, Inc., 81
English China Clays Ltd., 15 (upd.); 40
   (upd.)
Entegris, Inc., 112
Envirodyne Industries, Inc., 17
EP Henry Corporation, 104
Feldmuhle Nobel A.G., III
Fibreboard Corporation, 16
Filtrona plc, 88

Florida Rock Industries, Inc., 46
FLSmidth & Co. A/S, 72
Foamex International Inc., 17
Formica Corporation, 13
GAF Corporation, 22 (upd.)
Geon Company, The, 11
Gerresheimer Glas AG, 43
Giant Cement Holding, Inc., 23
Gibraltar Steel Corporation, 37
Glaverbel Group, 80
Granite Rock Company, 26
GreenMan Technologies Inc., 99
Groupe Sidel S.A., 21
Harbison-Walker Refractories Company,
   24
Harrisons & Crosfield plc, III
HeidelbergCement AG, 109 (upd.)
Heidelberger Zement AG, 31
Hexcel Corporation, 28
Holderbank Financière Glaris Ltd., III
Holnam Inc., 8; 39 (upd.)
Holt and Bugbee Company, 66
Homasote Company, 72
Howmet Corp., 12
Huttig Building Products, Inc., 73
Ibstock Brick Ltd., 14; 37 (upd.)
Imerys S.A., 40 (upd.)
Imperial Industries, Inc., 81
Internacional de Ceramica, S.A. de C.V.,
   53
International Shipbreaking Ltd. L.L.C., 67
Jaiprakash Associates Limited, 101
Joseph T. Ryerson & Son, Inc., 15
K-Tron International Inc., 115
Knauf Gips KG, 100
La Seda de Barcelona S.A., 100
Lafarge Cement UK, 28; 54 (upd.)
Lafarge Coppée S.A., III
Lafarge Corporation, 28
Lehigh Portland Cement Company, 23
Loma Negra C.I.A.S.A., 95
Lyman-Richey Corporation, 96
Manville Corporation, III; 7 (upd.)
Material Sciences Corporation, 63
Matsushita Electric Works, Ltd., III; 7
   (upd.)
McJunkin Corporation, 63
Medusa Corporation, 24
Mitsubishi Materials Corporation, III
Monarch Cement Company, The, 72
National Gypsum Company, 10
Nevamar Company, 82
Nippon Sheet Glass Company, Limited,
   III
North Pacific Group, Inc., 61
Nuplex Industries Ltd., 92
OmniSource Corporation, 14
Onoda Cement Co., Ltd., III
Otor S.A., 77
Owens-Corning Fiberglass Corporation,
   III
Pacific Clay Products Inc., 88
Pilkington Group Limited, III; 34 (upd.);
   87 (upd.)
Pioneer International Limited, III
PMC Global, Inc., 110
PolyOne Corporation, 87 (upd.)

## Mining & Metals

## Nonprofit & Philanthropic Organizations

## Paper & Forestry

## Publishing & Printing

## Real Estate

Sumitomo Realty & Development Co., Ltd., IV
Sun Communities Inc., 46
Sunterra Corporation, 75
Tanger Factory Outlet Centers, Inc., 49
Tarragon Realty Investors, Inc., 45
Taubman Centers, Inc., 75
Taylor Woodrow plc, 38 (upd.)
Technical Olympic USA, Inc., 75
Tejon Ranch Company, 35
Thor Equities, LLC, 108
Tishman Speyer Properties, L.P., 47; 112 (upd.)
Tokyu Land Corporation, IV
Trammell Crow Company, 8; 57 (upd.)
Trendwest Resorts, Inc., 33
Tridel Enterprises Inc., 9
Trizec Corporation Ltd., 10
Trump Organization, The, 23; 64 (upd.)
Unibail SA, 40
United Dominion Realty Trust, Inc., 52
Vistana, Inc., 22
Vornado Realty Trust, 20; 112 (upd.)
W.P. Carey & Co. LLC, 49
Weingarten Realty Investors, 95
William Lyon Homes, 59
Woodbridge Holdings Corporation, 99

## Retail & Wholesale

A-Mark Financial Corporation, 71
A.C. Moore Arts & Crafts, Inc., 30
A.S. Watson & Company Ltd., 84
Aaron's, Inc., 14; 35 (upd.); 114 (upd.)
Abatix Corp., 57
ABC Appliance, Inc., 10
ABC Carpet & Home Co. Inc., 26
Abercrombie & Fitch Company, 15; 35 (upd.); 75 (upd.)
Academy Sports & Outdoors, 27
Ace Hardware Corporation, 12; 35 (upd.)
Action Performance Companies, Inc., 27
Adams Childrenswear Ltd., 95
AEON Co., Ltd., 68 (upd.)
After Hours Formalwear Inc., 60
Alain Afflelou SA, 53
Alimentation Couche-Tard Inc., 77
Alldays plc, 49
Allders plc, 37
Alliance Boots plc, 83 (upd.)
Allou Health & Beauty Care, Inc., 28
Altmeyer Home Stores Inc., 107
AMAG Group, 102
Amazon.com, Inc., 25; 56 (upd.)
AMCON Distributing Company, 99
American Coin Merchandising, Inc., 28; 74 (upd.)
American Eagle Outfitters, Inc., 24; 55 (upd.)
American Furniture Company, Inc., 21
American Girl, Inc., 69 (upd.)
Ames Department Stores, Inc., 9; 30 (upd.)
Amscan Holdings, Inc., 61
Anderson-DuBose Company, The, 60
AnnTaylor Stores Corporation, 13; 37 (upd.); 67 (upd.)
Anton Schlecker, 102
Arbor Drugs Inc., 12

Arcadia Group plc, 28 (upd.)
Army and Air Force Exchange Service, 39
Art Van Furniture, Inc., 28
Ashworth, Inc., 26
Au Printemps S.A., V
Audio King Corporation, 24
Auto Value Associates, Inc., 25
Autobytel Inc., 47
AutoNation, Inc., 50; 114 (upd.)
AutoTrader.com, L.L.C., 91
AutoZone, Inc., 9; 31 (upd.); 110 (upd.)
AVA AG (Allgemeine Handelsgesellschaft der Verbraucher AG), 33
Aviall, Inc., 73
Aviation Sales Company, 41
AWB Ltd., 56
B. Dalton Bookseller Inc., 25
Babbage's, Inc., 10
Baby Superstore, Inc., 15
Baccarat, 24
Bachman's Inc., 22
Bailey Nurseries, Inc., 57
Ball Horticultural Company, 78
Banana Republic Inc., 25
Barnes & Noble, Inc., 10; 30 (upd.); 75 (upd.)
Barnes & Noble College Booksellers, Inc., 115
Barnett Inc., 28
Barneys New York Inc., 28; 104 (upd.)
Barrett-Jackson Auction Company L.L.C., 88
Bass Pro Shops, Inc., 42
Baumax AG, 75
Beacon Roofing Supply, Inc., 75
Beate Uhse AG, 96
bebe stores, inc., 31; 103 (upd.)
Bed Bath & Beyond Inc., 13; 41 (upd.); 109 (upd.)
Belk, Inc., V; 19 (upd.); 72 (upd.)
Ben Bridge Jeweler, Inc., 60
Benetton Group S.p.A., 10; 67 (upd.)
Berean Christian Stores, 96
Bergdorf Goodman Inc., 52
Bergen Brunswig Corporation, V; 13 (upd.)
Bernard Chaus, Inc., 27
Best Buy Co., Inc., 9; 23 (upd.); 63 (upd.)
Bestseller A/S, 90
Bhs plc, 17
Big 5 Sporting Goods Corporation, 55
Big A Drug Stores Inc., 79
Big Dog Holdings, Inc., 45
Big Lots, Inc., 50; 110 (upd.)
Big O Tires, Inc., 20
Birks & Mayors Inc., 112
Birthdays Ltd., 70
Blacks Leisure Group plc, 39
Blair Corporation, 25; 31 (upd.)
Blish-Mize Co., 95
Blokker Holding B.V., 84
Bloomingdale's Inc., 12
Blue Nile Inc., 61
Blue Square Israel Ltd., 41
Bluefly, Inc., 60
BlueLinx Holdings Inc., 97
Bob's Discount Furniture LLC, 104

Bombay Company, Inc., The, 10; 71 (upd.)
Bon Marché, Inc., The, 23
Bon-Ton Stores, Inc., The, 16; 50 (upd.)
Booker Cash & Carry Ltd., 68 (upd.)
Books-A-Million, Inc., 14; 41 (upd.); 96 (upd.)
Bookspan, 86
Boots Company PLC, The, V; 24 (upd.)
Borders Group, Inc., 15; 43 (upd.)
Boscov's Department Store, Inc., 31
Boulanger S.A., 102
Bowlin Travel Centers, Inc., 99
Bradlees Discount Department Store Company, 12
Bricorama S.A., 68
Brodart Company, 84
Broder Bros. Co., 38
Brooks Brothers Inc., 22; 115 (upd.)
Brookstone, Inc., 18
The Buckle, Inc., 18; 115 (upd.)
Buhrmann NV, 41
Build-A-Bear Workshop Inc., 62
Burdines, Inc., 60
Burlington Coat Factory Warehouse Corporation, 10; 60 (upd.)
Buttrey Food & Drug Stores Co., 18
buy.com, Inc., 46
C&A, V; 40 (upd.)
C&J Clark International Ltd., 52
Cabela's Inc., 26; 68 (upd.)
Cablevision Electronic Instruments, Inc., 32
Cache Incorporated, 30
Cactus S.A., 90
Caldor Inc., 12
Calloway's Nursery, Inc., 51
Camaïeu S.A., 72
Camelot Music, Inc., 26
Campeau Corporation, V
Campmor, Inc., 104
Campo Electronics, Appliances & Computers, Inc., 16
Car Toys, Inc., 67
Carphone Warehouse Group PLC, The, 83
Carrefour SA, 10; 27 (upd.); 64 (upd.)
Carson Pirie Scott & Company, 15
Carter Hawley Hale Stores, Inc., V
Carter Lumber Company, 45
Cartier Monde, 29
Casas Bahia Comercial Ltda., 75
Casey's General Stores, Inc., 19; 83 (upd.)
Castorama-Dubois Investissements SCA, 104 (upd.)
Castro Model Ltd., 86
Casual Corner Group, Inc., 43
Casual Male Retail Group, Inc., 52
Catherines Stores Corporation, 15
CDW Computer Centers, Inc., 16
Celebrate Express, Inc., 70
Celebrity, Inc., 22
CellStar Corporation, 83
Cencosud S.A., 69
Central European Distribution Corporation, 75
Central Garden & Pet Company, 23

## Rubber & Tires

## Telecommunications

Western Wireless Corporation, 36
Westwood One Inc., 23; 106 (upd.)
Williams Communications Group, Inc., 34
Williams Companies, Inc., The, 31 (upd.)
Wipro Limited, 43; 106 (upd.)
Wisconsin Bell, Inc., 14
Working Assets Funding Service, 43
Worldwide Pants Inc., 97
XM Satellite Radio Holdings, Inc., 69
Young Broadcasting Inc., 40
Zain, 102
Zed Group, 93
Zoom Technologies, Inc., 53 (upd.)

## Textiles & Apparel

Acorn Products, Inc., 55
adidas Group AG, 14; 33 (upd.); 75 (upd.)
Adolfo Dominguez S.A., 72
Aéropostale, Inc., 89
Albany International Corp., 8
Alba-Waldensian, Inc., 30
Alexandra plc, 88
Alexon Group PLC, 107
Algo Group Inc., 24
Allen-Edmonds Shoe Corporation, 61
Alpargatas S.A.I.C., 87
American & Efird, Inc., 82
American Apparel, Inc., 90
American Safety Razor Company, 20
Amoskeag Company, 8
Andin International, Inc., 100
Angelica Corporation, 15; 43 (upd.)
Annin & Co., 100
AR Accessories Group, Inc., 23
Aris Industries, Inc., 16
ASICS Corporation, 57
AstenJohnson Inc., 90
Athlete's Foot Brands LLC, The, 84
Authentic Fitness Corporation, 20; 51 (upd.)
Avon Products, Inc., 109 (upd.)
Babolat VS, S.A., 97
Banana Republic Inc., 25
Bardwil Industries Inc., 98
Bata Ltd., 62
Bauer Hockey, Inc., 104
bebe stores, inc., 31; 103 (upd.)
Belleville Shoe Manufacturing Company, 92
Benetton Group S.p.A., 10; 67 (upd.)
Betsey Johnson Inc., 100
Bill Blass Group Ltd., 32; 115 (upd.)
Billabong International Limited, 44; 112 (upd.)
Birkenstock Footprint Sandals, Inc., 12; 42 (upd.)
Blundstone Pty Ltd., 76
Body Glove International LLC, 88
Boss Holdings, Inc., 97
Boston Apparel Group, 112 (upd.)
Brannock Device Company, 48
Brazos Sportswear, Inc., 23
Brioni Roman Style S.p.A., 67
Brooks Brothers Inc., 22; 115 (upd.)
Brooks Sports Inc., 32
Brown Group, Inc., V; 20 (upd.)

Bruce Oakley, Inc., 107
Brunschwig & Fils Inc., 96
Bugle Boy Industries, Inc., 18
Burberry Group plc, 17; 41 (upd.); 92 (upd.)
Burke Mills, Inc., 66
Burlington Industries, Inc., V; 17 (upd.)
Calcot Ltd., 33
Calvin Klein, Inc., 22; 55 (upd.)
Candie's, Inc., 31
Canstar Sports Inc., 16
Capel Incorporated, 45
Capezio/Ballet Makers Inc., 62
Carhartt, Inc., 30, 77 (upd.)
Cato Corporation, 14
Chargeurs International, 6; 21 (upd.)
Charles Vögele Holding AG, 82
Charming Shoppes, Inc., 8
Cherokee Inc., 18
CHF Industries, Inc., 84
Chic by H.I.S, Inc., 20
Chico's FAS, Inc., 45
Chorus Line Corporation, 30
Christian Dior S.A., 19; 49 (upd.); 110 (upd.)
Christopher & Banks Corporation, 42
Cia Hering, 72
Cintas Corporation, 51 (upd.)
Citi Trends, Inc., 80
Claire's Stores, Inc., 17
Coach Leatherware, 10
Coats plc, V; 44 (upd.)
Collins & Aikman Corporation, 13; 41 (upd.)
Columbia Sportswear Company, 19; 41 (upd.)
Companhia de Tecidos Norte de Minas - Coteminas, 77
Compañia Industrial de Parras, S.A. de C.V. (CIPSA), 84
Concord Fabrics, Inc., 16
Cone Mills LLC, 8; 67 (upd.)
Conso International Corporation, 29
Converse Inc., 9; 31 (upd.)
Cotton Incorporated, 46
Courtaulds plc, V; 17 (upd.)
Crocs, Inc., 80
Croscill, Inc., 42
Crown Crafts, Inc., 16
Crystal Brands, Inc., 9
Culp, Inc., 29
Cutter & Buck Inc., 27
Cygne Designs, Inc., 25
Damartex S.A., 98
Dan River Inc., 35; 86 (upd.)
Danskin, Inc., 12; 62 (upd.)
Davis Service Group PLC, 45
DC Shoes, Inc., 60
Deckers Outdoor Corporation, 22; 98 (upd.)
Delta and Pine Land Company, 59
Delta Woodside Industries, Inc., 8; 30 (upd.)
Designer Holdings Ltd., 20
Diadora SpA, 86
Dixie Group, Inc., The, 20; 80 (upd.)
Dogi International Fabrics S.A., 52
Dolce & Gabbana SpA, 62

Dominion Textile Inc., 12
Donna Karan International Inc., 15; 56 (upd.)
Donnkenny, Inc., 17
Dooney & Bourke Inc., 84
Duck Head Apparel Company, Inc., 42
Dunavant Enterprises, Inc., 54
Dyersburg Corporation, 21
Eastland Shoe Corporation, 82
Ecco Sko A/S, 62
Echo Design Group, Inc., The, 68
Eddie Bauer Holdings, Inc., 9; 36 (upd.); 87 (upd.)
Edison Brothers Stores, Inc., 9
Eileen Fisher Inc., 61
Ellen Tracy, Inc., 55
Ennis, Inc., 21; 97 (upd.)
Eram SA, 51
Ermenegildo Zegna SpA, 63
ESCADA AG, 71
Esprit de Corp., 8; 29 (upd.)
Etam Developpement SA, 44
Etienne Aigner AG, 52
Evans, Inc., 30
Fab Industries, Inc., 27
Fabri-Centers of America Inc., 16
Farah Incorporated, 24
Fat Face Ltd., 68
Fechheimer Brothers Company, Inc., 110
Fieldcrest Cannon, Inc., 9; 31 (upd.)
Fila Holding S.p.A., 20
Fishman & Tobin Inc., 102
Florsheim Shoe Group Inc., 9; 31 (upd.)
Foot Petals L.L.C., 95
Fossil, Inc., 17; 112 (upd.)
Fred Perry Limited, 105
Frederick's of Hollywood Inc., 16
French Connection Group plc, 41
Fruit of the Loom, Inc., 8; 25 (upd.); 115 (upd.)
Fubu, 29
G&K Services, Inc., 16
Galey & Lord, Inc., 20; 66 (upd.)
Garan, Inc., 16; 64 (upd.)
Gerry Weber International AG, 63
Gianni Versace S.p.A., 22; 106 (upd.)
G-III Apparel Group, Ltd., 22
Gildan Activewear, Inc., 81
Giorgio Armani S.p.A., 45
Gitano Group, Inc., The, 8
GoldToeMoretz, LLC, 102
Gottschalks, Inc., 18; 91 (upd.)
Grandoe Corporation, 98
Great White Shark Enterprises, Inc., 89
Greenwood Mills, Inc., 14
Grendene S.A., 102
Groupe André, 17
Groupe DMC (Dollfus Mieg & Cie), 27
Groupe Yves Saint Laurent, 23
Gucci Group NV, 15; 50 (upd.); 115 (upd.)
Guess, Inc., 15; 68 (upd.)
Guilford Mills Inc., 8; 40 (upd.)
Gymboree Corporation, 15; 69 (upd.)
Haggar Corporation, 19; 78 (upd.)
Hampshire Group Ltd., 82
Hampton Industries, Inc., 20
Hanesbrands Inc., 98

## Utilities

## Waste Services

# Geographic Index

# Germany

Land and Houses PCL, 104
Pranda Jewelry plc, 70
PTT Public Company Ltd., 56
Siam Cement Public Company Limited,
The, 56
Thai Airways International Public
Company Limited, 6; 27 (upd.)
Thai Union Frozen Products PCL, 75
Thanulux Public Company Limited, 86
Topaz Group, Inc., The, 62

## Trinidad and Tobago
Angostura Holdings Ltd., 114
Guardian Holdings Limited, 111

## Tunisia
Société Tunisienne de l'Air-Tunisair, 49

## Turkey
Akbank TAS 79
Anadolu Efes Biracilik ve Malt Sanayii
A.S., 95
Dogan Sirketler Grubu Holding A.S., 83
Haci Omer Sabanci Holdings A.S., 55
Koç Holding A.S., I; 54 (upd.)
Turkish Airlines Inc. (Türk Hava Yollari
A.O.), 72
Turkiye Is Bankasi A.S., 61
Türkiye Petrolleri Anonim Ortakliği, IV

## Ukraine
Antonov Design Bureau, 53
National Bank of Ukraine, 102

## United Arab Emirates
Abu Dhabi National Oil Company, IV;
45 (upd.); 114 (upd.)
Al Habtoor Group L.L.C., 87
DP World, 81
Emirates Group, The, 39; 81 (upd.)
Etihad Airways PJSC, 89
Gulf Agency Company Ltd., 78
Jumeirah Group, 83
Rotana Hotel Management Corporation
LTD., 114

## United Kingdom
A. F. Blakemore & Son Ltd., 90
A. Nelson & Co. Ltd., 75
Aardman Animations Ltd., 61
Abbey National plc, 10; 39 (upd.)
Acergy SA, 97
Adams Childrenswear Ltd., 95
Admiral Group, PLC, 109
Aegis Group plc, 6
AG Barr plc, 64
Aga Foodservice Group PLC, 73
Aggregate Industries plc, 36
Aggreko Plc, 45
AgustaWestland N.V., 75
Air Partner PLC, 93
Airtours Plc, 27
Albert Fisher Group plc, The, 41
Alexandra plc, 88
Alexon Group PLC, 107
All England Lawn Tennis & Croquet
Club, The, 54

Alldays plc, 49
Allders plc, 37
Alliance and Leicester plc, 88
Alliance Boots plc, 83 (upd.)
Alliance Trust PLC, 109
Allied Domecq PLC, 29
Allied-Lyons PLC, I
Alpha Airports Group PLC, 77
Alvis Plc, 47
AMEC plc, 112
Amersham PLC, 50
Amey Plc, 47
Amnesty International, 50
Amstrad plc, III; 48 (upd.)
AMVESCAP PLC, 65
Anglo American PLC, 50 (upd.)
Anker BV, 53
Antofagasta plc, 65
Apax Partners Worldwide LLP, 89
Apple Corps Ltd., 87
Arcadia Group plc, 28 (upd.)
Arena Leisure Plc, 99
Argyll Group PLC, II
Arjo Wiggins Appleton p.l.c., 34
Arriva PLC, 69
Arsenal Holdings PLC 79
ASDA Group Ltd., II; 28 (upd.); 64
(upd.)
Ashtead Group plc, 34
Associated British Foods plc, II; 13 (upd.);
41 (upd.)
Associated British Ports Holdings Plc, 45
Aston Villa plc, 41
AstraZeneca PLC, 50 (upd.)
AT&T Istel Ltd., 14
Avecia Group PLC, 63
Aviva PLC, 50 (upd.)
Avon Rubber p.l.c., 108
BAA plc, 10; 33 (upd.)
Babcock International Group PLC, 69
BAE Systems plc, 108 (upd.)
Balfour Beatty plc, 36 (upd.)
Barclays plc, II; 20 (upd.); 64 (upd.)
Barings PLC, 14
Barratt Developments plc, I; 56 (upd.)
Bass PLC, I; 15 (upd.); 38 (upd.)
Bat Industries PLC, I; 20 (upd.)
Baxi Group Ltd., 96
Baxters Food Group Ltd., 99
BBA Aviation plc, 90
Beggars Group Ltd., 99
Belleek Pottery Ltd., 71
Bellway Plc, 45
Belron International Ltd., 76
Benfield Greig Group plc, 53
Bernard Matthews Ltd., 89
Bettys & Taylors of Harrogate Ltd., 72
Bhs plc, 17
BICC PLC, III
Biffa plc, 92
Big Food Group plc, The, 68 (upd.)
Birse Group PLC, 77
Birthdays Ltd., 70
Blacks Leisure Group plc, 39
Blackwell Publishing Ltd., 78
Bloomsbury Publishing PLC, 114
Blue Circle Industries PLC, III
BOC Group plc, I; 25 (upd.); 78 (upd.)

Body Shop International plc, The, 11; 53
(upd.)
Bodycote International PLC, 63
Bonhams 1793 Ltd., 72
Booker Cash & Carry Ltd., 13; 31 (upd.);
68 (upd.)
Boots Company PLC, The, V; 24 (upd.)
Bowater PLC, IV
Bowthorpe, 33
BP p.l.c., 45 (upd.); 103 (upd.)
BPB plc, 83
Bradford & Bingley PLC, 65
Brake Bros plc, 45
Brammer PLC, 77
Bristow Helicopters Ltd., 70
Britannia Soft Drinks Ltd. (Britvic), 71
British Aerospace plc, I; 24 (upd.)
British Airways PLC, I; 14 (upd.); 43
(upd.); 105 (upd.)
British American Tobacco PLC, 50 (upd.);
114 (upd.)
British Broadcasting Corporation Ltd., 7;
21 (upd.); 89 (upd.)
British Coal Corporation, IV
British Energy Plc, 49
British Film Institute, The, 80
British Gas plc, V
British Land Plc, 54
British Midland plc, 38
British Museum, The, 71
British Nuclear Fuels plc, 6
British Petroleum Company plc, The, IV;
7 (upd.); 21 (upd.)
British Railways Board, V
British Sky Broadcasting Group plc, 20;
60 (upd.)
British Steel plc, IV; 19 (upd.)
British Sugar plc, 84
British Telecommunications plc, V; 15
(upd.)
British United Provident Association
Limited (BUPA) 79
British Vita plc, 9; 33 (upd.)
British World Airlines Ltd., 18
British-Borneo Oil & Gas PLC, 34
BT Group plc, 49 (upd.); 114 (upd.)
BTG Plc, 87
BTR PLC, I
BTR Siebe plc, 27
Budgens Ltd., 59
Bunzl plc, IV; 31 (upd.)
Burberry Group plc, 17; 41 (upd.); 92
(upd.)
Burmah Castrol PLC, IV; 30 (upd.)
Burton Group plc, The, V
Business Post Group plc, 46
C&J Clark International Ltd., 52
C. Hoare & Co., 77
C.I. Traders Limited, 61
Cable and Wireless plc, V; 25 (upd.)
Cadbury plc, 105 (upd.)
Cadbury Schweppes PLC, II; 49 (upd.)
Caffè Nero Group PLC, 63
Caffyns, PLC, 105
Cains Beer Company PLC, 99
Camelot Group plc, 110

ACNielsen Corporation, 13; 38 (upd.)
Acorn Products, Inc., 55
Acosta Sales and Marketing Company, Inc., 77
Acsys, Inc., 44
ACT, Inc., 114
Action Performance Companies, Inc., 27
Activision, Inc., 32; 89 (upd.)
Actuant Corporation, 94 (upd.)
Acuity Brands, Inc., 90
Acushnet Company, 64
Acuson Corporation, 10; 36 (upd.)
Acxiom Corporation, 35
Adams Express Company, The, 86
Adams Golf, Inc., 37
Adaptec, Inc., 31
ADC Telecommunications, Inc., 10; 30 (upd.); 89 (upd.)
A-dec, Inc., 53
Adelman Travel Group, 105
Adelphia Communications Corporation, 17; 52 (upd.)
ADESA, Inc., 71
Administaff, Inc., 52
Adobe Systems Inc., 10; 33 (upd.); 106 (upd.)
Adolor Corporation, 101
Adolph Coors Company, I; 13 (upd.); 36 (upd.)
ADT Security Services, Inc., 12; 44 (upd.)
Adtran Inc., 22
Advance Auto Parts, Inc., 57
Advance Publications Inc., IV; 19 (upd.); 96 (upd.)
Advanced Circuits Inc., 67
Advanced Fibre Communications, Inc., 63
Advanced Marketing Services, Inc., 34
Advanced Medical Optics, Inc. 79
Advanced Micro Devices, Inc., 6; 30 (upd.); 99 (upd.)
Advanced Neuromodulation Systems, Inc., 73
Advanced Technology Laboratories, Inc., 9
Advanstar Communications, Inc., 57
Advanta Corporation, 8; 38 (upd.)
Advantica Restaurant Group, Inc., 27 (upd.)
Adventist Health, 53
Advertising Council, Inc., The, 76
Advisory Board Company, The, 80
Advo, Inc., 6; 53 (upd.)
Advocat Inc., 46
AECOM Technology Corporation 79
AEI Music Network Inc., 35
AEP Industries, Inc., 36
AeroGrow International, Inc., 95
Aerojet-General Corp., 63
Aeronca Inc., 46
Aéropostale, Inc., 89
Aeroquip Corporation, 16
Aerosonic Corporation, 69
AeroVironment, Inc., 97
AES Corporation, The, 10; 13 (upd.); 53 (upd.)
Aetna Inc., III; 21 (upd.); 63 (upd.)
AFC Enterprises, Inc., 32; 83 (upd.)
Affiliated Computer Services, Inc., 61
Affiliated Foods Inc., 53

Affiliated Managers Group, Inc. 79
Affiliated Publications, Inc., 7
Affinity Group Holding Inc., 56
Affymetrix Inc., 106
Aflac Incorporated, 10 (upd.); 38 (upd.); 109 (upd)
Africare, 59
After Hours Formalwear Inc., 60
Aftermarket Technology Corp., 83
Ag Services of America, Inc., 59
Ag-Chem Equipment Company, Inc., 17
AGCO Corporation, 13; 67 (upd.)
Agere Systems Inc., 61
Agilent Technologies Inc., 38; 93 (upd.)
Agilysys Inc., 76 (upd.)
AGL Resources Inc., 116
Agland, Inc., 110
Agri Beef Company, 81
Agway, Inc., 7; 21 (upd.)
AHL Services, Inc., 27
Air & Water Technologies Corporation, 6
Air Express International Corporation, 13
Air Methods Corporation, 53
Air Products and Chemicals, Inc., I; 10 (upd.); 74 (upd.)
Air T, Inc., 86
Air Wisconsin Airlines Corporation, 55
Airborne Freight Corporation, 6; 34 (upd.)
Airborne Systems Group, 89
Airgas, Inc., 54
AirTouch Communications, 11
AirTran Holdings, Inc., 22
AK Steel Holding Corporation, 19; 41 (upd.)
Akamai Technologies, Inc., 71
Akeena Solar, Inc., 103
Akin, Gump, Strauss, Hauer & Feld, L.L.P., 33
Akorn, Inc., 32
Alabama Farmers Cooperative, Inc., 63
Alabama National BanCorporation, 75
Alamo Group Inc., 32
Alamo Rent A Car, 6; 24 (upd.); 84 (upd.)
ALARIS Medical Systems, Inc., 65
Alaska Air Group, Inc., 6; 29 (upd.)
Alaska Communications Systems Group, Inc., 89
Alaska Railroad Corporation, 60
Albany International Corporation, 8; 51 (upd.)
Albany Molecular Research, Inc., 77
Albaugh, Inc., 105
Alba-Waldensian, Inc., 30
Albemarle Corporation, 59
Alberici Corporation, 76
Albert Trostel and Sons Company, 113
Alberto-Culver Company, 8; 36 (upd.); 91 (upd.)
Albert's Organics, Inc., 110
Albertson's, Inc., II; 7 (upd.); 30 (upd.); 65 (upd.)
Alco Health Services Corporation, III
Alco Standard Corporation, I
Alcoa Inc., 56 (upd.)
Aldila Inc., 46
Aldus Corporation, 10

Aleris International, Inc., 110
Alex Lee Inc., 18; 44 (upd.)
Alexander & Alexander Services Inc., 10
Alexander & Baldwin, Inc., 10; 40 (upd.)
Alexander's, Inc., 45
Alexandria Real Estate Equities, Inc., 101
Alfa Corporation, 60
Alico, Inc., 63
Alienware Corporation, 81
Align Technology, Inc., 94
All American Communications Inc., 20
Allbritton Communications Company, 105
Alleghany Corporation, 10; 60 (upd.)
Allegheny Energy, Inc., 38 (upd.)
Allegheny Ludlum Corporation, 8
Allegheny Power System, Inc., V
Allegheny Technologies Incorporated, 112 (upd.)
Allegiant Travel Company, 97
Allegis Group, Inc., 95
Allen Brothers, Inc., 101
Allen Canning Company, 76
Allen Foods, Inc., 60
Allen Organ Company, 33
Allen Systems Group, Inc., 59
Allen-Edmonds Shoe Corporation, 61
Allergan, Inc., 10; 30 (upd.); 77 (upd.)
Alliance Capital Management Holding L.P., 63
Alliance Entertainment Corp., 17
Alliance Laundry Holdings LLC, 102
Alliance Resource Partners, L.P., 81
Alliant Energy Corporation, 106
Alliant Techsystems Inc., 8; 30 (upd.); 77 (upd.)
Allied Defense Group, Inc., The, 65
Allied Healthcare Products, Inc., 24
Allied Products Corporation, 21
Allied Signal Engines, 9
Allied Waste Industries, Inc., 50
Allied Worldwide, Inc., 49
AlliedSignal Inc., I; 22 (upd.)
Allison Gas Turbine Division, 9
Allmerica Financial Corporation, 63
Allou Health & Beauty Care, Inc., 28
Alloy, Inc., 55
Allscripts-Misys Healthcare Solutions Inc., 104
The Allstate Corporation, 10; 27 (upd); 116 (upd.)
ALLTEL Corporation, 6; 46 (upd.)
Alltrista Corporation, 30
Allwaste, Inc., 18
Almost Family, Inc., 93
Aloha Airlines, Incorporated, 24
Alpha Natural Resources Inc., 106
Alpharma Inc., 35 (upd.)
Alpine Confections, Inc., 71
Alpine Lace Brands, Inc., 18
Alside Inc., 94
AltaVista Company, 43
Altera Corporation, 18; 43 (upd.); 115 (upd.)
Alternative Tentacles Records, 66
Alterra Healthcare Corporation, 42
Alticor Inc., 71 (upd.)
Altiris, Inc., 65

Geon Company, The, 11
GeoResources, Inc., 101
George A. Hormel and Company, II
George F. Cram Company, Inc., The, 55
George P. Johnson Company, 60
George S. May International Company, 55
George W. Park Seed Company, Inc., 98
Georgia Gulf Corporation, 9; 61 (upd.)
Georgia-Pacific LLC, IV; 9 (upd.); 47 (upd.); 101 (upd.)
Geotek Communications Inc., 21
Gerald Stevens, Inc., 37
Gerber Products Company, 7; 21 (upd.)
Gerber Scientific, Inc., 12; 84 (upd.)
German American Bancorp, 41
Gertrude Hawk Chocolates Inc., 104
Getty Images, Inc., 31
Gevity HR, Inc., 63
GF Health Products, Inc., 82
Ghirardelli Chocolate Company, 30
Giant Cement Holding, Inc., 23
Giant Eagle, Inc., 86
Giant Food LLC, II; 22 (upd.); 83 (upd.)
Giant Industries, Inc., 19; 61 (upd.)
Gibraltar Steel Corporation, 37
Gibson Greetings, Inc., 12
Gibson Guitar Corporation, 16; 100 (upd.)
Gibson, Dunn & Crutcher LLP, 36
Giddings & Lewis, Inc., 10
Gifts In Kind International, 101
G-III Apparel Group, Ltd., 22
Gilbane, Inc., 34
Gilead Sciences, Inc., 54
Gillett Holdings, Inc., 7
Gillette Company, The, III; 20 (upd.); 68 (upd.)
Gilman & Ciocia, Inc., 72
Gilmore Entertainment Group L.L.C., 100
Girl Scouts of the USA, 35
Gitano Group, Inc., The, 8
Glacier Bancorp, Inc., 35
Glacier Water Services, Inc., 47
Glamis Gold, Ltd., 54
Glazer's Wholesale Drug Company, Inc., 82
Gleason Corporation, 24
Glidden Company, The, 8
Global Berry Farms LLC, 62
Global Cash Access Holdings, Inc., 111
Global Crossing Ltd., 32
Global Hyatt Corporation, 75 (upd.)
Global Imaging Systems, Inc., 73
Global Industries, Ltd., 37
Global Marine Inc., 9
Global Outdoors, Inc., 49
Global Partners L.P., 116
Global Payments Inc., 91
Global Power Equipment Group Inc., 52
GlobalSantaFe Corporation, 48 (upd.)
Globe Newspaper Company Inc., 106
Glu Mobile Inc., 95
Gluek Brewing Company, 75
GM Hughes Electronics Corporation, II
GMAC, LLC, 109
GMH Communities Trust, 87

GNC Corporation, 98 (upd.)
Go Daddy Group Inc., The, 102
Godfather's Pizza Incorporated, 25
Godiva Chocolatier, Inc., 64
Goetze's Candy Company, Inc., 87
Gold Kist Inc., 17; 26 (upd.)
Golden Belt Manufacturing Co., 16
Golden Books Family Entertainment, Inc., 28
Golden Corral Corporation, 10; 66 (upd.)
Golden Enterprises, Inc., 26
Golden Krust Caribbean Bakery, Inc., 68
Golden Neo-Life Diamite International, Inc., 100
Golden State Foods Corporation, 32
Golden State Vintners, Inc., 33
Golden Valley Electric Association, 110
Golden West Financial Corporation, 47
Goldman Sachs Group, Inc., The, II; 20 (upd.); 51 (upd.); 110 (upd.)
Gold'n Plump Poultry, 54
Gold's Gym International, Inc., 71
GoldToeMoretz, LLC, 102
Golin/Harris International, Inc., 88
Golub Corporation, 26; 96 (upd.)
Gomez Inc., 104
Gonnella Baking Company, 40; 102 (upd.)
Good Guys, Inc., The, 10; 30 (upd.)
Good Humor-Breyers Ice Cream Company, 14
Goodby Silverstein & Partners, Inc., 75
Goodman Holding Company, 42
GoodMark Foods, Inc., 26
Goodrich Corporation, 46 (upd.); 109 (upd.)
GoodTimes Entertainment Ltd., 48
Goodwill Industries International, Inc., 16; 66 (upd.)
Goody Products, Inc., 12
Goodyear Tire & Rubber Company, The, V; 20 (upd.); 75 (upd.)
Goody's Family Clothing, Inc., 20; 64 (upd.)
Google, Inc., 50; 101 (upd.)
Gordmans, Inc., 74
Gordon Biersch Brewery Restaurant Group, Inc., 93
Gordon Food Service Inc., 8; 39 (upd.); 111 (upd.)
Gorman-Rupp Company, The, 18; 57 (upd.); 114 (upd.)
Gorton's, 13
Goss Holdings, Inc., 43
Gottschalks, Inc., 18; 91 (upd.)
Gould Electronics, Inc., 14
Gould Paper Corporation, 82
Goulds Pumps Inc., 24
Gourmet Services, Inc., 113
Goya Foods Inc., 22; 91 (upd.)
GP Strategies Corporation, 64 (upd.)
GPU, Inc., 27 (upd.)
Grace & Wild, Inc., 115
Graco Inc., 19; 67 (upd.)
Gradall Industries, Inc., 96
Graeter's Manufacturing Company, 86
Graham Corporation, 62

Graham Packaging Holdings Company, 87
GranCare, Inc., 14
Grand Casinos, Inc., 20
Grand Piano & Furniture Company, 72
Grand Traverse Pie Company, 98
Grand Union Company, The, 7; 28 (upd.)
Grandoe Corporation, 98
Granite Broadcasting Corporation, 42
Granite City Food & Brewery Ltd., 94
Granite Construction Incorporated, 61
Granite Industries of Vermont, Inc., 73
Granite Rock Company, 26
Granite State Bankshares, Inc., 37
Grant Prideco, Inc., 57
Grant Thornton International, 57
Graphic Industries Inc., 25
Graphic Packaging Holding Company, 96 (upd.)
Gray Communications Systems, Inc., 24
Graybar Electric Company, Inc., 54
Great American Management and Investment, Inc., 8
Great Atlantic & Pacific Tea Company, Inc., The, II; 16 (upd.); 55 (upd.); 114 (upd.)
Great Dane L.P., 107
Great Harvest Bread Company, 44
Great Lakes Bancorp, 8
Great Lakes Cheese Company, Inc., 111
Great Lakes Chemical Corporation, I; 14 (upd.)
Great Lakes Dredge & Dock Company, 69
Great Plains Energy Incorporated, 65 (upd.)
Great Western Financial Corporation, 10
Great White Shark Enterprises, Inc., 89
Great Wolf Resorts, Inc., 91
Greatbatch Inc., 72
Greater Washington Educational Telecommunication Association, 103
Grede Foundries, Inc., 38
Green Bay Packers, Inc., The, 32
Green Dot Public Schools, 99
Green Mountain Coffee Roasters, Inc., 31; 107 (upd.)
Green Tree Financial Corporation, 11
Green Tree Servicing LLC, 109
Greenberg Traurig, LLP, 65
Greenbrier Companies, The, 19
Greene, Tweed & Company, 55
GreenMan Technologies Inc., 99
GreenPoint Financial Corp., 28
Greenwood Mills, Inc., 14
Greg Manning Auctions, Inc., 60
Greif Inc., 15; 66 (upd.)
Grey Advertising, Inc., 6
Grey Global Group Inc., 66 (upd.)
Grey Wolf, Inc., 43
Greyhound Lines, Inc., I; 32 (upd.)
Greylock Partners, 116
Greyston Bakery, Inc., 101
Griffin Industries, Inc., 70
Griffin Land & Nurseries, Inc., 43
Griffith Laboratories Inc., 100
Griffon Corporation, 34

Stanley Works, The, III; 20 (upd.); 79 (upd.)
Staple Cotton Cooperative Association (Staplcotn), 86
Staples, Inc., 10; 55 (upd.)
Star Banc Corporation, 11
Star of the West Milling Co., 95
Starbucks Corporation, 13; 34 (upd.); 77 (upd.)
Starcraft Corporation, 30; 66 (upd.)
Starent Networks Corp., 106
Starkey Laboratories, Inc., 52
StarKist Company, 113
Starrett Corporation, 21
StarTek, Inc. 79
Starter Corp., 12
Starwood Hotels & Resorts Worldwide, Inc., 54
Starz LLC, 91
Stash Tea Company, The, 50
State Auto Financial Corporation, 77
State Farm Mutual Automobile Insurance Company, III; 51 (upd.)
State Financial Services Corporation, 51
State Street Corporation, 8; 57 (upd.)
Staten Island Bancorp, Inc., 39
Stater Bros. Holdings Inc., 64
Station Casinos, Inc., 25; 90 (upd.)
Staubach Company, The, 62
Steak n Shake Company, The, 41; 96 (upd.)
Stearns, Inc., 43
Steel Dynamics, Inc., 52
Steel Technologies Inc., 63
Steelcase, Inc., 7; 27 (upd.); 110 (upd.)
Stein Mart Inc., 19; 72 (upd.)
Steiner Corporation (Alsco), 53
Steinway Musical Instruments, Inc., 19; 111 (upd.)
Stemilt Growers Inc., 94
Stepan Company, 30; 105 (upd.)
Stephan Company, 60
Stephens Inc., 92
Stephens Media, LLC, 91
Stericycle, Inc., 33; 74 (upd.)
Sterilite Corporation, 97
STERIS Corporation, 29
Sterling Chemicals Inc., 16; 78 (upd.)
Sterling Drug, Inc., I
Sterling Electronics Corp., 18
Sterling Financial Corporation, 106
Sterling Software, Inc., 11
Steve & Barry's LLC, 88
Stevedoring Services of America Inc., 28
Steven Madden, Ltd., 37
Stew Leonard's, 56
Stewart & Stevenson Services Inc., 11
Stewart Enterprises, Inc., 20
Stewart Information Services Corporation, 78
Stewart's Beverages, 39
Stewart's Shops Corporation, 80
Stiefel Laboratories, Inc., 90
Stillwater Mining Company, 47
Stimson Lumber Company, 78
Stock Yards Packing Co., Inc., 37
Stone & Webster, Inc., 13; 64 (upd.)
Stone Container Corporation, IV

Stone Manufacturing Company, 14; 43 (upd.)
Stonyfield Farm, Inc., 55
Stop & Shop Supermarket Company, The, II; 24 (upd.); 68 (upd.)
Storage Technology Corporation, 6
Storage USA, Inc., 21
Stouffer Corp., 8
Strand Book Store Inc., 114
StrataCom, Inc., 16
Stratagene Corporation, 70
Stratasys, Inc., 67
Strattec Security Corporation, 73
Stratus Computer, Inc., 10
Strauss Discount Auto, 56
Strayer Education, Inc., 53
StreamServe Inc., 113
Stride Rite Corporation, The, 8; 37 (upd.); 86 (upd.)
Strine Printing Company Inc., 88
Strober Organization, Inc., The, 82
Stroh Brewery Company, The, I; 18 (upd.)
Strombecker Corporation, 60
Strongwell Corporation, 110
Stroock & Stroock & Lavan LLP, 40
Strouds, Inc., 33
Structure Tone Organization, The, 99
Stryker Corporation, 11; 29 (upd.); 79 (upd.)
Stuart C. Irby Company, 58
Stuart Entertainment Inc., 16
Student Loan Marketing Association, II
Stuller Settings, Inc., 35
Sturm, Ruger & Company, Inc., 19
Stussy, Inc., 55
Sub Pop Ltd., 97
Suburban Propane Partners, L.P., 30
Subway, 32
Sub-Zero Freezer Co., Inc., 31
Successories, Inc., 30
Sudbury Inc., 16
Suffolk Construction Company, Inc., 114
Suiza Foods Corporation, 26
Sullivan & Cromwell, 26
Summit Bancorporation, The, 14
Summit Family Restaurants, Inc. 19
Sun Communities Inc., 46
Sun Company, Inc., IV
Sun Country Airlines, 30
Sun Distributors L.P., 12
Sun Healthcare Group Inc., 25
Sun Hydraulics Corporation, 74
Sun Microsystems, Inc., 7; 30 (upd.); 91 (upd.)
Sun Sportswear, Inc., 17
Sun Television & Appliances Inc., 10
Sun World International, LLC, 93
SunAmerica Inc., 11
Sunbeam-Oster Co., Inc., 9
Sunburst Hospitality Corporation, 26
Sunburst Shutter Corporation, 78
Sun-Diamond Growers of California, 7
Sundstrand Corporation, 7; 21 (upd.)
Sundt Corp., 24
SunGard Data Systems Inc., 11
Sunglass Hut International, Inc., 21; 74 (upd.)

Sunkist Growers, Inc., 26; 102 (upd.)
Sun-Maid Growers of California, 82
Sunoco, Inc., 28 (upd.); 83 (upd.)
SunPower Corporation, 91
Sunrider Corporation, The, 26
Sunrise Greetings, 88
Sunrise Medical Inc., 11
Sunrise Senior Living, Inc., 81
Sunterra Corporation, 75
Suntron Corporation, 107
SunTrust Banks Inc., 23; 101 (upd.)
SunWize Technologies, Inc., 114
Super 8 Motels, Inc., 83
Super Food Services, Inc., 15
Supercuts Inc., 26
Superior Energy Services, Inc., 65
Superior Essex Inc., 80
Superior Industries International, Inc., 8
Superior Uniform Group, Inc., 30
Supermarkets General Holdings Corporation, II
SUPERVALU INC., II; 18 (upd.); 50 (upd.); 114 (upd.)
Suprema Specialties, Inc., 27
Supreme International Corporation, 27
Susan G. Komen Breast Cancer Foundation, 78
Susquehanna Pfaltzgraff Company, 8
Susser Holdings Corporation, 114
Sutherland Lumber Company, L.P., 99
Sutter Home Winery Inc., 16
SVB Financial Group, 109
Sverdrup Corporation, 14
SVP Worldwide LLC, 113
Swales & Associates, Inc., 69
Swank, Inc., 17; 84 (upd.)
SwedishAmerican Health System, 51
Sweet Candy Company, 60
Sweetbay Supermarket, 103 (upd.)
Sweetheart Cup Company, Inc., 36
Swett & Crawford Group Inc., The, 84
SWH Corporation, 70
Swift & Company, 55
Swift Energy Company, 63
Swift Transportation Co., Inc., 42
Swinerton Inc., 43
Swisher International Group Inc., 23
Swiss Colony, Inc., The, 97
Swiss Valley Farms Company, 90
Sybase, Inc., 10; 27 (upd.)
Sybron International Corp., 14
Sycamore Networks, Inc., 45
Sykes Enterprises, Inc., 45
Sylvan Learning Systems, Inc., 35
Sylvan, Inc., 22
Symantec Corporation, 10; 82 (upd.)
Symbol Technologies, Inc., 15
Syms Corporation, 29; 74 (upd.)
Symyx Technologies, Inc., 77
Synaptics Incorporated, 95
Synchronoss Technologies, Inc., 95
Syniverse Holdings Inc., 97
SYNNEX Corporation, 73
Synopsys, Inc., 11; 69 (upd.)
SynOptics Communications, Inc., 10
Synovus Financial Corp., 12; 52 (upd.)
Syntax-Brillian Corporation, 102
Syntel, Inc., 92

Vectren Corporation, 98 (upd.)
Veeco Instruments Inc., 32
Veit Companies, 43; 92 (upd.)
Velocity Express Corporation, 49; 94 (upd.)
Venator Group Inc., 35 (upd.)
Vencor, Inc., 16
Venetian Casino Resort, LLC, 47
Ventana Medical Systems, Inc., 75
Ventura Foods LLC, 90
Venture Stores Inc., 12
VeraSun Energy Corporation, 87
Verbatim Corporation, 14; 74 (upd.)
Veridian Corporation, 54
VeriFone Holdings, Inc., 18; 76 (upd.)
Verint Systems Inc., 73
VeriSign, Inc., 47
Veritas Software Corporation, 45
Verity Inc., 68
Verizon Communications, 43 (upd.); 78 (upd.)
Vermeer Manufacturing Company, 17
Vermont Country Store, The, 93
Vermont Pure Holdings, Ltd., 51
Vermont Teddy Bear Co., Inc., The, 36
Vertex Pharmaceuticals Incorporated, 83
Vertis Communications, 84
Vertrue Inc., 77
VF Corporation, V; 17 (upd.); 54 (upd.)
VHA Inc., 53
Viacom Inc., 7; 23 (upd.); 67 (upd.)
Viad Corp., 73
ViaSat, Inc., 54
Viasoft Inc., 27
VIASYS Healthcare, Inc., 52
Viasystems Group, Inc., 67
Viatech Continental Can Company, Inc., 25 (upd.)
Vicarious Visions, Inc., 108
Vicon Industries, Inc., 44
VICORP Restaurants, Inc., 12; 48 (upd.)
Victory Refrigeration, Inc., 82
Videojet Technologies, Inc., 90
Vienna Sausage Manufacturing Co., 14
Viewpoint International, Inc., 66
ViewSonic Corporation, 72
Viking Office Products, Inc., 10
Viking Range Corporation, 66
Viking Yacht Company, 96
Village Super Market, Inc., 7
Village Voice Media, Inc., 38
Vilter Manufacturing, LLC, 105
Vinson & Elkins L.L.P., 30
Vintage Petroleum, Inc., 42
Vinton Studios, 63
Virbac Corporation, 74
Virco Manufacturing Corporation, 17
Virginia Dare Extract Company, Inc., 94
Visa Inc., 9; 26 (upd.); 104 (upd.)
Vishay Intertechnology, Inc., 21; 80 (upd.)
Vision Service Plan Inc., 77
Viskase Companies, Inc., 55
Vista Bakery, Inc., 56
Vista Chemical Company, I
Vistana, Inc., 22
Visteon Corporation, 109
VISX, Incorporated, 30

Vita Food Products Inc., 99
Vita Plus Corporation, 60
Vitacost.com Inc., 116
Vital Images, Inc., 85
Vitalink Pharmacy Services, Inc., 15
Vitamin Shoppe Industries, Inc., 60
Vitesse Semiconductor Corporation, 32
Vitro Corp., 10
Vivra, Inc., 18
Vizio, Inc., 100
Vlasic Foods International Inc., 25
VLSI Technology, Inc., 16
VMware, Inc., 90
VNUS Medical Technologies, Inc., 103
Volcom, Inc., 77
Volkert and Associates, Inc., 98
Volt Information Sciences Inc., 26
Volunteers of America, Inc., 66
Von Maur Inc., 64
Vonage Holdings Corp., 81
Vons Companies, Inc., The, 7; 28 (upd.); 103 (upd.)
Vornado Realty Trust, 20; 112 (upd.)
Vought Aircraft Industries, Inc., 49
VSE Corporation, 108
Vulcan Materials Company, 7; 52 (upd.)
W.A. Whitney Company, 53
W. Atlee Burpee & Co., 27
W.B Doner & Co., 56
W.B. Mason Company, 98
W.C. Bradley Co., 69
W.H. Brady Co., 17
W.H. Braum, Inc., 80
W.L. Gore & Associates, Inc., 14; 60 (upd.)
W.P. Carey & Co. LLC, 49
W.R. Berkley Corporation, 15; 74 (upd.)
W.R. Grace & Company, I; 50 (upd.)
W.S. Badcock Corporation, 107
W.W. Grainger, Inc., V; 26 (upd.); 68 (upd.)
W.W. Norton & Company, Inc., 28
Waban Inc., 13
Wabash National Corp., 13
Wabtec Corporation, 40
Wachovia Bank of Georgia, N.A., 16
Wachovia Bank of South Carolina, N.A., 16
Wachovia Corporation, 12; 46 (upd.)
Wachtell, Lipton, Rosen & Katz, 47
Wackenhut Corporation, The, 14; 63 (upd.)
Waddell & Reed, Inc., 22
Waffle House Inc., 14; 60 (upd.)
Wagers Inc. (Idaho Candy Company), 86
Waggener Edstrom, 42
Wah Chang, 82
Wahl Clipper Corporation, 86
Wahoo's Fish Taco, 96
Wakefern Food Corporation, 33; 107 (upd.)
Walbridge Aldinger Co., 38
Walbro Corporation, 13
Waldbaum, Inc., 19
Waldenbooks, 17; 86 (upd.)
Walgreen Co., V; 20 (upd.); 65 (upd.)
Walker Manufacturing Company, 19
Wall Drug Store, Inc., 40

Wall Street Deli, Inc., 33
Wallace Computer Services, Inc., 36
Wal-Mart Stores, Inc., V; 8 (upd.); 26 (upd.); 63 (upd.)
Walsworth Publishing Co., 78
Walt Disney Company, The, II; 6 (upd.); 30 (upd.); 63 (upd.)
Walter E. Smithe Furniture, Inc., 105
Walter Industries, Inc., II; 22 (upd.); 72 (upd.)
Walton Monroe Mills, Inc., 8
Wang Laboratories, Inc., III; 6 (upd.)
Warnaco Group Inc., The, 12; 46 (upd.)
Warner Communications Inc., II
Warner Music Group Corporation, 90 (upd.)
Warner-Lambert Co., I; 10 (upd.)
Warners' Stellian Inc., 67
Warrantech Corporation, 53
Warrell Corporation, 68
Warwick Valley Telephone Company, 55
Washington Companies, The, 33
Washington Federal, Inc., 17
Washington Football, Inc., 35
Washington Gas Light Company, 19
Washington Mutual, Inc., 17; 93 (upd.)
Washington National Corporation, 12
Washington Natural Gas Company, 9
Washington Post Company, The, IV; 20 (upd.); 109 (upd.)
Washington Scientific Industries, Inc., 17
Washington Water Power Company, 6
Waste Connections, Inc., 46
Waste Holdings, Inc., 41
Waste Management, Inc., V; 109 (upd.)
Water Pik Technologies, Inc., 34; 83 (upd.)
Waterhouse Investor Services, Inc., 18
Waters Corporation, 43
Watkins-Johnson Company, 15
Watsco Inc., 52
Watson Pharmaceuticals Inc., 16; 56 (upd.)
Watson Wyatt Worldwide, 42
Watts Water Technologies, Inc., 19; 115 (upd.)
Wausau-Mosinee Paper Corporation, 60 (upd.)
Waverly, Inc., 16
Wawa Inc., 17; 78 (upd.)
WAXIE Sanitary Supply, 100
Waxman Industries, Inc., 9
WD-40 Company, 18; 87 (upd.)
WE: Women's Entertainment LLC, 114
Weather Central Inc., 100
Weather Channel Companies, The, 52
Weather Shield Manufacturing, Inc., 102
Weatherford International, Inc., 39
Weaver Popcorn Company, Inc., 89
Webasto Roof Systems Inc., 97
Webber Oil Company, 61
Weber-Stephen Products Co., 40
WebEx Communications, Inc., 81
WebMD Corporation, 65
Webster Financial Corporation, 106
Weeres Industries Corporation, 52
Wegmans Food Markets, Inc., 9; 41 (upd.); 105 (upd.)